SELF-REGULATION AND EGO CONTROL

Dedication

This book is dedicated to the loving memory of my big sister Gera (Hirt) Jacobs, who taught us all so beautifully how to make a difference in the world through love. Your spirit and your smile will forever live on in our hearts.

—**Edward R. Hirt**

SELF-REGULATION AND EGO CONTROL

Edited by

Edward R. Hirt
Joshua J. Clarkson
Lile Jia

ELSEVIER

AMSTERDAM • BOSTON • HEIDELBERG • LONDON
NEW YORK • OXFORD • PARIS • SAN DIEGO
SAN FRANCISCO • SINGAPORE • SYDNEY • TOKYO
Academic Press is an imprint of Elsevier

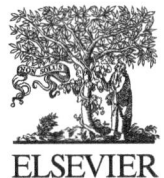

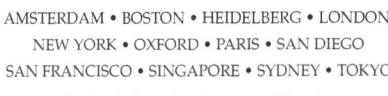

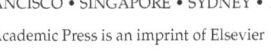

Academic Press is an imprint of Elsevier
125 London Wall, London EC2Y 5AS, United Kingdom
525 B Street, Suite 1800, San Diego, CA 92101-4495, United States
50 Hampshire Street, 5th Floor, Cambridge, MA 02139, United States
The Boulevard, Langford Lane, Kidlington, Oxford OX5 1GB, United Kingdom

Copyright © 2016 Elsevier Inc. All rights reserved.

No part of this publication may be reproduced or transmitted in any form or by any means, electronic or mechanical, including photocopying, recording, or any information storage and retrieval system, without permission in writing from the publisher. Details on how to seek permission, further information about the Publisher's permissions policies and our arrangements with organizations such as the Copyright Clearance Center and the Copyright Licensing Agency, can be found at our website: www.elsevier.com/permissions.

This book and the individual contributions contained in it are protected under copyright by the Publisher (other than as may be noted herein).

Notices
Knowledge and best practice in this field are constantly changing. As new research and experience broaden our understanding, changes in research methods, professional practices, or medical treatment may become necessary.

Practitioners and researchers must always rely on their own experience and knowledge in evaluating and using any information, methods, compounds, or experiments described herein. In using such information or methods they should be mindful of their own safety and the safety of others, including parties for whom they have a professional responsibility.

To the fullest extent of the law, neither the Publisher nor the authors, contributors, or editors, assume any liability for any injury and/or damage to persons or property as a matter of products liability, negligence or otherwise, or from any use or operation of any methods, products, instructions, or ideas contained in the material herein.

Library of Congress Cataloging-in-Publication Data
A catalog record for this book is available from the Library of Congress

British Library Cataloguing-in-Publication Data
A catalogue record for this book is available from the British Library

ISBN: 978-0-12-801850-7

For information on all Academic Press publications visit our website at https://www.elsevier.com/

 Working together to grow libraries in developing countries

www.elsevier.com • www.bookaid.org

Publisher: Nikki Levy
Acquisition Editor: Emily Ekle
Editorial Project Manager: Timothy Bennett
Production Project Manager: Susan Li
Designer: Matthew Limbert

Typeset by TNQ Books and Journals

Contents

List of Contributors — xiii
Preface — xv

1. Limited Resources for Self-Regulation: A Current Overview of the Strength Model
   R.F. BAUMEISTER

   Basic Idea and Early Thoughts — 2
   Building the Strength Model — 3
   Beyond Metaphor? Glucose Dynamics — 4
   Beyond Self-Control and Toward Free Will — 5
   Some Main Applications — 6
   Overcoming or Counteracting Depletion — 9
   State and Trait — 10
   Recent Challenges and Advances — 11
   Conclusion — 14
   References — 15

1
MODERATORS OF EGO CONTROL

2. Moderators of the Ego Depletion Effect
   D.D. LOSCHELDER AND M. FRIESE

   Organizing Grid: Timing and Leverage Point — 22
   Moderators Activated After the First Demanding Task — 24
   Moderators Already Activated Before the First Task — 30
   General Discussion — 35
   Concluding Thoughts — 38
   References — 38

3. Decoupling Goal Striving From Resource Depletion by Forming Implementation Intentions
   F. WIEBER AND P.M. GOLLWITZER

   The Resource Model of Self-Regulation — 44
   Self-Regulation by Goals and Implementation Intentions—Effects and Processes — 45

Mitigating the Seven "Deadly" Threats to Self-Regulation	47
Self-Regulatory Resource Depletion	47
Cue Exposure and Impulse Control	52
Emotional and Social Distress	53
Lapse-Activated Pattern and Abstinence Violations	54
Impairments of Self-Monitoring and Self-Awareness	55
The Influence of Other People	56
Alcohol Intoxication	57
Implementation Intentions and the Effects of Relevant Self-States on Self-Regulation	58
Implications	58
Conclusion	60
Acknowledgments	60
References	60

4. On Enhancing and Diminishing Energy Through Psychological Means: Research on Vitality and Depletion From Self-Determination Theory
F. MARTELA, C.R. DEHAAN AND R.M. RYAN

Introduction	67
Vitality Defined	69
Distinct Forms of Self-Regulation: Self-Control and Autonomous Regulation	70
Integrating the Ego-Depletion Model and Self-Determination Theory's Model of Vitality	73
Psychological Sources of Vitality	76
Conclusion	80
References	81

5. What Does Ego-Depletion Research Reveal About Self-Control? A Conceptual Analysis
J.J. CARNEVALE AND K. FUJITA

What Is Self-Control?	88
What Is Ego Depletion?	94
Ego Depletion's Lessons for Self-Control and Self-Regulation	100
Conclusion	103
References	104

2
MOTIVATIONAL FACTORS IN EGO CONTROL

6. Exercising Self-Control Increases Approach-Motivated Impulse Strength
B.J. SCHMEICHEL AND A. CROWELL

Strength Model of Self-Control	111
Impulse Strength and Self-Control Strength	112

Evidence That Exercising Self-Control Strength Increases Impulse Strength	113
Evidence That Exercising Self-Control Strength Increases Approach-Related Brain Activity	116
Additional Evidence That Trait Approach Motivation Moderates the Aftereffects of Self-Control	118
Does Increased Approach-Motivated Impulse Strength Explain the Ego Depletion Effect?	119
Future Directions and Conclusion	121
References	122

7. Self-Control and Motivation: Integration and Application
B.C. AMPEL, E.E. O'MALLEY AND M. MURAVEN

Hedonic Sampling and Depletion	127
Integration	130
Application	135
Conclusion	137
References	138

8. Motivational Tuning in Response to Ego Depletion
L. JIA, R. YU, E.R. HIRT AND A. FISHBACH

A Gap Between Conclusion and Empirical Evidence	144
Motivational Tuning of Depletion	146
The Antecedent Postulate: Individuals Activate a Prioritization Mind-Set in Response to Depletion	147
The Main Process Postulate: Individuals Motivationally Tune the Evaluation of the Accessible Goal Depending on Their Chronic Goal Commitment	149
Moderator Postulate: Motivational Tuning is Primarily Observed Among Individuals Who Are More Successful in Pursuing the Long-Term Goal	151
Revisiting the Antecedent Postulate	153
Neuroscience Model of Depletion-Induced Prioritization	154
Implications	156
Ongoing Goal Pursuit Process	157
Ultimate Accounts: Capacity View Versus Opportunity Cost Versus Homeostatic View	158
Implication for Goal Pursuit	159
Potential Practical Implications	160
Conclusion	160
References	161

9. Taming the Impulsive Beast: Understanding the Link Between Self-Regulation and Aggression
C.N. DEWALL AND D.S. CHESTER

Major Theories of Self-Regulation and Aggression	166
Aggression: From Top to Bottom	168
Balancing Aggression From the Bottom-Up	171
The Balance Between Aggressive Impulses and Inhibition	171

How to Use Knowledge of Ego Depletion to Reduce Aggression? 176
Concluding Remarks 177
References 177

3
THE ROLE OF PERCEPTIONS, EXPECTANCIES, AND LAY BELIEFS IN EGO CONTROL

10. Perceived Mental Fatigue and Self-Control
J.J. CLARKSON, A.S. OTTO, R. HASSEY AND E.R. HIRT

Perceptions of Mental Fatigue 186
Antecedents of Perceived Mental Fatigue 190
Points of Clarification 194
An Analysis of Effect Size 195
Conclusion 198
Conceptual Implications 198
Concluding Remarks 199
References 200

11. Implicit Theories About Willpower
V. JOB

Implicit Theories: Theoretical Background and
    Measurement 204
Moderating the Ego-Depletion Effect 206
Mechanisms 207
Effects of Implicit Theories About Willpower in Everyday Life 213
Boundaries and Possible Negative Consequences 217
Conclusion 221
References 221

12. Restoration Effects Following Depletion: Adventures in the Uncanny Resilience of Man
E.R. HIRT, J.J. CLARKSON, P.M. EGAN AND J.R. EYINK

The Underlying Role of Perceptual Processes 229
Expectancies of Restoration 230
The Restorative Effect of Mood: The Role of Expectancies of Mental
    Energy Change 233
The Restorative Effect of Interpersonal Power: The Moderating Influence
    of Belief Strength 237
Emerging Questions 244
Coda 247
References 248

4
MULTIPLE SYSTEM APPROACHES TO EGO CONTROL

13. Valuation as a Mechanism of Self-Control and Ego Depletion
E.T. BERKMAN, L.E. KAHN AND J.L. LIVINGSTON

Definitions of Central Constructs: Self-Regulation, Self-Control, and Subjective Value	256
The Critical Gap in the Literature: What Is the Mechanism?	258
Valuation as a Mechanism of Self-Control Conflict Resolution	259
Ego Depletion Explained by the Valuation Model	269
A New Horizon for Self-Control Research	272
References	274

14. What Can Cognitive Neuroscience Tell Us About the Mechanism of Ego Depletion?
D.D. WAGNER AND T.F. HEATHERTON

Brief Overview of Cognitive Neuroscience Methods	282
The Cognitive Neuroscience of Ego Depletion	289
Alternative Theories of Ego Depletion	292
Conclusion	293
References	294

15. Cognitive Control Processes Underlying Individual Differences in Self-Control
B.M. WILKOWSKI AND M.D. ROBINSON

What Is Self-control?	302
Cognitive Control Models—A Preliminary Sketch	303
Individual Differences in Error Monitoring	305
Individual Differences in Cognitive Control Operations	308
Diversity Across Different Domains of Self-Control	312
Improving Self-Control	316
Comparison to the Strength Model	318
Summary and Conclusion	319
References	319

16. Linking Diverse Resources to Action Control
E.J. MASICAMPO AND M.L. SLEPIAN

Linking Mental and Nonmental Resources	326
Linking Nonmental Resources to Action Control	332
Moving Forward: Looking Beyond Mental Resources in Understanding Action Control	341
Conclusion	343
References	343

17. On the Relation Between "Mental" and "Physical" Self-Control
P.M. EGAN AND E.R. HIRT

On the Relation Between "Mental" and "Physical" Self-Control	347
Metaphysical Perceptions and Self-Control	349
Discussion	359
Conclusion	364
References	364
Appendices	369

5
NEWER MODELS OF EGO CONTROL

18. Proximate and Ultimate Causes of Ego Depletion
Z.L. FRANCIS AND M. INZLICHT

Introduction	373
Ultimate Causes	376
Proximate Causes	381
Consequences of This Account	388
Alternative Accounts	389
Conclusion	391
References	392

19. How Depletion Operates in an Integrative Theory of Self-Control
H.P. KOTABE AND W. HOFMANN

Self-Control Theory in a Nutshell	400
Depletion Increases Desire Strength	402
Depletion Reduces Control Motivation	404
Fluctuations in Control Motivation	409
Depletion Decreases Control Capacity	410
Some Ways to Study Motivation Versus Capacity	414
Integrating Motivation and Capacity Into a Model of Control Effort Investment	414
Depletion and Control Effort	418
Concluding Remarks	419
References	420

20. Understanding Self-Regulation Failure: A Motivated Effort-Allocation Account
D.C. MOLDEN, C.M. HUI AND A.A. SCHOLER

Defining Self-Regulation Failure	426
Capacity-Based Explanations for Self-Regulation Failure	428
Limitations of Capacity Explanations	429

Emerging Alternatives to Capacity Explanations 430
A Motivated Effort-Allocation Model of Self-Regulation Failure 432
Advantages of a Motivated Effort-Allocation Model 443
Implications of a Motivated Effort-Allocation Model for Capacity
 Explanations of Self-Regulation Failure 447
Summary and Conclusions 453
References 454

Index 461

List of Contributors

B.C. Ampel University at Albany, Albany, NY, United States
R.F. Baumeister Florida State University, Tallahassee, FL, United States
E.T. Berkman University of Oregon, Eugene, OR, United States
J.J. Carnevale Purchase College SUNY, Purchase, NY, United States
D.S. Chester University of Kentucky, Lexington, KY, United States
J.J. Clarkson University of Cincinnati, Cincinnati, OH, United States
A. Crowell Texas A&M University, College Station, TX, United States
C.R. DeHaan University of Rochester, Rochester, NY, United States
C.N. DeWall University of Kentucky, Lexington, KY, United States
P.M. Egan Kendall College, Chicago, IL, United States
J.R. Eyink Indiana University, Bloomington, IN, United States
A. Fishbach The University of Chicago, Chicago, IL, United States
Z.L. Francis University of Toronto Scarborough, Toronto, ON, Canada
M. Friese Saarland University, Saarbrücken, Germany
K. Fujita The Ohio State University, Columbus, OH, United States
P.M. Gollwitzer University of Konstanz, Konstanz, Germany; New York University, New York, NY, United States
R. Hassey University of Cincinnati, Cincinnati, OH, United States
T.F. Heatherton Dartmouth College Hanover, New Hampshire, United States
E.R. Hirt Indiana University, Bloomington, IN, United States
W. Hofmann University of Cologne, Cologne, Germany
C.M. Hui Chinese University of Hong Kong, Shatin, Hong Kong
M. Inzlicht University of Toronto Scarborough, Toronto, ON, Canada
L. Jia National University of Singapore, Singapore, Singapore
V. Job University of Zurich, Zurich, Switzerland
L.E. Kahn University of Oregon, Eugene, OR, United States
H.P. Kotabe University of Chicago, Chicago, IL, United States
J.L. Livingston University of Oregon, Eugene, OR, United States
D.D. Loschelder Leuphana University Lüneburg, Germany
F. Martela University of Helsinki, Helsinki, Finland
E.J. Masicampo Wake Forest University, Winston Salem, NC, United States
D.C. Molden Northwestern University, Evanston, IL, United States
M. Muraven University at Albany, Albany, NY, United States

E.E. O'Malley University at Albany, Albany, NY, United States

A.S. Otto Baylor University, Waco, TX, United States

M.D. Robinson North Dakota State University, Fargo, ND, United States

R.M. Ryan University of Rochester, Rochester, NY, United States; Australian Catholic University, Strathfield, NSW, Australia

B.J. Schmeichel Texas A&M University, College Station, TX, United States

A.A. Scholer University of Waterloo, Waterloo, ON, Canada

M.L. Slepian Columbia University, New York, NY, United States

D.D. Wagner The Ohio State University, Columbus, OH, United States

F. Wieber Zurich University of Applied Sciences, Winterthur, Switzerland; University of Konstanz, Konstanz, Germany

B.M. Wilkowski University of Wyoming, Laramie, WY, United States

R. Yu National University of Singapore, Singapore, Singapore

Preface

The concept of self-regulation and self-control has a rich and fascinating history. Its roots stem from the classic philosophers of Ancient Greece (if not earlier), but the concept was not significantly advanced theoretically until Sigmund Freud at the turn of the 20th century. Freud proposed his structural model of the psyche (1923–61), a model that detailed three aspects of the psyche (the id, ego, and superego) and the role of the ego in regulating the often competing desires of the other two aspects. Decades later, and in direct contradiction to the abstract theorizing of Freud, BF Skinner published his classic survey of self-control techniques which focused heavily on behavior modification methods that seek to control our actions and environments to eschew our desires (Skinner, 1965). Groundbreaking work by Walter Mischel and his colleagues (eg, Mischel & Ebbesen, 1970) using his classic delay of gratification paradigm (the infamous marshmallow studies) offered an important shift in the study of self-control by exploring the cognitive and developmental processes, as well as environmental contexts, that dictate success in self-regulation.

However, despite its rich history, diverse theoretical perspectives, and clear practical relevance, the concept had not received a great deal of attention within the field of social psychology. Outside of the cybernetic models of self-regulation posited by Carver and Scheier (1981) and others, research within social psychology seemed to place greater emphasis on the self more broadly. This focus generated a wealth of insights into domains such as self-esteem, self-identity, and self-motivations, yet little insight into self-control.

This lack of emphasis changed dramatically in the 1990s when Roy Baumeister and his colleagues proposed a novel and revolutionary model of self-control based on a muscle metaphor. In short, our muscles get tired after prolonged use and need rest to sustain physical performance over long periods of time. Interestingly, our mental strength or "will" appears to have similar limitations, getting fatigued after the expenditure of self-control and resulting in compromised performance on subsequent tasks. In a classic set of experiments testing this new perspective on self-control, Baumeister et al. showed that after expending self-control in an initial task (such as resisting freshly baked chocolate chip cookies in favor of peeled radishes in a taste test), performance on later tasks requiring self-control (such as persistence on a challenging set of anagrams) was significantly reduced (Baumeister, Bratslavsky, Muraven, & Tice, 1998). These authors coined the term "ego depletion" to describe the deleterious consequences of prior expenditure of self-control on subsequent task performance.

Since that seminal article, work on ego depletion and its effects on self-control performance has proliferated, with well over 200 empirical studies documenting that prior exertion of self-control in one context impairs future efforts at self-control in subsequent contexts (see Hagger, Wood, Stiff, & Chatzisarantis, 2010, for a review). Indeed, the field had become enamored with "depletion effects," with researchers all over the world elaborating on its implications for outcomes ranging from aggression and prejudice to overeating, addiction, impulse spending, decision making, and implicit attitudes. Moreover, the influence of this depletion work has extended beyond the scientific community with the publication of the recent New York Time best seller entitled *Willpower: Rediscovering the Greatest Human Strength* (Baumeister & Tierney, 2012).

***

The predominant explanation for these effects has been a "strength model" which posits that humans have a limited pool of mental resources which are taxed (or "depleted") by initial acts of self-control and thus render individuals unable to devote sufficient resources to subsequent tasks. This characterization of the ebb and flow of self-regulation resonates well with our own phenomenological experience, nicely depicted by the cover photo of the Titan Atlas from Greek mythology embraced in the eternal struggle to hold the weight of the heavens on his broad shoulders. We are acutely aware of our limitations, feeling as if we have "hit a wall" or are unable to muster the necessary mental energy or resources to persist at demanding tasks.

Yet despite the anecdotal support and intuitive analog to physical exertion, a critical question facing researchers involves the search for the concrete nature of these limited resources. In response, an influential paper by Gailliot et al. (2007) provided evidence for changes in blood glucose level as the signature marker of depletion and, consequently, offered a clear physiological basis for depletion effects. However, a number of more recent papers (Beedie & Lane, 2012; Molden et al., 2012) have challenged these effects by offering convincing evidence that blood glucose changes cannot account for many depletion effects. Soon thereafter, as theoretical and empirical work accumulated that questioned the plausibility of blood glucose as the metric for mental energy, critics began to question other assumptions of the strength model. In a short time, a body of research developed that showed individuals' motivations, perceptions, lay beliefs, and psychological state (eg, positive mood, self-affirmation, power) moderate depletion effects and, in doing so, cast concerns over whether the muscle metaphor could adequately account for these emerging complexities.

Indeed, some researchers have interpreted this developing literature as evidence that depletion effects are not real (Carter & McCullough, 2014) or merely in our heads (Job, Dweck, & Walton, 2010).

***

At the 2014 SPSP meeting, amidst the rising tide of conflicting findings, we discussed the possibility of editing a book. The goal, we decided, would be to invite researchers currently embroiled in this controversy to contribute in an effort to collaboratively assess the current state of the construct of ego depletion and, as a consequence, the current state of the field. We believed the time was right for attempts to integrate these disparate results that have been appearing in the literature within existing models of self-regulation, with the hope of offering guidance for future efforts within this intriguing area of research. Convinced others would see the need for this type of contribution, we approached Elsevier with a book proposal. Elsevier, much to our appreciation, supported this project from its inception.

One important element of our book proposal was the plan to hold a conference for chapter contributors prior to the chapter submission deadline. The conference was designed to give authors the chance to present to each other, discuss issues, denote areas of agreement/disagreement, and identify important key questions and future directions for work in this area. By holding this conference prior to chapter submission deadlines, we aimed to achieve a more integrated and cohesive volume. The conference was held at Indiana University on July 27–28, 2015 and included 17 of the 20 chapter author teams. From our vantage point, this conference was an unequivocal success; it served to provide those in attendance with an opportunity to hear about each other's work, receive feedback on ideas, and establish a greater rapport with scholars from all over the world conducting research in this area. It is rare in our field that we have the experience to spend time in such an intense small group environment with other researchers engaged in a common venture and, based on the postconference feedback, it is clear this type of gathering needs to happen again in the near future—if not on a regular basis.

From the outset, we targeted this book as a resource for fellow researchers (faculty and graduate students) in social, cognitive, developmental, and clinical psychology with an interest in self-regulation and self-control. However, because of the broad implications of these topics for a variety of disciplines, we believe that professionals interested in the applications of self-control in areas such as addictions, counseling, eating disorders, motivational and sensitivity training will also find this book informative, insightful, and helpful, as the experience of depletion is at the heart of a number of these maladaptive behaviors.

***

The primary goals of this book are (1) to document and review recent research in the domain of self-control depletion that call into question some of the assumptions inherent in the dominant resource or "strength" model; and (2) to respond to the challenge of recent articles (cf. Inzlicht & Schmeichel, 2012; Kurzban, Duckworth, Kable, & Myers, 2013) calling for efforts to broaden the scope of theories of self-control change and to provide a more thorough and precise account of the existing findings. To accomplish these goals, we identified and contacted a set of potential contributors who were actively researching relevant topics related to self-regulation and depletion. Enthusiasm for this book was high, and nearly everyone that we asked was willing to contribute a chapter. Clearly, the timeliness of this project had a lot to do with the buy-in we received from our fellow self-regulation researchers. For that we are indebted.

Given these goals, the chapters reflect a breadth of topics related to contemporary and classic perspectives on self-regulation and ego control. In an attempt to offer a structure to these diverse topics, we organized the book thusly. We open with a foundational chapter by Roy Baumeister who provides the history and background of the resource/strength model. Building upon that foundation, the book then consists of five sections.

The first section outlines various factors known to moderate depletion effects. This section begins with a chapter by Loschelder and Friese that provides a taxonomy of different moderators using dimensions of timing and leverage point to organize this literature. We follow with a chapter by Weiber and Gollwitzer, which discusses the effects of implementation intentions in reducing the pejorative consequences of depletion. Martela, de Haan, and Ryan's chapter then utilizes self-determination theory to discuss the energizing effects of autonomous self-regulation for defusing depletion. We close this first section with a chapter by Carnavale and Fujita, which emphasizes the importance in distinguishing among key terms such as self-control, self-regulation, executive function, and inhibition for understanding ego depletion and its boundary conditions.

The second section addresses the role of motivation and goal pursuit in self-control exertion. One important contribution of this section is to imbed depletion research within the broader context of ongoing goal pursuit and various impulses. To date, much of the research has focused on experimenter-provided tasks in a largely goal-absent context. This section begins with a chapter by Schmeichel and Crowell, which explores how depletion increases approach motivation and impulse strength. Hence, self-control failures are not only a result of diminished capacity for control but also a consequence of the increased allure of temptations and indulgences. Ampel, O'Malley, and Muraven's chapter follows, and further argues that the motivational effect of depletion is, at its core, both a hedonic increase in temptations as well as a hedonic devaluation of effort investment. Jia, Yu, Hirt, and Fishbach's chapter then details the function of depletion as a signal to prioritize one's goal based on importance. This section then closes with DeWall and Chester's chapter highlighting the role of depletion in fueling aggressive impulses.

The third section introduces the roles of expectancies, lay beliefs, and individual differences in self-control exertion. This section kicks off with a chapter by Clarkson, Otto, Hassey, and Hirt that outlines the extent to which expectancies and perceptions of one's state of depletion lead to the observed performance effects, over and above actual levels of depletion. Job's chapter illustrates the powerful role that beliefs about limited versus nonlimited theories of willpower play on susceptibility to depletion effects. This section closes with Hirt, Clarkson, Egan, and Eyink's chapter describing how lay theories of replenishment determine restoration following depletion and introduces a model of spontaneous resource recovery through psychological (vs physiological) means.

The fourth section details multiple systems approaches to the phenomenon of depletion. Berkman, Kahn, and Livingston's chapter leads off this section by highlighting the central role of a valuation process of integrating multiple sources of subjective value for a given choice option as a mechanism of self-control. Wagner and Heatherton's chapter follows with a discussion of the cognitive neuroscience of self-regulation failure by examining the central roles of control and reward in modulating behavior. Robinson and Wilkowski's chapter then delves into the different facets of cognitive control that are responsible for self-control and modulate depletion effects. Masicampo and Slepian's chapter introduces the notion that individuals may draw upon other personal resources—social resources, money, bodily resources, or time—to achieve their self-regulation goals. Interestingly, this chapter discusses the potential substitutability of these different resources and its implications for the expenditure of mental resources. The final chapter of this section by Egan and Hirt devotes its attention more explicitly to the distinction between physical and mental depletion. This chapter builds upon dualistic beliefs of the interaction between mind and body to demonstrate the impact that framing tasks as requiring physical as opposed to mental resources may have for depletion effects.

In the final section of the book, we include three chapters which document recent efforts to develop more inclusive and integrative models of self-control exertion. Francis and Inzlicht's chapter kick starts this section with a discussion of the innate balance between immediate and long-term needs and the implications of this balance for different underlying causes of ego depletion. Next, Kotabe and Hoffman's chapter presents their dual-process model of depletion. This model outlines two central internal forces, represented in an activation cluster and an exertion cluster, which nicely capture both the conflict between desires and higher order goals as well as the elements of self-control utilized to enact one's volitional actions. Furthermore, this model includes a concern with enactment constraints, which captures the external forces that can moderate one's success in implementing self-control in vivo. Molden, Hui, and Scholer's chapter concludes the book with their motivated effort allocation (MEA) model, which incorporates a recursive assessment of motives and allocation of effort and attention based on these motives as key elements. These models represent attempts to build upon the strength model in ways that abate issues and concerns about the nature of the underlying resource, redirecting attention toward the complex interplay among psychological, motivational, and physiological elements that contribute to self-regulation. We feel that these latter models open up a plethora of new research questions and directions that can further our understanding of this seminal function of the active self.

***

They say it takes a village to raise a child. Well, it certainly takes that and more to edit a book! Thus, in closing, we would like to acknowledge the contributions of so many who have helped us in this endeavor. Thanks first to our editorial team at Elsevier: Emily Ekle and Tim Bennett. They have helped to shape this project into the final product it has become and have believed in this book from its inception. We would also like to express our gratitude and sincere appreciation to Mary Morgan and the team at IU Conferences for their help in hosting the conference in support of this book in July 2015 at Indiana University Bloomington. Mary took the reins in the planning and organization of the conference, and her calm demeanor and meticulous attention to detail made it go incredibly smoothly. Much of the success of that conference can be attributed to her efforts. We also acknowledge the financial support provided by the College of Arts and Sciences and the Department of Psychological and Brain Sciences at Indiana University to defray the cost of the conference. We thank Ross Crooks for recording the conference talks and assisting with the video production.

Thanks also go out to our mentors and colleagues who have influenced our thinking and shaped many of the ideas that motivated this book: Jim Sherman, Russ Fazio, Eliot Smith, Frank Kardes, Mary Murphy, Anne Krendl, Michelle VanDellen, Kathleen Vohs, Joshua Ackerman, Robert (BJ) Rydell, David Pisoni and Shinobu Kitayama. We are particularly grateful for the advice and wise counsel of Abraham Tesser, who along with his partner in crime Lenny Martin, hosted a conference back in 1995 in support of a book entitled *Striving and Feeling: Interactions among goals, affect, and self-regulation*. That experience served as a template from which we modeled our proposal. Though he now spends the majority of his time working as a master furniture craftsman, Abe continues to serve as a mentor and role model in more ways than we can fathom. We also want to thank our graduate students and colleagues who have helped out with our research, read drafts of chapters, and provided support to this effort: Julie Eyink, Cony Ho, Sam Karpen, and Alethea Koh.

Finally, we would like to dedicate this book to our families. Thank you for your love and support throughout this project.

For Ed, to my dear wife Kathy McTigue for her kindness, friendship, and support throughout the entirety of this process; to my daughters Molly and Maureen Hirt, for being such special young women who continue to be an endless source of joy and comfort in my life; to our beloved corgis Sammy and Tucker, for their unconditional love and unbridled passion for playing frisbee. To my parents, Charles and Charlotte Hirt, and to my siblings Chuck, Bill, Gina, and Gera, I think about you every day and continue to be inspired by your generous and caring spirits. To all of the brilliant and engaging contributors to this book, thank you for your willingness to bring your knowledge and expertise to this project. And finally to my fellow editors, who have been such dear friends and wonderful colleagues over the years, it was my pleasure to be a part of this collective effort with you two.

For Josh, to the Marketing Department at the University of Cincinnati who continues to support my intellectual pursuits, to my friends (Diesel, Chris, Adam) who remind me to stay balanced, to my parents for their endless encouragement, and to my brothers (Jordan and Judson) for their work ethic, my gratitude exceeds any words; just know I am grateful. And to the contributors and my fellow editors, a special thank you for an engaging and enjoyable experience.

For Lile, to my wife Melanie for your steadfast faith and support for always keeping me centered; to my daughter Leona for being my constant source of joy; and to my parents for the generous sharing of your positive outlook in life. My heartfelt gratitude also goes to all the contributors and my fellow editors. Thank you all for this memorable and illuminating journey.

We have thoroughly enjoyed the process of putting together this volume and we hope this enthusiasm fuels the curiosity of our readers who, in time, might forge the next step in the long and decorated history of self-control.

References

Baumeister, R. F., Bratslavsky, E., Muraven, M., & Tice, D. M. (1998). Ego depletion: Is the active self a limited resource? *Journal of Personality and Social Psychology, 74*(5), 1252–1265.

Baumeister, R. F., & Tierney, J. (2012). *Willpower: Rediscovering the greatest human strength*. New York: Penguin Books.

Beedie, C. J., & Lane, A. M. (2012). The role of glucose in self-control: Another look at the evidence and an alternative conceptualization. *Personality and Social Psychology Review, 16*, 143–153.

Carter, E. C., & McCullough, M. E. (2014). Publication bias and the limited strength model of self-control: Has the evidence for ego depletion been overestimated? *Frontiers in Psychology, 5*(823), 1–11.

Carver, C. S., & Scheier, M. P. (1981). *Attention and self-regulation: a control-theory approach to human behavior*. New York: Springer-Verlag.

Freud, S. (1961). The ego and the id. In J. Strachey (Ed.), *The standard edition of the complete psychological works of Sigmund Freud* (vol. 19) (pp. 3–66). London: Hogarth Press. Original work published 1923.

Gailliot, M. T., Baumeister, R. F., DeWall, C. N., Maner, J. K., Plant, E. A., Tice, D. M., ... Schmeichel, B. J. (2007). Self-control relies on glucose as a limited energy source: willpower is more than a metaphor. *Journal of Personality and Social Psychology, 92*(2), 325–336.

Hagger, M. S., Wood, C., Stiff, C., & Chatzisarantis, N. L. (2010). Ego depletion and the strength model of self-control: a meta-analysis. *Psychological Bulletin, 136*(4), 495–525.

Inzlicht, M., & Schmeichel, B. J. (2012). What is ego depletion?: Toward a mechanistic revision of the resource model of self-control. *Perspectives on Psychological Science, 7*, 450–463.

Job, V., Dweck, C. S., & Walton, G. M. (2010). Ego depletion — is it all in your head? Implicit theories about willpower affect self-regulation. *Psychological Science, 21*, 1686–1693.

Kurzban, R., Duckworth, A. L., Kable, J. W., & Myers, J. (2013). An opportunity cost model of subjective effort and task performance. *Behavioral & Brain Sciences, 36*, 661–726.

Mischel, W., & Ebbesen, E. B. (1970). Attention in delay of gratification. *Journal of Personality and Social Psychology, 16*(2), 329–337.

Molden, D. C., Hui, C. M., Scholer, A. A., Meier, B. P., Noreen, E. E., D'Agostino, P. R., & Martin, V. (2012). Motivational versus metabolic effects of carbohydrates on self-control. *Psychological Science, 23*, 1137–1144.

Skinner, B. F. (1965). *Science and human behavior*. Simon and Schuster.

CHAPTER 1

Limited Resources for Self-Regulation: A Current Overview of the Strength Model

R.F. Baumeister
Florida State University, Tallahassee, FL, United States

Understanding the nature of human selfhood and personal identity has been a preoccupation of multiple fields of inquiry and many thousands of scholars. My own ongoing interest in that topic led me in the 1980s to the study of self-regulation, which I thought might provide important keys. Regulating itself is not just one more thing that the self does: It is often a basic part of almost everything the self does.

The central importance of self-regulation to the theory of self is, to be sure, hardly the only reason to study self-regulation. Many other researchers have been attracted by its practical and applied benefits. Inadequate, misguided, or otherwise failing self-regulation has been linked to a breathtakingly broad assortment of personal and societal problems, including overeating and obesity, cigarette addiction, alcohol and drug addiction, violence and crime, prejudice, underachievement in school and work, lack of compliance with medicine, inadequate physical exercise, debt and bankruptcy, spousal abuse, failure to save money, and premature death.

This chapter is intended to provide an overview of the evolution of my inquiries and thoughts about self-regulation. It will feature the strength model, which has gradually grown into a highly influential but also controversial account of how self-regulation functions. For a thorough treatment of the findings, theoretical developments, and rival accounts, see Baumeister and Vohs (2016).

BASIC IDEA AND EARLY THOUGHTS

I started to study self-regulation as a potentially useful platform to help understand the self. Not having any clear understanding of self-regulation beyond the Carver and Scheier (1981, 1982) feedback loop, I began by reading lots of work. My practice in these things is to read more data than theory, so I mostly skipped other accounts of how self-regulation might work in process and instead read studies on people trying to quit smoking, overeating, spending too much, and the like. Along with two colleagues, we pulled the material together into a book, *Losing Control: How and Why People Fail at Self-regulation* (Baumeister, Heatherton, & Tice, 1994). In it, we concluded that many findings seemed to fit the idea that self-control depended on a limited energy supply akin to the folk notion of willpower, but certainly there was nothing conclusive, and other theories were still viable.

I completed the book while on sabbatical and sent it back to my graduate students who were working away, temporarily orphaned as it were by my (and Tice's) absence. Mark Muraven was then a graduate student in our laboratory, and he decided to try some experimental tests of the idea. I do not remember how much we communicated on this, and so the first studies may have been mainly his work or may have been developed in discussions with Dianne Tice. But his experiments worked well, indeed better than his previous studies on other topics, and so he latched onto this line of work.

Muraven was indeed the first author on the original paper on regulatory depletion (Muraven, Tice, & Baumeister, 1998). It established the methodological basis for much subsequent work, which has come to be described as the "dual task paradigm." It involves two different tasks that both require self-regulation. The first one is used to deplete the participant's willpower, so to speak. The second one measures the consequences.

In our early writings (Muraven et al., 1988; also Baumeister, Bratslavsky, Muraven, & Tice, 1998), we presented the studies as testing three competing models of self-regulation. One was that it depends on a limited energy supply. Another was that it was essentially an information-processing system. The third was that it was a skill. All these views had been advocated in the literature (as reviewed by Baumeister et al., 1994), and all were inherently plausible. They made competing predictions about how people would fare on a second self-regulation task as a result of having already done a different one. As we reasoned, if self-control depended on energy or strength, then the first one would deplete it to some degree, so performance would suffer on the second task. If self-regulation were mainly a cognitive process, then the first task should activate the self-regulating modules in mind and brain, and so performance should be facilitated and improved on the second task. And skill does not change from one trial to the next but should only show gradual improvements over considerable practice. Our results have consistently favored the strength model, but the early studies were done with an acute sense that things could go differently.

BUILDING THE STRENGTH MODEL

The idea that the self consisted partly of some kind of energy was quite radical in the early 1990s (and still is, in many quarters). Information-processing models reigned everywhere. To find a theorist who had taken seriously the idea that energy dynamics were central to understanding the self, we had to go back to Freud. Hence, we used the term *ego depletion* (using Freud's term "ego" to refer to the self) to refer to the state following exertion of self-control, marked by diminished capacity for further self-regulation. The idea was that some kind of energy resource gets depleted when one exerts self-control, leaving less available for further exertions.

The analogy of a muscle becoming fatigued was helpful from the start and over the years has been a useful heuristic. One exerts a muscle, and afterward it is tired and weak. In apparently similar fashion, one exerts self-control, and afterward the capacity for self-control likewise seems tired and weak. (Reports of fatigue and tiredness have been one subjective sign of ego depletion; see Hagger, Wood, Stiff, & Chatzisarantis, 2010, for a metaanalysis; Chapter 10.)

The muscle analogy was extended in two important ways in subsequent work. One is that the effects of fatigue show up long before the muscle is so exhausted that it is incapable of further responses. Athletes follow initial exertion by conserving their strength. In a similar fashion, self-controllers may follow initial exertion of self-control by conserving their remaining resources. The alternative (car engine) metaphor, that ego depletion indicates that the brain has run out of gas, does not correspond to observations. Muraven and Slessareva (2003) showed that people could overcome ego depletion if they were sufficiently motivated. Muraven, Shmueli, and Burkley (2006) provided abundant evidence that ego depletion effects are conservation effects: People skimp more on current self-control if they anticipate further demands for self-control, and so forth.

The other key aspect of the muscle analogy is that muscles can become strengthened over time by frequent exercise. The short-term effect of exertion is to tire the muscle, but after it recovers from fatigue, it is a little bit stronger. Muraven, Baumeister, and Tice (1999) contributed some preliminary findings indicating that people who exercised self-control regularly for 2 weeks (mainly trying to improve their posture as they went about their daily activities) showed improvements on laboratory tests of self-control (unrelated to posture). Their baseline performance was unchanged, but they showed slower decrements in response to ego-depleting tasks. In physical terms, the improvement was not so much in the muscle's raw power as in its stamina. Various other studies have shown improvements in self-control performance as a result of regular exercise (for a review, see Baumester, Gailliot, DeWall, & Oaten, 2006). Perhaps most impressively, Muraven (2010) showed that smokers were more successful at quitting smoking after having exercised their self-control "muscle" for 2 weeks.

BEYOND METAPHOR? GLUCOSE DYNAMICS

A failed study by Matt Gailliot opened a new perspective on ego depletion and suggested that it might be possible to move beyond metaphors of strength and energy to invoke genuine, observable physiological processes. Like presumably everyone else working on self-regulation, I assume that it has physiological bases, even though identifying the precise brain circuits has been remarkably difficult to do (see Chapters 13 and 14). The original hypothesis was as follows: Given that resisting temptation weakens self-control, then perhaps indulging in temptation would improve or strengthen it. Participants were depleted first, and then some had an ice cream treat before the second task. Consistent with that hypothesis, the ice cream did lead to improved self-control—but so did an unappetizing milk shake, made with half-and-half (milk and cream), no real ice cream, and no sugar, and thus consisting of a large dose of unsweetened dairy glop. Thus the pleasure of eating the ice cream was not necessary to counteract ego depletion. Reflecting on this, Gailliot and I began to think; perhaps it was the calories? Calories from food are, after all, energy.

Gailliot began to read up on glucose. Psychologists had not found glucose interesting, but nutritionists had documented various changes in behavior associated with glucose problems, and many of these suggested low self-control. A review of this literature concluded that low glucose impaired self-control (Gailliot & Baumeister, 2007a). We also undertook a program of laboratory studies to illuminate how glucose might work in the laboratory.

The experiments yielded three tentative conclusions about glucose and self-control (Gailliot et al., 2007). First, blood glucose levels drop from before to after ego-depleting tasks. (This one has not consistently replicated, however, and we no longer believe this to be generally true; at least, the picture is much more complicated.) Second, low levels of blood glucose predict poor performance on self-control tests. (This confirms what the abundant data from studies of nutrition, diabetes, and related areas had already suggested.) Third, getting a dose of glucose counteracts ego depletion. This was a novel prediction (although in a sense the milk shake study had shown it), but it has held up well in subsequent studies in our and others' labs.

The idea that glucose was the resource behind self-control, the active ingredient in willpower, was seductive, but almost certainly the picture is far more complicated than that. Molden et al. (2012) had participants swish a glucose drink in their mouths and spit it out—and that too counteracted ego depletion (see Chapter 20). Thus, they did not actually consume glucose (beyond the small amount absorbed through the mouth).

Another crucial point is that the human body has ample stores of glucose. Beedie and Lane (2012) proposed that ego depletion effects are less about an exhaustion of the resource than about allocation of it. When the task is important, people continue to allocate resources even if they have already expended some. The Molden et al. (2012) finding that the mere taste of glucose counteracted depletion could be explained by assuming that the body allocates glucose more readily when it anticipates that more will be coming in. (Usually, what one tastes in the mouth is coming to the stomach.)

The debate about the role of glucose has grown complex and interesting, and I anticipate further progress in unforeseeable directions. It seems hard to deny that glucose has a significant role, but it seems unlikely that glucose will provide a full explanation. In particular, adenosine may also play a key role. Adenosine is a by-product of glucose metabolism, and its accumulation seems to provide signals of fatigue. In other words, the body may find it easier to keep track of adenosine than to keep track of glucose quantities.

BEYOND SELF-CONTROL AND TOWARD FREE WILL

Assuming that there is one common resource used for self-regulation, what else might use the same resource? Insofar as glucose is part of the resource, self-regulation would be tied in to most of the body's mental and physical activities. Glucose is the body's (and brain's) energy supply. Even apart from that, however, an effective theory must recognize what other activities can cause ego depletion or suffer (or, indeed, benefit) as a result of it.

The initial ego depletion findings were emerging just as I was struggling to compile a thorough overview of social psychology's research on the self. I had grouped choice in the same category as self-regulation on conceptual grounds, and this led to the hypothesis that perhaps the same resource would be used in both. An initial study with a cognitive dissonance paradigm found some evidence that making choices depletes the self (resulting in impaired self-regulation afterward; Baumeister et al., 1998), but the method invited alternative explanations. After some years of work and many experiments, Vohs et al. (2008) showed that making decisions and choices does indeed produce the same decrements that initial exertion of self-control does. Choice is depleting.

Further studies confirmed that the effect works in reverse also. After exerting self-control, decision-making is impaired, in the sense that people shift to low-effort styles of deciding (Pocheptsova et al., 2009). Taken together, these findings pushed us to start thinking more broadly about executive function than about self-regulatory resource depletion.

What else, then, might make use of the same resource and be linked to ego depletion? Insofar as ego depletion weakens top–down control over mental processes, it should make the person generally more passive. Sure enough, multiple studies with different methods have confirmed the general passivity of depleted persons (Vohs, Baumeister, Vonasch, et al., 2014). We also think that planning should be depleting, but further research on this is needed.

The link between choice and self-control brought us into contact with philosophers, for whom those two phenomena are prototypical, often used examples of free will and hence must be either integrated into a theory of free will or explained away as not properly deserving that label. Proving or disproving the existence of free will is not likely to be something psychology experiments can resolve (although plenty seem intent on trying!). But this offered a fresh approach to the debate. In my view, these psychological processes involving ego depletion, glucose, choice, and self-regulation are the reality behind the popular concept of free will. If free will exists, these are what constitute it. If free will does not exist, then these constitute what is mistaken for it.

SOME MAIN APPLICATIONS

While some researchers have focused on the core phenomena of ego depletion and debated the underlying processes and mechanisms, and a few have even used dubious statistical methods to try to argue that there is no such thing as ego depletion (see Carter et al., 2015), a great many other researchers have found applications of ego depletion to a remarkably broad range of phenomena. Here, I offer merely a sampling.

Many people associate self-control mainly with impulse control, specifically eating (dieting), smoking, and spending. (Note, I use the terms self-control and self-regulation interchangeably, but some authors have made a good case that there are some forms of self-regulation that go beyond self-control; see Chapters 5 and 13.) There is ample evidence of increases in such impulsive behavior during the depleted state (see Chapter 6). As already noted, dieters eat more food, especially fattening food such as candy, when they are depleted (Vohs & Heatherton, 2000). Vohs and Faber (2007) found that depletion increased how much money people were willing to pay for products and also made people choose to buy more goods impulsively. Smoking cigarettes has also been linked to ego depletion, at least in the sense that when smokers resist the urge to smoke, they deplete their willpower (Hagger et al., 2013). Smokers also smoke more when depleted (Shmueli & Prochaska, 2012). People with alcohol problems drink more alcohol when depleted (Muraven, Collins, & Neinhaus, 2002).

Other impulses also seem to gain strength, or at least increase their chances of shaping behavior, when ego depletion weakens top–down control and the associated restraints. Aggressive impulses, for example, increase when people are depleted (DeWall, Baumeister, Stillman, & Gailliot, 2007; see also Chapter 9). This does not mean that depletion itself makes people more aggressive. Rather, the increase was found only among people who were provoked, suggesting that depletion weakened the normal inhibitions and restraints, rather than giving rise to the impulse. In a similar fashion, ego depletion does not itself seem to increase sexual desires, but it weakens restraints, thereby leading people to perform more overtly sexual and especially inappropriately sexual acts (Gailliot & Baumeister, 2007b).

In some of the most elegant work on the topic, Hofmann, Rauch, and Gawronski (2007) showed that people's unconscious, implicit attitudes guide behavior when people are depleted (see Chapter 19). In contrast, when people are not depleted and thus remain in more or less full possession of their powers of self-regulation, their actions are guided by their conscious, explicit attitudes rather than the unconscious ones. These fit the view that ego depletion weakens central control, allowing automatic or unconscious processes to influence behavior unchecked by conscious restraint.

But impulse control is only one aspect of self-regulation. A very different and provocative aspect concerns its relationship to intellectual performance. Intelligence tests were designed to measure a person's ability to think, so as to predict school performance. Some authors such as Duckworth and Seligman (2005) have tried to pit self-control against brainpower to predict school achievement, with self-control doing at least as well as IQ. Taking a different approach, Schmeichel, Vohs, and Baumeister (2003) showed that performance on IQ tests is itself heavily influenced by self-regulation. They found that ego depletion caused substantial drops in IQ test performance. It was also revealing to note which sorts of tests were affected. Those corresponding to automatic processes such as memory retrieval (eg, tests of vocabulary or general knowledge) were unaffected. In contrast, those requiring reasoning, inference, induction, or extrapolation suffered substantial decrements. These findings again link ego depletion and self-regulation to central, top–down control. Depletion does not impair the automatic processes such as encoding into memory and retrieving from it, but it affects the sort of thinking that requires central control to move, by means of reasoning or other rules, from one set of information to formulate other thoughts.

Performing well on intellectual tests may be a particular problem for some people, specifically those with test anxiety. Bertrams, Englert, Dickhäuser, and Baumeister (2013) noted abundant evidence that people with test anxiety perform worse than others on school tests—but also plenty of evidence that test anxiety has no effect on school performance. They reasoned that depletion might be one moderator. Sure enough, the experiments found that test-anxious people performed worse than others on tests when depleted but performed just as well as others when not depleted.

The effects of ego depletion on affect regulation generally have not received nearly as much attention as its effects on impulse control, but they are genuine. Muraven et al. (1998) had participants try to stifle their emotional reactions to funny film clips, including trying to maintain a "poker face" with no sign of emotion. Depleted people were less successful at hiding their mirth.

More generally, depleted persons report their emotions as stronger than otherwise. Vohs, Baumeister, Ramanthan, et al. (2014) found a broad range of feelings were intensified during depletion (see also Chapter 6). These included both positive and negative feelings. Desires were also felt more strongly by depleted than nondepleted persons. The intensification of subjective feelings guided behavior. In one study, participants had to submerge a hand in ice-cold water for as long as they could. Depleted persons felt the water as more painful than nondepleted persons, and this mediated their quicker withdrawal from the cold water. It is not entirely clear exactly why depletion intensifies feelings, but one hypothesis is that modern citizens routinely damp down their emotions, and ego depletion weakens this process.

Self-regulation is highly relevant to interpersonal relations. I already mentioned the findings of increased sexual and aggressive behavior. Vohs and Baumeister (2003) found a variety of effects of depletion on behavior in close relationships, including greater time spent exposing oneself to tempting photos of attractive members of the opposite sex (ie, not one's partner). They found that when couples were given randomly assigned bogus feedback on a task they had done together, the individuals tended to assign more credit to each other while taking the blame on themselves. This pattern clearly seems supportive of good relationships. However, when depleted, those patterns reversed, and the individuals blamed each other while hogging more credit for themselves. On a more ominous note, Finkel et al. (2009) showed that depleted persons were more likely than others to perpetrate intimate partner violence.

Overall, self-control seems a powerful aid to maintaining good quality relationships. Vohs, Finkenauer, and Baumeister (2011) wondered what configuration of trait self-control scores would yield the highest levels of relationship satisfaction. Most work on partner traits has debated whether similarity or complementarity is best, and these correspond to finding the smallest or largest possible difference between the partners' scores. Vohs et al. found no effect of the difference between partner scores on self-control on any measure of relationship satisfaction in three quite different samples. They did, however, find that the sum (rather than the difference) predicted significantly, and indeed above and beyond the independent contributions of the two individuals' scores. Thus the more self-control two partners have, the stronger and more satisfying their relationship will be.

OVERCOMING OR COUNTERACTING DEPLETION

Multiple sorts of interventions and manipulations have been shown to counteract the negative effects of ego depletion, thereby enabling people to perform well at self-control tasks despite having previously exerted self-control and expended some willpower. Chapter 2 claims to have identified over a 100 moderators of ego depletion effects. These complicate the development of the theory, and indeed multiple authors of those reports have been tempted to conclude that ego depletion does not really involve expenditure of energy but rather indicates some kind of shift in whatever variable they manipulated to restore performance.

Then again, most of these findings have pertained to slight or incipient levels of ego depletion. When depletion is more extensive, these restorative manipulations fail to restore and indeed in some cases have been counterproductive (Vohs, Baumeister, & Schmeichel, 2013). My view is that these resemble the patterns found with physical fatigue. When people are only slightly tired after mild exertion, various incentives or interventions can enable them to perform as well as usual. However, extensive fatigue following prolonged, strenuous exertion is much less amenable to overcoming, and people may fail to perform effectively despite such incentives or interventions.

Here is a partial list of manipulations that have negated the effects of ego depletion (see also Chapter 12). A dose of positive emotion following the initial depleting task restored good regulatory performance (Tice, Baumeister, Shmueli, & Muraven, 2007). A cash or a social incentive for good performance elicited good performance among depleted persons (Muraven & Slessareva, 2003). Assignment to a position of power and leadership improved self-regulatory performance and made people resistant to ego depletion—though later, these leaders were all the more depleted (DeWall, Baumeister, Mead, & Vohs, 2011). Persuading people that they had unlimited willpower made people immune to mild depletion (Job et al., 2010; also Chapter 11). Forming implementation intentions to guide action ("If X, I should do Y") enabled people to perform well despite depletion (see Chapter 3).

If self-regulation depended directly on a limited fuel supply, and a first exertion of self-control exhausted that supply, none of these procedures would succeed. However, even physical exertion does not conform to that pattern, and it is doubtful that self-regulatory exertion does either. Rather, the pattern appears to be that the natural response is to conserve energy after some has been expended, but one can overcome this conservationist impulse with motivation or other factors.

My current thinking is that only ingesting a dose of glucose truly replenishes the resource (eg, Gailliot et al., 2007). The others simply persuade people to continue expending the resource despite being depleted. The finding that severe depletion wipes out the benefits of some of those other effects suggests that the body does continue to monitor its energy use. With mild depletion, the body can be encouraged or even fooled into continuing to expend energy, but with more severe depletion, the energy deficit becomes harder to ignore, and the tendency to conserve becomes that much stronger.

STATE AND TRAIT

The strength model characterizes a person's capacity for self-regulation as a fluctuating state. There are, however, also trait aspects to self-control, in the sense that some people are habitually better than others at self-control. These differences may reflect different quantities of self-regulatory energy, different strategies for using it effectively, more effective monitoring of behaviors that one seeks to regulate, higher motivation to conform to self-regulatory standards, or other possible factors (see Chapter 20).

Currently the most widely used trait measure of self-control was the one developed by Tangney, Baumeister, and Boone (2004). Several features of this individual difference measure deserve mention. First, the authors factor analyzed the scale and came up with a set of factors that permitted the construction of subscales. But they all performed about the same and predicted the same things. The factor structure did not replicate all that strongly either. Hence, most researchers have abandoned the idea of subscales and instead use the scale to measure a single, general factor. This fits the view of self-control as a domain-general resource.

Second, the scale predicted a wide range of outcomes, including academic performance, mental health, adjustment, avoidance of problem behaviors (eg, binge eating and binge drinking), and good relationship quality. Third, the authors ran a host of statistical tests seeking quadratic or curvilinear effects—with no success. Put another way, the effects of good self-control appear to be linear, with no sign of a downturn at very high levels. There was no evidence that too much self-control had negative effects. The more self-control one has, the better.

A recent metaanalysis of the effects of trait self-control yielded one surprising finding that has changed my thinking (see de Ridder, Lensvelt-Mulders, Finkenauer, Stok, & Baumeister, 2012). Its main and rather unsurprising finding was that people with high self-control do better than those with low self-control on a broad range of outcomes (and no reversals were found, in which people with low self-control were better off). The effect sizes varied by domains, however. When the researchers coded the variables and compared effect sizes, the surprise emerged: Trait self-control had much more impact on variables classified as "automatic" than those classified as "controlled." How could self-control facilitate controlling automatic behaviors better than controllable ones?

The answer emerged after reexamining the codings. Behaviors labeled as automatic tended to be the ones involving habits. Thus, trait self-control produces better outcomes by way of habits (see also Neal, Wood, & Drolet, 2013), contrary to some stereotypes that depict self-control as functioning mainly in moments of extreme temptation and crisis. In particular, de Ridder et al. (2012) found that trait self-control had the most consistent and strongest effects on performance in work and school. This is presumably not because people use their self-control strength to pull all-nighters when faced with a deadline in the morning. Rather, they get to work on things in plenty of time so they are rarely faced with the crisis of having to work all night to meet a deadline.

Perhaps, then, the key to effective use of self-control over long periods of time is to use it to break bad habits and form good ones. If this tentative conclusion holds up, it would certainly strengthen the strength model. Habits are effective precisely because they require less energy and top–down control, so they can be regarded as strategies to conserve willpower. Conserving is of course only important insofar as a resource is limited.

Good habits can also help one avoid temptation, rather than having to resist it. Hofmann, Baumeister, Förster, and Vohs (2012) found that people with high scores on self-control had fewer problematic desires and were less likely than other people to report resisting desires.

RECENT CHALLENGES AND ADVANCES

The initial findings indicative of ego depletion in the late 1990s have led to considerable work by authors in various disciplines. Indeed, as I write this in early October 2015, Google Scholar reports that the original empirical report by Baumeister et al. (1998) has been cited 2763 times in the scientific literature, and Muraven and Baumeister (2000) has been cited 2388 times. Put another way, these numbers average out to suggest that roughly once every day, a new scientific article is published that cites one of these papers. Even the book in which these ideas were first tentatively suggested has garnered 1683 citations (Baumeister et al., 1994). Many subsequent works have used the idea to extend the field's understanding of diverse phenomena. Some have added important new aspects to the theory. And some have questioned the theory, even raising alternative accounts. Here, I briefly summarize some of these key theoretical developments. (For extended treatment, see Baumeister & Vohs, 2016.)

One highly important and insightful challenge was raised by Beedie and Lane (2012). They suggested that ego depletion effects do not reflect exhaustion of resource, insofar as glucose is the resource, because the human body has essentially unlimited stores of glucose. (Well, there are limits, but certainly nobody in a psychology experiment ever comes close to these limits.) Instead, they proposed that the effects are about allocation of the resource. The person (possibly by means of unconscious regulatory processes) decides whether to allocate energy to the current activity or not.

Allocation solves several of the problems raised above, and so I think the strength model should be revised to emphasize allocation rather than running out of fuel (see also Chapter 20). For example, the finding by Molden et al. (2012) that ego depletion's detrimental effects on performance can be eliminated by having people swish glucose in the mouth and spit it out rules out the suggestion that the new glucose replenishes the supply (because the person spit it out). It could, however, encourage allocation of the depleted resource, because the oral taste of glucose is probably a well-established cue that more resources are coming, so it is safe to abandon conservation and expend more.

Still, allocation only makes sense in the context of a limited resource. There is no need to be judicious and selective in allocating a resource that is truly unlimited. Hence, I see the allocation idea as a new version of the strength model rather than a replacement for it.

A recent and very popular theory has proposed that the idea of limited resources can be abandoned (Inzlicht & Schmeichel, 2012; Inzlicht, Schmeichel, & Macrae, 2014; also Chapter 18). Instead, they propose that all phenomena can be explained based on changes in motivation and attention. The idea that motivational and attentional processes affect self-regulation seems quite compelling, but it is fully compatible with a limited resource model. Indeed, the reason that one would be motivated to withdraw effort from self-regulation is presumably that one has already expended some resources and wants to conserve what remains. Without that assumption, the idea that exerting self-control leads to a motivation to not exert self-control (the central point of the motivation theory) loses much of its plausibility. In a sense, the motivation theory becomes a variant on the perennial idea that too much self-control is bad, so that after exerting self-control, it is adaptive to exert less self-control.

The motivation theory has multiple other problems and drawbacks. Empirically, it suffers from a sweeping lack of support. There are multiple studies that have measured motivation to perform well on the second task, and they generally find no sign that depletion reduces that motivation (eg, Boucher & Kofos, 2012; Clarkson, Hirt, Jia, & Alexander, 2010; Muraven, Rosman, & Gagné, 2007; see also Chapter 10). Even if changes were found, they would hardly contradict the strength model, because changes in motivation could be spurred by resource depletion. But changes in motivation are essential to any theory that emphasizes motivation change as the central factor in ego depletion effects. The rising tide of contrary evidence is thus a serious problem for that theory.

Apart from the problem of contrary evidence, the motivation theory would also need to stretch and accommodate in multiple ways before it could even hope to serve as a viable replacement for resource depletion. It would have to account for the beneficial effects of glucose ingestion and the longitudinal improvement of self-regulation by regular exercise. The attempt to paint depletion effects as adaptive motivational shifts would likewise have to explain in what sense it is adaptive for depleted people to perpetrate violence against romantic partners, to allow anxiety to impair test-taking performance, to refuse to help others, and the like. More generally, why do depletion effects carry over from one task to a different one? Inzlicht and Schmeichel (2012) propose that exerting self-control can be overdone, so that it is adaptive to shift away to do something else. Perhaps, but why should having exerted self-control on one task make it beneficial to withhold regulatory effort on a different task?

The most recent and, in my view, most profound revision of the strength model was recently put forward by Evans, Boggero, and Segerstrom (2015), based on Noakes' (1997) central governor theory. As I have frequently (but only informally) done, these authors look to physical fatigue as a helpful model to understand self-regulatory fatigue. It seems simple to propose that muscles get tired and when tired do not perform as well, but evidence has not backed up that simple model. Muscles show fatigue and impaired performance long before there is any discernible physiological change that genuinely impairs the muscle's ability to function. Noakes proposed that there is a central governor that creates feelings of fatigue that are at most very loosely tied to the body's and muscles' physiological status. Yes, physical exertion does consume energy. But the muscles feel tired before the body runs out of energy and before the muscle is incapacitated (for example, by a build-up of lactic acid).

By analogy, then, a central governor may keep track of self-regulatory exertion and start to curtail further self-control after a period. Again, it is true that energy is consumed, but the feelings of fatigue and the behavioral effects of ego depletion are largely independent of the actual state of the body's energy stores.

One possible explanation for the loose link is that it is not easy for the central governor to keep abreast of the current state of all energy stores. Instead, it may attend to the by-products of exertion, so that it simply knows how much energy it has recently expended. Adenosine, for example, has been proposed as an internal cue. Adenosine is a by-product of glucose metabolism. To put it metaphorically, instead of surveying how much willpower fuel is left, the body simply notes how much ashes there are and estimates whether it can afford to continue burning fuel at that rate. If something is important, or if it is confident that more fuel is coming, it is willing to burn more, but then it sees even more ashes and becomes increasingly inclined to conserve.

CONCLUSION

The self-regulatory strength model has attracted considerable interest. Right from the start, the notion of incorporating energy into psychological theory has encountered resistance, and many still resist it. Yet efforts to dispense with energy have not in my view been successful (see Baumeister & Vohs, 2016). To be sure, efforts to find a simple and clear process of energy consumption and equate it with the behavioral manifestations of ego depletion have also fallen far short of success. There is yet much to be learned. At present, the central governor idea by Evans et al. (2015) seems a promising way forward, because it both allows that energy is actually consumed but explains why actual energy consumption is not very closely linked to behavioral and other psychological effects. In effect, it says the human mind, body, and brain act as if they operate on a limited energy supply, which they seek to conserve and use judiciously.

I strongly suspect that there will be more advances and refinements to the field's understanding of self-regulation. The self is more than a cognitive structure. It consists in part of energy dynamics. Self-regulation is vital for an effective, functioning self, and at present the best guess is that self-regulation operates as if it depends on a limited supply of strength or energy, akin to the folk notion of willpower. And probably it does really depend on a limited energy supply—even if the processes that govern willpower conservation and ego depletion are only indirectly guessing at what remains of the self's energy supplies.

References

Baumeister, R. F., & Vohs, K. D. (2016). Strength model of self-regulation as limited resource: assessment, controversies, update. In J. Olson, & M. Zanna (Eds.). J. Olson, & M. Zanna (Eds.), *Advances in experimental social psychology: (vol. 54)*. (pp. 67–127). Elsevier; Oxford, UK.

Baumeister, R. F., Heatherton, R. F., & Tice, D. M. (1994). *Losing control: How and why people fail at self-regulation*. San Diego, CA: Academic Press.

Baumeister, R. F., Bratslavsky, E., Muraven, M., & Tice, D. M. (1998). Ego depletion: is the active self a limited resource? *Journal of Personality and Social Psychology, 74*, 1252–1265. http://dx.doi.org/10.1037/0022-3514.74.5.1252.

Baumeister, R. F., Gailliot, M., DeWall, C. N., & Oaten, M. (2006). Self-regulation and personality: how interventions increase regulatory success, and how depletion moderates the effects of traits on behavior. *Journal of Personality, 74*, 1773–1801. http://dx.doi.org/10.1111/j.1467-6494.2006.00428.x.

Beedie, C. J., & Lane, A. M. (2012). The role of glucose in self-control: another look at the evidence and an alternative conceptualization. *Personality and Social Psychology Review, 16*, 143–153. http://dx.doi.org/10.1177/1088868311419817.

Bertrams, A., Englert, C., Dickhäuser, O., & Baumeister, R. F. (2013). Role of self-control strength in the relation between anxiety and cognitive performance. *Emotion, 13*, 668–680. http://dx.doi.org/10.1037/a0031921.

Boucher, H. C., & Kofos, M. N. (2012). The idea of money counteracts ego depletion effects. *Journal of Experimental Social Psychology, 48*, 804–810. http://dx.doi.org/10.1016/j.jesp.2012.02.003.

Carter, E. C., Kofler, L. M., Forster, D. E., & McCullough, M. E. (2015). A series of meta-analytic tests of the depletion effect: self-control does not seem to rely on a limited resource. *Journal of Experimental Psychology: General*. http://dx.doi.org/10.1037/xge0000083 advance online publication.

Carver, C. S., & Scheier, M. (1981). *Attention and self-regulation: A control-theory approach to human behavior*. New York, NY: Springer-Verlag.

Carver, C. S., & Scheier, M. (1982). Control theory: a useful conceptual framework for personality – social, clinical, and health psychology. *Psychological Bulletin, 92*, 111–135. http://dx.doi.org/10.1037/0033-2909.92.1.111.

Clarkson, J. J., Hirt, E. R., Jia, L., & Alexander, M. B. (2010). When perception is more than reality: the effects of perceived versus actual resource depletion on self-regulatory behavior. *Journal of Personality and Social Psychology, 98*, 29–46. http://dx.doi.org/10.1037/a0017539.

DeWall, C. N., Baumeister, R. F., Stillman, T. F., & Gailliot, M. T. (2007). Violence restrained: effects of self-regulation and its depletion on aggression. *Journal of Experimental Social Psychology, 43*, 62–76. http://dx.doi.org/10.1016/j.jesp.2005.12.005.

DeWall, C. N., Baumeister, R. F., Mead, N. L., & Vohs, K. D. (2011). How leaders self-regulate their task performance: evidence that power promotes diligence, depletion, and disdain. *Journal of Personality and Social Psychology, 100*, 47–65. http://dx.doi.org/10.1037/a0020932.

Duckworth, A. L., & Seligman, M. E. P. (2005). Self-discipline outdoes IQ in predicting academic performance of adolescents. *Psychological Science, 16*, 939–944.

Evans, D. R., Boggero, I. A., & Segerstrom, S. C. (2015). The nature of self-regulatory fatigue and "ego depletion": lessons from physical fatigue. *Personality and Social Psychology Review*. http://dx.doi.org/10.1177/1088868315597841 advance online publication.

Finkel, E. J., DeWall, C. N., Slotter, E. B., Oaten, M., & Foshee, V. A. (2009). Self-regulatory failure and intimate partner violence perpetration. *Journal of Personality and Social Psychology, 97*, 483–499. http://dx.doi.org/10.1037/a0015433.

Gailliot, M. T., & Baumeister, R. F. (2007a). The physiology of willpower: linking blood glucose to self-control. *Personality and Social Psychology Review, 11*, 303–327. http://dx.doi.org/10.1177/1088868307303030.

Gailliot, M. T., & Baumeister, R. F. (2007b). Self-regulation and sexual restraint: dispositionally and temporarily poor self-regulatory abilities contribute to failures at restraining sexual behavior. *Personality & Social Psychology Bulletin, 33,* 173–186. http://dx.doi.org/10.1177/0146167206293472.

Gailliot, M. T., Baumeister, R. F., DeWall, C. N., Maner, J. K., Plant, E. A., Tice, D. M., ... & Schmeichel, B. J. (2007). Self-control relies on glucose as a limited energy source: willpower is more than a metaphor. *Journal of Personality and Social Psychology, 92,* 325–336. http://dx.doi.org/10.1037/0022-3514.92.2.325.

Hagger, M. S., Wood, C., Stiff, C., & Chatzisarantis, N. L. (2010). Ego depletion and the strength model of self-control: a meta-analysis. *Psychological Bulletin, 136,* 495–525. http://dx.doi.org/10.1037/a0019486.

Hagger, M. S., Leaver, E., Esser, K., Leung, C., Pas, N. T., Keatley, D. A., ... & Chatzisarantis, N. L. (2013). Cue-induced smoking urges deplete cigarette smokers' self-control resources. *Annals of Behavioral Medicine, 46,* 394–400.

Hofmann, W., Rauch, W., & Gawronski, B. (2007). And deplete us not into temptation: automatic attitudes, dietary restraint, and self-regulatory resources as determinants of eating behavior. *Journal of Experimental Social Psychology, 43,* 497–504. http://dx.doi.org/10.1016/j.jesp.2006.05.004.

Hofmann, W., Baumeister, R. F., Förster, G., & Vohs, K. D. (2012). Everyday temptations: an experience sampling study of desire, conflict, and self-control. *Journal of Personality and Social Psychology, 102,* 1318–1335. http://dx.doi.org/10.1037/a0026545.

Inzlicht, M., & Schmeichel, B. J. (2012). What is ego depletion? Toward a mechanistic revision of the resource model of self-control. *Perspectives on Psychological Science, 7,* 450–463. http://dx.doi.org/10.1177/1745691612454134.

Inzlicht, M., Schmeichel, B. J., & Macrae, C. N. (2014). Why self-control seems (but may not be) limited. *Trends in Cognitive Sciences, 18,* 127–133. http://dx.doi.org/10.1016/j.tics.2013.12.009.

Job, V., Dweck, C. S., & Walton, G. M. (2010). Ego depletion—Is it all in your head? Implicit theories about willpower affect self-regulation. *Psychological Science, 21,* 1686–1693. http://dx.doi.org/10.1177/0956797610384745.

Molden, D. C., Hui, C. M., Scholer, A. A., Meier, B. P., Noreen, E. E., D'Agostine, P. R., & Martin, V. (2012). Motivational versus metabolic effects of carbohydrates on self-control. *Psychological Science, 23,* 1137–1144. http://dx.doi.org/10.1177/0956797612439069.

Muraven, M., & Baumeister, R. F. (2000). Self-regulation and depletion of limited resources: does self-control resemble a muscle? *Psychological Bulletin, 126,* 247–259. http://dx.doi.org/10.1037//0033-2909.126.2.247.

Muraven, M., & Slessareva, E. (2003). Mechanisms of self-control failure: motivation and limited resources. *Personality & Social Psychology Bulletin, 29,* 894–906. http://dx.doi.org/10.1177/0146167203029007008.

Muraven, M., Tice, D. M., & Baumeister, R. F. (1998). Self-control as a limited resource: regulatory depletion patterns. *Journal of Personality and Social Psychology, 74,* 774–789. http://dx.doi.org/10.1037/0022-3514.74.3.774.

Muraven, M., Baumeister, R. F., & Tice, D. M. (1999). Longitudinal improvement of self-regulation through practice: building self-control strength through repeated exercise. *The Journal of Social Psychology, 139,* 446–457. http://dx.doi.org/10.1037/0022-3514.74.3.774.

Muraven, M., Collins, R. L., & Neinhaus, K. (2002). Self-control and alcohol restraint: an initial application of the self-control strength model. *Psychology of Addictive Behaviors, 16,* 113–120. http://dx.doi.org/10.1037/0893-164X.16.2.113.

Muraven, M., Shmueli, D., & Burkley, E. (2006). Conserving self-control strength. *Journal of Personality and Social Psychology, 91,* 524–537. http://dx.doi.org/10.1037/0022-3514.91.3.524.

Muraven, M., Rosman, H., & Gagné, M. (2007). Lack of autonomy and self-control: performance contingent rewards lead to greater depletion. *Motivation and Emotion, 31,* 322–330. http://dx.doi.org/10.1007/s11031-007-9073-x.

Muraven, M. (2010). Practicing self-control lowers the risk of smoking lapse. *Psychology of Addictive Behaviors, 24*, 446–452. http://dx.doi.org/10.1037/a0018545.

Neal, D. T., Wood, W., & Drolet, A. (2013). How do people adhere to goals when willpower is low? the profits (and pitfalls) of strong habits. *Journal of Personality and Social Psychology, 104*, 959–975. http://dx.doi.org/10.1037/a0032626.

Noakes, T. D. (1997). Challenging beliefs: ex Africa semper aliquid novi. *Medicine and Science in Sports and Exercise, 29*, 571–590.

Pocheptsova, A., Amir, O., Dhar, R., & Baumeister, R. F. (2009). Deciding without resources: resource depletion and choice in context. *Journal of Marketing Research, 46*, 344–355. http://dx.doi.org/10.1509/jmkr.46.3.344.

de Ridder, D., Lensvelt-Mulders, G., Finkenauer, C., Stok, F. M., & Baumeister, R. F. (2012). A meta-analysis of how trait self-control relates to a wide range of behaviors. *Personality and Social Psychology Review, 16*, 76–99. http://dx.doi.org/10.1177/1088868311418749.

Schmeichel, B. J., Vohs, K. D., & Baumeister, R. F. (2003). Intellectual performance and ego depletion: role of the self in logical reasoning and other information processing. *Journal of Personality and Social Psychology, 85*, 33–46. http://dx.doi.org/10.1037/0022-3514.85.1.33.

Shmueli, D., & Prochaska, J. J. (2012). A test of positive affect induction for countering self-control depletion in cigarette smokers. *Psychology of Addictive Behaviors, 26*, 157–161. http://dx.doi.org/10.1037/a0023706.

Tangney, J. P., Baumeister, R. F., & Boone, A. L. (2004). High self-control predicts good adjustment, less pathology, better grades, and interpersonal success. *Journal of Personality, 72*, 271–324. http://dx.doi.org/10.1111/j.0022-3506.2004.00263.x.

Tice, D. M., Baumeister, R. F., Shmueli, D., & Muraven, M. (2007). Restoring the self: positive affect helps improve self-regulation following ego depletion. *Journal of Experimental Social Psychology, 43*, 379–384. http://dx.doi.org/10.1016/j.jesp.2006.05.007.

Vohs, K. D., & Baumeister, R. F. (2003). *Unpublished findings on ego depletion and romantic relationships*. University of Minnesota.

Vohs, K. D., Baumeister, R. F., Ramanthan, S., Mead, N. L., Schmeichel, B. J., & Hofmann, W. (2014). *Depletion enhances urges and feelings* (Unpublished manuscript). Minneapolis, MN: University of Minnesota.

Vohs, K. D., Baumeister, R. F., & Schmeichel, B. J. (2013). Motivation, personal beliefs, and limited resources all contribute to self-control. *Journal of Experimental Social Psychology, 49*, 184–188. http://dx.doi.org/10.1016/j.jesp.2012.08.007.

Vohs, K. D., Baumeister, R. F., Schmeichel, B. J., Twenge, J. M., Nelson, N. M., & Tice, D. M. (2008). Making choices impairs subsequent self-control: a limited resource account of decision making, self-regulation, and active initiative. *Journal of Personality and Social Psychology, 94*, 883–898. http://dx.doi.org/10.1037/0022-3514.94.5.883.

Vohs, K. D., Baumeister, R. F., Vonasch, A., Pocheptsova, A., & Dhar, R. (2014). *Self-control resource depletion impairs active initiative and thus produces passivity* (Unpublished manuscript). Minneapolis, MN: University of Minnesota.

Vohs, K. D., & Faber, R. J. (2007). Spent resources: self-regulatory resource availability affects impulse buying. *Journal of Consumer Research, 33*, 537–547. http://dx.doi.org/10.1086/510228.

Vohs, K. D., Finkenauer, C., & Baumeister, R. F. (2011). The sum of friends' and lovers' self-control scores predicts relationship quality. *Social Psychological and Personality Science, 2*, 138–145. http://dx.doi.org/10.1177/1948550610385710.

Vohs, K. D., & Heatherton, T. F. (2000). Self-regulatory failure: a resource-depletion approach. *Psychological Science, 11*, 249–254. http://dx.doi.org/10.1111/1467-9280.00250.

SECTION 1

MODERATORS OF EGO CONTROL

CHAPTER 2

Moderators of the Ego Depletion Effect

D.D. Loschelder*[1], M. Friese*[2]
[1]Leuphana University Lüneburg, Germany; [2]Saarland University, Saarbrücken, Germany

A plethora of studies shows that exerting self-control can lead to impairments in subsequent attempts at self-control. For example, controlling thoughts or emotions (Muraven, Tice, & Baumeister, 1998), solving arithmetic problems (Schmeichel, 2007), or resisting temptations (Baumeister, Bratslavsky, Muraven, & Tice, 1998) was followed by increased intake of unhealthy food and alcohol (Otten et al., 2014; Vohs & Heatherton, 2000), less control of sexual impulses (Gailliot & Baumeister, 2007), and more aggressive behavior (Stucke & Baumeister, 2006; see Carter, Kofler, Forster, & McCullough, 2015; Hagger, Wood, Stiff, & Chatzisarantis, 2010; for metaanalyses). This state of impaired self-control performance is commonly labeled as *ego depletion* (see Chapter 1).

Although the ego depletion effect has been demonstrated numerous times and in various domains, there is considerable debate about the underlying psychological mechanism(s). The *strength model of self-control* posits that any exertion of self-control draws on a limited and domain-independent resource (Baumeister, 2014; Muraven & Baumeister, 2000). Engaging in self-control partially depletes this resource and impairs performance in subsequent self-control attempts. The *process model of self-control* (Inzlicht & Schmeichel, 2012; Inzlicht, Schmeichel, & Macrae, 2014; see also, Chapter 18) postulates that engaging in a demanding task reduces the motivation to exert further control and directs attention away from

---

*D. D. Loschelder and M. Friese contributed equally to this chapter. Preparation of this chapter was supported by a grant from the Swiss National Science Foundation to Malte Friese and Björn Rasch (138630) and a grant from the German Research Foundation to Malte Friese, David Loschelder, and Veronika Job (FR 3605/2-1).

cues associated with control toward gratifying cues related to, for example, palatable food, sex, or leisure.

In many situations, the strength model and the process model make similar predictions. The bulk of the published research is therefore compatible with both models. Several studies have tested boundary conditions that counteract, buffer, or exacerbate the ego depletion effect (Masicampo, Martin, & Anderson, 2014). These moderator studies are not only interesting from an applied perspective, but may also be informative with respect to the underlying processes of ego depletion: Indeed, some of the moderation findings seem compatible with one model, but difficult to reconcile with the other. Other findings may in principle be compatible with both models, but the models would offer different interpretations for how the findings emerged. In turn, these different interpretations offer new empirically testable hypotheses that may shed further light on the mechanisms underlying ego depletion effects.

In the present chapter, we propose an organizing grid that helps to structure the quickly growing literature on moderators of the ego depletion effect. Filling this grid, we review a necessarily selected subsample of empirically demonstrated moderators. At various points, we turn to the theoretical implications that these moderator studies have with respect to the strength model and the process model of self-control.

ORGANIZING GRID: TIMING AND LEVERAGE POINT

To structure and review the literature, we propose two organizing factors of moderators—namely, *timing* and *leverage point* (see Table 2.1). The first factor pertains to the *timing* of the moderating variables. Research has investigated both moderators that are already active before the beginning of the first demanding task (experimental manipulations, trait differences). Others are only activated between the first and the second demanding task. In the latter case, it is clear that the respective moderators *counteract* the ego depletion effect (ie, alleviate the symptoms). In the former case, this is less clear. Moderators that are already active before task 1 could exert their influence in the way people work on the first, the second, or both demanding tasks. Thus, they may in principle counteract, but also *buffer* the ego depletion effect (ie, prevent the effect from arising in the first place).

The second factor of the organizing grid pertains to the *leverage point* of the moderators: Research has addressed moderating factors that relate to (1) situational state differences of a person in a given situation, (2) the first or second demanding task itself by affecting the ease or difficulty with which a task is performed, and (3) the self-controlling person in terms of interpersonal trait differences (Table 2.1).

We use this *timing* by *leverage point* organizing grid to review a nonexhaustive selection of moderators of the ego depletion effect. For each of

TABLE 2.1 Organizing Grid for Moderators of the Ego Depletion Effect in Terms of *Timing* (Moderator Active Before vs After Task 1) and *Leverage Point* (Situation, Task, and Person)

	Moderator Activated After Task 1			Moderator Active Before Task 1		
	Explanation	Examples	Exemplary Reference	Explanation	Examples	Exemplary Reference
Situation (states)	Situational factors thwart depleted resources by fostering relaxation or increasing motivation.	Construal level Mindfulness Praying Social identities Incentives	Agrawal and Wan (2009) Friese et al. (2012) Friese et al. (2014) Loschelder et al. (2016) Muraven and Slessareva (2003)	Situational factors determine how much individuals are depleted from the first of two subsequent self-control tasks.	Praying Theories about willpower	Friese and Wänke (2014) Job et al. (2010)
Task (ease)	Task factors facilitate the ease with which self-control is exerted *after* individuals are already depleted—thereby counteracting depletion.	Implementation intentions Task similarity Money priming	Webb and Sheeran (2003) Dewitte et al. (2009) Boucher and Kofos (2012)	Task factors facilitate the ease with which self-control is exerted in the first of two subsequent tasks—thereby buffering ego depletion.	Implementation intentions Autonomy	Webb and Sheeran (2003) Muraven et al. (2008)
Person (traits)	Personality trait differences cannot be experimentally manipulated between tasks			Interpersonal trait differences buffer the depletion of self-control resources.	Trait self-control Theories about willpower Action orientation Trait anxiety Age	Imhoff et al. (2014) Job et al. (2010) Gröpel et al. (2014) Bertrams, Englert, Dickhäuser, and Baumeister (2013) Dahm et al. (2011)

the resulting cells of the organizing grid, we discuss selected key moderators. Some of these received more attention in the past than others, which is partly reflected in the depth in which we discuss these moderators. To structure this review, we start with antidotes located in the situation and the task that counteract ego depletion effects. The next section discusses how factors that are already active or activated at the beginning of the studies alleviate ego depletion effects—either by buffering or counteracting ego depletion. These factors can refer to situational manipulations affecting the person, the ease with which a demanding task is performed, or interpersonal trait differences. The concluding discussion reviews how some of the moderating findings speak differentially to the underlying mechanisms that are proposed by the strength model and the process model of self-control. Avenues for future research are outlined and we review how moderation findings may allow researchers to make causal inferences about underlying processes.

MODERATORS ACTIVATED AFTER THE FIRST DEMANDING TASK

This section reviews experimental manipulations that affect the person state or the ease with which the second demanding task can be performed to counteract ego depletion effects. The verb *counteract* indicates that, in terms of the *timing* variable, these factors operate after the first demanding task and help to overcome the state of ego depletion. By definition, stable trait variables cannot be experimentally manipulated between tasks and are thus only reviewed in the second section of the chapter.

Situational Factors Affecting the Person State

The bulk of research on moderators of ego depletion effects has examined levers that reside in the situation and can thus be experimentally manipulated as state factors. The section on situational factors therefore assumes a prominent position in this chapter. However, we can review only a small selection of these moderators—namely construal level, mindfulness, prayer, social identities, and performance incentives. Due to space restrictions, we refrain from discussing other prominent moderators belonging to this cell of the organizing grid such as positive mood (Egan, Clarkson, & Hirt, 2015; Tice, Baumeister, Shmueli, & Muraven, 2007; see also Chapter 7) and increased self-awareness (Alberts, Martijn, & de Vries, 2011).

Construal level: People differ in construal level depending on whether they focus on abstract, higher-level, decontextualized aspects (high construal level) or on concrete, lower-level, specific aspects (low construal level) of an object or event (Trope & Liberman, 2010). Some researchers have argued that upon having exerted self-control, individuals focus more on low-level aspects of the situation (eg, feelings of tiredness) and less on high-level aspects (eg, personal goals). Focusing on personal goals rather than subjective feelings of tiredness arguably increases the motivation to exert further control. In line with this reasoning, assuming a high construal level after an initial demanding task counteracts the ego depletion effect (Agrawal & Wan, 2009; see also Schmeichel & Vohs, 2009). For instance, depleted participants at a low construal level were less persistent while reading about dental health and flossing their teeth (Study 1) or while reading about an unfamiliar disease (Study 2) compared to nondepleted participants. This difference, however, disappeared and at times even reversed when participants were primed with a high construal level following the first depleting task.

Mindfulness: Mindfulness refers to the nonjudgmental, accepting, and present-focused awareness of one's inner and outer experiences (Kabat-Zinn, 1990). When mindful, people experience their present bodily sensations, thoughts, and feelings clearly, without evaluating and without feeling the urge to act on these sensations. If you were to close your eyes for a moment, focus your attention entirely on your breath, on how your chest rises and falls, on how the air enters and leaves your nostrils, mouth, and lungs, and on the many sensations that breathing evokes in different parts of your body, you have briefly engaged in a prominent mindfulness exercise. Mindfulness varies both as a state within and as a trait between persons (Baer, Smith, Hopkins, Krietemeyer, & Toney, 2006; Brown, Ryan, & Creswell, 2007).

Some evidence suggests that mindfulness may help to deal with ego depletion. For instance, after a brief mindfulness intervention, people withstood the impulse to aggress against a person who socially rejected them more effectively than participants in a control condition (Heppner et al., 2008). Dealing with a social rejection is a mentally strenuous, self-control reducing task that may be functionally similar to an ego depletion manipulation (see Chapter 9, for more information about the link between self-regulation and aggression).

More direct evidence comes from a field study in which participants of a mindfulness introduction seminar were either depleted or not (Friese, Messner, & Schaffner, 2012). Depleted participants showed poorer performance on a d2 test of attention (Brickenkamp, 1981) as compared to those in a control condition. However, depleted participants who had engaged in a brief mindfulness meditation after the initial depleting task performed just as well as nondepleted participants (Friese et al., 2012).

This effect was recently conceptually replicated in a study on aggression with participants who were naïve with regard to mindfulness (Yusainy & Lawrence, 2015). In this study, participants who had exerted self-control were more aggressive (ie, delivered more intensive noise blasts in a competitive reaction time task) than participants in a nondepleted control condition. Engaging in a brief mindfulness breathing exercise after the initial self-control exertion eliminated this effect. Mindfulness also improved persistence in a handgrip task, but this occurred independently of prior self-control exertion.

Together, these studies suggest that brief mindfulness exercises can counteract ego depletion effects. However, the specific processes that help to achieve these effects are yet unknown. It is of importance for future research to investigate these processes, particularly because on a priori grounds, one could have assumed that for inexperienced meditators engaging in a mindfulness exercise would be a rather demanding task (ie, repeatedly purposefully redirecting attention), leading to more pronounced instead of reduced ego depletion (Masicampo & Baumeister, 2007).

Prayer: Around the globe, praying is a central part in many major religions—Christianity, Judaism, Islam, and Hinduism. Millions of people pray daily. Praying regularly over an extended period of time appears to strengthen self-control (Lambert, Fincham, Marks, & Stillman, 2010). Research has also examined brief personal prayer as a short-term means to counteract ego depletion. Praying evokes feelings of inner strength, rest, and relief (Bänziger, van Uden, & Janssen, 2008; Janssen, Dehart, & Dendraak, 1990) and thus appears to be a promising antidote to ego depletion. This idea was corroborated in one experimental study (Friese, Schweizer, Arnoux, Sutter, & Wänke, 2014). Participants who had exerted self-control in a first task showed lower self-control performance in a subsequent Stroop task than participants in a control condition. Praying for 5 min (as compared to free thought) counteracted this ego depletion effect (see Rounding, Lee, Jacobson, & Ji, 2012, for a similar effect of priming of religious concepts counteracting ego depletion).

In a similar vein, praying helps people to better manage anger and control aggressive impulses after a provocation (Bremner, Koole, & Bushman, 2011). Dealing with provocations is commonly associated with subsequent impulsive (aggressive) behavior (Denson, DeWall, & Finkel, 2012). To the extent that managing anger and controlling aggressive responses upon provocation requires self-control, these studies may be regarded as further examples of praying counteracting ego depletion effects.

Social identity: Whereas prior research on ego depletion and its moderators has predominantly assumed an individual-level perspective, a large body of research from other fields shows manifold benefits of salient social identities (Jetten, Haslam, & Haslam, 2012). Social identities are the individual's knowledge that "he [or she] belongs to certain social groups together with some emotional and value significance to him [or her] of this group membership" (Tajfel, 1972, p. 292).

In line with the argument that a sense of social connectedness has numerous benefits (Cruwys, Haslam, Dingle, Haslam, & Jetten, 2014; Jones & Jetten, 2011), recent research suggests that after a complicated arithmetic task (Kirschbaum, Pirke, & Hellhammer, 1993) or a strenuous stimulus detection task (Baumeister et al., 1998) activating a group membership can counteract ego depletion effects (Loschelder, Gieseler, Job, & Friese, 2016). Depleted participants who identified with an actual real-world group (ie, their academic major), or an arbitrary positive group, which they had never encountered before (a fictitious nonprofit organization), showed similar Stroop performance as a nondepleted control condition. Follow-up analyses indicated that this effect was mediated by participants' elevated sense of social connectedness with the group (eg, "I felt as a group member during the task") but not by an increase in self-reported motivation.

Performance incentives: When people are motivated by incentives to perform well on a second demanding task, they counteract ego depletion effects (Muraven & Slessareva, 2003; see also Chapter 7). For instance, participants who had suppressed their emotions while watching a funny film clip consumed less of a bitter tasting beverage. However, when they were financially incentivized to consume the beverage, this effect was eliminated. In fact, incentivized, depleted participants consumed even more than incentivized, nondepleted participants (Muraven & Slessareva, 2003).

From the perspective of the strength model, increasing the motivation to perform well on the second task should counteract ego depletion effects, but at the cost of an even greater reduction of the self-control resource. Because the resource has been partly depleted, achieving similar performance levels as nondepleted participants may be more difficult and require more effort from depleted participants. From the perspective of the process model, there are no differences between depleted and nondepleted participants except for decreased motivation and possible downstream consequences on attention processes. Therefore, incentives reestablish motivation, rebalance the relation of investment and return, and eliminate any differences between depleted and nondepleted persons.

A recent study used monetary incentives for good performance to counteract the ego depletion effect and measured Stroop task performance, self-reported motivation, and systolic blood pressure as dependent variables (Friese, Loschelder, Peyk, & Job, 2015). Systolic blood pressure is a valid and established indicator of mental effort invested into a task (Wright, 2014). As expected, monetary incentives eliminated the ego depletion effect on Stroop performance. There was no drop in self-reported motivation to perform well in the Stroop task in depleted, nonincentivized participants that would have been predicted by the process model. Instead, all incentivized participants reported a higher motivation to perform well in the Stroop task—independent from the depletion condition. The psychophysiological indicator of mental effort invested into the Stroop task (systolic blood pressure) also showed no indication of depleted, nonincentivized participants slacking off. However, incentivized depleted participants invested more effort into the task (higher blood pressure reactivity) than any other group, as if it was particularly hard for them to reach the same level of performance.

From the perspective of the process model, the increased mental effort in incentivized, depleted participants may indicate that these participants wanted the dangling reward more than any other group, because the depletion made them seek rewards more strongly. This possibility cannot be ruled out by these data.

Another study sheds light on this question (Luethi et al., 2015). The study had a similar 2 (Depletion yes/no) × 2 (Motivation regular/high) design and used functional magnetic resonance imaging (fMRI) to investigate the neural processes associated with the interplay of depletion and motivation. Results revealed an interaction effect of brain activity in the left ventrolateral prefrontal cortex (VLPFC). This area is closely implicated in inhibitory processes (Nee, Wager, & Jonides, 2007). Nonincentivized, depleted participants showed less activity in this area than nondepleted participants. Whether participants could not or were not motivated to activate this area to the same degree as nondepleted participants is impossible to say based on these data (see also Friese, Binder, Luechinger, Boesiger, & Rasch, 2013). Importantly, the left VLPFC was more strongly activated in incentivized, depleted participants than in any other group, as if they needed to activate this area more strongly to achieve similar performance levels as nondepleted participants (see the systolic blood pressure reactivity results summarized above). Again, this could in principle be due to increased reward sensitivity. The authors also analyzed activity in the nucleus accumbens, an area closely involved in reward-related processing (eg, Liu, Hairston, Schrier, & Fan, 2011). The nucleus accumbens results revealed a main effect of the motivation factor: Performing well in the Stroop task was associated with more nucleus accumbens activity in incentivized than in regularly motivated participants. However, this effect was not particularly pronounced in depleted participants, suggesting that there were no important differences in reward sensitivity between the depleted and the nondepleted group. (For an in-depth discussion of the neural bases of ego depletion, see Chapter 14.)

Interim discussion: What do the studies reviewed in this section reveal about the processes underlying ego depletion effects? Several studies suffer from the fact that it remains unknown which factors drive the moderation effect in the first place. Increased motivation, relaxation, subjective feelings of strength, and other processes may explain why certain moderators counteract ego depletion effects. This view is in principle compatible with both the strength model and the process model. The strength model speaks about a partial depletion of a self-control resource that may be counteracted in the short-term (Baumeister, 2014). From this model's perspective, the price will be an even more depleted resource, which should become visible in the long run (but this is hardly ever tested). Any factor that counteracts ego depletion effects and does not fuel the resource (whatever the resource may be) necessarily drains it further. For the process model, any factors increasing the willingness to exert further control after initial self-control attempts are reasonable moderators of the ego depletion effect and should not leave any aftereffects once motivation is reestablished at baseline levels.

Few moderator studies directly tested the process model's core premise of reduced motivation after the initial exertion of self-control (eg, Friese et al., 2015; Loschelder et al., 2016). Self-reports found no support for this assumption, but may have suffered from a lack of introspective insight (Wilson & Dunn, 2004) or biased self-presentation tendencies (Silvia & Gendolla, 2001). Systolic blood pressure, a psychophysiological indicator of mental effort invested into a task that does not rely on self-report, also found no indication of people slacking off after the first self-control task (Friese et al., 2015). The data patterns in this study and a further study using fMRI as an indicator of the neural correlates of ego depletion (Luethi et al., 2015) may be reconcilable with predictions based on the strength model. Yet, this evidence obviously remains indirect because no self-control resource has been directly measured in these studies. Clearly, more research is needed on the underlying mechanisms that account for the counteracting effects of the discussed moderators and on the implications they may have for the more general question, namely, which processes drive ego depletion.

Factors Affecting the Second Self-Control Task

Moderators reviewed in this section affect the second demanding task in the dual-task paradigm (see Table 2.1). In particular, they affect the ease with which the second task is performed.

Implementation intentions: Implementation intentions delegate control over behavior to anticipated environmental cues (Gollwitzer, 1999). Specifically, implementation intentions assume the general form of, "When situation X occurs, then I will initiate behavior Y." They thus specify the when, where, and how of behavior initiation and reduce the cognitive effort and resources necessary to foster effective self-regulation. When applied to the dual-task paradigm, implementation intentions can counteract ego depletion by increasing the ease with which self-control is exerted (Bayer, Gollwitzer, & Achtziger, 2010; Webb & Sheeran, 2003; see also Chapter 3). Participants who had exerted self-control in a first task showed impaired Stroop task performance as compared to control participants. Forming an implementation intention on how to exert self-control in the Stroop task—that is, "As soon as I see the word I will ignore its meaning (for example, by concentrating on the second letter only) and I will name the color ink it is printed in" (Webb & Sheeran, 2003)—proved to be an effective means to increase the ease of Stroop performance (and thereby to counteract ego depletion).

Task similarity: Engaging in a first demanding task from one of various domains impairs subsequent self-control performance. Some research suggests that the dissimilarity of the first and the second task can magnify the ego depletion effect. In other words, the more similar the requirements of the two self-control tasks, the less pronounced the ego depletion effect. For instance, when people inhibited their food intake in a first task, they subsequently showed *improved* self-control in the domain of food intake control, but not when solving difficult anagrams (Dewitte, Bruyneel, & Geyskens, 2009; see also Dang, Dewitte, Mao, Xiao, & Shi, 2013). It appears that people get used to the requirements they are facing, which explains why self-regulation is enhanced when the second self-control task causes similar response conflicts and thus requires similar control processes as the first task.

Money priming: Activating the concept of money by means of a sentence descrambling task alleviates ego depletion (Boucher & Kofos, 2012). Across two experiments, participants who were reminded of money performed better in a Stroop task (Study 1) and in solving difficult anagrams (Study 2) than participants who were reminded of neutral concepts. While it can be argued that implementation intentions and task similarity affect the *objective* difficulty of a task, process analyses in this latter work indicated that reminders of money reduced the *subjective* difficulty and the effort required to succeed in the second demanding task (Boucher & Kofos, 2012; Study 2).

MODERATORS ALREADY ACTIVATED BEFORE THE FIRST TASK

The majority of research on moderating factors has examined means to counteract the ego depletion effect with experimental manipulations between the first and second demanding task. These manipulations either placed a self-regulatory lever at the situation or altered the difficulty of a task, and thereby counteracted ego depletion. Less research has looked at moderators that are already active *before* the first task. Following the organizing grid depicted in Table 2.1, we next review situational factors affecting the person state, task factors, and individual trait differences.

Situational Factors Affecting the Person State

Theories about willpower: A simple and brief questionnaire can bias people to believe (in the short-term) that the ability to exert willpower is limited versus nonlimited (see Chapter 11). People adopting a limited theory about willpower believe that exerting self-control will lead to fatigue and an increased need for rest and relaxation. People with a nonlimited willpower theory believe that exerting control in one task will only make them more prepared to exert further control in subsequent tasks (Job, Dweck, & Walton, 2010; see also Martijn, Tenbult, Merckelbach, Dreezens, & de Vries, 2002; Salmon, Adriaanse, De Vet, Fennis, & De Ridder, 2014, for similar ideas). Most relevant for present purposes, people holding a limited willpower theory show the regular ego depletion effect—impaired performance in a demanding task after the initial exertion of self-control. By contrast, people holding a nonlimited willpower theory do not show the ego depletion effect—if anything, they tend to excel under demanding conditions such as after initial exertions of self-control (Job et al., 2010). How this reduced susceptibility to ego depletion in people with a nonlimited willpower theory is brought about is not yet fully clear. Recent research suggests that exerting self-control activates a rest-goal in people with a limited willpower theory, but not in people with a nonlimited willpower theory (Job, Bernecker, Miketta, & Friese, 2015). The rest-goal is acted upon in that persons with a limited willpower theory who take longer breaks between strenuous tasks, as well as favor and use rest-conducive objects more than persons with a nonlimited willpower theory. Whether or not this leads nonlimited willpower theorists to exert relatively more effort in the second task compared to rest-seeking limited willpower theorists is currently unknown.

Somewhat related to theories about willpower, people's subjective mental fatigue also moderates the depletion effect. Irrespective of the amount of control they actually exerted, individuals who perceived themselves as less (vs more) depleted showed superior self-control performance in a subsequent task (Clarkson, Hirt, Chapman, & Jia, 2011; Clarkson, Hirt, Jia, & Alexander, 2010; see also Chapter 10).

Prayer: A brief period of personal prayer not only counteracts self-control depletion, but also proactively prevents it (Friese & Wänke, 2014). Participants who prayed privately for 5 min showed subsequent Stroop task performance that was less impaired from having suppressed emotions than participants who had engaged in free thought instead of praying before the Stroop task.

Factors Affecting the First Demanding Task

The following studies have examined how a first self-control task needs to be framed and approached to foster the subjective ease with which individuals succeed at this task. The lever to buffer self-control is thus placed at the task itself rather than the self-regulating person.

Implementation intentions: In line with the work showing that implementation intentions can counteract ego depletion effects, they also buffer the emergence of depletion in the first place (Webb & Sheeran, 2003; Chapter 3). Participants who formed an implementation intention on how to perform in a first Stroop task (see previous paragraphs) showed less-impaired self-control performance. They were more persistent with unsolvable puzzles than participants who had not formed an implementation intention and did not differ from a nondepleted control group. Presumably, the implementation intentions helped to make the Stroop task objectively less demanding, because it provided a strategy on how to circumvent the typical Stroop interference. In line with this, participants provided with implementation intentions reported less fatigue after the Stroop task compared to control participants.

Autonomy: Higher autonomy during a first demanding task prevents the depletion effect from unfolding and leads to improved performance in a subsequent task relative to control groups. This effect was found for dependent variables such as problem-solving (Moller, Deci, & Ryan, 2006), tennis serve accuracy (Englert & Bertrams, 2015), or concentration tasks (Muraven, Gagne, & Rosman, 2008; for an overview, see Chapter 4). Process analyses suggest that these benefits of exerting self-control autonomously in a first task can be traced back to higher perceived self-determination (Moller et al., 2006) and increased feelings of vitality (Muraven et al., 2008). In sum, this research suggests that means which make the exertion of self-control during a first task subjectively easier alleviate the ego depletion effect.

Interpersonal Trait Differences

Several interpersonal trait variables have been shown to moderate the ego depletion effect. The two trait differences that have likely received the most attention are subjective theories about willpower (Job et al., 2010) and trait self-control (Tangney, Baumeister, & Boone, 2004). In addition to these, we also briefly discuss the moderating impact of action orientation (Kuhl, 2008).

Theories about willpower: Subjective theories about willpower have already been discussed in the section relating to situational factors affecting the person state. Importantly, theories about willpower also vary as a stable interpersonal trait between persons. These trait differences in willpower beliefs have profound implications for self-regulation both in laboratory dual-task paradigms and in the real world (see Chapter 11). Most central for present purposes, people believing that the ability to exert willpower is limited are more likely to show the ego depletion effect than people who believe their willpower is nonlimited (Job et al., 2010). In these people, an initial exertion of self-control activates a rest-goal that also translates into more resting behavior as compared to people holding a nonlimited willpower theory (Job, Bernecker, Miketta, & Friese, 2015).

Trait self-control: Trait self-control can be defined "as the capacity to alter or override dominant response tendencies and to regulate behavior, thoughts, and emotions" (de Ridder, Lensvelt-Mulders, Finkenauer, Stok, & Baumeister, 2012, p. 77). Individual differences in trait self-control relate positively to a range of desirable outcomes (eg, academic achievement, stable social relationships, good health) and negatively to a range of undesired outcomes (eg, financial problems, aggression, crime, Moffitt et al., 2011; de Ridder et al., 2012).

Different hypotheses can be brought forward with regard to a potential moderating role of trait self-control. On one hand, one may suspect that high trait self-control persons have abundant self-control capacity and a positive history of controlling themselves, making them more immune to self-control failures after brief initial exertions of control. Indeed, some evidence is consistent with this assumption (DeWall, Baumeister, Stillman, & Gailliot, 2007; Dvorak & Simons, 2009). On the other hand, evidence suggests that high trait self-control persons actually inhibit dominant responses *less* often in daily life than low trait self-control persons, but manage to avoid many temptations in the first place (Hofmann, Baumeister, Förster, & Vohs, 2012). Due to this relative lack in inhibition training, they may even be more susceptible to ego depletion effects. Results of a different series of studies are consistent with this latter reasoning (Imhoff, Schmidt, & Gerstenberg, 2014).

Taken together, the evidence regarding the moderating role of trait self-control is inconclusive. There is some evidence that high trait self-control persons are less susceptible to the ego depletion effect. Other evidence suggests the opposite. Future research needs to investigate the reasons for these conflicting findings and delineate both theoretically and empirically the boundary conditions that predict the direction of trait self-control's moderating influence.

Action orientation: The personality characteristic of action versus state orientation reflects how people deal with demanding situations (Koole, Jostmann, & Baumann, 2012). Action-oriented people respond to increasing demands with initiative and decisiveness, whereas state-oriented people tend to remain in the situation as is and refrain from actively instigating changes to the current mental and behavioral state. Therefore, action-oriented people are more successful in flexibly allocating resources to task demands (Diefendorff, Hall, Lord, & Strean, 2000), while state-oriented people tend to remain passive. As a consequence, action-oriented people outperform state-oriented people under demanding circumstances (Koole et al., 2012).

Performing a strenuous self-control task just after having engaged in a first strenuous task is a demanding situation. Gröpel, Baumeister, and Beckmann (2014) reasoned that action-oriented people would be less likely to show ego depletion effects and found empirical evidence for this prediction in a series of three studies. Compared to state-oriented individuals, action-oriented athletes performed better in a d2 test of attention after engaging in strenuous physical exercise for 15 min (Study 1), showed better detection in light changes after 25 min of depleting vigilance tasks (Study 2), and action-oriented college students showed better Stroop performance after 20 min of a strenuous sensorimotor task (Gröpel et al., 2014; Study 3).

Interim Discussion

A number of moderators that are already active *before* the first demanding task have been investigated. These moderators comprise a smaller number as compared to those activated *after* the first task, but their number is increasing. Similar to the section on moderators that are activated after the first task, the mechanisms underlying the effects discussed in the present section are not yet fully understood in most cases. In fact, it is unclear for most moderators in this section whether they prevent depletion effects from unfolding in the first place, or whether they counteract those depletion effects after they emerged. (An exception are moderators that arguably decrease the objective difficulty of the first task, such as implementation intentions: these should buffer the effect.)

If moderators buffered ego depletion effects, one would have to show that people are more or less depleted after a first demanding task as a function of the respective moderator. If moderators counteracted ego depletion effects, one would have to show (1) that depletion after the initial task does not vary as a function of the moderator, and (2) that the moderator helps people to perform better in a subsequent second task. To this end, a valid and reliable measure of the degree of depletion would be necessary, which is currently not available.

Preliminary evidence suggests that limited and nonlimited willpower theorists experience the initial depleting task as similarly exhausting (Job et al., 2010; Study 3). This at least tentatively suggests that all people were similarly depleted, but those with a nonlimited willpower theory counteracted depletion, whereas those with a limited willpower theory did not. Future research should test whether manipulating willpower theories after the completion of the first task (but before the second) also helps to counteract ego depletion effects.

In a similar vein, there were no performance differences as a function of action orientation in the initial demanding task, nor in nondepleting contexts in the studies by Gröpel et al. (2014). The authors reasoned that action-oriented persons continued to allocate resources such as glucose or mental effort into the second task, while state-oriented individuals did so to a lesser extent but rather opted to conserve resources. This reasoning could be tested directly by measuring blood glucose levels at baseline and directly before the second task (Beedie & Lane, 2012), or by using psychophysiological indicators of invested effort into a task (eg, systolic blood pressure, Wright, 2014). (See also Chapter 20, for a theoretical model in which effort allocation plays a central role.)

Together, the findings discussed in this section tentatively suggest that at least some of the moderators exert their influence by how people approach the second task rather than by how they approach the first task. These moderators would thus qualify as counteracting rather than buffering the ego depletion effect. The question of leverage point needs to be addressed, however, for each of the discussed (and further) moderators separately (eg, age, Dahm et al., 2011; or trait anxiety, Bertrams, Englert, & Dickhauser, 2010).

Various moderators known to counteract ego depletion effects have not yet been examined as potential moderators activated before task 1 (eg, mindfulness meditation, performance incentives, activated social identity). Such studies may provide interesting insights, given that the strength model and the process model of self-control put forth competing predictions here. For instance, performance incentives for task 1 should motivate participants to try particularly hard and thus drain a greater share of the limited resource according to the strength model. This should lead—everything else being equal—to more pronounced ego depletion effects on the second task. By contrast, the process model suggests that monetary incentives for task 1 hinder the drop of motivation (and therefore the ego depletion effect), because (financial) compensation for invested effort during task 1 prevents the perception of an imbalance between leisure and labor (Inzlicht & Schmeichel, 2012).

GENERAL DISCUSSION

From the plethora of research on moderators of the ego depletion effect, we have reviewed a selected subset. These moderators (1) are either active before the start of the first demanding task or are experimentally activated after the first demanding task (ie, the timing differs), and (2) exert their moderating influence through (experimentally created) differences in the person state, the subjective or objective difficulty of the (first or second) self-control task, or through interpersonal trait differences (ie, different leverage points; see Table 2.1).

What can we learn from these moderator studies with respect to the processes underlying the ego depletion effect? Spencer and colleagues

(Spencer, Zanna, & Fong, 2005; see also Sigall & Mills, 1998) convincingly argued that to illuminate a process, it is not always necessary to measure it and statistically test for its mediating role in a traditional mediation analysis (Baron & Kenny, 1986; Preacher & Hayes, 2004). In fact, these *measurement-of-mediation* designs remain correlational and thus do not provide unequivocal causal evidence for a central role of the mediator. Instead, the authors suggest different study designs to investigate a proposed underlying process—depending on whether or not the process is easy versus difficult to measure and easy versus difficult to manipulate. Only when measuring the process is easy and manipulating it is difficult does measurement-of-mediation qualify as the most adequate option. When both measuring and manipulating the process is feasible, Spencer et al. (2005) suggest an *experimental-causal-chain* design. Given an effect (eg, exerting self-control leads to subsequent self-control impairment), this implies showing, first, that manipulating the independent variable (eg, amount of self-control needed on the first task) leads to changes on the process variable [eg, availability of a resource (strength model) or motivation to exert control (process model)]. In a next step, the process variable (resource or motivation) is experimentally manipulated and causes changes on the dependent variable (eg, self-control performance). This experimental-causal-chain design delivers reasonable evidence that the proposed process indeed underlies the effect under investigation.

Now, with respect to the process proposed by the strength model—reduction of a limited resource—this design is difficult to implement, because there is no established way of either directly measuring or manipulating the self-control resource. Hence, it is difficult, if not impossible, to come up with convincing evidence for the proposed process at all (Spencer et al., 2005). From the perspective of the strength model, this reasoning underlines the importance of developing a better understanding of the limited resource, so that it will become possible to directly measure and/or manipulate it to provide direct causal evidence.

On the conceptual level, the previous reasoning points to an asymmetry with respect to the falsifiability of the strength model and the process model, respectively. It appears impossible to directly test the strength model's central assumption about the self-control resource as long as this resource remains unspecified in its nature. Evidence in support of the strength model has to remain indirect ("If a resource existed, the expected pattern of results would have to look like this").

By contrast, it is possible to both measure and manipulate motivation—the central mechanism proposed by the process model. However, attempts at showing reductions in motivation after the initial exertion of self-control were largely unsupportive (eg, Boucher & Kofos, 2012; Loschelder et al., 2016). Mental effort invested into a task—a more indirect indicator than self-reported motivation—also showed no effect of people slacking off after self-control exertion (Friese et al., 2015). Maybe it is not so easy to measure motivation after all. In any case, future research should strive to realize experimental-causal-chain designs to test process assumptions underlying the ego depletion effect.

The third form of mediation analysis proposed by Spencer et al. (2005) is called a *moderation-of-process* design. This approach lends itself when manipulating a proposed process is easy, but measuring it is difficult. In a moderation-of-process design, a proposed mediator is experimentally manipulated together with the independent variable, leading to result patterns that show an interaction (moderation) effect. For instance, this approach has been applied in the studies that directly manipulated the motivation to exert control—the central mediating variable according to the process model—by promising rewards for good performance (Friese et al., 2015; Luethi et al., 2015; Muraven & Slessareva, 2003). In these studies, increasing motivation through incentives counteracted the ego depletion effect. Note, however, that a moderation-of-process design does not provide unequivocal evidence for a mediating process. First, if increasing factor A counteracts ego depletion effects, this does not necessarily mean that a shortage of factor A was the cause of the depletion effect in the first place. For example, increasing blood glucose counteracts ego depletion effects (Gailliot et al., 2007), but there is by now consensus that a shortage of blood glucose is not the central mediator underlying ego depletion effects (see also Chapter 1). Similarly, when performance incentives eliminate depletion, this suggests that motivation plays an important role in ego depletion (Baumeister & Vohs, 2007), but is not conclusive evidence that a lack of motivation is the sole causal factor leading to ego depletion in the first place. Second, although psychological experiments in principle allow for causal conclusions, it is not always easy to ensure that what is manipulated is indeed the intended construct and this intended construct only (Roethlisberger & Dickson, 1939).

Although many moderator effects of the ego depletion effect have been established in the literature, it often remains unclear which psychological processes were tapped and then causally led to the obtained effect. Thus, we do not know the processes underlying most of the moderator effects discussed in this chapter and beyond (eg, Masicampo et al., 2014; but see Chapter 12, for recent evidence on this issue). The informative value of these studies with respect to processes underlying ego depletion more generally is therefore quite limited in many cases. Several studies are compatible with the assumption that the experimental manipulations affected people's motivation to exert effort—but this remains a tentative conclusion. Many findings are in principle compatible with both the strength model and the process model. For instance, whether performance incentives lead participants to mobilize remaining resources (strength model) or instead reestablish motivation to baseline levels (process models) is difficult to say. To be fair, most of these moderation studies did not seek to test specific and competing predictions of the strength and the process models or other theoretical accounts. Nevertheless, it would be desirable to learn more from future moderation research about the vexing question of which processes account for ego depletion.

CONCLUDING THOUGHTS

Numerous factors moderate the ego depletion effect. In the present chapter, we have attempted to structure this plethora of research with an organizing grid that differentiates the *timing* (moderator active before vs after the first task) and the *leverage point* (situational state, difficulty of tasks, trait differences) of these moderators. Ego depletion is easily counteracted or buffered by a multitude of different factors. For many if not most of these moderators, the effect is established but underlying mechanisms remain unknown. With respect to the ego depletion effect more generally, these studies provide some, yet admittedly limited, evidence. Conclusive evidence for the strength model seems impossible to obtain because the nature of the proposed self-control resource to date remains unspecified. Direct tests of the process model's assumptions are currently rare, and the evidence has been mixed. Clearly, more research is needed to understand the mechanisms that account for the impairment and restoration of self-control. As is amply evident in this book, a new wave of self-control models are about to enter the stage that will further elucidate processes underlying ego depletion and other phenomena in self-control research (eg, see Chapters 13, 16, 19 and 20). When testing these models, researchers will be careful to provide more direct process evidence. We are convinced they will do so not solely, but certainly also, by relying on moderator studies.

References

Agrawal, N., & Wan, E. W. (2009). Regulating risk or risking regulation? Construal levels and depletion effects in the processing of health messages. *Journal of Consumer Research*, 36, 448–462.

Alberts, H. J. E.M., Martijn, C., & de Vries, N. K. (2011). Fighting self-control failure: overcoming ego depletion by increasing self-awareness. *Journal of Experimental Social Psychology*, 47, 58–62.

Baer, R. A., Smith, G. T., Hopkins, J., Krietemeyer, J., & Toney, L. (2006). Using self-report assessment methods to explore facets of mindfulness. *Assessment*, 13, 27–45.

Bänziger, S., van Uden, M., & Janssen, J. (2008). Praying and coping: the relation between varieties of praying and religious coping styles. *Mental Health, Religion & Culture*, 11, 101–118.

REFERENCES

Baron, R. M., & Kenny, D. A. (1986). The moderator-mediator variable distinction in social psychological research: conceptual, strategic, and statistical considerations. *Journal of Personality and Social Psychology, 51*, 1173–1182.

Baumeister, R. F. (2014). Self-regulation, ego depletion, and inhibition. *Neuropsychologia, 65*, 313–319.

Baumeister, R. F., Bratslavsky, M., Muraven, M., & Tice, D. M. (1998). Ego depletion: Is the active self a limited resource? *Journal of Personality and Social Psychology, 74*, 1252–1265.

Baumeister, R. F., & Vohs, K. D. (2007). Self-regulation, ego depletion, and motivation. *Social and Personality Psychology Compass, 1*, 115–128.

Bayer, U. C., Gollwitzer, P. M., & Achtziger, A. (2010). Staying on track: planned goal striving is protected from disruptive internal states. *Journal of Experimental Social Psychology, 46*, 505–514.

Beedie, C. J., & Lane, A. M. (2012). The role of glucose in self-control: another look at the evidence and an alternative conceptualization. *Personality and Social Psychology Review, 16*, 143–153.

Bertrams, A., Englert, C., & Dickhauser, O. (2010). Self-control strength in the relation between trait test anxiety and state anxiety. *Journal of Research in Personality, 44*, 738–741.

Bertrams, A., Englert, C., Dickhäuser, O., & Baumeister, R. F. (2013). Role of Self-Control Strength in the Relation Between Anxiety and Cognitive Performance. *Emotion, 13*, 668–680. http://dx.doi.org/10.1037/a0031921.

Boucher, H. C., & Kofos, M. N. (2012). The idea of money counteracts ego depletion effects. *Journal of Experimental Social Psychology, 48*, 804–810.

Bremner, R. H., Koole, S. L., & Bushman, B. J. (2011). "Pray for those who mistreat you": effects of prayer on anger and aggression. *Personality & Social Psychology Bulletin, 37*, 830–837.

Brickenkamp, R. (1981). *Test d2: Aufmerksamkeits-Belastungs-Test [D2 Test of Attention]* (7th ed.). Göttingen: Hogrefe.

Brown, K. W., Ryan, R. A., & Creswell, J. D. (2007). Mindfulness: theoretical foundations and evidence for its salutary effects. *Psychological Inquiry, 18*, 211–237.

Carter, E. C., Kofler, L. M., Forster, D. E., & McCullough, M. E. (2015). A series of meta-analytic tests of the depletion effect: self-control does not seem to rely on a limited resource. *Journal of Experimental Psychology-General, 144*, 796–815.

Clarkson, J. J., Hirt, E. R., Chapman, D. A., & Jia, L. L. (2011). The impact of illusory fatigue on executive control: do perceptions of depletion impair working memory capacity? *Social Psychological and Personality Science, 2*, 231–238.

Clarkson, J. J., Hirt, E. R., Jia, L., & Alexander, M. B. (2010). When perception is more than reality: the effects of perceived versus actual resource depletion on self-regulatory behavior. *Journal of Personality and Social Psychology, 98*, 29–46.

Cruwys, T., Haslam, S. A., Dingle, G. A., Haslam, C., & Jetten, J. (2014). Depression and social identity: an integrative review. *Personality and Social Psychology Review, 18*, 215–238.

Dahm, T., Neshat-Doost, H. T., Golden, A.-M., Horn, E., Hagger, M. S., & Dalgleish, T. (2011). Age shall not weary us: deleterious effects of self-regulation depletion are specific to younger adults. *PLoS One, 6*, e26351.

Dang, J. H., Dewitte, S., Mao, L. H., Xiao, S. S., & Shi, Y. C. (2013). Adapting to an initial self-regulatory task cancels the ego depletion effect. *Consciousness and Cognition, 22*, 816–821.

Denson, T. F., DeWall, C. N., & Finkel, E. J. (2012). Self-control and aggression. *Current Directions in Psychological Science, 21*, 20–25.

DeWall, C. N., Baumeister, R. F., Stillman, T. F., & Gailliot, M. T. (2007). Violence restrained: effects of self-regulation and its depletion on aggression. *Journal of Experimental Social Psychology, 43*, 62–76.

Dewitte, S., Bruyneel, S., & Geyskens, K. (2009). Self-regulating enhances self-regulation in subsequent consumer decisions involving similar response conflicts. *Journal of Consumer Research, 36*, 394–405.

Diefendorff, J. M., Hall, R. J., Lord, R. G., & Strean, M. L. (2000). Action-state orientation: construct validity of a revised measure and its relationship to work-related variables. *Journal of Applied Psychology, 85,* 250–263.

Dvorak, R. D., & Simons, J. S. (2009). Moderation of resource depletion in the self-control strength model: differing effects of two modes of self-control. *Personality & Social Psychology Bulletin, 35,* 572–583.

Egan, P. M., Clarkson, J. J., & Hirt, E. R. (2015). Revisiting the restorative effects of positive mood: an expectancy-based approach to self-control restoration. *Journal of Experimental Social Psychology, 57,* 87–99.

Englert, C., & Bertrams, A. (2015). Autonomy as a protective factor against the detrimental effects of ego depletion on tennis serve accuracy under pressure. *International Journal of Sport and Exercise Psychology, 13,* 121–131.

Friese, M., Binder, J., Luechinger, R., Boesiger, P., & Rasch, B. (2013). Suppressing emotions impairs subsequent stroop performance and reduces prefrontal brain activation. *PLoS One, 8,* e60385.

Friese, M., Loschelder, D., Peyk, P., & Job, V. (2015). *Ego depletion, motivation, and mental effort* (Unpublished data).

Friese, M., Messner, C., & Schaffner, Y. (2012). Mindfulness meditation counteracts self-control depletion. *Consciousness and Cognition, 21,* 1016–1022.

Friese, M., Schweizer, L., Arnoux, A., Sutter, F., & Wänke, M. (2014). Personal prayer counteracts self-control depletion. *Consciousness and Cognition, 29,* 90–95.

Friese, M., & Wänke, M. (2014). Personal prayer buffers self-control depletion. *Journal of Experimental Social Psychology, 51,* 56–59.

Gailliot, M. T., & Baumeister, R. F. (2007). Self-regulation and sexual restraint: dispositionally and temporarily poor self-regulatory abilities contribute to failures at restraining sexual behavior. *Personality & Social Psychology Bulletin, 33,* 173–186.

Gailliot, M. T., Baumeister, R. F., DeWall, C. N., Maner, J. K., Plant, E. A., Tice, D. M., ... Schmeichel, B. J. (2007). Self-control relies on glucose as a limited energy source: willpower is more than a metaphor. *Journal of Personality and Social Psychology, 92,* 325–336.

Gollwitzer, P. M. (1999). Implementation intentions: strong effects of simple plans. *American Psychologist, 54,* 493.

Gröpel, P., Baumeister, R. F., & Beckmann, J. (2014). Action versus state orientation and self-control performance after depletion. *Personality & Social Psychology Bulletin, 40,* 476–487.

Hagger, M. S., Wood, C., Stiff, C., & Chatzisarantis, N. L. D. (2010). Ego depletion and the strength model of self-control: a meta-analysis. *Psychological Bulletin, 136,* 495–525.

Heppner, W. L., Kernis, M. H., Lakey, C. E., Campbell, W. K., Goldman, B. M., Davis, P. J., & Cascio, E. V. (2008). Mindfulness as a means of reducing aggressive behavior: dispositional and situational evidence. *Aggressive Behavior, 34,* 486–496.

Hofmann, W., Baumeister, R. F., Förster, G., & Vohs, K. D. (2012). Everyday temptations: an experience sampling study of desire, conflict, and self-control. *Journal of Personality and Social Psychology, 102,* 1318–1335.

Imhoff, R., Schmidt, A. F., & Gerstenberg, F. (2014). Exploring the interplay of trait self-control and ego depletion: empirical evidence for ironic effects. *European Journal of Personality, 28,* 413–424.

Inzlicht, M., & Schmeichel, B. J. (2012). What is ego depletion? Toward a mechanistic revision of the resource model of self-control. *Perspectives on Psychological Science, 7,* 450–463.

Inzlicht, M., Schmeichel, B. J., & Macrae, C. N. (2014). Why self-control seems (but may not be) limited. *Trends in Cognitive Sciences, 18,* 127–133.

Janssen, J., Dehart, J., & Dendraak, C. (1990). A content-analysis of the praying practices of Dutch youth. *Journal for the Scientific Study of Religion, 29,* 99–107.

Jetten, J., Haslam, C., & Haslam, S. A. (Eds.). (2012). *The social cure: Identity, health and well-being.* New York, NY: Psychology Press.

Job, V., Bernecker, K., Miketta, S., & Friese, M. (2015). Implicit theories about willpower predict the activation of a rest goal following self-control exertion. *Journal of Personality and Social Psychology, 109,* 694–706.

Job, V., Dweck, C. S., & Walton, G. M. (2010). Ego depletion-Is it all in your head? Implicit theories about willpower affect self-regulation. *Psychological Science, 21,* 1686–1693.

Jones, J. M., & Jetten, J. (2011). Recovering from strain and enduring pain: multiple group memberships promote resilience in the face of physical challenges. *Social Psychological and Personality Science, 2,* 239–244.

Kabat-Zinn, J. (1990). *Full catastrophe living: Using the wisdom of your mind and body to face stress, pain, and illness.* New York, NY: Delacorte.

Kirschbaum, C., Pirke, K. M., & Hellhammer, D. H. (1993). The Trier Social Stress Test – a tool for investigating psychobiological stress responses in a laboratory setting. *Neuropsychobiology, 28,* 76–81.

Koole, S. L., Jostmann, N. B., & Baumann, N. (2012). Do demanding conditions help or hurt self-regulation? *Social and Personality Psychology Compass, 6,* 328–346.

Kuhl, J. (2008). Individual differences in self-regulation. In J. Heckhausen, & H. Heckhausen (Eds.), *Motivation and action* (2nd ed.) (pp. 296–322). New York, NY: Cambridge University Press.

Lambert, N. M., Fincham, F. D., Marks, L. D., & Stillman, T. F. (2010). Invocations and intoxication: does prayer decrease alcohol consumption? *Psychology of Addictive Behaviors, 24,* 209–219.

Liu, X., Hairston, J., Schrier, M., & Fan, J. (2011). Common and distinct networks underlying reward valence and processing stages: a meta-analysis of functional neuroimaging studies. *Neuroscience and Biobehavioral Reviews, 35,* 1219–1236.

Loschelder, D. D., Gieseler, K., Job, V., & Friese, M. (2016). *Identification with a group counteracts the ego depletion effect* (Unpublished manuscript).

Luethi, M., Friese, M., Binder, J., Luechinger, R., Boesiger, P., & Rasch, B. (in press). Motivational incentives lead to a strong increase in lateral prefrontal activity after self-control exertion. Social Cognitive and Affective Neuroscience. http://dx.doi.org/10.1093/scan/nsw073.

Martijn, C., Tenbult, P., Merckelbach, H., Dreezens, E., & de Vries, N. K. (2002). Getting a grip on ourselves: challenging expectancies about loss of energy after self-control. *Social Cognition, 20,* 441–460.

Masicampo, E. J., & Baumeister, R. R. (2007). Relating mindfulness and self-regulatory processes. *Psychological Inquiry, 18,* 255–258.

Masicampo, E. J., Martin, S. R., & Anderson, R. A. (2014). Understanding and overcoming self-control depletion. *Social and Personality Psychology Compass, 8,* 638–649.

Moffitt, T. E., Arseneault, L., Belsky, D., Dickson, N., Hancox, R. J., Harrington, H., ... Capsi, A. (2011). A gradient of childhood self-control predicts health, wealth, and public safety. *Proceedings of the National Academy of Sciences of the United States of America, 108,* 2693–2698.

Moller, A. C., Deci, E. L., & Ryan, R. M. (2006). Choice and ego-depletion: the moderating role of autonomy. *Personality & Social Psychology Bulletin, 32,* 1024–1036.

Muraven, M., & Baumeister, R. F. (2000). Self-regulation and depletion of limited resources: does self-control resemble a muscle? *Psychological Bulletin, 126,* 247–259.

Muraven, M., Gagne, M., & Rosman, H. (2008). Helpful self-control: autonomy support, vitality, and depletion. *Journal of Experimental Social Psychology, 44,* 573–585.

Muraven, M., & Slessareva, E. (2003). Mechanisms of self-control failure: motivation and limited resources. *Personality & Social Psychology Bulletin, 29,* 894–906.

Muraven, M., Tice, D. M., & Baumeister, R. F. (1998). Self-control as a limited resource: regulatory depletion patterns. *Journal of Personality and Social Psychology, 74,* 774–789.

Nee, D. E., Wager, T. D., & Jonides, J. (2007). Interference resolution: insights from a meta-analysis of neuroimaging tasks. *Cognitive Affective & Behavioral Neuroscience, 7,* 1–17.

Otten, R., Cladder-Micus, M. B., Pouwels, J. L., Hennig, M., Schuurmans, A. A. T., & Hermans, R. C. J. (2014). Facing temptation in the bar: counteracting the effects of self-control failure on young adults' ad libitum alcohol intake. *Addiction, 109,* 746–753.

Preacher, K. J., & Hayes, A. F. (2004). SPSS and SAS procedures for estimating indirect effects in simple mediation models. *Behavior Research and Methods, Instruments, & Computers, 36,* 717–731.

de Ridder, D. T. D., Lensvelt-Mulders, G., Finkenauer, C., Stok, F. M., & Baumeister, R. F. (2012). Taking stock of self-control: a meta-analysis of how trait self-control relates to a wide range of behaviors. *Personality and Social Psychology Review, 16,* 76–99.

Roethlisberger, F., & Dickson, W. (1939). *Management and the worker.* Cambridge: Harvard University Press.

Rounding, K., Lee, A., Jacobson, J. A., & Ji, L. J. (2012). Religion replenishes self-control. *Psychological Science, 23,* 635–642.

Salmon, S. J., Adriaanse, M. A., De Vet, E., Fennis, B. M., & De Ridder, D. T. D. (2014). When the going gets tough, who keeps going? Depletion sensitivity moderates the ego-depletion effect. *Frontiers in Psychology, 5.*

Schmeichel, B. J. (2007). Attention control, memory updating, and emotion regulation temporarily reduce the capacity for executive control. *Journal of Experimental Psychology: General, 136,* 241–255.

Schmeichel, B. J., & Vohs, K. D. (2009). Self-affirmation and self-control: affirming core values counteracts ego depletion. *Journal of Personality and Social Psychology, 96,* 770–782.

Sigall, H., & Mills, J. (1998). Measures of independent variables and mediators are useful in social psychology experiments: but are they necessary? *Personality and Social Psychology Review, 2,* 218–226.

Silvia, P. J., & Gendolla, G. H. E. (2001). On introspection and self-perception: does self-focused attention enable accurate self-knowledge? *Review of General Psychology, 5,* 241–269.

Spencer, S. J., Zanna, M. P., & Fong, G. T. (2005). Establishing a causal chain: why experiments are often more effective than mediational analyses in examining psychological processes. *Journal of Personality and Social Psychology, 89,* 845–851.

Stucke, T. S., & Baumeister, R. F. (2006). Ego depletion and aggressive behavior: is the inhibition of aggression a limited resource? *European Journal of Social Psychology, 36,* 1.

Tajfel, H. (1972). Social categorization [English manuscript of 'La catégorisation sociale']. In S. Moscovici (Ed.), *Introduction à la Psychologie Sociale* (Vol. 1), (pp. 272–302). Paris: Larousse.

Tangney, J. P., Baumeister, R. F., & Boone, A. L. (2004). High self-control predicts good adjustment, less pathology, better grades, and interpersonal success. *Journal of Personality, 72,* 271–324.

Tice, D. M., Baumeister, R. F., Shmueli, D., & Muraven, M. (2007). Restoring the self: positive affect helps improve self-regulation following ego depletion. *Journal of Experimental Social Psychology, 43,* 379–384.

Trope, Y., & Liberman, N. (2010). Construal-level theory of psychological distance. *Psychological Review, 117,* 440–463.

Vohs, K. D., & Heatherton, T. F. (2000). Self-regulatory failure: a resource-depletion approach. *Psychological Science, 11,* 249–254.

Webb, T. L., & Sheeran, P. (2003). Can implementation intentions help to overcome ego-depletion? *Journal of Experimental Social Psychology, 39,* 279–286.

Wilson, T. D., & Dunn, E. (2004). Self-knowledge: its limits, value, and potential for improvement. *Annual Review of Psychology, 55,* 493–518.

Wright, R. A. (2014). Presidential address 2013: fatigue influence on effort—considering implications for self-regulatory restraint. *Motivation and Emotion, 38,* 183–195.

Yusainy, C., & Lawrence, C. (2015). Brief mindfulness induction could reduce aggression after depletion. *Consciousness and Cognition, 33,* 125–134.

CHAPTER 3

Decoupling Goal Striving From Resource Depletion by Forming Implementation Intentions

F. Wieber[1,2], P.M. Gollwitzer[2,3]
[1]Zurich University of Applied Sciences, Winterthur, Switzerland;
[2]University of Konstanz, Konstanz, Germany; [3]New York University, New York, NY, United States

Is it a good idea to do some painful paperwork before attending a difficult meeting, to start dieting and to quit smoking at the same time, or to make important investment decisions after a strenuous day at work? One theory that offers clear-cut answers to these questions is the strength model of self-control (see Chapter 1). According to this theory, self-control is a limited resource. Exerting self-control in a first task should thus reduce the self-control that is available for a second task. In other words, exerting self-control leaves individuals in a state of ego depletion that in turn reduces the likelihood of succeeding at subsequent self-control tasks.

In the present chapter, we focus on if–then planning (ie, forming implementation intentions; IIs) as an easily applicable self-regulation tool that can help individuals and groups to overcome major threats to self-regulation such as being ego depleted. We start with a short overview of research on ego depletion, addressing the moderators of the depletion effect and recent suggestions to revise the conceptual basis of the ego-depletion theory. We then present an action control perspective on the ego-depletion phenomenon. To this end, we examine research on goal intentions and the limits of intentional action by goal intentions and introduce IIs. Next, we review studies that have directly tested II effects on ego depletion. We differentiate between studies that investigate whether IIs can be applied to avoid becoming depleted from studies that explore whether IIs are effective in helping participants to overcome the negative consequences of being depleted in subsequent self-control tasks. Because the self-regulation threat of being depleted often cooccurs with other self-regulation threats, we then expand our view to determine whether IIs can have beneficial effects not only on self-regulatory resource depletion but also the other six major threats to self-regulation that have been identified by Wagner and Heatherton (2015): impulse control and cue exposure, emotional and social distress, lapse-activated pattern and abstinence violations, impairments of self-monitoring and self-awareness, the influence of other people, and alcohol intoxication. We also review research on the regulation of detrimental self-states (such as self-definitional incompleteness) by IIs, in addition to research on ways to strengthen self-regulation by combining IIs with strategies that have also been found to reduce depletion effects (such as self-affirmation and setting autonomous goals). Finally, we discuss these findings and their implications for both the original and more recent explications of the ego-depletion phenomenon as well as for II research, and point to venues for future investigation.

THE RESOURCE MODEL OF SELF-REGULATION

In 1998, Baumeister, Bratslavsky, Muraven, and Tice suggested that active self-control can be costly in the sense that it depletes one's self-regulatory resources. The authors hypothesized that the same self-regulatory resource is used for many different tasks, including regulating thoughts, controlling emotions, inhibiting impulses, sustaining physical stamina, persisting in complex cognitive tasks, regulating self-impression, and dealing with stigmas or being the subject of prejudice. After an act of self-control, this resource becomes exhausted, and an individual experiences a state of ego-strength depletion. A metaanalysis conducted by Hagger, Wood, Stiff, and Chatzisarantis (2010) of 83 experimental studies with more than 10,500 participants observed a medium-to large-sized ego-depletion effect (Cohen, 1992) of $d^+ = 0.62$. Although the small sample sizes of many studies have been criticized (eg, Carter & McCullough, 2014) and the growing number of ways that have been discovered to reduce depletion effects (see Chapter 2; Masicampo, Martin, & Anderson, 2014) suggests that they are not as inevitable as initially thought, recent modifications of the original theory (Inzlicht & Schmeichel, 2012; Inzlicht, Schmeichel, & Macrae, 2014; Kurzban, Duckworth, Kable, & Myers, 2013) open up promising venues for future research. These approaches allow a refinement of the basic idea, the application of new methods for testing the processes underlying depletion effects in greater detail, and for developing intentional strategies to overcome depletion effects and depletion-related self-regulation failure.

SELF-REGULATION BY GOALS AND IMPLEMENTATION INTENTIONS—EFFECTS AND PROCESSES

When it comes to ways to reduce the ego-depletion effect, three strategies have been discussed. First, one can increase one's motivation to increase effort. Second, one can decrease the perceived task effort (see Chapter 4). A third option, which is the focus of the present chapter, is to counteract depletion by decreasing the actual task effort by automating the actions in the depletion task (ie, Task 1) or the subsequent task (ie, Task 2). In line with this argument, Goto and Kusumi (2013) observed that participants who engaged in reinforcement learning of habitual actions for a card selection task improved their performance in a subsequent Stroop task. Similar to these habit-formation effects, IIs should reduce the degree of self-control required to perform either the depleting task or subsequent task. However, although both strategies are assumed to automate action control, the acquisition of this automation differs. Whereas automating one's responses in self-control situations by reinforcement learning requires numerous repetitions, the II strategy is thought to be established by a single act of will (Gollwitzer, 1993).

One might argue that forming goal intentions such as "I want to attain goal X!" (eg, Ajzen, 2012) suffice to ensure successful goal attainment and that the automation of action control is not needed. However, research indicates that action control by goals mainly depend on effortful reflective processes, which are known to be slow and effortful (Strack & Deutsch, 2004) and that a substantial gap between even strong goal commitment and subsequent goal attainment exists (eg, Sheeran, 2002). For instance, a medium-to-large-sized change in goal commitment ($d=0.66$) led to only a small-to-medium-sized change ($d=0.33$) in behavior in Webb and Sheeran's (2006) metaanalysis. Thus, an alternative strategy is needed to help people to close the gap between their commitment to and their enactment of personal goals.

One effective strategy is the formation of IIs (Gollwitzer, 1999). These IIs support individuals (Gollwitzer & Sheeran, 2006) and groups (Thürmer, Wieber, & Gollwitzer, 2015a; Wieber, Thürmer, & Gollwitzer, 2012) in the translation of their intentions into action. Various metaanalyses have demonstrated that IIs have medium-to large-sized effects on healthy eating (Adriaanse, Vinkers, De Ridder, Hox, & De Wit, 2011), exercising (Bélanger-Gravel, Godin, & Amireault, 2013), prospective memory (Chen et al., 2015), and goal pursuit in individuals with mental-health problems (Toli, Webb, & Hardy, 2015). Recent research shows that they can even help individuals to change their personality attributes (Hudson & Fraley, 2015).

It has been demonstrated in various ways (Gollwitzer, 2014) that action control by IIs is fast and efficient; this makes it possible to effectively shield a focal goal pursuit from many different threats to successful self-regulation. IIs spell out the when, where, and how of goal striving in advance using the format of an if (*critical situation*)–then (*goal-directed response*) plan. For instance, if an individual has the goal of performing well on a series of tasks, she or he could form the if–then plan "And if I finish one task, then I will immediately start working on the next task!" to avoid procrastinating between the tasks. Thus, rather than simply committing to a desired end state (ie, forming a strong goal intention to finish as many tasks as possible), making an if–then plan commits the person to performing a certain goal-directed behavior (the then-part) when the specified critical situation (the if-part) is encountered.

IIs facilitate the attainment of personal goals through psychological mechanisms that pertain to the specified situation in the if-part, as well as to the mental link forged between the if-part and the specified goal-directed response in the then-part of the plan (overview by Wieber, Thürmer, & Gollwitzer, 2015b). Because forming an II entails the selection of a critical future situation, the mental representation of this situation becomes highly activated and hence more accessible. This heightened accessibility of the if-part of the plan has been observed in several studies using different cognitive task paradigms such as lexical decision and flanker tasks (eg, Aarts, Dijksterhuis, & Midden, 1999; Wieber & Sassenberg, 2006). Forming IIs not only heightens the activation (and thus the accessibility) of the mental representation of the situational cue specified in the if-component, but also forges a strong associative link between the mental representation of this cue and the mental representation of the specified response. These associative links are quite stable over time (Papies, Aarts, & de Vries, 2009) and ensure that the critical situational cues specified in the if-component will—when encountered—activate the mental representations of the responses specified in the then-component (eg, Webb & Sheeran, 2007).

As a consequence of the strong associative links between the if-part (situational cue) and the then-part (goal-directed response) created by forming IIs, the initiation of the goal-directed response exhibits features of automaticity. These features include immediacy, efficiency, and redundancy of conscious intent (Bargh, 1994). Compared to goal intentions, IIs have been found to facilitate the immediate initiation of goal-directed responses (eg, presenting counterarguments to racist comments more quickly; Gollwitzer & Brandstätter, 1997, Study 3) and to help people to deal more efficiently with cognitive demands (ie, speed-up effects are still evident under high cognitive load; eg, Brandstätter, Lengfelder, & Gollwitzer, 2001). Moreover, action control by IIs does not require a conscious intent to act in the critical moment (eg, II effects are still evident when the critical cue is presented subliminally or when the respective goal is activated outside of awareness; Bayer, Achtziger, Gollwitzer, & Moskowitz, 2009; Sheeran, Webb, & Gollwitzer, 2005). This strategic automation hypothesis (ie, in a conscious act of will, the person delegates action control to situational cues that produce fast and efficient action initiation without the need for further conscious intent) has recently received further support from brain studies on the localization and timing of action control by IIs and from studies addressing the modification of already existing automatic responses (Schweiger Gallo, Cohen, Gollwitzer, & Oettingen, 2013; Wieber et al., 2015b).

Together, these findings suggest that IIs indeed lead to strategic automation of the specified goal-directed response when the critical cue is encountered. This automation of action control should allow individuals to strategically decouple their goal pursuits from limited self-regulatory resources. IIs should reduce the amount of self-control required to perform a task, which should in turn help to (1) avoid depletion when IIs are directed at Task 1, and (2) avoid the negative consequences of being depleted when IIs are directed at Task 2. We now review the empirical evidence for this proposition in the context of critical self-regulation threats.

MITIGATING THE SEVEN "DEADLY" THREATS TO SELF-REGULATION

The detrimental self-state of depletion has been classified as one of the seven "deadly" threats to successful self-regulation (Wagner & Heatherton, 2015). As these threats commonly emerge bundled together rather than occurring in succession, it seems crucial to determine whether each of them can be successfully overcome by IIs. In the following section, we will therefore review studies that have tested II effects on each of these threats, starting with ego depletion and continuing with impulse control and cue exposure, emotional and social distress, lapse-activated pattern and abstinence violations, impairments of self-monitoring and self-awareness, the influence of other people, and alcohol intoxication.

SELF-REGULATORY RESOURCE DEPLETION

The threat to self-regulation most central to the present chapter is the depletion of individuals' self-regulation resources. As with other self-regulation threats, II studies have tested (1) whether IIs empower individuals to avoid depletion effects, and (2) whether the negative consequences of being depleted on subsequent goal pursuits can be counteracted.

Avoiding a State of Depletion Through Implementation Intentions

Using a sequential task paradigm, Webb and Sheeran (2003) investigated whether forming IIs allows individuals to overcome the ego-depletion effect. Building on the idea that exerting cognitive control in a first task will impair individuals' performance in a second task, they selected a paper-based Stroop task as their first task. In each single-participant session, participants received a list of 154 words. Each word was printed in an ink color (ie, green, red, yellow, or blue) that was incompatible with the meaning of the respective word (ie, "green," "red," "yellow," or "blue"). The participants' task was to correctly name the ink color of as many words as possible in 10min. This task requires one to override the automatic habitual response to read the words (see horse race model of response inhibition; eg, Verbruggen & Logan, 2009). Because IIs have been found to effectively change even automatic associations (eg, Adriaanse, Gollwitzer, De Ridder, de Wit, & Kroese, 2011) and to shift information processing from effortful top-down to automatic bottom-up action control (eg, Gilbert, Gollwitzer, Cohen, Oettingen, & Burgess, 2009), participants should be less depleted after having performed the Stroop task when bolstered by IIs rather than mere goal intentions.

Before actually working on the Stroop task, participants were randomly assigned to one of three experimental conditions that differed only in the Stroop task instructions. Participants in the depletion condition with goal intentions were asked to name the ink color of each word as quickly as possible (ie, they should try to override the automatic response). II participants in the depletion condition received the same goal instructions but added the if–then plan "As soon as I see a word, I will ignore its meaning (eg, by concentrating on the second letter only) and I will name the color of ink the word is printed in!" Participants in the no-depletion control condition were asked to simply read the words (ie, not fight against the automatic response).

The differences in depletion were measured in an unsolvable puzzle task that followed the Stroop task. This puzzle task, adapted from Baumeister et al. (1998), sought to measure participants' persistence. Because the participants did not know that the task was in fact unsolvable, being more persistent qualifies as adaptive goal-directed behavior, given that maintaining or increasing effort in the face of obstacles most often increases one's chances of successful goal attainment (eg, Brandstätter & Schüler, 2013; Heckhausen, 1991). In each of the three puzzles presented, participants were asked to trace the lines of a geometric shape. They were not allowed to retrace any line or to remove their pen from the piece of paper. To familiarize participants with the task, the experimenter demonstrated a solvable puzzle to them and explained that only the number of puzzles they finished would be judged, not the number of their unsuccessful attempts. Participants were also told that they could knock on the table when they solved all the puzzles or wanted to stop before they finished. While performing the puzzle task, participants listened to a 15-s loop of loud experimental music through a set of headphones; this served to increase the demands on their self-regulation.

Participants' self-reports indicated the success of the depletion manipulation. Those in the depletion conditions rated the difficulty of the Stroop task and the required effort as higher than those in the no-depletion control condition. The persistence results showed that ego-depletion participants fortified with a goal intention were less persistent in the puzzle task (16.55 min) than both no-depletion control participants (23.77 min) and II depletion participants (23.11 min). Although all participants reported lower motivation after the second task than after the first task, those in the goal-intention depletion condition reported being more tired on the physical fatigue subscale of the multidimensional fatigue inventory (Smets, Garssen, Bonke, & de Haes, 1995) than those in the II depletion and no-depletion conditions.

In sum, in comparison to simply reading the words in the Stroop task, naming the ink color of the words was found to reduce performance in a subsequent persistence task. Importantly, however, this reduction was diminished when individuals had formed IIs to automate their response to name the ink color, but not when participants had only formed mere goal intentions. In line with these findings, participants with mere goal intentions to name the ink color also reported being more depleted after the two tasks than II participants. Thus, forming IIs allowed individuals to successfully overcome the depletion effect.

The question of whether IIs directed at a first task can reduce depletion effects in a subsequent task has also been addressed by Bayer, Gollwitzer, and Achtziger (2010, Study 2). Extending the Webb and Sheeran findings, the authors applied an emotion-regulation depletion manipulation and a cognitive performance test (ie, an anagram task) as a second task. In a replication of the classic ego-depletion effect, participants who had to control their emotions in the first task aided by a mere goal intention were predicted to perform worse in the second anagram task in comparison to a control condition in which participants were not asked to control their emotions. However, because IIs have been found to automate emotion regulation (eg, Schweiger Gallo, Keil, McCulloch, Rockstroh, & Gollwitzer, 2009), it was expected that participants who added an II to their goal intention would not exhibit an ego-depletion effect in the second task but would instead perform at the level of control participants. Participants were invited to take part in two ostensibly unrelated experiments. Experiment 1 was purported to investigate mood effects on long-term memory, and experiment 2 was introduced as a concentration test that had to be performed twice for reasons of reliability and validity.

All participants first worked on a paper-based anagram task. Ten difficult anagrams had to be solved in 160 s. The number of correct solutions served as a baseline measure to control for interindividual differences in anagram performance. An adapted version of the emotion regulation task developed by Baumeister et al. (1998, Study 1) followed. Participants were randomly assigned to one of three experimental conditions that differed only in the task instructions. Participants in the depletion condition with goal intentions formed the goal to not show any emotions ("I do not want to laugh or to show any emotional response during the movie!") while watching a funny movie for 10 min (ie, overriding their impulse to laugh at funny scenes). Participants in the depletion condition with IIs set the same goal but added the if–then plan "And if I see a funny scene, then I will tell myself: These are only silly and ridiculous jokes!" Participants in the no-depletion control condition received no further instructions (ie, they could freely express their emotions).

With their consent, the participants were recorded on videotape while watching the movie. After the movie, participants filled out a questionnaire measuring mood, vivacity, and anger to rule out differences in participants' affects as an alternative explanation. Finally, all participants were again asked to work on anagram tasks for 10 min and to find as many solutions as possible. This time, the tasks were presented on a computer screen. The number of correct solutions served as the dependent variable. At the end of the experiment, all participants filled out a final questionnaire on the subjective experience of the second task (ie, task difficulty and commitment).

The analysis of participants' emotional expressions during the first task revealed that all participants followed the respective task instructions: Independent raters confirmed that those in the goal and II conditions smiled and laughed less often than those in the free expression control condition. Regarding performance in the second task, the analysis of the mean number of correctly solved anagram tasks demonstrated the expected differences between the experimental conditions. Replicating the classic-depletion effect, participants in the emotion control condition with mere goal intentions solved fewer anagrams ($M=4.73$) than those in the free expression condition ($M=7.35$). Importantly, this depletion was not found in the emotion control with II condition ($M=7.66$). These differences between the three experimental conditions were also observed when adjusting for individual differences by including baseline anagram performance as a covariate. Moreover, participants in all conditions rated the difficulty of the anagram task as high and reported being highly committed to performing well on the anagram tasks, thus confirming that the anagram task required participants to exert cognitive control and ruling out motivational differences as an alternative explanation.

In sum, participants performed worse on a subsequent anagram task if they had tried to control their emotional responses to a humorous movie in comparison to participants in a no-emotion regulation control condition, replicating the classic ego-depletion effect (Baumeister et al., 1998; Muraven, Tice, & Baumeister, 1998). Emotion regulation, however, did not impair participants' performance on the subsequent anagram task when the participants had planned in advance how they wanted to control their emotions using IIs. These findings provide support for both the ego-depletion effect and the power of IIs in helping to avoid depletion.

Avoiding the Consequences of Being Depleted Through Implementation Intentions

Webb and Sheeran (2003, Study 2) addressed the complementary question of whether IIs can also mitigate the depletion effect of exerting cognitive control in a first task by automating action control in the subsequent second task. To manipulate depletion in their first task, they adapted a test that is used to measure automation deficits in dyslexics (Fawcett, Nicolson, & Dean, 1996). In the depletion condition, participants were asked to stand on their weaker leg and to count down in sevens from 1000. In the control condition, participants were asked to stand normally and count to 1000 in multiples of five. After this depletion manipulation, the intention manipulation and paper-based Stroop task that had been used in their first study followed (see above; Webb & Sheeran, 2003; Study 1). In contrast to the first study, Study 2 applied a full 2×2 design with goal intentions versus IIs and depletion versus no depletion as between-subject factors, thus allowing an investigation of the II effect in the no-depletion condition. Finally, participants were asked to report their mood, the perceived difficulty of the first task, and their level of physical fatigue after the second task.

In support of the success of the depletion manipulation, both the goal intention and II-depletion conditions rated the difficulty of the first math task and their physical fatigue as higher than those in the no-depletion control condition. Replicating the classic depletion effect, goal intention participants in the depletion conditions took longer to perform the Stroop task ($M = 13.91$ min) and made more errors ($M = 27.57$) than those in the no-depletion control condition ($M = 10.88$ min and $M = 15.71$, respectively). Importantly, IIs successfully reduced this impact of being depleted on Stroop performance. II participants in the depletion conditions were as fast ($M = 11.62$ min) and made as few errors ($M = 17.15$) as those in the no-depletion condition. Interestingly, no II effects on speed ($M = 11.12$ min) or errors ($M = 15.38$) in the Stroop task were observed in the no-depletion condition. Most likely, it was easy enough for participants in the no-depletion conditions to perform well on the Stroop task that IIs were not necessary.

The formation of an II thus removed the drain on cognitive control that is usually imposed by the Stroop task. Although participants in the depletion conditions were in a more negative mood after the second task, adjusting for these differences by including mood as a covariate did not change the observed effects. In sum, these findings show that IIs can be used to avoid the negative effects of being depleted on subsequent task performance. This is especially remarkable because participants formed the IIs when they were already depleted, rather than before the actual depletion task. Thus, the formation of IIs as well as the execution of IIs is not limited by the state of being depleted. We now turn to the other critical threats to self-regulation that have been outlined by Wagner and Heatherton (2015) and examine whether IIs can also be used to overcome them.

CUE EXPOSURE AND IMPULSE CONTROL

Controlling impulses has been found to be the most frequent self-regulation task. About 75% of the time during the day, people report experiencing desires that conflict with their goals (eg, leisure, media use; Hofmann, Vohs, & Baumeister, 2012). Whereas most of these impulses, such as the urge to have a cup of coffee or to relax, have a fairly high probability of being successfully controlled (about 90% of the time), others, such as eating or media use, are less-easily controlled (about 75% of the time or less).

Studies on IIs have addressed many of these impulses by focusing on elementary cognitive processes, as well as by examining the ecological validity of II effects in applied contexts. With regard to cognitive processes, for instance, IIs have been shown to help individuals to improve the executive control demanded by task switching and the Simon task (Cohen, Bayer, Jaudas, & Gollwitzer, 2008) and to gain control over the activation and expression of attitudes (Webb, Sheeran, & Pepper, 2012), stereotypes (eg, Stewart & Payne, 2008), and priming effects (eg, Gollwitzer, Sheeran, Trötschel, & Webb, 2011). In addition, with the assistance of IIs, young children managed to better resist tempting distractions while working on a tedious categorization task (Wieber, Suchodoletz, Heikamp, Trommsdorff, & Gollwitzer, 2011).

With regard to II effects in applied contexts, IIs have been found to help individuals to overcome unhealthy eating patterns and to increase physical exercise (metaanalyses by Adriaanse, Vinkers, et al., 2011; Bélanger-Gravel et al., 2013). IIs have also been shown to improve self-regulation with respect to behaviors that are known to be affected by impulsivity, such as drinking alcohol (eg, Hagger et al., 2012), smoking (eg, Armitage, 2008), engaging in unprotected sex (eg, Martin, Sheeran, Slade, Wright, & Dibble, 2011), and spending money (Wieber, Gollwitzer, & Sheeran, 2014; Study 2).

In addition to these investigations of impacts on situations and cues that foster impulsive behaviors, II effects have also been examined in samples that suffer from impaired impulse control. For example, children with ADHD improved their performance in delay-of-gratification (Gawrilow, Gollwitzer, & Oettingen, 2011) and go/no-go tasks (Gawrilow & Gollwitzer, 2008), and these improvements in self-regulation by IIs are also reflected in physiological correlates such as increased P300 responses in

EEG measurements (Paul et al., 2007). Moreover, drug users (Nydegger, Keeler, Hood, Siegel, & Stacy, 2013) and opiate addicts undergoing withdrawal (Brandstätter et al., 2001; Study 1) were found to improve their self-regulation with the help of IIs. However, some findings suggest that trait impulsivity levels moderate these II effects. Whereas IIs successfully increased the fruit and vegetable intake in participants with low and moderate scores on the "urgency" impulsivity subscale, they did not affect the intake of those with high scores (Churchill & Jessop, 2010, 2011). Nonetheless, research also indicates that IIs can be used to boost self-control in response to temptations. In a cleverly designed set of studies, van Koningsbruggen, Stroebe, Papies, and Aarts (2011) demonstrate that an II to think of one's dieting goal when encountering chocolate, cookies, pizza, french fries, or chips successfully activated participants' dieting goals when they were exposed to tempting food cues (Study 1), and it helped them to reduce their calorie intake across 2 weeks (Study 2). Thus, the combination of IIs that act as (dieting) goal primes and IIs that specify an intended response (eg, "then I will grab an apple!") might be effective in reducing self-regulation failure even in impulsive individuals.

EMOTIONAL AND SOCIAL DISTRESS

Emotional and social distress has been pointed to as a major threat to self-regulation. Being in a negative mood increases the likelihood of self-regulation failure, such that dieters eat more, alcoholics report a greater craving for alcohol, and smokers experience a greater desire to smoke. Emotionally distressed people are generally more likely to engage in unprotected sex or problematic gambling, spend too much money, and behave aggressively (see Wagner & Heatherton, 2015; Chapter 9).

However, II studies have found that the detrimental effects of negative moods can be overcome or avoided by forming if–then plans. For example, IIs to control one's mood helped participants to overcome the detrimental effects of negative moods on risky behavioral choices (eg, willingness to drive a car despite knowing that the brakes may suddenly fail; Webb, Sheeran, Totterdell, et al., 2012, Study 1). Moreover, IIs aimed at focusing on the odds of winning in a gambling task reduced the maladaptive effects of being aroused on participants' betting behavior: Participants were more aware of risks and made better decisions in the gambling task (Webb, Sheeran, Totterdell, et al., 2012; Study 2). In addition to self-regulating the effects of negative moods and arousal, IIs have also been observed to diminish the detrimental effects of positive moods on goal pursuit (Bayer et al., 2010; Study 1). In participants who added an II to their goal intention to ignore a person's gender when forming an impression of women depicted in hand-painted sketches, positive moods did not increase stereotyping, whereas being in a positive mood led participants who were not assigned any goal to form a nonstereotypical impression as well as those who formed a mere goal intention to select more stereotypical descriptions of the women's activities than participants in a neutral mood. Other studies have shown that IIs can also be used to avoid slipping into a negative mood in the first place (eg, Schweiger Gallo et al., 2009).

In addition to mood effects, studies have examined the effectiveness of IIs when emotional distress and an additional threat to self-regulation endanger individuals' goal attainment. These studies, however, have observed mixed results. When cue exposure and impulse control threats challenge individuals' self-regulation, IIs have been found to improve response inhibition, but only when emotional activation is low (Burkard, Rochat, & Van der Linden, 2013). Thus, the combination of two threats (ie, impulse control and emotional distress) may overextend the capability of IIs to prevent self-regulation failure.

In addition to the regulation of emotional distress, studies have also tested whether IIs protect self-regulation when social distress threatens goal pursuit. For example, in a study conducted by Palayiwa, Sheeran, and Thompson (2010), female participants received either negative appearance-related comments or not, and either formed IIs or mere goal intentions to ignore these comments during an ongoing d2 attention-concentration task (Brickenkamp, 1994). Whereas negative comments impaired goal intention participants' performance, II participants performed as well as those who were not confronted with negative comments. Thus, IIs allowed the female participants in the study to shield their task performance from the stigmatizing comments.

Finally, in addition to mood and social distress, the impact of being stressed on II effects has also been investigated. For example, planning to eat healthy snack alternatives in stressful situations helped participants in a study on stress-related unhealthy snacking (O'Connor, Armitage, & Ferguson, 2015). Whereas daily stressors were associated with the consumption of unhealthy snacks in the control condition, no such correlation was observed for II participants, who managed to increase their consumption of healthy snacks on stressful days. In line with these findings, being stressed (as indicated by higher cortisol and heart rate levels) did not compromise the beneficial effects of IIs on go/no-go task performance (Scholz et al., 2009).

LAPSE-ACTIVATED PATTERN AND ABSTINENCE VIOLATIONS

The well-known "what the hell effect" (eg, Heatherton, Herman, & Polivy, 1991) whereby dieters are more likely to indulge in forbidden food once they break their diet is a well-established threat to self-regulation. Although there are no studies that have directly tested whether IIs can offset the negative consequences of violating one's abstinence rules, there is indirect evidence that IIs can be used to counteract the threat of violating one's abstinence intentions. For example, there are studies showing that IIs can help people to overcome unhealthy eating patterns (meta-analysis by Adriaanse, Vinkers, et al., 2011) such as breaking unwanted snacking habits (Adriaanse, Gollwitzer, et al., 2011); attempting to overcome unhealthy eating patterns can be assumed to involve some sort of abstinence violations. Moreover, because distress is assumed to be one of the mediators of the effects of abstinence violations on subsequent self-regulation failure, studies that demonstrate II effects even under stressful conditions (eg, O'Connor et al., 2015; Scholz et al., 2009) provide indirect evidence for the hypothesis that IIs should also mitigate the detrimental consequences of lapses and abstinence violations. However, future research should test whether IIs can strengthen one's self-control voice when there is the temptation to simply declare "What the hell!"

IMPAIRMENTS OF SELF-MONITORING AND SELF-AWARENESS

In addition to issues of impulse control, reduced self-monitoring and self-awareness have been suggested as a second axis of threats that contribute to self-regulation failure (Wagner & Heatherton, 2015). When addressing these threats, two routes seem viable from an action control perspective: IIs may either be used to raise self-awareness in a critical situation or to improve self-regulation under conditions of low self-awareness.

With regard to the first route mentioned earlier (ie, increasing self-awareness), recent II research provides indirect evidence by showing that IIs can trigger self-relevant processes. In a study on the escalation of commitment, IIs helped groups to successfully initiate a self-distancing response when making important decisions in an escalation of commitment situation (Wieber, Thürmer, & Gollwitzer, 2015a). IIs to take the perspective of a neutral observer helped groups to reduce their commitment to a self-chosen project after negative feedback. Similarly, the use of IIs as goal primes (van Koningsbruggen et al., 2011) that trigger deliberative thoughts about one's goals exemplifies how IIs may be used to increase self-awareness.

With respect to the second route (ie, improving self-regulation under conditions of low self-awareness), II studies that have attempted to boost self-regulation when individuals are not consciously aware of a critical situation indicate that this method of overcoming the threat of low self-awareness through IIs is also possible. For example, Bayer et al. (2009) examined whether the actions specified in IIs are triggered when the stimulus is presented subliminally. Participants who were insulted by an experimenter and formed IIs to complain read aloud instrumental words related to complaining more quickly after the subliminal presentation of a photo of the experimenter (Study 1). They were also faster at categorizing geometric shapes by pressing different buttons when subliminally presented shapes preceded the categorization trial (Study 2). These results suggest that IIs trigger actions automatically without individuals being aware of it, thus potentially triggering self-regulation responses even when individuals are not self-aware.

THE INFLUENCE OF OTHER PEOPLE

Despite the benefits and importance of social support (eg, reducing stress; Eisenberger, Taylor, Gable, Hilmert, & Lieberman, 2007), the influence of other people may also represent a threat to self-regulation. For instance, when individuals become immersed in a group (ie, deindividuation), they become more likely to break social norms not to steal, cheat, or act aggressively (see Wagner & Heatherton, 2015). Such deindividuation is hypothesized to endanger self-regulation by inhibiting individual standards and strengthening the respective group norms that guide people's actions instead (Reicher, Spears, & Postmes, 1995). Moreover, seeing others indulging (eg, in smoking, eating, or drinking alcohol; Hofmann, Baumeister, Förster, & Vohs, 2012) or breaking social norms (Keizer, Lindenberg, & Steg, 2008), or simply being primed with socializing (Sheeran, Aarts, et al., 2005) can increase the likelihood of self-regulation failure. Finally, behavioral mimicry contributes to self-regulation failure when individuals mimic the eating and drinking behavior of their food companions (Hermans et al., 2012).

Although the number of II studies on curbing the negative impact of social groups in terms of self-regulation is still limited, several of the social phenomena described earlier have been examined experimentally. For instance, IIs were found to help groups to improve their decisions by considering more unshared information (Thürmer, Wieber, & Gollwitzer, 2015b), helped individuals to emancipate themselves from unwanted mimicry effects (Wieber et al., 2014), and socially anxious individuals to reduce the attentional bias toward social threat words and to not underestimate their performance in social contexts from (Webb, Ononaiye, Sheeran, Reidy, & Lavda, 2010). Finally, studies have also found that IIs can be used to change social behavior directed at others. For example, IIs have been observed to increase prosocial behavior (Gollwitzer et al., 2011; Study 2), speed up counterarguing in response to racist comments (Gollwitzer & Brandstätter, 1997), and help men or women to defend their intimate relationships in response to threats (Lydon, Menzies-Toman, Burton,

& Bell, 2008). In sum, IIs have been demonstrated to successfully control the potentially negative influence of other people on self-regulation.

ALCOHOL INTOXICATION

Another major threat to successful self-regulation is alcohol intoxication (see Wagner & Heatherton, 2015). Alcohol is involved in about half of the criminal acts in the United States, and increases the likelihood of all of the self-regulatory failures, from smoking to behaving aggressively (see Steele & Josephs, 1990). In addition, it is known to reduce self-awareness and to narrow attention to the immediate situational context (eg, Sevincer, Oettingen, & Lerner, 2012).

Several studies have investigated whether IIs can reduce the frequency and quantity of alcohol consumption. For example, in an intervention study seeking to reduce alcohol consumption according to the recommendations of the World Health Organization, IIs helped undergraduate students from the UK and Estonia to reduce their consumption over the course of 4 weeks, and the intervention reduced the frequency of binge drinking in UK students (Hagger et al., 2012). As a limitation, however, there was no effect on alcohol consumption for students in Finland, and no reduction in binge drinking occasions for students in Estonia and Finland. Moreover, whereas Estonian students managed to meet the WHO recommendations, students in the UK and Finland still drank more units than recommended. Interestingly, although mentally simulated successful coping with critical prospective events has previously been found to enhance action control (eg, Knäuper et al., 2011), combining the II intervention with mental simulation did not improve the effectiveness of the intervention.

Significant effects of IIs on alcohol consumption were also observed in women who were moderate drinkers (but not men; Murgraff, Abraham, & McDermott, 2007) and in the general population in the UK (Armitage, 2009). The latter study also indicated that self-generated IIs were as effective as the IIs provided by the experimenter, allowing for cost-efficient standardized interventions. Thus, with some exceptions, IIs have been shown to help individuals to improve the self-regulation of their drinking behavior. The fact that IIs reduced the frequency of binge drinking also suggests that people succeeded in self-regulating their alcohol intake even after having a number of drinks. Thus, rather than giving in to the "what the hell" justification, individuals managed to successfully halt the escalation of their dinking despite their already reduced self-regulation capacity. These findings are also in line with the observation that individuals with high planning ability and inhibition control exhibit less of a gap between their intentions to reduce their binge-drinking behavior and their actions than those with low planning ability and inhibition control (Mullan, Wong, Allom, & Pack, 2011), and they highlight the power of planning in tackling the self-regulation threat of drinking.

IMPLEMENTATION INTENTIONS AND THE EFFECTS OF RELEVANT SELF-STATES ON SELF-REGULATION

In addition to the seven deadly threats to self-regulation, IIs have also been tested with regard to their effectiveness to decouple individuals' self-regulation from the consequences of detrimental inner states. For instance, IIs have been shown to mitigate the unwanted effects whereby feeling incomplete with respect to an aspired-to identity goal increases social insensitivity (Bayer et al., 2010; Study 3) and whereby low self-efficacy limits goal attainment (eg, Wieber, Odenthal, & Gollwitzer, 2010). Moreover, IIs counteracted the negative effects of self-handicapping on performance (Thürmer, McCrea, & Gollwitzer, 2013) and even diminished deficits in prospective memory in individuals suffering from early-stage psychosis (Khoyratty et al., 2015).

Complementary to this demonstrated ability to block the influence of detrimental states on self-regulation, a number of studies also indicate that II effects can benefit from certain self-states. For example, forming self-concordant goals (Chatzisarantis, Hagger, & Wang, 2010), combining self-affirmation and IIs (eg, Harris et al., 2014), or combining IIs and mental contrasting (MCII; eg, Oettingen, 2014; Oettingen, Wittchen, & Gollwitzer, 2013) seem very promising venues for the design of more powerful behavior change interventions. However, future research must explore how such combinations can be best structured to achieve maximum behavior change.

IMPLICATIONS

As a conceptual implication of the reported findings on II effects with regard to ego depletion, it can be concluded that these effects and the assumed processes are congruent with the shift from a "have to" to a "want to" motivation, an explanation that has recently been suggested by Inzlicht et al. (2014; see Chapter 18). Because performing the Stroop task or an emotion regulation task subsequent to forming an II should require less self-control (ie, draw less on the "have to" motivation), the shift to a subsequent reluctance to exert self-control (ie, acting in terms of the "have to" motivation) rather than engaging in "want to" activities should be less pronounced. Similarly, the II effects and processes are congruent with the change in the cost–benefit calculations that has been suggested by Kurzban et al. (2013). IIs should reduce the effort required to perform a self-control task, and consequently there should be no reduction in the deployment of computational mechanisms such as those associated with executive functions in subsequent self-control tasks.

Moreover, comparing II research to depletion research would seem to further our knowledge of the effects, processes, and physiological correlates of successful self-regulation (see Chapter 14), as well as facilitate the conceptual integration and the development of effective interventions. For example, comparing the research findings on the neurological correlates of depletion effects (eg, Inzlicht, Berkman, & Elkins-Brown, 2016) and those of II effects on emotion regulation suggest that IIs should mitigate the detrimental impact of depletion on emotion regulation. Whereas depletion has been found to increase the reactivity of the left amygdala and to reduce the functional connectivity between the left amygdala and the prefrontal cortex during the processing of negative scenes (Wagner & Heatherton, 2012), forming IIs is associated with a more effective modulation of the left amygdala and an improved coupling of the amygdala and the orbitofrontal cortex that is involved in automatic processing (Hallam et al., 2015). Similarly, depletion has been found to impair top-down control of action (Wagner, Altman, Boswell, Kelley, & Heatherton, 2013), whereas IIs have been observed to reduce the need for top-down control, since they establish bottom-up action control (Gilbert et al., 2009).

In addition to directly comparing II and depletion research, the combination of IIs and self-regulation strategies that have been found to moderate ego depletion seems a promising venue for further improving the effectiveness of self-regulation interventions, especially when more than one self-regulation threat is present. For instance, self-affirmation and self-concordant goals have both been found to reduce depletion effects and to boost II effects (see Chapter 4), suggesting that the combination of self-affirmation, self-concordant goals, and IIs should be especially effective in reducing the impact of ego depletion. Similarly, strengthening the belief that willpower is unlimited (see Chapter 11) in individuals who tend to think of willpower as a limited resource should help them to overcome depletion effects. Believing that willpower is limited has been found to activate a rest goal after the exertion of self-control (Job, Bernecker, Miketta, & Friese, 2015). To counteract the effects of this rest goal, people could use IIs to directly address their willpower-related beliefs ("And if I think of quitting my studies, then I will tell myself: Your willpower is unlimited!") or the consequences of these beliefs ("And if I have finished one task, then I will immediately start the next one!").

CONCLUSION

The concept of energy conservation brings together a variety of research areas, such as the formerly separate fields of sleeping habits and self-control (Pilcher, Morris, Donnelly, & Feigl, 2015) and clinical psychology research on addictive behaviors (Baumeister & Vonasch, 2015). This transphenomenal use of the self-control model represents a significant integrative potential to unite different research traditions, as well as an opportunity to refine a theory that can be used both to inspire new research questions and address applied challenges. The present chapter focused on the capability of the self-regulation strategy of forming IIs to decouple individuals' goal pursuits from the state of self-regulatory resources. IIs have been proven to be an easily applicable strategy: A single act of will is sufficient to allow an individual to successfully avoid depletion effects or the consequences of being depleted. The reviewed findings show that IIs can effectively address major threats to self-regulation such as low impulse control and cue exposure, high emotional and social distress, lapse-activated pattern and abstinence violations, impairments in self-monitoring and self-awareness, the influence of other people, and alcohol intoxication. Thus, the likelihood of self-regulation failure might be reduced not only by strategies such as proactive self-regulation (ie, preventing critical situations in the first place) or by performing self-control exercises over an extensive time period, but also by the simple planning strategy of forming IIs.

Acknowledgments

We thank Ute Bayer for her helpful comments on earlier drafts of this chapter. Correspondence concerning this chapter should be addressed to Frank Wieber (frank.wieber@zhaw.ch).

References

Aarts, H., Dijksterhuis, A. P., & Midden, C. (1999). To plan or not to plan? Goal achievement of interrupting the performance of mundane behaviors. *European Journal of Social Psychology, 29*, 971–979.

Adriaanse, M. A., Gollwitzer, P. M., De Ridder, D. T. D., de Wit, J. B. F., & Kroese, F. M. (2011). Breaking habits with implementation intentions: a test of underlying processes. *Personality and Social Psychology Bulletin, 37*, 502–513.

Adriaanse, M. A., Vinkers, C. D. W., De Ridder, D. T. D., Hox, J. J., & De Wit, J. B. F. (2011). Do implementation intentions help to eat a healthy diet? A systematic review and meta-analysis of the empirical evidence. *Appetite, 56*, 183–193.

Ajzen, I. (2012). The theory of planned behavior. In P. A. M. Van Lange, A. W. Kruglanski, & E. T. Higgins (Eds.), *Handbook of theories of social psychology* (Vol. 1) (pp. 438–459). Thousand Oaks, CA: Sage Publications Ltd.

Armitage, C. J. (2008). A volitional help sheet to encourage smoking cessation: a randomized exploratory trial. *Health Psychology, 27*, 557–566.

REFERENCES

Armitage, C. J. (2009). Effectiveness of experimenter-provided and self-generated implementation intentions to reduce alcohol consumption in a sample of the general population: a randomized exploratory trial. *Health Psychology, 28*, 545.

Bargh, J. A. (1994). The four horsemen of automaticity: awareness, intention, efficiency, and control in social cognition. In R. S. Wyer, Jr., & T. K. Srull (Eds.), *Handbook of social cognition* (2nd ed.) *Basic processes: Vol. 1.* (pp. 1–40). New York, NY: Psychology Press.

Baumeister, R. F., Bratslavsky, E., Muraven, M., & Tice, D. M. (1998). Ego depletion: is the active self a limited resource? *Journal of Personality and Social Psychology, 74*, 1252–1265.

Baumeister, R. F., & Vonasch, A. J. (2015). Uses of self-regulation to facilitate and restrain addictive behavior. *Addictive Behaviors, 44*, 3–8.

Bayer, U. C., Achtziger, A., Gollwitzer, P. M., & Moskowitz, G. B. (2009). Responding to subliminal cues: do if-then plans facilitate action preparation and initiation without conscious intent? *Social Cognition, 27*, 183–201.

Bayer, U. C., Gollwitzer, P. M., & Achtziger, A. (2010). Staying on track: planned goal striving is protected from disruptive internal states. *Journal of Experimental Social Psychology, 46*, 505–514.

Bélanger-Gravel, A., Godin, G., & Amireault, S. (2013). A meta-analytic review of the effects of implementation intentions on physical activity. *Health Psychology Review, 7*, 23–54.

Brandstätter, V., Lengfelder, A., & Gollwitzer, P. M. (2001). Implementation intentions and efficient action initiation. *Journal of Personality and Social Psychology, 81*, 946–960.

Brandstätter, V., & Schüler, J. (2013). Action crisis and cost–benefit thinking: a cognitive analysis of a goal-disengagement phase. *Journal of Experimental Social Psychology, 49*, 543–553.

Brickenkamp, R. (1994). *Test d2: Aufmerksamkeits-Belastungs-test.* Göttingen: Hogrefe.

Burkard, C., Rochat, L., & Van der Linden, M. (2013). Enhancing inhibition: How impulsivity and emotional activation interact with different implementation intentions. *Acta Psychologica, 144*, 291–297.

Carter, E. C., & McCullough, M. E. (2014). Publication bias and the limited strength model of self-control: has the evidence for ego depletion been overestimated? *Frontiers in Psychology, 5*.

Chatzisarantis, N. L. D., Hagger, M. S., & Wang, J. C. K. (2010). Evaluating the effects of implementation intention and self-concordance on behaviour. *British Journal of Psychology, 101*, 705–718.

Chen, X.-J., Wang, Y., Liu, L.-L., Cui, J.-F., Gan, M.-Y., Shum, D. H. K., & Chan, R. C. (2015). The effect of implementation intention on prospective memory: a systematic and meta-analytic review. *Psychiatry Research, 226*, 14–22.

Churchill, S., & Jessop, D. C. (2010). Spontaneous implementation intentions and impulsivity: can impulsivity moderate the effectiveness of planning strategies? *British Journal of Health Psychology, 15*, 529–541.

Churchill, S., & Jessop, D. C. (2011). Too impulsive for implementation intentions? Evidence that impulsivity moderates the effectiveness of an implementation intention intervention. *Psychology and Health, 26*, 517–530.

Cohen, A.-L., Bayer, U. C., Jaudas, A., & Gollwitzer, P. M. (2008). Self-regulatory strategy and executive control: implementation intentions modulate task switching and Simon task performance. *Psychological Research, 72*, 12–26.

Cohen, J. (1992). A power primer. *Psychological Bulletin, 112*, 155–159.

Eisenberger, N. I., Taylor, S. E., Gable, S. L., Hilmert, C. J., & Lieberman, M. D. (2007). Neural pathways link social support to attenuated neuroendocrine stress responses. *Neuroimage, 35*, 1601–1612.

Fawcett, A. J., Nicolson, R. I., & Dean, P. (1996). Impaired performance of children with dyslexia on a range of cerebellar tasks. *Annals of Dyslexia, 46*, 259–283.

Gawrilow, C., & Gollwitzer, P. M. (2008). Implementation intentions facilitate response inhibition in children with ADHD. *Cognitive Therapy and Research, 32*, 261–280.

Gawrilow, C., Gollwitzer, P. M., & Oettingen, G. (2011). If-then plans benefit delay of gratification performance in children with and without ADHD. *Cognitive Therapy and Research, 35*, 442–455.

Gilbert, S. J., Gollwitzer, P. M., Cohen, A.-L., Oettingen, G., & Burgess, P. W. (2009). Separable brain systems supporting cued versus self-initiated realization of delayed intentions. *Journal of Experimental Psychology: Learning, Memory, and Cognition, 35*, 905–915.

Gollwitzer, P. M., & Brandstätter, V. (1997). Implementation intentions and effective goal pursuit. *Journal of Personality and Social Psychology, 73*, 186–199.

Gollwitzer, P. M., & Sheeran, P. (2006). Implementation intentions and goal achievement: a meta-analysis of effects and processes. *Advances in Experimental Social Psychology, 38*, 69–119.

Gollwitzer, P. M., Sheeran, P., Trötschel, R., & Webb, T. L. (2011). Self-regulation of priming effects on behavior. *Psychological Science, 22*, 901–907.

Gollwitzer, P. M. (1993). Goal achievement: the role of intentions. *European Review of Social Psychology, 4*, 141–185.

Gollwitzer, P. M. (1999). Implementation intentions: strong effects of simple plans. *American Psychologist, 54*, 493–503.

Gollwitzer, P. M. (2014). Weakness of the will: is a quick fix possible? *Motivation and Emotion, 38*, 305–322.

Goto, T., & Kusumi, T. (2013). How can reward contribute to efficient self-control? Reinforcement of task-defined responses diminishes ego-depletion. *Motivation and Emotion, 37*, 726–732.

Hagger, M. S., Lonsdale, A., Koka, A., Hein, V., Pasi, H., Lintunen, T., & Chatzisarantis, N. L. (2012). An intervention to reduce alcohol consumption in undergraduate students using implementation intentions and mental simulations: a cross-national study. *International Journal of Behavioral Medicine, 19*, 82–96.

Hagger, M. S., Wood, C., Stiff, C., & Chatzisarantis, N. L. D. (2010). Ego depletion and the strength model of self-control: a meta-analysis. *Psychological Bulletin, 136*, 495–525.

Hallam, G. P., Webb, T. L., Sheeran, P., Miles, E., Wilkinson, I. D., Hunter, M. D., ... Farrow, T. F. D. (2015). The neural correlates of emotion regulation by implementation intentions. *PLoS One, 10*, 1–21.

Harris, P. R., Brearley, I., Sheeran, P., Barker, M., Klein, W. M., Creswell, J. D., ... Bond, R. (2014). Combining self-affirmation with implementation intentions to promote fruit and vegetable consumption. *Health Psychology, 33*, 729–736.

Heatherton, T. F., Herman, C. P., & Polivy, J. (1991). Effects of physical threat and ego threat on eating behavior. *Journal of Personality and Social Psychology, 60*, 138–143.

Heckhausen, H. (1991). *Motivation und action*. New York, NY: Springer.

Hermans, R. C. J., Lichtwarck-Aschoff, A., Bevelander, K. E., Herman, C. P., Larsen, J. K., & Engels, R. C. (2012). Mimicry of food intake: the dynamic interplay between eating companions. *PLoS One, 7*, e31027.

Hofmann, W., Baumeister, R. F., Förster, G., & Vohs, K. D. (2012). Everyday temptations: an experience sampling study of desire, conflict, and self-control. *Journal of Personality and Social Psychology, 102*, 1318–1335.

Hofmann, W., Vohs, K. D., & Baumeister, R. F. (2012). What people desire, feel conflicted about, and try to resist in everyday life. *Psychological Science, 23*, 582–588.

Hudson, N. W., & Fraley, R. C. (2015). Volitional personality trait change: can people choose to change their personality traits? *Journal of Personality and Social Psychology, 109*, 490–507.

Inzlicht, M., Berkman, E. T., & Elkins-Brown, N. (2016). The neuroscience of "ego depletion" or: how the brain can help us understand why self-control seems limited. In E. Harmon-Jones, & M. Inzlicht (Eds.), *Social neuroscience: biological approaches to social psychology*. New York, NY: Psychology Press., in press.

Inzlicht, M., & Schmeichel, B. J. (2012). What is ego depletion? toward a mechanistic revision of the resource model of self-control. *Perspectives on Psychological Science, 7*, 450–463.

Inzlicht, M., Schmeichel, B. J., & Macrae, C. N. (2014). Why self-control seems (but may not be) limited. *Trends in Cognitive Sciences, 18*, 127–133.

REFERENCES

Job, V., Bernecker, K., Miketta, S., & Friese, M. (2015). Implicit theories about willpower predict the activation of a rest goal following self-control exertion. *Journal of Personality and Social Psychology*.

Keizer, K., Lindenberg, S., & Steg, L. (2008). The spreading of disorder. *Science, 322*, 1681–1685.

Khoyratty, N.-B., Wang, Y., O'Gorman, J. G., Lloyd, C., Williams, P. L., Chan, R. C. K., Shum, D. H. K. (2015). Forming implementation intentions improves prospective memory in early psychosis. *Psychiatry Research, 228*, 265–271.

Knäuper, B., McCollam, A., Rosen-Brown, A., Lacaille, J., Kelso, E., & Roseman, M. (2011). Fruitful plans: adding targeted mental imagery to implementation intentions increases fruit consumption. *Psychology and Health, 26*, 601–617.

Kurzban, R., Duckworth, A., Kable, J. W., & Myers, J. (2013). An opportunity cost model of subjective effort and task performance. *Behavioral and Brain Sciences, 36*, 661–679.

Lydon, J. E., Menzies-Toman, D., Burton, K., & Bell, C. (2008). If-then contingencies and the differential effects of the availability of an attractive alternative on relationship maintenance for men and women. *Journal of Personality and Social Psychology, 95*, 50–65.

Martin, J., Sheeran, P., Slade, P., Wright, A., & Dibble, T. (2011). Durable effects of implementation intentions: reduced rates of confirmed pregnancy at 2 years. *Health Psychology, 30*, 368–373.

Masicampo, E. J., Martin, S. R., & Anderson, R. A. (2014). Understanding and overcoming self-control depletion. *Social and Personality Psychology Compass, 8*, 638–649.

Mullan, B., Wong, C., Allom, V., & Pack, S. L. (2011). The role of executive function in bridging the intention-behaviour gap for binge-drinking in university students. *Addictive Behaviors, 36*, 1023–1026.

Muraven, M., Tice, D. M., & Baumeister, R. F. (1998). Self-control as a limited resource: regulatory depletion patterns. *Journal of Personality and Social Psychology, 74*, 774–789.

Murgraff, V., Abraham, C., & McDermott, M. (2007). Reducing friday alcohol consumption among moderate, women drinkers: evaluation of a brief evidence-based intervention. *Alcohol and Alcoholism, 42*, 37–41.

Nydegger, L. A., Keeler, A. R., Hood, C., Siegel, J. T., & Stacy, A. W. (2013). Effects of a one-hour intervention on condom implementation intentions among drug users in Southern California. *AIDS Care – Psychological and Socio-Medical Aspects of AIDS/HIV, 25*, 1586–1591.

O'Connor, D. B., Armitage, C. J., & Ferguson, E. (2015). Randomized test of an implementation intention-based tool to reduce stress-induced eating. *Annals of Behavioral Medicine, 49*, 331–343.

Oettingen, G. A. (2014). *Rethinking positive thinking: Inside the new science of motivation*. New York, NY: Penguin Random House.

Oettingen, G. A., Wittchen, M., & Gollwitzer, P. M. (2013). Regulating goal pursuit through mental contrasting with implementation intentions. In A. E. Locke, & G. Latham (Eds.), *New developments in goal setting and task performance* (pp. 523–548). New York, NY: Routledge.

Palayiwa, A., Sheeran, P., & Thompson, A. (2010). "Words will never hurt me!": implementation intentions regulate attention to stigmatizing comments about appearance. *Journal of Social and Clinical Psychology, 29*, 575–598.

Papies, E. K., Aarts, H., & de Vries, N. K. (2009). Planning is for doing: implementation intentions go beyond the mere creation of goal-directed associations. *Journal of Experimental Social Psychology, 45*, 1148–1151.

Paul, I., Gawrilow, C., Zech, F., Gollwitzer, P., Rockstroh, B., Odenthal, G., … Wienbruch, C. (2007). If-then planning modulates the P300 in children with attention deficit hyperactivity disorder. *Neuroreport, 18*, 653–657.

Pilcher, J. J., Morris, D. M., Donnelly, J., & Feigl, H. B. (2015). Interactions between sleep habits and self-control. *Frontiers in Human Neuroscience, 9*.

Reicher, S. D., Spears, R., & Postmes, T. (1995). A social identity model of deindividuation phenomena. *European Review of Social Psychology, 6*, 161–198.

Scholz, U., La Marca, R., Nater, U. M., Aberle, I., Ehlert, U., Hornung, R., ... Kliegel, M. (2009). Go no-go performance under psychosocial stress: beneficial effects of implementation intentions. *Neurobiology of Learning and Memory, 91*, 89–92.

Schweiger Gallo, I., Keil, A., McCulloch, K. C., Rockstroh, B., & Gollwitzer, P. M. (2009). Strategic automation of emotion regulation. *Journal of Personality and Social Psychology, 96*, 11–31.

Schweiger Gallo, I., Cohen, A.-L., Gollwitzer, P. M., & Oettingen, G. (2013). Neurophysiological correlates of the self-regulation of goal pursuit. In P. A. Hall (Ed.), *Social neuroscience and public health* (pp. 19–33). New York, NY: Springer.

Sevincer, A. T., Oettingen, G., & Lerner, T. (2012). Alcohol affects goal commitment by explicitly and implicitly induced myopia. *Journal of Abnormal Psychology, 121*, 524–529.

Sheeran, P. (2002). Intention-behavior relations: a conceptual and empirical review. *European Review of Social Psychology, 12*, 1–36.

Sheeran, P., Aarts, H., Custers, R., Rivis, A., Webb, T. L., & Cooke, R. (2005). The goal-dependent automaticity of drinking habits. *British Journal of Social Psychology, 44*, 47–63.

Sheeran, P., Webb, T. L., & Gollwitzer, P. M. (2005). The interplay between goal intentions and implementation intentions. *Personality and Social Psychology Bulletin, 31*, 87–98.

Smets, E. M. A., Garssen, B., Bonke, B., & de Haes, J. C. (1995). The Multidimensional Fatigue Inventory (MFI) psychometric qualities of an instrument to assess fatigue. *Journal of Psychosomatic Research, 39*, 315–325.

Steele, C. M., & Josephs, R. A. (1990). Alcohol myopia: its prized and dangerous effects. *American Psychologist, 45*, 921–933.

Stewart, B. D., & Payne, B. K. (2008). Bringing automatic stereotyping under control: implementation intentions as efficient means of thought control. *Personality and Social Psychology Bulletin, 34*, 1332–1345.

Strack, F., & Deutsch, R. (2004). Reflective and impulsive determinants of social behavior. *Personality and Social Psychology Review, 8*, 220–247.

Thürmer, J. L., McCrea, S. M., & Gollwitzer, P. M. (2013). Regulating self-defensiveness: if–then plans prevent claiming and creating performance handicaps. *Motivation and Emotion, 37*, 712–725.

Thürmer, J. L., Wieber, F., & Gollwitzer, P. M. (2015a). Planning high performance: can groups and teams benefit from implementation intentions? In M. D. Mumford, & M. Frese (Eds.), *The psychology of planning in organizations: Research and applications* (pp. 123–146). New York, NY: Routledge.

Thürmer, J. L., Wieber, F., & Gollwitzer, P. M. (2015b). A self-regulation perspective on hidden-profile problems: if–then planning to review information improves group decisions. *Journal of Behavioral Decision Making, 28*, 101–113.

Toli, A., Webb, T. L., & Hardy, G. (2015). Does forming implementation intentions help people with mental health problems to achieve goals? A meta-analysis of experimental studies with clinical and analogue samples. Advance online publication *British Journal of Clinical Psychology*.

van Koningsbruggen, G. M., Stroebe, W., Papies, E. K., & Aarts, H. (2011). Implementation intentions as goal primes: boosting self-control in tempting environments. *European Journal of Social Psychology, 41*, 551–557.

Verbruggen, F., & Logan, G. D. (2009). Models of response inhibition in the stop-signal and stop-change paradigms. *Neuroscience and Biobehavioral Reviews, 33*, 647–661.

Wagner, D. D., Altman, M., Boswell, R. G., Kelley, W. M., & Heatherton, T. F. (2013). Self-regulatory depletion enhances neural responses to rewards and impairs top-down control. *Psychological Science, 24*, 2262–2271.

Wagner, D. D., & Heatherton, T. F. (2012). Self-regulatory depletion increases emotional reactivity in the amygdala. *Social Cognitive and Affective Neuroscience, 8*, 410–417.

Wagner, D. D., & Heatherton, T. F. (2015). Self-regulation and its failure: the seven deadly threats to self-regulation. In M. Mikulincer, P. R. Shaver, E. Borgida, & J. A. Bargh (Eds.), *APA handbook of personality and social psychology Attitudes and social cognition: Vol. 1.* (pp. 805–842). Washington, DC: American Psychological Association.

Webb, T. L., Ononaiye, M. S. P., Sheeran, P., Reidy, J. G., & Lavda, A. (2010). Using implementation intentions to overcome the effects of social anxiety on attention and appraisals of performance. *Personality and Social Psychology Bulletin, 36,* 612–627.

Webb, T. L., & Sheeran, P. (2003). Can implementation intentions help to overcome ego-depletion? *Journal of Experimental Social Psychology, 39,* 279–286.

Webb, T. L., & Sheeran, P. (2006). Does changing behavioral intentions engender behaviour change? A meta-analysis of the experimental evidence. *Psychological Bulletin, 132,* 249–268.

Webb, T. L., & Sheeran, P. (2007). How do implementation intentions promote goal attainment? A test of component processes. *Journal of Experimental Social Psychology, 43,* 295–302.

Webb, T. L., Sheeran, P., & Pepper, J. (2012). Gaining control over responses to implicit attitude tests: implementation intentions engender fast responses on attitude-incongruent trials. *British Journal of Social Psychology, 51,* 13–32.

Webb, T. L., Sheeran, P., Totterdell, P., Miles, E., Mansell, W., & Baker, S. (2012). Using implementation intentions to overcome the effect of mood on risky behaviour. *British Journal of Social Psychology, 51,* 330–345.

Wieber, F., Gollwitzer, P. M., & Sheeran, P. (2014). Strategic regulation of mimicry effects by implementation intentions. *Journal of Experimental Social Psychology, 53,* 31–39.

Wieber, F., Odenthal, G., & Gollwitzer, P. M. (2010). Self-efficacy feelings moderate implementation intention effects. *Self and Identity, 9,* 177–194.

Wieber, F., & Sassenberg, K. (2006). I can't take my eyes off of it – attention attraction effects of implementation intentions. *Social Cognition, 24,* 723–752.

Wieber, F., Suchodoletz, A. V., Heikamp, T., Trommsdorff, G., & Gollwitzer, P. M. (2011). If-then planning helps school-aged children to ignore attractive distractions. *Social Psychology, 42,* 39–47.

Wieber, F., Thürmer, J. L., & Gollwitzer, P. M. (2012). Collective action control by goals and plans: applying a self-regulation perspective to group performance. *American Journal of Psychology, 125,* 275–290.

Wieber, F., Thürmer, J. L., & Gollwitzer, P. M. (2015a). Attenuating the escalation of commitment to a faltering project in decision-making groups: an implementation intention approach. *Social Psychological and Personality Science, 6,* 587–595.

Wieber, F., Thürmer, J. L., & Gollwitzer, P. M. (2015b). Promoting the translation of intentions into action by implementation intentions: behavioral effects and physiological correlates. *Frontiers in Human Neuroscience, 9.*

CHAPTER 4

On Enhancing and Diminishing Energy Through Psychological Means: Research on Vitality and Depletion From Self-Determination Theory

F. Martela[1], C.R. DeHaan[2], R.M. Ryan[2,3]

[1]University of Helsinki, Helsinki, Finland; [2]University of Rochester, Rochester, NY, United States; [3]Australian Catholic University, Strathfield, NSW, Australia

INTRODUCTION

Vitality is one of the most phenomenally accessible variables in psychology. People can readily report on the available energy they have (Ryan & Frederick, 1997; Thayer, 2001). Even young children define wellness in terms of energy to do what one wants (eg, Natapoff, 1978). Many intellectual traditions also place concepts of energy at the heart of their definitions of health and wellness. For example, Chinese traditions refer to such vital energy as *chi*, and see it as a source of life, creativity, and organismic health. The Japanese concept of *Ki* carries similar implications. Among Western traditions, Freud (1923) proposed that humans have a limited supply of psychic energy, the availability or accessibility of which was defining of ego-strength and wellness. Selye (1956), a pioneer of stress research, conceptualized *adaptation energy* as a source of resilience, and argued that it could be depleted by stressful life events.

Recent research in social psychology has focused on the blocking and depletion of energy. Most notably, the *resource strength model* (Baumeister, Muraven, & Tice, 2000) proposes that the regulation or self-control of behavior requires energy. Self-control works "like a muscle" and thus draws upon resources that become depleted through use. The resulting state of ego depletion is "a temporary reduction in the self's capacity or willingness to engage in volitional action..., caused by prior exercise of volition" (Baumeister, Bratslavsky, Muraven, & Tice, 1998, p. 1253). In other words, it is the energy available for volitional activity that is undermined. Various experiments have indeed shown that self-control can deplete energy, and have connected this depletion to objective outcomes such as behavioral persistence and changes in blood glucose levels (eg, Baumeister & Vohs, 2007; Gailliot et al., 2007).

Research on ego depletion can tell us much about what diminishes energy. However, the processes that drain a person of energy are only one side of the coin. In addition to researching forms of regulation that deplete energy, we need complementary research on vitality and invigoration—on the processes that maintain or enhance energy. Whereas ego depletion is the state where a limited resource "akin to energy or strength is expended" (Tice, Baumeister, Shmueli, & Muraven, 2007, p. 379), *vitality* is its opposite, representing "the positive feeling of having energy available to the self" (Nix, Ryan, Manly, & Deci, 1999, p. 266).

Using the perspective of *self-determination theory* (SDT; Deci & Ryan, 2000; Ryan & Deci, 2000), researchers have been exploring factors associated with the maintenance and enhancement of subjective vitality and its behavioral manifestations. SDT distinguishes between autonomous and controlled forms of regulation, the former of which are felt to be volitional and self-endorsed, and the latter of which are felt to be externally regulated (Deci & Ryan, 2000). Autonomous motivation, as used here, thus does not imply any distinction between whether goal pursuit is implicit or explicit, but is rather about whether the motivation is felt to be self-determined or externally controlled.

Herein we integrate research on subjective vitality based on SDT with research on ego depletion and self-control, aiming to show that they are "tapping into the same phenomenon" (Ryan & Deci, 2008, p. 711). We further argue that the ability to allocate energy to behavior is a function of both physical and psychological factors. Specifically, our SDT formulation suggests that controlled forms of motivation are particularly depleting, lowering available energy and subjective vitality, whereas autonomous activities can maintain or even enhance available energy. Moreover, experiences of basic need satisfactions for relatedness, competence, and autonomy (eg, falling in love as a relatedness satisfaction, finding a sense of purpose as an autonomy satisfaction, discovering a new skill as a competence satisfaction) can all enhance vitality precisely because they invigorate self-functioning. In fact, basic psychological need satisfactions mediate the effects of many factors on energetic and health outcomes. Such results have both basic science import, as well as practical implications for schools, workplaces, and sports, among other applied domains.

VITALITY DEFINED

Subjective vitality is defined as the accessible "experience of having positive energy available to or within the regulatory control of one's self" (Ryan & Frederick, 1997, p. 530). Vitality describes the positive feeling of aliveness, energy, enthusiasm, and spirit. As a sense that energy is available to the self, subjective vitality is predicted to support volitional activity and performance, among other salutary effects. Ryan and Frederick (1997) developed a subjective vitality scale (SVS) to measure subjective vitality. This construct is differentiated from generalized energy in three main ways. First, it represents a subjective appraisal rather than a physiological condition, even though physical states such as fatigue or blood glucose levels impact this experience. Many effortful activities require, for example, the expenditure of caloric energy, yet some of these activities can be experienced as vitalizing, particularly when they are fun or enjoyable, whereas others, though requiring equal physical effort, feel particularly draining and tiring. Thus although subjective vitality is impacted by both somatic factors such as diet, sleep, or exercise, psychological factors such as autonomous motivation or social relatedness can strongly moderate or buffer such effects. As such, subjective vitality is a reflection of both biologic and psychological factors (Ryan & Frederick, 1997) and these self-perceptions of available energy are generally predictive of persistence, performance, and relevant health outcomes (Muraven, Gagné, & Rosman, 2008; Ryan & Deci, 2008; see also Chapter 10).

Secondly, vitality is specifically about energy that is *available to the self*. Thus the mere presence of arousal or energies that are not typically associated with volition, such as anger, anxiety, pressure, or jitteriness, are expected (and have been found) to be unrelated (or even negatively related) to vitality (Ryan & Frederick, 1997). Vitality is thus distinct from activation or energy per se, which includes also such negatively toned states and varied types of arousal. As such, vitality is related to the concepts of vigor (McNair, Lorr, & Droppleman, 1971), activated positive affect (Yik, Russell, & Feldman Barrett, 1999), and calm (vs tense) energy (Thayer, 1996), which all entail positively toned, actively energized states. It is in these states a person can most effectively *mobilize* and *intentionally regulate* energy, as experimental evidence will show.

Third, it is important to note that vitality is distinct from happiness or mere positive affect. Although both happiness and vitality are positive and pleasant states, the latter is characterized by high energy or activation (Nix et al., 1999). As a number of distinct researchers have shown, positive affect as such includes both high-activation dimensions (eg, feeling active, energetic, vigorous) and low-activation dimensions (eg, feeling content, satisfied, pleased), and vitality as a construct is associated only with the former (eg, McNair et al., 1971; Nowlis & Green, 1964; Purcell, 1982; Thayer, 1987; Yik et al. 1999). We add, however, that vitality is experienced only when positively toned vigor and energy are seen as self-organized or within autonomous control. For example, obsessively passionate individuals, while often vigorous, are vulnerable to depletion effects relative to more autonomously engaged people (Vallerand, 2015).

Although vitality is a subjectively accessible state, it has been associated with behavioral and objective health outcomes (Hirsch, Molnar, Chang, & Sirois, 2014). When in more vital states, people are more active and productive, report greater mental health, and cope better with stress and challenge (eg, Penninx et al., 2000; Ryan & Frederick, 1997; Tremblay, Blanchard, Pelletier, & Vallerand, 2006). Activated forms of positive affect that are associated with vitality have also been shown to render people more resilient to physical and viral stressors and less vulnerable to illness (eg, Benyamini, Idler, Leventhal, & Leventhal, 2000; Cohen, Alper, Doyle, Treanor, & Turner, 2006; Polk, Cohen, Doyle, Skoner, & Kirschbaum, 2005).

Kasser and Ryan (1999) studied elderly persons in a nursing facility, showing that vitality was positively associated with perceived physical health and psychological well-being, and negatively associated with depression and anxiety. Moreover, it has been suggested that vitality is associated with specific configurations of brain activation (Barrett, Della-Maggiore, Chouinard, & Paus, 2004) and positive response mechanisms to life challenges (Rozanski, Blumenthal, Davidson, Saab, & Kubzansky, 2005). In addition to being a desirable phenomenological state in itself, vitality thus has important physical and psychological consequences that make it an important focus of research.

DISTINCT FORMS OF SELF-REGULATION: SELF-CONTROL AND AUTONOMOUS REGULATION

An important insight arising from research on subjective vitality is that whereas efforts to control oneself drain psychological energy and vitality, autonomous self-regulation typically does not. In fact, instead of resulting in ego depletion, autonomous self-regulation has in some experiments predicted increases in subjective vitality and the behavioral indicators of energy (or nondepletion) associated with it (eg, see Kazén, Kuhl, & Leicht, 2015). Although ego-depletion models typically equate the concepts of self-control and self-regulation, suggesting that all acts of self-regulation entail energy expenditure and depletion, SDT has long maintained that these concepts should be clearly differentiated (Ryan, 1982). Motivation is considered *self-controlling* when based in external and introjected regulations, whereas *autonomous self-regulation* refers to a situation where a behavior is maintained due to being intrinsically motivating or integrated with a person's sense of self. Self-control is thus highly effortful: One part of one's personality must override and suppress another. In fact, self-control, is defined in ego-depletion models as "the capacity to alter or override dominant response tendencies and to regulate behavior, thoughts, and emotions" (de Ridder, Lensvelt-Mulders, Finkenauer, Stok, & Baumeister, 2012, p. 77) and thus seems similar to SDT's self-controlling forms of regulation. SDT would thus concur with the ego-depletion model that in cases where self-control is "controlling" in nature, behavioral regulation will be more effortful and result in the depletion of energy as well as subjective vitality. Yet because autonomous forms of self-regulation involve behavior that is more self-congruent and expressive of one's interests and values, SDT would argue that they do not require the same need for exhausting internal control or vigilant inhibition of competing motives.

Studies both by depletion model and SDT researchers have in fact well demonstrated that self-controlling forms of regulation clearly deplete energy as. For example, Vohs and Heatherton (2000) placed people adjacent to a bowl of candy where they had to control their urge to eat the candy. They showed that the performance on a subsequent activity demanding cognitive resources was worse for dieters sitting near the candy (who presumably needed to control themselves) than for either dieters sitting farther from the candy or participants not on a diet who sat near the candy. In another study, suppressing emotions while watching a sad movie decreased subsequent stamina in squeezing a handgrip exerciser (Muraven, Tice, & Baumeister, 1998). The decreased performance on subsequent tasks is interpreted as evidence of ego depletion, and a line of similar studies have shown that self-control used in one kind of task makes it less available in a subsequent task, even if that task would be of a completely different kind (for recent metaanalyses, see Hagger, Wood, Stiff, & Chatzisarantis, 2010; de Ridder et al., 2012).

SDT's studies of the undermining effects of self-controlling states on intrinsic motivation and autonomous persistence are longstanding (Deci & Ryan, 1985; 2000). SDT's approach to vitality and depletion makes the additional, and corollary, prediction that autonomous self-regulation, which involves less inhibition and control, is less depleting than the same activities when controlled by external or internal forces (Ryan & Frederick, 1997). The more the *perceived locus of causality* (de Charms, 1968) for actions is external to the self, the more that activity feels forced and thus more draining of energy. For example, Nix et al. (1999) performed three experiments to examine the difference between autonomous and nonautonomous regulation on their effect on vitality. In the first experiment, one group of participants were able to freely work on a cognitive problem-solving task, while other group had to enact identical behaviors through external directives. Whereas the vitality of other-directed participants dropped significantly from pre- to postexperiment, self-directed participants maintained same levels of vitality. In the second experiment, participants were asked to solve puzzles in two conditions: in the task-involving condition participants were told to solve the puzzles without any emphasis on evaluation, while in the ego-involving condition performance was emphasized, for example, by stating that the puzzles are used as a measure of intelligence in many places. The rationale was that emphasizing performance would make the participants feel more controlled and less self-determined (Ryan, 1982). A manipulation check showed that this indeed was the case, and results showed more positive change in vitality in the task-involving condition relative to the ego-involving condition. In a third study, participants were asked to imagine their reactions to success in a class they had either taken voluntarily or in one they were required to take and rate the expected feelings, including vitality. Again, vitality was higher in the voluntary group. Interestingly, in all three studies the post-study levels of happiness of the participants did not differ between the autonomous and controlled group. In other words, the data demonstrated the distinctiveness of vitality from happiness, showing that although success on a task might engender happiness (which happened in all three experiments), it was success with a more internal locus of causality that leads to greater vitality.

Diverse studies have been corroborating these findings. Rouse, Ntoumanis, and Duda (2013) showed that while a cognitively demanding task decreased vitality for people low in autonomous motivation (as compared to a control group with less demanding task), levels of vitality were maintained for participants high in autonomous motivation. Thoman, Smith, and Silvia (2011) found that engaging in an interesting task (which suggests greater autonomy) replenished more resources than a positive or a neutral task, even though the interesting task was more complex and required more effort than the other tasks. In field research, Gagne, Ryan, and Bargmann (2003) measured elite level female gymnasts' vitality both before and after practice. It turned out that intrinsic motivation predicted increased subjective vitality after practice. Even though practices were physically demanding, the energetic activation and vitality of the athletes was enhanced when they were intrinsically motivated. Kasser and Ryan (1999) showed that residents of a nursing care environment for older adults who reported more autonomous regulation of daily activities had more vitality. Perceived nursing care staff autonomy support was also strongly associated with vitality. Studies in the domain of work (Baard, Deci, & Ryan, 2004), teaching (Núñez, Fernández, León, & Grijalvo, 2015), and friendship (Deci, Guardia, Moller, Scheiner, & Ryan, 2006), have all similarly found that people report greater vitality in the presence of autonomy support. These and other diverse studies support SDT's view that autonomous forms of self-regulation are markedly less depleting than external- or self-controlling regulations.

Beyond the issue of autonomous and controlled forms of regulation, SDT suggests that energy fluctuations are predicted by physical supports such as food intake or resting (eg, Visser, Hirsch, Brown, Ryan, & Moynihan, 2015), but also by psychological factors—in particular the satisfaction or frustration of basic psychological needs for autonomy, competence, and relatedness (Ryan & Deci, 2008). When people engage in activities that satisfy these psychological needs, they show less depletion, and may experience increased vitality or energy available to the self.

INTEGRATING THE EGO-DEPLETION MODEL AND SELF-DETERMINATION THEORY'S MODEL OF VITALITY

The different and yet potentially complementary theoretical assumptions and predictions made by SDT and the regulatory strength model are illustrated by two early studies on choice and ego depletion. The first was by Baumeister, Bratslavsky, Muraven, and Tice (1998), who hypothesized that the process of making a choice would be depleting, relative to not making a choice, as the former involved cognitive effort. In contrast, SDT would suggest that a meaningful choice would facilitate autonomous self-regulation and would be less depleting than no choice. Nonetheless results from Baumeister et al. (1998, Study 2) initially supported their hypothesis. In the study, participants were told they would have to tape an argument for one side of a controversial issue, and they were asked to decide which side of the debate they would like to defend. However, the experimenter then told each person in the "high-choice" condition that enough participants had already chosen a specified side of the argument, so it would be very helpful if the participant would choose the other side, adding, however, that it really was "up to them to decide." This "high-choice" condition was compared with a "no-choice" condition in which participants were simply assigned one of the two sides of the issue. Before any speeches were taped, all participants were given an unsolvable puzzle task and ego depletion was assessed by how long time participants persisted with the puzzle. Results showed that high-choice participants persisted for a shorter period of time compared to no-choice participants, suggesting that choice had depleted their energy.

Coming from the SDT lens, however, a different interpretation of these results seemed plausible. In this "high-choice" condition, instead of participants experiencing a meaningful choice to select the side they wanted, they might have felt controlled in a subtle way. They were first told they had choice, but then softly pressured to pick a specific option, as it would "help the study a great deal" (Baumeister et al., 1998, p. 1257). The likelihood that participants did not experience choice, was also indicated by the fact that all of them, without exception, agreed to take the side that the experimenter suggested. But even more specifically, a prior experiment testing SDT by Pittman, Davey, Alafat, Wetherill, and Kramer (1980) had used just such a manipulation as a *controlling condition*, which they showed undermined an internal perceived locus of causality for the task, and subsequent intrinsic motivation. Moreover, a large number of studies have shown that making a meaningful choice should enhance autonomous motivation (see Patall, Cooper, & Robinson, 2008) and energy for tasks (Meng & Ma, 2015). Therefore it seemed that while true and meaningful choice should be less ego depleting, pressured choice (such as this "high-choice" manipulation of Baumeister et al. 1998) would be experienced as controlling and be ego depleting.

To test this, Moller, Deci, and Ryan (2006) conducted an experiment using methods that paralleled those used by Baumeister et al. (1998, Study 2). However, in the new experiment there were now three conditions. In a "true-choice" condition, participants were told about the two sides of a controversial issue, and were free to choose whichever side they wanted, without pressure from the experimenter. The "compelled-choice" condition was identical to the "high-choice" condition of Baumeister et al. (1998), that is, participants were told that they were free to make the choice, but also that it would be very helpful if they chose a specific side. In a third, "no-choice" condition, participants were simply assigned to one side. Results of this study were in line with Baumeister et al. (1998) results insofar that people in the "compelled-choice" condition again showed more ego depletion as compared to the "no-choice" participants. However, participants in the "true-choice" condition persisted significantly longer than participants in the "compelled-choice" participants, showing that it was not choice itself, but the controlled motivation that was ego depleting.

Other research has further connected the strength model and research on vitality. In one experiment, Muraven et al. (2008) asked participants to complete a brief, potentially depleting exercise (retyping a paragraph but omitting es and spaces). However, participants in the controlling condition had to do this in more pressuring conditions, where they were reminded about the time pressure and the demand to do well on the task. Subsequently, all participants had to engage in another task (hitting a key when certain numbers appeared on screen) that measured their ability to concentrate. The results showed that those in the pressuring condition performed worse on this task, missing more targets. In addition, this relation was mediated by subjective vitality: feeling pressure to exert self-control led to lower levels of subjective vitality, which in turn were related to poorer self-control performance. In another experiment, Muraven et al. (2008)

also showed that subjective vitality as measured with the SVS mediated the link between more or less autonomy-supportive experimental condition and depletion outcomes in subsequent tasks. These results directly linked subjective vitality and the behavioral measure of ego depletion: People in autonomy-supportive environments experience more vitality, and therefore exhibit less depletion. In yet another relevant paper, Muraven, Rosman, and Gagné (2007) reasoned that performance-contingent rewards to exert self-control might undermine autonomous motivation (a well-documented effect within SDT, see Deci, Koestner, & Ryan, 1999), resulting in depletion. They indeed found this effect, manifest as poorer performance during a subsequent task. Finally, Muraven (2008), rather than manipulating people's sense of autonomy, simply placed a bowl of cookies in front of them and asked them to complete a questionnaire that measured the relative autonomy of their reasons for not eating the cookies. Results showed that more autonomous reasons to regulate behavior as regards the cookies predicted better performance on a subsequent task than more controlled reasons for abstaining.

In a particularly interesting and potentially important study, Kazén et al. (2015) gave participants either self-motivating or self-controlling instructions to perform a cognitively demanding version of the Stroop task, and then measured both their performance on a second task, and their blood glucose levels. Basing their hypotheses on both *personality systems interaction* (PSI; Kuhl, 2000) as well as SDT, they predicted that whereas self-controlled actions would deplete energy, autonomously motivated actions would invigorate. Furthermore based on Beedie and Lane's (2012) resource allocation model of self-control, they suggested that blood glucose levels would follow the same patterns: Instead of being simply depleted by mental effort as suggested by Gailliot and Baumeister (2007), the redirection of glucose to brain would be governed by an appraisal of the importance of the situation, such that in personally relevant situations blood glucose levels would be maintained or even increased. Results showed that, consistent with the ego-depletion model, blood glucose levels of the self-control group did indeed drop during the experiment. However, the self-motivating group did not only perform better on the subsequent task compared to the self-control group, they showed a *rise* in their blood glucose levels. The researchers noted that such increments in blood glucose after performing tasks requiring executive control "are *not* expected by the strength model of ego depletion," but are congruent with both PSI and SDT (Kazén et al., 2015). This research thus provides evidence that performing tasks with autonomous regulation might not only maintain one's levels of energy, but could even increase them.

Together these studies demonstrate how subjective vitality and behavioral assessments of ego depletion are tapping into the same phenomenon (Ryan & Deci, 2008). Both depletion and invigoration effects seem to be mediated by changes in subjective sense of vitality, and both reflect the sense of energy available to the self. More particularly, while self-control leads to depletion, autonomy-supportive contexts, and autonomous reasons for regulation lead to less depletion and in some cases even increased energy. Naturally sense of autonomy and control vary in degrees, and a singular situation can involve both factors that enhance autonomy and factors that suppress it, so how depleting the regulation of any given behavior would be is a relative issue. Nevertheless the suggestion that some psychological factors can maintain and even enhance our sense of vitality, leads us to ask what factors could have such positive effect on human sense of energy. We have already seen that autonomous forms of regulation have such positive effects, but also other factors can be important. It is to these factors that we turn next.

PSYCHOLOGICAL SOURCES OF VITALITY

In their early studies on vitality, Ryan and Frederick (1997) showed that vitality was associated with physical factors. Physical activity, especially when autonomous, can enhance vitality. In contrast, when physically fatigued or ill, or when experiencing uncontrollable pain, people experience a lower sense of subjective vitality. Clearly there are many physical influences on available energy, including diet, exercise and health status. However, Ryan and Frederick (1997) also investigated psychological factors connected to vitality, showing that it was positively connected to self-actualization, self-determination, self-motivation, and varied indicators of mental health. Based on SDT, they suggested that the basic psychological needs for autonomy, competence, and relatedness provide important nutriments for the self (Deci & Ryan, 2000), and thus that satisfactions of these basic needs should lead to maintained or enhanced vitality. They found preliminary support for this notion in several studies, and since then a number of researchers have examined this relation directly. It is such psychological factors on which we focus in this review (see also Chapter 12).

Basic Psychological Needs and Vitality

Among the most potent psychological factors impacting vitality and depletion are basic psychological need satisfactions and frustrations. Based on SDT, a number of studies have looked at daily fluctuations in people's sense of need satisfaction and vitality. For example, Reis, Sheldon, Gable, Roscoe, and Ryan (2000) showed that daily vitality was higher on days when psychological needs for autonomy, competence, and relatedness were satisfied and that each of these three needs had an independent influence on vitality. These results have been corroborated by similar findings in other experienced sampling studies (Martela & Ryan, in press; Sheldon, Ryan, & Reis, 1996).

In contexts of physical activity, many studies have shown links between psychological need satisfactions and vitality indicators, independent of level of activity. In their study of elite gymnasts, Gagne et al. (2003) showed that satisfaction of all three needs during practice separately predicted positive pre- to postpractice changes in vitality. Vlachopoulos and Karavani (2009) subsequently examined predictors of vitality in a sample of Greek exercise participants. They reported a robust main effect between the experience of coaches autonomy support and the athlete's vitality, as well as a positive relation between vitality and all three psychological need satisfactions. In a mediation analysis, they found that the positive relations of autonomy support and vitality were most strongly mediated by *competence satisfaction*, which makes sense in this domain of activity where psychological needs for competence are so salient (see also Quested & Duda, 2010). Finally, Reinboth and Duda (2006) followed university athletes in the UK, assessing the coaching climate, basic need satisfactions, and both subjective vitality and physical symptoms. In line with their SDT-based hypothesis, an increase in perceptions of a task-involving climate positively predicted an increased satisfaction of the needs for autonomy, competence, and relatedness. In turn, changes in the satisfaction of the needs for autonomy and relatedness emerged as significant predictors of changes in subjective vitality.

The study of vitality and need satisfaction in organizational settings has been another active area of research (see Spreitzer, Sutcliffe, Dutton, Sonenshein, & Grant, 2005). In varied work contexts, all three needs have been found to be positively associated with vigor and negatively associated with exhaustion (Van den Broeck, Vansteenkiste, Witte, Soenens, & Lens, 2010), and combined need satisfaction was found to mediate the relationship between job resources, job demands, and employees' exhaustion and vigor (Van den Broeck, Vansteenkiste, De Witte, & Lens, 2008). In fact, Ryan, Bernstein, and Brown (2010) reported an experience sampling study of American workers and found that people reported lower vitality when in the work contexts as compared to their nonwork contexts. Further fluctuations in vitality were mediated by changes in autonomy and relatedness, which for most workers were needs not well satisfied in the workplace. Vitality for most of those full time employees rose on weekends, an effect accounted for by both increased choice of activities and greater relatedness satisfactions.

Insofar as work involves effortful regulation of behavior and cognition, how people conserve and regenerate energy surrounding work has also been a focus of research. For example, when workers engage in autonomous activities or autonomous forms of social relations during lunch breaks, recovery and revitalization are enhanced (eg, Trougakos, Hideg, Cheng, & Beal, 2013). In addition, workers who experience more autonomy and social support at work are more likely to employ strategies that effectively maintain energy across the day (Kinnunen, Feldt, de Bloom, & Korpela, 2015).

The management climate of workplaces in fact predicts vitality and well-being, and this relationship is strongly mediated by employees' basic psychological need satisfactions and frustrations in the workplace (Deci & Ryan, 2014; Schultz, Ryan, Niemeic, Legate, & Williams, 2015). For example, Graves and Luciano (2013), in a study of leadership communication and work climates, found that satisfaction of autonomy and competence needs on the job was associated with greater subjective vitality and organizational commitment. Quinn and Dutton (2005) argued that high-quality interpersonal connections at work engender a feeling of vitality, and a sense of eagerness and capability to act. Drawing on SDT, they proposed that energy and vitality are enhanced when people interpret interpersonal interactions at work as increasing their autonomy, competence, or relatedness. Kark and Carmeli (2009) similarly suggested that a sense of *psychological safety* is at the core of such high-quality connections. The climate of safety they describe is one of autonomy and relatedness supports—one where people feel safe to speak up, report mistakes and errors, and take risks without fearing a loss of status, or of feeling humiliated or rejected. Accordingly, Kark and Carmeli found that feelings of psychological safety directly affected employees' subjective vitality. Subjective vitality, in turn, partially mediated the relation between psychological safety and greater involvement in creative work. Together, such results suggest that the three basic needs for autonomy, competence, and relatedness, when satisfied, can be an important source of vitality for people, within and between tasks at work. These psychological need satisfactions can *engender* energy and, in interaction with physical influences on the individual, determine the overall energy available to the self.

Nature and Vitality

Human beings evolved in natural environments, and pervasive exposure to human-made and highly artifact-laden environments is, in evolutionary terms, a very recent phenomenon. Nature, in fact, still represents an important source of recreation, as people actively seek encounters with outdoor nature. Many people seem to think that natural environments can replenish their sense of vigor and vitality. It is possible that natural settings allow people to be more open and relaxed instead of engaging in effortful and directed attention. These everyday experiences led Ryan et al. (2010) to examine whether there is some specific connection between nature and vitality in the sense that nature would provide or catalyze positive energy.

Some data already existed to support this possibility (see, eg, Kaplan & Kaplan, 1989). For example, Greenway (1995, p. 128), reported that 90% of participants in an outdoor experience described "an increased sense of aliveness, well-being, and energy." To test this connection more directly, Ryan, Bernstein, and Brown (2010) and Ryan et al. (2010) conducted five studies utilizing survey, experimental, and diary methods that all assessed the effects of being outdoors or around natural elements on subjective vitality. In a vignette study where participants had to rate how they would feel in various scenarios, they showed that people expected to experience more vitality when outdoors, even when effects for physical activity and social interactions were accounted for. In the second study, participants walked the same distance either indoors or outdoors, and the latter led to greater pre–post change in vitality. Third study asked participants to look at photographic scenes of either natural or built environments, and imagine themselves in these scenes. Results showed that exposure to nature scenes enhanced subjective vitality from pre-to-post exposure, while pictures of built environment did not have this effect. Finally, a diary methodology was used in studies 4 and 5 to examine within-person variations in vitality as a function of being outdoors, controlling for physical and social interactions. The results showed that being outdoors was associated with greater vitality, and furthermore, this relation was mediated by the presence of natural elements. This means that the more participants were exposed to natural surroundings while being outdoors, the greater the positive effect on vitality. In other studies Weinstein, Przybylski, and Ryan (2009) showed that exposure to nature not only increases our sense of vitality, it also makes us more prosocial, more valuing of intrinsic goals, and increases our sense of autonomy and relatedness to nature. Together, these studies utilizing multiple methods thus found a reliable association between exposure to outdoor natural environments and enhanced vitality. This is a conclusion that should be taken seriously in a time when longer working hours and increased "screen time" in front of TV's and computers (Rigby & Ryan, 2011) increasingly separate people from nature.

Mindful Attention to Present

Another potential source of vitality is *mindfulness*, conceptualized as an open and receptive awareness and attention to present moment (Brown & Ryan, 2003). As vitality is understood to be calm and positive energy instead of tense and negative energy (Ryan & Frederick, 1997; Thayer, 2001), it is suggested that mindfulness might help people to calm and thus better tap into their sources of positive energy. Furthermore, mindful attention makes one more aware of various dimensions of experience—potentially also one's intrinsic needs—and could thus lead to behavior that is more autonomously regulated and thus enhancing of vitality (Brown, Ryan, & Creswell, 2007). Indeed, Brown and Ryan (2003) showed that subjectively evaluated mindful attention was positively associated with vitality, and Fayad and Kazarian (2013) similarly showed using a Lebanese sample that vitality was associated with experiential self-knowledge, a form of awareness close to mindfulness. Another study examined older adults and found that this positive relation between mindfulness and vitality was partially mediated by the enhanced sleep quality of persons higher in mindfulness (Visser et al., 2015). As with attention in nature, mindful attention is open and receptive, without the constraints or inhibitions required for more controlled forms of cognition and directed awareness (Deci, Ryan, Schultz, & Niemiec, 2015), which may in part explain its positive relations to vitality.

Benevolence and Vitality

Finally, we suggest that people feel more energy and vitality when they engage in eudaimonic activities such as benevolent and prosocial acts. In a series of experiments on helping, Weinstein and Ryan (2010) demonstrated that when persons helped others for autonomous rather than controlled reasons they showed enhanced vitality, and this effect was mediated by the three basic psychological needs. Similarly, Deci et al. (2006) found evidence that giving autonomy support to best friends was associated with enhanced vitality not only for the receiver, but also for the giver of support. In a study of Finnish employees, de Bloom, Kinnunen, and Korpela (2015) found that helping a coworker was associated with increased vigor. Martela and Ryan (in press), in turn, directly assessed the sense of beneficence—the feeling that one is having a positive impact in the lives of others—and found out that this sense of beneficence was associated with vitality in both cross-sectional and daily diary settings. Although a large part of this effect was mediated by SDT's three basic psychological needs, there also was independent effect of beneficence on vitality. In a further experimental study, Martela and Ryan (2016) asked participants to play a simple computer game that either had or did not have a prosocial impact, and found out that participants who were able to contribute through their gameplay experienced an increased sense of vitality, an effect that was mediated by sense of beneficence and the satisfaction of autonomy, competence, and relatedness.

CONCLUSION

Vitality and ego depletion are two concepts representing states of energy available to the self, with depletion referring to a state where energy available to the self is low, and vitality a state when that energy is high. Importantly, these two concepts seem to be directly linked. In one set of studies, vitality mediated the effects of engaging in a more or less strenuous experimental condition on subsequent task performance, a standard measure of ego depletion (Muraven et al., 2008). It is also crucial to distinguish between self-regulation and self-control. Whereas self-regulation refers to the management of one's actions to be in line with one's intentions and goals, not all self-regulation is controlling (Baumeister, Vohs, & Tice, 2007; Ryan & Deci, 2008). SDT highlights that behavior can also be autonomously motivated, such as when the person feels positively and wholeheartedly motivated to act toward a goal (Deci & Ryan, 2000). In contrast to self-control, autonomous self-regulation does not represent forcing behavior to align with expectations, but rather the individual is volitionally and willingly engaged, leading to less ego depletion. When autonomous, motivation for activities is high, as evidenced by both self report and electrophysiological data (Meng & Ma, 2015), and some evidence even suggests increases in blood glucose as well as subjective vitality when people act autonomously (eg, Kazén et al., 2015). Even engaging in physically exhausting activities can be experienced as energizing when autonomy is high (Gagne et al., 2003). In addition we saw evidence that events that satisfy basic psychological needs for autonomy, competence, and relatedness also can enhance vitality, as these invigorate the sense of self. Additionally, exposure to nature, mindful attention to the present, and benevolent acts can similarly yield positive, energizing effects.

Our intent on this review is to trigger more engagement between research on self-regulation, self-control, and ego depletion on the one hand and self-determination, autonomous regulation, and vitality on the other hand. We believe that combining these two approaches can lead to a more complete understanding of both what drains and what maintains and enhances the energy that is available to, and can be harnessed by, the self. Such studies have implications both for the understanding of recovery and the replenishment of energetic resources depleted during work or stress, as well as our understanding of the processes that support human well-being and health more generally.

References

Baard, P. P., Deci, E. L., & Ryan, R. M. (2004). Intrinsic need satisfaction: a motivational basis of performance and well-being in two work settings. *Journal of Applied Social Psychology*, 34, 2045–2068.

Barrett, J., Della-Maggiore, V., Chouinard, P. A., & Paus, T. (2004). Mechanisms of action underlying the effect of repetitive transcranial magnetic stimulation on mood: behavioral and brain imaging studies. *Neuropsychopharmacology: Official Publication of the American College of Neuropsychopharmacology*, 29(6), 1172–1189.

Baumeister, R. F., Bratslavsky, E., Muraven, M., & Tice, D. M. (1998). Ego depletion: is the active self a limited resource? *Journal of Personality and Social Psychology*, 74(5), 1252–1265.

Baumeister, R. F., Muraven, M., & Tice, D. M. (2000). Ego depletion: a resource model of volition, self-regulation, and controlled processing. *Social Cognition*, 18, 130–150.

Baumeister, R. F., & Vohs, K. D. (2007). Self-regulation, ego depletion, and motivation. *Social and Personality Psychology Compass, 1,* 115–128.

Baumeister, R. F., Vohs, K. D., & Tice, D. M. (2007). The strength model of self-control. *Current Directions in Psychological Science, 16,* 351–355.

Beedie, C. J., & Lane, A. M. (2012). The role of glucose in self-control: another look at the evidence and an alternative conceptualization. *Personality and Social Psychology Review, 16,* 143–153.

Benyamini, Y., Idler, E. L., Leventhal, H., & Leventhal, E. A. (2000). Positive affect and function as influences on self-assessments of health expanding our view beyond illness and disability. *The Journals of Gerontology Series B: Psychological Sciences and Social Sciences, 55*(2), P107–P116.

de Bloom, J., Kinnunen, U., & Korpela, K. (2015). Recovery processes during and after work: associations with health, work engagement, and job performance. *Journal of Occupational and Environmental Medicine, 57*(7), 732–742.

Brown, K. W., & Ryan, R. M. (2003). The benefits of being present: mindfulness and its role in psychological well-being. *Journal of Personality and Social Psychology, 84*(4), 822–848.

Brown, K. W., Ryan, R. M., & Creswell, J. D. (2007). Mindfulness: theoretical foundations and evidence for its salutary effects. *Psychological Inquiry, 18*(4), 211–237.

de Charms, R. (1968). *Personal causation.* New York: Academic Press.

Cohen, S., Alper, C. M., Doyle, W. J., Treanor, J. J., & Turner, R. B. (2006). Positive emotional style predicts resistance to illness after experimental exposure to rhinovirus or influenza A virus. *Psychosomatic Medicine, 68*(6), 809–815.

Deci, E. L., Koestner, R., & Ryan, R. M. (1999). A meta-analytic review of experiments examining the effects of extrinsic rewards on intrinsic motivation. *Psychological Bulletin, 125,* 627–668.

Deci, E. L., La Guardia, J. G., Moller, A. C., Scheiner, M. J., & Ryan, R. M. (2006). On the benefits of giving as well as receiving autonomy support: mutuality in close friendships. *Personality & Social Psychology Bulletin, 32*(3), 313–327.

Deci, E. L., & Ryan, R. M. (1985). *Intrinsic motivation and self-determination in human behavior.* New York: Plenum.

Deci, E. L., & Ryan, R. M. (2000). The "what" and "why" of goal pursuits: human needs and the self-determination of behavior. *Psychological Inquiry, 11*(4), 227–268.

Deci, E. L., & Ryan, R. M. (2014). The importance of universal psychological needs for understanding motivation in the workplace. In M. Gagne (Ed.), *The Oxford handbook of work engagement, motivation, and self-determination theory* (pp. 13–32). New York, NY: Oxford University Press.

Deci, E. L., Ryan, R. M., Schultz, P. P., & Niemiec, C. P. (2015). Being aware and functioning fully: mindfulness and interest-taking within self-determination theory. In K. W. Brown, R. M. Ryan, & J. D. Creswell (Eds.), *Handbook of mindfulness* (pp. 112–129). New York, NY: Guilford Press.

Fayad, Y. I., & Kazarian, S. S. (2013). Subjective vitality of Lebanese adults in Lebanon: validation of the Arabic version of the subjective vitality scale. *Social Indicators Research, 114,* 465–478.

Freud, S. (1923). *The ego and the id.* New York: W.W. Norton.

Gagne, M., Ryan, R. M., & Bargmann, K. (2003). Autonomy support and need satisfaction in the motivation and well-being of gymnasts. *Journal of Applied Sport Psychology, 15,* 372–390.

Gailliot, M. T., & Baumeister, R. F. (2007). The physiology of willpower: linking blood glucose to self-control. *Personality and Social Psychology Review, 11,* 303–327.

Gailliot, M. T., Baumeister, R. F., DeWall, C. N., Maner, J. K., Plant, E. A., Tice, D. M., … Schmeichel, B. J. (2007). Self-control relies on glucose as a limited energy source: willpower is more than a metaphor. *Journal of Personality and Social Psychology, 92,* 325–336.

Graves, L. M., & Luciano, M. M. (2013). Self-determination at work: understanding the role of leader-member exchange. *Motivation and Emotion, 37*, 518–536.

Greenway, R. (1995). The wilderness effect and ecopsychology. In T. Roszak, M. E. Gomes, & A. D. Kanner (Eds.), *Ecopsychology: Restoring the Earth, healing the mind* (pp. 122–135). San Francisco, CA: Sierra Club Books.

Hagger, M. S., Wood, C., Stiff, C., & Chatzisarantis, N. L. D. (2010). Ego depletion and the strength model of self-control: a meta-analysis. *Psychological Bulletin, 136*, 495–525.

Hirsch, J. K., Molnar, D., Chang, E. C., & Sirois, F. M. (2014). Future orientation and health quality of life in primary care. *Quality of Life Research, 24*, 1653–1659.

Kaplan, R., & Kaplan, S. (1989). *The experience of nature – A psychological perspective*. Cambridge: Cambridge University Press.

Kark, R., & Carmeli, A. (2009). Alive and creating: the mediating role of vitality and aliveness in the relationship between psychological safety and creative work involvement. *Journal of Organizational Behavior, 30*, 785–804.

Kasser, V. G., & Ryan, R. M. (1999). The relation of psychological needs for autonomy and relatedness to vitality, well-being, and mortality in a nursing home. *Journal of Applied Social Psychology, 29*, 935–954.

Kazén, M., Kuhl, J., & Leicht, E.-M. (2015). When the going gets tough…: self-motivation is associated with invigoration and fun. *Psychological Research, 79*(6), 1064–1076.

Kinnunen, U., Feldt, T., de Bloom, J., & Korpela, K. (2015). Patterns of daily energy management at work: relations to employee well-being and job characteristics. *International Archives of Occupational and Environmental Health, 88*(8), 1077–1086.

Kuhl, J. (2000). A functional-design approach to motivation and self-regulation: the dynamics of personality systems and interactions. In M. Boekaerts, & P. R. Pintrich (Eds.), *Handbook of self-regulation* (pp. 111–169). San Diego, Ca: Academic Press.

Martela, F., & Ryan, R. M. The benefits of benevolence: basic psychological needs, beneficence and the enhancement of well-being. *Journal of Personality*, (in press).

Martela, F., & Ryan, R. M. (2016). Prosocial behavior increases well-being and vitality even without contact with the beneficiary: causal and behavioral evidence. *Motivation and Emotion, 40*(3), 351–357.

McNair, D. M., Lorr, M., & Droppleman, L. F. (1971). *Profile of mood states*. San Diego, CA: Educational and Industrial Testing Service.

Meng, L., & Ma, Q. (2015). Live as we choose: the role of autonomy support in facilitating intrinsic motivation. *International Journal of Psychophysiology, 98*(3), 441–447.

Moller, A. C., Deci, E. L., & Ryan, R. M. (2006). Choice and ego-depletion: the moderating role of autonomy. *Personality & Social Psychology Bulletin, 32*(8), 1024–1036.

Muraven, M. (2008). Autonomous self-control is less depleting. *Journal of Research in Personality, 42*(3), 763–770.

Muraven, M., Gagné, M., & Rosman, H. (2008). Helpful self-control: autonomy support, vitality, and depletion. *Journal of Experimental Social Psychology, 44*(3), 573–585.

Muraven, M., Rosman, H., & Gagné, M. (2007). Lack of autonomy and self-control: performance contingent rewards lead to greater depletion. *Motivation and Emotion, 31*, 322–330.

Muraven, M., Tice, D. M., & Baumeister, R. F. (1998). Self-control as a limited resource: regulatory depletion patterns. *Journal of Personality and Social Psychology, 74*(3), 774–789.

Natapoff, J. N. (1978). Children's views of health: a developmental study. *American Journal of Public Health, 68*, 995–1000.

Nix, G. A., Ryan, R. M., Manly, J. B., & Deci, E. L. (1999). Revitalization through self-regulation: the effects of autonomous and controlled motivation on happiness and vitality. *Journal of Experimental Social Psychology, 35*(3), 266–284.

Nowlis, V., & Green, R. F. (1964). *Factor analytic studies of mood*. Technical Report. Office of Naval Research. Contract No. Nonr-668(12).

Núñez, J. L., Fernández, C., León, J., & Grijalvo, F. (2015). The relationship between teachers' autonomy support and students' autonomy and vitality. *Teachers and Teaching, 21*, 191–202.

Patall, E. A., Cooper, H., & Robinson, J. C. (2008). The effects of choice on intrinsic motivation and related outcomes: a meta-analysis of research findings. *Psychological Bulletin, 134*, 270–300.

Penninx, B. W., Guralnik, J. M., Bandeen-Roche, K., Kasper, J. D., Simonsick, E. M., Ferrucci, L., & Fried, L. P. (2000). The protective effect of emotional vitality on adverse health outcomes in disabled older women. *Journal of the American Geriatrics Society, 48*, 1359–1366.

Pittman, T. S., Davey, M. E., Alafat, K. A., Wetherill, K. V., & Kramer, N. A. (1980). Informational versus controlling verbal rewards. *Personality & Social Psychology Bulletin, 6*, 228–233.

Polk, D. E., Cohen, S., Doyle, W. J., Skoner, D. P., & Kirschbaum, C. (2005). State and trait affect as predictors of salivary cortisol in healthy adults. *Psychoneuroendocrinology, 30*, 261–272.

Purcell, A. T. (1982). The structure of activation and emotion. *Multivariate Behavioral Research, 17*(2), 221–251.

Quested, E., & Duda, J. L. (2010). Exploring the social-environmental determinants of well- and ill-being in dancers: a test of basic needs theory. *Journal of Sport & Exercise Psychology, 32*(1), 39–60.

Quinn, R. W., & Dutton, J. E. (2005). Coordination as energy-in-conversation. *Academy of Management Review, 30*, 36–57.

Reinboth, M., & Duda, J. L. (2006). Perceived motivational climate, need satisfaction and indices of well-being in team sports: a longitudinal perspective. *Psychology of Sport and Exercise, 7*, 269–286.

Reis, H. T., Sheldon, K. M., Gable, S. L., Roscoe, J., & Ryan, R. M. (2000). Daily well-being: the role of autonomy, competence, and relatedness. *Personality & Social Psychology Bulletin, 26*(4), 419–435.

de Ridder, D. T., Lensvelt-Mulders, G., Finkenauer, C., Stok, F. M., & Baumeister, R. F. (2012). Taking stock of self-control a meta-analysis of how trait self-control relates to a wide range of behaviors. *Personality and Social Psychology Review, 16*, 76–99.

Rigby, S., & Ryan, R. M. (2011). *Glued to games: How video games draw us in and hold us spellbound*. Santa Barbara, CA: Praeger.

Rouse, P. C., Ntoumanis, N., & Duda, J. L. (2013). Effects of motivation and depletion on the ability to resist the temptation to avoid physical activity. *International Journal of Sport and Exercise Psychology, 11*(1), 39–56.

Rozanski, A., Blumenthal, J. A., Davidson, K. W., Saab, P. G., & Kubzansky, L. (2005). The epidemiology, pathophysiology, and management of psychosocial risk factors in cardiac practice: the emerging field of behavioral cardiology. *Journal of the American College of Cardiology, 45*(5), 637–651.

Ryan, R. M. (1982). Control and information in the intrapersonal sphere: an extension of cognitive evaluation theory. *Journal of Personality and Social Psychology, 43*(3), 450–461.

Ryan, R. M., Bernstein, J. H., & Brown, K. W. (2010). Weekends, work, and well-being: psychological need satisfactions and day of the week effects on mood, vitality, and physical symptoms. *Journal of Social and Clinical Psychology, 29*, 95–122. http://dx.doi.org/10.1521/jscp.2010.29.1.95.

Ryan, R. M., & Deci, E. L. (2000). Self-determination theory and the facilitation of intrinsic motivation, social development, and well-being. *American Psychologist, 55*, 68–78.

Ryan, R. M., & Deci, E. L. (2008). From ego depletion to vitality: theory and findings concerning the facilitation of energy available to the self. *Social and Personality Psychology Compass, 2*(2), 702–717.

Ryan, R. M., & Frederick, C. (1997). On energy, personality, and health: subjective vitality as a dynamic reflection of well-being. *Journal of Personality, 65*(3), 529–565.

Ryan, R. M., Weinstein, N., Bernstein, J., Brown, K. W., Mistretta, L., & Gagne, M. (2010). Vitalizing effects of being outdoors and in nature. *Journal of Environmental Psychology, 30,* 159–168.

Schultz, P., Ryan, R. M., Niemeic, C., Legate, N., & Williams, G. C. (2015). Mindfulness, work climate, and psychological need satisfaction in employee well-being. *Mindfulness, 6*(5), 971–985.

Selye, H. (1956). *The stress of life.* New York: McGraw-Hill.

Sheldon, K. M., Ryan, R. M., & Reis, H. T. (1996). What makes for a good day? Competence and autonomy in the day and in the person. *Personality & Social Psychology Bulletin, 22,* 1270–1279.

Spreitzer, G., Sutcliffe, K., Dutton, J., Sonenshein, S., & Grant, A. M. (2005). A socially embedded model of thriving at work. *Organization Science, 16,* 537–549.

Thayer, R. E. (1987). Energy, tiredness, and tension effects of a sugar snack versus moderate exercise. *Journal of Personality and Social Psychology, 52*(1), 119–125.

Thayer, R. E. (1996). *The origin of everyday moods.* New York: Oxford University Press.

Thayer, R. E. (2001). *Calm energy.* New York: Oxford University Press.

Thoman, D. B., Smith, J. L., & Silvia, P. J. (2011). The resource replenishment function of interest. *Social Psychological and Personality Science, 2*(6), 592–599.

Tice, D. M., Baumeister, R. F., Shmueli, D., & Muraven, M. (2007). Restoring the self: positive affect helps improve self-regulation following ego depletion. *Journal of Experimental Social Psychology, 43,* 379–384.

Tremblay, M. A., Blanchard, C. M., Pelletier, L. G., & Vallerand, R. J. (2006). A dual route in explaining health outcomes in natural disaster. *Journal of Applied Social Psychology, 36,* 1502–1522.

Trougakos, J., Hideg, I., Cheng, B., & Beal, D. (2013). Lunch breaks unpacked: the role of autonomy as a moderator of recovery during lunch. *Academy of Management Journal, 57,* 405–421.

Vallerand, R. J. (2015). *The psychology of passion.* New York, NY: Oxford.

Van den Broeck, A., Vansteenkiste, M., De Witte, H., & Lens, W. (2008). Explaining the relationships between job characteristics, burnout, and engagement: the role of basic psychological need satisfaction. *Work & Stress, 22*(3), 277–294.

Van den Broeck, A., Vansteenkiste, M., Witte, H., Soenens, B., & Lens, W. (2010). Capturing autonomy, competence, and relatedness at work: construction and initial validation of the work-related basic need satisfaction scale. *Journal of Occupational and Organizational Psychology, 83,* 981–1002.

Visser, P. L., Hirsch, J. K., Brown, K. W., Ryan, R., & Moynihan, J. A. (2015). Components of sleep quality as mediators of the relation between mindfulness and subjective vitality among older adults. *Mindfulness, 6*(4), 723–731.

Vlachopoulos, S. P., & Karavani, E. (2009). Psychological need and subjective vitality in exercise: a cross-gender situational test of the needs universality hypothesis. *Hellenic Journal of Psychology, 6,* 207–222.

Vohs, K. D., & Heatherton, T. F. (2000). Self-regulatory failure: a resource-depletion approach. *Psychological Science, 11*(3), 249–254.

Weinstein, N., Przybylski, A. K., & Ryan, R. M. (2009). Can nature make us more caring? Effects of immersion in nature on intrinsic aspirations and generosity. *Personality & Social Psychology Bulletin, 35*(10), 1315–1329.

Weinstein, N., & Ryan, R. M. (2010). When helping helps: autonomous motivation for prosocial behavior and its influence on well-being for the helper and recipient. *Journal of Personality and Social Psychology, 98*(2), 222–244.

Yik, M., Russell, J., & Feldman Barrett, L. (1999). Structure of self-reported current affect: integration and beyond. *Journal of Personality and Social Psychology, 77*(3), 600–619.

CHAPTER 5

What Does Ego-Depletion Research Reveal About Self-Control? A Conceptual Analysis

J.J. Carnevale[1], K. Fujita[2]

[1]Purchase College SUNY, Purchase, NY, United States; [2]The Ohio State University, Columbus, OH, United States

Although researchers have studied self-control—the ability to regulate one's thoughts, feelings, and behavior to secure future benefits—for decades, interest in the topic has surged in recent years (eg, Baumeister & Heatherton, 1996; Baumeister & Vohs, 2004; Metcalfe & Mischel, 1999; Mischel, Shoda, & Rodriguez, 1989). Much of this surge in interest can be attributed to research on ego depletion—the apparent diminished capacity or willingness to exert self-control following a previous self-control act (Muraven & Baumeister, 2000). In one of the earliest studies to document this effect, research participants who resisted the impulse to eat chocolates and instead ate radishes persisted less on a difficult cognitive task (ie, solving unsolvable anagrams) than did participants who ate chocolates instead of radishes or skipped the food task (Baumeister, Bratslavsky, Muraven, & Tice, 1998). This shocking finding (and similar others), along with the implication that self-control may be a limited resource, has spawned a voluminous body of empirical research (eg, Hagger, Wood, Stiff, & Chatzisarantis, 2010).

In this chapter, we provide a conceptual analysis of self-control and its relationship to ego depletion. We do not cast doubt on the existence of ego depletion as a phenomenon (cf. Carter, Kofler, Forster, & McCullough, 2015), but argue that conceptual confusion about the terms self-control and ego depletion leads many to draw erroneous and unwarranted conclusions. Specifically, whether self-control is a necessary and sufficient condition for producing ego depletion warrants conceptual (and empirical) scrutiny. At the heart of our argument is a warning to others that they should not assume that the two terms are synonymous and interchangeable. We conclude by discussing what ego depletion can teach us about self-control and self-regulation in light of this caveat.

WHAT IS SELF-CONTROL?

Before we can discuss the relationship between self-control and ego depletion, we must first define self-control, a term that some have used interchangeably with related terms such as self-regulation, executive function, delay of gratification, and willpower. Let us first define self-regulation. Self-regulation is an umbrella term used to describe the collection of processes entailed in setting and managing goals, as well as guiding thoughts, feelings, and behavior to attain those goals (eg, Carver & Scheier, 1982, 1990; Gollwitzer, 1990; Mann, de Ridder, & Fujita, 2013). Self-regulation entails addressing a number of challenges, which include not only selecting desirable and feasible goals, but also identifying which goals to pursue at a given time, executing the necessary behaviors to attain those goals, finding ways around obstacles, and coping with setbacks.

The term executive function is often used in the cognitive science literature to refer to much the same processes and challenges (eg, Hofmann, Schmeichel, & Baddeley, 2012; Miyake & Friedman, 2012). Unsurprisingly, however, much of the focus in executive function has been on assessing the various cognitive operations necessary in regulating thoughts, feelings, and behavior (eg, updating, inhibition, task switching; Chapter 15). Whereas executive function is understood in largely cognitive terms, self-regulation attempts to integrate the dynamic interplay between cognitive, motivational, and behavioral processes involved in goal pursuit. More recent self-regulation research has, moreover, increasingly emphasized interpersonal processes as well (Fitzsimons, Finkel, & van Dellen, 2015).

Historically, self-control has generally been defined as a preference for larger delayed over smaller immediate rewards (eg, Ainslie, 1975; Hoch & Loewenstein, 1991; Kirby & Herrnstein, 1995; Mischel, 1974; Mischel et al., 1989; Rachlin, 1995; Rachlin & Green, 1972; Schelling, 1978; Strotz, 1955; Thaler & Shefrin, 1981). This conceptualization of self-control is the basis for research on delay of gratification and delay discounting. In Walter Mischel and colleagues' classic "marshmallow studies" (see Metcalfe & Mischel, 1999; Mischel et al., 1989; for reviews), for example, children were presented with a single marshmallow which they could eat immediately. However, they were also told that if they could resist eating it for 15min, they would receive two instead. The duration of time children are able to wait (ie, delay of gratification) constituted an assessment of self-control. Research on delay discounting similarly presents participants with choices between smaller immediate versus larger delayed rewards. Participants, for example, might be asked to choose between receiving $10 now versus $100 a year from now. Research suggests that people tend to prefer the former over the latter, even when traditional economic theory suggests that latter is more prescriptively normative (eg, Green, Fristoe, & Myerson, 1994; Kirby & Herrnstein, 1995). Thus self-control has traditionally been defined as prioritizing larger delayed over smaller immediate outcomes.

Fujita (2011) more recently proposed that this traditional behavioral conceptualization of self-control can be understood in motivational or self-regulatory terms as a dual-motive or dual-goal conflict. That is, people want both the smaller immediate and larger delayed rewards, but only one of these two motivations can be satisfied in any one moment. Self-control refers to those processes that allow people to prioritize and preferentially advance their more distal over proximal motivations. The immediate salience and proximity of the smaller immediate rewards, however, makes this task challenging.

What is important to note is that understood either behaviorally or motivationally, self-control is a specific self-regulatory challenge—one in which the pursuit of distal outcomes is threatened by more readily attainable proximal rewards. Although self-control is a type of self-regulatory challenge, not all self-regulation entails self-control (Fujita, 2011). Consider, for example, the situation in which a basketball player must sink free throws to win a championship game. This action requires very careful regulation of thoughts, feelings, and behavior. Yet, it does not entail self-control; the basketball player is not tempted to miss. Instead, his or her focus is on the proper execution of behavior, which is a self-regulatory challenge distinct from self-control. A distinguishing feature of self-control then is the presence of competing wants—a feature that not all self-regulation challenges present.

Effortful Inhibition

One way people overcome the challenge of self-control is by actively inhibiting the thoughts, feelings, and behavioral tendencies potentiated by their proximal motivations in the presence of temptations, a term sometimes referred to as willpower (eg, Mann et al., 2013; Mischel & Ayduk, 2004). An extensive body of research suggests that the ability to inhibit or restrain one's tendencies to indulge in immediate rewards is a critical cognitive mechanism in self-control (eg, Baumeister & Heatherton, 1996; Hofmann, Friese, & Strack, 2009; Hofmann, Schmeichel et al., 2012; Loewenstein, 1996; Metcalfe & Mischel, 1999; Wiers & Stacy, 2006). Critically, two properties of this inhibitory process are important to note (eg, Wegner, 1994, 2009).

First, inhibition is reactive—it is a process that is initiated after the detection of impulsive tendencies—tendencies to indulge in the smaller immediate reward. Second, inhibition is theorized to be effortful, requiring sufficient cognitive and motivational resources to enact.

Numerous studies have supported these assertions. Research suggests, for example, that when people are not alert, temptations can "fly under the radar" —leading them to indulge without appreciating the negative consequences for their valued long-term goals (eg, Do Vale, Pieters, & Zeelenberg, 2008; Magen, Dweck, & Gross, 2008; Myrseth & Fishbach, 2009). Moreover, burdens on cognitive resources, such as cognitive load, impair self-control (eg, Hinson, Jameson, & Whitney, 2003; Hofmann, Rauch, & Gawronski, 2007; Shiv & Fedorikhin, 1999; Ward & Mann, 2000). For example, people are more likely to choose unhealthy chocolate cake rather than healthy fruit salad as a snack when rehearsing a seven-digit rather than two-digit number string (Shiv & Fedorikhin, 1999). We might also add that effortful inhibition can cause ego depletion, providing additional evidence of how resource-intensive inhibiting impulsive thoughts, feelings, and behavior can be (eg, Baumeister & Heatherton, 1996; Muraven & Baumeister, 2000).

Conflating Effortful Inhibition With Self-Control

It is fairly uncontroversial to state that effortful inhibition can serve as a means to advance distal over proximal outcomes—that is, to promote self-control. Some researchers, however, have gone a step further and suggested that self-control can be defined as the effortful inhibition of impulsive thoughts, feelings, and behavior. Defining self-control in terms of effortful inhibition unfortunately introduces a number of conceptual problems. By equating a means of promoting self-control with the act itself, this conceptualization of self-control leads researchers to overlook the other means by which people enhance their self-control.

Recall that effortful inhibition is a reactive process that is initiated in response to temptation impulses. Research suggests that people can also engage in proactive forms of self-control, strategies invoked to prevent temptation impulses in the first place (eg, Ainslie, 1975; Ariely & Wertenbroch, 2002; Hoch & Loewenstein, 1991; Trope & Fishbach, 2000; Wertenbroch, 1998). Consider, for example, the strategies that dieters might use to promote their weight-loss efforts. They could engage in effortful inhibition of the various thoughts and feelings that they experience when they step into a bakery, willfully directing their attention instead to less calorie dense options. Alternatively, they could just avoid going to the bakery in the first place. Whereas the former is a reactive strategy—one that is initiated in response to the detection of undesired thoughts, feelings, and behavior, the latter is a proactive strategy—one that is initiated in anticipation of a self-control conflict to prevent those psychological reactions. Research suggests that people do indeed engage in such proactive efforts. For example, people deposit money into so-called "Christmas savings accounts" that pay no interest yet charge steep early withdrawal fees (Thaler & Shefrin, 1981). These accounts confer no financial advantages, but effectively deter impulsive withdrawal of the deposited funds. Children as young as 5 years of age, moreover, appear to recognize that occlusion of immediate rewards, rather than exposure to them, promotes self-control (eg, Mischel & Mischel, 1983).

The empirical literature also suggests that there may be efficient forms of self-control, those that do not require extensive cognitive resources to enact. Research suggests, for example, that those who are more successful at self-control develop what might be considered cognitive habits that advance their distal goals in the face of immediate temptations. Fishbach, Friedman, and Kruglanski (2003) demonstrated that those who are more successful at self-control evidence an asymmetric pattern of cognitive associations, whereby thinking about proximal temptations facilitates thinking about one's distal goals, but thinking about one's distal goals does not reciprocally facilitate thinking about proximal temptations. In other words, while thoughts about cookies activate a dieter's weight-loss goals, thinking of weight loss does not trigger thoughts about cookies. Such asymmetric associations are functional because they bias thoughts in favor of one's distal rather than proximal concerns (Fishbach et al., 2003; Papies, Stroebe, & Aarts, 2008). These asymmetric associations, moreover, are efficient—evident even when people are under cognitive load, thus providing people with a means of advancing their distal goals even in suboptimal processing conditions (Fishbach et al., 2003).

One might assume from the literature on skill learning that such cognitive habit learning might take lengthy repeated practice over time. Research on implementation intentions, however, suggests that such protracted practice may not be necessary. This work suggests that the generation of simple if-then plans can automatize responses to temptations to benefit distal goals (eg, Gollwitzer, 1990). For example, a dieter might commit to a plan such as "IF I am offered dessert, THEN I will refuse it." These if-then plans create cognitive links between the undesired temptation and the preferred behavior. When the critical situation specified by the "if" component is encountered, the behavior specified by the "then" component is automatically initiated without requiring any deliberative effort or monitoring (eg, Brandstätter, Lengfelder, & Gollwitzer, 2001). An extensive literature indicates that implementation intentions can be used as an effective means by which to instantiate efficient self-control (eg, Gollwitzer & Sheeran, 2006; see also Chapter 3).

Research on the role of subjective construal in self-control suggests that simply changing how one interprets or understands an event may also serve as an efficient way to promote one's distal yet valued goals (eg, Fujita, 2008; Fujita & Carnevale, 2012). Consider a piece of chocolate cake. Dieters can construe this stimulus as a tasty treat versus as a fattening overindulgence. The positive connotations of chocolate cake as a tasty treat may necessitate inhibitory processes to promote weight-loss goals. By contrast, the negative connotations of chocolate cake as a fattening overindulgence obviate the need for inhibition—the implied lack of positive qualities prevents the individual from being tempted in the first place. Research from construal level theory suggests that cognitive abstraction plays a key role in this meaning-making process (Fujita, 2008; Fujita & Carnevale, 2012). By highlighting the more abstract, essential, and invariant features of a stimulus (rather than more concrete, secondary, and idiosyncratic features), high-level (vs low-level) construal promotes sensitivity to the broader implications of single behaviors (Trope & Liberman, 2010). This sensitivity enhances self-control because it leads people to evaluate individual behaviors (eg, eating a second helping of dessert) in the context of broader, distal goals (eg, losing weight). Research demonstrates that high-level construal, by changing what temptations mean to people, can enhance self-control, and can do so without requiring effortful inhibition (eg, Carnevale, Fujita, Han, & Amit, 2015; Fujita & Han, 2009; Fujita & Sasota, 2011).

Self-Control Versus Self-Regulation

Proponents of defining self-control as effortful inhibition might respond to the discussion above by acknowledging that effortful inhibition represents only one of many means by which to advance distal over proximal goals. They might, however, suggest that there is something unique about effortful inhibition and that it is deserving of special attention in the form of its own distinct term; specifically, "self-control." All of the other means of promoting distal over proximal goals might be considered some other form of "self-regulation."

Although at first glance this might appear to be a reasonable reconciliation of terms, further analysis suggests that it creates more conceptual problems than it might resolve. The notion that self-control entails the effortful inhibition of temptations adopts a cognitive definition of self-control. To appreciate the implications of this change in approach, consider the following thought experiment. Imagine that a participant indicates that chocolate is tasty, and on another measure indicates that he is concerned about weight loss. Then, we observe that the participant forgoes an opportunity to eat a piece of chocolate cake. From the perspective of both traditional behavioral and more recent dual-motive definitions, this clearly constitutes a successful act of self-control: the dieter has preferred a distal relative to proximal outcome (weight loss over eating this particular cake). By contrast, the cognitive perspective must remain silent as to whether this act is successful self-control or not. This is because the dieter might have come to the conclusion to not eat the cake through a variety of potential mechanisms, of which only one can be considered successful self-control; namely, effortful inhibition. A researcher adopting a cognitive definition of self-control must confirm that the effortful inhibition was responsible for this outcome, and not some alternative mechanism such as asymmetric temptation–goal associations, implementation intentions, and subjective construal. Defining self-control cognitively thus renders behavior nondiagnostic of self-control. The need to confirm effortful inhibition as the specific mechanism for a given behavior would appear to put unnecessary conceptual and empirical demands on any researcher who purports to study self-control.

Defining self-control as effortful inhibition also narrows the explanatory breadth of self-control as a conceptual variable. Many researchers study self-control due to its association with important life outcomes like academic achievement, income, mental and physical health, and delinquency (eg, Duckworth & Seligman, 2005; Moffitt et al., 2011; Rodriguez, Mischel, & Shoda, 1989; Shoda, Mischel, & Peake, 1990; Tangney, Baumeister, & Boone, 2004). Although effortful inhibition can impact real-world behavior (see Miyake & Friedman, 2012; for review), more recent work suggests that it may not play as central a role in everyday self-control decision-making as some might assume.

Consider the results of a recent large-scale experience sampling study conducted by Hofmann, Schmeichel et al. (2012). They asked participants to wear a beeper for a week and asked them to report their feelings of immediate desires and effortful resistance to those desires at random points during each day (Hofmann, Baumeister, Förster, & Vohs, 2012). One might predict from theorizing about effortful inhibition that those with high trait self-control would be those who most frequently and effectively engage in effortful resistance. Instead, people highest in trait self-control were the least likely to report engaging in this process. What appeared to account for the success of those high in trait self-control is the absence of feeling tempted, a finding that is consistent with engaging instead in proactive and efficient forms of self-control (eg, avoidance, cognitive habits, subjective construal). Research by Galla and Duckworth (2015) provides evidence for this interpretation, demonstrating that efficient cognitive and behavioral habits (and not effortful inhibition) mediate the relationship between trait self-control and positive life outcomes. This finding also accords with a recent metaanalysis that concluded that trait self-control operates through effective habits and routines that allow people to avoid temptations rather than engaging in effortful resistance (de Ridder, Lensvelt-Mulders, Finkenauer, Stok, & Baumeister, 2012). Effortful inhibition therefore does not appear to play the critical role in people's everyday advancement of distal over proximal goals as one might expect from the inhibition literature. One might similarly observe that some of the most effective interventions to help people advance distal over proximal goals in the domains of retirement savings (eg, Thaler & Benartzi, 2004), food choice (eg, Adriaanse, Vinkers, De Ridder, Hox, & De Wit, 2011; Redden et al., 2015), and academics (eg, Duckworth, Kirby, Gollwitzer, & Oettingen, 2013), bypass effortful inhibition processes entirely, and instead engage proactive and cognitively efficient mechanisms.

Defining self-control as effortful inhibition requires self-control researchers to conclude that they are studying a process that has very little to say about what the most effective self-regulators do in their everyday lives and how the most effective interventions operate. By contrast, a broader definition of self-control—one couched in behavioral or motivational terms—provides researchers with the conceptual framework with which to integrate results like these and to expand the explanatory scope of the concept. Given this, and the conceptual and empirical hurdles imposed by a cognitive definition, it would appear disadvantageous to define self-control in terms of effortful inhibition.

Implications for Ego-Depletion Research

What we hope is clear from the discussion above is that defining self-control as effortful inhibition is a departure from traditional conceptualizations, creates a number of conceptual problems for researchers, and artificially constrains the explanatory scope of the concept. Nonetheless we might observe that much of the ego-depletion literature is grounded in the notion that self-control entails this effortful inhibition process (eg, Baumeister & Heatherton, 1996; Hagger et al., 2010; Muraven & Baumeister, 2000). What we explore in the next section are some of the implications this might have in how we interpret what ego depletion is and what its relationship to self-control might be.

WHAT IS EGO DEPLETION?

To assess the relationship between ego depletion and self-control, we must first define ego depletion in a manner that does not invite circularity. Unfortunately, ego depletion is frequently defined in self-control terms. Specifically, ego depletion is often described as a state of diminished "strength" or reduced resources that results from an initial act of self-control, which hampers subsequent self-control efforts (eg, Baumeister, Vohs, & Tice, 2007; Hagger et al., 2010).

We might observe, however, that the definition of ego depletion has shifted and evolved, and has not always referred specifically to self-control.

In one early conceptualization, Baumeister et al. (1998) proposed a broad definition of ego depletion based on the notion of the "active self." They proposed that the active self refers to an agentic self that acts autonomously on its own behalf, and encompasses many processes beyond self-control including making choices, modifying responses, and other volitional acts. Ego depletion from this perspective was defined as a reduction in the self's "capacity or willingness to engage in volitional action caused by prior exercise of volition" (Baumeister et al., 1998). From this perspective, any self-regulatory act—whether it entails setting appropriate goals, planning, executing goal-directed behavior, evaluating one's goal progress, or advancing distal over proximal outcomes—should cause ego depletion. It is important to note, however, that all of the manipulations designed to produce ego depletion in the actual empirical work that tested this conceptualization can be considered inductions of effortful inhibition. Thus, although Baumeister et al. (1998) defined ego depletion broadly, the empirical tests assumed a much narrower definition.

This focus on effortful inhibition is evident in other early ego-depletion studies. Around the same time as the Baumeister et al. (1998) paper was published, Muraven, Tice, and Baumeister (1998) proposed a narrower conceptualization of ego depletion focused on "self-regulation" specifically, rather than on the active self more generally. They defined self-regulation as "the capacity of the human organism to override, interrupt, and otherwise alter its own responses." Although this definition may encompass a number of different processes, Muraven et al. (1998) specifically focused on effortful inhibition as the means by which people enact self-regulation. It is therefore not particularly surprising that they then use the terms self-regulation and self-control interchangeably. Similar interchangeable use of the terms self-regulation, self-control, and effortful inhibition in the conceptualization of ego depletion can be seen in other early and influential papers in the literature. Vohs and Heatherton (2000), for instance, focused their analysis specifically on "effortful self-regulation" as a drain on limited regulatory resources, which then led to decrements in self-control (as assessed by dieters' eating behavior). Subsequent papers have largely followed suit, defining ego depletion in self-regulation or self-control terms, rather than referring to the "active self" more broadly. Moreover, they have focused exclusively on effortful inhibition as the means by which self-regulation and self-control are enacted (for reviews, see Baumeister et al., 2007; Hagger et al., 2010; Muraven & Baumeister, 2000).

We might instead define ego depletion behaviorally as the apparent diminished capacity or willingness to regulate thoughts, feelings, and behavior following some initial act. This definition makes no assumptions about the resource demands or regulatory nature of the initial act; instead, these assumptions can be empirically tested and validated. With this definition in mind, together with our discussion of the terms self-regulation, self-control, and effortful inhibition, we are now in a position to be able to evaluate the relationship between ego depletion and self-control.

The Relationship Between Ego Depletion and Self-Control: Do Acts of Self-Control Cause Ego Depletion?

There is compelling empirical evidence to suggest that there is a relationship between effortful inhibition and ego depletion. Numerous studies demonstrate that engaging in effortful inhibition can produce apparent decrements in people's ability or willingness to regulate in subsequent tasks (eg, Hagger et al., 2010). As described earlier, participants who inhibited the impulse to eat chocolates and instead ate less palatable radishes evidenced reduced persistence on a challenging task than did participants who ate chocolates instead of radishes or skipped the food task (Baumeister et al., 1998). Similarly, suppressing thoughts about white bears (vs completing three digit by three digit multiplication problems, an equally difficult task that did not require effortful inhibition) led participants to comply less successfully with instructions to mask their emotions while watching a humorous video (Muraven et al., 1998). These and other similar findings suggest that it is fairly noncontroversial to conclude that effortful inhibition is ego depleting.

That acts of self-control produce ego depletion, however, may be a more controversial assertion. To the extent that one defines self-control as effortful inhibition, the answer may be affirmative. Yet the effortful inhibition entailed in classic ego-depletion manipulations frequently lacks the conflict between competing larger distal versus smaller proximal wants that distinguishes self-control from other self-regulatory challenges. Consider, for example, suppressing thoughts about white bears (eg, Wegner, Schneider, Carter, & White, 1987; Muraven et al., 1998). Although this is certainly a manipulation of effortful inhibition, it is less clear for what ends one is engaging in this process. That is, what larger distal outcome do people achieve by successfully completing this exercise? Although participants in ego-depletion experiments are undoubtedly engaging in effortful inhibition, many of the manipulations do not appear to involve resolving a conflict between competing wants—the very kind of goal-directed effortful inhibition about which the researchers are attempting to draw conclusions.

There are, nevertheless, studies in the ego-depletion literature where the conflict between smaller proximal versus larger distal outcomes is more explicitly clear. Vohs and Heatherton (2000), for example, manipulated ego depletion by offering dieters the opportunity to help themselves to junk foods that were placed in a spatially proximal versus distant location while they watched a movie. As the forgoing of tempting junk food requires dieters to prioritize long-term weight loss over more short-term hedonic eating, this manipulation of ego depletion appears to capture all of the traditional elements of self-control. Moreover, the immediacy of the spatially proximal relative to spatially distant junk food makes it more tempting to dieters, thereby increasing the demand for self-control. After the movie, in an ostensibly separate study, participants were given an opportunity to eat ice cream. Results revealed that dieters who were presented with spatially proximal (vs distant) junk food during the movie subsequently ate more ice cream. Findings such as this suggest that acts of self-control can cause ego depletion.

Are Acts of Self-Control Necessary for Ego Depletion?

Although there are empirical studies that suggest that there is a relationship between self-control and ego depletion, it is less clear that one can make the assertion that ego depletion is specific to self-control. In other words, it is debatable whether self-control is a necessary condition for ego depletion. Research suggests that self-control can produce depletion effects, but so too can other actions that do not fall into either the effortful inhibition definition of self-control or more traditional behavioral or dual-motive definitions. Recall that the early "active self" conceptualization of ego depletion left room for the notion that actions other than effortful inhibition and/or self-control can produce ego-depletion effects, defining ego depletion as a "temporary reduction in the self's capacity or willingness to engage in volitional action caused by prior exercise of volition" (Baumeister et al., 1998). Many actions other than self-control may be considered volitional and research has shown that these actions can cause depletion. For example, participants who made many choices between consumer products persisted less in a cold pressor task (eg, holding one's arms in unpleasantly cold water) than did participants who merely recorded their responses to advertisements but did not choose between them (Vohs et al., 2014). Although making choices is certainly a volitional act, it does not immediately appear to entail the same effortful inhibition processes that are involved in typical ego-depletion manipulations (eg, suppressing thoughts about white bears), nor does it involve choosing between a smaller proximal versus larger distal outcomes. That some acts that do not fit into the definitions of self-control (both those proposed in terms of effortful inhibition or other perspectives on what constitutes self-control) produce ego depletion suggests that self-control is not a necessary condition for ego depletion.

Some might counterargue by asserting that volitional acts such as making choices must involve self-control because doing so leads to depletion (Vohs et al., 2014). It is problematic, however, to determine that an action requires self-control by measuring that action's influence on depletion, particularly if that action, such as making choices, does not fall into the definition of self-control a priori. The reasoning behind this claim is based on the converse of the premise that self-control causes ego depletion, which is logically faulty. That acts of self-control can cause ego depletion does not necessarily imply that states of ego-depletion signal acts of self-control.

More troubling for the assertion that self-control is necessary for ego depletion is research that indicates that nonvolitional acts can also be sufficient to cause depletion. For example, people appear to be able to experience depletion vicariously—by watching others engage in volitional acts, including self-control. In one study, participants read a story about a character engaging in self-control (Ackerman, Goldstein, Shapiro, & Bargh, 2009). Half were asked to adopt the perspective of the story's character while the other half were simply instructed to read the story. Those who adopted the perspective of someone engaging in self-control displayed worse self-control in the form of impulsive overspending on a subsequent task. A follow-up study similarly found that taking the perspective of someone engaging in self-control (as compared to someone not engaging in self-control) impaired performance on a subsequent cognitive performance task, suggesting that the effects of the first study were not due to the instructions to adopt another's perspective. Research by Clarkson and colleagues (Clarkson, Hirt, Chapman, & Jia, 2011; Clarkson, Hirt, Jia, & Alexander, 2010; see also Chapter 10) further demonstrates that when people are falsely led to believe that they have engaged in effortful inhibition, they evidence depletion, even when they have objected not engaged in anything depleting. Taken together, these findings suggest that people can experience ego depletion effects without actually engaging in any acts of volition and suggest that while it may be sufficient, it is not necessary for individuals to engage in self-control to experience depletion.Chapter 19

Are Acts of Self-Control Sufficient to Produce Ego Depletion?

Many researchers appear to assume that acts of self-control are sufficient to produce ego depletion. This assumption is problematic for two reasons. First, a myriad of findings suggest that although engaging in self-control *can* lead to depletion, it need not necessarily do so. Research highlights a host of factors that appear to moderate whether acts of self-control—or more specifically, acts of effortful inhibition—cause ego depletion (see Masicampo, Martin, & Anderson, 2014; for review; see also Chapter 2). Moller, Deci, and Ryan (2006), for example, demonstrated that the same act of effortful inhibition does not produce ego depletion when it is intrinsically rather than extrinsically motivated (see also Muraven, 2008; Muraven, Gagné, & Rosman, 2008; see also Chapter 4). Research by Job, Dweck, and Walton (2010) and Job, Walton, Bernecker, and Dweck (2013, see also Chapter 11) demonstrates that depletion effects are dependent on a person's beliefs about whether or not self-control resources are finite. The same manipulation that produces the typical ego-depletion effect among those who believe that self-control is a limited resource has no impact on those who believe that self-control resources are unlimited (Job et al., 2010). Similarly, those who were induced to believe that self-control capacity was unlimited through a laboratory manipulation did not show diminished performance on a second self-control task (Job et al., 2010). These and many other moderator studies suggest that self-control is not a sufficient condition for producing ego depletion.

Second, as noted earlier, much of the ego-depletion literature has focused on effortful inhibition, rather than self-control more broadly defined, as the cause of ego depletion. As such, researchers have largely overlooked the effect of engaging in other types of more proactive and/or efficient forms of self-control on depletion. It remains to be empirically tested whether engaging in some alternative self-control process produces ego depletion. We might observe, however, that one experiment by Webb and Sheeran (2003) suggests that implementation intentions—a form of efficient self-regulation—does not appear to produce ego depletion in the same way that effortful inhibition does. Participants first completed a manipulation of ego depletion—a Stroop interference task in which they were asked to identify the color of a word's font when the word itself referred to a different color (eg, the word "green" in red font; Stroop, 1935). Some of the participants, however, were furnished with an implementation intention—they were instructed to tell themselves "As soon as I see the word I will ignore its meaning and I will name the color ink it is printed in." Participants who were provided with implementation intentions showed no evidence of ego depletion on a subsequent persistence task. This then suggests that some forms of self-control, particularly those that are more efficient, may not cause ego depletion—a conclusion inconsistent with the notion that self-control is sufficient to cause ego depletion.

Summary of the Relationship Between Ego Depletion and Self-Control

Our analysis of the relationship between ego depletion and self-control reveals several surprising findings. First, most ego depletion studies do not examine self-control per se—they focus instead on the cognitive process of effortful inhibition. Although people often use effortful inhibition to prioritize larger distal over smaller proximal outcomes, the operationalization of effortful inhibition in many ego-depletion studies lacks this dynamic of competing wants. Thus the relevance of many ego-depletion studies to self-control is somewhat unclear. Second, although some studies indicate that self-control may produce ego depletion, research indicates that so too do a number of other factors—including those that do not entail effortful inhibition, such as imagining the behavior of others. Self-control is therefore not a necessary condition for ego depletion. Third, although self-control can produce ego depletion, it does not necessarily do so. A number of factors moderate the classic effect of effortful inhibition on ego depletion, suggesting that the same task may not be consistently depleting under all conditions for all individuals. Moreover, although research has yet to test directly the impact of efficient forms of self-control, research suggests that efficient forms of self-regulation more broadly do not produce depletion. Self-control therefore does not appear to be a sufficient condition for ego depletion. Taken as a whole, it appears that the relationship between ego depletion and self-control is more nuanced than many assume when they use the terms synonymously and interchangeably.

EGO DEPLETION'S LESSONS FOR SELF-CONTROL AND SELF-REGULATION

Although we argue that it is a mistake to consider self-control as a necessary and sufficient condition for ego depletion, the depletion literature nonetheless makes important contributions to our understanding of self-control and self-regulation. Here we discuss some of the lessons, as well as underexplored questions that might represent the basis of exciting future research.

Effortful Inhibition as a Costly and Fallible Self-Regulation Strategy

One important lesson of ego-depletion research is that effortful inhibition is a fallible self-regulation mechanism. Such attempts are not always successful, particularly if the individual does not have sufficient cognitive and motivational resources from which to draw. Although research has suggested that burdens on people's cognitive resources might impair performance on effortful inhibition tasks (eg, Hinson et al., 2003; Hofmann et al., 2007; Shiv & Fedorikhin, 1999; Ward & Mann, 2000), ego-depletion research is the first work to highlight the deleterious impact of these burdens on subsequent unrelated tasks (eg, Baumeister et al., 1998; Muraven et al., 1998). Effortful inhibition therefore presents a double vulnerability in that it is likely to fail without sufficient resources while at the same time further drawing down that same limited resource. As a regulatory strategy, effortful inhibition may represent an even more costly and demanding regulatory strategy than once believed.

Conceptual confusion about the relationship between effortful inhibition, self-control, and ego depletion, however, has had important consequences for how people understand self-control and how best to improve it. By assuming self-control is a sufficient condition for depletion, many researchers have assumed ego depletion is an inevitable and unavoidable consequence of goal pursuit. As such, research has focused on finding ways to overcome or counteract the drain that effortful inhibition has on people's regulatory resources. These include training to improve people's effortful inhibition abilities (Gailliot, Plant, Butz, & Baumeister, 2007; Muraven, Baumeister, & Tice, 1999; Oaten & Cheng, 2006), resting and recuperating following effortful inhibition (Muraven & Baumeister, 2000; Tyler & Burns, 2008), and conserving energy in anticipation of self-control demands (Muraven, Shmueli, & Burkley, 2006). As ego depletion is assumed to be inevitable, the general strategy of these studies is to induce some state of depletion, introduce some mitigating factor, and then observe the consequences for subsequent regulatory performance (eg, Hagger et al., 2010; Masicampo et al., 2014)—all while focusing on how to prevent and recover from depletion (see Chapter 12).

We might argue that this focus on prevention and recovery puts all of a self-regulator's eggs in a basket that is highly vulnerable to environmental influences. Missing from this discussion is the fact that people might use a myriad of more proactive and efficient forms of self-control to avoid a depleted state in the first place. As noted earlier, some research suggests that ego depletion can be avoided entirely by enacting efficient forms of self-regulation such as implementation intentions (Webb & Sheeran, 2003; see Chapter 3). Thus rather than start the self-control process with a state of ego depletion, we might instead ask what people might do to avoid engaging in effortful inhibition at all?

What makes framing the discussion in this way particularly problematic is that by defining self-control as effortful inhibition and by concluding that self-control is sufficient for ego depletion, researchers have focused exclusively on a process that few successful self-regulators use (eg, Galla & Duckworth, 2015; Hofmann, Schmeichel et al., 2012; de Ridder, de Boer, Lugtig, Bakker, & van Hooft, 2011). Rather than reflect dedicated efforts at self-control, one might suggest that regular experience of depletion indicates overreliance on a failed strategy. Thus, rather than serve as a hallmark of effective self-control, depletion may instead represent a predictor of poor self-control skill.

Rather than focus on mitigating depletion, we would argue that more research needs to be conducted to assess critically the conclusion that self-control is a sufficient condition for ego depletion. Do, for example, individuals who use efficient cognitive habits to resist temptations, such as those who evidence asymmetric temptation–goal associations, evidence ego depletion? We might note that construal levels have been shown to mitigate the deleterious effects of ego depletion (eg, Agrawal & Wan, 2009; Schmeichel & Vohs, 2009; see also Bruyneel & Dewitte, 2012), but might they help people avoid feeling depleted in the first place? By questioning the assumption that ego depletion is unavoidable and inevitable, we might come to better understand what role ego depletion plays (if any) in successful self-control.

Questioning the conclusion that self-control is a sufficient condition for depletion may also allow us paradoxically to embrace states of depletion as opportunities to promote goal-directed behavior. Research indicates that although depletion typically inhibits regulatory behavior on subsequent tasks, it can be used to advance valued goals under certain conditions. States of depletion have been found to enhance the salience of immediate, environmental influences. When these influences are cues that push people toward self-control failure, depletion makes people more likely to fail (Bruyneel, Dewitte, Vohs, & Warlop, 2006; Hofmann, Strack, & Deutsch, 2008). When on the other hand, salient local cues push people toward decisions that are more in line with distant goals, they are more likely to succeed in their self-control attempts (Salmon et al., 2015; Salmon, Fennis, de Ridder, Adriaanse, & de Vet, 2014). For example, depleted participants were more likely to make healthy food choices when the environment promoted selection of the healthy option through a social proof heuristic (ie, cues that indicate that the majority prefers the healthy product; Salmon et al., 2014). Under the right condition, then, depletion may serve to advance rather than undermine people's long-term goals—a possibility that deserves additional future empirical inquiry (see also Chapter 8).

The Importance of Subjective Feelings of Fatigue

By concluding that self-control is a necessary condition for ego depletion, researchers may have inadvertently narrowed the conceptual insights one might draw from ego-depletion research. That is, the concept of depletion may extend beyond self-control to other self-regulatory and motivational phenomena more broadly. As highlighted in early work (Baumeister et al., 1998; Baumeister & Heatherton, 1996), the experience of energy (or lack thereof) appears commonplace in everyday behavior, yet energy or resource depletion is poorly understood conceptually and theoretically by researchers. This may in large part be due to the dominance of social-cognitive models in our understanding of self-regulation (eg, Carver & Scheier, 1982, 1990; Gollwitzer, 1990; Kruglanski et al., 2012). There is little discussion in these models of the subjective experiences people have in the pursuit of goals. There is a long tradition of "energy dynamics" in motivation and self-regulation, yet much of it is focused on the mobilization of resources in the exertion of effort rather than the consequences of having exerted that effort (eg, Gendolla & Richter, 2010; Tomaka, Blascovich, Kelsey, & Leitten, 1993; Wright, 1996). As such, self-regulation research has had little to say about why people often feel "tired," and what this depleted state reveals about the processes underlying self-regulation and motivated behavior. Ego-depletion research illuminates the fact that beyond the narrower phenomenon of self-control, self-regulation and goal pursuit more broadly is very hard, not just from a cognitive standpoint, but also from a motivational and emotional perspective (see Chapter 7).

To fully explore this broader potential insight, more work needs to be done to understand ego depletion as a subjective state. There is some controversy about the nature of depletion and its relation to feeling fatigued. Some have suggested that the experience of depletion does not signal the reduction of actual resources, but that it instead serves as a signal to pursue other goals or better opportunities (Kurzban, Duckworth, Kable, & Myers, 2013; see also Chapter 18; Inzlicht & Schmeichel, 2012; Muraven et al., 2006). Others have suggested that depletion may not be reducible to fatigue alone. Vohs, Glass, Maddox, and Markman (2010) induced states of ego depletion among participants who were either sleep deprived (ie, had not slept for 24h) or not. They found that whereas sleep deprivation had no apparent effects of subsequent regulatory performance, those in the depletion (vs control) condition did show poorer regulation. This suggests some dissociation between physical and mental fatigue (see Chapter 17). Similarly, just as it is possible for one to become depleted by observing someone else engage in self-control (Ackerman et al., 2009), so too is it possible for one to recover from depletion's effects by observing someone else's restoration. For example, depleted participants who took the perspective of a narrative character who replenished resources with a nap persisted longer on a difficult anagram solving task as compared to those who took the perspective of someone who did not nap or those who read either story without perspective-taking (Egan, Hirt, & Karpen, 2012; see also Chapter 12). Key to advancing insights about depletion to self-regulation and motivation research more generally will require resolving what this depletion is and clarifying its role in effort expenditure (see also Chapter 1).

CONCLUSION

In this chapter, we have provided a conceptual analysis of ego depletion and its relationship with self-control. We first noted the considerable conceptual disagreement around the term "self-control" and attempted to clarify its relationship to related terms such as "self-regulation," "executive function," and "effortful inhibition." We have pointed out that many researchers have equated these terms, potentially leading some to make unwarranted conclusions about the relationship between ego depletion and self-control. Although self-control can cause ego depletion, it is neither a necessary nor sufficient condition. Moreover, by itself, states of ego depletion do not imply acts of self-control. By clarifying this relationship, we hope to resolve apparent controversies in the literature, and to inspire new research. We encourage and look forward to these developments.

References

Ackerman, J. M., Goldstein, N. J., Shapiro, J. R., & Bargh, J. A. (2009). You wear me out: the vicarious depletion of self-control. *Psychological Science, 20*, 326–332.

Adriaanse, M. A., Vinkers, C. D., De Ridder, D. T., Hox, J. J., & De Wit, J. B. (2011). Do implementation intentions help to eat a healthy diet? A systematic review and meta-analysis of the empirical evidence. *Appetite, 56*, 183–193.

Agrawal, N., & Wan, E. W. (2009). Regulating risk or risking regulation? Construal levels and depletion effects in the processing of health messages. *Journal of Consumer Research, 36*, 448–462.

Ainslie, G. (1975). Specious reward: a behavioral theory of impulsiveness and impulse control. *Psychological Bulletin, 82*, 463–496.

Ariely, D., & Wertenbroch, K. (2002). Procrastination, deadlines, and performance: self-control by precommitment. *Psychological Science, 13*, 219–224.

Baumeister, R. F., Bratslavsky, E., Muraven, M., & Tice, D. M. (1998). Ego depletion: is the active self a limited resource? *Journal of Personality and Social Psychology, 74*, 1252–1265.

Baumeister, R. F., & Heatherton, T. F. (1996). Self-regulation failure: an overview. *Psychological Inquiry, 7*, 1–15.

Baumeister, R. F., & Vohs, K. D. (2004). Four roots of evil. In A. G. Miller (Ed.), *The social psychology of good and evil* (pp. 85–101). New York: Guilford.

Baumeister, R. F., Vohs, K. D., & Tice, D. M. (2007). The strength model of self-control. *Current Directions in Psychological Science, 16*, 351–355.

Brandstätter, V., Lengfelder, A., & Gollwitzer, P. M. (2001). Implementation intentions and efficient action initiation. *Journal of Personality and Social Psychology, 81*, 946–960.

Bruyneel, S. D., & Dewitte, S. (2012). Engaging in self-regulation results in low-level construals. *European Journal of Social Psychology, 42*, 763–769.

Bruyneel, S. D., Dewitte, S., Vohs, K. D., & Warlop, L. (2006). Repeated choosing increases susceptibility to affective product features. *International Journal of Research in Marketing, 23*, 215–225.

Carnevale, J. J., Fujita, K., Han, H. A., & Amit, E. (2015). Immersion versus transcendence: how pictures and words impact evaluative associations assessed by the Implicit Association Test. *Social Psychological and Personality Science, 6*, 92–100.

Carter, E. C., Kofler, L. M., Forster, D. E., & McCullough, M. E. (2015). A series of meta-analytic tests of the depletion effect: self-control does not seem to rely on a limited resource. *Journal of Personality and Social Psychology, 144*(4), 796–815.

Carver, C. S., & Scheier, M. F. (1982). Control theory: a useful conceptual framework for personality–social, clinical, and health psychology. *Psychological Bulletin, 92*, 111–135.

Carver, C. S., & Scheier, M. F. (1990). Origins and functions of positive and negative affect: a control-process view. *Psychological Review, 97*, 19–35.

Clarkson, J. J., Hirt, E. R., Chapman, D. A., & Jia, L. (2011). The impact of illusory fatigue on executive control: do perceptions of depletion impair working memory capacity? *Social Psychological and Personality Science, 2*(3), 231–238.

REFERENCES

Clarkson, J. J., Hirt, E. R., Jia, L., & Alexander, M. B. (2010). When perception is more than reality: the effects of perceived versus actual resource depletion on self-regulatory behavior. *Journal of Personality and Social Psychology, 98*(1), 29–46.

Do Vale, R. C., Pieters, R., & Zeelenberg, M. (2008). Flying under the radar: perverse package size effects on consumption self-regulation. *Journal of Consumer Research, 35*, 380–390.

Duckworth, A. L., Kirby, T. A., Gollwitzer, A., & Oettingen, G. (2013). From fantasy to action: mental contrasting with implementation intentions (MCII) improves academic performance in children. *Social Psychological and Personality Science, 4*, 745–753.

Duckworth, A. L., & Seligman, M. E. (2005). Self-discipline outdoes IQ in predicting academic performance of adolescents. *Psychological Science, 16*, 939–944.

Egan, P. M., Hirt, E. R., & Karpen, S. C. (2012). Taking a fresh perspective: vicarious restoration as a means of recovering self-control. *Journal of Experimental Social Psychology, 48*, 457–465.

Fishbach, A., Friedman, R. S., & Kruglanski, A. W. (2003). Leading us not into temptation: momentary allurements elicit overriding goal activation. *Journal of Personality and Social Psychology, 84*, 296–309.

Fitzsimons, G. M., Finkel, E. J., & van Dellen, M. R. (2015). Transactive goal dynamics. *Psychological Review, 122*, 648–673.

Fujita, K. (2008). Seeing the forest beyond the trees: a construal-level approach to self-control. *Social and Personality Psychology Compass, 2*, 1475–1496.

Fujita, K. (2011). On conceptualizing self-control as more than the effortful inhibition of impulses. *Personality and Social Psychology Review, 15*, 352–366.

Fujita, K., & Carnevale, J. J. (2012). Transcending temptation through abstraction the role of construal level in self-control. *Current Directions in Psychological Science, 21*, 248–252.

Fujita, K., & Han, H. A. (2009). Moving beyond deliberative control of impulses the effect of construal levels on evaluative associations in self-control conflicts. *Psychological Science, 20*, 799–804.

Fujita, K., & Sasota, J. A. (2011). The effects of construal levels on asymmetric temptation-goal cognitive associations. *Social Cognition, 29*, 125–146.

Gailliot, M. T., Plant, E. A., Butz, D. A., & Baumeister, R. F. (2007). Increasing self-regulatory strength can reduce the depleting effect of suppressing stereotypes. *Personality & Social Psychology Bulletin, 33*, 281–294.

Galla, B. M., & Duckworth, A. L. (2015). More than resisting temptation: beneficial habits mediate the relationship between self-control and positive life outcomes. *Journal of Personality and Social Psychology, 109*(3), 508–525.

Gendolla, G. H., & Richter, M. (2010). Effort mobilization when the self is involved: some lessons from the cardiovascular system. *Review of General Psychology, 14*, 212–226.

Gollwitzer, P. M. (1990). Action phases and mind-sets. *Handbook of Motivation and Cognition: Foundations of Social Behavior, 2*, 53–92.

Gollwitzer, P. M., & Sheeran, P. (2006). Implementation intentions and goal achievement: a meta-analysis of effects and processes. *Advances in Experimental Social Psychology, 38*, 69–119.

Green, L., Fristoe, N., & Myerson, J. (1994). Temporal discounting and preference reversals in choice between delayed outcomes. *Psychonomic Bulletin & Review, 1*, 383–389.

Hagger, M. S., Wood, C., Stiff, C., & Chatzisarantis, N. L. (2010). Ego depletion and the strength model of self-control: a meta-analysis. *Psychological Bulletin, 136*, 495–525.

Hinson, J. M., Jameson, T. L., & Whitney, P. (2003). Impulsive decision making and working memory. *Journal of Experimental Psychology: Learning, Memory, and Cognition, 29*, 298–306.

Hoch, S. J., & Loewenstein, G. F. (1991). Time-inconsistent preferences and consumer self-control. *Journal of Consumer Research, 17*, 492–507.

Hofmann, W., Baumeister, R. F., Förster, G., & Vohs, K. D. (2012). Everyday temptations: an experience sampling study of desire, conflict, and self-control. *Journal of Personality and Social Psychology, 102*, 1318–1335.

Hofmann, W., Friese, M., & Strack, F. (2009). Impulse and self-control from a dual-systems perspective. *Perspectives on Psychological Science, 4*, 162–176.

Hofmann, W., Rauch, W., & Gawronski, B. (2007). And deplete us not into temptation: automatic attitudes, dietary restraint, and self-regulatory resources as determinants of eating behavior. *Journal of Experimental Social Psychology, 43*, 497–504.

Hofmann, W., Schmeichel, B. J., & Baddeley, A. D. (2012). Executive functions and self-regulation. *Trends in Cognitive Sciences, 16*, 174–180.

Hofmann, W., Strack, F., & Deutsch, R. (2008). Free to buy? Explaining self-control and impulse in consumer behavior. *Journal of Consumer Psychology, 18*, 22–26.

Inzlicht, M., & Schmeichel, B. J. (2012). What is ego depletion? Toward a mechanistic revision of the resource model of self-control. *Perspectives on Psychological Science, 7*, 450–463.

Job, V., Dweck, C. S., & Walton, G. M. (2010). Ego depletion—is it all in your head? Implicit theories about willpower affect self-regulation. *Psychological Science, 21*, 1686–1693.

Job, V., Walton, G. M., Bernecker, K., & Dweck, C. S. (2013). Beliefs about willpower determine the impact of glucose on self-control. *Proceedings of the National Academy of Sciences, 110*, 14837–14842.

Kirby, K. N., & Herrnstein, R. J. (1995). Preference reversals due to myopic discounting of delayed reward. *Psychological Science, 6*, 83–89.

Kruglanski, A. W., Belanger, J. J., Chen, X., Kopetz, C., Pierro, A., & Manneti, L. (2012). The energetics of motivated cognition: a force-field analysis. *Psychological Review, 119*, 1–20.

Kurzban, R., Duckworth, A., Kable, J. W., & Myers, J. (2013). An opportunity cost model of subjective effort and task performance. *The Behavioral and Brain Sciences, 36*, 661–679.

Loewenstein, G. (1996). Out of control: visceral influences on behavior. *Organizational Behavior and Human Decision Processes, 65*, 272–292.

Magen, E., Dweck, C. S., & Gross, J. J. (2008). The hidden-zero effect representing a single choice as an extended sequence reduces impulsive choice. *Psychological Science, 19*, 648–649.

Mann, T., de Ridder, D., & Fujita, K. (2013). Self-regulation of health behavior: social psychological approaches to goal setting and goal striving. *Health Psychology, 32*, 487–498.

Masicampo, E. J., Martin, S. R., & Anderson, R. A. (2014). Understanding and overcoming self-control depletion. *Social and Personality Psychology Compass, 8*(11), 638–649.

Metcalfe, J., & Mischel, W. (1999). A hot/cool-system analysis of delay of gratification: dynamics of willpower. *Psychological Review, 106*, 3–19.

Mischel, W. (1974). Processes in delay of gratification. In L. Berkowitz (Ed.), *Advances in experimental social psychology* (Vol. 7) (pp. 249–292). New York: Academic Press.

Mischel, W., & Ayduk, O. (2004). Willpower in a cognitive-affective processing system. *Handbook of Self-Regulation: Research, Theory, and Applications, 83*, 99–129.

Mischel, H. N., & Mischel, W. (1983). The development of children's knowledge of self-control strategies. *Child Development, 54*, 603–619.

Mischel, W., Shoda, Y., & Rodriguez, M. I. (1989). Delay of gratification in children. *Science, 244*, 933–938.

Miyake, A., & Friedman, N. P. (2012). The nature and organization of individual differences in executive functions four general conclusions. *Current Directions in Psychological Science, 21*, 8–14.

Moffitt, T. E., Arseneault, L., Belsky, D., Dickson, N., Hancox, R. J., Harrington, H., … Caspi, A. (2011). A gradient of childhood self-control predicts health, wealth, and public safety. *Proceedings of the National Academy of Sciences, 108*, 2693–2698.

Moller, A. C., Deci, E. L., & Ryan, R. M. (2006). Choice and ego-depletion: the moderating role of autonomy. *Personality & Social Psychology Bulletin, 32*, 1024–1036.

Muraven, M. (2008). Autonomous self-control is less depleting. *Journal of Research in Personality, 42*, 763–770.

Muraven, M., & Baumeister, R. F. (2000). Self-regulation and depletion of limited resources: does self-control resemble a muscle? *Psychological Bulletin, 126*, 247–259.

REFERENCES

Muraven, M., Baumeister, R. F., & Tice, D. M. (1999). Longitudinal improvement of self-regulation through practice: building self-control strength through repeated exercise. *The Journal of Social Psychology, 139*, 446–457.

Muraven, M., Gagné, M., & Rosman, H. (2008). Helpful self-control: autonomy support, vitality, and depletion. *Journal of Experimental Social Psychology, 44*, 573–585.

Muraven, M., Shmueli, D., & Burkley, E. (2006). Conserving self-control strength. *Journal of Personality and Social Psychology, 91*, 524–537.

Muraven, M., Tice, D. M., & Baumeister, R. F. (1998). Self-control as a limited resource: regulatory depletion patterns. *Journal of Personality and Social Psychology, 74*, 774–789.

Myrseth, K. O. R., & Fishbach, A. (2009). Self-control a function of knowing when and how to exercise restraint. *Current Directions in Psychological Science, 18*, 247–252.

Oaten, M., & Cheng, K. (2006). Improved self-control: the benefits of a regular program of academic study. *Basic and Applied Social Psychology, 28*, 1–16.

Papies, E. K., Stroebe, W., & Aarts, H. (2008). Healthy cognition: processes of self-regulatory success in restrained eating. *Personality & Social Psychology Bulletin, 34*, 1290–1300.

Rachlin, H. (1995). Self-control: beyond commitment. *Behavior and Brain Sciences, 18*, 109–159.

Rachlin, H., & Green, L. (1972). Commitment, choice, and self-control. *Journal of the Experimental Analysis of Behavior, 17*, 15–22.

Redden, J. P., Mann, T., Vickers, Z., Mykerezi, E., Reicks, M., & Elsbernd, S. (2015). Serving first in isolation increases vegetable intake among elementary schoolchildren. *PLoS One, 10*, 1–14.

de Ridder, D. T., de Boer, B. J., Lugtig, P., Bakker, A. B., & van Hooft, E. A. (2011). Not doing bad things is not equivalent to doing the right thing: distinguishing between inhibitory and initiatory self-control. *Personality and Individual Differences, 50*, 1006–1011.

de Ridder, D. T., Lensvelt-Mulders, G., Finkenauer, C., Stok, F. M., & Baumeister, R. F. (2012). Taking stock of self-control: a meta-analysis of how trait self-control relates to a wide range of behaviors. *Personality and Social Psychology Review, 16*, 76–99.

Rodriguez, M. L., Mischel, W., & Shoda, Y. (1989). Cognitive person variables in the delay of gratification of older children at risk. *Journal of Personality and Social Psychology, 57*, 358–367.

Salmon, S. J., De Vet, E., Adriaanse, M. A., Fennis, B. M., Veltkamp, M., & De Ridder, D. T. (2015). Social proof in the supermarket: promoting healthy choices under low self-control conditions. *Food Quality and Preference, 45*, 113–120.

Salmon, S. J., Fennis, B. M., de Ridder, D. T., Adriaanse, M. A., & de Vet, E. (2014). Health on impulse: when low self-control promotes healthy food choices. *Health Psychology, 33*, 103–109.

Schelling, T. C. (1978). Egonomics, or the art of self-management. *The American Economic Review, 68*, 290–294.

Schmeichel, B. J., & Vohs, K. (2009). Self-affirmation and self-control: affirming core values counteracts ego depletion. *Journal of Personality and Social Psychology, 96*, 770.

Shiv, B., & Fedorikhin, A. (1999). Heart and mind in conflict: the interplay of affect and cognition in consumer decision making. *Journal of Consumer Research, 26*, 278–292.

Shoda, Y., Mischel, W., & Peake, P. K. (1990). Predicting adolescent cognitive and self-regulatory competencies from preschool delay of gratification: identifying diagnostic conditions. *Developmental Psychology, 26*, 978–986.

Stroop, J. R. (1935). Studies of interference in serial verbal reactions. *Journal of Experimental Psychology, 18*, 643–662.

Strotz, R. H. (1955). Myopia and inconsistency in dynamic utility maximization. *The Review of Economic Studies, 23*, 165–180.

Tangney, J. P., Baumeister, R. F., & Boone, A. L. (2004). High self-control predicts good adjustment, less pathology, better grades, and interpersonal success. *Journal of Personality, 72*, 271–324.

Thaler, R. H., & Benartzi, S. (2004). Save more tomorrow: using behavioral economics to increase employee saving. *Journal of Political Economy, 112*, S164–S187.

Thaler, R., & Shefrin, H. M. (1981). An economic theory of self-control. *Journal of Political Economy, 39,* 392–406.

Tomaka, J., Blascovich, J., Kelsey, R. M., & Leitten, C. L. (1993). Subjective, physiological, and behavioral effects of threat and challenge appraisal. *Journal of Personality and Social Psychology, 65,* 248–260.

Trope, Y., & Fishbach, A. (2000). Counteractive self-control in overcoming temptation. *Journal of Personality and Social Psychology, 79,* 493–506.

Trope, Y., & Liberman, N. (2010). Construal-level theory of psychological distance. *Psychological Review, 117,* 440–463.

Tyler, J. M., & Burns, K. C. (2008). After depletion: the replenishment of the self's regulatory resources. *Self and Identity, 7,* 305–321.

Vohs, K. D., Baumeister, R. F., Schmeichel, B. J., Twenge, J. M., Nelson, N. M., & Tice, D. M. (2014). Making choices impairs subsequent self-control: a limited-resource account of decision making, self-regulation, and active initiative. *Journal of Personality and Social Psychology, 94,* 883–898.

Vohs, K. D., Glass, B. D., Maddox, W. T., & Markman, A. B. (2010). Ego depletion is not just fatigue: evidence from a total sleep deprivation experiment. *Social Psychological and Personality Science, 2,* 166–173.

Vohs, K. D., & Heatherton, T. F. (2000). Self-regulatory failure: a resource-depletion approach. *Psychological Science, 11,* 249–254.

Ward, A., & Mann, T. (2000). Don't mind if I do: disinhibited eating under cognitive load. *Journal of Personality and Social Psychology, 78,* 753–763.

Webb, T. L., & Sheeran, P. (2003). Can implementation intentions help to overcome ego-depletion? *Journal of Experimental Social Psychology, 39,* 279–286.

Wegner, D. M. (1994). Ironic processes of mental control. *Psychological Review, 101,* 34–52.

Wegner, D. M. (2009). How to think, say, or do precisely the worst thing for any occasion. *Science, 325,* 48–50.

Wegner, D. M., Schneider, D. J., Carter, S. R., & White, T. L. (1987). Paradoxical effects of thought suppression. *Journal of Personality and Social Psychology, 53,* 5–13.

Wertenbroch, K. (1998). Consumption self-control by rationing purchase quantities of virtue and vice. *Marketing Science, 17,* 317–337.

Wiers, R. W., & Stacy, A. W. (2006). Implicit cognition and addiction. *Current Directions in Psychological Science, 15,* 292–296.

Wright, R. A. (1996). Brehm's theory of motivation as a model of effort and cardiovascular response. In P. M. Gollwitzer, & J. A. Bargh (Eds.), *The psychology of action: Linking cognition and motivation to behavior* (pp. 424–453). New York: Guilford Press.

SECTION 2

MOTIVATIONAL FACTORS IN EGO CONTROL

CHAPTER 6

Exercising Self-Control Increases Approach-Motivated Impulse Strength

B.J. Schmeichel, A. Crowell

Texas A&M University, College Station, TX, United States

When a person works hard, they expect to be rewarded for it. This relationship between effort and reward is relevant for the psychology of self-control. People restrict their food intake, persist at boring chores, or otherwise exercise self-control to gain some other benefit. The benefits of self-control (eg, longer life, bigger paychecks) may be less probable and more delayed in time than the benefits of eating freely or quitting a boring chore, but they also tend to be larger and more lasting. The current chapter reviews evidence pertaining to the effect of exercising self-control on sensitivity to reward (a corollary of approach motivation) and traces the implications for the strength model of self-control.

STRENGTH MODEL OF SELF-CONTROL

Self-control refers to the capacity persons have to override or alter their predominant response tendencies (cf. Chapter 5). For example, a smoker who wants to stop smoking must override the impulse to light up another cigarette and do something else instead. According to the strength model of self-control, overriding or altering an impulse requires an inner strength to counteract the force of the predominant response tendency. Such exertions of inner strength are costly in the sense that they consume and temporarily deplete the capacity for further self-control, resulting in a state of *ego depletion*. Under ego depletion, a quitting smoker is more susceptible to other temptations, such as delicious but unhealthy foods.

Any weight gain during a smoking cessation attempt may be due in part to a temporary reduction in self-control strength from trying not to smoke (eg, Muraven, 2010).

But any weight gain that occurs when a person tries to break a smoking habit may also stem from an increased motivation to consume food. The outcome—weight gain—by itself does not reveal why a person puts on pounds. It could be because overriding impulses to smoke reduces the inner strength needed to control eating behavior. But it could also be because trying not to smoke increases the motivation to eat.

IMPULSE STRENGTH AND SELF-CONTROL STRENGTH

The ambiguity underlying the mechanisms of weight gain in this example stems from the fact that self-control outcomes are the product of at least two opposing forces: the motivational force that compels an impulse to find expression in thought, feeling, or behavior (ie, *impulse strength*) versus the inner capacity the person has to control their impulses (ie, *self-control strength*).

The strength model of self-control and the voluminous body of research it has inspired have focused on the control side of this equation. Accordingly, experiments that have found poorer self-control at time 2 as a result of having exercised self-control at time 1 have been interpreted as evidence that exercising self-control temporarily reduces self-control strength. However, the same behavioral outcomes would be expected if one assumed that exercising self-control increases impulse strength—particularly approach-motivated impulses and reward sensitivity.

Numerous findings in the literature on ego depletion suffer from this interpretational ambiguity. More precisely, numerous findings interpreted as evidence of depleted self-control strength may also be interpreted as evidence of increased approach-motivated impulse strength. After exercising self-control, dieters have been found to eat more ice cream (Vohs & Heatherton, 2000), social drinkers have been found to consume more alcohol (Muraven, Collins, & Nienhaus, 2002), insulted persons have been found to behave more aggressively (Stucke & Baumeister, 2006; see also DeWall, Baumeister, Stillman, & Gailliot, 2007), men have been found to perceive themselves more likely to engage in sexual infidelity (Gailliot & Baumeister, 2007), and risk taking in general has been found to increase (Fischer, Kastenmuller, & Asal, 2012; Freeman & Muraven, 2010; cf. Kostek & Ashroufioun, 2013; Yan, 2014). Prior acts of self-control have also been found to increase impulsive spending (Vohs & Faber, 2007) and to exacerbate preferences for immediate over-delayed rewards (Schmeichel & Vohs, 2009).

Crucially, each of the behaviors discussed in the previous paragraph (ie, the behaviors that were found to increase under ego depletion) may be linked to heightened approach motivation. Approach motivation can be defined as physical or psychological orienting toward reward and incentive (see Elliot, Eder, & Harmon-Jones, 2013) and has been linked to aggression (eg, Harmon-Jones & Sigelman, 2001), drug and alcohol consumption (eg, Baker, Morse, & Sherman, 1986), food consumption (Davis et al., 2007), risk taking (eg, Cavallo, Fitzsimons, & Holmes, 2009), and several other behaviors featured in studies of ego depletion.

So do the findings identified in the previous paragraphs reveal a reduction in self-control strength, or an increase in approach-motivated impulse strength? This question cannot be answered by studying behaviors (like alcohol consumption or aggression) that are influenced by both approach motivation and self-control. Rather, to isolate the possible effects on approach motivation, studies must probe the aftereffects of self-control on approach-motivated responses that themselves entail little or no self-control.

EVIDENCE THAT EXERCISING SELF-CONTROL STRENGTH INCREASES IMPULSE STRENGTH

To test the hypothesis that exercising self-control increases approach-motivated impulse strength, independent of or above and beyond any possible reductions in self-control strength, we must identify approach-motivated behaviors that people have no interest or inclination to control. Insofar as exercising self-control increases such behaviors, this would support the increased approach motivation hypothesis and would be difficult to explain in terms of reduced self-control strength. (Note that such findings would supplement—not supplant—the depleted strength hypothesis.)

As a first test of the increased approach hypothesis, we had participants exercise self-control (or not) before completing a measure of approach motivation (Schmeichel, Harmon–Jones, & Harmon–Jones, Study 1). Specifically, participants viewed an emotionally charged film clip under instructions either to suppress their emotional reactions or to express whatever they felt, a manipulation used numerous times in previous research to induce a state of ego depletion (eg, Vohs & Heatherton, 2000). Immediately after the film clip participants completed the behavioral activation system (BAS) sensitivity scale (Carver & White, 1994), a well-validated and widely used self-report measure of approach motivation.

The results revealed evidence of increased approach motivation after exercising self-control. Specifically participants who had suppressed their responses during the emotional film clip reported higher approach motivation compared to participants who viewed the same film clip without suppressing their emotional responses. This first study represents initial support for the hypothesis that exercising self-control can increase approach motivation.

A second experiment tested the same hypothesis using different methods and measures. We were particularly interested to move beyond self-reports and measure approach-motivated behavior. We also wanted to ensure that the behavior was influenced by approach motivation but relatively uninfluenced by self-control (unlike drinking and eating in the studies cited above). We therefore conducted pilot testing to identify a behavior that was sensitive to variations in trait approach motivation but was not sensitive variations in trait self-control. We found a behavior to fit the bill—risk-taking on a low-stakes gambling game (Schmeichel, Harmon-Jones, & Harmon-Jones, 2010; Study 2a).

Specifically we found that participants higher in trait approach motivation were more likely to take risks on a simple gambling game that involved fake money (ie, Monopoly money), whereas trait self-control was unrelated to risk taking. The game was simple. At the start of each round, participants received $20 in Monopoly money. Then they had to make a choice. They could either keep the $20 bill and advance to the next round of the game, or they could flip a virtual coin for a "double-or-nothing" bet. If the coin flip landed heads up, participants doubled their money and ended the round with $40. However, if the coin came up tails, the $20 was lost and participants ended the round with $0. In this scenario the safe choice was to forego the coin flip and keep the original $20, whereas the risky gamble was to flip the coin and take a chance on doubling up.

Participants played 20 rounds of this low-stakes gambling game with the goal of amassing as much Monopoly money as possible. Adopting the conservative, risk-free strategy yielded $400 in Monopoly money by the end of the game, but the risky option promised much more. We found that participants higher (versus lower) in trait approach motivation opted for the risky coin flip more often. Not coincidentally, participants higher in trait approach motivation also ended up with more money at the end of the game and reported having more fun playing it. Trait self-control was unrelated to the number of risky choices participants made and how much fun they had.

Why was trait self-control irrelevant to the decision to flip the coin in this simple gambling game? We believe it is because participants were not playing for real money. They had no expectations that the Monopoly money stood in for anything of consequence. In fact, we made it clear to participants that they were playing for fake money no tangible rewards were at stake in the game. Given these low stakes, there was no need for participants to override or alter a predominant response tendency. If a person had the impulse to gamble, there was nothing to stop them. *Go for it!* Note that things may have turned out differently if actual money had been at stake. With real money, it may be prudent to restrain the impulse to gamble because valuable assets could be lost. This was not the case with our gambling task, however. The stakes could not have been lower. Participants had nothing of consequence to lose (or gain).

Having established that low-stakes gambling behavior was sensitive to variations in trait approach motivation (higher approach participants did it more) but insensitive to variations in trait self-control (higher and lower self-controllers did it with equal frequency), we set out to test our key prediction: Exercising self-control will increase risk taking on the gambling game (Schmeichel et al., 2010; Study 2b). At the start of the experiment participants wrote a story. In the controlled writing condition, participants had to exercise self-control by writing the story without using two commonly used letters in the English language—*a* and *n*. In the free writing condition, participants wrote freely and without restrictions. This task has been used to induce ego depletion in numerous experiments (eg, Schmeichel, 2007).

Immediately after the writing manipulation participants played the low-stakes gambling game. We found that participants opted to take risks (ie, to flip the coin for a chance to double their Monopoly $20) more often in the controlled writing condition relative to the free writing condition. Hence, participants engaged in the approach-motivated gambling behavior more if they had previously exercised self-control. This result is difficult to explain in terms of a reduction in self-control capacity insofar as variations in self-control were irrelevant for this particular behavior. By contrast, high trait approach motivation predicted more gambling on this task, and the effect of our experimental manipulation was similar to the effect of having high trait approach motivation.

A third experiment tested the hypothesis in yet another way (Schmeichel et al., 2010; Study 3). One well-known consequence of motivation is heightened sensitivity to motive-relevant stimuli. As one example, a hungry person is more likely to notice food-related stimuli (eg, the Taco Bell sign along the highway) compared to a person who is not hungry (eg, Mogg, Bradley, Hyare, & Lee, 1998). We built on this fact by predicting that an approach-motivated person would be more likely to detect a ubiquitous reward-related stimulus—the dollar sign ($)—compared to a person who is not approach motivated, because approach-oriented persons are more sensitive to reward-related cues.

At the start of the experiment participants either did or did not exercise self-control while writing a story (as in the previous experiment). Then all participants completed a perceptual acuity task that involved viewing images that flashed on-screen for a very short period of time (70 ms). The task was to identify whether a dollar sign had been presented in the preceding image. A dollar sign did in fact appear in half of the images. We found that participants in the controlled writing condition correctly identified the presence of dollar signs more often than did participants in the free writing condition. Thus participants were more perceptually attuned to the reward-related cue if they had previously exercised self-control. This result is difficult to explain in terms of a reduction in the capacity for self-control, because little or no self-control was required for the task. The goal of the task was simply to determine if one had seen a dollar sign or not. The increased sensitivity to the presence of dollar signs in the controlled writing condition is thus supportive of the idea of increased reward sensitivity after exercising self-control.

Taken together the three studies reported by Schmeichel et al. (2010) represented the first evidence that exercising self-control could influence the impulse side of the self-control struggle. The ego depletion effect was thus not limited to the reduction of self-control strength; "being depleted" also appears to entail an increase in approach-motivated impulse strength.

EVIDENCE THAT EXERCISING SELF-CONTROL STRENGTH INCREASES APPROACH-RELATED BRAIN ACTIVITY

A more recent study found further support for the increased approach hypothesis using brain measures. Previous research had suggested that patterns of electrical activity in the prefrontal cortex covary with a person's motivational orientation. Specifically, persons higher in BAS sensitivity and approach motivation exhibit relatively more activity in the left versus right side of the prefrontal cortex (see review by Harmon-Jones, Gable, & Peterson, 2010), whereas persons higher in behavioral inhibition system (BIS) sensitivity, withdrawal motivation, and anxiety have been found to exhibit relatively more activity in the right side of the prefrontal cortex (eg, Davidson, Marshall, Tomarken, & Henriques, 2000; cf. Coan & Allen, 2003; Harmon-Jones & Allen, 1997; Hewig, Hagemann, Seifert, Naumann, & Bartussek, 2006).

If exercising self-control increases approach-motivated impulse strength, then relative left frontal cortical activity should increase after participants exercise (versus do not exercise) self-control. This hypothesis was put to the test in a study by Schmeichel, Crowell, and Harmon-Jones (2016). Participants completed the self-control manipulation described above by writing a story either with or without restrictions about using particular letters. Then participants viewed hedonically positive, negative, or neutral pictures while electroencephalographic (EEG) activity was recorded at the scalp. The results revealed that exercising self-control increased relative left frontal cortical activity, but only for some participants and only during some pictures. Specifically participants both higher in trait approach motivation (BAS) and lower in trait BIS sensitivity showed the increase in relative left frontal cortical activity, but only when they were looking at positive images (ie, pictures depicting individuals involved in fun or exciting activities, including erotica) or negative images (ie, pictures depicting acts of violence or mutilation); patterns of electrical activity in the prefrontal cortex did not change during neutral picture viewing.

This EEG study suggests three implications for understanding the aftereffects of self-control—implications that are not readily accommodated by the strength model. First, the results from this study and from Schmeichel et al. (2010) indicate that exercising self-control can influence responding that entails little or no self-control. This is notable insofar as the strength model of self-control is mute about responding that does not entail self-control. In the study by Schmeichel et al. (2016) the dependent measure (ie, frontal EEG activity) was assessed as participants sat passively and viewed pictures; self-control was irrelevant. One may suggest that participants spontaneously downregulated their responses while viewing aversive images, in which case the viewing task may have required some degree of self-control when aversive images appeared on-screen, but there is little reason to believe participants spontaneously attempted to downregulate their responses while viewing positive images. Yet it was precisely during the positive pictures that the aftereffects of self-control were expected to (and did) emerge, consistent with the increased approach hypothesis.

Second, this study is one of only a small handful of studies that has examined the aftereffects of self-control in patterns of electrical activity in the brain. The observed shifts in relative left prefrontal cortical activity observed by Schmeichel et al. (2016) complement the results of one of the only other EEG studies of ego depletion. Inzlicht and Gutsell (2007) found that exercising self-control caused a subsequent reduction in the magnitude of the error-related negativity (ERN). The ERN is a spike in neural activity following the commission of an error (Botvinick, Cohen, & Carter, 2004). Viewed together the two EEG studies suggest that exercising self-control can reduce electrocortical activity associated with action monitoring and increase activity associated with approach motivation, respectively. Not coincidentally, these patterns of brain activity (ie, reduced ERNs and increased relative left frontal activation) have been correlated in previous research (Nash, Inzlicht, & McGregor, 2012), which raises the possibility that approach-related brain activity and control-related brain activity operate in a reciprocal fashion, with increases in one corresponding with decreases in the other (eg, Maier, Makwana, & Hare, 2015; Wagner, Altman, Boswell, Kelley, & Heatherton, 2013; see Chapter 14).

Third, this study found that the aftereffects of self-control were moderated by individual differences in approach motivation. It was specifically those individuals reporting both higher trait approach motivation and lower behavioral inhibition who showed the largest increases in relative left frontal cortical activity after exercising self-control. This pattern of moderation by individual differences in approach motivation is congruent with the idea that approach motivation is an important key to understanding the aftereffects of self-control. We elaborate on this idea in the following section.

ADDITIONAL EVIDENCE THAT TRAIT APPROACH MOTIVATION MODERATES THE AFTEREFFECTS OF SELF-CONTROL

One strategy for identifying mechanisms underlying the effect of an experimental manipulation is to assess the contribution of individual difference variables that influence the tendency to engage the proposed mechanism (eg, Gohm & Clore, 2000; Underwood, 1975). The line of research at issue in this chapter concerns the aftereffects of exercising (versus not exercising) self-control (ie, the ego depletion effect), and one mechanism we presume to underlie the depletion effect is increased approach motivation. Accordingly evidence that trait approach motivation moderates the aftereffects of self-control lends support to the idea that increased approach motivation may be one mechanism by which exercising self-control influences subsequent behavior.

This line of reasoning was tested in pair of studies by Crowell, Kelley, and Schmeichel (2014). In the first study, participants exercised self-control (or not) during the now-familiar writing task. Then all participants completed a measure of optimism by rating the personal likelihood of succumbing to six different negative health outcomes (eg, cancer, diabetes; borrowed from Perloff & Fetzer, 1986). The results revealed that exercising self-control causes a subsequent increase in personal optimism, but this effect emerged only among individuals higher in trait approach motivation (ie, BAS). Neither trait self-control nor trait BIS moderated the aftereffects of self-control on optimism.

A second study found similar results using a different dependent measure. As in the first study participants exercised self-control (or not) during a writing task. Then all participants completed a measure of visual attentional bias borrowed from Kimchi and Palmer (1982). This task assessed the extent to which participants attend to the global, abstract features of a stimulus array versus the narrow, concrete features of the array. The results revealed that exercising self-control causes a subsequent increase in global attentional bias, but only among individuals higher in BAS.

Here again, neither trait self-control nor trait BIS moderated the increase in global attentional bias, suggesting that approach motivation was more relevant for the observed aftereffects of exercising self-control.

The results reported by Crowell et al. (2014) provided novel support for the increased approach hypothesis. The observed increases in optimism and global attentional bias after exercising self-control were most prominent among individuals prone to high levels of approach motivation (ie, those higher in BAS), consistent with the idea that individuals who are most likely to engage the proposed mechanism of the ego depletion effect (ie, increased approach motivation) are the most prone to showing the aftereffects. Neither trait self-control nor trait behavioral inhibition moderated the aftereffects of self-control in the same way, which suggests that the results were likely not due to self-control or behavioral inhibition. Indeed the key dependent measures in the studies by Crowell et al. were selected precisely because they had been found to vary with trait approach motivation in previous studies, but had not been found to relate to self-control or BIS.

DOES INCREASED APPROACH-MOTIVATED IMPULSE STRENGTH EXPLAIN THE EGO DEPLETION EFFECT?

The findings reviewed in this chapter suggest that exercising self-control increases impulse strength, particularly for impulses associated with approach motivation. This conclusion stands in contrast to the conclusion researchers typically derive from experiments on the aftereffects of self-control, namely that exercising self-control temporarily reduces self-control strength. The question arises: Does increased approach motivation explain the patterns typically attributed to reduced self-control strength and ego depletion?

The evidence needed for a definitive answer to this question has yet to accumulate. The crucial piece of information is still missing: Evidence that increases in approach motivation statistically mediate the ego depletion effect. The findings reviewed above reveal that (1) exercising self-control can increase approach motivation and (2) individual differences in trait self-control moderate some ego depletion effects. These findings are consistent with the idea that increased approach motivation explains the aftereffects of self-control, but they fall short of providing direct evidence that approach motivation mediates the ego depletion effect. Additional research is required. Ironically, perhaps, no direct evidence of mediation by a depleted resource exists, either. The most promising evidence of this type (regarding glucose; Galliot et al., 2007) has been challenged on multiple grounds (eg, Molden et al., 2012; see Inzlicht & Schmeichel, 2012).

Even if (or when) evidence of mediation of the aftereffects of self-control by approach motivation emerges, it seems unlikely that increased approach motivation would be able to explain *all* the ego depletion findings. Some findings would be difficult to explain in terms of increased approach motivation. For example, a series of studies by Schmeichel, Vohs, and Baumeister (2003) observed that exercising self-control causes decrements in intellectual performance and logical reasoning. These findings were interpreted in light of the typical depletion view: The capacity to arrive at logical conclusions from factual premises and to extrapolate from known information to generate accurate estimates for unknown quantities requires controlled cognitive processing, and ego depletion undermines such processing.

It is not obvious how an increase in approach motivation would explain poorer cognitive performance, at least not without making some additional assumptions. For example, one could assume that thinking lightly or taking the easy way out was more desirable and rewarding than thinking carefully and logically; this may be the case particularly when no tangible benefit accrues from thinking carefully or logically (as was true in the studies by Schmeichel et al., 2003). Rest may become particularly salient or desirable after exercising self-control, at least for some individuals (Job, Bernecker, Miketta, & Friese, 2015; see Chapter 11). In this view an increase in approach motivation may tilt the scales in favor of easy (versus hard) mental work. But we are aware of no independent evidence to support such an assumption. Evidence that increased approach motivation reduces engagement in cognitive labor (perhaps especially cognitive labor that promises no tangible benefits) is needed to interpret ego depletion findings such as these in terms of increased approach-motivated impulse strength.

According to the increased approach view, it may be the case that "depleted" individuals work harder on the second of two self-control tasks (ie, the dependent measure in a typical ego depletion experiment) if performance on the second task is rewarded in some way. That is, because individuals exhibit a shift toward greater approach motivation after exercising self-control, they may be more motivated to work hard to earn rewards. We are aware of only one set of experiments that has manipulated the opportunity to be rewarded for performance on the second of two self-control tasks, and the results were suggestive but not conclusive. A series of studies by Muraven and Slessareva (2003) manipulated the presence of an incentive for participants to perform well on the second of two self-control tasks, and they found that depleted participants performed better than other participants on the second task when an incentive for performance was offered, but the differences were not statistically significant. Perhaps individual differences in approach motivation moderate possible improvements in performance under ego depletion, such that persons more prone to high approach motivation perform better when they have an opportunity to earn a reward for the second of two self-control tasks. Additional research on this possibility is warranted.

Other findings may be harder still to explain in terms of increased approach-motivated impulse strength. For example, one series of studies found that individuals were more cautious and self-protective after exercising self-control, particularly in contexts that emphasize threat and danger (Lisjak & Lee, 2014). It seems unlikely that increased approach motivation could explain more cautious and self-protective responding. But these types of findings (ie, findings that ego depletion increase caution or avoidance) are relatively rare in the literature, and the opposite patterns (ie, reduced caution and increased risk taking under ego depletion) have also been observed (eg, Freeman & Muraven, 2010). Evidence that ego depletion leads to more approach-motivated responding is more common than evidence of increased caution or avoidance, as observed in the findings of increased aggression, increased alcohol consumption, more impulsive buying, increased ice cream consumption, and an increased preference for immediate (versus delayed) gratification under ego depletion.

At this stage the most conservative conclusion would seem to be that both reduced self-control strength and increased approach-motivated impulse strength contribute to the ego depletion effect. Despite our skepticism that some physical resource becomes depleted as a person exercises self-control (see Inzlicht & Schmeichel, 2012; Inzlicht, Schmeichel, & Macrae, 2014), it may be that individuals behave *as if* they have limited resources for self-control (eg, Job, Dweck, & Walton, 2010), and hence they may try to conserve or carefully allocate effort on this basis—in addition to the effects of shifts in motivational orientation toward increased approach. In this view, both (belief in) limited resources and shifts in motivation are relevant to understanding the ego depletion effect.

FUTURE DIRECTIONS AND CONCLUSION

The research reviewed in this chapter suggests the need for an alternate conceptualization of the aftereffects of self-control; the strength model of self-control is insufficient. Exercising self-control causes a temporary increase in approach-motivated impulse strength, in addition to any aftereffects on self-control strength. A model that incorporates both impulse strength and self-control strength is needed.

We close by speculating why approach motivation may increase after a person exercises self-control. One possibility is that approach motivation helps to regulate emotion. Exercising self-control is aversive (eg, Kool, McGuire, Rosen, & Botvinick, 2010), and because individuals generally favor pleasant emotional states over aversive ones, they may become motivated to seek pleasure and reward after expending effort to control themselves. In this view, an increase in approach motivation facilitates the return to a more pleasant emotional state after the unpleasantness of exercising self-control.

The second possibility hinges on the association between self-control and reward. As noted at the open of this chapter people typically expect to gain some benefit when they exercise self-control (ie, short-term "pain" yields long-term gain). To extent that this association stems from repeated pairings of self-control with (the expectation of) reward throughout one's lifetime, exercise self-control should increase the salience of reward and potentially also increase approach motivation.

The mood regulation view and the simple associative view, either alone or in combination, may account for increases in approach motivation of the type reviewed in this chapter. Of course, other possibilities exist and deserve to be explored. If research on the impulse side of the self-control equation is even a fraction as fecund as research on the self-control strength side has been, then evidence for more comprehensive models of self-control are just around the corner.

References

Baker, T. B., Morse, E., & Sherman, J. E. (1986). The motivation to use drugs: a psychobiological analysis of urges. *Nebraska Symposium on Motivation, 34*, 257–323.

Botvinick, M. M., Cohen, J. D., & Carter, C. S. (2004). Conflict monitoring and anterior cingulate cortex: an update. *Trends in Cognitive Sciences, 8*, 539–546.

Carver, C. S., & White, T. L. (1994). Behavioral inhibition, behavioral activation, and affective responses to impending reward and punishment: the BIS/BAS scales. *Journal of Personality and Social Psychology, 67*, 319–333.

Cavallo, J. V., Fitzsimons, G. M., & Holmes, J. G. (2009). Taking chances in the face of threat: romantic risk regulation and approach motivation. *Personality & Social Psychology Bulletin, 35*, 737–751.

Coan, J. A., & Allen, J. J. B. (2003). Frontal EEG asymmetry and the behavioral activation and inhibition systems. *Psychophysiology, 40*, 106–114.

Crowell, A., Kelley, N. J., & Schmeichel, B. J. (2014). Trait approach motivation moderates the aftereffects of self-control. *Frontiers in Psychology, 5*, 1112.

Davidson, R. J., Marshall, J. R., Tomarken, A. J., & Henriques, J. B. (2000). While a phobic waits: regional brain electrical and autonomic activity in social phobics during anticipation of public speaking. *Biological Psychiatry, 47*, 85–95.

Davis, C., Patte, K., Levitan, R., Reid, C., Tweed, S., & Curtis, C. (2007). From motivation to behaviour: a model of reward sensitivity, overeating, and food preferences in the risk profile for obesity. *Appetite, 48*, 12–19.

DeWall, C. N., Baumeister, R. F., Stillman, T. F., & Gailliot, M. T. (2007). Violence restrained: effects of self-regulation and its depletion on aggression. *Journal of Experimental Social Psychology, 43*, 62–76.

Elliot, A. J., Eder, A. B., & Harmon-Jones, E. (2013). Approach and avoidance motivation and emotion: convergence and divergence. *Emotion Review, 5*, 308–311.

Fischer, P., Kastenmuller, A., & Asal, K. (2012). Ego depletion increases risk-taking. *Journal of Social Psychology, 152*, 623–638.

REFERENCES

Freeman, N., & Muraven, M. (2010). Self-control depletion leads to increased risk taking. *Social Psychological and Personality Science, 2,* 175–181.

Gailliot, M. T., & Baumeister, R. F. (2007). Self-regulation and sexual restraint: dispositionally and temporarily poor self-regulatory abilities contribute to failures at restraining sexual behavior. *Personality & Social Psychology Bulletin, 33,* 173–186.

Gailliot, M. T., Baumeister, R. F., DeWall, C. N., Maner, J. K., Plant, E. A., Tice, D. M., & Schmeichel, B. J. (2007). Self-control relies on glucose as a limited energy source: willpower is more than a metaphor. *Journal of Personality and Social Psychology, 92,* 325–336.

Gohm, C. L., & Clore, G. L. (2000). Individual differences in emotional experience: mapping available scales to processes. *Personality & Social Psychology Bulletin, 26,* 679–697.

Harmon-Jones, E., & Allen, J. J. (1997). Behavioral activation sensitivity and resting frontal EEG asymmetry: covariation of putative indicators related to risk for mood disorders. *Journal of Abnormal Psychology, 106,* 159–163.

Harmon-Jones, E., Gable, P. A., & Peterson, C. K. (2010). The role of asymmetric frontal cortical activity in emotion-related phenomena: a review and update. *Biological Psychology, 84,* 451–462.

Harmon-Jones, E., & Sigelman, J. (2001). State anger and prefrontal brain activity: evidence that insult-related relative left-prefrontal activation is associated with experienced anger and aggression. *Journal of Personality and Social Psychology, 80,* 797–803.

Hewig, J., Hagemann, D., Seifert, J., Naumann, E., & Bartussek, D. (2006). The relation of cortical activity and BIS/BAS on the trait level. *Biological Psychology, 71,* 42–53.

Inzlicht, M., & Gutsell, J. N. (2007). Running on empty neural signals for self-control failure. *Psychological Science, 18,* 933–937.

Inzlicht, M., & Schmeichel, B. J. (2012). What is ego depletion? Toward a mechanistic revision of the resource model of self-control. *Perspectives on Psychological Science, 7,* 450–463.

Inzlicht, M., Schmeichel, B. J., & Macrae, C. N. (2014). Why self-control seems (but may not be) limited. *Trends in Cognitive Sciences, 18,* 127–133.

Job, V., Bernecker, K., Miketta, S., & Friese, M. (2015). Implicit theories about willpower predict the activation of a rest goal following self-control exertion. *Journal of Personality and Social Psychology, 109,* 694–706.

Job, V., Dweck, C. S., & Walton, G. M. (2010). Ego depletion—is it all in your head? Implicit theories about willpower affect self-regulation. *Psychological Science, 21,* 1686–1693.

Kimchi, R., & Palmer, S. E. (1982). Form and texture in hierarchically constructed patterns. *Journal of Experimental Psychology: Human Perception and Performance, 8,* 521–535.

Kool, W., McGuire, J. T., Rosen, Z. B., & Botvinick, M. M. (2010). Decision making and the avoidance of cognitive demand. *Journal of Experimental Psychology: General, 139,* 665–682.

Kostek, J., & Ashroufioun, L. (2013). Tired winners: the effects of cognitive resources and prior winning on risky decision making. *Journal of Gambling Studies, 30,* 423–434.

Lisjak, M., & Lee, A. Y. (2014). The bright side of impulse: depletion heightens self-protective behavior in the face of danger. *Journal of Consumer Research, 41,* 55–70.

Maier, S. U., Makwana, A. B., & Hare, T. A. (2015). Acute stress impairs self-control in goal-directed choice by altering multiple functional connections within the brain's decision circuits. *Neuron, 87,* 621–631.

Mogg, K., Bradley, B. P., Hyare, H., & Lee, S. (1998). Selective attention to food-related stimuli in hunger: are attentional biases specific to emotional and psychopathological states, or are they also found in normal drive states? *Behavioural Research and Therapy, 36,* 227–237.

Molden, D. C., Hui, C. M., Scholer, A. A., Meier, B. P., Noreen, E. E., D'Agostino, P. R., & Martin, V. (2012). Motivational versus metabolic effects of carbohydrates on self-control. *Psychological Science, 23,* 1137–1144.

Muraven, M. (2010). Practicing self-control lowers the risk of smoking lapse. *Psychology of Addictive Behaviors, 24,* 446–452.

Muraven, M., Collins, R. L., & Nienhaus, K. (2002). Self-control and alcohol restraint: an initial application of the self-control strength model. *Psychology of Addictive Behaviors, 16,* 113–120.

Muraven, M., & Slessareva, E. (2003). Mechanisms of self-control failure: motivation and limited resources. *Personality & Social Psychology Bulletin, 29*, 894–906.

Nash, K., Inzlicht, M., & McGregor, I. (2012). Approach-related left prefrontal EEG asymmetry predicts muted error-related negativity. *Biological Psychology, 91*, 96–102.

Perloff, L. S., & Fetzer, B. K. (1986). Self-other judgments and perceived vulnerability to victimization. *Journal of Personality and Social Psychology, 50*, 502–510.

Schmeichel, B. J. (2007). Attention control, memory updating, and emotion regulation temporarily reduce the capacity for executive control. *Journal of Experimental Psychology: General, 136*, 241–255.

Schmeichel, B. J., Crowell, A., & Harmon-Jones, E. (2016). Exercising self-control increases relative left frontal cortical activation. *Social Cognitive and Affective Neuroscience, 11*, 282–288.

Schmeichel, B. J., Harmon-Jones, C., & Harmon-Jones, E. (2010). Exercising self-control increases approach motivation. *Journal of Personality and Social Psychology, 99*, 162–173.

Schmeichel, B. J., & Vohs, K. (2009). Self-affirmation and self-control: affirming core values counteracts ego depletion. *Journal of Personality and Social Psychology, 96*, 770–782.

Schmeichel, B. J., Vohs, K. D., & Baumeister, R. F. (2003). Intellectual performance and ego depletion: role of the self in logical reasoning and other information processing. *Journal of Personality and Social Psychology, 85*, 33–46.

Stucke, T. S., & Baumeister, R. F. (2006). Ego depletion and aggressive behavior: is the inhibition of aggression a limited resource? *European Journal of Social Psychology, 36*, 1–13.

Underwood, B. J. (1975). Individual differences as a crucible in theory construction. *American Psychologist, 30*, 128–134.

Vohs, K. D., & Faber, R. J. (2007). Spent resources: self-regulatory resource availability affects impulse buying. *Journal of Consumer Research, 33*, 537–547.

Vohs, K. D., & Heatherton, T. F. (2000). Self-regulatory failure: a resource-depletion approach. *Psychological Science, 11*, 249–254.

Wagner, D. D., Altman, M., Boswell, R. G., Kelley, W. M., & Heatherton, T. F. (2013). Self-regulatory depletion enhances neural responses to rewards and impairs top-down control. *Psychological Science, 11*, 2262–2271.

Yan, X.-H. (2014). The effect of self-control resource on risk preference. *Social Behavior and Personality, 42*, 1335–1344.

CHAPTER

7

Self-Control and Motivation: Integration and Application

B.C. Ampel, E.E. O'Malley, M. Muraven

University at Albany, Albany, NY, United States

In 2006, a teacher in Nevada stopped a student with a gun by approaching him and giving him a hug ('Hero' Teacher Stopped Shooting with Hug, 2006). This was an amazing act of courage and self-control. As the police detective commented, "That's not a natural reaction, to hear gunfire and walk toward that gunfire." On the other hand, there are also horrible stories of lives gone awry because the person could not even maintain enough self-control to overcome weak or momentary impulses. Understanding why people can overcome some impulses some of the time but fail at other times is a critical and daunting question. The goal of this chapter is to shine some light on this question by integrating existing research on the role of motivation in self-control failure.

One of the most influential bodies of work on self-control failure in the last two decades is the resource model of self-control, which proposed that self-control operates as a transient, energy-based resource that, like a muscle, is fatigued through exertion (Muraven, Tice, & Baumeister, 1998). The resource model was initially well received. It offered a simple, testable hypothesis, as well as a concrete and parsimonious explanation for self-control failure. Initial results were overwhelmingly supportive of the resource model. Having previously exerted self-control, participants exhibited poorer performance on ensuing self-control tasks, but not on tasks that did not require self-control. This effect was dubbed "ego depletion" in homage to Freudian accounts of psychic energy, and a copious body of research supported the basic depletion effect (for a metaanalysis, see Hagger, Wood, Stiff, & Chatzisarantis, 2010). Despite its strengths, evidence has begun to accumulate that the resource model is oversimplifying a complex process, and in doing so, neglecting vital aspects of self-control. For example, Job, Dweck, and Walton (2010) found that the implicit beliefs concerning whether or not self-control was depletable was an important factor behind whether or not self-control was actually depleted. Additional research found that positive affect could reduce and even eliminate the depletion effect. Depleted participants watched a humorous video or received a surprise gift performed as well as participants who had not underwent self-control depletion (Tice, Baumeister, Shmueli, & Muraven, 2007). Other studies found that shifting attention away from the depletion task could mitigate the depleting effect (Alberts, Martijn, Nievelstein, Jansen, & de Vries, 2008). Likewise, depletion could also be reversed by plan making (Walsh, 2014); implementation intentions (Webb & Sheeran, 2003); or priming with self-awareness, money, or God (Alberts, Martijn, & de Vries, 2011; Boucher & Kofos, 2012; Rounding, Lee, Jacobson, & Ji, 2012).

Any proposed mechanism for the depletion effect must be able to explain the diversity of depletion effects. Several motivational accounts have risen to the challenge. The most prominent of these are the process model and the opportunity-cost model. The process model proposes that depletion is the product of system-wide changes in motivation and attention. These shifts direct attention away from efforts at suppression and control and toward immediate gratification (Inzlicht & Schmeichel, 2012). The opportunity-cost model takes an alternative though not irreconcilable perspective. The model assumes a computational model of processing, arguing that mental resources are divisible, but not depletable. Accordingly, self-control depletion is argued to be a result of mechanisms that function to weigh potential utility returns of continued effort against the cost of sacrificing alternative opportunities (Kurzban, Duckworth, Kable, & Myers, 2013). The opportunity-cost model views these evaluative mechanisms as resulting in motivational outputs that are weighed against each other which then leads a choice concerning continued investment or cessation for the sake of alternative opportunities.

The purpose of this chapter is to examine the mechanism responsible for motivational shifts during self-control depletion. We believe that both models have built the foundation required for a more thorough exploration of the motivational shifts responsible for depletion. The process model is likely correct in its assertion that motivational shifts are integral to the observed depletion effect. Likewise, we agree with the opportunity-cost model that the output of a comparative mechanism functions as input into assessments of whether to continue to exert effort. We supplement these models with a deeper analysis of the motivational shifts responsible for depletion. We argue that these motivational shifts are a result of a type of affective forecasting which we term "hedonic sampling." Finally, we apply hedonic sampling to work on depletion, self-control training, and motivational aspects of behavioral change.

HEDONIC SAMPLING AND DEPLETION

We hold that the motivational shift that is critical to both the process model and the opportunity-cost model is, at its core, an affective shift. When making decisions regarding potential behaviors (including the prospect of continuing a current behavior), individuals mentally simulate potential outcomes that result in brief affective responses (a process we refer to as hedonic sampling). These responses are then used as evaluative information concerning the value of each simulated possibility. Notably, this process leaves some residual affect that imbues subsequent simulations, leading to increasingly negative appraisals of further investment, and thus resulting in the depletion effect.

To illustrate, an original depletion study asked individuals to report to the lab for a supposed taste-testing experiment. Participants in the depletion condition were exposed to the aroma of freshly baked cookies, and then instructed that they were taste-testing raw radishes. Following this, subjects were given an unsolvable puzzle, their persistence on which was measured as the primary outcome measure (Baumeister, Bratslavsky, Muraven, & Tice, 1998; experiment 1). Our model proposes that a participant asked not to eat the cookies creates a mental simulation of two potential prospects (not eating versus eating the cookies) and then samples the affect from each of those mental simulations. In this situation, the motivation to continue with the study (for the extra credit or to merely avoid embarrassment) is stronger, and thus results in not eating the cookies. However, the affect produced from foregoing the cookies instead of the previously simulated and more attractive alternative of eating the cookies leaves a residual change in mood, and this mood is carried over into assessments of the cost of persistence on the unsolvable puzzle.

Evidence for Hedonic Sampling in Self-control

Evidence suggests that humans use mental simulations to make decisions, and further, that these simulations result in affective responses. For example, Gilbert and Wilson (2007) argue that, "simulations allow people to 'preview' events and to 'prefeel' the pleasures and pains those events will produce" (p. 1352). Consistent with the view that individuals rely on hedonic affect from mental simulation to make decisions, research utilizing fMRI imaging suggests that individuals exhibit neural activity resembling that of experiencing a reward when assessing possibly winning during a gambling task (Breiter, Aharon, Kahneman, Dale, & Shizgal, 2001). It is also likely that the simulation of tasks requiring the exertion of self-control results in negative affect. Self-control is often viewed as suffering short-term discomfort or foregoing temptation to reach a long-term reward (see Chapter 5). Indeed, giving into temptation leads to positive affect (Hofmann, Kotabe, & Luhmann, 2013). Furthermore, resisting a temptation often leads to negative feelings and people often relapse on goals simply to avoid negative affect (Baker, Piper, McCarthy, Majeskie, & Fiore, 2004). Even situations that do not directly involve giving up a temptation may result in negative affect. Mental effort itself is often rated as unpleasant to downright aversive, and negative affect may be produced through ongoing exertion of mental effort (Hockey, 1997; Kool, McGuire, Rosen, & Botvinick, 2010; Salomon, 1984). Incongruent words on the Stroop task result in neutral words directly after to be judged as more negative (Fritz & Dreisbach, 2013), and individuals report an increased desire to change tasks after incongruent trials (Lynn, Riddle, & Morsella, 2012). While we have up to this point focused on the mental simulation of hypothetical actions, in cases where one is in the process of a behavior the hedonic affect is likely being generated by the activity itself. This generation of negative affect is then being compared to the potential affect of alternative behaviors.

This reliance on affective information is not altogether surprising; affect serves a vital role in many aspects of human behavior, including decision-making. A large body of research reveals the high degree of reliance on affective information for decision-making processes (eg, the affect heuristic; Slovic, Finucane, Peters, & MacGregor, 2007). One of the more prominent models espousing this position is the feeling-as-information model, in which affective states are used as informational sources (for a thorough review, see Schwarz, 2010). This model emphasizes that, "emotions exist for the sake of signaling states of the world that have to be responded to, or that no longer need response and action" (Frijda, 1988, p. 345), suggesting that humans rely on affective responses to mental simulations when making choices about motivationally conflicting opportunities.

There is also evidence that mental simulation is integral to the development of the depletion. Studies have found that merely forming a concrete simulation of a self-control task results in depletion for areas such as emotional regulation, action control, and resisting tempting foods (Macrae et al., 2014). Further research by Ackerman, Goldstein, Shapiro, and Bargh (2009) suggests that even simulating the perspective of another individual exerting self-control results in depleted self-control in monetary spending (experiment 1) and lexical generation (experiment 2). Subsequent research extended these findings for mentally simulating squeezing a handgrip (Graham, Sonne, & Bray, 2014), and being exposed to tempting stimuli (Hagger et al., 2013). The opportunity-cost model and the process model are unable to explain findings such as these in which the participant exerts no actual self-control. However, if hedonic sampling is a pivotal ingredient in motivational conflict and functions as input in decisions concerning which activities we invest in, then the weighing of opportunity costs and shifts in motivation are essential to the depletion process and can be caused by the self-control decision itself.

Our model argues that the process of repeated hedonic sampling leaves behind residual affect that is utilized in subsequent self-control decisions. There is indeed some evidence that depletion results in an increase in negative affect. However, it is possible that the increase in negative affect is subtle enough that it is only evident in metaanalytic analyses with sufficiently high power (Hagger et al., 2010). One reason negative affect may be hard to detect in depleted participants is that our current measures are designed to examine explicit affect. However, evidence suggests that implicit affect impacts moods and often does not show up on explicit affect measures such as the brief mood introspection scale (BMIS) or the positive and negative affect schedule (PANAS) (eg, see Hu & Kaplan, 2013).

This negative affect, even if it is implicit, may alter subsequent self-control performance. For example, it is a well-established result that negative affect influences individuals' willingness to exert effort and overcome barriers (eg, Ellis, Thomas, & Rodriguez, 1984). Likewise, participants who were subliminally shown smiling faces or action words rode an exercise bike longer and reported less subjective feelings of fatigue (Quirin, Bode, & Kuhl, 2011). More directly, evidence suggests a role of this implicit hedonic affect in depletion. For example, Blanchfield, Hardy, and Marcora (2014) found that depleted participants exhibited greater positive implicit responses to energy words in the implicit association task (Dovidio, Kawakami, Johnson, Johnson, & Howard, 1997). Furthermore, a set of studies by Buczny, Layton, and Muraven (2015) found that neutral images were judged as more negative by depleted participants than by nondepleted participants. This suggests that hedonic sampling results in some residual affective state that is not visible with explicit measures due to its implicit nature. A series of studies by Aarts, Custers, and Holland (2007) further supports the impact of residual negative affect on goal-directed behavior. Across five studies, participants exposed to stimuli designed to produce negative affect also exhibited less goal desire as a response to goal priming.

Summary

To summarize, the assessment of behavioral choices causes shifts in motivation that result in the depletion effect. These motivational shifts are due to the process in which individuals create mental simulations of potential behaviors and utilize the affect that is produced as information concerning the value of each action. Importantly, the process of sampling possible simulations necessitates the experience of negative affect, which leaves a residual imprint on the individual's mood. This residual affect is then included in subsequent mental simulations. Negative affect experienced by the mental simulation of not indulging one's immediate desire likely then serves as the basis for depletion and self-control failure.

INTEGRATION

A number of depletion outcomes can be explained through incorporating hedonic sampling into current models, and it demonstrates a high level of flexibility. For example, the negative affect experienced by the mental simulation of not indulging one's immediate desire may serve as the basis for depletion and eventual self-control failure, but a different affective source (eg, positive affect from the mental simulation of achieving a goal) could also be the basis for situations in which depletion can be overcome or avoided. Hedonic sampling is therefore capable of explaining a number of outcomes associated with motivation and self-control. In the next section we apply hedonic sampling to current findings on depletion. Unfortunately, the number of variables found to interact with depletion is too large for the scope of this chapter. Instead, we focus on explaining those findings which have proven to be particularly difficult to explain.

Hedonic Sampling and Motivation to Conserve

Hedonic sampling may offer an explanation for the finding that individuals appear motivated to conserve self-control resources. Early studies on depletion and motivation discovered that individuals exhibited poorer self-control performance when they believed they would soon be asked to complete subsequent tasks that required self-control. For example, Muraven, Shmueli, and Burkley (2006) found that when depleted participants were informed about a future self-control task, they persisted on a cold-pressor task for less time than depleted nonanticipating participants (experiment 1). Likewise, Graham, Bray, and Ginis (2014) found that participants who anticipated having to exert self-control on four tasks (in order; a handgrip task, Stroop task, and two final handgrip tasks) completed fewer words on the Stroop task as compared to participants who did not anticipate having to complete four tasks. However, when participants were depleted and informed that the task they were going to engage in would not require self-control, they showed little difference from participants who were not told about any future task (experiment 2). When participants believe the study to be ending soon they cease conservation behavior and their self-control performance returns to normal (Tyler & Burns, 2009).

Conservation behavior can be explained with hedonic sampling through making future self-control tasks seem harder, more unpleasant, and less desirable. We propose that the prospect of completing multiple rigorous tasks generates negative affect that does not simply disappear after the sampling process is complete, but instead leaves some amount of residual affect. This affective information is then diagnostic in evaluating spending energy, time, or attention on subsequent behaviors requiring self-control.

It is thusly that the negative assessments resulting from hedonic sampling of multiple tasks may increase the motivation to conserve rather than expend self-control resources.

Hedonic Sampling and Positive Affect

Until now we have paid little attention to the role of positive affect in the hedonic sampling process; yet, evidence suggests that it plays a sizable part in determining whether individuals will fail or be successful when exerting self-control. Early investigations into the moderating role of affect on depletion supported this. Depleted participants who are randomly assigned to positive affect induction exhibit no reduction in self-control. For example, watching a comedic video or receiving a surprise gift negates the depletion effect; negative affect induction or neutral distraction do not (Tice et al., 2007). Smokers who exerted self-control followed by positive affect induction are less likely to give in to the temptation to smoke during a 10-min break than smokers in a neutral affect condition (Shmueli & Prochaska, 2012). Moreover, explicit awareness of positive affect does not seem to be necessary, as it appears to ameliorate depletion even when implicitly produced (Ren, Hu, Zhang, & Huang, 2010).

Positive affect may also act similarly to negative affect in that it is carried over into the generation of mental simulations. Accordingly, when positive affect is increased, the mental simulation of a task may be positive (or merely less negative). This more positive simulation represents an increase in motivation and results in better self-control performance. This may explain why reward increases resistance to depletion. For example, participants who have undergone a self-control depletion task but are paid to drink a noxious beverage exhibit no difference from nondepleted participants (Muraven & Slessareva, 2003). While this was attributed to an increase in motivation, we propose that this motivational difference is a result of positive affect produced by a mental simulation of receiving monetary compensation.

Research on depletion and self-determination theory also fits in this framework. When people exert self-control for intrinsic reasons, they perform better on subsequent tests of self-control compared to people who engage in the same self-control for extrinsic reasons (Chapter 4; Moller, Deci, & Ryan, 2006; Muraven, 2008; Muraven, Rosman, & Gagné, 2007). Subsequent research suggests that intrinsic motivation increased feelings of vitality, a positive emotion and that feeling is what led to the better self-control outcome (Muraven, Gagne, & Rosman, 2008).

Positive affect may explain other findings that are seemingly at odds with a strict resource account of depletion. For example, one of the biggest lines of research antithetical to the resource model of depletion argues that implicit beliefs about the transient nature of self-control moderates depletion; both innate and induced implicit beliefs that self-control is immutable and eliminates the depletion effect (Job et al., 2010). Job, Walton, Bernecker, and Dweck (2015) extended these findings longitudinally by demonstrating that participants with high regulatory need (eg, high course load) were better able to self-regulate if they believed that self-control was nonlimited. One possible explanation for these findings is that implicit beliefs about self-control lead to higher self-efficacy, and this may lead to less negative affect accrual during the hedonic sampling process. Consistent with the link between self-efficacy and positive affect, Schutte (2013) found that longitudinal interventions that increase positive affect also lead to higher self-efficacy.

Individual Differences in Motivation

Differential effects of depletion have also been attributed to shifts in approach and avoidance motivation. Studies have shown that in contrast to a reduction in self-control strength, increases in approach motivation may explain the effects of depletion. For example, betting behavior following a self-control task was associated with sensitivity to incentives, but not with trait self-control (Schmeichel, Harmon-Jones, & Harmon-Jones, 2010). Similarly, it has been shown that exercising self-control can affect responses that are associated with increased approach motivation (eg, optimism) but that require little or no self-control. Furthermore, these effects are more prominent in individuals high in trait approach motivation, whereas trait self-control had no moderating effect (Crowell, Kelley, & Schmeichel, 2014).

A hedonic sampling account would posit that during a self-control conflict, affect associated with mental simulations of outcomes predicts self-control performance. Because approach motivation decreases conflict detection (ie, conflict between immediate desires and self-control goals) in subsequent self-control tasks, the diagnosticity of positive affect associated with immediate gratification would likely also increase (Schmeichel et al., 2010). Differences in approach motivation may therefore increase reliance on positive affect associated with immediate gratification produced by this hedonic sampling, thus reducing self-control performance. In other words, individual differences in approach motivation could affect the nature of the hedonic sampling process, and therefore alters subsequent self-control performance. Such an interpretation would allow for an explanation of systematic differences in self-control performance between chronically approach-oriented and more avoidant individuals.

An interesting corollary to this finding is that by reducing this reliance on positive affect produced by hedonic sampling, self-control performance may actually be improved. Consistent with this assertion, participants who made concrete plans for how they would respond to specific contingencies were able to avoid being depleted by an initial self-control task (Webb & Sheeran, 2003). This may be due to the fact that implementation intentions modify implicit affective responses by overriding the momentary assessment of affect in mental simulations (Eder, 2011). Others have proposed that implementation intentions may increase automaticity, facilitating the formation of new behaviors (eg, Webb & Sheeran, 2003; Chapter 3). By creating automatic behavior patterns, the process of hedonic sampling is no longer employed to make self-control decisions in the moment, and thus depletion is averted. This ability to offset the hedonic sampling process may be crucial to understanding self-control training.

Hedonic Sampling and Self-control Training

While the resource model of self-control was integral to developing new insight into the facets of behavioral change, one of its biggest contributions is a relatively unexplored avenue: self-control training. In particular, the resource model of self-control predicts that through regular practice self-control can be strengthened, leaving individuals less susceptible to depletion. Tests of the resource model of self-control have provided strong evidence in favor of the phenomenon. Muraven, Baumeister, and Tice (1999) randomly assigned participants to practice one of the four tasks for 2 weeks: monitoring and improving posture; consistently trying to improve their mood; maintaining an extensive food diary; or a no-task control. Participants in all of the three self-control conditions exhibited significantly less depletion as measured on a handgrip-persistence task than participants who did not practice any task. Other lines of inquiry have found the training effect for a variety of tasks. For example, regular self-control exertion in the form of utilizing the nondominant hand for 2 weeks causes a decrease in aggressive responding to provocation (Denson, Capper, Oaten, Friese, & Schofield, 2011). Participants who practice self-control in the form of cutting back on sweets or regularly squeezing a handgrip exhibit better performance on a stop-signal task (Muraven, 2010a). Participants attempting to quit smoking who practiced self-control by avoiding sweets or squeezing a handgrip were significantly less likely to relapse than if they merely filled out a diary or completed nightly simple math problems (tasks which do not require substantial self-control; Muraven, 2010b). The self-control training literature has also been well validated in terms of the phenomenon's generalizability. For example, practicing self-control in the form of increasing financial monitoring (Oaten & Cheng, 2007), maintaining a structured academic study schedule (Oaten & Cheng, 2006), and going to the gym regularly (Oaten & Cheng, 2010) all lead to better resilience to depletion.

Despite the intrinsic value that self-control training holds, it is a relatively unexplored facet of the resource model, with a dearth of explanative models. One of the models to date, proposed by Berkman, Graham, and Fisher (2012), posits that practicing inhibitory control in one area may alter connectivity and functioning in the right inferior frontal gyrus, which would then possibly lead to better inhibitory control in different domains. A hedonic sampling account, however, offers further insight into the mechanism behind self-control training. In line with the previously discussed possibility that implementation intentions buffer against depletion by shifting the reliance on mental simulation, a hedonic sampling account interprets self-control building as the product of changes in the reliance on affect produced from hedonic sampling. In other words, training self-control increases the automaticity of engaging in a self-control task without relying on the hedonic affect generated by mental simulations. Rather, individuals who engage automatically in self-control tasks may cease simulating potential task outcomes altogether.

Individuals who practice self-control regularly may gain automaticity toward approaching self-control tasks, and thus spend less time simulating potential choices and engage more quickly in the undesirable task. As evidence of this, studies do suggest that the mere mental simulation of a self-control activity is enough to leave individuals in a depleted state (Graham, Sonne, et al., 2014; Macrae et al., 2014), although this is not the case for pleasant mental simulations not requiring self-control (eg, Hagger & Chatzisarantis, 2013; Knauper, Pillay, Lacaille, McCollam, & Kelso, 2011). Furthermore, it has also been shown that participants who were instructed to form implementation intentions or were given a cognitive load showed no indication of depletion (Knauper et al., 2011). Similarly, when individuals do not dwell on a task but instead begin it without thinking there is no depletion effect (Walsh, Mantonakis, & Joordens, 2015). Thus, altering the affective nature of mental simulations, whether by increasing positively sampled affect or by decreasing the reliance on sampled affect altogether, appears to alter self-control outcomes.

Summary

Motivation is an integral aspect of self-control that is not easily separated for study in isolation. This is may be due to its inherent presence in self-control; self-control is not necessary without the presence of motivational conflict. Our investigation into motivation has taken the general view that motivation in self-control is built upon hedonic affect that is sampled from mental simulations of potential task outcomes. We further argue that depletion can be understood as a tendency for these affective reactions to influence feelings and behavior about subsequent tasks. Depletion is therefore understandable as the result of negatively sampled affect that is generated by the simulation of task outcomes (eg, simulating the experience of unpleasant or effortful tasks), and which influences future behavior through the motivational shifts proposed by the process model (Inzlicht & Schmeichel, 2012). Using a hedonic sampling approach, various findings concerning depletion can be integrated and explained. Implicit beliefs, affect-based interventions, and self-control training are interpreted as products of adjustments to the basic hedonic sampling process.

APPLICATION

Introducing a hedonic sampling approach to motivation and self-control has some fairly interesting implications. For example, it suggests paramount importance for the Alcoholics Anonymous maxim, "one day at a time." If hedonic affect carries over into future assessments of temptations and unpleasant tasks, simulating one moment at a time may increase success rates during lengthy behavioral change processes. However, the authors found little research that assessed Alcoholics Anonymous' emphasis on the 24-cycle as a fixation point and its exact impact on alcohol cessation. Another interesting implication of hedonic sampling is the importance of maintaining positive affect. As previously discussed, research indicates that the sampling of positive affect may lead to more positive affective evaluations of future behavioral options. This suggests that interventions that induce long-lasting positive affect states may be beneficial (eg, self-affirmation, Schmeichel, 2009).

Given the proposition that mood impacts the affective forecasting of mental simulations, another interesting implication for a hedonic sampling is the importance of positive affect during in-the-moment temptations. For example, previous studies have found that cigarette smokers attempting to quit are left depleted by temptations to smoke (Hagger et al., 2013). This would suggest that leveraging positive affect during temptation may be successful in countering the impulse to succumb to those temptations. Indeed, interventions such as positive affect (Shmueli & Prochaska, 2012) and glucose tablets (Harakas & Foulds, 2002) are found to increase resilience to temptations to smoke. Given that it is unlikely that a glucose tablet is entering the brain in the time delay between consumption and temptation, it is probable that glucose is acting to leverage previous affective states against forecasted affective states by increasing current hedonic affect. In support, research has found that glucose causes a relief of tension (Benton & Owens, 1993). Furthermore, glucose causes a change in brain activity that is distinct from activity associated with artificial sweeteners and indicative of a pleasure response (Frank et al., 2008; Smeets, Weijzen, de Graaf, & Viergever, 2011).

Conversely, where positive affect may benefit the hedonic sampling process and increase self-control performance, hedonic sampling predicts that negative affect may be detrimental to the hedonic sampling process by contributing to negative moods more generally following self-control tasks. There is some preliminary evidence to support this. For example, Vohs, Baumeister, Mead, Ramanathan, and Hofmann (2014; Experiments 1,2) found that assessments of neutral images were more negative for depleted participants than for nondepleted participants. This is in general confirmation with metaanalytic findings that participants exhibit mild increases in negative affect when depleted (Hagger et al., 2010). Such negative moods may be the result of negative affect carried over from the hedonic sampling process.

Hedonic sampling also has interesting implications for the formation of interventions to increase self-control and enhance the behavioral change process in general. We suggest that increased reliance on the hedonic sampling process decreases subsequent self-control performance. Prioritizing a "colder" system of processing that reduces reliance on affect then may have positive implications for increasing self-control performance. Research investigating "hot," emotion-dependent versus "cold," emotion-independent systems of processing would appear to be consistent with this (Peters, Vastfjall, Garling, & Slovic, 2006). Similarly, increasing the automaticity of behavior may reduce the need for moment-to-moment assessments, thus overriding the hedonic sampling process and potentially increasing self-control performance.

A similar line of research would suggest that bypassing the self-control conflict itself (and thus also bypassing the affective sampling of yet-undecided outcomes) would result in greater self-control performance. Interestingly, some research has found that the inclination to bypass self-control conflicts ahead of time has also been correlated with trait self-control (de Ridder, Lensvelt-Mulders, Finkenauer, Stok, & Baumeister, 2012). The avoidance of self-control conflicts ahead of time may ironically creates less of a need to expend self-control in the moment. The same sentiment is echoed by a hedonic sampling account, where bypassing the evaluative affective processes inherent in a self-control conflict reduces the need for self-control, and therefore reduces the risk of depletion. Anticipatory behaviors that address ways of reducing the reliance on the hedonic sampling process therefore have implications for increasing self-control and encouraging behavior change.

An Alternative Account

An alternative mechanism for depletion to the negative affect accumulation we propose may be the motive to regulate the hedonic affect itself. Studies suggest that individuals suffer regulatory failure when in a negative affective state because they are attempting to hedonistically self-soothe. For example, Leith and Baumeister (1996) utilized a mood-freezing paradigm and found that individuals who are in a negative mood and who believe that they are unable to change their current mood state ate fewer fatty snacks (experiment 1), preferred long-term gratification over short term (experiment 2), and engaged in less procrastination (experiment 3). They argue that when in a negative mood, individuals give priority to affect regulation over self-restraint and attempt to use pleasure as a method of mood repair. Similarly, Tice, Bratslavsky, and Baumeister (2001) replicated this effect and argued that negative affect must be regulated, and that individuals attempt to regulate by giving in to self-control. Some additional evidence lends an interesting addendum to this proposition. Namely, some new research has begun to suggest that emotional regulation ability declines during mental fatigue (Grillon, Quispe-Escudero, Mathur, & Ernst, 2015). Evidence also suggests that these feelings of fatigue may be less effectively regulated in depleted individuals. For example, in restrained eaters who had undergone negative affect induction, seeing appetizing food caused brain activity that was related to increased reward salience (Wagner, Boswell, Kelley, & Heatherton, 2012), suggesting that hedonic impulses are underregulated in the presence of negative affect. Whether these findings fall in line with a hedonic sampling or a mood-repair model is yet unclear, and further research is needed.

CONCLUSION

Motivation is an integral and complex component of self-control. Previous models such as the process model (Inzlicht & Schmeichel, 2012) and the opportunity-cost model (Kurzban et al., 2013) have attempted to incorporate motivational shifts into research on self-control depletion. We agree with the basic tenets of both models, but suggest an integral role of hedonic sampling. More specifically, we posit that self-control depletion is the product of a process in which individuals create mental simulations of alternative tasks and sample the hedonic affect produced by those simulations; a process we refer to as hedonic sampling. Furthermore, we suggest that the hedonic affect produced by this process leaves lasting impacts on mood, which colors subsequent assessments of future choices. This view is compatible with the opportunity-cost model in that current tasks are compared with alternatives, and the phenomenal aspect of this comparison process comes in the form of input that is used for effort-based decision-making. It is also compatible with the process model in that the hedonic sampling process is our proposed mechanism for motivational shifts during depletion. More specifically, we posit that shifts in the affect generated by mental simulation following the exertion of self-control lead to the lower likelihood of self-control success that the depletion effect describes. When various depletion effects are viewed in light of hedonic sampling, the effects of self-affirmation, implementation intentions, and implicit beliefs about self-control may be readily explained.

References

Aarts, H., Custers, R., & Holland, R. W. (2007). The nonconscious cessation of goal pursuit: when goals and negative affect are coactivated. *The Journal of Personality and Social Psychology, 92*(2), 165–178.

Ackerman, J. M., Goldstein, N. J., Shapiro, J. R., & Bargh, J. A. (2009). You wear me out: the vicarious depletion of self-control. *Psychological Science, 20*(3), 326–332.

Alberts, H. J. E.M., Martijn, C., & de Vries, N. K. (2011). Fighting self-control failure: overcoming ego depletion by increasing self-awareness. *Journal of Experimental Social Psychology, 47*(1), 58–62.

Alberts, H. J. E.M., Martijn, C., Nievelstein, F., Jansen, A., & de Vries, N. K. (2008). Distracting the self: shifting attention prevents ego depletion. *Self and Identity, 7*(3), 322–334.

Baker, T. B., Piper, M. E., McCarthy, D. E., Majeskie, M. R., & Fiore, M. C. (2004). Addiction motivation reformulated: an affective processing model of negative reinforcement. *Psychological Review, 111*, 33.

Baumeister, R. F., Bratslavsky, E., Muraven, M., & Tice, D. M. (1998). Ego depletion: is the active self a limited resource? *Journal of Personality and Social Psychology, 74*(5), 1252–1265.

Benton, D., & Owens, D. (1993). Is raised blood glucose associated with the relief of tension? *Journal of Psychosomatic Research, 37*(7), 723–735.

Berkman, E. T., Graham, A. M., & Fisher, P. A. (2012). Training self-control: a domain-general translational neuroscience approach. *Child Development Perspectives, 6*(4), 374–384.

Blanchfield, A., Hardy, J., & Marcora, S. (2014). Non-conscious visual cues related to affect and action alter perception of effort and endurance performance. *Frontiers in Human Neuroscience, 8*, 967.

Boucher, H. C., & Kofos, M. N. (2012). The idea of money counteracts ego depletion effects. *Journal of Experimental Social Psychology, 48*(4), 804–810.

Breiter, H. C., Aharon, I., Kahneman, D., Dale, A., & Shizgal, P. (2001). Functional imaging of neural responses to expectancy and experience of monetary gains and losses. *Neuron, 30*(2), 619–639.

Buczny, J., Layton, R. L., & Muraven, M. (2015). The role of implicit affective responses and trait self-control in ego resource management. *Motivation and Emotion, 39*(5), 669–679.

Crowell, A., Kelley, N. J., & Schmeichel, B. J. (2014). Trait approach motivation moderates the aftereffects of self-control. *Frontiers in Psychology, 5*, 1112.

Denson, T. F., Capper, M. M., Oaten, M. M., Friese, M., & Schofield, T. P. (2011). Self-control training decreases aggression in response to provocation in aggressive individuals. *Journal of Research in Personality, 45*(2), 252–256.

Dovidio, J. F., Kawakami, K., Johnson, C., Johnson, B., & Howard, A. (1997). On the nature of prejudice: automatic and controlled processes. *Journal of Experimental Social Psychology, 33*(5), 510–540.

Eder, A. B. (2011). Control of impulsive emotional behaviour through implementation intentions. *Cognition & Emotion, 25*(3), 478–489.

Ellis, H. C., Thomas, R. L., & Rodriguez, I. A. (1984). Emotional mood states and memory: elaborative encoding, semantics processing, and cognitive effort. *Journal of Experimental Psychology: Learning, Memory, and Cognition, 10*, 470.

Frank, G. K., Oberndorfer, T. A., Simmons, A. N., Paulus, M. P., Fudge, J. L., Yang, T. T., ... Kaye, W. H. (2008). Sucrose activates human taste pathways differently from artificial sweetener. *Neuroimage, 39*(4), 1559–1569.

Frijda, N. H. (1988). The laws of emotion. *American Psychologist, 43*, 349–358.

Fritz, J., & Dreisbach, G. (2013). Conflicts as aversive signals: conflict priming increases negative judgments for neutral stimuli. *Cognitive, Affective, & Behavioral Neuroscience, 13*(2), 311–317.

Gilbert, D. T., & Wilson, T. D. (2007). Prospection: experiencing the future. *Science, 317*(5843), 1351–1354.

REFERENCES

Graham, J. D., Bray, S. R., & Ginis, K. A. M. (2014). "Pay the piper": it helps initially, but motivation takes a toll on self-control. *Psychology of Sport and Exercise, 15*(1), 89–96.

Graham, J. D., Sonne, M. W., & Bray, S. R. (2014). It wears me out just imagining it! Mental imagery leads to muscle fatigue and diminished performance of isometric exercise. *Biological Psychology, 103*, 1–6.

Grillon, C., Quispe-Escudero, D., Mathur, A., & Ernst, M. (2015). Mental fatigue impairs emotion regulation. *Emotion (Washington, DC), 15*(3), 383–389.

Hagger, M. S., & Chatzisarantis, N. L. (2013). The sweet taste of success: the presence of glucose in the oral cavity moderates the depletion of self-control resources. *Personality & Social Psychology Bulletin, 39*(1), 28–42.

Hagger, M. S., Leaver, E., Esser, K., Leung, C. M., Te Pas, N., Keatley, D. A., … Chatzisarantis, N. L. (2013). Cue-induced smoking urges deplete cigarette smokers' self-control resources. *Annals of Behavioral Medicine, 46*(3), 394–400.

Hagger, M. S., Wood, C. W., Stiff, C., & Chatzisarantis, N. L. D. (2010). Ego depletion and the strength model of self-control: a meta-analysis. *Psychological Bulletin, 136*(4), 495–525.

Harakas, P., & Foulds, J. (2002). Acute effects of glucose tablets on craving, withdrawal symptoms, and sustained attention in 12-h abstinent tobacco smokers. *Psychopharmacology, 161*(3), 271–277.

'Hero' teacher stopped shooting with hug. (March 16, 2006). Retrieved July 7, 2015, from http://abcnews.go.com/GMA/story?id=1732518&page=1#.

Hockey, G. R. J. (1997). Compensatory control in the regulation of human performance under stress and high workload: a cognitive-energetical framework. *Biological Psychology, 45*, 73–93.

Hofmann, W., Kotabe, H., & Luhmann, M. (2013). The spoiled pleasure of giving in to temptation. *Motivation and Emotion, 37*, 733–742.

Hu, X., & Kaplan, S. (2013). The effects of unconsciously derived affect on task satisfaction and performance. *Journal of Business and Psychology, 30*(1), 119–135.

Inzlicht, M., & Schmeichel, B. J. (2012). What is ego depletion? Toward a mechanistic revision of the resource model of self-control. *Personality & Social Psychology Bulletin, 7*(5), 450–463.

Job, V., Dweck, C. S., & Walton, G. M. (2010). Ego depletion—is it all in your head? Implicit theories about willpower affect self-regulation. *Psychological Science, 21*(11), 1686–1693.

Job, V., Walton, G. M., Bernecker, K., & Dweck, C. S. (2015). Implicit theories about willpower predict self-regulation and grades in everyday life. *Journal of Personality and Social Psychology, 108*(4), 637–647.

Knauper, B., Pillay, R., Lacaille, J., McCollam, A., & Kelso, E. (2011). Replacing craving imagery with alternative pleasant imagery reduces craving intensity. *Appetite, 57*(1), 173–178.

Kool, W., McGuire, J. T., Rosen, Z. B., & Botvinick, M. M. (2010). Decision making and the avoidance of cognitive demand. *Journal of Experimental Psychology: General, 139*, 665.

Kurzban, R., Duckworth, A. L., Kable, J. W., & Myers, J. (2013). An opportunity cost model of subjective effort and task performance. *Behavioral and Brain Sciences, 36*(6), 661–679.

Leith, K. P., & Baumeister, R. F. (1996). Why do bad moods increase self-defeating behavior? Emotion, risk taking, and self-regulation. *Journal of Personality and Social Psychology, 71*(6), 1250–1267.

Lynn, M. T., Riddle, T. A., & Morsella, E. (2012). The phenomenology of quitting: effects from repetition and cognitive effort. *Korean Journal of Cognitive Science, 23*, 25–46.

Macrae, C. N., Christian, B. M., Golubickis, M., Karanasiou, M., Troksiarova, L., McNamara, D. L., … Miles, L. K. (2014). When do i wear me out? Mental simulation and the diminution of self-control. *Journal of Experimental Psychology: General, 143*(4), 1755–1764.

Moller, A. C., Deci, E. L., & Ryan, R. M. (2006). Choice and ego-depletion: the moderating role of autonomy. *Personality & Social Psychology Bulletin, 32*, 1024–1036.

Muraven, M. (2008). Autonomous self-control is less depleting. *Journal of Research in Personality, 42*, 763–770.

Muraven, M. (2010a). Building self-control strength: practicing self-control leads to improved self-control performance. *Journal of Experimental Social Psychology, 46*(2), 465–468.

Muraven, M. (2010b). Practicing self-control lowers the risk of smoking lapse. *Psychology of Addictive Behaviors, 24*(3), 446–452.

Muraven, M., Baumeister, R. F., & Tice, D. M. (1999). Longitudinal improvement of self-regulation through practice: building self-control strength through repeated exercise. *Journal of Personality and Social Psychology, 139*(4), 446–457.

Muraven, M., Gagne, M., & Rosman, H. (2008). Helpful self-control: autonomy support, vitality, and depletion. *Journal of Experimental Social Psychology, 44*, 573–585.

Muraven, M., Rosman, H., & Gagné, M. (2007). Lack of autonomy and self-control: performance contingent rewards lead to greater depletion. *Motivation and Emotion, 31*, 322–330. http://dx.doi.org/10.1007/s11031-007-9073-x.

Muraven, M., Shmueli, D., & Burkley, E. (2006). Conserving self-control strength. *Journal of Personality and Social Psychology, 91*(3), 524–537.

Muraven, M., & Slessareva, E. (2003). Mechanisms of self-control failure: motivation and limited resources. *Personality & Social Psychology Bulletin, 29*(7), 894–906.

Muraven, M., Tice, D. M., & Baumeister, R. F. (1998). Self-control as a limited resource: regulatory depletion patterns. *Journal of Personality and Social Psychology, 74*(3), 774–789.

Oaten, M., & Cheng, K. (2006). Improved self-control: the benefits of a regular program of academic study. *Basic and Applied Social Psychology, 28*(1), 1–16.

Oaten, M., & Cheng, K. (2007). Improvements in self-control from financial monitoring. *Journal of Economic Psychology, 28*(4), 487–501.

Oaten, M., & Cheng, K. (2010). Longitudinal gains in self-regulation from regular physical exercise. *British Journal of Health Psychology, 11*(4), 717–733.

Peters, E., Vastfjall, D., Garling, T., & Slovic, P. (2006). Affect and decision making: a "hot" topic. *Journal of Behavioral Decision Making, 19*(2), 79–85.

Quirin, M., Bode, R. C., & Kuhl, J. (2011). Recovering from negative events by boosting implicit positive affect. *Cognition & Emotion, 25*(3), 559–570.

Ren, J., Hu, L., Zhang, H., & Huang, Z. (2010). Implicit positive emotion counteracts ego depletion. *Social Behavior and Personality, 38*(7), 919–928.

de Ridder, D. T., Lensvelt-Mulders, G., Finkenauer, C., Stok, F. M., & Baumeister, R. F. (2012). Taking stock of self-control: a meta-analysis of how trait self-control relates to a wide range of behaviors. *Personality and Social Psychology Review: An Official Journal of the Society for Personality and Social Psychology, Inc., 16*(1), 76–99.

Rounding, K., Lee, A., Jacobson, J. A., & Ji, L. J. (2012). Religion replenishes self-control. *Psychological Science, 23*(6), 635–642.

Salomon, G. (1984). Television is "easy" and print is "tough": the differential investment of mental effort in learning as a function of perceptions and attributions. *Journal of Educational Psychology, 76*, 647.

Schmeichel, B. J. (2009). Self-affirmation and self-control: affirming core values counteracts ego depletion. *Journal of Personality and Social Psychology, 96*(4), 770–782.

Schmeichel, B. J., Harmon-Jones, C., & Harmon-Jones, E. (2010). Exercising self-control increases approach motivation. *Journal of Personality and Social Psychology, 99*(1), 162–173.

Schutte, N. S. (2013). The broaden and build process: positive affect, ratio of positive to negative affect and general self-efficacy. *The Journal of Positive Psychology, 9*(1), 66–74.

Schwarz, N. (2010). Feelings-as-information. In P. Van Lange, A. W. Kruglanski, & E. T. Higgins (Eds.), *Handbook of theories of social psychology*. Sage.

Shmueli, D., & Prochaska, J. J. (2012). A test of positive affect induction for countering self-control depletion in cigarette smokers. *Psychology of Addictive Behaviors, 26*(1), 157–161.

Slovic, P., Finucane, M. L., Peters, E., & MacGregor, D. G. (2007). The affect heuristic. *European Journal of Operational Research, 177*(3), 1333–1352.

Smeets, P. A., Weijzen, P., de Graaf, C., & Viergever, M. A. (2011). Consumption of caloric and non-caloric versions of a soft drink differentially affects brain activation during tasting. *Neuroimage, 54*(2), 1367–1374.

Tice, D. M., Baumeister, R. F., Shmueli, D., & Muraven, M. (2007). Restoring the self: positive affect helps improve self-regulation following ego depletion. *Journal of Experimental Social Psychology, 43*(3), 379–384.

Tice, D. M., Bratslavsky, E., & Baumeister, R. F. (2001). Emotional distress regulation takes precedence over impulse control: if you feel bad, do it! *Journal of Personality and Social Psychology, 80*(1), 53–67.

Tyler, J. M., & Burns, K. C. (2009). Triggering conservation of the self's regulatory resources. *Basic and Applied Social Psychology, 31*(3), 255–266.

Vohs, K., Baumeister, R. F., Mead, N. L., Ramanathan, S., & Hofmann, W. (2014). *Engaging in self-control heightens urges and feelings*. University of Minnesota (submitted for publication).

Wagner, D. D., Boswell, R. G., Kelley, W. M., & Heatherton, T. F. (2012). Inducing negative affect increases the reward value of appetizing foods in dieters. *Journal of Cognitive Neuroscience, 24*(7), 1625–1633.

Walsh, D. (2014). Attenuating depletion using goal priming. *Journal of Consumer Psychology, 24*(4), 497–505.

Walsh, D., Mantonakis, A., & Joordens, S. (2015). Is "getting started" an effective way for people to overcome the depletion effect? *Canadian Journal of Administrative Sciences, 32*(1), 47–57.

Webb, T. L., & Sheeran, P. (2003). Can implementation intentions help to overcome ego-depletion? *Journal of Experimental Social Psychology, 39*(3), 279–286.

CHAPTER 8

Motivational Tuning in Response to Ego Depletion

L. Jia[1], R. Yu[1], E.R. Hirt[2], A. Fishbach[3]

[1]National University of Singapore, Singapore, Singapore; [2]Indiana University, Bloomington, IN, United States; [3]The University of Chicago, Chicago, IL, United States

> I count him braver who overcomes his desires than him who conquers his enemies; for the hardest victory is over self. *Aristotle (384–322 BC)*
>
> He who controls others may be powerful, but he who has mastered himself is mightier still. *Lao Tzu (571–531 BC)*

Philosophers from both the West and the East have long recognized the importance of one's capacity to rein over the self; its desires, impulses, and inertia. While their focus on self-control is centered on character development, modern social scientists have linked self-control to successful long-term goal pursuit. For example, children's ability to engage in self-control positively predicts their financial, career, and relationship success in adolescence (Mischel, Shoda, & Rodriguez, 1989) and adulthood (Moffitt et al., 2011). Because pursuing long-term goals such as academic success, career advancement, financial stability, good health, and harmonious relationships requires self-control to forego temptations and overcome obstacles (Baumeister, Heatherton, & Tice, 1994), sustained output of self-control is crucial for long-term success.

Unfortunately, research on ego depletion has demonstrated that our capacity for repeated self-control seems limited (see Baumeister, Vohs, & Tice, 2007; Hagger, Wood, Stiff, & Chatzisarantis, 2010 for reviews). After exerting self-control, individuals seem to be "depleted" of some centralized strength for further control and display subsequent self-control failures in an impressive range of domains, ranging from impaired intellectual performance (Schmeichel, Vohs, & Baumeister, 2003), impulsive spending (Vohs & Faber, 2007), to increased aggression (Stucke & Baumeister, 2006).

The strength model of depletion (Baumeister et al., 2007; Muraven & Baumeister, 2000; Vohs & Heatherton, 2000) thus proposes that one's self-control acts metaphorically like a muscle, which fatigues from repeated use. This conclusion, paired with findings from experience sampling demonstrating the prevalence of depletion in everyday life (Hofmann, Vohs, & Baumeister, 2012), has led scholars to claim that the limited capacity for self-control, and its frequent depletion, is a major hindrance to long-term goal pursuit (eg, Baumeister et al., 2007; Vohs, Kaikati, Kerkhof, & Schmeichel, 2009).

In this chapter, we argue that the interplay between depletion and long-term goal pursuit is more nuanced. Specifically, we propose a motivational tuning process that underscores the dynamic role depletion plays in long-term goal pursuit. We first highlight a gap in the literature that has motivated our conceptualization and investigation. We then proceed to describing our framework and the related evidence. After a brief speculation of the neuroscience foundation of the proposed process, we end the chapter by discussing the implications of our framework with regard to the potentially adaptive function of depletion.

A GAP BETWEEN CONCLUSION AND EMPIRICAL EVIDENCE

Although researchers conclude that depletion limits long-term goal pursuit, most depletion research in the past was conducted in goal-absent contexts (see Hagger et al., 2010; Inzlicht & Schmeichel, 2012). By goal-absent, we do not mean that participants are devoid of all motivation during the experiments (it is likely that some may be motivated to impress the experimenter or complete the tasks quickly). Instead, we emphasize that long-term goals are often not made salient in those experiments.

In fact, even in situations where a long-term goal is directly relevant, researchers try their best to downplay its relevance. Take depletion research on dieting behavior, for example. Researchers are interested in whether prior exertion of self-control reduces dieters' ability to restrain from copious eating (eg, Hagger et al., 2013; Vohs & Heatherton, 2000). Although the long-term goal of dieting is the conceptual cornerstone for this research, the experiments were designed to appear irrelevant to the dieting context. Participants' consumption of tempting foods, for example, was assessed in what ostensibly were taste-testing or product evaluation tasks. This downplay of the dieting goal was also evident in neuroscience research on depletion. When participants' brain reactivity to palatable foods was assessed via fMRI, their focal task was to judge the pictures as either indoor or outdoor stimuli (Wagner, Altman, Boswell, Kelley, & Heatherton, 2013), again highlighting a task goal irrelevant to dieting.

These efforts at masking the overarching, long-term goals are certainly not methodological flaws. Quite to the contrary, they are driven by sound methodological and theoretical concerns. For starters, masking the purpose of the experiments minimizes demand characteristics. Perhaps more importantly, downplaying the relevance of long-term goals minimizes the modulating influence of an overarching goal on depletion processes. Since research on depletion, for quite a long time, aims to establish that self-control is a centralized, limited, and depletable capacity (Hagger et al., 2010), minimizing the interference from the operation of other goal-directed processes on depletion makes perfect sense.

This consideration in past research, however, also means that we rarely conceptualize or study the effect of depletion in conjunction with an accessible long-term goal. As a result, the claim that depletion limits long-term goal pursuit (Vohs et al., 2009) paints only half of the story. Given the impressive body of empirical research on the phenomenon of depletion, accumulated by different labs using varying methodologies (eg, Hagger et al., 2010; Inzlicht, Schmeichel, & Macrae, 2014), we believe that the effect of depletion certainly places some general limit on goal pursuit. Especially when we consider the protracted nature of long-term goal pursuit, even if an accessible overarching goal modulates the effect somewhat, the limited nature of self-control can still constrain maximal goal pursuit.

On the other hand, this general conclusion underestimates the dynamic role depletion may play in long-term goal pursuit. Underlying the claim that depletion limits long-term goal pursuit is an implicit assumption that goal-directed processes interacts with self-control capacity in a passive way. That is, effective pursuit of long-term goals rises and ebbs monotonously with the amount of remaining, deployable self-control capacity (see Chapter 19 for discussions on the distinction between remaining versus deployable self-control capacity). More self-control capacity means more fuel for goal pursuit, and depleted self-control means the goal pursuit mechanism runs "dry" and less effective. However, goal-directed processes can also operate *dynamically*, or more actively, in response to changes in self-control capacity. That is, one's self-control capacity could be an informational input of a self-regulatory system, such that the system recruits *different* processes depending on the level of self-control capacity. When the fuel runs low, the individual may actively switch to a different way to run the engine.

In this chapter, we are interested in putting forth at least one way in which depletion can dynamically interplay with goal-directed processes. Given the prevalence of depletion in everyday life (Hofmann et al., 2012), we are particularly interested in how individuals cope with the potentially debilitating effect of depletion. We propose that when there is an accessible goal in mind, individuals can actively respond to depletion with motivational tuning: shifts in evaluations to facilitate the prioritization of important over less important goals. Specifically, depleted individuals would increase their evaluation of the goal if their chronic commitment to the goal is high and decrease the evaluations of it if their chronic commitment to the goal is low. Our approach resonates well with recent calls to move beyond the strength model and explore the underlying processes an act of prior self-control activates (eg, Clarkson, Hirt, Jia, & Alexander, 2010; Inzlicht & Schmeichel, 2012; Job, Dweck, & Walton, 2010; Kurzban, Duckworth, Kable, & Myers, 2013; Molden et al., 2012).

MOTIVATIONAL TUNING OF DEPLETION

We adopt a Person × Situation framework (Buss, 1979; Trevino, 1986) to understand the motivational tuning process (Fig. 8.1).

First, we highlight two situation-level factors—depletion and goal accessibility—as relevant for activating motivational tuning. Based on past

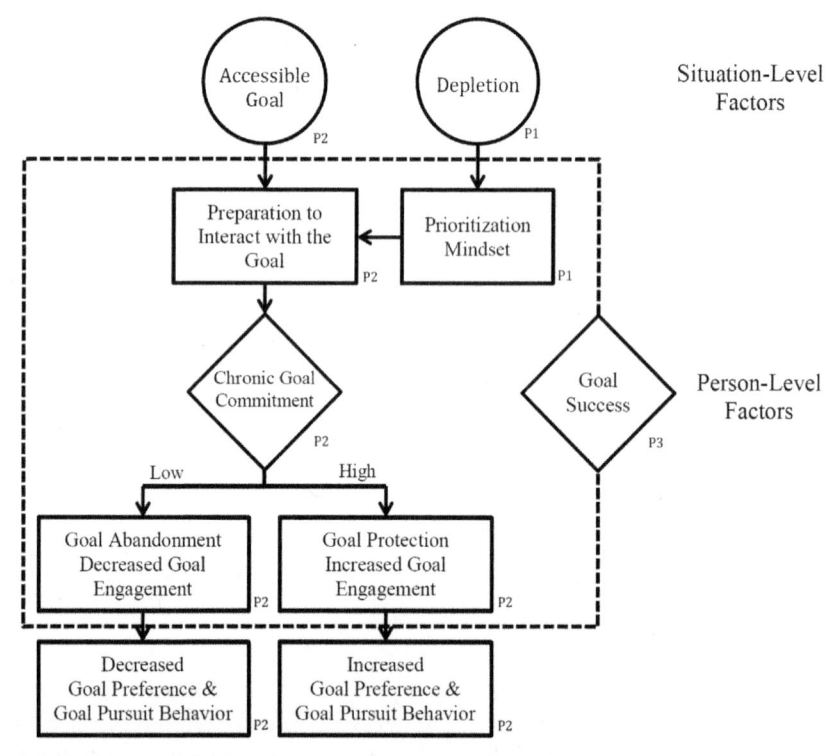

FIGURE 8.1 Motivational Tuning of Depletion. The conceptual framework consists of three main postulates: antecedent postulate (P1), main process postulate (P2), and moderator postulate (P3). The dotted region indicates the potential stages at which goal success moderates the tuning effect.

demonstrations that depleted individuals strategically utilize their subsequent self-control (Muraven, Shmueli, & Burkley, 2006; Tyler & Burns, 2009), we argue that individuals can adaptively respond to depletion by activating a prioritization mind-set: depleted individuals become more selective with how to spend their remaining self-control capacity. When a goal is accessible, depleted individuals should incorporate this prioritization mind-set as they mentally prepare for and decide on the level of goal engagement. This makes the individual highly selective about whether a goal is worth pursuing or not and, subsequently, tune their evaluation to prepare for goal (dis)engagement.

While depletion and goal accessibility constitute situational factors that activate motivational tuning, we posit that person-level factors should determine the direction and presence of tuning. We highlight two person-level factors: chronic goal commitment and goal success. We argue that individuals under the prioritization mind-set rely on their chronic commitment to the accessible goal to determine the direction of tuning: they decrease the evaluation of the goal if they consider it as a low-commitment goal and increase the goal evaluation if they consider it as a high-commitment goal. These shifts in goal preference serve to facilitate the abandonment of a low-commitment goal and the protection of a high-commitment goal.

Finally, we argue that not everyone is equally like to show motivational tuning. Just as physically healthy individuals tend to possess better biological defense mechanism, we propose that individuals who are more successful at pursuing long-term goals are more likely to possess and demonstrate motivational tuning.

We organize the ensuing discussion of the model with the following three specific postulates:

Antecedent postulate (P1): Depleted individuals can activate a prioritization mind-set, the prerequisite for motivational tuning.
Main process postulate (P2): Depleted individuals motivationally tune the evaluation of the accessible goal depending on their chronic goal commitment.
Moderator postulate (P3): Motivational tuning is primarily observed among individuals who are more successful in pursuing the long-term goal.

THE ANTECEDENT POSTULATE: INDIVIDUALS ACTIVATE A PRIORITIZATION MIND-SET IN RESPONSE TO DEPLETION

The most critical step of our framework is that people activate a prioritization mind-set in response to depletion. This step compels the self-regulatory system to select the appropriate process to counteract depletion. Counteracting is an active response to depletion. This active response stands in comparison with the scenario when a goal-directed process simply becomes less effective and has reduced output under depletion, which would be a passive reaction to depletion. In other words, activating a prioritization mind-set is the key stage at which depletion can provide input to a dynamic self-regulatory mechanism.

Evidence for antecedent process postulate: The most direct evidence for the notion that depletion can lead to prioritization of one's action planning comes from research on resource conservation (eg, Muraven et al., 2006; Tyler & Burns, 2009). In one experiment (Muraven et al., 2006; Study 1), after some depletion manipulation, participants anticipated a self-control challenge while working on an intermediate task. Depleted participants strategically withdrew their efforts on the intermediate task and ended up performing at a comparable level as nondepleted participants. On the other hand, nondepleted participants did not demonstrate such a strategic allocation of their self-control efforts. In another experiment (Muraven et al., 2006; Study 3), participants under depletion only withdrew self-control effort when they anticipated more self-control challenges later during that day. Again, nondepleted participants' self-control efforts did not show such sensitivity to their future self-control needs.

Research on moderators of the typical depletion effect provides indirect evidence on the prioritization mind-set which depletion triggers. Several variables have been found to restore the self-control performance of depleted individuals (Masicampo, Martin, & Anderson, 2014; Chapter 2). For example, depleted individuals' self-control performance can be restored to a level comparable to that of nondepleted individuals through positive mood (Tice, Baumeister, Shmueli, & Muraven, 2007), extrinsic motivation (Muraven & Slessareva, 2003), and self-affirmation (Schmeichel & Vohs, 2009). Interestingly, in all these studies, these variables did not improve nondepleted individuals' self-control. The common explanation is that nondepleted participants were performing at a ceiling level of self-control, and these variables cannot further improve uncompromised self-control. We readily acknowledge the viability of this explanation. Nonetheless, we offer an alternative, supplementary account. We argue that these findings also suggest that depletion makes individuals more sensitive to situational factors would inform their action planning. More specifically, nondepleted individuals may be less attuned to the rewards attached to their action planning (extrinsic motivation), whether the environment is safe to pursue the action planning (positive mood), or whether themselves have adequate resources (self-affirmation). Heightened sensitivity to these factors is consistent with a prioritization mind-set.

THE MAIN PROCESS POSTULATE: INDIVIDUALS MOTIVATIONALLY TUNE THE EVALUATION OF THE ACCESSIBLE GOAL DEPENDING ON THEIR CHRONIC GOAL COMMITMENT

We propose that the prioritization mind-set activated in response to depletion is then incorporated in one's preparation to interact with an accessible goal. With a salient goal in mind (consciously or unconsciously), individuals view their social environment in relation to the goal (Austin & Vancouver, 1996; Custers & Aarts, 2010). They focus on the affordances and opportunities provided by both internal states and external contexts pertinent to the salient goal. This shift in perceiving the social world in a goal-relevant way prepares the individual to interact with the goal. It is at this stage of goal preparation, we argue, that the individual takes the depletion-triggered prioritization mind-set into consideration and determines how to interact with the goal.

Goal commitment directs motivational tuning. As the individual prioritizes subsequent action planning, he or she should be especially concerned with factors that indicate the priority or importance of the goal. While goals are desirable end states that people strive toward (eg, Austin & Vancouver, 1996; Custers & Aarts, 2010; Fishbach & Ferguson, 2007; Kruglanski & Kopetz, 2009; Locke & Latham, 1990), not all goals are created equal. The classic value × expectancy model (Feather, 1982) suggests that depending on the value and likelihood of goal achievement, which may result from past social experiences with the goal, various long-term goals differ in their priority to the person and are pursued with different zest (eg, Geers, Wellman, & Lassiter, 2009). We propose that chronic goal commitment, the strength or determination of goal pursuit (Kruglanski et al., 2002; Shah, Friedman, & Kruglanski, 2002), provides the summary information about the priority of a goal. Hence, when the accessible goal is a low-commitment goal, individuals under a prioritization mind-set would disengage from it (goal abandonment); when the accessible goal is a high-commitment goal, individuals would prioritize it by increasing goal engagement (goal protection). Under depletion, thus, individuals' chronic goal commitment would positively predict their level of engagement in the accessible goal.

Our emphasis on chronic goal commitment as a summary index of goal priority is consistent with past research showing that individuals have a self-regulatory mechanism to protect high-commitment goal pursuit at the expense of low-commitment goal pursuit. For example, research on *goal shielding* finds that individuals can automatically inhibit the activation of alternative goals when pursuing a focal goal (Shah et al., 2002). This mechanism is adaptive for pursuing the focal goal because it can reduce the loss of attentional resources to intrusive alternative goals (eg, Shah

& Kruglanski, 2002). More important, goal shielding is found to be more pronounced for high- than for low-commitment goals. Similarly, research on temptation-activated control demonstrates that individuals mentally represent the relationship between important long-term goals and less important short-term goals (temptations) in a way that favors the pursuit of the former (Fishbach, Friedman, & Kruglanski, 2003; Fishbach, Zhang, & Trope, 2010). While temptations facilitate the activation of overarching goals, goals inhibit the activation of temptations. The asymmetric associations between goals and temptations are, again, instrumental in protecting the pursuit of the high-commitment goals.

Goal preference: evaluative manifestation of motivational tuning. We propose that individuals tune their evaluation of the accessible goal to facilitate the prioritization of high-commitment over low-commitment goals. The close relationship between motivation and evaluation has been demonstrated by a large body of past research. When individuals are motivated to fulfill their biological needs, such as hunger (Seibt, Häfner, & Deutsch, 2007), thirst (Ferguson & Bargh, 2004), or nicotine-deprivation (Sherman, Rose, Koch, Presson, & Chassin, 2003), they display evaluative preference for objects that help them fulfill those needs (eg, water, juice) over irrelevant objects (eg, chair, trees) that hinder the satiation of the need (eg, thirst). Even for abstract goals, increased goal engagement is associated with an evaluative preference for goal-congruent objects over goal-incongruent objects. For example, individuals motivated to pursue an athletic goal showed more positive attitudes toward concepts such as *strong, agile*, than concepts such as *scholarly, studious*. Conversely, more negative evaluation of goal-related concepts is related to goal disengagement (Aarts, Custers, & Holland, 2007).

Our framework focuses on the evaluative preference for goal-congruent over goal-incongruent concepts: *goal preference*. Conceptually, a shift toward increased goal preference could be driven by an increased evaluation of goal-congruent concepts, a decreased evaluation of goal-incongruent objects, or both. We treat these finer distinctions as common representative of the relative shift in evaluation between goal-congruent and goal-incongruent concepts. A shift toward the former facilitates increased goal engagement and a shift toward the later facilitates decreased goal engagement.

Evidence for Main Process Postulate. We first gathered evidence of this motivational tuning in the domain of dietary restraint (Jia, Hirt, & Fishbach, 2016; Study 1). After female participants went through a typical depletion manipulation, they were either reminded of the dieting goal with a completion of the dietary restraint scale (Polivy, Herman, & Warsh, 1978) or not (participants in this condition completed the scale at the end of the experiment). All participants were then asked to indicate their preferences between pairs of parting gifts for similar future experiments. Among a dozen pairs, three critical pairs contained a healthy versus unhealthy food option (apple/chips, tea/soda, Twix/granola bar). Participants' choices reflected their goal preference, given that healthy and unhealthy foods were goal-congruent and goal-incongruent objects, respectively. We found that when the goal was made accessible, depleted but not nondepleted participants' preference was well predicted by their goal commitment (measured by the dietary restraint scale). This indicates that depleted participants tune their goal preference according to their goal commitment. Furthermore, compared to nondepletion, depletion reduced goal preference among participants who rated the dieting goal as a low-commitment goal, but it increased goal preference among those who deemed the dieting goal as a high-commitment goal. This suggests that motivational tuning facilitates both the abandonment of a low-commitment goal and the protection of a high-commitment goal as a response to depletion. By contrast, this pattern of motivational tuning did not occur when the goal was not made accessible.

In two follow-up studies (Studies 2 and 5), we found the same pattern of motivational tuning with an implicit attitude measure (Fazio, Jackson, Dunton, & Williams, 1995) in both the dieting and athletic domains. Importantly, we found behavioral consequences of motivational tuning when the dieting goal was made accessible through subliminal priming. Specifically, depletion led to more copious consumption when the dieting goal was a low-commitment goal, but it led to more restraint consumption when the dieting goal was a high-commitment goal. In other words, as individuals motivationally tune their evaluation of the accessible goal, they also display corresponding shifts in their goal pursuit behavior (Fig. 8.1, P2).

These findings are particularly encouraging because they showcase the two aspects of an adaptive self-regulation mechanism: a downplay of low-priority components and an augmentation of high-priority components. Where past research on strategic allocation of self-control efforts following depletion demonstrate only reduced effort toward less important tasks (Muraven et al., 2006), our findings reveal both reduced engagement of low-commitment goals and an increased engagement of high-commitment goals. This is exactly what should happen if depletion can be a trigger for adaptive self-regulation mechanism.

MODERATOR POSTULATE: MOTIVATIONAL TUNING IS PRIMARILY OBSERVED AMONG INDIVIDUALS WHO ARE MORE SUCCESSFUL IN PURSUING THE LONG-TERM GOAL

We propose that the motivational tuning of depletion does not occur equally across individuals. Much research suggests that people who are better at goal pursuit are equipped with more effective self-regulatory mechanisms. For example, goal shielding is found to occur more readily for those who are more tenacious in their goal pursuit (Shah et al., 2002). In the domain of academic achievement, students with higher grade point averages (GPA) also showed greater automatic tendency to approach study-related concepts and to avoid temptation-related concepts (Fishbach & Shah, 2006). Similarly, in the domain of dietary restraint, more successful dieters, compared to less successful ones, showed more adaptive responses to palatable food, which would assist them in resisting the temptations (Papies, Stroebe, & Aarts, 2008). We consider the motivational tuning process as an adaptive self-regulatory mechanism, and we too propose that high goal success individuals should show more pronounced tuning.

Evidence for moderator postulate. We first tested this prediction within the academic achievement domain. Both past research (Fishbach et al., 2003) and our pilot study strongly indicate that doing well in school is a highly important goal for almost all of our college student participants. For this high-commitment goal, our framework predicts that individuals under the prioritization mind-set should tune their evaluation to facilitate the protection of goal pursuit. The moderating role of goal success, thus, should be such that only high goal success individuals show this pattern of tuning.

In one study (Jia et al., 2016; Study 3), college students were asked to rate their enjoyment of various leisure activities after going through a depletion manipulation. Before they viewed the list of leisure activities, we either highlighted to them that these leisure activities were temptations from academic achievements (high goal accessibility) or not (low goal accessibility). In this case, an increase in goal preference should be evident through the devaluation of leisure activities, as they are goal-incongruent concepts. After a series of filler tasks (20 min), we asked participants about their general ease with resisting these leisure activities. As individuals who are highly successful in goal pursuit should resisting temptations easily (Fishbach et al.; 2003), we took this reported subjective ease as a measure of goal success. Indeed, we found that participants under depletion reported lower enjoyment of leisure activities than non-depleted participants. More important, this increase in goal preference was primarily observed among high goal success students.

We observed the same moderating role of goal success when we measured it in a more objective way. In the domain of academic achievement, we asked for participants' GPA and found that the pattern of motivational tuning was mostly observed among students with higher GPA, consistent with our prediction (Jia et al., 2016; Studies 4 and 6). In the dieting domain (Study 5), we used individuals' body mass index (BMI) to represent their goal success (Papies et al., 2008). Again, the pattern of motivational tuning with both implicit attitude measure and chocolate consumption, which are described in the previous section, was moderated by BMI, such that individuals with low BMI showed more pronounced motivational tuning than those with high BMI.

REVISITING THE ANTECEDENT POSTULATE

Since high goal success individuals show more pronounced tuning than low success individuals, an immediate question is how such a difference emerges. Although our framework (Fig. 8.1) leaves open the possibility that goal success moderates the motivational tuning process at multiple stages, we are particularly interested in its role with relation to the antecedent postulate. For our framework, it is critical for individuals to be able to activate a prioritization mind-set in response to depletion. Part of this process entails extraction of some form of signal from the state of depletion, or having exerted self-control, to necessitate the prioritization of actions. Hence, is it plausible that high and low goal success individuals differ in their ability to detect and extract information from depletion?

In the same study that higher GPA individuals demonstrated a more pronounced motivational tuning (Jia et al., 2016; Study 6), we also found that higher GPA individuals had more aversive feelings following depletion. Specifically, high GPA individuals were more mentally fatigued and felt a more negative mood following a depletion task than a nondepletion task. By contrast, low GPA individuals' subjective feelings did not differ much between the depletion and nondepletion conditions. This finding is particularly interesting because all individuals, regardless of their GPA, felt that the depletion task demanded more self-control from them than the nondepletion task. In other words, the difference between high and low GPA students in their subjective feelings following depletion cannot be attributed to differences in the self-control they exerted. Together, these findings suggest that high goal success individuals are better at detecting depletion than low goal success individuals, which may pave way for increased readiness to activate the prioritization mind-set.

The next question is, then, *Are the two aversive feelings, mental fatigue and negative mood, conducive for activating a prioritization mind-set?* The notion that mental fatigue activates a prioritization mind-set sits well with recent theorizations that fatigue provides informational value for goal switching (Hockey, 2011; Kurzban et al., 2013). In these models, the primary function of the subjective feeling of fatigue is to signal to the individual to reconsider the worthwhileness of the current action and consider alternative, more rewarding behavioral plans. In light of this, our findings suggest that high goal success individuals are more likely to feel the sense of fatigue and enter a consideration of various behavioral plans. With a salient focal goal, fatigue would then prompt the individual to assess the importance or priority of this goal and decide to (dis)engage accordingly.

Research on mood as information (Schwarz & Clore, 2003) also suggests that feeling a negative mood can trigger a prioritization mind-set. As opposed to a positive mood, which suggests that the immediate environment is safe and the potential cost of a suboptimal behavioral plan is low, a negative mood signals that there may be potential threats in the surroundings. As a result, individuals in a negative mood tend to be more vigilant and have a higher threshold in adopting any currently accessible goal than those in a positive mood (Fishbach & Labroo, 2007). The fact that, following depletion, high goal success individuals evoke a negative mood more readily than low goal success individuals suggests that they are more likely to enter this vigilant mind-set and scrutinize the priority of the accessible goal. This, again, is consistent with a prioritization mind-set.

NEUROSCIENCE MODEL OF DEPLETION-INDUCED PRIORITIZATION

Having reviewed theories and evidence related to the notion that depletion can induce a prioritization mind-set, albeit with differing effectiveness among individuals, we explore and propose a neural pathway that could possibly support the depletion-induced prioritization, from depletion to negative mood and mental fatigue sensation, and finally, to goal prioritization.

Psychologists and neuroscientists have long been interested in how the human brain keeps track of mental effort and fatigue. A series of functional neuroimaging studies have identified that the insula and posterior cingulate cortex (PCC) are related to the fatigue sensation. The insula cortex, especially the anterior part, is believed to be involved in human awareness and plays an important role in the regulation of the body's homeostasis (Craig, 2009). Earlier research suggests that integration of information about somatic state changes is crucial for the self-evaluation of mental effort investment. Patients with damage to the anterior cingulate cortex (ACC) experienced no conscious feeling of mental effort and showed no skin-conductance responses (Naccache, Dehaene, et al., 2005). A recent fMRI study found stronger activation of the anterior insular cortex during evaluation of mental effort in a mentally fatiguing cognitive task (Otto, Zijlstra, et al., 2014). It is thus believed that the ACC conveys information about somatic state changes to the insula which generates self-evaluation of mental effort investment.

The PCC forms a central node in the default mode network of the brain and has also been implicated in human awareness (Raichle, MacLeod, et al., 2001). Recent studies found that activation in the PCC was related to the level of the fatigue sensation (Cook, O'Connor, Lange, & Steffener, 2007; Ishii, Tanaka, Yamano, & Watanabe, 2014; Jouanin, Peres, et al., 2009). The

PCC was activated when participants imagined that they were fatigued or viewed others who displayed fatigued facial expressions (Caseras, Mataix-Cols, et al., 2008; Ishii, Tanaka, et al., 2012). Taken together, several brain regions, such as insula and PCC, seem to be actively monitoring the level of mental fatigue.

Negative emotions may signal the presence of unexpected threats. There is a wealth of evidence to suggest that the amygdala is one of the most important brain regions underpinning the processing of negative emotions such as fear and threat (Pessoa & Adolphs, 2010). It was found that the amygdala connectivity with the dorsolateral prefrontal cortex (DLPFC) was significantly weaker among individuals who experience burnout at work, indicating a reduced ability to downregulate the response to emotional stress (Golkar et al., 2014). The amygdala–prefrontal coupling plays a crucial role for successful regulation of negative emotion and its dysfunction has been implicated in a variety of psychiatric disorders (Kim, Loucks, et al., 2011). Ego depletion may, thus, elicit negative mood in the amygdala in response to the threat of inadequate mental resource.

When individuals' emotions or mental resources change, it might be evolutionarily adaptive to have the appropriateness of active goals changed as well. Updating goals in a flexible manner could be adaptive for allowing individuals respond to changing emotional and mental states. Goal management in a dynamic environment might be represented via an integration of mood change and fatigue sensation information in the DLPFC (see Fig. 8.2). The DLPFC receives rich projections from the amygdale and other

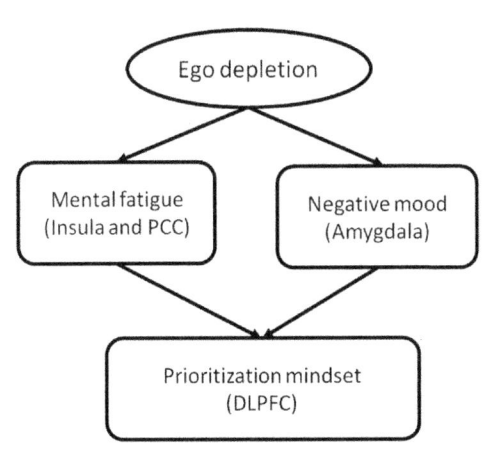

FIGURE 8.2 A social neuroscience model of depletion-induced prioritization. Ego depletion leads to mental fatigue sensation in the insula and posterior cingulate cortex (PCC) as well as negative mood registered in the amygdala. The dorsolateral prefrontal cortex (DLPFC) integrates information from both mental fatigue sensation and negative mood brain circuits and represents a prioritization mind-set.

parts of the limbic system including the insula, which places the DLPFC in an ideal position to communicate with other brain regions implicated in ego depletion (Cieslik, Zilles, et al., 2013). The DLPFC may thus receive and integrate information about all major aspects of an individual's emotional and mental state, which would enable it to determine the changes in this state due to mental effort investment. It has been consistently shown that the DLPFC is involved in cognitive control that allows individuals to resist distraction or interference and to update goals in a flexible manner (Crockett, Braams, et al., 2013; Hare, Camerer, & Rangel, 2009). We propose that the DLPFC a key area for the integration of emotional and mental state information as well as dynamic prioritization mind-set. Future neuroimaging studies could directly test this model and further examine the neural mechanisms underlying adaptive prioritization of goals. A depiction of the proposed neural pathway is represented in Fig. 8.2.

IMPLICATIONS

Understanding Depletion as a Potential Trigger for Adaptive Self-regulation

The present framework highlights the adaptive role depletion plays in a dynamic self-regulatory mechanism. Past theories and empirical studies on depletion have focused mostly on its limiting nature in the context of self-regulation and goal pursuit (eg, Baumeister et al., 2007; Muraven & Baumeister, 2000; Vohs & Heatherton, 2000). While such an emphasis has inspired an impressive range of studies bringing the executive branch of the self to the foreground of social psychology research, there is a recent call to better understand the underlying processes related to ego depletion (Inzlicht & Schmeichel, 2012; Inzlicht et al., 2014; Kurzban et al., 2013). The present framework conceptualizes and demonstrates an important way that depletion can provide informational input to a dynamic goal pursuit process. Not only does our framework show that depletion can lead to disengagement from less important goals, but it also reveals that the disengagement is part of an adaptive prioritization process that prepares and protects the engagement of high-commitment goals.

This perspective has important implications on how we can interpret past depletion findings. Past research mostly focuses on the debilitating effects of depletion, that it reduces self-control efforts and impairs task performance. Although works on resource conservation have emphasized the strategic nature of effort withdrawal (Muraven et al., 2006; Tyler & Burns, 2009), they are usually silent on whether any upward regulation of goal-directed process is part of such strategic allocation. In light of our framework, past findings on the debilitating effects of depletion may also be part of an adaptive self-regulatory mechanism, with possibly undiscovered benefits.

This finding also challenges the definition of self-control failures in past research. If the apparent decrease in self-control efforts following depletion is part of strategic resource allocation (see Chapter 20) or an adaptive prioritization process as we propose, does it still make sense to call it a failure? This concern resonates with a broader discussion on the general definition of active inhibition, self-control, and self-regulation, which is elaborated in greater detail and thoughtfulness in Chapter 5.

ONGOING GOAL PURSUIT PROCESS

Although our framework suggests that depletion benefits the pursuit of an important goal, we do not reject the general claim that depletion is a major limiting factor for goal pursuit (Vohs et al., 2009). Our investigation captures only a "slice" of what usually is an extended process of long-term goal pursuit. This has two implications. First, like many other works on depletion, we examine only "slight" levels of depletion. In protracted effortful pursuit of long-term goals, individuals are more likely to experience extended and extensive depletion. Under such high level of depletion, factors that have been shown to counteract depletion become ineffective or, worse, counterproductive (Vohs, Baumeister, & Schmeichel, 2013). Hence, it is likely that motivational tuning facilitates effortful pursuit of important goals only under mild, transient forms of depletion.

Second, maintaining high goal accessibility throughout the extended pursuit of long-term goals can be difficult. Note that one main precursor of the motivational tuning effect is goal accessibility. Within the duration of long-term goal pursuit, the focal goal may not always be salient. Research on mind wandering, for example, has demonstrated that even within a span of an experimental session, individuals are likely to experience multiple incidents of *goal neglect*, whereby their mind acts as if it forgets the focal goal (eg, Kane & Engle, 2003). In these lapses of goal focus, the long-term goal is unlikely to be accessible to drive the motivational tuning process. Sustaining high goal accessibility becomes even more challenging when we consider the dynamic way individuals pursue goals (eg, Carver & Scheier, 1998; Fishbach & Dhar, 2005). The classic cybernetic model of self-regulation (Carver & Scheier, 1998), for example, suggests that individuals may "coast" or disengage from goal pursuit altogether when they perceive that their goal progress has been satisfactory. In these situations, goal accessibility is likely to be low and the limiting effect of depletion may take the helm in guiding one's goal pursuit. Hence, it is a fruitful avenue for future research to explore the fluctuation and interaction of different processes that depletion is involved throughout the course of long-term goal pursuit. Such research on the course instead of "slices" of goal pursuit, however, has been woefully rare.

ULTIMATE ACCOUNTS: CAPACITY VIEW VERSUS OPPORTUNITY COST VERSUS HOMEOSTATIC VIEW

It is also important to note that the present framework offers a proximate, not an ultimate, account of depletion (Inzlicht et al., 2014; also see Chapter 18 for a thorough treatment on the distinction between proximate and ultimate accounts of depletion). Our conceptual framework hinges upon the notion that depletion can provide informational value to activate an adaptive self-regulation mechanism. As a proximate account, however, our framework is silent on how depletion, or having exerted prior control, can achieve its signaling function. Ultimate accounts, on the other hand, are very much concerned with such a question. As a result, our framework puts the various ultimate accounts to the challenge of making sense of the signaling function of depletion.

First off, the strength model (Baumeister et al., 2007; Muraven & Baumeister, 2000; Vohs & Heatherton, 2000) is intuitively compatible with our framework. Consistent with past works on resource conservation, the strength model suggests that a reduction, and not necessarily exhaustion, in self-control resources or capacity can lead individuals to be judicious in subsequent expenses of self-control efforts (Muraven et al., 2006). This perspective suggests that the reduction of self-control resources or capacity is the source of the informational value. The challenge for the traditional strength model is thus to identify the underlying physiological or neurological correlate of this capacity, which has been elusive in several past attempts (Gailliot et al., 2007; cf. Molden et al., 2012).

The opportunity cost model (Kurzban et al., 2013) goes well with our framework in that it, too, emphasizes the informational value of depletion. Inspired by the motivational model of fatigue (Hockey, 2011), it posits that the individual is constantly computing the opportunity cost (ie, the rewards from other alternative behavioral plans) of pursuing the current action. When the computation determines that the opportunity costs exceed the benefits of the current action, a sense of depletion or mental fatigue is evoked to signal the individual to reprioritize their behavioral planning. In other words, the signaling function is the primary function of the depletion or fatigue feeling.

Finally, homeostatic models of depletion (eg, Inzlicht et al., 2014) may at first glance seem incompatible with the notion that depletion signals a prioritization of long-term goals. Inzlicht and colleagues argue that people are constantly balancing between labor and leisure activities. Prior exertion of self-control is considered a laborious activity that increases one's need for leisure, "want-to," activities. Hence, depleted individuals are inclined to perform more leisure activities and less labor activities to restore an equilibrium. How can a shift in the labor–leisure balance toward leisure instigate prioritization of laborious long-term goal pursuit? We argue that the reduced inclination for labor activities means that individuals are more selective of any labor activity they will engage in. If a labor activity is a low-priority course of action, people should be even less inclined toward pursuing it. Only when a labor activity is highly important should individuals with a diminishing need for labor activities engage in it.

In fact, we can make a new prediction based on the model of labor–leisure tradeoff. If a shift in balance away from labor activities indeed leads to the prioritization of labor, it stands to reason that a shift toward leisure activities should lead to a more liberal choice of leisure activities. In other words, depleted individuals should be inclined to engage in all leisure activities indiscriminately. Indeed, research has shown that depleted individuals are content with engaging in passive or simple resting behaviors that do not seem to offer significant rewards (see Chapter 11).

In sum, our framework is useful in generating hypotheses with regard to the various ultimate accounts of depletion. Future research that simultaneously tests both proximate and ultimate accounts may prove to be particularly fruitful.

IMPLICATION FOR GOAL PURSUIT

Huang and Bargh (2014) have recently proposed an influential view of goal pursuit. Drawing parallels with the notion that genes self-perpetuate with a total disregard for the specific organisms that carry them, they argue that goals, too, operate in a similarly selfish manner. Goals, as long as they are activated, operate to perpetuate actions toward their fulfillment, often without awareness, or interference from the self. In other words, they argue that the executive branch of the self serves only to provide the necessary structure and mechanisms to serve goal perpetuation. Their view of goal pursuit is thus a bottom-up one, highlighting the autonomous operation of individual goals and downplaying the organizing role of the self.

Our framework supports a different perspective. While we agree that bottom-up processes are highly important in goal pursuit, we suggest the self is crucial in negotiating among multiple goals (cf. Fishbach, 2014 for a more detailed discussion). In our framework, when a goal is made accessible, the goal does not inexorably drive the individual to its completion. Instead, the self, particularly if it is under depletion, determines whether the accessible goal should be engaged depending on its priority. Hence, our model underscores the organizing role of the self and its top-down influence in goal pursuit. We believe that future research examining the interplay between bottom-up and top-down processes would provide a more holistic understanding of goal pursuit.

POTENTIAL PRACTICAL IMPLICATIONS

One practical implication of our framework is to improve long-term goal pursuit by training individuals to be better at detecting depletion. Since high goal success individuals can detect depletion better than low goal success individuals, which may underlie their effectiveness in activating motivational tuning, training low goal success individuals to be sensitive to the state of depletion could allow them to also benefit from motivational tuning. One caveat for this training is that making individuals attuned to depletion is only the first step in improving people's adaptive responses to depletion. Individuals may also differ in later stages of the motivational tuning process, such as recruiting evaluative shift for goal prioritization (Fishbach et al., 2010; Geers et al., 2009). Merely activating a prioritization mind-set, thus, may or may not be enough to activate the later stages of the motivational tuning process. This is an empirical question that is worth pursuing in the future.

CONCLUSION

In this chapter, we highlight a gap between existing empirical findings and the theoretical argument that ego depletion is a limiting factor of long-term goal pursuit. We offer and test a framework to conceptualize a dynamic self-regulatory mechanism, of which ego depletion is part in goal-present contexts. Our analysis and evidence suggest that ego depletion can activate a motivational tuning process that prioritizes goal pursuit. In other words, the limited nature of one's self-control capacity may impose an overall debilitating effect on long-term goal pursuit, and depletion can trigger an adaptive self-regulatory process to facilitate the pursuit of important goals. Our findings also emphasize the importance of recognizing and capitalizing on the signaling value of depletion. The traditional strength model of depletion highlights exactly why both Aristotle and Lao Tzu lamented on the difficulty for self-control. We suggest that being aware of and adaptively responding to the state of ego depletion makes mastering the self, a trying and noble challenge, slightly easier.

References

Aarts, H., Custers, R., & Holland, R. (2007). On the cessation of nonconscious goal pursuit: when goals and negative affect are coactivated. *Journal of Personality and Social Psychology, 92*, 165–1178.

Austin, J. T., & Vancouver, J. B. (1996). Goal constructs in psychology: structure, process, and content. *Psychological Bulletin, 120*, 338–375.

Baumeister, R. F., Heatherton, R. F., & Tice, D. M. (1994). *Losing control: How and why people fail at self-regulation*. San Diego, CA: Academic Press.

Baumeister, R. F., Vohs, K. D., & Tice, D. M. (2007). The strength model of self-control. *Current Directions in Psychological Science, 16*, 351–355.

Buss, A. R. (1979). The trait-situation controversy and the concept of interaction. *Personality & Social Psychology Bulletin, 5*, 191–195.

Carver, C. S., & Scheier, M. F. (1998). *On the self-regulation of behavior*. New York, NY: Cambridge University Press.

Caseras, X., Mataix-Cols, D., Rimes, K. A., Giampietro, V., Brammer, M., Zelaya, F., ... Godfrey, E. (2008). The neural correlates of fatigue: an exploratory imaginal fatigue provocation study in chronic fatigue syndrome. *Psychological Methods, 38*, 941–951.

Cieslik, E. C., Zilles, K., Caspers, S., Roski, C., Kellermann, T. S., Jakobs, O., ... Eickhoff, S. B. (2013). Is there "one" DLPFC in cognitive action control? Evidence for heterogeneity from co-activation-based parcellation. *Cerebral Cortex, 23*, 2677–2689.

Clarkson, J. J., Hirt, E. R., Jia, L., & Alexander, M. B. (2010). When perception is more than reality: the effects of perceived versus actual resource depletion on self-regulatory behavior. *Journal of Personality and Social Psychology, 98*, 29–46.

Cook, D. B., O'Connor, P. J., Lange, G., & Steffener, J. (2007). Functional neuroimaging correlates of mental fatigue induced by cognition among chronic fatigue syndrome patients and controls. *Neuroimage, 36*, 108–122.

Craig, A. D. (2009). How do you feel—now? the anterior insula and human awareness. *Nature Review Neuroscience, 10*, 59–70.

Crockett, M. J., Braams, B. R., Clark, L., Tobler, P. N., Robbins, T. W., & Kalenscher, T. (2013). Restricting temptations: neural mechanisms of precommitment. *Neuron, 79*, 391–401.

Custers, R., & Aarts, H. (2010). The unconscious will: how the pursuit of goals operates outside of conscious awareness. *Science, 329*, 47–50.

Fazio, R. H., Jackson, J. R., Dunton, B. C., & Williams, C. J. (1995). Variability in automatic activation as an unobtrusive measure of racial attitudes. A bona fide pipeline? *Journal of Personality and Social Psychology, 69*, 1013–1027.

Feather, N. T. (1982). In *Expectations and actions: Expectancy–value models in psychology*. Hillsdale, NJ: Erlbaum.

Ferguson, M. J., & Bargh, J. A. (2004). Liking is for doing: effects of goal pursuit on automatic evaluation. *Journal of Personality and Social Psychology, 88*, 557–572.

Fishbach, A. (2014). The motivational self is more than the sum of its goals. *Behavioral and Brain Sciences, 37*, 143–144.

Fishbach, A., & Dhar, R. (2005). Goals as excuses or guides: The liberating effect of perceived goal progress on choice. *Journal of Consumer Research, 32*, 370–377.

Fishbach, A., & Ferguson, M. F. (2007). The goal construct in social psychology. In A. W. Kruglanski, & T. E. Higgins (Eds.), *Social psychology: Handbook of basic principles* (pp. 490–515). NY: Guilford.

Fishbach, A., Friedman, R. S., & Kruglanski, A. W. (2003). Leading us not unto temptation: momentary allurements elicit overriding goal activation. *Journal of Personality and Social Psychology, 84*, 296–309.

Fishbach, A., & Labroo, A. A. (2007). Be better or be merry: how mood affects self-control. *Journal of Personality and Social Psychology, 93*, 158–173.

Fishbach, A., & Shah, J. Y. (2006). Self-control in action: implicit dispositions toward goals and away from temptations. *Journal of Personality and Social Psychology, 90*, 820–832.

Fishbach, A., Zhang, Y., & Trope, Y. (2010). Counteractive evaluation: asymmetric shifts in the implicit value of conflicting motivations. *Journal of Experimental Social Psychology, 46*, 29–38.

Gailliot, M. T., Baumeister, R. F., DeWall, C. N., Maner, J. K., Plant, E. A., Tice, D. M., ... Schmeichel, B. J. (2007). Self-control relies on glucose as a limited energy source: willpower is more than a metaphor. *Journal of Personality and Social Psychology, 92*, 325–333.

Geers, A. L., Wellman, J. A., & Lassiter, G. D. (2009). Dispositional optimism and engagement: the moderating influence of goal prioritization. *Journal of Personality and Social Psychology, 96*, 913–932.

Golkar, A., Johansson, E., Kasahara, M., Osika, W., Perski, A., & Savic, I. (2014). The influence of work-related chronic stress on the regulation of emotion and on functional connectivity in the brain. *PLoS One, 9*, e104550.

Hagger, M. S., Panetta, G., Leung, C. M., Wong, G. G., Wang, J. C. K., Chan, D. K. C., ... Chatzisarantis, N. L. D. (2013). Chronic inhibition, self-control and eating behavior: test of a 'Resource Depletion' model. *PLoS One, 8*, 1–8.

Hagger, M. S., Wood, C., Stiff, C., & Chatzisarantis, N. L. D. (2010). Ego depletion and the strength model of self-control: a meta-analysis. *Psychological Bulletin, 136*, 495–525.

Hare, T. A., Camerer, C. F., & Rangel, A. (2009). Self-control in decision-making involves modulation of the vmPFC valuation system. *Science, 324*, 646–648.

Hockey, G. R. J. (2011). A motivational control theory of cognitive fatigue. In P. L. Ackerman (Ed.), *Cognitive fatigue: Multidisciplinary perspectives on current research and future applications* (pp. 167–188). Washington, DC: American Psychological Association.

Hofmann, W., Vohs, K. D., & Baumeister, R. F. (2012). What people desire, feel conflicted about, and try to resist in everyday life. *Psychological Science, 23*, 582–588.

Huang, J. Y., & Bargh, J. A. (2014). The Selfish Goal: autonomously operating motivational structures as the proximate cause of human judgment and behavior. *Behavioral and Brain Sciences, 37*, 121–135.

Inzlicht, M., & Schmeichel, B. J. (2012). What is ego depletion? towards a mechanistic revision of the resource model of self-control. *Perspectives on Psychological Science, 7*, 450–463.

Inzlicht, M., Schmeichel, B. J., & Macrae, C. N. (2014). Why self-control seems (but may not be) limited. *Trends in Cognitive Sciences, 18*, 127–133.

Ishii, A., Tanaka, M., Yamano, E., & Watanabe, Y. (2014). The neural substrates of physical fatigue sensation to evaluate ourselves: a magnetoencephalography study. *Neuroscience, 261*, 60–67.

Ishii, A., Tanaka, M., et al. (2012). Neural substrates activated by viewing others expressing fatigue: a magnetoencephalography study. *Brain Research, 1455*, 68–74.

Jia, L., Hirt, E. R., & Fishbach, A. (2016). *The motivational-tuning hypothesis: Abandoning low- and protecting high-commitment goals in response to depletion* (under review).

Job, V., Dweck, C. S., & Walton, G. M. (2010). Ego depletion–is it all in your head? Implicit theories about willpower affect self-regulation. *Psychological Science, 21*, 1686–1693.

Jouanin, J. C., Peres, M., et al. (2009). A dynamic network involving M1-S1, SII-insular, medial insular, and cingulate cortices controls muscular activity during an isometric contraction reaction time task. *Human Brain Mapping, 30*(2), 675–688.

Kane, M. J., & Engle, R. W. (2003). Working-memory capacity and the control of attention: the contributions of goal neglect, response competition, and task set to Stroop interference. *Journal of Experimental Psychology: General, 132*, 47–70.

Kim, M. J., Loucks, R. A., Palmer, A. L., Brown, A. C., Solomon, K. M., Marchante, A. N., & Whalen, P. J. (2011). The structural and functional connectivity of the amygdala: from normal emotion to pathological anxiety. *Behavioural Brain Research, 223*, 403–410.

Kruglanski, A. W., & Kopetz, C. (2009). The role of goal-systems in self-regulation. In J. Bargh, P. Goallwitzer, & E. Morsella (Eds.), *The psychology of action The mechanisms of human action: Vol. 2.* (pp. 350–361). New York: Oxford University Press.

REFERENCES

Kruglanski, A. W., Shah, J. Y., Fishbach, A., Friedman, R., Chun, W. Y., & Sleeth-Keppler, D. (2002). A theory of goal systems. In M. P. Zanna (Ed.), *Advances in experimental social psychology* (34) (pp. 331–378). New York: Academic Press.

Kurzban, R., Duckworth, A., Kable, J. W., & Myers, J. (2013). An opportunity cost model of subjective effort and task performance. *Behavioral and Brain Sciences, 36*, 661–679.

Locke, E. A., & Latham, G. P. (1990). *A theory of goal setting and task performance*. Englewood Cliffs, NJ: Prentice-Hall.

Masicampo, E. J., Martin, S. R., & Anderson, R. A. (2014). Understanding and overcoming self-control depletion. *Social and Personality Psychology Compass, 8*, 638–649.

Mischel, W., Shoda, Y., & Rodriguez, M. L. (1989). Delay of gratification in children. *Science, 244*, 933–938.

Moffitt, T. E., Arseneault, L., Belsky, D., Dickson, N., Hancox, R. J., Harrington, H., ... Caspi, A. (2011). A gradient of childhood self-control predicts health, wealth, and public safety. *Proceedings of the National Academy of Sciences of the United States of America, 108*, 2693–2698.

Molden, D. C., Hui, C. M., Scholer, A. A., Meier, B. P., Noreen, E. E., D'Agostino, P. R., ... Martin, V. (2012). The motivational versus metabolic effects of carbohydrates on self-control. *Psychological Science, 23*, 1137–1144.

Muraven, M., & Baumeister, R. F. (2000). Self-regulation and depletion of limited resources: does self-control resemble a muscle? *Psychological Bulletin, 126*, 247–259.

Muraven, M., Shmueli, D., & Burkley, E. (2006). Conserving self-control strength. *Journal of Personality and Social Psychology, 91*, 524–537.

Muraven, M., & Slessareva, E. (2003). Mechanisms of self-control failure: motivation and limited resources. *Personality & Social Psychology Bulletin, 29*, 894–906.

Naccache, L., Dehaene, S., Cohen, L., Habert, M. O., Guichart-Gomez, E., Galanaud, D., & Willer, J. C. (2005). Effortless control: executive attention and conscious feeling of mental effort are dissociable. *Neuropsychologia, 43*, 1318–1328.

Otto, T., Zijlstra, F. R., & Goebel, R. (2014). Neural correlates of mental effort evaluation–involvement of structures related to self-awareness. *Social Cognitive and Affective Neuroscience, 9*, 307–315.

Papies, E. K., Stroebe, W., & Aarts, H. (2008). Healthy cognition: processes of self-regulatory success in restrained eating. *Personality & Social Psychology Bulletin, 34*, 1290–1300.

Pessoa, L., & Adolphs, R. (2010). Emotion processing and the amygdala: from a 'low road' to 'many roads' of evaluating biological significance. *Nature Review Neuroscience, 11*, 773–783.

Polivy, J., Herman, C. P., & Warsh, S. (1978). Internal and external components of emotionality in restrained and unrestrained eaters. *Journal of Abnormal Psychology, 87*, 497–504.

Raichle, M. E., MacLeod, A. M., Snyder, A. Z., Powers, W. J., Gusnard, D. A., & Shulman, G. L. (2001). A default mode of brain function. *Proceedings of National Academy of Science of the United States of America, 98*, 676–682.

Schmeichel, B. J., & Vohs, K. D. (2009). Self-affirmation and self-control: affirming core values counteracts ego depletion. *Journal of Personality and Social Psychology, 96*, 770–782.

Schmeichel, B. J., Vohs, K. D., & Baumeister, R. F. (2003). Ego depletion and intelligent performance: role of the self in logical reasoning and other information processing. *Journal of Personality and Social Psychology, 85*, 33–46.

Schwarz, N., & Clore, G. L. (2003). Mood as information: 20 years later. *Psychological Inquiry, 14*, 296–303.

Seibt, B., Häfner, M., & Deutsch, R. (2007). Prepared to eat: how immediate affective and motivational responses to food cues are influenced by food deprivation. *European Journal of Social Psychology, 37*, 359–379.

Shah, J. Y., Friedman, R., & Kruglanski, A. W. (2002). Forgetting all else: on the antecedents and consequences of goal shielding. *Journal of Personality and Social Psychology, 83*, 1261–1280.

Shah, J. Y., & Kruglanski, A. W. (2002). Priming against your will: how accessible alternatives affect goal pursuit. *Journal of Experimental Social Psychology, 38*, 368–383.

Sherman, S. J., Rose, J. S., Koch, K., Presson, C. C., & Chassin, L. (2003). Implicit and explicit attitudes toward cigarette smoking: the effects of contexts and motivation. *Journal of Social and Clinical Psychology, 22*, 13–39.

Stucke, T. S., & Baumeister, R. F. (2006). Ego depletion and aggressive behavior: is the inhibition of aggression a limited resource? *European Journal of Social Psychology, 36*, 1–13.

Tice, D. M., Baumeister, R. F., Shmueli, D., & Muraven, M. (2007). Restoring the self: positive affect helps improve self-regulation following ego depletion. *Journal of Experimental Social Psychology, 43*, 379–384.

Trevino, L. K. (1986). Ethical decision making in organizations: a person-situation interactionist model. *The Academy of Management Review, 11*, 601–617.

Tyler, J. M., & Burns, K. C. (2009). Triggering conservation of the self's regulatory resources. *Basic and Applied Social Psychology, 31*, 255–266.

Vohs, K. D., Baumeister, R. F., & Schmeichel, B. J. (2013). Motivation, personal beliefs, and limited resources all contribute to self-control. *Journal of Experimental Social Psychology, 49*, 184–188.

Vohs, K. D., & Faber, R. J. (2007). Spent resources: self-regulatory resource availability affects impulse buying. *Journal of Consumer Research, 33*, 537–547.

Vohs, K. D., & Heatherton, T. F. (2000). Self-regulatory failure: a resource-depletion approach. *Psychological Science, 11*, 249–254.

Vohs, K. D., Kaikati, A. M., Kerkhof, P., & Schmeichel, B. J. (2009). Self-regulatory resource depletion: a model for understanding the limited nature of goal pursuit. In G. B. Moskowitz, & G. Heidi (Eds.), *The psychology of goals* (pp. 423–446). New York: Guilford Press.

Wagner, D. D., Altman, M., Boswell, R. G., Kelley, W. M., & Heatherton, T. F. (2013). Self-regulatory depletion enhances neural responses to rewards and impairs top-down control. *Psychological Science, 11*, 2262–2271.

CHAPTER

9

Taming the Impulsive Beast: Understanding the Link Between Self-Regulation and Aggression

C.N. DeWall, D.S. Chester
University of Kentucky, Lexington, KY, United States

Is studying aggression a fool's errand? We have never lived in a more peaceful time (Pinker, 2011). Unlike previous eras, people rarely watch others get tortured, have family members who are murdered, or participate in duels. Most people will never hit, choke, or stab another person. They might never even threaten someone with violence. With such a low rate of aggression, we need to question why researchers continue to devote their lives to studying such an elusive behavior.

Aggression might be dwindling, but aggressive urges have not gone away. We still get grumpy when other people insult us; our blood boils when someone swipes our snort of cocaine; and swerving drivers make us wish that the punishment for texting and driving is a swift kick to solitary confinement. Many people feel the urge to aggression, but people rarely follow up on their impulses (Finkel, DeWall, Slotter, Oaten, & Foshee, 2009). What puts the brakes on an aggressive urge from becoming an aggressive action?

That is precisely what this chapter is about. We propose that self-regulation, defined as changing our responses to remain in agreement with what is appropriate (Baumeister, 1998, 2016), helps us act peaceful when we want to act vengeful. When we experience an aggressive urge, we use self-regulation to restrain ourselves from acting aggressively. Most research has focused on this restraining process.

But where this research has succeeded in identifying factors that increase and decrease restraint, it has failed to explain why aggressive urges spur aggression. Without a full understanding of aggressive urges that need to be restrained, researchers will continue to explore only half of the puzzle about why aggression persists. Explicating the role of desires in problematic behaviors such as aggression is a crucial task to understanding and reducing such acts (Kotabe & Hofmann, 2016; Schmeichel & Crowell, 2016). This chapter seeks to partially fill this gap.

The chapter is divided into five main sections. First, we review major theories of aggression that emphasize the importance of self-regulation in understanding why people act aggressively. Second, we show that self-regulation helps to inhibit aggression, especially when people experience an aggressive urge. Third, we discuss why aggressive urges increase aggression—and how the balance of such urges can cause behavior to teeter between helpful and hurtful. Fourth, we review evidence that aggressive urges cause aggression because such behavior is associated with hedonic reward. When the prospect of the reward of aggression outweighs the need to inhibit, people become more likely to lash out. The fifth section discusses practical implications for aggression-reducing interventions.

MAJOR THEORIES OF SELF-REGULATION AND AGGRESSION

Many social psychological theories are influenced by other disciplines and subareas. The study of self-regulation and aggression is no exception. In 1990, two criminologists, Michael Gottfredson and Travis Hirschi, published an influential book with an ambitious title, *A General Theory of Crime*. Their mission was to provide a wide-ranging explanation of criminal behavior by offering ideas that would organize and synthesize observations. To collect such observations, they combed through hundreds of studies. Their meticulous efforts resulted in two main conclusions. The first was uninteresting: Criminal behavior becomes more likely when opportunity increases. For example, if you leave your door unlocked, your chances of getting robbed are higher than if you lock your door. Crime also rises on the weekends, when the criminals are not working and have more opportunity to break the law.

The second, and more impactful, finding was that many criminal acts result from poor self-control. Consider the case of violent crime. Movies and true-crime books often portray violent criminals as cold-hearted and methodical. The data paint a different picture. Many times the violent assailant is nearly asleep from mental exhaustion (Gottfredson & Hirschi, 1990). Very few people wake up, eat breakfast, and start attacking people. And instead of using an unmarked cargo van to transport the stolen booty, the sleepy assailant merely walks a few blocks and impulsively burglarizes the first apartment that seems like a safe bet. Subsequent research has supported Gottfredson and Hirschi's *General Theory of Crime*. Indeed, one metaanalysis concluded that poor self-control is one of the "strongest known correlates of crime" (Pratt & Cullen, 2000, p. 952.)

The General Theory of Crime motivated an extension of the dominant social psychological theory of aggression, namely the General Aggression Model (GAM) (Anderson & Bushman, 2002; DeWall, Anderson, & Bushman, 2011). The GAM is a dynamic, social-cognitive, developmental model that provides an integrative framework for domain-specific aggression theories. This model shares many features of the GAM provides a useful framework for understanding how aggression operates under the control of internal psychological processes that restrain aggressive urges. Specifically, individual differences in self-control and situational factors that undermine or bolster self-control produce a state characterized by varying levels of self-control fatigue.

The current internal state of self-control fatigue should have direct consequences for the appraisal and decision process component (see Fig. 9.1). The internal state of self-control fatigue leads people to engage in impulsive rather than thoughtful actions. Crucially, if people improve their self-control through regular practice or receive a boost of energy, they should have sufficient resources to engage in cognitive reappraisal processes, which should in turn lead to a thoughtful, non-aggressive action. These predictions derived from the GAM are consistent with the strength model of self-control (Baumeister, Bratslavsky, Muraven, & Tice, 1998; Muraven & Baumeister, 2000), which is a main focus of this book.

A third theoretical model, I^3 metatheory (pronounced I-cubed; Finkel, 2007, 2014), was born out of a motivation to explain behavior as a function of three interdependent processes. (Each process begins with the letter *I*. Hence, the name I^3 metatheory.) Using principles of statistical moderation,

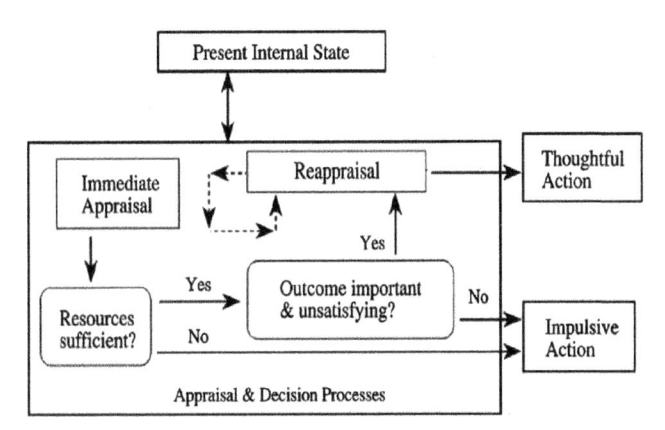

FIGURE 9.1 Appraisal and decision processes component of the General Aggression Model (Anderson & Bushman, 2002).

I³ metatheory proposes that a combination of instigation, impellance, and inhibition influence the likelihood of aggression. Instigation refers to any event that triggers an aggressive urge, such as a verbal insult or physical pain. Impellance is any factor that prepares a person to experience an aggressive urge. For example, people high in trait physical aggressiveness are more prone to experience an aggressive urge compared with their less-aggressive counterparts (Denson, Pedersen, Ronquillo, & Nandy, 2009; Suls & Wan, 1993). Inhibition refers to any factor that increases the likelihood that a person will override an aggressive urge.

Perfect Storm Theory, derived from the I³ metatheory, asserts that the probability and severity of aggression is highest when instigation is high, impellance is high, and inhibition is low compared to "any of the situations formed by the other seven possible combinations" (Finkel, 2014, p. 33). A main reason why this is the preferred combination is that it offers the most opportunities for falsification (Popper, 1959).

The General Theory of Crime, GAM, and I³ metatheory take distinct approaches to understanding the causes of aggression. But they share a common interest in the importance of overriding aggressive urges via self-regulation in predicting aggressive and violent behavior. In this way, these theories take a top-down approach to understanding aggression. In the next section, we briefly review some evidence that tested this top-down approach.

AGGRESSION: FROM TOP TO BOTTOM

It is tough and downright unethical to have people commit violent acts in a laboratory. The criminological data benefit from the use of archival data, in which researchers can obtain reports of actual aggression and violent behavior. But criminologists often come up short when it comes to cause and effect. We know that most violent crime occurs late at night (Safe Horizon, 2015). This does not mean that late nights cause fistfights.

To establish cause and effect, researchers started with simple experiments (DeWall, Baumeister, Stillman, & Gailliot, 2007). In one study, participants arrived at a laboratory for a supposed taste-testing study. First, they wrote an essay about a personally relevant topic. Next, the experimenter told them they would taste some food before preparing a food sample for another study participant. By the flip of a coin, participants were assigned to either taste a donut or a radish. In reality, this constituted the self-regulation fatigue manipulation.

Participants were given their food and a food-taste questionnaire. Their job was to taste the food and then report how the food tasted. Once participants lifted the food to take their first bite, the experimenter explained, "Wait! You're not supposed to eat it." The experimenter confessed to flubbing this part of the experiment, but reassured participants that they would still receive credit. They just needed to wait in the room while the experimenter fixed the mistake. And so they waited alone, with the plate of forbidden food, for about 7 min.

Imagine what those 7 min were like. If you were in the donut condition, they would be grueling. You had to look at a tasty food you came close to eating but was now forbidden. Such waiting would have taxed your mental energy more than resisting the less-tempting radish. With less mental energy, the donut-resisting participants might give into their aggressive urges.

To trigger an aggressive urge, participants received insulting essay feedback from the person who would consume the food sample they would prepare. The feedback even contained the handwritten comment, "This is one of the worst essays I've read!" To measure aggression, participants decided how much hot sauce the insulting participant had to eat—and they were made aware that their soon-to-be-victim disliked hot and spicy food. Many studies have validated this measure of aggression (Lieberman, Solomon, Greenberg, & McGregor, 1999).

Who behaved the most aggressively? Participants who resisted eating a tempting food, thereby using up some of their self-control energy. Follow-up studies confirmed that mental energy is needed to override aggressive urges. In the absence of an aggressive urge, fatigued people do not become prone to aggression. These findings jibe with those reviewed in Gottfredson and Hirschi's (1990) *A General Theory of Crime*. They also add some nuance. Yes, most violent crime occurs when people are mentally fatigued. But the odds are that sleepy criminals act aggressively in response to a triggering event. If you keep people awake all night, as one group of researchers did, you do not create a cauldron of criminality (Vohs, Glass, Maddox, & Markman, 2011). You only produce passive zombies.

A wave of research extended these findings in intricate ways. The first set of findings showed that self-control fatigue had implications for intimate partner violence (IPV; Finkel et al., 2012). IPV occurs at alarmingly high rates. A review of dating violence at 31 colleges in 16 countries revealed physical dating violence perpetration rates between 17% and 45%, with similar rates for men and women (Straus, 2004). Rates go down as people mature, but the rate among married and cohabiting adults still hovers at approximately 16% (Schafer, Caetano, & Clark, 1998; Straus & Gelles, 1986).

This line of research yielded three main findings. First, people experience relatively frequent aggressive urges toward their romantic partner, but they rarely act on them. Put another way, people regularly feel the need to inhibit their aggressive urges toward loved ones. Second, a mixture of self-control fatigue and provocation also increases aggression toward romantic partners. Stimulate an aggressive urge and it takes ample self-control energy to override it, regardless of whether the target of aggression is a stranger or a romantic partner. The third, and most novel, finding was that regularly practicing self-control buffered people against depletion-induced aggression.

A second set of findings identified dispositional factors that enhance or reduce the relationship between self-control and aggression. Trait aggressiveness, defined as having a heightened propensity to think, feel, and act aggressively, increases the link between self-control fatigue and aggression (Finkel et al., 2012). People with low trait self-control, who generally struggle to plan and follow through on goals, also express the highest levels of aggressive intentions when they are depleted of their self-control energy (DeWall et al., 2007). On the flipside, highly religious people are buffered from the effects of self-control fatigue on aggression (Pond, DeWall, & Keller, 2015). Religious people's higher levels of self-control may help explain why they are so adept at controlling their aggressive urges (DeWall et al., 2014; McCullough & Willoughby, 2009).

The third set of findings delved into a biological process that might help explain the relationship between self-control and aggression. Beyond being a mere metaphor, physiological energy may help explain when the risk for aggression is high or low. Glucose is fuel for the brain. Although the brain represents 2% of our mass, it consumes 20% of our energy. To complete self-control tasks, it helps when you have adequate physiological energy and hurts when you do not.

In one study, married people pricked their fingers at the end of each day to provide a measure of their blood glucose levels (Bushman, DeWall, Pond, & Hanus, 2014). Participants also stabbed a voodoo doll that represented their spouse, which is a valid and reliable measure of aggressive inclinations (DeWall et al., 2013). On days when participants experienced low glucose levels, they expressed greater aggressive inclinations toward their partner. Our findings confirmed that when people feel hangry—that dangerous combination of hunger and anger—they are prone toward aggression.

Rather than raise aggression, other research examined whether boosting physiological energy may reduce aggression. It did. People who drank a glucose-laden beverage behaved less aggressively than did people who drank a sweet beverage that did not contain glucose (DeWall, Deckman, Gailliot, & Bushman, 2011).

Follow-up research has replicated and extended these findings in three ways. First, glucose reduces aggression primarily among people who are at heightened risk for aggression. For example, glucose has its strongest aggression-reducing effect among people high in trait aggressiveness and high in rejection sensitivity (Denson, von Hippel, Kemp, & Teo, 2010; Pfundmair et al., 2016). Second, glucose reduces aggression primarily in situations when an aggressive urge has been stimulated, such as through provocation (Denson et al., 2010) or rejection (Pfundmair et al., 2016). Third, glucose likely reduces aggression through its influence on neural rather than metabolic processes. Therefore, people need not ingest glucose to experience some of its beneficial effects (Molden et al., 2012). Gargling a little glucose in your mouth is enough to enhance self-control (Sanders, Shirk, Burgin, & Martin, 2012). This effect may be due to glucose's ability to activate regulatory brain structures in the prefrontal cortex and other areas (for a review of these neural regions see Wagner & Heatherton, 2016).

The bottom line: Top-down processes help explain why people succeed and fail to control their aggressive urges. But we can gain much by starting our investigation before people interpret that need to override an aggressive urge. What happens the moment that people experience an aggression urge? The next section discusses how the balance between aggressive and peaceful behavior hinges on the amount of pleasure people perceive they will experience by behaving aggressively.

BALANCING AGGRESSION FROM THE BOTTOM-UP

Whereas previous research on aggression and ego depletion has focused on the ability of top-down inhibition to constrain aggression, we argue for another, complimentary focus. Classic aggression research placed a substantial emphasis on the impulses that resulted in aggression. These include transient internal states, such as frustration (Berkowitz, 1989), the accessibility of aggressive constructs and associations (Dollard, Miller, Doob, Mowrer, & Sears, 1939), internalized scripts for aggressive acts (Huesmann, 1986), arousal (Zillmann, Katcher, & Milavsky, 1972), and many others. However, contemporary research on aggression has not maintained this focus on bottom-up aspects of the aggressive equation. Nor has this research examined how ego depletion might affect aggressive impulses, and through them, aggression itself. In what follows, we call for an increase in focus on bottom-up impulses that motivate aggressive acts and how ego depletion might alter them.

THE BALANCE BETWEEN AGGRESSIVE IMPULSES AND INHIBITION

Whether aggression occurs is likely due to two inputs: impulses that motivate aggressive acts and inhibitory control over aggressive behavior. Two theoretical frameworks support this argument: I^3 metatheory (Finkel, 2014) and balance theory (Heatherton & Wagner, 2011; Kotabe & Hofmann, 2016). Balance theory draws heavily from literature on cognitive neuroscience, in which inhibitory regions of the prefrontal cortex exist in a tenuous

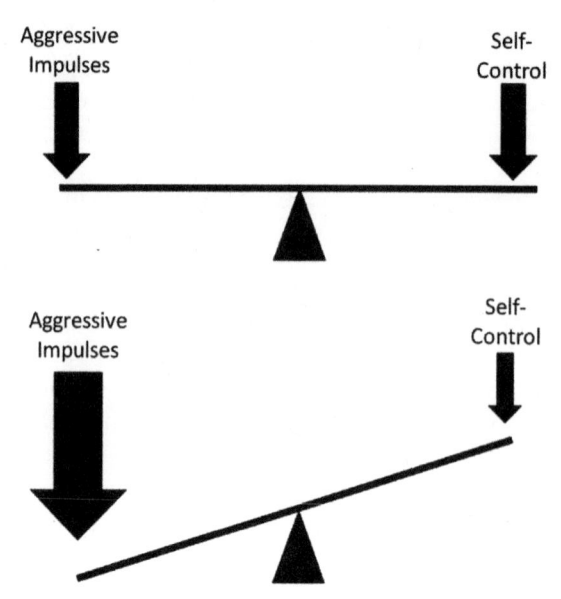

FIGURE 9.2 Balance model of aggression, in which aggression occurs due to an imbalance in which aggressive impulses are magnified while self-control is impaired.

regulatory balance with subcortical brain regions such as the amygdala and nucleus accumbens that assist in the generation of impulses that undermine self-control goals. Although some have questioned this line of reasoning (eg, Lindquist, Wager, Kober, Bliss-Moreau, & Barrett, 2012), the balance perspective is at least a useful heuristic (Fig. 9.2).

According to this perspective, aggression occurs when the balance between impulses and inhibition is tipped toward aggressive impulses by (1) increases to impulses, (2) decreases to inhibition, or (3) both. Self-regulation need not always arise from this interplay between impulses and inhibition (Carnevale & Fujita, 2016; Fujita, 2011), but a wealth of research has suggested that much if not most of self-regulatory processes map well onto this model (eg, Heatherton & Wagner, 2011).

Our research has demonstrated that ego depletion and aggressive impulses are often not enough on their own to elicit aggression, and instead, must often interact with one another to cause aggressive acts (DeWall et al., 2007). As such, our balance model holds that aggression will only reliably arise when ego depletion coincides with aggressive urges.

What Constitutes an Aggressive Impulse?

Having established that aggressive impulses are a crucial element to the determination of whether an aggressive act will occur, the constitutional elements of aggressive impulses have yet to be fully explicated.

Aggression is a highly complex behavior, as reflected in the inherent intricacies built into theories of aggressive behavior (eg, GAM; Anderson & Bushman, 2002). As such, there are likely multiple psychological mechanisms that mediate person and situation inputs that yield aggressive outcomes. In this section, we detail affective, cognitive, and motivational processes that have been linked to aggressive behavior.

Arousal

Physiological arousal often motivates aggressive acts. This mechanism was championed by Excitation Transfer Theory (Zillmann et al., 1972). Drawing heavily from the Two-Factor Theory of emotion (Schachter, 1964), this theoretical approach posited that physiological arousal from one event feeds into subsequent interactions and can be misattributed in a manner that increases aggression. For example, a cup of coffee's excitatory effects might, through well-established appraisal mechanisms, render a harmless slight into an infuriating provocation, increasing the likelihood of aggression.

Cognitive Processes

Not all aggressive impulses are "hot," some are attributable to relatively "cold" cognitive mechanisms. Hostile cognitions are characterized by the perception that neutral stimuli are potentially threatening, that aggression is a ubiquitous feature of the environment, and is subserved by the chronic accessibility of aggressive concepts in semantic association networks (Anderson & Bushman, 2002). Such hostile perceptual distortions are potent in their ability to cause aggressive behavior (Castro, Veerman, Koops, Bosch, & Monshouwer, 2002) and often mediate aggressive phenomena (DeWall, Twenge, Gitter, & Baumeister, 2009). Indeed, one recent study showed that a hostile attribution bias consistently mediated the relationship between perceived provocation and aggressive inclinations among children from nine countries (Dodge et al., 2015). These findings suggest that a hostile attribution bias represents a universal cognitive process underlying aggression.

Social Mimicry and Scripts

Humans are consummately social beings. As such, we display a pronounced tendency to use the behavior of others as a guide to our own. From the classic "Bobo Doll" studies, we learned that humans have an innate tendency to mimic others' aggressive behavior (Bandura, Ross, & Ross, 1963). From these interpersonal observations, we internalize guides for our behaviors called scripts, which can promote aggressive reactions to situations (Huesmann, 1986). Indeed, watching others act aggressively, even if through media such as violent video games can magnify and even create aggressive impulses where none previously existed (Anderson & Bushman, 2001).

Negative Affect

Perhaps the most reliably invoked proximate cause of aggression is negative affect. Aggressive acts are often preceded by and cooccur with aversive sensations such as anger (Denson, Capper, Oaten, Friese, & Schofield, 2011), frustration (Berkowitz, 1989), excessive heat (Anderson, 2001), physical pain (Berkowitz, Cochran, & Embree, 1981), social pain (Chester et al., 2014), shame (Thomaes, Bushman, Stegge, & Olthof, 2008), and others. But not all negative affect increases aggression, as demonstrated by disgust's negative association with aggressive behavior across multiple contexts (Pond et al., 2012). In spite of this, the aggression literature has concluded that people tend to aggress when they feel bad.

Positive Affect

Aversive states reliably produce aggression, but what about pleasant sensations? People tend to report that retaliatory, but not nonretaliatory, aggression as pleasant (Ramírez, Bonniot-Cabanac, & Cabanac, 2005). Such revenge also is reliably correlated with a bias in brain activity that favors the left hemisphere of the prefrontal cortex over the right hemisphere, a neural signature of approach orientation (Harmon-Jones & Sigelman, 2001). Such approach orientations are linked to the experience of positive affect. Retaliatory aggression is also associated with an impairment in the brain's ability to regulate the experience of pleasure (Chester & DeWall, 2016b). Extending beyond the brain to personality, individuals who experience the pleasant sensation of self-esteem (eg, narcissists) have heightened aggressive tendencies (Baumeister, Bushman, & Campbell, 2000). Taken together, there is ample evidence that positive affect plays a central role in motivating retaliatory aggressive behavior.

Emotion-Regulation Motivation and Anticipated Affect

Individuals seek to maintain an affective homeostasis in which negative and positive affect are in balance with one another (Larsen, 2000). This emotion-regulation motivation may shed light on how affective states produce aggression. Reliable causes of aggression are also causes of negative affect (eg, frustrated goals, insults, threats). Individuals may then turn to aggression to harness its associated positive affect to regulate their emotions and improve their mood. People readily believe in Freudian notions of cathartic aggression, in which violent acts will serve to regulate and improve their moods, though this tends not to be the case (Bushman, 2002). People who expect that aggression is an effective means to improve their mood also tend to be the most aggressive in response to such aversive experiences as provocation (Bushman, Baumeister, & Phillips, 2001).

We have replicated this effect with aggressive responses to social rejection (Chester & DeWall, 2016a). Building upon these findings, we demonstrated that the initial increase in negative affect and decrease in positive affect that rejection entails is effectively eliminated after an aggressive act. Thus it appears that people leverage the sweetness of revenge to combat the sting of daily life and this motivation may impel people to aggress.

Evolutionary Motives

Aggression is a behavioral tendency we humans share with almost every other organism on the planet. From single-celled organisms to our close relatives the chimpanzee, attempts to harm others abound in the animal kingdom. Such ubiquity of aggression suggests that it is an evolutionary adaptation that serves to solve recurring problems throughout organisms' life histories. What evolutionary motives might aggression serve to solve? According to evolutionary psychologists, aggression can serve several functions that include self-protection from acquiring resources, bodily threats, gaining social status, and preventing mate defection to sexual rivals (Buss & Shackelford, 1997). Aggression against intrasexual rivals may even serve to attract potential mates (Griskevicius et al., 2009). Such ancient tendencies may yet explain the seemingly intractable impulses humans have to harm each other. Indeed, evolutionary forces play a substantial role in the regulation of human behavior (Francis & Inzlicht, 2016).

How Does Depletion Alter Aggressive Impulses?

It is clear that ego depletion functions to impair inhibitory, top-down control of aggression. Yet it remains almost completely unknown how depletion influences aggressive impulses. Below we discuss some possibilities.

Arousal

Tasks that tax self-control (eg, eating carrots while resisting eating cookies), have been shown to initially reduce biomarkers of arousal (eg, heart rate) which then rebound in the form of greater galvanic skin responses (Segerstrom & Nes, 2007). Thus ego depletion may also contribute to aggression by ultimately exacerbating physiological arousal.

Cognitive Processes

Though few studies have directly tested the effect of ego depletion on aggressive cognitions, research from related fields can provide us with an idea of how depletion may alter hostility, scripts, and social mimicry. Each of these processes is often construed as heuristic forms of biased thought, which occur automatically and without much conscious awareness.

Ego depletion readily impairs the ability to inhibit heuristic thought processes and results in cognitive processing that is heavily driven by such automatic biases (eg, social influence; Janssen, Fennis, Pruyn, & Vohs, 2008). By magnifying the role of automatic cognition, ego depletion may enhance the heuristic biases that promote aggressive behavior.

Affective Processes

Impairments in general self-regulatory resources predict impairments in emotion regulation (Schmeichel & Tang, 2015). Thus ego depletion is likely to exacerbate the negative affect individuals experience in response to such aggression-increasing inputs such as provocations and heat. Poorly regulated positive affect predicts greater retaliatory aggression (Chester & DeWall, 2016b). By increasing both the negative affect that arises from provocations and the positive affect of aggression, both of these forces may interact to magnify the motivation to use aggression to regulate emotions (Bushman et al., 2001). Such a perfect storm of exacerbated affect may then go on to promote aggressive behavior.

Summary

Ego depletion has conventionally been thought to promote aggression by operating on one side of the balance model we propose: by reducing inhibitory control over aggressive impulses. However, we argue that the other side of the balance model has largely been ignored. In this section, we have sought to articulate the constituents of the aggressive impulse, an ignored realm of aggression research, and outlined how ego depletion might influence these various facets of the drive to harm others.

HOW TO USE KNOWLEDGE OF EGO DEPLETION TO REDUCE AGGRESSION?

Understanding how self-regulation works is a useful academic exercise. To leverage our understanding further, we can design interventions that seek to strengthen inhibition and weaken aggressive impulses. Aggression arises from many factors. Hence, interventions will have the highest degree of success when they tackle multiple components that increase the risk for aggression.

Thus far, most aggression interventions have aimed to improve inhibition. For example, some studies have assigned people to regularly practice self-regulation (Denson et al., 2011; Finkel et al., 2009). Compared with people who do not practice self-regulation, those who do are less prone to depletion-induced aggression. Other research has enhanced psychological processes related to inhibition of aggressive impulses, such as empathy

(Day, Casey, & Gerace, 2010). These interventions suggest that strengthening inhibition provides one avenue for reducing aggression.

But inhibition offers only half of the story about why people behave aggressively. To reduce aggression, researchers need to reduce the pleasure that people experience when they hurt those who have harmed them. The drug naltrexone may fill this need. Naltrexone is an opioid antagonist. By blocking opioid receptors, it reduces the pleasure that people experience when they engage in behaviors that normally give them a sense of euphoria. For example, naltrexone reduces alcohol consumption among heavy drinkers and gambling among people who have gambling compulsions (Anton et al., 2008; Kim, Grant, Adson, & Shin, 2001). We predict that naltrexone will reduce aggression among highly aggressive people by reducing the pleasure they experience by behaving aggressively. Instead of blunting pleasure, it may also be fruitful to imbue nonaggressive acts (eg, altruism) with such positive affect, as doing so recruits motivational neural circuitry that can be brought to bear (Berkman, Kahn, & Livingston, 2016).

CONCLUDING REMARKS

The limited resource model of self-regulation has renewed interest in one of humanity's greatest strengths. It has spawned hundreds of studies that attempted to explain why humans often fail at what they are capable of doing so well—changing one response in favor of another to achieve a desired outcome. We might live in one of most peaceful periods in human history, but we still experience aggressive urges. When we feel mentally fatigued, we have difficulty inhibiting our aggressive urges. And no matter how much we consider ourselves nonaggressive, giving into our aggressive urges can feel good. There is no blueprint for creating a completely peaceful society. The best we can do is learn to limit aggressive urges and strengthen our ability and motivation to override them when they crop up.

References

Anderson, C. A. (2001). Heat and violence. *Current Directions in Psychological Science, 10*(1), 33–38.

Anderson, C. A., & Bushman, B. J. (2001). Effects of violent video games on aggressive behavior, aggressive cognition, aggressive affect, physiological arousal, and prosocial behavior: a meta-analytic review of the scientific literature. *Psychological Science, 12*(5), 353–359.

Anderson, C. A., & Bushman, B. J. (2002). Human aggression. *Annual Review of Psychology, 53*(1), 27–51.

Anton, R. F., Oroszi, G., O'Malley, S., Couper, D., Swift, R., Pettinati, H., & Goldman, D. (2008). An evaluation of μ-Opioid receptor (OPRM1) as a predictor of naltrexone response in the treatment of alcohol dependence: results from the Combined Pharmacotherapies and Behavioral Interventions for Alcohol Dependence (COMBINE) Study. *Archives of General Psychiatry, 65*, 135–144.

Bandura, A., Ross, D., & Ross, S. A. (1963). Imitation of film-mediated aggressive models. *The Journal of Abnormal and Social Psychology*, 66(1), 3–11.

Baumeister, R. F. (1998). The self. In D. T. Gilbert, S. T. Fiske, & G. Lindzey (Eds.), *Handbook of social psychology* (4th ed.) (pp. 680–740). New York: McGraw-Hill.

Baumeister, R. F. (2016). Chapter 1: Does willpower exist? In E. Hirt (Ed.), *Self-regulation and ego control*. San Diego, CA: Elsevier, (in press).

Baumeister, R. F., Bratslavsky, E., Muraven, M., & Tice, D. M. (1998). Ego depletion: is the active self a limited resource? *Journal of Personality and Social Psychology*, 74, 1252–1265.

Baumeister, R. F., Bushman, B. J., & Campbell, W. K. (2000). Self-esteem, narcissism, and aggression does violence result from low self-esteem or from threatened egotism? *Current Directions in Psychological Science*, 9(1), 26–29.

Berkman, E. T., Kahn, L. E., & Livingston, J. L. (2016). Chapter 13: Valuation as a mechanism of self-control and ego depletion. In E. Hirt (Ed.), *Self-regulation and ego control*. San Diego, CA: Elsevier, (in press).

Berkowitz, L. (1989). Frustration-aggression hypothesis: examination and reformulation. *Psychological Bulletin*, 106(1), 59–73.

Berkowitz, L., Cochran, S. T., & Embree, M. C. (1981). Physical pain and the goal of aversively stimulated aggression. *Journal of Personality and Social Psychology*, 40(4), 687–700.

Bushman, B. J. (2002). Does venting anger feed or extinguish the flame? Catharsis, rumination, distraction, anger, and aggressive responding. *Personality & Social Psychology Bulletin*, 28(6), 724–731.

Bushman, B. J., Baumeister, R. F., & Phillips, C. M. (2001). Do people aggress to improve their mood? Catharsis beliefs, affect regulation opportunity, and aggressive responding. *Journal of Personality and Social Psychology*, 81(1), 17–32.

Bushman, B. J., DeWall, C. N., Pond, R. S., Jr., & Hanus, M. D. (2014). Low glucose relates to greater aggression in married couples. *Proceedings of the National Academy of Science*, 111, 6254–6257.

Buss, D. M., & Shackelford, T. K. (1997). Human aggression in evolutionary psychological perspective. *Clinical Psychology Review*, 17(6), 605–619.

de Castro, B. O., Veerman, J. W., Koops, W., Bosch, J. D., & Monshouwer, H. J. (2002). Hostile attribution of intent and aggressive behavior: a meta-analysis. *Child Development*, 73(3), 916–934.

Carnevale, J., & Fujita, K. (2016). Chapter 5: What does ego depletion reveal about self-control? In E. Hirt (Ed.), *Self-regulation and ego control*. San Diego, CA: Elsevier, (in press).

Chester, D. S., & DeWall, C. N. (2016a). *Combating the sting of rejection with the pleasure of revenge: A new look at how emotion shapes aggressive responses to rejection* Manuscript in preparation.

Chester, D. S., & DeWall, C. N. (2016b). The pleasure of revenge: retaliatory aggression arises from a neural imbalance toward reward. *Social Cognitive and Affective Neuroscience*, 11, 1173–1182.

Chester, D. S., Eisenberger, N. I., Pond, R. S., Richman, S. B., Bushman, B. J., & DeWall, C. N. (2014). The interactive effect of social pain and executive functioning on aggression: an fMRI experiment. *Social Cognitive and Affective Neuroscience*, 9(5), 699–704.

Day, A., Casey, S., & Gerace, A. (2010). Interventions to improve empathy awareness in sexual and violent offenders: conceptual, empirical, and clinical issues. *Aggression and Violent Behavior*, 15, 201–208.

Denson, T. F., Capper, M. M., Oaten, M., Friese, M., & Schofield, T. O. (2011). Self-control training decreases aggression in response to provocation in aggressive individuals. *Journal of Research in Personality*, 45, 252–256.

Denson, T. F., von Hippel, W., Kemp, R. I., & Teo, L. S. (2010). Glucose consumption decreases impulse aggression in response to provocation in aggressive individuals. *Journal of Experimental Social Psychology*, 46, 1023–1028.

Denson, T. F., Pedersen, W. C., Ronquillo, J., & Nandy, A. S. (2009). The angry brain: neural correlates of anger, angry rumination, and aggressive personality. *Journal of Cognitive Neuroscience*, 21(4), 734–744.

REFERENCES

Denson, T. F., Pedersen, W. C., Friese, M., Hahm, A., & Roberts, L. (2011). Understanding impulsive aggression: angry rumination and reduced self-control capacity are mechanisms underlying the provocation-aggression relationship. *Personality & Social Psychology Bulletin, 37*(6), 850–862.

DeWall, C. N., Anderson, C. A., & Bushman, B. J. (2011). The general aggression model: theoretical extensions to violence. *Psychology of Violence, 1*, 245–258.

DeWall, C. N., Baumeister, R. F., Stillman, T. F., & Gailliot, M. T. (2007). Violence restrained: effects of self-regulation and its depletion on aggression. *Journal of Experimental Social Psychology, 43*(1), 62–76.

DeWall, C. N., Deckman, T., Gailliot, M. T., & Bushman, B. J. (2011). Sweetened blood cools hot tempers: physiological self-control and aggression. *Aggressive Behavior, 37*, 73–80.

DeWall, C. N., Finkel, E. J., Lambert, N. J., Slotter, E. B., Bodenhausen, G. V., Pond, R. S., Jr., ... Fincham, F. D. (2013). The voodoo doll task: introducing and validating a novel method for studying aggressive inclinations. *Aggressive Behavior, 39*, 419–439.

DeWall, C. N., Pond, R. S., Jr., Carter, E. C., McCullough, M. E., Lambert, N. M., Fincham, F. D., & Nezlek, J. B. (2014). Explaining the relationship between religiousness and substance use: self-control matters. *Journal of Personality and Social Psychology, 107*, 339–351.

DeWall, C. N., Twenge, J. M., Gitter, S. A., & Baumeister, R. F. (2009). It's the thought that counts. *Journal of Personality and Social Psychology, 96*(1), 45–59.

Dodge, K. A., Malone, P. S., Lansford, J. E., Sorbring, E., Skinnera, A. T., Tapanya, S., ... Pastorelli, C. (2015). Hostile attribution bias and aggressive behavior in global context. *Proceedings of the National Academy of Sciences, 112*, 9310–9315.

Dollard, J., Miller, N. E., Doob, L. W., Mowrer, H. O., & Sears, R. R. (1939). *Frustration and aggression* (Vol. viii). New Haven, CT, US: Yale University Press.

Finkel, E. J., DeWall, C. N., Slotter, E. B., Oaten, M., & Foshee, V. A. (2009). Self-regulatory failure and intimate partner violence perpetration. *Journal of Personality and Social Psychology, 97*, 483–499.

Finkel, E. J. (2007). Impelling and inhibiting forces in the perpetration of intimate partner violence. *Review of General Psychology, 11*, 193–207.

Finkel, E. J. (2014). The I^3 model: metatheory, theory, and evidence. *Advances in Experimental Social Psychology, 49*, 1–104.

Finkel, E. J., DeWall, C. N., Slotter, E. B., McNulty, J. K., Pond, R. S., Jr., & Atkins, D. C. (2012). Using I3 theory to clarify when dispositional aggressiveness predicts intimate partner violence perpetration. *Journal of Personality and Social Psychology, 102*, 533–549.

Francis, Z., & Inzlicht, M. (2016). Chapter 18: Proximate and ultimate causes of ego depletion. In E. Hirt (Ed.), *Self-regulation and ego control*. San Diego, CA: Elsevier, (in press).

Fujita, K. (2011). On conceptualizing self-control as more than the effortful inhibition of impulses. *Personality and Social Psychology Review, 15*(4), 352–366.

Gottfredson, M. R., & Hirschi, T. (1990). *A general theory of crime*. Palo Alto, CA: Stanford University Press.

Griskevicius, V., Tybur, J. M., Gangestad, S. W., Perea, E. F., Shapiro, J. R., & Kenrick, D. T. (2009). Aggress to impress: hostility as an evolved context-dependent strategy. *Journal of Personality and Social Psychology, 96*(5), 980–994.

Harmon-Jones, E., & Sigelman, J. (2001). State anger and prefrontal brain activity: evidence that insult-related relative left-prefrontal activation is associated with experienced anger and aggression. *Journal of Personality and Social Psychology, 80*(5), 797–803.

Heatherton, T. F., & Wagner, D. D. (2011). Cognitive neuroscience of self-regulation failure. *Trends in Cognitive Sciences, 15*(3), 132–139.

Huesmann, L. R. (1986). Psychological processes promoting the relation between exposure to media violence and aggressive behavior by the viewer. *Journal of Social Issues, 42*(3), 125–139.

Janssen, L., Fennis, B. M., Pruyn, A. T. H., & Vohs, K. D. (2008). The path of least resistance: regulatory resource depletion and the effectiveness of social influence techniques. *Journal of Business Research, 61*(10), 1041–1045.

Kim, S. W., Grant, J. E., Adson, D. E., & Shin, Y. C. (2001). Double-blind naltrexone and placebo comparison study in the treatment of pathological gambling. *Biological Psychiatry, 49*, 914–921.

Kotabe, H. P., & Hofmann, W. (2016). Chapter 19: How depletion operates in a unified model of self-control. In E. Hirt (Ed.), *Self-regulation and ego control*. San Diego, CA: Elsevier, (in press).

Larsen, R. J. (2000). Toward a science of mood regulation. *Psychological Inquiry, 11*(3), 129–141.

Lieberman, J. D., Solomon, S., Greenberg, J., & McGregor, H. A. (1999). A hot new way to measure aggression: hot sauce allocation. *Aggressive Behavior, 25*, 331–348.

Lindquist, K. A., Wager, T. D., Kober, H., Bliss-Moreau, E., & Barrett, L. F. (2012). The brain basis of emotion: a meta-analytic review. *Behavioral and Brain Sciences, 35*(03), 121–143.

McCullough, M. E., & Willoughby, B. L. B. (2009). Religion, self-regulation, and self-control: associations, explanations, and implications. *Psychological Bulletin, 135*, 69–93.

Molden, D. C., Hui, C. H., Scholer, A. A., Meier, B. P., Noreen, E. E., D'Agostino, P. R., & Martin, V. (2012). Motivation versus metabolic effects of carbohydrates on self-control. *Psychological Science, 23*, 1137–1144.

Muraven, M., & Baumeister, R. F. (2000). Self-regulation and depletion of limited resources: does self-control resemble a muscle? *Psychological Bulletin, 126*, 247–259.

Pfundmair, M., DeWall, C. N., Fries, V., Geiger, B., Krämer, T., Krug, S., … Aydin, N. (2016). Sugar or spice: using I^3 metatheory to understand how and why glucose reduces rejection-related aggression. *Aggressive Behavior, 41*, 537–543.

Pinker, S. (2011). *The better angels of our nature*. New York: Viking.

Pond, R. S., Jr., DeWall, C. N., & Keller, P. S. (2015). *Practicing what you preach: Self-control mediates the association between religiosity and aggression* Manuscript in preparation.

Pond, R. S., Jr., DeWall, C. N., Lambert, N. M., Deckman, T., Bonser, I. M., & Fincham, F. D. (2012). Repulsed by violence: disgust sensitivity buffers trait, behavioral, and daily aggression. *Journal of Personality and Social Psychology, 102*(1), 175–188.

Popper, K. (1959). *The logic of scientific discovery*. New York: Hutchinson & Co.

Pratt, T. C., & Cullen, F. T. (2000). The empirical status of Gottfredson and Hirschi's general theory of crime: a meta-analysis. *Criminology, 38*, 931–964.

Ramírez, J. M., Bonniot-Cabanac, M.-C., & Cabanac, M. (2005). Can aggression provide pleasure? *European Psychologist, 10*(2), 136–145.

Safe Horizon. (2015). Retrieved on September 3, 2015 from http://www.safehorizon.org/page/domestic-violence-statistics–facts-52.html.

Sanders, M. A., Shirk, S. D., Burgin, C. J., & Martin, L. L. (2012). The gargle effect: rinsing the mouth with glucose enhances self-control. *Psychological Science, 23*, 1470–1472.

Schachter, S. (1964). The interaction of cognitive and physiological determinants of emotional state. *Advances in Experimental Social Psychology, 1*, 49–80.

Schafer, J., Caetano, R., & Clark, C. L. (1998). Rates of intimate partner violence among U.S. couples. *American Journal of Public Health, 88*, 1702–1704.

Schmeichel, B. J., & Crowell, A. (2016). Chapter 6: Exercising self-control increases approach-motivated impulse strength. In E. Hirt (Ed.), *Self-regulation and ego control*. San Diego, CA: Elsevier, (in press).

Schmeichel, B. J., & Tang, D. (2015). Individual differences in executive functioning and their relationship to emotional processes and responses. *Current Directions in Psychological Science, 24*(2), 93–98.

Segerstrom, S. C., & Nes, L. S. (2007). Heart rate variability reflects self-regulatory strength, effort, and fatigue. *Psychological Science, 18*(3), 275–281.

Straus, M. A. (2004). Prevalence of violence against dating partners by male and female university students worldwide. *Violence Against Women, 10*(7), 790–811.

Straus, M. A., & Gelles, R. J. (1986). Societal change and change in family violence from 1975 to 1985 as revealed by two national surveys. *Journal of Marriage and the Family, 48*, 465–479.

Suls, J., & Wan, C. K. (1993). The relationship between trait hostility and cardiovascular reactivity: a quantitative review and analysis. *Psychophysiology, 30*, 615–626.

Thomaes, S., Bushman, B. J., Stegge, H., & Olthof, T. (2008). Trumping shame by blasts of noise: narcissism, self-esteem, shame, and aggression in young adolescents. *Child Development, 79*(6), 1792–1801.

Vohs, K. D., Glass, B. D., Maddox, W. T., & Markman, A. B. (2011). Ego depletion is not just fatigue: evidence from a total sleep deprivation experiment. *Social Psychological and Personality Science, 2,* 166–173.

Wagner, D. D., & Heatherton, T. F. (2016). Chapter 14: What can cognitive neuroscience tell us about the mechanism of ego depletion? In E. Hirt (Ed.), *Self-regulation and ego control.* San Diego, CA: Elsevier, (in press).

Zillmann, D., Katcher, A. H., & Milavsky, B. (1972). Excitation transfer from physical exercise to subsequent aggressive behavior. *Journal of Experimental Social Psychology, 8*(3), 247–259.

SECTION 3

THE ROLE OF PERCEPTIONS, EXPECTANCIES, AND LAY BELIEFS IN EGO CONTROL

CHAPTER 10

Perceived Mental Fatigue and Self-Control

J.J. Clarkson[1], A.S. Otto[2], R. Hassey[1], E.R. Hirt[3]

[1]University of Cincinnati, Cincinnati, OH, United States; [2]Baylor University, Waco, TX, United States; [3]Indiana University, Bloomington, IN, United States

Pause for a moment and consider your level of mental alertness—that is, how well can you focus and concentrate right now? Are you rather energized and able to focus or are you struggling to regulate your attention? We can all relate to the ebb and flow of mental alertness throughout the day, transitioning from feeling alert, focused, and energized to tired, exhausted, and drained. As such, this question of mental alertness is one with which we all are not only very familiar but also tend to consider with sufficient regularity.

Yet while these questions may seem rather mundane, recent research has shown that the manner in which individuals respond to these types of questions has immense impact on their subsequent abilities for self-control. That is, individuals' observations of their own mental alertness define their *perceptions of mental fatigue,* a label that can be more formally characterized as a subjective assessment of one's ability to engage in mental activity (Clarkson, Hirt, Chapman, & Jia, 2011; Clarkson, Hirt, Jia, & Alexander, 2010; see also Smets, Garssen, Bonke, & De Haes, 1995). Of most importance, however, these perceptions of mental fatigue have been shown to have immense consequence for individuals' ability to regulate attention, stifle impulses, delay gratification, and otherwise engage in self-control.[1]

---

[1] We use the term *self-control* in this chapter to reflect a multitude of cognitive and motivational regulatory processes. However, we recognize the ongoing debate regarding definitional issues surrounding terms such as self-control (Fujita, 2011; see Chapter 5) and acknowledge that, while our work does not speak to this debate, it is important to consider the implications of mental fatigue for different regulatory processes.

The purpose of this chapter is to outline the empirical work to date regarding the importance of these subjective perceptions of mental fatigue for self-control. We first review existing research on the causal link between perceptions of mental fatigue and self-control. Next, we discuss factors shown to impact or alter individuals' perceptions of mental fatigue. We then present a meta-analysis to provide insight into the direct impact of perceived mental fatigue on self-control. Finally, we speak to the implications of this research for the manner in which self-control is conceptualized within a limited resource model specifically as well as models of self-control more broadly.

PERCEPTIONS OF MENTAL FATIGUE

In the early work on the phenomenon of ego depletion, researchers often used ad hoc measures of subjective fatigue as checks for their resource depletion manipulations. The consistent finding was that those exposed to a high depletion manipulation reported feeling more fatigued than did those exposed to a low depletion manipulation (eg, Baumeister, Bratslavsky, Muraven, & Tice, 1998; Muraven, Tice, & Baumeister, 1998; Schmeichel, Vohs, & Baumeister, 2003). These individuals then exhibited differential levels of self-control. Thus, this early work offers direct evidence that perceptions of mental fatigue covary with variations in resource depletion. However, this work only provides indirect evidence that these perceptions might exert their own impact on self-control performance. That is, though this early research showed that perceptions of mental fatigue covary with actual resource availability, these findings are unable to disambiguate the effects of perceived versus actual mental fatigue on self-control.

To offer insight into the extent to which perceptions of mental fatigue could impact self-control performance independent of individuals' actual resource availability, Clarkson et al. (2010) relied on a classic misattribution paradigm to tease apart the effect of what they believed to be two separate constructs. Specifically, they had participants complete a classic depletion manipulation (ie, the e-crossing task) on yellow paper and afterward told participants that the color yellow generally had either a depleting or a replenishing effect on people. They found that those in the low depletion condition perceived themselves as less fatigued and subsequently performed better when told that the paper color was replenishing (versus depleting). Conversely, those in the high depletion condition perceived themselves as less fatigued and subsequently performed better when told that the paper color was depleting (versus replenishing).

Importantly, then, individuals who reported being less mentally fatigued elicited greater self-control performance, and this performance was independent of their actual resource availability. Indeed, this effect was demonstrated across various well-documented manipulations of resource depletion and different indices of self-control. For instance, perceptions of mental fatigue impacted individuals' persistence, attention regulation, and elaborative thought.

The Malleability of Working Memory

Documenting the role of perceptions in altering self-control performance, researchers next turned to understanding the means by which perceptions impact self-control. That is, by what means or mechanisms does this shift in perception result in enhanced or undermined self-control?

To address this question, Clarkson et al. (2011) focused on the role of *working memory*—formally defined as the capacity to temporarily store and manipulate information (Baddeley, 1986; Just & Carpenter, 1992). Research has demonstrated a clear link between working memory capacity and self-control performance (Hofmann, Gschwender, Friese, Wiers, & Schmitt, 2008; Schmeichel, Volokhov, & Demaree, 2008; Shamosh & Gray, 2007; see Hofmann, Schmeichel, & Baddeley, 2012). Indeed, Schmeichel (2007) demonstrated that manipulations of ego depletion directly impacted working memory capacity, such that those high in resource depletion showed less resource availability in the form of a more restricted working memory capacity than did those low in resource depletion. To that end, Clarkson et al. (2011) wondered if altering individuals' perceptions of their mental fatigue was sufficient to vary the accessibility of regulatory resources in the form of working memory capacity.

In many ways, this *resource allocation hypothesis* stands in direct contrast to the dominant perspective on working memory capacity, a perspective that conceptualizes working memory capacity as a stable individual difference (see Engle, 2002). However, external cues have been shown to alter individuals' working memory capacity. For instance, heightened salience of demographics associated with aversive stereotypes (eg, age, race, gender) has been shown to restrict working memory capacity and reduce cognitive performance (Rydell, McConnell, & Beilock, 2009; Schmader & Johns, 2003). Additionally, increasing performance expectations has been shown to expand working memory capacity and improve cognitive performance (Beilock & Carr, 2005). Thus, while working memory may reflect a rather stable individual difference, external cues are clearly capable of expanding and constricting resource availability (in the form of working memory capacity; Schmeichel, 2007) and consequently impacting subsequent performance.

To offer direct insight into the possibility that perceptions of mental fatigue are sufficient to impact working memory capacity, Clarkson et al. (2011) presented individuals with the same misattribution paradigm used in their original research (Clarkson et al., 2010) but made two critical changes. First, rather than focusing on self-control consequences, they presented participants with a popular measure of working memory capacity—the automated operation span task (*Aospan*; Unsworth, Heitz, Schrock, & Engle, 2005). This change was driven by the desire to demonstrate that differences in working memory capacity were responsible for the previously documented differences in self-control performance. Second, after receiving the misattribution feedback concerning the yellow paper, they asked participants to complete the mental fatigue subscale of the multidimensional fatigue inventory (*MFI*; Smets et al., 1995). This change was driven by the desire to utilize a formal index of mental fatigue to explore the mediating role of perceptions of mental fatigue on working memory.

With respect to findings, Clarkson et al. (2011) demonstrated a pattern for individuals' working memory capacity that mirrored the performance data observed in prior research. That is, those in the low depletion condition exhibited greater working memory capacity when told that the paper color was replenishing (versus depleting), whereas those in the high depletion condition exhibited greater working memory capacity when told that the paper color was depleting (versus replenishing). Moreover, the same pattern was observed on the mental fatigue subscale of the MFI, and these perceptions of mental fatigue both predicted working memory scores and mediated the effect of the misattribution manipulation on working memory. Consistent with other research on external cues and working memory, then, the perception of mental fatigue was shown to alter accessibility to resources critical for self-control performance (see also Egan, Clarkson, & Hirt, 2015; Egan & Hirt, 2015).

Of course, working memory capacity could be argued as an alternative performance index of self-control. However, as argued by other researchers (see Schmeichel, 2007), working memory capacity represents a cognitive instantiation of what could more broadly be construed as self-regulatory resources. That is, working memory capacity reflects the means or resources by which individuals are subsequently able to engage (or not) in successful self-control. These findings then illustrate a seemingly minor but important distinction for self-control, as perceptions of mental fatigue influence the availability of regulatory resources but not necessarily the subsequent allocation of those resources to a specific task of self-control. Indeed, the extent to which this expanded or constricted capacity of resources is allocated to a specific task could depend on factors beyond perceptions (Inzlicht & Schmeichel, 2012), such as the desire to conserve resources for future self-control tasks (Muraven, Shmueli, & Burkley, 2006).

That said, subsequent research has shown that the effect of perceived mental fatigue on self-control performance can be driven by differences in working memory capacity (Egan et al., 2015). Through exploring the

```
Perceived Mental Fatigue  →  Working Memory Capacity  →  Self-Control Performance
```

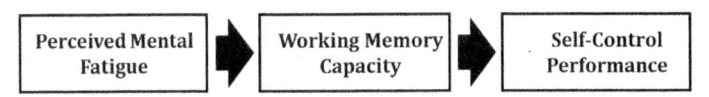

FIGURE 10.1 Path model of perceived mental fatigue on self-control performance through working memory capacity.

effects of positive mood on self-control, Egan and colleagues had participants complete indices of perceived mental fatigue, working memory capacity, and self-control and demonstrated the mediation model that has become the dominant empirical explanation for the effect of perceived mental fatigue on self-control performance (see Fig. 10.1). Thus, while the distinction between resource availability and allocation is critical to acknowledge, the data appear to suggest that the effect of perceived mental fatigue on resource availability subsequently impacts resource allocation (Egan et al., 2015; see also Egan & Hirt, 2015).

Alternative Mechanisms

Importantly, while research supports this resource allocation hypothesis, other potential mechanisms apart from working memory capacity are certainly plausible. For instance, the perception of being mentally fatigued could elicit negative feelings in general, and research shows that negative mood can undermine self-control performance (Tice, Baumeister, Shmueli, & Muraven, 2007; see also Egan et al., 2015). Similarly, the perception of being mentally fatigued could either undermine individuals' motivation to perform well or, more likely, elicit a desire to conserve one's remaining resources for future tasks (Muraven et al., 2006). However, research has not found any effect of perceptions of mental fatigue on individuals' subsequent mood (Clarkson et al., 2010, 2011), direct or indirect motivation to perform well (Clarkson et al., 2010, 2011; Egan et al., 2015), or desire to engage in resource conservation (Clarkson et al., 2010, 2011; Egan et al., 2015).

Of course, these findings do not mean these mechanisms could not exert an influence under specifiable conditions or that they could not have a direct effect on perceptions of mental fatigue. For instance, heightened perceptions of mental fatigue might elicit greater resource conservation when individuals have an explicit reason to hold back their effort—such as when completing a series of tasks that end with a task of high importance. Moreover, these findings do not rule out additional constructs that could account for the impact of perceptions of mental fatigue on self-control, such as individuals' confidence in their ability to self-regulate (ie, self-efficacy; Bandura, 1977) or an inaction goal (Albarracín et al., 2008; Albarracín, Hepler, & Tannenbaum, 2011). That is, heightened perceptions of mental fatigue could undermine individuals' confidence in their ability to successfully perform a task of self-control or heighten a general inaction goal. However, the collective empirical support at this time points toward the malleability of working memory capacity in driving the effect of individuals' perceptions of mental fatigue on subsequent self-control performance.

ANTECEDENTS OF PERCEIVED MENTAL FATIGUE

Given the importance of individuals' perceptions of mental fatigue for self-control, research has focused on identifying the factors that alter these perceptions. We outline several factors that have been shown to impact individuals' self-control performance by altering their perceptions of mental fatigue.

State Feedback

The work by Clarkson et al. (2010, 2011) provided participants with false feedback concerning the impact of a specific aspect of a prior task on their mental abilities. Specifically, participants completed a task on yellow paper and were then later told that the color yellow has been consistently shown to either exhaust or restore people's mental abilities. Though one might suppose the feedback would be taken at face value, such that those in the exhaust condition reported being more fatigued and those in the replenish condition reported being less fatigued, it turned out that the manner in which the task feedback was interpreted depended on individuals' actual state of resource availability. Individuals attributed the feedback to their mental abilities differently as a function of whether they were high or low in resource depletion, and these different attributions resulted in different implications for individuals' perceptions of their mental resources.

Though not intuitive, this finding is consistent with the *resource attribution hypothesis* posited by Clarkson et al. (2010). This hypothesis states that the manner in which individuals use situational cues (such as task feedback) to inform their perceptions of mental fatigue varies as a function of the ambiguity of their mental state and thus provides the basis for a clear distinction between two categories of attributions. In particular, they argued that individuals seek out information to help **explain** concrete states but to **interpret** ambiguous states. Moreover, they showed that individuals report high-resource depletion as a more concrete state than low-resource depletion. Consequently, those high in resource depletion are more likely to engage in an *explanation* attribution, whereas those low in resource depletion are more likely to engage in an *interpretation* attribution.

This distinction is important because, as noted, the same task feedback is then interpreted in different ways depending on whether individuals are high or low in resource depletion. For those high in resource depletion, they seek an *explanation* for their mental fatigue. Thus, when provided with the depleting feedback, the fatigue is now explained and—given the depleting stimulus (eg, the yellow paper) is now absent—they now perceive themselves as less fatigued. Yet when provided with the replenishing feedback, the fatigue is not explained—in fact, their state is incongruent with the feedback. As such, the only explanation must be that they are so fatigued that even the paper could not help them and—even with the replenishing stimulus absent—they perceive themselves as highly fatigued (for a similar rationale, see Schachter & Singer, 1962).

However, for those low in resource depletion, they seek an *interpretation* for their current state. Thus, when given any feedback, they engage in a form of biased hypothesis confirmation whereby they identify instances beyond the yellow paper that confirm the feedback. For instance, those in the depleting feedback condition recall instances that reinforce being depleted (eg, not getting a good night's sleep), whereas those in the replenishing feedback condition recall instances that reinforce being replenished (eg, eating a good breakfast). Consequently, their perceptions are consistent with the feedback and persist even when the stimulus (eg, the yellow paper) is removed, as they have now generated a list of alternative reasons consistent with the feedback (for a similar rationale, see Ross, Lepper, & Hubbard, 1975).

Theories of Willpower Capacity

Researchers have demonstrated that individuals hold very different lay beliefs or theories concerning the extent to which their capacity for available resources is limited (Job, Dweck, & Walton, 2010, 2013, 2015; Job, Bernecker, Miketta, & Friese, 2015; Martijn, Tenbült, Merckelbach, Dreezens, & De Vries, 2002; Miller et al., 2012). Specifically, Job and colleagues distinguish between those who believe self-control resources are relatively exhaustible (*limited theorists*) and those who believe self-control resources are relatively inexhaustible (*nonlimited theorists*). This research has focused largely on the ability of nonlimited theorists to overcome the deleterious effects of resource depletion on self-control relative to limited theorists. Specifically, nonlimited theorists are relatively immune to the traditional depletion effect, presumably due to their belief that their resources are, in fact, not depletable (for a more in-depth review of this construct, see Chapter 11).

Interestingly, this work offers evidence that individuals' perceptions of mental fatigue serve an important role in predicting the performance of willpower theorists. Specifically, Job et al. (2010) argued that perceptions of mental fatigue serve as a signal to individuals that they are running out of resources critical to success. Consistent with this argument, they further showed that perceptions of mental fatigue mediated the self-control performance of limited, but not nonlimited, theorists. The rationale for this mediation pattern, they argued, is that limited theorists are more sensitive to perceptions of mental fatigue than are nonlimited theorists, as only limited theorists believe that their resources can be depleted.

However, recent work suggests perceptions of mental fatigue can impact both limited and nonlimited willpower theorists when not experiencing resource depletion (Clarkson, Otto, Hirt, & Egan, 2016). Specifically, this research argues that nonlimited theorists may implicitly perceive themselves as less mentally depleted than limited theorists. That is, due to their belief in what could be argued as a larger storehouse of regulatory resources, nonlimited theorists may hold to a lower baseline level of perceived mental fatigue than limited theorists, and that this baseline difference in perceptions can drive subsequent self-control. In support of these hypotheses, this work demonstrates that nonlimited theorists do indeed perceive themselves as generally less mentally fatigued than do limited theorists, and that this perceptual difference predicted individuals' cognitive abilities, impulsivity, and delayed gratification.

Moreover, Clarkson, Hirt, and Jia (2016) further show that these baseline perceptions of these implicit theories are not fixed. Across a series of experiments, they demonstrate that the efficacy of these willpower theories vary as a function of the fluency—and thus confidence—associated with these theories. For instance, when individuals doubted their *nonlimited* theory, they reported elevated levels of mental fatigue and reduced self-control. Conversely, when individuals doubted their *limited* theory, they reported reduced levels of mental fatigue and elevated self-control. Thus, while unlimited theorists may naturally exhibit a lower baseline perception of mental fatigue, these perceptions—and the self-control consequences they elicit—are malleable (here, as a function of individuals' confidence in their willpower theory).

Positive Mood

Positive mood has been shown to impact self-control (Fredrickson, Mancuso, Branigan, & Tugade, 2000; Leith & Baumeister, 1996) and, in particular, individuals' self-control recovery (Tice et al., 2007). Specifically, Tice et al. (2007) showed that individuals initially depleted of their regulatory resources replenished those resources faster when in a positive mood. That is, when mentally depleted, individuals exposed to a positive mood induction performed better on a subsequent task of self-control relative to a control condition. Indeed, those initially depleted but then exposed to a positive mood induction performed as well as those never initially depleted. Positive mood, then, appears to accelerate self-control recovery.

Tice et al. (2007) argued that the positive mood induction restores self-control resources by elevating individuals' arousal, though no evidence was presented in support of this mechanism. In response, Egan et al. (2015) posited that psychological factors might explain the restorative effects of positive mood independent of any potential physiological factors (eg, elevations in arousal). Specifically, they argued that positive mood elicits expectations of energy restoration (see Chapter 12 for a more detailed discussion of the importance of expectations for self-control), which leads individuals experiencing a positive mood to perceive themselves as less mentally fatigued than those in a negative mood. In support of this psychological-based perspective, these researchers demonstrated that individuals presented with a positive (versus negative) mood induction reported feeling less mentally fatigued as well as greater working memory capacity and restored self-control. Furthermore, the effect of positive mood on individuals' working memory capacity and self-control performance was predicted by individuals' perceptions of mental fatigue.

Power

Researchers have documented the beneficial impact of interpersonal power for several constructs related to self-control, such as higher action tendencies (Galinsky, Gruenfeld, & Magee, 2003), greater creativity (Galinsky, Magee, Gruenfeld, Whitson, & Liljenquist, 2008), and decreased procrastination (Judge & Bono, 2001). While various reasons exist for the effects of power on these diverse indices of self-control, recent work demonstrates that feelings of power can impact executive functioning (Egan & Hirt, 2015). Indeed, across several studies, Egan and Hirt (2015) show that heightened feelings of power have a direct and positive impact on individuals' self-control performance.

Importantly, however, this effect of power on self-control performance was moderated by social dominance orientation (SDO; see Pratto, Sidanius, Stallworth, & Malle, 1994). That is, Egan and Hirt (2015) showed that SDO affected individuals' expectations of mental restoration and subsequent perceptions of mental fatigue. SDO focuses on individuals' belief in the importance of status and social hierarchy, with those high in this belief viewing power as a necessary and important component to effective functioning (see Altemeyer, 1998). Given the importance attributed to interpersonal power for general efficacy by those high in SDO, Egan and Hirt reasoned and subsequently showed that those high in SDO expected power to be mentally energizing and thus reported themselves less mentally fatigued following a power manipulation than did those low in SDO. As a result, these changes in mental fatigue altered working memory capacity and subsequent self-control performance.

POINTS OF CLARIFICATION

The research discussed in this chapter provides a novel lens by which to consider strength in self-control. Yet this work tends to consistently raise a handful of questions. For instance, how aware are individuals of their state of mental fatigue? In the work described here, the effects occurred regardless of whether individuals' perceptions of mental fatigue were assessed or not, which suggests that individuals are impacted by their perceptions even without being prompted to reflect on them. Yet presumably these effects are contingent on these perceptions being salient to individuals, and we certainly believe there are aspects of the situation that can impact the salience and thus awareness of individuals' state of mental fatigue. For instance, in the e-crossing depletion task (Baumeister et al., 1998), participants are instructed to complete two tasks—one as a baseline (to establish a habit) and a second to either continue or to disrupt that habit. In this and other dual-task paradigms, we would suspect completing the second task in light of a baseline task increases the salience of mental fatigue. Thus, while individuals seem to exhibit a general awareness of their mental fatigue, certainly facets of the self-control context should heighten this awareness and thus the impact of these perceptions on subsequent performance.

Additionally, individuals might be more or less predisposed to be aware of their mental fatigue. We spoke earlier in this chapter about work on individuals' implicit theories concerning the limits of their willpower capacity (see Chapter 11). Research within this stream has shown that while both limited and nonlimited theorists report similar levels of awareness regarding their perceptions of mental fatigue, only limited theorists are responsive to their level of mental fatigue (see Job et al., 2010). Given the diagnosticity of these perceptions for subsequent performance, it seems to reason that limited theorists might place greater weight on their perceptions of mental fatigue that results in a heightened salience across multiple self-control contexts relative to nonlimited theorists. Similarly, the subjective vitality scale (Ryan & Frederick, 1997) measures perceptual differences in the amount of energy available to the self (see Chapter 4 for further discussion of this construct), and this scale could presumably serve as a dispositional index of individuals' awareness of their mental fatigue.

Finally, individuals should use different information as the basis for their perceptions. That is, individuals should not necessarily rely on the same information when formulating their perceptions of mental fatigue. Indeed, Clarkson, Hirt, et al. (2016) directly addressed this question by presenting individuals high and low in need for cognition (Cacioppo & Petty, 1982) with the misattribution paradigm described in Clarkson et al. (2010). Consistent with the findings reported herein, they found that perceptions of mental fatigue predicted self-control performance, irrespective of individuals' need for cognition. Interestingly, however, these perceptions were based on different information. Specifically, those high in need for cognition based their perceptions on the implied effect of the yellow paper on their mental resource capacity, whereas those low in need for cognition based their perceptions solely on the depletion manipulation. In other words, the misattribution feedback only affected those high in need for cognition. This finding is consistent with work showing those high in need for cognition are more likely to engage in effortful, metacognitive thought (Petty, Briñol, Tormala, & Wegener, 2007). Yet as a result of this motivational difference in reflection, those low in need for cognition were less susceptible to the misattribution paradigm and thus more accurate in forming perceptions that were consistent with their actual level of available resources. Thus, while perceptions of mental fatigue continued to exert a consistent influence on self-control performance, the basis of these perceptions can and do vary in systematic ways.

AN ANALYSIS OF EFFECT SIZE

While the consequences of perceived mental fatigue on self-control performance have been well documented, we sought to offer some level of appreciation for the overall relationship between perceptions of mental fatigue and self-control. For instance, in a key meta-analysis on the resource depletion model, Hagger and colleagues (Hagger, Wood, Stiff, & Chatzisarantis, 2010) reported that measures of subjective fatigue elicit a medium effect size (*Cohen's* $d = 0.44$). Though valuable, this analysis was based on indirect measures of perceived mental fatigue (often used as manipulation checks) as opposed to an analysis of direct manipulations of these perceptions.

What then can be gleaned about the strength of the relationship between perceptions of mental fatigue and self-control through an analysis of the existing body of research that directly tests this relationship? To offer insight into this question, we conducted a meta-analysis of the research looking at the direct effect of perceived mental fatigue on self-control performance (Fig. 10.2).

Method

Inclusion criteria. Studies relevant to the meta-analysis were those that empirically tested the relationship between perceived mental fatigue and self-control performance. Appropriate studies were those that directly manipulated perceived mental fatigue and assessed the associative effects

Paper	Study Number	Self-control Index	Perceived Depletion Manipulation	Study N	High Depletion Correlation	Low Depletion Correlation
Clarkson, Hirt, Jia, and Alexander (2010)	1	Anagram persistence	State feedback	96	0.42	0.42
Clarkson, Hirt, Jia, and Alexander (2010)	2	Anagram persistence	State feedback	66	0.42	0.36
Clarkson, Hirt, Jia, and Alexander (2010)	2	Anagram performance	State feedback	66	0.5	0.39
Clarkson, Hirt, Jia, and Alexander (2010)	3	Response latencies	State feedback	52	0.5	0.41
Clarkson, Hirt, Chapman, and Jia (2011)	1	Working memory capacity	State feedback	91	0.29	0.4
Egan and Hirt (2015)	3	Anagram performance	Power	80	0.55	0.27
Egan, Clarkson, and Hirt (2015)	4	Working memory capacity	Mood	150	0.31	0.26
Egan, Clarkson, and Hirt (2015)	4	Anagram performance	Mood	150	0.5	0.34

FIGURE 10.2 Summary of articles in meta-analysis.

on an index of self-control. Studies that used indirect measures (eg, manipulation checks) of perceived mental fatigue were not included in the meta-analysis (see Hagger et al., 2010).

Data Coding. In total, 16 effects examining the relationship between perceptions of mental fatigue and self-control performance met the inclusion criteria outlined earlier. A review of the studies revealed that correlations were an appropriate metric for the meta-analysis, as the respective data were reported using metrics that could be readily converted to correlations (see Borenstein, Hedges, Higgins, & Rothstein, 2009; Peterson & Brown, 2005). Because multiple effects were reported in single studies, the effects were coded and thus analyzed to assess whether dependency was meaningfully present in the data set for that particular association. Importantly, assessments of dependency are necessary to ensure that the variance within the studies and the variance between the effects are appropriately captured. Finally, all correlations were adjusted for sample size estimates and corrected for attenuation (for further discussion of the rationale for these procedures, see Borenstein et al., 2009).

Descriptive Analysis. The analysis of the perceived mental fatigue correlations began with estimating the weighted Fisher's Z values (Hedges & Pigott, 2001). Analysis of weighted Fisher's Z values and their conversion back to correlations for reporting purposes was done to minimize the bias in the distribution of effects when correlations depart significantly from zero. Weighting Fisher's Z values by its unconditional variance was done to minimize bias from sampling error. To account for the variance between effects, random-effect modeling was used throughout the meta-analysis. A random-effect model is argued as preferable to a fixed-effect model for both bivariate and model-driven meta-analyses (Becker, 2009; Borenstein et al., 2009).

Additional Analyses. As the data included relationships between perceived mental fatigue and self-control performance for both high- and low-resource depletion manipulations, it was important to assess measures of central tendency and its dispersion to develop insights as to whether level of resource depletion should be treated as a meaningful moderator. If the variance of the synthesized effect is judged substantial (based primarily on Cochran's Q statistic for heterogeneity and the I^2 estimate of true heterogeneity; Higgins Thompson, Deeks, & Altman, 2003), the analysis should focus on identifying moderators—here, this would mean parsing the data by level of resource depletion.

Results

Preliminary Analyses. The results of the effect-wise analysis (ie, intraclass correlation, ICC) with study as the grouping variable suggest meaningful dependency among the reported effects is not present in the database (ICC = 0.09). Furthermore, the nonsignificant Q test for heterogeneity

($Q = 16.60$, $p < .34$) and the low percentage of true variance in the perceived depletion–self-control correlations ($I^2 = 6.62\%$) suggests that the perceived mental fatigue—self-control effects are not meaningfully stronger under high- or low-resource depletion conditions. The data were therefore collapsed across all conditions.

Perceived Mental Fatigue and Self-control Analysis. The data support a positive and statistically significant mean correlation between perceptions of mental fatigue and self-control. The mean of the effect size distribution for perceptions and self-control is equal to 0.36 ($p < .001$), an equivalent Cohen's d of 0.74. The fail-safe N of 853 (the number of missing, null effects necessary for the mean effect to be nonsignificant) suggests the estimate is likely absent meaningful publication bias.

CONCLUSION

In summary, the mean perceived mental fatigue—self-control effect is relatively large (*Cohen's* $d = 0.74$) and positively statistically significant. Importantly, this effect is robust, as it was shown to occur above and beyond differences in actual levels of resource depletion and generalizes to a variety of self-control indices. In turn, the results of the meta-analysis only further bolster the importance of perceptions of mental fatigue in predicting self-control behavior.

CONCEPTUAL IMPLICATIONS

This chapter focused on extant research on the consequence of perceptions of mental fatigue. These perceptions, once shown to covary with resource depletion manipulations as manipulation checks, now not only exert an independent influence apart from individuals' actual resource availability but are affected by factors beyond resource depletion manipulations (eg, mood states, lay beliefs of willpower capacity). Furthermore, research details the importance of executive functioning—and working memory capacity in particular—in driving the effects of perceived mental fatigue on self-control performance. Thus, the mounting body of research offers consistent evidence for the importance of perceived mental fatigue for individuals' self-control abilities.

Yet from a limited strength model of self-control (Baumeister et al., 1998; Vohs & Baumeister, 2011; see Chapter 1), should we be surprised that these perceptions of mental fatigue can exert such a significant impact on self-control performance? On one hand, perhaps so. Baumeister and colleagues' model of ego depletion argues that self-control constitutes a single process of resource availability. Here, self-control performance ebbs and flows as a direct function of the amount of resources available to exert self-control. Yet the findings from the Clarkson et al. (2010, 2011) studies could be construed as in direct opposition to a strict resource availability hypothesis. For instance, in those studies, a limited resource model would predict that only the resource depletion manipulation should impact self-control and that the information about the effects of the paper color should have no impact on individuals' performance. However, not only did the manipulation of resource depletion interact with state feedback to predict self-control performance, but no main effect of the depletion manipulation was observed in any of the studies.

However, in a less dogmatic sense, perhaps not. After all, both actual (Schmeichel, 2007) and perceived (Clarkson et al., 2010; 2011) mental fatigue impact working memory capacity, and working memory capacity has been shown to be central to the cognitive processes underlying self-control (Schmeichel et al., 2008; see also Ilkowska & Engle, 2010). Moreover, research shows that factors can immediately restore a depleted resource capacity (see Chapter 12 on restoration). Thus, perceptions of mental fatigue might offer an important revision to the conceptualization of strength within this model. That is, conceptualizing regulatory strength in terms of perceptions as well as actual abilities still explains the ebb and flow of performance as a function of resource exertion (recall perceptions tend to covary with actual resource depletion) while also accounting for dramatic shifts in resource availability not readily explained by motivational processes.

CONCLUDING REMARKS

This review sought to detail existing research on the impact of individuals' perceptions of mental fatigue for subsequent self-control. As models of self-control continue to evolve, it will be interesting to see what role individuals' subjective assessments of mental fatigue have in elucidating the underlying processes responsible for successful self-control. From our perspective, these perceptions offer potential to exert a significant influence at multiple stages of the self-control process. For instance, the perception of mental fatigue might impact the *agency* (ie, how we use our regulatory resources; Muraven et al., 2006; see also Chapter 7), *allocation* (ie, where we use our regulatory resources; Inzlicht & Schmeichel, 2012), and/or *efficacy* (ie, our confidence in our resources to incite successful regulation; Bandura, 1977) of our self-regulatory resources to maximize the process of goal pursuit. For now, though, it is clear that the role of perceived mental fatigue exerts a significant influence that must be taken into account if we hope to grasp the intricacies of the self-control process.

Now pause again, only this time reflect on how mentally alert, focused, and energized you feel. A silly exercise, perhaps, but—given the extant literature on mental fatigue reviewed in this chapter—one that can hold significant consequence for your ability to successfully engage in self-control.

References

Albarracín, D., Handley, I. M., Noguchi, K., McCulloch, K. C., Li, H., Leeper, J., ... Hart, W. P. (2008). Increasing and decreasing motor and cognitive output: a model of general action and inaction goals. *Journal of Personality and Social Psychology, 95*, 510–523.

Albarracín, D., Hepler, J., & Tannenbaum, M. (2011). General action and inaction goals: their behavioral, cognitive, and affective origins and influences. *Current Directions in Psychological Science, 20*, 119–123.

Altemeyer, B. (1998). *The other "authoritarian personality"*. San Diego: Academic Press, 47–92.

Baddeley, A. D. (1986). *Working memory*. New York: Clarendon Press.

Bandura, A. (1977). Self-efficacy: toward a unifying theory of behavioral change. *Psychological Review, 84*, 191–215.

Baumeister, R. F., Bratslavsky, E., Muraven, M., & Tice, D. M. (1998). Ego depletion: is the active self a limited resource? *Journal of Personality and Social Psychology, 74*, 1252–1265.

Becker, B. J. (2009). Model-based meta-analysis. In H. M. Cooper, L. V. Hedges, & J. Valentine (Eds.), *The handbook of research synthesis and meta-analysis* (2nd ed.) (pp. 377–395). New York: Russell Sage Foundation.

Beilock, S. L., & Carr, T. H. (2005). When high-powered people fail: working memory and "choking under pressure" in math. *Psychological Science, 16*, 101–105.

Borenstein, M., Hedges, L. V., Higgins, J., & Rothstein, H. R. (2009). *Introduction to meta-analysis*. Chichester (UK): John Wiley & Sons.

Cacioppo, J. T., & Petty, R. E. (1982). The need for cognition. *Journal of Personality and Social Psychology, 42*, 116–131.

Clarkson, J. J., Hirt, E. R., Chapman, D. A., & Jia, L. (2011). The impact of illusory fatigue on executive control: do perceptions of depletion impair working memory capacity? *Social Psychological and Personality Science, 2*, 231–238.

Clarkson, J. J., Hirt, E. R., & Jia, L. (2016). *The influence of need for closure on the formation of regulatory perceptions*, Working paper.

Clarkson, J. J., Hirt, E. R., Jia, L., & Alexander, M. B. (2010). When perception is more than reality: the effects of perceived versus actual resource depletion on self-regulatory behavior. *Journal of Personality and Social Psychology, 98*, 29–46.

Clarkson, J. J., Otto, A. S., Hirt, E. R., & Egan, P. M. (2016). *The malleable efficacy of willpower theories*, Working paper.

Egan, P. M., Clarkson, J. J., & Hirt, E. R. (2015). Revisiting the restorative effects of positive mood: an expectancy-based approach to self-control restoration. *Journal of Experimental Social Psychology, 57*, 87–99.

Egan, P. M., & Hirt, E. R. (2015). Flipping the switch: power, social dominance, and expectancies of mental energy change. *Personality & Social Psychology Bulletin, 41*, 336–350.

Engle, R. W. (2002). Working memory capacity as executive attention. *Current Directions in Psychological Science, 11*, 19–23.

Fredrickson, B. L., Mancuso, R. A., Branigan, C., & Tugade, M. M. (2000). The undoing effect of positive emotions. *Motivation and Emotion, 24*, 237–258.

Fujita, K. (2011). On conceptualizing self-control as more than the effortful inhibition of impulses. *Personality and Social Psychology Review, 15*, 352–366.

Galinsky, A. D., Gruenfeld, D. H., & Magee, J. C. (2003). From power to action. *Journal of Personality and Social Psychology, 85*, 453–466.

Galinsky, A. D., Magee, J. C., Gruenfeld, D. H., Whitson, J. A., & Liljenquist, K. A. (2008). Power reduces the press of the situation: implications for creativity, conformity, and dissonance. *Journal of Personality and Social Psychology, 95*, 1450–1466.

Hagger, M. S., Wood, C., Stiff, C., & Chatzisarantis, N. L. D. (2010). Ego depletion and the strength model of self-control: a meta-analysis. *Psychological Bulletin, 136*, 495–525.

Hedges, L. V., & Pigott, T. D. (2001). The power of statistical tests in meta-analysis. *Psychological Methods, 6*, 203–217.

Higgins, J. P., Thompson, S. G., Deeks, J. J., & Altman, D. G. (2003). Measuring inconsistency in meta-analyses. *Bmj: British Medical Journal, 327*, 557–560.

Hofmann, W., Gschwender, T., Friese, M., Wiers, R. W., & Schmitt, M. (2008). Working memory capacity and self-regulatory behavior: toward an individual differences perspective on behavior determination by automatic versus controlled processes. *Journal of Personality and Social Psychology, 95*, 962–977.

Hofmann, W., Schmeichel, B. J., & Baddeley, A. D. (2012). Executive functions and self-regulation. *Trends in Cognitive Sciences, 16*, 174–180.

Ilkowska, M., & Engle, R. W. (2010). Working memory capacity and self-regulation. In R. H. Hoyle (Ed.), *Handbook of personality and self-regulation* (pp. 265–290). Oxford, UK: Wiley-Blackwell.

Inzlicht, M., & Schmeichel, B. J. (2012). What is ego depletion? toward a mechanistic revision of the resource model of self-control. *Perspectives on Psychological Science, 7*, 450–463.

Job, V., Bernecker, K., Miketta, S., & Friese, M. (2015). Implicit theories about willpower predict the activation of a rest goal following self-control exertion. *Journal of Personality and Social Psychology, 109*, 694–706.

Job, V., Dweck, C. S., & Walton, G. M. (2010). Ego depletion-is it all in your head? Implicit theories about willpower affect self-regulation. *Psychological Science, 21*, 1686–1693.

Job, V., Walton, G. M., Bernecker, K., & Dweck, C. S. (2013). Beliefs about willpower determine the impact of glucose on self-control. *Proceedings of the National Academy of Sciences, 110*, 14837–14842.

Job, V., Walton, G. M., Bernecker, K., & Dweck, C. S. (2015). Implicit theories about willpower predict self-regulation and grades in everyday life. *Journal of Personality and Social Psychology, 108*, 637–647.

Judge, T. A., & Bono, J. E. (2001). Relationship of core self-evaluation traits – self-esteem, generalized self-efficacy, locus of control, and emotional stability with job satisfaction and job performance: a meta-analysis. *Journal of Applied Psychology, 86*, 80–92.

Just, M. A., & Carpenter, P. A. (1992). A capacity theory of comprehension: individual differences in working memory. *Psychological Review, 99*, 122–149.

Leith, K. P., & Baumeister, R. F. (1996). Why do bad moods increase self-defeating behavior? Emotion, risk taking, and self-regulation. *Journal of Personality and Social Psychology, 71*, 1250–1267.

Martijn, C., Tenbült, P., Merckelbach, H., Dreezens, E., & De Vries, N. K. (2002). Getting a grip on ourselves: challenging expectancies about loss of energy after self-control. *Social Cognition, 20*, 441–460.

Miller, E. M., Walton, G. M., Dweck, C. S., Job, V., Trzesniewski, K. H., & McClure, S. M. (2012). Theories of willpower affect sustained learning. *PLoS One, 7*, e38680.

Muraven, M., Shmueli, D., & Burkley, E. (2006). Conserving self-control strength. *Journal of Personality and Social Psychology, 91*, 524–537.

Muraven, M., Tice, D. M., & Baumeister, R. F. (1998). Self-control as limited resource: regulatory depletion patterns. *Journal of Personality and Social Psychology, 74*, 774–789.

Peterson, R. A., & Brown, S. P. (2005). On the use of beta coefficients in meta-analysis. *Journal of Applied Psychology, 90*, 175–181.

Petty, R. E., Briñol, P., Tormala, Z. L., & Wegener, D. T. (2007). The role of meta-cognition in social judgment. In A. W. Kruglanski, & E. Tory Higgins (Eds.), *Social psychology: Handbook of basic principles* (2nd ed.) (pp. 254–284). New York: Guilford Press.

Pratto, F., Sidanius, J., Stallworth, L. M., & Malle, B. F. (1994). Social dominance orientation: a personality variable predicting social and political attitudes. *Journal of Personality and Social Psychology, 67*, 741–763.

Ross, L., Lepper, M. R., & Hubbard, M. (1975). Perseverance in self-perception and social perception: biased attributional processes in the debriefing paradigm. *Journal of Personality and Social Psychology, 32*, 880–892.

Ryan, R. M., & Frederick, C. (1997). On energy, personality, and health: subjective vitality as a dynamic reflection of well-being. *Journal of Personality, 65*, 529–565.

Rydell, R. J., McConnell, A. R., & Beilock, S. L. (2009). Multiple social identities and stereotype threat: imbalance, accessibility, and working memory. *Journal of Personality and Social Psychology, 96,* 949–966.

Schachter, S., & Singer, J. (1962). Cognitive, social, and physiological determinants of emotional state. *Psychological Review, 69,* 379–399.

Schmader, T., & Johns, M. (2003). Converging evidence that stereotype threat reduces working memory capacity. *Journal of Personality and Social Psychology, 85,* 440–452.

Schmeichel, B. J. (2007). Attention control, memory updating, and emotion regulation temporarily reduce the capacity for executive control. *Journal of Experimental Psychology: General, 136,* 241–255.

Schmeichel, B. J., Vohs, K. D., & Baumeister, R. F. (2003). Intellectual performance and ego depletion: role of the self in logical reasoning and other information processing. *Journal of Personality and Social Psychology, 85,* 33–46.

Schmeichel, B. J., Volokhov, R. N., & Demaree, H. A. (2008). Working memory capacity and the self-regulation of emotional expression and experience. *Journal of Personality and Social Psychology, 95,* 1526–1540.

Shamosh, N. A., & Gray, J. R. (2007). The relation between fluid intelligence and self-regulatory depletion. *Cognition & Emotion, 21,* 1833–1843.

Smets, E. M. A., Garssen, B., Bonke, B., & De Haes, J. C. J.M. (1995). The multidimensional fatigue inventory (MFI) psychometric qualities of an instrument to assess fatigue. *Journal of Psychosomatic Research, 39,* 315–325.

Tice, D. M., Baumeister, R. F., Shmueli, D., & Muraven, M. (2007). Restoring the self: positive affect helps improve self-regulation following ego depletion. *Journal of Experimental Social Psychology, 43,* 379–384.

Unsworth, N., Heitz, R. P., Schrock, J. C., & Engle, R. W. (2005). An automated version of the operation span task. *Behavior Research Methods, 37,* 498–505.

Vohs, K. D., & Baumeister, R. F. (Eds.). (2011). *Handbook of self-regulation: Research, theory, and applications.* New York: Guilford Press.

CHAPTER 11

Implicit Theories About Willpower

V. Job

University of Zurich, Zurich, Switzerland

Over a century ago, William James (1907) argued that "ideas set free beliefs, and that beliefs set free our wills" (p. 14). James was convinced that many people live at low levels of power and engagement because they habitually, based on their beliefs, yield to feelings of fatigue (Bernecker, 2015). Recent research supports his notion and argues that people's beliefs—*their implicit theories*—about their willpower are an important determinant of their actual willpower and, as a result their engagement. In particular, the belief that willpower is a limited resource that is easily depleted seems to undermine self-control and cause people to fall short of their potential (Job, Dweck, & Walton, 2010). In this chapter, I will provide an overview of research my collaborators and I, as well as other research groups, have conducted to examine the effects of people's implicit theories about willpower on self-control. We show these effects on people's ability to maintain high performance on consecutive tasks in the laboratory and on their ability to maintain optimal self-regulatory, emotional, and performance outcomes in the face of high demands in everyday life.

The strength model of self-control suggests that acts of self-control, indeed, consume a limited resource, leaving people in a state of *ego depletion* and making them less able to exert self-control on subsequent tasks (eg, Baumeister, Bratslavsky, Muraven, & Tice, 1998; Baumeister, Vohs, & Tice, 2007). Therefore, our research started out as a challenge to the strength model by suggesting that ego depletion is not an inevitable state determined by physiological processes. Instead, it is, at least in part, created by people's beliefs and expectations about willpower. However, since these first findings continuing research on implicit theories about willpower reached beyond a mere critique to the strength model. It also informed our knowledge about processes (eg, self-efficacy or rest-goal activation) accounting for reduced self-regulatory performance after previous self-control exertion and in the face of high self-control demands.

IMPLICIT THEORIES: THEORETICAL BACKGROUND AND MEASUREMENT

The research on implicit theories about willpower highlights the power of people's beliefs to determine their experiences and their behavior. It is grounded in the broader research framework on implicit theories about personal attributes, which has a long tradition in social psychology (Dweck, 1986; Dweck & Leggett, 1988; Hong, Chiu, Dweck, Lin, & Wan, 1999; Molden & Dweck, 2006). Implicit theories are "people's basic assumptions about themselves and their world" (Dweck, 1996, p. 69). Similar to scientists who develop theories to explain phenomena in the world, laypersons hold theories and beliefs about different personal characteristics, such as intelligence, personality, or health (Burnette, O'Boyle, VanEpps, Pollack, & Finkel, 2013; Dweck, Chiu, & Hong, 1995). In contrast to scientific theories, laypersons' theories are often implicit in the sense that their holders are not aware of them and how they affect their behavior. However, people are typically capable of recognizing their theories when they are made explicit on questionnaires.

The study of personal beliefs goes back to Jean Piaget who argued that children develop so-called meaning systems that guide their behavior (Piaget, 1964; Piaget & Garcia, 1991). Likewise, George Kelly (1955) proposed that each individual has a unique set of conceptual representations that he or she uses to construct meaning in their world. Building on these theoretical traditions, Carol Dweck and her colleagues began to examine children's beliefs about intelligence—whether it is a fixed versus malleable trait—and their effect on persistence in difficult tasks and helpless reactions to setbacks (Dweck, 1986; Dweck & Leggett, 1988). This line of research built the groundwork for the social-cognitive framework of motivation and self-regulation (Dweck, 1999; Molden & Dweck, 2006). The framework proposes that implicit theories about intelligence or other personal attributes channel different cognitive, affective, and behavioral patterns in relevant situations by shaping peoples' goals, expectations, and interpretations. Numerous studies showed that implicit theories have an effect on outcomes in different life areas such as academic performance (Blackwell, Trzesniewski, & Dweck, 2007), romantic relationships (Knee, 1993), health (Crum & Langer, 2007), or intergroup conflict (Halperin et al., 2012) by shaping peoples goals and motivational orientations and, consequentially, their behavior.

Recently, the idea of implicit theories that shape people's motivation and behavior was applied to the context of self-control (Job et al., 2010; Martijn,

Tenbult, Merckelbach, Dreezens, & De Vries, 2002; Mukhopadhyay & Johar, 2005). The core hypothesis was that people differ in the degree in which their beliefs about willpower correspond with the strength model of self-control—whether they think that self-control is a limited resource—and that these beliefs determine their self-control capacity.

Carolien Martijn et al. (2002) proposed a precursor of this idea. They developed a 20-item scale that articulated diverse beliefs about the relation between self-control exertion and tiredness ("After trying to control my emotions, I feel tired") and about self-control being a matter of motivation ("If I am really motivated, I always manage to control myself"). They showed that participants on average agreed more with the belief that self-control is tiring. However, they did not investigate whether their scale predicted actual self-control performance.

Following up on these initial steps, we developed a scale that focused on the belief in willpower as a limited and easily depleted resource (*limited-resource theory*; eg, "After a strenuous mental activity your energy is depleted and you must rest to get it refueled again"). Thereby, the reverse-coded items (eg, "After a strenuous mental activity, you feel energized for further challenging activities") refer to the opposite believe. They reject the idea that willpower is highly constraint and, instead, propose that exerting willpower can even be energizing. We called the latter belief a *nonlimited* theory of willpower. We intentionally do not use the term "unlimited." People with a nonlimited theory may not believe that willpower is infinite or that they can engage in self-control tasks endlessly without needing to rest and sleep eventually. However, they reject the view that willpower is easily depleted by any act of self-control.

The scale assessing implicit theories about willpower with regard to strenuous mental activity proved to predict self-control on mental tasks in the laboratory (Job et al., 2010; Job, Walton, Bernecker, & Dweck, 2013) and self-regulation in the academic context (Job, Walton, Bernecker, & Dweck, 2015). An analysis over multiple datasets collected in the United States, Switzerland, and Germany, confirms measurement invariance and speaks to adequate psychometric properties (Napolitano & Job, 2016).

In line with the study reported by Martijn et al. (2002), our data show that participants from US and European samples on average agree more with a limited-resource theory (Napolitano & Job, 2016). Typically, the mean is significantly different from the scale midpoint. However, as a recent set of studies suggest, this is not the case in all cultures. In the Indian cultural context people tend to agree less with a limited theory about willpower and, instead, think that engaging in strenuous mental activity can be energizing and facilitating for consecutive performance (Savani & Job, 2016).

Depending on the research question and the purpose of a study, later research included additional scales assessing beliefs about resistance to temptation, emotion control, and physical exertion (Bernecker & Job, 2015a). The subscales represent distinct factors that best predict specific behavior when they are matched to the behavior in question. For example, in a study conducted with diabetes 2 patients, a limited-resource theory in the domain of resisting temptations was related to a less-healthy diet and a limited-resource theory with regard to strenuous physical activity to a less-physical activity (Bernecker & Job, 2015a).

The implicit theories about willpower scales we used so far are certainly not exhaustive and it is up to future research to include other possible self-control domains. Further, thinking in terms of a limited versus nonlimited resource does not represent the only dimension in which people can think about willpower. Mukhopadhyay and Johar (2005) proposed that besides believing that willpower can be a limited versus nonlimited resource people also think of it as fixed versus malleable. I will return to their research later in the chapter.

MODERATING THE EGO-DEPLETION EFFECT

The first set of studies about implicit theories about willpower that my collaborators Carol Dweck, Greg Walton, and I conducted aimed at challenging the strength model of self-control or at least its prediction of rapid, universal ego depletion and its explanation for the ego-depletion effect. We asked the question whether ego depletion is "all in your head," whether it occurs only if people believe that willpower is a limited resource (Job et al., 2010).

In a first study, we tested the hypothesis that peoples' habitual implicit theories about willpower, as assessed with the implicit theories about strenuous mental activity scale, would moderate the ego-depletion effect. After filling in the implicit theories about willpower scale, participants completed an "e-crossing task," a procedure adopted from previous research to manipulate depletion (Baumeister et al., 1998; Tice, Baumeister, Shmueli, & Muraven, 2007; Wheeler, Brinol, & Hermann, 2007). As a dependent measure of subsequent self-control performance, the Stroop task was administered (Inzlicht, McKay, & Aronson, 2006; Webb & Sheeran, 2003). Analyses showed that we replicated the traditional ego-depletion effect since there was a main effect of depletion condition on the number of mistakes in the Stroop task. However, the results also supported the hypothesis that implicit theories about willpower moderate ego depletion. Only participants who held a limited-resource theory showed ego depletion as indicated by making more mistakes on the Stroop task after the initial depleting task than after the nondepleting task.

Recently, these results were replicated in a study by Stefanie Salmon and colleagues (Salmon, Adriaanse, de Vet, Fennis, & de Ridder, 2014). They assessed people's beliefs about willpower with a slightly broader measure (Depletion Sensitivity Scale), which contains items that are similar to our strenuous mental activities scale ("I have difficulties focusing my attention after I exerted a lot of effort"). Participants were depleted with the same e-crossing manipulation and subsequent cognitive performance was assessed with a complex reasoning task. The results showed that the more participants indicated a belief that their self-control capacity is limited, the more they were prone to show the ego-depletion effect. Participants who did not hold this belief were not affected by the depletion manipulation.

Since in the abovementioned studies implicit theories about willpower were only measured, they cannot rule out the possibility that third variables (eg, trait self-control or glucose metabolism) are responsible for the effects. Hence, in a next step it was important to test the causal effect of implicit theories about willpower and to investigate whether manipulated theories moderate ego depletion too.

To temporarily manipulate people's theories about willpower, we developed two biased questionnaires containing easy-to-agree-with items that either endorsed a limited or a nonlimited resource theory (eg, "Working on a strenuous mental task can make you feel tired such that you need a break before accomplishing a new task" versus "Sometimes, working on a strenuous mental task can make you feel energized for further challenging activities"). Two experimental studies found that this manipulation of theories about willpower has the same effect on self-control performance following depletion as the measured theories had. Whereas participants who had been led to endorse the limited resource theory showed ego depletion, participants who had been led to endorse the nonlimited theory showed no such evidence—their self-control performance did not drop following the initial depleting task and, if anything, it tended to rise.

In sum, in the classic dual task paradigm, only people who thought of or who were led to think of willpower as a limited resource showed ego depletion. By contrast, for people who had or were led to adopt a nonlimited-resource theory, a demanding initial task did not undermine subsequent performance. These results indicated that ego depletion results not from a true lack of resources after a demanding task, but from people's beliefs about their resources.

MECHANISMS

The initial studies indicated that theories about willpower moderate ego depletion, that is, they predict self-control performance following previous self-control exertion. How exactly does this happen? What are the processes explaining the effect of willpower theories on actual performance that looks like a self-fulfilling prophecy? So far, several mechanisms that may be involved in the effects of willpower theories on performance have been explored: perceived fatigue, sensitivity to cues about the availability of resources, activation of a rest goal, and self-efficacy. I will describe them in the following paragraphs.

Perceived Exhaustion

The first mechanism that we explored was perceived exhaustion. A series of experiments conducted by Joshua Clarkson and colleagues suggest, that whether people show ego depletion or not depends on whether they perceive that a previous task exhausted their resources rather than whether they really exerted self-control or not (Clarkson, Hirt, Jia, & Alexander, 2010; see Chapter 7). Hence, one may wonder whether implicit theories about willpower determine how exhausting people experience a self-control task to be. It could be that a limited theory about willpower makes people experience self-control exertion as more exhausting evoking a stronger feeling of exhaustion and in turn reducing subsequent performance. To test this assumption, we included self-report questions about perceived exhaustion ("How exhausting was the task?") in one of the abovementioned experiments, where implicit theories about willpower were manipulated. The results showed, first, that theories about willpower did not affect the experience of the depleting task as exhausting. People with a nonlimited-resource theory experienced the depleting task as just as exhausting as those with a limited-resource theory (Job et al., 2010; Study 3). Later studies confirmed this finding showing that implicit theories about willpower have no effect on depletion manipulation checks (perceived amount of required self-control and perceived exhaustion) administered after the depletion manipulation (Job, Bernecker, Miketta, & Friese, 2015).

However, perceived exhaustion proved to be involved in the effect of willpower theories on ego depletion. Mediation analyses showed that perception of exhaustion mediated the effects of the depletion manipulation in participants with a limited-resource theory, but not for participants with a nonlimited-resource theory. That is, implicit theories about willpower affect the relationship between the experience of exhaustion and subsequent self-control performance. People with a nonlimited-resource theory feel just as exhausted after the depleting task as those with a limited-resource theory but for them exhaustion does not undermine subsequent performance. This result indicates that only for people with a limited theory exhaustion is a sign to reduce effort whereas nonlimited people are much less responsive to perceptions of exhaustion.

Sensitivity to Cues About the Availability of Resources

The findings on perceived exhaustion provide initial evidence that people with a limited resource theory perform worse after a demanding task because they are sensitive to cues about the availability of mental resources. This resource sensitivity hypothesis is supported by another set of studies, which link the theories about willpower to the finding that ingested glucose too, buffers the ego-depletion effect (Job, Walton, Bernecker, & Dweck, 2013).

Recent research on the performance enhancing effect of glucose suggests that ingested glucose serves as a cue about the availability of resources. It is assumed that peripheral sensory receptors in the mouth and digestive system specifically sensitive to glucose activate reward regions in the brain (Chambers, Bridge, & Jones, 2009; Kringelbach, 2004; Kurzban, 2010). For example, studies showed that even a mere glucose mouth rinse boosts physical performance and buffers the ego-depletion effect (Hagger & Chatzisarantis, 2013; Molden et al., 2012; Sanders, Shirk, Burgin, & Martin, 2012). Thus, people who have ingested glucose may perform better because these peripheral cues signal the likely availability of energy, motivating them to sustain effort on difficult tasks. Because we assumed that only people with a limited theory about willpower would be sensitive to signals about the availability of resources, we postulated that theories about willpower would moderate the effect of glucose on subsequent performance.

Three experiments tested the joint effect of implicit theories about willpower and glucose ingestion on self-control performance following an initial demanding task. Implicit theories about willpower were either measured (Study 1) or manipulated (Studies 2 and 3) and participants drank and evaluated lemonade sweetened with either sugar or a sugar substitute. A Stroop task measured self-control capacity following previous self-control exertion on an unrelated task. The results confirmed our hypothesis and showed that the effect of glucose on self-control performance after a demanding task depends on people's theories about willpower. Only participants with a limited-resource theory performed better after consuming sugar. They showed the typical glucose-enhancement effect on performance. However, participants with a nonlimited theory showed no difference between the sugar and nonsugar conditions—they performed well in both cases.

These results provided further evidence against the theory that self-control relies on a limited physiological resource that is depleted by even brief acts of self-control and is restored by glucose consumption (Gailliot & Baumeister, 2007; Gailliot et al., 2007). Again, only those who believe that willpower relies on a limited resource showed poor performance without sugar and a replenishment effect with sugar. The results support the assumption that people with a limited-resource theory are responsive to cues about the availability of resources. Interestingly, they were responsive to glucose even without being able to tell it apart from the sugar-substitute drink. This result documents how top-down beliefs interact with physiological bottom-up information in influencing peoples' self-control capacity. Future research may further analyze and test these mechanisms.

Activation of a Rest Goal

In another line of studies, we asked the question about concrete motivational processes accounting for the differences in self-control performance between people holding a limited versus nonlimited theory about willpower as a response to previous self-control exertion (Job et al., 2015). We grounded our reasoning in the process model of self-control (Inzlicht & Schmeichel, 2012; Inzlicht, Schmeichel, & Macrae, 2014). It proposes that after they exert self-control, people are no longer motivated to exert themselves further and therefore perform worse on subsequent self-control tasks. Akin to this theorizing, we proposed that the effect of implicit theories about willpower on self-control performance can be explained by a change in the motivational orientation, triggered by the initial exertion of self-control and the perception of low availability of resources. We postulated that specifically for people with a limited-resource theory, as compared to people with a nonlimited-resource theory, exerting self-control activates the goal to preserve and replenish mental resources (rest goal), which translates into actual resting behavior.

Because it is well documented that people possess limited introspective abilities that often lead to invalid self-reports about inner motivational states (eg, Silvia & Gendolla, 2001; Wilson & Dunn, 2004), we used indirect implicit and behavioral indicators to assess a motivational shift toward rest after depletion. We relied on procedures to assess manifestations of rest goal activation based on reaction times (RTs), object evaluations, and actual resting behavior.

A first study was designed to test this hypothesis with accessibility of rest-related concepts as an indicator of rest goal activation. Previous research has indicated that active, unfulfilled goals enhance the accessibility of goal-related concepts (eg, Aarts & Dijksterhuis, 2003; Förster, Liberman, & Higgins, 2005). For example, Förster et al. (2005) showed that participants who had the goal to find a specific target stimulus showed enhanced accessibility of target-related words prior to finding the target and reduced accessibility after finding it. Therefore, we figured that an active rest goal should manifest as higher accessibility of rest-related concepts in the semantic network. Our first study tested the hypothesis that theories about willpower predict the accessibility of a rest goal following self-control exertion. Theories about willpower were measured with the strenuous mental activity scale. Next, ego depletion was manipulated with a thought suppression task (Muraven, Tice, & Baumeister, 1998). Finally, accessibility of a rest goal was measured using a lexical-decision task (Meyer & Schvaneveldt, 1971), one of the most widely used tasks to measure cognitive accessibility in the semantic network (Higgins, 1996). A series of letter strings was presented in the center of a screen and participants were asked to decide as quickly as possible whether a letter string was a real word. The results confirmed out hypothesis. In the depletion condition, the more participants endorsed a limited-resource theory, the faster they were in recognizing rest-related words as words. Hence, whereas previous research has documented that individuals with a limited-resource theory show impaired performance on self-control tasks following self-control exertion (Job et al., 2010), their performance regarding rest words was better (ie, shorter RTs) after self-control exertion in this study.

Next, two studies were run to conceptually replicate this finding and to provide evidence for the proposed causal relationship. For that purpose, we drew on the previous finding that activated goals affect how people evaluate objects. Specifically, objects that are means to a current goal are evaluated more positively than goal irrelevant objects (Ferguson & Bargh, 2004; Fishbach, Shah, & Kruglanski, 2004). In our studies, we tested whether people with a limited-resource theory would more strongly value means to reach the goal to rest and recover after they exerted self-control. We created a set of pictures depicting objects that are helpful for getting rest (bed, sofa, hammock, cup of tea, bathtub, TV screen) and pictures depicting objects that are used for physical or mental exertion (barbell, racing bicycle, punching bag, treadmill, sneakers, Sudoku puzzles). After filling in the theories about willpower scale and completing the depletion manipulation, participants were asked for each of the objects how much they liked it. Results showed that in the high-depletion condition, endorsement of a limited-resource theory was associated with more positive evaluations of rest-conducive objects. Furthermore, participants with a limited-resource theory devaluated objects conducive to physical and mental exertion. This result indicates that after self-control exertion, a limited-resource theory about willpower may affect motivational orientation in both directions; that is, people are inclined to value rest and recovery and devalue activities that involve high effort and exertion. A second study with the same paradigm manipulating theories about willpower confirmed this result. Participants who were led to adopt a limited-resource theory evaluated objects conducive to rest more positively when they were depleted than when they were not depleted.

Finally, an activated rest goal should translate into actual resting behavior. Therefore, two further studies tested the question of whether participants with a limited-resource theory would engage in more resting behavior after depletion. The first study had a correlational design, testing whether theories about willpower predicted the length of a break participants took after an initial depleting task. That was exactly the case. The more participants endorsed a limited-resource theory, the longer they rested before continuing with another task. A second study tested the causal effect of theories about willpower in interaction with depletion on resting behavior. Theories about willpower were manipulated with the biased questionnaire and participants were randomly assigned to a low- versus high-depletion condition. Consecutive resting behavior was assessed with an ostensible product-testing task: Participants were asked to take a seat on several chairs and to rate them later. A hidden camera filmed the product-testing session and participants' sitting times on each chair were recorded. We used the length of time sitting on the chairs as the indicator for the need to rest after self-control exertion given that it provides an opportunity to relax and to fulfill one's rest goal. The results supported our hypothesis. Only participants with a limited-resource theory sat longer on the chairs of the ostensible product-testing task after they had worked on a previously depleting self-control task. Participants with a nonlimited-resource theory showed no difference between the two depletion conditions.

These data show that exerting self-control in an initial task causes a motivational shift toward rest in individuals who believe that willpower is a limited resource. The findings support the process model of self-control, which denies the existence of a specialized self-control resource and explains ego depletion effects by shifts in motivation and attention (Inzlicht & Schmeichel, 2012; Inzlicht et al., 2014). It postulates that after having expended effort in a strenuous task, people are less motivated to expend further effort. Our research adds one important specification to the model: Only individuals who believed (or were led to believe) that the ability to self-control is limited showed the motivational shift toward rest.

The results of the rest-goal studies suggest that the limited-resource theory makes people seek rest after they exerted self-control. We assume that it is this motivational orientation toward rest that undermines their subsequent self-control performance. Hence, a nonlimited-resource theory buffers the ego-depletion effect because it breaks a process that undermines self-control performance by turning people's attention toward rest and inaction. For this reason, a nonlimited-resource theory about willpower cannot simply be grouped with factors that boost motivation after depletion, such as monetary incentives to perform well on a second task (Muraven & Slessareva, 2003). Strong incentives may cause people to exert high effort on a task even when they feel tired. In this case, they might conquer the need for rest and inhibit their activated rest goal. On the contrary, the belief that willpower is not limited does not make people more motivated to engage in self-control despite the desire for rest. Rather, they show better self-control performance because they are not oriented toward resting in the first place.

Changes in Self-efficacy

A recent line of research suggests a further mechanism involved in the ego-depletion effect and in the effect of people's implicit theories about willpower: Changes in self-efficacy. Self-efficacy refers to "judgment of how well one can execute courses of action required to deal with prospective situations" (Bandura, 1982, p. 122). It is an important determinant of task engagement, since people tend to engage effort in tasks that they perceive to have high self-efficacy and withdraw from tasks that seem too difficult to them. Jason Chow and colleagues (Chow, Hui, & Lau, 2015) proposed that when people exert self-control their self-efficacy for upcoming tasks is temporarily reduced, which in turn impairs their further performance. Concretely, they argued that self-efficacy is strategically reduced if individuals are motivated to preserve their resources. Since this is particularly the case if people hold a limited theory about willpower, it should be only limited theorists who report reduced self-efficacy after they exerted self-control. For people with a nonlimited theory about willpower, this should not be the case. Accordingly, Chow and colleagues predicted that only people with a limited theory would exhibit reduced self-efficacy for future self-control exertion, which would mediate the ego-depletion effect.

The results of three experiments supported their assumption. First, they showed that participants who were depleted by an initial self-control task reported reduced self-efficacy in domains that require self-control. A second study confirmed that this reduction in self-efficacy mediated the effect of a depletion manipulation on subsequent self-control performance. Finally, a third experiment confirmed that only people with a limited theory about willpower showed this drop in self-efficacy following self-control exertion. In this experiment, self-efficacy mediated the moderating effect of implicit theories about willpower on ego depletion.

This research adds further evidence for the moderating effect of theories about willpower on self-control after previous depletion. It also provides evidence for the motivational-shift assumption postulated in the process model of self-control (Inzlicht & Schmeichel, 2012; Inzlicht et al., 2014) with the extension that these motivational shifts do not only refer to values and incentives (what would I like to do?) but also the expectations (what am I able to do?). Our research and that of Chow and colleagues suggest that both are determined by people's implicit theories about willpower.

EFFECTS OF IMPLICIT THEORIES ABOUT WILLPOWER IN EVERYDAY LIFE

The laboratory experiments showed that implicit theories about willpower predict remaining self-control capacity after participants completed a task that put high demands on their self-control. Only people who believe that willpower is a limited resource show impaired self-control after they exert themselves on an unrelated self-control task. The next question was: Do people's implicit theories about willpower have an effect on their everyday behavior? And if so, what theory is functional for people's goal striving and as a consequence for their psychological adjustment? The strength model would suggest that understanding the limits of self-control capacity should help people to use their resources wisely and overall, improve self-regulation and well-being especially when demands are high (Vohs, Baumeister, & Schmeichel, 2012). However, we expected the opposite. As the previously described studies suggest, people with a limited resource theory act as though their self-control capacity is depleted long before they reach any actual limit. As a consequence, these people should reduce their effort on everyday tasks and engage in overindulgent behavior especially when they face high demands in their everyday life. In contrast, people with a nonlimited theory might stay engaged for a longer time. Even a little more persistence and less indulgence should, accumulated over a day, improve their everyday self-regulation, make them more successful in their goal striving, and, eventually, promote their subjective well-being.

Self-regulation

We expected that paralleling the laboratory findings, people with a limited theory about willpower would show impaired self-regulation in everyday life specifically when they face high demands. To test this assumption, we ran a first longitudinal study with college students (Job et al., 2010; Study 4). We tracked them across three time points, the last of which was during final exams. As indicators of everyday self-regulation, we assessed procrastination (eg, "How often did you watch TV instead of studying?") and eating behavior (how often in the previous week they had consumed several high fat or high sugar foods and drinks). The results showed that a limited-resource theory predicted worse self-regulation on both measures at the stressful time point (controlling for baseline self-regulation). During the week before their final exams students with a limited theory ate more unhealthy food and procrastinated more than students with a nonlimited theory. This was not the case with regard to self-regulation for the more relaxed time point in the middle of the term. These results were the first to support the hypothesis that the nonlimited-resource theory of willpower, compared with the limited-resource theory, predicts better self-regulation during periods of heightened stress.

The first study simply assumed that self-regulatory demands were high for all students at a particular time; that is, as final exams approached. Therefore, we conducted a second study where we assessed the level of self-regulatory demands for each student on a week-by-week basis so we could identify the students who faced consistently high demands and those who faced lower demands (Job et al., 2015). We hypothesized that a nonlimited theory about willpower would predict better self-regulatory outcomes among students who contended with high self-regulatory demands but not necessarily among students who faced low self-regulatory demands. The results confirmed this assumption. Students with a limited and a nonlimited theory reported similar self-regulatory demands. But only students with a limited theory responded to high demands with more self-regulation failures. Besides self-reported self-regulatory failure, this study included participants' end-of-term grade point average (GPA) as a further outcome that is determined in part by self-regulation and that is not self-report. What we found is that among students who took a heavy course load, students with the nonlimited theory earned higher grades than students with the limited theory.

A recent study extended this research to the context of diabetes (Bernecker & Job, 2015a). Patients diagnosed with this disease face particularly high self-control challenges because they have to follow a rigorous diabetes regimen. To control their blood sugar levels, patients have to adhere to a complex therapy throughout their entire life (American Diabetes Association, 2008). The daily prescription typically involves regular blood sugar testing, taking medication, following a low-glycemic diet, and engaging in physical exercise (Boule, Haddad, Kenny, Wells, & Sigal, 2001; Brand-Miller, Petocz, Hayne, & Colagiuri, 2003). We expected implicit theories about willpower to be related to how well patients adhere to their therapy. In a correlational study, type 2 diabetes patients completed the theories about willpower scale and filled in various questionnaires assessing therapy adherence (ie, self-care activities, diet, exercise) and psychological adjustment (ie, emotional distress, well-being, life quality). The findings suggest that among people with type 2 diabetes, endorsing a limited theory about willpower is associated with lower therapy adherence and poorer psychological adjustment. Participants with a limited theory reported fewer self-care activities, a less-healthy diet, and lower levels of physical activity than people with a nonlimited theory. They further reported higher emotional distress from the disease and experienced lower subjective well-being and life quality. Overall, the belief that willpower is nonlimited seems to be more adaptive for the adjustment to diabetes than the belief that willpower is limited. Further, the effect of willpower theories on self-care activities was moderated by diabetes duration. The pattern of the interaction suggests that the impact of willpower theories decreased with longer diabetes duration. We suspect that over time, self-care activities such as regular blood sugar monitoring become habitual, which means that they are more automatically enacted and less dependent on reflective processes like self-control (Rothman, Sheeran, & Wood, 2009).

Personal Goal Striving

Previous research has applied the implicit theories about willpower perspective to the context of personal goal striving. Mukhopadhyay and

Johar (2005) showed that measured and manipulated theories about willpower as being a limited versus nonlimited resource and as either malleable versus fixed affected the number of new year resolutions people set. Moreover, an experimental study showed that a manipulation of implicit theories about willpower affected people's success in the keeping of their resolutions. In their study, participants with a limited theory about willpower were less likely to succeed 4 months later, specifically if they had low self-efficacy. Hence, their studies provided first evidence for an effect of implicit theories about willpower on goal striving as indicated by goal setting as well as by goal attainment.

In our research, we further looked at what is happening in between goal setting and goal attainment. We tested the hypothesis that people with a limited theory about willpower would display impaired goal-related self-regulation specifically in the face of accumulating demands. In one of the abovementioned longitudinal studies (Job et al., 2010; Study 4), we assessed self-regulation with respect to a personal achievement–related goal. At T1, participants listed a personal goal that involved challenge and achievement. This goal was presented to participants at each time point, and they were asked how well they had regulated themselves in pursuing it (eg, "I was often not in the mood to do something for this goal"). The results showed that theories about willpower predicted a change in goal-related self-regulation in the week prior to students' final exams. Those who had a limited theory about willpower reported worse goal-related self-regulation as compared to students with a nonlimited theory.

A recent study, conducted by Katharina Bernecker, aimed to test whether willpower theories predict effective goal striving on a day-to-day basis depending on how many demands participants faced during the previous day. To that purpose, she used a daily diary method (Bernecker & Job, 2015b). She found that people with a nonlimited theory reported more effective goal striving throughout a day when their previous day was more versus less demanding. Additionally, she examined the role of day-specific expectations regarding progress and exhaustion (reported in the morning). A limited theory predicted lower expected progress on unpleasant tasks (but not on pleasant tasks) and higher expected exhaustion from unpleasant tasks (but not on pleasant tasks). Again, willpower theories predicted these expectations on the next day only when the previous day was highly demanding.

Well-Being

Personal goal progress is an important predictor for subjective well-being (Brunstein, 1993; Diener, Suh, Lucas, & Smith, 1999). As outlined earlier, viewing willpower as a nonlimited resource helps people to successfully strive for their personal goals, particularly as self-regulatory demands increase, and, thereby, promotes progress toward these goals. Therefore, in a next set of studies, we proposed that endorsing a nonlimited theory about willpower would be further related to higher subjective well-being (Bernecker, Herrmann, Brandstätter, & Job, 2015). A first correlational study found a strong relationship between theories about willpower and life satisfaction as well as affective well-being. The more participants endorsed a limited theory about willpower, the lower was their subjective well-being.

Next, a longitudinal study was conducted to test whether willpower theories predict a change in subjective well-being over the course of students' first year in college. Based on previous research, we assumed that demands increase over the course of the first year when final exams approach (Job et al., 2015; Oaten & Cheng, 2005). As expected, a limited theory about willpower predicted a negative trend in subjective well-being from a period with low demands (ie, beginning of the first year) to a period with high demands (ie, final exam period at the end of the first year).

A final longitudinal study replicated the finding that a limited theory predicts lower levels of well-being using a daily diary method to measure subjective well-being in a nondemanding phase (ie, beginning of a term) and in a demanding phase (ie, final exam period). The results confirmed that a limited theory about willpower predicts lower subjective well-being during a final-exam period. In addition, this study tested the proposed mechanism. Indeed, students with a nonlimited theory reported more effective goal striving (assessed in the diary phase) at the end of the term than students with a limited theory. They further reported more progress on three personal goals over the course of the term. Change in effective goal striving (from beginning to end) and change in personal goal progress (from beginning to end of term) were both positively related to change in life satisfaction (Bernecker et al., 2015, Study 3).

To sum, these findings suggest that the previously documented functionality of the nonlimited theory for self-control performance and academic achievement can be extended to well-being. A nonlimited theory about willpower encourages people to successfully strive for and make progress toward personally meaningful goals, and this investment pays off in terms of higher subjective well-being.

BOUNDARIES AND POSSIBLE NEGATIVE CONSEQUENCES

The findings I have presented thus far on self-regulation on consecutive tasks in the laboratory and on everyday self-regulation, goal striving, and well-being suggest that a nonlimited theory about willpower is more beneficial than a limited theory about willpower. However, some research points toward the possible boundary conditions for the positive effects of a nonlimited theory. Specifically, it has been argued that a nonlimited theory might be counterproductive under conditions of severe depletion and that it might have negative consequences in child-rearing practice. Finally, studies about related willpower theories (entity vs incremental) might suggest possible downsides of a nonlimited theory in the interpersonal context.

Overuse of Resources

Extending the research on implicit theories about willpower, Kathleen Vohs et al. (2012) raised an important question: Will the positive effect of a nonlimited theory hold when self-control demands are especially high? Vohs and colleagues hypothesized that a nonlimited theory about willpower could lead people to overuse their resources and that the positive effects that seem to emerge from that theory might simply reflect temporarily compensation for depleted resources. They suggested that people can compensate effectively in the face of mild or moderate self-control demands but not in the face of high demands. They assumed that "severe" depletion would eventually take its toll. In a laboratory experiment, they included three experimental conditions: a "no-depletion" condition in which participants completed no initial self-control tasks; a "mild-depletion" condition in which participants completed two initial self-control tasks; and a "severe-depletion" condition in which participants completed four initial self-control tasks. In addition, theories about willpower were manipulated with the biased questionnaire used in previous research. First, Vohs and colleagues replicated the finding that a nonlimited theory of willpower improves self-control in the "mild-depletion" condition. But in the "severe-depletion" condition, there was no positive effect of a nonlimited theory. Moreover, on one of two measures of self-control performance, the effect even reversed: participants led to adopt a limited-resource theory performed better. Vohs and colleagues concluded that a nonlimited theory can be counterproductive. Thinking that willpower is nonlimited, they write, "might undermine the normal tendency to conserve resources (Muraven, Shmueli, & Burkley, 2006) so that people find themselves severely depleted after multiple tasks" (p. 186).

One important aspect of the experiment conducted by Vohs and colleagues has to be stressed: the three conditions did not vary only in the level of self-control demands, they were also confounded by duration. Participants in the control condition participated in a much shorter experiment than participants in the severe depletion condition. Hence, it is possible that participants in the severe-depletion condition were no longer willing to exert further effort for the study. They might have decided that the study was no longer interesting or consequential enough. Another possible explanation is that the subtle manipulation of implicit theories about willpower vanished after the longer period of time. The biased questionnaire is a subtle procedure to prime theories about willpower without the intention to create lasting changes. A simple explanation for the findings reported by Vohs and colleagues is that as time goes by people return to their own dispositional theory about willpower washing out any effects of an experimental manipulation. Therefore, further research is warranted to solve the question about effects of willpower on self-control tasks in the laboratory over time.

Importantly, our research on effects of implicit theories about willpower in everyday life contradicts the idea that a nonlimited theory is counterproductive especially when demands are high. To the contrary, examining students' self-regulatory success and failure in a highly demanding academic environment, we found that the nonlimited theory was most predictive of better outcomes among students who faced the greatest demands on their self-regulation (Job et al., 2015). Further, in a group of people that face very high self-regulatory demands, patients with type 2 diabetes, willpower theories predicted therapy adherence (Bernecker & Job, 2015a). In sum, looking at important outcomes in people's lives, we do not find evidence for negative effects of a nonlimited theory about willpower under high demands.

However, we cannot rule out that under extreme conditions, when people with a limited and nonlimited theory are brought into situation of extreme physical or psychological exhaustion (eg, under torture) the pattern might change. It is further important to stress that implicit theories about willpower perspective do not imply that people can continue controlling themselves and exert effort infinitely without needing rest, sleep, or food. What the research on implicit theories shows is, that compared to people who believe that willpower is a limited resource, people who think of it as not limited simply stay engaged for a longer time. Or put the other way around: it is the limited-resource theory that undermines peoples' self-control capacity by making them reduce effort and conserve their "limited resource" far before they reach any true limits.

Interpersonal Consequences

The abovementioned research was merely concerned with the effects of people's theories about willpower on their own self-control capacity, performance, and well-being. The majority of this research documented positive effects of a nonlimited theory about willpower, with the mere exception of the Vohs et al. (2012) assumption about a change in the pattern after severe depletion.

Still one may wonder whether there is a downside of thinking about willpower as a nonlimited resource. Some research suggests that there might be negative consequences in the interpersonal context. If a person believes that willpower is not limited this might affect what this person expects not only from him/herself but also from other people. It is plausible to assume that a nonlimited theory makes people expect greater self-control performance in others. If other people fail to control themselves, nonlimited theorists might be less understanding and harsher in their judgments. There is indirect evidence supporting this assumption with regard to implicit theories about the malleability willpower (Freeman, Shmueli, & Muraven, 2013). In this research, peoples' beliefs about willpower as either malleable or a fixed trait were measured and manipulated. Participants were then asked to report their impressions of target persons whose self-regulatory failure (weight loss or smoking) were made salient. Results indicate that a malleable theory about willpower caused harsher judgments when self-control failure was made salient.

Further, research conducted by Anirban Mukhopadhyay and Catherine Yeung (2010) was dedicated to the question of how parents' implicit theories about willpower affect their self-control-related parenting behavior. They assumed that parents who think of willpower as a nonlimited resource would not sufficiently prioritize the development of self-control skills in their children. They expected that parents with a limited theory about willpower, who in addition believe that the limited capacity can be enlarged (limited, but malleable theorists), would engage most in behaviors that are functional in developing their children's self-control. Indeed, a series of studies showed that parents who believed that willpower is limited but malleable were more likely to restrict unhealthy snacking and fast-food consumption in their children as compared to nonlimited-malleable theorists. They were further more likely to choose educational and not entertaining television programs for their children. A manipulation of theories about willpower further confirmed their causal effect. Adults who were led to believe that willpower is nonlimited were more likely to choose gifts for a child that provided instant pleasure. On the contrary, adults who were led to believe that willpower is limited but malleable choose gifts that would deliver greater value in the long run. They were further convinced that their choice would have a positive effect on the child's development. People with a nonlimited theory did not emphasize the development of children's self-control in their choice. Apparently, they did not think it necessary to foster the development of something that is already plentiful.

In summary, there is initial evidence suggesting that the belief that willpower is not limited might have some negative interpersonal consequences. However, it is important to keep in mind that the capacity for self-control, which is enhanced by the nonlimited willpower theory, is overall a positive predictor of outcomes in the interpersonal context (eg, Moffitt et al., 2011; Tangney, Baumeister, & Boone, 2004). Being able to control one's impulses and regulate one's emotions in the face of high demands is particularly crucial in conflict situations and therefore contributes to relationship quality and functional parenting (Deater-Deckard, 2014; Valiente, Lemery-Chalfant, & Reiser, 2007). If a nonlimited theory about willpower helps people to stay controlled in the face of high demands, one may expect that overall a nonlimited theory about willpower should contribute to the quality of relationships and parenting. Further, adults with a nonlimited theory might promote good self-control in their children by modeling. However, an important task for future research is to understand how to promote a nonlimited theory without potential drawbacks. For example, it is possible for parents to learn that although self-control is nonlimited, it nonetheless needs to be fostered in children. Or, it is possible for people in general to learn that although self-control can be nonlimited, not everyone understands and operates according to this belief.

CONCLUSION

The research on implicit theories about willpower suggests that when people fail to control themselves or when they have trouble to reach their personal goals this may result from their beliefs about self-control resources and not from a true lack of them. Thereby, the willpower theories approach does not deny that a person is in part an energy-based system. Obviously, people need food to function well, they get tired, and they must sleep some portion of their time. The point is, that in the normal range of self-regulatory demands in everyday life and the experimental settings used to explore the ego-depletion effect, there is not a narrow energy-based constraint on self-control capacity. But, if people believe that there is such a constraint, eg, because they learned about the strength model of self-control, the belief itself limits their willpower.

References

Aarts, H., & Dijksterhuis, A. (2003). The silence of the library: environment, situational norm, and social behavior. *Journal of Personality and Social Psychology*, 84, 18–28.
American Diabetes Association. (2008). Diagnosis and classification of diabetes mellitus. *Diabetes Care*, 31, S55–S60.
Bandura, A. (1982). Self-efficacy mechanism in human agency. *American Psychologist*, 37, 122–147.
Baumeister, R. F., Bratslavsky, E., Muraven, M., & Tice, D. M. (1998). Ego depletion: is the active self a limited resource? *Journal of Personality and Social Psychology*, 74, 1252–1265.
Baumeister, R. F., Vohs, K. D., & Tice, D. M. (2007). The strength model of self-control. *Current Directions in Psychological Science*, 16, 351–355.
Bernecker, K. (2015). *Implicit theories about willpower and their consequences for achievement, health, and well-being* (Unpublished doctoral dissertation). Zurich, Switzerland: University of Zurich.
Bernecker, K., Hermann, M., Brandstätter, V., & Job, V. (2015). Implicit theories about willpower predict subjective well-being. *Journal of Personality* (in press). http://dx.doi.org/10.1111/jopy.12225.

Bernecker, K., & Job, V. (2015a). Beliefs about willpower are related to therapy adherence and psychological adjustment in patients with type 2 Diabetes. *Basic and Applied Social Psychology, 37*, 188–195.

Bernecker, K., & Job, V. (2015b). Beliefs about willpower moderate the effect of previous day demands on next day's expectations and effective goal striving. *Frontiers in Psychology, 6*(1496), 1–10.

Blackwell, L. S., Trzesniewski, K. H., & Dweck, C. S. (2007). Implicit theories of intelligence predict achievement across an adolescent transition: a longitudinal study and an intervention. *Child Development, 78*, 246–263.

Boule, N. G., Haddad, E., Kenny, G. P., Wells, G. A., & Sigal, R. J. (2001). Effects of exercise on glycemic control and body mass in type 2 diabetes mellitus: a meta-analysis of controlled clinical trials. *Journal of the American Medical Association, 286*, 1218–1227.

Brand-Miller, J., Petocz, P., Hayne, S., & Colagiuri, S. (2003). Low-glycemic index diets in the management of diabetes: a meta-analysis of randomized controlled trials. *Diabetes Care, 26*, 2261–2267.

Brunstein, J. C. (1993). Personal goals and subjective well-being: a longitudinal study. *Journal of Personality and Social Psychology, 65*, 1061–1070.

Burnette, J. L., O'Boyle, E. H., VanEpps, E. M., Pollack, J. M., & Finkel, E. J. (2013). Mind-sets matter: a meta-analytic review of implicit theories and self-regulation. *Psychological Bulletin, 139*, 655–701.

Chambers, E. S., Bridge, M. W., & Jones, D. A. (2009). Carbohydrate sensing in the human mouth: effects on exercise performance and brain activity. *The Journal of Physiology, 587*, 1779–1794.

Chow, J. T., Hui, C. M., & Lau, S. (2015). A depleted mind feels inefficacious: ego-depletion reduces self-efficacy to exert further self-control. *European Journal of Social Psychology, 45*, 754–768.

Clarkson, J. J., Hirt, E. R., Jia, L., & Alexander, M. B. (2010). When perception is more than reality: the effects of perceived versus actual resource depletion on self-regulatory behavior. *Journal of Personality and Social Psychology, 98*, 29–46.

Crum, A. J., & Langer, E. J. (2007). Mind-set matters: exercise and the placebo effect. *Psychological Science, 18*, 165–171.

Deater-Deckard, K. (2014). Family matters: intergenerational and interpersonal processes of executive function and attentive behavior. *Current Directions in Psychological Science, 23*, 230–236.

Diener, E., Suh, E. M., Lucas, R. E., & Smith, H. L. (1999). Subjective well-being: three decades of progress. *Psychological Bulletin, 125*, 276–302.

Dweck, C. S. (1986). Motivational processes affecting learning. *American Psychologist, 41*, 1040–1048.

Dweck, C. S. (1996). Implicit theories as organizers of goals and behavior. In P. M. Gollwitzer, & J. A. Bargh (Eds.), *The psychology of action: Linking cognition and motivation to behavior*. New York, NY: The Guilford Press.

Dweck, C. S. (1999). *Self-theories*. Lillington, NC: Taylor & Francis.

Dweck, C. S., Chiu, C., & Hong, Y. (1995). Implicit theories and their role on judgements and reactions: a world from two perspectives. *Psychological Inquiry, 6*, 267–285.

Dweck, C. S., & Leggett, E. L. (1988). A social-cognitive approach to motivation and personality. *Psychological Review, 95*, 256–273.

Ferguson, M. J., & Bargh, J. A. (2004). Liking is for doing: the effects of goal pursuit on automatic evaluation. *Journal of Personality and Social Psychology, 87*, 557–572.

Fishbach, A., Shah, J. Y., & Kruglanski, A. W. (2004). Emotional transfer in goal systems. *Journal of Experimental Social Psychology, 40*, 723–738.

Förster, J., Liberman, N., & Higgins, E. T. (2005). Accessibility from active and fulfilled goals. *Journal of Experimental Social Psychology, 41*, 220–239.

Freeman, N., Shmueli, D., & Muraven, M. (2013). Lay theories of self-control influence judgments of individuals who have failed at self-control. *Journal of Applied Social Psychology, 43*, 1418–1427.

Gailliot, M. T., & Baumeister, R. F. (2007). The physiology of willpower: linking blood glucose to self-control. *Personality and Social Psychology Review, 11*, 303–327.

Gailliot, M. T., Baumeister, R. F., DeWall, C. N., Maner, J. K., Plant, E. A., Tice, D. M., ... Schmeichel, B. J. (2007). Self-control relies on glucose as a limited energy source: willpower is more than a metaphor. *Journal of Personality and Social Psychology, 92*, 325–336.

Hagger, M. S., & Chatzisarantis, N. L. D. (2013). The sweet taste of success: the presence of glucose in the oral cavity moderates the depletion of self-control resources. *Personality & Social Psychology Bulletin, 39*, 28–42.

Halperin, E., Crisp, R. J., Husnu, S., Trzesniewski, K. H., Dweck, C. S., & Gross, J. J. (2012). Promoting intergroup contact by changing beliefs: group malleability, intergroup anxiety, and contact motivation. *Emotion (Washington, DC), 12*, 1192–1195.

Higgins, E. T. (1996). Knowledge activation: accessibility, applicability, and salience. In E. T. Higgins, & A. W. Kruglanski (Eds.), *Social psychology: Handbook of basic principles* (pp. 133–168). New York, NY: Guilford Press.

Hong, Y., Chiu, C., Dweck, C. S., Lin, D. M. -S., & Wan, W. (1999). Implicit theories, attributions, and coping: a meaning system approach. *Journal of Personality and Social Psychology, 77*, 588–599.

Inzlicht, M., McKay, L., & Aronson, J. (2006). Stigma as ego depletion: how being the target of prejudice affects self-control. *Psychological Science, 17*, 262–269.

Inzlicht, M., & Schmeichel, B. J. (2012). What is ego depletion? toward a mechanistic revision of the resource model of self-control. *Perspectives on Psychological Science, 7*, 450–463.

Inzlicht, M., Schmeichel, B. J., & Macrae, C. N. (2014). Why self-control seems (but may not be) limited. *Trends in Cognitive Sciences, 18*, 127–133.

James, W. (1907). The energy of men. *The Philosophical Review, 16*, 1–20.

Job, V., Bernecker, K., Miketta, S., & Friese, M. (2015). Implicit theories about willpower predict the activation of a rest goal following self-control exertion. *Journal of Personality and Social Psychology, 109*, 694–706.

Job, V., Dweck, C. S., & Walton, G. M. (2010). Ego depletion–is it all in your head? implicit theories about willpower affect self-regulation. *Psychological Science, 21*, 1686–1693.

Job, V., Walton, G. M., Bernecker, K., & Dweck, C. S. (2013). Beliefs about willpower determine the impact of glucose on self-control. *Proceedings of the National Academy of Sciences, 110*, 14837–14842.

Job, V., Walton, G. M., Bernecker, K., & Dweck, C. S. (2015). Implicit theories about willpower predict self-regulation and grades in everyday life. *Journal of Personality and Social Psychology, 108*, 637–647.

Kelly, G. A. (1955). *The psychology of personal constructs*. New York, NY: Norton.

Knee, C. R. (1993). Implicit theories of relationships: assessment and prediction of romantic relationship initiation, coping, and longevity. *Journal of Personality and Social Psychology, 74*, 360–370.

Kringelbach, M. L. (2004). Food for thought: hedonic experience beyond homeostasis in the human brain. *Neuroscience, 126*, 807–819.

Kurzban, R. (2010). Does the brain consume additional glucose during self-control tasks? *Evolutionary Psychology, 8*, 244–259.

Martijn, C., Tenbult, P., Merckelbach, H., Dreezens, E., & De Vries, N. K. (2002). Getting a grip on ourselves: challenging expectancies about loss of energy after self-control. *Social Cognition, 20*, 441–460.

Meyer, D. E., & Schvaneveldt, R. W. (1971). Facilitation in recognizing pairs of words: evidence of a dependence between retrieval operations. *Journal of Experimental Psychology, 90*, 227–234.

Moffitt, T. E., Arseneault, L., Belsky, D., Dickson, N., Hancox, R. J., & Harrington, H. (2011). A gradient of childhood self-control predicts health, wealth, and public safety. *Proceedings of the National Academy of Sciences, 108,* 2693–2698.

Molden, D. C., & Dweck, C. S. (2006). Finding "meaning" in psychology: a lay theories approach to self-regulation, social perception, and social development. *The American Psychologist, 61,* 192–203.

Molden, D. C., Hui, C. M., Scholer, A. A., Meier, B. P., Noreen, E. E., D'Agostino, P. R., & Martin, V. (2012). Motivational versus metabolic effects of carbohydrates on self-control. *Psychological Science, 23,* 1137–1144.

Mukhopadhyay, A., & Johar, G. V. (2005). Where there is a will, is there a way? effects of lay theories of self-control on setting and keeping resolutions. *Journal of Consumer Research, 31,* 779–786.

Mukhopadhyay, A., & Yeung, C. W. (2010). Building character: effects of lay theories of self-control on the selection of products for children. *Journal of Marketing Research, 47,* 240–250.

Muraven, M., Shmueli, D., & Burkley, E. (2006). Conserving self-control strength. *Journal of Personality and Social Psychology, 91,* 524–537.

Muraven, M., & Slessareva, E. (2003). Mechanisms of self-control failure: motivation and limited resources. *Personality & Social Psychology Bulletin, 29,* 894–906.

Muraven, M., Tice, D. M., & Baumeister, R. F. (1998). Self-control as limited resource: regulatory depletion patterns. *Journal of Personality and Social Psychology, 74,* 774–789.

Napolitano, C. M., & Job, V. (2016). *Validating the implicit theories of willpower scale: Multigroup and cross-cultural measurement invariance and convergent and divergent validity.* Manuscript in preparation.

Oaten, M., & Cheng, K. (2005). Academic examination stress impairs self-control. *Journal of Social and Clinical Psychology, 24,* 254–279.

Piaget, J. (1964). *Judgment and reasoning in the child.* Patterson, NJ: Littlefield, Adams (Original work published 1928).

Piaget, J., & Garcia, R. (1991). *Toward a logic of meanings.* New York, NY: Viking.

Rothman, A. J., Sheeran, P., & Wood, W. (2009). Reflective and automatic processes in the initiation and maintenance of dietary change. *Annals of Behavioral Medicine, 38,* 4–17.

Salmon, S. J., Adriaanse, M. A., De Vet, E., Fennis, B. M., & De Ridder, D. T. D. (2014). "When the going gets tough, who keeps going?" Depletion sensitivity moderates the ego-depletion effect. *Frontiers in Psychology, 5.*

Sanders, M. A., Shirk, S. D., Burgin, C. J., & Martin, L. L. (2012). The gargle effect: rinsing the mouth with glucose enhances self-control. *Psychological Science, 23,* 1470–1472.

Savani, K., & Job, V. (2016). *Is ego-depletion a cultural phenomenon? Acts of self-control improve subsequent performance in cultures in which willpower exertion is believed to be energizing.* Manuscript in preparation.

Silvia, P. J., & Gendolla, G. H. E. (2001). On introspection and self-perception: does self-focused attention enable accurate self-knowledge? *Review of General Psychology, 5,* 241–269.

Tangney, J. P., Baumeister, R. F., & Boone, A. L. (2004). High self-control predicts good adjustment, less pathology, better grades, and interpersonal success. *Journal of Personality, 72,* 271–324.

Tice, D., Baumeister, R., Shmueli, D., & Muraven, M. (2007). Restoring the self: positive affect helps improve self-regulation following ego depletion. *Journal of Experimental Social Psychology, 43,* 379–384.

Valiente, C., Lemery-Chalfant, K., & Reiser, M. (2007). Pathways to problem behaviors: chaotic homes, parent and child effortful control, and parenting. *Social Development, 16,* 249–267.

Vohs, K. D., Baumeister, R. F., & Schmeichel, B. J. (2012). Motivation, personal beliefs, and limited resources all contribute to self-control. *Journal of Experimental Social Psychology, 48,* 943–947.

Webb, T. L., & Sheeran, P. (2003). Can implementation intentions help to overcome ego-depletion? *Journal of Experimental Social Psychology, 53*, 5–13.

Wheeler, S., Brinol, P., & Hermann, A. (2007). Resistance to persuasion as self-regulation: ego-depletion and its effects on attitude change processes. *Journal of Experimental Social Psychology, 43*, 150–156.

Wilson, T. D., & Dunn, E. W. (2004). Self-knowledge: its limits, value, and potential for improvement. *Annual Review of Psychology, 55*, 493–518.

CHAPTER 12

Restoration Effects Following Depletion: Adventures in the Uncanny Resilience of Man

E.R. Hirt[1], J.J. Clarkson[2], P.M. Egan[3], J.R. Eyink[1]

[1]Indiana University, Bloomington, IN, United States; [2]University of Cincinnati, Cincinnati, OH, United States; [3]Kendall College, Chicago, IL, United States

One of the more intriguing aspects of mental depletion is its ubiquity; we can all relate to the experience of depletion in our professional and personal lives. As academics, we routinely feel depleted as we write journal articles (and book chapters!), develop grant proposals, review manuscripts, prepare talks, give lectures, and grade assignments. Furthermore, in spite of the obvious importance of these tasks, we collectively share in the consequences of this mental depletion. For instance, we are all familiar with the experience of realizing we have no memory of the last few pages we have been reading or of being unable to maintain a consistent train of thought—and we collectively label these ubiquitous experiences with such colorful phrases such as "my brain is fried" and "my mind is on strike."

How then do we respond when we become aware of this experience of mental depletion? In some situations, as when we are under a strict and imminent deadline, we may have to simply "push through" and attempt as best we can to maintain our productivity despite our depleted mental faculties. Indeed, despite the robustness of the deleterious effects of depletion on subsequent task performance, evidence suggests that with sufficient incentives and motivation, we can overcome the effects of mental depletion (Muraven & Slessareva, 2003), at least temporarily (Vohs, Baumeister, & Schmeichel, 2012).

More often, though, we simply feel the need to stop and take a break. That is, we decide that it would be in our best long-term interest to pursue efforts to rest and/or replenish our mental resources, as replenishment offers the potential to return to the task at hand with renewed focus and vigor. Thus, rather than trying to fight through the difficulties with concentration and mental fatigue resulting from depletion, we disengage from our current activity and seek out available means to restore our mental energy. Though seemingly straightforward, the process of mental restoration is much more complex than mere rest, food consumption, and/or sleep. Indeed, what has intrigued us and our collaborators for several years are the range of activities that people pursue to restore their mental resources (see Chapter 4 for further insights in factors that influence mental restoration).

In our earliest foray into this area of work, we gave students several scenarios in which they might experience mental fatigue and asked them to indicate what method or methods they would use to restore their mental energies and reengage in mental tasks. As might be expected, there were some obvious methods that respondents consensually believed would serve as effective mechanisms for mental restoration. For instance, respondents consistently referenced the use of caffeinated beverages (eg, coffee, soda, energy drink), with the logic that caffeine would provide a sufficient mental energy boost to both stave off mental fatigue and complete the task.

Similarly, the bulk of respondents indicated that a nap would be helpful. However, this consensual response was not without a considerable amount of variation. First, while many respondents raved about the effectiveness of naps for mental restoration, several directly stated doubts about their efficacy. For instance, some individuals believed that naps would leave them feeling even more tired and groggy than they were before the nap (and thus counterproductive for mental restoration). Second, even among the majority of those who indicated a nap would be helpful, we saw considerable variation in the duration of the nap that was deemed "optimal" for mental restoration. For instance, some reported 20 min as the optimal duration for replenishment, whereas others reported 60 min or longer.

Finally, there were activities for which respondents were unequivocally split. A prototypical example here was physical exercise (eg, going for a run, working out). Interestingly, though there were a considerable number of respondents who believed that exercise would rejuvenate their mental energy, an equal number of respondents believed that exercise would only exacerbate their mental fatigue by increasing their physical fatigue.

Thus, we witnessed certain activities for which there was clear consensus concerning their restorative potential. However, even with consensus, there were other activities where we witnessed immense diversity in respondents' beliefs about the optimal conditions for the activity to achieve restoration. Additionally, there were activities where respondents were strongly divided to a point that the same activity was viewed as either productive or counterproductive for mental restoration. For us, then, these data were striking in that they illustrated the subjective nature of people's lay beliefs about the process of mental restoration and the means used to attain it.

THE UNDERLYING ROLE OF PERCEPTUAL PROCESSES

So far, we have illustrated the idiosyncratic nature of what devices individuals pursue to restore their mental energies. However, the choice of which solution will effectively achieve one's goal of restoration is only one facet of the problem; researchers must also consider how long one must engage in these activities to get the desired outcome. If I sleep too long, will it backfire on me and ruin me for the rest of the day? If I exercise too hard, will I end up mentally as well as physically drained? What is the correct dosage level for these activities to restore me back to my baseline level of mental energy?

While a full consideration of these issues is beyond the scope of the current chapter, this analysis highlights critical questions about the degree of introspective awareness we have about our own level of mental energy. In other words, how well can we assess our own level of mental depletion?

Early work on ego depletion found that people's ability to self-report their own level of depletion and mental fatigue was relatively mixed. Indeed, although it was commonplace for depletion studies to include manipulation checks following depletion manipulations, many studies failed to find reliable differences on these self-report measures, suggesting that people may not be very good at introspecting about their own depletion (cf. Baumeister, 2014; Hagger, Wood, Stiff, & Chatzisarantis, 2010). We should not find this result particularly surprising, given the wealth of evidence detailing people's limitations in accurately introspecting about their own attitudes and decision-making processes (Nisbett & Wilson, 1977; Wilson et al., 1993). Moreover, when it comes to reporting our own emotional states, there is plenty of research to show that we often misattribute the source of our emotional arousal to plausible extraneous causes like the weather (Schwarz & Clore, 1983), the lighting in the room (Gonzalez & Cooper, 1976), or are influenced by the responses of others around us (Hatfield, Cacioppo, & Rapson, 1993; Schachter & Singer, 1962).

Our early foray into this area of work centered on the role that perceptions play in driving our self-regulatory behavior. When someone says "you look tired," we tend to engage in biased hypothesis testing processes (Trope & Liberman, 1996) and can more often than not recruit evidence from memory that supports the current hypothesis (eg, did not sleep well last night, worked out hard earlier in the day). However, given the same actual state of depletion, someone given the hypothesis that they look energized rather than tired can recruit evidence consistent with that hypothesis, resulting in a completely different assessment of their current level of mental energy. Thus, we argued that individuals' perceptions of depletion, independent of their actual level of depletion, should determine their subsequent self-control performance.

To test these predictions, Clarkson, Hirt, Jia, and Alexander (2010) manipulated participants' level of depletion using the "e-crossing" task (Baumeister, Bratslavsky, Muraven, & Tice, 1998). Importantly, the passages used for the task were printed on yellow paper, and we later provided participants with feedback about the alleged effects of the yellow paper on their level of mental energy. Half of the participants were told that the yellow paper should make them feel energized and alert, whereas the other half were told that the same yellow paper should make them feel lethargic and tired. After the feedback manipulation, participants were asked to perform a self-control task, ranging from persistence at a multiple solution anagram to evaluation of a persuasive counterargument.

Our results consistently indicated that, independent of one's *actual level of depletion*, participants who perceived themselves to be depleted showed poorer subsequent performance than did participants who perceived themselves to be replenished. Importantly, those who had actually been depleted but could blame their depletion on the yellow paper (and thus could misattribute their depletion to an external cause) outperformed participants who had not been depleted but were told that the paper should make them feel lethargic and tired. Indeed, this work was also able to show that perceptions of depletion served as the critical mediator of these downstream performance consequences. Moreover, later work (Clarkson, Hirt, Chapman, & Jia, 2011) illustrated that these perceptions of depletion manipulations served to expand or contract participants' working memory capacity, a pivotal component for self-control performance that Schmeichel (2007) has shown to be profoundly affected by depletion (for a more detail discussion of this research, see Chapter 10).

EXPECTANCIES OF RESTORATION

Given that perceptions of depletion seemed to be so powerfully altered by our feedback manipulation, we then hypothesized that perceptions of recovery or replenishment should be similarly malleable. Consistent with this perspective, the depletion literature is replete with instances of manipulations that have been shown to enable previously depleted individuals to recover unavailable or otherwise inaccessible resources. For instance, research has illustrated that positive mood (Tice, Baumeister, Shmueli, &

Muraven, 2007), interpersonal power (DeWall, Baumeister, Mead, & Vohs, 2011), self-affirmation (Schmeichel & Vohs, 2009), and exposure to nature (Kaplan & Berman, 2010) only sample the factors shown to rapidly restore the subsequent performance of previously depleted individuals to a level commensurate with that of nondepleted controls.

These demonstrations of spontaneous resource recovery (SRR) are no doubt intriguing and certainly beg the question of the mechanism(s) responsible for these effects. In searching for explanations, researchers have posited (and at times demonstrated) a range of different physiological and psychological mechanisms for these results. Some of these mechanisms make intuitive sense. For instance, the idea that certain factors can heighten individuals' state of physiological arousal (Tice et al., 2007) or the manner in which the self-control task is construed (Schmeichel & Vohs, 2009) seem plausible. However, other mechanisms are less intuitive. For instance, blood glucose (Gailliott et al., 2007) has been thought to be a physiological correlate on depletion. Yet the amount of time necessary to metabolize glucose renders it implausible as the primary mechanism responsible for these instances of SRR. Moreover, recent studies have effectively challenged the validity of the glucose hypothesis (Beedie & Lane, 2012; Molden et al., 2012) and in doing so provide a motivational mechanism for the presence of SRR.

Notwithstanding the potential validity of any or all of these hypothesized mechanisms, we offer the possibility that expectancies derived from shared lay beliefs about the energetic consequences of these different manipulations may be a common mechanism at the root of these findings. Consistent with the work of Job, Dweck, and Walton (2010; see also Chapter 11), which has illustrated that lay theories of willpower moderate susceptibility to depletion effects, we argue that specific lay beliefs about the effects of specific experiences (eg, positive mood, interpersonal power) could serve as the basis for expectancies of their restorative consequences.

To address this possibility, we embarked on a series of studies to see whether people did in fact share consensual beliefs about the energetic effects of these SRR manipulations. This initial study explored four such inductions (ie, positive mood, interpersonal power, self-affirmation, and immersion in nature). Specifically, we asked participants to respond to a set of four questions ($\alpha=.95$) of the format "____ gives me more mental energy than normal." We found that there was considerable consensus among participants that positive mood, high power, and immersion in a natural setting reliably led to increased mental energy, whereas negative mood, low power, and immersion in an urban setting reliably led to decreased mental energy (see Table 12.1). The same pattern held true (albeit to a lesser—though still significant—extent) for self-affirmation. Thus, our initial results suggested that there was considerable agreement among

TABLE 12.1 Expectancy of Mental Energy Change as a Function of Spontaneous Resource Recovery Variable

Variable	Mean (SD)
Positive mood	7.33 (0.88)
Negative mood	3.69 (1.21)
High power	7.40 (1.84)
Low power	2.00 (1.41)
Self-affirmation	5.86 (1.57)
No affirmation	4.33 (1.37)
Natural setting	7.14 (1.56)
Urban setting	3.28 (1.93)

Note. Responses were given on a 9-pt scale ranging from 1 (Strongly disagree) to 9 (Strongly agree).

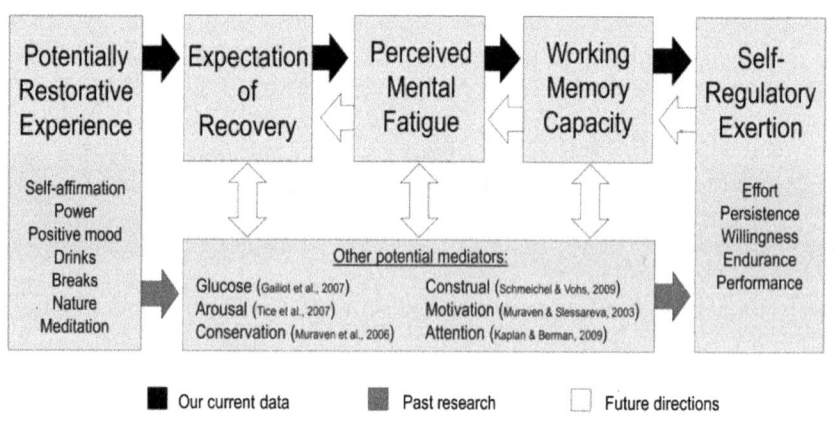

FIGURE 12.1 Model of spontaneous resource recovery.

individuals in their expectancies of the mental energy consequences of these variables critical to the emergence of (spontaneous) replenishment.

From this promising vantage point, we then sought to explicate our model of the SRR process (see Fig. 12.1). Building upon the past work by Clarkson et al. (2010), and Clarkson, Hirt, et al. (2011), we propose that these instances of spontaneous resource recovery are rooted in expectations of replenishment derived from lay beliefs about mental energy change. These expectations, in turn, should elicit a systematic influence on mental restoration. That is, depleted individuals who expect a particular experience to lead to mental restoration should subsequently experience a reduction in perceived mental fatigue or depletion. Moreover, as we have shown (Clarkson, Hirt, et al., 2011), lower perceived depletion drives expansion of working memory capacity, which then culminates in improved subsequent self-regulatory performance. While our model does not (nor is intended to) preclude the potential contributions of other mediators, it serves to unify the litany of observed instances of SRR under a single umbrella, arguing that the effectiveness of these SRR experiences results at least in part from individuals' beliefs in their mentally restorative effects.

To explore the sequelae of our model, we embarked on a series of studies to elucidate the role of expectancies of recovery in documented instances of SRR. Given that we had already documented that people share consensual beliefs about the mental energetic consequences about these effects, our general approach in these investigations was to then replicate the SRR effect and index that these expectations of recovery lead to corresponding changes in perceptions of mental fatigue. From there, we examined the consequences of these changes in perceptions of depletion for both working memory capacity and self-regulatory performance.

THE RESTORATIVE EFFECT OF MOOD: THE ROLE OF EXPECTANCIES OF MENTAL ENERGY CHANGE

In one of the most well-cited instances of SRR, Tice et al. (2007) demonstrated that exposing depleted individuals to a positive mood induction can counteract depletion effects, restoring their performance on subsequent self-control tasks to a level commensurate with nondepleted controls. These authors posited that the general emotional arousal (Thayer, 1989) associated with positive mood may counteract the negative effects of depletion and lead to replenishment. However, recall that we found that individuals shared the consensual belief that positive mood led to increased mental energy, whereas negative mood led to decreased mental energy. Thus, in our initial test of our model, we examined the extent to which the restorative effects of positive mood can stem from individuals' expectancies about the restorative properties of positive mood (see Table 12.1).

Specifically, Egan, Clarkson, and Hirt (2015, Study 3) had participants complete a thought-listing task for 5 min in which they were allowed to think freely about anything they wanted, except for a white bear. This thought-suppression task, modeled after the famous work of Dan Wegner and his colleagues (Wegner, 1994; Wegner, Schneider, Carter, & White, 1987), has been shown in past work to successfully induce depletion given the self-control required to inhibit the unwanted thought (see Clarkson et al., 2010; Muraven, Tice, & Baumeister, 1998). Following this depletion induction, participants were given an autobiographical memory task in which they were asked to write about either a positive or negative emotional experience. This procedure has been used in past research to

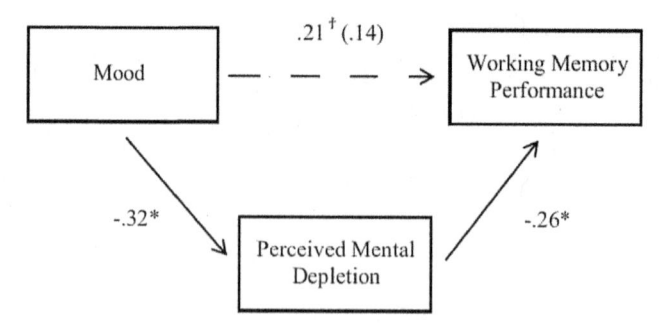

FIGURE 12.2 Path analysis of positive mood and working memory capacity through perceptions of mental fatigue. *Reproduced from Egan, P.M., Clarkson, J.J., & Hirt, E.R. (2015). Revisiting the restorative effects of positive mood: an expectancy-based approach to self-control restoration.* Journal of Experimental Social Psychology, 57, 87–99, Study 3.

reliably induce changes in mood (Bless et al., 1996; Fishbach & Labroo, 2007; Schwarz & Clore, 1983). We then measured participants' perceived mental fatigue and their working memory capacity. In particular, we were interested in demonstrating whether the restorative effects of positive mood on working memory capacity were mediated by changes in perceptions of mental fatigue.

As predicted, inducing a positive mood reduced depleted participants' perceived mental fatigue, relative to negative mood participants. Interestingly, the amount of perceived mental fatigue of positive mood participants did not differ significantly from that of nondepleted control participants, whereas the perceived mental fatigue of negative mood participants remained at a level consistent with that of depleted control participants. Thus, the positive mood induction appeared to restore depleted participants back to their baseline level of mental energy. Furthermore, examination of the effects of our mood induction on working memory capacity revealed that positive mood participants showed enhanced working memory capacity compared to their negative mood counterparts. Again, the working memory capacity exhibited by positive mood participants was commensurate with the nondepleted controls, suggesting that the positive mood restored working memory capacity back to baseline. Finally, a test of the mediational role of perceived mental fatigue in the observed changes in working memory capacity as a function of mood indicated that perceptions did mediate these effects (see Fig. 12.2).

While these results were clearly quite promising, we sought a more stringent test of our model by directly manipulating participants' expectancies about the restorative effects of *positive* and *negative* mood. That is, if we could actually manipulate participants' lay beliefs about the effects of both mood states on mental energy (rather than rely on their own idiosyncratic beliefs about the effects of these states), we could more confidently illustrate the causal role that these beliefs and expectancies play in SRR.

Of course, we wondered if these lay beliefs would be so firmly held that they would be relatively immune to experimental manipulation. However, past research has illustrated that lay beliefs can be successfully manipulated experimentally (Job et al., 2010; Molden & Dweck, 2006; Nussbaum & Dweck, 2008; Petrocelli, Clarkson, Tormala, & Hendrix, 2010). For instance, in Nussbaum and Dweck (2008, Study 1), participants were given a brief *Psychology Today*-style scientific article that either supported an entity or incremental theory of intelligence. The entity theory passage described research which reliably showed that "almost all of a person's intelligence is either inherited or determined at a very young age"; conversely, the incremental theory passage described parallel but opposite research which reliably showed that "intelligence can be increased substantially over the lifespan." Thus, based on past precedent, we were confident that we could devise similar passages to manipulate participants' beliefs about the restorative effects of positive and negative mood.

Indeed, in Egan et al. (2015, Study 4), we ambitiously attempted to orthogonally manipulate initially depleted participants' mood state and their mood-relevant expectancies. As in our earlier studies (see Egan et al., 2015), we manipulated mood via an autobiographical memory task in which they recalled either a positive or negative experience. The mood-relevant belief manipulation used passages modeled after those of Nussbaum and Dweck (2008). Specifically, half of the participants read a passage describing research that reliably showed positive mood is beneficial for mental energy (eg, it makes people optimistic, willing to explore their environment and take risks) whereas negative mood is detrimental to mental energy (eg, it makes people pessimistic, leads to rumination about past failures and transgressions). Conversely, the other half of participants read a passage describing research that reliably showed positive mood is detrimental to mental energy (eg, it makes people complacent, focusing only on maintaining and basking in their good mood, using low effort and heuristic strategies for decision-making) whereas negative mood is beneficial for mental energy (eg, it signals danger and threat, mobilizing resources aimed at problem solving and safety, using effortful and systematic processing strategies for decision-making).

Readers will note that these effects refer directly to actual research findings in the mood literature, and pretesting revealed that they were highly effective at manipulating participants' expectancies about the restorative consequences of either positive or negative mood (depending on condition). Armed with this potent expectancy manipulation, we sought to demonstrate the causal effect of these expectancies on perceived mental depletion, working memory capacity, and self-control performance (here, measured by performance on a multiple solution anagram task).

Importantly, we predicted that in the positive mood is restorative condition, we should replicate the findings of Tice et al. (2007) and our earlier study (Egan et al., 2015, Study 3), illustrating the restorative effects of positive mood. Negative mood, on the other hand, should not restore participants' mental energy back to baseline levels. Conversely, in the negative mood is restorative condition, we expected to find a complete reversal of these prior results, such that now negative mood should restore participants' mental energy back to baseline levels. Positive mood, on the other hand, should not restore participants since participants should hold the expectancy that positive mood is detrimental to mental energy.

Consistent with these hypotheses, we observed a significant interaction between mood state and expectancy condition for perceived mental fatigue. In short, when positive mood was expected to restore mental resources, the induction of a positive mood led to less mental fatigue than did the induction of a negative mood; however, the reverse pattern was illustrated when negative mood was expected to restore mental resources, as here the induction of a negative mood led to less mental fatigue than did the induction of a positive mood. These results are important as they demonstrate any psychological or physiological effects associated with positive mood are independent (or at least can be superseded by) the effect of individuals' expectations of restoration on mental fatigue.

Further examination of the implications of these changes in perceived mental depletion for working memory capacity and anagram performance revealed that the downstream consequences of our manipulations translated to self-control performance. Enhanced working memory capacity and anagram performance was observed for participants induced into a positive (versus negative) mood when positive mood was expected to be restorative. These findings directly replicated the results obtained in Egan et al. (2015, Study 3) and the anagram performance data are conceptually consistent with Tice et al. (2007). Nonetheless, these findings were reversed when negative mood was expected to restore mental resources, as those in the negative (as opposed to positive) mood condition now showed enhanced working memory capacity and anagram performance.

We believe that these findings provide strong support for our proposed model of SRR effects more broadly and the efficacy of expectancies about restorative experiences in particular. Indeed, participants who held the expectancy that positive mood is conducive to mental energy restoration displayed reduced perceptions of mental depletion following a positive mood induction. These changes in perceived depletion, in turn, led to enhanced working memory capacity, which could then be applied to a subsequent self-control task (resulting in better anagram performance). Moreover, recall this expectancy was consensually shared by participants in our initial exploration of the restorative expectancies associated with several experiences (Table 12.1). Indeed, the consistency of results across the studies reported in Egan et al. (2015) provides a cogent rationale why the Tice et al. (2007) findings related to the restorative consequences of positive mood appear to be so robust.

However, when we manipulated participants' expectancies such that we led them to believe that negative (rather than positive) mood is restorative, we found that positive mood no longer displayed any restorative effects, whereas negative mood suddenly exhibited restorative consequences. Specifically, those who experienced a negative mood induction reported less mental fatigue than did those who experienced a positive mood induction—and these changes in perceptions of depletion resulted in corresponding reversals in working memory capacity and subsequent anagram performance. Through this expectancy perspective, then, we were able to not only eliminate the documented effects of positive mood for mental restoration but also demonstrate when negative mood can be beneficial for mental restoration. Indeed, although our initial results indicated that most individuals personally believe negative mood undermines mental restoration, we were able to show that these expectancies are both malleable and manipulable (eg, Job et al., 2010; Nussbaum & Dweck, 2008), such that we can directly observe the powerful role that these expectancies play in instances of SRR.

THE RESTORATIVE EFFECT OF INTERPERSONAL POWER: THE MODERATING INFLUENCE OF BELIEF STRENGTH

While we were pleased to find such strong and consistent support for our model in the case of the efficacy of positive mood as an avenue for SRR, we wanted to replicate these findings for other instances of SRR to establish the ubiquity of these effects. Thus, in our next set of studies, we embarked on an exploration of the restorative effects of interpersonal power. DeWall et al. (2011, Study 2) demonstrated that a power manipulation can successfully counteract the effects of depletion. In their research, they had participants complete an attention regulation task adapted from Gilbert, Pelham, and Krull (1988), in which they watched a video clip (without audio) of a woman being interviewed by an off-camera interviewer. While participants watched the interview, neutral words irrelevant to the interview were presented in the bottom corner of the screen. Participants were instructed to ignore the words and to direct their attention to the woman being interviewed. Thus, they had to exert self-control to regulate their attention. Following this depletion induction, DeWall et al. manipulated power by placing participants into either a high power (manager) or low power (subordinate) position on a group task, a procedure used successfully in past research on power (Anderson & Berdahl, 2002;

Galinsky, Gruenfeld, & Magee, 2003). Subsequent self-regulatory performance was measured using a dichotic listening task in which participants were asked to ignore the incoming information presented to their right ear and write down each word spoken in his or her left ear that contained the letters *m* or *p*.

These authors found that while depletion undermined the performance of low power participants, it had no effects on the performance of the high power participants. Thus, high power seemed to make participants immune to depletion effects. DeWall et al. (2011) posit that these effects might be due to either the increased motivation level of participants in the high power condition (a condition associated with greater action orientation, cf. Galinsky et al., 2003) or the tendency for high power to be associated with a higher, more abstract construal level (Fujita, Trope, Liberman, & Levin-Sagi, 2006; Lammers, Galinsky, Gordijn, & Otten, 2008; Magee & Smith, 2013). While power may indeed have these effects on participants, we would argue that the SRR effects of power may simply reflect the consensual expectancy that high power leads to increased mental energy. Thus, to test this hypothesis, we followed the approach we utilized in Egan et al. (2015) regarding the restorative effects of positive mood, but instead examined the role of expectancies about the energetic effects of interpersonal power.

Importantly, although we found that there was a considerable amount of consensus in people's lay beliefs about the energetic effects of conditions like positive mood, power, immersion in natural environments, and self-affirmation, we readily acknowledge that there is likely to be considerable variability in the ***strength*** with which these particular beliefs are held. For instance, the literature on attitude strength has highlighted the fact that there are individual differences in the degree to which particular attitudes are chronically accessible (Bargh, Bond, Lombardi, & Tota, 1986), held with greater extremity (Jarvis & Petty, 1996), and vary in their stability (see Krosnick & Petty, 1995). Thus, it seemed incredibly naïve of us to ignore the potential moderating influence of individual differences in belief strength as we moved forward in this line of research.

A perusal of the interpersonal power literature revealed a number of relevant individual difference variables that have been shown to moderate the effects of an experimental power manipulation, including power motivation (Magee & Langer, 2008), personal dominance (Maner & Mead, 2010), relationship orientation (Chen, Lee-Chai, & Bargh, 2001), dispositional anxiety (Maner, Gailliot, Menzel, & Kunstman, 2012), and approach/avoidance tendencies (Sassenberg, Ellemers, & Scheepers, 2012). However, the factor that served as the focus of our interpersonal power work has been social dominance orientation (*SDO*; Pratto, Sidanius, Stallworth, & Malle, 1994).

High SDO individuals legitimize status differential as a necessary part of society and effective group organization, and thus value powerful social roles to a significantly greater extent than do low SDO individuals. Given high SDO individuals place greater value on interpersonal power, we hypothesized they might also have stronger and more stable (ie, less malleable) beliefs in the positive effects of power for mental energy. We further posited that these differences in belief strength would then translate into more pronounced SRR effects among high SDO individuals. Indeed, Maner et al. (2012) showed that low anxiety individuals expected power-inducing actions to be more rewarding than did high anxiety individuals. Furthermore, these expectancies then mediated the downstream effects of interpersonal power on such measures as greater willingness to take risks and greater sexual attraction to a partner. Thus, there seemed to be past precedent to the notion that expectancies based on individual difference variables might moderate the effects of interpersonal power on subsequent outcomes.

To address these hypotheses, we first sought to directly assess whether individual differences in SDO predicted expectancies about the restorative effects of interpersonal power. In an initial study (Egan & Hirt, Study 1), we assessed participants' level of SDO and then presented them with a series of power-inducing experiences (eg, being a leader) and power-reducing experiences (eg, following orders). Participants were asked to simply report their expectancies of mental energy change resulting from each experience [on a 1–7 scale anchored from 1 (very mentally depleting) to 7 (very mentally restorative)] as well as their confidence in these beliefs [again, on a 1–7 scale anchored at 1 (not at all confident) to 7 (extremely confident)].

Our results supported our intuitions and indicated that SDO significantly predicted participants' expectancies of power-inducing tasks, such that higher SDO scores were associated with stronger beliefs in the restorative potential of interpersonal power ($\beta = .41$, $p < .001$). In addition, SDO predicted participants' confidence in their expectancies regarding these power-inducing tasks, with higher SDO scores corresponding to increased confidence ($\beta = .23$, $p = .05$). Importantly, in this same study, we assessed participants' expectancies concerning the mental energy impact of several other experiences, including positive mood, self-affirmation, and consuming an energy drink, as well as their confidence in those expectancies. We found that SDO did not predict the expectancies or expectancy confidence in these other domains, suggesting that the relationship of SDO to our expectancy and confidence data was unique to power-relevant experiences and not simply a reflection of greater belief of strength or confidence (regardless of domain) on the part of high SDO individuals.

Given that high SDO participants appear to hold stronger expectancies that power restores mental energy, we then tested whether SDO moderates the SRR effects of power. Adopting a paradigm similar to Egan et al. (2015, Study 3), we first had all participants complete a standard depletion task, and then exposed them to a power manipulation, in which they were assigned to assume the role of the leader (high power condition) or a follower (low power condition) on a joint task (cf. Galinsky et al., 2003). In this joint task, the leader and follower each independently answered a set of difficult problems (taken from the Culture Fair Intelligence Test; Cattell & Cattell, 1960), but the leader ultimately had the final say in terms of which response was given by the team. After this power manipulation, participants completed a perceived depletion measure and then performed a computerized Stroop task as our key index of subsequent self-control performance.

Regression analyses performed on the perceived depletion measure revealed a main effect of condition, such that the high power condition predicted less overall perceived depletion ($\beta=-.20$, $p=.06$). However, this main effect was qualified by an interaction between condition and our individual difference measure of SDO ($\beta=-.29$, $p=.01$). To interpret this interaction, we broke down participants into those high (+1 SD), medium (0 SD), and low (−1 SD) in SDO, and looked at the effects of the power manipulation for each group of participants. For high and medium SDO participants, higher power predicted less perceived depletion (high SDO $\beta=-.54$, $p=.001$; medium SDO $\beta=-.22$, $p=.03$). For low SDO participants, however, the power manipulation had no effect on perceived depletion ($\beta=.09$, ns). Indeed, a closer examination of these data revealed that for high SDO participants, not only did high power lead to a decrease in perceived depletion, but also low power led to an increase in perceived mental depletion. Clearly, then, these results suggest that the stronger expectancies held by individuals higher in SDO influenced their perceived level of depletion more robustly and intensely than it did for individuals lower in SDO.

Did these changes in perceived depletion then translate into differences in subsequent self-control performance? To address this question, we calculated a measure of Stroop performance by subtracting the mean response time on incongruent trials [in which the font color did not match the word name (eg, the word "red" printed in green font)] from the mean response time on the congruent trials [in which the font color matched the word name (eg, the word "red" printed in red font) using only trials for which the participant provided a correct response]. Past work in the depletion literature has often used such a measure of Stroop interference as an index of self-control performance (eg, Clarkson et al., 2015; Job et al., 2010; Webb & Sheeran, 2003), with lower scores reflecting better self-control performance. Paralleling the findings on our measure of perceived depletion, we found that high power predicted less Stroop interference ($\beta=-.22$, $p=.04$), nicely replicating and extending the findings obtained by DeWall et al. (2011). However, as we saw with the perceived depletion data, this effect was qualified by an interaction between condition and SDO ($\beta = -.26$, $p = .01$), such that again it was only the high ($\beta = -.51$, $p = .001$) and medium ($\beta = -.24$, $p = .02$) who showed improved Stroop performance in the high power condition. No effect of power was observed among low SDO participants ($\beta = .04$, ns).

Finally, consistent with our model, mediational analyses performed on these data indicated that, as in Egan et al. (2015, Study 3) investigating the SRR effects of positive mood, the self-control performance differences observed as a function of the power manipulation and SDO were mediated by the changes in perceived depletion. Thus, it appears that the SRR effects of interpersonal power, like those of positive mood, are a consequence of the expectancies of mental energy change and the corresponding changes in perceived depletion that result from those expectancies. However, this particular investigation added another important wrinkle to that account, attesting to the role that individual differences play in the magnitude of these effects. Specifically, the present work powerfully showed that the SRR effects of interpersonal power only apply for high and medium SDO individuals, who hold stronger and more confident expectations about the beneficial aspects of power for mental energy.

While we were encouraged by these findings, we again sought to experimentally manipulate (rather than simply measure) expectancies of mental energy change concerning interpersonal power to demonstrate the robustness of expectancies in driving these effects. Thus, in Egan and Hirt (2015, Study 3), we followed a similar approach to that detailed earlier in Egan et al. (2015, Study 4) and orthogonally manipulated both power (high/low power condition) as well as expectancies toward power (high power is restorative/high power is depleting) to more thoroughly examine the role that expectancies play in these perceptual and performance-based consequences of mental restoration.

As in Egan et al. (2015, Study 4), all participants were first depleted and then given the power manipulation. In this study, we used a widely used experiential writing task (cf. Smith, Jostmann, Galinsky, & van Dijk, 2008) in which participants wrote for 5 min about an experience in which they either controlled one or more other people (high power condition), or were controlled by one or more other people (low power condition). Following the power manipulation, participants received the power-relevant expectancy manipulation, again modeled after Nussbaum and Dweck (2008).

Specifically, participants read a passage of information regarding recent research concerning power's effects. In the power is restorative version, participants read that high power has been shown to be associated with increased mental energy and improved cognitive performance, whereas low power is associated with decreased mental energy and diminished cognitive performance. In the power is depleting version, participants read the opposite—that high power is associated with decreased mental energy and diminished cognitive performance, whereas low power is associated with increased mental energy and improved cognitive performance. Pretesting had again revealed that these passages were highly effective at manipulating participants' expectancies about the mental energetic consequences of high and low power.

Armed with this potent expectancy manipulation, we sought to demonstrate the causal effect of these expectancies on perceived mental depletion, working memory capacity, and self-control performance (here, measured by performance on a multiple solution anagram task: Baumeister et al., 1998; Egan, Hirt, & Karpen, 2012). Importantly, we predicted that in the power is restorative condition, we should replicate the findings of DeWall et al. (2011) and those of our earlier study (Egan & Hirt, 2015, Study 2), illustrating the restorative effects of high (but not low) power. Conversely, in the power is depleting condition, we again expected to see a reversal of the pattern observed in past studies, such that low (but not high) power should restore participants' mental energy back to baseline levels.

However, the intriguing question raised by Egan and Hirt (2015, Study 2) was whether this power expectancy manipulation would be equally effective for individuals at high and low levels of SDO. That is, would this situational manipulation be powerful enough to overwhelm and replace the strong expectancy between high power and mental restoration held by those high in SDO (Egan & Hirt, Study 1)? Although to our knowledge, past research has not directly explored the interaction between situationally induced and individual difference-based expectancies, the robustness of these situational manipulations would seem to imply that they should hold for individuals at all levels of this and other relevant personality dimensions. The present study hence provided us with an ideal opportunity to explore this potential interaction.

Looking first at the perceived depletion measure, we found the predicted two-way interaction between power and expectancy ($\beta=.25$, $p=.03$), such that when participants in the high power condition reported less mental depletion (ie, felt restored) when they were told that power is restorative rather than power is depleting. Conversely, when participants were in the low condition, they reported less mental depletion when they were told that power is depleting rather than restorative. Thus, our situational manipulation of power-relevant expectancy led to corresponding changes in perceived depletion among participants in response to the power manipulation. However, these findings were qualified by a significant three-way interaction between power, expectancy, and SDO ($\beta=-.29$, $p=.01$). As can be seen in Fig. 12.3 (top panel), the predicted interaction between power and expectancy only held for individuals who were low in SDO. That is, low SDO participants were sensitive to the expectancy manipulation and perceived their level of depletion in a manner that matched their expectancy. High SDO participants, on the other hand, were unaffected by the expectancy manipulation. Instead, they simply reported

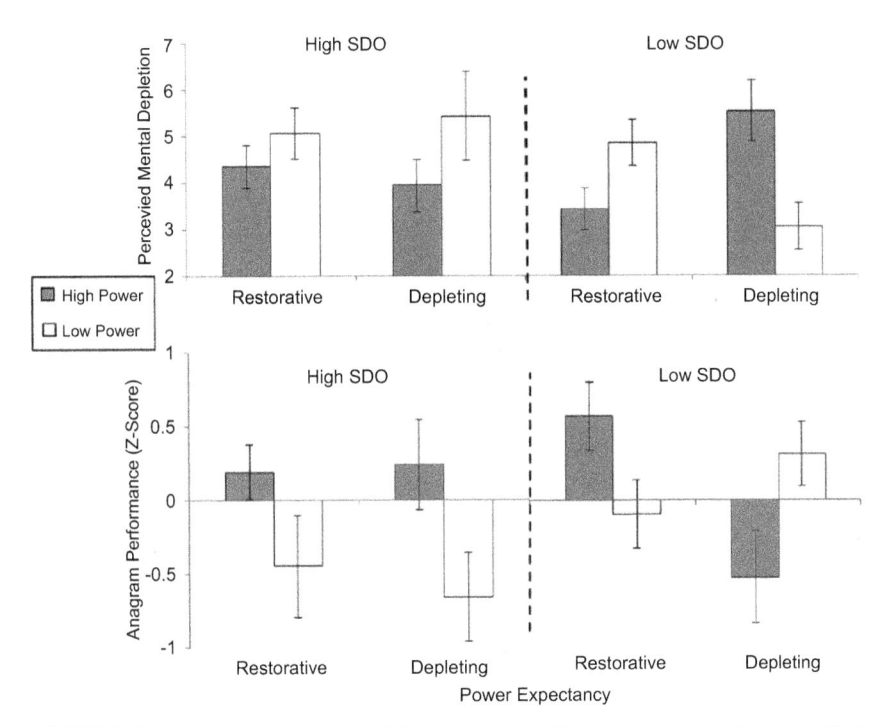

FIGURE 12.3 Perceptions of mental fatigue (top panel) and anagram performance (bottom panel) as a function of interpersonal power, expectancy, and social dominance orientation. *Reproduced from Egan, P.M., & Hirt, E.R. (2015). Flipping the switch: power, social dominance, and expectancies of mental energy change.* Personality & Social Psychology Bulletin, 41, 336–350, Study 3.

less mental depletion in the high power condition, regardless of whether they were told that power is restorative or depleting.

This same pattern of results was revealed on the anagram measure, our key index of self-regulatory performance (see Fig. 12.3, bottom panel). Again, we found a significant two-way interaction between power and expectancy ($\beta = .23$, $p = .04$), with high power participants exhibiting better anagram performance when they read that power was restorative rather than depleting (the performance of low power participants was basically equivalent in the power is depleting and power is restorative conditions). However, we again obtained a three-way interaction between power, expectancy, and SDO ($\beta = -.21$, $p = .06$), which indicated that the expectancy manipulation only influenced the self-regulatory performance of the low SDO participants (see Fig. 12.1, bottom panel). The anagram performance of the high SDO participants was unaffected by the expectancy information; high SDO individuals consistently exhibited better anagram performance when in the high power than the low power condition.

Consistent with our model, this research provided supporting evidence for hypothesized role that expectancies of mental energy change play in the SRR effects of interpersonal power. By directly manipulating participants' expectancies about the restorative or depleting effects of power, we were able to illustrate corresponding changes not only in participants' perception of their own state of mental depletion, but also their subsequent self-regulatory performance. Importantly, as we found in our past studies, these performance differences were again mediated by changes in perceived depletion, attesting to their power of perception to drive the cognitive and behavioral sequelae associated with depletion (see Clarkson et al., 2010).

Nonetheless, while this research fits well within our model and nicely replicates the findings of Egan et al. (2015) regarding the SRR effects of positive mood, the findings adds a critical caveat to our model by highlighting the importance of belief strength as a moderator of SRR effects. That is, we found individual differences in the strength of participants' expectancies alter the magnitude of SRR effects. Specifically, high SDO individuals, shown to hold stronger and more confident beliefs about the restorative effects of interpersonal power, exhibited greater changes in perceived depletion and performance following a power manipulation. Furthermore, unlike their low SDO counterparts, these high SDO individuals were quite resistant to a situational manipulation of their expectancies.

How such individuals were able to counterargue and dismiss such a strong persuasive message is an interesting and important question for future research. It may be that these high SDO individuals have had more direct experience with high power situations, and direct experience has been shown to result in stronger and more accessible attitudes that are highly resistant to change (Fazio & Zanna, 1978). Alternatively, perhaps these individuals may be willing to admit that power may be depleting for others (after reading the power is depleting manipulation) but still staunchly defend the belief that in their own personal experience power has restorative effects for me (cf. Hendrix & Hirt, 2009)? Regardless of the mechanism by which these individuals are able to resist the situational manipulation, our work highlights an important boundary condition to the efficacy of these (and similar) expectancy manipulations (Egan et al., 2015; Job et al., 2010; Molden & Dweck, 2006; Nussbaum & Dweck, 2008).

EMERGING QUESTIONS

We believe that the present work provide nice support for our model of expectancy-based processes driving the SRR effects observed in the literature. As we noted earlier, many potential psychological and physiological mechanisms have been suggested to underlie various examples of these

SRR effects. While we would clearly agree that these mechanisms may play a contributing role in some of these cases, our evidence provides initial evidence that lay beliefs about mental energy change and the expectancies that derive from these beliefs are sufficient to produce SRR effects. To date, we have investigated two of these SRR variables (positive mood, interpersonal power) in detail, but we hypothesize that these same expectancy-based processes should be operative for any of the other SRR effects noted in the literature. Obviously, direct empirical testing of this hypothesis awaits future research. However, based on our model, we would further conjecture that these same processes can and should underlie the success of any other potentially restorative experience. Thus, we hope that this model can serve as a springboard for the exploration and identification of other heretofore unidentified variables that produce SRR effects.

Expectations of Restoration versus Exhaustion. The astute reader will note that our model denotes lay beliefs about mental energy *change* and the expectancies derived from them. Notably, changes in mental energy can be in the positive (restorative) or negative (depleting) direction. In the present work, we have focused primarily on positive changes in mental energy that result in the restoration of individuals' mental energy following depletion. Indeed, we initiated this line of work with the explicit purpose of understanding the role of perceptions in instances of SRR. However, it is important to point out that our model is far broader than this and encompasses instances of lay beliefs of negative (as well as positive) mental energy change. That is, such beliefs should result in expectations of depletion and the corresponding changes in (greater) perceived mental depletion, (impaired) working memory capacity, and (poorer) performance on subsequent self-regulatory tasks. In fact, we have found evidence of these same expectancy-based processes in the creation and maintenance of depletion with the feedback manipulation of Clarkson et al. (2010), as well as in the negative mood conditions of Egan et al. (2015) and the low power conditions of Egan and Hirt (2015) discussed earlier. Furthermore, our model could be further expanded to include other instance of depleting experiences, experiences already noted in the literature such as ostracism/social exclusion (Ciarocco, Sommer, & Baumeister, 2001) or thought/stereotype suppression (Macrae, Bodenhausen, Milne, & Jetten, 1994; Wegner et al., 1987), or ones that have yet to be identified and studied. Hence, we think that our model could prove useful in not only integrating and explaining documented instances of depletion and restoration effects, but also could be generative for the exploration of novel instances of these same phenomena.

The Impact of Awareness. One question that we have yet to address to this point is how conscious and aware people are of these effects. Indeed, we directly asked people about their lay beliefs of mental energy change and they seem to be quite able to self-report their beliefs and expectancies accurately. But recall that we began the chapter by alluding to situations in which people perceive themselves to be depleted and actively choose activities that they believe will restore them. Such situations reflect not only that people can accurately self-report their beliefs and expectancies when queried, but actually access and utilize them when making choices about what activities to pursue when they are or are not feeling depleted. While we have yet to tackle this question directly, the work of Michelle vanDellen and her colleagues (vanDellen, Shah, Leander, Delose, & Bornstein, 2015) suggests that people are at least somewhat aware of the resource demands of various tasks during their day and actively plan their day according to the anticipated level of depletion at particular times of the day. Furthermore, Jia, Hirt, and Fishbach (2016; Chapter 8) find evidence that depletion serves as signal for individuals that their ability to complete future tasks may be compromises, and thus motivates counteractive control processes (Fishbach & Trope, 2007) to prioritize goal pursuit and redirect their limited resources toward their most important goal(s). As Carnevale and Fujita (Chapter 5) noted, individuals can and do engage in many types of proactive and/or efficient forms of self-control to successfully pursue their goals. Extrapolating from this work, we might surmise that people may in fact actively consult their lay beliefs and expectancies when depleted to select and pursue activities that might effectively restore them. These are questions that we hope to address in our future research efforts.

Expectancies or Placebos? Whenever we have talked about our model and its account for these SRR effects, one consistent comment that gets raised is whether our expectancy-based process reduces this phenomenon to another example of placebo effects. That is, we have known for decades that patient's expectancies about the efficacy of some treatment (eg, a sugar pill), even if it has no actual physiological effects, can seemingly produce observable positive physiological and behavioral outcomes (Colloca & Benedetti, 2005; Finniss, Kaptchuk, Miller, & Benedetti, 2010; Meissner et al., 2011; Morton, El-Deredy, Watson, & Jones, 2010; Stewart-Williams & Podd, 2004). For instance, restorative expectancies concerning a particular medical treatment predict analgesic responses rivaling direct physiological intervention (Aslaksen & Flaten, 2008; Morton et al., 2010). Furthermore, these types of expectancy effects are found across multiple domains, such as sleep recovery (Draganich & Erdal, 2014), cardiovascular improvement (Crum & Langer, 2007; Stoate, Wulf, & Lewthwaite, 2012), pain reduction (Kam-Hansen et al., 2014), and hunger satiation (Crum, Corbin, Brownell, & Salovey, 2011).

Certainly, our model and its predictions have some clear links to the work on placebo effects. Our work makes a compelling case that people's expectancies about the energetic effects of these SRR manipulations determine their efficacy. However, this observation does not preclude the possibility that these manipulations may and likely do have actual physiological or psychological effects on their own. Thus, the extent to which these expectancies merely document the actual or perceived effects of these manipulations from an individual's own past experiences is clearly an important question that we must address. Indeed, the fact that high SDO participants illustrated resistance to the "power is depleting" expectancy manipulation in Egan and Hirt (2015, Study 3) suggests that individuals do relate a given expectancy to their own personal experience in determining whether they believe that particular expectancy applies to them. If there is a clear mismatch between their own experience and the implication of the manipulation, participants will not blindly accede to the manipulated expectancy, but will instead adhere to their own strongly held and confident beliefs. Thus, there seems to be a potentially complex interplay of processes that may determine the success of any particular expectancy induction in driving perceptions of depletion and subsequent changes in working memory capacity and/or self-regulatory behavior.

CODA

What do these perceptual effects mean for the dominant resource model of depletion? Collectively, our research suggests that independent of the actual amount of cognitive resources available to individuals, their perceptions of their state of depletion and/or restoration will determine their subsequent self-regulatory performance. As was true for the classic models of misattribution (Schachter & Singer, 1962), to the extent that people's perceptions of their state of depletion are accurate and isomorphic with their actual state of resource availability, our model makes similar predictions to the resource model. However, as we have seen from this research, there are many situations in which actual and perceived state of depletion and restoration diverge. Moreover, the inherent ambiguity of our internal state of mental energy affords the possibility that our expectancies will shape our interpretation of our own subjective experience. In this way, our model seems entirely consistent with Inzlicht and Schmeichel's (2012) process model, which posits that motivational and/or attentional shifts occur following depletion that drive subsequent self-regulatory behavior. Individuals' perceived amount of available resources are likely to determine both when the motivation to exert (Muraven & Slessareva, 2003) or conserve (Muraven, Shmueli, & Burkley, 2006) their self-control resources as well as the prioritization of those resources (Inzlicht & Schmeichel, 2012; see Chapters 18, 8). While the specific details of how these models interface awaits future research, we believe that the dynamic ways by which perceptions of mental energy guide self-regulatory behavior is an important lens by which we will be able to progress further in our understanding of the psychology of restoration.

References

Anderson, C., & Berdahl, J. L. (2002). The experience of power: examining the effects of power on approach and inhibition tendencies. *Journal of Personality and Social Psychology, 83,* 1362–1377.

Aslaksen, P., & Flaten, M. A. (2008). The roles of physiological and subjective stress in the effectiveness of a placebo on experimentally induced pain. *Psychosomatic Medicine, 70,* 811–818.

Bargh, J. A., Bond, R. N., Lombardi, W. J., & Tota, M. E. (1986). The additive nature of chronic and temporary sources of construct accessibility. *Journal of Personality and Social Psychology, 50,* 869–878.

Baumeister, R. F. (2014). Self-regulation, ego depletion, and inhibition. *Neuropsychologica, 65,* 313–319.

Baumeister, R. F., Bratslavsky, E., Muraven, M., & Tice, D. M. (1998). Ego depletion: is the active self a limited resource? *Journal of Personality and Social Psychology, 74,* 1252–1265.

Baumeister, R. F., Muraven, M., & Tice, D. M. (2000). Ego depletion: a resource model of volition, self-regulation, and controlled processing. *Social Cognition, 18,* 130–150.

Beedie, C. J., & Lane, A. M. (2012). The role of glucose in self-control: another look at the evidence and an alternative conceptualization. *Personality and Social Psychology Review, 16,* 143–153.

Bless, H., Clore, G. L., Schwarz, N., Golisano, V., Rabe, C., & Wölk, M. (1996). Mood and the use of scripts: does a happy mood really lead to mindlessness? *Journal of Personality and Social Psychology, 71,* 665–679.

Cattell, R. B., & Cattell, A. K. S. (1960). *Culture Fair Intelligence Test: A measure of "g".* Bobbs-Merrill.

Chen, S., Lee-Chai, A. Y., & Bargh, J. A. (2001). Relationship orientation as a moderator of the effects of social power. *Journal of Personality and Social Psychology, 80,* 173–187.

Ciarocco, N. J., Sommer, K. L., & Baumeister, R. F. (2001). Ostracism and ego depletion: the strains of silence. *Personality & Social Psychology Bulletin, 27,* 1156–1163.

Clarkson, J. J., Hirt, E. R., Chapman, D. A., & Jia, L. (2011). The impact of illusory fatigue on executive control: do perceptions of depletion impair working memory capacity? *Social Psychological and Personality Science, 2,* 231–238.

Clarkson, J. J., Hirt, E. R., Jia, L., & Alexander, M. B. (2010). When perception is more than reality: the effects of perceived versus actual resource depletion on self-regulatory behavior. *Journal of Personality and Social Psychology, 98,* 29–46.

Colloca, L., & Benedetti, F. (2005). Placebos and painkillers: is mind as real as matter? *Nature Reviews Neuroscience, 6,* 545–552.

Crum, A. J., Corbin, W. R., Brownell, K. D., & Salovey, P. (2011). Mind over milkshakes: mindsets, not just nutrients, determine ghrelin response. *Health Psychology, 30,* 424–429.

Crum, A. J., & Langer, E. J. (2007). Mind-set matters: exercise and the placebo effect. *Psychological Science, 18,* 165–171.

vanDellen, M. R., Shah, J. Y., Leander, N. P., Delose, J. E., & Bornstein, J. X. (2015). In good company: managing interpersonal resources that support self-regulation. *Personality & Social Psychology Bulletin, 41,* 869–882.

DeWall, C. N., Baumeister, R. F., Mead, N. L., & Vohs, K. D. (2011). How leaders self-regulate their task performance: evidence that power promotes diligence, depletion, and disdain. *Journal of Personality and Social Psychology, 100,* 47–65.

Draganich, C., & Erdal, K. (2014). Placebo sleep affects cognitive functioning. *Journal of Experimental Psychology: Learning, Memory, and Cognition, 40*(3), 857–864.

Egan, P. M., Clarkson, J. J., & Hirt, E. R. (2015). Revisiting the restorative effects of positive mood: an expectancy-based approach to self-control restoration. *Journal of Experimental Social Psychology, 57,* 87–99.

REFERENCES

Egan, P. M., & Hirt, E. R. (2015). Flipping the switch: power, social dominance, and expectancies of mental energy change. *Personality & Social Psychology Bulletin, 41*, 336–350.

Egan, P. M., Hirt, E. R., & Karpen, S. C. (2012). Taking a fresh perspective: vicarious restoration as a means of recovering self-control. *Journal of Experimental Social Psychology, 48*, 457–465.

Fazio, R. H., & Zanna, M. P. (1978). On the predictive validity of attitudes: the roles of direct experience and confidence. *Journal of Personality, 46*(2), 228–243.

Finniss, D. G., Kaptchuk, T. J., Miller, F., & Benedetti, F. (2010). Biological, clinical, and ethical advances of placebo effects. *The Lancet, 375*, 686–695.

Fishbach, A., & Labroo, A. A. (2007). Be better or be merry: how mood affects self-control. *Journal of Personality and Social Psychology, 93*, 158.

Fishbach, A., & Trope, Y. (2007). Implicit and explicit mechanisms of counteractive self-control. In J. Y. Shah, & W. Gardner (Eds.), *Handbook of motivation science* (pp. 281–294). NY: Guilford.

Fujita, K., Trope, Y., Liberman, N., & Levin-Sagi, M. (2006). Construal levels and self-control. *Journal of Personality and Social Psychology, 90*, 351–367.

Gailliot, M. T., Baumeister, R. F., DeWall, C. N., Maner, J. K., Plant, E. A., Tice, D. M., … Schmeichel, B. J. (2007). Self-control relies on glucose as a limited energy source: willpower is more than a metaphor. *Journal of Personality and Social Psychology, 92*, 325–336.

Galinsky, A. D., Gruenfeld, D. H., & Magee, J. C. (2003). From power to action. *Journal of Personality and Social Psychology, 85*, 453–466.

Gilbert, D. T., Pelham, B. W., & Krull, D. S. (1988). On cognitive busyness: when person perceivers meet persons perceived. *Journal of Personality and Social Psychology, 54*, 733–740.

Gonzalez, A. E. J., & Cooper, J. (1976). What to do with leftover dissonance: blame it on the lights. Reported in Zanna, M. P., & Cooper, J. Dissonance and the attribution process. In J. H. Harvey, W. J. Ickes, & R. F. Kidd (Eds.), *New directions in attribution research* (Vol. 1). Hillsdale, NJ: Erlbaum.

Hagger, M. S., Wood, C., Stiff, C., & Chatzisarantis, N. L. D. (2010). Ego depletion and the strength model of self-control: a meta-analysis. *Psychological Bulletin, 136*, 495–525.

Hatfield, E., Cacioppo, J. L., & Rapson, R. L. (1993). Emotional contagion. *Current Directions in Psychological Sciences, 2*, 96–99.

Hendrix, K. S., & Hirt, E. R. (2009). Stressed out over possible failure: the role of regulatory fit on claimed self-handicapping. *Journal of Experimental Social Psychology, 45*, 51–59.

Inzlicht, M., & Schmeichel, B. J. (2012). What is ego depletion? toward a mechanistic revision of the resource model of self-control. *Perspectives on Psychological Science, 7*, 450–463.

Jarvis, W. B. G., & Petty, R. E. (1996). The need to evaluate. *Journal of Personality and Social Psychology, 70*, 172–194.

Jia, L., Hirt, E. R., & Fishbach, A. (2016). Spotlight model of depletion: Protecting high and abandoning low commitment goal pursuit in response to ego depletion. *Journal of Personality and Social Psychology*.

Job, V., Dweck, C. S., & Walton, G. M. (2010). Ego depletion—is it all in your head? Implicit theories about willpower affect self-regulation. *Psychological Science, 21*, 1–8.

Kam-Hansen, S., Jakubowski, M., Kelley, J. M., Kirsch, I., Hoaglin, D. C., Kaptchuk, T. J., & Burstein, R. (2014). Altered placebo and drug labeling changes the outcome of episodic migraine attacks. *Science Translational Medicine, 6*, 218ra5.

Kaplan, S., & Berman, M. G. (2010). Directed attention as a common resource for executive functioning and self-regulation. *Perspectives on Psychological Science, 5*, 43–57.

Krosnick, J. A., & Petty, R. E. (1995). Attitude strength: an overview. *Attitude strength: Antecedents and consequences, 1*, 1–24.

Lammers, J., Galinsky, A. D., Gordijn, E. H., & Otten, S. (2008). Illegitimacy moderates the effects of power on approach. *Psychological Science, 19*, 558–564.

Macrae, C. N., Bodenhausen, G. V., Milne, A. B., & Jetten, J. (1994). Out of mind but back in sight: stereotypes on the rebound. *Journal of Personality and Social Psychology, 67*, 808–817.

Magee, J. C., & Langer, C. A. (2008). How personalized and socialized power motivation facilitate antisocial and prosocial decision-making. *Journal of Research in Personality, 42*, 1547–1559.

Magee, J. C., & Smith, P. K. (2013). The social distance theory of power. *Personality and Social Psychology Review, 17*, 158–186.

Maner, J. K., Gailliot, M. T., Menzel, A. J., & Kunstman, J. W. (2012). Dispositional anxiety blocks the psychological effects of power. *Personality & Social Psychology Bulletin, 38*, 1383–1395.

Maner, J. K., & Mead, N. L. (2010). The essential tension between leadership and power: when leaders sacrifice group goals for the sake of self-interest. *Journal of Personality and Social Psychology, 99*, 482–497.

Meissner, K., Bingel, U., Colloca, L., Wager, T. D., Watson, A., & Flaten, M. A. (2011). The placebo effect: advances from different methodological approaches. *The Journal of Neuroscience, 31*, 16117–16124.

Molden, D. C., & Dweck, C. S. (2006). Finding "meaning" in psychology: a lay theories approach to self-regulation, social perception, and social development. *American Psychologist, 61*, 192–203.

Molden, D. C., Hui, C. M., Scholer, A. A., Meier, B. P., Noreen, E. E., D'Agostino, P. R., & Martin, V. (2012). The motivational versus metabolic effects of carbohydrates on self-control. *Psychological Science, 23*, 1137–1144.

Morton, D. L., El-Deredy, W., Watson, A., & Jones, A. K. P. (2010). Placebo analgesia as a case of a cognitive style driven by prior expectation. *Brain Research, 1359*, 137–141.

Muraven, M., Shmueli, D., & Burkley, E. (2006). Conserving self-control strength. *Journal of Personality and Social Psychology, 91*, 524–537.

Muraven, M., & Slessareva, E. (2003). Mechanisms of self-control failure: motivation and limited resources. *Personality & Social Psychology Bulletin, 29*, 894–906.

Muraven, M., Tice, D. M., & Baumeister, R. F. (1998). Self-control as a limited resource: regulatory depletion patterns. *Journal of Personality and Social Psychology, 74*, 774–789.

Nisbett, R. E., & Wilson, T. D. (1977). Telling more than we can know: verbal reports on mental processes. *Psychological Review, 84*, 231–259.

Nussbaum, A. D., & Dweck, C. S. (2008). Defensiveness versus remediation: self-theories and modes of self-esteem maintenance. *Personality & Social Psychology Bulletin, 34*, 599–612.

Petrocelli, J. V., Clarkson, J. J., Tormala, Z. L., & Hendrix, K. S. (2010). Perceiving stability as a means to attitude certainty: the role of implicit theories of attitudes. *Journal of Experimental Social Psychology, 46*, 874–883.

Pratto, F., Sidanius, J., Stallworth, L. M., & Malle, B. F. (1994). Social dominance orientation: a personality variable predicting social and political attitudes. *Journal of Personality and Social Psychology, 67*, 741–763.

Sassenberg, K., Ellemers, N., & Scheepers, D. (2012). The attraction of social power: the influence of construing power as opportunity versus responsibility. *Journal of Experimental Social Psychology, 48*, 550–555.

Schachter, S., & Singer, J. (1962). Cognitive, social, and physiological determinants of emotional state. *Psychological Review, 69*, 379–399.

Schmeichel, B. J. (2007). Attention control, memory updating, and emotional regulation temporarily reduce the capacity for executive control. *Journal of Experimental Psychology: General, 136*, 241–255.

Schmeichel, B. J., & Vohs, K. (2009). Self-affirmation and self-control: affirming core values counteracts ego depletion. *Journal of Personality and Social Psychology, 96*, 770–782.

Schwarz, N., & Clore, G. L. (1983). Mood, misattribution, and judgments of well-being: informative and directive functions of affective states. *Journal of Personality and Social Psychology, 45*, 513–523.

Smith, P. K., Jostmann, N., Galinsky, A. D., & van Dijk, W. W. (2008). Lacking power impairs executive functions. *Psychological Science, 16*, 785–791.

REFERENCES

Stewart-Williams, S., & Podd, J. (2004). The placebo effect: dissolving the expectancy versus conditioning debate. *Psychological Bulletin, 130,* 324–340.

Stoate, I., Wulf, G., & Lewthwaite, R. (2012). Enhanced expectancies improve movement efficiency in runners. *Journal of Sports Sciences, 30,* 815–823.

Thayer, R. E. (1989). *The biopsychology of mood and arousal.* New York: Oxford University Press.

Tice, D. M., Baumeister, R. F., Shmueli, D., & Muraven, M. (2007). Restoring the self: positive affect helps improve self-regulation following ego depletion. *Journal of Experimental Social Psychology, 43,* 379–384.

Trope, Y., & Liberman, A. (1996). Social hypothesis-testing: cognitive and motivational mechanisms. In E. T. Higgins, & A. W. Kruglanski (Eds.), *Social psychology: Handbook of basic principles* (pp. 239–270). New York: Guilford Press.

Vohs, K. D., Baumeister, R. F., & Schmeichel, B. J. (2012). Motivation, personal beliefs, and limited resources all contribute to self-control. *Journal of Experimental Social Psychology, 48,* 943–947.

Webb, T. L., & Sheeran, P. (2003). Can implementation intentions help to overcome ego-depletion? *Journal of Experimental Social Psychology, 53,* 5–13.

Wegner, D. M. (1994). Ironic processes of mental control. *Psychological Review, 101,* 34–52.

Wegner, D. M., Schneider, D. J., Carter, S. R., & White, T. L. (1987). Paradoxical effects of thought suppression. *Journal of Personality and Social Psychology, 53,* 5–13.

Wilson, T. D., Lisle, D., Schooler, J., Hodges, S. D., Klaaren, K. J., & LaFleur, S. J. (1993). Introspecting about reasons can reduce post-choice satisfaction. *Personality and Social Psychology Bulletin, 19,* 331–339.

SECTION 4

MULTIPLE SYSTEM APPROACHES TO EGO CONTROL

CHAPTER

13

Valuation as a Mechanism of Self-Control and Ego Depletion

E.T. Berkman, L.E. Kahn, J.L. Livingston
University of Oregon, Eugene, OR, United States

This chapter presents a mechanistic account of self-control that provides a parsimonious explanation of many phenomena related to self-control including ego depletion. We propose that valuation—the process of integrating multiple sources of subjective value for a given choice option—is a mechanism of self-control. The sources of subjective value can be "hot," such as impulses or temptations, or "cold," such as health concerns or long-term goals. A given choice option can have an arbitrary number of value sources, the sources of value for the response options can be heterogeneous, and the value sources can shift over time depending on situational or intrapersonal constraints. In this way, the valuation mechanism extends classic "dual process" models of self-control by specifying a mechanism for self-control conflict resolution that has well-studied behavioral and neural properties. This *valuation model* of self-control draws upon the extensive insights from the decision-making and neuroeconomics literature about the dynamic nature of valuation to account for the ego-depletion phenomenon and other effects related to how self-control fluctuates over time.

We begin by defining the central-related constructs of self-regulation and self-control. These definitions are not perfunctory, but rather are necessary to get to the core of current debate about the nature of self-control and why it apparently "fatigues" with use. We will then describe the key gap in the present literature, which is the lack of a specific mechanism or process by which self-control conflicts come to be resolved. Following on that background, we will present the valuation model and explain how valuation is a viable candidate mechanism for self-control. Next, we will provide a stepwise, mechanistic explanation for the ego-depletion phenomenon based on the valuation model. We close by arguing that the valuation model can enable the field to move beyond descriptive research and provide tangible prescriptive tools to help people improve self-control.

DEFINITIONS OF CENTRAL CONSTRUCTS: SELF-REGULATION, SELF-CONTROL, AND SUBJECTIVE VALUE

This volume contains a number of definitions of the constructs, and this chapter does not intend to focus mostly on definitions, let alone provide the definitive ones (see Chapter 5, for a detailed discussion of definitional issues). Nonetheless clear definitions of the constructs are a prerequisite for a theory that purports to explain how those constructs interact with each other. Beyond that, often clear definitions can help elucidate theoretical issues, which we believe is the case here. Specifically, defining self-regulation and self-control in terms of (observable) behavioral outcomes instead of (unobservable) mental processes broadens the scope of possible explanations for self-control and enables connections to be made between the self-control literature and other literature that would appear to be unrelated when focusing only on the underlying processes.

What Do We Mean by Self-regulation and Self-control?

Self-regulation is defined here as purposefully directing one's actions, thoughts, and feelings toward a goal (Carver & Scheier, 2011). A goal is a cognitive construct that specifies an intended outcome, typically one that is relatively long in duration and wide in scope compared to immediate or hedonic desires. Goals are embedded in a mental hierarchy with long-term, abstract, "be" actions at the top and short-term, concrete, "do" actions at the bottom (Carver & Scheier, 1998). It is of note that self-regulation can proceed with relatively little conflict as long as goal-counter impulses or temptations are avoided. In this sense, self-regulation can, but does not always, rely upon self-control. For example, "quit smoking" is a self-regulatory goal for a smoker that would require self-control only when the goal conflicts with the low-level goal to "smoke a cigarette"; effective self-regulation can be achieved without self-control if situations that trigger the low-level goal are anticipated and avoided.

We define self-control as the set of processes that promote the enactment of psychologically distant goals when they conflict with psychologically proximal ones. It is noteworthy that in this definition self-control includes not only overriding or inhibiting prepotent responses (typically referred to as inhibitory control, an avoidance action) but also biasing behavior toward desired responses, usually in the face of prepotent alternative responses or mere inertia (sometimes referred to as goal striving, an approach action). This definition implies that there are many ways to resolve self-control conflicts, with inhibitory control or other forms of cognitive control as only one possibility. Another might be to strengthen the motivation to enact the long-term oriented behavior, for example, through high-level construal (Fujita & Carnevale, 2012) or by directly incentivizing it (Muraven & Slessareva, 2003). For example, self-control on a Stroop task might involve maximizing performance instead of giving in to the temptation to slack off, and one way to perform well would be to engage attentional control to focus on the color of the first letter of each word. Self-control success is thus "equifinal" when it is defined by enacting a behavior that favors long-term outcomes because there are many ways to do so. In contrast, self-control failure in a given situation is usually tied to one behavior (eg, acting on a specific temptation).

What Do We Mean by "Subjective Value"?

Value has been given a variety of definitions in the research literature, but here we use it to refer to a subjective sense of net reward or utility (positive value) or punishment, disutility, or cost (negative value) associated with a given behavior (Camerer & Loewenstein, 2004; Kahneman, 2003). Subjective value bears on self-control to the extent that choices about behaviors relevant to goals are adjudicated by a value comparison process: the perceived response options in a given situation are each assigned a value and the option with the greatest value is enacted. Value is continuous as opposed to categorical, and can fluctuate from moment to moment (Busemeyer & Townsend, 1993). Subjective value is the "common currency" that enables a comparison among qualitatively different outcomes (Georgescu-Roegen, 1968; Glimcher & Rustichini, 2004). For example, in deciding whether or not to smoke a cigarette, a smoker might compare the anticipated positive value derived from hedonic experience against the anticipated negative value associated with failing to live up to social expectations and his or her long-term goals and self-concept.

The term "value" is sometimes used synonymously with "reward"; however, reward generally refers to the outcome of a decision, whereas value refers to the **expected** outcome (Montague, King-Casas, & Cohen, 2006). As such, subjective value is computed in the prechoice period, after options have been considered but before a decision has been made. In the behavioral economics and neuroeconomics literature, this kind of value is called "decision value" because it represents a key input to the decision-making process (Chib, Rangel, Shimojo, & O'Doherty, 2009).

The calculation of subjective value in decision contexts (ie, when the individual must make a choice between two or more options) has been investigated primarily within the economics literature. This research has a century-long history that is beyond the scope of this chapter, although later we review work from the field of behavioral economics that is relevant to the valuation model of self-control. For now, three discoveries about subjective value are pertinent. The first is that the process of valuation involves translating heterogeneous inputs about a particular option, and integrating them into a cumulative summary that can be compared to other options. This process has been modeled extensively by economists (eg, Philiastides, Biele, & Heekeren, 2010), and can be captured with a stochastic evidence accumulator model that compiles noisy data until a threshold is reached and a decision can be made (De Martino, Fleming, Garrett, & Dolan, 2013; Smith & Ratcliff, 2004). The second is that, though valuation is used to model conscious choice, the process itself occurs implicitly and automatically (Lebreton, Jorge, Michel, Thirion, & Pessiglione, 2009). Explicit processes can modulate the process, for example, by volitionally drawing attention to certain features of the stimulus, but valuation occurs continuously even without explicit attention. Finally, valuation deviates in predictable ways from strict gain-maximization principles, displaying several characteristic "anomalies" that we detail later (Kahneman, Knetsch, & Thaler, 1991). These anomalies are relatively stable within persons, which can explain cross-situational stability of valuation and choice within an individual.

Another way that researchers have sought to understand the processes behind the unified value calculation is by identifying its neuroanatomical substrates. With remarkable consistency, these researchers have found that activity in the ventromedial prefrontal cortex (vmPFC) (and closely associated mesolimbic dopamine structures such as the orbitofrontal cortex, OFC, and the ventral striatum, VS; Wallis, 2007) tracks closely with the subjective value of a variety of stimuli including food, goods, money, and charitable donations (Chib et al., 2009; Gallagher, McMahan, & Schoenbaum, 1999; Hare, Camerer, Knoepfle, O'Doherty, & Rangel, 2010; Izuma, Saito, & Sadato, 2008; Levy & Glimcher, 2011; O'Doherty, 2007). We will also review this evidence in more detail in subsequent sections, where we argue that the vmPFC is the locus of value integration and therefore is instrumental in studying and improving self-control.

THE CRITICAL GAP IN THE LITERATURE: WHAT IS THE MECHANISM?

Regardless of precisely how self-regulation and self-control are defined, prominent psychological models of self-regulation focus on self-control as a critical component of self-regulation. Self-control is usually assumed to operate through a competition between two opposing processes: one control process that promotes successful self-regulation by impelling behavior toward a goal and a second impulsive process that promotes failed self-regulation by impelling behavior toward an alternative behavior that is counter to the goal (Hofmann, Friese, & Strack, 2009). For example, in the classic dieter's dilemma, the impulsive process is a craving for a tasty but high-calorie snack and the control process is the ability to resist the craving (eg, through attentional deployment, cognitive control, or some other top-down process). These "dual process" models explain the outcome of a given self-control effort as the product of a competition between the two processes, whereby the stronger "wins out" to enact the behavior.

There are two problematic aspects of this approach. First is that the dominant process is nearly always inferred by observation. For example, if a hungry participant does not eat a tempting food, then his or her behavior is attributed to effective self-control; but if he or she eats it, his or her behavior is attributed to poor self-control and/or excessive impulsiveness. Using this logic to infer a mental process from observed behavior is a key limitation of studies on dual process models because it is somewhat circular; if there are only two outcomes, then only two processes can be inferred. Thus, no pattern of observations can falsify dual process models in studies following this template.

Equally problematic is the lack of a specific mechanism by which the conflict between the two processes is resolved. The dual process model is a useful analogy, but the search for neural systems that clearly map on to the two psychological systems has thus far been unsuccessful (Kelley, Wagner, & Heatherton, 2015). Instead, a variety of neural systems appear to be activated in self-control conflicts depending on the situational constraints, individual differences, and other factors (Kelley et al., 2015). Thus it is far from apparent in this early stage of inquiry whether there are only two processes that feed into self-control conflict resolution. And, perhaps more critically, even if the number of processes does turnout to be two, it is not clear exactly how the conflict between them becomes resolved at a neural or computational level. The details of that conflict resolution are important because they will provide clues about why repeated attempts to resolve the conflict lead to ego depletion and other self-control phenomena.

VALUATION AS A MECHANISM OF SELF-CONTROL CONFLICT RESOLUTION

As noted earlier, the predominant assumption is that self-control conflicts are the result of two competing processes. However, these processes are only inferred based on behavioral responses, and when researchers use neuroimaging to directly measure their neural activation, no clear evidence of two separable systems has been found. An alternative approach, found within economics, is to model self-control conflict resolution as a "revealed preference" derived from an underlying valuation process (Gul & Pesendorfer, 2004; Samuelson, 1948). From this perspective, what can be inferred from an observable behavior is merely that the chosen option was preferred, or valued, to a greater degree than the unchosen option, though the reasons behind this preference are unknowable from the behavior alone. Self-control success or failure, therefore, is a result of the relative value placed on the choice options in the moment.

A valuation-based model of self-control addresses the problems described earlier related to the processes and the mechanism of conflict resolution. If automatic and controlled processes serve as inputs to a common valuation process instead of interacting directly with one another, then additional (third, fourth, etc.) processes can contribute to self-control conflict resolution simply by also contributing to the value calculation. And the extensive work from behavioral economics and neuroeconomics about subjective value and its neural underpinnings (reviewed later) provides an increasingly detailed model of the computations involved in the calculation of subjective value, which can be leveraged to inform how self-control conflicts are resolved.

As applied to self-control, the valuation model predicts that each option in a self-control conflict accumulates subjective value based on an arbitrary number of value inputs (Fig. 13.1). In psychology studies, there are usually only two choice options, but in the real world there can be many more (though Fig. 13.1 shows only two options for simplicity). Similarly, each option can have many value inputs. The value inputs can fluctuate dynamically depending on the organism's changing needs, available resources, and attentional focus. For example, the relative value of choice options can change as a function of which options are included in the choice set (Tversky & Simonson, 1993). Which options are noticed and evaluated and which are ignored or unseen is therefore a major factor in determining self-control outcomes. (The processes that determine which choice options are included in the choice set is beyond the scope of the present chapter, but interested readers can refer to Gross (2015) for a thoughtful discussion of this topic.) Additionally, the reference point against which values are assigned is not an absolute value, but rather a relative value that can change depending on psychological factors such as framing (Kahneman & Tversky, 1979). Therefore, the outcome of a self-control conflict is a product not only of the value inputs, but also of the context, the choice set, and the reference point, all of which can change from moment to moment.

In the following sections, we consider the implications if, in fact, self-control conflicts are resolved through a general valuation process. We first describe several anomalies in valuation that have been documented by research in economics, drawing parallels to the psychology literature, and then discuss research from neuroeconomics that has established the neural systems for valuation, outlining how this same system might be a mechanism of self-control.

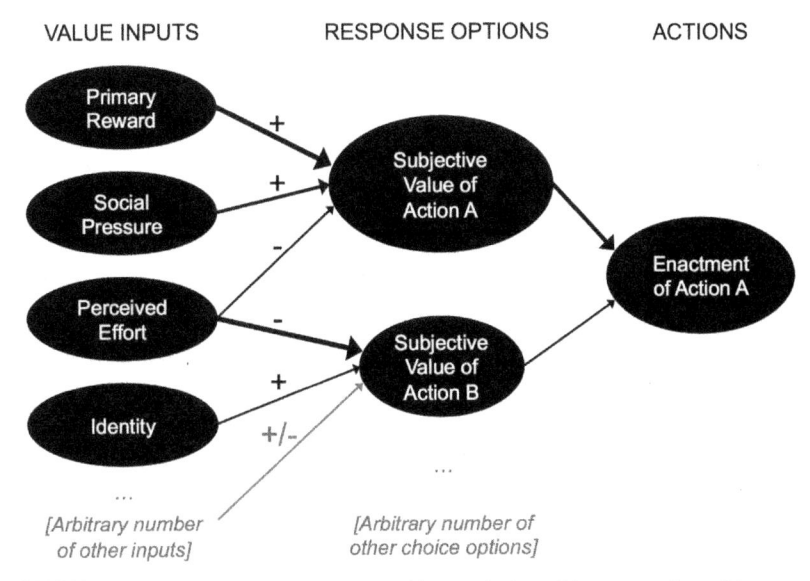

FIGURE 13.1 The valuation model of self-control. An arbitrary number of input processes such as primary/secondary rewards, social pressures, effort costs, and identity (left) contribute to the subjective value (middle) of the response options (eg, the "self-controlled" and "impulsive" actions). There can be an arbitrary number of input sources and response options depending on the context and the actions that are perceived as available, and the input sources and options can change across time. The option with the highest cumulative subjective value is enacted (right). Self-control success occurs when one of the actions that align with the long-term goal accumulates the greatest amount of subjective value.

Valuation Anomalies Relevant to Self-control

Research using economic games has documented an assortment of anomalies in value-based choice. For the most part, the anomalous behavior involves cases where people's behavior does not maximize objective gains or is inconsistent across time even though the gains and losses do not change (eg, Kahneman et al., 1991; Loewenstein & Thaler, 1989). These anomalies are of interest to economists because they violate classical economic models such as expected utility theory (von Neumann & Morgenstern, 1953), which hypothesizes that people make choices that maximize expected utility and are not influenced by irrelevant details such as when the gain will occur. The field of "behavioral economics" emerged to study these anomalies using empirical means and to update economic models based on predictable, if suboptimal, patterns of human behavior during economic choice (Camerer & Loewenstein, 2004).

Since the inception of the field in the 1970s, researchers in behavioral economics developed tools to evoke these behavioral anomalies in the lab and, thereby, rapidly generated a body of work that illustrates when these anomalies occur and describes them with formal models. This work assumes that economic choice is driven by a subjective value (or utility) calculation, and that the anomalies can be explained by predictable ways that objective gains and losses are translated into subjective value. If this same valuation process underlies self-control, then the results and models from behavioral economics should apply not only to economic choice but also to self-control conflict resolution. Below, we outline three anomalies in economic choice and explain how they can be understood as general phenomena that apply directly to the specific domain of self-control conflict.

Endowment

The endowment effect refers to the asymmetry in value people place on the same object when they sell it versus when they buy it: people ask a higher price as owners than they are willing to pay as buyers (Thaler, 1980). Even studies that control for the obvious reasons for the asymmetry, such as the seller's loss aversion, still reveal an endowment effect (Morewedge, Shu, Gilbert, & Wilson, 2009), suggesting that humans place some inherent value on mere ownership.

The explanation proposed by social psychologists is that owned objects can be viewed as part of the "extended self" (Belk, 1989; Wicklund & Gollwitzer, 1982) and therefore have more subjective value than objects that are not. This is supported by evidence that the endowment effect is greater for objects that have been owned for a longer time (Strahilevitz & Loewenstein, 1998) and objects that are easier to associate with the self such as coffee mugs featuring a college insignia (Tom, 2004). This explanation is further supported by extensive research in social psychology showing that people are motivated to maintain a positive self-image (Rosenberg, 1979; Taylor & Brown, 1988), and that one way they do so is by imbuing their beliefs, identities, possessions, and so forth with increased value (Abelson & Prentice, 1989; Crocker & Wolfe, 2001; Gawronski, Bodenhausen, & Becker, 2007; Pelham, 1995; Pelham & Swann, 1989).

In terms of the valuation mechanism of self-control, the endowment effect suggests that goals that are seen as part of the self or extended self will have higher value than those that are not, and are thus more likely to be enacted when they conflict with other actions or behaviors. This prediction has not yet been tested directly (eg, by comparing self-relevant versus non-self-relevant goals), but there is a variety of research that supports it indirectly. Most prominently, research testing self-determination theory (Deci & Ryan, 1985; Ryan & Deci, 2000; see Chapter 4) shows that goals that are consistent with the intrinsic motives for competence, relatedness, and autonomy are more successful than goals that are pursued for extrinsic reasons. For example, a self-control task that was chosen by participants (invoking the intrinsic motive of autonomy) was less depleting than a self-control task that was assigned to them by the experimenter (Moller, Deci, & Ryan, 2006).

Another line of research also provides indirect support for the prediction that ownership would improve goal pursuit. Studies in this line leverage the fact that identity is reflected in—and affected by—language, and specifically draw upon the subtle semantic effect of using a noun instead of a verb to describe the same action (eg, becoming "a quitter" versus attempting "to quit"). Indeed, the strength of smokers' "quitter" identities at baseline predicts smoking abstinence even when controlling for baseline smoking rates (Shadel & Mermelstein, 1996; Van Den Putte, Yzer, Willemsen, & De Bruijn, 2009). Similarly, using a noun ("being a voter") instead of a verb ("voting") in questions about the likelihood of voting increased voting intentions and actual turnout in statewide elections (Bryan, Walton, Rogers, & Dweck, 2011). In another study, participants were less likely to cheat by claiming money they were not entitled to if that behavior was described using a (negative) noun ("being a cheater") instead of a verb ("cheating"; Bryan, Adams, & Monin, 2013). All of these results are consistent with the prediction that ownership (of an identity) can increase self-control by increasing the subjective value of behaviors related to the identity.

Temporal Discounting

One of the most perplexing violations of pure economic utility maximization is that humans tend to "discount" gains as a function of time such that the equivalent amount of money is apparently worth less to us in the future than it is in the present (Ainslie, 1975; Green & Myerson, 2004). This anomaly is most apparent when people make choices between options that vary in both time and nominal value, known as "intertemporal choices." For example, most people would choose to gain $101 in 13 months instead of $100 in 12 months, and also choose $100 now instead of $101 1 month from now, even though both choices involve a gain of $1 in 1 month. Strict gain-maximization models incorrectly predict that people should choose the larger amount regardless of the delay.

The standard explanation for this phenomenon is that subjective value (relative to objective value) is discounted over time, typically following a hyperbolic function (Kirby & Marakovic, 1995). An ultimate cause of temporal discounting may be probability: later rewards are inherently more uncertain than sooner rewards because future events becomes more unpredictable as time increases (similar to the logic of the folk wisdom, "a bird in the hand is worth two in the bush"; Stevenson, 1986). Indeed, formal modeling supports the notion that people use the same underlying process to transform delayed rewards and probabilistic rewards into subjective value (Green & Myerson, 2004; Prelec & Loewenstein, 1991). Similarly, though Prospect Theory (Kahneman & Tversky, 1979) is technically a model of choice under uncertainty as opposed to time, the model's central claim that the calculation of subjective value involves a nonlinear transformation of objective value based on probability also applies to transformations of time (Rachlin, Raineri, & Cross, 1991).

The explanation from behavioral economics that time and probability are mentally interchangeable is consistent with construal level theory (CLT; Trope & Liberman, 2003, 2010) from social psychology. CLT states that various forms of distance—physical, temporal, probabilistic, and so forth—represent "psychological distances" that can all be overcome through the same process of creating abstract mental construals of psychologically distant objects. According to CLT, the process of making an intertemporal choice or an "interprobabilistic" choice (ie, one between options with differing numerical values and probabilities) involves computing the psychological distance of both options before comparing them. The relative strength of the more distal representation depends on a number of factors specified by the CLT including its perceptual features and the level of abstraction at which it is considered, or its "action identification" (Vallacher & Wegner, 1989).

The implication for self-control is that, all else being equal, the subjective value of psychologically distal options—those that are less likely, physically further away, and more intangible—will be less than the subjective value of psychological proximal options. Manipulations that counteract that asymmetry by reducing the psychological distance to the distal option, or by increasing the psychological distance to the proximal option, should thus change self-control behavior. Perhaps the most vivid example of this is the classic marshmallow studies in which most children had difficulty choosing two later, unseen, marshmallows in favor of one immediate, visible one, but directing attention away from the immediately visible marshmallow promoted self-control (eg, Mischel & Ebbesen, 1970). More recently, Fujita and colleagues have shown that construing a goal in terms of its high-level meaning and implications (eg, thinking about why you want to be healthy) increases self-control related to that goal, presumably because drawing attention to the goal increases its salience and reduces the psychological distance to a long-term goal that would otherwise feel distal and intangible (Fujita, Trope, Liberman, & Levin-Sagi, 2006). The valuation model predicts that any manipulation that reduces psychological distance should produce similar effects to the extent that the manipulation elicits changes in the appraisal of the possible responses and their relative subjective values.

Another implication for self-control is that individual differences in discounting will relate to real-world behaviors where the choice options consistently differ in time delay. This is the case, for example, in substance use, where the reward derived from the substance is immediate and certain, and the reward derived from abstinence is delayed and uncertain. Even if the two rewards were objectively equivalent, the subjective value of the delayed reward would be discounted because it is psychologically distant, so people who temporally discount more are expected to be more likely to choose the more immediate reward. Consistent with this, people who tend to discount delayed hypothetical rewards are more likely to use a variety of substances including nicotine, alcohol, cocaine, and heroin (Bickel, Odum, & Madden, 1999; Kirby & Petry, 2004; Petry, 2001) and are also more likely to have problems with gambling (Holt, Green, & Myerson, 2003). Additionally, a metaanalysis revealed the effect size of the relationship between addictive behaviors and delay discounting as indexed by multiple hypothetical choices to be $d=0.58$ (MacKillop et al., 2011). The fact that a relationship exists between discounting and a variety of problem behaviors supports the notion that valuation anomalies such as temporal discounting are "transdisease processes" (Bickel & Mueller, 2009), or general phenomena that apply to a range of behaviors.

Diminishing Marginal Utility

Diminishing marginal utility refers to the phenomenon that each additional unit of gain leads to an ever-smaller increase in subjective value. For example, three bites of candy are better than two bites, but the twentieth bite does not add much to the experience beyond the nineteenth (and could even make it worse). This effect is so well established that it is referred to as the "law of diminishing marginal utility" in economics (Gossen, 1854/1983), and is reflected in the concave shape of most subjective utility functions (eg, Kahneman & Tversky, 1979; Rabin, 2000; see Fig. 13.2). An important consequence of diminishing marginal utility is that subjective value changes most dynamically near the zero point, and quickly levels off as gains (or losses) accumulate.

Within the psychology literature, diminishing marginal utility is akin to the phenomena of affective habituation (Dijksterhuis & Smith, 2002) and hedonic adaptation (Brickman & Campbell, 1971). The general finding in these lines of work is that people quickly adjust to affective experiences, so that repeated exposures to the same stimulus are less potent (habituation) and major events do not generally change people's baseline affect (adaptation). Psychological models of adaptation have been updated and qualified in recent years, and may apply differently to short-term and long-term changes (see, for example, Diener, Lucas, & Scollon, 2006), but the general pattern holds: humans acclimate to events, particularly small events, as their novelty subsides. From a psychology perspective, diminishing marginal utility of short-term gains can be understood in terms of habituation—the first bite of chocolate tastes better than the second, and so forth—and long-term gains can be understood in terms of adaptation

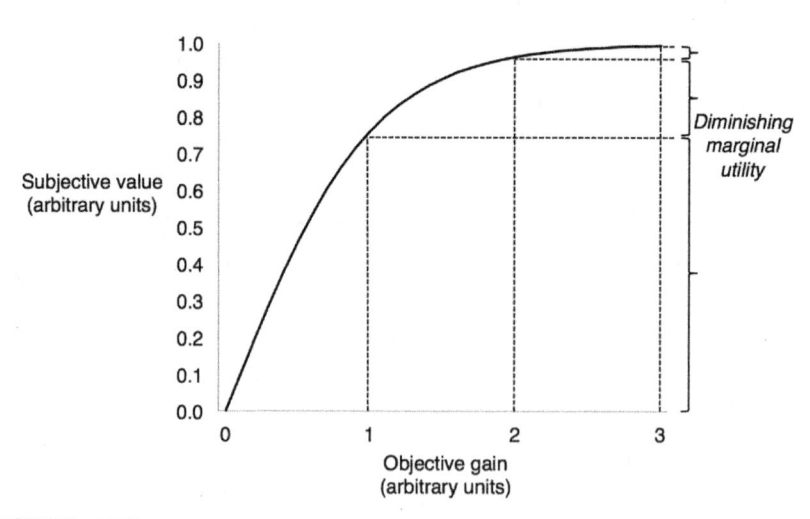

FIGURE 13.2 Diminishing marginal utility of gains. Given a concave relationship between objective gains (x-axis) and subjective value (y-axis), each one-unit gain produces a smaller increase in subjective value than the previous gain of an equal unit. The marginal utility, or the change in subjective value above the existing level, diminishes as gains increase (shown on the y-axis to the right).

to a new zero point—winning the lottery does not permanently increase happiness but instead resets one's reference point so that the subjective value of stimuli are evaluated with respect to that new starting point.

The tendency for returns on subjective value to diminish with repetition is relevant to how self-control plays out over time. By our definition, self-control is required when there is a conflict between a high-level goal and a low-level goal or impulse. Both options have some degree of subjective value, even if that value is derived from a different source (such as the immediate physical gratification associated with a positive experience or the sense of accomplishment that accompanies goal completion). Therefore, recent positive experiences that diminish the subjective value of one but not the other goal will influence self-control. Take, for example, the case of a smoker who is trying to quit and experiences a self-control conflict between the desire to smoke a cigarette (hedonic value) and the desire to quit (abstract goal value). According to the law of diminishing marginal utility, the subjective value of smoking an additional cigarette will be diminished if the smoker has just had a cigarette. Indeed, smokers are less likely to light up if they have recently smoked than if they were abstinent (and this effect also holds for food for most people; Epstein, Bulik, Perkins, Caggiula, & Rodefer, 1991). Apart from physiological factors such as dependency, the subjective value of a temptation (such as a cigarette for a smoker) is diminished with sequential consumption. Similarly, the subjective value of abstinence should be lower when a quitter makes progress than when he or she feels that he or she is falling short. As expected by diminishing marginal utility, motivation to attain a goal decreases if one focuses on the progress made toward that goal, particularly for goals to which an individual is highly committed (Fishbach, Eyal, & Finkelstein, 2010).

The law of diminishing marginal utility also applies to the case of ego depletion, a claim we will argue in a section later. First, however, we present neuroscientific data in support of the valuation model of self-control.

Neural Systems of Valuation

In addition to the extensive knowledge about choice anomalies that economics research has provided, the study of "neuroeconomics" has also established the neural systems that support the calculation of subjective value and how activity in those systems tracks with behavior. Identifying these systems is important because the valuation model assumes that there must be some region or set of brain regions that translate various inputs into a common mental currency in the form of subjective value so they can be integrated and compared to each other. Additionally, localizing these systems is the first step in understanding how to develop targeted interventions to improve self-regulation (Fisher & Berkman, 2015).

Neuroeconomics research overwhelmingly implicates regions in the mesolimbic dopaminergic system including the vmPFC, OFC, and VS in the computation of subjective value. Consistent with the common currency idea, this research suggests that the vmPFC is involved in the computation of subjective value of both appetitive and aversive stimuli (Bartra, McGuire, & Kable, 2013; Tom, Fox, Trepel, & Poldrack, 2007). In a series of studies, Rangel and colleagues have found that the vmPFC integrates information across a range of properties about a stimulus to produce a final value signal that includes stimulus properties, active goals, costs, and other types of choice-relevant information (Rangel & Hare, 2010). Not only does vmPFC integrate various sources of value for a stimulus, but activity in the vmPFC also tracks the subjective value of a range of stimulus types (Padoa-Schioppa & Assad, 2006). For example, vmPFC activity predicts choice regardless of whether the stimuli in question are food or money (Levy & Glimcher, 2011). A related study found that activity in vmPFC scales with the subjective value of a monetary gain for oneself and another person (Zaki, Lopez, & Mitchell, 2014). These findings converge in identifying the vmPFC as playing a central role in the integration of subjective value.

Activity in the vmPFC also tracks with the anomalies observed in the behavioral economics studies described earlier. This fact is important because it suggests that vmPFC codes for subjective value even when it deviates from objective reward value. For example, activity in vmPFC (and in the nearby medial prefrontal cortex) correlates with "mere ownership" (Kim & Johnson, 2014, 2015), which is suggestive that this region might be associated with endowment effects in valuation. Also, activity in vmPFC is related hyperbolically (as opposed to linearly) to the magnitude of both delayed and probabilistic rewards, and correlates highly with participants' delay discounting curves (Peters & Büchel, 2009). Furthermore, lesions to the vmPFC cause sharp increases in delay discounting, suggesting that the vmPFC is not merely involved in responses to immediate rewards (Sellitto, Ciaramelli, & di Pellegrino, 2010). Finally, activity in vmPFC appears to track marginal utility above and beyond discounting and accordingly diminishes as gains accumulate within a session (Pine et al., 2009).

The presumptive purpose of this vmPFC "unified valuation" system that integrates across disparate outcomes is to facilitate choice among them (Levy & Glimcher, 2011; Peters & Büchel, 2010). For example, the vmPFC value signal predicts decisions regardless of whether they appear to be driven by impulsive or self-controlled processes (eg, keeping money vs giving it to charity, or eating unhealthy vs healthy foods; Hare et al., 2010; Hare, Malmaud, & Rangel, 2011a). In another study, participants separately rated the tastiness and healthiness of a series of food stimuli, and then made choices about whether or not to eat each food (with one choice randomly selected at the conclusion of the study and given to the participant to eat). Activity in the vmPFC predicted the participants' subsequent choices regardless of whether the choice on a given trial was driven by health or taste concerns (Hare, Camerer, & Rangel, 2009). The vmPFC thus appears to be a point of convergence for value-related information during choice.

The valuation model predicts that the common value calculation integrates inputs from a variety of sources depending on the context. Consistent with this idea, the vmPFC receives inputs from other brain regions depending on the contextual cues and available response options. For example, the dorsolateral prefrontal cortex is functionally connected with the vmPFC when higher order goals such as health concerns or social factors are made salient (Hare et al., 2010, 2011a; Hutcherson, Plassmann, Gross, & Rangel, 2012). There is also evidence that the value of potential response options are reflected in the vmPFC before specific action plans are selected (Wunderlich, Rangel, & O'Doherty, 2010), and that value signals provide input to downstream brain regions that are responsible for selecting and implementing motor plans (Hare, Schultz, Camerer, O'Doherty, & Rangel, 2011b). And, like subjective value during choice, activity in the vmPFC in the moments before a decision also fits a stochastic evidence accumulator model (De Martino et al., 2013), presenting the possibility that its activity can be modeled at a relatively fine-grained level. Taken together, then, the emerging view from the neuroeconomics literature is that the vmPFC represents a point of convergence for a variety of input signals that are relevant to the decision at hand, and its activation reflects a dynamic value integration process that subsequently biases behavior toward high-valued actions.

Earlier, we have reviewed evidence showing that activity in the vmPFC and related regions (1) represents the subjective value of a variety of stimuli, (2) parallels subjective value anomalies in behavior such as endowment, temporal discounting, and diminishing marginal utility, (3) temporally precedes and predicts choice, and (4) receives input from other brain regions depending on the context and choice options. The evidence reviewed earlier strongly implicates the vmPFC as the neuroanatomical locus of an integration of heterogeneous inputs into a "neural currency" (Montague & Berns, 2002) of subjective value that drives decisions.

EGO DEPLETION EXPLAINED BY THE VALUATION MODEL

As described throughout this volume, "ego depletion" refers to the phenomenon that self-control performance declines from an initial self-control task to a subsequent one repetition (Baumeister, Bratslavsky, Muraven, & Tice, 1998). Ego depletion is studied in the laboratory typically using a sequential task paradigm in which participants complete an initial task that either requires a high or low amount of self-control (Time 1) and then another, supposedly unrelated self-control task (Time 2). Participants in the high self-control condition at Time 1 perform worse at Time 2 than participants in the low self-control condition. Having been observed in more than 200 studies (Hagger, Wood, Stiff, & Chatzisarantis, 2010), the fact that self-control performance wanes over time with use is not in doubt. What is lacking is an explanation for why it does so. Given the robustness of ego depletion, any proposed theory or mechanism of self-control must provide an account of ego depletion. Accordingly, the valuation model presents an explanation for ego depletion that is grounded in scientific knowledge about how subjective value is calculated.

The overarching valuation process hypothesis is that self-control outcomes are dictated by the relative subjective value of the choice options. In the specific case of ego depletion, the valuation model predicts that the subjective value of persistence on the task is initially higher than the alternatives, but then eventually becomes lower than the alternatives for the experimental participants. The first step in unpacking this prediction is to consider what the perceived choice options are in most ego-depletion studies. Participants complete a self-control task at Time 1. Notably, most people are capable of completing the task, so performance is attributed to motivation rather than ability per se. One choice option is to try to complete the task to the best of one's abilities ("maximizing"; Schwartz et al., 2002). A second option is to complete the task but in a halfhearted or otherwise relaxed way, investing enough work to fulfill the minimum requirements of the situation but no more, sometimes called "satisficing" (Simon, 1955, 1956).

Given this set of two choice options, and acknowledging that many more exist but are not chosen by most people, the next step is to consider the possible sources of subjective value for each. What is the utility of each option for participants? The empirical literature on ego depletion is moot on this point, for the most part making the blanket assumption that participants are motivated to engage in our studies. Fig. 13.3A depicts several plausible sources of subjective value for each option at Time 1. People might maximize to demonstrate their competence (Ryan & Deci, 2000), to fulfill an implied social contract with the experimenter ("I have agreed to participate so I will arrive and complete the experiment to the best of my ability"; Arrow, 1972), or perhaps out of curiosity, interest, or novelty seeking (Kashdan, Rose, & Fincham, 2004; Loewenstein, 1994). There are also costs, the most notable of which is effort (Kool & Botvinick, 2014; Kool, McGuire, Wang, & Botvinick, 2013; Westbrook & Braver, 2015). The option to satisfice requires less effort but does not fulfill competence needs and potentially violates the social contract, though it might have similar curiosity value. On balance, participants in most published ego-depletion studies appear to decide that the value of maximizing at Time 1 is at least slightly greater than the value of satisfying.

However, the value of each of those options changes over time because of diminishing marginal utility (Fig. 13.3B). Having demonstrated competence on Time 1, the value of putting in the same amount of work to continue to demonstrate competence on Time 2 is diminished. Additionally, some participants might have found value in demonstrating competence to the experimenter; this motive would have been fulfilled by good performance at Time 1. The social contract is at least partially fulfilled. This is particularly likely because many psychology studies involve only one task, but ego-depletion studies usually draw the participants' attention to the fact that they are being asked to do a separate, second task as part of the same study. (Performance actually improves on two highly similar, sequential self-control tasks, which could be due to participants perceiving them as part of the same task; Dewitte, Bruyneel, & Geyskens, 2009.) The value of novelty is marginally diminished or worse; participants might feel their curiosity about the experiment was amply satisfied after one (usually quite boring) task, and are actively *un*interested to learn more about a second. Finally, the cost of effort is the same or potentially greater. Some economists have noted the increasing marginal cost of effort (Mortensen, 1986), which is reflected in the vmPFC during decisions related to persistence on an effortful task (McGuire & Kable, 2015).

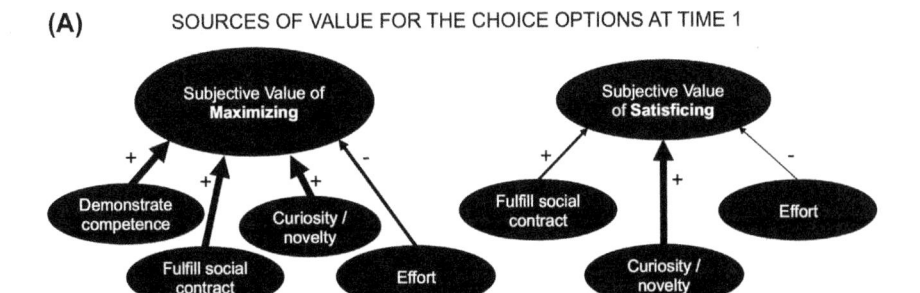

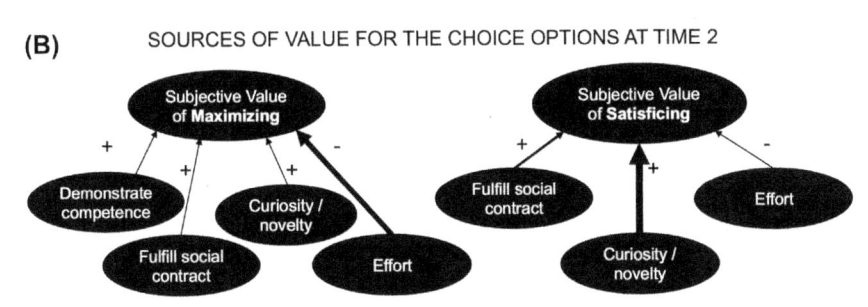

(A) SOURCES OF VALUE FOR THE CHOICE OPTIONS AT TIME 1

(B) SOURCES OF VALUE FOR THE CHOICE OPTIONS AT TIME 2

FIGURE 13.3 The valuation model explanation of ego depletion. At Time 1, the cumulative value of maximizing performance on the task is higher than the value of satisficing (A). But, at Time 2, the subjective value of maximizing is reduced because of the diminishing marginal utility of its value sources and the increasing marginal cost of effort (B). The net effect is that an individual is less likely to maximize performance at Time 2 than at Time 1.

All together, then, the sources of subjective value of maximizing at Time 2 are diminished or eliminated, and the costs are equal or greater. The increased relative value of satisficing can explain why many participants choose that option at Time 2.

A valuation explanation also explains some notable moderators of the ego-depletion effect (see Chapter 2 for further discussion of moderators). Anything that adds to the total subjective value of maximizing—either by increasing the value of that action or reducing its perceived costs—will increase its likelihood. This explains why incentives eliminate the ego-depletion effect (Muraven & Slessareva, 2003). Affirming core values is likely to involve intrinsic motives for maximizing autonomy and competence (Ryan & Deci, 2000) and also engages high-level construal (Fujita et al., 2006), both of which reframe the decision with respect to the self and frame attention around sources of value for the maximize option. It is not surprising, then, that self-affirmation reduces ego depletion (Schmeichel & Vohs, 2009). Beliefs that a task is not difficult or that resources are available might reduce the perceived cost of effort (Clarkson, Hirt, Jia, & Alexander, 2010). Likewise, individuals who believe that their self-control resources are unlimited (Job, Dweck, & Walton, 2010) may derive value from verifying that aspect of their identity to themselves and others (Swann & Read, 1981), which would explain why they maximize at Time 2. Similarly, reframing the Time 2 task as a measure of personal willpower eliminates the ego-depletion effect (Magen & Gross, 2007), and reframing it as a measure of physical strength instead of mental strength increases the effect (see Chapter 17), presumably because the task's diagnosticity gives participants a reason to value good performance.

The valuation model provides a mechanistic explanation for how ego depletion occurs in terms of shifts in subjective value. The explanation is grounded in a theoretical model supported by extensive behavioral and neural data, and accounts for many of the known moderators of the depletion effect. Additionally, the model draws a connection between research on self-control and ego depletion and the literature on behavioral economics and neuroeconomics. In the final section, we describe a key benefit of this connection, which is that it allows the field to leverage knowledge about the valuation system to improve self-control and self-regulation.

A NEW HORIZON FOR SELF-CONTROL RESEARCH

The forefather of social psychology Kurt Lewin is reported to have challenged psychologists in saying that "if you truly want to understand something, try to change it." Many theories of self-regulation fall short of this standard. They describe empirical phenomena, and perhaps indicate the conditions under which self-control is likely to succeed or fail. Recent theorizing and research on the resource model, for example, focuses mostly on defining the nature of the resource that is apparently depleted (such as whether it is physiological or motivational). Despite a handful of studies showing a modest effect of training on self-control (Inzlicht & Berkman, 2015), fewer than 10 studies have been prescriptive rather than descriptive.

The imbalance between descriptive and prescriptive research is understandable. It is prudent to study something thoroughly before attempting to change it. But, as Lewin's quote suggests, an intervention can be a strong test of a theory, and social science faces a dearth of advice for people seeking help with self-control deficits. The valuation model of self-control lends itself well to prescriptive tests because it specifies a mechanistic process (valuation) with a well-characterized neuroanatomical system (the vmPFC and related regions) for a behavioral phenotype (self-control) that relates to a broad range of socially costly outcomes. The next step is to develop intervention studies that target valuation at the psychological and, ideally, neural levels (Fisher & Berkman, 2015).

In some ways, this research has already begun. Noting that sharp temporal discounting seems to confer risk for a variety of disorders related to self-control, researchers have attempted to reduce discounting as a therapeutic and preventive intervention for substance use and other disorders (Bickel, Quisenberry, Moody, & Wilson, 2015). Others have taken a similar approach in targeting "inhibitory control," or the ability to prevent an unwanted behavioral response (Berkman, Graham, & Fisher, 2012). However, these lines of work focus on neurocognitive skills such as working memory or inhibition, which interact with the valuation system, but they do not target the valuation system itself. The next generation of interventions could focus directly on the valuation system itself, which would be not only a more robust test of the valuation mechanism hypothesis, but also a way to more fully capitalize on the knowledge available about valuation from the related literature described earlier.

What might interventions to improve self-control based on the valuation model look like? One is to add subjective value to self-control in a rather direct way—paying for it. This intervention is known as "contingency management" and is an effective treatment for a range of substance use disorders (Bigelow & Silverman, 1999). Similarly, imposing a monetary cost for self-control failures can also be effective in changing behavior (Schwartz et al., 2014). Another potential source of subjective value is identity (Berkman, Livingston, & Kahn, 2015). As noted earlier, the endowment effect follows from the fact that people value themselves and their attributes and property, and people actively seek to verify their beliefs about themselves. Given this, it may be the case that aspects of identity could become self-fulfilling, so an identity intervention to target people's self-concept would be effective. For instance, calling someone conscientious might make him or her disposed to act in a conscientious way, which might eventually turn into full-blown conscientiousness (Alfano, 2016). In one study, labeling children as "tidy" prompted them to conform to this label to a greater degree than merely asking them to be tidier (Miller, Brickman, & Bolen, 1975); in another, calling adults helpful led them to see themselves as altruistic, which in turn increased their willingness to volunteer (Burger & Caldwell, 2003). To our knowledge, nobody has yet tried this with self-control ("you are good at self-control"); this is a promising avenue for future research.

More generally, considering how to improve self-control based on the valuation model involves thinking through the myriad possible sources of value for self-control. This is relatively new territory for the field, but we believe it could be highly impactful. A complete model of self-regulation requires that we understand not just when people meet their goals and the skills that are necessary, but also the reasons why people pursue the goals they do in the first place.

References

Abelson, R. P., & Prentice, D. A. (1989). Beliefs as possessions: a functional perspective. In Anthony R. Pratkanis, Steven James Breckler, & Anthony G. Greenwald (Eds.), *Attitude structure and function* (pp. 361–381). Hillsdale, NJ: Erlbaum.

Ainslie, G. (1975). Specious reward: a behavioral theory of impulsiveness and impulse control. *Psychological Bulletin*, 82(4), 463–496.

Alfano, M. (2016). How one becomes what one is called. *Journal of Nietzsche Studies*, 46(2), 261–269. http://dx.doi.org/10.5325/jnietstud.46.2.0261.

Arrow, K. J. (1972). Gifts and exchanges. *Philosophy and Public Affairs*, 1(4), 343–362. http://dx.doi.org/10.2307/2265097.

Bartra, O., McGuire, J. T., & Kable, J. W. (2013). The valuation system: a coordinate-based meta-analysis of BOLD fMRI experiments examining neural correlates of subjective value. *Neuroimage*, 76, 412–427. http://dx.doi.org/10.1016/j.neuroimage.2013.02.063.

Baumeister, R. F., Bratslavsky, E., Muraven, M., & Tice, D. M. (1998). Ego depletion: is the active self a limited resource? *Journal of Personality and Social Psychology*, 74(5), 1252–1265.

Belk, R. W. (1989). Extended self and extending paradigmatic perspective. *Journal of Consumer Research*, 16(1), 129–132. http://dx.doi.org/10.2307/2489310.

Berkman, E. T., Graham, A. M., & Fisher, P. A. (2012). Training self-control: a domain-general translational neuroscience approach. *Child Development Perspectives*, 6(4), 374–384. http://dx.doi.org/10.1111/j.1750-8606.2012.00248.x.

Berkman, E., Livingston, J. L., & Kahn, L. E. (2015). Finding the "self" in self-regulation: the identity-value model. *SSRN Electronic Journal*. http://dx.doi.org/10.2139/ssrn.2621251.

Bickel, W. K., & Mueller, E. T. (2009). Toward the study of trans-disease processes: a novel approach with special reference to the study of co-morbidity. *Journal of Dual Diagnosis*, 5(2), 131–138. http://dx.doi.org/10.1080/15504260902869147.

Bickel, W. K., Odum, A. L., & Madden, G. J. (1999). Impulsivity and cigarette smoking: delay discounting in current, never, and ex-smokers. *Psychopharmacology*, 146(4), 447–454. http://dx.doi.org/10.1007/PL00005490.

Bickel, W. K., Quisenberry, A. J., Moody, L., & Wilson, A. G. (2015). Therapeutic opportunities for self-control repair in addiction and related disorders: change and the limits of change in trans-disease processes. *Clinical Psychological Science*, 3(1), 140–153. http://dx.doi.org/10.1177/2167702614541260.

Bigelow, G. E., & Silverman, K. (1999). Theoretical and empirical foundations of contingency management treatments for drug abuse. In S. T. Higgins, & K. Silverman (Eds.), *Motivating behavior change among illicit-drug abusers: Research on contingency management interventions* (pp. 15–31). Washington, DC: American Psychological Association.

Brickman, P., & Campbell, D. T. (1971). Hedonic relativism and planning the good society. In M. H. Appley (Ed.), *Adaptation level theory: A symposium* (pp. 287–302). New York: Psychology Press.

Bryan, C. J., Adams, G. S., & Monin, B. (2013). When cheating would make you a cheater: implicating the self prevents unethical behavior. *Journal of Experimental Psychology: General*, 142(4), 1001–1005. http://dx.doi.org/10.1037/a0030655.supp.

Bryan, C. J., Walton, G. M., Rogers, T., & Dweck, C. S. (2011). Motivating voter turnout by invoking the self. *Proceedings of the National Academy of Sciences*, 108(31), 12653–12656. http://dx.doi.org/10.1073/pnas.1103343108.

Burger, J. M., & Caldwell, D. F. (2003). The effects of monetary incentives and labeling on the foot-in-the-door effect: evidence for a self-perception process. *Basic and Applied Social Psychology*, 25(3), 235–241. http://dx.doi.org/10.1207/S15324834BASP2503_06.

Busemeyer, J. R., & Townsend, J. T. (1993). Decision field theory: a dynamic-cognitive approach to decision making in an uncertain environment. *Psychological Review*, 100(3), 432.

Camerer, C. F., & Loewenstein, G. (2004). Behavioral economics: past, present, future. In C. F. Camerer, G. Loewenstein, & M. Rabin (Eds.), *Advances in behavioral economics* (Vol. 1) (pp. 3–51). Princeton: Princeton University Press.

Carver, C., & Scheier, M. (1998). *On the self-regulation of behavior.* New York, NY: Cambridge University Press.

Carver, C. S., & Scheier, M. F. (2011). Self-regulation of action and affect. In (2nd ed.) K. D. Vohs, & R. F. Baumeister (Eds.), *Handbook of self-regulation* (Vol. 1) (pp. 3–21). New York: The Guilford Press.

Chib, V. S., Rangel, A., Shimojo, S., & O'Doherty, J. P. (2009). Evidence for a common representation of decision values for dissimilar goods in human ventromedial prefrontal cortex. *The Journal of Neuroscience, 29*(39), 12315–12320. http://dx.doi.org/10.1523/JNEUROSCI.2575-09.2009.

Clarkson, J. J., Hirt, E. R., Jia, L., & Alexander, M. B. (2010). When perception is more than reality: the effects of perceived versus actual resource depletion on self-regulatory behavior. *Journal of Personality and Social Psychology, 98*(1), 29–46. http://dx.doi.org/10.1037/a0017539.

Crocker, J., & Wolfe, C. T. (2001). Contingencies of self-worth. *Psychological Review, 108*(3), 593–623. http://dx.doi.org/10.1037//0033-295X.108.3.593.

De Martino, B., Fleming, S. M., Garrett, N., & Dolan, R. J. (2013). Confidence in value-based choice. *Nature Neuroscience, 16*(1), 105–110. http://dx.doi.org/10.1038/nn.3279.

Deci, E. L., & Ryan, R. M. (1985). *Intrinsic motivation and self-determination in human behavior.* New York: Plenum.

Dewitte, S., Bruyneel, S., & Geyskens, K. (2009). Self-regulating enhances self-regulation in subsequent consumer decisions involving similar response conflicts. *Journal of Consumer Research, 36*(3), 394–405.

Diener, E., Lucas, R. E., & Scollon, C. N. (2006). Beyond the hedonic treadmill: revising the adaptation theory of well-being. *The American Psychologist, 61*(4), 305–314. http://dx.doi.org/10.1037/0003-066X.61.4.305.

Dijksterhuis, A., & Smith, P. K. (2002). Affective habituation: subliminal exposure to extreme stimuli decreases their extremity. *Emotion, 2*(3), 203–214. http://dx.doi.org/10.1037/1528-3542.2.3.203.

Epstein, L. H., Bulik, C. M., Perkins, K. A., Caggiula, A. R., & Rodefer, J. (1991). Behavioral economic analysis of smoking: money and food as alternatives. *Pharmacology, Biochemistry, and Behavior, 38*(4), 715–721.

Fishbach, A., Eyal, T., & Finkelstein, S. R. (2010). How positive and negative feedback motivate goal pursuit. *Social and Personality Psychology Compass, 4*(8), 517–530.

Fisher, P. A., & Berkman, E. T. (2015). Designing Interventions Informed by Scientific Knowledge About Effects of Early Adversity: a Translational Neuroscience Agenda for Next-Generation Addictions Research. *Current Addiction Reports, 2*(4), 347–353. http://dx.doi.org/10.1007/s40429-015-0071-x.

Fujita, K., & Carnevale, J. J. (2012). Transcending temptation through abstraction: the role of construal level in self-control. *Current Directions in Psychological Science, 21*(4), 248–252. http://dx.doi.org/10.1177/0963721412449169.

Fujita, K., Trope, Y., Liberman, N., & Levin-Sagi, M. (2006). Construal levels and self-control. *Journal of Personality and Social Psychology, 90*(3), 351–367. http://dx.doi.org/10.1037/0022-3514.90.3.351.

Gallagher, M., McMahan, R. W., & Schoenbaum, G. (1999). Orbitofrontal cortex and representation of incentive value in associative learning. *The Journal of Neuroscience, 19*(15), 6610–6614.

Gawronski, B., Bodenhausen, G. V., & Becker, A. P. (2007). I like it, because I like myself: associative self-anchoring and post-decisional change of implicit evaluations. *Journal of Experimental Social Psychology, 43*(2), 221–232. http://dx.doi.org/10.1016/j.jesp.2006.04.001.

Georgescu-Roegen, N. (1968). Utility. In *International encyclopedia of social sciences* (Vol. 16) (pp. 236–267) New York.

Glimcher, P. W., & Rustichini, A. (2004). Neuroeconomics: the consilience of brain and decision. *Science, 306*(5695), 447–452. http://dx.doi.org/10.1126/science.1102566.

Gossen, H. H. (1983). *The laws of human relations and the rules of human action derived therefrom.* Cambridge, MA: MIT Press.

Green, L., & Myerson, J. (2004). A discounting framework for choice with delayed and probabilistic rewards. *Psychological Bulletin, 130*(5), 769–792. http://dx.doi.org/10.1037/0033-2909.130.5.769.

Gross, J. J. (2015). Emotion regulation: current status and future prospects. *Psychological Inquiry, 26*(1), 1–26. http://dx.doi.org/10.1080/1047840X.2014.940781.

Gul, F., & Pesendorfer, W. (2004). Self-control, revealed preference and consumption choice. *Review of Economic Dynamics, 7*(2), 243–264. http://dx.doi.org/10.1016/j.red.2003.11.002.

Hagger, M. S., Wood, C., Stiff, C., & Chatzisarantis, N. L. D. (2010). Ego depletion and the strength model of self-control: a meta-analysis. *Psychological Bulletin, 136*(4), 495–525. http://dx.doi.org/10.1037/a0019486.

Hare, T. A., Camerer, C. F., Knoepfle, D. T., O'Doherty, J. P., & Rangel, A. (2010). Value computations in ventral medial prefrontal cortex during charitable decision making incorporate input from regions involved in social cognition. *The Journal of Neuroscience, 30*(2), 583–590. http://dx.doi.org/10.1523/JNEUROSCI.4089-09.2010.

Hare, T. A., Camerer, C. F., & Rangel, A. (2009). Self-control in decision-making involves modulation of the vmPFC valuation system. *Science, 324*(5927), 646–648. http://dx.doi.org/10.1126/science.1168450.

Hare, T. A., Malmaud, J., & Rangel, A. (2011a). Focusing attention on the health aspects of foods changes value signals in vmPFC and improves dietary choice. *Journal of Neuroscience, 31*(30), 11077–11087. http://dx.doi.org/10.1523/JNEUROSCI.6383-10.2011.

Hare, T. A., Schultz, W., Camerer, C. F., O'Doherty, J. P., & Rangel, A. (2011b). Transformation of stimulus value signals into motor commands during simple choice. *Proceedings of the National Academy of Sciences of the United States of America, 108*(44), 18120–18125. http://dx.doi.org/10.1073/pnas.1109322108.

Hofmann, W., Friese, M., & Strack, F. (2009). Impulse and self-control from a dual-systems perspective. *Perspectives on Psychological Science, 4*(2), 162–176.

Holt, D. D., Green, L., & Myerson, J. (2003). Is discounting impulsive? *Behavioural Processes, 64*(3), 355–367. http://dx.doi.org/10.1016/S0376-6357(03)00141-4.

Hutcherson, C. A., Plassmann, H., Gross, J. J., & Rangel, A. (2012). Cognitive regulation during decision making shifts behavioral control between ventromedial and dorsolateral prefrontal value systems. *The Journal of Neuroscience, 32*(39), 13543–13554. http://dx.doi.org/10.1523/JNEUROSCI.6387-11.2012.

Inzlicht, M., & Berkman, E. T. (2015). Six questions for the resource model of control (and some answers). *Social and Personality Psychology Compass.* http://dx.doi.org/10.1111/spc3.12200.

Izuma, K., Saito, D. N., & Sadato, N. (2008). Processing of social and monetary rewards in the human striatum. *Neuron, 58*(2), 284–294. http://dx.doi.org/10.1016/j.neuron.2008.03.020.

Job, V., Dweck, C. S., & Walton, G. M. (2010). Ego depletion—is it all in your head? Implicit theories about willpower affect self-regulation. *Psychological Science, 21*(11), 1686–1693. http://dx.doi.org/10.1177/0956797610384745.

Kahneman, D. (2003). Maps of bounded rationality: psychology for behavioral economics. *The American Economic Review, 93*(5), 1449–1475.

Kahneman, D., Knetsch, J. L., & Thaler, R. H. (1991). Anomalies: the endowment effect, loss aversion, and status quo bias. *The Journal of Economic Perspectives, 5*(1), 193–206. http://dx.doi.org/10.2307/1942711.

Kahneman, D., & Tversky, A. (1979). Prospect theory: an analysis of decision under risk. *Econometrica, 47*(2), 263–292.

Kashdan, T. B., Rose, P., & Fincham, F. D. (2004). Curiosity and exploration: facilitating positive subjective experiences and personal growth opportunities. *Journal of Personality Assessment, 82*(3), 291–305. http://dx.doi.org/10.1207/s15327752jpa8203_05.

Kelley, W. M., Wagner, D. D., & Heatherton, T. F. (2015). In search of a human self-regulation system. *Annual Review of Neuroscience, 38,* 389–411. http://dx.doi.org/10.1146/annurev-neuro-071013-014243.

Kim, K., & Johnson, M. K. (2014). Extended self: spontaneous activation of medial prefrontal cortex by objects that are "mine". *Social Cognitive and Affective Neuroscience, 9*(7), 1006–1012. http://dx.doi.org/10.1093/scan/nst082.

Kim, K., & Johnson, M. K. (2015). Distinct neural networks support the mere ownership effect under different motivational contexts. *Social Neuroscience, 10*(4), 376–390. http://dx.doi.org/10.1080/17470919.2014.999870.

Kirby, K. N., & Marakovic, N. N. (1995). Modeling myopic decisions: evidence for hyperbolic delay-discounting within subjects and amounts. *Organizational Behavior and Human Decision Processes, 64*(1), 22–30.

Kirby, K. N., & Petry, N. M. (2004). Heroin and cocaine abusers have higher discount rates for delayed rewards than alcoholics or non-drug-using controls. *Addiction, 99*(4), 461–471. http://dx.doi.org/10.1111/j.1360-0443.2003.00669.x.

Kool, W., & Botvinick, M. (2014). A labor/leisure tradeoff in cognitive control. *Journal of Experimental Psychology: General, 143*(1), 131–141. http://dx.doi.org/10.1037/a0031048.

Kool, W., McGuire, J. T., Wang, G. J., & Botvinick, M. M. (2013). Neural and behavioral evidence for an intrinsic cost of self-control. *PLoS One, 8*(8), e72626. http://dx.doi.org/10.1371/journal.pone.0072626.

Lebreton, M., Jorge, S., Michel, V., Thirion, B., & Pessiglione, M. (2009). An automatic valuation system in the human brain: evidence from functional neuroimaging. *Neuron, 64*(3), 431–439. http://dx.doi.org/10.1016/j.neuron.2009.09.040.

Levy, D. J., & Glimcher, P. W. (2011). Comparing apples and oranges: using reward-specific and reward-general subjective value representation in the brain. *The Journal of Neuroscience, 31*(41), 14693–14707. http://dx.doi.org/10.1523/JNEUROSCI.2218-11.2011.

Loewenstein, G. (1994). The psychology of curiosity: a review and reinterpretation. *Psychological Bulletin, 116*(1), 75–98. http://dx.doi.org/10.1037/0033-2909.116.1.75.

Loewenstein, G., & Thaler, R. H. (1989). Anomalies: intertemporal choice. *The Journal of Economic Perspectives, 3*(4), 181–193. http://dx.doi.org/10.2307/1942918.

MacKillop, J., Amlung, M. T., Few, L. R., Ray, L. A., Sweet, L. H., & Munafò, M. R. (2011). Delayed reward discounting and addictive behavior: a meta-analysis. *Psychopharmacology, 216*(3), 305–321. http://dx.doi.org/10.1007/s00213-011-2229-0.

Magen, E., & Gross, J. J. (2007). Harnessing the need for immediate gratification: cognitive reconstrual modulates the reward value of temptations. *Emotion, 7*(2), 415–428. http://dx.doi.org/10.1037/1528-3542.7.2.415.

McGuire, J. T., & Kable, J. W. (2015). Medial prefrontal cortical activity reflects dynamic re-evaluation during voluntary persistence. *Nature Neuroscience, 18*(5), 760–766. http://dx.doi.org/10.1038/nn.3994.

Miller, R. L., Brickman, P., & Bolen, D. (1975). Attribution versus persuasion as a means for modifying behavior. *Journal of Personality and Social Psychology, 31*(3), 430–441. http://dx.doi.org/10.1037/h0076539.

Mischel, W., & Ebbesen, E. B. (1970). Attention in delay of gratification. *Journal of Personality and Social Psychology, 16*(2), 329–337.

Moller, A. C., Deci, E. L., & Ryan, R. M. (2006). Choice and ego-depletion: the moderating role of autonomy. *Personality and Social Psychology Bulletin, 32*(8), 1024–1036. http://dx.doi.org/10.1177/0146167206288008.

Montague, P. R., & Berns, G. S. (2002). Neural economics and the biological substrates of valuation. *Neuron, 36*(2), 265–284.

Montague, P. R., King-Casas, B., & Cohen, J. D. (2006). Imaging valuation models in human choice. *Annual Review of Neuroscience, 29,* 417–448. http://dx.doi.org/10.1146/annurev.neuro.29.051605.112903.

Morewedge, C., Shu, L., Gilbert, D., & Wilson, T. D. (2009). Bad riddance or good rubbish? Ownership and not loss aversion causes the endowment effect. *Journal of Experimental Social Psychology, 45,* 947–951.

Mortensen, D. T. (1986). Job search and labor market analysis. In O. C. Ashernfelter, & R. Layard (Eds.), *Handbook of labor economics* (pp. 849–919). UK: Oxford.

Muraven, M., & Slessareva, E. (2003). Mechanisms of self-control failure: motivation and limited resources. *Personality and Social Psychology Bulletin, 29*(7), 894–906. http://dx.doi.org/10.1177/0146167203029007008.

Neumann, von J., & Morgenstern, O. (1953). *Theory of games and economic behavior.* Princeton, NJ: Princeton University Press.

O'Doherty, J. P. (2007). Lights, Camembert, action! The role of human orbitofrontal cortex in encoding stimuli, rewards, and choices. *Annals of the New York Academy of Sciences, 1121*(1), 254–272. http://dx.doi.org/10.1196/annals.1401.036.

Padoa-Schioppa, C., & Assad, J. A. (2006). Neurons in the orbitofrontal cortex encode economic value. *Nature, 441*(7090), 223–226. http://dx.doi.org/10.1038/nature04676.

Pelham, B. W. (1995). Self-investment and self-esteem: evidence for a Jamesian model of self-worth. *Journal of Personality and Social Psychology, 69*(6), 1141–1150.

Pelham, B. W., & Swann, W. B. (1989). From self-conceptions to self-worth: on the sources and structure of global self-esteem. *Journal of Personality and Social Psychology, 57*(4), 672–680.

Peters, J., & Büchel, C. (2009). Overlapping and distinct neural systems code for subjective value during intertemporal and risky decision making. *The Journal of Neuroscience, 29*(50), 15727–15734. http://dx.doi.org/10.1523/JNEUROSCI.3489-09.2009.

Peters, J., & Büchel, C. (2010). Neural representations of subjective reward value. *Behavioural Brain Research, 213*(2), 135–141. http://dx.doi.org/10.1016/j.bbr.2010.04.031.

Petry, N. M. (2001). Delay discounting of money and alcohol in actively using alcoholics, currently abstinent alcoholics, and controls. *Psychopharmacology, 154*(3), 243–250. http://dx.doi.org/10.1007/s002130000638.

Philiastides, M. G., Biele, G., & Heekeren, H. R. (2010). A mechanistic account of value computation in the human brain. *Proceedings of the National Academy of Sciences, 107*(20), 9430–9435. http://dx.doi.org/10.1073/pnas.1001732107.

Pine, A., Seymour, B., Roiser, J. P., Bossaerts, P., Friston, K. J., Curran, H. V., & Dolan, R. J. (2009). Encoding of marginal utility across time in the human brain. *The Journal of Neuroscience, 29*(30), 9575–9581. http://dx.doi.org/10.1523/JNEUROSCI.1126-09.2009.

Prelec, D., & Loewenstein, G. (1991). Decision making over time and under uncertainty: a common approach. *Management Science, 37*(7), 770–786. http://dx.doi.org/10.2307/2632534.

Rabin, M. (2000). Risk aversion and expected-utility theory: a calibration theorem. *Econometrica, 68*(5), 1281–1292. http://dx.doi.org/10.2307/2999450.

Rachlin, H., Raineri, A., & Cross, D. (1991). Subjective probability and delay. *Journal of the Experimental Analysis of Behavior, 55*(2), 233–244. http://dx.doi.org/10.1901/jeab.1991.55-233.

Rangel, A., & Hare, T. (2010). Neural computations associated with goal-directed choice. *Current Opinion in Neurobiology, 20*(2), 262–270. http://dx.doi.org/10.1016/j.conb.2010.03.001.

Rosenberg, M. (1979). *Conceiving the self.* New York: Basic Books.

Ryan, R. M., & Deci, E. L. (2000). Self-determination theory and the facilitation of intrinsic motivation, social development, and well-being. *American Psychologist, 55*(1), 68–78.

Samuelson, P. A. (1948). Consumption theory in terms of revealed preference. *Economica, 15*(60), 243–253. http://dx.doi.org/10.2307/2549561.

Schmeichel, B. J., & Vohs, K. (2009). Self-affirmation and self-control: affirming core values counteracts ego depletion. *Journal of Personality and Social Psychology, 96*(4), 770–782. http://dx.doi.org/10.1037/a0014635.

Schwartz, J., Mochon, D., Wyper, L., Maroba, J., Patel, D., & Ariely, D. (2014). Healthier by precommitment. *Psychological Science, 25*(2), 538–546. http://dx.doi.org/10.1177/0956797613510950.

Schwartz, B., Ward, A., Monterosso, J., Lyubomirsky, S., White, K., & Lehman, D. R. (2002). Maximizing versus satisficing: happiness is a matter of choice. *Journal of Personality and Social Psychology*, 83(5), 1178–1197. http://dx.doi.org/10.1037//0022-3514.83.5.1178.

Sellitto, M., Ciaramelli, E., & di Pellegrino, G. (2010). Myopic discounting of future rewards after medial orbitofrontal damage in humans. *The Journal of Neuroscience*, 30(49), 16429–16436. http://dx.doi.org/10.1523/JNEUROSCI.2516-10.2010.

Shadel, W. G., & Mermelstein, R. (1996). Individual differences in self-concept among smokers attempting to quit: validation and predictive utility of measures of the smoker self-concept and abstainer self-concept. *Annals of Behavioral Medicine*, 18(3), 151–156.

Simon, H. A. (1955). A behavioral model of rational choice. *The Quarterly Journal of Economics*, 69(1), 99–118. http://dx.doi.org/10.2307/1884852.

Simon, H. A. (1956). Rational choice and the structure of the environment. *Psychological Review*, 63(2), 129–138.

Smith, P. L., & Ratcliff, R. (2004). Psychology and neurobiology of simple decisions. *Trends in Neurosciences*, 27(3), 161–168. http://dx.doi.org/10.1016/j.tins.2004.01.006.

Stevenson, M. K. (1986). A discounting model for decisions with delayed positive or negative outcomes. *Journal of Experimental Psychology: General*, 115(2), 131–154.

Strahilevitz, M. A., & Loewenstein, G. (1998). The effect of ownership history on the valuation of objects. *Journal of Consumer Research*, 25(3), 276–289. http://dx.doi.org/10.1086/209539.

Swann, W. B., & Read, S. J. (1981). Self-verification processes: how we sustain our self-conceptions. *Journal of Experimental Social Psychology*, 17(4), 351–372. http://dx.doi.org/10.1016/0022-1031(81)90043-3.

Taylor, S. E., & Brown, J. D. (1988). Illusion and well-being: a social psychological perspective on mental health. *Psychological Bulletin*, 103(2), 193–210.

Thaler, R. (1980). Toward a positive theory of consumer choice. *Journal of Economic Behavior & Organization*, 1(1), 39–60. http://dx.doi.org/10.1016/0167-2681(80)90051-7.

Tom, G. (2004). The endowment-institutional affinity effect. *Journal of Psychology Interdisciplinary and Applied*, 138(2), 160–170.

Tom, S. M., Fox, C. R., Trepel, C., & Poldrack, R. A. (2007). The neural basis of loss aversion in decision-making under risk. *Science*, 315(5811), 515–518. http://dx.doi.org/10.1126/science.1134239.

Trope, Y., & Liberman, N. (2003). Temporal construal. *Psychological Review*, 110(3), 403–421.

Trope, Y., & Liberman, N. (2010). Construal-level theory of psychological distance. *Psychological Review*, 117(2), 440–463. http://dx.doi.org/10.1037/a0018963.

Tversky, A., & Simonson, I. (1993). Context-dependent preferences. *Management Science*, 39(10), 1179–1189. http://dx.doi.org/10.2307/2632953.

Vallacher, R. R., & Wegner, D. M. (1989). Levels of personal agency: individual variation in action identification. *Journal of Personality and Social Psychology*, 57(4), 660–671.

Van Den Putte, B., Yzer, M., Willemsen, M. C., & De Bruijn, G.-J. (2009). The effects of smoking self-identity and quitting self-identity on attempts to quit smoking. *Health Psychology*, 28(5), 535–544. http://dx.doi.org/10.1037/a0015199.

Wallis, J. D. (2007). Orbitofrontal cortex and its contribution to decision-making. *Annual Review of Neuroscience*, 30(1), 31–56. http://dx.doi.org/10.1146/annurev.neuro.30.051606.094334.

Westbrook, A., & Braver, T. S. (2015). Cognitive effort: a neuroeconomic approach. *Cognitive, Affective, and Behavioral Neuroscience*, 15(2), 395–415. http://dx.doi.org/10.3758/s13415-015-0334-y.

Wicklund, R. A., & Gollwitzer, P. M. (1982). *Symbolic self-completion*. Hillsdale, NJ: Lawrence Erlbaum.

Wunderlich, K., Rangel, A., & O'Doherty, J. P. (2010). Economic choices can be made using only stimulus values. *Proceedings of the National Academy of Sciences*, 107(34), 15005–15010. http://dx.doi.org/10.1073/pnas.1002258107.

Zaki, J., Lopez, G., & Mitchell, J. P. (2014). Activity in ventromedial prefrontal cortex co-varies with revealed social preferences: evidence for person-invariant value. *Social Cognitive and Affective Neuroscience*, 9(4), 464–469. http://dx.doi.org/10.1093/scan/nst005.

CHAPTER

14

What Can Cognitive Neuroscience Tell Us About the Mechanism of Ego Depletion?

D.D. Wagner[1], T.F. Heatherton[2]

[1]The Ohio State University, Columbus, OH, United States; [2]Dartmouth College Hanover, New Hampshire, United States

The last decade has seen an ever-increasing interest in using the tools and methods of cognitive neuroscience to examine the brain systems involved in self-regulation and its failure (Heatherton & Wagner, 2011). Although the study of related topics, such as cognitive control, response inhibition, and the executive functions, have long been mainstays of cognitive neuroscience, research on self-regulation and self-regulation failure is a more recent phenomenon. Findings from this work have not only helped specify the brain mechanisms that underlie successful self-regulation, but they have also resulted in new ways of thinking about self-control and the reasons why it sometimes breaks down. Indeed, it is already the case that research findings from cognitive neuroscience are whittling their way back into psychological theory as evidenced by the increasing use of neuroscientific research in contemporary theories of self-regulation (Denson, DeWall, & Finkel, 2012; Hofmann, Schmeichel, & Baddeley, 2012; Inzlicht, Elkins-Brown, & Berkman, 2015; Inzlicht, Legault, & Teper, 2014; Inzlicht, Schmeichel, & Macrae, 2014; Kelley, Wagner, & Heatherton, 2015, Chapter 13).

As prior research has consistently shown, the ability to self-regulate is impaired following prior bouts of effortful self-control (Baumeister, Bratslavsky, Muraven, & Tice, 1998; Vohs & Heatherton, 2000; for a meta-analysis see Hagger, Wood, Stiff, & Chatzisarantis, 2010). However, there remains much debate concerning the mechanism for this phenomenon (Inzlicht & Berkman, 2015; Inzlicht & Schmeichel, 2012; Inzlicht, Schmeichel, & Macrae, 2014; Job, Dweck, & Walton, 2010, Chapter 11, Chapter 20). In this chapter, we review findings from cognitive neuroscience on the brain systems involved in ego depletion and how these may inform discussions of the mechanisms of ego depletion. We begin our chapter by first presenting an overview of several cognitive neuroscience methods and how they might be applied to the study of self-regulation failure and ego depletion. We then examine the extant neuroscience research on ego depletion, looking at how brain systems involved in self-control and reward processing are affected by ego depletion. Finally, we review recent neuroscience informed models of ego depletion that seek either to challenge or extend the limited resource model of self-regulation.

BRIEF OVERVIEW OF COGNITIVE NEUROSCIENCE METHODS

There are many tools in the cognitive neuroscience toolbox that have been used to study self-regulation and related topics. These tools can be grouped into three categories: those based on measuring or perturbing the electrical activity of the brain [eg, electroencephalography (EEG), magnetoencephalography (MEG), transcranial magnetic stimulation (TMS)], those based on detecting regional changes in blood flow (PET, fMRI) and those designed to assess anatomy and anatomical connectivity (MRI, DTI). In general, there is a trade-off between spatial and temporal resolution, such that measures of electrical activity are ideal for detecting the temporal dynamics of psychological processes but are comparatively poor at determining the precise location. Conversely, measures based on detecting blood flow changes are optimized for locating activity in the brain but suffer from poor temporal resolution. In this section, we give a brief overview of several of these methods, along with examples of how they have been, or may be, used to study ego depletion.

Electroencephalography and Magnetoencephalography

EEG is a method aimed at directly measuring the electrical potentials generated by ongoing neural activity with a temporal resolution in the milliseconds. Although providing a wealth of information about the timing of global brain activity, EEG's ability to localize brain activity to distinct regions is hampered by relatively poor spatial resolution and difficulty in localizing subcortical sources that lie below the surface of the brain. MEG is a related technique that, rather than measuring electrical potentials, uses an array of sensitive magnometers to measure the magnetic fields generated by the electrical activity of the brain. One advantage of this is that MEG measurements are not as distorted by the skull and surrounding tissue as those in EEG, thus considerably improving the localization of the source of neural activity.

To examine the precise timing of psychological processes, researchers general employ event-related averaging of different trials of a task to generate a comparatively noise-free waveform representing task-induced brain activity during an experiment. This method, known as event-related potentials (ERPs), has been used to investigate the relative timing of different psychological processes such as face perception (Bentin, Allison, Puce, Perez, & McCarthy, 1996), memory recognition (Curran, Schacter, Johnson, & Spinks, 2001), as well as social categorization and prejudice (Ito, Thompson, & Cacioppo, 2004). With respect to research on self-regulation, various ERP components have been found to be associated with different self-control processes. For instance, there are ERP components that reliably index conflict monitoring (Botvinick, Braver, Barch, Carter, & Cohen, 2001; Nieuwenhuis, Yeung, van den Wildenberg, & Ridderinkhof, 2003), response inhibition (Fallgatter & Strik, 1999), and the emotionally aversive side of self-control conflict and performance errors (Hobson, Saunders, Al-Khindi, & Inzlicht, 2014). ERP has also been used to identify differences between successful and unsuccessful self-regulators. For example, in a study of dieters freely viewing images of tempting food, those who were incentivized to regulate their food choices to lose weight demonstrated ERP evidence of both increased attentional control and reduced value given to unhealthy foods (Harris, Hare, & Rangel, 2013).

Transcranial Magnetic Stimulation

TMS is a noninvasive technique that allows for the creation of temporary "lesions" in relatively circumspect brain regions by disrupting the ongoing electrical activity of a patch of cortex. This is achieved via a powerful magnetic field that, when rapidly switched on and off, induces an electrical current in a small area of the brain directly beneath the magnetic coil. One commonly used technique, known as repetitive TMS, delivers multiple pulses over a short period of time, thereby temporarily disrupting a given area of the brain following the stimulation. One of the advantages of this method over other techniques is its ability to show the causal role that different brain regions play in perceptual, motor, or cognitive processes. For instance, whereas studies using fMRI have shown that a region of the brain known as the intraparietal sulcus is implicated in action observation and planning, TMS was used to demonstrate a direct role for this region in action planning, namely, by showing that transient disruption of the intraparietal sulcus impairs the ability to form the appropriate hand configurations for grasping objects (Tunik, Frey, & Grafton, 2005).

With respect to research on self-regulation, TMS has been used to demonstrate a causal role for the lateral prefrontal cortex (PFC) in impulsive decision-making (Chambers et al., 2006; Knoch, Pascual-Leone, Meyer, Treyer, & Fehr, 2006) and the preference for immediate rewards over larger delayed ones (Figner et al., 2010). Other studies have shown that deactivation of this region impairs the ability to resist monetary temptations and turn down unfair monetary offers (Baumgartner, Knoch, Hotz, Eisenegger, & Fehr, 2011; Knoch, Schneider, Schunk, Hohmann, & Fehr, 2009).

Magnetic Resonance Imaging of Brain Anatomy

High-resolution magnetic resonance imaging allows for the noninvasive measurement of neuroanatomical structures and connections between structures. Analysis of brain morphometry refers to the measurement of the size, volume, and shape characteristics of different brain structures and tissue types. For example, morphometric methods have been used to study the volume and density of gray matter, where most of the neuronal computations occur, but also of white matter, a tissue type composed primarily of myelinated axons that connect different gray matter areas. Historically the analysis of brain morphometry has been instrumental in much of the successes of MRI in identifying and localizing brain pathologies. Although there are multiple types of analyses that can be carried out on anatomical imaging data, two popular approaches are the morphometric analysis of brain anatomy (including gray matter density, cortical thickness, and volumetric measurements of brain structures) and the analysis of white matter connectivity using diffusion tensor imaging (DTI) (see next section).

With regards to the former, studies have shown that the size and volume of different neural structures are correlated with learning and experience. For instance, musicians have been found to have increased gray matter density in Broca's area (a region important for language) compared to nonmusicians (Sluming et al., 2002), London taxi cab drivers have a larger posterior hippocampus than matched control subjects (Maguire et al., 2000), and experienced meditation practitioners have increased cortical thickness in brain regions involved in attention (Lazar et al., 2005) and lateral prefrontal regions implicated in cognitive control (Kang et al., 2013).

Several studies have examined the relationship between brain morphometry and individual differences in self-regulation abilities. Research on fear extinction, for example, demonstrates that individual differences in the cortical thickness of the ventromedial PFC is positively correlated with the ability to extinguish conditioned fear memories (Milad et al., 2005;

Rauch et al., 2005). Meanwhile, research in other domains has shown that reduced cortical thickness in the lateral PFC is associated with impulsivity (Schilling et al., 2012) and emotional reactivity (Foland-Ross et al., 2010). With respect to what these findings mean for self-regulation more generally, what these studies suggest is that individual differences in self-regulatory success may in part be attributable to differences in the cortical thickness of brain regions important for self-control and executive function.

Diffusion Tensor Imaging

Unlike morphometric methods which can only provide information regarding size and volume of gray and white matter regions, DTI along with methods for determining the direction and integrity of the white matter tracts that connect different brain regions (ie, tractography) allows for inferences regarding the strength and amount of connections linking different brain areas together. Analysis of the white matter connectivity between prefrontal brain regions involved in self-control and striatal regions implicated in reward processing have resulted in novel findings regarding how the connectivity between these systems supports self-regulation-related abilities. For example, individual differences in the ability to forgo immediate rewards for future larger ones (eg, delay discounting) is associated with increased integrity in a fronto-striatal white matter track connecting the striatum to the medial prefrontal (Peper et al., 2013) and lateral prefrontal (van den Bos, Rodriguez, Schweitzer, & McClure, 2014) cortices. Finally, recent work has also demonstrated that the integrity of a white matter pathway between the lateral PFC and a region of the orbitofrontal cortex (OFC) involved in reward processing has been shown to be inversely related to overall body mass index (BMI). What these data suggest is that long-term weight control is associated with individual differences in the strength of the pathway connecting brain areas involved in self-control and those involved in reward processing. One somewhat speculative interpretation of this finding is that the strength of the white matter pathway linking brain regions involved in self-regulation and those related to reward may be just as important as self-regulatory capacity or reward reactivity (Chen, Chavez & Heatherton, unpublished).

Functional Magnetic Resonance Imaging

Although many readers will no doubt be familiar with functional MRI as a means of localizing brain activity associated with stimulus or task conditions, there are many other methods that rely on the same measurement but go beyond basic brain activation studies. For instance, fMRI measurements can be used to make inferences regarding functional connectivity changes associated with different psychological processes or task parameters. In this type of analysis, it is not the overall magnitude of a brain region that is being measured but rather how the connectivity between a brain region and the rest of the brain changes as a function of different psychological processes. There are also methods for investigating how the brain encodes stimulus properties or task parameters in multivariate patterns of brain activity as well as studies aimed at decoding stimulus properties or psychological processes from fMRI measurements. There is also research that seeks to relate parameters derived from computational models of behavior to levels of brain activity within discrete regions. Finally, there is an entire field devoted to studying the human connectome that relies on resting fluctuation in brain activity to make inferences regarding the network properties of different brain systems (Sporns, 2013). Each of these vastly different approaches relies on the same underlying measure of brain activity, namely, the blood oxygen level–dependent response.

A large proportion of the research on the brain basis of self-regulation is based on brain activation studies carried out with fMRI, and in the following sections, we review this work by looking at brain systems implicated in craving and reward processing, as well as those involved in self-control and response inhibition.

Functional Neuroimaging Studies of Reward

In both animals and humans, a system of brain regions comprising the ventral striatum, OFC, and the ventral tegmental area (VTA) has been associated with reward-related processes (Berridge & Robinson, 2003; Haber & Knutson, 2010; Kringelbach, 2005). For instance, during reward learning in animals, neurons in the VTA show an increased firing rate for unexpected or novel rewards, and after learning to associate these with a cue, VTA neurons shift their response toward the reward-predicting cue (Schultz, Dayan, & Montague, 1997). In humans, functional neuroimaging research has shown that the OFC and ventral striatum show increased brain activity to reward receipt and appear to be sensitive to momentary changes in the subjective value or pleasantness of rewards. For example, when participants consume an appetizing food, their ratings of pleasantness decrease as they approach satiety and this decrease in pleasantness is correlated with decreasing activity in the OFC (Kringelbach, O'Doherty, Rolls, & Andrews, 2003; Small, Zatorre, Dagher, Evans, & Jones-Gotman, 2001).

The OFC and ventral striatum responds not only to reward receipt but also to cues associated with rewards such as money, attractive faces, or food images (Cloutier, Heatherton, Whalen, & Kelley, 2008; Knutson, Taylor, Kaufman, Peterson, & Glover, 2005; van der Laan, de Ridder, Viergever, & Smeets, 2011). For example, the reward system shows heightened activity when listening to preferred passages of music

(Blood & Zatorre, 2001), viewing restaurant menus containing desired food items versus undesired food items (Arana et al., 2003), when smokers view smoking paraphernalia (David et al., 2005) or smoking behavior (Wagner, Dal Cin, Sargent, Kelley, & Heatherton, 2011), and when people view attractive faces from the opposite sex (Aharon et al., 2001; Cloutier et al., 2008; O'Doherty et al., 2003). Learning about cues that can predict reward is vitally important for animals and humans alike, as it helps to guide behavior toward those aspects of the environment that are important for survival (eg, food, water, conspecifics) and motivate behaviors that are evolutionary important (eg, reproduction). As humans are constantly bombarded by cues signaling potential rewards (from television and online advertisements to the sight and smell of high-calorie foods at restaurants and food courts), there has been a long-standing interest in examining the relationship between reactivity to cues and addictive or otherwise unhealthy behaviors (eg, Carter & Tiffany, 1999; Sayette, Martin, Wertz, Shiffman, & Perrott, 2001). For instance, research has demonstrated that reward cues capture people's attention (Castellanos et al., 2009; Lochbuehler, Voogd, Scholte, & Engels, 2011) and can elicit craving and positive hedonic thoughts about the desired items (Hofmann, van Koningsbruggen, Stroebe, Ramanathan, & Aarts, 2010; Sayette & Hufford, 1997).

With respect to neural cue reactivity, there have been a number of studies examining the relationship between brain activity to reward cues and various potential markers of poor self-regulation (eg, addiction, BMI, smoking relapse, weight gain). For example, research has demonstrated a link between individual differences in cue reactivity to food and BMI (Rapuano, Huckins, Sargent, Heatherton, & Kelley, 2015). Other work has attempted to use neural cue-reactivity measures to predict poor self-regulation behavior. For example, Demos, Heatherton, and Kelley (2012) used a food–cue reactivity paradigm to investigate whether individual differences in reward-related brain activity was associated with weight gain during the first year of college (eg, the infamous "freshman 15"). The authors found that food cue-related activity in the ventral striatum prospectively predicted the magnitude of weight gain 6 months later. Moreover, this effect was specific to food images, as the ventral striatal response to other image categories (eg, alcohol, erotic images) was not predictive of the amount of weight gained (Demos et al., 2012).

More recently, Lopez, Hofmann, Wagner, Kelley, and Heatherton (2014) extended this work by combining functional neuroimaging of cue reactivity with an experience sampling paradigm to better understand how cue reactivity is associated with those daily behaviors that contribute to weight gain. In this study, participants first took part in a functional neuroimaging session whereby they viewed images of highly appetizing food items. Subsequent to this, they underwent a period of experience sampling whereby their daily food desires, amount eaten, and ability to resist acting upon their food desires was measured. The authors found that individual difference in ventral striatal activity to food images predicted both daily food desires and the likelihood of giving in to those desires. Taken together, the results of these studies suggest that individual differences in reward reactivity may be an important source of variance in self-regulatory ability.

Functional Neuroimaging Studies of Self-Regulation

Research on the brain systems involved in the effortful regulation of cravings, emotions, and behavior have largely converged on a system of prefrontal brain regions comprised of regions of the lateral PFC (including the inferior frontal gyrus and ventrolateral PFC) and, particularly in studies of emotion regulation, the ventromedial PFC [for reviews, see (Aron, Robbins, & Poldrack, 2014; Cohen & Lieberman, 2010; Kelley et al., 2015; Ochsner, Silvers, & Buhle, 2012)]. Across multiple tasks and domains, these regions are associated with downregulating reward-related responses to cigarettes (Kober et al., 2010), food (Giuliani, Mann, Tomiyama, & Berkman, 2014; Hare, Camerer, & Rangel, 2009), drugs (Volkow et al., 2010), and monetary rewards (Delgado, Gillis, & Phelps, 2008), and also in downregulating emotional responses to negative emotional stimuli (Johnstone, van Reekum, Urry, Kalin, & Davidson, 2007; Ochsner et al., 2004; Urry et al., 2006). The flip side of these findings is that people suffering from self-regulation impairments will often show enhanced reward or emotion reactivity in conjunction with reduced recruitment of the lateral or ventromedial PFC (eg, Johnstone et al., 2007; New et al., 2007; Silbersweig et al., 2007; Yoo, Gujar, Hu, Jolesz, & Walker, 2007). However, this pattern of findings is not always consistent across the literature, with several studies also showing enhanced lateral or ventromedial PFC activity among those demonstrating self-regulation impairments [see Kelley et al. (2015) for further discussion of the difficulties inherent in attempting to describe self-regulation failure in terms of simple increases or decreases in PFC activity].

More recent work has explored the possibility that individual differences in the recruitment of prefrontal structures involved in self-control may underlie real-world self-regulation impairments. For instance, in a study examining regular smokers attempting to quit smoking, activity in the lateral PFC during a response inhibition task was found to predict reductions in cigarette craving and consumption during a 3-week period (Berkman, Falk, & Lieberman, 2011). In another study, this time in dieters, lateral PFC activity in a similar response inhibition task involving appetitive food images predicted dieters' success at regulating daily food desires over the subsequent week (Lopez et al., 2014). Together with studies demonstrating that inhibiting the electrical activity of the lateral PFC activity with TMS increases impulsivity during decision-making (reviewed in a previous section), these findings point to the lateral PFC as being vitally important for the regulation of behavior during daily life. Indeed, patients with damage to this area struggle with planning, and are easily distracted by competing cues or task demands (Petrides & Milner, 1982; Shallice & Burgess, 1991).

THE COGNITIVE NEUROSCIENCE OF EGO DEPLETION

Cognitive neuroscience research on ego depletion is still in its relative infancy; however, in the last several years, there have been a number of studies designed to investigate how ego depletion impacts brain system that involves in self-control, affect, and reward. The first of these studies (Inzlicht & Gutsell, 2007) used ERP (for a brief overview of this method, see an earlier section of this chapter) and examined error-related negativity, an index of conflict monitoring thought to originate in the anterior cingulate cortex. In this study, participants performed a standard sequential task paradigm whereby a subset of participants engaged in an effortful emotion regulation task followed by a Stroop task. Relative to a control group, depleted participants showed a decrement in behavioral performance on the Stroop task (ie, an increase in the reaction time difference between incongruent and congruent trials) and a reduced error-related negativity signal. Moreover, the reduction in error-related negativity mediated the relationship between ego depletion and Stroop performance. Based on these findings, the authors suggest that ego depletion is a result of an impaired conflict monitoring process, and thus depleted participants' impaired performance is because they are less able to monitor for commission of an error (Inzlicht & Gutsell, 2007). However, a subsequent study using fMRI instead suggests that depletion appears not so much to reduce conflict monitoring but to disrupt the ability to implement self-control (Hedgcock, Vohs, & Rao, 2012). In this study, half of the participants were assigned to perform an effortful attention control task, whereas the other half performed a similar task that did not require effortful self-control. Following this depletion manipulation, participants engaged in a choice task whereby they were asked to make decisions between various items. Their principal finding was a reduction in right dorsolateral PFC among the depleted group; however, there was no difference in activity between depleted and control participants in the anterior cingulate cortex. The authors interpret this finding as indicating that depletion impairs the ability to implement self-control rather than impairing conflict monitoring (Hedgcock et al., 2012). One possibility for the discrepancy between the prior study and this one is that different self-control tasks tax conflict monitoring and self-control differentially. Whereas performance in the Stroop task used in the prior study may be predicated on an ability to detect the response conflict between the color of the word and the word itself, the choice task used to assess ego depletion in this study may not be contingent on the ability to successfully monitor for errors but rather is weighted more toward the ability to implement effortful self-control. Indeed, an examination of the behavioral data showed that participants in the depletion condition made faster decisions during the choice task, suggesting that they spent less time deliberating over those decisions (Hedgcock et al., 2012).

Similar findings were observed in another study in which participants engaged in a verb generation task after being assigned to either a depletion condition (consisting of an effortful working memory task) or a control condition. Here, the authors found that activity in the left lateral PFC was reduced in depleted participants compared to the control group, and this reduction in activity was associated with poor performance among the depleted group (Persson, Larsson, & Reuter-Lorenz, 2013). Around the same time, Friese, Binder, Luechinger, Boesiger, and Rasch (2013) published a study demonstrating ego depletion's impact on activity in the lateral PFC by investigating how activity in the same patch of cortex changes during a sequential task paradigm. As in Inzlicht and Gutsell (2007), participants in this study were first tasked with suppressing their emotions, followed by a Stroop task. Whereas ego depletion led to increased reaction times on incongruent trials for the depletion group in the Inzlicht and Gutsell study (2007), here depletion led to higher error rates on incongruent trials but no reaction time differences between depleted and control participants (Friese et al., 2013). With respect to ego depletion's effects on brain activity, the authors found an interaction in the dorsolateral PFC between task and group such that this region showed more activity in the depleted group relative to the control group during the emotion suppression task, but less activity in the depleted group during the Stroop task. Of particular note is that, hitherto, most studies have examined the aftereffects of depletion on the brain; however, this study examined the same area of the lateral PFC during both the depletion task and the subsequent task, thereby demonstrating that the same area of lateral PFC is involved in both tasks and is differentially affected by prior effort.

All of the above studies have primarily examined the aftereffects of ego depletion on cognitive tasks (eg, the Stroop or a choice-making task). However, recent experimental work has suggested that ego depletion may have independent effects on self-control and impulse strength, both impairing self-control and intensifying desires and emotions. For instance, prior work by Schmeichel, Harmon-Jones, and Harmon-Jones (2010) showed the ego depletion increases attention to rewards in the absence of any self-control task (Schmeichel et al., 2010). The idea that depletion may independently increase the strength of impulses and rewards is consistent with prior work showing that ego depletion leads people to eat more food (Hofmann, Rauch, & Gawronski, 2007; Vohs & Heatherton, 2000), drink more alcohol (Muraven, Collins, & Nienhaus, 2002), and show difficulty regulating their emotions (Schmeichel, 2007). Although the findings in each of these studies were initially interpreted as being the result of impaired self-regulation capacity, it is also possible to view these findings as examples of increased impulse strength.

Two neuroimaging studies of ego depletion have sought to address the possibility that depletion affects not only the self-control side of the equation but also the impulse side. In the first of these, participants completed a simple emotional scene categorization task, followed by either an effortful attention control task or noneffortful version of the same task. Subsequent to this, they completed another set of emotion scene categorizations (Wagner & Heatherton, 2013). Of interest here is whether depletion resulted in an exaggerated response in regions of the brain that are sensitive to emotional valence and intensity (ie, the amygdala). Compared to their pre-depletion baseline, depleted participants demonstrated an increased amygdala response to negative emotional scenes but not to neutral or positive scenes. Moreover, the difference between depleted and control participants was significant for negative emotional scenes, but not for neutral or positive scenes. Importantly, by assessing amygdala reactivity to emotional scenes prior to depletion, the authors were able to demonstrate that there was no pre-existing difference between the groups. In addition to these findings, this study also examined the functional connectivity between the amygdala and a region of the ventral medial PFC that has been implicated in emotion regulation (Johnstone et al., 2007; Somerville et al., 2013). The results showed that, relative to controls, depleted participants exhibited a reduced coupling between the amygdala and VMPFC (Wagner & Heatherton, 2013) suggesting the possibility that, unlike controls, depleted participants fail to spontaneously recruit the VMPFC to downregulate reactivity to negative and aversive emotional scenes.

A second functional neuroimaging (ie, Wagner, Altman, Boswell, Kelley, & Heatherton, 2013) showed a conceptually similar finding, this time in the domain of dieting and food cue reactivity. Here, chronic dieters were exposed to appetizing food images following the same ego depletion manipulation as in the above study. Compared to nondepleted dieters, those that underwent ego depletion demonstrated a heightened reward-related response to food images in the OFC. Moreover, analysis of the functional connectivity between this region and the lateral PFC found evidence of reduced connectivity between these areas relative to a control group (Wagner et al., 2013). These two studies suggest that, even in the absence of explicit self-control tasks, ego depletion may serve to heighten impulses and emotions (see also Chapter 6 for an extended discussion of this possibility). Moreover, it appears that the mechanism for this increased reactivity is due to a decoupling between regulatory regions in the PFC and the cortical and subcortical regions involved in emotion and reward.

Taken together, all the ego-depletion studies reviewed earlier are generally consistent with a balance model of self-regulation failure (eg, Heatherton & Wagner, 2011). In this framework, prefrontal regions involved in self-regulation are common across many form of self-regulation, however, the target of prefrontal control differ according to the individual's regulatory context. For instance, if an individual is regulating fear or anger, then a prefrontal–amygdala pathway may be involved, whereas if an individual is regulating food cravings, this may instead involve a prefrontal and ventral striatal/orbitofrontal circuit. In this model, self-regulation failure occurs whenever the strength of an impulse (represented in the reward or emotional systems) outmatches current self-regulatory capacity, or whenever self-regulatory capacity is itself diminished, be it due to depletion, prefrontal brain damage, distraction, or alcohol. The studies reviewed here are consistent both with the notion that ego depletion somehow disrupts the ability to recruit prefrontal mechanisms for self-control, but also that depletion may decouple this system from those involved in representing reward value or emotional salience. Once uncoupled, these regions become sensitized to the rewarding properties of stimuli, which in turn can lead to further difficulties engaging in self-regulation.

Finally, it is worth noting that although the results across these few ego-depletion studies are generally consistent with each other, there are still some issues remaining to be resolved. For example, the first set of studies used primarily cognitive tasks (eg, the Stroop task) to assess the aftereffect of depletion. These studies have generally shown that ego depletion leads to reduced recruitment of the anterior cingulate cortex (Inzlicht & Gutsell, 2007) or the lateral PFC, although there remains some ambiguity as to the laterality of these effects, with some studies demonstrating reductions in left lateral PFC (Persson et al., 2013) and others in right lateral PFC (Friese et al., 2013; Hedgcock et al., 2012). Moreover, in other studies (Wagner et al., 2013; Wagner & Heatherton, 2013), depletion does not act directly on the overall amount of activity in a region, but rather appears to reduce the connectivity between regulatory regions in the PFC and their targets in the reward or emotion brain systems. Whether these differences represent separate phenomena or are instead due to differences in tasks or analysis methodology remains an ongoing question.

ALTERNATIVE THEORIES OF EGO DEPLETION

Recently, a number of alternative explanations for the ego-depletion effect have been proposed (Beedie & Lane, 2012; Inzlicht & Schmeichel, 2012; Job et al., 2010; Kurzban, Duckworth, Kable, & Myers, 2013). Common among them is the notion that self-regulation failure following depletion may reflect not so much a lack of self-control capacity, but rather a decision to avoid engaging in further effortful task performance in favor of expending less effort. Underlying this theory is the notion that expending effort is itself aversive and to be avoided, unless the rewards are sufficient. For instance, research has shown that, all things being equal, people will invariably prefer tasks that they perceive as requiring less effort (Kool, McGuire, Rosen, & Botvinick, 2010). These new ways of thinking about depletion recast the classic tug-of-war between impulses and self-control capacity as a labor dispute whereby effortful cognitive work will be performed by the individual only as long as the payment is sufficient. In this framework, the after-effects of depletion are due to insufficient reward for cognitive services rendered. Functional neuroimaging work has provided evidence that the lateral PFC may be involved in registering the cost of engaging in effortful tasks. For instance, when participants were given a choice to choose between tasks that differed in the overall effort required to complete them, participants came to prefer the low-effort task, and activity in the LPFC during the task block was associated with subsequent ratings of how much they wanted to avoid the effortful task (McGuire & Botvinick, 2010).

That is not to say these accounts are not without some issues of their own when it comes to attempts to utilize them to explain the constellation of previously reported depletion effects. For instance, given a fixed reward for participants, it would be sensible for them to avoid additional effort on self-control tasks after depletion (assuming minimally motivated experimental participants). However, it is difficult to reconcile this view with findings showing that depletion precipitates self-regulation failure in circumstances for which individuals are highly motivated to continue exerting effort irrespective of the task rewards. For example, restrained eaters are highly motivated to avoid the overconsumption of unhealthy food, and yet self-regulatory depletion can lead to disinhibited eating (Vohs & Heatherton, 2000) and increased reward cue reactivity (Wagner et al., 2013). Similarly, people are typically motivated to give a good impression; however, research has shown that, following an effortful self-control task, they become less thoughtful during social interactions, thereby appearing arrogant or socially awkward (Vohs, Baumeister, & Ciarocco, 2005). It is, on the surface, difficult to reconcile these findings with the notion that these participants are, following depletion, choosing to avoid the effortful task of maintaining their diet or not appearing like a schmuck in a social interaction simply because they have been insufficiently rewarded. It instead appears less a case of *will not* and more a case of *cannot*.

CONCLUSION

The last several years have seen a surge of research on brain basis of self-regulatory failure; by and large, this work is consistent with the view that self-regulation may result from a strong impulse or insufficient self-control capacity. Recent theorizing has suggested that many examples of self-regulation failure may instead be conceived of not as a lack of self-control capacity, but rather as a shift in motivation, as individuals opt to focus on rewards and leisure (Inzlicht & Schmeichel, 2012; Inzlicht, Schmeichel, et al., 2014) or determine that the cost of self-control is too great and therefore decide to avoid expending any more effort (Kool & Botvinick, 2014). Current findings from functional neuroimaging studies are not yet in a position to arbitrate between these different accounts of self-regulation failure, as findings of reduced prefrontal activity (Friese et al., 2013; Hedgcock et al., 2012; Persson et al., 2013) or of alternations in functional connectivity between the PFC and the reward system (eg, Wagner et al., 2013; Wagner & Heatherton, 2013) following depletion are consistent both with the strength model of self-control but also with the various alternative accounts (Inzlicht, Schmeichel, et al., 2014; Kurzban et al., 2013). As the many chapters in this book will attest, there is much more work to be done to elucidate the mechanisms of ego depletion. Given the increasing importance of social and cognitive neuroscience findings in contemporary theories of self-regulation failure and ego depletion, we have no doubt that a neuroscience approach will continue to play an important if not decisive role in our understanding of the phenomena of ego depletion.

References

Aharon, I., Etcoff, N., Ariely, D., Chabris, C. F., O'Connor, E., & Breiter, H. C. (2001). Beautiful faces have variable reward value: fMRI and behavioral evidence. *Neuron*, 32(3), 537–551. http://dx.doi.org/10.1016/S0896-6273(01)00491-3.

Arana, F. S., Parkinson, J. A., Hinton, E., Holland, A. J., Owen, A. M., & Roberts, A. C. (2003). Dissociable contributions of the human amygdala and orbitofrontal cortex to incentive motivation and goal selection. *The Journal of Neuroscience*, 23(29), 9632–9638.

Aron, A. R., Robbins, T. W., & Poldrack, R. A. (2014). Inhibition and the right inferior frontal cortex: one decade on. *Trends in Cognitive Sciences*, 18(4), 177–185. http://dx.doi.org/10.1016/j.tics.2013.12.003.

Baumeister, R. F., Bratslavsky, E., Muraven, M., & Tice, D. M. (1998). Ego depletion: is the active self a limited resource? *Journal of Personality and Social Psychology*, 74(5), 1252–1265.

Baumgartner, T., Knoch, D., Hotz, P., Eisenegger, C., & Fehr, E. (2011). Dorsolateral and ventromedial prefrontal cortex orchestrate normative choice. *Nature Neuroscience*, 14(11), 1468–1474. http://dx.doi.org/10.1038/nn.2933.

Beedie, C. J., & Lane, A. M. (2012). The role of glucose in self-control: another look at the evidence and an alternative conceptualization. *Personality and Social Psychology Review: An Official Journal of the Society for Personality and Social Psychology, Inc.*, 16(2), 143–153. http://dx.doi.org/10.1177/1088868311419817.

Bentin, S., Allison, T., Puce, A., Perez, E., & McCarthy, G. (1996). Electrophysiological studies of face perception in humans. *Journal of Cognitive Neuroscience*, 8(6), 551–565. http://dx.doi.org/10.1162/jocn.1996.8.6.551.

Berkman, E. T., Falk, E. B., & Lieberman, M. D. (2011). In the trenches of real-world self-control. *Psychological Science*, 22(4), 498–506. http://dx.doi.org/10.1177/0956797611400918.

REFERENCES

Berridge, K. C., & Robinson, T. E. (2003). Parsing reward. *Trends in Neurosciences*, 26(9), 507–513. http://dx.doi.org/10.1016/S0166-2236(03)00233-9.

Blood, A. J., & Zatorre, R. J. (2001). Intensely pleasurable responses to music correlate with activity in brain regions implicated in reward and emotion. *Proceedings of the National Academy of Sciences*, 98(20), 11818–11823. http://dx.doi.org/10.1073/pnas.191355898.

van den Bos, W., Rodriguez, C. A., Schweitzer, J. B., & McClure, S. M. (2014). Connectivity strength of dissociable striatal tracts predict individual differences in temporal discounting. *The Journal of Neuroscience*, 34(31), 10298–10310. http://dx.doi.org/10.1523/JNEUROSCI.4105-13.2014.

Botvinick, M. M., Braver, T. S., Barch, D. M., Carter, C. S., & Cohen, J. D. (2001). Conflict monitoring and cognitive control. *Psychological Review*, 108(3), 624–652. http://dx.doi.org/10.1037/0033-295X.108.3.624.

Carter, B. L., & Tiffany, S. T. (1999). Meta-analysis of cue-reactivity in addiction research. *Addiction (Abingdon, England)*, 94(3), 327–340.

Castellanos, E. H., Charboneau, E., Dietrich, M. S., Park, S., Bradley, B. P., Mogg, K., & Cowan, R. L. (2009). Obese adults have visual attention bias for food cue images: evidence for altered reward system function. *International Journal of Obesity*, 33(9), 1063–1073. http://dx.doi.org/10.1038/ijo.2009.138.

Chambers, C. D., Bellgrove, M. A., Stokes, M. G., Henderson, T. R., Garavan, H., Robertson, I. H., ... Mattingley, J. B. (2006). Executive "Brake Failure" following deactivation of human frontal lobe. *Journal of Cognitive Neuroscience*, 18(3), 444–455. http://dx.doi.org/10.1162/jocn.2006.18.3.444.

Cloutier, J., Heatherton, T. F., Whalen, P. J., & Kelley, W. M. (2008). Are attractive people rewarding? Sex differences in the neural substrates of facial attractiveness. *Journal of Cognitive Neuroscience*, 20(6), 941–951. http://dx.doi.org/10.1162/jocn.2008.20062.

Cohen, J. R., & Lieberman, M. D. (2010). The common neural basis of exerting self-control in multiple domains. In R. R. Hassin, K. N. Ochsner, & Y. Trope (Eds.), *Self control in society, mind, and brain* (pp. 141–160). New York, NY, US: Oxford University Press.

Curran, T., Schacter, D. L., Johnson, M. K., & Spinks, R. (2001). Brain potentials reflect behavioral differences in true and false recognition. *Journal of Cognitive Neuroscience*, 13(2), 201–216. http://dx.doi.org/10.1162/089892901564261.

David, S. P., Munafò, M. R., Johansen-Berg, H., Smith, S. M., Rogers, R. D., Matthews, P. M., & Walton, R. T. (2005). Ventral striatum/nucleus accumbens activation to smoking-related pictorial cues in smokers and nonsmokers: a functional magnetic resonance imaging study. *Biological Psychiatry*, 58(6), 488–494. http://doi.org/16/j.biopsych.2005.04.028.

Delgado, M. R., Gillis, M. M., & Phelps, E. A. (2008). Regulating the expectation of reward via cognitive strategies. *Nature Neuroscience*, 11(8), 880–881. http://dx.doi.org/10.1038/nn.2141.

Demos, K. E., Heatherton, T. F., & Kelley, W. M. (2012). Individual differences in nucleus accumbens activity to food and sexual images predict weight gain and sexual behavior. *The Journal of Neuroscience*, 32(16), 5549–5552. http://dx.doi.org/10.1523/JNEUROSCI.5958-11.2012.

Denson, T. F., DeWall, C. N., & Finkel, E. J. (2012). Self-control and aggression. *Current Directions in Psychological Science*, 21(1), 20–25. http://dx.doi.org/10.1177/0963721411429451.

Fallgatter, A. J., & Strik, W. K. (1999). The NoGo-anteriorization as a neurophysiological standard-index for cognitive response control. *International Journal of Psychophysiology: Official Journal of the International Organization of Psychophysiology*, 32(3), 233–238.

Figner, B., Knoch, D., Johnson, E. J., Krosch, A. R., Lisanby, S. H., Fehr, E., & Weber, E. U. (2010). Lateral prefrontal cortex and self-control in intertemporal choice. *Nature Neuroscience*, 13(5), 538–539. http://dx.doi.org/10.1038/nn.2516.

Foland-Ross, L. C., Altshuler, L. L., Bookheimer, S. Y., Lieberman, M. D., Townsend, J., Penfold, C., ... Thompson, P. M. (2010). Amygdala reactivity in healthy adults is correlated with prefrontal cortical thickness. *The Journal of Neuroscience: The Official Journal of the Society for Neuroscience*, 30(49), 16673–16678. http://dx.doi.org/10.1523/JNEUROSCI.4578-09.2010.

Friese, M., Binder, J., Luechinger, R., Boesiger, P., & Rasch, B. (2013). Suppressing emotions impairs subsequent stroop performance and reduces prefrontal brain activation. *PLoS One, 8*(4), e60385. http://dx.doi.org/10.1371/journal.pone.0060385.

Giuliani, N. R., Mann, T., Tomiyama, A. J., & Berkman, E. T. (2014). Neural systems underlying the reappraisal of personally craved foods. *Journal of Cognitive Neuroscience, 26*(7), 1390–1402. http://dx.doi.org/10.1162/jocn_a_00563.

Haber, S. N., & Knutson, B. (2010). The reward circuit: linking primate anatomy and human imaging. *Neuropsychopharmacology: Official Publication of the American College of Neuropsychopharmacology, 35*(1), 4–26. http://dx.doi.org/10.1038/npp.2009.129.

Hagger, M. S., Wood, C., Stiff, C., & Chatzisarantis, N. L. D. (2010). Ego depletion and the strength model of self-control: a meta-analysis. *Psychological Bulletin, 136*(4), 495–525. http://doi.org/37/a0019486.

Hare, T. A., Camerer, C. F., & Rangel, A. (2009). Self-control in decision-making involves modulation of the vmPFC valuation system. *Science (New York, NY), 324*(5927), 646–648. http://dx.doi.org/10.1126/science.1168450.

Harris, A., Hare, T., & Rangel, A. (2013). Temporally dissociable mechanisms of self-control: early attentional filtering versus late value modulation. *The Journal of Neuroscience, 33*(48), 18917–18931. http://dx.doi.org/10.1523/JNEUROSCI.5816-12.2013.

Heatherton, T. F., & Wagner, D. D. (2011). Cognitive neuroscience of self-regulation failure. *Trends in Cognitive Sciences, 15*(3), 132–139. http://dx.doi.org/10.1016/j.tics.2010.12.005.

Hedgcock, W. M., Vohs, K. D., & Rao, A. R. (2012). Reducing self-control depletion effects through enhanced sensitivity to implementation: evidence from fMRI and behavioral studies. *Journal of Consumer Psychology, 22*(4), 486–495. http://dx.doi.org/10.1016/j.jcps.2012.05.008.

Hobson, N. M., Saunders, B., Al-Khindi, T., & Inzlicht, M. (2014). Emotion down-regulation diminishes cognitive control: a neurophysiological investigation. *Emotion, 14*(6), 1014–1026. http://dx.doi.org/10.1037/a0038028.

Hofmann, W., van Koningsbruggen, G. M., Stroebe, W., Ramanathan, S., & Aarts, H. (2010). As pleasure unfolds. Hedonic responses to tempting food. *Psychological Science, 21*(12), 1863–1870. http://dx.doi.org/10.1177/0956797610389186.

Hofmann, W., Rauch, W., & Gawronski, B. (2007). And deplete us not into temptation: automatic attitudes, dietary restraint, and self-regulatory resources as determinants of eating behavior. *Journal of Experimental Social Psychology, 43*(3), 497–504. http://dx.doi.org/10.1016/j.jesp.2006.05.004.

Hofmann, W., Schmeichel, B. J., & Baddeley, A. D. (2012). Executive functions and self-regulation. *Trends in Cognitive Sciences, 16*(3), 174–180. http://dx.doi.org/10.1016/j.tics.2012.01.006.

Inzlicht, M., & Berkman, E. (2015). Six questions for the resource model of control (and some answers). *Social and Personality Psychology Compass, 9*(10), 511–524. http://dx.doi.org/10.1111/spc3.12200.

Inzlicht, M., Elkins-Brown, N., & Berkman, E. T. (2015). The neuroscience of "ego depletion" or: how the brain can help us understand why self-control seems limited. In E. Harmon-Jones, & M. Inzlicht (Eds.), *Social neuroscience: Biological approaches to social psychology*. New York: Psychology Press.

Inzlicht, M., & Gutsell, J. N. (2007). Running on empty: neural signals for self-control failure. *Psychological Science, 18*(11), 933–937. http://dx.doi.org/10.1111/j.1467-9280.2007.02004.x.

Inzlicht, M., Legault, L., & Teper, R. (2014). Exploring the mechanisms of self-control improvement. *Current Directions in Psychological Science, 23*(4), 302–307. http://dx.doi.org/10.1177/0963721414534256.

Inzlicht, M., & Schmeichel, B. J. (2012). What is ego depletion? Toward a mechanistic revision of the resource model of self-control. *Perspectives on Psychological Science, 7*(5), 450–463. http://dx.doi.org/10.1177/1745691612454134.

Inzlicht, M., Schmeichel, B. J., & Macrae, C. N. (2014). Why self-control seems (but may not be) limited. *Trends in Cognitive Sciences, 18*(3), 127–133. http://dx.doi.org/10.1016/j.tics.2013.12.009.

REFERENCES

Ito, T. A., Thompson, E., & Cacioppo, J. T. (2004). Tracking the timecourse of social perception: the effects of racial cues on event-related brain potentials. *Personality & Social Psychology Bulletin*, 30(10), 1267–1280. http://dx.doi.org/10.1177/0146167204264335.

Job, V., Dweck, C. S., & Walton, G. M. (2010). Ego depletion–is it all in your head? Implicit theories about willpower affect self-regulation. *Psychological Science*, 21(11), 1686–1693. http://dx.doi.org/10.1177/0956797610384745.

Johnstone, T., van Reekum, C. M., Urry, H. L., Kalin, N. H., & Davidson, R. J. (2007). Failure to regulate: counterproductive recruitment of top-down prefrontal-subcortical circuitry in major depression. *The Journal of Neuroscience*, 27(33), 8877–8884. http://dx.doi.org/10.1523/JNEUROSCI.2063-07.2007.

Kang, D.-H., Jo, H. J., Jung, W. H., Kim, S. H., Jung, Y.-H., Choi, C.-H., … Kwon, J. S. (2013). The effect of meditation on brain structure: cortical thickness mapping and diffusion tensor imaging. *Social Cognitive and Affective Neuroscience*, 8(1), 27–33. http://dx.doi.org/10.1093/scan/nss056.

Kelley, W. M., Wagner, D. D., & Heatherton, T. F. (2015). Search of a human self-regulation system. *Annual Review of Neuroscience*, 38(1). http://dx.doi.org/10.1146/annurev-neuro-071013-014243 null.

Knoch, D., Pascual-Leone, A., Meyer, K., Treyer, V., & Fehr, E. (2006). Diminishing reciprocal fairness by disrupting the right prefrontal cortex. *Science*, 314(5800), 829–832. http://dx.doi.org/10.1126/science.1129156.

Knoch, D., Schneider, F., Schunk, D., Hohmann, M., & Fehr, E. (2009). Disrupting the prefrontal cortex diminishes the human ability to build a good reputation. *Proceedings of the National Academy of Sciences*, 106(49), 20895–20899. http://dx.doi.org/10.1073/pnas.0911619106.

Knutson, B., Taylor, J., Kaufman, M., Peterson, R., & Glover, G. (2005). Distributed neural representation of expected value. *Journal of Neuroscience*, 25(19), 4806–4812. http://dx.doi.org/10.1523/JNEUROSCI.0642-05.2005.

Kober, H., Mende-Siedlecki, P., Kross, E. F., Weber, J., Mischel, W., Hart, C. L., & Ochsner, K. N. (2010). Prefrontal–striatal pathway underlies cognitive regulation of craving. *Proceedings of the National Academy of Sciences*, 107(33), 14811–14816. http://dx.doi.org/10.1073/pnas.1007779107.

Kool, W., & Botvinick, M. (2014). A labor/leisure tradeoff in cognitive control. *Journal of Experimental Psychology. General*, 143(1), 131–141. http://dx.doi.org/10.1037/a0031048.

Kool, W., McGuire, J. T., Rosen, Z. B., & Botvinick, M. M. (2010). Decision making and the avoidance of cognitive demand. *Journal of Experimental Psychology: General*, 139(4), 665–682. http://dx.doi.org/10.1037/a0020198.

Kringelbach, M. L. (2005). The human orbitofrontal cortex: linking reward to hedonic experience. *Nature Reviews. Neuroscience*, 6(9), 691–702. http://dx.doi.org/10.1038/nrn1747.

Kringelbach, M. L., O'Doherty, J., Rolls, E. T., & Andrews, C. (2003). Activation of the human orbitofrontal cortex to a liquid food stimulus is correlated with its subjective pleasantness. *Cerebral Cortex (New York, NY: 1991)*, 13(10), 1064–1071.

Kurzban, R., Duckworth, A., Kable, J. W., & Myers, J. (2013). An opportunity cost model of subjective effort and task performance. *Behavioral and Brain Sciences*, 36(06), 661–679. http://dx.doi.org/10.1017/S0140525X12003196.

van der Laan, L. N., de Ridder, D. T. D., Viergever, M. A., & Smeets, P. A. M. (2011). The first taste is always with the eyes: a meta-analysis on the neural correlates of processing visual food cues. *NeuroImage*, 55(1), 296–303. http://dx.doi.org/10.1016/j.neuroimage.2010.11.055.

Lazar, S. W., Kerr, C. E., Wasserman, R. H., Gray, J. R., Greve, D. N., Treadway, M. T., … Fischl, B. (2005). Meditation experience is associated with increased cortical thickness. *Neuroreport*, 16(17), 1893–1897.

Lochbuehler, K., Voogd, H., Scholte, R. H. J., & Engels, R. C. M.E. (2011). Attentional bias in smokers: exposure to dynamic smoking cues in contemporary movies. *Journal of Psychopharmacology (Oxford, England)*, 25(4), 514–519. http://dx.doi.org/10.1177/0269881110388325.

Lopez, R. B., Hofmann, W., Wagner, D. D., Kelley, W. M., & Heatherton, T. F. (2014). Neural predictors of giving in to temptation in daily life. *Psychological Science, 25*(7), 1337–1344. http://dx.doi.org/10.1177/0956797614531492.

Maguire, E. A., Gadian, D. G., Johnsrude, I. S., Good, C. D., Ashburner, J., Frackowiak, R. S. J., & Frith, C. D. (2000). Navigation-related structural change in the hippocampi of taxi drivers. *Proceedings of the National Academy of Sciences, 97*(8), 4398–4403. http://dx.doi.org/10.1073/pnas.070039597.

McGuire, J. T., & Botvinick, M. M. (2010). Prefrontal cortex, cognitive control, and the registration of decision costs. *Proceedings of the National Academy of Sciences, 107*(17), 7922–7926. http://dx.doi.org/10.1073/pnas.0910662107.

Milad, M. R., Quinn, B. T., Pitman, R. K., Orr, S. P., Fischl, B., & Rauch, S. L. (2005). Thickness of ventromedial prefrontal cortex in humans is correlated with extinction memory. *Proceedings of the National Academy of Sciences of the United States of America, 102*(30), 10706–10711. http://dx.doi.org/10.1073/pnas.0502441102.

Muraven, M., Collins, R. L., & Nienhaus, K. (2002). Self-control and alcohol restraint: an initial application of the self-control strength model. *Psychology of Addictive Behaviors: Journal of the Society of Psychologists in Addictive Behaviors, 16*(2), 113–120.

New, A. S., Hazlett, E. A., Buchsbaum, M. S., Goodman, M., Mitelman, S. A., Newmark, R., ... Siever, L. J. (2007). Amygdala–prefrontal disconnection in borderline personality disorder. *Neuropsychopharmacology: Official Publication of the American College of Neuropsychopharmacology, 32*(7), 1629–1640. http://dx.doi.org/10.1038/sj.npp.1301283.

Nieuwenhuis, S., Yeung, N., van den Wildenberg, W., & Ridderinkhof, K. R. (2003). Electrophysiological correlates of anterior cingulate function in a go/no-go task: effects of response conflict and trial type frequency. *Cognitive, Affective & Behavioral Neuroscience, 3*(1), 17–26.

Ochsner, K. N., Ray, R. D., Cooper, J. C., Robertson, E. R., Chopra, S., Gabrieli, J. D. E., & Gross, J. J. (2004). For better or for worse: neural systems supporting the cognitive down- and up-regulation of negative emotion. *NeuroImage, 23*(2), 483–499. http://dx.doi.org/10.1016/j.neuroimage.2004.06.030.

O'Doherty, J., Winston, J., Critchley, H., Perrett, D., Burt, D. M., & Dolan, R. J. (2003). Beauty in a smile: the role of medial orbitofrontal cortex in facial attractiveness. *Neuropsychologia, 41*(2), 147–155. http://dx.doi.org/10.1016/S0028-3932(02)00145-8.

Ochsner, K. N., Silvers, J. A., & Buhle, J. T. (2012). Functional imaging studies of emotion regulation: a synthetic review and evolving model of the cognitive control of emotion. *Annals of the New York Academy of Sciences, 1251*(1), E1–E24. http://dx.doi.org/10.1111/j.1749-6632.2012.06751.x.

Peper, J. S., Mandl, R. C. W., Braams, B. R., Water, E. de, Heijboer, A. C., Koolschijn, P. C. M.P., & Crone, E. A. (2013). Delay discounting and frontostriatal fiber tracts: a combined DTI and MTR study on impulsive choices in healthy young adults. *Cerebral Cortex, 23*(7), 1695–1702. http://dx.doi.org/10.1093/cercor/bhs163.

Persson, J., Larsson, A., & Reuter-Lorenz, P. A. (2013). Imaging fatigue of interference control reveals the neural basis of executive resource depletion. *Journal of Cognitive Neuroscience, 25*(3), 338–351. http://dx.doi.org/10.1162/jocn_a_00321.

Petrides, M., & Milner, B. (1982). Deficits on subject-ordered tasks after frontal- and temporal-lobe lesions in man. *Neuropsychologia, 20*(3), 249–262.

Rapuano, K. M., Huckins, J. F., Sargent, J. D., Heatherton, T. F., & Kelley, W. M. (2015). Individual differences in reward and somatosensory-motor brain regions correlate with adiposity in adolescents. *Cerebral Cortex (New York, NY: 1991)*. http://dx.doi.org/10.1093/cercor/bhv097.

Rauch, S. L., Milad, M. R., Orr, S. P., Quinn, B. T., Fischl, B., & Pitman, R. K. (2005). Orbitofrontal thickness, retention of fear extinction, and extraversion. *NeuroReport: For Rapid Communication of Neuroscience Research, 16*(17), 1909–1912. http://dx.doi.org/10.1097/01.wnr.0000186599.66243.50.

Sayette, M. A., & Hufford, M. R. (1997). Effects of smoking urge on generation of smoking-related information1. *Journal of Applied Social Psychology, 27*(16), 1395–1405. http://dx.doi.org/10.1111/j.1559-1816.1997.tb01604.x.

Sayette, M. A., Martin, C. S., Wertz, J. M., Shiffman, S., & Perrott, M. A. (2001). A multidimensional analysis of cue-elicited craving in heavy smokers and tobacco chippers. *Addiction, 96*(10), 1419–1432. http://dx.doi.org/10.1046/j.1360-0443.2001.961014196.x.

Schilling, C., Kühn, S., Romanowski, A., Schubert, F., Kathmann, N., & Gallinat, J. (2012). Cortical thickness correlates with impulsiveness in healthy adults. *Neuroimage, 59*(1), 824–830. http://dx.doi.org/10.1016/j.neuroimage.2011.07.058.

Schmeichel, B. J. (2007). Attention control, memory updating, and emotion regulation temporarily reduce the capacity for executive control. *Journal of Experimental Psychology: General, 136*(2), 241–255. http://dx.doi.org/10.1037/0096-3445.136.2.241.

Schmeichel, B. J., Harmon-Jones, C., & Harmon-Jones, E. (2010). Exercising self-control increases approach motivation. *Journal of Personality and Social Psychology, 99*(1), 162–173. http://dx.doi.org/10.1037/a0019797.

Schultz, W., Dayan, P., & Montague, P. R. (1997). A neural substrate of prediction and reward. *Science, 275*(5306), 1593–1599. http://dx.doi.org/10.1126/science.275.5306.1593.

Shallice, T., & Burgess, P. W. (1991). Deficits in strategy application following frontal lobe damage in man. *Brain, 114*(2), 727–741. http://dx.doi.org/10.1093/brain/114.2.727.

Silbersweig, D., Clarkin, J. F., Goldstein, M., Kernberg, O. F., Tuescher, O., Levy, K. N., ... Stern, E. (2007). Failure of frontolimbic inhibitory function in the context of negative emotion in borderline personality disorder. *The American Journal of Psychiatry, 164*(12), 1832–1841. http://dx.doi.org/10.1176/appi.ajp.2007.06010126.

Sluming, V., Barrick, T., Howard, M., Cezayirli, E., Mayes, A., & Roberts, N. (2002). Voxel-based morphometry reveals increased gray matter density in Broca's area in male symphony orchestra musicians. *NeuroImage, 17*(3), 1613–1622.

Small, D. M., Zatorre, R. J., Dagher, A., Evans, A. C., & Jones-Gotman, M. (2001). Changes in brain activity related to eating chocolate: from pleasure to aversion. *Brain: A Journal of Neurology, 124*(Pt 9), 1720–1733.

Somerville, L. H., Wagner, D. D., Wig, G. S., Moran, J. M., Whalen, P. J., & Kelley, W. M. (2013). Interactions between transient and sustained neural signals support the generation and regulation of anxious emotion. *Cerebral Cortex (New York, NY: 1991), 23*(1), 49–60. http://dx.doi.org/10.1093/cercor/bhr373.

Sporns, O. (2013). The human connectome: origins and challenges. *NeuroImage, 80*, 53–61. http://dx.doi.org/10.1016/j.neuroimage.2013.03.023.

Tunik, E., Frey, S. H., & Grafton, S. T. (2005). Virtual lesions of the anterior intraparietal area disrupt goal-dependent on-line adjustments of grasp. *Nature Neuroscience, 8*(4), 505–511. http://dx.doi.org/10.1038/nn1430.

Urry, H. L., van Reekum, C. M., Johnstone, T., Kalin, N. H., Thurow, M. E., Schaefer, H. S., ... Davidson, R. J. (2006). Amygdala and ventromedial prefrontal cortex are inversely coupled during regulation of negative affect and predict the diurnal pattern of cortisol secretion among older adults. *The Journal of Neuroscience, 26*(16), 4415–4425. http://dx.doi.org/10.1523/JNEUROSCI.3215-05.2006.

Vohs, K. D., Baumeister, R. F., & Ciarocco, N. J. (2005). Self-regulation and self-presentation: regulatory resource depletion impairs impression management and effortful self-presentation depletes regulatory resources. *Journal of Personality and Social Psychology, 88*(4), 632–657. http://dx.doi.org/10.1037/0022-3514.88.4.632.

Vohs, K. D., & Heatherton, T. F. (2000). Self-regulatory failure: a resource-depletion approach. *Psychological Science, 11*(3), 249–254. http://dx.doi.org/10.1111/1467-9280.00250.

Volkow, N. D., Fowler, J. S., Wang, G.-J., Telang, F., Logan, J., Jayne, M., ... Swanson, J. M. (2010). Cognitive control of drug craving inhibits brain reward regions in cocaine abusers. *NeuroImage, 49*(3), 2536–2543. http://dx.doi.org/10.1016/j.neuroimage.2009.10.088.

Wagner, D. D., Altman, M., Boswell, R. G., Kelley, W. M., & Heatherton, T. F. (2013). Self-regulatory depletion enhances neural responses to rewards and impairs top-down control. *Psychological Science*, 24(11), 2262–2271. http://dx.doi.org/10.1177/0956797613492985.

Wagner, D. D., Dal Cin, S., Sargent, J. D., Kelley, W. M., & Heatherton, T. F. (2011). Spontaneous action representation in smokers when watching movie characters smoke. *The Journal of Neuroscience: The Official Journal of the Society for Neuroscience*, 31(3), 894–898. http://dx.doi.org/10.1523/JNEUROSCI.5174-10.2011.

Wagner, D. D., & Heatherton, T. F. (2013). Self-regulatory depletion increases emotional reactivity in the amygdala. *Social Cognitive and Affective Neuroscience*, 8(4), 410–417. http://dx.doi.org/10.1093/scan/nss082.

Yoo, S.-S., Gujar, N., Hu, P., Jolesz, F. A., & Walker, M. P. (2007). The human emotional brain without sleep — a prefrontal amygdala disconnect. *Current Biology*, 17(20), R877–R878. http://dx.doi.org/10.1016/j.cub.2007.08.007.

CHAPTER

15

Cognitive Control Processes Underlying Individual Differences in Self-Control

B.M. Wilkowski[1], M.D. Robinson[2]

[1]University of Wyoming, Laramie, WY, United States; [2]North Dakota State University, Fargo, ND, United States

The strength model of self-control (Baumeister, Vohs, & Tice, 2007) proposes that individual differences in general self-control strength can explain why some people excel or struggle in multiple domains of life. Consider Alvin Wong, who was identified in a 2011 Gallup poll as one of the happiest people in the United States (Rampell, 2011). At age 69, Wong is extremely healthy, married, and has children. As a devout Jew, he maintains a strict kosher diet. He owns his own health-care business and makes $120,000 a year. In terms of emotional well-being, physical health, interpersonal relations, and financial success, Wong is thriving.

Now compare Wong to Chris Farley, the American comedian who died of a drug overdose at age 33 (Chris Farley's Death, 1998). Beyond his addiction, Farley's poor diet led to obesity and advanced heart disease. He never married or had children. Although Farley had friends, many of them publically expressed concerns about his lifestyle and well-being. Just as Wong thrived in many areas of life, Farley struggled.

One of the great accomplishments of the strength model (Baumeister et al., 2007) is that it pointed to individual differences in self-control as a parsimonious explanation for functioning across different domains. While fully acknowledging this accomplishment, one major emphasis of this chapter is that individual differences in self-control are not entirely unitary across domains. Returning to our example, one must acknowledge Chris Farley was enormously successful in his career. It is difficult to imagine how this could have happened without him refining his talents meticulously, persisting in the face of obstacles, overcoming fatigue to memorize his lines, etc. In short, it appears that Farley could, and did, exert a great deal of self-control in career-related efforts. How can we explain this sort of domain specificity? This chapter seeks to provide relevant answers.

In more particular terms, we review research by ourselves and others seeking to understand both domain-general and domain-specific individual differences in self-control. In doing so, we adopt a process-oriented perspective by focusing on the cognitive control processes underlying individual differences in self-control. As we will show, this approach gives rise to some precise, testable predictions concerning dispositional self-control.

After reviewing some definitional issues, we introduce a family of cognitive control models that are useful in thinking about how self-control is likely to operate. We then review three lines of work pertaining to error-monitoring, cognitive control performance, and self-control outcomes. Finally, we discuss how the cognitive control perspective can help to improve interventions designed to boost self-control and understand ego depletion effects.

WHAT IS SELF-CONTROL?

Before beginning, it is important to be clear about what self-control is and how it differs (or does not differ) from the related constructs of self-regulation and cognitive control. Self-regulation is involved in the pursuit of any goal (Carver & Scheier, 2012). Thus, self-regulation occurs both when we satisfy short-term impulses (eg, eating a candy bar) and when we achieve fairly difficult long-term objectives (eg, losing 10 pounds). Self-control, by contrast, is a term typically reserved for cases in which a person overcomes momentary desires in favor of a more valuable long-term goal (Chapter 5; Hofmann, Schmeichel, & Baddeley, 2012). Restraining from unhealthy food to maintain physical health is one example. Persisting at a difficult task (eg, studying) that could result in long-term benefits (eg, academic and career success) is another. As should be apparent, self-regulation and self-control are related but distinct constructs. Although our main focus is self-control, it is often not meaningful to discuss self-control without a consideration of the wider self-regulation context.

Cognitive control overlaps with self-control in that it involves overcoming immediate reactions in favor of a longer-term goal (or task) of the individual. Cognitive control, however, is defined in more process-oriented terms. Along these lines, Botvinick and Braver (2015, p. 85) defined cognitive control as: "[T]hat set of superordinate functions that encode and maintain a representation of the current task—ie, contextually relevant stimulus-response associations, action-outcome contingencies, and target states or goals—marshaling to that task subordinate functions including working, semantic, and episodic memory; perceptual attention; and action selection and inhibition." Other terms for cognitive control include executive function and effortful control, which are defined and assessed in very similar ways (Miyake & Friedman, 2012). Following these definitions, we use the term *cognitive control* to describe psychological processes, while we use the term *self-control* to describe outcomes consistent with resisting momentary temptation in favor of long-term goals (eg, healthy eating, academic success).

COGNITIVE CONTROL MODELS—A PRELIMINARY SKETCH

Cognitive control models (Botvinick, Braver, Barch, Carter, & Cohen, 2001; Holroyd & Coles, 2002) share a great deal in common with cybernetic models of self-regulation (Carver & Scheier, 2012). As depicted in Fig. 15.1, a monitoring system determines whether there is a need for control by monitoring for discrepancies between what is desired and what is happening. If a discrepancy is detected, the operating systems seek to reduce it.

The Monitoring System

Multiple theories suggest that the *Monitoring* system is neurologically located in the anterior cingulate cortex (ACC) and monitors for diverse events which signal the need for control (Botvinick & Braver, 2015; Holroyd & Yeung, 2012). First, this system monitors for the simultaneous

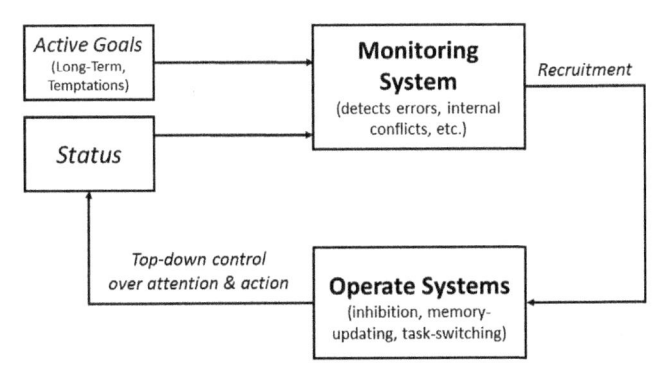

FIGURE 15.1 A cognitive control model of the processes underlying self-control.

activation of conflicting responses (Botvinick et al., 2001). This system would thus detect the conflicting responses activated by momentary temptations (eg, "Eat the chocolate!") and long-term goals (eg, "No, have a radish instead!"). In addition, this system also monitors for errors in task performance. The theory of Holroyd and Coles (2002) suggests that the basal ganglia compares expected responses and outcomes to those which actually occurred. When this result is worse than expected, this information is fed to the monitoring system in the ACC, signaling the need for control.

At a broader level, the monitoring system is sensitive to aversive events that run counter to goal attainment (Botvinick & Braver, 2015). Thus, it is a "hot" system which supports goal pursuit, rather than a "cold" information processing system. Errors and conflict are aversive events (Hajcak & Foti, 2008; Hofmann, Luhmann, Fisher, Vohs, & Baumeister, 2013), and this aversion is instrumental to subsequent control (Inzlicht & Al-Khindi, 2012). Furthermore, monitoring only occurs if the motivation for control is present. When people are unmotivated to do well on a task, error monitoring is reduced (Gehring, Goss, Coles, Meyer, & Donchin, 1993). Further, if a person knows that valued goals can be obtained, cognitive control resources can be proactively recruited ahead of time to obtain the desired goal (Jimura, Locke, & Braver, 2010).

The Operate Systems

Like the strength model (Baumeister et al., 2007), cognitive control models propose that the *Operations* underlying effective self-control depend on limited capacity resources (Botvinick et al., 2001; Holroyd & Coles, 2002). These resources are invariably identified with regions of the prefrontal cortex (ie, dorsolateral; inferior frontal junction; frontopolar). When response conflicts, errors, or other relevant signals are detected, these limited capacity resources are recruited to perform the "work" of self-control.

While the strength model contends that all acts of self-control rely on a single resource (Baumeister et al., 2007), cognitive control models propose that different cognitive control operations are supported by several distinct but overlapping neural areas. Critical to current concerns, individual differences in cognitive control performance cannot be explained by a single factor (Miyake & Friedman, 2012). Rather, three separate factors are often found. Individual differences in *inhibition* refer to the ability to override dominant responses in favor of subdominant (but contextually appropriate) response. Individual differences in *updating* refer to the ability to dynamically update the contents of memory as events change. Finally, individual differences in *task-switching* refer to the ability to flexibly switch back and forth between different tasks. Beyond this, neuroimaging studies indicate that different cognitive control tasks activate overlapping but distinct neural areas (Nee, Wager, & Jonides, 2007). Furthermore, cognitive control recruitment on one task only benefits performance on other control tasks under certain conditions (Enger, 2008).

INDIVIDUAL DIFFERENCES IN ERROR MONITORING

The cognitive control models just reviewed provide specific and testable hypotheses concerning the processes underlying individual differences in self-control. In this section, we focus on two such predictions. While the strength model has emphasized the *Operate* phase (eg, Tangney, Baumeister, & Boone, 2004), cognitive control models suggest that *Monitoring* is also critical to self-control. Furthermore, cognitive control models suggest that monitoring operations critically depend on the goals of the individual. Thus, a person can control themselves better in a particular domain if they are motivated to do so. We review research on individual differences in monitoring in light of these points. As research has mainly focused on error monitoring, we focus mainly on this aspect of monitoring as well.

Basic Research on Error Monitoring

The *error-related negativity* (ERN: Gehring et al., 1993) is an event-related potential generated by the ACC which peaks roughly 100 ms following errors on many speeded reaction time (RT) tasks (eg, the Stroop, flanker). Multiple theories (eg, Holroyd & Coles, 2002) suggest that it reflects the detection of errors by the monitoring system, triggering subsequent control. Consistent with this, posterror ACC activity is closely linked to subsequent prefrontal activity (eg, Kerns, 2006). These prefrontal regions instantiate control in part through slowed responding following errors (Gehring et al., 1993), ultimately allowing individuals to improve their subsequent performance (see Botvinick & Braver, 2015).

Error-Monitoring and Self-control Outcomes

Cognitive control models suggest that individuals higher in error monitoring should display better self-control in a variety of domains. To test this, studies have examined whether individual differences in the ERN or the posterror slowing of RTs predict self-control outcomes.

Studies have found that error monitoring is linked to greater self-control across many domains. Students who display a more robust ERN achieve a higher grade point average (Hirsch & Inzlicht, 2010). Conversely, individuals with problems related to substance abuse (Olvet & Hajcak, 2008) or obesity (Skoranski et al., 2013) display less robust ERNs. Furthermore, individuals who are prone to antisocial behavior (Wilkowski & Robinson, 2008a) and aggression (Chang, Davies, & Gavin, 2010) display less robust posterror slowing and ERNs.

Error monitoring is also linked to a variety of constructs which measure self-control more broadly construed, including externalizing (Hall, Bernat, & Patrick, 2007) and impulsivity (Potts, George, Martin, & Barratt, 2006). Moeller and Robinson (2010) also found that females display a more robust posterror slowdown in RTs than males, consistent with well-documented gender difference in self-control (eg, Else-Quest, Hyde, Goldsmith, & van Hulle, 2006).

Given the regulatory benefits of error monitoring, it is reasonable to suspect that it may lead to greater emotional well-being. This would occur because cognitive control processes are involved in emotion regulation (Ochsner & Gross, 2005) and because error monitoring is likely to facilitate goal achievement (Carver & Scheier, 2012). Consistent with this, Robinson (2007) found that individuals who show a more robust posterror slowing of RTs displayed less depression and greater happiness. Robinson, Ode, Wilkowski, and Amodio (2010) also found error monitoring was especially useful at reducing negative affect for individuals high in neuroticism. Finally, Compton et al. (2008) found that participants who displayed a more robust ERN on a Stroop task were more capable of downregulating anxious reactions to daily stressors.

Motivation and Error Monitoring

In summary, error monitoring is linked to self-control across domains. It is important to remember, however, that the monitoring system's function is to facilitate goal achievement. Accordingly, error monitoring increases when incentives are offered (Gehring et al., 1993). This suggests that when individuals are motivated to control themselves in a particular domain, they should exhibit greater error monitoring and self-control than they would otherwise.

For example, individuals who are particularly motivated to obtain rewards monitor for incentives that can be obtained through cognitive control exertion (Jimura et al., 2010). When monetary incentives were offered on working memory tasks, these individuals displayed increased activity in the prefrontal cortex.

Individual differences have also figured prominently in another line of research focused on the intrinsic motivation to control prejudice (Amodio, Devine, & Harmon-Jones, 2008). Individuals high in this motivation display more robust ERNs following errors indicative of implicit prejudice (ie, weapon misidentifications following African-American primes). This increase in the ERN was highly specific and did not generalize to other types of errors on the same or other tasks. Furthermore, it was instrumental in reducing prejudicial responding.

Finally, motivation can also help explain apparent exceptions to the general link between error-monitoring and beneficial outcomes. While there is evidence linking error monitoring to greater self-control across many domains, it is also related to greater worry and anxious apprehension (Moser, Moran, Schroder, Donnellan, & Yeung, 2013). People who habitually worry do so because they believe it serves a functional purpose (Tamir, 2005). Consistent with this, Moser et al. (2013) found that more robust ERNs were especially useful in boosting academic performance among worry-prone undergraduate students. Since these individuals believe worry is useful, they do not monitor for "errors" in mood regulation. In fact, once the risk of errors has passed, these individuals redirect their cognitive control resources to the task of worrying itself (Moser et al., 2013). Thus, both the functional and dysfunctional features of worry are consistent with a motivation-to-control analysis (Matthews & Wells, 2000).

Conscious Awareness and Monitoring

While motivation can explain domain-specific differences in monitoring, other individual differences related to conscious awareness appear to support domain-general monitoring. First, a longstanding literature has linked individual differences in *self-consciousness* to monitoring processes (Carver & Scheier, 2012). Self-consciousness is defined as the tendency to focus attention on one's self. By doing so, one's goals are maintained in an active state and goal comparisons are more likely to occur. Research has shown that people high in dispositional self-consciousness are more likely to behave in accordance with their goals (Carver & Scheier, 2012), due to increased monitoring (Scheier & Carver, 1983). Related research has shown that higher levels of self-consciousness are useful in overcoming ego depletion effects (Wan & Sternthal, 2008).

A newer literature on *mindfulness* also suggests that awareness promotes domain-general monitoring and self-control. Mindfulness is defined as a nonjudgmental awareness of one's current environment (eg, Teper, Segal, & Inzlicht, 2013). Individuals high in mindfulness accrue multiple benefits consistent with self-control. They are less anxious and depressed, experience greater satisfaction with life, report more satisfying social relationships (Brown, Ryan, & Creswell, 2007), engage in better eating habits (Jordan, Wang, Donatoni, & Meier, 2014), and are more persistent (Evans, Baer, & Segerstrom, 2009). Important for present purposes, mindfulness has also been linked to improved performance on cognitive control tasks involving inhibition (Teper et al., 2013), working memory (Jha, Krompinger, & Baime, 2007), and emotion regulation (Chambers, Gullone, & Allen, 2009). Finally, mindfulness meditation ameliorates ego depletion effects (Friese, Messner, & Schaffner, 2012).

The benefits of mindfulness appear to be due to increased monitoring and awareness of goal-relevant stimuli. For example, mindfulness has been shown to increase perceptual awareness of visual stimuli (MacLean et al., 2010) and internal physiological states (Farb, Segal, & Anderson, 2013). Furthermore, it is linked to more robust ERNs (see Teper et al., 2013).

While research on self-consciousness and mindfulness point to the importance of conscious awareness, future research should examine individual differences in *unconscious* monitoring processes. The ERN has been detected even when participants are not consciously aware of committing an error (Nieuwenhuis, Ridderinkhof, Blom, Band, & Kok, 2001), and people can automatically compare their goals to outcomes (Moors, de Houwer, & Eelen, 2003). As cognitive control models do not require consciousness (Botvinick & Braver, 2015), unconscious monitoring processes, too, should increase self-control. However, we could locate no research directly testing this hypothesis.

Section Summary

In summary, research indicates that error monitoring is typically associated with greater self-control across a variety of domains. These domain-general outcomes are likely due to processes closely related to the nature of monitoring itself, such as mindful awareness and active goal representations. Despite these domain-general differences, individuals differ in motivation across different domains, and this creates domain-specific differences in monitoring and self-control.

INDIVIDUAL DIFFERENCES IN COGNITIVE CONTROL OPERATIONS

Cognitive control models suggest that *Monitoring* is necessary but not sufficient for self-control. In this section, we therefore turn to the *Operate* phase of cognitive control. While the strength model has emphasized the unitary nature of self-control operations (Baumeister et al., 2007; Tangney et al., 2004), cognitive control abilities are not entirely unitary (Miyake & Friedman, 2012). This section reviews these differences and their consequences.

The Unity and Diversity of Cognitive Control

According to Miyake and Friedman's (2012) influential account, individual differences in cognitive control exhibit both unity and diversity across different tasks. This model proposes a *general* factor to account for the modest positive correlations found across many cognitive control tasks. Nonetheless, the model also proposes that distinct types of cognitive control can be isolated as well.

To test this account, Miyake, Friedman, Emerson, Witzki, and Howerter (2000) gave participants a battery of nine cognitive control tasks. Three were hypothesized to represent *inhibition*, including the well-known Stroop task. Three other tasks were hypothesized to represent the ability to *update* working memory contents. For example, they administered the two-back task, which asks participants if the current stimulus matches a stimulus presented two trials prior. Finally, three other paradigms were hypothesized to represent capacities to *switch* between different tasks. In addition to these three separable factors, they hypothesized a higher-order *general* factor. Analyses using structural equation modeling provided clear support for the unity-and-diversity perspective. The hypothesized model fit the data better than models positing one unitary factor, three unrelated factors, and alternative loadings of cognitive control tasks.

More recent research indicates that the *general* factor can fully explain individual differences in *inhibition* but not *updating* or *switching*. Friedman et al. (2008) found that, after accounting for individual differences in *general* cognitive control, individual differences in the *inhibition*-specific factor were no longer significant. This suggests that psychological processes which underlie inhibition also contribute generally to updating and switching. By contrast, there appear to be unique processes involved in updating and switching.

Inhibition and Self-control Outcomes

Researchers have frequently used measures of inhibition to predict self-control outcomes (Hofmann, Schmeichel, et al., 2012). For example, the stop-signal task has frequently been used, which measures how quickly a participants can stop an initiated key press response when they are signaled to do so (Verbruggen & Logan, 2008). Individuals who perform better on inhibitory tasks are less likely to overuse drugs (eg, Houben & Wiers, 2009), overeat (Nederkoorn, Houben, Hofmann, Roefs, & Jansen, 2010), commit infidelity (Karremans, Pronk, & van der Wal, 2016), or unintentionally stereotype (eg, Payne, 2005). Similarly, children who perform better on these tasks exhibit fewer problems with attention (Friedman et al., 2007), externalizing (eg, conduct disorder: Young et al., 2009), and restraint (ie, touching a forbidden toy; Friedman, Miyake, Robinson, & Hewitt, 2011).

Because individual differences in *inhibition* can be explained in terms of *general* cognitive control (Miyake & Friedman, 2012), these effects should reflect this general factor. All studies administering a battery of cognitive control tasks have found support for this idea. This has been true in studies examining the control of implicitly prejudiced errors (Ito et al., 2015), attention problems, externalizing disorder symptoms, and self-restraint (see Herd et al., 2014).

Memory Updating and Self-control Outcomes

Updating tasks also tell us something important about a person's capacity for control (Hofmann, Schmeichel, et al., 2012). People who perform better on these tasks are more capable of regulating their emotions (Schmeichel, Volokhov, & Demaree, 2008), resisting temptations (eg, Hofmann, Friese, & Roefs, 2009), controlling ruminative thought (Brewin & Smart, 2005), and lessening explicit prejudice (Ito et al., 2015).

An important question is whether the apparent benefits of *updating* are due to these abilities in particular or to the *general* cognitive control factor. The few studies which have included a larger battery of cognitive control tasks have found that updating has unique benefits. Updating predicts healthier eating (Hofmann et al., 2009), greater problem-solving ability (Friedman et al., 2008), and reduced explicit prejudice (Ito et al., 2015), even after controlling for inhibition or general cognitive control. Although more research would be useful, we tentatively conclude that updating uniquely contributes to self-control.

Switching and Self-control Outcomes

There have been comparatively fewer studies examining whether task-switching abilities predict self-control outcomes. Among the established findings is that better switching ability predicts lower implicit prejudice scores on the implicit association test (IAT; Ito et al., 2015; Klauer, Schmitz, Teige-Mocigemba, & Voss, 2010). Zero-order correlations also link greater *switching* ability to fewer attentional problems (Friedman et al., 2007) and to fewer externalizing behaviors (Young et al., 2009).

While these findings may suggest that switching is linked to improved self-control, a closer examination warns against such a conclusion. Klauer et al. (2010) points out that the IAT procedure requires people to switch between two different categorization tasks. Thus, switching may be related to implicit prejudice only because of common method variance. In support of this, improved *switching* performance is related to lower IAT scores even when self-control is quite irrelevant to the cognitive associations examined (eg, flowers vs insects) (Klauer et al., 2010). Similarly, Ito et al. (2015) found that relations between *switching* and implicit prejudice did not generalize beyond the IAT to other measures of implicit prejudice.

Of even greater interest, studies demonstrate that greater *switching* performance actually predicts lower self-control once *general* cognitive control abilities are accounted for. Such paradoxical relationships have been found for problem-solving outcomes (Friedman et al., 2008), restraint, and externalizing problems (Herd et al., 2014). This suggests that the unique variance in switching performance is actually related to worse self-control outcomes.

Processes Underlying Different Components of Cognitive Control

To summarize, research suggests that *general* and *updating*-specific components of cognitive control lead to greater self-control; while the *switching*-specific component actually leads to lower self-control once general cognitive control is accounted for. How can we explain these findings? One promising framework is the prefrontal basal ganglia working memory (PBWM) model (Hazy, Frank, & O'Reilly, 2007). This computational model is neurologically realistic and has been used to explain performance on a number of cognitive control tasks. Of further importance, the model provides insights into individual differences in cognitive control (Herd et al., 2014).

According to the PBWM model (Hazy et al., 2007), the basal ganglia is first responsible for gating information into working memory. This includes representations of goals, means of achieving these goals, and other task-relevant information. Once information is in working memory, the prefrontal cortex is responsible for maintaining it in an active state. Recurrent excitatory connections in the PFC serve this function. Finally, control itself is implemented through top-down biasing signals sent to other neural regions involved in perception and action. Through such processes, behavioral responses can be aligned with current goals.

Herd et al. (2014) recently used the PBWM to simultaneously model individual differences in Stroop and task-switching performance. The analysis suggested that the strength of the PFC's top-down influence is likely an important process underlying the *general* cognitive control factor. As the strength of top-down influence was increased in their computational model, the size of both the Stroop effect and the task-switching cost diminished, suggesting improved cognitive control on both tasks.

By contrast, the ability to actively maintain information in working memory contributed differentially to inhibitory and switching performance. As Herd et al. (2014) increased this parameter in their computational model, the Stroop incongruency effect decreased. This finding is quite sensible, as the Stroop task requires participants to continually maintain one goal (ie, name the font color) throughout the task. Interestingly, though, increasing this parameter led to *greater* task-switching costs. Although not as obvious, this finding is also quite sensible. If the cognitive representation of a task is maintained in a more active state, it will be harder for participants to switch away from it to another task.

This computational model can help explain the complex relationships between *general* cognitive control, *switching*-specific cognitive control, and self-control outcomes (Friedman et al., 2008). As strong top-down signals appear to underlie the general factor of cognitive control, they may underlie this factor's salutary effects on self-control outcomes. Once these processes are stripped away from task-switching performance, what may be left is a measure of quickly decaying goal representations. Such effervescent representations may appear to add flexibility when a person is completing a task-switching paradigm, but may lead people to forget or neglect their long-term goals in real life (see Hofmann, Schmeichel, et al., 2012, for a related analysis).

Clearly, the use of the PBWM model to understand individual differences in cognitive control is in an early stage. A more complete analysis of cognitive control tasks is needed. It would also be useful if computational work led to procedures for calculating individual difference parameters for use in empirical research. Finally, this model has not integrated monitoring processes yet. Nonetheless, we believe that the model provides a valuable tool for researchers as they begin to study the cognitive processes underlying self-control.

Section Summary

In summary, research indicates that individual differences in cognitive control are not entirely unitary. *General* cognitive control can fully account for individual differences on inhibition and partially account for updating and switching performance. Nonetheless, *updating* and *switching* clearly exist as independent factors. Furthermore, these distinctions are important. General and updating factors uniquely contribute to greater self-control, but lower residual switch costs are actually predictive of worse self-control. These insights would be missed if cognitive control was treated as a monolithic entity.

DIVERSITY ACROSS DIFFERENT DOMAINS OF SELF-CONTROL

The strength model has presented two sources of evidence to support the unitary nature of trait self-control. First, scales designed to measure trait self-control predict self-controlled behavior across a variety of domains. Second, behavior is often correlated across very different self-control domains (eg, good grades can predict prosocial behavior). We first review these two sources of evidence and then suggest that unity across different domains is far from complete. Second, we present evidence that motivation and monitoring processes can explain how a person could effectively control themselves in one domain but not others.

The Predictive Ability of General Self-control Scales

Tangney et al. (2004) created a dispositional self-control scale and showed that higher levels of it were associated with better grades, better eating habits, less aggression, and higher emotional well-being. Many subsequent studies have used this scale to predict other life outcomes and behaviors. In a recent metaanalysis, de Ridder, Lensvelt-Mulders, Finkenauer, Stok, and Baumeister (2012) found that the self-control scale significantly predicted a number of self-control outcomes.

In addition to the trait self-control scale, there is a much longer tradition in personality psychology of using trait impulsivity measures to predict self-control outcomes (Sharma, Markon, & Clark, 2014). As discussed in further detail below, a weakness of this tradition is that different researchers have conceptualized impulsivity in dramatically different ways. Nonetheless, Sharma et al.'s (2014) metaanalysis clearly indicates that diverse aspects of impulsivity predict many self-control outcomes.

Processes Underlying Trait Self-control's Effects

Tangney et al. (2004) proposed that their scale measures individual differences in self-control strength. According to this account, individuals high in trait self-control should be more capable of resisting temptations. Consistent with this original account, Schmeichel and Zell (2009) found that individuals high on this scale could resist the urge to blink and tolerate pain more effectively. Friese and Hofmann (2009) also found that these individuals were more capable of resisting automatic unhealthy impulses.

However, a number of more recent findings question the effortful inhibition account of trait self-control. Duckworth and Kern (2011) were unable to successfully link scores on the trait self-control scale with objective cognitive control performance. In addition, Hofmann, Baumeister, Forster, and Vohs (2012) were unable to support the idea that trait self-control predicts success in resisting temptations encountered in daily life. Instead, it appears that people high in trait self-control structure their lives so that temptations are less likely to be encountered. Consistent with this, studies indicate that high self-control individuals report less conflict between goals and desires (Hofmann et al., 2013), take proactive steps to avoid temptations (Ent, Baumeister, & Tice, 2014), and develop habits which allow them to achieve desired goals effortlessly (Galla & Duckworth, 2015).

While more research is clearly needed, these studies suggest that high self-control individuals proactively avoid temptations. While this is certainly an interesting and important aspect of self-control (Fujita, 2011), it suggests that many other individual difference variables are related to self-control. In other words, we encourage a broader perspective on individual differences in self-control than can be assessed using the Tangney et al. (2004) scale.

Consistency in Behavior Across Self-control Domains

Beyond research related to the trait self-control scale, consistencies in behavior across self-control domains have been offered as evidence for the unified view of trait self-control. For example, the criminologists Gottfredson and Hirschi (1990) noted that the same individuals who commit criminal acts also tend to engage in other behaviors suggestive of lesser self-control. They drink and smoke too much. They show up late for work or school. This tends to be true regardless of relevant behaviors' legality.

Clinical psychologists have uncovered similar covariations (see Markon, Kruger, & Watson, 2005). Factor analyses have led to the identification of two factors of clinical symptoms. The first has been labeled *internalizing* and primarily consists of anxiety and mood disorders (eg, depression, generalized anxiety). This factor appears to reflect the pathological end of the neuroticism dimension (Markon et al., 2005). More pertinent to current concerns, the second factor has been labeled *externalizing* and primarily consists of substance abuse and conduct disorders. This factor appears to reflect pathological levels of the normal disinhibition continuum. Disinhibition represents a higher-order personality trait that combines low conscientiousness and low agreeableness from the Big Five model of personality (Markon et al., 2005).

Despite the existence of this general externalizing factor, clinical researchers have posited more specific forms of disinhibition. Multiple studies have found that externalizing includes two lower-order constructs related to overt aggression and covert, nonaggressive behaviors (Markon et al., 2005). These appear to correspond to disagreeable and unconscientious forms of disinhibition, respectively. Below these facets, the more traditional diagnoses represent even more specific types of disinhibition.

Research on normal variations in human personality also points to similar conclusions, in that there are a number of distinct forms of impulsivity. In a metaanalytic factor analysis of published impulsivity scales, Sharma et al. (2014) discovered three relatively distinct traits. The first factor has been labeled sensation seeking. It describes a tendency to engage in dangerous, thrill-seeking activities and is related to extraversion in the Big Five tradition. The second factor has been labeled negative urgency. It describes an inability to think or control one's actions when distressed and is related to neuroticism. The third factor has been labeled disinhibition. It describes a lack of planning and persistence and is related to low conscientiousness.

Sharma et al. (2014) also found that the different forms of impulsivity were all valid in predicting daily impulsive behaviors. Sensation seeking was related to alcohol use and delinquency; Negative urgency predicted substance use more broadly, as well as aggression and delinquency; and disinhibition was widely predictive of all the impulsive behaviors examined. In short, individual differences in self-control cannot be fully captured by one factor.

The Motivation and Ability to Control

How can we make sense of the heterogeneity reviewed earlier? One possibility is that the various types of self-control map onto the various types of cognitive control. However, metaanalyses indicate little to no correlation between self-report questionnaires of self-control/impulsivity and laboratory cognitive control tasks. Sharma et al. (2014) found an overall correlation of $r = 0.02$, and Duckworth and Kern (2011) found an overall correlation of $r = 0.10$. Moreover, these metaanalyses could not locate more precise aspects of self-control or cognitive control which were more consistently related.

Null findings of this type have led some theorists to suggest that self-reported measures of self-control and impulsivity may instead reflect the *motivation* to exert self-control (eg, Karremans et al., 2016). In this view, the higher-order factor of disinhibition (Markon et al., 2005) may reflect a willingness to exert effort toward long-term goals. Lower-level factors may, in turn, reflect more specific goals. For example, agreeable inhibition may reflect the motivation to maintain harmonious social relationships; while conscientious inhibition may reflect one's valuing of long-term achievements. This analysis suggests that both motivation and ability may be important to consider when predicting self-control outcomes.

Consistent with this view, Hofmann, Gschwendner, Friese, Wiers, and Schmitt (2008) found that participants' conscious self-control goals (in this case, related to negative explicit attitudes toward pornography, sweets, and aggression) only predicted self-controlled behavior for individuals high in working memory capacity. By contrast, the behavior of people low in working memory capacity was guided by their implicit attitudes. This pattern has subsequently been replicated for other behaviors such as weight loss (Nederkoorn et al., 2010) and with other indices of cognitive control such as inhibition (Nederkoorn et al., 2010). Cognitive control therefore seems to facilitate self-control by allowing people to act in accordance with their conscious (rather than implicit) goals.

Situation-Specific Recruitment of Cognitive Control

We are accustomed to thinking about cognitive control in terms of abilities (Miyake & Friedman, 2012). However, abilities will not matter if they are not used. Accordingly, the more pertinent question may be *when* people recruit cognitive control. Recent studies have pursued this idea.

Cognitive control models suggest that the most direct predictor of self-control in a specific domain is whether a person recruits cognitive control resources in that domain. To test this idea, we (Wilkowski & Robinson, 2008b) developed a paradigm in which participants are primed with hostile or nonhostile words before completing trials of a cognitive control task. In these studies, we found that individuals low in trait anger exhibit better cognitive control following hostile primes, whereas people high in trait anger do not. This interactive pattern has been found for the flanker task (which is quite similar to the classic Stroop incongruency task; Wilkowski & Robinson, 2008b, Study 2; Wilkowski, Robinson, & Troop-Gordon, 2010, Studies 1–2), the stop-signal task (Wilkowski, 2012), and a task-switching paradigm (Wilkowski & Robinson, 2008b, Study 1). In future research, it will be interesting to see if similar findings will hold in other self-control domains.

Section Summary

In summary, there is some evidence for the unity of individual differences in self-control across domains. Higher-order factors such as externalizing or disinhibition emerge in many factor analyses. Nonetheless, it is necessary to postulate more specific, lower-order factors to fully understand individual differences in self-control. Scales measuring self-control or impulsivity do not show clear correspondence with performance on cognitive control tasks, so they may instead reflect the motivation to engage in self-control. Consistent with this, motivation interacts with cognitive control in predicting self-control in specific domains. A person's tendencies to recruit cognitive control in a specific situation may prove to be the most direct predictor of self-control outcomes in the same domain.

IMPROVING SELF-CONTROL

Given what we have learned about individual differences in self-control, how can we use this knowledge to increase people's self-control? The strength model has suggested that repeatedly engaging in self-control tasks will eventually strengthen the resource underlying self-control (Baumeister et al., 2007). Several studies have tested this possibility by asking participants to engage in self-control training tasks (eg, using one's nondominant hand) for several weeks. While many studies have found improvements in self-control, Inzlicht and Berkman (2015) have presented a metaanalysis questioning the robustness of these results (see Shipstead, ReMiyakedick, & Engle, 2012, for evidence of a similar state of affairs in efforts to enhance working memory capacity). While a full consideration of these training protocols is beyond the scope of this chapter, we would like to briefly consider how a cognitive control framework may inform and improve self-control training protocols. In this connection, we present four points.

Importance of Monitoring

If the need for self-control goes unnoticed, efforts toward self-control will not be initiated. Thus, monitoring processes are critical to self-control. In support of this point, there is now a sizeable literature showing that mindfulness-based interventions effectively improve many self-control outcomes (Brown et al., 2007). These interventions aim to facilitate awareness of one's body and one's surroundings and are believed to work (at least in part) because they improve monitoring processes (Teper et al., 2013).

The Challenge of Cross-Domain Generalization

A major conclusion of our review is that individual differences in self-control are not entirely unitary. Thus, a critical question is whether self-control training in one domain will generalize to another domain. For example, asking participants to use their nondominant hand may cultivate their ability to maintain this goal in memory, recognize stimuli relevant to this goal (eg, doorknobs), recognize errors in achieving this goal (eg, "Oops! I almost used my right hand!"), and implement top-down control over behavior to support this goal (eg, left-hand usage). However, these processes may not transfer to other goals. This problem has clearly surfaced in the working memory training research, where practice on a spatial n-back memory task has sometimes failed to improve performance on the extremely similar verbal n-back task (see Shipstead et al., 2012). It has been suggested that continual practice at one idiosyncratic task may automatize strategies which improve performance only for that one narrow task. Similar generalization problems may occur with self-control training.

The Role of Motivation

If a person is unmotivated to control themselves in a particular domain, self-control training seems unlikely to have much of an effect. Even when people are motivated, one must consider the nature of the motivation. This point emerges from a recent series of studies by Denson et al. (2015). These authors administered self-control training protocols and examined their impact on aggression. When participants had nonaggressive goals (eg, to be compassionate to others), self-control training reduced aggression. However, when participants had aggressive goals (eg, to prevent others from taking advantage of them), self-control training actually *increased* aggression. Null effects for training may often occur because different people have different goals.

Domain-Specific Training

Given difficulties with cross-domain generalization and motivation, it may be more productive to improve self-control in one domain of interest. Along these lines, Wilkowski, Crowe, and Ferguson (2015) recently designed a procedure that trained participants to recruit cognitive control in aggressive situations specifically. This manipulation effectively reduced behavioral aggression among people automatically prone to such acts. Houben and colleagues developed similar procedures to target unhealthy eating (Houben, 2011) and heavy alcohol usage (Houben, Nederkoorn, Wiers, & Jansen, 2011). This work suggests that it may be more fruitful to encourage participants to control themselves in specific circumstances than to improve their domain-general self-control abilities.

COMPARISON TO THE STRENGTH MODEL

The strength model used an elegant metaphor to draw attention to an important aspect of human functioning (Baumeister et al., 2007). The model has been immensely successful. It has inspired volumes of research on an impressive array of variables, from Stroop performance to romantic relationships. This book is a further testament to the influence of the model.

As research progresses, though, it is increasingly important to understand the processes underlying self-control. Attempts to use the original muscle metaphor to do so have not always led to the expected results. For example, while glucose was once thought to be the source of self-control strength (Gailliot et al., 2007), recent evidence suggests that this is not the case (Molden et al., 2012). As researchers attempt to specify the processes underlying self-control, it may be useful to realize that the muscle metaphor is, in the end, just a metaphor. It sheds light on some aspects of self-control, but leaves other aspects of self-control in the dark.

In this connection, we offer the following suggestions for the broader literature on self-control. First, in agreement with the classic strength model, a cognitive control perspective suggests that self-control relies on limited resources. However, these limited capacity resources are not monolithic in nature. Furthermore, they are identified with the prefrontal cortex rather than glucose. Because this region uses recurrent excitatory connections to maintain task-relevant information in an active state (Hazy et al., 2007), it can only complete one cognitive control task at a time. This creates a bottleneck that is evident when participants seek to perform two cognitive control tasks simultaneously (see Enger, 2008).

Because the cognitive control perspective differs in its conceptualization of these resources, it does not suggest that resources grow smaller with use (cf. Kurzban, Duckworth, Kable, & Myers, 2013). Instead, this perspective suggests that ego depletion effects may be due to changes in motivation and monitoring. Because self-control relies on a limited resource, the continual use of this resource for one goal detracts from other goals. Thus, people's motivation and monitoring efforts shift from one goal (eg, completing a psychological study for course credit) to another goal (eg, daydreaming and planning for other upcoming events) (cf. Chapters 13, 18); Inzlicht & Berkman, 2016).

SUMMARY AND CONCLUSION

In this chapter, we reviewed research which has used cognitive control models to understand individual differences in self-control. This analysis suggests at least three important conclusions. First, monitoring is critically important to self-control. If one is oblivious of the need for control, control will not be implemented. Second, individual differences in self-control are not fully consistent across all domains. Chris Farley may have simply not cared to regulate his cravings for drugs, alcohol, or unhealthy foods, but he was motivated to use self-control to excel in his profession. Finally, the resources underlying self-control operations do not appear to be entirely unitary. For example, it is possible that Farley had excellent updating abilities but poor inhibition abilities. This could have allowed him to memorize lines and adapt his routine, but left him unable to control his impulses. We suggest that these three critical insights may have broader relevance to improving self-control training and understanding ego depletion effects.

References

Amodio, D. M., Devine, P. G., & Harmon-Jones, E. (2008). Individual differences in the regulation of intergroup bias: the role of conflict monitoring and neural signals for control. *Journal of Personality and Social Psychology, 94*, 60–74.

Baumeister, R. F., Vohs, K. D., & Tice, D. M. (2007). The strength model of self-control. *Current Directions in Psychological Science, 16*, 351–355.

Botvinick, M. M., & Braver, T. (2015). Motivation and cognitive control: from behavior to neural mechanism. *Annual Review of Psychology, 66*, 83–113.

Botvinick, M. M., Braver, T. S., Barch, D. M., Carter, C. S., & Cohen, J. D. (2001). Conflict monitoring and cognitive control. *Psychological Review, 108*, 624–652.

Brewin, C. R., & Smart, L. (2005). Working memory capacity and suppression of intrusive thoughts. *Journal of Behavioral Therapy and Experimental Psychiatry, 36*, 61–68.

Brown, K. W., Ryan, R. M., & Creswell, J. D. (2007). Mindfulness: theoretical foundations and evidence for its salutary effects. *Psychological Inquiry, 18,* 21–37.

Carver, C. S., & Scheier, M. F. (2012). *Attention and self-regulation: A control-theory approach to human behavior.* New York: Springer-Verlag.

Chambers, R., Gullone, E., & Allen, N. B. (2009). Mindful emotion regulation: an integrative review. *Clinical Psychology Review, 29,* 560–572.

Chang, W. P., Davies, P. L., & Gavin, W. J. (2010). Individual differences in error monitoring in healthy adults: psychological symptoms and antisocial personality characteristics. *European Journal of Neuroscience, 32,* 1388–1396.

Chris Farley's death laid to drug overdose. (January 3, 1998). *The New York Times.* www.newyorktimes.com.

Compton, R. J., Robinson, M. D., Ode, S., Quandt, L. C., Fineman, S. L., & Carp, J. (2008). Error-monitoring ability predicts daily stress regulation. *Psychological Science, 19,* 702–708.

de Ridder, D. T. D., Lensvelt-Mulders, G., Finkenauer, C., Stok, F. M., & Baumeister, R. F. (2012). Taking stock of self-control: a meta-analysis of how trait self-control relates to a wide range of behaviors. *Personality and Social Psychology Review, 16,* 76–99.

Denson, T. D., Wilkowski, B. W., DeWall, C. N., Friese, M., Hofmann, W., Ferguson, E. L., et al. (2015). *Boosting self-control capacity supports the aggressive and non-aggressive pursuit of distal goals* (Manuscript submitted for publication).

Duckworth, A. L., & Kern, M. L. (2011). A meta-analysis of the convergent validity of self-control measures. *Journal of Research in Personality, 45,* 259–268.

Else-Quest, N. M., Hyde, J. S., Goldsmith, H. H., & van Hulle, C. A. (2006). Gender differences in temperament: a meta-analysis. *Psychological Bulletin, 132,* 33–72.

Enger, T. (2008). Multiple conflict-driven control mechanisms in the human brain. *Trends in Cognitive Sciences, 12,* 374–380.

Ent, M. R., Baumeister, R. F., & Tice, D. M. (2014). Trait self-control and the avoidance of temptation. *Personality and Individual Differences, 74,* 12–15.

Evans, D. R., Baer, R. A., & Segerstrom, S. C. (2009). The effects of mindfulness and self-consciousness on persistence. *Personality and Individual Differences, 47,* 379–382.

Farb, N. A. S., Segal, Z. V., & Anderson, A. K. (2013). Mindfulness meditation training alters cortical representations of interoceptive attention. *Social Cognitive and Affective Neuroscience, 8,* 15–26.

Friedman, N. P., Haberstick, B. C., Willcutt, E. G., Miyake, A., Young, S. E., Corley, R. P., et al. (2007). Greater attention problems during childhood predict poorer executive functioning in late adolescence. *Psychological Science, 18,* 893–900.

Friedman, N. P., Miyake, A., Young, S. E., DeFries, J. C., Corley, R. P., & Hewitt, J. K. (2008). Individual differences in executive functions are almost entirely genetic in origin. *Journal of Experimental Psychology: General, 137,* 201–225.

Friedman, N. P., Miyake, A., Robinson, J. L., & Hewitt, J. K. (2011). Developmental trajectories in toddlers' self-restraint predict individual differences in executive functions 14 years later: a behavioral genetic analysis. *Developmental Psychology, 47,* 1410–1430.

Friese, M., & Hofmann, W. (2009). Control me or I will control you: impulses, trait self-control, and the guidance of behavior. *Journal of Research in Personality, 43,* 795–805.

Friese, M., Messner, C., & Schaffner, Y. (2012). Mindfulness meditation counteracts self-control depletion. *Consciousness and Cognition, 21,* 1016–1022.

Fujita, K. (2011). On conceptualizing self-control as more than the effortful inhibition of impulses. *Personality and Social Psychology Review, 15,* 352–366.

Gailliot, M. T., Baumeister, R. F., DeWall, C. N., Maner, J. K., Plant, A., Tice, D. M., et al. (2007). Self-control relies on glucose as a limited energy source: willpower is more than a metaphor. *Journal of Personality and Social Psychology, 92,* 325–336.

Galla, B. M., & Duckworth, A. L. (2015). More than resisting temptation: beneficial habits mediate the relationship between self-control and positive life outcomes. *Journal of Personality and Social Psychology, 109,* 508–525.

REFERENCES

Gehring, W. J., Goss, B., Coles, M. G. H., Meyer, D. E., & Donchin, E. (1993). A neural system for error detection and compensation. *Psychological Science, 4*, 385–390.

Gottfredson, M. R., & Hirschi, T. (1990). *A general theory of crime*. Stanford, CA: Stanford University Press.

Hajcak, G., & Foti, D. (2008). Errors are aversive: defensive motivation and the error-related negativity. *Psychological Science, 19*, 103–108.

Hall, J. R., Bernat, E. M., & Patrick, C. J. (2007). Externalizing psychopathology and the error-related negativity. *Psychological Science, 18*, 326–333.

Hazy, T. E., Frank, M. J., & O'Reilly, R. C. O. (2007). Toward an executive without a homunculus: computational models of the prefrontal cortex/basal ganglia system. *Philosophical Transactions of the Royal Society, Series B, Biological Sciences, 362*, 105–118.

Herd, S. A., O'Reilly, R. C. O., Hazy, T. E., Chantham, C. H., Brant, A. M., & Friedman, N. P. (2014). A neural network model of individual differences in task switching abilities. *Neuropsychologia, 62*, 375–389.

Hirsch, J. B., & Inzlicht, M. (2010). Error-related negativity predicts academic performance. *Psychophysiology, 47*, 192–196.

Hofmann, W., Gschwendner, T., Friese, M., Wiers, R. W., & Schmitt, M. (2008). Individual differences perspective on behavior determination by automatic versus controlled processes. *Journal of Personality and Social Psychology, 95*, 962–977.

Hofmann, W., Friese, M., & Roefs, A. (2009). Three ways to resist temptation: the independent contributions of executive attention, inhibitory control, and affect regulation to the impulse control of eating behavior. *Journal of Experimental Social Psychology, 45*, 431–435.

Hofmann, W., Schmeichel, B. J., & Baddeley, A. D. (2012). Executive functions and self-regulation. *Trends in Cognitive Science, 16*, 174–180.

Hofmann, W., Baumeister, R. F., Forster, G., & Vohs, K. D. (2012). Everyday temptations: an experience sampling study of desire, conflict, and self-control. *Journal of Personality and Social Psychology, 201*, 1318–1335.

Hofmann, W., Luhmann, M., Fisher, R. R., Vohs, K. D., & Baumeister, R. F. (2013). Yes, but are they happy?: effects of trait self-control on affective well-being and life satisfaction. *Journal of Personality, 82*, 265–277.

Holroyd, C. B., & Coles, M. G. H. (2002). The neural basis of human error processing: reinforcement learning, dopamine, and the error-related negativity. *Psychological Review, 109*, 679–709.

Holroyd, C. B., & Yeung, N. (2012). Motivation of extended behaviors by anterior cingulate cortex. *Trends in Cognitive Sciences, 16*, 122–128.

Houben, K., & Wiers, R. W. (2009). Response inhibition moderates the relationship between implicit associations and drinking behavior. *Alcoholism: Clinical and Experimental Research, 33*, 1–8.

Houben, K., Nederkoorn, C., Wiers, R. W., & Jansen, A. (2011). Resisting temptation: decreasing alcohol-related affect and drinking behavior by training response inhibition. *Drug and Alcohol Dependence, 116*, 132–136.

Houben, K. (2011). Overcoming the urge to splurge: influencing eating behavior by manipulating inhibitory control. *Journal of Behavior Therapy and Experimental Psychiatry, 42*, 384–388.

Inzlicht, M., & Al-Khindi, T. (2012). ERN and the Placebo: a misattribution approach to studying the arousal properties of the error-related negativity. *Journal of Experimental Psychology: General, 141*, 799–807.

Inzlicht, M., & Berkman, E. (2015). Six questions for the recourse model of control (and some answers). *Social and Personality Psychology Compass, 9*, 511–524.

Ito, T. A., Friedman, N. P., Bartholow, B. D., Correl, J., Loersch, C., Altamirano, L. J., et al. (2015). Toward a comprehensive understanding of executive cognitive function in implicit racial bias. *Journal of Personality and Social Psychology, 108*, 187–218.

Jha, A. P., Krompinger, J., & Baime, M. J. (2007). Mindfulness training modifies subsystems of attention. *Cognitive, Affective, and Behavioral Neuroscience, 7*, 109–119.

Jimura, K., Locke, H. S., & Braver, T. S. (2010). Prefrontal cortex mediation of cognitive enhancement in rewarding motivational contexts. *Proceeding of the National Academy of Science, 107*, 8871–8876.

Jordan, C. H., Wang, W., Donatoni, L., & Meier, B. P. (2014). Mindful eating: trait and state mindfulness predict healthier eating behavior. *Personality and Individual Differences, 68*, 107–111.

Karremans, J., Pronk, T., & van der Wal, R. (2015). Executive control and relationship maintenance processes: an empirical overview and theoretical integration. *Social and Personality Psychology Compass, 9*, 303–347.

Kerns, J. G. (2006). Anterior cingulate and prefrontal cortex activity in an fMRI study of trial-to-trial adjustments on the Simon task. *Neuroimage, 15*, 399–405.

Klauer, K. C., Schmitz, F., Teige-Mocigemba, S., & Voss, A. (2010). Understanding the role of executive control in the Implicit Association Test: why flexible people have small IAT effects. *Quarterly Journal of Experimental Psychology, 63*, 595–619.

Kurzban, R., Duckworth, A., Kable, J. W., & Myers, J. (2013). An opportunity cost model of subjective effort and task performance. *Behavioral and Brain Sciences, 36*, 661–726.

MacLean, K. A., Ferrer, E., Aichele, S. R., Bridwell, D. A., Zanesco, A. P., Jacobs, T. L., … & Saron, C. D. (2010). Intensive meditation training improves perceptual discrimination and sustained attention. *Psychological Science, 21*, 829–839.

Markon, K. E., Kruger, R. F., & Watson, D. (2005). Delineating the structure of normal and abnormal personality: an integrative hierarchical approach. *Journal of Personality and Social Psychology, 88*, 139–157.

Matthews, G., & Wells, A. (2000). Attention, automaticity, and affective disorder. *Behavior Modification, 24*, 69–93.

Miyake, A., & Friedman, N. P. (2012). The nature and organization of individual differences in executive functions: four general conclusions. *Current Directions in Psychological Science, 21*, 8–14.

Miyake, A., Friedman, N. P., Emerson, M. J., Witzki, A. H., Howerter, A., & Wager, T. D. (2000). The unity and diversity of executive functions and their contributions to complex "frontal lobe" tasks: a latent variable analysis. *Cognitive Psychology, 41*, 49–100.

Moeller, S. K., & Robinson, M. D. (2010). Sex differences in implicit punishment sensitivity: evidence from two cognitive paradigms. *Personality and Individual Differences, 48*, 283–287.

Molden, D. C., Hui, C. M., Scholer, A. A., Meier, B. P., Noreen, E. E., D'Agostino, P. R., et al. (2012). Motivational versus metabolic effects of carbohydrates on self-control. *Psychological Science, 23*, 1137–1144.

Moors, A., de Houwer, J., & Eelen, P. (2003). Automatic stimulus-goal comparisons: support from motivational affective priming studies. *Cognition & Emotion, 18*, 29–54.

Moser, J. S., Moran, T. P., Schroder, H. S., Donnellan, M. B., & Yeung, N. (2013). On the relationship between anxiety and error monitoring: a meta-analysis and conceptual framework. *Frontiers in Human Neuroscience, 7*, 1–19.

Nederkoorn, C., Houben, K., Hofmann, W., Roefs, A., & Jansen, A. (2010). Control yourself or just eat what you like?: weight gain over a year is predicted by an interactive effect of response inhibition and implicit preference for snack foods. *Health Psychology, 29*, 389–393.

Nee, D. E., Wager, T. D., & Jonides, J. (2007). Interference resolution: insights from a meta-analysis of neuroimaging tasks. *Cognitive, Affective & Behavioral Neuroscience, 7*, 1–17.

Nieuwenhuis, S., Ridderinkhof, K. R., Blom, J., Band, G. P. H., & Kok, A. (2001). Error-related brain potentials are differently related to awareness of response errors: evidence from an antisaccade task. *Psychophysiology, 38*, 752–760.

Ochsner, K. N., & Gross, J. J. (2005). The cognitive control of emotion. *Trends in Cognitive Sciences, 9,* 242–249.

Olvet, D. M., & Hajcak, G. (2008). The error-related negativity (ERN) and psychopathology: toward an endophenotype. *Clinical Psychology Review, 28,* 1343–1354.

Payne, B. K. (2005). Conceptualizing control in social cognition: how executive functioning modulates the expression of automatic stereotyping. *Journal of Personality and Social Psychology, 89,* 488–503.

Potts, G. F., George, M. R. M., Martin, L. E., & Barratt, E. S. (2006). Reduced punishment sensitivity in neural systems of behavior monitoring in impulsive individuals. *Neuroscience Letters, 397,* 130–134.

Rampell, C. (March 5, 2011). *The happiest man in America*. The New York Times. www.newyorktimes.com.

Robinson, M. D., Ode, S., Wilkowski, B. M., & Amodio, D. M. (2010). Neurotic contentment: a self-regulation view of neuroticism-linked distress. *Emotion, 7,* 579–591.

Robinson, M. D. (2007). Gassing, braking, and self-regulating: error self-regulation, well-being, and goal-related processes. *Journal of Experimental Social Psychology, 43,* 1–16.

Scheier, M. F., & Carver, C. S. (1983). Self-directed attention and the comparison of self with standards. *Journal of Experimental Social Psychology, 19,* 205–222.

Schmeichel, B. J., & Zell, A. (2009). Trait self-control predicts performance on behavioral tests of self-control. *Journal of Personality, 75,* 743–756.

Schmeichel, B. J., Volokhov, R. N., & Demaree, H. A. (2008). Working memory capacity and the self-regulation of emotional expression and experience. *Journal of Personality and Social Psychology, 95,* 1526–1540.

Sharma, L., Markon, K. E., & Clark, L. A. (2014). Toward a theory of distinct types of "impulsive" behaviors: a meta-analysis of self-report and behavioral measures. *Psychological Bulletin, 140,* 374–408.

Shipstead, Z., ReMiyakedick, T. S., & Engle, R. W. (2012). Is working memory training effective? *Psychological Bulletin, 138,* 628–654.

Skoranski, A. M., Most, S. B., Lutz-Stehl, M., Hoffman, J. E., Hassink, S. G., & Simons, R. F. (2013). Response monitoring and cognitive control in childhood obesity. *Biological Psychology, 92,* 199–204.

Tamir, M. (2005). Don't worry, be happy? Neuroticism, trait-consistent affect regulation, and performance. *Journal of Personality and Social Psychology, 89,* 449–461.

Tangney, J. P., Baumeister, R. F., & Boone, A. L. (2004). High self-control predicts good adjustment, less pathology, better grades, and interpersonal success. *Journal of Personality, 72,* 271–324.

Teper, R., Segal, Z. V., & Inzlicht, M. (2013). Inside the mindful mind: how mindfulness enhances emotion regulation through improvements in executive control. *Current Directions in Psychological Science, 22,* 449–454.

Verbruggen, F., & Logan, G. D. (2008). Response inhibition in the stop-signal paradigm. *Trends in Cognitive Sciences, 12,* 418–424.

Wan, E. W., & Sternthal, B. (2008). Regulating the effects of depletion through monitoring. *Personality & Social Psychology Bulletin, 34,* 32–46.

Wilkowski, B. M., & Robinson, M. D. (2008a). Putting the brakes on antisocial behavior: secondary psychopathy and post-error adjustments in reaction time. *Personality and Individual Differences, 44,* 1807–1818.

Wilkowski, B. M., & Robinson, M. D. (2008b). Guarding against hostile thoughts: trait anger and the recruitment of cognitive control. *Emotion, 8,* 578–583.

Wilkowski, B. M., Robinson, M. D., & Troop-Gordon, W. (2010). How does cognitive control reduce anger and aggression?: the role of conflict monitoring and forgiveness processes. *Journal of Personality and Social Psychology, 98,* 830–840.

Wilkowski, B. M., Crowe, S. E., & Ferguson, E. L. (2015). Learning to keep your cool: reducing aggression through the experimental modification of cognitive control. *Cognition & Emotion, 13*, 774–781.

Wilkowski, B. M. (2012). Responding to social signals for response reversal: a psychological process underlying trait anger. *Social Psychological and Personality Science, 3*, 72–79.

Young, S. E., Friedman, N. P., Miyake, A., Willcutt, E. G., Corley, R. P., Haberstick, B. C., et al. (2009). Behavioral disinhibition: liability for externalizing spectrum disorders and its genetic and environmental relation to response inhibition across adolescence. *Journal of Abnormal Psychology, 118*, 117–130.

CHAPTER 16

Linking Diverse Resources to Action Control

E.J. Masicampo[1], M.L. Slepian[2]

[1]Wake Forest University, Winston Salem, NC, United States; [2]Columbia University, New York, NY, United States

The capacity to make decisions and exert control over one's behaviors is one of the defining features of human life. This capacity for control, however, seems limited. Over the past two decades, research in psychology has yielded evidence that the capacity for control operates as if relying on a limited resource (eg, Baumeister, Bratslavsky, Muraven, & Tice, 1998). Many dozens of psychological studies have yielded evidence that after people exert self-control, an apparent state of self-control fatigue ensues, causing decrements in self-control performance on subsequent tasks (Hagger, Wood, Stiff, & Chatzisarantis, 2010).

This pattern of self-control fatigue has been the subject of much theorizing in recent years. The main aim of these theories has been to explain the mechanism underlying self-control fatigue effects (eg, Beedie & Lane, 2012; Gailliot & Baumeister, 2007; Inzlicht, Schmeichel, & Macrae, 2014; Kurzban, Duckworth, Kable, & Myers, 2013). While the various theories are in general agreement that self-control diminishes with use, they disagree on precisely why that occurs and on whether an actual limited resource (blood glucose) is involved. The starting point for the present chapter is in the place where the theories agree, rather than where they disagree. The general consensus is that people's self-control behaviors do operate *as if* relying on a limited resource (although for a contrary view, see Carter, Kofler, Forster, & McCullough, 2015). Furthermore, people generally report believing that their own self-control ability diminishes with use (though a minority diverges from this view; see Job, Dweck, & Walton, 2010). Given that self-control is treated as, and operates as if, it relies on a limited resource, we considered in the present chapter how other, nonmental resources may affect the willingness to exert self-control. The present chapter considers how self-control fatigue effects—independent of how they arise—are influenced by factors beyond those directly implicated in self-control processes—specifically, other, nonmental resources.

Action control is merely one means by which a person may achieve desired outcomes. A person may draw on other personal resources as well to achieve desired ends, including social or monetary resources. We argue that the various resources people draw on are, to a degree, substitutable. Furthermore, given this substitutability, we argue that the availability of nonmental resources may influence whether a person is willing to engage in mentally effortful action control. In this chapter, we will review the evidence consistent with this line of thought, discuss possible future work on this topic, and explore implications of this theory for action control.

LINKING MENTAL AND NONMENTAL RESOURCES

People cultivate a wide range of mental capacities, including intelligence, creativity, social aptitude, and memory. However, our main focus in this chapter is on self-control capacity as a mental resource, primarily because this is the mental capacity that people most commonly conceive of as a limited resource. The empirical evidence suggests that self-control behavior diminishes with use as if relying on a limited resource (Baumeister et al., 1998; Muraven, Tice, & Baumeister, 1998), and people's lay beliefs also assume that self-control relies on a limited resource (see Chapter 9 for further discussion). Self-control thus operates and is treated as a resource, even if there is no tangible, exhaustible resource underlying it (eg, Kurzban, 2009).

Self-control also provides numerous benefits. By drawing on the capacity for self-control, people are able to avoid unwanted impulses, regulate their emotions, focus in the face of distraction, and resist short-term rewards in favor of larger, long-term benefits. As a result, people high in self-control tend to have better physical health, mental health, social relationships, academic success, and career success than people low in self-control (Moffitt et al., 2011; Tangney, Baumeister, & Boone, 2004). Self-control represents a highly beneficial commodity.

In this section, we explore mental resources (ie, self-control resources) and nonmental resources and draw links between the two. While people may achieve desired ends by drawing on limited mental resources, they may also achieve desired ends by drawing on other, nonmental resources, such as family, friends, or finances. Furthermore, we propose that mental and nonmental resources are substitutable. A student who wants to excel in school may draw on personal self-control efforts by focusing and persisting on schoolwork; alternatively, the student may draw on social resources by asking friends to serve as study partners or monetary resources by hiring a tutor. If self-control and other resources are interchangeable, the availability or lack thereof of any one resource may influence the willingness to conserve or use up the others.

Limited Mental Resources

Making decisions, exerting self-control, or engaging in other volitions operates as if drawing on a common resource that becomes exhausted with use (Baumeister et al., 1998; Muraven et al., 1998). Initial studies in support of this view demonstrated that exerting effortful control for as little as 5 min can lead to a temporary state in which people are less willing or less able to exert self-control, a state often referred to as "ego depletion" (Baumeister et al., 1998). In the nearly three decades since the initial demonstrations of ego depletion, hundreds of studies have documented evidence of ego depletion's effects (Hagger et al., 2010).

The limited capacity for control constrains a wide range of mental faculties. Self-control behaviors such as controlling thoughts, regulating emotions, and resisting impulses have all been shown to produce ego depletion effects. Ego depletion effects are also produced by making decisions (Vohs et al., 2008), memory updating, and inhibiting responses (Schmeichel, 2007). Regardless of the type of executive function being used, using control leads to a state of ego depletion, and control suffers when people are in a depleted state (see Chapter 6).

Explaining Ego Depletion

There have been numerous, often competing theories for *why* mental resources seem limited. The glucose model argues that the limited resource on which control relies is glucose in the bloodstream (Gailliot et al., 2007). Across several studies, Gailliot and colleagues found that blood glucose levels dropped significantly more after self-control tasks than after other tasks; low blood glucose levels after initial self-control exertion predicted decreases in performance on subsequent self-control tasks; and boosts in blood glucose via sugary drinks counteracted the ego depletion effect. The authors concluded that self-control and other volitional acts rely on the limited availability of glucose in the blood and brain.

The glucose model has, however, been challenged on numerous fronts. First, it has been argued that the glucose model is not neurophysiologically feasible (Kurzban, 2009). Second, the studies that Gailliot and colleagues published in support of the glucose model have been argued to suffer from numerous methodological deficiencies (Kurzban, 2009; Schimmack, 2012). Third, numerous empirical findings have cast doubt on the glucose model. Some of this work has found that self-control tasks do not significantly decrease blood glucose (Molden et al., 2012; Study 1).

Other work has demonstrated that simply tasting sugary drinks without swallowing them can counteract ego depletion (Hagger & Chatzisarantis, 2013; Molden et al., 2012; Sanders, Shirk, Burgin, & Martin, 2012), suggesting that metabolization of sugar is unnecessary to restore self-control. These challenges have prompted numerous alternative accounts of ego depletion.

Most alternative theories have emphasized a motivational account of ego depletion patterns. One theory, termed the process model, argues that ego depletion occurs because people seek to balance labor and leisure (Inzlicht et al., 2014). Another model, the opportunity cost model, argues that ego depletion occurs when people withdraw working memory resources from demanding self-control tasks that are deemed not to be worth the investment (Kurzban et al., 2013). Both theories explain ego depletion effects as occurring not from the limited availability of some self-control resource but instead from the motivational switching to alternative tasks.

Another alternative account to the glucose model is the notion that lay beliefs underlie ego depletion effects. Many people endorse the theory that willpower is limited, and when these people exert self-control, they show the standard depletion effect (Job et al., 2010). In contrast, the minority of people who hold the view that willpower is nonlimited tend *not* to show the ego depletion effect. Experimental work confirms a causal effect of these beliefs (see Chapter 9).

The idea that people's beliefs about self-control depletion are the key driver of depletion effects has also received support in other work. Perceived self-control exertion has been shown to be more predictive of subsequent self-control decrements than actual self-control exertion (Clarkson, Hirt, Jia, & Alexander, 2010; see also Chapter 19). Moreover, the mere belief that an event or object can restore willpower has been shown to eliminate ego depletion effects (see Chapter 20). Thus, some evidence suggests that ego depletion occurs, in part, because people expect it to.

Convergence Across Models

As is clear from the number and variety of models attempting to explain ego depletion, the notion of limited mental resources is a controversial one. Our aim is not to propose a resolution of this controversy but instead to focus on where the different perspectives converge. Regardless of whether the mechanism underlying ego depletion is one of glucose availability (Gailliot & Baumeister, 2007), motivated task switching (eg, Inzlicht et al., 2014; Kurzban et al., 2013), or consequential lay beliefs (Job et al., 2010), it is apparent that self-control acts *as if* mentally effortful tasks rely on a limited resource. Indeed, people generally view self-control in this way (Job et al., 2010).

The various models overlap in other respects as well. There is agreement that ego depletion is a domain-general phenomenon, affecting a wide range of mental faculties. Indeed, numerous tasks that involve mental effort (self-control, decision-making, executive functions, etc.) are diminished with continued use. There is also agreement that successful use of these mental faculties affords numerous positive benefits, such as healthfulness, happiness, achievement, and good relationships (Moffitt et al., 2011; Tangney et al., 2004).

Thus, we assume that every individual has mental capacities that are experienced and treated as limited (ie, self-control and other executive functions), and that are helpful for achieving desirable outcomes. If this is true, then these mental resources should be perceived of and managed in ways that are similar to other kinds of resources.

Other Limited Resources

Mental resources are only one of many resources that individuals may use to achieve desirable outcomes. We focus on three nonmental resources that share certain features with mental resources: each is helpful for achieving desirable outcomes and the availability of each fluctuates over time. These resources are bodily resources, social resources, and money.

Bodily Resources

The body is the most basic means by which animals, including humans, satisfy needs and goals. If wanting to achieve some desired end, a person can often bring that about through sheer physical work. This seems a truism for countless, quotidian acts, such as showering or pouring a bowl of cereal. Likewise, larger goals such as moving into a new home, which are often accomplished by recruiting help from or hiring others, can be accomplished through self-imposed manual labor.

Bodily resources are limited and fluctuate across time. A primary constraint on the body is physical energy, which waxes and wanes throughout the day. If people are sleep deprived, physically fatigued, hungry, or ill, then physical energy may be low. In contrast, if they are well rested, well fed, and in good health, physical energy may be high. Bodily resources are also affected by physical capacities. People who are physically strong, fit, and able have more bodily resources at their disposal than those who are relatively weak, unfit, or incapacitated.

Social Resources

The notion that humans are inherently social creatures, whose biological imperative is to connect with and rely on others, has become a common axiom in psychology (eg, Baumeister & Leary, 1995). Thus, for any individual, other people are an essential resource. People go to family, friends, and others in their social networks for many kinds of help, including help with physical labor, emotional support, information, and advice.

Crucially, the availability of social resources fluctuates over time. As people enter into marriages, grow their families, and develop strong friendships, social resources increase. Likewise, as people ascend the hierarchies of their various social groups, they wield greater power over others. Social resources can just as easily decrease. People may move to new cities or start new jobs, or lose friends and partners, in which case social capital may be in short supply.

Money

Money is essentially a type of social resource. That is, money is an alternative means by which one can obtain goods and services from others in the absence of any prior social relationship, such as an ongoing friendship. Thus, rather than ask for social favors, one can use money to pay other people for what one needs.

As with social resources, however, the availability of money is prone to fluctuations. People generally begin their lives with little access to money and gradually accumulate money over time when they start their careers, acquire higher salaries, invest, and save. Of course, the availability of money can be quickly diminished with large expenses, job loss, investments that depreciate, or other major life changes.

Substitutability Between Resources

We propose that the resources people draw from to satisfy their goals are partly substitutable. Substitutability between resources has important implications for action control. A person whose only resource is money will likely be a penny pincher. But if the person amasses far reaching social influence, then money will become less needed and the person may be more willing to spend it. Likewise, a person who is relatively rich in various resources may be more willing to spend rather than conserve limited mental resources. The relative scarcity or abundance of any resource will affect the value placed on other, substitutable resources.

It is easy to think of everyday examples of substitutability between the various nonmental resources of bodily resources, social resources, and money. Take a person whose lawn needs mowing. If he has the strength and energy, he can do it himself. Alternatively, he can ask a friend to do it for him, or he can hire a professional landscaping company to do it for pay. Thus, bodily resources, social resources, and money can be substituted for the same end.

There are many examples in which bodily resources, social resources, and money can be substituted with each other. There are also many examples in which these nonmental resources can be substituted with mental resources, which we review later.

Bodily Resources

Recent empirical work points to the substitutability between mental resources and bodily resources. Rosenbaum, Gong, and Potts (2014) assigned participants a simple task: pick up a heavy bucket and carry it to the end of an alley. Participants could choose between two buckets, the only difference between them being that one was farther from the participant and thus closer to the end of the alley. One might predict that participants would choose the bucket nearest the end of the alley, because that would mean carrying it a shorter distance. However, across several variants of this paradigm, participants repeatedly chose the bucket that was closer to their starting point, which meant having to carry the bucket a farther distance. In other words, participants were voluntarily doing more work than was necessary. The authors' explanation for this phenomenon was that participants wanted to reduce the cognitive load involved in remembering their assigned goal. Rather than hold the task in mind, people preferred to start the task earlier, even though it meant exerting extra physical work.

This parallels common, everyday decisions. A person might carry around a book, gym clothes, and extra pair of shoes inside her bag wherever she goes, even on days when not needing any of these items. Rather than take the time to think about and decide what she might specifically need, she can avoid mental effort by grabbing the items, and not thinking further.

Social Resources

Recent work suggests that people rely on help from others as a substitute for one form of mental effort: self-control exertion (Fitzsimons & Finkel, 2011). In that work, participants withdrew self-regulatory efforts at maintaining good health if reminded of a supportive other who helps them to achieve that goal. Thus, if a close other will ensure successful pursuit of health, then there is no need to spend the mental energy doing so one's self.

Transactive memory, the idea of shared memory between people, is another example of people outsourcing mental efforts (Wegner, 1987). Memorization takes considerable effort, insofar as long-term retention of information requires elaborate encoding processes (Craik & Tulving, 1975). One study on transactive memory gave romantic couples a collaborative memory task in which they had to memorize a series of facts. In the study, participants scaled back efforts at remembering facts from domains that their romantic partners knew well (Wegner, Erber, &

Raymond, 1991). Thus, people may draw on social resources as a substitute for expending mental effort.

Money

Money may also substitute for mental resources. While we are not aware of direct tests of this process, modern life offers numerous examples of people paying money to achieve goals that others attain via mental effort. For example, people hire personal trainers at the gym, which reduces the need for self-motivation and effortful planning. People also pay for cosmetic surgeries such as liposuction and bariatric surgeries such as stomach stapling, which reduce the need for self-restraint in eating.

One indirect link between mental resources and money comes from research linking poverty to decrements on cognitive functioning (Mani, Mullainathan, Shafir, & Zhao, 2013). The authors found that people who were poor tended to perform worse than those who were well-off on a number of cognitive tasks. The authors' reasoning was that people with little money are forced to use up mental resources when making difficult financial decisions that the relatively wealthy do not have to make (eg, being able only to spend a certain amount at the grocery store, and figuring out how to meet that budget). In this way, money serves for the wealthy as a substitute for what would otherwise be a tiresome and effortful mental process—making difficult decisions about limited finances. For the poor, what they are unable to afford with money they must pay for with mental work, which then impairs their mental performance elsewhere.

Summary

For each of the nonmental resources we have reviewed, there are at least some instances in which that resource can substitute for mental effort. Thus, rather than spend mental resources to achieve some desired end, people can often draw on bodily resources, social resources, or money. Due to this degree of substitutability between mental and nonmental resources, we propose that the abundance and scarcity of nonmental resources can influence people's willingness to exert mental effort and, ultimately, to engage in action control.

LINKING NONMENTAL RESOURCES TO ACTION CONTROL

Due to the substitutability between resources, we make two predictions about how nonmental resources might affect mental resources, or more specifically how they might affect action control. First, we predict that as nonmental resources become scarce, people will conserve mental resources and therefore be less willing to control their behaviors. We refer to this as the *linked scarcity hypothesis*. Second, we predict that as nonmental resources become abundant, people will be more willing to use up mental resources and therefore be more willing to control their behaviors. We refer to this as the *linked abundance hypothesis*.

The Linked Scarcity Hypothesis

The linked scarcity hypothesis predicts that when any one resource is low, the other resources will increase in value. In other words, people will become less willing to spend and more motivated to replenish the other resources. This is intuitively true when considering any one resource in isolation. If a person is low on money, then every dollar the person has will take on greater value (eg, Cialdini, 1993). Moreover, the person should be less willing to spend money and more motivated to gain money. Likewise, we predict that in the context of multiple resources, if one resource is low, then the other resources become more valuable.

There is evidence to support the linked scarcity hypothesis when looking at interactions between the various nonmental resources. Research suggests that money and bodily resources are linked in this way (Briers, Pandelaere, Dewitte, & Warlop, 2006). When bodily resources are low (eg, people are hungry), people become less willing to part with their money. Conversely, when people are manipulated into desiring money, they tend to consume more food. Thus, monetary resources and bodily resources (more specifically, caloric resources) are linked. When one is scarce, the other is more valued.

There have also been many demonstrations of linked scarcity between mental resources and nonmental resources. We review such evidence later. In most cases, the original findings we describe were not explained by the original authors in terms of linked scarcity of resources, but the data nevertheless follow the basic pattern of the linked scarcity hypothesis.

Scarce Bodily Resources

There are numerous kinds of evidence of linked scarcity between mental resources and bodily resources. Some of this work has examined people with Type 2 diabetes, a disorder in which metabolization of glucose is impaired. Common symptoms include fatigue and constant hunger. Among Type 2 diabetics, then, bodily resources are chronically low. Furthermore, consistent with the linked scarcity hypothesis, people exhibiting Type 2 diabetic symptoms show evidence of low self-control. They exhibit greater aggressiveness, seemingly due to impaired self-control (DeWall, Deckman, Gailliot, & Bushman, 2011). They also exhibit less forgiveness and less cooperation, which are both prosocial acts that require self-control (DeWall, Pond, & Bushman, 2010).

Other work has examined natural fluctuations in blood glucose, with lower levels indicating lower bodily energy. Here too, numerous findings support the linked scarcity hypothesis. Low blood glucose levels predict increased aggression in married couples (Bushman, DeWall, Pond, & Hanus, 2014), so that when bodily resources are low, people are less likely to control their aggressive impulses (see also Chapter 5). Likewise, when blood glucose levels are low, people are more likely to prioritize small immediate rewards over larger long-term rewards (Wang & Dvorak, 2010). Thus, when bodily resources are low, people are less likely to favor the long-term over the short-term, a defining feature of successful self-control (Fujita, 2011).

Other evidence for linked scarcity comes from the literature on physical fatigue. A large number of studies have manipulated physical fatigue via periods of intense exercise and tested the effects on mental functioning. The literature contains many apparently contradictory findings, with some studies suggesting that physical exercise facilitates cognitive functioning (eg, Aks, 1998; Arcelin, Brisswalter, & Delignieres, 1997) and others suggesting that it impairs it (eg, Cian et al., 2000). Recent theorizing has attempted to reconcile the contradiction. Specifically, one theory proposes that the link between physical exercise and cognitive functioning fits an inverted-U pattern (Tomporowski, 2003), such that brief periods of intense exercise (eg, 20–40 min) improve cognitive functioning and extended periods of intense exercise (eg, 1–2 h or more) impair it. One reason for this pattern is that brief periods of exercise may actually energize and invigorate the body and therefore the mind, whereas extended periods of exercise may induce fatigue and therefore impair the mind. Thus, when a person is fatigued and thus bodily resources are scarce, performance on mental tasks suffers.

Even more consistent with the linked scarcity hypothesis, research suggests that extended periods of intense exercise impair not all cognitive functions but specifically the type that is resource limited—effortful cognitive control. After an hour of intense exercise, impairments are seen in tasks requiring cognitive control but not in similar tasks that do not require cognitive control (Dietrich & Sparling, 2004). When bodily resources are low, it is specifically the tasks that require considerable mental resources that are impaired.

There is also indirect evidence of linked scarcity between bodily resources and mental resources in research on time-of-day effects. Research suggests that people exert less self-control late in the day as fatigue sets in. People are less ethical as the day wears on (Kouchaki & Smith, 2013), which is a characteristic behavior of those low in self-control. Judges also rely on decision defaults more as the day wears on (Danziger, Levav, & Avnaim-Pesso, 2011), thus making easy rather effortful decisions. During times of day when bodily resources are low, people seem to conserve mental resources.

Scarce Social Resources

People also seem to conserve mental resources when social resources are low. Much of the evidence for this comes from research on social exclusion. When people are socially excluded, and so they are low in social resources, they exhibit reduced self-control in diverse laboratory tests of self-control (Baumeister, DeWall, Ciarocco, & Twenge, 2005). Socially excluded people are also more likely to behave aggressively, due perhaps to failing to restrain aggressive impulses (Twenge, Baumeister, Tice, & Stucke, 2001). Socially excluded people are less likely to act prosocially (Twenge, Baumeister, DeWall, Ciarocco, & Bartels, 2007), which prior work has shown requires mental effort (DeWall, Baumeister, Gailliot, & Maner, 2008). Thus, across a wide range of behaviors, those low in social resources (ie, socially excluded people) seem to conserve rather than expend mental resources.

Another situation in which social resources are scarce is when people lack power (ie, influence over others). Being low in power is linked to decreased executive functioning, which could be the by-product of conserving mental resources (Smith, Jostmann, Galinsky, & van Dijk, 2008). Participants who were manipulated to feel low (vs high) in power were less effective at an n-back task requiring information updating, a Stroop task requiring response inhibition, and the Tower of Hanoi task that requires planning and problem solving.

Scarce Money

Empirical work linking scarce money to engagement in mentally effortful tasks is almost nonexistent. However, what little work we found was supportive of the linked scarcity hypothesis. Spears (2011) manipulated whether people felt relatively rich or poor in a simulated store task. He found that people in the poor condition exhibited less cognitive control than people in the rich condition on subsequent tests, a Stroop task and a hand grip persistence task. This is consistent with the notion that when money is scarce, people are less willing to expend mental effort.

Scarce Mental Resources

If nonmental resource scarcity causes the value of mental resources to increase, then the reverse should also be true: mental resources scarcity should cause the value of nonmental resources to increase. Stated differently, when people are mentally depleted, they should value bodily resources, social resources, and money more.

Here the evidence is sparse, but there is some evidence that people value money more when they are mentally depleted (Schmeichel, Harmon-Jones, & Harmon-Jones, 2010). In that work, mentally depleted people showed greater attentional tuning than nondepleted individuals to dollar signs but not to other symbols. Elsewhere, evidence suggests being mentally depleted can lead to interest in products that can increase bodily resources (ie, those that might restore energy). Specifically, recent work found that mentally depleted people showed greater interest in rest and in rest-conducive objects (eg, comfortable armchairs) than nondepleted people (Job, Bernecker, Miketta, & Friese, 2015).

Summary

There are numerous kinds of evidence for linked scarcity between mental resources and nonmental resources. Whenever any nonmental resource is low, people seem less willing to expend mental effort. When bodily resources, social resources, and money are scarce, decisions and behaviors become more automatic and less controlled.

The Linked Abundance Hypothesis

Just as one scarce resource should increase the value of other resources, one abundant resource should *decrease* the value of other resources. This is the idea behind the linked abundance hypothesis. Namely, if a person is rich in any one resource, then that person should be more willing to spend the other resources and less motivated to conserve or acquire them.

There is evidence for linked abundance between the various nonmental resources. Perhaps the most direct evidence draws connections between social resources and money. When people are randomly assigned to feel high (vs low) in social support, those people subsequently report caring less about making money and are more willing to part with their money (Vohs, Lasaleta, & Chaplin, 2015). At the same time, the wealthier people are (as measured by household income), the less time they report spending with family (Bianchi & Vohs, 2016). According to the authors of that work, having ample money means not needing to invest in supportive family relationships. As the linked abundance hypothesis suggests, when one resource is abundant, other resources lose value. People are more willing to spend those resources and less motivated to acquire and conserve them.

In this section, we focus on the linked abundance between mental and nonmental resources. Specifically, we review the evidence that when any one nonmental resource is abundant, people are less motivated to conserve mental resources. If this is true, then when any nonmental resource is plentiful, it should mean that people are more willing to engage in mentally effortful acts such as making effortful decisions and exerting self-control.

Abundant Bodily Resources

Evidence for linked abundance between mental resources and bodily resources comes from a variety of sources. Several studies have now linked consumption of sugary drinks, which increases physical energy, to increased willingness to exert mental effort. Specifically, drinking a sugary drink, but not a similar drink containing artificial sweeteners, has been shown to eliminate the ego depletion effect, thereby restoring self-control performance (Gailliot et al., 2007) and effortful decision-making (Masicampo & Baumeister, 2008). Thus, a boost in bodily resources motivates people to expend greater mental effort.

Recent experiments have demonstrated that simply tasting sugary drinks, but not drinks containing artificial sweeteners, can eliminate the ego depletion effect (Hagger & Chatzisarantis, 2013; Molden et al., 2012; Sanders et al., 2012). These experiments are also consistent with the linked abundance hypothesis. The mouth senses whether an incoming beverage contains sugar or not. The detection of sugar in the oral cavity is a fairly reliable signal that energy is incoming and bodily resources are being replenished. Consistent with the linked abundance hypothesis, bodily energy is on the rise, and so the person is more willing to use up mental resources.

Evidenced of linked abundance between bodily resources and mental resources has also been found in court decisions by judges (Danziger et al., 2011). An analysis of judges' parole decisions indicated that as the day wears on, judges relied more and more on the easy, default decision not to grant parole. However, after a food break, the odds of being granted parole returned to its original level. Thus, when bodily resources were restored with food, judges were more willing to make the effortful and risky decision of granting people parole.

Abundant Social Resources

There is some empirical evidence that having plentiful social resources promotes exertion of mental effort. This evidence comes from the finding that reminders of family promote better self-control (Stillman, Tice, Fincham, & Lambert, 2009). When people were exposed to family-related words or to images of their families, they exhibited greater persistence and performance on a difficult problem-solving task and greater restraint in eating unhealthy snacks. Reminders of social resources promoted spending mental resources.

Research on power also supports the idea that abundant social resources predict greater expenditure of mental resources. When participants were experimentally induced to perceive themselves as high in power (ie, having social influence over others), they increased their efforts and performance on various self-control tasks (DeWall, Baumeister, Mead, & Vohs, 2011). Thus, again, abundance in social resources promoted expenditure of mental resources.

Abundant Money

The most direct evidence of linked abundance between money and mental resources comes from the same work that we described previously as offering support for the linked scarcity hypothesis. Specifically, Spears (2011) manipulated participants into feeling relatively rich or poor, and those feeling relatively rich performed better on two self-control. Ample monetary resources seem to promote spending mental resources.

Other, more indirect evidence of linked abundance comes from research on the effects of mere reminders of money. Recent work demonstrated that simply reminding people of money is sufficient to eliminate the ego depletion effect (Boucher & Kofos, 2012). To be sure, reminding a person of money is not the same as making a person feel as though they have abundant access to money. However, other work does suggest that mere reminders of money can make people feel greater vitality (eg, Zhou, Vohs, & Baumeister, 2009) and make them rely less on nonmonetary resources, such as social support (Vohs, Mead, & Goode, 2006). Thus, the effects of money reminders seem more consistent with making people feel rich than with making them feel poor. If so, then the fact that mere reminders of money (and potentially the perception of monetary wealth) cause people to expend more mental effort (Boucher & Kofos, 2012) is consistent with the linked abundance hypothesis.

Abundant Mental Resources

If mental and nonmental resources are experienced as substitutable, then it may also be the case that when mental resources are abundant, people become more willing to spend nonmental resources. One way in which mental resources might increase is through self-control exercise. A common metaphor invoked for the benefits of such exercise is that of physical exercise. With repeated physical exercise, muscles can grow, leading a physical task that once was extremely effortful (picking up a heavy weight) to eventually become less effortful and fatiguing. Likewise, with repeated self-control, self-control might become less effortful and fatiguing (Baumeister et al., 1998; Muraven & Baumeister, 2000). Thus, with repeated exercise of spending mental resources, a task that was once mentally effortful and fatiguing (eg, solving an algebra problem), can become less so. Indeed, this kind of mental exercise (such as from repeated studying; Oaten & Cheng, 2006) leads people to perform better at a cognitive task following a depletion manipulation. Moreover, after undergoing this exercise to increase mental resources, individuals were more willing to spend nonmental resources, such as bodily resources, by doing more household chores and increasing physical exercise (Oaten & Cheng, 2006).

Mindfulness interventions are another form of self-control exercise that might increase mental resources (Masicampo & Baumeister, 2007). Mindfulness interventions encourage people to control and alter their default responses to certain stimuli, and thus correspondingly encourage self-control practice. Mindfulness leads people to be more willing to spend nonmental resources. For example, when people high in mindfulness intend to exercise, they actually engage in physical exercise more than do people low in mindfulness who have the same exercise intentions (Chatzisarantis & Hagger, 2007). Thus, the mindful who may have more mental resources are more willing to spend bodily resources toward a goal of improved health.

Summary

As with the linked scarcity hypothesis, there seem to be a large number of diverse findings consistent with the linked abundance hypothesis. When any nonmental resource is high, regardless of the resource, evidence suggests that people are more willing to expend greater mental effort.

Explaining the Links Between Resources

There seems to be ample evidence in support of both the linked scarcity and the linked abundance hypotheses. However, what remains unclear is whether the resources truly are linked in terms of sharing some underlying mechanism. It is possible that there is some general phenomenon by which the abundance versus scarcity of a person's resources affects behavior, and that this applies across types of resources (eg, Shah, Mullainathan, & Shafir, 2012). One alternative possibility is that the various resources are linked by a shared mechanism but that the mechanism is not specific to resource regulation and, in fact, is much broader. A second alternative possibility is that the numerous resources only appear to be linked and that there are many, distinct mechanisms occupying the different spaces between linked resources, with each pair of resources being linked through a different underlying process.

Possible Shared Mechanisms

One possibility is that there is a shared subjective component to the experiences of scarcity and abundance across the various resources. When any of a person's resources is scarce, the person may feel tired, fatigued, or otherwise unwilling to act. When resources are abundant, the person may feel energetic and active. These subjective experiences seem undeniably true for bodily resources. When bodily resources are low, people experience fatigue; when bodily resources are abundant, people experience vitality. For mental resources as well, the intuition seems to be that scarcity and abundance are experienced via fatigue and vitality. For the other resources (money and social), the subjective experience may be a bit more difficult to imagine. However, there is some empirical evidence of similar subjective experiences here as well. Social exclusion, an extreme case in which social resources are low, has been demonstrated to cause lethargy (Twenge, Catanese, & Baumeister, 2003). Likewise, counting large sums of money, thus creating a sense of monetary abundance, has been shown to increase sense of vitality (Zhou et al., 2009). Thus, all resources may influence how energetic and active people feel, thereby affecting the motivation to spend versus conserve resources.

Another candidate for a shared mechanism across resources is approach and avoidance motivations. Approach and avoidance motivations refer to the drives toward success and away from failure, respectively. Approach and avoidance orientations are fundamentally about one's resourcefulness. When a person has high expectations of success, then an approach orientation is endorsed; when a person has low expectations of success, an avoidance orientation is endorsed (Elliot & Church, 1997). In terms of resource availability, people are more likely to adopt approach orientations when resources are abundant and avoidance orientations when resources are scarce (Schnelle, Brandstätter, & Knöpfel, 2010). Furthermore, when people are in an avoidance mind-set, they are more motivated to conserve resources than when they are in an approach mind-set (Roskes, Elliot, Nijstad, & De Dreu, 2013). Thus, the various resources may each be linked via this shift toward motivational avoidance during times of resource scarcity and toward motivational approach during times of resource abundance. When a resource like money is low, this may heighten avoidant tendencies, which may in turn motivate conservation of social resources, bodily resources, and mental resources.

General and Nonresource-Specific Mechanisms

It may also be the case that a shared mechanism explains the various links between resources but that the mechanism is not specific to resource regulation. For example, it may be the case that acquiring and maintaining valuable resources is rewarding and results in a positive emotional state, whereas spending or losing resources is aversive and results in a negative emotional state. Moreover, people who are in positive moods seem more willing spend resources. Happy people are more willing to spend time and energy to help others (Isen & Levin, 1972; Weyant, 1978); more willing than other people to spend money (Spies, Hesse, & Loesch, 1997); and more willing to exert effortful self-control (Tice, Baumeister, Shmueli, & Muraven, 2007).

Thus, it may be that resource abundance (vs scarcity) induces positive emotions, which then increases spending of other resources. This would qualify as a shared mechanism across resources. However, it is not unique to resource regulation. For example, watching a funny movie does not alter one's resources, but it can induce a positive emotional state and may therefore increase willingness to spend resources. If emotional experiences are driving the linked abundance and scarcity patterns, then those patterns are not unique but rather are a special case of a much broader phenomenon.

Numerous Distinct Mechanisms

Another possible explanation for the linked scarcity and abundance patterns is that there are many distinct mechanisms driving the various links between resources. We reviewed evidence that whenever any nonmental resource is scarce, people become less willing to expend mental resources. Thus, due to linked scarcity, whenever bodily resources, social resources, or money are scarce, the desire to conserve across resources increases, and people exert less mental effort. However, it is possible that the links between nonmental resource scarcity and reduced mental effort are different across nonmental resources. When social resources are scarce (eg, people have been socially excluded), self-control efforts may wane due to the fact that people are ashamed and avoid thinking about themselves, which is difficult, thus making it difficult to exert self-control (Baumeister et al., 2005). When money is scarce, self-control efforts may wane due to the fact that poor people have more difficult decisions to make than wealthy people (Mani et al., 2013), thereby resulting in decision fatigue (Vohs et al., 2008). Thus, the reductions in mental effort that occur under scarcity may not be due to a central scarcity process but instead to numerous, disparate processes.

Other Issues With a Linked Resource Approach

There are a variety of factors that are likely to be relevant to the connectedness between mental resources, nonmental resources, and action control. These other factors are beyond the scope of the current chapter, but they do bear mentioning at least briefly. First, situational factors could influence the connectedness between resources. For example, the substitutability between resources is more apparent for certain goals than for others. Second, there may be stable individual differences in terms of the resources people think about or draw from. For example, extraverts or people high in status seeking may be especially attuned to other people as a social resource and so may be more sensitive than others to shifts in social resource availability. Third, there may of course be other resources that we have overlooked. Potentially any valuable means toward achieving desired ends, if limited, can be thought of and treated as a limited resource. If that resource can furthermore be interpreted as substitutable with mental resources and other resources, then linked scarcity and abundance effects may be likely to occur.

MOVING FORWARD: LOOKING BEYOND MENTAL RESOURCES IN UNDERSTANDING ACTION CONTROL

We proposed that the availability of nonmental resources may influence a person's willingness to expend mental resources or, in other words, to exert self-control. When nonmental resources are abundant, people may be more willing to exert self-control. When nonmental resources are scarce, they may be less willing to exert self-control.

The present chapter thus presents a new approach to thinking about the link between limited resources and action control. Much of the recent work on effortful control has focused on the underlying cause of self-control depletion effects, with the main point of contention involving whether an actual limited resource underlies effortful mental processing and if so, what it is (Beedie & Lane, 2012; Gailliot & Baumeister, 2007; Inzlicht et al., 2014; Job et al., 2010; Kurzban et al., 2013). Our starting point for the current chapter was at the place in which the competing theories converge, which is the notion that effortful control declines with use and is at least thought of and treated by people *as if* it relies on a mental resource (Job et al., 2010). Our work thus seeks to expand the discussion of mental resources and action control by taking a broad view rather than by narrowing in.

The framework we have proposed of connectedness between mental and nonmental resources provides numerous hypotheses to test. First, there are many testable predictions that follow from the linked scarcity and linked abundance hypotheses. Though we reviewed multiple kinds of evidence for these hypotheses, the evidence was sparse for the link between certain resources, and much of the evidence was indirect. Future work can provide direct tests of whether perceived scarcity or abundance of any given nonmental resource has a direct causal effect on expenditure of mental resources. Given the number and variety of resources that may be substitutable with mental resources, there are many novel predictions to test.

Second, there are many potential mechanisms underlying the linked scarcity and linked abundance patterns that remain to be tested. As reviewed earlier, there are multiple candidates for a shared underlying mechanism between the various resources. Future work can test whether such a shared mechanism exists, be it subjective experiences of fatigue and vitality, shifts in approach and avoidance motivations, or some other process. Future work can also test whether there are other, distinct mechanisms linking unique pairs of resources. There might be an underlying process linking mental resources to social resources that is specific to those two resources. Here too, there are a large number of novel predictions to test.

The present framework also holds numerous real-world applications. Self-control capacity is predictive of many important life outcomes, and decrements in self-control are at the heart of many serious life problems, such as drug abuse, obesity, criminality, and issues with relationships, school, work, and finances (Elfhag & Morey, 2008; Moffitt et al., 2011; Perry & Carroll, 2008; Tangney et al., 2004). If the willingness to exert self-control is linked not only to perceived mental resources but also to the perceived availability of other resources—bodily resources, social resources, and monetary resources—then the current framework exposes many new problems as well as potential new solutions to a range of life challenges.

CONCLUSION

Self-control is essential for a life well lived. People who are successful at exercising self-control are happier, healthier, more successful and have better relationships than people who are less successful at exercising self-control (Moffitt et al., 2011; Tangney et al., 2004; Vohs, Finkenauer, & Baumeister, 2011). Most people seem limited in their ability to exert self-control, however. After initial self-control exertions, subsequent self-control behavior typically suffers (Muraven et al., 1998). Self-control thus operates as if relying on a limited mental resource (Muraven & Baumeister, 2000). A major challenge for people seeking to control their behaviors is finding ways to manage and cope with these limited mental resources.

Mental resources are just one of many diverse resources people draw from to pursue their goals. To the extent that these diverse resources are substitutable, the availability of any one resource may influence a person's willingness to conserve versus spend the other resources. Thus, scarce resources elsewhere may motivate a person to conserve mental resources, while abundant resources elsewhere may make a person more willing to expend mental resources. The amount of resources at a person's disposal—whether bodily resources, social resources, monetary resources, or otherwise—may have a profound influence on a person's willingness to exert self-control.

References

Aks, D. J. (1998). Influence of exercise on visual search: implications for mediating cognitive mechanisms. *Perceptual and Motor Skills*, 87(3), 771–783.

Arcelin, R., Brisswalter, J., & Delignieres, D. (1997). Effect of physical exercise duration on decisional performance. *Journal of Human Movement Studies*, 32(3), 123–140.

Baumeister, R. F., Bratslavsky, E., Muraven, M., & Tice, D. M. (1998). Ego depletion: is the active self a limited resource? *Journal of Personality and Social Psychology*, 74(5), 1252–1265.

Baumeister, R. F., DeWall, C. N., Ciarocco, N. J., & Twenge, J. M. (2005). Social exclusion impairs self-regulation. *Journal of Personality and Social Psychology*, 88(4), 589–604.

Baumeister, R. F., & Leary, M. R. (1995). The need to belong: desire for interpersonal attachments as a fundamental human motivation. *Psychological Bulletin*, 117(3), 497–529.

Beedie, C. J., & Lane, A. M. (2012). The role of glucose in self-control another look at the evidence and an alternative conceptualization. *Personality and Social Psychology Review*, 16(2), 143–153.

Bianchi, E. C., & Vohs, K. D. (2016). Social class and social worlds: income predicts the frequency and nature of social contact. *Social Psychological and Personality Science*, 7(5), 479–486.

Boucher, H. C., & Kofos, M. N. (2012). The idea of money counteracts ego depletion effects. *Journal of Experimental Social Psychology*, 48(4), 804–810.

Briers, B., Pandelaere, M., Dewitte, S., & Warlop, L. (2006). Hungry for money the desire for caloric resources increases the desire for financial resources and vice versa. *Psychological Science, 17*(11), 939–943.

Bushman, B. J., DeWall, C. N., Pond, R. S., & Hanus, M. D. (2014). Low glucose relates to greater aggression in married couples. *Proceedings of the National Academy of Sciences, 111*(17), 6254–6257.

Carter, E. C., Kofler, L. M., Forster, D. E., & McCullough, M. E. (2015). A series of meta-analytic tests of the depletion effect: self-control does not seem to rely on a limited resource. *Journal of Experimental Psychology: General, 144*(4), 796–815.

Chatzisarantis, N. L., & Hagger, M. S. (2007). Mindfulness and the intention-behavior relationship within the theory of planned behavior. *Personality and Social Psychology Bulletin, 33*, 663–676.

Cialdini, R. B. (1993). *Influence: Science and practice*. New York: Harper Collins.

Cian, C., Koulmann, N., Barraud, P. A., Raphel, C., Jimenez, C., & Melin, B. (2000). Influences of variations in body hydration on cognitive function: effect of hyperhydration, heat stress, and exercise-induced dehydration. *Journal of Psychophysiology, 14*(1), 29–36.

Clarkson, J. J., Hirt, E. R., Jia, L., & Alexander, M. B. (2010). When perception is more than reality: the effects of perceived versus actual resource depletion on self-regulatory behavior. *Journal of Personality and Social Psychology, 98*(1), 29–46.

Craik, F. I., & Tulving, E. (1975). Depth of processing and the retention of words in episodic memory. *Journal of experimental Psychology: General, 104*(3), 268–294.

Danziger, S., Levav, J., & Avnaim-Pesso, L. (2011). Extraneous factors in judicial decisions. *Proceedings of the National Academy of Sciences, 108*(17), 6889–6892.

DeWall, C. N., Baumeister, R. F., Gailliot, M. T., & Maner, J. K. (2008). Depletion makes the heart grow less helpful: helping as a function of self-regulatory energy and genetic relatedness. *Personality and Social Psychology Bulletin, 34*(12), 1653–1662.

DeWall, C. N., Baumeister, R. F., Mead, N. L., & Vohs, K. D. (2011). How leaders self-regulate their task performance: evidence that power promotes diligence, depletion, and disdain. *Journal of Personality and Social Psychology, 100*(1), 47–65.

DeWall, C. N., Deckman, T., Gailliot, M. T., & Bushman, B. J. (2011). Sweetened blood cools hot tempers: physiological self-control and aggression. *Aggressive Behavior, 37*(1), 73–80.

DeWall, C. N., Pond, R. S., & Bushman, B. J. (2010). Sweet revenge: diabetic symptoms predict less forgiveness. *Personality and Individual Differences, 49*(7), 823–826.

Dietrich, A., & Sparling, P. B. (2004). Endurance exercise selectively impairs prefrontal-dependent cognition. *Brain and Cognition, 55*(3), 516–524.

Elfhag, K., & Morey, L. C. (2008). Personality traits and eating behavior in the obese: poor self-control in emotional and external eating but personality assets in restrained eating. *Eating Behaviors, 9*(3), 285–293.

Elliot, A. J., & Church, M. A. (1997). A hierarchical model of approach and avoidance achievement motivation. *Journal of Personality and Social Psychology, 72*(1), 218–232.

Fitzsimons, G. M., & Finkel, E. J. (2011). Outsourcing self-regulation. *Psychological Science, 22*(3), 369–375.

Fujita, K. (2011). On conceptualizing self-control as more than the effortful inhibition of impulses. *Personality and Social Psychology Review, 15*(4), 352–366.

Gailliot, M. T., & Baumeister, R. F. (2007). The physiology of willpower: linking blood glucose to self-control. *Personality and Social Psychology Review, 11*(4), 303–327.

Gailliot, M. T., Baumeister, R. F., DeWall, C. N., Maner, J. K., Plant, E. A., Tice, D. M., … Schmeichel, B. J. (2007). Self-control relies on glucose as a limited energy source: willpower is more than a metaphor. *Journal of Personality and Social Psychology, 92*(2), 325–336.

Hagger, M. S., & Chatzisarantis, N. L. (2013). The sweet taste of success the presence of glucose in the oral cavity moderates the depletion of self-control resources. *Personality and Social Psychology Bulletin, 39*(1), 28–42.

REFERENCES

Hagger, M. S., Wood, C., Stiff, C., & Chatzisarantis, N. L. (2010). Ego depletion and the strength model of self-control: a meta-analysis. *Psychological bulletin*, *136*(4), 495–525.

Inzlicht, M., Schmeichel, B. J., & Macrae, C. N. (2014). Why self-control seems (but may not be) limited. *Trends in Cognitive Sciences*, *18*(3), 127–133.

Isen, A. M., & Levin, P. F. (1972). Effect of feeling good on helping: cookies and kindness. *Journal of Personality and Social Psychology*, *21*(3), 384–388.

Job, V., Bernecker, K., Miketta, S., & Friese, M. (2015). Implicit theories about willpower predict the activation of a rest goal following self-control exertion. *Journal of Personality and Social Psychology*, *109*(4), 694–706.

Job, V., Dweck, C. S., & Walton, G. M. (2010). Ego depletion—is it all in your head? Implicit theories about willpower affect self-regulation. *Psychological Science*, *21*(11), 1686–1693.

Kouchaki, M., & Smith, I. H. (2013). The morning morality effect: the influence of time of day on unethical behavior. *Psychological Science*, *25*(1), 95–102.

Kurzban, R. (2009). Does the brain consume additional glucose during self-control tasks? *Evolutionary Psychology*, *8*(2), 244–259.

Kurzban, R., Duckworth, A., Kable, J. W., & Myers, J. (2013). An opportunity cost model of subjective effort and task performance. *Behavioral and Brain Sciences*, *36*(6), 661–679.

Mani, A., Mullainathan, S., Shafir, E., & Zhao, J. (2013). Poverty impedes cognitive function. *Science*, *341*(6149), 976–980.

Masicampo, E. J., & Baumeister, R. F. (2007). Relating mindfulness and self-regulatory processes. *Psychological Inquiry*, *18*(4), 255–258.

Masicampo, E. J., & Baumeister, R. F. (2008). Toward a physiology of dual-process reasoning and judgment: lemonade, willpower, and expensive rule-based analysis. *Psychological Science*, *19*(3), 255–260.

Moffitt, T. E., Arseneault, L., Belsky, D., Dickson, N., Hancox, R. J., Harrington, H., ... Caspi, A. (2011). A gradient of childhood self-control predicts health, wealth, and public safety. *Proceedings of the National Academy of Sciences*, *108*(7), 2693–2698.

Molden, D. C., Hui, C. M., Scholer, A. A., Meier, B. P., Noreen, E. E., D'Agostino, P. R., & Martin, V. (2012). Motivational versus metabolic effects of carbohydrates on self-control. *Psychological Science*, *23*(10), 1137–1144.

Muraven, M., & Baumeister, R. F. (2000). Self-regulation and depletion of limited resources: does self-control resemble a muscle? *Psychological Bulletin*, *126*(2), 247–259.

Muraven, M., Tice, D. M., & Baumeister, R. F. (1998). Self-control as a limited resource: regulatory depletion patterns. *Journal of Personality and Social Psychology*, *74*(3), 774–789.

Oaten, M., & Cheng, K. (2006). Improved self-control: the benefits of a regular program of academic study. *Basic and Applied Social Psychology*, *28*, 1–16.

Perry, J. L., & Carroll, M. E. (2008). The role of impulsive behavior in drug abuse. *Psychopharmacology*, *200*(1), 1–26.

Rosenbaum, D. A., Gong, L., & Potts, C. A. (2014). Pre-crastination: hastening subgoal completion at the expense of extra physical effort. *Psychological Science*, *25*(7), 1487–1496.

Roskes, M., Elliot, A. J., Nijstad, B. A., & De Dreu, C. K. (2013). Avoidance motivation and conservation of energy. *Emotion Review*, *5*(3), 264–268.

Sanders, M. A., Shirk, S. D., Burgin, C. J., & Martin, L. L. (2012). The gargle effect: rinsing the mouth with glucose enhances self-control. *Psychological Science*, *23*(12), 1470–1472.

Schimmack, U. (2012). The ironic effect of significant results on the credibility of multiple-study articles. *Psychological Methods*, *17*(4), 551–566.

Schmeichel, B. J. (2007). Attention control, memory updating, and emotion regulation temporarily reduce the capacity for executive control. *Journal of Experimental Psychology: General*, *136*(2), 241–255.

Schmeichel, B. J., Harmon-Jones, C., & Harmon-Jones, E. (2010). Exercising self-control increases approach motivation. *Journal of Personality and Social Psychology*, *99*(1), 162–173.

Schnelle, J., Brandstätter, V., & Knöpfel, A. (2010). The adoption of approach versus avoidance goals: the role of goal-relevant resources. *Motivation and Emotion*, *34*(3), 215–229.

Shah, A. K., Mullainathan, S., & Shafir, E. (2012). Some consequences of having too little. *Science, 338*(6107), 682–685.

Smith, P. K., Jostmann, N. B., Galinsky, A. D., & van Dijk, W. W. (2008). Lacking power impairs executive functions. *Psychological Science, 19*(5), 441–447.

Spears, D. (2011). Economic decision-making in poverty depletes behavioral control. *The BE Journal of Economic Analysis & Policy, 11*(72), 1–42.

Spies, K., Hesse, F., & Loesch, K. (1997). Store atmosphere, mood and purchasing behavior. *International Journal of Research in Marketing, 14*(1), 1–17.

Stillman, T. F., Tice, D. M., Fincham, F. D., & Lambert, N. M. (2009). The psychological presence of family improves self-control. *Journal of Social and Clinical Psychology, 28*, 498–530.

Tangney, J. P., Baumeister, R. F., & Boone, A. L. (2004). High self-control predicts good adjustment, less pathology, better grades, and interpersonal success. *Journal of Personality, 72*(2), 271–324.

Tice, D. M., Baumeister, R. F., Shmueli, D., & Muraven, M. (2007). Restoring the self: positive affect helps improve self-regulation following ego depletion. *Journal of Experimental Social Psychology, 43*(3), 379–384.

Tomporowski, P. D. (2003). Effects of acute bouts of exercise on cognition. *Acta Psychologica, 112*(3), 297–324.

Twenge, J. M., Baumeister, R. F., DeWall, C. N., Ciarocco, N. J., & Bartels, J. M. (2007). Social exclusion decreases prosocial behavior. *Journal of Personality and Social Psychology, 92*(1), 56–66.

Twenge, J. M., Baumeister, R. F., Tice, D. M., & Stucke, T. S. (2001). If you can't join them, beat them: effects of social exclusion on aggressive behavior. *Journal of Personality and Social Psychology, 81*(6), 1058–1069.

Twenge, J. M., Catanese, K. R., & Baumeister, R. F. (2003). Social exclusion and the deconstructed state: time perception, meaninglessness, lethargy, lack of emotion, and self-awareness. *Journal of Personality and Social Psychology, 85*(3), 409–423.

Vohs, K. D., Baumeister, R. F., Schmeichel, B. J., Twenge, J. M., Nelson, N. M., & Tice, D. M. (2008). Making choices impairs subsequent self-control: a limited resource account of decision making, self-regulation, and active initiative. *Journal of Personality and Social Psychology, 94*, 883–898.

Vohs, K. D., Finkenauer, C., & Baumeister, R. F. (2011). The sum of friends' and lovers' self-control scores predicts relationship quality. *Social Psychological and Personality Science, 2*(2), 138–145.

Vohs, K. D., Lasaleta, J. D., & Chaplin, L. N. (2015). *With friends like these, who needs money? Feeling socially supported weakens the desire for money* (Manuscript submitted for publication).

Vohs, K. D., Mead, N. L., & Goode, M. R. (2006). The psychological consequences of money. *Science, 314*(5802), 1154–1156.

Wang, X. T., & Dvorak, R. D. (2010). Sweet future fluctuating blood glucose levels affect future discounting. *Psychological Science, 21*(2), 183–188.

Wegner, D. M. (1987). Transactive memory: a contemporary analysis of the group mind. In B. Mullen, & G. R. Goethals (Eds.), *Theories of group behavior* (pp. 185–208). New York: Springer-Verlag.

Wegner, D. M., Erber, R., & Raymond, P. (1991). Transactive memory in close relationships. *Journal of Personality and Social Psychology, 61*, 923–929.

Weyant, J. M. (1978). Effects of mood states, costs, and benefits on helping. *Journal of Personality and Social Psychology, 36*(10), 1169–1176.

Zhou, X., Vohs, K. D., & Baumeister, R. F. (2009). The symbolic power of money reminders of money alter social distress and physical pain. *Psychological Science, 20*(6), 700–706.

CHAPTER 17

On the Relation Between "Mental" and "Physical" Self-Control

P.M. Egan[1], E.R. Hirt[2]
[1]Kendall College, Chicago, IL, United States; [2]Indiana University, Bloomington, IN, United States

ON THE RELATION BETWEEN "MENTAL" AND "PHYSICAL" SELF-CONTROL

In understanding what forces govern our behavior, much philosophical and scientific inquiry has been devoted to the debate over mind–body dualism. One end of this debate contends that particular psychological and emotional experiences cannot be fully explained by the operation of physiological systems, whereas the other end contends that all psychological and emotional experiences are completely attributable to underlying physiology. Among contemporary scientists, there exists ever-increasing support for the latter perspective, regardless of whether this support is assessed (1) directly via self-report surveys (Clark, 2010; Farah & Murphy, 2009; Larson & Witham, 1998; for dissenting views, see Klein, 2012; Miller, 2010) or (2) indirectly via scientific domains exploring the interdependence between psychological and physiological systems. Among others, domains such as cognitive neuroscience (Cacioppo, Berntson, Ernst, & Ito, 2000; Lieberman, 2007; Ochsner & Lieberman, 2001), embodied cognition (Carney, Cuddy, & Yap, 2010; Jostmann, Lakens, & Schubert, 2009; Niedenthal, Barsalou, Winkielman, Krauth-Gruber, & Ric, 2005; Strack, Martin, & Stepper, 1988), pain perception (DeWall et al., 2010; Eisenberger & Lieberman, 2004, 2005; Eisenberger, Lieberman, & Williams, 2003; MacDonald, Kingsbury, & Shaw, 2005; MacDonald & Leary, 2005; Price, 2000; Randles, Heine, & Santos, 2013), and fatigue onset (Ackerman, 2011; Bray, Ginis, & Woodgate, 2011; Bray, Graham, Martin Ginis, & Hicks,

2012; Gailliot & Baumeister, 2007; Heatherton & Wagner, 2011; Inzlicht & Gutsell, 2007) all underscore the fact that psychological processes have physiological substrates and physiological outcomes are altered by psychological experience.

Although the scientific viability of mind–body dualism is rather limited (see also Gervais & Norenzayan, 2012; Larson & Witham, 1998), dualistic perspectives nonetheless receive subjective support across a broad range of human populations. Indeed, developmental psychologists have shown that children are "natural born theists" who endorse a multitude of mind–body separations (Bering & Bjorklund, 2004; Bloom, 2004; Gottfried, Gelman, & Schultz, 1999; Hood, Gjersoe, & Bloom, 2012; Johnson, 1990; Kelemen, 2004; Legare, Evans, Rosengren, & Harris, 2012). Furthermore, dualistic belief systems persist into adulthood, with populations ranging from university students (Demertzi et al., 2009), to everyday citizens (Cohen, Burdett, Knight, & Barrett, 2011), to cross-cultural samples (Legare et al., 2012) all indicating various levels of support for a fundamental distinction between mental and physical systems. Interestingly, this support is observed among contemporary scientific communities as well, with various disciplines (eg, clinical psychologists, Miresco & Kirmayer, 2006; medical doctors, Sharpe & Walker, 2012; National Academy of Sciences, Larson & Witham, 1997) exhibiting beliefs consistent with an inherent separation between mind and body.[1]

If dualistic beliefs are widely endorsed in the population, it follows that *metaphysical perceptions* (ie, whether one construes a given phenomenon in physiological or psychological terms) should play a critical role in cognitive and behavioral processes. A multitude of studies support this notion, with specific categories of metaphysical perception having a notable impact on important subjective and objective outcomes. Neuroscientific studies have shown that different brain areas are active when considering the physical processes underlying behavior or the mental processes motivating behavior (Lieberman, 2007; Ochsner et al., 2004; Spunt, Falk, & Lieberman, 2010; Van Overwalle & Baetens, 2009). Morality research has found that focusing on a target's physical or mental properties alters one's attentional and attributional processes (Gray, Knobe, Sheskin, Bloom, & Barrett, 2011; see also Loughnan et al., 2010). Metascientific work has suggested that physiological explanations for a given outcome are perceived as more believable and exacting than are equivalent psychological explanations (Beck, 2010; Keehner, Mayberry,

---

[1] In understanding why dualism persists in modern populations, both systemic factors (eg, religion—Preston, Ritter, & Hepler, 2013; health care—Park, 2013) and individual factors (eg, existential threat, terror management—Pyszczynski, Greenberg, & Solomon, 1999; belief in free will—Paulhus & Carey, 2011; need for perceived human uniqueness—Haslam et al., 2008) would appear to play pivotal roles.

& Fischer, 2011; McCabe & Castel, 2008; but see Hook & Farah, 2013). Finally, social–psychological theory suggests that focusing on the physical versus mental properties of a stimulus leads to distinct cognitive mind-sets; mind-sets which catalyze divergent psychological and behavioral outcomes (Spunt et al., 2010; Trope & Liberman, 2010).

Considering the role that metaphysical perceptions have in other domains, our lab has recently begun considering the role of metaphysical perceptions within the domain of self-control. Because there are a multitude of self-control processes that invoke both mental and physical terminology (eg, energy, effort, focus, inhibition, endurance), we sought to systematically investigate how situational and individual factors influence one's metaphysical perception of self-control contexts; perceptions that should presumably impact cognitive and behavioral systems underlying self-control exertion (eg, Clarkson, Hirt, Jia, & Alexander, 2010; Egan, Hirt, & Karpen, 2012; Job, Dweck, & Walton, 2010). In terms of situational factors, we reasoned that individuals should show sensitivity to experimental manipulations that focus on physical or mental processes, such that the same self-control context could be altered or framed in ways that cause one's behavior to be perceived in more physical or mental terms. In terms of individual factors, we reasoned that self-control perceptions and behavior should correspond to one's personally endorsed metaphysical beliefs, such that the same task could be construed and performed differently as a function of one's beliefs concerning the interrelation between body and mind.

The remainder of the present chapter discusses some preliminary findings on the relation between metaphysical perceptions and self-control exertion (Egan, 2015). Upon explicating these findings, we elaborate on the potential importance of metaphysical perceptions in research on self-control processes, and identify several areas in which the application of these ideas might produce new discoveries concerning the relationship between perceptual and behavioral self-control aspects. By the end of this chapter, we hope that readers are motivated to both critique and expand upon our initial work in ways that strengthen extant theory surrounding self-control depletion, restoration, and exertion.

METAPHYSICAL PERCEPTIONS AND SELF-CONTROL

Situational Cues and Metaphysical Perceptions

As we began considering the relationship between metaphysical perceptions and self-control, one central question drove our initial approach: What cues in the immediate environment cause individuals to perceive the same self-control task in different metaphysical terms? In other words, could we change certain aspects of a self-control context such that individuals perceive performance as reliant on physical or mental processes? As mentioned in the introduction—and as demonstrated in the various chapters comprising this volume—there exist numerous self-control components that can be described in either physical or mental terms (eg, effort, pain, fatigue, endurance). For instance, a person might perceive effort as a product of psychological or physiological influence, they might experience pain as a mental or physical symptom, or they might expect endurance to rely upon mental or physical resources. Although most lay people may not consider these dichotomies explicitly in all situations, we reasoned that if they generally differentiate between mental and physical processes, then experimental manipulations might push perceptions toward one side of the metaphysical continuum. Assuming that such metaphysical perceptions of self-control contexts are malleable, we reasoned that such perceptual changes could drive subsequent alterations in self-control exertion.

Our lab therefore began focusing on contextual manipulations that could alter one's metaphysical perceptions of self-control tasks. As is summarized throughout this volume, there exist a wide array of contexts employed to gauge self-control, regardless of whether one considers research in the area of ego depletion (Hagger, Wood, Stiff, & Chatzisarantis, 2010), cognitive fatigue (Ackerman, 2011), or human physiology (Bray et al., 2011). From these myriad possibilities, we selected a task highly representative of self-control research across multiple domains: *handgrip persistence*. Handgrip tasks have been utilized to study how multiple psychophysiological systems influence self-control, with the assumption that greater fatigue in a given system predicts lesser persistence on an extended handgrip task. Experimental research on handgrip exertion has highlighted several systems that influence task persistence, including prior effort expenditure on both physiological (Bray et al., 2011, 2012) and psychological (Egan et al., 2012; Martijn, Tenbült, Merckelbach, Dreezens, & de Vries, 2002; Muraven, Tice, & Baumeister, 1998) tasks. With an established relationship to both "physical" and "mental" systems, a handgrip paradigm represents a context in which metaphysical perceptions are highly malleable. That is, this task has been studied in both purely physiological and purely psychological contexts, which affords the possibility to realistically frame handgrip exertion in physical or mental terms.

In considering cues that could effectively prime mental or physical construals of this handgrip paradigm, we observed several past experiments that employed highly salient psychophysiological measurements to track ongoing task performance. For instance, in the human physiology literature, participants have electrodes attached to their arm as they persist on handgrip persistence tasks, such that researchers can measure muscle fatigue as a mediating process of behavioral output (Bray et al., 2011).

Because electrodes can viably detect activity in both the arm (ie, electromyography) and brain (ie, electroencephalography), we reasoned that their placement could effectively focus participants on arm activity or brain activity—both of which are theorized to drive effective task performance. In general, we anticipated that participants with electrodes on their biceps would be more likely to focus on the physical nature of handgrip persistence (eg, muscle activity, hand pressure), whereas participants with electrodes on their temples would be more likely to focus on the psychological nature of handgrip persistence (eg, brain activity, willpower). Pilot work reinforced this general expectation, in that participants who read about a hypothetical handgrip paradigm were more likely to believe the grip task measured mental constructs when electrodes were attached to the subject's temples, as opposed to the subject's biceps.

From this pilot work, we constructed an experimental paradigm that could both measure handgrip persistence and manipulate metaphysical perceptions of such persistence simultaneously (see Appendix 1). To this end, we recruited undergraduate participants and randomly assigned them to one of three conditions (*mental*—electrodes on temples; *physical*—electrodes on biceps; *control*—no electrodes). All participants were exposed to an electronic handgrip system assessing both maximum grip strength (Phase 1) and grip persistence (Phase 2).[2] In Phase 1, participants received an introduction to the system, completed a measure of maximum grip strength (two 10s trials), and completed a short set of questions concerning their current mood. In Phase 2, participants were asked to stabilize their grip strength at 40% of their maximum Phase 1 performance, and then to hold their performance slightly above this threshold for as long as possible. Just prior to beginning this second phase, participants were informed that electrodes would be attached during this portion of the experiment—ostensibly to measure their internal state during the persistence task. Upon obtaining verbal consent, electrodes were attached to each temple (ie, approximately 1 inch above and outside the lateral end of each eye) or each bicep (ie, approximately 3 inches above the inside of each elbow). A control condition without any form of electrode attachment was also included for comparison purposes. During Phase 2, all

---

[2] Handgrip exertion data were assessed and retained using Vernier Human Physiology software, which consists of an electronic handgrip dynamometer attached to a desktop computer. The software allows for the dynamic representation of handgrip exertion on the computer monitor, such that handgrip output is measured at a rate of four times per second. All data in the present experiment were saved in electronic spreadsheets as a function of trial, which were then analyzed either during (Phase 1—to set performance threshold) or after (Phase 2—to assess overall persistence) the experiment.

participants reported their subjective pain at 20-s increments using a scale ranging from 1 (*no pain at all*) to 10 (*extreme pain*).

Our results yielded several patterns of findings suggestive of a relationship between metaphysical perceptions and self-control exertion. For one, we asked participants to reflect on their performance following Phase 2, such that they provided open-ended responses concerning how they perceived the task. Upon coding these responses, we examined differences in the types of constructs mentioned. Consistent with pilot data, we found that participants with electrodes attached to their temples during the task mentioned more mental constructs (eg, willpower, motivation, brain) and fewer physical constructs (eg, muscle, blood flow, bicep) than did participants with electrodes attached to their biceps. Thus, participants in the mental condition reflected on their performance with a greater amount of psychological terminology and a lesser amount of physiological terminology. These findings bolstered our confidence that the experimental manipulation was effective in varying participants' metaphysical perceptions in the intended direction.

Upon confirming the efficacy of our electrode placement manipulation, we assessed how this manipulation affected subjective and objective outcomes during Phase 2. On the subjective side, we examined whether the electrode attachment influenced self-reported pain on the persistence task. In particular, we calculated each participant's pain slope by computing how rapidly their subjective pain rating rose throughout the persistence task. Given that pain and discomfort can undermine performance on extended exercise persistence tasks, we reasoned that participants with lower pain slopes were demonstrating more effective self-control by regulating their subjective experience. Using this pain slope metric, we found that participants in the mental condition showed a less rapid rise in pain across the persistence task, suggesting that they were less responsive and/or more resistant to psychophysiological cues of pain.

On the objective side, we examined whether the electrode attachment influenced on the length of time participants maintained their performance above the performance threshold. To ensure that this time-on-task measurement was as valid as possible, we included both maximum hand-grip strength (ie, the metric obtained in Phase 1) and overall performance quality (ie, the number of times participants temporarily fell below the threshold) as covariates in all analyses.[3] Results showed significant differences in self-control exertion as a function of electrode placement, such that participants in the mental condition lasted longer on the persistence task than did participants in either the physical condition or the no electrode control condition (see Fig. 17.1, Panel A). In understanding why these conditional differences emerged, we observed that pain slope

---

[3] Mood, motivation, and perceived depletion were also included as covariates in all analyses. We found no effect of these metrics on task performance.

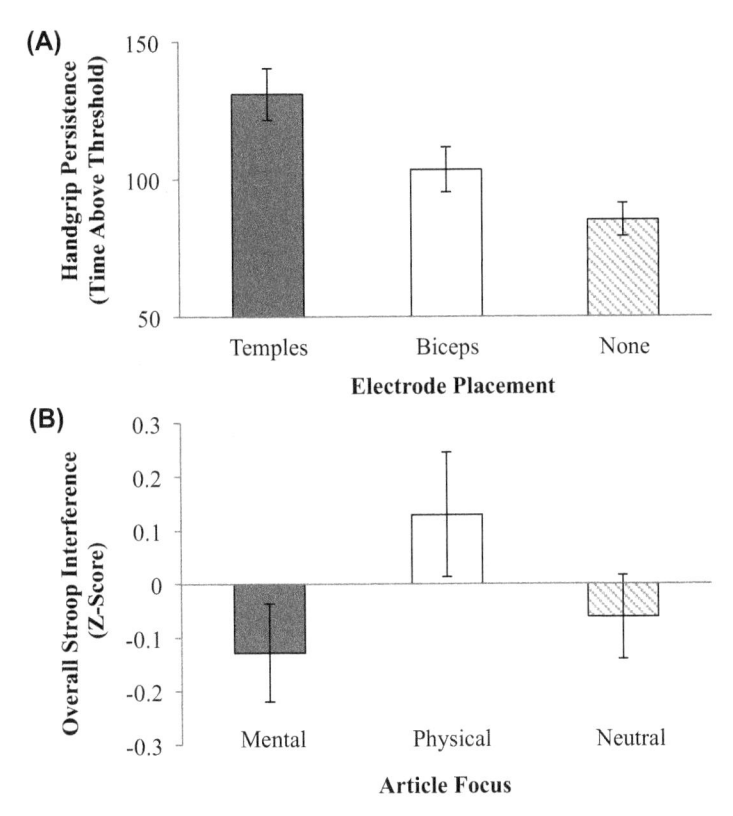

FIGURE 17.1 Effect of metaphysical perception manipulations on self-control performance in a handgrip persistence context (Panel A, top) and a Stroop interference context (Panel B, bottom). In the handgrip experiment, participants were exposed to an electrode placement manipulation; in the Stroop experiment, participants were exposed to a reading prime manipulation. In both experiments, a significant performance advantage was observed for participants in the mental—as opposed to the physical—condition. Error bars indicate standard error.

strongly predicted persistence (ie, lower pain slope = higher persistence), and fully controlling for differences in subjective pain accounted for the behavioral differences across conditions.

Overall, these findings offer several novel extensions of extant research on self-control exertion. For one, they suggest that subtle situational manipulations might be an effective manner by which metaphysical perceptions of self-control exertion can be altered. Thus, even if a particular task can be construed as a complex combination of mental and physical inputs, environmental factors that heighten the salience of particular task components can shift metaphysical perceptions in manners predictive of self-control performance. In the present context, our electrode placement manipulation allowed an examination of whether handgrip persistence differs as a function of how such persistence is perceived from a metaphysical standpoint. Thus, even though it is reasonable to perceive various types of self-control tasks as reliant on a dynamic interplay between physical (ie, muscle endurance) and mental (ie, inhibition) processes, cues that differentially focus individuals on specific categories of processes may facilitate distinct patterns of effort exertion.

In addition to outlining the power of situational cues in altering metaphysical perceptions, our findings suggest that framing a task in psychological terms may benefit self-control to a greater extent than framing a task in physiological terms. There exist myriad possible explanations for this conclusion, including differences in construal level emerging from abstract versus concrete perceptions (Fujita, Trope, Liberman, & Levin-Sagi, 2006), differences in task motivation emerging from the potential implications of positive and negative performance (Muraven & Slessareva, 2003), and differences in lay theories concerning the limitations of physical versus mental energy (Job et al., 2010). Nonetheless, before delineating any broader explanations for a link between particular metaphysical perceptions and self-control performance, it is critical to replicate these types of findings across other self-control tasks and perceptual manipulations. In this vein, our lab found a similar positive impact of mental (as opposed to physical) task framing on a Stroop interference task, thus offering the possibility that the benefits associated with psychological task framings are applicable across a diverse range of contexts.[4]

Not only does our work suggest an advantage to psychological— versus physiological—framings of self-control tasks, it also suggests

---

[4] Participants read a story about the difficulties experienced by student-athletes in college (eg, long schedules, grueling practices, injuries), which was manipulated such that some participants read about these difficulties as either physical or mental challenges. For instance, when reading about the effects of long schedules on student-athletes, participants in the physical condition were presented with several physiological ailments that these schedules promoted (eg, blood glucose levels, stress hormone changes, aching body), whereas participants in the mental condition were presented with equivalent psychological ailments (eg, intellectual performance levels, self-reported stress changes, anxious mind). A pilot study indicated that the mental story increased the propensity for individuals to perceive various self-control tasks in psychological terms. In the main experiment, participants completed a set of 120 Stroop trials following exposure to this reading prime. Results showed that individuals exposed to the mental story exhibited significantly better self-control performance than did participants primed with the physical story, with the performance of a neutral control condition falling in-between. That is, participants in the mental condition showed the least evidence of Stroop interference on incongruent trials, and participants in the physical condition showed the greatest evidence of Strop interference (see Fig. 17.1, Panel B). This pattern of findings is consistent with results obtained within our handgrip experiment.

that such advantages are explained via perceptual mechanisms. For instance, when the handgrip persistence task's mental nature was emphasized via electrode placement on the temples, this placement promoted improved effort exertion via the alteration of subjective pain. It follows that particular metaphysical frames may not only shift one's thoughts about the task in question, they may also alter one's thoughts about internal processes engaged by the task. From this, we theorize that an individual's metaphysical task perceptions should be most impactful on behavioral output when such perceptions also alter the construal of ongoing transient states. In other words, even if a given framing manipulation changes how a participant thinks about the task (eg, "This handgrip task is testing my psychological willpower"), behavioral alterations are most likely when such task-level perceptions alter the construal of performance-relevant subjective states (eg, "If this task is testing my willpower, then this pain I'm feeling is mostly mental"). There exist a broad range of transient states that both (1) emerge during self-control exertion and (2) can be experienced in different metaphysical terms (eg, pain, effort, hunger, fatigue, endurance, focus), suggesting that subjective states offer a window into understanding how metaphysical task perceptions influence behavior (See Chapters 13, 4, 7, & 10).

Individual Differences and Metaphysical Perceptions

Concurrent to investigating contextual factors that influence metaphysical perceptions of self-control tasks, we have also begun investigating individual difference factors that impact such perceptions. Past research suggests that humans have a general tendency to differentiate between mental and physical phenomena, but we reasoned that individual-level variability in this tendency could influence metaphysical perceptions in manners relevant to self-control exertion. To examine this individual-level variability in metaphysical beliefs, we developed a measurement of *lay interactionism (LI), which assesses the perceived amount of overlap between physical and mental processes.* Using this measurement, we have examined how beliefs about mental–physical interaction impact metaphysical perceptions of self-control contexts.

Our development of LI emerged from an examination of extant individual difference measures concerned with capturing metaphysical beliefs. Although many scholars have constructed such measures, there exists little evidence that they assess constructs which are either (1) accessible to lay populations or (2) relevant to self-control contexts. For one, the majority of metaphysical belief measures rely on asking participants highly complex philosophical questions about the nature of the mind and body. While certainly interesting from an academic perspective, it stands to reason that the majority of the population has not considered these philosophical perspectives in great depth. Furthermore, even if particular individuals have an adequate grasp of such topics, the multifaceted nature of metaphysical belief (eg, the existence of a soul, the independence of mind and body, the possibility of free will) suggests that many aspects of their belief are not directly relevant to self-control contexts.

Based on these observations, we sought to develop our own individual difference measurement that assesses the extent to which individuals perceive overlap between physical and mental systems. Our measurement includes a series of items considering the intersection between ubiquitous psychological and physiological systems, such that individuals are asked to respond in terms of the extent to which they believe particular "mental" processes impact "physical" outcomes (and vice versa). As can be observed in Appendix 2, these items are chiefly concerned with the capability for physiological and psychological processes to interact in everyday human experience. For instance, can psychological stress impact physical health; does a person's body posture alter their emotional state; will regular exercise improve mental functioning? Together, we reasoned that asking individuals about how common mental and physical processes influence one another could effectively capture the extent to which they perceive self-control as reliant on psychological or physiological forces.

In the course of developing this construct, we have conducted numerous surveys assessing both the reliability and validity of LI (see Fig. 17.2). These surveys suggest that LI is an effective method by which to measure metaphysical beliefs about the mind–body interaction, as well as an index that predicts individual differences related to physiological–physiological overlap. For one, LI shows moderate levels of statistical reliability across various populations, ranging from adult MTurk samples ($N=340$; $\alpha=0.68$) to traditional college student samples ($N=126$; $\alpha=0.74$). Second, LI shows significant correspondence with extant measures of metaphysical belief (*Mental-Physical Overlap*—Forstmann, Burgmer, & Mussweiler, 2012; *Mind-Body Dualism*—Preston et al., 2013). Third, LI shows no discernible relationship to general measures of personality (*Big Five*—Digman, 1989), cognitive processing (*Categorical Thinking*—Epstein & Meier, 1989), or spiritual beliefs (*Religiosity*—Koenig & Büssing, 2010). Finally, LI predicts the extent to which individuals report integration between psychological and physiological experiences in various contexts (*Perspective-Taking*—Davis, 1983; *Private Body Consciousness*—Miller, Murphy, & Buss, 1981; *Private Self-consciousness*—Fenigstein, Scheier, & Buss, 1975; *Connectedness to Nature*—Mayer & Frantz, 2004).

In our surveys of LI, we have also attempted to examine how this construct corresponds to individual difference measurements concerned

MTurk Sample, N = 340		Student Sample, N = 126	
Lay Theory of Willpower	.00	Lay Theory of Willpower	.13
Trait Self-Control	.11*	Trait Self-Control	.00
Faith in Intuition	.25**	Faith in Intuition	.11
Connectedness to Nature	.19**	Connectedness to Nature	.15†
Private Body Consciousness	.18**	Private Body Consciousness	.28**
Religiosity	.13*	Religiosity	.11
Mental-Physical Overlap	.25**	Mental-Physical Overlap	.55**
		Self-Control as Energy	.24**
		Self-Control as State of Mind	.25**
		Generalized Self-Efficacy	.25**
		Free Will	.13
		Categorical Thinking	-.02
		Mind-Body Dualism	.21*
		Perspective-Taking	.27**
		Lay Theory of Intelligence	.21*
		Grit	-.03
		Need for Cognition	.31**
		Need for Closure	.10
		Private Self-Consciousness	.26**
		Self-Esteem	.11
		Self-Monitoring	.12
		Openness to Experience	.05
		Conscientiousness	.01
		Extraversion	.09
		Agreeableness	.01
		Neuroticism	.05

FIGURE 17.2 Presents pairwise correlations (r) between lay interactionism and other individual difference measurements. Left column shows results from our earliest pilot study conducted with a MTurk sample, whereas the right column shows a follow-up study conducted with an introductory psychology sample. In both columns, significance of the correlations is indicated by the following: †$p<.10$, *$p<.05$, **$p<.01$.

chiefly with self-control. In terms of abstract beliefs about self-control, LI positively predicts the extent to which participants endorse *self-control as energy* (Martijn et al., 2002) and *self-control as a state of mind* (Martijn et al., 2002). That is, participants who perceive a stronger overlap between mental and physical processes are more likely to believe that self-control can be construed as both a physiological construct (ie, requiring energy) and a psychological construct (ie, requiring motivated effort). However, with such a multifaceted construal of self-control's determinants, high LI individuals show no preference for a particular perspective on the limitations of self-control (*Lay Theories of Willpower*—Job et al., 2010). In terms of concrete beliefs about one's self-control abilities,

LI shows no statistical relationship with perceptions of personal self-control effectiveness (*Trait Self-control*—Tangney, Baumeister, & Boone, 2004; *Grit*—Duckworth, Peterson, Matthews, & Kelly, 2007) but does show a significant positive relationship with personal self-efficacy (*Generalized Self-efficacy*—Schwarzer & Jerusalem, 1995).

Aside from exploring relationships between LI and other individual difference measures, we have included LI within experimental contexts to assess how these beliefs impact metaphysical perceptions of self-control tasks. Interestingly, we have found that high LI individuals endorse a more balanced metaphysical perception of self-control tasks, such that they are more likely than low interactionists to emphasize both the mental and physical inputs required for effective self-control. We have identified this pattern across various contexts, including handgrip persistence, cold pressor immersion, and Stroop interference—all of which are commonly used to index self-control effectiveness. For instance, although both high and low interactionists perceive handgrip persistence tasks as very physically taxing, high interactionists perceive such tasks as more mentally taxing that do low interactionists. This pattern of findings suggests that high LI individuals believe effective self-control is reliant on both mental and physical systems, whereas low LI individuals believe that self-control is more reliant on one primary system.

At a general level, this pattern suggest that high LI individuals are more flexible in their metaphysical interpretation of self-control tasks; a flexibility that may allow for better performance in diverse self-control contexts. For example, the ability to reconstrue one's performance or subjective state in different metaphysical terms affords an enhanced possibility for heightened distraction or motivation when self-control exertion becomes increasingly aversive. Thus, if an individual is persisting on a difficult exercise task, an understanding that this task is reliant on both physical and mental processes allows a more rapid and effective reconstrual of the task when primary fatigue onset occurs. Following from the observation that physiological task framings may more clearly undermine self-control effectiveness (see previous section), it is possible that such perceptual flexibility is especially valuable during self-control conflicts that are initially construed in physical terms. That is, rather than continuing to ruminate on the physiological nature of an increasingly difficult self-control conflict (eg, dieting in the face of salient hunger cues), high LI individuals may show a greater propensity toward reframing this conflict in psychological terms; a reframing with the potential to decrease the likelihood of self-control failure.

In addition to examining how LI affects general metaphysical perceptions of self-control conflicts, our inclusion of this metric in experimental work has also shown that LI moderates the efficacy of cues intended to shift one's metaphysical perceptions toward particular tasks. For instance, in the handgrip experiment discussed previously, we found a significant interaction between LI and the electrode placement manipulation on participant's metaphysical task perceptions. Specifically, although low LI individuals reported task perceptions that corresponded to the placement of the electrodes (ie, temples = more mental; biceps = more physical), this pattern was reversed for high LI individuals. Thus, high LI individuals were more likely to perceive the task in physical terms when electrodes were attached to their temples.

Such findings imply that high LI participants have a more complex interpretation of cues intended to focus attention on the mental or physical aspects of a given task. Rather than assimilate to the singular process implied by a situational cue, the presentation of this cue may activate a more nuanced representation of the self-control task among high LI individuals. Thus, people who perceive high mental–physical overlap may interpret electrodes on their temples as assessing how the brain and body interact, whereas people who perceive low mental–physical overlap may interpret such electrodes as assessing how the brain drives performance irrespective of the body. As such, situational primes of particular metaphysical processes may have very different effects as a function of how someone thinks the mind and body relate. On one hand, if the mind and body are perceived as separate entities with minimal interaction, we should expect to observe strong perceptual and behavioral differences between self-control tasks framed in divergent metaphysical terms. In contrast, if the mind and body are perceived as a singular system with perpetual interaction, we should expect to observe minimal differences between self-control tasks framed in divergent metaphysical terms. This conclusion implies that the inclusion of individual differences is central to understanding how metaphysical perceptions affect self-control, such that person-level features may determine the absolute benefits and decrements associated with particular metaphysical framings.

DISCUSSION

In arguing that metaphysical representations influence self-control outcomes, our work follows in the wake of contemporary research on the power of perceptions in guiding self-control behavior. As can be garnered from other chapters within the present volume, a multitude of perceptual processes have been identified as relevant in self-control exertion, including beliefs about limitations of willpower (see Chapter 11), and beliefs about mental energy change (see Chapter 10). These processes point to the influence of personal beliefs—regardless of whether such beliefs are assessed as individual differences or manipulated experimentally—in driving the emotional, perceptual, and behavioral consequences of self-control engagement. We believe that studying metaphysical perceptions offers a novel extension of this recent work by promoting the investigation of questions sitting firmly at the intersection of psychology, philosophy, and physiology. While the separation of body and mind is a potentially contentious topic to debate among friends and colleagues, it certainly represents an area ripe for inquiry within psychological science—particularly within the domain of self-control.

One primary question that emerges from this initial work concerns the types of metaphysical representations that have the most positive and negative effects on self-control effectiveness. Preliminary findings suggest that a psychological frame offers greater self-control benefits than an equivalent physiological frame, and these findings may be partly attributable to alterations in construal level, motivation, and/or regulatory fit. For one, psychological frames may broaden one's construal level within a self-control context, and this type of broadened construal may indirectly drive enhanced self-control engagement (Fujita et al., 2006; Maglio & Trope, 2012; but see Schmeichel, Vohs, & Duke, 2011; Wan & Agrawal, 2011). Second, it is possible that individuals deem mental abilities more important to their sense of self than corresponding physical abilities (Haslam, Loughnan, Kashima, & Bain, 2008), thus motivating individuals to exhibit greater self-control exertion (Muraven & Slessareva, 2003). Third, psychological frames may be the default method by which many self-control tasks are construed, such that individuals experience greater regulatory fit when a task is framed in psychological terms; fit that ultimately drives enhanced task engagement and behavioral effectiveness (Higgins, 2000).

In contrast to a positive influence of psychological framings, it is also possible that our findings can be explained via a negative influence of physiological framings. For instance, perceiving self-control in physiological terms may heighten the presumed realism of subjective states inherent in extended self-control exertion (McCabe & Castel, 2008). As such, when prolonged self-control tasks produce aversive subjective experiences such as pain, fatigue, or difficulty, construing these experiences in physical terms may suggest that they are more severe or debilitating than if they were construed in mental terms. It follows that perceiving a self-control task as physically-based may heighten the perceived limitations of self-control (Job et al., 2010), increase one's motivation to conserve energy (Muraven, Shmueli, & Burkley, 2006), decrease behavioral self-efficacy (Sniehotta, Scholz, & Schwarzer, 2005), or direct attention toward other somatic markers of exhaustion (Eccleston & Crombez, 1999). In any of these cases, one would expect a dampening effect on behavioral self-control output as a function of perceiving such output in physiological terms.

Regardless of whether one hypothesizes a positive effect of psychological frames or a negative effect of physiological frames, it is critical to understand the specific links between one's metaphysical task perceptions and downstream behavioral output. Although we have obtained some evidence suggesting that ongoing subjective experiences play a critical role, it remains to be seen exactly why subjective experience differs when a task is construed in physical or mental terms. For instance, when considering the effect of our electrode placement manipulation on subjective pain, we failed to assess precisely what aspect of pain differed as a function of condition. One possibility is that the electrode placement altered the conceptual meaning of "pain," such that participants with electrodes on their temples defined pain as a psychological experience, whereas participants with electrodes on their biceps defined pain as a physical symptom. Another possibility is that participants with electrodes attached to their temples obscured or delayed the onset of pain via mental strategies (eg, distraction; goal setting), whereas participants with electrodes attached to their biceps employed physical strategies (eg, repositioning; muscle engagement). It follows that understanding how subjective experiences change as a function of metaphysical perceptions will facilitate the development of stronger theory concerning the behavioral influences of mental and physical task construals.

Future Directions

Although the findings presented in this chapter offer some promising possibilities, we would be remiss to argue that they provide a firm understanding of the relationship between metaphysical task perceptions and self-control. Indeed, there are many more questions than answers provided in the present work; questions we hope that other researchers will consider when building integrative theories concerning the influence of perceptual factors on self-control.

As outlined elsewhere in the present volume, numerous works have identified distinct perceptual processes that influence self-control effectiveness, such as perceptions concerning the limitations of willpower (see Chapter 11), perceptions concerning the energy value of a given task (see Chapter 10), or perceptions concerning one's personal self-control abilities (Duckworth et al., 2007; Tangney et al., 2004). We believe that our work can extend these types of findings, such that metaphysical task perceptions should interact with other perceptual features to produce nuanced patterns of self-control exertion. For instance, although perceiving willpower as an unlimited resource can benefit self-control performance (Job et al., 2010), this pattern may not hold when the self-control task under study is perceived to rely upon physiological—rather than psychological—effort. That is, believing in unlimited willpower should be most functional when willpower can presumably exert a strong influence on task performance. It follows that individual differences and/or situational cues which weaken the perceived correspondence between willpower and task performance can undermine the utility of willpower beliefs in self-control contexts.

Similar possibilities exist concerning recent studies on informational cues of mental energy depletion and restoration (Clarkson et al., 2010; Egan, Clarkson, & Hirt, 2015; see Chapters 10, 12). In these studies, feedback about the depleting and/or restorative nature of previous tasks has been shown to drive subsequent self-control performance via changes in perceived mental energy. Given that such studies have focused on how informational feedback alters perceived mental energy, it is possible that the behavioral patterns identified in these works could be moderated by how the subsequent self-control task is framed metaphysically. That is, when the self-control task under study is construed as reliant upon physical—as opposed to mental—energy, beliefs about one's current state of mental energy availability may be wholly irrelevant to self-control performance. Put another way, perceptions of mental energy should predict self-control exertion most clearly when task performance is perceived to be reliant upon psychological—rather than physiological—resources.

Just as metaphysical task perceptions may alter the relationship between self-control and personal beliefs (eg, lay theories of willpower) or self-perceptions (eg, perceived mental depletion), these same types of personal beliefs and self-perceptions may also alter the relationship between self-control and metaphysical task perceptions. In terms of personal beliefs, there exists a robust literature linking spiritual engagement and self-control performance, such that both that mindfulness mediation (Bowlin & Baer, 2012; Friese, Messner, & Schaffner, 2012; Zainal, Booth, & Huppert, 2012) and religious thought (Friese & Loschelder; Friese & Wänke, 2014; McCullough & Willoughby, 2009; Rounding, Lee, Jacobson, & Ji, 2012) have been shown to increase self-control output in various contexts. In explaining this relationship, one possibility is that mindful and/or religious individuals frame self-control conflicts in increasingly psychological and/or spiritual terms, and these particular task conceptualizations promote more effective self-control exertion. It follows that highly religious or highly mindful individuals may be insensitive to the impact of particular metaphysical task framings, such that they will perceive self-control in relatively psychological terms regardless of how a particular task is presented.

In terms of self-perceptions, it is possible that one's current subjective state can influence the effect of metaphysical task framings, such that perceptions of energy availability may moderate how a given framing impacts behavioral output. Thus, when individuals believe they have ample mental resources available, situational cues emphasizing the psychological nature of this task may be particularly beneficial to self-control outcomes. Such conclusions also apply to more generalized self-perceptions, such that individuals who believe that they are highly skilled at mental (eg, high-achieving students) or physical (eg, high-achieving athletes) tasks may benefit from task framings that emphasize the centrality of such skills in task performance.

Given that the focus of many chapters within the present volume concerns the topic of "ego depletion," it is also important to consider how our ideas about metaphysical perceptions function within conventional ego depletion paradigms. Generally speaking, depletion effects are observed in multitask paradigms, such that self-control exertion on an initial task affects self-control exertion on a subsequent task (Hagger et al., 2010). With two distinct tasks presented to the participant, there exists the possibility for metaphysical perceptions of these tasks to converge or diverge in ways that drive particular behavioral outcomes. Assuming that individuals distinguish energy resources into distinct mental and physical categories, self-control depletion may be most pronounced when both tasks are perceived as relying upon similar psychophysiological processes (Dewitte, Bruyneel, & Geyskens, 2009). For instance, if an individual is exposed to consecutive self-control tasks framed in similar metaphysical terms, depletion effects may be observed simply because both tasks are perceived to rely upon a singular resource pool. In contrast, if this same individual is exposed to consecutive self-control tasks framed in divergent metaphysical terms, depletion effects may not be observed simply because each task is perceived to rely upon a separate resource pool. Such possibilities reinforce the potential for perceptual processes to impact self-control dynamics (Clarkson et al., 2010; Job et al., 2010), and point to the potential utility of measuring/manipulating metaphysical perceptions within conventional depletion paradigms.

Finally, although the present chapter is inherently concerned with the influence of metaphysical perceptions within the domain of self-control, exploring these perceptions presents intriguing possibilities within other domains concerned with the interaction between psychological and physiological states. As social–psychological theories increasingly explore the complex interplay between cognitive, affective, physiological, and behavioral mechanisms, there exists increasing opportunity to explore how an individual's perceptions of such mechanisms influence downstream behavior. As but one example, psychologists have identified an array of processes underlying the generation and modulation of human attitudes (Amodio et al., 2004; Greenwald, McGhee, & Schwartz, 1998; Judd, Drake, Downing, & Krosnick, 1991; Phelps et al., 2000), ranging from those implicating primarily psychological processes (eg, semantic networks) to those implicating primarily physiological processes (ie, neurological activity). Although such processes clearly interact with one another to form complex theoretical possibilities, their inherent perceptual distinctiveness allows researchers to explore how particular metaphysical representations impact attitudinal outcomes. In other words, researchers can utilize differential task framings, differential measurement techniques, or particular individual differences to understand whether metaphysical perceptions of attitudes impact corresponding cognitions and behavior. This same type of logic applies to numerous other areas of psychology, including metaphysical perceptions of pain, emotion, health, attraction, and any other constructs that can be described in relatively physiological or psychological terms.

CONCLUSION

By exploring the role of metaphysical perceptions, the present work offers a novel perspective by which to consider self-control at the intersection of psychology, philosophy, and physiology. Although our work is in its early stages, we believe it offers numerous implications for current and future theorizing on the perceptual determinants of self-control exertion. We hope this chapter highlights the ubiquity of metaphysical perceptions in everyday self-control conflicts and helps readers consider how such perceptions interact with other cognitive, affective, and behavioral determinants to produce highly nuanced self-control outcomes.

References

Ackerman, P. L. (2011). *Cognitive fatigue: Multidisciplinary perspectives on current research and future applications.* American Psychological Association.

Amodio, D. M., Harmon-Jones, E., Devine, P. G., Curtin, J. J., Hartley, S. L., & Covert, A. E. (2004). Neural signals for the detection of unintentional race bias. *Psychological Science, 15,* 88–93.

Beck, D. M. (2010). The appeal of the brain in the popular press. *Perspectives on Psychological Science, 5,* 762–766.

Bering, J. M., & Bjorklund, D. F. (2004). The natural emergence of reasoning about the afterlife as a developmental regularity. *Developmental Psychology, 40,* 217–233.

Bloom, P. (2004). *Descartes' baby: How the science of child development explains what makes us human.* New York: Basic Books.

Bowlin, S. L., & Baer, R. A. (2012). Relationships between mindfulness, self-control, and psychological functioning. *Personality and Individual Differences, 52*, 411–415.

Bray, S. R., Ginis, K. A. M., & Woodgate, J. (2011). Self-regulatory strength depletion and muscle-endurance performance: a test of the limited-strength model in older adults. *Journal of Aging and Physical Activity, 19*, 177–188.

Bray, S. R., Graham, J. D., Martin Ginis, K. A., & Hicks, A. L. (2012). Cognitive task performance causes impaired maximum force production in human hand flexor muscles. *Biological Psychology, 89*, 195–200.

Cacioppo, J. T., Berntson, G. G., Ernst, J. M., & Ito, T. A. (2000). Social neuroscience. In A. E. Kazdin (Ed.), *Encyclopedia of psychology*. New York: Oxford University Press.

Carney, D. R., Cuddy, A. J. C., & Yap, A. J. (2010). Power posing: brief nonverbal displays affect neuroendocrine levels and risk tolerance. *Psychological Science, 21*, 1363–1368.

Clark, A. (2010). There is no non-materialist neuroscience. *Cortex: A Journal Devoted to the Study of the Nervous System and Behavior, 46*, 147–149.

Clarkson, J. J., Hirt, E. R., Jia, L., & Alexander, M. B. (2010). When perception is more than reality: the effects of perceived versus actual resource depletion on self-regulatory behavior. *Journal of Personality and Social Psychology, 98*, 29–46.

Cohen, E., Burdett, E., Knight, N., & Barrett, J. (2011). Cross-cultural similarities and differences in person-body reasoning: experimental evidence from the United Kingdom and Brazilian Amazon. *Cognitive Science, 35*, 1282–1304.

Davis, M. H. (1983). Measuring individual differences in empathy: evidence for a multidimensional approach. *Journal of Personality and Social Psychology, 44*, 113–126.

Demertzi, A., Liew, C., Ledoux, D., Bruno, M., Sharpe, M., Laureys, S., & Zeman, A. (2009). Dualism persists in the science of the mind. *Disorders of Consciousness, 1157*, 1–9.

DeWall, C., MacDonald, G., Webster, G. D., Masten, C. L., Baumeister, R. F., Powell, C., ... Eisenberger, N. I. (2010). Acetaminophen reduces social pain: behavioral and neural evidence. *Psychological Science, 21*, 931–937.

Dewitte, S., Bruyneel, S., & Geyskens, K. (2009). Self-regulation enhances self-regulation in subsequent consumer decisions involving similar response conflicts. *Journal of Consumer Research, 36*, 394–405.

Digman, J. M. (1989). Five robust trait dimensions: development, stability, and utility. *Journal of Personality, 57*, 195–214.

Duckworth, A. L., Peterson, C., Matthews, M. D., & Kelly, D. R. (2007). Grit: perseverance and passion for long-term goals. *Journal of Personality and Social Psychology, 9*, 1087–1101.

Eccleston, C., & Crombez, G. (1999). Pain demands attention: a cognitive–affective model of the interruptive function of pain. *Psychological Bulletin, 125*, 356.

Egan, P. M. (2015). *The effects of physical and mental foci on self-regulatory persistence* (Doctoral dissertation).

Egan, P. M., Clarkson, J. J., & Hirt, E. R. (2015). Revisiting the restorative effects of positive mood: an expectancy-based approach to self-control restoration. *Journal of Experimental Social Psychology, 57*, 87–99.

Egan, P. M., Hirt, E. R., & Karpen, S. C. (2012). Taking a fresh perspective: vicarious restoration as a means of recovering self-control. *Journal of Experimental Social Psychology, 48*, 457–465.

Eisenberger, N. I., & Lieberman, M. D. (2004). Why rejection hurts: a common neural alarm system for physical and social pain. *Trends in Cognitive Sciences, 8*, 294–300.

Eisenberger, N. I., & Lieberman, M. D. (2005). Why it hurts to be left out: the neurocognitive overlap between physical and social pain. In K. D. Williams, J. P. Forgas, & W. von Hippel (Eds.), *The social outcast: Ostracism, social exclusion, rejection, and bullying* (pp. 109–127). New York: Psychology Press.

Eisenberger, N. I., Lieberman, M. D., & Williams, K. D. (2003). Does rejection hurt? an fMRI study of social exclusion. *Science, 302,* 290–292.

Epstein, S., & Meier, P. (1989). Constructive thinking: a broad coping variable with specific components. *Journal of Personality and Social Psychology, 57,* 332–350.

Farah, M. J., & Murphy, N. (2009). Neuroscience and the soul. *Science, 323,* 1168.

Fenigstein, A., Scheier, M. F., & Buss, A. H. (1975). Public and private self-consciousness: assessment and theory. *Journal of Consulting and Clinical Psychology, 43,* 522–527.

Forstmann, M., Burgmer, P., & Mussweiler, T. (2012). "The mind is willing, but the flesh is weak": the effects of mind-body dualism on health behavior. *Psychological Science, 23,* 1239–1245.

Friese, M., Messner, C., & Schaffner, Y. (2012). Mindfulness meditation counteracts self-control depletion. *Consciousness and Cognition, 21,* 1016–1022.

Friese, M., & Wänke, M. (2014). Personal prayer buffers self-control depletion. *Journal of Experimental Social Psychology, 51,* 56–59.

Fujita, K., Trope, Y., Liberman, N., & Levin-Sagi, M. (2006). Construal levels and self-control. *Journal of Personality and Social Psychology, 90,* 351–367.

Gailliot, M. T., & Baumeister, R. F. (2007). The physiology of willpower: linking blood glucose to self-control. *Personality and Social Psychology Review, 11,* 303–327.

Gervais, W. M., & Norenzayan, A. (2012). Analytic thinking promotes religious disbelief. *Science, 336,* 493–496.

Gottfried, G. M., Gelman, S. A., & Schultz, J. (1999). Children's understanding of the brain: from early essentialism to biological theory. *Cognitive Development, 14,* 147–174.

Gray, K., Knobe, J., Sheskin, M., Bloom, P., & Barrett, L. F. (2011). More than a body: mind perception and the nature of objectification. *Journal of Personality and Social Psychology, 101,* 1207–1220.

Greenwald, A. G., McGhee, D. E., & Schwartz, J. L. (1998). Measuring individual differences in implicit cognition: the implicit association test. *Journal of Personality and Social Psychology, 74,* 1464–1480.

Hagger, M. S., Wood, C., Stiff, C., & Chatzisarantis, N. L. D. (2010). Ego depletion and the strength model of self-control: a meta-analysis. *Psychological Bulletin, 136,* 495–525.

Haslam, N., Loughnan, S., Kashima, Y., & Bain, P. (2008). Attributing and denying humanness to others. *European Review of Social Psychology, 19,* 55–85.

Heatherton, T. F., & Wagner, D. D. (2011). Cognitive neuroscience of self-regulation failure. *Trends in Cognitive Science, 15,* 132–139.

Higgins, E. T. (2000). Making a good decision: value from fit. *American Psychologist, 55,* 1217–1233.

Hood, B., Gjersoe, N. L., & Bloom, P. (2012). Do children think that duplicating the body also duplicates the mind? *Cognition, 125,* 466–474.

Hook, C. J., & Farah, M. J. (2013). Look again: effects of brain images and mind-brain dualism on lay evaluations of research. *Journal of Cognitive Neuroscience, 25,* 1397–1405.

Inzlicht, M., & Gutsell, J. N. (2007). Running on empty: neural signals for self-control failure. *Psychological Science, 18,* 933–937.

Job, V., Dweck, C. S., & Walton, G. M. (2010). Ego depletion-is it all in your head? Implicit theories about willpower affect self-regulation. *Psychological Science, 21,* 1686–1693.

Johnson, C. N. (1990). If you had my brain, where would I be? Children's understanding of the brain and identity. *Child Development, 61,* 962–972.

Jostmann, N. B., Lakens, D., & Schubert, T. W. (2009). Weight as an embodiment of importance. *Psychological Science, 20,* 1169–1174.

Judd, C. M., Drake, R. A., Downing, J. W., & Krosnick, J. A. (1991). Some dynamic properties of attitude structures: context-induced response facilitation and polarization. *Journal of Personality and Social Psychology, 60,* 193–202.

Keehner, M., Mayberry, L., & Fischer, M. H. (2011). Different clues from different views: the role of image format in public perceptions of neuroimaging results. *Psychonomic Bulletin & Review*, *18*, 422–428.

Kelemen, D. (2004). Are children 'intuitive theists'? *Psychological Science*, *15*, 295–301.

Klein, S. B. (2012). The self and science: is it time for a new approach to the study of human experience? *Current Directions in Psychological Science*, *21*(4), 253–257.

Koenig, H. G., & Büssing, A. (2010). The Duke University Religion Index (DUREL): a five-item measure for use in epidemiological studies. *Religions*, *1*, 78–85.

Larson, E. J., & Witham, L. (1997). Scientists are still keeping the faith. *Nature*, *386*, 435–436.

Larson, E. J., & Witham, L. (1998). Leading scientists still reject God. *Nature*, *395*, 313.

Legare, C. H., Evans, E. M., Rosengren, K. S., & Harris, P. L. (2012). The coexistence of natural and supernatural explanations across cultures and development. *Child Development*, *83*, 779–793.

Lieberman, M. D. (2007). Social cognitive neuroscience: a review of core processes. *Annual Review of Psychology*, *58*, 259–289.

Loughnan, S., Haslam, N., Murmane, T., Vaes, J., Reynolds, C., & Suitner, C. (2010). Objectification leads to depersonalization: the denial of mind and moral concern to objectified others. *European Journal of Social Psychology*, *40*, 709–717.

MacDonald, G., Kingsbury, R., & Shaw, S. (2005). Adding insult to injury: social pain theory and response to social exclusion. In K. D. Williams, J. P. Forgas, & W. von Hippel (Eds.), *The social outcast: Ostracism, social exclusion, rejection, and bullying*. New York: Psychology Press.

MacDonald, G., & Leary, M. R. (2005). Why does social exclusion hurt? the relationship between social and physical pain. *Psychological Bulletin*, *131*, 202–223.

Maglio, S. J., & Trope, Y. (2012). Disembodiment: abstract construal attenuates the influence of contextual bodily state in judgment. *Journal of Experimental Psychology: General*, *141*, 211–216.

Martijn, C., Tenbült, P., Merckelbach, H., Dreezens, E., & de Vries, N. K. (2002). Getting a grip on ourselves: challenging expectancies about loss of energy after self-control. *Social Cognition*, *20*, 441–460.

Mayer, F. S., & Frantz, C. M. (2004). The connectedness to nature scale: a measure of individuals' feeling in community with nature. *Journal of Environmental Psychology*, *24*, 503–515.

McCabe, D. P., & Castel, A. D. (2008). Seeing is believing: the effect of brain images on judgments of scientific reasoning. *Cognition*, *107*, 343–352.

McCullough, M. E., & Willoughby, B. L. (2009). Religion, self-regulation, and self-control: associations, explanations, and implications. *Psychological Bulletin*, *135*, 69.

Miller, G. A. (2010). Mistreating psychology in the decades of the brain. *Perspectives on Psychological Science*, *5*, 716–743.

Miller, L. C., Murphy, R., & Buss, A. H. (1981). Consciousness of body: private and public. *Journal of Personality and Social Psychology*, *41*, 397–406.

Miresco, M. J., & Kirmayer, L. J. (2006). The persistence of mind-brain dualism in psychiatric reasoning about clinical scenarios. *American Journal of Psychiatry*, *163*, 913–918.

Muraven, M., Shmueli, D., & Burkley, E. (2006). Conserving self-control strength. *Journal of Personality and Social Psychology*, *91*, 524–537.

Muraven, M., & Slessareva, E. (2003). Mechanism of self-control failure: motivation and limited resources. *Personality & Social Psychology Bulletin*, *29*, 894–906.

Muraven, M., Tice, D. M., & Baumeister, R. F. (1998). Self-control as a limited resource: regulatory depletion patterns. *Journal of Personality and Social Psychology*, *74*, 774–789.

Niedenthal, P. M., Barsalou, L. W., Winkielman, P., Krauth-Gruber, S., & Ric, F. (2005). Embodiment in attitudes, social perception, and emotion. *Personality and Social Psychology Review*, *9*, 184–211.

Ochsner, K. N., Knierim, K., Ludlow, D. H., Henelin, J., Ramachandra, T., Glover, G., & Mackey, S. C. (2004). Reflecting upon feelings: an fMRI study of neural systems supporting the attribution of emotion to self and other. *Journal of Cognitive Neuroscience, 16*, 1746–1772.

Ochsner, K. N., & Lieberman, M. D. (2001). The emergence of social cognitive neuroscience. *American Psychologist, 56*, 717–734.

Park, C. (2013). Mind-Body CAM Interventions: current status and consideration for integration into clinical health psychology. *Journal of Clinical Psychology, 69*, 45–63.

Paulhus, D. L., & Carey, J. M. (2011). The FAD–Plus: measuring lay beliefs regarding free will and related constructs. *Journal of Personality Assessment, 93*, 96–104.

Phelps, E. A., O'Connor, K. J., Cunningham, W. A., Funayama, E. S., Gatenby, J. C., Gore, J. C., & Banaji, M. R. (2000). Performance on indirect measures of race evaluation predicts amygdala activation. *Journal of Cognitive Neuroscience, 12*, 729–738.

Preston, J. L., Ritter, R. S., & Hepler, J. (2013). Neuroscience and the soul: competing explanations for the human experience. *Cognition, 127*, 31–37.

Price, D. D. (2000). Psychological and neural mechanisms of the affective dimension of pain. *Science, 288*, 1769–1772.

Pyszczynski, T., Greenberg, J., & Solomon, S. (1999). A dual-process model of defense against conscious and unconscious death-related thoughts: an extension of terror management theory. *Psychological Review, 106*, 835–845.

Randles, D., Heine, S. J., & Santos, N. (2013). The common pain of surrealism and death: acetaminophen reduces compensatory affirmation following meaning threats. *Psychological Science, 24*, 966–973.

Rounding, K., Lee, A., Jacobson, J. A., & Ji, L. J. (2012). Religion replenishes self-control. *Psychological Science, 23*, 635–642.

Schmeichel, B. J., Vohs, K. D., & Duke, S. C. (2011). Self-control at high and low levels of mental construal. *Social Psychological and Personality Science, 2*, 182–189.

Schwarzer, R., & Jerusalem, M. (1995). Generalized self-efficacy scale. *Measures in Health Psychology: A User's Portfolio. Casual and Control Beliefs, 1*, 35–37.

Sharpe, M., & Walker, J. (2012). Mind-body dualism, psychiatry, and medicine. In M. Gelder, N. Andreasen, J. Lopez-Ibor, & J. Geddes (Eds.), *New Oxford Textbook of Psychiatry*. Oxford University Press.

Sniehotta, F. F., Scholz, U., & Schwarzer, R. (2005). Bridging the intention–behaviour gap: planning, self-efficacy, and action control in the adoption and maintenance of physical exercise. *Psychology & Health, 20*, 143–160.

Spunt, R. P., Falk, E. B., & Lieberman, M. D. (2010). Dissociable neural systems support retrieval of how and why action knowledge. *Psychological Science, 21*, 1593–1598.

Strack, F., Martin, L. L., & Stepper, S. (1988). Inhibiting and facilitating conditions of the human smile: a nonobtrusive test of the facial feedback hypothesis. *Journal of Personality and Social Psychology, 54*, 768–777.

Tangney, J. P., Baumeister, R. F., & Boone, A. L. (2004). High self-control predicts good adjustment, less pathology, better grades, and interpersonal success. *Journal of Personality, 72*, 271–322.

Trope, Y., & Liberman, N. (2010). Construal level theory of psychological distance. *Psychological Review, 117*, 440–463.

Van Overwalle, F., & Baetens, K. (2009). Understanding others' actions and goals by mirror and mentalizing systems: a meta-analysis. *Neuroimage, 48*, 564–584.

Wan, E. W., & Agrawal, N. (2011). Carryover effects of self-control on decision making: a construal-level perspective. *Journal of Consumer Research, 38*, 199–214.

Zainal, N. Z., Booth, S., & Huppert, F. A. (2012). The efficacy of mindfulness-based stress reduction on mental health of breast cancer patients: a meta-analysis. *Psycho-oncology, 22*, 1457–1465.

APPENDICES

Appendix 1

Handgrip Paradigm and Electrode Placement

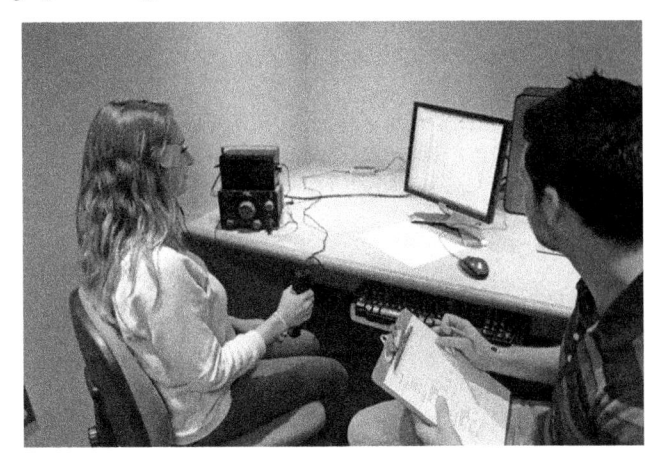

Picture shows participant completing a handgrip persistence assessment (ie, performance is tracked dynamically on screen; failure threshold is based upon 40% of individual's maximum handgrip strength) with electrodes attached to their temples. In other conditions, participants completed the same handgrip task with electrodes attached to their biceps or did not have electrodes attached at all.

Appendix 2

Lay Interactionism Scale
1. A person's body posture influences their mental state.
2. A person's mind needs regular intellectual exercise to stay fit.
3. Positive thinking can speed up a person's recovery from health problems.
4. A person's thought patterns do not directly affect their susceptibility to disease. Reverse-coded (R)
5. Intense mental work does not require as much energy as intense physical work. (R)
6. What someone eats does not influence their intellectual abilities. (R)
7. Eating nonnutritious food can cause lowered mental focus.
8. Experiencing stress and anxiety can directly cause health problems.
9. Mental exhaustion indicates that a person's body needs rest.
10. The mind and body require similar nutrition to perform at a high level.

11. Rigorous physical exercise does not require a strong mental focus. (R)
12. A person's thoughts cannot immediately impact their bodily state. (R)
13. Getting in better shape does not improve a person's intellectual abilities. (R)
14. Physical illnesses are rarely caused by psychological problems. (R)
15. A person's mood "leaks out" through their body language.

Assessed on a 1 (strongly disagree) to 7 (strongly agree) scale. Score on scale predicts metaphysical perception of self-control tasks, such that participants with greater beliefs in mind–body interactionism perceive conventional experimental measures of self-control (eg, handgrip, Stroop) as more mentally—as opposed to physically—demanding.

SECTION 5

NEWER MODELS OF EGO CONTROL

CHAPTER 18

Proximate and Ultimate Causes of Ego Depletion

Z.L. Francis, M. Inzlicht

University of Toronto Scarborough, Toronto, ON, Canada

INTRODUCTION

Self-regulation is fundamental to long-term success. Although automatic responses correctly guide us through much of our daily lives, these impulses are imperfect and sometimes need to be suppressed or overridden. Most familiar situations have an automatic response or habit attached: when presented with delicious food, you want to eat it; when presented with discomfort, you want to avoid it; when presented with your computer, you want to play games or go on social media. Automatic responses are cognitively quick, efficient, and sometimes beneficial, especially when habits align with future goals (Adriaanse, Kroese, Gillebaart, & De Ridder, 2014; Galla & Duckworth, 2015). However, automatic responses are sometimes misaligned with long-term goals, such as losing weight or finishing school work, and people must self-regulate to inhibit the automatic response and replace it with a different behavior. This act of inhibition requires mental effort (Baumeister, Bratslavsky, Muraven, & Tice, 1998; Kool, McGuire, Rosen, & Botvinick, 2010).

Mental effort, however, appears exhaustible. Mental ability gradually weakens with use of cognitive effort, resulting in temporary fatigue (Hagger, Wood, Stiff, & Chatzisarantis, 2010; Warm, Parasuraman, & Matthews, 2008). Mental fatigue has been extensively documented during prolonged tasks, especially when the tasks are cognitively demanding (Boksem & Tops, 2008; Warm et al., 2008). When a person is asked to do a single task for an extended period of time, they report feeling mentally tired and their performance on the task starts to decrease. Fatigued people make more errors, are less attentive, and are slower to respond (Lorist, Boksem, & Ridderinkhof, 2005; Lorist et al., 2000).

In vigilance tasks, mental fatigue limits participants' ability or willingness to complete the fatiguing task successfully. However, these fatigue effects are not only due to the monotony of doing a single task (Pattyn, Neyt, Henderickx, & Soetens, 2008)—the deleterious effects of mental fatigue also cross over between tasks, so that fatigue from one effortful act leaves people in an error-prone and less competent state for a second, subsequent task (eg, Webster, Richter, & Kruglanski, 1996). We have known about fatigue spilling over to unrelated tasks for over 100 years. Back in 1904, Carl Seashore commented, "the fatigue through a particular activity also reduces the capacity for such work as is brought about through quite different mental activities" (p. 98). Mental fatigue, including fatigue originating in one task and affecting performance on a second one, is a long-known phenomenon[1].

Given that exerting mental effort generally results in a temporary state of mental fatigue, effortful self-control should also induce mental fatigue and all of its accompanying detriments on subsequent task performance. Indeed, a plethora of studies show that using self-control at Time 1 often reduces performance on various other self-control tasks immediately following at Time 2 (Hagger et al., 2010). This decrease in self-control due to previously using self-control is commonly referred to as *ego depletion* (Baumeister et al., 1998). We consider ego depletion to be a form of mental fatigue, centering on the sequential task paradigm and the use of self-control. It should be noted, however, that not all self-regulation is necessarily fatiguing or depleting. People with high trait self-control may only rarely engage in depleting inhibition, and instead cultivate beneficial, goal-compatible habits (Gillebaart & De Ridder, 2015). People with the right kinds of motivation seem to accomplish their goals effortlessly and are not tempted by goal-inconsistent behaviors (Milyavskaya, Inzlicht, Hope, & Koestner, 2015). Thus, these individuals frequently perform self-regulation without having to actively and effortfully suppress unwanted automatic responses and do not become depleted afterward. Ego depletion seems restricted to situations where the exertion of self-control is perceived as effortful (Clarkson, Hirt, Jia, & Alexander, 2010; Werle, Wansink, & Payne, 2014).

Understanding the causes of ego depletion—and of mental fatigue broadly—can help researchers discover the boundary conditions of fatigue, when it can or cannot be prevented, and ultimately how to encourage self-regulation in society. Not every situation or every experiment results in depletion. Indeed, there are many known moderators of the effect

---

[1] The phenomenon that we now call ego depletion has long been known, but never undisputed. Edward Thorndike (1900) insisted that previous cognitive work "did not decrease one jot or tittle the ability of the scholars to do [subsequent] mental work" (p. 547).

(Baumeister et al., 1998; Job, Dweck, & Walton, 2010; Tice, Baumeister, Shmueli, & Muraven, 2007) and no doubt additional unknown moderators, some of which may account for situations where depletion is expected but not found (Converse & Deshon, 2009; Dewitte, Bruyneel, & Geyskens, 2009; Xu et al., 2014). Understanding the theory behind depletion can inform our methods to more reliably detect the depletion effect, which has sometimes proved illusive (Carter, Kofler, Forster, & Mccullough, 2015). Improvements of theory, methods, and research practices can improve our grasp of ego depletion and allow researchers to move forward and answer new questions.

Overview

In this chapter, we explore the ultimate and proximate causes of ego depletion, expanding and updating the framework setup by Inzlicht, Schmeichel, and Macrae (2014). The shifting-priorities process model was previously introduced as an alternative explanation of ego depletion, an explanation which does not rely on a limited resource. The model primarily explains *changes* in self-control across time. Why can someone resist unhealthy snacks for a short of time, but then give up and binge after a difficult day at work? Why does one previous activity reduce some people's willingness to perform a second difficult task?

In this extension of the process model, we first ask: from an evolutionary perspective, why are failures of self-control ever permissible? Various lines of evidence suggest that we have two drives: one to satisfy immediate, leisurely urges and one to perform effortful work to prepare for our future. Although we frequently feel that denying immediate pleasure for long-term benefits is the hallmark of success, it is evolutionarily advantageous to ensure that your immediate needs are constantly taken care of (by exploiting known resources), prior to taking care of your future self. Gathering knowledge and resources for the future is important, but only in moderation, as time spent preparing for the future is time that could otherwise be spent on more immediately prosperous activities. We first explain this trade-off in terms of an exploration–exploitation conflict, where we will introduce how the perception of effort accompanies unpleasant delayed gratification. We then parallel the exploration–exploitation trade-off with finding a balance between labor and leisure and discuss ego depletion as the craving for leisure that occurs after an excess of effortful work.

Next, what are the proximate mechanisms of depletion? In the second half of this chapter, we discuss how the labor and leisure balance leads to decisions between have-to and want-to goals, and how construal of any task as effortful or enjoyable is subjective. When an activity requires the use of executive functions (particularly sustained attention and inhibition) and is not perceived as immediately rewarding, it is perceived as effortful and fatiguing. As this effortful task is performed, motivation and attention shift so that reward-related neural areas are additionally activated and control-related areas are less responsive. A depleted person experiences increased approach motivation, an aversion toward additional effort, and a subjective feeling of fatigue. This proposed mechanism for depletion, the shifting-priorities process model, allows for other motivational influences to compensate for depletion and also allows for individual variation in levels of depletion, as depletion relies on the previous task being perceived as effortful by that specific person. Finally, we discuss consequences and predictions of this account and briefly compare the shifting-priorities process model with two other theories of ego depletion.

ULTIMATE CAUSES

First, why is effort aversive, why does it lead to fatigue (Kurzban, 2016)? Evolution is imperfect, and many inefficient or impractical traits will continue to proliferate in a species if not harmful enough to be consistently selected against (Kurzban, Duckworth, Kable, & Myers, 2013), but a trait with negative consequences and no reciprocal benefit is unlikely to survive across thousands of generations. Impaired physical endurance (Dorris, Power, & Kenefick, 2012; Marcora, Staiano, & Manning, 2009; Molden et al., 2012), decision-making (Pocheptsova, Amir, Dhar, & Baumeister, 2008), vigilance, and reaction times are clearly unfavorable in almost all environments and cultures (and for many species), and any mechanism that causes these impairments should be selected against. Yet—even when there is no physical fatigue—both humans and other animals put less effort into tasks when they are mentally tired (eg, Weary, Krebs, Eddyshaw, McGregor, & Horn, 1988). Mental fatigue should thus also have an advantageous purpose, which outweighs the occasional loss in productivity that occurs when fatigued. Instead of fatigue causing an overall decrease in ability (presumably evolutionarily disadvantageous), it may instead cause a reallocation of ability and attention. Fatigue may be the signal to switch tasks, to stop doing an unpleasant future-oriented task and instead engage in an immediately rewarding task. Survival emphasizes meeting your short-term needs; preparing for the future (by fulfilling long-term goals) is a luxury to be engaged in only once your immediate needs are met.

Later, we discuss two broad categories of decisions that are frequently made by animals, both human and nonhuman: between exploration and exploitation, and between labor and leisure. The ability to balance between these broad categories of behaviors should be rewarded by natural selection and, importantly, each individual decision point is dependent on the decisions that came previously. Given free ability, people and other animals will sample between exerting future-focused "self-control" options and easier rewarding options. The mechanisms that evolved to monitor the equality between these options—such as the phenomenology of fatigue and effort—may be a source of mental fatigue and ego depletion today.

Exploration and Exploitation

One of the first situations that sets immediate rewards and longer-term goals against each other is when a foraging animal decides whether to exploit or explore. *Exploitation* behaviors take advantage of opportunities that will provide immediate known rewards, while *exploration* prepares the organism for future successes by searching for novel sources of future rewards and reducing uncertainty by gathering information (Cohen, McClure, & Yu, 2007). Exploitation is the more conservative behavior, such as getting food from a familiar source—a human going to a favorite restaurant, or a squirrel foraging nuts from a much-frequented tree. Exploration involves some risk; you may discover a new restaurant or tree that is superior to the familiar one, but you may also be disappointed. The optimal balance between exploitation and exploration is difficult to determine because (1) the risk to benefit ratio of the exploration option is inherently unknown and (2) even the known exploitation option has a degree of uncertainty, since rarely does our environment stay exactly the same across time (Cohen et al., 2007). Given this, it is difficult to know exactly when to switch from one strategy to another.

Regardless, it is necessary to find some balance between exploitation and exploration. Exploring indefinitely does not allow for an animal to gather the benefits from any resource, since they will not keep their attention focused long enough to be productive. Constant exploitation in the same locations is also problematic; the known option may gradually become less desirable relative to other options, particularly if the resource is nonrenewable, and becomes more difficult to exploit as time passes (Kurzban et al., 2013). The longer that you try to find berries on a single bush, the more difficult it becomes since there are fewer and fewer berries. Similarly, when doing a literature search, the longer you spend using the identical key search terms, the less relevant the papers will be that you find. At some point, you are best served to go to a different bush, or try different search terms.

Deciding when to leave a feeding area to explore is easier for animals with a single homogeneous, readily available food source—an approximate solution to the explore–exploit problem is to explore once the current location's resources diminish to the area's average (Hayden, Pearson, & Platt, 2011). Humans, in contrast, evolved with diverse omnivorous diets and are able to eat foods of differing nutritional value and accessibility. Effectively deciding between varied food sources is possibly one of the driving evolutionary selection pressures for developing general self-control—sometimes it is better to spend extra effort to acquire a higher-quality food, instead of eating a more readily available lower-nutrition food. Across 36 nonhuman animal species, breadth of dietary resources is the second strongest predictor of performance on experimental inhibitory self-control tasks, after brain volume (MacLean et al., 2014), and animals that eat food that takes longer to materialize also have better self-regulation (Stevens, Hallinan, & Hauser, 2005). Abandoning one readily available food source in search of alternative higher-yield food might be one origin of self-control, the ability to pursue a long-term goal at the cost of giving up short-term reward.

While regulation between exploration and exploitation may have originally evolved to optimize food gathering, the ability to navigate the exploration–exploitation conflict can be used in any situation requiring balance between short-term rewards and long-term goals. Even animals that are capable of enacting self-control to delay gratification—from humans to monkeys—do not always choose to do so (Evans & Beran, 2007). The individual who always waits or goes searching for better food will starve. Each decision to explore or exploit thus is dependent on previous actions. Repeatedly deciding to explore results in more knowledge about the environment, but it also creates "time-on-task" neural changes that gauge how much time has been spent on the unrewarding activity (Hayden et al., 2011; Lorist et al., 2005). This "time-on-task" monitoring then may be used in calculations to determine when it is time to change tasks, to ensure that the exploit–explore balance is maintained and the current self is not neglected.

Humans have evolved to balance short-term and long-term interests in many domains, including ones without edible stakes. The mechanisms that evolved to weigh options of *now or later*—while taking into account variables such as accessibility, immediate need, reward size, and uncertainty—have a built-in bias toward diversity; sometimes now and sometimes later. To balance the explore/exploit conundrum, people should sometimes, but not always, decide to exert self-control, forgo the benefits in front of them, and explore the world to find other options. According to the exploration/exploitation account, people who have previously engaged in self-control, as in during an ego depletion task, become less likely to engage self-control in the future and instead would prefer to gratify their immediate needs (exploitation)[2].

[2] Earlier versions of the ultimate account of the process model (Inzlicht et al., 2014) suggested that self-control tasks corresponded to exploitation (not exploration). In this revision, we recognize that although the term "exploration" sounds like fun from our human standpoint, from the perspective of a foraging animal it shares more commonalities with delayed gratification and self-control. Exploration and exploitation still do not directly map onto labor and leisure in humans; for example, novelty itself is perceived as rewarding by humans.

Delayed or Immediate Rewards

There are other choices between immediate and delayed rewards, which are not tied to exploring and exploiting. Nonhuman animals plan for the future through performing instinctive behaviors such as storing food. However, animals will always prioritize their current needs over any future planning. There is no use saving food for the winter if you are at risk of starving in the summer. While humans frequently use our overdeveloped prefrontal cortex to plan for the future, we also retain the natural bias toward putting immediate needs first.

Immediate rewards are processed differently and more strongly in the brain than delayed rewards. There is evidence for two different neural systems, one for immediate outcomes and one for other delayed outcomes (McClure, Laibson, Loewenstein, & Cohen, 2004). The midbrain dopaminergic pathways of the limbic system create the motivation for immediate outcomes, for seeking rewards and hedonic pleasure. The response strength in these regions even correlates with individual differences in impulsivity (Hariri et al., 2006). Meanwhile, prefrontal and posterior parietal cortexes respond consistently to time-delayed rewards (McClure et al., 2004). Behaviorally, immediate rewards are generally hyperbolically preferred over delayed future rewards in both humans and other animals, a preference called delay discounting (Cohen et al., 2007; Matta, Gonçalves, & Bizarro, 2012). In most cases, a smaller reward now is chosen over a larger reward later. This bias toward immediate rewards makes choosing immediate gratification feel easy and rewarding, and going against the impulse is effortful. Experiencing discomfort (such as refusing a delicious snack) in exchange for a long-term reward (such as losing weight) goes against this bias toward preferring immediate gratification.

Effort Avoidance

While seeking immediate rewards is neurologically encouraged, engaging in nonrewarding acts of self-control is discouraged through the feeling of effort. Use of executive functions such as inhibition, as well as sustained attention and working memory, often feel subjectively effortful, particularly when there is no accompanying reward (see section *Subjective Effort*). Effort itself, both cognitive and physical, is considered mildly aversive or unpleasant (Kool et al., 2010) and may originate in the negative affect arising when conflicts are detected during cognitive control (Inzlicht, Bartholow, & Hirsh, 2015; Saunders & Inzlicht, 2015). The negative feeling of effort creates a cost for an activity, which the perceived benefits must outweigh for someone to engage in the activity. Additionally, when given the choice between an easy task and a difficult task, we will choose the easy task (assuming that the benefits are equal between the two; Hull, 1943). Organisms generally follow the *law of least effort* by avoiding unnecessary use of executive functions (Kool et al., 2010)—the law of least effort is complementary to the preference for immediate rewards. Although humans and nonhuman animals can engage in self-control and delayed gratification, performing them without countervailing rewards tasks is perceived as effortful and aversive.

Labor and Leisure

Another common choice in behaviors involves choosing between doing work and taking a break. Deciding to perform work in exchange for a reward, termed *labor*, involves putting up with the discomfort of effort to get the associated reward (Kool & Botvinick, 2014). Alternatively, you might choose to quit the activity, forego both the reward and the aversive effort, and choose *leisure*. People—and maybe some animals—seem to gravitate toward a balance between labor and leisure (Kool & Botvinick, 2014), paralleling the balance between exploration and exploitation, and the general balance between seeking short-term and long-term rewards. An individual decision to perform the laborious effortful behavior instead of the option to stop and satisfy the immediate needs of avoiding effort is not decided in isolation. The longer that someone spends on one task, the more activated are leisurely goals.

Ego Depletion

The proposed shifting-priorities mechanism ensures a balance between short-term gratification and long-term rewards, and, in so doing, explains the phenomenon of fatigue and ego depletion. A traditional ego depletion paradigm, the sequential task paradigm, involves participants completing one self-control task followed by a second. The self-control tasks that are used are varied and include the Stroop task, solving anagrams, resisting food, suppressing stereotypes, suppressing displays of aggression, among many others. All of these tasks have a few things in common: they require exertion of effort, they are not immediately rewarding, and they are extrinsically motivated. Self-control tasks are aversive and are reported to be difficult or effortful (Hagger et al., 2010). Like mental vigilance tasks, they require heightened executive functioning, generally some type of inhibition. The tasks have only the potential for future rewards, but with the certainty of present costs, including foregoing a current gratification.

Performance on the second self-control task is poorer, and self-control appears to "run out" because it is evolutionarily disadvantageous to spend excessive time on tasks with only future rewards and present costs. We evolved to balance between immediate and delayed rewards, with a preferential bias toward immediately gratifying activities. After the first self-control task, our attention switches toward more leisurely or exploitative goals. Just because we can engage in self-control and think of our future selves, does not mean that we should do so to the exclusion of our current desires and needs. The more effort that participants spend on the first task, the more important that it is to equalize the balance between short-term and long-term needs by engaging in immediately rewarding tasks. The feelings of fatigue signal that it is time to change tasks to a more rewarding activity.

Summary of Ultimate Causes

Hedonistic drives and approach motivations necessarily evolved to ensure that organisms take care of their immediate needs. Many complex animals, including humans, have also evolved behaviors to prepare for the future: deciding to wait for a reward that will grow in time, or to engage in an effortful activity that should eventually result in a benefit. These long-term preparations are particularly risky when immediate needs are not already satiated, so long-term preparation behaviors that are not accompanied by immediate benefits (such as effortful self-control behaviors) are perceived as increasingly effortful and unpleasant as they continue to be pursued. Eventually, the future-focused behavior is perceived as so effortful and difficult that the behavior is stopped, and an immediately rewarding action is performed instead. This results in a balance being maintained between short-term and long-term needs, between leisure and labor, or between exploitation and exploration. This "ultimate" cause is one piece of how ego depletion and mental fatigue occur in humans today, but this mechanism of trading-off between the two sets of needs is complicated by additional factors of human cognition. In the next section, we discuss how the construal of goals, subjective perception, and autonomy impact the experience of this labor/leisure trade-off, as well as how this mechanism is reflected in the brain.

PROXIMATE CAUSES

Obligatory and Intrinsic Goals

One way that we may construe our behaviors are as actions that we have to do and actions that we want to do. These two types of drives—referred to as *should* and *wants* (Milkman, Rogers, & Bazerman, 2008) or as have-tos and want-tos (Inzlicht et al., 2014)—are personally subjective and dynamic. Whether an action is a *have-to* or a *want-to* is a combination of the when you receive the reward (now or in the future) and whether it is high effort or low effort. In broad terms, we generally want to do things with immediate rewards or things that require no work at all. We generally feel that we should do things that require work, especially for a delayed benefit. Have-to goals are created out of a sense of obligation, either to others or obligation to oneself, while want-to goals are intrinsically meaningful and rewarding as you perform them. Ultimately, we tend to choose to work toward both have-to and want-to goals (Read, Loewenstein, & Kalyanaraman, 1999) in various proportions. Even perceiving the fulfillment of have-to goals can bias people further toward want-to goals (Tobin, Greenaway, McCulloch, & Crittall, 2015).

To complicate the matter, it is not always clear what goal is a have-to and what is a want-to (Sheldon & Elliot, 1998). People's conscious construal of behaviors is not always obvious and does not always match up with researcher's assumptions. For example, saving money for the future is often assumed to be a have-to goal, something that requires self-control and effort (Baumeister, 2002; Milkman et al., 2008). But there are different reasons why people save money, including as a precaution, to enhance self-esteem, or out of pure-miserliness (Canova, Rattazzi, & Webley, 2005). Someone who remembers their growing bank account at the moment when they choose to save money, instead of spend it, might receive an immediate reward of a sense of satisfaction, safety, accomplishment, or even feeling superior to others. On the other hand, personally selected goals and activities are not always intrinsically enjoyable, and sometimes are perceived to be obligations (Sheldon & Elliot, 1998). Even playing video games, the perfect example of a *want-to*, is occasionally reversed; some gamers report "gaming fatigue" where they feel unmotivated to continue their activities, pushed on only to maintain their identity as a gamer, or to play the games they have already paid for (eg, Fahey, 2012).

In the sequential task paradigm, participants first engage in an obligatory, have-to task that is perceived as difficult (Hagger et al., 2010), unpleasant to perform, and provides no direct sense of reward. After engaging in this have-to task, participants are more interested in engaging in their own leisurely and enjoyable want-to tasks. Instead of being focused on doing work, participants become selectively attentive to pleasurable stimuli like pictures of food (Wagner, Altman, Boswell, Kelley, & Heatherton, 2013) or pictures of objects related to rest (Job, Bernecker, Miketta, & Friese, 2015). When they are then subsequently asked to do an additional cognitive control task, their motivation and attentional biases are mismatched with the task requirements. This results in poorer performance on cognitive tasks (eg, Inzlicht & Gutsell, 2007; Vohs, Baumeister, & Schmeichel, 2012) and more selection of immediate rewards such as food (eg, Baumeister et al., 1998; Werle et al., 2014).

Autonomy

Goals may be perceived as "have-to" or "want-to" goals largely on the basis of perceived autonomy. If someone performs a behavior freely, without external pressure, they will feel more intrinsically interested in that action and the behavior will feel less effortful (Ryan & Deci, 1987). When participants are made to feel more autonomous, the initial task feels easier and less fatiguing, so they are more able to engage in self-control subsequently; autonomy manipulations thus significantly moderate ego depletion (Englert & Bertrams, 2015; Moller, Deci, & Ryan, 2006; Muraven, Gagné, & Rosman, 2008). In the reverse scenario, when someone is made to feel explicitly out of control (nonautonomous), their approach motivation and desire to complete their own personal goals increases (Greenaway et al., 2015), paralleling the want-to-seeking motivation of depleted individuals. The role of autonomy and self-determination in depletion is further discussed in Chapter 4.

Perceived (Not Objective) Effort

The critical characteristic that separates fatiguing "have-to" goals from energizing "want-to" goals is whether the activity creates feelings of effort. An activity, such as checking your email, might be simultaneously something that you *have to* do and that you *want to* do. In this case, if you truly want to check your email and enjoy yourself while doing it, then you will not experience it as effortful and it will not cause fatigue. The *want-to* attributes supersedes the *have-to* attributes.

Creation of Subjective Effort

The subjective feeling of effort is dissociable from actual cognitive control and is critical for the creation of fatigue. Some studies find that the degree of depletion is primarily caused by the experience of subjective effort (Christiansen, Cole, & Field, 2012) and can even override whether a participant was originally assigned to a depletion or control condition (Thompson, Sanchez, Wesley, & Reber, 2014). Naccache et al. (2005) reported on a clinical patient with a lesion in the left mediofrontal cortex that encompassed the anterior cingulate cortex (ACC), who experienced no subjective effort even when performing normally on executive control tasks, confirming that phenomenal effort must not necessarily exist whenever inhibition or attention is required. Indeed, the existence of phenomena such as *flow*—times of intense, but enjoyable, concentration on a difficult task (Csikszentmihalyi, 1990)—also shows that not all difficult tasks feel subjectively effortful.

When does something feel effortful? There does seem to be some initial values of phenomenal effort, given constant construal and motivation levels. Subjective effort is differentially experienced for different types of tasks: tasks with high sustained attention are reported to be most effortful, evaluations are moderately effortful, and random action is least effortful (Robinson & Morsella, 2014), and some tasks are more effortful when performed visually or audibly (Szalma et al., 2004). This suggests that some constant cost values are assigned to various executive functions.

When construal of a task changes, however, the feeling of effort changes with it (Laran & Janiszewski, 2011; Deci & Ryan, 1987; Werle et al., 2014). Feelings of effort may be produced when the gained immediate rewards are lower than the standard cost of the executive functions, as balanced by the nucleus accumbens and ACC (Botvinick, Huffstetler, & McGuire, 2009). In other words, the degree of subjective effort may be represented by the following equation:

Objective Demand − Immediate Rewards = Subjective Effort (& Fatigue)

Objectively difficult and demanding activities that are also highly rewarding, such as playing video games (Hoeft, Watson, Kesler, Bettinger, & Reiss, 2008; Koepp et al., 1998), are not perceived as effortful and can thus be performed for hours at a time. An immediate reward does not have to be in the form of food or physical pleasure—feeling compassion for others or succeeding at a competition are similarly rewarding (Fliessbach et al., 2007; Kim et al., 2009). An intrinsically motivated task is perceived as less fatiguing than a have-to task, because the intrinsically motivated task provides immediate feelings of reward. Any task that has immediately perceived rewards—assuming that those rewards are salient—can be effortless. A task that is not immediately enjoyable is then effortful, even if it is rationally deemed to be the best choice for the future.

Subjective Effort Drives Depletion

Particular activities can be construed as either have-to or want-to goals and can be perceived as either effortful or easy. The potentially rewarding characteristics can be either salient or ignored. Research has suggested that the perception of effort, not the objective task characteristics, dictates the levels of depletion. This suggests a motivational account of depletion that is dependent on mental categorization along the continuum of labor (not immediately rewarding) to leisure (rewarding). Critical experiments have manipulated perceptions of Time 1 tasks without changing the actual substance of the task. Laran and Janiszewski (2011) manipulated the construal of a candy-rating task as either fun or obligatory and found that such framing affected participants' self-control. Similarly, Werle et al. (2014) manipulated the framing of physical activity to be considered work (exercise) or fun (scenic walk). The construal of the activity as "work" increased participants' self-reported levels of fatigue, decreased their subjective mood, and resulted in reduced self-control as measured by increased consumption of unhealthy food immediately afterward. In these cases, the external construal of the task likely changed the saliency of different task characteristics—increasing participants' focus on the scenery meant that they found the activity more appealing, compared to participants who focused on the physical exertion.

Self-perceptions of one's own fatigue or energy levels influences subsequent task performance, sometimes overriding the effects of objective previous exertion (see Chapter 10; Clarkson, Hirt, Chapman, & Jia, 2011). A series of experiments have found that falsely believing that an easy task is depleting results in subsequently impaired performance, to the extent that perceptions of exerted effort override the effects of actual exerted effort (Clarkson et al., 2010, 2011). Other research has found that even imagining performing effortful tasks may hurt subsequent task performance when the imagined scenario is realistic and concrete, both temporally and spatially nearby (Macrae et al., 2014).

Additional evidence of the importance of construal comes from work on lay theories of willpower (see Chapter 11; Job et al., 2010). Every person may have their own beliefs about willpower and doing work—while some people believe that work is depleting and fatiguing (a view of limited willpower), some people believe that performing work is energizing and vitalizing (unlimited willpower). Self-reported beliefs in willpower moderate ego depletion as in a self-fulfilling prophecy; people who believe willpower is limited experience depletion more than those who believe in unlimited willpower. Beliefs in unlimited willpower also attenuate self-reported fatigue (Francis, Milyavskaya, & Inzlicht, 2016; Job et al., 2010). Implicit beliefs in willpower can also be experimentally manipulated; priming participants with belief in unlimited willpower increases their self-control and focused attention compared to priming them with limited willpower beliefs (Job et al., 2010; Miller et al., 2012). People with theories of limited willpower—either held or induced—seem to more acutely experience the desire for leisure after effortful labor (Job et al., 2015).

This evidence collectively suggests that one's construal of an action significantly determines the effortfulness and depleting nature of that given activity. This is not surprising, given that basic sensory processes, such as visual and auditory perceptions, are meaningfully influenced by top-down beliefs (Balcetis & Dunning, 2006; Bruner, 1957; Eberhardt, Dasgupta, & Banaszynski, 2003; Gilbert & Sigman, 2007). Preexisting motivations or beliefs impact preconscious processing and what environmental information is available to conscious awareness (Balcetis & Dunning, 2006). If someone expects a task to be fun and enjoyable, they will selectively attend to enjoyable characteristics of the task. If someone expects to feel exhausted and frustrated by a task, they will selectively notice both the difficult aspects of the task and signs that their own internal state is tired. The underlying neural markers of fatigue keep track of fatigue by using this perceived information, not by an objective and static measure of the difficulty of the activity. Perceiving something to be effortful then makes that activity effortful.

Neural Representations of Depletion

The decision to engage in something immediately rewarding or effortful is a computation of values and risk, often done via heuristic short cuts

(Evans & Stanovich, 2013; Inzlicht & Schmeichel, 2013). Critically for the understanding of ego depletion, some of the values involved in the computation change as a function of time-on-task, and specific brain areas become more or less reactive as effort continues to be applied. These neural correlates of mental fatigue and of time-on-task then impact how the outcome of the decision is calculated.

Fatigue Markers

There are converging lines of evidence that the brain monitors fatigue and time-on-task, and that at least some of these neural changes can be observed in depletion paradigms. Both the ACC and the prefrontal cortex are implicated in self-control, and both exhibit less responsiveness with increasing fatigue (Cohen et al., 2007; Kurzban et al., 2013). As a task continues, the ACC becomes progressively less active according to both fMRI BOLD signals (Moeller, Tomasi, Honorio, Volkow, & Goldstein, 2012) and less responsive to errors, as measured by the error-related negativity (Boksem, Meijman, & Loris, 2006; ERN; Lorist et al., 2005), a scalp-recorded electric signal thought to be produced by the ACC in reaction to response conflict (Carter & van Veen, 2007). Diminished ERNs have also been observed in classical ego depletion paradigms, where depleted participants have significantly smaller ERNs in response to errors than control participants (Inzlicht & Gutsell, 2007).

Areas of the prefrontal cortex, also intimately involved in self-control, exhibit reduced BOLD activity during second tasks of the sequential task paradigm (Hedgcock, Vohs, & Rao, 2012; Persson, Welsh, Jonides, & Reuter-Lorenz, 2007), and other measures of engagement such as cortisol levels and pupil diameter also decrease (Hopstaken, van der Linden, Bakker, & Kompier, 2014; Tops, Boksem, Wester, Lorist, & Meijman, 2006). Consistent with our understanding of exploration as a self-control process, frontal areas are also increasingly active when strategically employing exploration instead of exploiting a known source of reward (Cavanagh, Figueroa, Cohen, & Frank, 2012). Lastly, the degree to which the ERN decreases with time-on-task varies as a function of personality traits (Tops & Boksem, 2010), paralleling the findings that some people are more susceptible to depletion effects.

Not only do inhibition-related areas seem to become less responsive as fatigue progresses, but reward-related areas—such as the midbrain and orbitofrontal cortex (OFC)—seem to become increasingly active in response to rewarding stimuli (Heatherton & Wagner, 2012; Wagner et al., 2013). The mesolimbic dopamine pathway is associated with immediate rewards and pleasure, including choosing immediate financial rewards instead of delayed and responding to drug or food cues (McClure et al., 2004; Salamone, Correa, Farrar, & Mingote, 2007). fMRI results have shown increased midbrain activity as fatigue increases and

ACC activity decreases (Moeller et al., 2012), consistent with a balancing account between inhibition and gratification. The OFC, which may monitor the reward value and emotional valence of a situation, also has been observed to have more BOLD activity in depleted participants compared to nondepleted participants (Wagner et al., 2013; also see Chapter 14).

Attention does seem to shift as a result of these changing motivational states. Behaviorally, Schmeichel, Harmon-Jones, and Harmon-Jones (2010) found that depleted individuals were more approach-oriented and had increased attention to reward-relevant stimuli (dollar signs). Vohs et al. (2012) also found that depletion increases the strength of desires (as cited in Wagner et al., 2013), and Job et al. (2015) found that rest-conducive objects were liked more after depletion. Schmeichel presents additional evidence of strengthened impulses in Chapter 6. On the other hand, mental fatigue, and perhaps ego depletion, leads to decreased discrimination between task-relevant and irrelevant stimuli on obligatory self-control tasks (Boksem, Meijman, & Lorist, 2005). Reduced attention toward the experimental demands and more attention to appetitive stimuli may be a primary explanation of reduced performance after the use of self-control.

Dopamine

Depletion and fatigue may reflect changes in dopamine activity or sensitivity, both in areas related to self-control—such as the prefrontal cortex and ACC—and areas involved in reward seeking (Holroyd & Coles, 2002). Experimental and correlational evidence in both humans and rats suggests that dopamine is centrally involved in effort-reward decisions, and that shifting tonic (baseline) levels of dopamine activity can result in changes in self-control behaviors. Rats given dopamine antagonists selectively choose a low-reward/low-effort option (leisure) instead of a high-reward/high-effort action, while rats given dopamine agonists selectively choose the high-effort option (Bardgett, Depenbrock, Downs, & Green, 2009; Salamone, Correa, Farrar, Nunes, & Pardo, 2009). Similarly in humans, artificially decreased dopamine impairs performance at inhibition tasks as well as decreased ACC activity (Luijten et al., 2013), while pharmacologically increased dopamine improves self-control (Nandam et al., 2011). Most applicably, a recent pharmacological study found that increasing dopamine with methylphenidate (Ritalin) eliminates the effect of depletion, and this effect seemed specific to cognitive control instead of due to general increases in alertness (Sripada, Kessler, & Jonides, 2014).

Dopamine has previously been linked to cognitive control and error processing in the ACC; the ERN seems to result from a phasic drop in dopamine, a momentary decrease in the release of dopamine in response to the negative stimuli (Holroyd & Coles, 2002). Interestingly, at the same time that dopamine agonists increase tonic dopamine, they decrease phasic dopamine (Cohen, Braver, & Brown, 2002; Frank & O'Reilly, 2006).

Reducing tonic dopamine with the antagonist haloperidol—which is expected to also increase the phasic spike of dopamine released—weakens the ERN in humans (Zirnheld et al., 2004). The increased phasic dopamine obscures the phasic drop in dopamine that normally results in an ERN. We could speculate, then, that fatigue and depletion, characterized by weakened ERNs and poorer cognitive control, may be partially caused by reduced tonic dopamine in brain areas associated with cognitive control, which in turn reduces sensitivity to phasic drops in dopamine (the proposed source of the ERN).

CONSEQUENCES OF THIS ACCOUNT

Limitless Self-Control?

Often, motivational accounts are taken as a sign that self-control is theoretically limitless. Indeed, in a hypothetical situation where the motivation to perform self-control rose exponentially, to constantly exceed the motivational pressure to engage in leisurely activities, then self-control might continue indefinitely. However, practical limitations make this unlikely to occur in the real world (or even in experimental settings). First, the shift in motivation from have-to to want-to goals is not binary—the desire to seek intrinsically rewarding activities likely continues to increase the longer it is denied, while the feeling of fatigue also increases constantly (eg, linearly across a 4-h task; Wascher et al., 2014). Thus, in situations where the external incentive to engage in self-control remains constant (eg, for air traffic controllers) eventually the motivation toward immediate pleasure will overwhelm even the greatest motivation. Second, the shifts in motivation drive a change in attention away from potential external motivating factors. Even if increasing amounts of money and importance are linked to completing a self-control task, the person will attend less and less to those considerations and be increasingly distracted by their desire to switch tasks to something more intrinsically rewarding. Third, some problems that may sometimes be attributed to ego depletion—such as attention lapses during monotonous vigilance tasks such as truck driving—are exacerbated by problems such as sleepiness (for differentiation from depletion see Vohs, Glass, Maddox, & Markman, 2010) or the task's monotony causing habituation to external signals (Pattyn et al., 2008).

The motivational process account of depletion does not mean that self-control will be limitless in practice, at least not without pharmacological intervention. The shift in motivation toward intrinsically rewarding and leisurely activities likely becomes continuously stronger as it is denied, and "willing" oneself to continue in self-control will still eventually be overcome. However, the shifting-priorities process account also suggests that when a given task is perceived as leisurely, intrinsically rewarding, and fun, it will not be depleting. Thus, convincing reconstrual of a given activity may help increase persistence and performance.

Not Enough Effortful Labor? Contrafreeloading

The shifting-priorities process model revolves around maintaining a balance between immediate rewards and future self-control behaviors. Depletion and fatigue occur after an excess of future-oriented self-control behaviors, but what does the opposite phenomena look like? Can excess pleasure or immediate gratification cause increased motivation for engaging in effortful tasks? There are situations where human and nonhuman animals choose the more effortful option, opposing the law of least effort. For example, rats, pigs, and bears sometimes choose to press a lever (perform work) to eat food, instead of eating the identical, freely available food (for review see Inglis, Forkman, & Lazarus, 1997; Osborne, 1977). Monkeys will sometimes repeatedly press a screen to watch a movie, even when the identical movies are freely available (Ogura, 2011). This behavior, called contrafreeloading, goes directly against the principle of effort avoidance.

Even humans sometimes engage in contrafreeloading, preferring to eat snacks that require a button press, reminiscent of Pez candy dispensers, instead of eating a snack from a bowl (Tarte, 1981). The preference for the mildly effortful task seems to be due to the novelty of the activity—and indeed, it has been theorized that contrafreeloading occurs so that animals can gain more information about their environment and their various food sources, which is ultimately an example of exploration future-oriented behaviors (Inglis et al., 1997; Inglis, Langton, Forkman, & Lazarus, 2001). Always taking food from the easily available source would perpetuate the lack of knowledge about alternate sources and might be detrimental to the future self. The pursuit of a balance between exploration and exploitation results in novelty seeking and exploration, even though it requires additional work. Sometimes, a desire for autonomy and control can also override the law of less work, such as when people choose to complete a task manually instead of have a computer do it automatically (Osiurak, Wagner, Djerbi, & Navarro, 2013). Fatigue is more commonly experienced than contrafreeloading, due to our innate bias toward the immediately pleasurable, but there is some evidence that the priority-balancing mechanism is bidirectional.

ALTERNATIVE ACCOUNTS

Other models of ego depletion exist and many have strongly influenced the theory presented here. The field of self-control research is gradually acknowledging the central role that motivation plays in depletion, and others have proposed models based on decision-making and motivational research. Here we briefly discuss two common alternative accounts of ego depletion and the relative strengths of the shifting-priorities process model.

Resource Model

The original, most widely known theory is the resource (or strength) model of self-control. Baumeister et al. (1998) first understood ego depletion as the result of a limited self-control resource that existed in the brain, which all cognitive control tasks drew upon. Once someone performed a previous self-control task, they had less of the resource available for the second self-control task. Although widely appealing and embraced, the original resource model was not compatible with subsequent research that showed how motivational and perceptual factors eliminate or strengthen the depletion effect, as discussed earlier (Inzlicht & Schmeichel, 2012). If self-control relied on a physical resource, then receiving payment (Muraven & Slessareva, 2003), watching videos (Tice et al., 2007), or merely believing in unlimited willpower (Job et al., 2010) should not eliminate the depletion effect. The revised strength model of self-control states that depletion symptoms occur to preemptively ensure that the self-control resource never does run out, and that daily experienced fatigue is mediated by this motivation to conserve the resource (Baumeister, 2014). Given that the physical content of the self-control research has yet to be identified, alternative motivational models that do not rely on a resource may be more useful to lead researchers in creating novel hypotheses and predictions (for additional response, see Inzlicht & Berkman, 2015; Inzlicht et al., 2014).

Opportunity Cost Model and Decision-Making Models

The opportunity cost model, proposed by Kurzban et al. (2013), states that mental effort is an indicator of the opportunity cost of engaging in one's current cognitive task, given that each moment spent on that task is unavailable to be spent on other activities. When the benefits of a given activity no longer outweigh the costs (of forgone activities), then we disengage from that activity in favor of an alternative. Although the opportunity cost model has greatly contributed to other motivational accounts of depletion, a strict benefit–cost calculation cannot account for experimental evidence in the depletion and mental-effort literature. In particular, the explicit comparison between the current task and potentially available alternative tasks seems problematic. For example, people do not always choose to engage in the most "rational" behavior; Kool & Botvinick, 2014 found that participants disproportionally choose an easier task when the pay of a laborious task increased, diverging from the predicted outcome of a cost–benefit calculation and suggesting that there is an inherent drive toward leisure regardless of the alternative opportunities available.

Additionally, the opportunity cost model and other decision-making models only partially explain the change in utility over time, particularly across two-task designs. These models state that performance decrements on the second task are due to participants having gradually fulfilled obligations to the researchers; however, failures of self-control due to depletion also seem to happen outside of laboratory experiments (eg, Job et al., 2010; Werle et al., 2014). Decision-making models further explain that performance declines are due to decreasing utility of that activity, but then why is the utility of a second self-control task dependent on one's previous engagement in a prior unrelated self-control task? We think that the shifting-motivation process model better addresses the change in task utility over time, particularly across tasks, and is especially compatible with evidence of neurological and motivational changes that occur as fatigue progresses.

Broader models of self-control and decision-making (eg, Chapters 13 and 19) contribute much to our understanding of when self-control will or will not be engaged in; human behavior is impacted by numerous variables not discussed here. The shifting-priorities model is complementary with these frameworks, and specifically fills a gap by explicitly addressing why the "control capacity" changes after an effortful task, why fatigue occurs.

CONCLUSION

Humans have multiple priorities—we care about our current happiness and pleasure a great deal, but we are also interested in maintaining stability and happiness for the future. Finding the balance between immediate gratification and immediate discomfort for future benefit is a long-experienced problem. The problem occurs when an animal decides between exploiting resource and exploring for information, or when a student decides between a comfortable couch and an uncomfortable study desk. Generally, we have an aversion to work that is effortful and not intrinsically rewarding (*labor* or *have-tos*). It is evolutionarily disadvantageous to spend the majority of your time planning for the future, particularly at the cost of taking care of your current self. Thus, although we can engage in laborious cognitive–control activities when they are deemed appropriate, they are experienced as effortful and gradually lead to fatigue. This fatigue, or depletion, further shifts our motivation away from laborious extrinsically motivated activities and toward things that make us feel good—things that we want to do—to restore the balance.

Whether something is experienced as fatiguing or not, however, depends on whether the activity is truly rewardless. Feeling entertainment, competition, compassion, or interest in an activity makes it rewarding and the use of executive functions is no longer experienced as effortful. Only when an activity is done out of a sense of obligation, without any directly experienced satisfaction, is it fatiguing. Effort is situationally construed, but all of us have perceived limits on how much effort we are willing to exert before it is time for a break. Although there is no biological limit to self-control, the more effort that is experienced and the more fatigue that is builtup, the stronger the urge toward immediately pleasing activities and the more attention is directed toward pleasurable stimuli. Effortful self-control has practical limits in the real world. Effortless self-regulation, good habits, and engaging in difficult but equally rewarding activities, however—those are limitless.

References

Adriaanse, M. A., Kroese, F. M., Gillebaart, M., & De Ridder, D. T. D. (2014). Effortless inhibition: habit mediates the relation between self-control and unhealthy snack consumption. *Frontiers in Psychology*, 5, 444. http://dx.doi.org/10.3389/fpsyg.2014.00444.

Balcetis, E., & Dunning, D. (2006). See what you want to see: motivational influences on visual perception. *Journal of Personality and Social Psychology*, 91(4), 612–625. http://dx.doi.org/10.1037/0022-3514.91.4.612.

Bardgett, M. E., Depenbrock, M., Downs, N., & Green, L. (2009). Dopamine modulates effort-based decision-making in rats. *Behavioral Neuroscience*, 123(2), 242–251. http://dx.doi.org/10.1037/a0014625.Dopamine.

Baumeister, R. F. (2002). Yielding to temptation: self-control failure, impulsive purchasing, and consumer behavior. *Journal of Consumer Research*, 28(4), 670–676. http://dx.doi.org/10.1086/338209.

Baumeister, R. F. (2014). Self-regulation, ego depletion, and inhibition. *Neuropsychologia*. http://dx.doi.org/10.1016/j.neuropsychologia.2014.08.012.

Baumeister, R. F., Bratslavsky, E., Muraven, M., & Tice, D. M. (1998). Ego depletion: is the active self a limited resource? *Journal of Personality and Social Psychology*, 74(5), 1252–1265.

Boksem, M. A. S., Meijman, T. F., & Lorist, M. M. (2005). Effects of mental fatigue on attention: an ERP study. *Brain Research. Cognitive Brain Research*, 25(1), 107–116. http://dx.doi.org/10.1016/j.cogbrainres.2005.04.011.

Boksem, M. A. S., Meijman, T. F., & Lorist, M. M. (2006). Mental fatigue, motivation andaction monitoring. *Biological Psychology*, 72(2), 123–132. http://dx.doi.org/10.1016/j.biopsycho.2005.08.007.

Boksem, M. A. S., & Tops, M. (2008). Mental fatigue: costs and benefits. *Brain Research Reviews*, 59(1), 125–139. http://dx.doi.org/10.1016/j.brainresrev.2008.07.001.

Botvinick, M. M., Huffstetler, S., & McGuire, J. T. (2009). Effort discounting in human nucleus accumbens. *Behavioural Neuroscience*, 9(1), 22. http://dx.doi.org/10.3758/CABN.9.1.16.Effort.

Bruner, J. S. (1957). On perceptual readiness. *Psychological Review*, 64(2), 123–152. http://dx.doi.org/10.1037/h0043805.

Canova, L., Rattazzi, A. M. M., & Webley, P. (2005). The hierarchical structure of saving motives. *Journal of Economic Psychology*, 26(1), 21–34. http://dx.doi.org/10.1016/j.joep.2003.08.007.

Carter, C. S., & van Veen, V. (2007). Anterior cingulate cortex and conflict detection: an update of theory and data. *Cognitive, Affective & Behavioral Neuroscience, 7*(4), 367–379. http://dx.doi.org/10.3758/cabn.7.4.367.

Carter, E. C., Kofler, L. M., Forster, D. E., & Mccullough, M. E. (2015). A series of meta-analytic tests of the depletion effect: self-control does not seem to rely on a limited resource. *Journal of Experimental Psychology: General, 144*(4), 796–815.

Cavanagh, J. F., Figueroa, C. M., Cohen, M. X., & Frank, M. J. (2012). Frontal theta reflects uncertainty and unexpectedness during exploration and exploitation. *Cerebral Cortex, 22*(11), 2575–2586. http://dx.doi.org/10.1093/cercor/bhr332.

Christiansen, P., Cole, J. C., & Field, M. (2012). Ego depletion increases ad-lib alcohol consumption: investigating cognitive mediators and moderators. *Experimental and Clinical Psychopharmacology, 20*(2), 118–128. http://dx.doi.org/10.1037/a0026623.

Clarkson, J. J., Hirt, E. R., Chapman, D. A., & Jia, L. (2011). The impact of illusory fatigue on executive control. Do perceptions of depletion impair working memory capacity? *Social Psychological and Personality Science, 2*(3), 231–238. http://dx.doi.org/10.1177/1948550610386628.

Clarkson, J. J., Hirt, E. R., Jia, L., & Alexander, M. B. (2010). When perception is more than reality: the effects of perceived versus actual resource depletion on self-regulatory behavior. *Journal of Personality and Social Psychology, 98*(1), 29–46. http://dx.doi.org/10.1037/a0017539.

Cohen, J. D., Braver, T. S., & Brown, J. W. (2002). Computational perspectives on dopamine function in prefrontal cortex. *Current Opinion in Neurobiology, 12*(2), 223–229. http://dx.doi.org/10.1016/S0959-4388(02)00314-8.

Cohen, J. D., McClure, S. M., & Yu, A. J. (2007). Should I stay or should I go? How the human brain manages the trade-off between exploitation and exploration. *Philosophical Transactions of the Royal Society of London. Series B, Biological Sciences, 362*(1481), 933–942. http://dx.doi.org/10.1098/rstb.2007.2098.

Converse, P. D., & Deshon, R. P. (2009). A tale of two tasks: reversing the self-regulatory resource depletion effect. *The Journal of Applied Psychology, 94*(5), 1318–1324. http://dx.doi.org/10.1037/a0014604.

Csikszentmihalyi, M. (1990). *Flow: The psychology of optimal experience*. New York: Harper Perennial.

Deci, E. L., & Ryan, R. M. (1987). The support of autonomy and the control of behavior. *Journal of Personality and Social Psychology, 53*(6), 1024–1037. http://dx.doi.org/10.1037//0022-3514.53.6.1024.

Dewitte, S., Bruyneel, S., & Geyskens, K. (2009). Self-regulating enhances self-regulation in subsequent consumer decisions involving similar response conflicts. *Journal of Consumer Research, 36*(3), 394–405. http://dx.doi.org/10.1086/598615.

Dorris, D. C., Power, D. A., & Kenefick, E. (2012). Investigating the effects of ego depletion on physical exercise routines of athletes. *Psychology of Sport and Exercise, 13*(2), 118–125. http://dx.doi.org/10.1016/j.psychsport.2011.10.004.

Eberhardt, J. L., Dasgupta, N., & Banaszynski, T. L. (2003). Believing is seeing: the effects of racial labels and implicit beliefs on face perception. *Personality & Social Psychology Bulletin, 29*(3), 360–370. http://dx.doi.org/10.1177/0146167202250215.

Englert, C., & Bertrams, A. (2015). Autonomy as a protective factor against the detrimental effects of ego depletion on tennis serve accuracy under pressure. *International Journal of Sport and Exercise Psychology, 13*(2), 121–131. http://dx.doi.org/10.1080/1612197X.2014.932828.

Evans, T. A., & Beran, M. J. (2007). Delay of gratification and delay maintenance by rhesus macaques (*Macaca mulatta*). *The Journal of General Psychology, 134*(2), 199–216. http://dx.doi.org/10.3200/GENP.134.2.199-216.

Evans, J. S. B.T., & Stanovich, K. E. (2013). Dual-process theories of higher cognition: advancing the debate. *Perspectives on Psychological Science, 8*(3), 223–241. http://dx.doi.org/10.1177/1745691612460685.

Fahey, M. (2012). *Sometimes you just get tired of playing video games*. Kotaku. Retrieved from http://kotaku.com/5926474/sometimes-you-just-get-tired-of-playing-video-games.

Fliessbach, K., Weber, B., Trautner, P., Dohmen, T., Sunde, U., Elger, C. E., ... Falk, A. (2007). Social comparison affects reward-related brain activity in the human ventral striatum. *Science*, *318*(5854), 1305–1308. http://dx.doi.org/10.1126/science.1145876.

Francis, Z., Milyavskaya, M., & Inzlicht, M. (2016). A novel within-subject paradigm to examine self-control's refractory period. Toronto, Canada: Department of Psychology, University of Toronto (Unpublished manuscript).

Frank, M. J., & O'Reilly, R. C. (2006). A mechanistic account of striatal dopamine function in human cognition: psychopharmacological studies with cabergoline and haloperidol. *Behavioral Neuroscience*, *120*(3), 497–517. http://dx.doi.org/10.1037/0735-7044.120.3.497.

Galla, B. M., & Duckworth, A. L. (2015). More than resisting temptation : beneficial habits mediate the relationship between self-control and positive life outcomes. *Journal of Personality and Social Psychology*, *109*(3), 508–525.

Gilbert, C. D., & Sigman, M. (2007). Brain states: top-down influences in sensory processing. *Neuron*, *54*(5), 677–696. http://dx.doi.org/10.1016/j.neuron.2007.05.019.

Gillebaart, M., & De Ridder, D. T. D. (2015). Effortless self-control: a novel perspective on response conflict strategies in trait self-control. *Social and Personality Psychology Compass*, *9*(2), 88–99. http://dx.doi.org/10.1111/spc3.12160.

Greenaway, K. H., Storrs, K. R., Philipp, M. C., Louis, W. R., Hornsey, M. J., & Vohs, K. D. (2015). Loss of control stimulates approach motivation. *Journal of Experimental Social Psychology*, *56*, 235–241. http://dx.doi.org/10.1016/j.jesp.2014.10.009.

Hagger, M. S., Wood, C., Stiff, C., & Chatzisarantis, N. L. D. (2010). Ego depletion and the strength model of self-control: a meta-analysis. *Psychological Bulletin*, *136*(4), 495–525. http://dx.doi.org/10.1037/a0019486.

Hariri, A. R., Brown, S. M., Williamson, D. E., Flory, J. D., de Wit, H., & Manuck, S. B. (2006). Preference for immediate over delayed rewards is associated with magnitude of ventral striatal activity. *The Journal of Neuroscience : The Official Journal of the Society for Neuroscience*, *26*(51), 13213–13217. http://dx.doi.org/10.1523/JNEUROSCI.3446-06.2006.

Hayden, B. Y., Pearson, J. M., & Platt, M. L. (2011). Neuronal basis of sequential foraging decisions in a patchy environment. *Nature Neuroscience*, *14*(7), 933–939. http://dx.doi.org/10.1038/nn.2856.

Heatherton, T. F., & Wagner, D. D. (2012). Cognitive neuroscience of self-regulation failure. *Trends in Cognitive Sciences*, *15*(3), 132–139. http://dx.doi.org/10.1016/j.tics.2010.12.005.Cognitive.

Hedgcock, W. M., Vohs, K. D., & Rao, A. R. (2012). Reducing self-control depletion effects through enhanced sensitivity to implementation: evidence from fMRI and behavioral studies. *Journal of Consumer Psychology*, *22*(4), 486–495. http://dx.doi.org/10.1016/j.jcps.2012.05.008.

Hoeft, F., Watson, C. L., Kesler, S. R., Bettinger, K. E., & Reiss, A. L. (2008). Gender differences in the mesocorticolimbic system during computer game-play. *Journal of Psychiatric Research*, *42*(4), 253–258. http://dx.doi.org/10.1016/j.jpsychires.2007.11.010.

Holroyd, C. B., & Coles, M. G. H. (2002). The neural basis of human error processing: reinforcement learning, dopamine, and the error-related negativity. *Psychological Review*, *109*(4), 679–709. http://dx.doi.org/10.1037//0033-295X.109.4.679.

Hopstaken, J. F., van der Linden, D., Bakker, A. B., & Kompier, M. a. J. (2014). A multifaceted investigation of the link between mental fatigue and task disengagement. *Psychophysiology*, *52*(3), 305–315. http://dx.doi.org/10.1111/psyp.12339.

Hull, C. (1943). *Principles of behaviour*. New York: Appleton–Century–Crofts.

Inglis, I. R., Forkman, B., & Lazarus, J. (1997). Free food or earned food? A review and fuzzy model of contrafreeloading. *Animal Behaviour*, *53*(6), 1171–1191. http://dx.doi.org/10.1006/anbe.1996.0320.

Inglis, I. R., Langton, S., Forkman, B., & Lazarus, J. (2001). An information primacy model of exploratory and foraging behaviour. *Animal Behaviour*, *62*(3), 543–557. http://dx.doi.org/10.1006/anbe.2001.1780.

Inzlicht, M., Bartholow, B. D., & Hirsh, J. B. (2015). Emotional foundations of cognitive control. *Trends in Cognitive Sciences*, *19*(3), 1–7. http://dx.doi.org/10.1016/j.tics.2015.01.004.

Inzlicht, M., & Berkman, E. (2015). Six questions for the resource model of control (and some answers). *Social and Personality Psychology Compass*, 9(10), 511–524.

Inzlicht, M., & Gutsell, J. N. (2007). Running on empty: neural signals for self-control failure. *Psychological Science*, 18(11), 933–937. http://dx.doi.org/10.1111/j.1467-9280.2007.02004.x.

Inzlicht, M., & Schmeichel, B. J. (2012). What is ego depletion? Toward a mechanistic revision of the resource model of self-control. *Perspectives on Psychological Science*, 7(5), 450–463. http://dx.doi.org/10.1177/1745691612454134.

Inzlicht, M., & Schmeichel, B. J. (2013). Beyond simple utility in predicting self-control fatigue: a proximate alternative to the opportunity cost model. *The Behavioral and Brain Sciences*, 36(6), 695–696. http://dx.doi.org/10.1017/S0140525X13001076 discussion 707–726.

Inzlicht, M., Schmeichel, B. J., & Macrae, C. N. (2014). Why self-control seems (but may not be) limited. *Trends in Cognitive Sciences*, 18(3), 127–133. http://dx.doi.org/10.1016/j.tics.2013.12.009.

Job, V., Bernecker, K., Miketta, S., & Friese, M. (2015). Implicit theories about willpower predict the activation of a rest goal following self-control exertion. *Journal of Personality and Social Psychology*, 109(4), 694–706. http://dx.doi.org/10.1037/pspp0000042.

Job, V., Dweck, C., & Walton, G. M. (2010). Ego depletion—Is it all in your head? Implicit theories about willpower affect self-regulation. *Psychological Science*, 21(11), 1686–1693. http://dx.doi.org/10.1177/0956797610384745.

Kim, J. W., Kim, S. E., Kim, J. J., Jeong, B., Park, C. H., Son, A. R., ... Ki, S. W. (2009). Compassionate attitude towards others' suffering activates the mesolimbic neural system. *Neuropsychologia*, 47(10), 2073–2081. http://dx.doi.org/10.1016/j.neuropsychologia.2009.03.017.

Koepp, M., Gunn, R., Lawrence, A., Cunningham, V., Dagher, A., Brooks, D., ... Grasby, P. (1998). Evidence for striatal dopamine release during a video game. *Nature*, 393, 453–455.

Kool, W., & Botvinick, M. (2014). A labor/leisure tradeoff in cognitive control. *Journal of Experimental Psychology: General*, 143(1), 131–141. http://dx.doi.org/10.1037/a0031048.

Kool, W., McGuire, J. T., Rosen, Z. B., & Botvinick, M. M. (2010). Decision making and the avoidance of cognitive demand. *Journal of Experimental Psychology. General*, 139(4), 665–682. http://dx.doi.org/10.1037/a0020198.

Kurzban, R. (2016). The sense of effort. *Current Opinion in Psychology*, 7, 67–70. http://dx.doi.org/10.1016/j.copsyc.2015.08.003.

Kurzban, R., Duckworth, A. L., Kable, J. W., & Myers, J. (2013). An opportunity cost model of subjective effort and task performance. *The Behavioral and Brain Sciences*, 36(6), 661–679. http://dx.doi.org/10.1017/S0140525X12003196.

Laran, J., & Janiszewski, C. (2011). Work or fun? How task construal and completion influence regulatory behavior. *The Journal of Consumer Research*, 37(6), 967–983. http://dx.doi.org/10.1086/656576.

Lorist, M. M., Boksem, M. A. S., & Ridderinkhof, K. R. (2005). Impaired cognitive control and reduced cingulate activity during mental fatigue. *Cognitive Brain Research*, 24(2), 199–205. http://dx.doi.org/10.1016/j.cogbrainres.2005.01.018.

Lorist, M. M., Klein, M., Nieuwenhuis, S., De Jong, R., Mulder, G., & Meijman, T. F. (2000). Mental fatigue and task control: planning and preparation. *Psychophysiology*, 37(5), 614–625. http://dx.doi.org/10.1111/1469-8986.3750614.

Luijten, M., Veltman, D. J., Hester, R., Smits, M., Nijs, I. M. T., Pepplinkhuizen, L., ... Franken, I. H. A. (2013). The role of dopamine in inhibitory control in smokers and non-smokers: a pharmacological fMRI study. *European Neuropsychopharmacology*, 23(10), 1247–1256. http://dx.doi.org/10.1016/j.euroneuro.2012.10.017.

MacLean, E. L., Hare, B., Nunn, C. L., Addessi, E., Amici, F., Anderson, R. C., ... Zhao, Y. (2014). The evolution of self-control. *Proceedings of the National Academy of Sciences of the United States of America*, 111(20), E2140–E2148. http://dx.doi.org/10.1073/pnas.1323533111.

Macrae, C. N., Christian, B. M., Golubickis, M., Karanasiou, M., Troksiarova, L., McNamara, D. L., ... Miles, L. K. (2014). When do I wear me out? Mental simulation and the diminution of self-control. *Journal of Experimental Psychology. General*, 143(4), 1755–1764. http://dx.doi.org/10.1037/a0036100.

Marcora, S. M., Staiano, W., & Manning, V. (2009). Mental fatigue impairs physical performance in humans. *Journal of Applied Physiology, 106*(3), 857–864. http://dx.doi.org/10.1152/japplphysiol.91324.2008.

Matta, A., Gonçalves, F., & Bizarro, L. (2012). Delay discounting: concepts and measures. *Psychology and Neuroscience, 5*(2), 135–146. http://dx.doi.org/10.3922/j.psns.2012.2.03.

McClure, S. M., Laibson, D. I., Loewenstein, G., & Cohen, J. D. (2004). Separate neural systems value immediate and delayed monetary rewards. *Science (New York, N.Y.), 306*(5695), 503–507. http://dx.doi.org/10.1126/science.1100907.

Milkman, K. L., Rogers, T., & Bazerman, M. H. (2008). Harnessing our inner angels and demons: what we have learned about want-should conflicts and how that knowledge can help us reduce short-sighted decision making. *Perspectives on Psychological Science, 3*(4), 324–338. http://dx.doi.org/10.1111/j.1745-6924.2008.00083.x.

Miller, E. M., Walton, G. M., Dweck, C. S., Job, V., Trzesniewski, K. H., & McClure, S. M. (2012). Theories of willpower affect sustained learning. *PLoS One, 7*(6), e38680. http://dx.doi.org/10.1371/journal.pone.0038680.

Milyavskaya, M., Inzlicht, M., Hope, N., & Koestner, R. (2015). Saying "No" to temptation : want-to motivation improves self-regulation by reducing temptation rather than by increasing self-control. *Journal of Personality and Social Psychology, 109*, 677–693.

Moeller, S. J., Tomasi, D., Honorio, J., Volkow, N. D., & Goldstein, R. Z. (2012). Dopaminergic involvement during mental fatigue in health and cocaine addiction. *Translational Psychiatry, 2*(10), e176. http://dx.doi.org/10.1038/tp.2012.110.

Molden, D. C., Hui, C. M., Scholer, A. A., Meier, B. P., Noreen, E. E., D'Agostino, P. R., … Martin, V. (2012). Motivational versus metabolic effects of carbohydrates on self-control. *Psychological Science, 23*(10), 1137–1144. http://dx.doi.org/10.1177/0956797612439069.

Moller, A. C., Deci, E. L., & Ryan, R. M. (2006). Choice and ego-depletion: the moderating role of autonomy. *Personality & Social Psychology Bulletin, 32*(8), 1024–1036. http://dx.doi.org/10.1177/0146167206288008.

Muraven, M., Gagné, M., & Rosman, H. (2008). Helpful self-control: autonomy support, vitality, and depletion. *Journal of Experimental Social Psychology, 44*(3), 573–585. http://dx.doi.org/10.1016/j.jesp.2007.10.008.

Muraven, M., & Slessareva, E. (2003). Mechanisms of self-control failure: motivation and limited resources. *Personality and Social Psychology Bull, 29*(7), 894–906. http://dx.doi.org/10.1177/0146167203253209.

Naccache, L., Dehaene, S., Cohen, L., Habert, M.-O., Guichart-Gomez, E., Galanaud, D., … Willer, J.-C. (2005). Effortless control: executive attention and conscious feeling of mental effort are dissociable. *Neuropsychologia, 43*(9), 1318–1328. http://dx.doi.org/10.1016/j.neuropsychologia.2004.11.024.

Nandam, L. S., Hester, R., Wagner, J., Cummins, T. D. R., Garner, K., Dean, A. J., … Bellgrove, M. A. (2011). Methylphenidate but not atomoxetine or citalopram modulates inhibitory control and response time variability. *Biological Psychiatry, 69*(9), 902–904. http://dx.doi.org/10.1016/j.biopsych.2010.11.014.

Ogura, T. (2011). Contrafreeloading and the value of control over visual stimuli in Japanese macaques (*Macaca fuscata*). *Animal Cognition, 14*(3), 427–431. http://dx.doi.org/10.1007/s10071-010-0377-y.

Osborne, S. R. (1977). The free food (contrafreeloading) phenomenon: a review and analysis. *Animal Learning & Behavior, 5*(3), 221–235. http://dx.doi.org/10.3758/BF03209232.

Osiurak, F., Wagner, C., Djerbi, S., & Navarro, J. (2013). To do it or to let an automatic tool do it? The priority of control over effort. *Experimental Psychology, 60*(6), 453–468. http://dx.doi.org/10.1027/1618-3169/a000219.

Pattyn, N., Neyt, X., Henderickx, D., & Soetens, E. (2008). Psychophysiological investigation of vigilance decrement: boredom or cognitive fatigue? *Physiology & Behavior, 93*(1–2), 369–378. http://dx.doi.org/10.1016/j.physbeh.2007.09.016.

Persson, J., Welsh, K. M., Jonides, J., & Reuter-Lorenz, P. A. (2007). Cognitive fatigue of executive processes: interaction between interference resolution tasks. *Neuropsychologia, 45*(7), 1571–1579. http://dx.doi.org/10.1055/s-0029-1237430.Imprinting.

Pocheptsova, A., Amir, O., Dhar, R., & Baumeister, R. F. (2008). Deciding without resources: psychological depletion and choice in context. *Journal of Marketing Research, 46,* 344–355.

Read, D., Loewenstein, G., & Kalyanaraman, S. (1999). Mixing virtue and vice: combining the immediacy effect and the diversification heuristic. *Journal of Behavioral Decision Making, 12*(4), 257–273. http://dx.doi.org/10.1002/(SICI)1099-0771(199912)12:4<257::AID-BDM327>3.0.CO;2–6.

Robinson, M. M., & Morsella, E. (2014). The subjective effort of everyday mental tasks: attending, assessing, and choosing. *Motivation and Emotion, 38*(6), 832–843. http://dx.doi.org/10.1007/s11031-014-9441-2.

Salamone, J. D., Correa, M., Farrar, A., & Mingote, S. M. (2007). Effort-related functions of nucleus accumbens dopamine and associated forebrain circuits. *Psychopharmacology, 191*(3), 461–482. http://dx.doi.org/10.1007/s00213-006-0668-9.

Salamone, J. D., Correa, M., Farrar, A. M., Nunes, E. J., & Pardo, M. (September 2009). Dopamine, behavioral economics, and effort. *Frontiers in Behavioral Neuroscience, 3,* 13. http://dx.doi.org/10.3389/neuro.08.013.2009.

Saunders, B., & Inzlicht, M. (2015). Vigour and fatigue: how variation in affect underlies effective self-control. In T. Braver (Ed.), *Motivation and cognitive control.* New York: Taylor & Francis/Routledge.

Schmeichel, B. J., Harmon-Jones, C., & Harmon-Jones, E. (2010). Exercising self-control increases approach motivation. *Journal of Personality and Social Psychology, 99*(1), 162–173. http://dx.doi.org/10.1037/a0019797.

Seashore, C. E. (1904). The experimental study of mental fatigue. *Psychological Bulletin, I*(4), 97–101.

Sheldon, K. M., & Elliot, A. J. (1998). Not all personal goals are personal: comparing autonomous and controlled reasons for goals as predictors of effort and attainment. *Personality & Social Psychology Bulletin, 24*(5), 546–557. http://dx.doi.org/10.1177/0146167298245010.

Sripada, C., Kessler, D., & Jonides, J. (2014). Methylphenidate blocks effort-induced depletion of regulatory control in healthy volunteers. *Psychological Science, 25*(6), 1227–1234. http://dx.doi.org/10.1177/0956797614526415.

Stevens, J. R., Hallinan, E. V., & Hauser, M. D. (2005). The ecology and evolution of patience in two New World monkeys. *Biology Letters, 1*(2), 223–226. http://dx.doi.org/10.1098/rsbl.2004.0285.

Szalma, J. L., Warm, J. S., Matthews, G., Dember, W. N., Weiler, E. M., Meier, A., … Eggemeier, F. T. (2004). Effects of sensory modality and task duration on performance, workload, and stress in sustained attention. *Human Factors: The Journal of the Human Factors and Ergonomics Society, 46*(2), 219–233.

Tarte, R. D. (1981). Contrafreeloading in humans. *Psychological Reports, 49,* 859–866. http://dx.doi.org/10.2466/pr0.1981.49.3.859.

Thompson, K. R., Sanchez, D. J., Wesley, A. H., & Reber, P. J. (2014). Ego depletion impairs implicit learning. *PLoS One, 9*(10), e109370. http://dx.doi.org/10.1371/journal.pone.0109370.

Thorndike, E. (1900). Mental fatigue I. *Psychological Review, 7*(6), 547–579. http://dx.doi.org/10.1126/science.9.229.712.

Tice, D. M., Baumeister, R. F., Shmueli, D., & Muraven, M. (2007). Restoring the self: positive affect helps improve self-regulation following ego depletion. *Journal of Experimental Social Psychology, 43*(3), 379–384. http://dx.doi.org/10.1016/j.jesp.2006.05.007.

Tobin, S. J., Greenaway, K. H., McCulloch, K. C., & Crittall, M. E. (2015). The role of motivation for rewards in vicarious goal satiation. *Journal of Experimental Social Psychology, 60,* 137–143. http://dx.doi.org/10.1016/j.jesp.2015.05.010.

Tops, M., & Boksem, M. A. S. (2010). Absorbed in the task: personality measures predict engagement during task performance as tracked by error negativity and asymmetrical frontal activity. *Cognitive, Affective & Behavioral Neuroscience, 10*(4), 441–453. http://dx.doi.org/10.3758/CABN.10.4.441.

Tops, M., Boksem, M. A. S., Wester, A. E., Lorist, M. M., & Meijman, T. F. (2006). Task engagement and the relationships between the error-related negativity, agreeableness, behavioral shame proneness and cortisol. *Psychoneuroendocrinology, 31*(7), 847–858. http://dx.doi.org/10.1016/j.psyneuen.2006.04.001.

Vohs, K. D., Baumeister, R. F., & Schmeichel, B. J. (2012). Motivation, personal beliefs, and limited resources all contribute to self-control. *Journal of Experimental Social Psychology, 48*(4), 943–947. http://dx.doi.org/10.1016/j.jesp.2012.03.002.

Vohs, K. D., Glass, B. D., Maddox, W. T., & Markman, A. B. (2010). Ego depletion is not just fatigue: evidence from a total sleep deprivation experiment. *Social Psychological and Personality Science, 2*(2), 166–173. http://dx.doi.org/10.1177/1948550610386123.

Wagner, D. D., Altman, M., Boswell, R. G., Kelley, W. M., & Heatherton, T. F. (2013). Self-regulatory depletion enhances neural responses to rewards and impairs top-down control. *Psychological Science.* http://dx.doi.org/10.1177/0956797613492985.

Warm, J. S., Parasuraman, R., & Matthews, G. (2008). Vigilance requires hard mental work and is stressful. *Human Factors: The Journal of the Human Factors and Ergonomics Society, 50*(3), 433–441. http://dx.doi.org/10.1518/001872008X312152.

Wascher, E., Rasch, B., Sänger, J., Hoffmann, S., Schneider, D., Rinkenauer, G., ... Gutberlet, I. (2014). Frontal theta activity reflects distinct aspects of mental fatigue. *Biological Psychology, 96*(1), 57–65. http://dx.doi.org/10.1016/j.biopsycho.2013.11.010.

Weary, D. M., Krebs, J. R., Eddyshaw, R., McGregor, P. K., & Horn, A. (1988). Decline in song output by great tits: exhaustion or motivation? *Animal Behaviour, 36*(3), 1242–1244.

Webster, D., Richter, L., & Kruglanski, A. (1996). On leaping to conclusions when feeling tired: mental fatigue effects on impressional primacy. *Journal of Experimental Social Psychology, 195,* 181–195.

Werle, C. O. C., Wansink, B., & Payne, C. R. (2014). Is it fun or exercise? The framing of physical activity biases subsequent snacking. *Marketing Letters.* http://dx.doi.org/10.1007/s11002-014-9301-6.

Xu, X., Demos, K. E., Leahey, T. M., Hart, C. N., Trautvetter, J., Coward, P., ... Wing, R. R. (2014). Failure to replicate depletion of self-control. *PLoS One, 9*(10), e109950. http://dx.doi.org/10.1371/journal.pone.0109950.

Zirnheld, P. J., Carroll, C. A., Kieffaber, P. D., O'Donnell, B. F., Shekhar, A., & Hetrick, W. P. (2004). Haloperidol impairs learning and error-related negativity in humans. *Journal of Cognitive Neuroscience, 16*(6), 1098–1112. http://dx.doi.org/10.1162/0898929041502779.

CHAPTER 19

How Depletion Operates in an Integrative Theory of Self-Control

H.P. Kotabe[1], W. Hofmann[2]
[1]University of Chicago, Chicago, IL, United States; [2]University of Cologne, Cologne, Germany

Self-control research is fragmented, resulting in definitional, organizational, and integrational problems. Integrating the key components of self-control can be useful for understanding important self-control phenomena, such as "ego depletion" (Baumeister, Bratslavsky, Muraven, & Tice, 1998). In this chapter, we outline integrative self-control theory (SCT) (Kotabe & Hofmann, 2015) on which we base our approach to explaining the depletion effect. We first spell out the key assumptions of SCT in detail. Then, we explain how depletion operates within this theoretical framework. In short, we argue that depletion affects effort-related processes by increasing desire strength, decreasing control motivation, and decreasing control capacity. These mechanisms separately increase the likelihood that after self-control at Time 1, control effort at Time 2 is insufficient to effectively control temptation.

SCT is an integrative model of self-control which applies to self-control cases which involve intrapsychic conflict between desire and a higher-order goal (cf. see Chapter 5). Myriad human behavioral phenomena are included such as the dieter tempted by a mouthwatering desert, the designated driver tempted by free cocktails, the faithful spouse tempted by an attractive colleague, the ex-smoker tempted by a pack of cigarettes, the frugal consumer tempted by fashionable but expensive clothes, and the student tempted to sleep in after another long day of exam preparations. The thread entwining these cases is that they revolve around what we call *desire–goal (D-G) conflicts*. Although D-G conflicts are key to self-control, it is worth mentioning conflicts between desires can conflict with each other and so can goals. There can be *desire–desire (D-D) conflicts* (ie, conflicts between two desires such as to one party or another) as well as *goal–goal (G-G) conflicts* (ie, conflicts between two goals such as to study versus to exercise). In the case of self-control and depletion, we propose that focusing on the "asymmetric" (Hofmann, Friese, & Strack, 2009; Scholer & Higgins, 2010) case has several benefits including stimulating discussion of the characteristics and determinants of two qualitatively different psychological "forces" (Lewin, 1951), their neuropsychological foundations (eg, triggers and mechanisms of reward processing in the case of desire; executive operations in the case of higher-order goal pursuit), and how they conflict; drawing attention to possible differences in how people deal with asymmetric D-G conflicts versus symmetric D-D or G-G conflicts (eg, Hofmann, Fisher, Luhmann, Vohs, & Baumeister, 2014); presenting qualitatively different ways through which self-control can fail or succeed (eg, desire may be mentally overwhelming—a "hot" route—or commitment to higher-order goals may be too weak—a "cold" route); and highlighting novel ways to improve self-control in the long run (eg, changing desire experiences through evaluative conditioning or motivational retraining while boosting goal commitment through risk education programs).

SELF-CONTROL THEORY IN A NUTSHELL

SCT proposes that the behavioral outcome of a self-control episode is determined by the interplay of seven core psychological components which could be represented as nodes in a graph (see Fig. 19.1):

1. **Desire**. A driving force which begins as a subcortically mediated visceral state of "wanting" (as defined by Berridge, Robinson, & Aldridge, 2009), often followed by cognitive elaboration, which directs a person toward immediate reward-related stimuli.
2. **Higher-order goal**. A more cortically mediated and largely cognitive construct associated with an endorsed end state that motivates instrumental psychological (cognitive, affective, and behavioral) activity. Unlike desires, higher-order goals are often pursued intentionally and associated with declarative expectations of long-term benefits.
3. **D-G conflict**. A form of response conflict caused by the coactivation of a given desire and an at least partly incompatible higher-order goal. D-G conflict turns desire into temptation and the higher-order goal into a self-control goal.
4. **Control motivation**. The aspiration to control desire. As such, control motivation is determined by the self-control goal as well as additional factors that increase this aspiration.

SELF-CONTROL THEORY IN A NUTSHELL

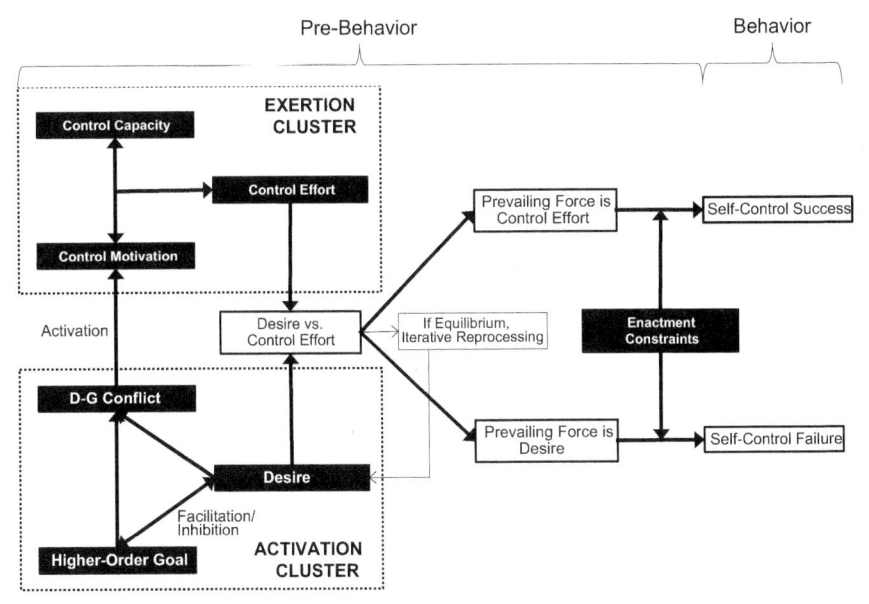

FIGURE 19.1 A diagram of self-control theory. The coactivation of desire and an at least partly incompatible higher-order goal induces desire–goal (D-G) conflict, which triggers self-control exertion processes by yielding control motivation. Control motivation and control capacity determine the upper limit of control effort (see Fig. 19.3 for further explanation). If control effort prevails over desire, then self-control will succeed provided that enactment constraints do not prevent higher-order goal enactment. If desire prevails over control effort, then self-control will fail provided that enactment constraints do not prevent desire enactment. *Adapted from Kotabe, H. P., & Hofmann, W. On integrating the components of self-control. Perspectives on Psychological Science, 10, 618–638. Copyright 2015 by H. P. Kotabe and W. Hofmann. Reprinted with permission.*

5. **Control capacity**. All the potential nonmotivational cognitive resources a person can use to facilitate the control of temptation (eg, directed attention and inhibitory capacity).
6. **Control effort**. The effective use of control capacity.
7. **Enactment constraints**. Environmental factors that limit one's behavioral options.

In a nutshell, SCT proposes that the first three components—desire, higher-order goal, and D-G conflict—are involved in activating self-control (*activation cluster*): A desire (eg, for relaxation) in itself is unproblematic and perhaps fully endorsed. It is only when an incompatible higher-order goal (eg, to meet a tight deadline) is present that the desire *becomes* a temptation and the higher-order goal *becomes* a self-control goal. The extent of D-G conflict experienced is a function of the strength of the desire, the strength of the higher-order goal, and the degree to which they are incompatible. D-G conflict activates self-control exertion by triggering control motivation. Control motivation and control capacity are major determinants of control effort. Together, these three components form the *exertion cluster*. Higher control motivation and control capacity yield higher *potential* control effort—the amount of control effort that one is *prepared* to spend toward combating temptation. SCT proposes that the strength of temptation, the perceived skill with which one can handle said temptation, and competing goals determine *actual* control effort—the amount of control effort that one actually uses to effectively combat temptation. If the investment of actual control effort reaches a threshold to prevail over desire strength, then self-control will "succeed" (ie, temptation will not be enacted), provided that enactment constraints do not prevent success. If actual control effort does not reach this threshold, then self-control will fail (ie, temptation will be enacted), provided that enactment constraints do not prevent failure.

How Depletion Operates in Integrative Self-Control Theory

One of the major benefits of this integrative approach is that it facilitates a rigorous, mechanistic approach to explaining important self-control phenomena such as the depletion effect. To include the wide range of research on this topic, we define depletion as an effect according to which *the investment of self-control effort at Time 1 reduces self-control success at a proximate Time 2*. In this section, we apply SCT to explaining the depletion effect, taking a perspective from which depletion can have multiple effects on multiple components of SCT. Specifically, we argue that, within the realm of D-G motivational conflicts, depletion may operate via three separable mechanisms: (1) an increase in desire strength, (2) a decrease in control motivation, and (3) a decrease in control capacity.

DEPLETION INCREASES DESIRE STRENGTH

Desire is a psychological driving force that varies in strength and is rooted in innate or learned need states (eg, for food, alcohol, drugs, sex, rest, social connection, gambling, etc.). It directs a person toward immediate, rewarding stimuli. A person can experience desire even without being cognizant of why he or she is experiencing desire (eg, imagine the gambler who desires to gamble even when he is certain that he is done for the night). Desire originates as a state of "wanting" (Berridge et al., 2009) when subcortical reward processing regions such as the nucleus accumbens are involved in evaluating external stimuli against the backdrop of internal need states and one's learning history (Hofmann & Kotabe, 2013). Relatively fast associative processes give rise to spontaneous, intrusive thoughts about the appetitive target. When those intrusive thoughts signal the possibility of pleasure or relief, cognitive elaboration usually ensues (Kavanagh, Andrade, & May, 2005). Through cognitive elaboration, desires can "crowd out" concurrent cognitive activity associated with higher-order goals (Hofmann, Friese, Schmeichel, & Baddeley, 2011; Hofmann & Van Dillen, 2012; Kavanagh et al., 2005). Cognitive elaboration also maintains the desired target in working memory over an extended period.

There is mounting evidence that depletion increases desire strength (the *desire-based depletion hypothesis*) (see Chapter 6). Recent research lending support to this hypothesis suggests that depletion heightens urges and feelings. In an experience sampling study and two follow-up experiments, Vohs et al. (2013) showed that depletion led to stronger desires, not only when measured at one moment in time after a depletion manipulation but also when measured continuously for 2 min, suggesting that depletion may increase desire strength not just momentarily but for an extended period. Furthermore, in three additional experiments, they showed that manipulating depletion led to more extreme evaluations of pleasant and unpleasant images, as well as unfamiliar Chinese character. We should note here that although desire is not always correlated with pleasantness or "liking," it usually is, and likewise, although dread is not always correlated with unpleasantness or "disliking," it usually is. Thus, these bidirectionally valenced results suggest that depletion might induce not only stronger desires, but also stronger dread, though this requires further research. These intense motivational states may share similar physiological underpinnings (Faure, Reynolds, Richard, & Berridge, 2008; Reynolds & Berridge, 2008).

Relatedly, a standard depletion manipulation that utilizes a task that demands attentional control over an extended period (the *extended-attentional-control task*) (see Schmeichel, Vohs, & Baumeister, 2003; Experiment 1) has been shown to cause brain activity in dieters that is associated with increased sensitivity to rewards (Wagner, Altman, Boswell, Kelley, & Heatherton, 2013) (see also Chapter 14). Compared with nondepleted dieters, depleted dieters exhibited greater activity in the orbitofrontal cortex in response to images of appetizing foods. This brain area has been associated with encoding the reward value and pleasantness of various sensory experiences including taste (Rolls, 2000).

Our research on anticipated emotions and self-control also supports that depletion increases desire strength (Kotabe, Righetti, & Hofmann, 2016). In one experiment, we manipulated depletion with the extended-attentional-control task before participants read vignettes portraying common self-control scenarios. They then forecasted the pleasure and guilt they would experience if they were to enact the temptation described in the scenario and the pride and frustration they would experience if they were to resist enacting this temptation. Next, they indicated how likely they would be to exert self-control in these scenarios. Compared to the nondepleted group, those who were depleted weighted anticipated pleasure more and anticipated guilt less into these self-control judgments. And as predicted, anticipated pleasure was related with judgments calling for less self-control, and anticipated guilt was related with judgments calling for more self-control. These results align with Inzlicht and Schmeichel's (2012) process model of depletion (see Chapter 18), and they also suggest one possible mechanism underlying the observed increase in reward sensitivity under depletion.

Also relevant here is that depletion may lower construal level, which may increase desire strength according to early self-control research by Mischel and Baker (1975). Mischel and Baker (1975) showed that low-level consummatory ideation directed at relevant rewarding stimuli hindered effective delay in the delay of gratification paradigm, presumably because such ideation increases desire strength. In contrast, higher-level ideation of relevant rewards which focused on their nonconsummatory qualities facilitated delay behavior, presumably because such ideation decreases desire strength. Therefore, if depletion lowers construal level, it may decrease desire strength. Recent research suggests depletion lowers construal level. Wan and Agrawal (2011) inferred this based on the effects of using self-control at Time 1 on construal-dependent judgments and choices at Time 2 in six experiments. Bruyneel and Dewitte (2012) showed across four experiments that people who used self-control at Time 1 (vs. those who did not) provided lower egocentric spatial distance estimates, formed more groups when categorizing objects, and used more concrete language when describing the behavior of cartoon characters at Time 2.

Collectively, these results begin to corroborate that depletion increases desire strength, which is one mechanism by which depletion via self-control at Time 1 could reduce self-control at Time 2. In SCT, an increase in desire strength would necessitate an increase in actual control effort to effectively control temptation. This may require an increase in potential control effort—a function of both control motivation and control capacity. The problem is that, at the same time, depletion seems to reduce control motivation and control capacity, thus limiting potential control effort. We elaborate on this next.

DEPLETION REDUCES CONTROL MOTIVATION

There is now substantial evidence that self-control exertion at Time 1 decreases control motivation at Time 2 (the *motivation-based depletion hypothesis*). An early test of this hypothesis comes from Muraven and Slessareva (2003). The three experiments they reported suggest that incentivizing people after they are depleted counteracts the effect of depletion on self-control performance. In Experiment 1, after a depleting task, they led one group to believe that their performance on a following task would provide useful data for the development of new therapies for patients with Alzheimer's disease. Compared to another depleted group who was not presented with this performance incentive, people in the experimental group tended to persist longer on unsolvable puzzles suggesting greater control motivation. In contrast, the Alzheimer's information did not have a significant effect on people who did a nondepleting control task. In Experiment 2, after a different depleting task, they led one group to believe that practice at a frustrating task would improve performance on that task. Compared to another group who was led to believe that practice would have little benefit, the experimental group practiced longer at the frustrating task, again suggesting greater control motivation. In contrast, there was no significant effect of the practice-efficacy manipulation on people who performed a nondepleting control task. In Experiment 3, after another different depleting task, they had people consume a relatively unpleasant beverage (Kool-Aid containing vinegar). They manipulated incentives by giving one group only $0.01 per ounce of bad-tasting beverage consumed whereas another group was given $0.25 per ounce consumed. People in the $0.25 group drank significantly more of the bad-tasting beverage suggesting increased motivation to control the temptation to stop, which would result in less monetary gain. There was no significant effect of incentives in a nondepleted control group, nor within the group who drank a relatively pleasant beverage (Kool-Aid containing sugar) which presumably required less self-control to drink, suggesting that stronger incentives specifically counteracted effects of depletion on self-control.

Another area of research relevant to the motivation-based depletion hypothesis suggests that effects of depletion on self-control performance can be counteracted by believing that self-control can be used limitlessly (Job, Dweck, & Walton, 2010; Mukhopadhyay & Johar, 2005) (see Chapter 11). Job et al. (2010) conducted a correlational study, two experiments, and a longitudinal field study to test whether a "limitless-resource theory" would play a role in counteracting the effect of depletion on self-control performance. In one of their experiments, they manipulated self-control beliefs prior to a standard depletion manipulation. Subsequently, participants self-reported their subjective exhaustion, and then they performed a Stroop task and eight challenging IQ problems. The limited-resource theory group showed depletion effects on the Stroop task and IQ task whereas the limitless-resource theory group did not show detectable depletion effects. Interestingly, there was no main effect of implicit-theory condition or an interactive effect of depletion condition and implicit-theory condition on self-reported exhaustion. Despite this, self-reported exhaustion predicted performance on the Stoop and IQ tasks in the limited-resource theory group but not in the limitless-resource theory group. This suggests that people in the two theory conditions did not differ much, on average, in terms of how exhausted they felt by the depletion task. Nevertheless, those in the limitless-theory group did not show the depletion effect, suggesting that they had more control motivation.

Closely related to research on self-control beliefs, there is another area of research that concerns how an illusory sense of depletion affects self-control (see Chapter 10). Clarkson, Hirt, Jia, and Alexander (2010) conducted four experiments that suggest that people who perceive themselves as not depleted, regardless of whether they are actually depleted, tend to exert self-control more than people who perceive themselves as more depleted. To illustrate, in one experiment they had people do a task which involves inhibiting a learned response over an extended period (the *perceptual-vigilance task*, also known as the "e-crossing" task) (Baumeister et al., 1998; Experiment 4) before some of them were told that the color of the paper used for task was replenishing whereas others were told that it was depleting. Next, they all worked on an anagram task until they decided to quit. People who perceived themselves as depleted did not persist as long at solving anagrams. Note that they argued that these are not motivational effects; however, they did not directly assess in these experiments whether people in the low-perceived-depletion group were specifically less motivated to *control* themselves. We think it is plausible that—regardless of whether one is actually depleted—perceiving oneself as depleted may decrease control motivation.

What the research reviewed in this section demonstrates is that depletion may not be just about a reduction of control capacity (the classical view) but also a reduction of control motivation. In simple words, whereas earlier models argued that people would not be *able* to control themselves anymore, more recent approaches argue that people do not *try* to control themselves anymore. More generally, several psychologists have recently argued that resource allocation (a motivational process, see Chapter 20) is as important as or more important than resource depletion (a capacity process) when it comes to explaining depletion phenomena (eg, Beedie & Lane, 2012; Inzlicht, Schmeichel, & Macrae, 2014; Kurzban, Duckworth, Kable, & Myers, 2013; Molden et al., 2012). In particular, these psychologists cast doubt on the "glucose hypothesis" which proposes that single acts of self-control cause reductions in blood glucose which then impairs self-control (Gailliot et al., 2007).

Beedie and Lane (2012) argued against the glucose hypothesis from three perspectives: first, the evolution of self-control at the species level; second, the adaptation of self-control at the individual level; and third, the physiology of glucose transport. From the first perspective, they suggest that we ask, why would humans evolve to have an energy-expensive ability to self-control without an adequate energy supply for it? From the second perspective, they suggest we ask, why would the physiological systems involved in self-control not have adapted to the repeated demands for self-control? From the third perspective, the suggest we ask, would the body really not replenish glucose as fast as it is used by the brain for self-control, especially considering that the amount of glucose used by the brain per unit time is extremely small compared to the amount used by the whole body (see Kurzban, 2010)?

Some empirical support for the resource-allocation account comes from Molden et al. (2012). Across four experiments, they showed both that using self-control had minimal effect on blood glucose levels and that rinsing with a carbohydrate solution increased self-control without significantly affecting blood glucose levels. In Experiment 1, they manipulated depletion with the perceptual-vigilance task before making precise measurements of blood glucose levels. This widely used manipulation of depletion did not significantly affect blood glucose levels. In Experiment 2, they manipulated depletion the same way, then randomly assigned participants to rinse their mouths either with a carbohydrate solution or a solution without carbohydrates before measuring persistence on a task involving squeezing a high-tension handgrip. Persisting on this task despite growing discomfort has been widely used as an index of self-control (Hagger, Wood, Stiff, & Chatzisarantis, 2010). The carbohydrate rinse reduced the effect of the depletion manipulation on persistence—there was a significant effect of depletion on persistence in the noncarbohydrate-rinse group but not in the carbohydrate-rinse group. In Experiment 3, everyone was depleted with the attentional-control depletion task. Then they manipulated the rinsing procedure used in Experiment 2 before assessing reaction time in a Stroop task. On average, people in the carbohydrate-rinse condition responded faster to incongruent trials, suggesting quicker resolution to response conflicts. In Experiment 4, they provided evidence that the carbohydrate rinse did not release substantial endogenous energy stores.

Inzlicht et al. (2014) proposed the elaborated process model of self-control to explain such results that are inconsistent with a purely capacity-based depletion model. In this model, apparent self-control failures reflect "the motivated switching of task priorities as people strive to strike an optimal balance between engaging cognitive labor to pursue 'have-to' goals versus preferring cognitive leisure in the pursuit of 'want-to' goals." After self-control exertion at Time 1, the model proposes that there are shifts in attention, emotion, and motivation away from "have-to" tasks and toward "want-to" tasks resulting in what *appears* to be self-control failure at Time 2.

Another area of research relevant to how depletion may reduce control motivation concerns a phenomenon called "motivated reasoning." Motivated reasoning is a kind of reasoning that biases people toward particular desired conclusions by making thoughts that support the desired conclusions more accessible (De Witt Huberts, Evers, & De Ridder, 2013; Kunda, 1990). For example, a dieter who lapses once at self-control by drinking a milkshake with dinner may think, "oh what the hell, dieting is done for today," then subsequently indulge again by eating ice cream for dessert (Herman & Mack, 1975). Or, a person may rationalize indulgence in the here and now by instilling a sense of deservingness or justify why controlling oneself is unwarranted by augmenting the costs of self-control and/or downplaying possible risks of desire enactment. It follows from the elaborated process model of self-control (Inzlicht et al., 2014) that depletion may result in motivated reasoning that disfavors pursuing the "have-to" task. In other words, depletion-induced motivated reasoning may decrease higher-order goal strength which, holding all else equal, would reduce control motivation. Such motivated reasoning may lead to arguably insensible behaviors—for example, a depleted dieter may not control the desire to order a ridiculously unhealthy entrée, justifying it because it came with a salad (Chernev, 2011).

Perhaps subsumed under motivated reasoning, "self-licensing"—the phenomena in which, after a self-attributed virtuous act, people are more likely to indulge due to a sense of deservingness (Khan & Dhar, 2006; Mukhopadhyay & Johar, 2009; see also Fishbach & Dhar, 2005)—lends support to the motivation-based depletion hypothesis. Because self-control in itself is thought to be a virtue (Baumeister & Juola Exline, 1999; Hofmann, Wisneski, Brandt, & Skitka, 2014; Read, Loewenstein, & Kalyanaraman, 1999), a prior act of self-control could reduce control motivation via a self-licensing effect. Although not traditionally considered in relation to depletion, this view suggests that this is one way depletion could operate.

Germaine to the motivation-based depletion hypothesis, De Witt Huberts, Evers, and De Ridder (2012) conducted two experiments that aimed to rule out capacity-based explanations for self-licensing effects in favor of the view that self-licensing is a motivational phenomenon. For these experiments, they manipulated self-licensing by making people feel as if they put high effort or low effort into a task. Perceiving that one put high effort into the task was presumed to grant the "license to indulge" later. In both conditions, people were told that they would be doing a validation task for a new dyslexia screener. The task involved indicating the first letter of 240 words. Halfway through, there was a 1-min break in which participants in the high-effort group were led to believe that they might randomly be selected to do the task again to establish its reliability when really all of them were asked to finish the second half of the task. People in the low-effort group also had a 1-min break but they simply were told that they were to take a short break before continuing to the second half of the task. A pilot experiment confirmed that people in the high-effort group perceived themselves as having exerted more effort than people in the low-effort group. Importantly, the pilot experiment also showed that this manipulation had no detectable effect on control capacity as indexed by Stroop performance. In their follow-up experiment, they utilized this manipulation before having people do a bogus taste test which was actually a test of how much people would eat after the manipulation. They showed that people ate more after manipulating perceptions of high effort than after manipulating perceptions of low effort. Assuming this manipulation had a minimal effect on control capacity, it would suggest that self-licensing occurred because of control motivation was decreased by the sense that one already had exerted much effort.

FLUCTUATIONS IN CONTROL MOTIVATION

According to SCT, there are at least three key moderators of control motivation beyond the higher-order goal and desire strength as mediated by D-G conflict. First, as one of the axioms of psychology is that people generally aspire to feel *effective and in control* (Bandura, 1977; Deci & Ryan, 1985; Higgins, 2011; White, 1959), SCT holds that this basic motive is superordinate and independent of the strength of the higher-order goal in conflict with desire. Second, it holds that expectations of future higher-order-goal-consistent behaviors and beliefs regarding how D-G conflicts should be balanced over time also affect control motivation. Third, it holds that people aspire to control temptations to experience positive self-conscious emotions such as pride or to not experience negative self-conscious emotions such as guilt. There could be additional sources of control motivation. Basically, anything that moderates the value of controlling temptation should result in corresponding fluctuations in control motivation.

We speculate that depletion could reduce control motivation by way of these three sources of control motivation. For example, depletion might temporarily reduce people's chronic need to feel in control. There is at least one study suggesting that a threat to one's sense of control decreases self-control (Chae & Zhu, 2014); however, it is possible that a threat to one's sense of control due to depletion could result in attempts to restore that sense of control (Kay, Whitson, Gaucher, & Galinsky, 2009). The question of whether threats to personal control decrease or increase motivation to control is debatable may depend on some key moderator. Depletion might affect people's beliefs concerning how to best balance D-G conflicts over time—with a bias toward allowing desire to run its course more frequently. This idea resonates with the idea of a fluctuating "optimal balance" between engaging in cognitive labor to pursue "have-to" goals and engaging in cognitive leisure to pursue "want-to" goals put forward by Inzlicht et al. (2014). Or depletion may increase the extent to which anticipated pleasure guides judgments concerning whether to self-control while decreasing the influence of anticipated guilt (Kotabe et al., 2016). Such possibilities present potential directions for future research.

DEPLETION DECREASES CONTROL CAPACITY

The classical view of depletion was that prior exertion of self-control impairs subsequent self-control by drawing on a person's *exhaustible and replenishable* capacity for self-control (the *capacity-based depletion hypothesis*) (see Chapter 1)—thus the term "depletion." Despite the arguments supporting a motivational account that we reviewed earlier, we think there is insufficient evidence to abandon capacity-based mechanisms of depletion altogether (the baby might be thrown out with the bathwater). There is some empirical evidence supporting that capacity-based mechanisms are at work too, though there is definitely room for improvement in this area of research. Also, are we to think that human ability really does not matter in the realm of self-control (or even more far-fetched, that it does not exist)? And that, out of pure motivation, people can endlessly exert self-control?

Consider this thought experiment: Sam is a talented journalist working on a highly important report late into the night. He is facing a tight deadline so despite a strong desire to take a break, he keeps on pushing himself to write more. He notices that the quality of his writing has seriously deteriorated. His sentences lack coherence and his reasoning is increasingly flawed. Thirty minutes pass in which he finds himself in a cycle of writing a poor sentence, deleting it, and repeating. He has run into more than one mental roadblock. The report is due early in the morning so he has no option but to continue or fail to finish in time. If he fails to finish in time, he might lose his job. Even if Sam mustered all the motivation in the world (imagine he has a gun to his head), would his writing suddenly flow with the grace and skill that he has when not severely depleted? Even if endogenous energy stores could restore his mental state temporarily, how long could this really last before maintaining peak performance became physically impossible?

Although the point of a thought experiment is to learn about reality without empirical evidence, we will review select empirical evidence anyway to bolster the argument for control capacity. First, what should we think about observations of self-control impairment following lesions to frontal and prefrontal regions of the brain if not a capacity-based impairment? As a classic example, take Phineas Gage—neuroscience's most famous patient. In 1848, Gage, 25, was laying railroad bed in Cavendish, Vermont. He was packing explosive powder into a hole with a tamping iron. The powder detonated, launching the meter long tamping iron through his left cheek, ripping through his left frontal lobe (and possibly part of the right), and exiting through the top of his skull. Gage survived but his friends saw him as "no longer Gage." The doctor who treated him observed that Gage could not stick to plans, he uttered gross profanities, and he was offensive and disrespectful. In short, Gage seemed to be driven by primitive animal propensities with little to no restraint. He lost the *faculty* of self-control. If Gage were motivated enough, would he have been able to keep his primitive impulses at bay?

Phineas Gage is not the only person to show behavioral changes after damage to frontal brain regions. Many studies of patients with closed head injuries, brain tumors, stroke lesions, and focal epilepsy have demonstrated a correspondence between damage or dysfunction to frontal regions and behavioral disinhibition (Clark, Manes, Antoun, Sahakian, & Robbins, 2003; Shallice & Burgess, 1991; Starkstein & Robinson, 1997; Tranel, Bechara, & Denburg, 2002). Relatedly, disruption to brain activity using repetitive transcranial magnetic stimulation over the course of several minutes has been used to provide evidence that prefrontal regions are causally involved in self-control-relevant behaviors such as risk taking (Knoch & Fehr, 2007) and intertemporal choice (Figner et al., 2010).

Another implication of a purely motivation-based depletion hypothesis that is hard to reconcile with reality is the prediction that if incentives are strong enough, there would not be individual differences in self-control performance. Simply put, given enough motivation, everyone would do equally well at self-control. Research relating individual differences in executive functioning to self-control suggests that this is not true (for a review, see Hofmann, Schmeichel, & Baddeley, 2012). A more plausible reality is that there are natural boundaries based on individual differences in control capacity.

A lot of the early work on ego depletion inferred that control capacity was affected by self-control at Time 1 based on self-control performance at Time 2. Recent debates about the role of motivation have made it clear that it is hard to tease apart the effects of motivation and capacity effects based on such observations. In fact, most of the research on depletion does not clearly show effects of motivation versus capacity. There are a few exceptions that are better than others at making this distinction. We review these exceptional studies later, then in the following section we propose a few new ways to study the relative effects of depletion on control motivation and control capacity.

One study on the separable effects of motivation and capacity was conducted by Vohs, Baumeister, and Schmeichel (2012). They noticed that recent studies showed that the depletion effect could be counteracted by incentives or implicit beliefs. However, they also noted that all of these experiments only manipulated mild depletion. They asked, can increasing motivation counteract *any* amount of depletion? They randomly depleted some participants to a more severe degree than is reached in the typical depletion experiment, then tested whether implicit beliefs or incentives could still fully counteract the severe depletion manipulation. In short, it seems not. In Experiment 1, they followed procedures used by Job et al. (2010) in their investigation of the role of implicit beliefs in counteracting depletion effects. The main difference was that they added a "severe depletion" condition in which participants had to complete four self-control tasks at Time 1 as a depletion manipulation prior to two more self-control tasks at Time 2 as a depletion assessment. In the "mild depletion" condition, participants completed two self-control tasks at Time 1, and in the control condition, participants did not do any self-control tasks at Time 1. For the depletion assessment, all participants were tested on delay of gratification using the intertemporal choice paradigm (Loewenstein, Thaler, Goldstein, & Hogarth, 1997) and the cognitive estimation test (Bullard et al., 2004) which is thought to involve active, logical thinking and extrapolation. They found that a limitless-resource theory counteracted depletion in the "mild depletion" group but not in the "severe depletion" group. In fact, after the strong depletion manipulation, people in the limitless-resource theory group showed *worse* cognitive estimation test scores than people in the limited-resource theory group—perhaps because having a limitless-resource theory promoted relatively nonconservative resource expenditure (Muraven, Shmueli, & Burkley, 2006). In addition, holding a limitless-resource theory counteracted depletion effects on delay of gratification in the "mild depletion" group but not in the "severe depletion" group. In contrast, self-control beliefs did not have significant effects in the control group, consistent with what was found by Job et al. (2010). In Experiment 2, they followed a procedure used by Muraven and Slessareva (2003) to manipulate incentives for self-control. They also manipulated mild and strong depletion—this time, by having participants do one or three self-control tasks prior to the depletion assessment (the control group did no self-control tasks). The depletion assessment was the same as in Experiment 1. They found that the incentivization counteracted depletion in the "mild depletion" group but not in the "strong depletion" group. Similar to Experiment 1, and consistent with what was found by Muraven and Slessareva (2003), there were no significant effects of incentives in the control group. The results of these experiments suggest that notions that self-control is a purely motivational phenomena should be tempered.

More evidence for a role of control capacity comes from Schmeichel (2007), who conducted four experiments that suggest that using various executive functions impaired subsequent executive function performance and provided evidence against noncapacity-based mechanisms such as motivation, mood, and task difficulty. In one of his experiments, he had people do an attentional-control depletion task or a control task before they were assessed on working memory span with an operation span test or a sentence span test. (The attentional-control task requires sustained directed attention which seems to be a key cognitive resource depleted and shared by self-control and executive functioning, Kaplan and Berman (2010).) On average, people in the depletion group did worse at both the operation span test and the sentence span test as indexed by number of word sets recalled, longest set recalled, number of words in correct sets, and total words recalled. The effect does not seem to be due to motivation or mood. People in both groups worked similarly long at the working memory span tasks, suggesting that neither group rushed through due to a lack of control motivation. Furthermore, statistically controlling for mood did not change the main pattern of results.

Coping with stress requires self-control (Muraven & Baumeister, 2000). Schoofs, Preuß, and Wolf (2008) conducted an experiment to test whether a social stress task impairs working memory—that is, does it deplete this *cognitive ability* rather than having some sort of motivational effect. They randomly assigned people to do the trier social stress test (Kirschbaum, Pirke, & Hellhammer, 1993) or a comparable control task before an n-back task (Kirchner, 1958) that assess working memory performance. One should note that worsened performance on the n-back task could be due to depletion or a motivational shift—that is, resource depletion or resource allocation, respectively. Thus, importantly, they found that regardless of condition, most participants seemed to be motivated in the n-back task. Only 4 of the 40 participants showed lack of motivation (as indicated by highly repetitive single-key pressing the n-back task) and only one of them was in the depletion group. One of their key results was that the reduction in working memory performance due to depletion was evident only at the beginning of the n-back task. This might be due to an interaction between depletion and practice. Or, it could reflect the gradual restoration of energy to active working memory regions of the brain as blood is diverted to those regions from less active regions. Again, this would be consistent with the view that self-control relies on an exhaustible and replenishable capacity, and it would add nuance to what it takes to replenish this resource.

The addition of control capacity to a coherent integrative model of self-control is theoretically justified, particularly with regard to depletion at group and individual levels, in that it adds substantial explanatory power while adding only one additional component. Researchers often prefer and are attracted to simple explanations such as a purely capacity-based or purely motivation-based model and the pendulum seems to be swinging from one extreme to the other. Perhaps there is some danger in holding a one-sided view (eg, theory-induced blindness). We believe that the future of self-control research will best be served by integrative models, not unlike the integrative models of the past which have proved to be generative for their respective fields (eg, Fazio's (1990) MODE model of attitude-behavior relations; Gross's (1998) process model of emotion regulation).

SOME WAYS TO STUDY MOTIVATION VERSUS CAPACITY

It is clear that empirically disentangling motivation and capacity is a major challenge. For example, as alluded to above, there is a general problem underlying inferences concerning the relative effects of motivation versus capacity in any achievement-oriented tasks such as those used extensively in research on executive functions. Namely, if one were to observe a decrement in performance at some achievement-oriented task at *one time* following *mild depletion*, how can one possibly attribute it to motivation or capacity? A few useful approaches may be to assess performance *across time*, or by *comparing mild versus severe depletion* (as in Vohs et al., 2012), or *some combination of these two approaches* in a depletion study involving incentivized performance (see Fig. 19.2). First, the multiple-times approach is like the standard depletion study except that performance is incentivized and effects of the depletion manipulation are observed not only at Time 2 but also several subsequent times. The prediction is that at Time 2, one may observe no significant difference in performance because of control motivation, but at subsequent times up to and including Time n, one may observe significant differences in performance because of control capacity. Second, the severe-depletion approach is also like the standard depletion study except performance is incentivized and there is an additional comparison group that is severely depleted at Time 1. The prediction is that at Time 2, one may observe no significant difference in performance in the mild depletion group because of control motivation, but may observe a significant difference in performance in the severe depletion group because of control capacity (as in Vohs et al., 2012). Lastly, the combined approach incorporates everything stated earlier about the multiple-times approach and the severe-depletion approach. In addition, one can observe differential effects of mild versus severe depletion on performance at times up to and including Time n.

INTEGRATING MOTIVATION AND CAPACITY INTO A MODEL OF CONTROL EFFORT INVESTMENT

SCT is, at its core, a model of control effort investment. Because of its ultimate focus on control effort as the countervailing "force" to desire strength, SCT is able to integrate both capacity-based and motivation-based limitations on how much control effort can be invested at any given point in time. In the following, we spell out this integration and then apply it to the depletion case.

Based on formulations of effort in cognitive energetics theory (Kruglanski et al., 2012), SCT proposes that control motivation and control capacity may

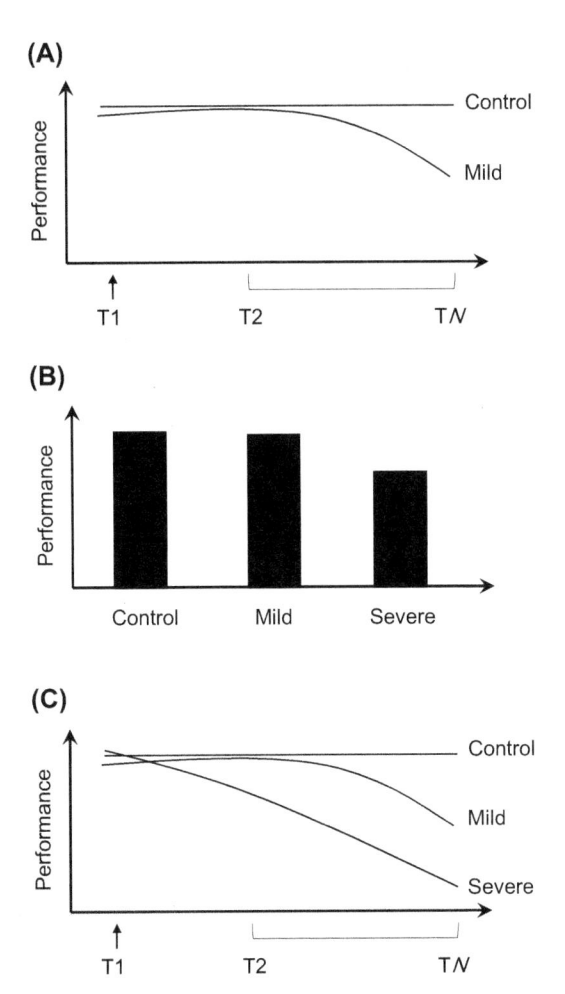

FIGURE 19.2 Three approaches to disentangling control motivation and control capacity in an incentivized-performance depletion study. (A) Multiple-times approach. (B) Server-depletion approach. (C) Combined approach.

determine the *potential* control effort that can be invested in a given moment. How much control capacity is *actually* used in battling desire is dynamically moderated by additional factors including desire strength, perceived skill, and competing goals. Potential control effort (E_P) is proposed to be proportional to the product of control motivation (M) and control capacity (C) at a given point in time:

$$E_P \sim M \times C, \text{ where } 0 < M < 1$$

The multiplicative relation implies that, in terms of determining the level of potential control effort, control motivation and control capacity are functionally interchangeable (see Fig. 19.3, row A). Further, the terms imply that

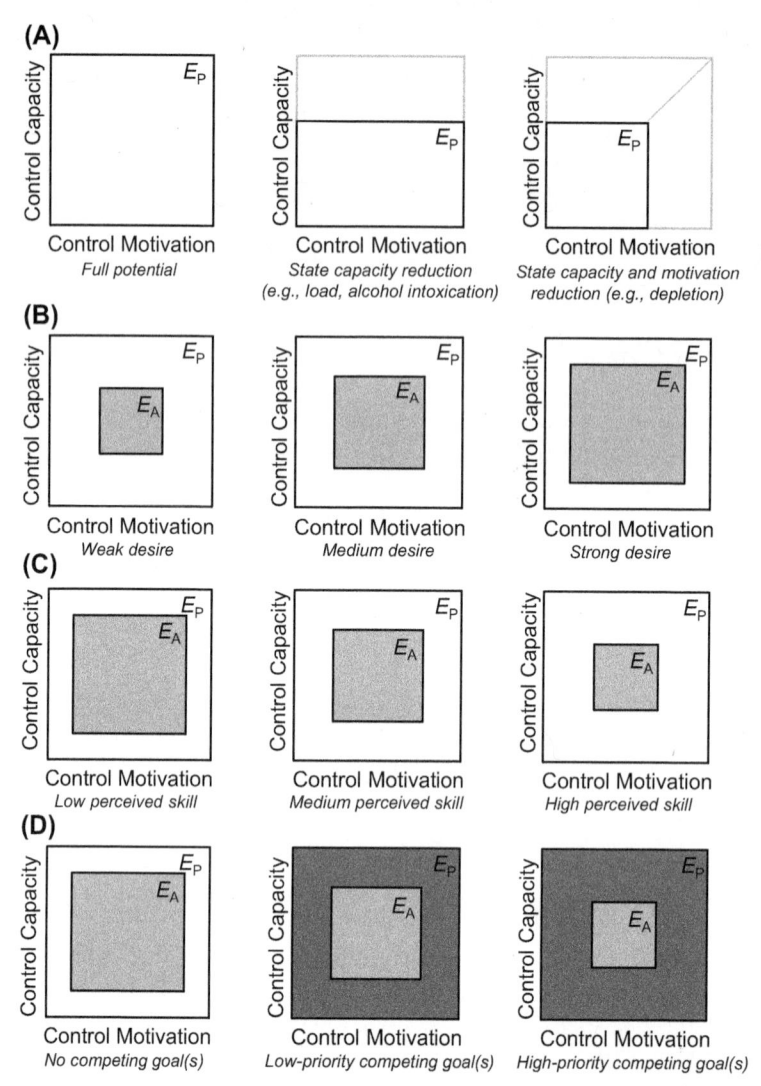

FIGURE 19.3 An illustration of the model assumptions regarding potential control effort (E_P) and actual control effort (E_A). State control motivation × state control capacity determines potential control effort, E_P, the upper limit of actual control effort, E_A (row A). E_A (*light gray area*) is further determined by moderators including desire strength (row B), perceived skill (row C), and competing goals (row D). *White areas* signify available mental resources not invested due to effort conservation. *Dark gray areas* represent mental resources allotted to competing goals.

how much control effort could be invested *in principle* is a joint function of the various sources that factor into control motivation and of trait differences (eg, in executive functions) and state influences (eg, cognitive load, alcohol intoxication, stereotype threat) that factor into control capacity. The range of M implies that potential effort is capped by the control capacity at a given time.

5. NEWER MODELS OF EGO CONTROL

Now, regarding why people do not always fully exert themselves, control motivation and control capacity determine how much control effort *can* be exerted, but how much control effort *is* actually exerted may depend on additional moderators. First, according to the effort mobilization literature, actual control effort investment should depend on the difficulty of controlling desire. Most centrally, effort allocation is assumed to be guided by a basic concern for energy conservation (Brehm & Self, 1989; Fiske & Taylor, 1991; Kruglanski et al., 2012). Further, recent research suggests that cognitive effort is intrinsically costly (Kool, McGuire, Wang, & Botvinick, 2013). These views support that, like the use of money or time, the use of effort should be economical and contingent on one's available "budget." In fact, Kool and Botvinick (2014) showed that labor/leisure decisions in humans (ie, choosing between using cognitive effort or "taking it easy") resemble labor/leisure decisions predicted by economic models of labor supply. The point is that multiple streams of research converge on the idea that people *try* to *efficiently* allocate control effort to *effectively* deal with the desire at hand. Thus, it follows that people usually allocate less effort to control weak desires than strong desires (row B) (Hofmann & Van Dillen, 2012; Kavanagh et al., 2005). However, this linear relationship holds up only to the point where the perceived strength of desire is too high in relation to one's potential control effort—resulting in (temporary) disengagement (see Brehm & Self, 1989; Gendolla & Richter, 2010).

A second moderator is perceived skill. Some people may see themselves as more tacitly able to use their available control capacity in the service of self-control than others (Reber, 1989; Wagner & Sternberg, 1985). Additionally, some people may believe they have more and/or better self-control strategies at their disposal in a given situation than others (see Sheppes & Meiran, 2008). In both cases, the degree of perceived skill would inversely vary with control effort engagement because of energy conservation concerns (row C). The emphasis on *perceived* skill suggests that people may downplay the difficulty of combating a given desire or make overly confident judgments about their skill in controlling it, perhaps due to unrealistic perceptions of self-efficacy. Such "control illusions" may lead them to actually allocate less control effort than required (leading to a mismatch between desire strength and actual control effort) and might thus lead to self-control failure (Nordgren, Van Harreveld, & Van Der Pligt, 2009).

Third, as self-control does not occur in a vacuum, one may (have to) allocate control resources, even unintentionally, to competing goals (row D) (Hassin, Bargh, & Zimerman, 2009; Kruglanski et al., 2012; Shah & Kruglanski, 2002). For example, imagine a person tempted to go to the next bar despite knowing he should go home to get rest for work the next day. However, he is simultaneously socializing with his clients which demands some cognitive resources that otherwise could be utilized in pursuit of his self-control goal to call it a night. In this example, even if potential control effort were high, a consequence of the competing goal may be insufficient available resources for the self-control goal.

In sum, whereas control capacity and control motivation factor into determining the potential amount of control effort that *can* be used at a given time, how much control effort *is* invested may depend on the additive effects of at least three moderators: desire strength, perceived skill, and competing goals. Accordingly, actual control effort expenditure would be highest when desire strength is high, perceived skill is low, and competing goals are absent. Oppositely, actual control effort expenditure would be lowest when desire strength is low, perceived skill is high, and competing goals are present.

DEPLETION AND CONTROL EFFORT

This model implies that depletion could reduce control effort in several ways (see Fig. 19.4). First, depletion could reduce control motivation and control capacity, thus reducing potential control effort. Reducing control effort places a restriction on the maximum actual control effort that can be exerted to combat temptation. So if desire strength increases, thus increasing task demands, then more control effort needs to be recruited

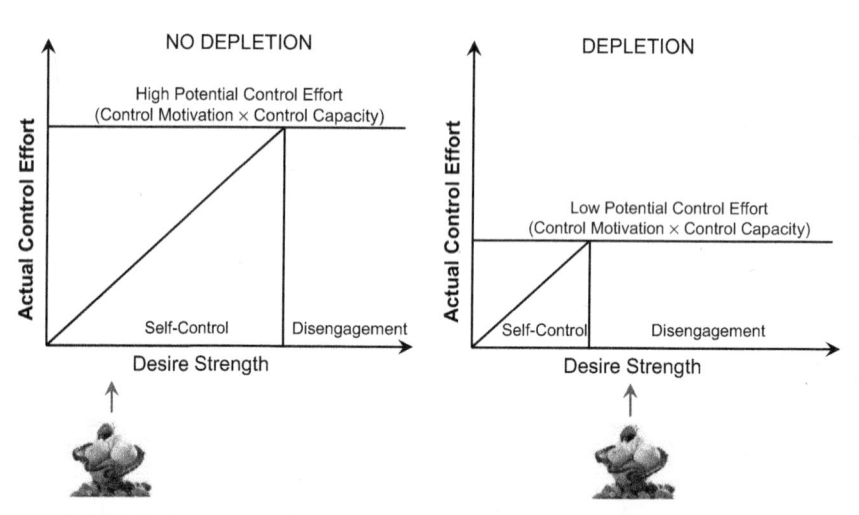

FIGURE 19.4 A diagram of how depletion could lead to self-control failure by decreasing control motivation and control capacity while increasing desire strength. As potential control effort is multiplicatively determined by control motivation and control capacity, a decrease in control motivation and control capacity decreases potential control effort (*dotted line*), thus lowering the upper limit of actual control effort (*y*-axis). Before depletion (*left panel*), self-control succeeds because desire strength is not past the point of disengagement, which is defined by the point at which desire strength demands the maximum control effort that one is prepared to invest (ie, where actual control effort = potential control effort). After depletion affects desire strength, control motivation, and control capacity (*right panel*), self-control fails because desire strength is past the point of disengagement.

to effectively deal with it. This may not be a problem when control motivation and control capacity are high (see Fig. 19.4, left panel). However, when control motivation is reduced and control capacity is exhausted, the same desire may almost reach a point of effort disengagement (where the actual effort needed to effectively control temptation exceeds the amount of effort one is prepared to invest). And if depletion increases desire strength even by a little, the temptation "tipping point" may be reached, resulting in self-control failure (see Fig. 19.4, right panel).

Implications and Future Directions

SCT, and in particular the central component of control effort, has important implications for how to operationalize and assess self-control. That is, one implication of the model is that perhaps the most useful and direct index of self-control is the extent to which people engage control effort relative to desire strength, rather than whether temptation was enacted or not (the ultimate behavioral level determined by the interplay of control effort, desire strength, and enactment constraints), or whether people were motivated or able to control themselves (antecedents of control effort). Regarding the former, observed self-control success—especially in field settings or when inferred from people's self-reports—has the problem of possibly being influenced or even determined by enactment constraints. To illustrate, imagine a student at a school cafeteria. He might *appear* to succeed at self-control because he chose an apple instead of a cookie when checking out at the cafeteria, when in fact, he was unprepared (not motivated and able) to resist the cookie but only chose the apple because the student in front of him took the last cookie. That is, the desire to effort ratio in this case was >1, but nevertheless, he did not enact temptation because of the fortuitous constraints imposed by the other student. Or imagine the student chose a cookie instead of an apple. He might *appear* to fail at self-control, when in fact, he was prepared (motivated and able) to resist the cookie but ended up choosing the cookie anyway because it was the only option left after the student in front of him took the apple. That is, the desire to effort ratio in this case was <1 but he nevertheless enacted temptation because of the unfortunate enactment constraints imposed by the other student.

CONCLUDING REMARKS

In this chapter, we demonstrated how SCT can be used to make sense of a complicated self-control phenomena—ego depletion. Our analysis suggests that future research on depletion would benefit from a stronger focus on control effort relative to desire strength. We argue that the most supported effects of depletion most directly concern these components. Depletion either decreases potential control effort (via effects on control motivation and control capacity) or it increases the actual control effort required for self-control success (via effects on desire strength). By applying SCT to the problem of depletion, we were able to see how important the effort component is for depletion research. This insight could only be gathered by looking at the forest.

References

Bandura, A. (1977). Self-efficacy: toward a unifying theory of behavioral change. *Psychological Review, 84*, 191–215.
Baumeister, R. F., Bratslavsky, E., Muraven, M., & Tice, D. M. (1998). Ego depletion: is the active self a limited resource? *Journal of Personality and Social Psychology, 74*, 1252–1265.
Baumeister, R. F., & Juola Exline, J. (1999). Virtue, personality, and social relations: self-control as the moral muscle. *Journal of Personality, 67*, 1165–1194.
Beedie, C. J., & Lane, A. M. (2012). The role of glucose in self-control: another look at the evidence and an alternative conceptualization. *Personality and Social Psychology Review, 16*, 143–153.
Berridge, K. C., Robinson, T. E., & Aldridge, J. W. (2009). Dissecting components of reward: 'Liking', 'wanting', and learning. *Current opinion in pharmacology, 9*, 65–73.
Brehm, J. W., & Self, E. A. (1989). The intensity of motivation. *Annual Review of Psychology, 40*, 109–131.
Bruyneel, S. D., & Dewitte, S. (2012). Engaging in self-regulation results in low-level construals. *European Journal of Social Psychology, 42*, 763–769.
Bullard, S. E., Fein, D., Gleeson, M. K., Tischer, N., Mapou, R. L., & Kaplan, E. (2004). The Biber cognitive estimation test. *Archives of Clinical Neuropsychology, 19*, 835–846.
Chae, B. G., & Zhu, R. J. (2014). Environmental disorder leads to self-regulatory failure. *Journal of Consumer Research, 40*, 1203–1218.
Chernev, A. (2011). The dieter's paradox. *Journal of Consumer Psychology, 21*, 178–183.
Clark, L., Manes, F., Antoun, N., Sahakian, B. J., & Robbins, T. W. (2003). The contributions of lesion laterality and lesion volume to decision-making impairment following frontal lobe damage. *Neuropsychologia, 41*, 1474–1483.
Clarkson, J. J., Hirt, E. R., Jia, L., & Alexander, M. B. (2010). When perception is more than reality: the effects of perceived versus actual resource depletion on self-regulatory behavior. *Journal of Personality and Social Psychology, 98*, 29–46.
De Witt Huberts, J. C., Evers, C., & De Ridder, D. T. D. (2012). License to sin: self-licensing as a mechanism underlying hedonic consumption. *European Journal of Social Psychology, 42*, 490–496.
De Witt Huberts, J. C., Evers, C., & De Ridder, D. T. (2013). "Because I am worth it": a theoretical framework and empirical review of a justification-based account of self-regulation failure. *Personality and Social Psychology Review, 18*(2), 119–138.
Deci, E. L., & Ryan, R. M. (1985). *Intrinsic motivation and self-determination in human behavior.* New York, NY: Plenum Press.
Faure, A., Reynolds, S. M., Richard, J. M., & Berridge, K. C. (2008). Mesolimbic dopamine in desire and dread: enabling motivation to be generated by localized glutamate disruptions in nucleus accumbens. *The Journal of Neuroscience, 28*, 7184–7192.
Fazio, R. H. (1990). The MODE model as an integrative framework. *Advances in Experimental Social Psychology, 23*, 75–109.
Figner, B., Knoch, D., Johnson, E. J., Krosch, A. R., Lisanby, S. H., Fehr, E., … Weber, E. U. (2010). Lateral prefrontal cortex and self-control in intertemporal choice. *Nature Neuroscience, 13*, 538–539.

REFERENCES

Fishbach, A., & Dhar, R. (2005). Goals as excuses or guides: the liberating effect of perceived goal progress on choice. *Journal of Consumer Research, 32*, 370–377.

Fiske, S. T., & Taylor, S. E. (1991). *Social cognition* (2nd ed.). New York, NY: McGraw-Hill Book Company.

Gailliot, M. T., Baumeister, R. F., DeWall, C. N., Maner, J. K., Plant, E. A., Tice, D. M., ... Schmeichel, B. J. (2007). Self-control relies on glucose as a limited energy source: willpower is more than a metaphor. *Journal of Personality and Social Psychology, 92*, 325–336.

Gendolla, G. H., & Richter, M. (2010). Effort mobilization when the self is involved: some lessons from the cardiovascular system. *Review of General Psychology, 14*, 212–226.

Gross, J. J. (1998). The emerging field of emotion regulation: an integrative review. *Review of General Psychology, 2*, 271–299.

Hagger, M. S., Wood, C., Stiff, C., & Chatzisarantis, N. L. (2010). Ego depletion and the strength model of self-control: a meta-analysis. *Psychological Bulletin, 136*, 495–525.

Hassin, R. R., Bargh, J. A., & Zimerman, S. (2009). Automatic and flexible: the case of nonconscious goal pursuit. *Social Cognition, 27*, 20–36.

Herman, C. P., & Mack, D. (1975). Restrained and unrestrained eating. *Journal of Personality, 43*, 647–660.

Higgins, E. T. (2011). *Beyond pleasure and pain: How motivation works*. New York, NY: Oxford University Press.

Hofmann, W., Fisher, R. R., Luhmann, M., Vohs, K. D., & Baumeister, R. F. (2014). Yes, but are they happy? Effects of trait self-control on affective well-being and life satisfaction. *Journal of Personality, 82*, 265–277.

Hofmann, W., Friese, M., Schmeichel, B. J., & Baddeley, A. D. (2011). Working memory and self-regulation. In K. D. Vohs, & R. F. Baumeister (Eds.), *Handbook of self-regulation: Research, theory, and applications* (Vol. 2) (pp. 204–225). New York, NY: Guilford Press.

Hofmann, W., Friese, M., & Strack, F. (2009). Impulse and self-control from a dual-systems perspective. *Perspectives on Psychological Science, 4*, 162–176.

Hofmann, W., & Kotabe, H. P. (2013). Desire and desire regulation: basic processes and individual differences. In J. J. Gross (Ed.), *Handbook of emotion regulation* (2nd ed.). New York, NY: Guilford Press.

Hofmann, W., Schmeichel, B. J., & Baddeley, A. D. (2012). Executive functions and self-regulation. *Trends in Cognitive Sciences, 16*, 174–180.

Hofmann, W., & Van Dillen, L. (2012). Desire: the new hot spot in self-control research. *Current Directions in Psychological Science, 21*, 317–322.

Hofmann, W., Wisneski, D. C., Brandt, M. J., & Skitka, L. J. (2014). Morality in everyday life. *Science, 345*, 1340–1343.

Inzlicht, M., & Schmeichel, B. J. (2012). What is ego depletion? Toward a mechanistic revision of the resource model of self-control. *Perspectives on Psychological Science, 7*, 450–463.

Inzlicht, M., Schmeichel, B. J., & Macrae, C. N. (2014). Why self-control seems (but may not be) limited. *Trends in Cognitive Sciences, 18*(3), 127–133.

Job, V., Dweck, C. S., & Walton, G. M. (2010). Ego depletion-is it all in your head? Implicit theories about willpower affect self-regulation. *Psychological Science, 21*, 1686–1693.

Kaplan, S., & Berman, M. G. (2010). Directed attention as a common resource for executive functioning and self-regulation. *Perspectives on Psychological Science, 5*, 43–57.

Kavanagh, D. J., Andrade, J., & May, J. (2005). Imaginary relish and exquisite torture: the elaborated intrusion theory of desire. *Psychological Review, 112*, 446–467.

Kay, A. C., Whitson, J. A., Gaucher, D., & Galinsky, A. D. (2009). Compensatory control: achieving order through the mind, our institutions, and the heavens. *Current Directions in Psychological Science, 18*, 264–268.

Khan, U., & Dhar, R. (2006). Licensing effect in consumer choice. *Journal of Marketing Research, 43*, 259–266.

Kirchner, W. K. (1958). Age differences in short-term retention of rapidly changing information. *Journal of experimental psychology, 55*, 352–358.

Kirschbaum, C., Pirke, K.-M., & Hellhammer, D. H. (1993). The 'Trier Social Stress Test': a tool for investigating psychobiological stress responses in a laboratory setting. *Neuropsychobiology, 28*, 76–81.

Knoch, D., & Fehr, E. (2007). Resisting the power of temptations. *Annals of the New York Academy of Sciences, 1104*, 123–134.

Kool, W., & Botvinick, M. (2014). A labor/leisure tradeoff in cognitive control. *Journal of Experimental Psychology: General, 143*, 131–141.

Kool, W., McGuire, J. T., Wang, G. J., & Botvinick, M. M. (2013). Neural and behavioral evidence for an intrinsic cost of self-control. *PLoS One, 8*, e72626.

Kotabe, H. P., & Hofmann, W. (2015). On integrating the components of self-control. *Perspectives on Psychological Science, 10*, 618–638.

Kotabe, H. P., Righetti, F., & Hofmann, W. (2016). *Anticipated emotions guide self-control judgments* (Manuscript submitted for publication).

Kruglanski, A. W., Belanger, J. J., Chen, X. Y., Kopetz, C., Pierro, A., & Mannetti, L. (2012). The energetics of motivated cognition: a force-field analysis. *Psychological Review, 119*, 1–20.

Kunda, Z. (1990). The case for motivated reasoning. *Psychological Bulletin, 108*, 480–498.

Kurzban, R. (2010). Does the brain consume additional glucose during self-control tasks? *Evolutionary Psychology, 8*, 244.

Kurzban, R., Duckworth, A. L., Kable, J. W., & Myers, J. (2013). An opportunity cost model of subjective effort and task performance. *Behavioral and Brain Sciences, 36*, 661–726.

Lewin, K. (1951). *Field theory in social science: Selected theoretical papers*. Oxford, UK: Harpers.

Loewenstein, G., Thaler, R. H., Goldstein, W. M., & Hogarth, R. M. (1997). *Intertemporal choice research on judgment and decision making: Currents, connections, and controversies*. Cambridge University Press, 365.

Mischel, W., & Baker, N. (1975). Cognitive appraisals and transformations in delay behavior. *Journal of Personality and Social Psychology, 31*, 254–261.

Molden, D. C., Hui, C. M., Scholer, A. A., Meier, B. P., Noreen, E. E., D'Agostino, P. R., ... Martin, V. (2012). Motivational versus metabolic effects of carbohydrates on self-control. *Psychological Science, 23*, 1137–1144.

Mukhopadhyay, A., & Johar, G. V. (2005). Where there is a will, is there a way? Effects of lay theories of self-control on setting and keeping resolutions. *Journal of Consumer Research, 31*, 779–786.

Mukhopadhyay, A., & Johar, G. V. (2009). Indulgence as self-reward for prior shopping restraint: a justification-based mechanism. *Journal of Consumer Psychology, 19*, 334–345.

Muraven, M., & Baumeister, R. F. (2000). Self-regulation and depletion of limited resources: does self-control resemble a muscle? *Psychological Bulletin, 126*, 247–259.

Muraven, M., Shmueli, D., & Burkley, E. (2006). Conserving self-control strength. *Journal of Personality and Social Psychology, 91*, 524–537.

Muraven, M., & Slessareva, E. (2003). Mechanisms of self-control failure: motivation and limited resources. *Personality & Social Psychology Bulletin, 29*, 894–906.

Nordgren, L. F., Van Harreveld, F., & Van Der Pligt, J. (2009). The restraint bias: how the illusion of self-restraint promotes impulsive behavior. *Psychological Science, 20*, 1523–1528.

Read, D., Loewenstein, G., & Kalyanaraman, S. (1999). Mixing virtue and vice: combining the immediacy effect and the diversification heuristic. *Journal of Behavioral Decision Making, 12*, 257–273.

Reber, A. S. (1989). Implicit learning and tacit knowledge. *Journal of Experimental Psychology: General, 118*, 219–235.

Reynolds, S. M., & Berridge, K. C. (2008). Emotional environments retune the valence of appetitive versus fearful functions in nucleus accumbens. *Nature Neuroscience, 11*, 423–425.

Rolls, E. T. (2000). The orbitofrontal cortex and reward. *Cerebral Cortex, 10*, 284–294.

Schmeichel, B. J. (2007). Attention control, memory updating, and emotion regulation temporarily reduce the capacity for executive control. *Journal of Experimental Psychology: General, 136*, 241–255.

Schmeichel, B. J., Vohs, K. D., & Baumeister, R. F. (2003). Intellectual performance and ego depletion: role of the self in logical reasoning and other information processing. *Journal of Personality and Social Psychology, 85,* 33–46.

Scholer, A., & Higgins, E. (2010). *Conflict and control at different levels of self-regulation self control in society, mind, and brain.* Oxford, UK: Oxford University Press, 312–334.

Schoofs, D., Preuß, D., & Wolf, O. T. (2008). Psychosocial stress induces working memory impairments in an n-back paradigm. *Psychoneuroendocrinology, 33,* 643–653.

Shah, J. Y., & Kruglanski, A. W. (2002). Priming against your will: how accessible alternatives affect goal pursuit. *Journal of Experimental Social Psychology, 38,* 368–383.

Shallice, T., & Burgess, P. W. (1991). Deficits in strategy application following frontal lobe damage in man. *Brain, 114,* 727–741.

Sheppes, G., & Meiran, N. (2008). Divergent cognitive costs for online forms of reappraisal and distraction. *Emotion, 8,* 870–874.

Starkstein, S. E., & Robinson, R. G. (1997). Mechanism of disinhibition after brain lesions. *The Journal of Nervous and Mental Disease, 185,* 108–114.

Tranel, D., Bechara, A., & Denburg, N. L. (2002). Asymmetric functional roles of right and left ventromedial prefrontal cortices in social conduct, decision-making, and emotional processing. *Cortex, 38,* 589–612.

Vohs, K. D., Baumeister, R. F., Mead, N. L., Hofmann, W., Ramanathan, S., & Schmeichel, B. J. (2013). *Engaging in self-control heightens urges and feelings* (Manuscript submitted for publication).

Vohs, K. D., Baumeister, R. F., & Schmeichel, B. J. (2012). Motivation, personal beliefs, and limited resources all contribute to self-control. *Journal of Experimental Social Psychology, 48,* 943–947.

Wagner, D. D., Altman, M., Boswell, R. G., Kelley, W. M., & Heatherton, T. F. (2013). Self-regulatory depletion enhances neural responses to rewards and impairs top-down control. *Psychological Science, 24,* 2262–2271.

Wagner, R. K., & Sternberg, R. J. (1985). Practical intelligence in real-world pursuits: the role of tacit knowledge. *Journal of Personality and Social Psychology, 49,* 436–458.

Wan, E. W., & Agrawal, N. (2011). Carryover effects of self-control on decision making: a construal-level perspective. *Journal of Consumer Research, 38,* 199–214.

White, R. W. (1959). Motivation reconsidered: the concept of competence. *Psychological Review, 66,* 297–333.

CHAPTER 20

Understanding Self-Regulation Failure: A Motivated Effort-Allocation Account

D.C. Molden[1], C.M. Hui[2], A.A. Scholer[3]

[1]Northwestern University, Evanston, IL, United States; [2]Chinese University of Hong Kong, Shatin, Hong Kong; [3]University of Waterloo, Waterloo, ON, Canada

> Refrain tonight;
> And that shall lend a kind of easiness
> To the next abstinence, the next more easy... *William Shakespeare, Hamlet*

When it comes to understanding people's failure and unhappiness in many different areas of their lives, psychologists have discovered few variables as important as self-regulation. People who fail to self-regulate—are less successful at monitoring and altering their own actions, thoughts, and emotions—have less satisfying relationships, achieve less in school and in their careers, are less happy, and suffer poorer mental and physical health (de Ridder, Lensvelt-Mulders, Finkenauer, Stok, & Baumeister, 2012). Thus, simply encouraging and improving self-regulation holds the promise of ameliorating a great many personal and societal problems.

Alas, despite having identified this seemingly critical variable for improving people's lives, researchers have made limited progress in helping people initiate and sustain self-regulation over time (Steel, 2007; Wu, Gao, Chen, & van Dam, 2009). Contrary to Hamlet's suggestion earlier, many studies suggest that even when people do manage to exert self-regulation in one instance, this frequently does not ease their further efforts. Instead, initiating self-regulation toward one particular set of concerns often *reduces* subsequent regulation even for separate sets of concerns that demand entirely different types of thought and action (Hagger, Wood, Stiff, & Chatzisarantis, 2010). As described by Baumeister, Heatherton, and Tice (1994) using the metaphor of a muscle, exerting control over one's thoughts and actions thus generally seems as if it consumes "energy," resulting in a state of self-regulatory "depletion" that hinders further efforts toward control. That is, people behave as if they have a fixed capacity of resources available for self-regulation that are consumed when used, leading to a diminishing ability to self-regulate over time.

Although this metaphor aptly describes the observed fragility of self-regulation and the limits of its application, recently, efforts have increased to go beyond such metaphors and better understand the precise psychological mechanisms responsible when regulation fails (eg, Baumeister & Vohs, 2007; Gailliot et al., 2007; Inzlicht, Schmeichel, & Macrae, 2014; Kurzban, Duckworth, Kable, & Myers, 2013; Molden et al., 2012; Robinson, Schmeichel, & Inzlicht, 2010; see also Chapters 7, 13, 14, 15, 18, and 19). Several different perspectives have emerged and made some progress in this endeavor, but much uncertainty still exists surrounding the mechanisms of such failure. The present chapter thus evaluates and integrates the developing perspectives on self-regulation failure to construct a broader model of self-regulation that (1) identifies the key processes needed to explain current findings on regulation failure and (2) highlights what research questions are most critical for finding more effective ways to successfully bolster self-regulation.

We begin by considering what defines self-regulation failure and reviewing the findings implying that such failure arises from the depletion of a broad self-regulatory capacity. We then briefly review emerging evidence inconsistent with this capacity metaphor of self-regulation and the new perspectives developed to explain such evidence. Next, we integrate these new perspectives by characterizing self-regulation as a motivated process of effort evaluation and allocation and discuss how this framework provides a more comprehensive account of regulation failure. Finally, in light of this motivated effort-allocation perspective, we reexamine whether limited capacities are still needed to explain self-regulation failure and suggest an agenda for future research.

DEFINING SELF-REGULATION FAILURE

In our analysis, we adopt a broad definition of self-regulation failure. We conceptualize *self-regulation* as any instance in which people attempt to monitor and alter their own thoughts and behaviors for some desired objective (Baumeister & Vohs, 2007) and define failure in terms of any disruption of this process. As detailed later, this definition of self-regulation is related to, but broader than, the concepts of either *self-control* or *executive function*.

In both the psychological literature and popular consciousness, the concept of self-regulation is often interchangeable with *self-control*. However, some researchers explicitly distinguish the two, most often with the objective of creating narrower definitions of self-control as a subset of broader self-regulatory process. These distinctions most often conceptualize self-control specifically as the effortful and conscious process of managing a conflict between incompatible goals or desires, such as when people are tempted by short-term impulses that interfere with their long-term goals (eg, Baumeister, Vohs, & Tice, 2007; Fujita, 2011; Inzlicht & Berkman, 2015). Thus, whereas our definition of self-regulation includes additional processes such as choosing which goals to pursue, evaluating goal progress, and deciding whether to continue pursuit or disengage (see Carver & Scheier, 2001), these processes are seen as separate from self-control.

Because our definition of self-regulation encompasses this broad range of processes, it also captures multiple aspects of what is termed executive function. Executive function describes a specific set of psychological mechanisms, which include (1) *inhibiting* dominant responses, (2) *monitoring*, sustaining, and updating the contents of attention and working memory, and (3) *shifting* flexibly between appraisals or mind-sets (Miyake & Friedman, 2012). Although these mechanisms all play a role in broader self-regulatory processes of setting and pursuing goals, researchers who study self-control often specifically focus on how self-control is primarily supported by the successful inhibition of dominant responses (Baumeister, 2014; Inzlicht & Berkman, 2015; but see Chapter 5). In contrast, we believe it is useful to consider the role of all components of executive function when examining the success or failure of self-regulation.

Thus, while we agree that self-control conflicts requiring the inhibition of immediate impulses to achieve long-term goals are prototypical cases of self-regulation failure, we regard them as only a subset of the broader processes of self-regulation. Therefore, we aspire to identify general mechanisms that explain when and why people not only fail to inhibit their impulses but also fail to sustain their effort and focus or effectively shift between appraisals when setting and pursuing their goals. Even if self-control conflicts have unique characteristics that deserve special attention (eg, Kotabe & Hoffman, Chapter 19), we believe that any account of self-control failure should ultimately also fit within a more general account of self-regulation failure. Consequently, as detailed later, we analyze the internal mental processes responsible for whether people succeed or fail at sustaining their motivations for dedicating effort and attention toward highly valued goals.

CAPACITY-BASED EXPLANATIONS FOR SELF-REGULATION FAILURE

Most people greatly value highly desirable outcomes such as forming relationships, achieving personal and professional success, and being in good health. But, if such outcomes are so highly prioritized, it seems puzzling that individuals would so often fail to sustain their motivation to achieve them or shift their attention to goals they assign less importance. Indeed, classic models of self-regulation based simply on people's expectations for and valuing of success (eg, Feather, 1982), or their monitoring of the progress they are making toward desired outcomes (eg, Carver & Scheier, 1982) do not provide any ready way of accounting for these types of failures.

The elegant proposal that engaging in self-regulation draws from a general, but limited, pool of mental resources (Baumeister et al., 1994), and that the consumption of these resources reduces one's capacity for further self-regulation, provides a nice solution to this puzzle. If people's broad capacity for self-regulation diminishes every time they utilize it, then it is no surprise that they often have trouble sustaining such regulation toward important goals over time. Moreover, due to the decreased amount of general self-regulatory resources that would remain available, this perspective on self-regulation failure suggests that any exertion of self-regulation toward one particular goal should also subsequently impair the exertion of self-regulation toward any other goal, regardless of how much these goals differ in their content or the behaviors they require. That is, with their metaphorical self-regulatory strength expended, people should be "too weak" to carry out further regulation without sufficient opportunity for recovery. As also noted earlier, this type of broad carryover effect—which has come to be known as *ego depletion*—has indeed been repeatedly observed across a wide variety of circumstances and behaviors (Hagger et al., 2010).[1]

---

[1] A more recent metaanalysis examining carryover effects only in the context of well-validated indices of executive function found similar support for these effects (Carter, Kofler, Forster, & Mccullough, 2015). However, this analysis also noted that when newly developed statistical tools designed to correct for publication bias were applied, there appeared to be no cumulative evidence for carryover effects. Yet, concerns have arisen that these new statistical tools often severely underestimate metaanalytic effect sizes and inappropriately suggest the absence of cumulative metaanalytic effects (Reed, Florax, & Poot, 2015). Thus, any conclusions that evidence for the interference of one act of self-regulation on subsequent acts of self-regulation in a different domain is generally lacking seem premature (see also Inzlicht & Berkman, 2015).

LIMITATIONS OF CAPACITY EXPLANATIONS

The idea that self-regulation relies upon some general mental capacity that depletes whenever utilized was a critical theoretical innovation; it provided a clear and parsimonious answer to the unaddressed question of why self-regulation so often fails and identified an entirely new set of phenomena involving the transfer of this failure from one endeavor to another. However, this type of capacity model, and the muscle metaphor on which it is based, does not directly specify the psychological processes involved in self-regulation failure. Thus, subsequent research has begun to carefully examine these processes to better understand when and why carryover effects in self-regulation failure occur. Yet, instead of clarifying the mechanisms by which self-regulatory capacity depletes, the results of this research have actually raised questions about the extent to which a limited capacity really plays a role in self-regulation failure at all.

The specific programs of research that challenge the notions of a limited capacity for self-control are detailed in several other chapters throughout this volume (Chapters 2, 4, 8, 10, 11, and 17), but a few findings are worth highlighting here. First, it has long been established that people's exertion of self-regulation is highly dependent upon their levels of motivation. Apparent instances of ego depletion can be readily counteracted if the objective toward which people are self-regulating is especially motivationally engaging (eg, Hong & Lee, 2008; Moller, Deci, & Ryan, 2006; Muraven, Gagné, & Rosman, 2008), associated with large enough incentives (eg, Muraven & Slessareva, 2003), or one that inspires a close monitoring of the progress being made (Alberts, Martijn, & de Vries, 2011; Wan & Sternthal, 2008).

More recent discussions of capacity models of self-regulation have thus often acknowledged that the "ego depletion" typically observed is unlikely to be due to a completely exhausted capacity for regulation and begun to describe carryover effects from one instance of self-regulation to another as more often reflecting motivations to preserve one's limited resources unless good reasons exist to expend them (Baumeister, 2014; Baumeister et al., 2007). That is, extending the muscle metaphor, people presumably prefer to conserve their self-regulatory strength unless some emergency or opportunity sufficiently inspires them to greater expenditures of energy. This motivational reconfiguration of carryover effects preserves the importance of limited capacity as the primary source of motivations to withdraw from self-regulation, but places it in an indirect role such that people are assumed to withdraw their effort from regulation as they sense reductions in their self-regulatory capacity and choose to conserve these limited resources.

However, other recent findings have further challenged even this more indirect role for limited capacity. Several studies have indicated that after engaging in self-regulation, people will not show carryover effects if they (1) misattribute the effort involved in their initial regulation to an irrelevant source (Clarkson, Hirt, Chapman, & Jia, 2011; Clarkson, Hirt, Jia, & Alexander, 2010; see Chapter 10) or reconstrue this effort as enjoyable (Laran & Janiszewski, 2011), (2) merely expect or imagine their capacity for self-regulation is expanded following some initial regulation (Egan, Clarkson, & Hirt, 2015; Egan, Hirt, & Karpen, 2012; see Chapter 17), or (3) simply do not believe their own self-regulation is limited in capacity (Job, Dweck, & Walton, 2010; Job, Walton, Bernecker, & Dweck, 2013; Martijn, Tenbült, Merckelbach, Dreezens, & de Vries, 2002; see Chapter 11). Similarly, several studies have also shown that people will show these carryover effects without having actually engaged in any self-regulation themselves if they (1) attribute extra effort to an easy initial task (eg, Clarkson et al., 2011, 2010) or (2) merely expect or imagine an upcoming strenuous task (eg, Macrae et al., 2014). What's more, even in the absence of such specific attributions about or expectations of engaging in self-regulation, experiences that simply increase relaxation or boost tolerance for effort—such as watching a humorous video clip or favorite television program (Derrick, 2013; Tice, Baumeister, Shmueli, & Muraven, 2007), affirming one's core values (Schmeichel & Vohs, 2009), meditating (Friese, Messner, & Schaffner, 2012), or praying (Friese & Wänke, 2014), to name just a handful of examples—can eliminate carryover effects and sustain self-regulation (for recent overviews of the many factors that reduce carryover effects in self-regulation, see Chapters 2, 12; Masicampo, Martin, & Anderson, 2014).

Together, this second set of findings strongly suggests that the types of effects labeled as "ego depletion" can arise independent of the amount of self-regulation that people have actually exerted. That is, self-regulation failures appear to depend as much on people's mere beliefs and perceptions about how much self-regulation they have already performed, how much regulation might be required in the future, or even simply how relaxed or mentally taxed they are currently feeling, as it does on the actual amount of self-regulation in which they have engaged thus far. Such findings are difficult to reconcile with any monitoring of or response to reductions in one's fixed capacity for self-regulation (see also Inzlicht & Schmeichel, 2015).

EMERGING ALTERNATIVES TO CAPACITY EXPLANATIONS

Thus, although explaining self-regulation failure in terms of a limited capacity for such regulation initially provided a powerful and succinct account of an impressive variety effects, after nearly two decades of further research, such explanations no longer appear to adequately capture the full range of this phenomena. Accordingly, alternative explanations of self-regulation failure have begun to appear. Space limitations prevent a detailed review of these alternatives, some of which are described elsewhere in this volume (Chapters 7, 13, 18, and 19), but, again, a few aspects are worth emphasizing. First, to incorporate the observed effects of people's motivations on their continued exertion of self-regulation, most updated accounts of self-regulation failure characterize this as a process of motivated allocation of attention and effort, but one that does not depend on perceptions of reduced capacity (cf., Baumeister, 2014; Baumeister & Vohs, 2007). These types of mechanisms explain how increased engagement, importance, or incentives associated with particular goals can bolster self-regulation and counteract any carryover effects of previous efforts at regulation (ie, reduce "depletion"). Second, to incorporate the observed effects of people's beliefs about or experiences of exerting self-regulation on their continued regulation, most updated accounts of self-regulation failure conceptualize these types of beliefs and experiences as directly influencing the motivations that determine the allocation of effort and attention. These types of mechanisms explain how factors such as beliefs about the source of one's effort, interpretations of the experience of effort, or any additional experiences that might offset the unpleasantness of effort can also bolster self-regulation and counteract carryover effects of previous regulation. Therefore, on the whole, these newly emerging perspectives on self-regulation failure do not rely on a limited capacity to explain such failure (see Masicampo et al., 2014) and some even reject the idea that such a capacity exists at all (eg, Inzlicht & Schmeichel, 2015; Kurzban et al., 2013).

For example, Kurzban et al. (2013) describe the role of motivation in self-regulation in terms of people's desires to exert and sustain self-regulation based on the perceived opportunity costs of continued exertion. They propose that people assess whether maintaining self-regulation toward one particular goal would interfere with allocating that regulation toward alternative goals and suggest that self-regulation failure represents a shift of effort and attention from one goal to others (see also Chapter 13). Similarly, Inzlicht and Schmeichel (2012, 2015) and Inzlicht et al. (2014) also place motivational dynamics at the center of people's choices to sustain self-regulation, but instead of focusing on perceived opportunity costs more generally, they propose that exerting self-regulation sensitizes people to specific types of opportunities that involve immediately rewarding outcomes. From this perspective, engaging in self-regulation actually alters people's motivations and shifts their priorities and attention in ways that often undermine their continued regulation until these more immediate concerns have been addressed.

Moreover, beyond their basic grounding in motivational processes, both of these accounts of self-regulation failure also give a prominent role to people's experiences during self-regulation as activating and directing these processes. In addition to proposing that perceived opportunity costs motivate choices to engage in self-regulation, Kurzban et al. (2013) further propose that the effort experienced during regulation directly informs the calculation of these perceived costs. Drawing on recent conceptualizations of mental effort and cognitive fatigue as states that inform and direct goal pursuit (see Hockey, 2013), they argue that the greater fatigue experienced during or greater effort attributed to self-regulation, the greater the perceived opportunity costs of continued regulation, and the more likely that effort will be withdrawn. Based on the same motivational conceptualizations of mental effort, Inzlicht and Schmeichel (2015) and Inzlicht et al. (2014) similarly propose that such effort is experienced as inherently aversive (Inzlicht, Bartholow, & Hirsh, 2015) and thus spurs people to shift their priorities to more enjoyable pursuits. That is, as negative feelings of exerting self-regulation accumulate, people are presumably less likely to choose to engage in further regulation and more likely to choose something that gives them pleasure or fulfills immediate desires without requiring effort (see also Chapter 7).

A MOTIVATED EFFORT-ALLOCATION MODEL OF SELF-REGULATION FAILURE

Whatever differences exist among these emerging accounts of self-regulation failure, the growing consensus is that processes associated both with shifting motivations regarding the value of continued self-regulation and with the perceived experience of engaging in regulation are central to such failure. Our own initial attempts to integrate all of the emerging perspectives into a more comprehensive account of self-regulation thus rest upon these two fundamental processes as well. However, in our *motivated effort-allocation* (MEA) model of self-regulation failure, we also further specify the particular mechanisms that should determine people's experiences of self-regulation and how these experiences should alter people's motivations for continued regulation. Drawing from classic models of goal selection and goal pursuit, we address some of the uncertainties remaining in the accounts described earlier and identify critical areas for further research.

Before we describe the MEA model further, it is important to note that although explaining self-regulation failure in terms of shifting motivations regarding the value of continued self-regulation and perceived experiences of engaging in regulation does not rely on any notion of a limited capacity for regulation, it does still prominently characterize self-regulation as difficult and requiring attention and mental effort. Indeed, although the various lines of evidence presented earlier challenge the notion that failures of self-regulation occur because of a depleted capacity for regulation, this evidence also clearly illustrates that people themselves often perceive limits to the levels of effort they can muster or sustain (Job et al., 2010; Martijn et al., 2002). That is, even if they are not directly sensing the approach of any true limits to their self-regulatory capacity, people tend to avoid fatigue and are motivated to conserve their expenditures of effort (Bijleveld, Custers, & Aarts, 2012; Kool & Botvinick, 2014; Kool, McGuire, Rosen, & Botvinick, 2010). Thus, any alternative perspective on self-regulation must explain such motivations in addition to all of the other mechanisms described thus far. As we discuss more fully in the final section of this chapter, while it may be tempting to assume a focus on conservation must reflect some real consumption of mental "energy," emerging perspectives on the nature of fatigue strongly question the validity of such assumptions and are completely consistent with alternative perspectives on self-regulation failure that do not rely on limited capacities for regulation (see Hockey, 2013).

The broad structure of the MEA model is presented in Fig. 20.1. This model involves a cyclical process with three main components: (1) the *assessment* of how strongly one is motivated to engage in self-regulation, (2) the *allocation* of effort and attention to self-regulation produced by this assessment, and (3) the *monitoring* of the consequences and experiences of

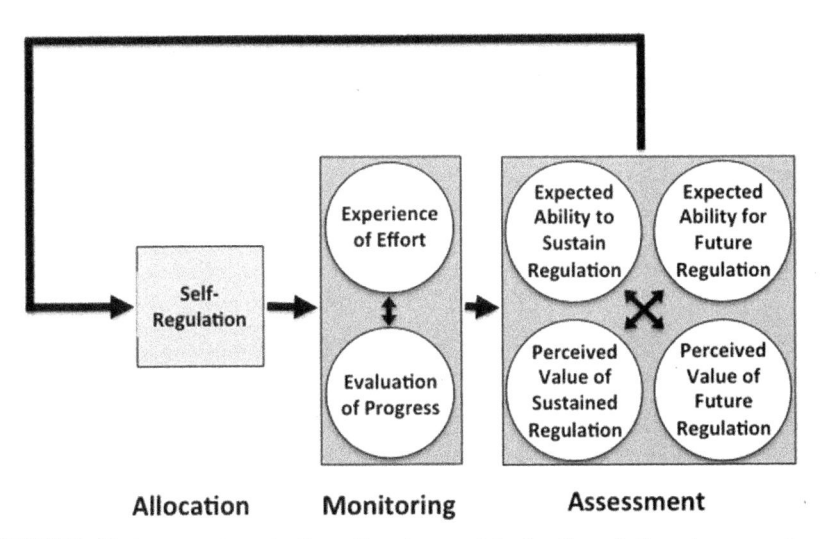

FIGURE 20.1 A motivated effort-allocation model of self-regulation. Assessments of motivations to exert self-regulation produce allocations of effort and attention to engage in regulation. The consequences of self-regulation are then monitored and motivations to continue regulation reassessed.

this allocation, which then spurs a reassessment of one's motivations to continue self-regulation.

Our account of self-regulation failure thus places experiences of engaging in self-regulation and motivations for continued regulation within the context of cybernetic control theories of this process (see also Chapter 15; Robinson et al., 2010). Control theories are defined by a continuous feedback loop that functions to assess and respond to discrepancies from a desired state (Carver & Scheier, 2001).[2] In the MEA model, we propose that people first assess whether engaging in self-regulation is indeed likely to produce this type of desired state. This assessment defines their motivation to engage in regulation and results in an allocation of attention and effort to pursuing appropriate actions proportional to that motivation. We further propose that, following this allocation, people monitor whether self-regulation is effectively bringing about the desired state by evaluating the costs and benefits of their current level of regulation and whether it is worth continuing. This monitoring defines their perceptions and experiences of pursuing such regulation. At any point, if these experiences suggest that current levels of self-regulation will not produce the desired state without the costs outweighing the benefits, then regulation will diminish or cease altogether. Thus, the MEA model also borrows extensively from Kurzban et al.'s (2013) perspective, but, as detailed later, also expands upon it in several important ways.

In the following sections, we elaborate more on how we conceptualize each of these processes and their ongoing interactions, but some general considerations are worth noting at the outset. Although the assessment, allocation, and monitoring processes in the MEA model may often involve conscious deliberation and intentional action, in contrast to some other emerging accounts of self-regulation failure (Inzlicht & Schmeichel, 2015; Inzlicht et al., 2014), this need not be the case. Accumulating evidence suggests that self-regulation can be initiated and pursued outside of intention and awareness (see Gillebaart & De Ridder, 2015; Chapter 3). Thus, in the MEA model, awareness and intention are conceptualized as potentially

---

[2] As Carver and Scheier (2001) have noted, control-theory accounts of self-regulation include goals that involve both reducing discrepancies with desired end-states and increasing discrepancies with undesired end-states. Although, for simplicity, we describe the assessment and monitoring processes of the MEA model as they apply to desired end-states, these processes are proposed to operate the same way with undesired end-states. That is, in the MEA model, the critical variables that determine motivations to engage in and sustain self-regulation and the mechanisms for monitoring this regulation are identical in either case; however, the unique cognitions and emotions arising from the assessment and monitoring of progress toward a desired end-state versus progress away from an undesired end-state (eg, Carver, Lawrence, & Scheier, 1999) should still affect the output of these mechanisms and the course of self-regulation overall.

altering when and how people may engage in self-regulation but not the types of evaluations and experiences that guide regulation. Instead, we assume that the assessments of perceived ability, assignments of value, and monitoring of effort and progress displayed in Fig. 20.1 and detailed later can all both occur outside of awareness or intention and be guided by conscious deliberation (see Bijleveld et al., 2012; Marien, Custers, Hassin, & Aarts, 2012). That is, although conscious attention to these processes may change how their specific outputs are weighted or interpreted during self-regulation, generating and integrating these outputs is not presumed to require such attention.

Another general consideration worth noting is that the monitoring and assessment processes describe by the MEA model in Fig. 20.1 concern people's motivations to engage in self-regulation toward some objective, but are not necessarily equivalent to their overall motivations to accomplish that objective itself. That is, the MEA model specifically describes the proximal regulation of effort or attention directed toward some goal rather than the ultimate engagement in the goal itself. Thus, if motivations for self-regulation shift and wane, people may temporarily cease actively pursuing a particular goal in the moment, but not disengage from this goal overall (eg, choosing to end a workout early does not mean that one has abandoned the goal to get in shape). This hierarchical distinction is essentially equivalent to one made by Duckworth and Gross (2014) between sustained goal pursuit in the moment (what they label *self-control*) and sustained goal pursuit over an extended period of time (what they label *grit*), and the MEA model primarily explains self-regulation failure of the former rather than the latter variety.

Assessing Motivations for Self-Regulation

The MEA model places emerging insights on the mechanisms of self-regulation failure within the motivational context of control theories of regulation, but it also integrates important features of other broad models of self-regulatory processes as well. First, as Fig. 20.1 illustrates, our specific account of people's assessments of whether to initiate, continue, or withdraw from self-regulation incorporates longstanding theories on the role of expectancy and value in goal setting and goal pursuit (Feather, 1982). That is, we conceptualize these assessments as depending upon both people's expectations concerning their ability to muster the effort and attention they believe self-regulating toward some outcome will require, and the total value they believe regulation will have for producing this outcome versus any alternative outcome to which such regulation might be dedicated. Also similar to traditional motivational theories of expectancy and value, the MEA model assumes a multiplicative relationship between these two factors, such that as either expected ability to engage in the self-regulation required or perceived value of what this regulation would accomplish becomes increasingly low, then the actual self-regulation allocated to some objective will rapidly diminish as well (but see Shah & Higgins, 1997).

However, the MEA model also extends traditional considerations of expectancy and value by including not only evaluations of the self-regulation they are currently pursuing, but also the potential regulation they believe they might pursue in the near future (see also Chapter 7). To capture the influence of people's perceptions of limited capacity, and the concerns with conservation this may produce (see Job, Bernecker, et al., 2015), the MEA model proposes that motivations for allocating self-regulation depend on their assessment of both the outcomes they could currently pursue and any outcomes they might want to pursue in the immediate future (or of just the possibility of immediately pursuing nonspecified future outcomes in general). As Fig. 20.1 further illustrates, we conceptualize this assessment of potential future outcomes as again relying both on people's expected ability to summon whatever effort and attention such outcomes might demand and the value they believe this future regulation would contribute toward accomplishing them. The MEA model assumes some inverse multiplicative relationship between these factors, such that as either anticipated ability to exert additional self-regulation toward future objectives becomes increasingly low or perceived value of what regulation would contribute to these future rather than the current objectives becomes increasingly high, then the self-regulation allocated to the current objective will, again, rapidly diminish.

Thus, overall, according to the MEA model, people's motivation to engage in self-regulation arises from their assessments of what this regulation can accomplish. This assessment depends on the combination of the expected ability for engaging in and the value placed on self-regulating toward the various objectives one might pursue in the present and, at the same time, on the combination of the expected ability for engaging in and the value placed on potentially self-regulating toward whatever objectives one might anticipate pursuing in the immediate future. In this way, the assessment stage of the MEA model captures the dynamic influence of both people's motivations to sustain effort on the current focus of their self-regulation and their motivations to conserve effort for any important demands for future regulation that might subsequently arise.

Monitoring the Consequences and Experiences of Self-Regulation

Once the assessment process activates motivations to engage in self-regulation toward a desired outcome, and these motivations evoke the allocation of effort and attention toward pursuing the outcome, the MEA model proposes that this then also activates a monitoring process to evaluate how effectively the current level of self-regulation is producing the desired outcome. As shown in Fig. 20.1, drawing heavily on control theories of self-regulation, we conceptualize the first major component of the monitoring process as an evaluation of the progress made toward the desired outcome. This evaluation includes not only how close one is to successfully achieving the outcome but also how quickly one is progressing in pursuit of the outcome (Carver & Scheier, 2001). This aspect of the monitoring process thus captures the perceived consequences of self-regulation and involves judgments of whether these consequences match what was intended.

Yet, once again, the MEA model extends traditional control theories by also including in the monitoring process evaluations of effort as well as progress. Drawing upon recent reconceptualizations of experiences of effort and mental fatigue as part of a motivational signaling process (Hockey, 2013; Kurzban et al., 2013), we propose that the second major component of the monitoring process is an evaluation of the effort required to self-regulate toward the desired outcome. This aspect of the monitoring process captures perceptions of the varying costs defined by the amount of effort and attention required to achieve different levels of progress.

Furthermore, as also shown in Fig. 20.1, although evaluations of effort and progress are independent, the MEA model proposes that these two evaluations are integrated during the monitoring process. The output of this integration is defined as a weighting of the benefits of perceived progress achieved through self-regulation by the costs of perceived effort required to sustain this level of progress. That is, monitoring processes produce a combined evaluation of the *worth* of maintaining current levels of self-regulation, which we suggest is based on the ratio of progress to effort. Thus, as the perceived progress produced by self-regulation becomes increasingly small or the perceived effort required to sustain self-regulation becomes increasingly large, then the overall worth of continued regulation will rapidly diminish as the costs of further self-regulation are perceived as quickly overwhelming the benefits.

As in Kurzban et al.'s (2013) opportunity cost perspective on self-regulation, the MEA model assumes judgments of worth that occur during monitoring produce specific phenomenological experiences of mental fatigue. As the judged worth of continuing self-regulation diminishes, experiences of mental fatigue grows. Note that we are conceptualizing such fatigue as distinct from mere effort. Whereas we define effort as arising from perceptions of the amount of attention and focus required by current acts of self-regulation, we define fatigue as arising from the accumulated effects of this effort on the judged worth of continued regulation (see Hockey, 2013).

Another important assumption of the MEA model is that even if effort and progress during self-regulation remain constant, over time the judged worth of self-regulation will decrease and mental fatigue will increase.

Much research has shown that on tasks requiring sustained effort and attention, performance steadily declines and reported fatigue increases (eg, Wascher et al., 2014). Although these effects are somewhat offset by introducing additional incentives for sustained performance after some time period, neither performance nor fatigue typically return to their original levels (eg, Lorist et al., 2009). Also, people evaluate engaging in the effort of self-regulation and cognitive control as inherently costly; they will forgo greater rewards and even spend more time performing a task to reduce the acute cognitive effort they must exert (Kool & Botvinick, 2014; Kool et al., 2010). Therefore, as effort toward engaging in self-regulation continues, this effort should be perceived as increasingly more costly (see also Inzlicht et al., 2014; Kurzban et al., 2013), fatigue should accumulate, and judgments of worth should decrease.[3]

Thus, according to the MEA model, people's evaluations of the consequences of engaging in self-regulation arise from their monitoring of what this regulation is worth. Judgments of worth depend on the ratio of the perceived benefits of the progress being made through self-regulation and the perceived costs of the effort required to sustain the amount of regulation producing this progress. Moreover, judgments of worth are assumed to directly affect experiences of mental fatigue, which progressively accumulate over the course of self-regulation due to the inherent perceived costs of continued effort. Thus, when the perceived progress produced by self-regulation outweighs accumulated experiences of the effort required to attain this progress, judged worth will be higher and experienced fatigue will be lower. However, once accumulated experiences of effort begin to outweigh perceived progress, judged worth will be lower and experienced fatigue will be higher. Also, as noted earlier, although experiences of effort and fatigue are critical components of the monitoring process, the basic computations of worth during monitoring and the subsequent effects of this judged worth need not be conscious or intentional and may result from more implicit and spontaneous evaluations (Bijleveld et al., 2012; Marien et al., 2012; see also Chapter 7; Kool et al., 2010). In this way, the monitoring stage of the MEA model captures how online evaluations of momentary fluctuations in the experiences of engaging in self-regulation, as well as how these experiences progress

---

[3] Vohs, Glass, Maddox, and Markman (2010) showed that whereas engaging in an initial self-regulation task reduced subsequent self-regulation in the form of aggression following provocation, sleep deprivation did not. Although Vohs et al. have argued that these findings demonstrate carryover effects in self-regulation distinct from experiences of fatigue, sleep deprivation creates a unique state that is not equivalent to mental fatigue (Hockey, 2013; Hossain, Reinish, Kayumov, Bhuiya, & Shapiro, 2003). Thus, such findings do not conclusively undermine the proposed role of experiences of fatigue in self-regulation failure (see Inzlicht & Berkman, 2015).

over time, dynamically affect ongoing impressions of whether regulation is producing desirable effects.

Reassessment and Reallocation

Following the initial assessments that motivate self-regulation and the monitoring of whether the attention and effort then allocated has proven worthwhile, the MEA model finally proposes a cyclical reassessment of whether sufficient motivations still exist to continue regulation. As Fig. 20.1 illustrates, the judged worth of sustaining self-regulation that emerges from evaluations of effort and progress reengages the assessment process detailed earlier and updates present motivations for regulation. That is, the experiences of fatigue emerging from judged worth function as motivational signals that may alter the perceived ability for and value of continued self-regulation (see also Hockey, 2013; Kurzban et al., 2013). If judged worth is high and fatigue is low, perceptions of ability and value for continued self-regulation should also generally remain high and produce sufficient motivations for sustaining regulation versus conserving effort for the future (or, if the judged worth is high enough, motivation for current regulation could even increase). But, if judged worth is low and fatigue is high, perceptions of either ability for or the value of continued regulation, or both, should decrease and motivations to continue self-regulation versus conserve effort for the future should diminish (see also Chapter 8).

In summary, the MEA model explains self-regulation failure as a disruption of motivations to exert this regulation toward valued goals. That is, even if overall motivations to accomplish some objective remain high, when the judged worth of continuing self-regulation to pursue this goal is currently diminished, such regulation may fail (cf. Duckworth & Gross, 2014). Furthermore, because the perceived costs of effort and experienced fatigue of self-regulation accumulate, after completing or withdrawing from self-regulation toward one objective, motivations to pursue regulation on subsequent tasks may still be diminished. Such motivational disruptions can thus explain not only failures to sustain self-regulation toward current goals, but also carryover effects of exerting regulation in one domain to subsequent self-regulation failures in another (see also Kool & Botvinick, 2014; Kurzban et al., 2013). Thus, in the MEA model, the carryover effects that capacity models of self-regulation define as "ego depletion" are a general motivational consequence of sustained self-regulation (see also Chapter 18; Inzlicht & Schmeichel, 2015).

Additional Influences on Monitoring and Assessment

The MEA model presented in Fig. 20.1 incorporates the two fundamental processes identified as important for understanding when and how self-regulation failure occurs by newly emerging accounts of this phenomena: motivations for and experiences of engaging in self-regulation. It also extends these emerging accounts by further specifying the critical components of these motivations and experiences and integrating elements from classic models of goal selection and goal pursuit. But, we believe the true value of the MEA model is how it incorporates and explains the effects on self-regulation of all the diverse incentives, attributions, lay theories, or subjective experiences reviewed earlier (see also Chapters 2, 10, 11, and 12; Masicampo et al., 2014). As illustrated in Fig. 20.2, additional variables arising from (1) the objectives toward which people are self-regulating, (2) how they represent or experience these objectives, or (3) whatever additional opportunities are present can affect self-regulation by altering the final output of both monitoring and assessment processes.

Monitoring

Many variables could affect the monitoring of the consequences of self-regulation by altering either the experiences of effort during regulation or the evaluations of the progress this regulation produces. Actions or environments that increase experiences of relaxation, tranquility, engagement,

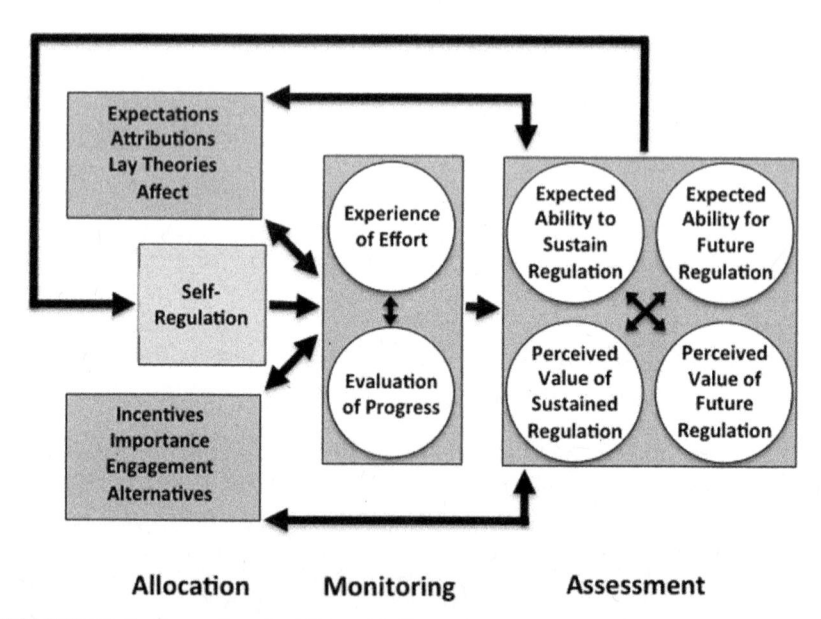

FIGURE 20.2 Examples of additional influences on motivated effort-allocation during self-regulation. A variety of cognitive and motivational processes can alter and interact with both the assessment of motivations for self-regulation and the monitoring of the consequences of the attention and effort allocated to regulation.

or just broad positive affect; such as taking a short rest (Tyler & Burns, 2008) or any of the other activities such as meditation, or prayer reviewed earlier; should help sustain self-regulation by counteracting the experiences of effort and fatigue associated with regulation (see also Chapter 4). Furthermore, as also reviewed earlier, what is most critical for these influences on monitoring processes is not the experiences themselves, but people's interpretations of how these experiences may offset the effortful costs of engaging in self-regulation (see Chapters 11, 12, and 17). In addition, circumstances that enhance attention to how well one is achieving a desired objective, such as the cues or expectations that encourage the monitoring of current task performance or boost the importance or self-relevance of this task, as reviewed earlier, should prolong regulation. Similarly, expectations or lay theories about how fast progress should occur or the amount of effort it should require could also affect these types of evaluations; beliefs that progress should be fast and easy may more quickly result in lower judgments of worth and reduced motivations for self-regulation if substantial effort is required, whereas beliefs that progress will not only demand effort but can also be measured by the effort expended may sustain judged worth and motivations for regulation (Labroo & Kim, 2009; Miele & Molden, 2010; see Molden, 2013). Thus, overall, any variables that independently alter how people either experience the act of engaging in self-regulation or evaluate the progress that regulation produces should also moderate the total judged worth of self-regulation produced by the monitoring process and, in turn, motivations for continued regulation.

Assessment

Beyond indirectly influencing motivations to continue self-regulation through effects on judged worth during monitoring, many variables could also directly affect the assessment of motivations to sustain self-regulation. For example, even if monitoring of progress and effort indicates low judged worth for continued self-regulation, as reviewed earlier, increased incentives associated with the personal importance of or the motivational engagement produced by the outcome of current regulation could still directly enhance the perceived value of this regulation and bolster assessed motivations to continue. Furthermore, high perceived efficacy for sustaining self-regulation or attributions of fatigue to motivationally irrelevant features of the environment could directly counteract effects of experienced fatigue and low judged worth of regulation on expected ability to sustain regulation, which could again independently bolster assessed motivations to continue (Chow, Hui, & Lau, 2015; Chapter 10).

In contrast, even if the monitoring of progress and effort indicate high judged worth for sustained self-regulation, perceived opportunities to pursue alternative highly valued goals or to obtain immediately desirable rewards could directly undermine the perceived value of the current regulation and independently impair assessed motivations to continue. Furthermore, beliefs that one's mental capacities are limited and quickly depleting or attributions of fatigue to one's capacity to continue could directly counteract high judged worth for regulation by undermining expected ability to sustain regulation in the present or to reinitiate regulation in the near future and again undermine assessed motivations to continue. Thus, overall, variables that independently affect any of the components of the assessment process in Fig. 20.2 should also moderate the ultimate impact of the motivational signals produced by monitoring processes on cumulative motivations to engage in self-regulation and allocations of effort and attention to sustain such regulation.

Other Important Features of the Motivated Effort-Allocation Model

Some additional implications of the expanded MEA model in Fig. 20.2 are also worth noting. First, any variable may conceivably inhibit or bolster self-regulation through both the monitoring and assessment processes. For example, the autonomy of the objective toward which people are self-regulating can bolster regulation both by increasing experiences of subjective vitality (eg, Muraven et al., 2008; see Chapter 4), which would improve the judged worth during monitoring, and by independently bolstering the personal importance of and engagement with this objective (eg, Moller et al., 2006). Thus, as Masicampo et al. (2014) noted, many variables may have the same effects on self-regulation whether they are introduced before any regulation has begun, thus potentially altering subsequent assessment of motivations for regulation, or only after some initial regulation, thus potentially altering subsequent monitoring and reassessment of motivations for continuing regulation toward the same or different objectives. However, some variables could have different effects on self-regulation depending upon which process they most directly affect; concrete, low-level mental construals may sustain regulation when they bolster the monitoring of progress toward maintaining a desired standard (Schmeichel, Vohs, & Duke, 2010), but hinder regulation when they increase the focus on immediate judgments of diminishing worth during assessment of motivations to continue and undermine a focus on broader, abstract values that may still support these motivations (Fujita & Carnevale, 2012). Thus, the MEA model emphasizes the importance of considering multiple routes through which various factors may affect the self-regulation process, and whether these effects will be complementary or offsetting.

Another important aspect of the MEA model worth noting is that, in Fig. 20.2, the variables that affect monitoring and assessment processes (which are not meant to represent a comprehensive list) are roughly divided into a set of more cognitive influences, such as expectations, attributions, and lay theories, toward the top of the figure and more motivational influences, such as incentives, engagement, and the value of alternative pursuits, toward the bottom. However, this is not intended to imply that the former variables are only expected to affect more cognitive processes such as perceptions of effort and expectations of ability to engage in self-regulation whereas the latter are only expected to affect more motivational processes such as evaluations of progress and the value of present or future efforts at regulation. It is likely that variables such as engagement or importance affect experiences of effort and expectations about abilities to sustain regulation, and variables such as lay theories and attributions affect variables such as perceived progress and the value placed on future progress. Thus, the MEA model incorporates the many known interactions between motivational and cognitive processes (see Molden & Higgins, 2005, 2012), and when one is applying this model to investigate the mechanisms by which a particular variable affects self-regulation, it is important to consider and empirically test all of the possible routes of this influence (cf. Chow et al., 2015; vanDellen, Shea, Davisson, Koval, & Fitzsimons, 2014).

A final feature of the MEA model worth nothing is that, although we have portrayed it as a series of separate stages, we assume that processes of assessment, allocation, monitoring, and reassessment are dynamically updated and can occur in parallel (eg, Ehret, Monroe, & Read, 2015). For example, changes in the judged worth of self-regulation during monitoring may instantaneously spur the online reassessment of motivations to continue, which in turn alters the allocation until an equilibrium is again reached and the current level of self-regulation stabilizes.

ADVANTAGES OF A MOTIVATED EFFORT-ALLOCATION MODEL

Our MEA model of self-regulation failure builds upon, and thus highly overlaps with, other recent perspectives (eg, Inzlicht & Schmeichel, 2015; Inzlicht et al., 2014; Kurzban, 2010). However, we believe that, because it integrates several key aspects of these other models, along with other classic perspectives on self-regulation, the MEA model has several unique advantages.

Common Mechanisms for Different Types of Self-Regulation Failure

The first advantage of the MEA model is its generality. As noted at the outset, many other accounts (eg, Inzlicht & Schmeichel, 2015; Chapter 19) focus only on explaining specific instances of conflict between short-term desires or temptations and long-term goals, which are typically labeled as involving self-control. The MEA model also captures these conflicts between incompatible desires or goals in that alternative priorities (or temptations) that arise can both temporarily increase the effort experienced while regulating toward the current focal goal and reduce the perceived value of sustained regulation toward this goal (see Fig. 20.2). However, within the same general framework, our model also describes (1) failures to muster sufficient effort or attention to attain desired levels of performance, in that any factors highlighting accumulating experiences of effort or perceptions of reduced progress undermine the judged worth of continued regulation and (2) failures to optimally shift regulation between different objectives, in that any factors reducing experiences of effort or enhancing experiences of progress increase the perceived value of continued regulation toward one pursuit at the expense of other important goals. Thus, the MEA model encompasses the full range of phenomena related to the deployment, maintenance, and withdrawal of effort and attention toward valued goals.

Another benefit of the generality of MEA model is that it need not distinguish conflicts involving short-term desires and long-term goals from other instances of competing motivations. Because some perspectives define only the former as involving self-control (Inzlicht & Schmeichel, 2015; Chapter 19), precise classification of what constitutes *desires* versus *goals* or what span of time counts as "short term" versus "long term" is ultimately required. Indeed, accumulating evidence suggests that people may often redefine what they have previously considered to be distracting temptations or desires as valued goals (see De Witt Huberts, Evers, & De Ridder, 2013), making such distinctions problematic. The MEA model avoids these problems by assuming that any alternative desires or objectives that might interfere with self-regulation toward a particular goal will affect this regulation through the processes outlined in Figs. 20.1 and 20.2.

Expanded Specification of Phenomenological and Motivational Processes

Elaborating on the Opportunity Costs Model

Because Kurzban et al.'s (2013) opportunity costs perspective on self-regulation failure is also a general model of motivated engagement and withdrawal of effort, the MEA model shares the same basic structure and many similar features. However, our model goes beyond an opportunity costs perspective in several important ways. Opportunity costs are presumed to motivate effort toward self-regulation through a simple utility calculation based on the anticipated costs and benefits of various actions requiring such effort. Moreover, experiences of effort and fatigue during self-regulation are presumed to be a direct signal of opportunity costs. We agree that considerations of alternative costs and benefits, as well as experiences of effort and fatigue are important for understanding self-regulation and the MEA model features them prominently. However, our model provides a more elaborate analysis of the phenomenological and motivational processes of engaging in self-regulation.

First, we further specify what the relative costs and benefits people experience during self-regulation entail: the effort of sustaining regulation versus the amount and rate of progress toward a valued goal that this regulation produces, respectively. In addition, we distinguish between the experience of *effort* during self-regulation and the experience of *fatigue*. In our view, whereas effort directly represents the perceived costs that regulation entails, fatigue reflects the progress effort produces, as well as how long this effort has continued, and constitutes the primary motivational input for assessing whether self-regulation should continue (cf. Hockey, 2013).

Furthermore, rather than assuming that the motivational signals produced by effort and fatigue are uniform, the MEA model specifies several variables that may modify these signals. As discussed earlier, people's expectations, attributions, and lay theories may influence how they interpret their experiences of effort as related to the progress they are making; when individuals view effort as nondiagnostic of progress (see Chapter 10), or even as a signal that they are creating opportunities for increased progress (Labroo & Kim, 2009; Miele & Molden, 2010), then experiences of mental fatigue no longer lower judgments of the worth of self-regulation or motivations to continue regulation, and in some cases can even increase it (see Molden, 2013).

Finally, beyond treating experiences of mental effort and fatigue simply as a signal for the utility of continued self-regulation, the MEA model places this signal in the broader motivational context of principles of goal selection and pursuit. That is, our model considers the effects that experiences of mental fatigue may have on both expected abilities for and the value placed on sustained regulation, and for both present and future objectives. In this way, the MEA model captures the dynamics of people's separate motivations to continue self-regulation in the present and beliefs they might need to conserve "mental energy" for the future. Therefore, overall, the MEA model does not contradict the core principles of Kurzban et al.'s (2013) opportunity–costs perspective, but it does specify additional mechanisms that explain a greater range of phenomena.

Clarifying the Shifting Priorities Perspective

In addition to elaborating upon opportunity costs perspectives, the MEA model expands and clarifies Inzlicht and Schmeichel's (2015) shifting priorities account of self-regulation failure. First, as discussed earlier, the shifting priorities account focuses on a narrower range of self-regulation failures involving conflicts between short-term desires and long-term goals. Also, as it has developed, the shifting priorities account has absorbed the basic structure of the opportunity costs perspective regarding how experienced effort alters motivations to exert self-regulation. Thus, the relative advantages we have already outlined for the MEA model regarding these two issues apply to the shifting priorities account as well.

However, the novel feature of the shifting priorities account is that it too goes beyond the simple utility calculation of the opportunity costs perspective by describing how experiences of effort and fatigue shift motivations away from (1) *exploiting* known incentives to *exploring* new incentives, (2) *laborious* pursuits that demand effort to *leisurely* pursuits that are free from effort, and (3) what people feel they *have* to do to what they feel they *want* to do (Chapter 18; Inzlicht et al., 2014). Furthermore, whereas increased concerns with exploration versus exploitation and leisure versus labor represent broader, ultimate causes of self-regulation failure, their effects are proposed to be mediated through the proximal cause of focusing on what one wants versus what one has to do. Thus, experiences of effort and fatigue shift attention and motivation toward alternative objectives that are perceived as more enjoyable and rewarding.

The MEA model is certainly consistent with both of these ultimate and proximal motivational consequences of self-regulation, but it clarifies what we see as important distinctions between the processes involved. As detailed earlier, we agree that exerting effort is experienced as unpleasant and costly (Inzlicht et al., 2015; Kool et al., 2010) and that carryover effects of self-regulation essentially reflect a reduced willingness to bear the perceived costs of further effort. However, we do not agree that this motivational process is equivalent to, or its effects directly mediated by, increased desires for immediate rewards (Inzlicht & Schmeichel, 2012) or for pursuing objectives people feel they want to rather than have to (Inzlicht et al., 2014).

Both immediate rewards and objectives people want to achieve can require high or low effort to realize, and thus these two priorities are conceptually independent of motivations to exert effort. Indeed, although accumulating evidence suggests that engaging in self-regulation does increase attention to the possibility of reward (see Chapters 6, 13, and 14), some research has suggested that the diminished motivations for effort that also follow self-regulation have priority such that people only increase reward-seeking behavior if little effort is required (Giacomantonio, Jordan, Fennis, & Panno, 2014). Thus, the MEA model provides separate pathways for the motivational influences of reward and effort. Perceived costs of effort and labor are defined as an inherent feature of the monitoring process, which is consistent with the argument of the shifting priorities account that these costs are a general product of human evolutionary history (Inzlicht et al., 2014). However, as shown in Fig. 20.2, other motivations concerning how people construe the importance, personal relevance, or autonomy of a particular objective are not an inherent part of the monitoring process and affect continued self-regulation through their own pathways. Thus, in the MEA model, although feeling one wants to self-regulate rather than one has to should certainly affect experiences of fatigue through the influence of these feelings on monitoring processes, the overall effects of such feelings will also depend upon their direct effects on assessments of the expected ability to and the perceived value of engaging in both current and future self-regulation. In this way, motivations concerning willingness to exert effort and engage in "labor" and motivations concerning what one wants to and has to do may still be related and interact, but the processes through which they affect continued self-regulation remain separate and their independent influences can be evaluated.

IMPLICATIONS OF A MOTIVATED EFFORT-ALLOCATION MODEL FOR CAPACITY EXPLANATIONS OF SELF-REGULATION FAILURE

On the whole, the MEA model of self-regulation failure incorporates the host of newly emerging lines of research on the different perceptions, experiences, and motivations that can help or hinder self-regulation. It also integrates, extends, and refines other recent attempts to bring together this new literature. But, beyond this, one of the most important aspects of the MEA model is its implications for capacity explanations of self-regulation failure.

In their own reconceptualization of "depletion" effects in which an initial instance of self-regulation reduces subsequent efforts at regulation, both Kurzban et al. (2013) and Inzlicht et al. (2014) suggest that the original capacity explanations of this reduction are no longer tenable. They argue that given the many factors moderating whether one act of self-regulation affects those that follow and the sufficiency of motivational mechanisms for explaining how and when this occurs, there is little evidence or theoretical justification for continuing to consider limited capacity as an important aspect of these effects. However, Baumeister (2014) has countered that, although the emerging evidence clearly reveals the influence of motivation on carryover effects of engaging in self-regulation, the concept of a limited resource is still required to explain the full range of related phenomena. Based on the MEA model, we agree with the former argument that, despite the critical role of capacity models in advancing research on self-regulation, the current evidence no longer justifies retaining the idea of limited self-regulatory resources when explaining, predicting, or attempting to improve such regulation. Indeed, we believe that the MEA model can explain the types of evidence that Baumeister cites as still demonstrating limited self-regulatory capacity within the framework of the monitoring and assessment processes displayed in Fig. 20.2.

Explaining Increases in Self-Regulation From Practice

The first type of evidence frequently cited to support the continued role of a limited capacity in carryover effects of self-regulation is that practicing acts of regulation over time appears to build this capacity (ie, in terms of the guiding strength metaphor of capacity models, it "strengthens the self-regulation muscle"). That is, people who engaged in small, regular actions of self-regulation, such as not eating sweets or using their non-dominant hands for everyday tasks, later sustained higher levels of regulation on unrelated tasks than people who monitored, but did not regulate their behavior (eg, Muraven, 2010; Oaten & Cheng, 2007). Moreover, these findings were not explained by expectancies about whether the practice would work, global self-efficacy, or emotional distress, which seems to support a broader capacity explanation.

Putting aside for the moment questions about how robust these types of practice effects are (see Inzlicht & Berkman, 2015), other findings do highlight the relevance of cognitive processes included in the MEA model that could explain such effects. Although practicing self-regulation might not increase global self-efficacy, it could increase expectations about abilities to sustain regulation both now and in the future when assessing motivations for continued regulation. Once recognizing that small efforts they are making to change their behavior are both possible and do not greatly interfere with self-regulation toward other important goals, people could develop increased efficacy for such regulation more specifically, which would then support motivations for sustained regulation. Indeed, a recent study has shown the direct role of these more specific perceptions of efficacy in continued self-regulation (Chow et al., 2015). Following difficult acts of sustained self-regulation, participants reported specific reduction in efficacy for performing a new task that also required regulation, and this reduction mediated decreases in subsequent regulation.

Explaining Effects of "Severe Depletion"

Another set of findings often cited to illustrate the continued need for limited capacity in explaining carryover effects in self-regulation is two studies by Vohs, Baumeister, and Schmeichel (2013), in which participants either initially performed a single self-regulation task or an extended series of several self-regulation tasks before completing the same final task. When participants performed only one initial task, increasing incentives for sustained self-regulation or instilling lay theories that mental capacity for such regulation is not limited did eliminate carryover effects from this initial task to the final task, as in other studies (eg, Job et al., 2010; Muraven & Slessareva, 2003). However, when participants performed an extended series of tasks, increasing incentives or instilling nonlimited lay theories did not eliminate the carryover effects to the final task. Vohs et al. thus argued that this latter finding demonstrates that enough self-regulation does stretch resources for regulation to their capacity and produces severe enough depletion that the processes outlined in the MEA model (and other alternative perspectives reviewed here) will no longer apply.

Although this is one logical interpretation of such findings, a closer examination raises questions that participants must truly be exhausting their capacity for continued self-regulation. First, the incentive manipulation used to potentially counteract "severe depletion" was neither particularly direct nor strong. Participants learned that the research in which they were participating was generally important and would "…aid consumer welfare, happiness, and health" (Vohs et al., 2013, p. 186). Thus, their efforts in the study did not promise immediate benefits to themselves (cf. Muraven & Slessareva, 2003) and could only eventually help society at large (and perhaps the experimenters) sometime in the future. Thus, although participants were more likely to be motivated in this condition than the no-incentive condition, as manipulation checks and performance following the single self-regulation task showed, their motivation likely waned as they performed the extended series of initial self-regulation tasks, which could explain the lack of sustained regulation in this condition. That is, the MEA model predicts that people continually monitor their effort and progress and reassess the value of sustained regulation; therefore it seems highly plausible that by the time participants reached the final task, it was the perceived value of any additional progress participants felt they could make in helping the experimenter relative to their continued effort—not their capacity for self-regulation—that was severely diminished.

Similarly, the expectations and beliefs created by the specific manipulation of lay theories used in these studies to counteract "severe depletion" were again not likely strong or lasting. As in previous studies of such theories (eg, Job et al., 2010), to instantiate the belief that "mental energy" is or is not a limited resource, Vohs et al. (2013) had participants rate their agreement with a short series of statements worded in a biased way to elicit agreement with one viewpoint or the other, and manipulation checks again indicated that moderate agreement with either theory was created, at best. Given this mild inducement—the success of which itself is an indication that people's lay theories of self-regulation can be rather dynamic and fluid—it again makes sense that such a shift in beliefs could encourage sustained effort following a single self-regulation task. However, when induced beliefs that exerting mental effort can be energizing were countered by the experiences produced by a series of seemingly unimportant tasks that required self-regulation, such experiences should have had at least as strong an effect on participants' beliefs as the original manipulation, and thus eliminated its influence. That is, as illustrated in Fig. 20.2, the MEA model suggests not only that expectations and beliefs influence experiences of self-regulation, but that these experiences can update beliefs and expectations. Thus, because they were in possession of only moderate theories about self-regulation that were recently formed, it is likely that participants' experiences of engaging in extended regulation were strong enough to counter whatever influences these initial beliefs might have had (see also Chapter 12).

Beyond these specific critiques based on the MEA model, perhaps more problematic for the idea that exerting continued self-regulation over time will produce more and more severe depletion as the limits of capacity are reached are the variety of directly contradictory findings. Some studies have shown that performing several self-regulation tasks in succession (eg, Converse & Deshon, 2009; Dewitte, Bruyneel, & Geyskens, 2009), or extending the time spent on one of a series of self-regulation tasks can actually lead to enhanced rather than reduced self-regulation (see Dang, Xiao, & Dewitte, 2014). Furthermore, other studies have shown that performing multiple self-regulation tasks simultaneously, which should also be more "severely depleting," can similarly facilitate self-regulation (Tuk, Zhang, & Sweldens, 2015). It is extremely difficult to reconcile these results with Vohs et al.'s (2013) claim that their findings reflect an exhausted capacity for regulation, but they are readily explainable by shifts in people's expectations for or the value they place on continued regulation, and their experiences of engaging in self-regulation, as outlined by the MEA model.

Explaining the Role of Glucose

Perhaps the biggest challenge for any model of self-regulation that questions whether there is a fixed capacity for self-regulation would be to address evidence of an actual physiological resource that both (1) is consumed during regulation and (2) can restore regulation when replenished. Initial findings by Gailliot et al. (2007) appeared to indicate that circulating levels of glucose in the bloodstream met both of these criteria, suggesting that glucose directly fuels self-regulation just as it does muscle function (see also Bushman, DeWall, Pond, & Hanus, 2014). However, these findings have subsequently been undermined in multiple ways. Regarding the physiological consumption of glucose during self-regulation, reanalyses of the original Gailliot et al. data by Kurzban (2010) suggest that these data do not actually provide good support for such an effect (see also Lange & Kurzban, 2014; Schimmack, 2012), and further studies testing this claim in the most precise manner possible failed to replicate it (Molden et al., 2012). Indeed, Baumeister (2014) now acknowledges that "…it seems unlikely that ego depletion's effects are caused by a shortage of glucose in the bloodstream" (p. 315).

Regarding the restoration of self-regulation by ingesting additional glucose, several other findings beyond the original Gailliot et al. (2007) studies have supported the idea that ingesting glucose can reduce carryover effects of exerting self-regulation and bolster continued regulation (DeWall, Baumeister, Gailliot, & Maner, 2008; Masicampo & Baumeister, 2008; McMahon & Scheel, 2010; Wang & Dvorak, 2010). However, whereas Baumeister (2014) argues that this is sufficient evidence to still regard glucose as a critical resource fueling self-regulation, further research has undermined this claim as well. Several independent replications have confirmed that the effects of glucose on improved self-regulation do not depend upon its metabolization and conversion to energy, but may instead rely on perceptual and motivational processes (Hagger & Chatzisarantis, 2013; Molden et al., 2012; Sanders, Shirk, Burgin, & Martin, 2012). These studies all showed that merely rinsing one's mouth with, but not ingesting, glucose-flavored drinks has the same bolstering effects on self-regulation. Furthermore, these effects are found not only for short-lived cognitive tasks, but also on tests of athletic endurance that require sustaining maximum effort for up to 1 h (a "severely depleting" circumstance if ever one existed; for recent reviews and meta-analyses see Jeukendrup, Rollo, & Carter, 2013; e Silva et al., 2014).

Research is still ongoing concerning the mechanisms of these mouth-rinsing effects, but the MEA model points to several possibilities. First, when glucose is detected in the mouth, this could influence monitoring processes by altering perceptions of effort. Fares and Kayser (2011) provided preliminary support for this idea by showing that people perceived the same amount of physical work as less effortful when rinsing their mouths with carbohydrate solutions. Alternatively, the presence of glucose in the mouth could directly affect expected ability for or the value placed on self-regulation, and thus could alter assessments of motivations to continue. Neuroimaging findings showing that carbohydrate mouth-rinses selectively engage dopaminergic pathways in the striatum, which are closely associated with responses to reward, provided preliminary support for this idea as well (Chambers, Bridge, & Jones, 2009). In addition, the presence of glucose in the mouth could also influence assessments of motivations to continue by affecting expectations about ability for future self-regulation. That is, because detection of carbohydrates in the mouth suggests imminent ingestion and an increase in the energy soon available, another function of the neurological signals initiated by this detection could be to offset motivations for conservation that might otherwise arise from prolonged self-regulation (cf. Baumeister, 2014).

In summary, engaging in self-regulation does not appear to physiologically consume glucose, and the positive effects of ingesting glucose on self-regulation do not appear to depend on the energy produced by its metabolization. Thus, at present, there is little remaining evidence to claim that glucose functions as a resource that places a capacity on self-regulation. Instead, as with the findings involving building self-regulatory "strength" and "severe depletion," even these effects can be explained equally well by the psychological processes outlined by the MEA model.

Explaining Perceptions of Limited Resources and Motivations to Conserve

One final argument often offered to support capacity models of self-regulation is that they most accurately represent how people experience and respond to exerting regulation. That is, because people often believe they have a limited capacity for self-regulation (Job et al., 2010; Job, Walton, Bernecker, & Dweck, 2015; Martijn et al., 2002) and behave as if they are conserving and allocating these resources carefully (Muraven, Shmueli, & Burkley, 2006; Tyler & Burns, 2008), this is a strong sign that there must be some actual limits to which they are responding (Baumeister, 2014).

Putting aside that people's introspections are typically not optimal foundations for determining what psychological mechanisms are operating, we believe that the MEA model can explain these typical patterns of thought and behavior as well. First, we agree with Kurzban et al. (2013) that the actual psychological limits people do face are they cannot simultaneously (1) consciously process and attend to every piece of information in their environment and (2) engage in every behavior currently possible. Therefore, people must constantly prioritize their concerns and objectives, which involves difficult trade-offs requiring sophisticated evaluations of when to engage or disengage in a variety of actions. We also broadly agree with Kurzban et al. and others (Hockey, 2013; Inzlicht et al., 2014) that experiences of mental fatigue function to facilitate such evaluations. As outlined earlier, the MEA model proposes that rising fatigue signals that the relative worth of the effort and attention devoted to self-regulation toward one objective is diminishing and indicates that a reevaluation of priorities is necessary. Moreover, the MEA model further proposes that to adequately guard against perseveration and missed opportunities and to balance attention between making continued progress toward attaining known objectives versus detecting new objectives that are worthy of pursuit (Cohen, McClure, & Yu, 2007), experiences of fatigue typically accumulate and increase over time (see Wascher et al., 2014).

In the MEA model, the primary function of fatigue is thus to ensure a motivational homeostasis between sustained self-regulation toward currently important goals and pauses in self-regulation to reassess what alterative goals might deserve attention and effort. Maintaining such a homeostasis requires a conservative system of effort allocation in which fatigue grows progressively more intense over time and can extend beyond task completion, which then triggers a break from self-regulation and ensures a more optimal distribution of effort overall. However, the immediate phenomenological experiences of rising intensity and extended duration that such a system of mental fatigue creates are readily appraised as feeling that one's "mental energy" is "depleted" and must be "conserved" for later use. Interestingly, some have even suggested that one reason for the frequency of these particular appraisals is that experiences of mental fatigue originally evolved out of the more basic phenomenology of physical fatigue, where a maximum capacity for energy expenditure does indeed exist (see Evans, Boggero, & Segerstrom, 2015). Nevertheless, whatever the reason for the frequency of such appraisals, the critical point is that a wealth of evidence reviewed throughout this chapter suggests that experiences of "depletion" are merely appraisals that may be altered by a variety of other factors. That is, on the whole, if common experiences of self-regulation are to be offered as evidence for an actual capacity of such regulation, the malleability of these experiences must then also be acknowledged as seriously challenging the idea that such a capacity plays a critical role in self-regulation failure.

SUMMARY AND CONCLUSIONS

We began this chapter by noting that self-regulation is both enormously beneficial and enormously difficult. The primary challenge of research on self-regulation is thus to understand this difficulty and to find ways to ameliorate it. For quite some time, because capacity explanations have been the primary source of understanding self-regulation, few possible options for facilitating regulation and allowing people to better realize its benefits have seemed to be available. That is, other than suggestions for a regular program of "exercise" to build this capacity (eg, Muraven, 2010) or vague recommendations to set aside time for regular periods of relaxation or to eat healthy, glucose-rich snacks to keep one's existing capacity as full as possible (eg, Baumeister, 2014), no other good means of sustaining self-regulation would have seemed to be viable.

However, the MEA model of self-regulation, and all of the other emerging perspectives that it integrates and extends (Chapters 4, 7, 13, and 18; Kurzban et al., 2013), forcibly redefine the challenge of facilitating self-regulation as a motivational problem. If failures of self-regulation arise from motivational deficiencies and misalignments, they may then potentially be solved by altering incentives, increasing engagement, eliminating distracting alternatives, or reinterpreting and reappraising the experiences that guide such regulation. Thus, transcending the notion of limited capacity offers a host of new psychological mechanisms as possible targets for interventions intended to bolster self-regulation and a wealth of promising avenues for future research.

Yet, by rejecting a fixed capacity for self-regulation, the MEA model does not necessarily make solving the existing challenges of self-regulation failure easier. Even if such regulation does not consume some specific resource, this does not mean that the motivations instead driving self-regulation are themselves unlimited. People must regularly manage a wide variety of motivational conflicts based on the dynamic opportunities, temptations, and obstacles they encounter, and the experiences of fatigue that accompany self-regulation accumulate and create their own powerful disincentives. Yet, by better defining the psychological processes that contribute to frequently observed instances of self-regulation failure, the MEA model creates a clearer path forward for studying attempts to overcome such failure. Further research may ultimately provide more compelling evidence that self-regulation does indeed have its own special limited capacity and force further reconceptualizations. But, until then, it will be much more fruitful for research on self-regulation to move beyond such theoretical limits. Thus, although Hamlet may have been mistaken about the typical consequences of self-regulation, perhaps research inspired by the MEA model and other new perspectives will help teach us how to encourage restraint and abstinence in a way that indeed grows progressively easier with their continued application.

References

Alberts, H. J. E. M., Martijn, C., & de Vries, N. K. (2011). Fighting self-control failure: overcoming ego depletion by increasing self-awareness. *Journal of Experimental Social Psychology*, 47(1), 58–62.

Baumeister, R. F. (2014). Self-regulation, ego depletion, and inhibition. *Neuropsychologia*, 65, 313–319.

Baumeister, R. F., Heatherton, T. F., & Tice, D. M. (1994). *Losing control: How and why people fail at self-regulation*. Waltham, MA: Academic Press.

Baumeister, R. F., & Vohs, K. D. (2007). Self-regulation, ego depletion, and motivation. *Social and Personality Psychology Compass*, 1(1), 115–128.

Baumeister, R. F., Vohs, K. D., & Tice, D. M. (2007). The strength model of self-control. *Current Directions in Psychological Science*, 16(6), 351–356.

Bijleveld, E., Custers, R., & Aarts, H. (2012). Adaptive reward pursuit: how effort requirements affect unconscious reward responses and conscious reward decisions. *Journal of Experimental Psychology: General*, 141(4), 728–742.

Bushman, B. J., DeWall, C. N., Pond, R. S., & Hanus, M. D. (2014). Low glucose relates to greater aggression in married couples. *Proceedings of the National Academy of Sciences*, 111(17), 6254–6257.

Carter, E. C., Kofler, L. M., Forster, D. E., & Mccullough, M. E. (2015). A series of meta-analytic tests of the depletion effect: self-control does not seem to rely on a limited resource. *Journal of Experimental Psychology: General*, 144(3).

REFERENCES

Carver, C. S., Lawrence, J. W., & Scheier, M. F. (1999). Self-discrepancies and affect: incorporating the role of feared selves. *Personality and Social Psychology Bulletin*, 25(7), 783–792.

Carver, C. S., & Scheier, M. F. (1982). Control theory: a useful conceptual framework for personality-social, clinical, and health psychology. *Psychological Bulletin*, 92(1), 111–135.

Carver, C. S., & Scheier, M. F. (2001). *On the self-regulation of behavior*. New York: Cambridge University Press.

Chambers, E. S., Bridge, M. W., & Jones, D. A. (2009). Carbohydrate sensing in the human mouth: effects on exercise performance and brain activity. *The Journal of Physiology*, 587(Pt 8), 1779–1794.

Chow, J. T., Hui, C. M., & Lau, S. (2015). A depleted mind feels inefficacious: ego-depletion reduces self-efficacy to exert further self-control. *European Journal of Social Psychology*, 45(6), 754–768.

Clarkson, J. J., Hirt, E. R., Chapman, D. A., & Jia, L. (2011). The impact of illusory fatigue on executive control: do perceptions of depletion impair working memory capacity? *Social Psychological and Personality Science*, 2(3), 231–238.

Clarkson, J. J., Hirt, E. R., Jia, L., & Alexander, M. B. (2010). When perception is more than reality: the effects of perceived versus actual resource depletion on self-regulatory behavior. *Journal of Personality and Social Psychology*, 98(1), 29–46.

Cohen, J. D., McClure, S. M., & Yu, A. J. (2007). Should I stay or should I go? How the human brain manages the trade-off between exploitation and exploration. *Philosophical Transactions of the Royal Society B: Biological Sciences*, 362(1481), 933–942.

Converse, P. D., & Deshon, R. P. (2009). A tale of two tasks: reversing the self-regulatory resource depletion effect. *The Journal of Applied Psychology*, 94(5), 1318–1324.

Dang, J., Xiao, S., & Dewitte, S. (2014). Self-control depletion is more than motivational switch from work to fun: the indispensable role of cognitive adaptation. *Frontiers in Psychology*, 5, 933.

De Witt Huberts, J. C., Evers, C., & De Ridder, D. T. D. (2013). "Because I am worth it": a theoretical framework and empirical review of a justification-based account of self-regulation failure. *Personality and Social Psychology Review*, 18(2), 119–138.

vanDellen, M. R., Shea, C. T., Davisson, E. K., Koval, C. Z., & Fitzsimons, G. M. (2014). Motivated misperception: self-regulatory resources affect goal appraisals. *Journal of Experimental Social Psychology*, 53, 118–124.

Derrick, J. L. (2013). Energized by television: familiar fictional worlds restore self-control. *Social Psychological and Personality Science*, 4(3), 299–307.

DeWall, C. N., Baumeister, R. F., Gailliot, M. T., & Maner, J. K. (2008). Depletion makes the heart grow less helpful: helping as a function of self-regulatory energy and genetic relatedness. *Personality and Social Psychology Bulletin*, 34(12), 1653–1662.

Dewitte, S., Bruyneel, S., & Geyskens, K. (2009). Self-regulating enhances self-regulation in subsequent consumer decisions involving similar response conflicts. *Journal of Consumer Research*, 36(3), 394–405.

Duckworth, A. L., & Gross, J. J. (2014). Self-control and grit: related but separable determinants of success. *Current Directions in Psychological Science*, 23(5), 319–325.

Egan, P. M., Clarkson, J. J., & Hirt, E. R. (2015). Revisiting the restorative effects of positive mood: an expectancy-based approach to self-control restoration. *Journal of Experimental Social Psychology*, 57, 87–99.

Egan, P. M., Hirt, E. R., & Karpen, S. C. (2012). Taking a fresh perspective: vicarious restoration as a means of recovering self-control. *Journal of Experimental Social Psychology*, 48(2), 457–465.

Ehret, P. J., Monroe, B. M., & Read, S. J. (2015). Modeling the dynamics of evaluation: a multilevel neural network implementation of the iterative reprocessing model. *Personality and Social Psychology Review: An Official Journal of the Society for Personality and Social Psychology, Inc*, 19(2), 148–176.

Evans, D. R., Boggero, I. A., & Segerstrom, S. C. (2015). The nature of self-regulatory fatigue and "ego depletion": lessons from physical fatigue. *Personality and Social Psychology Review*.

Fares, E.-J. M., & Kayser, B. (2011). Carbohydrate mouth rinse effects on exercise capacity in pre- and postprandial states. *Journal of Nutrition and Metabolism*, 2011, 385962.

Feather, N. T. (Ed.). (1982). *Expectations and actions: Expectancy-value models in psychology*. Hillsdale, NJ: Erlbaum.

Friese, M., Messner, C., & Schaffner, Y. (2012). Mindfulness meditation counteracts self-control depletion. *Consciousness and Cognition*, 21(2), 1016–1022.

Friese, M., & Wänke, M. (2014). Personal prayer buffers self-control depletion. *Journal of Experimental Social Psychology*, 51, 56–59.

Fujita, K. (2011). On conceptualizing self-control as more than the effortful inhibition of impulses. *Personality and Social Psychology Review*, 15(4), 352–366.

Fujita, K., & Carnevale, J. J. (2012). Transcending temptation through abstraction: the role of construal level in self-control. *Current Directions in Psychological Science*, 21(4), 248–252.

Gailliot, M. T., Baumeister, R. F., DeWall, C. N., Maner, J. K., Plant, E. A., Tice, D. M., ... Schmeichel, B. J. (2007). Self-control relies on glucose as a limited energy source: willpower is more than a metaphor. *Journal of Personality and Social Psychology*, 92(2), 325–336.

Giacomantonio, M., Jordan, J., Fennis, B. M., & Panno, A. (2014). When motivational consequences of ego depletion collide: conservation dominates over reward-seeking. *Journal of Experimental Social Psychology*, 55, 217–220.

Gillebaart, M., & De Ridder, D. T. D. (2015). Effortless self-control: a novel perspective on response conflict strategies in trait self-control. *Social and Personality Psychology Compass*, 9(2), 88–99.

Hagger, M. S., & Chatzisarantis, N. L. D. (2013). The sweet taste of success: the presence of glucose in the oral cavity moderates the depletion of self-control resources. *Personality and Social Psychology Bulletin*, 39(1), 28–42.

Hagger, M. S., Wood, C., Stiff, C., & Chatzisarantis, N. L. D. (2010). Ego depletion and the strength model of self-control: a meta-analysis. *Psychological Bulletin*, 136(4), 495–525.

Hockey, G. R. J. (2013). *The psychology of fatigue*. New York: Cambridge University Press.

Hong, J., & Lee, A. Y. (2008). Be fit and be strong: mastering self-regulation through regulatory fit. *Journal of Consumer Research*, 34(5), 682–695.

Hossain, J. L., Reinish, L. W., Kayumov, L., Bhuiya, P., & Shapiro, C. M. (2003). Underlying sleep pathology may cause chronic high fatigue in shift-workers. *Journal of Sleep Research*, 12(3), 223–230.

Inzlicht, M., Bartholow, B. D., & Hirsh, J. B. (2015). Emotional foundations of cognitive control. *Trends in Cognitive Sciences*, 19(3), 126–132.

Inzlicht, M., & Berkman, E. (2015). Six questions for the resource model of control (and some answers). *Social and Personality Psychology Compass*, 10, 1–14.

Inzlicht, M., & Schmeichel, B. J. (2012). What is ego depletion? toward a mechanistic revision of the resource model of self-control. *Perspectives on Psychological Science*, 7(5), 450–463.

Inzlicht, M., & Schmeichel, B. J. (2015). Beyond limited resources: self-control failure as the product of shifting priorities. In K. Vohs, & R. F. Baumeister (Eds.), *The handbook of self-regulation: Research, theory, and applications*. New York: Guilford Press, (in press).

Inzlicht, M., Schmeichel, B. J., & Macrae, C. N. (2014). Why self-control seems (but may not be) limited. *Trends in Cognitive Sciences*, 18(3), 127–133.

Jeukendrup, A., Rollo, I., & Carter, J. (2013). Carbohydrate mouth rinse: performance effects and mechanisms. *Sports Science*, 26(118), 1–8.

Job, V., Bernecker, K., Miketta, S., Friese, M., Job, V., & Bernecker, K. (2015). Implicit theories about willpower predict the activation of a rest goal following self-control exertion following self-control exertion. *Journal of Personality and Social Psychology*, 109(4), 694–706.

Job, V., Dweck, C. S., & Walton, G. M. (2010). Ego depletion—is it all in your head?: implicit theories about willpower affect self-regulation. *Psychological Science, 21*(11), 1686–1693.

Job, V., Walton, G. M., Bernecker, K., & Dweck, C. S. (2013). Beliefs about willpower determine the impact of glucose on self-control. *Proceedings of the National Academy of Sciences of the United States of America, 110*(37), 14837–14842.

Job, V., Walton, G. M., Bernecker, K., & Dweck, C. (2015). Implicit theories about willpower predict self-regulation and grades in everyday life. *Journal of Personality and Social Psychology, 108*(4), 637–647.

Kool, W., & Botvinick, M. (2014). A labor/leisure tradeoff in cognitive control. *Journal of Experimental Psychology: General, 143*(1), 131–141.

Kool, W., McGuire, J. T., Rosen, Z. B., & Botvinick, M. M. (2010). Decision making and the avoidance of cognitive demand. *Journal of Experimental Psychology: General, 139*(4), 665–682.

Kurzban, R. (2010). Does the brain consume additional glucose during self-control tasks? *Evolutionary Psychology, 8*(2), 244–259.

Kurzban, R., Duckworth, A., Kable, J. W., & Myers, J. (2013). An opportunity cost model of subjective effort and task performance. *Behavioral and Brain Sciences, 36*(6), 661–679.

Labroo, A. A., & Kim, S. (2009). The "instrumentality" heuristic: why metacognitive difficulty is desirable during goal pursuit. *Psychological Science, 20*(1), 127–134.

Lange, F., & Kurzban, R. (2014). Sugar levels relate to aggression in couples without supporting the glucose model of self-control. *Frontiers in Psychology, 5*, 572.

Laran, J., & Janiszewski, C. (2011). Work or fun? how task construal and completion influence regulatory behavior. *Journal of Consumer Research, 37*(6), 967–983.

Lorist, M. M., Bezdan, E., ten Caat, M., Span, M. M., Roerdink, J. B. T. M., & Maurits, N. M. (2009). The influence of mental fatigue and motivation on neural network dynamics; an EEG coherence study. *Brain Research, 1270*, 95–106.

Macrae, C. N., Christian, B. M., Golubickis, M., Karanasiou, M., Troksiarova, L., McNamara, D. L., & Miles, L. K. (2014). When do I wear me out? Mental simulation and the diminution of self-control. *Journal of Experimental Psychology. General, 143*(4), 1755–1764.

Marien, H., Custers, R., Hassin, R. R., & Aarts, H. (2012). Unconscious goal activation and the hijacking of the executive function. *Journal of Personality and Social Psychology, 103*(3), 399–415.

Martijn, C., Tenbült, P., Merckelbach, H., Dreezens, E., & de Vries, N. K. (2002). Getting a grip on ourselves: challenging expectancies about loss of energy after self-control. *Social Cognition, 20*(6), 441–460.

Masicampo, E. J., & Baumeister, R. F. (2008). Toward a physiology of dual-process reasoning and judgment: lemonade, willpower, and expensive rule-based analysis. *Psychological Science, 19*(3), 255–260.

Masicampo, E. J., Martin, S. R., & Anderson, R. A. (2014). Understanding and overcoming self-control depletion. *Social and Personality Psychology Compass, 8*(1), 638–649.

McMahon, A. J., & Scheel, M. H. (2010). Glucose promotes controlled processing: matching, maximizing, and root beer. *Judgment and Decision Making, 5*(6), 450–457.

Miele, D. B., & Molden, D. C. (2010). Naive theories of intelligence and the role of processing fluency in perceived comprehension. *Journal of Experimental Psychology. General, 139*(3), 535–557.

Miyake, A., & Friedman, N. P. (2012). The nature and organization of individual differences in executive functions: four general conclusions. *Current Directions in Psychological Science, 21*(1), 8–14.

Molden, D. C. (2013). An expanded perspective on the role of effort phenomenology in motivation and performance. *Behavioral and Brain Sciences, 36*(6), 699–700.

Molden, D. C., & Higgins, E. T. (2005). Motivated thinking. In K. Holyoak, & B. Morrison (Eds.), *Cambridge handbook of thinking and reasoning* (pp. 295–320). New York: Cambridge University Press.

Molden, D. C., & Higgins, E. T. (2012). Motivated thinking. In K. Holyoak, & B. Morrison (Eds.), *The Oxford handbook of thinking and reasoning* (pp. 390–406). New York: Oxford University Press.

Molden, D. C., Hui, C. M., Scholer, A. A., Meier, B. P., Noreen, E. E., D'Agostino, P. R., & Martin, V. (2012). Motivational versus metabolic effects of carbohydrates on self-control. *Psychological Science, 23*(10), 1137–1144.

Moller, A. C., Deci, E. L., & Ryan, R. M. (2006). Choice and ego-depletion: the moderating role of autonomy. *Personality and Social Psychology Bulletin, 32*(8), 1024–1036.

Muraven, M. (2010). Practicing self-control lowers the risk of smoking lapse. *Psychology of Addictive Behaviors, 24*(3), 446–452.

Muraven, M., Gagné, M., & Rosman, H. (2008). Helpful self-control: autonomy support, vitality, and depletion. *Journal of Experimental Social Psychology, 44*(3), 573–585.

Muraven, M., Shmueli, D., & Burkley, E. (2006). Conserving self-control strength. *Journal of Personality and Social Psychology, 91*(3), 524–537.

Muraven, M., & Slessareva, E. (2003). Mechanisms of self-control failure: motivation and limited resources. *Personality and Social Psychology Bulletin, 29*(7), 894–906.

Oaten, M., & Cheng, K. (2007). Improvements in self-control from financial monitoring. *Journal of Economic Psychology, 28*(4), 487–501.

Reed, W. R., Florax, R. J. G.M., & Poot, J. (2015). A Monte Carlo analysis of alternative meta-analysis estimators in the presence of publication bias. *Economics Discussion Papers* 2015-9.

de Ridder, D. T. D., Lensvelt-Mulders, G., Finkenauer, C., Stok, F. M., & Baumeister, R. F. (2012). Taking stock of self-control: a meta-analysis of how trait self-control relates to a wide range of behaviors. *Personality and Social Psychology Review, 16*(1), 76–99.

Robinson, M. D., Schmeichel, B. J., & Inzlicht, M. (2010). A cognitive control perspective of self-control strength and its depletion. *Social and Personality Psychology Compass, 4*(3), 189–200.

Sanders, M. A., Shirk, S. D., Burgin, C. J., & Martin, L. L. (2012). The gargle effect: rinsing the mouth with glucose enhances self-control. *Psychological Science, 23*(12), 1470–1472.

Schimmack, U. (2012). The ironic effect of significant results on the credibility of multiple-study articles. *Psychological Methods, 17*(4), 551–566.

Schmeichel, B. J., & Vohs, K. (2009). Self-affirmation and self-control: affirming core values counteracts ego depletion. *Journal of Personality and Social Psychology, 96*(4), 770–782.

Schmeichel, B. J., Vohs, K. D., & Duke, S. C. (2010). Self-control at high and low levels of mental construal. *Social Psychological and Personality Science, 2*(2), 182–189.

Shah, J., & Higgins, E. T. (1997). Expectancy x value effects: regulatory focus as determinant of magnitude and direction. *Journal of Personality and Social Psychology, 73*(3), 447–458.

e Silva, T. D. A., de Souza, M. E. D. C. A., de Amorim, J. F., Stathis, C. G., Leandro, C. G., & Lima-Silva, A. E. (2014). Can carbohydrate mouth rinse improve performance during exercise? A systematic review. *Nutrients, 6*, 1–10.

Steel, P. (2007). The nature of procrastination: a meta-analytic and theoretical review of quintessential self-regulatory failure. *Psychological Bulletin, 133*(1), 65–94.

Tice, D. M., Baumeister, R. F., Shmueli, D., & Muraven, M. (2007). Restoring the self: positive affect helps improve self-regulation following ego depletion. *Journal of Experimental Social Psychology, 43*(3), 379–384.

Tuk, M. A., Zhang, K., & Sweldens, S. (2015). The propagation of self-control: self-control in one domain simultaneously improves self-control in other domains. *Journal of Experimental Psychology: General, 144*(3), 639–654.

Tyler, J. M., & Burns, K. C. (2008). After depletion: the replenishment of the self's regulatory resources. *Self and Identity, 7*(3), 305–321.

Vohs, K. D., Baumeister, R. F., & Schmeichel, B. J. (2013). Motivation, personal beliefs, and limited resources all contribute to self-control. *Journal of Experimental Social Psychology, 49*(1), 184–188.

Vohs, K. D., Glass, B. D., Maddox, W. T., & Markman, A. B. (2010). Ego depletion is not just fatigue: evidence from a total sleep deprivation experiment. *Social Psychological and Personality Science, 2*(2), 166–173.

Wan, E. W., & Sternthal, B. (2008). Regulating the effects of depletion through monitoring. *Personality and Social Psychology Bulletin, 34*(1), 32–46.

Wang, X. T., & Dvorak, R. D. (2010). Sweet future: fluctuating blood glucose levels affect future discounting. *Psychological Science, 21*(2), 183–188.

Wascher, E., Rasch, B., Sänger, J., Hoffmann, S., Schneider, D., Rinkenauer, G., … Gutberlet, I. (2014). Frontal theta activity reflects distinct aspects of mental fatigue. *Biological Psychology, 96*, 57–65.

Wu, T., Gao, X., Chen, M., & van Dam, R. M. (2009). Long-term effectiveness of diet-plus-exercise interventions vs. diet-only interventions for weight loss: a meta-analysis. *Obesity Reviews, 10*(3), 313–323.

Index

'*Note*: Page numbers followed by "f" indicate figures and "t" indicate tables.'

A
Abstinence violations, 43–44, 47, 54–55
Academic performance, 204
Action orientation, 32
  effect on interpersonal trait differences, 33–34
Active self, 94–95
Adaptation energy, 67
Adaptive self-regulation, depletion as potential trigger for, 156–157
Affect
  anticipated, 174–175
  negative, 127–132, 135–137, 174, 176, 306
  positive, 125–128, 130–133, 135–136, 174, 176
Affective habituation, 265–266
Aggression, 168–171
  aggressive impulses and inhibition, balance between, 171–176, 172f
  arousal, 173, 175
  cognitive processes, 173, 175–176
  emotion-regulation motivation and anticipated affect, 174–175
  evolutionary motives, 175
  negative affect, 174, 176
  positive affect, 174, 176
  social mimicry and scripts, 173
  balancing, 171
  ego depletion for reducing, 176–177
  glucose's ability and, 170–171
  major theories of, 166–168
  self-control and, 167, 169–170
  self-regulation and, 165–182
Agreeableness, 314
Alcoholics Anonymous (AA), 135
Alcohol intoxication, 43–44, 47, 57–58
Amygdala
  and ego depletion, 291
  and negative emotions, 155, 155f
Anger, and aggression, 174
Anterior cingulate cortex (ACC)
  and fatigue sensation, 154, 155f
  monitoring system in, 303–305
  and subjective feeling of effort, 383–384, 387–388
Anticipated affect, 174–175
Anxiety, 116
Appraisal, subjective, 69
Approach/avoidance tendencies, 238
Approach-motivated impulse strength, 109–124
  after effects of self-control, 118–119
  ego depletion and, 119–121
  exercising, evidence of, 113–116
  future directions of, 121–122
  self-control effects on brain activity, 116–118
Approach motivation, 340. *See also* Motivation
Arousal, 69, 171, 173, 175, 193
  physiological, 231
Automatic responses, 373
Autonomous regulation, 70–73
Autonomy, 68–69, 73, 76–77, 382–383
  effect on first demanding task, 32
Aversion, 304
Avoidance
  effort, 379–380
  motivation, 340
Awareness, impact on restoration, 245–246

B
Balance theory, 171–172
Behavior, across self-control domains, 314–315
Behavioral activation system (BAS) sensitivity scale, 113, 116, 118–119
Behavioral disinhibition, 411
Behavioral economics, 261
Behavioral inhibition system (BIS) sensitivity, 116, 118
Benevolence, and vitality, 80
Big Five model of personality, 314
BMIS, 129

"Bobo Doll" studies, 173
Bodily resources, 329
 abundant, 336–337
 scarce, 333–334
 substitutability between resources, 331
Brain anatomy, magnetic resonance imaging of, 284–285

C

Capacity
 -based depletion hypothesis, 410
 -based explanations, for self-regulation failure, 428
  alternatives to, 430–432
  limitations of, 429–430
  and motivation, integrating, 414–418, 416f. *See also* Motivation
  versus motivation, 414, 415f
Causality, perceived locus of, 71–72
Choice, 255
 interprobabilistic, 264
 intertemporal, 263–264
CODA, 247
Cognition, embodied, 347–348
Cognitive control, 301–324
 comparison to strength model, 318–319
 defined, 302–303
 diversity across self-control domains, 312–316
  consistency in behavior, 314–315
  motivation and ability to control, 315
  predictive ability of general self-control scales, 313
  processes underlying trait self-control's effects, 313
  situation-specific recruitment of cognitive control, 315–316
 error monitoring, individual differences in, 305–308
  and self-control outcomes, 305–306
  basic research, 305
  conscious awareness and, 307–308
  motivation and, 306–307
 models, 303–305, 303f
  monitoring system, 303–304
  operate systems, 304–305
 operations, individual differences in, 308–312
  components of cognitive control, 311–312
  inhibition and self-control outcomes, 309–310
  memory updating and self-control outcomes, 310
  switching and self-control outcomes, 310–311
  unity and diversity of cognitive control, 308–309
 self-control, improving, 316–318
  cross-domain generalization, challenge of, 317
  domain-specific training, 318
  monitoring, importance of, 317
  role of motivation, 317–318
Cognitive estimation test (CET), 411–412
Cognitive labor, 407, 409–410
Cognitive leisure, 407, 409–410
Cognitive neuroscience, 281–300, 347–348
 diffusion tensor imaging, 285
 of ego depletion, 289–292
 electroencephalography, 282–283
 functional magnetic resonance imaging, 285–289
 magnetic resonance imaging of brain anatomy, 284–285
 magnetoencephalography, 282–283
 transcranial magnetic stimulation, 283–284
Cognitive processes, and aggression, 173, 175–176
Competence, 68–69, 73, 76–77, 80–81
 satisfaction, and vitality, 77
Conscientiousness, 314
Conscious awareness, and error-monitoring, 307–308
Construal level, effect on person state, 24–25
Construal level theory (CLT), 264
Contingency management, 273
Contrafreeloading, 389
Control capacity, 401–402
 depletion effect on, 410–413
Control effort, 401–402
 depletion effect on, 418–419, 418f
Control illusions, 417
Control motivation, 400–402, 409–410
 depletion effect on, 404–409
Coping with stress, 413
Cue exposure, 43–44, 47, 52–53
Cue reactivity paradigm, 287

D

Decision-making, 6, 376
 models, 390–391
Decision value, 257

INDEX

Delay discounting, 285, 379
Delayed gratification, 88–89, 185, 378–380, 404
Delayed or immediate rewards, 379
Depletion
  and control capacity, 410–413
  and control motivation, 404–409
  and desire strength, 402–404
  ego. *See* Ego depletion
  operation, in integrative self-control theory, 402
  severe, 448–450
Depletion Sensitivity Scale, 206–207
Desire, 400–402
  -based depletion hypothesis, 403
  strength, depletion effect on, 402–404
Desire–desire (D-D) conflicts, 399–400
Desire–goal (D-G) conflicts, 399–402, 401f, 409–410
Diffusion tensor imaging (DTI), 285
Diminishing marginal utility, 265–267, 266f
Disinhibition, 314–315
Dispositional anxiety, 238
Dopamine sensitivity, and ego depletion, 387–388
Dorsolateral prefrontal cortex (DLPFC)
  and negative emotions, 155–156, 155f
  and sequential task paradigm, 290
Dual-motive or dual-goal conflict, 89, 92–93
Dual task paradigm, 2

E

E-crossing depletion task, 186, 194, 206, 230, 406
Effort avoidance, 379–380
Effortful inhibition, 89–96, 98–99
  as self-regulation strategy, 100–102
Ego depletion, 3, 5–8, 11–14, 43–44, 67–68, 87–88, 111–112, 125–126, 186, 350, 371–399, 428, 430
  alternative accounts of, 389–391
    decision-making models, 390–391
    opportunity cost model, 390–391
    resource model, 390
  alternative theories of, 292–293
  and approach-motivated impulse strength, 119–121
  cognitive neuroscience of, 289–292
  conclusion and empirical evidence, gap between, 144–146
  consequences of, 388–389

contrafreeloading, 389
limitless self-control, 388–389
defined, 94–100
effect
  limited mental resources, 327–328
  moderating, 206–207
  moderators of, 19–42
  glucose dynamics and, 4–5
  integrating with self-determination theory, 73–76
  lessons for self-control and self-regulation, 100–103
    effortful inhibition, as self-regulation strategy, 100–102
    fatigue, subjective feelings of, 102–103
  motivational tuning of. *See* Motivational tuning of depletion
  overcoming or counteracting, 9–10
  proximate causes of, 381–388
    neural representations of depletion, 385–388
    obligatory and intrinsic goals, 381–383
    perceived (not objective) effort, 383–385
  for reducing aggression, 176–177
  research, implications for, 94
  restoration effects following, 227–252
  self-control acts for
    necessary of, 97–98
    sufficiency of, 98–99
  and self-control, relationship between, 96–100
  ultimate causes of, 376–381
    delayed or immediate rewards, 379
    effort avoidance, 379–380
    exploitation, 377–378
    exploration, 377–378
    labor and leisure, 380
  valuation model explanation of, 269–272, 271f
Electroencephalography (EEG), 282–283
Embodied cognition, 347–348
Emotional distress, 43–44, 47, 53–54
Emotion-regulation motivation, 174–175
Endowment effect, 262–263
Energy conservation, 60
Error-related negativity (ERN), 117, 305–308, 386–388
Event-related potentials (ERPs), 283, 289–290
Evolutionary motives, and aggression, 175
Excitation Transfer Theory, 173
Executive function, 88, 427

Exhaustion
  perceived, 208
  versus restoration, 245
Experimental-causal-chain design, 35–36
Exploitation, 377–378
Exploration, 377–378
Exposure to nature, 230–232, 238
Extended-attentional-control task, 403
Extended self, 262
Externalizing, 306, 314
Extrinsic motivation, 148

F

Fatigue
  cognitive, 350
  gaming, 382
  markers, 386–387
  mental, 373–374, 376
  onset, 347–348
  self-control, 167, 169–170, 325–326
  strength model of, 167
  subjective feelings of, 102–103
Feelings-as-information model, 128
Feelings of tiredness, 24–25
Flanker tasks, 46
Free will, 5–6
Frustration, and aggression, 171, 174
Functional magnetic resonance imaging (fMRI), 285–289
  of reward, 286–288
  of self-regulation, 288–289

G

Gage, Phineas, 410–411
Gaming fatigue, 382
General Aggression Model (GAM), 167
  appraisal and decision processes component of, 167f
Glucose
  and aggression, 170–171
  dynamics, 4–5
  hypothesis, 406–407
  model, 327–328
  role in self-regulation failure, 450–452
Goal(s)
  achievement, 306
  commitment, 149–151
  -directed response, 45–47
  higher-order, 400–402
  intentions, 46–47, 49
  intrinsic, 381–383
  long-term, 144–145, 151–153, 373, 376–377
  neglect, 157–158
  obligatory, 381–383
  preference, 150
  prioritization, 147–148, 153–154
  pursuit, 156–160
  self-regulation by, 45–47
  shielding, 149–150
  striving, willpower and, 215–216
Goal–goal (G-G) conflicts, 399–400

H

Handgrip persistence/paradigm, 350–351, 353f, 369, 369f
Happiness, 69–70
Hedonic adaptation, 265–266
Hedonic sampling approach, 126–129
  to motivation, 126–129
    application of, 135–137
    individual differences, 132–133
    motivation to conserve, 130–131
    positive affect, 131–132
    self-control training, 133–134
  in self-control, 127–129
Homeostatic models of depletion, 158–159
Horse race model of response inhibition, 47–48

I

If–then planning, 43–50, 53–54, 91
I^3 metatheory, 167–168, 171–172
Impaired physical endurance, 376
Implementation intentions (IIs), 99, 101
  consequences of being depleted through, avoiding, 51–52
  effect on first demanding task, 32
  effect on second self-control task, 29–30
  implications of, 58–59
  mental contrasting, 58
  self-regulation by, 45–47
  state of depletion through, avoiding, 47–51
Implicit association test (IAT), 310
Implicit theories, about willpower, 203–226
  boundaries of, 217–221
  effects in everyday life, 213–217
    personal goal striving, 215–216
    self-regulation, 214–215
    well-being, 216–217
  ego depletion effect, moderating, 206–207
  mechanisms, 207–213
    changes in self-efficacy, 212–213
    perceived exhaustion, 208

rest-goal activation, 210–212
sensitivity to cues about resource availability, 208–210
negative consequences of, 217–221
interpersonal consequences, 219–221
overuse of resources, 218–219
theoretical background and measurement, 204–206
Impulse control, 7–8, 43–44, 47, 52–53
Impulse inhibition, 185
Impulse strength, 112–113
approach-motivated, 109–124
Impulsivity, 306, 313–315
Incremental theory of intelligence, 235
Inhibition, 88, 304–305, 309, 315, 375–376
and aggressive impulses, balance between, 171–176, 172f
arousal, 173, 175
cognitive processes, 173, 175–176
emotion-regulation motivation and anticipated affect, 174–175
evolutionary motives, 175
negative affect, 174, 176
positive affect, 174, 176
social mimicry and scripts, 173
conflating with self-control, 90–92
effortful, 89–96, 98–99
and self-control outcomes, 309–310
Inhibitory control, 273
Integrative self-control theory. See Self-control theory (SCT)
Intelligence, 204
incremental theory of, 235
Intergroup conflict, 204
Internalizing, 314
Interpersonal power, 230–232
restorative effect of, 237–244, 243f
Interpersonal relations, stress-regulation and, 8–9
Interpersonal trait differences, 32–34
Interprobabilistic choice, 264
Intertemporal choice paradigm, 263–264, 411–412
Intimate partner violence (IPV), 169
Intrinsic motivation, 72–73

L

Labor, 380
Labor–leisure tradeoff model, 159
Lapse-activated pattern, 43–44, 47, 54–55
Lateral PFC
and ego depletion, 292–293
and self-regulation, 288–289
and sequential task paradigm, 290
Lay beliefs, 328
and restoration, 231–233, 235, 238, 244–246
Lay interactionism (LI), 355–359, 357f
Lay Interactionism Scale, 369–370
Lay theories of willpower, 385
Left mediofrontal cortex, and subjective feeling of effort, 383
Leisure, 375–376, 380
Lexical decision, 46
Limited mental resources, 328–329
convergence across models, 329–330
ego depletion effect, 327–328
Limitless-resource theory, 388–389, 411–412
Linked abundance hypothesis, 336–339
bodily resources, 336–337
mental resources, 338–339
money resources, 337–338
social resources, 337
Linked scarcity hypothesis, 333–336
bodily resources, 333–334
mental resources, 335–336
money resources, 335
social resources, 335
Long-term goal, 144–145, 151–153, 373, 376–377

M

Magnetic resonance imaging (MRI) of brain anatomy, 284–285
Magnetoencephalography (MEG), 282–283
Measurement-of-mediation design, 35–36
Memory updating, and self-control outcomes, 310
Mental contrasting implementation intention (MCII), 58
Mental energy change, restorative effect of, 233–237, 234f
Mental fatigue, 373–374, 376
Perceived. See Perceived mental fatigue
restorative effect of, 228–229, 232–234, 234f, 236, 243f
Mere positive affect, 69–70
Meta-analysis, 196f
Metaphysical perceptions, 349–359
individual differences in, 355–359
situational cues and, 349–355
Mind–body dualism, 347–348

Mindfulness
  effect on person state, 25–26
  and error-monitoring, 307–308
  interventions, 338–339
  and vitality, 79–80
Model of control effort investment, 414–418
MODE model of attitude-behavior relations, 413
Moderators, of ego depletion effect, 19–42
  activated after first demanding task, 24–30
    factors affecting second self-control task, 29–30
    situational factors affecting person state, 24–29
  activated before first demanding task, 30–35
    factors affecting second self-control task, 31–32
    interim discussion, 34–35
    interpersonal trait differences, 32–34
    situational factors affecting person state, 31
  general discussion, 35–38
  organizing grid, 22–24, 23t
Money priming, effect on second self-control task, 30
Money resources, 330
  abundant, 337–338
  scarce, 335
  substitutability between resources, 332
Monitoring
  error monitoring, individual differences in, 305–308
    and self-control outcomes, 305–306
    basic research, 305
    conscious awareness and, 307–308
    motivation and, 306–307
  and self-control, 317
  system, 303–304
Mood
  -freezing paradigm, 136–137
  negative, 153–155, 155f. *See also* Aggression
    and perceived mental fatigue, 189
    restorative effect of, 233–237
  positive, 148, 154, 188–189
    and perceived mental fatigue, 192–193
    restorative effect of, 230–238
  restorative effect of, 233–237, 234f
Motivated effort-allocation (MEA) model of self-regulation failure, 432–443, 433f
  additional influences on monitoring and assessment, 439–442, 440f
  advantages of, 443–447
    mechanisms, 443–444
    phenomenological and motivational processes, expanded specification of, 444–447
  features of, 442–443
  implications of, 447–453
  motivation assessment for self-assessment, 435–436
  reassessment and reallocation, 439
  self-regulation consequences and experiences, monitoring, 436–439
Motivated reasoning, 407–408
Motivation
  and ability to control, 315
  approach, 109–124, 340
  avoidance, 340
  -based depletion hypothesis, 405–406, 408, 411
  versus capacity, 414, 415f
    integrating, 414–418, 416f
  control, 400, 413
  emotion-regulation, 174–175
  and error-monitoring, 306–307
  extrinsic, 148
  hedonic sampling approach to, 126–129
    application of, 135–137
    individual differences, 132–133
    motivation to conserve, 130–131
    positive affect, 131–132
    self-control training, 133–134
  intrinsic, 72–73
  self-control and, 125–142, 317–318
  theory, 13
  withdrawal, 116
Motivational tuning of depletion, 146–147, 146f
  capacity view versus opportunity cost versus homeostatic view, 158–159
  goal commitment, 149–151
  goal pursuit, 157–158
    implications for, 159–160
  long-term goal, 151–153
  as potential trigger, for adaptive self-regulation, 156–157
  potential practical implications of, 160
  prioritization mind-set, activation of, 147–148, 153–154
Multidimensional fatigue inventory (MFI), 187–188

N

Negative affect, 127–132, 135–137, 306
  and aggression, 174, 176
Negative urgency, 314–315
Neural representations of depletion, 385–388
Neural systems of valuation, 267–269
Neuroeconomics, 267
Neuroscience
  cognitive. *See* Cognitive neuroscience
  model of depletion-induced prioritization, 154–156, 155f
Neuroticism, 314
Novelty seeking, 389
Nucleus accumbens, effect on performance incentives, 28

O

Operate systems, 304–305
Operation span test, 412–413
Opportunity-cost model, 126, 126, 128–129, 158, 328, 390–391, 444–445
Orbitofrontal cortex (OFC)
  effect on ego depletion, 386–387
  and reward processing, 285–287
Other people, influence on self-regulation, 43–44, 47, 56–57

P

Pain perception, 347–348
PANAS (measure), 129
Perceived (not objective) effort, 383–385
Perceived exhaustion, 208
Perceived locus of causality, 71–72
Perceived mental fatigue, 183–202
  antecedents of, 190–193
    positive mood, 192–193
    power, 193
    state feedback, 190–191, 196f
    willpower capacity, theories of, 191–192
  effect size analysis, 195–198
    method, 195–197
    results, 197–198
  implications of, 198–199
  perceptions of, 185–190
    alternative mechanisms, 189–190
    working memory, malleability of, 187–189, 189f
  points of clarification, 194–195
Perceived skill, 417

Perceptual-vigilance task. *See* E-crossing depletion task
Perfect Storm Theory, 168
Performance incentives, effect on person state, 27–28
Personal beliefs, and self-control, 362
Personal dominance, 238
Personality systems interaction (PSI), 75
Person state, situational factors affecting, 24–29, 31
Physical pain, and aggression, 174
Placebo effects of restoration, 246
Positive affect, 125–128, 130–133, 135–136
  and aggression, 174, 176
Posterior cingulate cortex (PCC), and fatigue sensation, 154–155
Power
  effect on self-control performance, 193
  interpersonal, 230–232, 237–244, 243f
  motivation, 238
Prayer, effect on person state, 26, 31
Prefrontal basal ganglia working memory (PBWM) model, 311–312
Prejudice, 306
  implicit, 310
Process model, 126, 328
  of depletion, 403–404
  of emotion regulation, 413
  of self-control, 21–22, 37–38
Prospect Theory, 263–264
Provocation, and aggression, 169–171, 173–174, 176
Psychological safety, 78
Psychological sources of vitality, 76–80
  basic needs and, 76–78
  benevolence and, 80
  mindful attention to present, 79–80
  nature and, 78–79

R

Reaction times, 376
Regulatory strength model, 73
Relatedness, 68–69, 73, 76–77, 80–81
Relationship orientation, 238
Resource allocation, 406–407
  hypothesis, 187
  model of self-control, 75
Resource attribution hypothesis, 190
Resource model, 390
  of self-regulation, 44

Resources to action control, linking, 325–346
  bodily resources, 329
  general and nonresource-specific mechanisms, 340
  individual differences, 341
  limited mental resources, 328–329, 341–343
    convergence across models, 328–329
    ego depletion effect, 327–328
  money, 330
  nonmental resources, 332–341
    linked abundance hypothesis, 336–339
    linked scarcity hypothesis, 333–336
    numerous distinct mechanisms, 340–341
    possible shared mechanisms, 339–340
  situational factors, 341
  social resources, 329–330
  substitutability between resources, 330–332
    bodily resources, 331
    money, 332
    social resources, 331–332
Rest-goal activation, 203–204, 210–212
Restoration effects following depletion, 227–252
  awareness, impact of, 245–246
  CODA, 247
  emerging questions, 244–247
  exhaustion versus, 245
  expectancies of, 230–233
  interpersonal power, 237–244, 243f
  mental energy change, 233–237, 234f
  perceptual processes, role of, 229–230
  placebo effects of, 246
Retaliatory aggression, 174
Revenge, and aggression, 174
Reward, 257
  delayed or immediate, 379
  functional magnetic resonance imaging studies of, 286–288
Risk-taking, 112, 114–115, 411
Romantic relationships, 204

S

Scripts, and aggression, 173
Self
  active, 94–95
  extended, 262
Self-actualization, 76
Self-affirmation, 43–44, 148, 230–232, 238
Self-awareness, impairments of, 43–44, 47, 55–56

Self-consciousness, and error-monitoring, 307
Self-control, 5–6, 70–73
  acts, for ego depletion
    necessary of, 97–98
    sufficiency of, 98–99
  cognitive control processes and, 301–324
  conceptual analysis of, 87–108
  conflating with effortful inhibition, 90–92
  defined, 256–257, 302–303
  domains, diversity across, 312–316
    consistency in behavior, 314–315
    motivation and ability to control, 315
    predictive ability of general self-control scales, 313
    processes underlying trait self-control's effects, 313
    situation-specific recruitment of cognitive control, 315–316
  ego depletion's lessons for, 100–103
    effortful inhibition, as self-regulation strategy, 100–102
    fatigue, subjective feelings of, 102–103
    relationship between, 96–100
  fatigue, 167, 169–170, 325–326
  glucose dynamics and, 4–5
  improving, 316–318
    cross-domain generalization, challenge of, 317
    domain-specific training, 318
    monitoring, importance of, 317
    role of motivation, 317–318
  limitless, 388–389
  mental and physical, relation between, 347–349
  outcomes
    error-monitoring and, 305–306
    inhibition and, 309–310
    memory updating and, 310
    switching and, 310–311
  performance, restorative effects of, 236
  process model of, 21–22, 37–38
  resource allocation model of, 75
  versus self-regulation, 92–94
  second task, factors affecting, 29–32
  strength model of, 21–22, 28–29, 37–38, 43, 111–113, 158, 203–204, 301, 318–319
  trait, 33
Self-control theory (SCT), 399–424, 401f. *See also* Self-determination theory (SDT)
  control capacity, depletion effect on, 410–413

control effort, depletion effect on,
    418–419, 418f
control motivation, depletion effect on,
    404–409
depletion operation in, 402
desire strength, depletion effect on,
    402–404
future directions of, 419
implications of, 419
motivation and capacity, integrating,
    414–418, 416f
motivation versus capacity, 414, 415f
psychological components of, 400
speculations and future directions,
    409–410
Self-determination, 76
Self-determination theory (SDT)
    integrating with ego-depletion model,
        73–76
    model of vitality, 67–86
Self-efficacy, 189–190, 203–204, 417
    changes in, 212–213
Self-esteem, 382. *See also* Self-determination
    theory (SDT)
    and aggression, 174
Self-licensing, 408–409
Self-monitoring, impairments of, 43–44, 47,
    55–56
Self-motivation, 76
Self-perceptions, 362–363
Self-regulation, 1–18, 88, 302, 373
    and aggression, 165–182
    applications of, 6–9
    basic idea and early thoughts, 2–3
    capacity, 452–453
    defined, 95, 256–257
    ego depletion's lessons for, 100–103
        effortful inhibition, as self-regulation
            strategy, 100–102
        fatigue, subjective feelings of, 102–103
    failure. *See* Self-regulation failure
    forms of, 70–73
    functional magnetic resonance imaging
        studies of, 288–289
    by goals, 45–47
    by implementation intentions, 45–47, 58
    major theories of, 166–168
    and perceived mental fatigue, 189–190
    recent challenges and advances, 11–14
    resource model of, 44
    self-states effect on, 58
    state and trait of, 10–11
    versus self-control, 92–94

threats to, mitigating, 47
willpower and, 214–215
Self-regulation failure, 425–460
    capacity-based explanations for, 428
        alternatives to, 430–432
        limitations of, 429–430
    defined, 426–428
    motivated effort-allocation model of,
        432–443, 433f
        additional influences on monitoring
            and assessment, 439–442, 440f
        advantages of, 443–447
        features of, 442–443
        implications of, 447–453
        mechanisms, 443–444
        motivation assessment for
            self-assessment, 435–436
        phenomenological and motivational
            processes, expanded specification
            of, 444–447
        reassessment and reallocation, 439
        self-regulation consequences and
            experiences, monitoring, 436–439
Self-regulatory resource depletion, 47–52
    consequences of being depleted through
        implementation intentions,
        avoiding, 51–52
    state of depletion through
        implementation intentions,
        avoiding, 47–51
Sensation seeking, 314–315
Sentence span test, 412–413
Sexual infidelity, 112
Shame, and aggression, 174
Situational cues, 46–47
    and metaphysical perceptions, 349–355
Situation-specific recruitment of cognitive
    control, 315–316
Social distress, 43–44, 47, 53–54
Social dominance orientation (SDO), 193,
    238–244, 246–247
Social identity, effect on person state, 26
Social mimicry, and aggression, 173
Social pain, and aggression, 174
Social–psychological theory, 348–349,
    363–364
Social resources, 329–330
    abundant, 337
    scarce, 335
    substitutability between resources,
        331–332
Spontaneous resource recovery (SRR),
    231–233, 232f, 232t, 237–238, 244–245

State feedback, on perceived mental fatigue, 190–191
Strength model
  building, 3–4
  regulatory, 73
  resource, 67–68
  of self-control, 21–22, 28–29, 37–38, 43, 111–112, 158, 167, 203–204, 301, 318–319
Subjective appraisal, 69
Subjective construal, role in self-control, 91–92
Subjective effort
  creation of, 383–384
  effect on ego depletion, 384–385
Subjective value, 263–264
  defined, 257–258
Subjective vitality scale (SVS), 69, 74–75
Sustained attention, 375–376
Switching, and self-control outcomes, 310–311

T

Task framing, 360
Task similarity, effect on second self-control task, 30
Task-switching, 88, 304–305, 311–312, 316, 328
Temporal discounting, 263–265
Threats to self-regulation, mitigating, 47
"Time-on-task" monitoring, 378
Tractography, 285
Traits
  interpersonal differences, 32–34
  self-control, 33, 313
Transactive memory, 331–332
Transcranial magnetic stimulation (TMS), 283–284
Transdisease processes, 264–265
Two-Factor Theory of emotion, 173

V

Valuation model of self-control, 253–280, 261f
  conflict resolution, 259–269
    anomalies, 261–267
    neural systems of valuation, 267–269
  ego depletion and, 269–272, 271f
  mechanism of, 258–259
  new horizon for research, 272–273
Ventral tegmental area (VTA), and reward processing, 286
Ventrolateral prefrontal cortex (VLPFC), effect on performance incentives, 28
Ventromedial prefrontal cortex (vmPFC)
  and ego depletion, 291
  and self-control, 258, 267–269
  and self-regulation, 288
Vigilance, 376
Vigor, 69
Vitality, 67–86
  defined, 69–70
  psychological sources of, 76–80

W

Well-being, and willpower, 216–217
Willpower, 89–90
  capacity, perceptions of perceived mental fatigue, 191–192
  implicit theories about, 203–226
  lay theories of, 385
  theory
    effect on interpersonal traits, 32–33
    effect on person state, 31
Withdrawal motivation, 116
Working memory
  defined, 187
  malleability of, 187–189

Peace Education in Conflict and Post-Conflict Societies

Previous Publications

Zvi Bekerman (Ed.)

Cultural Education-Cultural Sustainability: Identity, Tolerance, and Multicultural Issues in Minority, Diaspora, and Indigenous education (2008)

Mirror Images: Popular Culture and Education (2008)

Learning in Places: The Informal Educational Reader (2006)

Zvi Bekerman and Claire McGlynn (Eds.)

Addressing Ethnic Conflict through Peace Education: International Perspectives (2007)

Tony Gallagher

Education in Divided Societies (2004)

Michalinos Zembylas

The Politics of Trauma in Education (2008)

Five Pedagogies, A Thousand Possibilities: Struggling for Hope and Transformation in Education (2007)

Teaching with Emotion: A Postmodern Enactment (2005)

Peace Education in Conflict and Post-Conflict Societies
Comparative Perspectives

Edited by Claire McGlynn, Michalinos Zembylas,
Zvi Bekerman, and Tony Gallagher

palgrave
macmillan

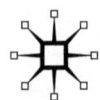

PEACE EDUCATION IN CONFLICT AND POST-CONFLICT SOCIETIES
Copyright © Claire McGlynn, Michalinos Zembylas, Zvi Bekerman, and Tony Gallagher, 2009.

All rights reserved.

First published in 2009 by PALGRAVE MACMILLAN® in the United States—a division of St. Martin's Press LLC, 175 Fifth Avenue, New York, NY 10010.

Where this book is distributed in the UK, Europe and the rest of the world, this is by Palgrave Macmillan, a division of Macmillan Publishers Limited, registered in England, company number 785998, of Houndmills, Basingstoke, Hampshire RG21 6XS.

Palgrave Macmillan is the global academic imprint of the above companies and has companies and representatives throughout the world.

Palgrave® and Macmillan® are registered trademarks in the United States, the United Kingdom, Europe and other countries.

ISBN-13: 978-0-230-60842-9
ISBN-10: 0-230-60842-6

> Peace education in conflict and post-conflict societies : comparative perspectives / edited by Claire McGlynn ... [et al.].
>   p. cm.
> Includes index.
> ISBN 0-230-60842-6
>   1. Peace—Study and teaching. 2. Conflict management. 3. Postwar reconstruction. I. McGlynn, Claire.

JZ5534.P4273 2009
303.6'6—dc22   2008034768

A catalogue record of the book is available from the British Library.

Design by Scribe Inc.

First edition: April 2009

10 9 8 7 6 5 4 3 2 1

Printed in the United States of America.

Contents

Acknowledgments — ix

Introduction — 1
Claire McGlynn

Part I Approaches to Peace Education: Comparative Lessons — 5
Tony Gallagher

1 Negotiating Cultural Difference in Divided Societies: An Analysis of Approaches to Integrated Education in Northern Ireland — 9
Claire McGlynn

2 Grassroots Voices of Hope: Educators' and Students' Perspectives on Educating for Peace in Post-conflict Burundi — 27
Elavie Ndura-Ouedraogo

3 The Emergence of Human Rights Education amid Ethnic Conflict in the Dominican Republic — 43
Monisha Bajaj and Cheila Valera Acosta

4 From Conflict Society to Learning Society: Lessons from the Peace Process in Northern Ireland — 59
Paul Nolan

5 Peace, Reconciliation, and Justice: Delivering the Miracle in Post-apartheid Education — 75
Pam Christie

Part II Peace Education and Contact: Introduction   89
Zvi Bekerman

6   Social Context and Contact Hypothesis: Perceptions and Experiences of a Contact Program for Ten- to Eleven-year-old Children in the Republic of Macedonia   93
Ana Tomovska

7   "Smoking Doesn't Kill; It Unites!": Cultural Meanings and Practices of "Mixing" at the Gymnasium Mostar in Bosnia and Herzegovina   109
Azra Hromadzic

8   The Cultural Psychology of American-based Coexistence Programs for Israeli and Palestinian Youth   127
Phillip L. Hammack

9   Toward the Development of a Theoretical Framework for Peace Education Using the Contact Hypothesis and Multiculturalism   145
Ulrike Niens

10   Promoting Reconciliation through Community Relations Work: A Comparison among Young People in Belfast, Northern Ireland, and Vukovar, Croatia   161
Ankica Kosic and Jessica Senehi

Part III Curriculum and Pedagogy: Introduction   179
Michalinos Zembylas

11   Inventing Spaces for Critical Emotional Praxis: The Pedagogical Challenges of Reconciliation and Peace   183
Michalinos Zembylas

12   Arab and Jewish Students' Participatory Action Research at the University of Haifa: A Model for Peace Education   199
Tamar Zelniker, Rachel Hertz-Lazarowitz, Hilla Peretz, Faisal Azaiza, and Ruth Sharabany

13   Deliberative History Classes for a Post-conflict Society: Theoretical Development and Practical Implication through International Education in United World College in Bosnia and Herzegovina   215
Pilvi Torsti and Sirkka Ahonen

14 "Yeah, It Is Important to Know Arabic—I Just Don't
   Like Learning It": Can Jews Become Bilingual in the
   Palestinian-Jewish Integrated Bilingual Schools? 231
   Zvi Bekerman

15 Teacher Preparation for Peace Education in
   South Africa and the United States: Maintaining
   Commitment, Courage, and Compassion 247
   Candice C. Carter and Saloshna Vandeyar

Contributors 263

Index 271

Acknowledgments

We want to express our deep gratitude to the World Council of Comparative Education Societies, which provided the venue in its Sarajevo Conference (September 2007) for presenting a number of symposia titled "Transition, Conflict and Post-Conflict Societies." These symposia constituted the initiation of this writing project. We are grateful to Palgrave Macmillan for undertaking this project and particularly to our editor, Julia Cohen, for providing support throughout all the stages of this effort.

Many thanks are also offered to our respective institutions for their continuing support and encouragement by providing us with the "space" to conduct our research and writing: the School of Education at Queen's University Belfast, the Open University of Cyprus, the Melton Centre for Jewish Education, and the Truman Institute for the Advancement of Peace at the Hebrew University in Jerusalem.

Introduction

Claire McGlynn

It is widely acknowledged that one model of peace education (Bekerman & McGlynn, 2007; Harris & Morrison, 2003; Salomon & Nevo, 2002) or educational response to conflict (Gallagher, 2004; Davies, 2004) cannot possibly fit all societies. Why then put together an edited collection of papers that represent widely differing contextual situations if models are not transferable? The answer is this: while the number and range of international peace programs continue to proliferate, there is a marked absence of interdisciplinary and comparative research to guide academic development and inform practice in this challenging arena. It is these deficits that the present volume aims to address. This book continues the project started with *Addressing Ethnic Conflict Through Peace Education: International Perspectives* (Bekerman & McGlynn, 2007) by drawing on a wide range of theoretical, methodological, and contextual perspectives and hence resisting the constraints and limitations of remaining only within one area of academic turf. Rather than focus on *ad hoc* peace education efforts, this book further investigates the need for long-term, systemic approaches and innovative pedagogies. While actively acknowledging and problematizing the complexity of human interaction and the restraints imposed by sociopolitical and historical contexts, it teases out not a blueprint for peace education, but rather principles, insights, and lessons learned that are of use to policy makers and practitioners in the development of peace education. In particular it considers the enactment of peace education, not just in conflict or low-conflict situations, but also in post-conflict and pre-conflict contexts. Fresh insights are provided into well-researched countries such as South Africa, Israel, and Northern Ireland, in addition to thought-provoking considerations of countries such as Burundi, Macedonia, the Dominican Republic, and Cyprus, which have been less well-represented in the peace education literature. Perspectives on formal, informal, and adult education are all offered, illustrating the various types as well as contexts of peace education.

This project was initiated with a series of papers presented at a number of symposia titled "Transition, Conflict and Post-conflict Societies" at a conference of the World Council of Comparative Education Societies Conference in Sarajevo in September 2007. A subsequent further call for papers allowed for an extensive peer-review process that has brought together a truly excellent group of scholars whose writing is richly illustrated by case studies of the very wide range of societies in which they work. As such, the volume engages directly with peace education practice in contexts variously affected by conflict.

The chapters are organized into three parts, namely, "Approaches to Peace Education: Comparative Lessons," "Peace Education and Contact," and "Curriculum and Pedagogy." Each part is introduced by an editorial commentary that clearly situates the chapters in a broader context and highlights the aspects that can be gleaned from these particular cross-country evaluations. As such, attention is drawn by the editors to a number of important transnational comparative issues relating to each of the three themes.

The first part, "Approaches to Peace Education: Comparative Lessons," presents optimistic and pessimistic views of peace education through the presentation of case studies from Northern Ireland (one study each from formal and informal education), Burundi, the Dominican Republic, and South Africa. Important questions regarding the role of education in peace making and peace building are thus asked. The five chapters reveal complex and nuanced challenges of dealing with difference in conflicted societies. Approaches to peace education, such as multicultural education and human rights, are critically evaluated, along with an exploration of the role of a raft of civil society activity in supporting peace. In the case of South Africa, the opportunities for an educational role in peace-building are shown to be constrained by broader economic policies that have sustained rather than challenged inequalities.

The second part of this volume, "Peace Education and Contact," directly addresses a criticized aspect of application of contact theory—that is, the accusation that the emphasis on positivist methodology fails to provide sufficient insight into the complexity of human interaction in educational intergroup encounters. This part offers critically evaluated case studies from Macedonia, Bosnia, Israel, Croatia, and Northern Ireland that focus our thoughts on the need to pay close attention to sociopolitical realities as well as to the complex processes involved. It considers also the limitation of contact theory as a singular theoretical frame for peace education and proposes a number of additional conceptual perspectives from the fields of sociology and political science that may, in combination, strengthen the potential of contact theory for underpinning peace education efforts.

The third part of the book, "Curriculum and Pedagogy," presents a range of ideas that challenge our thinking regarding the curriculum and pedagogy of peace education. Drawing on empirical research studies in Cyprus, Israel, Bosnia, South Africa, and the United States, the authors utilize a variety of methodological approaches, including ethnography and action research, to illuminate this area. A number of promising peace education tools, such as *critical emotional praxis* and *deliberative communication*, are presented and explored. In addition, our understanding is enriched by the wide range of theoretical perspectives that underpin these chapters. We readily acknowledge the limitations of this book. No doubt there are many theoretical, methodological, and contextual perspectives absent, and no claims of exclusivity are made. We trust that our interdisciplinary approach offers critical complexity without the loss of clarity. We also sincerely hope that this volume adds to knowledge and understanding of peace education. Above all, we trust that our edited collection offers encouragement and constructive help to all those involved in searching for context-sensitive and effective approaches in the challenging field of peace education.

REFERENCES

Bekerman, Z., & McGlynn, C. (Eds.). (2007). *Addressing ethnic conflict through peace education.* New York: Palgrave Macmillan.

Davies, L. (2004). *Education and conflict: Complexity and chaos.* London: Routledge Falmer.

Gallagher, T. (2004). *Education in divided societies.* Basingstoke: Palgrave Macmillan.

Harris, I., & Morrison, M. L. (2003). *Peace education.* Jefferson: North Carolina: McFarland.

Salomon, G., & Nevo, B. (2002). *Peace education: The concept, principles and practices around the world.* New York: Lawrence Erlbaum Associates.

Part I

Approaches to Peace Education
Comparative Lessons

Tony Gallagher

The central dilemma for education in divided societies lies in the way its schools engage with issues of difference. The historical role of education systems has been to promote social cohesion either by inculcating children into the national community through a process of assimilation, or by preparing them for their appropriate station in life within the ordered hierarchy of society, or, perhaps more often, both at the same time. Conflict arises when elites have to work hard to maintain a position of domination or when oppressed groups see a possibility of change; violent conflict emerges when there are no alternative routes to prosecuting these claims. What then of the role of education? Optimists might be those who believe that education can subvert the process to the extent that alternative and peaceful discourses of change can emerge and prevent violent conflict breaking out in the first place. Pessimists might be those who feel that the best we can hope for is that the experience of violent conflict will encourage people to see education as a route to the future. The five chapters in this part of the book provide examples of both, sometimes within the same chapter.

Using the framework above, we can see that the chapters by Claire McGlynn (on integrated schools in Northern Ireland), Elavie Ndura (on peace education in Burundi), and Monisha Bajaj and Cheila Valera (on human rights education in the Dominican Republic) fall firmly within the "optimist" camp. McGlynn's examination of the views of principals in integrated schools in Northern Ireland starkly illustrates the tensions being addressed in schools that developed out of a settled norm of division. That the routes to the future are unclear is hardly surprising as these educators are seeking to chart a map in largely unexplored terrain. McGlynn's analysis seeks to categorize their approaches using a complex interweave of plural, liberal, and critical discourses, but perhaps the most striking theme to emerge is that, in a pioneering endeavor, such as the one represented by the integrated schools movement, there are so many versions of the model.

Ndura's thesis offers a clearer prescription, but perhaps this is enabled by a more aspirational tone. For example, she offers the robust claim that multicultural education must yield agents of peace and peace education must be multicultural, but she offers little evidence to substantiate the claim. What is offered is startlingly clear evidence on how easy it is to divide people into ethnic silos and the desperate choices individuals face when the priority is survival. If education does provide the key to the future, it is likely, as Ndura suggests, that education will be characterized by interdependence, respect, and social justice, but even the very opening of her chapter ("much of the nation's tragic history has been skillfully kept out of reach throughout the educational system") serves as a reminder of the scale of this challenge: education is not an unambiguous social good but has been deployed in the service of indifference and hatred.

The third example of optimism focuses on the potential of human rights education in the Dominican Republic and also is heavily aspirational in tone. The aspiration this time is that human rights education can help prevent violent conflict from breaking out by providing a set of discourses through which education can promote inclusive practices. The difference in this example, however, is that the claims of effect are based on a body of experience arising from within civil society. The examples of liberation theology, feminism, and agitation to support landless peasants all highlight practical strategies through which the claims to a rights-based approach can be realized. Thus, even though Bajaj and Valera stoically recognize that, while human rights education is officially recognized, it is not implemented in any meaningful way, the prior example of civil society agitation provides proof of efficacy and hope for the future. Of course, a rights-based approach does not in itself solve the central dilemma—what do you do, for example, when the rights of two communities diverge—but at least it provides a core set of values and principles that, in the best of all possible worlds, will elevate debate above the narrow confines of particularism…maybe.

The "maybe" is underlined by Nolan's examination of the Northern Ireland experience. This analysis differs from McGlynn's in at least two ways: First, looking back to assess the impact of educational initiatives in the period before the peace process, it seems to offer the pessimistic conclusion that, while many factors help bring the violence to an end, educational initiatives probably did not play a large role. Second, echoing Bajaj and Valera, Nolan does highlight the role of various interweaves within civil society that perhaps helped to maintain some sense of better possible futures. As in the case of the Dominican Republic, the cast includes women's organizations, religious activists, and grassroots political projects. In this way, we see a more optimistic suggestion—emerging from Nolan's pessimism on the role of education as a vehicle to end war—that education, more broadly understood, might help secure the peace.

But even here, there remains a more pessimistic possibility, as highlighted by Pam Christie's sober analysis of the "miracle" of democratic South Africa. Of the three peace processes of the 1990s (South Africa, Northern Ireland, and the Middle East), it is perhaps South Africa that appears to have been the most successful. Certainly, as Christie points out, the triumph of the new democratic government was its compromise, as "erstwhile enemies of over forty years were able to commit themselves to peace, reconciliation, and justice." However, while one consequence was the progressive discourse of rights that were embedded in an undoubtedly radical constitution, there was another axis of influence through the impact of neoliberal economic priorities under globalizing pressures. The need to encourage inward investment meant that the egalitarian ambitions of the democratic government were steadily eroded. Thus, in the absence of material provision, rights remain largely symbolic and the political stability that appears to have been achieved has been at the cost of continuing inequality. And for education, we are left again with, on the one hand, a lost opportunity for nation building and, on the other hand, the aspiration for a new imaginary.

The central dilemma for education in divided societies lies in the way it engages with difference. The central dilemma for educators is that the way forward remains elusive, which is why the accumulation of experience, learning, and critical reflection remains so important.

Chapter 1

Negotiating Cultural Difference in Divided Societies
An Analysis of Approaches to Integrated Education in Northern Ireland

Claire McGlynn

Introduction

While political theorists contest issues of equality, culture, identity, and group rights and debate the relative merits of multiculturalism or egalitarianism, educators are left to navigate their own route when policies lag behind the urgent realities of meeting the needs of diverse groups of students. The challenge of appropriate educational responses to cultural diversity is a universal one, but it is arguably more urgent in countries that have suffered from protracted violence, where the rights of diverse societal groups are in conflict and where group affiliation is of critical importance.

This chapter is concerned with response to pupil diversity in integrated settings in societies where education is usually segregated. The case study explored is that of the integrated school sector in Northern Ireland, where Catholic, Protestant, and other children are educated together. Based on interviews with principals of integrated schools, this chapter examines

---

This study was made possible by a grant from the International Fund for Ireland, with grateful thanks to the Northern Ireland Council for Integrated Education and all participants.

the fundamental approaches to multicultural education reflected by these leaders and considers their potential implications in the context of the wider debate around multiculturalism and social cohesion. As such, the chapter raises questions relating to the role of schools in the development of cultural identities.

Multiculturalism Challenged

Irrespective of whether they endorse multiculturalism as a policy agenda or ideology, all modern states face the challenges of multiculturalism in that they need to respond to the conflicting claims of groups of people who share identities that differ from the majority (Kelly, 2002). Recent moves toward political models of pluralistic citizenship in which common societal goals provide cohesion while respecting the diverse cultural, ethnic, linguistic, and religious backgrounds of the population have been challenged by liberal egalitarian Barry (2001), who asserts that multiculturalist policies may inhibit beneficial universalistic measures. Multiculturalists, however, argue that the cultural neutrality of liberal egalitarianism neglects the role of culture and group identity in defining harms and cases of injustice. They contend that culture matters, and they endorse the communitarian social thesis—that is, that "individual identity is shaped by and provided through membership of groups, of which cultural groups are perhaps the most important" (Kelly, 2002, p. 7).

Indeed, Jenkins's (2004) concept of identity incorporates both individual and collective aspects in such a way that they interact crucially in the fluid process of identity construction. Jenkins concedes that we are powerless to resist the "socialising tyranny of categorization" (p. 183), and Taylor (1994) admits that, due to the politics of recognition, he favors collective over personal identification. However, he argues that people should not be compelled to organize their lives around their group identity. Kymlicka (1995) reconciles the social thesis with the primary liberal value of autonomy and maintains that collective identity and culture provide the moral resources from which an autonomous and valuable life can be constructed. Benhabib (2002) points out, "there are no easy ways to reconcile either in theory or practice rights of individual liberty with rights of collective cultural expression" (p. x).

She does, however, distinguish between positions that defend the demands of cultural groups in order to preserve minority cultures or that do so in the desire to promote democratic inclusion. In favoring the latter, Benhabib contends that cultures, like identities, are not fixed or distinct but rather are constantly evolving.

Conflict and Multicultural Education

The management of cultural diversity in education challenges our views on individual and collective rights, not least in divided countries with a legacy of conflict. While recent forms of multicultural education that promote diversity have been much criticized for essentializing identity, critical theory (Kincheloe & Steinberg, 1997; Mahalingham & McCarthy, 2000; Nieto, 2000; Sleeter & McLaren, 1995) proposes that an acknowledgment of diversity divorced from a serious questioning of social inequality may be fraudulent and potentially harmful. A critical, multicultural perspective questions the role of teachers and schooling in perpetuating dominant values and common culture.

Critical theorists maintain that liberal forms of multiculturalism supporting belief in a natural equality and a common humanity are flawed (Kincheloe & Steinberg, 1997). They argue that if commonalities are stressed rather than difference, the promotion of cultural invisibility will fail to address issues of race, sex, or class bias. Liberal multiculturalists counter this by claiming that criticism of dominance alone is inadequate and that positive ideals, such as liberty and equality, need to be endorsed. They contend that such a liberal standpoint gives hope for the stable coexistence of people with diverse values (Duarte & Smith, 2000). Kincheloe and Steinberg (1997) suggest that the mainstream articulation of multiculturalism in U.S. schools is not critical but pluralist, whereby diversity, history, and cultural heritage are celebrated and prized, but the context of politics and power is unchallenged.

Sen (2006) argues that the presumption that people can be uniquely categorized based on their religion or culture is not only inaccurate but actually constitutes a major source of conflict in the contemporary world. He rejects a plural monocultural approach that essentializes identity in favor of multicultural practice that endows the freedom to cultivate reasoned choice of identity priorities. As such, Sen distinguishes between two approaches to multiculturalism: "one which concentrates on the promotion of diversity as a value in itself; the other approach focuses on the freedom of reasoning and decision-making, and celebrates cultural diversity to the extent that it is as freely chosen as possible by the persons involved" (Sen, 2006, p. 150).

In a similar vein, Davies (2004) warns that attempts to preserve distinct cultures can present communities as homogenous and fixed rather than dynamic and emerging. Lappalainen (2006) agrees, suggesting that far from integrating different worldviews, multiculturalism can reify cultural difference and treat the hegemonic culture as natural. Adhering to Babha's concept of hybridity, Davies (2004) argues that education can resist confirming the essentialist identities that can be mobilized for conflict in two ways: firstly, by acknowledging the complexity and hybridity within a person, and secondly, by avoiding stereotyped portrayals of the other. In addition, in their description of the goals of peace education in intractable conflicts, Harris and Morrison (2004) contend that educators need not only to promote respect and acceptance but also to develop a caring disposition toward members of other groups.

According to Reich (2002), the challenge to educational theory is "to navigate successfully between the 'pluribus' whilst also promoting an 'unum'" (p. 116). His response is to propose an adapted liberal theory of multicultural education that tries not to ascribe cultural identity to an individual student but rather to treat them as an evolving, self-governing person. Hence, we return to the concept of autonomy: "The goal of liberal multicultural education is not to teach students who they already are, scripting them for a cultural identity; rather the goal is to enable children to decide who they want to become and to be able to participate as informed citizens in a democratic and diverse state" (Reich, 2002, p. 140). Although autonomy is clearly his goal, Reich readily concedes that education about alternative cultures is needed to address the narrow ethnocentric educational practices of the past. As such, the emphasis is not on the promotion of commonality but rather on the development of self-reflective individuals. Brighouse (2006) sees the possibility for promoting human flourishing through the development of autonomy. He views the model autonomy-promoting school as comprised of children from a diversity of backgrounds who are enabled to learn about new perspectives and alternative ways of living.

A powerful argument for desegregated education is provided by the American Educational Research Association (2006) research brief, which brings together extensive and compelling evidence for maintaining desegregated schools in the United States. Reich (2002) claims that "the efficacy of multicultural education likely increases to the degree that the school in which the children learn is integrated, not segregated, by cultures" (p. 131). The current trend, however, is educational resegregation (Orfield & Lee, 2006). In the United Kingdom, the chair of the Commission for Racial Equality warns of the dangers of sleepwalking to segregation (Phillips, 2005), and there are no doubts that community tensions are raised post-9/11 and post-7/7. Government policy of increasing the number of funded, faith-based schools has been questioned (McGlynn, 2005; Parker-Jenkins, Hartas, & Irving, 2004). Brighouse (2006) goes as far as to propose that faith schools undermine the opportunity for autonomy of those who do not attend them.

INTEGRATED EDUCATION IN NORTHERN IRELAND

This brings us to integrated education, defined here as the education, together, in equal numbers, of children who are more usually educated separately, providing an opportunity for them to develop respect and understanding for alternative cultures and perspectives. Integrated education was established in Northern Ireland with the opening of the first planned integrated postprimary school by parents in 1981. An additional fifty-seven primary and postprimary schools have since been established either by parent groups or by parental ballot, but education remains largely separate with children either attending Catholic-maintained schools or *de facto* Protestant-controlled schools. Newly planned, integrated schools are grant maintained (GMI), whereas existing controlled schools that transform to integrated status are known as controlled integrated (CI). Under Northern Ireland's 1989 Education Reform Order, the government has a duty to meet the needs of parents requesting integrated education where it is feasible. Only eighteen thousand children (6 percent of all pupils) attend integrated schools, and the phenomenon has been described as voluntary integration by parental consent rather than compulsory desegregation (Gallagher & Smith, 2002).

Progress toward a more peaceful and democratic society in Northern Ireland has been painstaking, characterized by a lack of trust on all sides and a struggle to reinstate local government rule. Indeed, some commentators have observed that the Good Friday Agreement of 1998 has served to institutionalize sectarianism, resulting in greater political and social segregation. Gallagher (2005) argues that the overprivileging of difference by the peace process has left little space for a discourse of the common good. The Policy and Strategic Framework for Good Relations in Northern Ireland "A Shared Future" has the potential to underpin such a goal for Northern Ireland (Office of the First Minister and Deputy First Minister [OFMDFM], 2005). With a key challenge of new policy being the building of cohesive communities, Shared Future critically states that "separate but equal is not an option" (OFMDFM, 2005, p. 20). This would appear to have implications for an education system still segregated along denominational lines, not least in the current climate of demographic decline, which is provoking a major rationalization of school provision (Bain, 2006).

Research evidence suggests that integrated education may impact positively on identity, outgroup attitudes, and forgiveness, with potential to heal division (McGlynn, Niens, Cairns, & Hewstone, 2004; Montgomery, Fraser, McGlynn, & Smith, 2003; McGlynn, 2001) and promote a less sectarian outlook (Hayes, McAllister, & Dowds, 2006). However, it would appear that, in some integrated schools, issues around religion and politics are avoided (Donnelly, 2004; Hughes & Donnelly, 2007). The evidence also suggests that integration often relies on the interpersonal contact that arises from sharing classrooms rather than intergroup contact (Niens & Cairns, in press). This passive approach was observed in a review of integrated education practice (Montgomery et al., 2003), although reactive and proactive models of integration were also noted. In a small-scale study of leadership in integrated schools, McGlynn (2008) contends that some principals adopt liberal rather than plural or critical approaches to multicultural education. In a further small study, Loughrey, Kidd, and Carlin (2003) suggest that integration practices are more substantial and sophisticated in planned than in transformed primary schools. However, Whitehead's (2006) ethnographic research in a transformed, postprimary school reports a concertedly proactive approach to integration.

This chapter is concerned with approaches to integrating pupils from diverse groups in shared schools. It explores a case study of the integrated school sector in Northern Ireland, which provides an opportunity to investigate approaches to integrated education in a segregated society. The theoretical perspectives on multiculturalism and identity outlined above will be brought to bear on the data collected.

Methods

Interviews were conducted with principals of planned and transformed integrated schools. All fifty-eight integrated principals were approached to participate in the research, and fifty-two agreed to be interviewed, of whom thirty-three were principals of planned schools and nineteen were principals of transformed schools. The principals were coded as follows: principals of planned primary schools, 1–21; principals of transformed primary schools, 22–36; principals of planned postprimary schools, 37–48; and principals of transformed postprimary schools, 49–52. Interviews lasted approximately one hour, were semistructured, and open-ended questions were asked that explored the principals' understandings of the concept of integration and their policies and practice regarding the integration of culturally diverse students. The majority of interviews were taped, and detailed field notes were also taken from which interview summaries were developed. Data were analyzed using qualitative methods, whereby units of relevant meanings were clustered and common themes determined before themes general and unique to all interviews were identified (Freebody, 2003; Mason, 1996; Punch, 1998).

Findings

Before considering the findings, there are two provisos that should be taken into account. Firstly, it should be noted that the breadth and depth of response to questions regarding vision and practice of integration varied greatly between principals, indicating a variation in the degree of importance allocated to the integrated status of the school. Some principals evidently keep integration more to the fore than others. In addition it was also clear that not all principals were happy with their current approach, indicating a desire to develop it. However, distinctive categories of approach to integration, characterized by the emphasis placed on cultural difference or by similarity and willingness to tackle inequalities, clearly emerged from the data. The categories of approach were highly consistent with the understandings and practice of integration as articulated by the school principals. Approaches to integration constituted five main categories, namely, liberal, plural, critical, liberal-plural, and liberal-critical, of which two categories were further self-divided (see Table 1.1). Each approach will be considered in turn.

Table 1.1 Approaches to integration shown by integrated school principals, where P = planned and T = transformed

Type of principal	Liberal proactive	Liberal passive	Plural inclusive	Plural limited	Critical	Liberal/ plural	Liberal/ critical	Total
P primary principals 1–21	2	1	3	1	3	5	6	21
T primary principals 22–36	2	6	4	2	0	1	0	15
P post-primary principals 37–48	3	2	5	0	0	0	2	12
T post-primary principals 49–52	2	0	1	0	1	0	0	4
Total	9	9	13	3	4	6	8	52

Liberal Integration

A total of eighteen principals described approaches to integration that could be categorized as liberal—that is, where the emphasis appeared to be on cultural commonality rather than difference, reflecting the liberal position that individuals from diverse groups share a natural equality and common humanity and endorsing the joint ideals of liberty and equality. However, the approaches reported could be further divided into *liberal proactive*, where the emphasis on commonality was deliberate (9 principals), and *liberal passive*, where it appeared coincidental (9 principals).

The *liberal proactive* approach is typified by the following comments: "Integration is everyone working together, all classes and all creeds. It should be all one family under the one sky. Respect is the core value. It is important how you treat people and children should experience how to deal with conflict" (Principal 2). In this principal's school, there was active work on developing conflict resolution skills, including a peer mediation program. This was reflected by other proactive liberal principals, for example, "Integration here is not too much in your face. It is about more than the things that divide us. A balanced celebration of events is difficult.…Conflict resolution is a central plank at the micro and macro level. Integration features through all levels in the school" (Principal 37).

Such comments not only reflect a conscious effort to find common ground ("we are all human first and foremost" [School 49]) but also indicate a deliberate reluctance to focus on difference. Instead, there is a desire to build a united school community: "We see integration as being welcoming, friendly and serving the wider community. It is about breaking down suspicions...we are seeking to encourage the sense of community within the school" (Principal 38).

By contrast the *liberal passive* approach was characterized by a belief that integration could happen "naturally" (Principal 25) and that there was no need to move from this position. Although integration was perceived as a child-friendly and welcoming concept, there was some evidence of the avoidance of divisive issues ("Do we look at symbols and emblems? No!"[Principal 27]) and also evidence of an acknowledgment that it was a challenge to keep integration to the fore. A typical comment illustrates the reluctance to prioritize integration: "Our core business is the education of children. We would love to have more time on the integrated ethos but it is a bit of a luxury being able to do that" (Principal 39).

Plural Integration

A pluralist approach to integration that embraced the celebration of diversity, history, and cultural heritage was exhibited by sixteen principals. However, these principals did not mention a need to challenge inequality and discrimination against diverse groups of people—that is, a critical, multicultural perspective was absent. The plural approach noted could also be further subdivided into *plural inclusive*, where the focus was on celebrating all aspects of difference (thirteen principals) and *plural limited*, where although world religions and ethnic minority groups were recognized, references to Catholic or Protestant differences were avoided (three principals).

Principals reflecting a *plural inclusive* approach articulated a clear focus on all forms of cultural and religious difference: "We recognize differences and encourage children to celebrate these differences. Everything should be out in the open—for discussion. We celebrate all religions" (Principal 31).

By contrast to the *liberal passive* approach, they described, "'in your face' integration. Everything should be informed by the fact that it is integrated. Respect should be paramount" (Principal 51). This approach to integration was clearly an intrinsic part of school development planning and was reflected in reports of both the formal and informal curricula. The celebration of cultural tradition and the expression of cultural identity was a priority: "We celebrate cultural diversity. You are not trying to take little loyalists and nationalists and make them Alliance voters...you should be proud of who you are and what you believe in but have respect for others' cultures" (Principal 45).

By contrast, three principals described an approach to integration that was *plural limited* in that overt references to Catholic or Protestant differences appeared to be avoided, although recognition was given to other diverse groups. These principals reported a range of curricular and other activities that celebrated "world religions and culture, for example, Ramadan" (Principal 7). Assemblies were seen as a particular opportunity to recognize world faiths, minority ethnic culture, and minority languages. While attempts were clearly made to celebrate these diverse traditions, at no point did these principals report a focus on denominational, cultural, or political differences between the Catholic or Protestant pupils.

Critical Integration

A small number (four) of principals exhibited a *critical* approach to integration. This was characterized not only by a policy of recognizing and celebrating all differences, both denominational and other, but also by a desire to tackle social injustice: "While we recognize and celebrate difference, we appreciate that school in not a neutral haven. Issues of prejudice must be addressed. We are inclusive in all respects…we address the needs of all faiths and we are challenged by supporting the needs of our ethnic minority pupils" (Principal 9).

These principals described a range of initiatives that promoted the celebration of difference, including the existence of integration committees and integration development plans; whole school celebration of the Catholic sacraments of confession, communion, and confirmation; the teaching of world faiths; visits to Christian and non-Christian places of worship; and displays of cultural symbols and emblems. What distinguished this approach from the *plural inclusive* approach was an accompanying emphasis on challenging inequality: "We are tackling controversial issues and conflict resolution. You need to be comfortable with difference. This is the challenge of an increasingly multicultural society. We have to confront racist attacks" (Principal 8). Principals also reported human rights and antibullying initiatives as central to their *critical* practice of integrated education.

Liberal/Plural Integration

An approach that could be described as incorporating aspects of both *liberal* and *plural* models of integration was reported by six principals. While cultural difference was acknowledged, commonality and equality was stressed, for example, "Integration is primarily about equal opportunity, all are welcome. School is safe and child-centred. All children are special and unique—we value and celebrate difference and promote tolerance and respect" (Principal 14).

While offering pupils "the freedom to be different" (Principal 34), the *liberal/plural* approach attempts to construct an inclusive school community where "children and staff feel valued" (Principal 34). The inclusion of diverse groups pivots on the liberal principle of equality: "Children come first. Everyone is welcome and all are treated with respect…all children are educated together. Children are treated equally. Our school tries to instill an attitude of respect" (Principal 15). As such, the *liberal/plural* approach appears to promote a model of integration that reconciles cultural difference within a common school community.

Liberal/Critical Integration

Likewise, the *liberal/critical* approach to integration reported by eight principals also seeks common ground between diverse groups. While also overtly acknowledging cultural difference, this approach also commits to challenging injustice such as sectarianism and racism head on: "Integration should drive all areas and the teaching should reflect this. Children will be looking at contentious issues...we have a constant awareness of anti-bias, anti-bullying and conflict resolution" (Principal 16).

A further principal, although clearly in favor of seeking commonality, saw initiatives on difference and injustice as a route to promoting equality: "The ideal is no awareness of Protestant or Catholic. We have a firm discipline policy on sectarianism...we tackle sectarian abuse" (Principal 47).

The construction of a common school community from both existing and new diverse groups was clearly an ongoing challenge: "There is a debate around ignoring or embracing differences...an increased number of people from other cultures in Northern Ireland will help people here address their own culture and identity. We have to think about how we acknowledge and celebrate minority faiths and cultures" (Principal 20).

The data indicated that these principals were reflecting on how they might bind together an eclectic school community comprised of Catholics, Protestants, those of other faiths and no faith, boys and girls of all abilities, social classes, and ethnic backgrounds. Proactive antibias and antiprejudice work was seen as vital. In addition, two principals reported on the importance of an emphasis on developing pupil autonomy. This was exemplified by the following comment: "Each child is special and should be given opportunities to develop good self-esteem and achieve success. There is a place in the sun for everyone" (Principal 17).

DISCUSSION

Previous research evidence not only points to positive outcomes for integrated education in Northern Ireland (Hayes et al., 2006; McGlynn, 2001; McGlynn et al., 2004; Montgomery et al., 2003) but also suggests that opportunities for proactive practice are missed in some schools (Donnelly, 2004; Hughes & Donnelly, 2007; Montgomery et al., 2003). A smaller study of leadership in integrated schools indicates that principals tend to adopt liberal rather than plural approaches to integration (McGlynn, 2008). This larger study reports a wider range of approaches, including liberal, plural, critical, liberal/plural, and liberal/critical. Although principals are seen elsewhere in the literature as having a crucial role in the leadership of effective and improving schools (Day, Harris, Hadfield, Tolley, & Beresford, 2000; Huber, 2004) and are considered here to have responsibility for integration policy, it must be remembered that their approach may not necessarily be reflected in the practice of individual teachers, nor in the experiences of the pupils themselves. In addition it would appear that the principals' views of integration are evolving, particularly with the advent of more ethnic minority children, and may develop from the approaches reported in this study.

An examination of the foundational principles of integrated education, as agreed by the integrated schools as members of the Northern Ireland Council for Integrated Education (NICIE; 2007) reveals statements, such as the following:

> We…define Integrated Education in the Northern Ireland context as "Education together in school of pupils drawn in approximately equal numbers from the two major traditions with the aim of providing for them an effective education that gives equal recognition to and promotes equal expression of the two major traditions.
>
> We affirm that children brought up in a plural and divided society should be nurtured in their parents' religious and national traditions and identity, whilst respecting the identity and appreciating the traditions of others." (NICIE, 2007)

These and the majority of the foundational principles of integrated education are unmistakably *plural inclusive* in nature, with the possible exception of statements that emphasize the Christian character of integrated schools, which might be perceived as exclusive to children of other faiths. In addition, only one out of the sixteen principles encourages an overtly *critical* perspective: "We affirm that children should be encouraged to identify with those less fortunate than themselves, the oppressed and victims of injustice" (NICIE, 2007).

Few also are the *liberal proactive* statements, such as the following: "There shall be equality of respect and treatment for all children, regardless of creed, culture, race, class, gender or ability" (NICIE, 2007). Rather, the guiding principles appear to focus on the role of integrated schools in the affirmation of existing identities—that is, reflecting a *plural* approach rather than promoting the development of new or common identities. The data from this study would suggest that some principals have a more *liberal* or *critical* or, indeed, *combined approach* to integration than that proposed by the NICIE statement of principles. Possible reasons for this might include the personal career history of the principal, the age of the school, the school context, and the restrictions imposed by the governing body of the school (McGlynn, 2008). It may also be significant that the statement of principles was written in conjunction with early integrated schools and predates not only many of the existing schools but also increasing societal ethnic diversity.

Loughrey et al. (2003) suggest that integration practice may be more substantial in planned than in transformed integrated primary schools. By this, Loughrey et al. (2003) were reporting on the extent to which their study schools reflected plural multicultural practice with respect to Catholic and Protestant pupil groups. The present data provide a more nuanced impression of variation in approach between planned and transformed schools (see Table 1.1). At primary level, although a higher proportion of transformed principals report a *liberal passive* rather than a *liberal proactive* approach, a number describe a *plural inclusive* interpretation of integration. However, while the majority of planned principals reflected *critical*, *liberal/plural*, or *liberal/critical* views, only one transformed principal matched these criteria. At the postprimary level, there were fewer transformed principals in the *liberal passive* and more in the *critical* categories than planned principals. However, more planned principals reported a *plural inclusive* approach. Thus, while at the primary level it could be argued that transformed principals tend to reflect more *passive*, more *limited*, and less *critical* approaches to integration, there are a range of approaches, including *plural inclusive*. At the postprimary level, the picture is less clear, incorporating a variety of approaches.

A number of principals expressed a desire to develop their integration policy, and it is here that recourse to theoretical perspectives may inform discussion of the merits and demerits of approaches to integration. Central here is the necessity to strike a balance between respecting group and individual rights, Reich's (2002) navigation between the "pluribus" and "unum" (p. 116). This is a complex challenge and Benhabib (2002) proposes evaluating group claims against their ability to further inclusion. In such a way, a degree of both recognition and unity could be achieved, but with unity as the primary goal. Likewise, Kymlicka (1995) reconciles the multiculturalists' social thesis with the liberal concept of autonomy by viewing cultural identity as a resource from which to build an individual life, giving dignity to collective and individual claims, but with the development of autonomy to the fore.

This brings us to competing ideologies regarding the purposes of education, namely for social reproduction or social transformation. There is something rather contrary in attempting to bring children together in integrated schools by adopting policies that affirm the very identities that may be complicit in the conflict—that is, by reproducing existing identity forms or categories, the possibilities for transformation and reconciliation may be reduced. However, in a divided society, parents may be unwilling or unable to see beyond the rights of their collectivity to distinctive treatment. Arguments around the potential impact of separate or integrated schools in Northern Ireland have been rehearsed elsewhere (McGlynn, 2005), and it would appear that, for some parents, their rights to separate schooling are an important expression of their group identity. The mainly *plural* nature of the statement of principles might thus reassure parents that integration does not mean assimilation. However, this is arguably in contrast to a view of cultural identity as impure, fluid, and constantly evolving (Benhabib, 2002).

It is clear that empirical evidence is needed of the impact of schooling on the development of identity. However, it is also important to consider the potential advantages and disadvantages of approaches to multicultural education. Kincheloe and Steinberg (1997) warn that *liberal* approaches may promote cultural invisibility and fail to challenge prejudice and injustice toward minority groups. However, *liberal proactive* endorsement of commonality, liberty, and equality might help to construct common ground between conflicting communities. The weaker *liberal passive* model, also reported in this study, may, at best, leave the building of such common ground to chance. More *plural* approaches that advocate the celebration of diversity also have limitations. It is difficult to defend a *plural limited* model that, while willing to recognize minorities, appears to deny recognition to the two majority groups, Catholics and Protestants. Although the *plural inclusive* approach may be more easily supported due to its willingness to acknowledge and celebrate all forms of diversity, without a critical edge, does it promise equality it cannot deliver? *Plural* approaches also risk the unintentional reification of difference by presenting group identities as homogeneous and fixed. This is also a difficulty for *critical* approaches, which, while challenging hegemonic culture, may also potentially reinforce cultural boundaries.

Sen (2006) resists oversimplistic categorization of people purely on the basis of their religion or culture. To him, conflict is sustained through the illusion of a choiceless identity, and he argues for the autonomy of the individual in celebrating whichever aspects of their culture they choose. Only two of the fifty-two principals interviewed reported that the development of pupil autonomy was a central aspect of their approach to integration. Of course, this does not imply that they think education cannot contribute to this, but rather that they tend to conceptualize integration in terms of bringing groups of pupils together.

Niens and Cairns (in press) suggest that the contact hypothesis (Allport, 1954; Pettigrew & Tropp, 2000) has been an unspoken guiding principle behind integrated education. However, developments of the contact hypothesis (Hewstone, 1996) indicate the importance of group salience in the process of prejudice reduction. This risks reifying difference. Whereas contact theory foregrounds difference, Sen's approach challenges us to reduce difference to the lowest common denominator. Indeed, to promote a culture of peace, he advocates the development of understanding of the pluralities of human identity (Sen, 2006). Davies (2004) suggests, "efforts to 'preserve' or 'celebrate' distinct cultures…

may be counterproductive: it would be better to acknowledge hybridity as a positive identity" (p. 87).

The challenge for educators then is to find a way of communicating that individuals form and reform their complex identities by combining a number of different markers. It is difficult to imagine how this might be translated into policy and practice in schools. It is also possible that children might receive mixed messages, particularly in a divided society where collective identification is thrust upon an individual.

Reich (2002) outlines a theory of liberal, multicultural education (and its pedagogical and policy implications) that promotes the development of self-reflective individuals who are empowered to make autonomous decisions about shaping their own lives. Although students would be critically exposed to alternative cultural perspectives, they would be treated as evolving and self-governing rather than being scripted for a predetermined cultural identity. Although the study principals rarely held up the development of autonomy as central to integration, the combined *liberal/plural* and *liberal/critical* approaches reported represent attempts to reconcile individual and group rights, the more critical model acknowledging the need to proactively challenge prejudice and injustice against individuals and minority groups.

Conclusion

The theoretical perspectives outlined can provide a valuable framework for discussions regarding the development of integrated education policy and practice. One thing must be remembered: the socializing role of schools is limited, and it remains to be seen whether educational initiatives, such as integrated education, can overcome the "socializing tyranny of categorization" (Jenkins, 2004, p. 183). Gallagher (2006) claims there are indications that the balance in the world is now shifting away from a privileging of difference and swinging back to a celebration of similarity over difference, providing an opportunity to develop inclusive, integrationist strategies rather than separatist, exclusionary ones. This will have profound implications for all forms of education, not just integrated education. This study reports a range of approaches to managing cultural difference. The motto "Ut sint unum" (Together we are one) of the first integrated school in Northern Ireland is a powerful rallying call to peace: its translation into practice is an ongoing challenge.

References

Allport, G. W. (1954). *The nature of prejudice*. London: Addison-Wesley.
American Educational Research Association. (2006). Brief of the American Educational Research Association as *Amicus Curiae* for the respondents. Retrieved February 19, 2007, from http://www.aera.net/uploadedFiles/News_Media/AERA_Amicus_Brief.pdf

Bain, G. (2006). *Schools for the future: Funding, strategy, sharing.* Report of the Independent Strategic Review of Education. Retrieved February 19, 2007, from http://www.deni.gov.uk/review_of_education.pdf

Barry, B. (2001). *Culture and equality: An egalitarian critique of multiculturalism* Cambridge: Polity Press.

Benhabib, S. (2002). *The claims of culture: Equality and diversity in the global era.* Princeton: Princeton University Press.

Brighouse, H. (2006). *On education.* Oxon: Routledge.

Day, C., Harris, A., Hadfield, M., Tolley, H., & Beresford, J. (2000). *Leading schools in times of change.* Buckingham: Open University Press.

Davies, L. (2004). *Education and conflict: Complexity and chaos.* London: Routledge Falmer.

Donnelly, C. (2004). What price harmony? Teachers' methods of delivering an ethos of tolerance and respect for diversity in an integrated school in Northern Ireland. *Educational Research, 46*(1), 3–16.

Duarte, E. M., & Smith, S. (2000). *Foundational perspectives in multicultural education.* New York: Longman.

Education Reform (Northern Ireland) Order (1989) S.I 1989, No. 2406 (NI20) (Belfast, Her Majesty's Stationery Office).

Freebody, P. (2003). *Qualitative research in education: Interaction and practice.* London: Sage.

Gallagher, T. (2005). Balancing difference and the common good: Lessons from a post conflict society. *Compare, 35*(4), 429–442.

Gallagher, T. (2006). *Has multiculturalism failed?* Paper presented to the British Association of International and Comparative Education conference, Queen's University, Belfast, September 8–10, 2006.

Gallagher, T., & Smith, A. (2002). Selection, integration and diversity in Northern Ireland. In A. M. Gray, K. Lloyd, P. Devine, G. Robinson, & D. Heenan (Eds.), *Social attitudes in Northern Ireland: The eighth report* (pp. 120–137). London: Pluto.

Government of the United Kingdom of Great Britain and Northern Ireland, the Government of Ireland. (1998). The Agreement; Agreement reached in the Multi-party Negotiations (Belfast, Northern Ireland Office).

Hayes, B. C., McAllister, I., & Dowds, L. (2006). In search of the middle ground: Integrated education and Northern Ireland politics. Research Update No. 42. ARK (Northern Ireland Social & Political Archive). Retrieved February 13, 2007, from http://www.ark.ac.uk/publications/updates/update42.pdf

Harris, I., & Morrison, M. L. (2004). *Peace education.* Jefferson, NC: McFarland and Company.

Hewstone, M. (1996). Contact and categorisation: Social psychological interventions to change intergroup relations. In C. N. Macrae, C. Stangor, & M. Hewstone (Eds.), *Foundations of stereotypes and stereotyping* (pp. 323–368). New York: Guilford.

Huber, S. G. (2004). School leadership and leadership development: Adjusting leadership theories and development programs to values and core purpose of school. *Journal of Educational Administration, 42*(6), 669–684.

Hughes, J., & Donnelly, C. (2007). Is the policy sufficient? An exploration of integrated education in Northern Ireland and bi-lingual/bi-national education in Israel. In Z. Bekerman & C. McGlynn (Eds.), *Addressing ethnic conflict through peace education* (pp. 121–133). New York: Palgrave Macmillan.

Jenkins, R. (2004). *Social identity*. London: Routledge.

Kelly, P. (2002). *Multiculturalism reconsidered*. Cambridge: Polity Press.

Kincheloe, J. L., & Steinberg, S. R. (1997). *Changing multiculturalism*. Buckingham, Philadelphia: Open University Press.

Kymlicka, W. (1995). *Multicultural citizenship*. Oxford: Clarendon Press.

Lappalainen, S. (2006). Liberal multiculturalism and national pedagogy in a Finnish preschool context: inclusion or nation-making? *Pedagogy, Culture and Society, 14*(1), 99–112.

Loughrey, D., Kidd, S., & Carlin, J. (2003). Integrated primary schools and community relations in Northern Ireland. *Irish Journal of Education*, xxxiv, 30–46.

McGlynn, C. (2005). Integrated schooling and faith-based schooling in Northern Ireland, *Irish Journal of Education, 36*, 49–62.

McGlynn, C. (2008). Leading integrated schools: A study of the multicultural perspectives of Northern Irish principals. *Journal of Peace Education, 5*(1), 3–16.

McGlynn, C. W. (2001). The impact of post primary integrated education in Northern Ireland on past pupils: A study. Unpublished doctoral thesis, University of Ulster at Jordanstown, Belfast.

McGlynn, C., Niens, U., Cairns, E., & Hewstone, M. (2004). Moving out of conflict: The contribution of integrated schools in Northern Ireland to identity, attitudes, forgiveness and reconciliation. *Journal of Peace Education, 1*(2), 147–163.

Mahalingham, R., & McCarthy, C. (2000). *Multicultural curriculum: New directions for social theory, practice and policy*. New York: Routledge.

Mason, J. (1996). *Qualitative researching*. London: Sage.

Montgomery, A., Fraser, G., McGlynn, C., Smith, A., & Gallagher, T. (2003). Integrated education in Northern Ireland: Integration in practice. Coleraine: UNESCO Centre, University of Ulster.

Niens, U., & Cairns, E. (in press). Integrated education in Northern Ireland: A review.

Nieto, S. (2000). *Affirming diversity: The sociopolitical context of multicultural education*. New York: Longman.

Northern Ireland Council for Integrated Education (NICIE). (2007). Statement of principles of integrated education. Retrieved February 13, 2007, from http://www.nicie.org/aboutus/default.asp?id=27

Office of the First Minister and Deputy First Minister (OFMDFM). (2005). *A shared future: Policy and strategic framework for good relations in Northern Ireland*. Belfast: Author.

Orfield, G., & Lee, C. (2006). *Racial transformation and the changing nature of segregation*. Retrieved February 19, 2007, from http://www.civilrightsproject.harvard.edu/research/deseg/Racial_Transformation.pdf

Parker-Jenkins, M., Hartas, D., & Irving, B. (2004). *In good faith: Schools, religion and public funding*. Abingdon: Ashgate Press.

Pettigrew, T. F., & Tropp, L. R. (2000). Does intergroup contact reduce prejudice? Recent metanalytic findings. In S. Oskamp (Ed.), *Reducing prejudice and discrimination* (pp. 93–114). Mahwah, NJ: Earlbaum.

Phillips, T. (2005). *After 7/7: Sleepwalking to segregation*. Speech given by Chair of the Commission for Racial Equality at the Manchester Council for Community Relations, September 22, 2005. Retrieved February 19, 2007, from http://www.cre.gov.uk/Default.aspx.LocID-0hgnew07s.RefLocID-0hg00900c002.Lang-EN.htm

Punch, K. F. (1998). *Introduction to social research: Quantitative and qualitative approaches*. London: Sage.

Reich, R. (2002). *Bridging liberalism and multiculturalism in American education*. Chicago: University of Chicago Press.

Sen, A. (2006). *Identity and violence*. New York: Norton.

Sleeter, C., & McLaren, P. (Eds.). (1995). *Multicultural education, critical pedagogy and the politics of difference*. New York: State University of New York Press.

Taylor, C. (1994). The politics of recognition. In A. Gutmann (Ed.), *Multiculturalism: Examining the politics of recognition* (pp. 25–73). Princeton: Princeton University Press.

Whitehead, J. (2006). *What's in a name? Insights into what it means for a school in Northern Ireland to become "integrated."* Paper presented to the British Association of International and Comparative Education conference, Queen's University, Belfast, September 8–10, 2006.

CHAPTER 2

GRASSROOTS VOICES OF HOPE
EDUCATORS' AND STUDENTS' PERSPECTIVES ON EDUCATING FOR PEACE IN POST-CONFLICT BURUNDI

Elavie Ndura-Ouedraogo

The beautiful tropical landscape, temperate climate, and rather reserved but warm people of Burundi stand in ominous contrast with the history of interethnic conflict and violence that characterize the postcolonial era of this small nation nested in the heart of Africa. Even though much of the nation's tragic history has been skillfully kept out of reach throughout the educational system, it is very much alive in people's individual and collective memories. In addition, a growing, albeit still limited, body of literature documents the complex nature, broad scope, and annihilating consequences of cyclical interethnic conflicts that have for decades polarized Hutu and Tutsi and crystallized ethnic borderlines (Chrétien, 1985, 2003; Lemarchand, 1994, 2004; Makoba & Ndura, 2006; Ndura, 2003, 2006a, 2006b; Scherrer, 2002; Uvin, 2002).

Much of the existing literature analyzes Burundi history of interethnic conflict in terms of its causes, most often agreeing that the Belgian colonial policies and practices that promoted Tutsi hegemony in all social, economic, and political sectors is at the root of the endless carnage (Lemarchand, 1994; Mamdani, 2001; Ndura, 2006a, 2006b). Still limited or even lacking in the literature, however, are discussions of sustained efforts to shift the interethnic discourse and move forward from the roots and scope paradigm to an inclusive, reconstructivist paradigm that would foster peaceful interethnic coexistence and help the people of Burundi reclaim their humanity. Initial attempts to lay the theoretical foundation for this new paradigm place education at the center of the quest for societal transformation (Ndura, 2003, 2004a, 2004b, 2006a, 2006b; Ndura & Makoba, 2008). Such efforts must be solidified with relevant data that reflect the narratives and understanding of the people whose communities are the targets of transformative and reconstructivist endeavors.

This chapter discusses the findings from a study that explored educators' and students' perceptions of the role of education in the quest for sustainable peace in Burundi, Africa. The limited available literature addressing the Burundian context paints a picture of a country where education has been part of the problem in the Hutu-Tutsi discord instead of providing a framework for collaboration, reconciliation, and peace. Scholars argue that inequality and exclusion begin with inequitable educational opportunity and access, which has for decades promoted Tutsi hegemony in the civil service, the army, and the judiciary (Chrétien, 1985, 2003; Lemarchand, 1994; Reyntjens, 2000). Scholars have also argued that, in the past, even the few Hutus who attempted to get an education often became alienated and disenfranchised from the system because of pervasive discriminatory attitudes, policies, and practices. Most damaging to the shaping of the Burundian ethnic landscape is that these discriminatory policies and practices have not been consistently exposed or questioned (Ndura, 2006a).

The goal of this chapter and of the research is to contribute to efforts to shift the Burundian interethnic discourse toward a transformative and reconstructivist paradigm, rooted in the intersection between multicultural education and peace education. The discussion of the theoretical framework that guides this chapter clarifies this intersection and highlights the importance of engaging the youth in these critical conversations. A description of the study and findings follows. The chapter concludes with a general discussion of the research questions and recommendations for further research and action.

THEORETICAL FRAMEWORK: TRANSFORMATIVE EDUCATION AND STUDENTS' VOICES

With the advent of a new coalition government after twelve years of civil war, there is reason to hope that the country's leaders and citizens will develop a united vision of reconciliation, societal transformation, and peace. The new government has taken the first step by declaring primary education universal and free for all Burundian children (Associated Press, 2005). Nevertheless, this step will produce limited results if existing educational programs and practices are not transformed to better address the pressing issues of ethnic diversity and peaceful interethnic coexistence. Transformative education empowers educators and students to become reflective agents of change who advocate for and labor to achieve equity, social justice, and peaceful coexistence in their interethnic communities and in the multicultural global community (Ndura, 2003, 2004a, 2004b).

Transformation education is defined and shaped by principles and practices drawn from the intersection between multicultural education and peace education. Effective multicultural education must yield agents of peace, and effective peace education must be multicultural in nature and scope (Ndura, in press). Therefore, in addition to becoming culturally competent agents of social transformation who labor to achieve equity and social justice by challenging all forms of discrimination (Nieto, 2000, 2004) and resisting all forms of oppressive social relationships (Sleeter, 1996), educators and students need to become agents of peaceful coexistence who validate others' narratives of suffering, take ownership of their group's actions toward other groups, are empathetic and trusting toward others, and have nonviolent dispositions (Salomon, 2002). The intersection between multicultural education and peace education is further clarified by Synott (2005), who argues, "The goals of peace education are towards social change and transformation, or…towards the formation of a world culture of peace" (p. 13). Therefore, educators must become transformative intellectuals who possess the dispositions, knowledge, and skills necessary to develop a discourse that unites the language of critique with the language of possibility. They must speak up against economic, political, and social injustices within and outside of schools (Giroux, 1988). They must also become ethnic border-crossers who understand the impact of their ethnic identities on their classroom practices and interactions. In addition, they must become critical pedagogues who can transform classrooms into critical spaces that question the obviousness of taken-for-granted assumptions. Educators must also become social activists who are at the forefront of the pursuit of true independence and national self-determination (Ndura, 2004b).

Seeking and listening to students' voices are prerequisites to transformative education. These prerequisites are particularly critical in the Burundian context where, as literature shows, youth's active involvement in interethnic violence has been notable. For instance, quoting observers of the 1972 genocide of the Hutu by the Tutsi government and military, Lemarchand (2004) states,

> Tutsi pupils prepared lists of their Hutu classmates to make identification by officials more straightforward…some of the most gruesome scenes took place on the premises of the university in Bujumbura, and in secondary and technical schools.…Scores of Hutu students were physically assaulted by their Tutsi classmates, and many beaten to death. In a scenario that would repeat itself again and again, groups of soldiers and members of the Uprona youth wing, the so-called Juenesses Revolutionnaires Rwangsore

(JRR), would suddenly appear in classrooms, call the Hutu students by name and take them away. Few ever returned. (p. 326)

Youth's active participation in interethnic conflicts is a significant aspect of Burundi's history of violence, as will be discussed in this chapter's findings section. It is therefore critical that youth's voices be included in the mapping of the transformative and reconstructivist paradigm. This is important not only because students and youth in general are integral members of society and are equally impacted (if not even worse) by its challenges but also because they contribute fresh and powerful insights to educational decision-making processes (Antrop-Gonzalez, 2006; Ivey & Broaddus, 2001).

Description of the Study

This qualitative study (Stake, 2000; Wolcott, 1994; Yin, 1994) is part of a larger research project that examined educators' perceptions of their roles and the role of education in the quest for sustainable peace in the African Great Lakes region, with particular emphasis on Burundi. The project sought to encourage educators to reflect on their roles and responsibilities as citizens and professionals in the process of peace building and societal reconstruction in their country and the region. The project also aimed at contributing to the scholarly discourse about the role of education in the pursuit for social change in Burundi, the African Great Lakes region, and other parts of the world. It rests on the belief that raising educators' consciousness of the critical role that education must play in the peace-building and social reconstruction processes in their post-war nation would help them clarify their own roles as agents of positive social change (Makoba & Ndura, 2006; Ndura, 2003, 2004a, 2004b, 2006a, 2006b; Ndura & Makoba, 2008). This part of the study addressed one overarching question: what do educators and students perceive to be the role of educational programs and practices in the peace-building process in Burundi? To answer this central question, three subquestions were addressed:

1. How have ethnic conflict and violence impacted educators' and students' lives in Burundi?
2. How do educators and students characterize the role of education in the quest for sustainable peace?
3. To what extent does educators' and students' involvement in a discourse surrounding peace reflect a promising step toward societal transformation?

The thirty-six participants who took part in the larger study consisted of a convenience criterion and snowball sample (Creswell, 1998) of thirty-three professional educators and three high school students. The participants were from three provinces. Twelve of the participants were female, and twenty-four were male. The educators included eleven administrators, twenty-one teachers, and one bookkeeper. Twenty-three participants were affiliated with elementary schools, twelve with secondary schools, and one worked in higher education. Seven of the participants identified themselves as Tutsi, twenty as Hutu, and one as mixed. The remaining eight did not identify their ethnic membership. Twenty-six of the participants were married; eight were single, and two were widows. The participants were mostly Burundians (one was a Congolese national), and they ranged in age from the early twenties to early fifties. The educators' length of experience in the profession ranged from novice to veteran.

Participants were initially contacted through the researcher's existing acquaintances in Burundi after securing the official permission to access schools from the Burundi Ministry of National Education and Culture. Being familiar with the participants' culture and fluent in their native language (Kirundi) and academic language (French) helped the researcher establish a sense of trust (Vásquez-Montilla et al., 2000), a prerequisite for credible data collection. The participants took part in semistructured interviews that lasted between one and two hours in the spring and early summer of 2006. The interviews were conducted in the participants' preferred language, Kirundi or French, or a mixture of both. The researcher also maintained a journal where she recorded her observations of the research environment.

The digitally recorded interviews were professionally transcribed and coded to facilitate analysis. Data from the interviews and field notes were analyzed separately during and after the data collection process to identify recurrent themes (Creswell, 1998; Marshall & Rossman, 2006) relevant to educators' perceptions of their roles and the role of education in the quest for sustainable peace in Burundi and the African Great Lakes region. The findings and conclusions were shared with selected participants for verification purposes.

Although the themes discussed in the findings are representative of the larger study, the examples used to illustrate them are drawn from six of the participants in order to maintain a sense of focus. Participants' names have been replaced with pseudonyms to protect their identities. Following is a brief profile of each of the six participants.

Pontien was a thirty-one-year-old Tutsi teacher, married, with no children. He had a D6 diploma (six years of secondary education). At the time of the interview, he had been teaching in elementary school for six years. Sounding almost embarrassed by his low educational achievement, he clarified that he was quite intelligent but that poverty had forced him to interrupt his educational pursuit. He had just entered secondary school when the civil war erupted in 1993.

Pamphile was a forty-two-year-old Tutsi Roman Catholic priest who graduated from the local seminary with a baccalaureate in philosophy and theology. At the time of the interview, he had been teaching in secondary school for three years after working in various positions within the

Church for twelve years. His experiences with and memories of interethnic conflict went back to the 1972 genocide. His father was killed during the recent civil war.

Liz was a Hutu school administrator in her late forties. She earned a bachelor's degree from the local university. She was married with three children. She barely escaped death on several occasions during the civil war. Her home was completely destroyed by grenade attacks in the early days of the civil war in 1993. She spent eight years of utter hardship in displacement. She fought hard to maintain her teaching position in secondary school through the war, risking her life in order to sustain her family. At the time of the interview, she had not yet been able to return to her home.

Langalanga was a nineteen-year-old Hutu student. He was the third in a family of eight children. He was in elementary school when the civil war began in 1993. Both his parents were educators. His father was killed during the war in 2003. Langalanga hoped to become a priest.

Fédor was a twenty-year-old Tutsi student, the second in a family of four boys and from a well-off family. His father worked for the government, and his mother was an accountant. He had attended private schools his entire life. He was in the second grade when the civil war erupted. Both his parents were still alive at the time of the interview. He hoped to become a lawyer.

Kijaba was a twenty-one-year-old Hutu student. He was the seventh in a family of nine children. His father was a construction worker, and his mother worked the fields. He was in the second grade when the civil war began. He had to change schools twice during the war. At the time of the interview, he was at his third secondary school. His parents were still alive. His memories of the war experiences were so fresh and vivid that he even remembered the days when many of the incidents happened.

Findings

Data analysis revealed five main themes, which are discussed individually in this section: (1) ethnic polarization, (2) youth involvement in interethnic violence, (3) suffering and trauma, (4) group-hopping for survival, and (5) education as the cradle of hope.

Ethnic Polarization

Ethnic polarization, a pervasive theme in the literature pertaining to the people and society of Burundi and the African Great Lakes region, impacted the participants' lived experiences, and it was a major cause of the civil war that ravaged Burundi from 1993 until 2005. The conflict robbed some of the participants of their innocence as they discovered ethnicity and its impact on human relations. Langalanga shared:

Children with whom we usually played and their parents rejected us.... The military came to gather the Tutsis from school, the community, everywhere...and then I heard gun shots...they began shooting at the fearless Hutus who wanted to go find those soldiers....It was difficult for us to go to the commune because that is where the Tutsis were gathered...prior to the war, I did not know if there was a Hutu, a Tutsi, or a Twa.

Fédor, who described his elementary school and first secondary school as dominated by Tutsis and his current institution as predominately Hutu, was also unaware of ethnic membership before the 1993 to 2005 civil war. He explained:

When the crisis erupted, they started to say these are Hutus and those are Tutsis. So, I asked "What side am I on?" Then they tell you...I am Tutsi...they told me, since I did not even know the criteria....In any case, I learned to differentiate ethnicity during the crisis...people were killed because of their ethnicity.

Kijaba related vivid memories of interethnic violence and affirmed, "My first experience is that I was able to understand what ethnicity is in Burundi." Pontien had just started the seventh grade when the civil war began. He indicated that, while the majority of the students were Hutu, the authorities (i.e., teachers and administrators) were Tutsi. He recounted his experiences as he and his classmates tried to escape an attack on their school but found themselves encircled by a Hutu mob:

A few kilometers away from the school, the people began to separate us. "You are Tutsi, you are Hutu...anyone who knows that he is Tutsi, go to the other side...whoever knows that he is Hutu...stand here." They separated us only by looking at us...the nose, size, height...he is a Tutsi...they mixed up [ethnicities] therefore, because there are no real criteria.

Liz recounted how Tutsi militias forced her and her family out of their home and into eight years of painful, dehumanizing displacement:

Our housekeeper warned us that our neighborhood was surrounded by Tutsi militias with knifes and bamboos....We settled in Kinama....We found ourselves under attack by the military who were avenging their fellow Tutsis killed in the countryside....They forced us out...shooting everywhere in Kinama....They finally forced us out of Kinama and Kamenge....When we reached Gatumba, there were so many [Hutu] refugees because at that time even the [Hutu] residents of Bwiza and Buyenzi had been forced out.

Pamphile's memories of and experiences with ethnic polarization went back to the 1972 genocide of the Hutus by the Tutsi-dominated government and military. He recounted,

> I lived an unhappy experience in 72....I was eight years old....We had to hide in the swamps every night....We would see a Jeep with soldiers.... They would take the Hutus, all Hutus...our teachers...and they would not come back....There were killings in 1995....So the displaced [Tutsis] came to take revenge, assisted by the military....The next day every Hutu person residing in the town center had been killed....Hutus could not come to [the] church [located in the town center] and I could not go to the [Church] branches, because I was Tutsi.

Suffering and Trauma

The experiences that the participants shared during the interviews showed that the conflict and violence witnessed during the twelve–year civil war had a scarring impact on their lives. Pontien shared how his school was under military attack,

> The military were shooting...armored vehicles...so we fled...we hid in the swamps by the river....We stayed there throughout the night, unable to sleep....I had no towel, no sheet over me....I slept on reed.... They sting....It is like poison....In the morning, my skin was swollen and I was trembling, trembling a lot.

Liz described her despicable living conditions in a small rental hut with dirt walls and dirt floor and no furniture in Gatumba, and recounts how, even there in internal exile, she and her fellow Hutus were constantly harassed by the military. She concluded, "The military were animals."

Langalanga recalled the killing of his father with palpable melancholy: "What hurt me the most was when they killed my father....This was a time of despair....There were bombings every day, and we had nowhere to seek refuge....And you know, the loss of a father is not an easy experience to endure." Kijaba, too, was traumatized by the war. He shared, "I learned what war is in general...spending several weeks outside the house...seeking shelter in the forest...when it rains, the rain falls on you... you suffer from several illnesses because of poor shelter."

Youth Involvement in Violence

Many participants related that young people in schools and communities actively participated in interethnic violence through intimidation, looting, and even killing. Pontien reported:

Sometimes they caught students with grenades, sometimes with daggers…but then the most bizarre thing happened.…It was a Sunday…every Tutsi student had purchased a sword or a dagger…they brought them to school and hid them in their bags.…When we Hutus saw that…we had to warn the [school] authorities.…We couldn't sleep for several days and nights.…One time we actually caught a student who was about to stab his classmate.…He [the victim] was going to the restroom and the other [the perpetrator] followed him with a dagger.…During a subsequent search, it was discovered that there were daggers and grenades in bags belonging to the Tutsis.

Liz recounted a similarly terrifying incident that occurred at her school where students had just murdered a person and were about to set the body on fire when a Red Cross crew arrived at the scene. She was so terrified by this incident that she did not return to work for three weeks. She talked further about the pervasive involvement of the youth in the conflict:

During the years 1995 and 1996…we often heard of secondary school children watching people burn in tires.…At the height of the crisis, young people would gather in hidden corners unknown to their parents in order to smoke marijuana. They would smoke drugs in order to be brave enough to ambush and murder people.…They looted, smoked drugs, drank a lot of alcohol.…They were stealing and stealing…after smoking drugs and mixing with alcohol, they would rape anybody that they saw.

Langalanga experienced interethnic mistrust and intimidation at school where Hutus and Tutsis constantly accused and feared each other.

Group-hopping for Survival

Although group-hopping appeared in the interview with only one of the six participants who are the focus of this paper, it holds particular meaning because it highlights the complexity of ethnic identity and problematizes people's motives for allegiance during the Burundi conflict. Pamphile discussed how he camouflaged his Tutsi identity in order to escape Hutu wrath and admitted, "I lied, of course, to save my life." He explained how people contributed money to opposing parties:

The rebels already had money because the Hutus gave financial contributions in order to survive…Tutsis contributed money [to the rebel movement] as well.…Whenever they pulled you over in your car, you would show them the contribution receipt…and they would let you go.…But the Tutsis contributed in secret…Hutus who did not have receipts were killed, accused of supporting the government…and if by accident Tutsis showed the receipts to the government military, they were also killed, accused of supporting the rebels.

Education as the Cradle of Hope

Many participants believed that education must play a central role in the quest for sustainable peace and that educators must become active agents of peace committed to reconciliation and peaceful interethnic coexistence. Thus, participants saw education as the cradle of hope for societal change and reconstruction and peace. Pamphile argued that ignorance and illiteracy are some of the handicaps to peace. He explained, "Intellectual culture reduces barbarism and [tempers] emotions....Education plays a critical role in human development...a society were everyone is educated has a better chance to live in peace...because education broadens people's frames of reference....Ignorance is really dangerous."

Education is very important because it helps shape the future leadership, as Langalanga observed,

> If the youth are not taught to develop peaceful dispositions or to work towards peace when they are still in school, and if they are not taught to uncover the wrong ideas which are in their hearts when still in school, I don't think they will change in their adult life when they start working.

Fédor echoed this sentiment by saying, "Education must teach students that they must respect one another regardless of their ethnic differences...to achieve sustainable peace without violence...teach them to tell the truth and fight for righteous justice, since without justice...there will never be peace." Education should also foster mutual understanding, as Kijaba posited, "Civic education which teaches patriotism among other things should foster self-exposure and facilitate the sharing and comparing of lived experiences among students from different clans or tribes.... Education should help [people] liberate themselves from ethnism."

The participants indicated that educators must become role models and guides who are committed to peace and who have the courage to engage in critical conversations surrounding ethnicity. Liz observed, "Educators [must] guide the youth, teach them the value of peace...show them that without peace we cannot progress...we only march backwards...because without peace, we destroy....Without peace, no one thinks about anybody else....We must insist on patriotism, human rights, [and] respect for the other." Arguing that educators need to practice what they preach, Pamphile explained, "Educators' primary role is to become role models and guides...true peace agents who are committed to the reconstruction of their nation....Their role is really vital to the development of the children's humane conscience."

Langalanga expressed a similar perception: "Educators should set a good example because here at school, they are our light; they are our role models. A good educator is one who loves peace, who teaches his students, from his lived experience, how to live in peace."

Educators must have the courage to engage their students in open discussions surrounding issues of ethnicity and foster reconciliation. Kijaba clarified, "Educators should teach the reconciliation process....They should not be afraid of discussing ethnicity and ethnic membership.... You should not be afraid of discussing your ethnic background even if there are some schools where you are expelled whenever you talk about ethnicity."

Discussion and Conclusion

In the conclusion to his discussion of the origins, nature, and broad consequences of Burundi's cyclical interethnic conflicts, Scherrer (2002) argues that the implementation of a future, comprehensive peace treaty in Burundi will require a process that, among other things, reaches the grass roots and addresses the root causes of the conflict. This research project represents an attempt to bring Burundi's interethnic discourse to the grass roots by seeking the perspectives of educators and students from elementary and secondary schools on how to educate the nation's youth for peace. The study drew upon the participants' lived experiences with interethnic discord to shift the discourse of mutual accusation toward a discourse of hope and possibilities inspired by a transformative and reconstructivist paradigm. The three research questions that guided the study are addressed in this section, followed by some recommendations for further research and action.

The first research question explored the extent to which ethnic conflict and violence had impacted the participants' lived experiences. It is clear from their accounts that all participants, educators and students alike, bore vivid memories of pain and suffering from the conflict. The students' innocence was shattered as they came to discover the hidden but deadly face of ethnicity in their schools and neighborhoods. For some of the educators, the civil war was a devastating reminder of the 1972 genocide as mostly unspoken, yet venomous, interethnic mistrust and mutual suspicion emerged like the deadly head of a sneaky viper now perilously exposed. The scars from the conflict were palpable, from the loss of family members and property, to disrupted education and pervasive economic hardship resulting from years of destruction.

The second research question sought the participants' insights about how education could contribute to the quest for sustainable piece. Both educators and students agreed that education should be the vehicle through which students and teachers engage in critical conversations about ethnicity and interethnic conflict in order to share and validate their individual and collective experiences and begin the process of reconciliation and peace building. Both groups acknowledged the vital role that educators must play as peace agents and role models.

The third research question looked at the extent to which educators' and students' involvement in a discourse surrounding peace reflected a promising step toward societal transformation. To address this question, the researcher drew upon her authentic knowledge and understanding of Burundian society and culture as a Burundi native, born and educated in Burundi. Knowing Burundians to be somewhat reserved, particularly when discussing sensitive personal experiences with nonfamily members, the participants' openness and candidness in sharing their stories were quite significant. They were all comfortable revealing their ethnic backgrounds, a topic formerly seen as taboo in public conversations, and discussing the different groups' involvement in the conflict, including their own. Of particular importance was the inclusive nature of the participants' portrayal of the roles that educators need to play to contribute to peace building. There were no interethnic blaming or accusations, and no indication that Hutu participants expected the Tutsis to work any harder to resolve the country's ethnic issues, or vice versa. Instead, all the participants believed that it is the responsibility of everyone, Tutsi and Hutu alike, as well as educators and students, to actively engage in the work necessary to achieve sustainable peace and transform society. Therefore, the experience reflected a promising step toward societal transformation as the participants were able to name and begin to reflect upon issues of ethnicity and interethnic conflict. This predisposition may facilitate efforts to engage in further critical reflection and exploration of individual and collective action necessary to reframe interethnic relations and work toward societal change.

What future action and research should then be undertaken to expound and capitalize on the findings discussed in this chapter? Some concluding thoughts and recommendations briefly address this important question. As Francis (2006) argues, the concept of peace is about security, development, and social justice. Closely linked to the quest for sustainable peace is the task of capacity building. Huang and Harris (2006) posit that in the context of post-conflict building, "efforts are made to build local capacity… so that individuals can better perform their jobs, but also in the hope that it would…[help] to build up durable state institutions with full ownership over their own affairs" (p. 85). The central role that education plays in this process cannot be debated. But the question is, what kind of education? One immediate recommendation would be to explore and to expound upon principles of critical and transformative multicultural education (Ndura, in press, 2006b; Ndura & Makoba, 2008). Johnson and Johnson (2006) posit that "peace building deals with structural issues and is aimed at creating long-term harmonious relationships based on positive interdependence, mutual respect and social justice" (p. 150). By challenging hegemony, affirming ethnic diversity, and seeking equity and social justice (Ndura, in press), critical and transformative multicultural education would effectively support and actualize the peace building process.

For any educational program development or reform effort to be effective, it must be inspired and shaped by local realities. Therefore, a second recommendation is to enhance research efforts throughout Burundi in order to gather educators' and students' perspectives on their experiences with and hopes for teaching and learning. Such efforts would engage them in critical conversations about their individual and collective responsibilities toward peace building and societal reconstruction and transformation. While it is important to engage leaders in divided societies, such as Burundi, in conversations that help them explore their conflicting as well as their shared interests (Wolpe & McDonald, 2006), it is equally important, if not more critical, to develop such endeavors at the grassroots level—that is, among educators and students—to help develop from an early age the dispositions, attitudes, behaviors, and relationships necessary to heal the wounds from years of interethnic conflict and violence and build a peaceful nation for all Burundians.

References

Antrop-Gonzalez, R. (2006). Toward the school as a sanctuary concept in multicultural urban education: Implication for small high school reform. *Curriculum Inquiry, 36*(3), 273–301.

Associated Press. (2005). *Burundi schools overflow with students.* Retrieved October 2, 2005, from http://www.cnn.com/2005/WORLD/africa/09/15/burundi.education.ap/index.html

Chrétien, J. P. (1985). Hutu and Tutsi au Rwanda et au Burundi. In J. L. Amselle & E. M'Bokolo (Eds.), *Aur cœur de l'éthnie, tribalisme et état en Afrique* (pp. 129–165). Paris: Editions la Découverte.

Chrétien, J. P. (2003). *The great lakes of Africa: Two thousand years of history.* New York: Zone Books.

Creswell. J. W. (1998). *Qualitative inquiry and research design: Choosing among five traditions.* Thousand Oaks, CA: Sage.

Francis, D. J. (2006). Linking peace, security and developmental regionalism: Regional economic and security integration in Africa. *Journal of Peacebuilding & Development, 2*(3), 7–20.

Giroux, H. A. (1988). *Teachers as intellectuals: Toward a critical pedagogy of learning* Westport, CT: Bergin & Garvey.

Huang, R., & Harris, J. (2006). The nuts and bolts of post-conflict capacity building: Practicable lessons from East Timor. *Journal of Peacebuilding & Development, 2*(3), 78–92.

Ivey, G., & Broaddus, K. (2001). "Just plain reading:" A survey of what makes students want to read in middle school classroom. *Reading Research Quarterly, 36*(4), 350–377.

Johnson, D. W., & Johnson, R. T. (2006). Peace education for consensual peace: The essential role of conflict resolution. *Journal of Peace Education, 3*(2), 147–174.

Lemarchand, R. (1994). *Burundi: Ethnocide as discourse and practice.* New York: Woodrow Wilson Center Press.
Lemarchand, R. (2004).The Burundi genocide. In S. Totten, W. S. Parsons, & I. W. Charny (Eds.), *Century of genocide: Critical essays and eyewitness accounts* (2nd ed., pp. 321–337). New York: Routledge.
Makoba, J. W., & Ndura, E. (2006). The roots of contemporary ethnic conflict and violence in Burundi. In S. C. Santosh (Ed.), *Perspectives on contemporary ethnic conflict: primal violence or the politics of conviction?* (pp. 295–310). Lanham: Lexington Books.
Mamdani, M. (2001). *When victims become killers: Colonialism, nativism, and the genocide in Rwanda.* Princeton, NJ: Princeton University Press.
Marshall, C., & Rossman, G. B. (2006). *Designing qualitative research* (4th ed.). Thousand Oaks, CA: Sage.
Ndura, E. (in press). Empowering citizens to achieve sustainable peace in Burundi through transformative multicultural education. In M. Meyer & J. Atiri (Eds.), *Seeds taking root: Pan-African peace action for the twenty-first century.* Trenton, NJ: Africa World/Red Sea Press.
Ndura, E. (2003). Peaceful conflict resolution: A prerequisite for social reconstruction in Burundi, Africa. In E. E. Uwazie (Ed.), *Conflict resolution and peace education in Africa* (pp. 151–160). Lanham: Lexington Books.
Ndura, E. (2004a). La contribution de l'éducation familiale et scolaire à la réalisation d'une paix durable au Burundi. *Tuj-i-Buntu, 40,* 4–7.
Ndura, E. (2004b). *Building a foundation for sustainable peace in Burundi: A transformative multicultural education framework.* Paper presented at the Annual Conference of the Peace and Justice Studies Association, San Francisco, CA.
Ndura, E. (2006a). Western education and African cultural identity in the Great Lakes Region of Africa: A case of failed globalization, *Peace and Change, 31*(1), 90–101.
Ndura, E. (2006b). Transcending the majority rights and minority protection dichotomy through multicultural reflective citizenship in the African Great Lakes region. *Intercultural Education, 17*(2), 195–205.
Ndura, E., & Makoba, J. W. (2008). Education for social change in Burundi and Rwanda: Creating a national identity beyond the politics of ethnicity. In S. C. Santosh (Ed.), *Ethnicity and sociopolitical change in Africa and other developing countries: A constructive discourse in state building* (pp. 59–76). Lanham: Lexington Books.
Nieto, S. (2000). Placing equity front and center: Some thoughts on transforming teacher education for a new century. *Journal of Teacher Education, 51*(3), 180–187.
Nieto, S. (2004). *Affirming diversity: The sociopolitical context of multicultural education* (4th ed.). Boston: Pearson.
Reyntjens, F. (2000). *Burundi: Prospects for peace.* London: Minority Rights Group International.
Salomon, G. (2002). The nature of peace education: Not all programs are created equal. In G. Salomon & B. Nevo (Eds.), *Peace education: The concept, principles, and practices around the world* (pp. 3–13). Mahwah, NJ: Lawrence Erlbaum Associates.
Scherrer, C. P. (2002). *Genocide and crisis in central Africa: Conflict roots, mass violence, and regional war.* London: Praeger.

Sleeter, C. E. (1996). *Multicultural education as social activism*. Albany: State University of New York Press.

Stake, R. E. (2000). Case studies. In N. K. Denzin & Y. S. Lincoln (Eds.), *Handbook of qualitative research* (2nd ed., pp. 435–454). Thousand Oaks, CA: Sage.

Synott, J. (2005). Peace education as an educational paradigm: Review of a changing field using an old measure. *Journal of Peace Education, 2*(1), 3–16.

Uvin, P. (2002). On counting, categorizing, and violence in Burundi and Rwanda. In D. I. Kertzer & D. Arel (Eds.), *Census and identity: The politics of race, ethnicity, and language in national censuses* (pp. 148–175). Cambridge: Cambridge University Press.

Vásquez-Montilla, E., Reyes-Blanes, M. E., Hyun, E., & Brovelli, E. (2000). Practices for culturally responsive interviews and research with Hispanic families. *Multicultural Perspective, 2*(3), 3–7.

Wolcott, H. F. (1994). Posturing in qualitative research. In M. D. LeCompte, W. L. Millroy, & J. Preissle (Eds.), *The handbook of qualitative research in education* (pp. 3–52). San Diego: Academic Press.

Wolpe, H., & McDonald, S. (2006). Burundi's transition: Training leaders for peace. *Journal of Democracy, 17*(1), 132–138.

Yin, R. K. (1994). *Case study research: Design and methods* (2nd ed.). Thousand Oaks, CA: Sage.

CHAPTER 3

THE EMERGENCE OF HUMAN RIGHTS EDUCATION AMID ETHNIC CONFLICT IN THE DOMINICAN REPUBLIC[1]

Monisha Bajaj and Cheila Valera Acosta

INTRODUCTION

While this volume discusses the role of peace education in conflict and post-conflict societies, this chapter asserts that the definition of "conflict" societies should be expanded to include those societies that, while not undergoing or emerging from armed conflict, have exhibited ethnic or other social conflict that results in the widespread and systematic denial of basic human rights. The situation of ethnic Haitians and Dominicans of Haitian descent in the Dominican Republic fits the description of that which might be found in a "conflict society" due to the routine violation of the basic human rights of this sizeable population, whose estimates range anywhere from 500,000 to one million, or between five and eleven percent of the Dominican population, depending on the criteria used for inclusion (Ferguson, 2003).[2]

While recent literature importantly focuses on peace education in "conflict" and "post-conflict" conditions (Davies, 2005; Bekerman and McGlynn, 2007), the Dominican Republic demonstrates many *pre-conflict* characteristics—such as impunity for extrajudicial killings, police abuse (Amnesty International, 2005), and rising ethnic tensions—that offer a strong rationale for its inclusion in discussions of conflict and peace education.

This chapter provides information about Haitian migration to the neighboring Dominican Republic, examines the rights abuses endured by migrants and their Dominican-born children and grandchildren, and explores the antecedents and emergence of human rights education in the Dominican Republic, which is, in part, focused on mitigating the adverse societal effects of xenophobia and discrimination. The goal of this chapter is to provide a context for understanding the limits and possibilities of peace education efforts—in this case, human rights education—in addressing ethnic conflict that is rooted in post/colonial, political, and economic histories. In order to better understand the possibility for human rights education (HRE) to expand definitions of citizenship and membership in conflict-ridden societies, it is worthwhile to first explore the origins of HRE and its emergence as part of broader peace building efforts.

Human rights education

Once at the periphery of both human rights and educational movements, HRE, or the incorporation of content and pedagogy with the aim of inculcating knowledge of international human rights norms in diverse educational settings, is now being adopted by governments across the globe, facilitated largely by funding and support from inter-governmental agencies.[3] Though popular education aimed at raising awareness of human rights issues has been a strategy utilized by non-governmental organizations (NGOs) since the 1950s in building their social movements (Kapoor, 2004), initiatives such as the United Nations Decade for Human Rights Education (1995-2004) have placed greater international pressure on governments to consider the importance of HRE in their national policy, pedagogy, and curricula in line with the tenets of international human rights documents. Indeed, the advancement of HRE national initiatives by more than 90 countries of the world today indicate that it has taken center stage in international educational policy discourse (UNHCHR, 2005).

Identified in the 1948 Universal Declaration of Human Rights (UDHR) as a component of universal rights, HRE as a field of practice and study has primarily emerged only within the past three decades. For the purpose of this discussion, the distinguishing characteristics of HRE will include: "learning *about* and learning *for* human rights" (Lohrenscheit, 2002, p. 176). Learning about human rights implies a transfer of knowledge, inclusion of subject matter pertaining to human rights in textbooks and on national exams, and awareness of international laws and organizations. The latter refers to inculcating the skills, values, and behaviors towards identifying human rights issues, acting in solidarity with victims, and advocating for social change towards greater human rights protection for all.

HRE is inextricably linked to the modern field of peace education, which currently includes the notions of 'positive' peace, as opposed to 'negative' peace (Galtung, 1969). Negative peace is the absence of organized, personal violence, or, in other words, the absence of war, while positive peace requires the absence of structural violence or the elimination of social inequalities that lead to disparities in the quality of life for distinct groups (Wiberg, in Brock-Utne, 1989). Whereas earlier peace education scholars focused on negative peace, the current inclusion of positive peace in the field creates an opportune link with education for the promotion of human rights: "Human rights are most readily adaptable to the study of positive peace, the social, political, and economic conditions most likely to provide the environment and process for social cohesion and nonviolent conflict resolution" (Reardon, 1997, p. 22).

HRE is increasingly becoming a cornerstone of peace education programs. The link between respect for human rights and sustainable peace is clear in international documents and declarations that highlight the importance of rights as the foundation of international peace, such as the UDHR framework that facilitates a deeper understanding and concretization of the sometimes abstract notions of peace. Reardon (1997) also emphasizes the role of HRE in using codified principles to elucidate multicultural, conflict resolution, development, and environmental education—all components of a comprehensive peace education approach.

Given the differing constructions of HRE in different contexts, it is important to note that programs will and should take on local modifications that appropriately adapt the information and mode of instruction for the specific learning community. While it is relevant to look at the national context in which curricula on human rights are often formulated, it is also important to note the differing experiences of human rights problems across communities, even within the same nation-state. As such, adaptation of curricula to local needs is essential (Tibbits, 2002). In order to examine the scope and reach of HRE in the Dominican Republic, it is therefore important to first explore the contextual realities that structure, limit, and enable such programs in their attempts to foster greater respect for human rights.

Human rights in the Dominican Republic

The Dominican Republic shares the Caribbean island of Hispaniola with Haiti and has a population of approximately 9.5 million residents. Since its independence from colonial rule, the Dominican Republic has had a series of authoritarian regimes, most notably the 31-year iron-fisted tenure of Trujillo, ended by his assassination in 1961. In addition to general repression against opponents, Trujillo, motivated by a racialized dislike of Afro-Haitian culture, ordered the massacre in 1937 of reportedly 15,000-20,000 Haitian cane-cutters along the border. Ironically, these workers had been contracted by the Dominican State, and approved by Trujillo himself, years earlier to work on its government-run sugar plantations (Turits, 2002).

The racist policies and ideology that were institutionalized during Trujillo's 31-year tenure in textbooks (Wigginton, 2005), historical reconstruction, and political discourse still endure today, distinguishing and valorizing in the Dominican political imagination the superiority of a

Catholic, Hispanicized Dominican Republic over its supposedly "inferior" Afro-Haitian, Creole-speaking, and Voudou-practicing neighbor (Balaguer, 1983). This construction of Haitian identity based on racial and cultural stereotypes belies the fact that, since colonial times, migration has been constant between the neighboring countries who have shared the island of Hispaniola, and that 90 percent of the Dominican population is of African descent, identifiable as black or mulatto/a (Torres-Saillant, 2000).

In the post-Trujillo era, little was done to counteract his ideological legacy or to demand justice for the tens of thousands of cases of state-sponsored murders, disappearances, and acts of torture reported to have occurred. For 22 of the 35 years following Trujillo's assassination, his one-time Foreign Minister and Vice-President, Balaguer held the presidency, originally backed by both the United States and the Roman Catholic Church (Wucker, 1999). Dominican scholars have deemed "the repression under the first six years of that regime even bloodier than the worst excesses under Trujillo," with Balaguer's paramilitary forces killing and intimidating leftists and political opponents (Wucker, 1999, p. 70). As such, even though notions of due process and legal protections have technically been part of the Dominican judicial system since the 1960s, they remain aspects that many people have seen violated or forgone given the many years of authoritarian rule and quasi-democracy.

The strong emergence of civil society and regular elections with independent candidates in recent years have been a countering force, but widespread belief in legal guarantees for human rights still does not exist. Current human rights problems include extensive police abuse, violence against women, child labor, and systemic discrimination and xenophobia against Haitians, Dominicans of Haitian descent, and dark-skinned Dominicans in the Dominican Republic.[4] These factors contribute to the Dominican Republic's inclusion in this volume on the role of peace education in "conflict" societies.

The Dominican government has come under international scrutiny for its treatment of Haitian immigrants and Dominicans of Haitian descent. Various international monitoring bodies have documented discrimination against these groups in the forms of illegal round-ups and deportations, as well as restricted access to identity documents when officials routinely carry out "racially discriminatory profiling" and deny Dominican children of Haitian descent their *cédulas*, or identity cards (Human Rights Watch, 2002). Without identification documents, young people cannot access public services such as healthcare or education.

Two legal cases against the Dominican Republic government that have come before the Inter-American Human Rights System have brought significant national and international attention to issues facing Haitians and Dominicans of Haitian descent: 1) the issue of deportations of any person suspected to be undocumented without due process and 2) the denial of birth certificates and access to public education to Dominican children of Haitian descent. While the first case on mass deportations of Haitian migrants and Dominicans of Haitian descent is still pending, in September 2005, the Inter-American Court handed down a decision against the Dominican government and in favor of two young girls who had been denied access to education. The government has yet to comply with the decision at the time of this writing, and inter-ethnic tensions have heightened, resulting in many vigilante killings and their reprisals between Dominicans and Haitian migrants and their descendants, also known as Dominico-Haitians. Given these discriminatory practices and pervasive contempt for Haitian immigrants and their children due to complex cultural and historical factors, including the 22-year occupation of the Dominican Republic by Haiti in the 19th century, many current human rights education initiatives include content related to discrimination and xenophobia.[5]

It is important to note that systemic and social discrimination towards Haitians and Dominico-Haitians is often based on skin color since legal processes are often bypassed; as a result, all of the abuses mentioned are also faced by dark-skinned Dominicans with no connection to Haiti, reinforcing unequal treatment across the country.

HRE in the Dominican Republic

It is interesting to note that while the Dominican government has come under fire for its disregard of its human rights obligations under international law, the previous presidential administration in the Dominican Republic put forth a comprehensive document in accordance with the United Nations Decade for Human Rights Education in 2003 that details governmental and non-governmental initiatives vis-à-vis human rights education in the Dominican Republic. This approach of government-led HRE has been called into question by scholars suggesting that it undermines the revolutionary potential of a critical human rights consciousness, since "state-led HRE [may] translate more into window dressing than into sustainable reform" (Cardenas, 2005, p. 364). According to these scholars, HRE must come from grassroots community efforts.

We argue in this chapter that simultaneous and complementary efforts from above (government efforts) and from below (grassroots social movements) must emerge in order to institutionalize the presence of HRE in the Dominican Republic. While government efforts are recent and seemingly lack the political will for comprehensive implementation at the present moment, this chapter traces the origins and current manifestations of HRE in the Dominican Republic today. Both government and grassroots efforts towards sustained HRE offer the promise of greater respect for human rights in the Dominican Republic, and especially the rights of those individuals, such as Haitian migrants and their descendants, who exist on the very margins of Dominican society today.

Educating about discrimination and xenophobia is only one component of HRE; it also has the potential to transform long-standing ethnic tensions if human rights norms are accepted and internalized among learners. This change in attitudes and beliefs was noted during a pilot human rights course offered to eighth graders in Santo Domingo, in which HRE students demonstrated greater agency in intervening in situations of abuse, greater solidarity with marginalized groups, and greater self-confidence in their abilities and identities after participating in the course (Bajaj, 2004). Little research and evaluation exists on HRE in general, and especially on HRE in the Dominican Republic and greater scholarly attention should be paid to it in policy and practice.

While HRE in the Dominican Republic has emerged primarily from the international community and through the United Nations system, local movements and organizations in the Dominican Republic have embraced HRE due to its resonance with many of the educational principles that existed long before the rise of HRE. In order to explore some of the civil society efforts towards sustained human rights and peace through education, it is important to explore several waves of social movements in the Dominican Republic, many of which have exerted long-term influence on the political process.

The objectives of each of these movements have been to bring about greater equity and justice, which are the underlying aims of rights-based approaches and educational initiatives carried out within them. While HRE is broader than just focusing on the situation of Dominico-Haitians, in this historical moment and as the most marginalized group in the Dominican Republic, HRE holds out the promise for fostering greater understanding and inter-ethnic cooperation that could stem the tide of social conflict that characterizes the country today. It is with this in mind that the focus now shifts to exploring the roots of HRE in the Dominican Republic as manifested through four waves of grassroots educational movements that are historical and contextual precursors to the current emergence of education for human rights.

The first wave: Liberation theology and religious movements

In the late 1960s and 1970s amidst repression by the Balaguer regime, social movements premised on human rights concepts emerged through progressive Church-based and religious communities primarily comprised of rural communities, students, women, and laborers. Among the most prominent movements was that based on liberation theology, inspired by the writings of Freire and which utilized popular education as a strategy for raising awareness of social inequalities. Mejia (1993) finds that popular education emerged in the 1960s as a way to unite social forces and provide a shared identity that could be consolidated through political action.

From 1979 onwards, a network of Catholic radio stations has worked to promote progressive social movements across the country. The objective of this network is to promote active citizenship that will contribute to the democratization of Dominican society and its institutions. Within this movement are grassroots organizations, primarily in marginalized rural and urban communities, that came together as a result of the messages about social justice infused by Latin American liberation theology (Pérez and Artiles, 1992). These community groups have had an important educational role in raising the awareness and mobilizing social action among impoverished communities, and when examined through the definition of education *for* and *about* human rights, while not self-identified as such, can be considered human rights education given the shared purposes of the approaches.

One of the results of popular education in the Dominican Republic has been, according to Fiallo (2000), the alternatives to development that grassroots communities have put forth that give greater voice to the needs and realities of disadvantaged communities in the larger political and economic discourse. Examples of these alternative development approaches are grassroots organizing to meet community needs, greater development of participatory approaches in policy-making, and the forging of international linkages with donor aid agencies directing resources to neglected communities often through Dominican-run non-governmental organizations.

The second wave: Popular education and Dominican NGOs

In 1970, the first Dominican non-governmental organization (NGO), the Center for Planning and Ecumenical Action (CEPAE), was born to address the right of landless rural Dominicans, particularly that of women, to land. From its establishment in 1973 until today, CEPAE has built 23 educational centers that have been dedicated to utilizing popular education, fostering the autonomy of rural social movements, developing equitable social relations, and building theory grounded in local practices and knowledges (CEPAE, 2007). In recent years, CEPAE has grounded its advocacy for the rights of landless Dominicans in a human rights framework through the development of trainings and educational materials related to the right to land and employment.

In 1979, another important non-governmental institution emerged dedicated to popular education, the Dominican Center for the Study of Education (CEDEE). CEDEE maintains a neo-Marxist analysis of social relations and accordingly, has produced materials that seek to explore the roots of economic production and exploitation. Focusing on economic and social rights, CEDEE has conducted popular education trainings and disseminated its materials to community groups and educational institutions to encourage an interrogation of social inequalities in Dominican society. CEDEE has continued to focus on adult and nonformal education around economic and social justice, but as with many NGOs, it has faced the challenge of inconsistent funding and lack of financial support (Edwards & Hulme, 1996).

In the 1980s, Latin America in general and the Dominican Republic in particular faced tremendous economic crises and nations were thus compelled to negotiate agreements with international financial institutions, such as the International Monetary Fund (IMF). The new economic model upon which financial assistance was conditioned represented a significant shift for many Latin American countries whose social programs had previously been based on a welfare state model (Segura-Ubiergo, 2007). The introduction of Structural Adjustment Programs (SAPs) to stimulate macroeconomic growth resulted in decreased social spending and educational budgets, and, as a result, produced greater inequality and limited educational opportunities for the poorest segments of the Dominican population (Itzigsohn, 2000).

The implementation of neoliberal economic policies without broad-based support of the Dominican population fostered the politicization of Dominican NGOs that organized and participated in widespread public protests (Itzigsohn, 2000). The confluence of economic crisis, the unification of social movements, and the proliferation of non-government organizations pushed the Dominican Republic towards greater political development, evidenced by the increasing independence of the press and the consolidation of regular elections [although these were not entirely free and fair until the late 1990s, according to reports] (Espinal, 1995). While external influences on Dominican policy still exist through international lending and intergovernmental relationships, what is notable for this discussion is the expanding social space for the participation of NGOs beginning in the 1980s and continuing to the present. Government reports indicate that some 10,000 NGOs currently operate in the Dominican Republic and while not all of these are visibly active (Blanc, 2007), they represent a significantly large civil society presence in a country of 9.5 million residents.

The 1980s also gave rise to many NGOs focused specifically on human rights that continue to operate today. As mentioned earlier, particularly endemic problems that these groups focus attention on include police abuse, judicial reform, violence against women, child labor, ethnic discrimination, and forced deportations of and the denial of access to basic services for Haitian migrants and their descendants. The NGOs and social movements that have emerged from the 1980s onwards have been a democratizing force in Dominican society, as well as an internationalizing force, consolidating the Dominican Republic's integration into the global community through people-to-people connections rather than just governmental ones. With NGO representatives attending international meetings sponsored by the United Nations and other international institutions, Dominican NGOs are increasingly holding their government accountable to its obligations under international human rights law (Freedman, 2003).

The third wave: Feminist perspectives on human rights

During the 1980s, the feminization of social movements occurred in the Dominican Republic with women organizing around reproductive rights and against patriarchy and machismo in Dominican culture (Baez & Arregui, 1989). Despite the increase in women's participation overall, women still remain under-represented in leadership positions of organizations and institutions, indicating that work still remains in the eradication of gender inequality in the Dominican Republic. Nonetheless, the human rights framework has informed women's movements in the Dominican Republic and the participation of Dominican delegates in the Mexico City (1975), Nairobi (1985), and Beijing (1995) women's conferences organized by the United Nations has influenced the subsequent localization of feminist human rights discourse.

The work of women's rights organizations in the Dominican Republic has infused the concept of gender as a social construct, challenging notions of biological determinism and patriarchy (Curiel, 2005). Feminist thought and movements have stimulated the rise of multiple gender-focused NGOs in the Dominican Republic, including one of the most well known organizations, the Center for Investigation and Feminist Action (CIPAF). CIPAF was founded in 1980 and has had a nationally- and internationally-recognized impact not only due to its effective research on women's realities, but also to its creative educational outreach around women's rights. It hosts a "non-sexist" and "peace education" program aimed at raising the awareness of young people about gender inequalities in Dominican society. Among its earliest projects in the 1980s was the publication of a series of curricular guides about education for gender equality.

CIPAF and its partners in the feminist movement have advanced the inclusion and consideration of feminist thought and platforms in national policymaking and legislative reform. Representatives of feminist movements have had a role in the implementation of certain policy recommendations, such as the establishment of a gender unit in the Dominican Ministry of Education, that have changed the curriculum, training, and approach of pre-university education to include an emphasis on gender and the importance of women's rights in all spheres. The collaborative approach of feminist movements in working with government, international organizations, and across NGOs, particularly in advancing education that guarantees and promotes gender equity, continues to contribute to the emergence and implementation of HRE in the Dominican Republic.

The fourth wave: Critical pedagogy and human rights education

Based on the earlier discussion of educational and social antecedents, critical pedagogy, intrinsically linked to popular education and human rights education, began to take root in the Dominican Republic in the 1980s, continuing into the 1990s and until the present day. While many organizations have projects related to peace or human rights education, certain institutions have incorporated HRE as a foundational principle of their operations.

The most noted institution working specifically towards HRE is the Poveda Cultural Center founded in 1985. Poveda is a "a center of training, research and socio-educational consultation prompted by an interdisciplinary team whose vision is to promote a humanizing movement that impacts in public policy and in the transformation of the Dominican reality" (Gonzalez, 2005). The Poveda Center has various components of their human rights education programs, including teacher training in the formal sector as well as community education around human rights and social justice. The main distinctions in Poveda's work from previous efforts are: (1) its expansive use of a human rights framework that incorporates civil, political, economic, social, and cultural rights; (2) its use of formal and nonformal education as a strategy for building greater human rights awareness; and (3) its sustained efforts over the past 20 years to institutionalize teacher training, the publication of textbooks integrating human rights, and regular publications about its work.

According to one of Poveda's founders, the Center has emphasized HRE to raise awareness of human rights norms in the context of neoliberal globalization and of deepening social inequalities (González, 2005). Poveda's activities include a diploma course for teachers on human rights, publication of human rights education textbooks, and participation in national and international networks of human rights educators.

While Poveda's work in human rights education is advancing the field forward in the Dominican Republic, other NGOs are also utilizing human rights education principles and materials. With greater global attention being paid to HRE beginning in the 1980s, the shift from previous forms of education around specific rights to an explicit mention of human rights education can be attributed to international linkages, funding, and, as mentioned above, the resonance of HRE with regional and local experiences with liberation theology, an emergent civil society focused on human rights concerns, and the increasing participation of Dominican organizations in global civil society meetings.

The four waves identified have advanced HRE, even if not self-identified as doing so, within the historical moment in which each was initiated. While the objectives may slightly differ from liberation theology to popular education to women's rights movements, each movement utilized education and collective action as a means for counter-hegemonic contestation in the public sphere. HRE and critical pedagogy in the present period in the Dominican Republic has bubbled up from below as a grassroots endeavor, but has the unique distinction as a movement whose goals are also valorized from above given the international pressure being placed on governments to adopt human rights curricular content. It is in this way that the current wave of HRE and the protagonists involved in it in the Dominican Republic and elsewhere, must consider and engage the state in meaningful ways such that the purpose and promise of HRE are sustained at the distinct levels of policy, pedagogy and practice. Coordinated and aligned efforts from above and below can work together to preempt the transition from a pre-conflict to a conflict society in nations, such as the Dominican Republic, that exhibit many of the perilous tendencies of exacerbating ethnic conflict.

Contextualising HRE and the Dominican state

Since the 1990s, several factors have emerged that suggest the limits of Dominican democracy despite advances that have been made to move away from the nation's authoritarian legacy and towards greater awareness of human rights. The Dominican Republic has experienced economic growth but without corresponding equity, as evidenced by an unequal distribution of wealth in Dominican society (UNDP, 2005; Sanchez, 2005). Authoritarian values continue to operate in Dominican society and the persistence of political patronage limits civic participation despite some expansion of the freedom of speech and increasing demands for institutional channels to express dissent (Brea et al., 1995).

Despite these limits, the importance of HRE has been officially recognized in the Dominican Republic at the highest levels, arguably though, without sustained political will for integrated implementation. The most comprehensive document to date on HRE in the Dominican Republic was compiled in 2003 through a joint initiative between UNESCO, the social science think tank FLACSO, and the Office of the First Lady of the Dominican Republic. In their 200-plus page document, strategies and practices of HRE were identified, proposed and presented at the highest levels of government. The main conclusions recognized progress and suggested future directions to consolidate the emergence of human rights education across sectors and levels in Dominican society.

With the election of President Leonel Fernandez in 2004, it is unclear whether the new administration will follow up on the recommendations made by the authors of the report. The refusal to implement policy changes indicated by the Inter-American Court's decision on the aforementioned case of the Dominican girls of Haitian descent who were denied access to education suggest that the Fernandez regime has yet to take up universal human rights as a centerpiece of their political platform.

Conclusion

The Dominican Republic's educational movements towards the incorporation of human rights education principles present a glimpse into the pressures from both grassroots communities and from national and international agencies that have exerted influence on Dominican policy and practice over the past five decades. In characterizing the Dominican Republic as a conflict society, though not one embroiled in violent conflict, the role of educational initiatives such as HRE are essential for the advancement of equity and the maintenance of peace.

The extent to which HRE has been implemented in the Dominican Republic thus far as discussed in this chapter is largely due to the ways in which human rights pedagogy and content has resonated with pre-existing local movements and ideologies. This is an important lesson for other contexts, given that the localization of peace and human rights education must take into account and root itself in historical and contextual realities. While the Dominican Republic is presented as a "pre-conflict" case vis-à-vis violent conflict—and it is hoped that such conflict is thwarted by initiatives such as human rights education—there are some lessons that can be gleaned for other societies who are entrenched in or emerging from conflict.

Many post-conflict nations have neglected to utilize the possibility that classrooms afford as places of healing and peacebuilding. For example, the teaching of history in Rwandan classrooms has been suspended at the national level since the genocide because of the inability to reach consensus on the content and approach (Weinstein et al., 2007). Recently, with the assistance of international actors, textbooks are being created for such purposes. In the interim, however, an entire generation of Rwandan youth has been schooled without engaging with the country's history and the ways in which human rights were systematically violated.

Other post-conflict nations present troubling evidence of the failure of schools to be used as sites to build solidarity and respect for difference. In the case of Bosnia and Herzegovina, schools have been segregated by ethnicity since the early 1990s and provide differentiated instruction to students based on their ethnic background. This has been cited as a "failed" post-conflict education strategy by high-ranking members of the U.N. Security Council (Pierce, 2007). In Northern Ireland, school segregation persists between Catholics and Protestants. The transformative potential of schooling to overcome social inequalities and ethnic tensions is often bypassed when difficult topics are ignored or when students and their perspectives are segregated into distinct spaces in a form of conflict avoidance. Despite the greater resources and training required for integrated schools, in that teachers must be well equipped to deal with a diverse student body and that an appropriate curriculum must be developed, the corresponding possibilities for peace and human rights awareness are exponentially magnified when differences are normalized and engaged in educative spaces.

The distinct contributions of Dominican civil society towards HRE, while limited, offer a glimpse into how one nation has begun to localize international principles. By charting the course that has been engaged upon thus far, it is hoped that new avenues for the further consolidation of human rights education in all social spheres and aimed at creating greater social equity can emerge. Engaging the differences of ethnic groups through dialogue and utilizing the foundation of human rights principles through education can only enhance the long-term potential for peaceful coexistence of different ethnic and racial groups not only in the Dominican Republic, but across the globe.

NOTES

1. Excerpts of this chapter are highly re-edited versions of information contained in Bajaj, M. (2004). Human Rights Education and student self-conception in the Dominican Republic, *Journal of Peace Education*, 1(1), 21–34, and Bajaj, M. & Valera, C. (forthcoming). Educación en Derechos Humanos en la República Dominicana. In A. Magendzo (Ed.) (forthcoming). *Ideas fuerzas y pensamiento en educación en derechos humanos en América Latina*. Santiago, Chile: UNESCO. Additionally, Belinda Chiu contributed to the development of this chapter.
2. According to Ferguson (2003), "The Haitian presence in the Dominican Republic is comprised of three groups: a small group of documented and legal migrants; a large community of long-term residents who were born in Haiti; and a floating, transient population of temporary Haitian migrant workers. Together they form a distinct minority within Dominican society, but each, with the exception of the documented group, faces its own particular problems. A significant and separate community is comprised of Dominico-Haitians, people of Haitian origin born in the Dominican Republic. This category includes differing generations, as well as individuals born to one or more Haitian parent. What they have in common is that they were born in the Dominican Republic, yet face problems in 'proving' their Dominican citizenship and accessing fundamental rights" (p. 8).
3. Among the agencies most active in advocating for and supporting the integration of human rights education into national curricula are UNESCO, the Council of Europe, the UN High Commission for Human Rights, and the World Programme for Human Rights Education, which was established in 2005 to build on the considerable momentum towards HRE generated during the UN Decade for Human Rights Education (1995–2004).
4. The Dominican Constitution grants citizenship to any individual who is born on Dominican territory except for those deemed to be 'in transit,' a clause intended for diplomats and tourists, but invoked in the case of Haitian workers who were historically brought to or arrived in the Dominican Republic as cane-cutters and now work in other sectors
5. See Wucker's (1999) book entitled *Why the Cocks Fight* for more information about the historical tensions between Haiti and the Dominican Republic.

References

Amnesty International. (2005). *Dominican Republic*. London, UK: Amnesty International.
Bajaj, M. (2004). Human Rights Education and student self-conception in the Dominican Republic. *Journal of Peace Education*, 1(1), 21–34.
Báez, C., & Arregui, M. (1989). *Las mujeres en el movimiento social urbano dominicano: El caso de la ciudad de Santo Domingo*. Santo Domingo: Centro Dominicano de Estudios de la Educación.
Balaguer, J. (1983). *La isla al revés: Haití y el destino Dominicano*. Santo Domingo, Dominican Republic: Fundación José Antonio Caro.
Blanc, C. L. (2007). Sólo 460 de 10,000 ONG declaran actividades a DGII. *Listin Diario*. Retrieved November 18, 2007, from: http://dcivil.lomerosenlinea.com/index.php?name=News&file=article&sid=382
Brea, Duarte, Tejada, & Báez. (1995). *Estado de Situación de la Democracia Dominicana (1978–1992)*. Santo Domingo: PUCMM-PID.
Brock-Utne, B. (1989) *Feminist perspectives on peace and peace education*. New York, NY: Pergamon Press.
Cardenas, S. (2005). Constructing rights? Human Rights Education and the state. *International Political Science Review*, 26(4), 363–379.
CEPAE. (2007). Centro de planificación y acción ecuménica. Retrieved October 10, 2007, from www.cepae.do.org
CIPAF. (2007). *Quehaceres*. Santo Domingo, Dominican Republic: Centro de Investigación Para la Acción Femenina
Curiel, O. (2005). Identidades esencialistas o construcción de identidades políticas: El dilema de las feministas. In G. Candelario (Ed.), *Miradas Desencadenantes: Los Estudios de Género en la República Dominicana al Inicio del Tercer Milenio*. Santo Domingo: INTEC.
Davies, L. (2005). Schools and war: Urgent agendas for comparative & international education. *Compare: A Journal of Comparative Education*, 35(4), 357–371.
Edwards, M. and Hulme, D. (Eds.). (1996). *Beyond the magic bullet: NGO performance and accountability in the post Cold War world*. West Hartford, CT: Kumarian Press.
Espinal, R. (1995). Economic restructuring, social protest, and democratization in the Dominican Republic. *Latin American Perspectives*, 22(3), 63–79.
Ferguson, J. (2003). *Migration in the Caribbean: Haiti, the Dominican Republic and beyond*. United Kingdom: Minority Rights Group International.
Fiallo, A. (2000). Identidades, movimientos sociales y acción política educativa. In *Para Una Nueva Ciudadanía en América Latina* (pp. 167–196). Santo Domingo, Dominican Republic: Novaamerica, Yachay Tinkuy y Centro Poveda.
Freedman, L. P. (2003). Human rights, constructive accountability and maternal mortality in the Dominican Republic. *International Journal of Gynecology and Obstetrics*, 82, 111–114.
Galtung, J. (1969). Violence, peace, and peace research. *Journal of Peace Research*, 6(3): 167–191.
González, R. (2005). Modos de intervención del Centro Cultural Poveda. In *En Educación Crítica: Retos y Aportes Para Que Otro Mundo Sea Posible, Anuario Pedagógico 8* (pp. 195–202). Santo Domingo, Dominican Republic: Centro Cultural Poveda.

Human Rights Watch. (2002) Citizenship and proof of identity. In *Illegal people: Haitians and Dominico-Haitians in the Dominican Republic*. New York, NY: Human Rights Watch.

Itzigsohn, J. (2000). *Developing poverty: The state, labor market deregulation, and the informal economy*. University Park, PA Penn State Press.

Kapoor, D. (2004). Popular education and social movements in India: State responses to constructive resistance for social justice. *Convergence, 37*(2), 55–63.

Lohrenscheit, C. (2002) International approaches in human rights education, *International Review of Education, 48*(3/4), 173–185.

Bekerman, Z. and McGlynn, C. (2007). (Eds) *Addressing ethnic conflict through peace education: International perspectives*. New York, NY: Palgrave MacMillan.

Pérez, C., & Artiles, L. (1992). *Movimientos sociales Dominicanos: Identidad y dilemas*. Santo Domingo, Dominican Republic: INTEC.

Pierce, K. (2007). Opening Remarks for a Panel on Teacher Training in Africa, British Consulate, New York.

Reardon, B. (1997). Human rights as education for peace. In G. Andreopoulos & R. P. Claude (Eds.), *Human Rights Education for the Twenty-First Century* (pp. 21–34). Philadelphia, PA: University of Pennsylvania Press.

Sánchez, D. (2005). Domestic capital, civil servants and the state: Costa Rica and the Dominican Republic under globalization. *Journal of Latin American Studies, 37*, 693–726.

Segura-Ubiergo, A. (2007). *The political economy of the welfare state in Latin America globalization, democracy, and development*. Cambridge, UK: Cambridge University Press.

Tibbits, F. (2002) Understanding what we can do: Emerging models for human rights education. *International Review of Education, 48*(3/4), 159–171.

Torres-Saillant, S. (2000). The tribulations of Blackness: Stages in Dominican racial identity. *Callaloo, 23*(3), 1086–1111.

Turits, R. (2002). World destroyed, a nation imposed: The 1937 Haitian Massacre in the Dominican Republic. *Hispanic American Historical Review, 82*(3), 589–636.

UNDP. (2005). *Informe nacional de desarrollo humano República Dominicana*. Santo Domingo, Dominican Republic: United Nations.

UNESCO & FLACSO. (2003). *Diagnostico: Hacia un plan nacional de derechos humanos*. Santo Domingo, Dominican Republic: UNESCO.

UNHCHR. (2005). *Database on human rights education and training*. Retrieved October 8, 2007, from http://hre.ohchr.org/hret/Intro.aspx?Lng=en

Weinstein, H. M., Freedman, S. W., & Hughson, H. (2007). School voices: Challenges facing education systems after identity-based conflicts. *Education, Citizenship and Social Justice, 2*(1), 41–71.

Wigginton, S. (2005). Character or caricature: Representations of Blackness in Dominican social science textbooks. *Race Ethnicity and Education, 8*(2), 191–211.

Wucker, M. (1999). *Why the cocks fight: Dominicans, Haitians, and the struggle for Hispaniola*. New York, NY: Hill & Wang. Including construction, domestic work, and other low-wage jobs (Ferguson, 2003).

Chapter 4

From Conflict Society to Learning Society
Lessons from the Peace Process in Northern Ireland

Paul Nolan

The political crisis in Northern Ireland from 1969 to 2008, the period known euphemistically as "the Troubles," can be seen as a crisis of learning, just as the political developments that led to the present settlement can be seen as part of the growth of a learning society. I use the phrase "learning society" advisedly, since it has been captured so successfully by government and recast to fit within the lexicon of economic need. In its original formulation, however, the potency of the term has to do with its meaning across a range of contexts, involving the broadest number of learning subjects, and I wish to retain that breadth in order to examine not just formal, structured, educational provision but the myriad informal ways in which the various partners to the conflict came to create the new, shared understandings that underpin the recent political settlement. It is possible that there are lessons here for other deeply divided societies, but that suggestion is offered cautiously. For many years the nature of the Northern Ireland conflict was obscured by misleading analogies with conflicts elsewhere and, as a consequence, so too was the search for a way forward. Northern Ireland was and remains a society with a very high degree of particularity, and there is little to be gained by reversing the direction of inappropriate analogies through an insistence that the template of this particular peace process can be applied elsewhere.

That said, the move out of violent conflict has been a remarkable story in its own terms, the lessons of which may well be of interest to those in other conflict societies. I am going to suggest ten lessons in all, a suspiciously round number that, I admit, I have chosen partly because of the challenge it presents, but, however the arguments are aggregated or disaggregated, the issues they highlight seem, to me, to be the important ones. The first three points are of a contextual kind, the next six bring the focus more closely to bear on educational issues, and the final point is used to indicate a general message about the peace process in Northern Ireland, which is, I think, of relevance to conflict societies everywhere. I begin, however, by attempting to clarify what I intend when I talk about a learning society.

Northern Ireland and the Learning Society

If one looks for exemplar models of what it means to be a learning society, empirical real-life case studies are hard to find; this is one of those concepts that is easier elucidated by pointing to negative examples. One can safely say that whatever definition is used, Northern Ireland has traditionally presented itself as the opposite of a learning society. Rather, the impression has been of a people who, like the Bourbons, learned nothing and forgot nothing. The learning cycle models developed by Lewin (1948) and Kolb (1984) show a transition from experience to reflection, followed by a further transition from reflection to theoretical knowledge and on to more sophisticated forms of action that incorporate the new learning. In the case of Northern Ireland's prolonged agony the various parties—not just the Catholic and Protestant communities but also the British and Irish governments—failed to gather the learning experiences, and therefore, the wheels spun hopelessly in the sands of experience. Trapped, it seemed, in history, the contending forces achieved a form of equilibrium that matched force against counterforce. What then provided the key to unlocking the problem? Much of the political-science literature on the 1998 Good Friday Agreement (otherwise known as the Belfast Agreement) concentrates on the intricate constitutional machinery created to allow this experiment in consociationalism to work (see, for example, Morgan, 2000; O'Leary,1999), but the reality is that neither the 1998 agreement nor its successor document, the 2007 St. Andrew's Agreement, differs in its main outline from a number of previous attempts to sketch out a solution. There were seven attempts in all, but the most significant one was the Sunningdale Agreement of 1973, which contained the same commitment to power sharing and to north-south constitutional arrangements and which, for a brief period of months, allowed the hope that a solution had been found. The nationalist politician and former school principal, Seamus Mallon, who participated in both the Sunningdale negotiations and the talks that led to the Good Friday/Belfast Agreement twenty-five years later, wryly characterized the latter as "Sunningdale for slow learners" (see BBC Web site, 2008).This much-quoted jibe has more than a tinge of bitterness, but it also recognizes a fundamentally important truth: learning had taken place. The immediate targets, the local politicians Mallon had in mind when he made his comments, were only some of the subjects involved in the learning process; in a broader sense, the whole society and the governmental actors were all caught up in this journey toward understanding. Is this what people mean when they talk about a learning society?

It is interesting to trace the genealogy of the idea and to find in its genesis the seeds of an idea about the enhancement of democratic political cultures. Welton (2005) identifies the first uncertain steps toward the learning society ideal as taking place at the first United Nations Educational Scientific and Cultural Organisation (UNESCO) conference on adult education, which took place at Elsinore in Denmark in 1949. UNESCO had only been created in 1946, and the 106 delegates from 47 countries who gathered at Elsinore met in the ruins of a Europe devastated by war, where they pledged to stimulate what J. Roby Kidd describes as a "genuine spirit of democracy and a genuine spirit of tolerance; restore a sense of community to people who live in an age of specialisation and isolation; cultivate an enlightened sense of belonging to a world community" (Kidd, 1974, cited in Welton, 2005, p. 29). The same humanistic impulse is evident, though in a more structured and programmatic way, in the UNESCO report edited by Delors (Ed. 1996), *Learning: The Treasure Within*. It was this document that gave birth to a succession of further reports and initiatives throughout the 1990s and that, drawing upon the language of the UNESCO report, spoke of the learning society, the learning region, the learning company, and the learning organization. Wales even decided to rebrand itself as the "learning country." The more profligate the use of the term, the more contested its meanings became. Outside of the academy, the main gravitational pull from government has been toward the skills needs of the economy and the concept of the learning society was increasingly linked to a series of overlapping concepts, such as the knowledge society and the information society. The rapidity with which this economy-based interpretation has achieved dominance tends to obscure the fact that other, more humanistic meanings were intended in the original UNESCO document. Given the pivotal nature of this report it is worth going back to see where the emphasis falls. Delors's report speaks of four "pillars" of learning: learning to live together, learning to understand, learning to do, and learning to be. The most important of these, the report says, is the first, learning to live together. The centrality of that idea may have been to do with the fact that at the time of writing, ethnic genocide was once again being attempted on the eastern borders of Europe. No specific reference was made to Northern Ireland, but as I shall attempt to show, Northern Ireland provides an interesting case study for the proposition that people from one of the world's most divided societies can in fact learn to coexist peacefully.

The Importance of Timing

Perhaps the simplest explanation of why Northern Ireland moved away from violence is that of war weariness. At the point when the Irish Republican Army (IRA) declared its ceasefire in 1994, the armed conflict had been underway for twenty-five years, more than twice as long as World War I and World War II put together. Sollenberg and Wallenstein (2001) record that fifty-six civil wars came to an end in the 1989 to 2000 period: twenty-two by peace agreements, and thirty-four by ceasefire or other methods. Commenting on these figures, Darby and McGinty (2002)state, "To a certain extent the high number of conflict terminations is merely a function of the high number of conflicts and the inability of antagonists to sustain their violent campaigns over extended time periods"(p. 1). Even if one were to accept this analysis, there is still the question of why the peace momentum gained traction in one particular period rather than another. Why did the initiative happen then rather than sooner or later? In Zartman's (2000) analysis, a moment of opportunity comes precisely at the point when things seem most hopeless, the point he describes as the mutually hurting stalemate. Working from a rational choice model, Zartman seeks to identify the moment of opportunity when the option of continuing to fight seems to offer all sides nothing but "a flat unpleasant terrain stretching into the future" (p. 268). To move from a temporary cessation of violence to lasting peace requires two other elements: as Zartman suggests, the ripe moment for conflict resolution must coincide with finding a formula that allows all parties to escape defeat and claim some honor. The presentation of a formula may come through third-party intervention, or it may be through indigenous political leadership. In the case of the Northern Ireland conflict, it was both, as the British, Irish, and American governments worked with local political and paramilitary leaders to build a web of trust sufficiently strong enough to support an international peace agreement. There is now a considerable body of literature within conflict resolution studies that focuses on the role of local leadership in conflict situations, with most attention on "ethnic entrepreneurs," those who manipulate ethnic identities in a quest for power: Slobodan Milosevic is often cited as being a particular case of the general category (see, for example, Silber & Little, 1996). While the malign effect of such individuals is well-attested, the Northern Ireland experience would seem to suggest that the converse can also be true: in order to move from a vicious to a virtuous spiral, there must be ethnic entrepreneurs who see opportunities for peace—let's call them peace entrepreneurs—who are prepared to work to find the formula, however elusive it might be.

Learning from Elsewhere

Despite its reputation as "a place apart," Northern Ireland was not impervious to developments elsewhere. On the republican side, there had always been an eagerness to identify with revolutionary anti-imperialist movements throughout the world—in particular, with the struggle of the African National Congress in South Africa, the cause of the Palestinians, and the long-running campaign of Euskadi Ta Askatasuna in the Basque country. The waning of the revolutionary tide at the end of the 1980s was therefore a cause of some difficulty. As Cox (2006) puts it, "In effect having become identified with and made cause alongside other national liberation movements, Irish republicanism could hardly avoid being affected by their effective collapse in the latter half of the 1980s" (p. 432). Cox (1998, 2006) argues further that the end of the cold war significantly altered the dynamic of the conflict in Northern Ireland, principally by exposing the IRA's armed struggle as a cul-de-sac. Dixon (2006) takes a more nuanced view, pointing out that the crucial first steps by the IRA in making secret contact with both the British and Irish governments were taken before 1989, and casts doubt on the degree of debate on international affairs within the Provisional movement. What he sees instead is a "script" about the changing international climate used by the IRA leadership to persuade grassroots republicans to give up the armed struggle

Republicans were not the only parties to the conflict who found themselves caught in the variable geometry of international politics. The European Union (EU)—far from being a model in itself of how seemingly permanent hostilities could be overcome—brought the British and Irish governments into a new, mediated relationship that allowed them to approach the governance of Northern Ireland from a shared perspective. As Meehan (2000) described it, "the language and conventions of EU policy-making have helped to open up a space for contending parties to talk about solutions to old problems in a new way—and to act upon that" (p. 96).

The Importance of Language

The EU brought not only a new vocabulary to bear on the conflict—words like *marginalization*, *inclusion*, and *cohesion*—it brought a new grammar and syntax to the consideration of national identities. Hitherto, the language of the conflict had been constructed on the binary structure—or what linguists would call the "discursive framework"—of two mutually excluding communities, a framework that measured every possible development on a zero-sum calculus where a gain by one party would automatically be understood as a loss by the other. From that standpoint, the vocabulary of the conflict became an inevitable site for battle. The most bitter of these engagements was the one that led to the hunger strikes of the early 1980s and the deaths of Bobby Sands and his comrades. Margaret Thatcher wished to withdraw political status from IRA prisoners in the jails; in her view, the correct term for those convicted of crimes was *criminal*; for the IRA, which regarded itself as an army waging a legitimate war against oppression, such a designation was insulting. The IRA demanded the retention of the term *political prisoner*. Much hung on this semantic dispute: in order to retain the name, the rights, and the entitlements of political prisoners, the prisoners embarked on a campaign of resistance that culminated in the deaths of ten hunger strikers and, in so doing, prompted the emergence of mass street protests and the reemergence of Sinn Fein as a political force.

To take another example, community relations practitioners in Northern Ireland have constantly emphasized the importance of language, stressing for example that they themselves are not involved in conflict *resolution*, a term that appears too maximalist in its ambitions, and prefer to talk instead in terms of conflict *transformation*. This latter formulation accepts the inevitability and, indeed, the desirability of conflict but seeks ways to drain it of its toxicity. The Mennonite peace activist and theorist Lederach (a frequent visitor to Northern Ireland; 1996) makes the point that "language is always more than a vehicle for communication. It is also a window into how people organise both their own understanding and expression of conflict, often in keeping with cultural patterns and ways of operating" (p. 78). The reframing of the political problems in Northern Ireland in such a way that solutions could be glimpsed was very much dependent upon a reframing of the language used to describe those problems.

What then of the role of education or, to put it in the broader formulation, the learning culture? I will now go on to examine the successes and the limitations, beginning first with the formal sector and then looking at informal modes of learning.

The Segregation of Schools

A counterfactual history of Northern Ireland could sketch an interesting scenario about what might have happened if the plans laid by the first minister for education, Lord Charles Londonderry, had come to pass. The vision he presented in 1925 to the first Stormont Parliament was for a secular and integrated schooling system. In a brief moment of unity, the Catholic and Protestant hierarchies combined to crush that hope, and by 1930 a segregated schooling system was in place and Lord Londonderry was back in the center of Westminster politics. The hope that an integrated schooling movement could arise and that such a movement could help overcome sectarian division has "aroused a good deal of interest among those involved in peace-building and conflict resolution throughout the world" (Stephen, 2006, p. 273). The big "if" in this scenario—if only all the children could be schooled together—is not actually counterfactual, as integrated schools do now exist, but the hope is still in advance of the achievement. The first school to consciously recruit both Catholics and Protestants, Lagan College, was a parent-led initiative, which opened its doors in 1981. Integrated schools are now a well-established presence, and the struggle to achieve that status is in many ways a heroic one, well-documented elsewhere (Gallagher, 2004; McGlynn, Niens, Cairns, & Hewstone, 2004; O'Connor, 2002).

It is, however, difficult to trace any causal link between their efforts and the creation of peace settlement in Northern Ireland. There are two reasons commonly cited for excluding the integrated schools movement from any serious political analysis: (1) that they are too few in number to be relevant and (2) that their composition is too middle-class to impact upon the hard core of the problem. (Stephen, 2006, p. 270). Neither of these seems, to me, to touch upon the crucial point, but let me deal briefly with each in turn. There are a total of sixty-two integrated schools that, between them, educate approximately 6 percent of the school population. This does not mean that 6 percent of the current adult population has received the benefit of mixed schooling; government figures show only 1.7 percent of adults report having attended schools that fit the official designation of integrated education (Hayes, MacAllister, & Dowds, 2006). Does that make them too statistically insignificant to expect any real, measurable impact? Not necessarily if the students were infused with a strong proselytizing sense of mission, but the research into the political attitudes of former pupils shows only weak evidence of center-ground political attitudes emerging from the experience of mixed education—particularly when consideration is given to the fact that these students tend to come from family backgrounds where there already is a commitment to more accommodationist politics (Hayes et al, 2006).

Demography—The Subversive Force

While integrated education may have left no clear imprint on voting behavior or on constitutional arrangements, there is no doubt that the "identity-widening" (Stryker & Serpe, 1982, pp. 199–218) aspects of shared experience do open up enlarged social spaces outside of the two blocs. The subterranean force that might transform the educational landscape may not be ideational, but rather the disruption that demography has in store for the segregated schools of Northern Ireland. Educational debates naturally tend to reflect educationalists' concerns with curriculum, selection, assessment, and all those other matters that fall within the compass of policy makers. Important as these are, it is, in fact, demography, more than any other factor, that determines the number of students in the classroom, the resources allocated to them and—a crucial factor in divided societies—the religious and ethnic mix in each local situation. As John Maynard Keynes contended, the slow changes of population shift are responsible for the most profound events in history (see Toye, 2000).

In Northern Ireland the subterranean movements that are reshaping the political landscape are those that are recasting the relative ratios of the two main blocs. Protestant dominance is no longer a fact in political, cultural, or numerical terms (the 2001 census showed the Protestant community at 53.13 percent, the Catholic at 43.76 percent). The near equivalence has brought forth a political arrangement that rests upon a legislative framework that guarantees equality of treatment, expressed through a raft of policy measures designed to ensure parity of esteem between the two communities. The restless dynamic of demographic change has further changes in store, ones that impact in unpredictable ways. There are two forces at work: the first has to do with educational policy making, and the second, over which government has no control, has to do with population decline. While the school rolls are set to fall dramatically, the government is committed to funding an ever-expanding range of provision, not just Protestant and Catholic schools but, in the spirit of cultural diversity, Irish language schools and, more recently, faith schools, such as those run by Rev. Ian Paisley's Free Presbyterian Church. The financial costs of running an educational system so willing to accommodate difference are not financially feasible in the long-term (Deloitte Consulting, 2007).

What then is to be done? The obvious solution, the creation of a single secular system, is the one most out of reach because of the opposition of the two main blocs. The best hope at present lies in the recommendations made in a radical report (Independent Strategic Review of Education, 2006), which sidesteps the issue of integration and calls instead for an organized system of sharing. The village with three schools might find that intercommunal arrangements allow them to share the same soccer pitch or employ one music teacher or find economies in contracting and purchasing. Incentives should be built in, the report argues, to reward cross-community cooperation. These recommendations, if acted upon, have the potential to significantly change the educational landscape. Demographic realities so important in dividing Northern Ireland may yet help to produce a more interdependent future.

Learning for Employment

The exhortation to become a learning society—repeated mantra-like in all government policy documents for a decade—appears to have most relevance to post-compulsory education. Adult education, which hitherto had been perceived to be a dusty little corner of provision, suddenly found itself propelled into the spotlight as a key priority for government after the events that took place in 1996, the European Year of Lifelong Learning. Northern Ireland joined in the effort then taking place throughout Europe, to fill the concept with content. The Department of Education (1998) issued a document titled *Lifelong Learning: A New Learning Culture For All*, which rehearsed the same themes that could be found in governmental policy documents in any other European state at this time: It spoke of globalization, the speed of technological change, and the need for learning to permeate all parts of existence. Belfast declared itself "a learning city"—significantly an initiative taken by Belfast City Council rather than a formal provider, and a sign that adult learning was to be seen as an engine for economic development.

Part of the attraction of the learning society idea was to do with the way these agendas—economic, political, and educational—could be telescoped into one. It wasn't just about learning, it was about tackling social inclusion. Tony Blair explained the logic quite neatly in an introduction to a publication on social exclusion: "The best defence against social exclusion is having a job, and the best way to get a job is to have a good education, with the right training and experience" (Social Exclusion Unit, 1999, p. 6). And in Northern Ireland, it wasn't just about tackling social exclusion, it was about dealing with political alienation. "If work can be found for 10,000 unemployed boys in West Belfast," remarked the British minister, Richard Needham, "that in itself will do more to impact on political and security areas than any other measure" (Needham, cited in Wilson, 1989, p. 6). Since that time, work has indeed been found for the boys—and, indeed, the girls—of West Belfast, and, at the time of writing, unemployment stands at 4.5 percent, the lowest level for three generations. Jobs grew by 30 percent in the 1990 to 2005 period, and, not only that, but the Northern Ireland economy, as measured by gross added value per head has risen by 50 percent faster than that of the UK as a whole. (Department for Employment and Learning, 2006).

As I have indicated previously, not everyone is happy with the dominance of the economic model. Reviews of learning society literature (Coffield, 2000; Field, 2000; Jarvis, 2007; Welton, 2005) show that there is discontent that sees social inclusion only in terms of the workplace and ignores the humanistic tradition of adult education: as Coffield puts it, "There's precious little society in the learning society" (p. 16). A false dichotomy can, and has, been created; there is, in fact, no need to set the two in opposition. In Northern Ireland, the skills agenda has been of pressing importance. The broken-backed economy that resulted from a combination of political violence and the collapse of traditional manufacturing industries was not assisted by a workforce that, at the time of the first ceasefires, was less qualified and less interested in gaining qualifications than any in Europe (Sargant et al, 1996). The economic recovery described above is not attributable to educational policies alone, but a new virtuous spiral has been created, which allows adult learning and economic growth to act positively on each other. It is still not possible for any simple deductions to be made about causality in the peace process, but, at minimum, it must be allowed that learning, employment, prosperity, and peace enjoy some natural form of companionship.

The Involvement of Civil Society

Civil society is usually described as a set of intermediate bodies between the state and the citizen, including voluntary organizations, business clubs, and other associational groupings. In the classic nineteenth-century study by Alexis de Tocqueville, *Democracy in America*,(Tocqueville, 2000), it was thought to be constitutive of democracy, an idea that was revived with urgency and some theoretical overclaiming following the rise of Solidarity in Poland and other "people's movements" in Eastern Europe. In Northern Ireland, there is a strong empirical basis to the civil society idea: There are, for example, more than 4,500 voluntary organizations listed by the Northern Ireland Council of Voluntary Organisations, operating within a population of only 1.7 million. Two claims are made for the role of civil society in the peace process: (a) that it was the network of voluntary associations that provided the invisible stitching that prevented the fraying of the whole social fabric during the worst periods of the Troubles and (b) that it was civil society that drove the peace process from below by putting pressure on the political elites to find a settlement (Cochrane & Dunn, 2002). At the theoretical level, the idea has been buttressed by the growth of interest in the related concept of social capital, and, at the practical level, the adoption by government of social capital as a key concept has ensured that civil society is given a key role in all peace building measures. Putnam's (2000) distinction between bonding and bridging forms of social capital and Woolcock's (1998) refinement of the theory have been seen as particularly helpful in creating a framework for community relations policy, and resource allocation has followed on from this. In short, there has been a major financial investment in voluntary bodies and cultural associations in the hope that they can deliver a more generous accommodation of communal differences.

The balance sheet to date shows a mixed return on that investment. Acheson, Cairns, Stringer, & Williamson (2007) show that voluntary bodies, while often presenting themselves as having an innocent relationship to politics, are often caught up intimately in communalist identities. If that is true, as Acheson et al. say in most cases, then allowance must still be made for the corollary, which is, in some particular cases, civil society organizations have been hugely important in building and maintaining contact networks that connect the two communities. The churches can be seen to play what David Stevens describes as a Janus role: while they are most frequently associated with the religious and social divisions at the heart of the conflict, the hierarchies of both sides have maintained an unbroken unity in their opposition to political violence (Stevens, 2004, pp. 80–92). There is also a steady traffic on the ecumenical routes through which the churches mobilize cross-community exchanges. Community-based women's organizations have also provided an alternative network that crisscrosses the usual borders and even helped inspire the briefly flowering Women's Coalition, which managed to introduce conciliatory politics into the drafting of the Good Friday Agreement. Perhaps the most important single initiative was the Opsahl Commission of the early 1990s. The inspiration of a group of liberal journalists, academics, and civil society activists, this was a 'people's commission,' overseen by the distinguished Norwegian judge, Torkel Opsahl, who tried to change the terms of political debate by holding public meetings and inviting submissions on the future of Northern Ireland. Such an enterprise fits well with the sort of reflexivity advocated by Anthony Giddens, Jurgen Habermas, and other social theorists, and, indeed, the opinions that resulted were very different from those dictated by political and paramilitary elites, and much more able to facilitate the politics of compromise.

Dealing with the Past

The Northern Ireland peace process will not be complete until ways have been found to deal with the weight of memory. A conventional view of Irish history is that, by failing to learn from it, we are doomed to relive it. By elision, this shades into what Vincent (1993) calls "the myth of atavism" (p. 123), or the belief that the recurrence of political conflict in Ireland is rooted in problems in the Irish psyche that erupt in periodic bursts of violence. The "ancient hatreds" theory of conflict has also been applied liberally by journalists to explain the politics of Eastern Europe and Africa, but it is as Nodia (2000) says, an interpretation that "virtually all serious scholars of nationalism rightly reject" (p. 172; see also Bowen, 1996 and Mann, 2005). The notion of a national psyche, however, finds a curious echo in the learning society discourse, where the tendency toward animism is most pronounced when dealing with memory. Much of the literature on the learning organization, for example, treats the company as though it were a sentient being with both conscious and unconscious memory. While it is accepted that learning can only take place through the consciousness of individuals, the appeal of the theory lies in the suggestion that the collective learning process is more than just the aggregate of the members' efforts and that the company—or the region, or the society—can store and mobilize knowledge when it is required (Starkey, Tempest, & McKinlay, 2004). The cultural patterning that determines the use of this knowledge has a metaphorical connection with the neurological pathways of human memory, and so long as the metaphor is not taken too literally, it can prove a useful way to view situations where whole collectives are engaged in the learning process. There have been repeated attempts to establish a South African-style Truth and Reconciliation Commission to allow for former antagonists to come together to reflect on their experiences. Such efforts usually draw upon the metaphor of healing the wound, but the sense that old wounds will simply be reopened by such an interrogation has proved more resilient, and no initiative of this kind has yet been launched.

It may be that the interrogation of history does not proceed by the creation of a new grand narrative. As Salomon (2002) argues in the context of the Middle East, the task is not to forge a single, shared history but to allow for the legitimation of competing narratives: to allow the

Jewish child to understand how the creation of the Israeli state can be viewed as the Nakbah, the great disaster, when seen from a Palestinian perspective, and to allow also for the converse to happen. Northern Ireland does not have such a long road to travel. This is not the Middle East where two worldviews collide, nor is it the former Yugoslavia where, in a situation that fits Sen's (2006) description of "plural monocultures" (p. 156), Serbian, Croatian, and Muslim children are taught how aggression was perpetrated by the *other*. Educationalists in Northern Ireland have already worked to address this problem by the creation of a shared history curriculum taught in both Catholic and Protestant schools. Alongside this are competing narratives, but one does not have to fall into a hopeless cultural relativism to accept that, rather than quash these alternative understandings, the task is, as Salomon (2002) suggests, to allow each side to accept the validity of other understandings.

The Business of Reconciliation

The concept of reconciliation has been marinated so long in religious doctrine that even notionally secular events like the South African Truth and Reconciliation Commission have been imbued with Christian notions of atonement and forgiveness. The same is true in Northern Ireland where a whiff of sanctimony still attaches to the term despite the fact that it has been adopted as a sort of offial-ese by governments and external funding bodies. In 1995, for example, the British and Irish governments announced their joint initiative, the Anglo-Irish Agreement as an instrument of reconciliation; subsequently, the signatories to the Good Friday Agreement dedicated themselves to "the achievement of reconciliation, tolerance and mutual trust" (Northern Ireland Office, 1998, p. 2). The EU's support for the peace process for Northern Ireland, which began in 1995 just after the first ceasefires, came under the title "The European Union Special Support Programme for Peace and Reconciliation in Northern Ireland and the Border Counties." The fact that resources have been attached to reconciliation work and that these required quite onerous reporting requirements led to a kickback against what is referred to pejoratively as the "reconciliation industry," and there is no doubt that the moral weight of the term has been diminished by its use as an administrative category, subject to audit.

What can not be dismissed though is that 15,016 projects were organized under the first EU peace program, which ran from 1995 to 1999, and a similar number were organized under the second program, which ran from 2000 to 2006. Education or training was not distinct categories for funding, but the Northern Ireland Council for Voluntary Action estimates that some 27 percent of projects funded had an educational character. One example here might suffice to demonstrate how learning is built into the reconciliation process. The Corrymeela Community on the North Antrim coast is residential center dedicated to reconciliation.

It was set up in 1966, that hopeful time before the Troubles, and its early operations were characterized by a willingness to experiment. The ecumenical ferment in Europe in that period had encouraged a radical spirit of reconciliation; Paulo Freire had taken up a position with the World Council of Churches in Geneva where, from 1970 to1980, he served as a consultant. The early Corrymeela founders met with him and with others who, in that restless period, wished to develop dialogue through unstructured group learning. All the ecumenists drank from the same well in that period, and, while Corrymeela cannot be described as Freirean (it does not, for instance, share his Manichean tendency to divide the world into oppressors and oppressed), a genealogical chart would show certain family resemblances between the experiments in adult learning conducted in the mountain villages of northeast Brazil and the group experiences at a residential center on the coast of North Antrim. Corrymeela has reconciliation and not education as its definition of purpose, but some six thousand people go through its programs each year, using radical adult learning processes to discover truths about their neighbors and themselves, and to overcome differences. In its own particular way, it is proof of how the commitment to peace is also a commitment to learning.

Progress Is Possible

In the 1990s, ethnic conflict—or intrastate wars, as these were sometimes described—became the new paradigm. A sort of *fin-de-siecle* gloom descended upon political analysts at the end of the millennium as the fragmentation of the former Yugoslavia, and the murderous conflict in Rwanda appeared to be no more than the most visible manifestations of the resurgence of a new primordialism that was consuming places as far apart as Azerbajian, Afghanistan, India, Kashmir, the Basque Country, Tibet, Burundi, Liberia, Chechnya, and Sierra Leone. One measure of the severity of such conflicts was the degree to which they could be deemed to be "intractable." Northern Ireland has always featured in the list of "intractable" quarrels (Richmond, 2002; Salomon, 2002). E. E. Azar's definition of an intractable region is one where there are "ethnic (racial, national, or religious) hostilities crossed with developmental inequities that have a long history and a bleak future." (Azar,1990, cited in Salomon, 2002, p.7). As one of the world's most intractable conflicts during the 1980s and early 1990s, the expectation that Northern Ireland's future would remain bleak was one that was generally shared—and, it would have to be said, shared as much inside Northern Ireland as outside. The fact that a violent conflict of this obduracy has been transformed must give hope to other conflict societies. It should also be borne in mind that the movement toward peace, particularly within the Irish republican movement, was itself inspired partly by the remarkable chain of events in the late 1980s, most notably the collapse of the Berlin Wall and the triumph of the African National Congress in South Africa. An alternative narrative can be constructed of late twentieth-century history, which foregrounds these political 'miracles' and argues that the laws of political gravity can occasionally allow for upward movement. Intractability is a construction, not a statement of destiny.

Are there not other lessons to be learned from Northern Ireland? This is by no means a definitive or exhaustive list but merely a starting point. Others may choose a different ordering or the inclusion of additional factors not noted here. Inevitably, any list becomes a procrustean bed. One obvious omission to my list is pointed up by a survey of Organisation for Security and Cooperation in Europe (OCSE) negotiators into the lessons learned from the Balkans crisis of the 1990s. (Sandole, 2006, pp. 111–127). The most important lesson for the respondents in that survey was conflict prevention—in other words, preventing the house from catching fire. Good advice, but too late for Northern Ireland. In terms of future research, though, it may be worth pointing out that the focus on crises and intractability is less illuminating than a focus on learning, and that those countries, like Belgium, Switzerland, and Canada, where different cultures have learned to live together have a lot to teach us. Northern Ireland may also be on its way to joining those ranks as a learning society.

References

Acheson, N., Cairns, E., Stringer, M., & Williamson, A. (2007). *Voluntary action and community relations in Northern Ireland*. Coleraine: Centre for Voluntary Action Studies, University of Ulster.

Azar, E. E. (1990). Correct year*The management of protracted social conflicts*. Hampshire, UK: Dartmouth.

BBC (2008) A State Apart http://www.bbc.co.uk/nothernireland/learning/history/stateapart/agreement/agreement/agreement3.shtml

Bowen, J. R. (1996). The myth of global ethnic conflict. *Journal of Democracy*, 7(4), 3–14.

Cochrane, F., & Dunn, S. (2002). *People power? The role of the voluntary and community sector in Northern Ireland* Cork; Cork University Press.

Coffield, F. (Ed.). (2000). The three stages of lifelong learning. In Coffield, F. (Ed.). *Differing versions of a learning society* (Vol. 2). Bristol: Policy Press.

Cox, M. (1998). Cinderella at the ball: Explaining the end of the war in Northern Ireland *Millennium, 27* (2): pp. 325–42.Cox, M. (2006). Rethinking the International and Northern Ireland. In M. Cox, A. Guelke & F. Stephen (Eds.), *A farewell to arms: Beyond the Good Friday Agreement* (pp. 427–443). Manchester: Manchester University Press.

Darby, J., & McGinty, R. (2002). *Contemporary peace-making: Conflict, violence and peace processes*. Basingstoke: Palgrave Macmillan.

Deloitte Consulting. (2007). *Research into the financial costs of the Northern Ireland divide*. Belfast: Office of the First Minister and Deputy First Minister.

Delors, J.(Ed.) (1996). *Learning: The treasure within*. Paris: United Nations Educational Scientific and Cultural Organisation.

Department of Education. (1998). *Lifelong learning: A new learning culture for all*. Belfast: Her Majesty's Stationery Office.

Department for Employment and Learning. (2006). *Success through skills* Belfast: HMSO.
Dixon, P. (2006). Rethinking the international and Northern Ireland: A critique. In M. Cox, A. Guelke, & F. Stephen (Eds.), *A farewell to arms: Beyond the Good Friday Agreement* (pp. 409–426). Manchester: Manchester University Press
Field, J. (2000). *Lifelong leaning and the new educational order*. Stoke-on-Trent: Trentham Books.
Independent Strategic Review of Education. (2006). *Schools for the future: Funding, strategy, sharing*. Belfast: Department of Education.
Gallagher, T. (2004). *Education in divided societies*. Basingstoke: Palgrave Macmillan.
Hayes, B., MacAllister, I., & Dowds, L. (2006). "In search of the middle ground: Integrated education and Northern Ireland politics," (January) 1–4. *ARK Social and Political Archive: Research Update 42* Belfast: Queen's University Belfast and University of Ulster.
Jarvis, P. (2007). *Globalisation, lifelong learning and the learning society*. London: Routledge.
Kolb, D. A. (1984). *Experiential learning*. Englewood Cliffs, NJ: Prentice Hall.
Lederach, J. P. (1996). *Preparing for peace: Conflict transformation across cultures*. New York: Syracuse University Press.
Lewin, K. (1948). *Resolving social conflicts: Selected papers on group dynamics* (D. Cartwright, ed.). New York: Harper and Row.
Mann, M. (2005). *The dark side of democracy*. Cambridge: Cambridge University Press.
McGlynn, C. (2007). Challenges in integrated education in Northern Ireland. In
McGlynn, C., Niens, U., Cairns, E., & Hewstone, M. (2004). Moving out of conflict: The contribution of integrated schools in Northern Ireland to identity, attitudes, forgiveness and reconciliation. *Journal of Peace Education, 1*(2), 147–163.
Meehan, E. (2000). Europe and the Europeanisation of the Irish question. In M. Cox, A. Guelke, & F. Stephen (Eds.), *A farewell to arms: Beyond the Good Friday Agreement* (pp. 338–356). Manchester: Manchester University Press.
Morgan, A. (2000). *The Belfast Agreement: A practical legal analysis*. London: Belfast Press.
Nodia, G. (2000). Nurturing nationalism. *Journal of Democracy, 11*(4), 169–173.
Northern Ireland Office. (2008). The Good Friday Agreement (Belfast Agreement). Belfast: Her Majesty's Stationery office.
O'Connor, F. (2002). *A shared childhood: The story of integrated schools in Northern Ireland*. Belfast: Blackstaff Press.
O'Leary, B. (1999). The nature of the Northern Ireland Agreement. *Fordham International Law Journal, 23*(4), 1628–1667.
Putnam, R. (2000). *Bowling alone: The collapse and revival of American community*. New York: Simon and Schuster.
Richmond, O. P. (2002). *Maintaining order, making peace*. Basingstoke, UK: Palgrave Macmillan.

Salomon, G. (2002). The nature of peace education: Not all programs are created equal. In Salomon, G. (Ed.), *Peace education: The concept, principles and practices around the world*. London: Lawrence and Earlbaum.

Sargant, N. with Field, J., Francis, H., Schuller, T., & Tuckett, A. (1997). The *learning divide: A report of the findings of a UK-wide survey on adult participation in education and training* Leicester: National Institute of Adult and Continuing Education.

Sandole, D. (2006). *Peace and security in the postmodern world: the OSCE and conflict resolution*. London: Routledge.

Sen, A. (2006). *Identity and violence: The illusion of destiny*. London: Allen Lane.

Silber, D., & Little, A. (1996). *The death of Yugoslavia*. London: Penguin BBC Books.

Social Exclusion Unit. (1999). *Bridging the gap: New opportunities for 16–18 year olds not in education, employment or training*. London: HMSO.

Sollenberg, M., & Wallenstein, P. (2000) Armed conflict 1989–1999. *Journal of Peace Research*, 37(5), pp. 635–645.

Starkey, K., Tempest, S., & McKinlay, A. (2004). *How organisations learn: Managing the search for knowledge* (3rd ed.). London: Thompson.

Stephen, F. (2006). Integrated schools: Myths, hopes and prospects. In M. Cox, A. Guelke, & F. Stephen (Eds.), *A farewell to arms: Beyond the Good Friday Agreement* (pp. 268–279). Manchester: Manchester University Press.

Stryker, S., & Serpe, R. (1982). Commitment, identity salience and role behaviour. In W. Ickes & E. S. Knowles (Eds.), *Personality, roles and social behaviour* (pp. 199–218). New York: Springer-Verlag.

Tocqueville, A..D. (2000) (Trans and Ed. Mansfield,H.C. and Winthrop, D.) *Democracy in America* Chicago: University of Chicago Press.

Toye, J. (2000). *Keynes on population*. Oxford: Oxford University Press

Vincent, S. (1993). Ethnicity and the state in Northern Ireland. In J. D. Toland (Ed.), *Ethnicity and the state* (pp.123–46. New Brunswick: Transaction.

Welton, M. (2005). *Designing the just learning society*. Leicester: National Institute for Adult and Continuing Education.

Wilson, R. (1989, September). If it moves, sell it. *Fortnight*, 276, 8.

Woolcock, M. (1998). Social capital and economic development: Toward a theoretical synthesis and policy framework. *Theory and Society*, 27(2), 151–208.

Zartman, I. W. (2000). Ripeness: The hurting stalemate and beyond. In P. C. Sterns & D. Druckman (Eds.), *International conflict resolution after the cold war* (pp. 225–250). Washington: National Academies Press.

CHAPTER 5

PEACE, RECONCILIATION, AND JUSTICE
DELIVERING THE MIRACLE IN POST-APARTHEID EDUCATION

Pam Christie

In the last decade of the twentieth century, the liberation struggle in South Africa bore its fruit. Apartheid was brought to an end through a negotiated settlement, and a new constitutional state was established, enshrining equality and human rights for all. In 1994, at the first democratic elections in South Africa, millions of people queued to exercise their first vote, and Nelson Mandela, once gaoled as a terrorist, was installed as president in a glorious ceremony rich with symbolism of the changing order. In an historic compromise where amnesty would be exchanged for truth-telling, the Truth and Reconciliation Commission provided a public process for coming to terms with the worst human rights abuses of apartheid. It was a limited record, addressing individual instances of gross abuse rather than the everyday suffering of ordinary people under the structural violence of apartheid. Nonetheless, in the spirit of compromise and national unity, restorative justice prevailed over retribution so that a new order could be forged from the old.

Peace, reconciliation, and justice are key concepts in the narrative of transformation in South Africa. The political violence spawned by apartheid gave way to largely peaceful, legitimate government. Formal reconciliation was achieved, at least at a national level. And the new constitution and bill of rights established a modernist state with the rule of law based on human rights, equal citizenship, and equal human dignity for all. These are enormous achievements—widely acclaimed as a "miracle."

Yet, as Mark Gevisser (cited in Kudla, 2004) evocatively articulates, more than ten years on from the historic elections of 1994, there was a sense in the national psyche of being still in transition—"going somewhere, suspended between two places" (p. 1)—an "interminable interregnum," in Arrighi's words. Gevisser identifies in South Africa "the Janus face of the miracle nation: a nation filled with hope and optimism, but under great pressure to transfer that optimism into progress and results" (Kudla, 2004, p. 1). While Mandela presided over a miracle nation, his successor, Thabo Mbeki, faced "a troublesome country, grim with poverty, grubby with politics." The transformation could be delivered, and the result was psychic distress. Gevisser points out that Mbeki quoted Hughes's "Montage of a Dream Deferred"(in Kudla, 2004, p.1). He talked of South Africa being divided into two nations: one prosperous and largely white and one poverty-stricken and largely black. And the national psyche of South Africa remained suspended in a sense of continuing transition.

This same scenario plays through in education: a noble framework of justice and equal rights—the product of peace and reconciliation—which seems not yet to have delivered change for the majority of black students who remain in segregated and unequally resourced schools. Education operates as if in a transitional space, seemingly still, serving two nations and unable to deliver on the Freedom Charter's historic promise in 1956 that "The Doors of Learning Shall Be Opened To All." How might the transition state be ended?

This chapter addresses the question of what happens after the moment when, at a formal level, peace has been achieved, reconciliation delivered, and justice declared. The challenge is to shift from a sense of the interminable interregenum of transition to acceptance that a destination has been reached and must be worked with. This requires a different imaginary: a move from dreams and miracles to active engagement, creativity, and responsibility. How might this be achieved? This chapter sets out the challenges and constraints facing post-apartheid reconstruction, both generally and in terms of education. Drawing on Jean Paul Lederach's (2005) notion of the moral imagination, it argues that the new imaginary must understand these challenges and work across the remaining apartheid divides to build a society and education system that give material expression to the ideals of justice, rights, and reconciliation. The chapter ends by setting out possibilities for peace education to play a part in constructing this new imaginary and building positive peace.

Peace, Justice, and the New Constitutional Order

The end of apartheid was brought about by negotiations in the context of a debilitating conflict that neither side could win outright (see Sparks,

1995; Truth and Reconciliation Commission of South Africa, 1998). The National Party, architect of apartheid and custodian of its crumbling power, was no longer able to hold at bay the pressures against it from the liberation movements backed by foreign powers, and a failing economy. The major liberation movements (African National Congress [ANC], Pan African Congress [PAC] and South African Communist Party [SACP]), banned since the 1960s, had built momentum externally and internally, with an intensified armed struggle and an internal campaign to make the country ungovernable. Secret negotiations prior to1990 brought about the unbanning of the ANC and other political groupings, and ushered in a period of intense and sometimes faltering negotiations. In the violent and uncertain days of negotiations, before a peaceful settlement could be guaranteed by either side, compromises were made for a future sharing of power. The compromise settlement agreed that a new constitution would be established, the ANC would lead the Government of National Unity (GNU), and a "sunset clause" would protect the tenure of senior members of the bureaucracy. A last-minute "postamble" tacked onto the constitutional agreements made provision for amnesty to be granted in respect of acts, omissions and offences with political objectives and committed in the course of the conflicts of the past. The triumph of the new government was its compromise, as erstwhile enemies of over forty years were able to commit themselves to peace, reconciliation, and justice. This was the miracle presided over by Mandela. However, the miracle had to be taken forward into results, which proved increasingly elusive as the new government was established and set to work (for accounts of this period, see, for example, Bond, 2000; Hirsch, 2005; Marais, 2001; Saul, 2005; Seekings & Nattrass, 2005.)

The GNU was multiply hybrid. The ANC led an alliance grouping of itself, the SACP, and the Congress of South African Trade Unions (COSATU). This involved an ideological spread with the ANC to the right of its alliance partners on economic policies. In addition, the GNU included members of the National Party and the major Zulu opposition party, Inkatha. Compromise and negotiation were the order of the day, as more radical visions for change gave way to what was possible under the circumstances. As well as the government itself, the bureaucracy, too, was hybrid. Public servants of the previous regime worked alongside new appointees. The former had expertise in how the system operated, which they could use to facilitate or block change. Most of the latter had "struggle" credentials rather than government experience.

Two axes structured the policy work of the new government. First, a political axis was provided by the new constitution of 1996, which exemplified the rights and rule of law for a liberal, modern state. Second, an economic axis was heavily influenced by policies to accommodate neoliberal globalization. These two axes not only opened up but also limited possibilities for change in the new South Africa.

Politically, the 1996 constitution laid the ground rules for a state that would be the antithesis of apartheid. The constitution intended to heal the divisions of the past by according equal rights and equal dignity to all citizens and by protecting rights to differences in language and culture in a shared common order. Whereas apartheid had enshrined identity politics based on race and ethnicity, the new constitution enshrined common citizenship and a bill of rights. Instead of apartheid's ten tribal homelands with degrees of self-government and pseudoindependence, the new state would be unitary with geographically based provinces. In the face of the fractured and unequal identity politics of apartheid, the new imaginary was a unitary state with common citizenship, which would be blind to race and ethnicity and which would provide constitutional rights. In reality, apartheid identities and inequalities had been cut deeply into the social fabric over forty years of systematic action. The result was a torn, if not unraveling, social fabric that could not be straightforwardly mended by simple sutures.

Indeed, nonracism and a common identity cannot be built simply through constitutional measures, such as granting citizenship rights, however important these may be in a democratic polity. This is well argued by the South African intellectual and activist, Neville Alexander (2000). Dismissing the metaphor of the "rainbow nation" as "ornamental" (p. 82), Alexander argues for the necessity of building a sense of common destiny—nation building—in the newly formed state in South Africa. He suggests that the arguments that nations precede states are Eurocentric; they do not apply in the African context where states were arbitrarily formed by colonial carve-up. In this context, nations must be imagined after states are formed. Under these conditions, nation-building projects across tribal, ethnic, and linguistic differences are crucial to the survival of a common destiny. There is an ever-present danger of ethnic consciousness intersecting with economic interests, or, in South Africa's case, of the persistence of inherited racial identities coming to prevail again. Alexander urges South Africa's political and cultural leaders to "devise and promote strategies which will reinforce the centripetal, not the centrifugal, tendencies in the social formation" (p. 84). This is not about fabrication of national identity, but the imagining and creating of it. Alexander's warning is strong: "In this country we face the real problem that if we do not promote national unity, that is, arrive at a core of common values, practices and national projects (regardless of the class character of the leadership for the moment), we shall, as in similar cases in recent historical experience in Europe, Africa and Asia, fall apart into warring ethnic groups, each with a more or less separatist agenda. If that were to happen, similar events to the north of us would pale into historical insignificance" (p. 91).

In the light of these points, it could be argued that allowing the sense of an interminable interregnum to prevail in South Africa is potentially a dangerous waste of time. Ethnic and economic interests do not stand still. Instead, in the interregnum, interests are consolidated, extended, won—and lost. Under the centrifugal metaphor of "two nations," opportunities for building "one nation" are not seized. A new imaginary does not transcend the divisions of the old. The political project of achieving peace, justice, and equality is left to its own devices, its possibilities opened but not realized.

Economic policies, which formed the second major axis of the policies of the new government, also show the ambiguity of the interregnum. They, too, faced major limitations in redressing the inequalities of apartheid. The new state was launched at a time of neoliberal globalization, which was harshly competitive and unsympathetic toward redistributive approaches. Early attempts to formulate a development strategy of growth through redistribution were set out in the Reconstruction and Development Program (RDP) in the Mandela years. By 1996, the RDP had given way to the Growth, Employment, and Redistribution Strategy (GEAR), which amounted to a form of self-imposed structural adjustment (see Bond, 2000; Marais, 2001). Under such policies, South Africa attempted macroeconomic stabilization, market-led growth, fiscal restraint, and reduced social spending (Hirsch, 2005). The goal was to produce job-creating economic growth on the basis of which social spending might alleviate the conditions of the poor. For the first ten years at least, growth was slower than anticipated and what growth there was did not produce jobs. What was achieved was pro-poor spending on child support and age grants, and the partial upgrading of infrastructure and social services to disadvantaged communities. The economy was not fundamentally restructured, though more black people moved into the middle classes (see Seekings & Nattrass, 2005). Those without employment—some 40 percent of the population—remained vulnerable to chronic poverty. And South Africa continued to have one of the highest measured rates of inequality in the world, as indicated by its Gini coefficient.

In short, ten years after independence, South Africa was an upper-middle-income country that had achieved a measure of macroeconomic stability. However, alongside this, there existed large-scale chronic and endemic poverty, and long-standing inequality. In the face of this, Mbeki famously lamented the existence of "two nations" in an address to parliament on May 29, 1998. He said,

> Material conditions have divided our country into two nations, one black, the other white. The smaller, white group is relatively prosperous and has ready access to a developed economic, physical, educational, communication and other infrastructure. The second, and larger, nation of South Africa is black and poor, and lives under conditions of a grossly underdeveloped infrastructure. (Statement on Reconciliation and Nation-Building, National Assembly, May 29 1998, modified)

However descriptively appealing such a picture may be in pointing to the continuing inequalities and injustices that are apartheid's legacy, it is analytically misleading, if not inaccurate (see Seekings & Nattrass, 2005). Its major flaw is that it neglects to analyze the changes that have been occurring and why they have occurred as they have. It depicts inequalities in static, commonsense, rural, and racial forms. Yet inequalities in post-apartheid South Africa are not static but changing, not at least while racial divisions are being infused with inequalities of social class. One of the most significant changes during this period is the growth of the black middle class, and hence the growing inequality among black people. Poverty and inequality are urban as well as rural phenomena. More importantly, the changes that have been occurring are not without cause or reason. They are, at least partly, consequences of specific neoliberal policies adopted by the government, which bring heightened inequalities in their wake. Complex though it is to steer the political economy of the country in demanding times of globalization, it would be wrong to assume that there is no one at the helm.

This is not to underestimate the enormity of the task facing the government, nor to make light of what was achieved during this period. Certainly, the first ten years of democracy in South Africa brought political peace and reconciliation and provided an alternative vision to the violence, enmity, and injustice of apartheid. This was an enormous achievement. The construction of an alternative society after the miracle of negotiated settlement is no small task. But it is not assisted by a social imaginary that yearns for more miracles as it looks at the incomplete task it faces.

This situation is paralleled in education, as the following section illustrates.

The Dream Deferred in Education

The new government inherited an education system scarred by the inequalities of forty years of apartheid and decades of segregation before that (see Chisholm, 1997; Christie, 2008). The apartheid education system was premised on racial differentiation and, consequently upon that, racially fragmented education systems that were separately administered and unequally funded. Across the country, nineteen different national, provincial, racial, and ethnic education departments delivered a formally similar core curriculum in schools that operated under vastly different conditions. "Two nations" would have been too simple a description for the hybrid and fragmented system that apartheid deliberately constructed. Whereas education for those classified "white" was free and compulsory to age fifteen, for other classification groups, education was not compulsory, resulting in enrolment patterns that resembled third-world countries alongside a first-world pattern for white students. In the heyday of apartheid, the per capita funding for white children was twelve times that of African children, with those classified Indian and Coloured receiving respectively less and less than whites. In the last decade of apartheid, secondary schooling for Africans expanded, and by the end of apartheid, the expenditure gap had reduced to four times more per white child. The starkness of underprovision in African schools was revealed in the Schools Register of Needs (1996), a mapping task undertaken by the new government shortly after taking power (see Bot, 1997). This revealed that 24 percent of schools had no water within walking distance, 13 percent had no toilet facilities at all, 57 percent had no electricity, 69 percent had no learning materials, 83 percent had no library facilities, 6 percent were in such poor condition that they are not suitable for education at all, and a further 11 percent were in serious need of repair. The greatest deprivation was in rural African schools and, consequently, in largely rural provinces.

In education, the first task of the new government was to restructure the system away from its fragmented, racial basis to a nonracial, provincial system (see Chisholm, 2004; Christie, 2008; Fleisch, 2002; Sayed & Jansen, 2001). The national Department of Education was responsible for providing norms and standards for the system as a whole, while schooling was delivered by provincial departments who received their funding from the national fiscus. This set in place a structural disjuncture between policy designers who had no direct responsibility for service delivery and school providers who had no say over what they were required to implement. The national department had no means of ensuring that designated funding was, in fact, spent on education, and provinces did not always have the capacity to spend their allocations. This is one instance of the gap between policy visions and conditions on the ground that characterized the terrain of educational change.

With its provisions for common citizenship in a unitary state, the 1996 constitution stated that education would be a basic right for all. In its words,

> Everyone shall have the right: (a) to basic education, including adult education; and (b) to further education, which the state, through reasonable measures, must make progressively available and accessible.

Yet statements of rights are largely symbolic unless accompanied by material provisions. Achieving the right to education in South Africa would require major investment and resource allocation if the majority of the population were to receive what had previously been available only to a minority. This investment was, in practice, not forthcoming. Instead, the prevailing approach was that expenditure on social services should be limited and that efficiencies should be sought within existing budgetary allocations. South Africa's overall spending on education was benchmarked against the spending of other countries—countries that did not have historical backlogs to address. Whether or not the country had the capacity to run an expanded schooling system remains a hypothetical question, given that funding was not present.

The first White Paper on Education and Training, issued in 1995, based itself firmly on the premises of the new constitution and committed itself to a set of new principles:

> It should be the goal of education and training policy to enable a democratic, free, equal, just and peaceful society to take root and prosper in our land, on the basis that all South Africans without exception share the same inalienable rights, equal citizenship, and common national destiny, and that all forms of bias (especially racial, ethnic and gender) are dehumanizing. (Department of Education, 1995, p. 22)

And:

> The education system must *counter the legacy of violence* by promoting the values underlying the democratic process and the charter of fundamental rights, the importance of due process of law and the exercise of civic responsibility, and by teaching values and skills for conflict management and conflict resolution, the importance of mediation, and the benefits of tolerance and co-operation. Thus peace and stability will become the normal condition of our schools and colleges, and citizens will be empowered to participate confidently and constructively in social and civic life. (p. 22)

Put in this way, the White Paper reads like a prospectus for a peace education program. Yet, ironically, peace did not feature as an explicit goal in subsequent education policies, nor were the ideal conditions for peace, as expressed in these statements, given priority attention.

It could be argued that the parameters of what is possible in terms of education for peace, equity, and justice are fundamentally enabled or constrained by decisions of political economy. In the case of the new South Africa, the government's commitment to neoliberal economic policies meant that justice and equity would be framed within market logics and parameters of fiscal restraint. Market logics do not reserve a role for the state to intervene through equity measures, particularly in circumstances where budgets are straitened (see Christie, 2008). However, given the extent of historical inequalities in education, unless substantial resources were earmarked for equity purposes, there would be no chance of improving the educational opportunities of those without private resources to pay for schooling. Leaving peace, equity, and justice to chance on an historically unequal playing field under conditions of globalization inevitably opened possibilities of not only continuing existing inequalities but also of increasing them.

The White Paper provided an idealistic vision and broad framework for a new education system, and over the next few years, a whole range of new policies were put in place to give effect to the framework. Many of these were ideal-type policies, too sophisticated to be implemented, particularly by disadvantaged schools. An unintended consequence of these policies was that most benefit went to those with resources and capacity—the formerly privileged schools that were historically white.

Of the new policies, those for funding and governance illustrate most clearly the unintended consequences that arose from idealist approaches that did not engage with the structurally unequal conditions that prevailed or the power relations that maintained them.

Funding and governance policies were addressed by the South African Schools Act (SASA) of 1996. Both of these were contested issues in the political transition (see Sayed & Jansen, 2001). In terms of funding, an early decision was taken that state resources could be supplemented by fees at individual school level. The reason for this was to hold the middle classes within the public system rather than have them seek quality education in a private system. Given that the state did not have the resources to provide free and compulsory education for all on the formula established for white schools under apartheid, fees would have the benefit of bringing additional private funding into the system to supplement state funding.

However, the result of this approach to education financing was that the majority of formerly white schools, the most privileged in the system, became a haven for the middle classes of all races, operating selectively through the high fees they were empowered to charge. Although the act provided fee exemptions for poor students, in practice, most poor children did not have access to this tier of elite schools. Moreover, while schools in wealthy communities were able to charge fees in the thousands of Rands, those in poor communities were hardly able to raise fees at all, and many were subsequently declared fee-free. Thus, a hierarchy of privilege and disadvantage was an inadvertent consequence of the new policy, which ironically increased inequalities within the system as a whole instead of reducing them.

The issue of governance was also a contested one for similar and different reasons. On the one hand were the demands by former white schools for as much autonomy as possible under the new government. In the dying days of apartheid, by sleight of hand, the previous government managed to pass ownership of white schools to parentally elected governing bodies under graduated conditions of self-management. The new government was thus confronted by a status quo of powerful, vested interests. On the other hand, in the last decades of apartheid, many black schools had become sites of opposition to apartheid where authority was contested by students and in some cases assumed by civic and parent bodies. For these groups, school-based management represented a desirable democracy. Faced with these two quite different pressures for devolution of power and influenced also by international trends, the government adopted the principles of school-based management, at first giving full powers only to schools that demonstrated financial capacity, with the idea of subsequently giving powers to all schools. The unintended consequence of this was that governing bodies were able to assume powers against the wishes of the state, particularly in matters of staffing and admissions, and have their rights upheld by the courts.

Thus, in both funding and governance, vested interests were able to exercise their rights to privilege. In both cases, inequalities in schooling were entrenched in different forms. That is not to say that policies were intentionally unjust. Rather, it is to illustrate the difficulties of working against entrenched inequalities in education where old, vested interests persist and are joined by new ones. It is to illustrate the conditions under which "the dream is deferred" and "two nations" becomes a mantra of disillusionment.

Certainly, the new government did legislate for equity measures in education. Its Equitable Shares Funding formula provided for redistribution of the nonpersonnel budget from the least poor to the poorest provinces and schools. It provided toilets, telephones, and other facilities to increasing numbers of schools. It took measures to regularize teachers' salaries and conditions of work, and it committed itself again and again in annual reports to the eradication of poverty and inequality in education. These and other measures are not to be dismissed. Above all, the government succeeded in running the education system during a time of massive change and putting in place a new vision and framework for future policies. But the quality of the system remained a continuing challenge (South Africa came last in both mathematics and science on the international Trends in International Mathematics and Science Study (TIMSS) tests) and the annual release of matriculation results spotlights the slow progress in changing the performance of the system.

Not surprisingly, "two nations" metaphors have been used to describe the education system, as is illustrated by the following statement made at the Public Hearing on the Right to Basic Education, held by the South African Human Rights Commission (2006) held in 2005: "The research clearly shows that if you are black—particularly if you are rural and poor—schooling and education does not work for you. For 60–80% of our children, education reinforces marginalisation, trapped in a second economy of unemployment and survival with few ways out. It may even be said that there exist 'two education systems' in South Africa, mirroring the problems of two economies" (p. 18).

Toward a New Imaginary

"Two nations," I suggest, is a metaphor that represents disappointment and powerlessness. It bemoans the seeming impossibility of achieving desired change and the inexplicable persistence of the old despite the birth of the new. Moreover, as stated earlier, it is a metaphor in which description—inaccurate at that—takes the place of rigorous analysis. It represents, I suggest, a failure in the social imaginary.

If peace, reconciliation, and justice are to be achieved in practice in South Africa, it is necessary to analyze the post-apartheid dispensation with greater accuracy and to work actively toward change. Instead of accepting existing inequalities as self-evident and inevitable, the task is to work against them and to challenge unconsidered assumptions and practices that have the effect of perpetuating them.

What I have been suggesting is the need for a different social imaginary, which embraces the task of building the new through creative and responsible action. Writing in the context of peace building, Lederach (2005) outlines the dimensions of a "moral imagination," which, I suggest, offer useful insights to the task required in South Africa, if it is transposed to suit that context: "The moral imagination requires the capacity to imagine ourselves in a web of relationships that includes our enemies; the ability to sustain a paradoxical curiosity that embraces complexity without reliance on dualistic polarity; the fundamental belief in and pursuit of the creative act; and the acceptance of the inherent risk of stepping into the mystery of the unknown that lies beyond the far too familiar landscape of violence" (p. 5).

Instead of a divided social imaginary, what I am proposing here is a version of Lederach's moral imagination of inclusivity. This imaginary would work from the assumption that all South Africans are in a shared web of relationships rather than in separate webs. Instead of falling back on familiar, old accounts of dualistic polarity, which accept the existence of inequalities and structural violence, the new imaginary would need to sustain a paradoxical curiosity about the society that is being created, in all its complexity. It would also need to embrace the spirit of creativity and risk that is required to leave behind the familiar landscape with its old contours of inequalities. Building a shared destiny across historic divides is far too urgent and important a project to defer.

Challenges for Peace Education

What role may peace education play in this? As Harris (2004) usefully points out, peace education has a dynamic relation with peace practice; it is both philosophy and process (Harris, 2003). Understandings of peace are varied, as are ideas about how best to achieve positive peace. In his overview of peace education theory, Ian Harris (2004) identifies five approaches (and arguably, more could be distinguished): international education, human rights education, development education, environmental education, and conflict-resolution education. However, as Betty Reardon (1997) and others (see Salomon & Nevo, 2002) point out, these different approaches may not, in practice, be overtly geared toward understanding or promoting peace.

For South Africans who have engaged in the struggle against apartheid, peace may all too easily be glossed over as having been achieved through the negotiated settlement, the Truth and Reconciliation Commission, the

1996 constitution, and the new governance structures and social institutions. This sense that the task is over may also prevail in other post-conflict situations as well. However, I suggest that this approach accords more with negative peace (as absence of violence) rather than positive peace. Positive peace, as Harris (2003) points out, "involves following standards of justice, living in balance with nature, and providing meaningful participation to citizens in their government" (p. 12). In the face of the continuing inequalities outlined in this chapter, it is clear that much remains to be done to achieve positive peace in South Africa, as well as social and economic justice.

What, then, might peace education address in the South African context? While it is correct to point to the achievements of state and civil society in achieving possibilities for peace in South Africa (as do Nkomo, Weber, & Malada, 2007), it is also important to note that "peace education is not widely understood in South Africa" (Maxwell, Enslin, & Maxwell, 2004, p. 116). Under such circumstances, its specific concerns could easily be engulfed by other change agendas and its dynamic relation to peace practice lost.

In terms of the broad field of peace education, the position adopted here is consonant with the quotation from the White Paper on Education provided earlier. It is that a legacy of violence needs to be actively countered by the promotion of democratic values and civic responsibility, by building a common present and shared future, and by promoting values of justice, respect, and care for the other. It assumes that in a complex society like South Africa, conflict and differences of identity need to be acknowledged and worked with in constructive ways rather than denied or avoided. It assumes that peace depends upon building a more just society where social and economic inequalities are actively worked against. It assumes an imagination of something different beyond the familiar landscape of violence, oppression, and social suffering—a creative act of "paradoxical curiosity" in relation to the "mystery of the unknown," in Lederach's (2005) words.

Elsewhere (Christie, 2005), I have argued for an ethical imagination in education, comprising three dimensions: an ethics of intellectual rigor, an ethics of civility, and an ethics of care. In terms of this framework, peace education would be based on rigorous analysis of the structural and cultural conditions of peace and violence in the past and the present, commitment to building a public sphere in which democratic participation and social and economic justice are the basis for building peace and resolving conflicts, and an acceptance of responsibility to care for others, which requires us to be open to their suffering as well as our own (following Levinas, 1998). All of this involves willingness to engage emotionally and imaginatively in praxis of change.

To achieve positive peace, justice and reconciliation—and for peace education to contribute to this—requires actively building a different imaginary, in which a just and inclusive future is embraced with hope, to be built by our own collective action, creativity, and responsibility. This is a task that South Africa—and, I suggest, other post-conflict societies—cannot afford to defer.

References

Alexander, N. (2002). *An ordinary country: Issues in the transition from apartheid to democracy in South Africa.* Pietermaritzburg: University of Natal Press.

Bond, P. (2000). *Elite transition: From apartheid to neo-liberalism in South Africa.* Pietermaritzburg: University of Natal Press.

Bot, M. (1997, August). Schools Register of Needs: A provincial comparison of school facilities, 1996. *Edusource Data News, 17.* Johannesburg: Education Foundation.

Chisholm, L. (1997). The restructuring of South African education and training in comparative context. In P. Kallaway, G. Kruss, A. Fataar, & G. Donn (Eds.), *Education after apartheid: South African education in transition* (pp. 50–67). Cape Town: University of Cape Town Press.

Chisholm, L. (Ed.). (2004). *Changing class: Education and social change in post-apartheid South Africa.* London: Zed Press.

Christie, P. (2005). Towards an ethics of engagement in education in global times. *Australian Journal of Education, 49*(3), 238–250.

Christie, P. (2008). *Opening the doors of learning: Changing schools in post-apartheid South Africa.* Johannesburg: Heinemann.

Department of Education. (1995). White Paper on education and training in South Africa: First steps to develop a new system (White Paper One). Pretoria: Government Gazette.

Fleisch, B. (2002). *Managing educational change: The state and school reform in South Africa.* Johannesburg: Heinemann.

Harris, I. (2003). *Peace education.* Jefferson: McFarland.

Harris, I. (2004). Peace education theory. *Journal of Peace Education, 1*(1), 5–20.

Hirsch, A. (2005). *Season of hope: Economic reform under Mandela and Mbeki.* Scottsville, South Africa: University of KwaZulu-Natal Press.

Kudla, J. (2004). Review of Mark Gevisser: Are we living in a dream deferred? Fifth Wolpe Memorial Lecture, University of KwaZulu Natal. Retrieved May 27, 2008, from http://www.ukzn.ac.za/ccs/default.asp?11,22,5, 439

Lederach, J. P. (2005). The moral imagination—The art and soul of building peace. [Electronic version]. New York: Oxford University Press. Retrieved March 23, 2007, from http://www.oxfordscholarship.com/oso/public/content/religion/9780195174540/toc.html

Levinas, E. (1998). *Entre nous: On thinking-of-the-other.* (M. B. Smith & B. Harshav, trans.) London: Athlone Press.

Marais, H. (2001). *South Africa—limits to change: The political economy of transition.* London: Zed Books Ltd.

Maxwell, A.-M., Enslin, P., & Maxwell, T. (2004). Educating for peace in the midst of violence: A South African experience. *Journal of Peace Education, 1*(1), 103–121.

Mbeki, T. (1998). Statement on reconciliation and nation-building, National Assembly, May 29. Cape Town, Hansard: Government Printers.

Nkomo, M., Weber, E., & Malada, B. (2007). Sustaining peace through school and civil society: Mortar, bricks and human agency. *Journal of Peace Education*, 4(1), 95–108.

Reardon, B. A. (1997). Human rights as education for peace. In G. J. Andrepoulos & R. P. Claude (Eds.), *Human rights education for the twenty-first century*. Philadelphia: University of Pennsylvania Press.

Salomon, G., & Nevo, B. (2002). *Peace education: The concepts, principles and practices around the world*. Mahwah NJ: Lawrence Erlbaum.

Saul, J. S. (2005). *The next liberation struggle: Capitalism, socialism and democracy in Southern Africa*. New York: Monthly Review Press.

Sayed, Y., & Jansen, J. (Eds.). (2001). *Implementing education policies: The South African experience*. Cape Town: University of Cape Town Press.

Seekings, J., & Nattrass, N. (2005). *Class, race and inequality in South Africa*. New Haven: Yale University Press.

South African Human Rights Commission. (2006). *Report of the Public Hearing on the Right to Basic Education, 12–14 October 2005*. Johannesburg: Author.

Sparks, A. (1995). *Tomorrow is another country: The inside story of South Africa's negotiated settlement*. Johannesburg: Jonathan Ball.

Truth and Reconciliation Commission of South Africa. (1998). *Report*. Cape Town: Author.

Part II

Peace Education and Contact
Introduction

Zvi Bekerman

The chapters in this part touch upon important issues related to the theoretical basis that support educational efforts geared toward the creation of positive conditions that will sustain a better world. The chapters also point to a method of inquiry that carries the promise of allowing for a better understanding of the educational processes undertaken and their potential effects. In short, the chapters deal with theoretical perspectives developed in dialogue with contact hypothesis and with qualitative or ethnographic approaches in the research of peace and coexistence education.

The contact hypothesis tradition (Allport, 1954), posits that social change can be attained through extensive integration toward the achievement of social stability and harmony. Allport's influential initial articulation has throughout the years evolved into a complex taxonomy of conditions for "good contact" to be possible. The main prescriptions recommended in the contact literature include the following: contact should be regular and frequent; it should involve a balanced ratio of in-group to out-group members while allowing for a genuine "acquaintance potential"; it should occur between individuals who share equality of status; and, while being institutionally sanctioned, it should be organized around cooperation toward the achievement of a super ordinate goal.

Research has shown that intergroup contact seems to generally promote intergroup acceptance, especially when appropriate conditions for the contact are being met (Hewstone, Tausch, Hughes, & Cairns, 2005; Pettigrew & Tropp, 2000). Yet research in this field has dealt with rather short-term interventions devised for dispute resolution, conflict management, and intergroup encounters. The research methodology frequently utilizes quantitative, positivist perspectives that deal with the manipulation of variables and graphical representations of relationship patterns but do not necessarily offer insights into the complexities of human activity, in general, and intergroup educational encounters, in particular. Exceptions are to be found (Bekerman, 2004, 2005; Helman, 2002; Maoz, Bar-On, Bekerman, & Jaber-Massarwa, 2004), but these critiques stand and have been recently raised again even from within the psychological literature (Dixon, Durheim, & Tredoux, 2005). It is from this critical perspective that the importance of the chapters that follow should be considered.

Tomovska's chapter, a case study of a contact-based program for ten- to eleven-year-old ethnic Macedonians, furthers our understanding on the importance of considering wider sociopolitical contexts on the implementation of contact-guided educational programs. Theoretically, the chapter contributes to our understanding of contact theory by drawing from the bioecological system theory posited by Bronfenbrenner and Bourdieu's notion of habitus. Tomovska shows how the bioecological system theory helps appreciate the complex developmental environment within which contact theory might or might not produce positive outcomes while Bourdieu's habitus helps explain developmental outcomes at an individual level. Methodologically, Tomovska adopts an ethnographic approach that provides evidence of the ways by which children seek information from their environments, thus becoming active agents in the formation of their perspectives and behaviors. Tomovska suggests that much could be gained by educators planning contact interventions by paying attention to events in their students' surrounding context. Using the events uncovered in the surrounding systems as opportunities for inquiry by the students might help them better understand their active coparticipation in the construction of their habitus rather than of having to deal with the idealistic, detached perspectives that adults and educators many times suggest as possible paths to change.

Hromadzic's chapter examines and interprets practices of mixing as instances of border-crossing among youth at the Gymnasium Mostar in Bosnia and Herzegovina. The ethnographic approach adopted helps Hromadzic illustrate the hows and whens of mixing so as to uncover its logic and map the emerging forms of social relations it allows for among the participants in the school context. Hromadzic shows how mixing practices, such as the ones implemented in the school to be acceptable, need to preserve a superficial character; yet, some mixing practices do become places of resistance or places were boundaries can be tested and stretched. Hromadzic suggests mixing as an analytical concept that can help us better understand phases of post-conflict social reconstruction, for it captures small, social interactional details that otherwise go unnoticed in traditional social research much dominated by powerful categories, such as identity and culture.

Hammack's chapter offers descriptive insights on two American-based coexistence programs for Israelis and Palestinian youth. His interpretative work uncovers the paradigmatic basis of this educational activity and shows them to be rooted in American folk psychological perspectives on identity and intergroup relations. The study points to the need for a greater reflectivity on the side of the organizers of educational interventions geared toward the alleviation of conflict about their own cultural assumptions and psychological perspectives. At the same time, the study is very attentive to the distinct sociopolitical realities that envelop the target populations of their educational work. Moreover, he encourages educators and theorists to consider the intricate relationships between individual psychological and social structural change as well as to become more critically conscious about the limitations of intergroup contact.

Nien's chapter sheds light on the conceptualizations of peace education and explores how theoretical frameworks, based on approaches from the political sciences (multiculturalism) and social psychology (contact hypothesis), may be used to underpin the design of education in conflict and post-conflict societies. The chapter suggests that the use of the contact hypothesis in conjunction with multiculturalism can strengthen and develop the effectiveness of educational initiatives that strive to secure a more peaceful future.

Kosic and Senehi's chapter provides a conceptual framework for mapping cross-community work designed to assist the process of reconciliation in conflict and post-conflict societies. As the basis for their analysis, they make use of interview data gathered from leaders of community programs implemented in Croatia and Northern Ireland, which try to promote intergroup contact among young people and to deal with salient ethnic and religious identities. They suggest that the main strategies used in such programs can be divided into two main categories—single-identity work and intergroup contact—and scrutinize their potential pros and cons. The chapter also raises some critical questions regarding the difficulties encountered by organizers in offering more longitudinal plans and projects, their concern with the recruitment and involvement of participants, and their continuous agonizing over the possibilities of obtaining funding. Lastly, the chapter suggests that more attention should be given to the issues of perception of victimhood and collective responsibility to promote reconciliation among conflicting parties.

From both theoretical and methodological perspectives, the chapters in this part add a welcomed critical complexity to our present knowledge on peace and coexistence educational processes. These complexities should help us problematize our present approaches and should encourage us to keep searching for new, pedagogical, context-sensitive strategies to better cope with the multiple and varied problems confronted by educators in conflict and post-conflict societies around the world.

We should not expect peace and coexistence educational initiatives to be able to offer solutions to long-standing and bloody conflicts whose roots are to be found on a very material, unequal allocation of resources. Unfortunately, many times societies and governments find it easier to support such initiatives rather than work hard toward structural change. Hoping this is not the situation in the contexts under study, the question becomes what can be realistically expected from such initiatives.

Salomon's (2004) proposal sounds partially true when affirming that though peace education cannot resolve intractable conflicts, it can prepare the ground for desirable political change. What needs to be clarified is what type of educational interventions can prepare the ground.

REFERENCES

Allport, G. W. (1954). *The nature of prejudice*. London: Addison-Wesley.

Bekerman, Z. (2004). Multicultural approaches and options in conflict ridden areas: Bilingual Palestinian-Jewish education in Israel. *Teachers College Record, 106*(3), 574–610.

Bekerman, Z. (2005). Complex contexts and ideologies: Bilingual education in conflict-ridden areas. *Journal of Language Identity and Education, 4*(1), 1–20.

Dixon, J., Durheim, K., & Tredoux, C. (2005). Beyond the optimal contact strategy. *American Psychologist, 60*(7), 697–711.

Helman, S. (2002). Monologic Results of Dialogue: Jewish-Palestinian Encounter Groupes as Sites of Essentialization. *Identities: Global Studies in Culture and Power, 9*, 327–354.

Hewstone, M., Tausch, N., Hughes, J., & Cairns, E. (2005). Prejudice, intergroup contact and identity: Do neighbourhoods matter? *Economic & Social Research Council* (RES-148-25-0045). Northern Ireland.

Maoz, I., Bar-On, D., Bekerman, Z., & Jaber-Massarwa, S. (2004). Learning about "good enough" through "bad enough": The story of a planned dialogue between Israeli Jews and Palestinians. *Human Relations, 57* (9), 1075–1101.

Pettigrew, T. F., & Tropp, L. R. (2000). Does intergroup contact reduce prejudice? Recent meta-analytic findings. In S. Oskamp (Ed.), *Reducing prejudice and discrimination* (pp. 93–114). Mahwah, NJ: Earlbaum.

Salomon, G. (2004). Does peace education make a difference in the context of an intractable conflict? *Journal of Peace Psychology, 10*, 257–274.

CHAPTER 6

SOCIAL CONTEXT AND CONTACT HYPOTHESIS

PERCEPTIONS AND EXPERIENCES OF A CONTACT PROGRAM FOR TEN- TO ELEVEN-YEAR-OLD CHILDREN IN THE REPUBLIC OF MACEDONIA

Ana Tomovska

INTRODUCTION

Educational systems can promote division and intolerance, which can have a negative impact on intergroup relations or can bridge the division and promote positive intergroup relations (Bush & Saltareli, 2000). Using education for promotion of tolerance and good interethnic relations is very important in conflict-affected countries faced with deep entrenched narratives about "the good us" versus "the bad them," such as in the Republic of Macedonia. Therefore, in such societies, it is important to create a more positive intergroup climate through an educational system that will lead the children away from the endemic violence, dangerous stereotypes, and conformity to intolerant behavior (Salomon, 2004; Shapiro, 2002). Although peace education has many different forms and different theoretical underpinnings (Bekerman & McGlynn, 2007), the contact hypothesis still underpins much of the peace education in schools. This usually involves organizing group encounters in face-to-face meetings in an attempt to alter participants' hostile views of each other and promote mutual understanding (Kupermintz & Salomon, 2005).

The contact hypothesis was first defined by Allport (1954), who stated that contact situations, which provide equal status between the participants, cooperation in pursuit of common goals, and institutional support, should lead to improved intergroup relations. Over the years the hypothesis has been redefined and a growing number of additional conditions have been added (Amir, 1969). However, most of the studies have been quantitative in nature and concentrated on testing and refining the relevant conditions. While this approach is useful to a certain extent, it runs the risk of turning the contact hypothesis into an "ever-expandable laundry list," which is very cumbersome and hard to implement (Pettigrew, 1998). It may be more helpful to look at the conditions proposed by the contact hypothesis in terms of facilitating change rather than as essential factors for change (Pettigrew & Tropp, 2006). As a result, attention has turned to consideration of not only when but also how and why contact works. The importance of both quantity and quality of contact has been accentuated. In addition, emotional, situational, and contextual variables alongside cognitive variables present before and during the contact situation have been emphasized (Hewstone & Brown, 2005; Stephan & Stephan, 1996). Quantitative studies that consider conflict-affected settings have pointed to the importance of emotional aspects and anxiety-reducing mechanisms (Niens, Cairns, & Hewstone, 2003; Paolini, Hewstone, Cairns, & Voci, 2004), as well as the broader context for the outcomes of contact (Bloomer & Weinreich, 2003; O'Connor, Hartop, & McCully, 2003; Smith & Dunn, 1990; Toner, 1995).

However, due to the nature of the research and the limited information gathered by quantitative methods, studies to date have not fully accounted for the importance of the contexts within which contact takes place (Salomon, 2004; Smith & Dunn, 1990). There has been some qualitative research that started to address and uncover the complexity and the meaning of the context in peace-promoting contact work. Nevertheless, this work has focused on older participants (Feuerverger, 1997; Sagy, 2002) or did not fully engage in consideration of younger children's perspectives of contact work (Kilpatrick & Leitch, 2004).

Relatively few studies have looked at the perspectives of primary school children. One such study was mainly exploratory and delineated ten- to eleven-year-old children's competency in engaging with issues of their everyday life (Connolly & Maginn, 1999). They concluded that the contact program was rather unsuccessful because children's previous experiences were not considered. Therefore, this chapter aims to contribute further to this body of knowledge by drawing upon a case study of a contact program for ten- to eleven-year-old ethnic Macedonian children in a city faced with interethnic tensions in the Republic of Macedonia, using ethnographic methodology. By drawing together the theoretical work of Bronfenbrenner (1992) and Bourdieu (1977), it suggests a theoretical framework that may be of use in helping to understand the importance of consideration of the wider context within which children and contact schemes are located.

This chapter will start by outlining the alternative theoretical frameworks. The data from the case study will then be used to support the theoretical implications for planned contact interventions. Drawing upon both data and theory, this chapter concludes by considering the implications of the findings for contact based peace education work.

Alternative Theoretical Frameworks

Bronfenbrenner's (1979) bioecological system theory helps us understand the multilayered and interrelated nature of the social contexts within which children are located. This is important for the present case study, which shows how children's experiences in the context of school, family, and elsewhere interrelate and play an important role in how children respond to a contact program. According to Bronfenbrenner (1992), human development is a result of two-way interplay between the characteristics of the active person and the characteristics of the dynamic environment because each person is tightly embedded within the environment. The developmental context is conceived as a "set of nested structures, each inside the other like a set of Russian dolls" (Bronfenbrenner, 1979, p. 3). Therefore, understanding the connections and interactions between different settings is important in comprehending a child's views and behaviors, as they form the basis of human development.

The first setting is the microsystem that contains the developing person and all the roles, activities, and interpersonal interaction in a given face-to-face setting, such as families, peer groups, and school classes. Within the microsystem, the change and development of one member can instigate change in the other members as well. In addition, each person is a part of many microsystems and they all interact with each other forming mesosystems. The personal characteristics, views, and behaviors are formed through the complex, synergistic, interactive effects that happen within the mesosystems. As a result of the different mesosystems formed between the classroom as a microsystem and the various other microsystems children belong to, each child has a different schooling experience.

Furthermore, the microsystems and mesosystems are in constant interaction with exosystems, which do not contain the developing person, but events in these systems can have indirect effects on the individual as they filter into the microsystems. Examples of exosystems systems are parents' jobs and peers' families. All these systems are influenced by the macrosystem, which sets the overall content, belief system, and interpersonal interactions as a societal blueprint of a certain culture or subculture (Bronfenbrenner, 1979, 1992).

In addition, each child is an active agent of their own development. They internalize the external information, during which the external content is transformed, according to the subjective human experience and perception of the context. The internal processes are called proximal processes. These interactive processes instigate activities slightly beyond the child's developmental level and drive the development forward (Bronfenbrenner & Ceci, 1994).

Although bioecological system theory can help in understanding the complex developmental environment and the factors stemming from it (Darling, 2007), it is lacking a clear notion of the structure of the developmental outcomes on an individual level. Bourdieu's (1977) notion of habitus can help fill the gap.

The habitus is a product of the social world and social relationships, but it is incorporated into the individual in a system of permanent dispositions (Bourdieu, 1990). As such, the habitus provides the much-needed internal reflection of the environmental context serving as an internal organizing structure that guides the human behavior, lacking in Bronfenbrenner's (1992) theory. The habitus provides the basis for the ways in which individuals approach, view, and act in the social world, developed through a constant interaction within a particular environment. The habitualized way of approaching the social world is reinforced over time by other individuals within the same mesosystems. However, that does not mean that the habitus is a simple reproduction of the social factors. It is powerfully generative because it transforms the social conditions of its own production in a relatively unpredictable and individual way (Bourdieu, 1993). For example, the understanding of ethnic relations and the pictures of each ethnic group are formed by drawing upon available information in the microsystems that a child inhabits coupled with their transformation and structuring inside the mind. When the habitus is formed, it guides future behavior and reactions toward people from different ethnic groups. However, the behavior in a particular situation of contact with members of the other group cannot be predicted, as the subjects are free to make decisions about their own behavior. Nevertheless, their choices are somewhat determined by what they already know and what they have already tried in similar situations.

Bourdieu's theory has been criticized for being too deterministic because the habitus can be seen as a system of durable dispositions closely tied to a social environment that limits individual's reactions (Jenkins, 1992). On the other hand, changes in the habitus are possible through experiences that will enable individuals to understand their dispositions and achieve a relative closure of the system of their dispositions before building new dispositions (Bourdieu & Wacquant, 1992).

As both theories emphasize, children are active agents of their own development and changes in their habitus are possible in carefully planned interventions. This is important because every contact program forms another microsystem for each child and it interacts with other microsystems that they are already part of to form different mesosystems. As such, the effects of the program will vary depending on the children's experiences in other contexts and their habitus. Successful changes can be achieved if the program engages with the broader context and children's habitus to provide opportunities for gradual change.

Consequently, to engage with the broader context and understand the children's experiences, this study adopted open ethnographic methods of study. Children were given the chance to express themselves. The study was conducted in a city in the Republic of Macedonia that experienced violent conflict in 2001 and is still experiencing tensions. It concentrated on exploring the context of the contact work with thirty-five Macedonian children (ten- to eleven-years-old). The work was carried out in the 2006 to 2007 school year over a period of four months. During that time, observations of the regular school days as well as the organized contact situation were carried out. In addition, semistructured interviews were carried out. These started with questions about what children like to do, how they feel during contact and similar ones, and moving onto exploring children's experiences. The interviews were conducted with groups of three or four children at a time. Each child was interviewed at least twice to capture children's experiences and perceptions of the program.

The data analysis was carried out in several stages. Initially, descriptive codes emerged and were assigned to the data. After connections between the descriptive codes were established, they were linked to theoretical framework to achieve better explanations and reach conclusions. A qualitative software package, MaxQda2, was used to achieve better systematization and rigor of the coding process.

In the next section, the broader context and the children's experiences of it will be outlined before presenting the children's views of the contact program.

The Context of the Work in the Republic of Macedonia

The Republic of Macedonia is a country inhabited by people from different ethnic, cultural, linguistic, and religious background. According to the census of population, households and dwellings (State Statistical Office, 2005), 64 percent of the whole population is comprised of Macedonians, 25 percent Albanians, and 11 percent other ethnic groups. The groups' ethnicities coincide with cultural, religious, and language differences, which make communication between people from different ethnicities difficult. Moreover, the structure of the population varies around the country. The majority of the Albanians live in the northwestern parts of the country, and in some parts they comprise more than 80 percent of the population. In some Eastern parts of the country, there are places with no Albanians. The residential segregation is becoming more obvious as time passes because people tend to live in ethnically homogenous neighborhoods.

This diversity and uneven distribution of the population combined with the lack of social interaction have made the Macedonians and the

Albanians "hostages" of ethnic tensions. Communication between the two groups is fairly limited and interethnic dialogue is marked by intolerance, suspicion, and mistrust. The tensions resulted in violent conflict in 2001. The main violence happened in the predominantly Albanian areas in the northwestern part of the country. The violent outburst ended with the signing of the Ohrid Framework Agreement (Balalovska, Silj, & Zucconi, 2002). However, tensions still exist in some regions as Macedonians and Albanians interpret and perceive the agreement differently (Brunnbauer, 2002). The situation in the country, as a macrosystem, provides the overall context in which different smaller systems are located and creates the overall atmosphere in which children develop.

The educational system itself has been largely influenced by politics in the country and by community relations. The educational system has long been one of the major contributors to the *de facto* ethnic segregation in the country. The minority students have attended classes in their mother language resulting in very limited contact between primary school Macedonian and Albanian children (Myhrvold, 2005). Studies have shown that primary school children appear to live in parallel worlds, knowing very little about the other group and showing very few signs of willingness to cooperate (Brusset & Otto, 2004; Najchevska, Simoska, & Gaber, 2001).

The primary school "Pitu Guli,"[1] which forms the microsystem for the children in this study, caters to Macedonian children. It is located in a city with a mixed population, which was deeply affected by the violent conflict outburst in 2001 and still experiences high interethnic tensions (Muzurovic, Frank, & Gurcinovski, 2002). It is important to note that the school shares the school building with another school that caters to Albanian children. Although the building is the same and the school yard is mutual, the corridor is separated by a metal door that has not been opened for years. The strategy that the two schools adopt is one of avoiding the problems rather than addressing them. For example, the schools have a specific schedule for who uses the yard in which period of the day and who keeps the children separated from each other during breaks, arrivals, and departure. The children from both schools arrive and leave the school fifteen minutes apart from each other so that they do not meet in the school yard. When I asked the staff about keeping the children apart, the majority mentioned that it is the only way of preventing incidents between the children. As one teacher explained, she tries to keep the children inside during break time because the Albanians sometimes try to take their football. She said that she has more peace of mind if they are inside because bigger incidents, such as fights, can be prevented.

While conducting the fieldwork, the author noted that the school was a tense environment and incidents occurred. The incidents tended to be the only experiences that the children have of the shared yard and of their peers from the other school. The situation within this microsystem is reflected in the children's perception and explanation of the situation and their relationship with the children from the other school. In this context most of the children appear to accept the segregation that exists. Thus, over time, the children from the neighboring school become "the other" and a threat, which becomes incorporated in their habitus. This can be seen in the following interview:

> *Ana*: How often do you play football?
> *Jovan*: Well, about half an hour.
> *Boban*: When the teacher lets us play.
> *Boban*: No. Rarely.
> *Toni*: No.
> *Ana*: Why does she not allow you to go out?
> *Boban*: Well, if it is cold, we don't go out.
> *Jovan*: Well, maybe we will start to argue with the Shiptari (derogatory term used for the ethnic Albanians).
> *Boban*: Yes, yes.
> *Ana*: Well, who are they? Why do you argue with each other?
> *Jovan*: Well, they are Shiptari; they hit us.
> *Boban*: They are big.
> *Jovan*: They want to hit us, and that is why we run away.
> *Ana*: And where are they from?
> *Jovan*: Well, they study in this school (points to the building next to them)
> *Boban*: They study in this other school next to us.
> *Ana*: Are they older than you?
> *Jovan*: Yes.
> *Boban*: Well, in our shift they are older, and our older children are in the same shift with their younger ones.
> *Ana*: Do you often fight with each other?
> *Boban*: Yes.
> *Toni*: Yes.
> *Jovan*: Yes.
> *Ana*: When was the last time it happened?
> *Jovan*: Well, three, few days ago.
> *Boban*: Four [or] five days ago.
> *Toni*: Well, today we were close to fighting but Marina and I escaped.

This schooling experience usually interacts with children's family microsystems forming mesosystems, and the results are visible in the children's habitus. Most of them are able to competently connect their own experience with the children from the other school with the prejudiced statement they are hearing in their families. Over time, children draw upon reinforcement of their own negative views received within such mesosystems. The majority of the children in this study have come to internalize their experiences in coherent and taken-for-granted ways of thinking and behaving toward the Albanians as a group, and that became incorporated in the children's habitus that has formed its habitus. The mesosystems they belong to provide fertile soil for internalizing and expressing prejudiced views. This can be seen in the following interview in which one child clearly connects the situation between the schools with what his grandmother says about Albanians:

> *Ana*: There is another school next to yours. Do you play with the children from that school?
> *Krste*: No.
> *Mite*: No.
> *Nenad*: No. Rarely. Maybe if we know someone.
> *Ana*: Why not?
> *Krste*: They will hit us.
> *Nenad*: They will make fun of us, tease us, and hit us.
> *Mite*: They are more numerous.
> *Nenad*: Sometimes they carry knives.
> *Ana*: Why do you think that happens?
> *Nenad*: Well because they are…I don't want to say it.
> *Mite*: They are taught that way.
> *Ana*: Nenad, tell me what you think. It is nothing to be afraid of.
> *Nenad*: They are animals. (He makes an angry expression on his face.)
> *Mite*: I think they are taught that way at home.
> *Ana*: What are they taught at home?
> *Nenad*: In Albania they are more polite, and here they carry knives, take drugs.
> *Ana*: You mentioned Albania. How are the children from the other school connected to Albania?
> *Nenad*: Well, they are Albanians.
> *Mite*: Oooh, they are not.
> *Ana*: You don't think they are Albanians. What are they then?
> *Mite*: There is a difference between Albanians and Shiptari.
> *Ana*: Can you explain the difference to me?
> *Mite*: The Shiptari came from the mountains during the war (he means the First and Second World War), and the Albanians stayed in their country. Shiptari are more like wild and Albanians are better. That is what my grandmother says.
> *Ana*: And who lives here?
> *Nenad*: Well, now they want to turn themselves into Albanians.

However, not all children had only negative experiences. For some children, their other microsystems, such as the family and their Albanian peers, provide positive experiences. Subsequently, their habitus incorporates a more diverse picture of the Albanians. For example, in the following extract, they try to reconcile their positive experiences with the negative experiences and information they receive from the environment:

> *Ana*: Now I want to talk about the people from this city. Can you tell me more?

Nenad: There are people which are bad, and there are people which are good.
Ana: There are good and bad people?
Nenad: Well, Macedonians are good. I mean, Macedonians are better than the Albanians.
Ana: Why are they better?
Nenad: Actually, no. Albanians are better than the Macedonians because an Albanian gave my father a tool box and some other present as well, another tool. He gave him, everything he gave him. There is no Macedonian that would do such a thing; instead, a Macedonian would fight with him.
Ana: Well, I don't understand [why] you said Albanians fight, now Macedonians fight…
Nenad (interrupts me): Yes, but the older Albanians, some of them are bad, some of them are good. It not that there are only bad Albanians.
Ana: So, there are bad and good Albanians?
Toni: When Albanians drive, they let us go first, they tell us with hands [that] we should go first, then they go.
Ana: So, there are good Albanians as well and you cooperate with them?
Nenad: Yes, we do. For example, Sedat and I today…Well, I have a computer and CD writer, and I will make copies of some games, and I will call that one Albanian Sedat we are friends [with], and we will sell something together, cooperation.

As such, these positive examples and experiences coming from the microsystems (i.e., peer groups), as well as exosystems (i.e., parent's job), are something that could potentially provide opportunities for exploration during educational peace programs. The programs could draw upon children's experiences in different contexts to exploit the contradictions that exist between different microsystems. In turn, this might help the children within the school to develop more inclusive ways of thinking and to gradually develop a more inclusive habitus. By giving the children time and space to share their positive experiences, drawing upon those and reconciling them with their negative experiences, the children could come to realize that each ethnic group is more diverse and that more positive mutual relations are possible. Contact programs could potentially aim at exploring those issues during contact encounters. However, as discussed in the next section, the task has proven difficult for the two neighboring schools.

The Contact Program

The fragile situation has made it difficult to organize any sort of contact program between the schools. They have experienced difficulty in maintaining the program due to the lack of cooperation between them. The first attempt to organize a contact program was part of a project organized by a nongovernmental organization that aimed to build networks of schools for multicultural understanding and that focused on interschool relations. However, the school catering for Albanian children withdrew from the 2005 to 2006 program after a few joint activities. As a result, the Pitu Guli school had to maintain the contact with an Albanian school from another city. The 2006 to 2007 program, which was studied and is presented in this paper, was an attempt to reestablish the 2005 to 2006 initiative between the two neighboring schools.

The planned contact has been motivated by the incidents in the playground and outside the schools between the children from both schools. The main idea was to use a planned contact program to help the children build more amicable relationships, but with a topic that will not touch upon interschool relations. Therefore, the work concentrated on raising nonsmoking awareness. The withdrawal of the Albanian school was used to support the 2006 to 2007 program's orientation toward issues that are less contrived. The program has been segregated from regular school activities, and not all staff and children are involved, breaking one of the Allport's (1954) conditions for institutional support of contact. Moreover, during the contact encounter, Macedonian language was used more frequently, as it is the language that both groups of children understand, giving the Macedonian children a slightly better status within the contact situation.

Even though the mutual encounters were brief and oriented toward accomplishment of certain tasks, such as origami ornaments, they provided a positive atmosphere. This was in stark contrast to many of the previous yard encounters, which the children recalled were filled with animosity. Therefore, the children tried to find out more about their peers from the other school by sitting next to them or trying to work on the same task. Their higher status, coupled with the positive encounter, resulted in initial excitement, which can be seen in the following interview:

> *Ana*: What did you like about most of the activities that you were involved in a while ago?
> *Jovan*: Well, we made cups, decorations.
> *Marija*: We made presents, we were having good time with the Albanians.
> *Ema*: Yes.
> *Ana*: Marija mentioned Albanians. Did you meet them?
> *Ema*: They were good.
> *Jovan*: Yes, and they were very good.
> *Ema*: They were also making presents.
> *Jovan*: They were helping us.
> *Ana*: Did you talk to them?
> *Jovan*: Yes.
> *Ema*: Yes, and I also helped her. She helped me. We were cutting together.

Dona: Well, we were writing on a board. She asked us some questions, translated some words in Albanian.
Ana: Did you talk about something else?
Jovan: Well, we talked, cut, glued together.
Ana: So, what do you think about the children from the other school?
Ema: Some of them are bad, and some of them are good.
Dona: Some of them are good.
Ema: Some are friendly.
Marija: Well, there are no bad children. If we tease them, they will tease back, I guess.

The contact provided the children with an opportunity to realize that mutual encounters with the children from the other school could be friendly. However, as it is evident in the interview, the children only talk about activities that they did together. Those activities did not involve much talking and, therefore, may have failed to provide the opportunities for development of closer friendships by lacking the acquaintance potential of contact that Allport (1954) emphasized. There was a lack of opportunity for getting to know each other better; however, the next interview suggests that this was something the children wanted:

Ana: Did you learn anything about those children?
Ilina: Well, no, we played games together. We didn't talk, we just played.
Ana: Did you ask them anything, did you make friends?
Ilina: Well, we were together for a short time. We were playing showing our masks, and then we had to go, because the older children had to come.
Ana: Did you want to know more about them?
Ilina: Yes, but unfortunately I couldn't.

In addition to not complying with all of the conditions for contact specified by Allport (1954), these experiences were relatively isolated from children's everyday life in their other microsystems. The children did not have enough opportunities to engage with their peers from the other school and to explore each other's views, ways of life, and behavior. They could not connect this isolated experience with their everyday schooling experience or their experience outside of school. Therefore, the program did not create a mesosystem for the children that could have given them opportunities to reconsider their old, habitualized ways of thinking about and behaving toward their peers from the other school. When back in their old microsystem of separated schooling, the children continued to use the derogative term *Shiptari* around their peers and did not share their experiences with their classmates. This may have occurred because they could not see how and why their experience was important or appropriate.

However, the children themselves recognize the need to be engaged in contact that will allow them to engage in deeper exploration of the issues and problems they are faced with in the everyday context of school life. The majority of the children want answers and solutions to their everyday problems with their neighbors. They want something that would help them have more peaceful relationships with their peers from the other school and put a stop to the incidents in the yard, leading to more amicable mutual relations and gradual changes in their habitus:

> *Ana*: Well, if you are together for longer, what would you like to talk about with them?
> *Sanja*: I would like to talk about kindness.
> *Ana*: Whose kindness?
> *Sanja*: Well, because they always tease us when we go on break. For example, the other day I went out with the boys, and some children from the other school tried to take our ball and make us play in a different part of the yard.
> *Ana*: So, why do you think it would help if you talk about kindness?
> *Sanja*: They would stop teasing us.
> *Ana*: So, what would you ask them about kindness?
> *Sanja*: Well, I would ask them why they tease us so much, why can't we be friends, how can we become friends instead of enemies.

Conclusion

This study provides some evidence that children are active agents of their own development. They tend to seek information from their environment that they deem relevant for their understanding and organize it in coherent units. The information that they receive comes from different sources, and there is certainly an interaction between the information from those sources, which shape children's habitus and their consequent understanding, views, and behavior.

The current study is limited in scope due to the small number of cases involved and concentrating only on the perspectives of one ethnic group. Nevertheless, the main aim was to gain a deeper understanding of children's perspectives, their perceptions of the context in which they develop, and the way in which that context interacts with their experiences of contact programs. As such, the study brings to light the limitations of change in relation to the broader relations between the groups that impact children's habitus and set the context of contact programs. It, therefore, emphasizes the need for a deeper understanding of the environment before any planned contact is organized and advocates contact situations that enable the children to gradually explore issues of their interest on their own terms. As a result of the current study, there may be several implications for the school-based peace education efforts for ten- to eleven-year-old children through contact programs in conflict-affected societies.

The limitations for contact work, which stem from the broader environment and the overall atmosphere in which contact happens, need to be understood as they are reflected in children's habitus and experiences of contact. Given that the importance of the overall context has been emphasized by both Bronfenbrenner (1979) and Bourdieu (1990) as well as authors exploring the contact hypothesis (Hewstone & Brown, 2005; Stephan & Stephan, 1996), contact programs should pay attention to the events happening in the environment. These can hamper or facilitate positive change and should be explored during contact, in a nonthreatening manner. Keeping in mind the children's active engagement in their own development, the contact should be organized in a way that will provide opportunities for each child to become involved in a process of exploration of the events in their environment, which provide the context for their reactions. It is therefore very important that the process is gradual and that it does not try to introduce something that is idealistic and too far away from the influences of the environment (Connnolly & Maginn, 1999) and the children's habitus.

The children should be helped to understand the events in the mesosystems they are part of, which provide the basis for the formation of their habitus. The process should also enable deconstruction of the habitualized pictures of other group and build on some of the children's positive experiences with the other group. In such a situation, sharing their different experiences in different contexts can be used as a starting point for deconstructing the picture of "the other." By organizing contact situations that satisfy Allport's (1954) conditions of contact and allow the children to explore issues of their interest on their own terms and pace, each child's positive experience and change can be used to guide their peer's thinking and motivate them toward more amicable and diversified thinking.

Note

1. For anonymity purposes, the names of the school and the children used in the chapter are pseudonyms.

References

Allport, G. W. (1954). *The nature of prejudice*. Reading: Addison-Wesley.
Amir, Y. (1969). Contact hypothesis in ethnic relations. *Psychological Bulletin, 71*(5), 319–342.
Balalovska, K., Silj, A., & Zucconi, M. (2002). *Minority politics in Southeastern Europe: Crisis in Macedonia*. Rome: Ethnobarometer, International Research Network on Interethnic Policies and Migration.
Bekerman, Z., & McGlynn, C. (2007). Introduction. In Z. Bekerman & C. McGlynn (Eds.), *Addressing ethnic conflict through peace education* (pp. 1–5). New York: Palgrave Macmillan.
Bloomer, F. & Weinreich, P. (2003). Cross-community relations projects and interdependent identities. In O. Hargie & D. Dickson (Eds.), *Researching the troubles: Social science perspectives on the Northern Ireland conflict* (pp. 141–161). Edinburgh: Mainstream.

Bourdieu, P. (1977). *Outline of a theory of practice*. Cambridge: Cambridge University Press.
Bourdieu, P. (1990). *The logic of practice*. Cambridge: Polity Press.
Bourdieu, P. (1993). *Sociology in question*. London: Sage.
Bourdieu, P., & Wacquant, L. J. D. (1992). *An invitation to reflexive sociology*. Cambridge: Polity Press.
Bronfenbrenner, U. (1979). *The ecology of human development: Experiments by nature and design*. Cambridge: Harvard University Press.
Bronfenbrenner, U. (1992). Ecological systems theory. In R. Vasta (Ed.), *Six theories of child development: Revised formulations and current issues* (pp. 187–249). London: Jessica Kingsley.
Bronfenbrenner, U., & Ceci, S. J. (1994). Nature-nurture reconceptualized in developmental perspective: A bioecological model. *Psychological review, 101*(4), 568–586.
Brunnbauer, U. (2002). The implementation of Ohrid Agreement: Ethnic Macedonian resentment. *Journal of Ethnopolitics and Minority Issues in Europe, 1*. Retrieved November, 8, 2007, from http://www.ecmi.de/jemie/download/Focus1-2002Brunnbauer.pdf
Brusset, E., & Otto, R. (2004). *Evaluation of Nashe Maalo: Design, implementation and outcomes: Social transformation through the media*. Retrieved November 1, 2005, from http://www.sfcg.org/sfcg/evaluations/nash2004.pdf
Bush, K. D., & Saltareli, D. (2000). *The two faces of education in ethnic conflict: Towards a peacebuilding education for children*. Florence: Innocenti Research Centre.
Connolly, P., & Maginn, P. (1999). *Sectarianism, children and community relations in Northern Ireland*. University of Ulster: Centre for the Study of Conflict.
Darling, N. (2007). Ecological system theory: The person in the center of the circles. *Research in human development, 4*(3/4), 203–217.
Feuerverger, G. (1997). An educational program for peace: Jewish-Arab conflict resolution in Israel. *Theory into Practice, 36*(1), 17–25.
Hewstone, M., & Brown, R. (2005). An integrative theory of intergroup contact. In M.P. Zanna (Ed.), *Advances in experimental social psychology vol. 37* (pp. 255–343). Oxford: Elsevier Academic Press.
Jenkins, R. (1992). *Key sociologists: Pierre Bourdieu*. London: Routledge.
Kilpatrick, R., & Leitch, R. (2004). Teachers' and pupils' educational experiences and school based responses to the conflict in Northern Ireland. *Journal of Social Issues, 60*(3), 563–586.
Kupermintz, H., & Salomon, G. (2005). Lessons to be learned from research on peace education in the context of intractable conflict. *Theory into Practice, 44*(4), 293–302.
Muzurovic, L., Frank, J., & Gurcinovski, S. (2002). *Fact finding mission to Macedonia*. Vienna: International Helsinki Federation for Human Rights. Retrieved November, 1, 2005, from http://www.ihf-hr.org/viewbinary/viewdocument.php?doc_id=829
Myhrvold, R. (2005). *Former Yugoslav Republic of Macedonia: Education as a political phenomenon*. Oslo: Norwegian Centre for Human Rights.
Najchevska, M., Simoska, E., & Gaber, N. (2001). *Sources and factors of ethnic tension in the educational process*. Skopje: Institute for Sociological, Political and Judicial Research.

Niens, U., Cairns, E., & Hewstone, M. (2003). Contact and conflict in Northern Ireland. In O. Hargie & D. Dickson (Eds.), *Researching the troubles: Social science perspectives on the Northern Ireland conflict* (pp. 123–139). Edinburgh: Mainstream.

O'Connor, U., Hartop, B., & McCully, A. (2003). *A research study of pupils perceptions of the schools community relations programme.* Belfast: Department of Education Northern Ireland.

Paolini, S., Hewstone, M., Cairns, E., & Voci, A. (2004). Effects of direct and indirect cross-group friendships on judgements of Catholic and Protestant in Northern Ireland: The mediating role of an anxiety-reduction mechanism. *Personality and Social Psychology Bulletin, 30*(6), 770–786.

Pettigrew, T. F. (1998). Intergroup contact theory. *Annual review of psychology, 49,* 65–85.

Pettigrew, T, F., & Tropp, L. R. (2006). A meta-analytic test of intergroup contact theory. *Journal of Personality and Social Psychology, 90*(5), 751–783.

Sagy, S. (2002). Intergroup encounters between Jewish and Arab students in Israel: Towards an interactionist approach. *Intercultural Education, 13*(3), 259–274.

Salomon, G. (2004). Does peace education make a difference in the context of an intractable conflict? *Peace and Conflict: Journal of Peace Psychology, 10*(3), 257–274.

Shapiro, S. (2002). Towards a critical pedagogy of peace education. In G. Salomon & B. Nevo (Eds.), *Peace education: The concept, principles, and practices around the world* (pp. 63–71). Mahwah: Lawrence Erlbaum Associates.

Smith, A., & Dunn, S. (1990). *Extending inter school links: An evaluation of contact between protestant and catholic pupils in Northern Ireland.* University of Ulster: Centre for the Study of Conflict.

State Statistical Office. (2005). *Census of population, households and dwellings in the Republic of Macedonia 2002, book XII.* Retrieved November, 26, 2007, from http://www.stat.gov.mk/pdf/kniga_13.pdf

Stephan, W. G., & Stephan, C. W. (1996). *Intergroup relations.* Boulder: Westview Press.

Toner, I. J. (1995). Temporary residential cohabitation of children from Northern Ireland. *Irish Journal of Psychology, 16*(1), 67–82.

Chapter 7

"Smoking Doesn't Kill; It Unites!"
Cultural Meanings and Practices of "Mixing" at the Gymnasium Mostar in Bosnia and Herzegovina

Azra Hromadzic

Introduction

This anthropological study examines the meanings and practices of "mixing" among youth at the Gymnasium Mostar in Bosnia and Herzegovina (B&H).[1] I use the local term *miješanje*, or mixing, to describe instances of "border-crossing" among youth of different ethnic groups at the school. Furthermore, I look at formal and informal spaces of *miješanje* and I portray novel boundaries of intimacy reflected in processes of making friends, coffee drinking, and dating. In addition, I describe fears, tensions, resistances, and obstacles to mixing that reflect changes in the social environment. I understand mixing as multileveled processes of interaction and relationship building among ethnically divided people in a post-conflict society. Processes of mixing simultaneously take place on the individual, communal, and societal levels, often with different intensities. For example, while some forms of mixing are tolerated or even encouraged in one context, they are socially or culturally forbidden in others. In what follows, I illustrate the *how, why, who, when,* and *where* of mixing in order to discover its local logic and to map out emerging forms of social relations among the youth in B&H.

A Brief Introduction to Bosnia and Herzegovina and the Gymnasium Mostar

Short History of B&H

The Socialist Federal Republic of Yugoslavia (SFRY; 1945–91) was a federation of six republics: Slovenia, Croatia, B&H, Serbia (with two autonomous regions Kosovo and Vojvodina), Montenegro, and Macedonia. The country emerged after the Second World War under the ironfist leadership of Tito, who spent most of his energy trying to balance the power between the two largest nations in SFRY, Serbia and Croatia. B&H was the most ethnically diverse of all Yugoslav republics. It included 43.5 percent Bosnian Muslims (Bosniaks)[2], 31.2 percent Bosnian Serbs, 17.4 percent Bosnian Croats and 7.9 percent others (Federalni Zavod za Statistiku, 1991).

After the death of Tito in 1980, the tension between the republics increased, culminating in the declaration of independence by Slovenia and Croatia in June of 1991. B&H found itself in a position where it had to choose between independence (supported by Bosniaks and Croats) and remaining in the Yugoslav federation (supported by the Serbs). B&H became an independent state on April 6, 1992 (Malcolm, 1996) On the same day that B&H was officially recognized, the Serbian paramilitary units and the Yugoslav People's Army (JNA) attacked the B&H's capital, Sarajevo. With the help of men and weapons from Serbia and its president Milošević, this army succeeded in conquering close to 70 percent of the country's territory. The seizing of territory included some of the most brutal acts of violence exercised against the non-Serb populations, which involved mass killings, ethnic cleansing, forced migration, and rape.

Toward the end of 1992, the war between previously cooperating armies of Croats and Bosniaks erupted in central B&H, causing additional bloodshed and damage (Malcolm, 1996). A quasi-state of Croats was established during the war in the Croat-dominated areas (Malcolm, 1996). One of the major sites of Bosniak-Croat violence was the city of Mostar (Malcolm,1996). In March 1994, the Washington Peace Agreement brought "peace" between Croats and Bosniaks, and it led to the creation of the Bosniak-Croat Federation (Lovrenović, 2001). The war in the rest of the country continued, however, causing further bloodshed and expulsions. After more than three years of bloody conflict, 200,000 deaths, and the displacing of 1.5 million people as refugees, on December 14, 1995, the Dayton Peace Agreement brought an end to the Bosnian war. While claiming to have as its objectives reconciliation, democracy, power-sharing, and ethnic pluralism, in the eyes of its critics, the agreement inscribed in law the ethnic partitioning of Serbs, Croats, and Bosniaks (Campbell, 1999; Chandler, 2000). It divided B&H into two entities: the Federation of B&H (FB&H), with a 51 percent share of the territory, and inhabited by mostly Bosniaks and Croats; and Republic Srpska (RS), with

49 percent of the territory, and populated almost exclusively by Serbs. Further, the agreement separated the FB&H into ten cantons, with little intermixing between the ethnic groups.[3] The collapse of Yugoslavia was particularly destructive in Mostar; the JNA attacked Mostar from the eastern hills of the city, driving the inhabitants to the western part of town in search of shelter. During this time, the greater part of Serbs left the town, leaving behind a few Serb families. After initially defending the city against JNA forces jointly, fighting then broke out between Croats and Bosniaks leading to the complete division of the town into a Croat-dominated western part and a Bosniak-dominated eastern side (Vetters, 2007). The destruction of the Old Bridge in November 1994 cemented this physical and symbolic segregation between the two communities, which continues until present.

Gymnasium Mostar

During the war, the centralized educational system became fragmented along ethnonational lines. Almost immediately, education was turned into a tool for the political control and advancement of nationalist ideologies. The Dayton Peace Agreement brought an end to the shelling of school buildings, but it also reinforced the fragmentation and decentralization in education created during the war. The International Community (IC),[4] in charge of the democratization efforts in B&H, made the reintegration of ethnically segregated schools and reconciliation among ethnically divided young people the main goals of successful nation building in B&H. Among the first schools to be integrated was the Mostar Gymnasium, which is my primary ethnographic site.

In 1999, when the city was still divided into Croat and Bosniak municipalities, the Croat-dominated city council transferred authority over the school to the Croat political leaders (Organization for Security and Co-operation in Europe [OSCE], 2005). The Croat leadership in Mostar almost immediately set about some small-scale repair work and began teaching 257 students using the Croat curricula and Croat language (OSCE, 2005). Meanwhile, the Bosniak leaders established a temporary high school in an old neighborhood on the east side (OSCE, 2005).

For the IC and a number of citizens of Mostar, the Gymnasium Mostar continues to rank among the most important symbols of prewar coexistence and postwar social reconstruction in B&H. In the Gymnasium Mostar, the IC saw an opportunity to reintegrate the school and "undo the Croat strategy of separation, to engineer the reunification of the city, and to establish a showcase example of the benefits of cross-communal coexistence and cooperation" (Wimmen, 2003 p. 5).

After several years of heated negotiations, demonstrations, petitions, and the investment of large sums of money in reconstruction, the school was finally reunited on an administrative level in February 2004. In September of the same year and for the first time since 1991, Bosniak and Croat students began attending the same school (OSCE, 2005). The two schools became one administratively unified school but with separate instruction in all subjects. In practice, this means that reunification has maintained separate national curricula for the students of the two ethnic groups, thus preserving ethnic segregation through unification. The rest of this chapter focuses on the relations among ethnically segregated youth at the school, and it illustrates uncertain but hopeful moments of making, breaking, stretching, exploring, and continuously reasserting boundaries of belonging in post-conflict countries struggling on their path to democracy.

Theorizing Mixing

Numerous scholars within the field of anthropology have been studying the nature of contact and exchange among groups of people differently positioned in relation to power. Recent interest in globalization in general and global and local dynamics in particular has spurred research in a variety of domains, notably on ethnicity and notions of belonging. Barth's (1969) seminal work on the "character of ethnic boundaries" (p. 9) that persist despite flows [of people] across them (Barth, 1969) initiated multiple works on the notions of ethnicity, identity, and group boundaries that continue into the present day. The notion of mixing, however, has been surprisingly absent from these studies. While philosophers and political scientists have been debating about moral obligations and political implications of ethnic mixing in liberal democracies (Taylor, 1994; Trappenburg, 2003), anthropologists have stayed outside of this debate and left the idea of mixing empirically and theoretically uncultivated. One exception is the work of Khan (2004) in which she examines the creation of the Trinidad's nation and where she argues that "the notion of mixing holds central importance in forming interpretations of identity and self-worth, of place in the world, and therefore interpreting the quality of relations among individuals, communities, nation-states, and religions" (p. 3). Building on Khan, in this chapter, I argue that the notions of mixing in B&H are not secondary to the primary interpretative categories, such as ethnicity and democracy, but rather they bring to life the categories that are supposed to give rise to them. In other words, practices and ideologies of (un)mixing and border-crossing give potency and significance to identity categories, such as Croat, Serb, or Bosniak.[5]

While there has been very little theorizing of mixing in anthropology, the term *miješanje* has, at least, a fifty-yearlong tradition in the studies of ex-Yugoslavia. Most frequently, it is related to the phenomenon of ethnically mixed marriages as indicators of social acceptance and lack of discrimination (see Botev & Wagner, 1993; Gagon, 1994. In his analysis of the geography of violence in ex-Yugoslavia, Hayden (1996) proposes that the wars have taken place almost entirely within regions that were among the most mixed ones. Furthermore, he argues that the wars have been about the forced *unmixing* of peoples whose continuing coexistence was counter to the nationalist political ideologies and their force as a dominant prescriptive culture (Hayden, 1996a). The imagined community of mixed Yugoslavs failed, and new, nationalist ideologies of ethnic homogeneity clashed with the ethnically heterogeneous social reality on the ground (Hayden, 1996a), causing bloodshed of enormous proportions. In addition to the bloody conflicts, this clash resulted in the change of the local *culture of mixing*, in terms of its ideology, meanings and practice. This transformation is the main topic of the rest of this paper.

Cultural Meanings and Practices of Mixing
Etymology of Mixing

Miješanje is a word in the Bosnian and Croat languages that is often translated into English as (to) *mix, alloy, blend, meddle, mingle, and stir*.[6] As a reflexive verb, *miješati se* is best translated as "to mix oneself." In addition to the words *miješanje* and *miješati se*, my informants used many other versions of this word, such as *umiješati se* ("to mix [oneself] into something"), *pomiješati* ("to mix two or more components together"), or *mješanac* (a noun, meaning, "the mixed one, the one coming from two different or ethnic parts"). Additionally, students and teachers at the reunified school often mentioned in passing that a certain teacher or student *voli da se miješa* ("likes or loves to mix").

After collecting numerous examples of spoken and unspoken instances of *miješanje*, I started to outline new meanings and boundaries of mixing that differed from the aforementioned studies and that reflected changes in the society since the Yugoslav times. While in the past "to mix" meant to enter a mixed marriage or to be a child from a mixed marriage, today, mixing has a less ambitious application. I collected the following definitions from the students at the school, which clearly demonstrate this change: "At this time and in this situation, to mix would be when I approach a group of students from the Federal Curricula, or if one of them would approach us," or "Mixing...that is when someone spends time with the people of the other ethnic group. That is a rough expression, and we use it in our local, Mostar jargon." In the next section, I move away from the etymology of mixing to spaces in which mixing takes place at the Gymnasium Mostar and beyond.

Spaces of Mixing

There are formal and informal spaces of mixing at the Gymnasium Mostar. Formal spaces of mixing are "no-man's-lands" designed as the "border-crossing" regions in the geography of the school. These spaces are the library, the computer lab, the student council room, the teachers' room, and the student duty room. In addition, there are activities usually initiated by the IC that take place outside the school building, such as extracurricular activities, seminars, and workshops. These places and the activities that occur in them are envisioned by the people in charge, mostly the IC, as *open-to-all*. Their more or less explicit agenda is to help people to confront stereotypes by engaging in common activities and eventually rebuilding the trust between the individuals and groups at the school.

Informal places of *miješanje* emerge spontaneously and often illegally, such as during the forbidden smoking activities in bathrooms.[7] Commenting on the increasing intermingling in the bathroom, one student stated enthusiastically, "Smoking does not kill, it unites!" I spent many hours inhaling illegally produced smoke in one of the two second-floor bathrooms, where Croat and Bosniak seniors have a quick smoke several times a day during the five-minute recesses. Even though mixing became a regular practice in this bathroom, it evolved slowly and carefully, as Dario[8] remembers, "I remember when they [Bosniaks] just came, we would all smoke in the bathroom—we were in the right part, smoking near the toilets, and they, a few Federal guys who smoked, were standing next to the sinks, on the left. Gradually, we all mixed." Little by little, the bathroom emerged as the central place for mixing, as it is captured in the text message I received from one of the students on a day I was absent from school: "Azra, where are you? Today we went to the bathroom, and everyone was there, Ana, Marijana, Ivan, and Jelica from their classroom and many students from our classroom...and we talked to them, and made jokes together. It was so cool! I was sad when the bell [indicating the end of recess] rang. The bathroom rules! Greetings from the best school in the world." During these short breaks, students manage to exchange many conversations, from comparing their class loads to more challenging talks about religion, ethnicity, divisions, and unification.

Spaces and time for informal mixing, however, are so limited that several students who wanted to mix went to the bathroom during the break even though they did not smoke, only "to hang out with them, and see what they are like." Some of the students were so eager to meet the students "from the other side" in spaces other than bathrooms that they asked me for help: "Azra, I thought about this...you sit both in our and their classes...I cannot just go to their classroom and say: 'Here I am.' Would you please introduce me to the guys from IVc [Croatian classroom next door] one of these days?"

This question saddened me, but it also helped me realize how little opportunity to mix and develop meaningful, informal interaction across ethnic lines exists for the youth willing to cross ethnic boundaries at the reunified school. As one student explains, "We have the best time in the bathroom, and I am so glad for it, and I would not exchange the bathroom for any room in the school, but that is not enough...it is not true mixing of thoughts and ideas, but it is just hanging out, not true friendship." The fine line between mixing and hanging out, on the one side, and true friendship, on the other, emerged as an important aspect of the new ethos of mixing.

Frequent seminars, workshops, and trips outside the divided city are potential places where more profound types of mixing could materialize. In the new contexts of seminars, usually a costal town or ski resort, students and teachers are encouraged to leave behind the pressures emerging from the life in the divided city in order to engage in less burdened interactions. These interactions attempt to transgress ethnic divisions by focusing on topics of a common interest, such as the reform of education, new teaching methods, or creation of joint student councils. In a new environment, these ethnically divided citizens can at least temporarily create new forms of a short-term solidarity. A fluid and limited sense of groupness develops based on common interests, similarities, and curiosity, which enables some individuals to, at least temporarily, cross the boundaries of ethnic separation more easily than they would do in their segregated city. While these opportunities open up new spaces for communication across ethnic divides, these meetings simultaneously bring about memories of violence and unresolved wrongdoings in the recent past. This combination of war memories, terror, and tension penetrate new exchanges and challenge the possibility of future friendships. To these fears and anxieties we turn next.

Fears, Memories, and Anxieties of Mixing

The school reunification provided an opportunity for youth to explore new domains of social relationships by interacting with the students of the other ethnic group whom they never had opportunity to meet. The first interactions often initiated the tearing apart of badly sealed wounds from the recent war, which then shaped the behavior of students, often subconsciously. Anisa, who was three-years-old when she was first imprisoned and then forced to walk for twenty miles to freedom, explains,

> *Anisa*: I do not know…I cannot establish any real contact with them. Maja [Anisa's friend] can and she does…I am not capable, not yet.
> *Azra*: What is stopping you?
> *Anisa*: Some feeling, undefined, which I never had before…is it fear, or mistrust, this or that, I simply feel uncomfortable and all I can do is say "hello" to them.

The spatial proximity brings about opportunities to say hello and maybe even start a conversation, as well as to project verbal or physical violence in the shared space of mixing. One day, Melita, who desperately wanted to meet students from the other curriculum, came to me visibly shaken: "Azra, you will not believe what has just happened to me. I walked in front of their classroom where a group of Croat boys were standing, looking at us. I looked back, and one of them told me *mrš* [piss off]! I froze." Melita's experience is not unique. Similarly to students, some teachers experience seminars as both possibilities for rebuilding trust and opportunities to revisit the violent past. A young Bosniak teacher explains her experience at one of the seminars organized for the teachers of both curricula in Neum, a small and impoverished coastal town in B&H. Here, the terror of the past did not come from confronting the teachers of the other curricula but from the presence of other guests at the hotel, which organizers from the IC did not take into account when they planned the seminar. Several teachers complained about this omission:

> I cannot remember exactly…but the name was I think….The Croat War Veterans. They also stayed at the hotel. You cannot imagine the scene…when we arrived, they were in those black shirts, on which it was written *Za dom spremni* ["Ready for the Homeland," the main slogan of the Croat Defense Forces during the Yugoslav wars], and they were holding signs…all cripples, in wheelchairs, without eyes, deformed, with scars marking their faces…initially I felt empathy…but [raises her voice], how deep their *Ustašluk* [Ustaša[9] sentiment] goes?! They started screaming *balija*[10] and cursing *Allah, Muhammad*…10 years passed since then [since the war] Azra, but all that stayed deep inside of them [unintelligible]…and some of the professors from the Croat curriculum felt uncomfortable because of the situation. Azra, that night we were too scared to go out, because they [Croat War Veterans] reserved the main part of the hotel. We circled around the hotel to avoid them. Until four or five in the morning they sang and played music, only *Ustaša* songs.…Every hair on my body was erect…so much fear, so much negative energy…so many years have passed, so much was forgotten, but they…still think like in 1993—crippled but ready to fight, for that something, I do not know what, for some idea of theirs. That is that *duh Ustaštva* [Ustaša spirit] I was telling you about.

In addition to instances of verbal violence, the conflict manifests itself in a shape of written messages, drawings, and graffiti that students write to each other on the bathroom walls or on the pieces of the school furniture they share. The messages are numerous, including the Ustašha signs engraved in the bathroom walls or chairs, and the message such as *Balije, Bog vas jebo* ("Balije, let God fuck you"). While the school management tries to minimize and quietly eliminate these signs as soon as they spot them, messages constantly reemerge, only to be removed again, usually with the hard labor of the cleaning ladies. The existence of these tensions and different forms of everyday violence shaped new relationships among students at *Gymnasium Mostar*. In what follows, I explore the types of relationships and practices subsumed under the category of *miješanje*, which will enable us to grasp its rules, scope, and potential.

New Boundaries and Rules of Mixing

Many students and teachers stressed that mixing does not lead to "true" friendship but that the interactions between the ethnically divided individuals stop at the level of a superficial friendship:

> *N*: Seminars also connected people, because after the official seminar we would go for coffee, drink coffee together. But, when we come back to Mostar, no one goes to coffee with anyone else. No one wants that. Because seminars…they are not about true friendships.
> *I*: And what is true friendship for you?
> *N*: True friendship is when I have a need to call you and have coffee with you, and that I do not have any secrets in front of you, and that I celebrate New Year's and birthday parties with that person and…that you can talk about anything, in a relaxed manner with that person…. Because, with them [Croats] I can talk about a lamp, how nice it is, or about cosmetics, and stuff like that…but about politics and the war you cannot talk to them, because our opinions differ. Because, there are three truths [the Serb, the Croat, and the Bosniak truth] here now, and you have one *narod* [people] whose 8,000 people were slaughtered in Srebrenica[11], but that very same *narod* killed 100 Croats in Drežnica[12], and everyone looks at his or her truth and pain.

This dialogue illustrates multiple dimensions and limitations of mixing. The traditional forms of trust building and mixing in the past, such as frequent coffee drinking, joint celebrations of birthdays and New Year's, and home visits, are not part of the post-conflict practices of mixing. In B&H, having coffee with someone means much more than just "having a coffee"—it stands for intimacy, trust building, and routine, all signs of (potential) friendship. Having a coffee with someone from the other side would therefore signal one's readiness to challenge the post-conflict divisions, to attempt to cross over the boundaries of divide, or even to reestablish the old relationships. The following statement from the school's principal demonstrates the symbolism attached to coffee drinking: "When I was thinking about taking this job, the minister called me in and told me: 'Do not take the job if you are not ready to have a coffee with B. [Bosniak vice principal].'"

To call someone on the phone and ask them to come over for coffee or to meet a person in town and say, "let's go for coffee," are common expressions of trust, friendship, and family relations that existed in many regions of the former Yugoslavia before the war and that still continue today. However, nowadays these invitations for coffee happen rarely across ethnic divides. As one teacher comments, "Do you know what it means to have a coffee with someone? I carefully pick who I can have coffee with!"

Before the war, coffee drinking was a practice that often included mixing with people from other ethnic groups, which included home visits, relaxed talk, and genuine friendship. The quotes above, however, clearly demonstrate the shrinking of this mixing space. This is due to several interrelated processes, including the collapse of trust between ethnic communities where trust is a necessary precondition for friendly coffee drinking. Additionally, the unresolved issues in the recent past obstruct true dialogue and relaxed conversation. Finally, the destruction of the common public spaces in which joint coffee drinking could take place, such as mixed coffee shops, together with the elimination of practices of home visits across ethnic lines remove possibilities for spending time with the people from the other side of town. All students I talked to had a clear idea about what was included and excluded from the cultural practices of mixing today. Having a coffee is one of the borderline activities that become the place of resistance or the place for testing and stretching new boundaries of belonging. In other words, mixing practices today, in order to be socially acceptable, have to fall below the line of a true friendship; they need to preserve a superficial character. Lana explains, "I have no problems with *miješanje* for as long as it stays on the level of *raja*,[13] but if it becomes more serious than that, then I would not do it." When I asked Lana and many others what "more serious than *raja*" would be, almost uniformly they responded that dating would be one of those practices that would push the boundaries of mixing beyond what is acceptable to people in post-conflict Mostar.

Mixing and Dating

In present-day Mostar, dating became one of the most carefully guarded activities; dating across ethnic divisions is socially undesirable and often forbidden by the rules of family, community, and society. When one says "mixing," almost no young person in Mostar today links the term to practices of dating:

> At this moment, very few people think of *miješanje* as a type of dating. Most of those who would dare to do that would be killed by their parents. Unfortunately, that [dating across ethnic divides] is not part of the mental make-up of most people here. One of my friends who was shortly seeing a Serb man never mentioned his name to her parents. I also have a friend who could not say to his parents that he is going out with a Muslim girl, I mean a Bosniak girl. One of our classmates, you know her, cannot go out with a boy she likes because he is Croat. That is so sad…I mean that it is OK to marry a German or an American but not someone who lives two meters away from you. We all lose so much with that separation, I mean with non-mixing.

As this quote suggests, some young people engage in dating across ethnic and religious divisions, even if they face serious consequences by their family and community. Fedja is one of those young Bosniak men who fell in love with a Croat girl. Fedja met Daria when he was a young boy, since the two families have been friends for a long time:

> I love her so much and she is the best for me. Our parents are also OK with it since they were friends before the war and they still visit each other at home. They and I, well, we do not have *podjela u glavi* [division in their heads], which is the main problem in this city today.... Yes, many people comment and criticize what we are doing, even the teachers, one of whom told me: "Could you not find a nice Bosniak girl?" Also, the other day, I was passing by a group of girls from IV2 [Federal classroom], and Selma and Emina said: "Why are you seeing that Latinka [folk term for Catholics]. But we do not care; it is those people with *podjela u glavi* that have problems.

Other students told me that they would engage in superficial romantic flirtation with boys and girls from the other side, but anything more then a month of flirtation would be too much. When I ask them to explain why one month was the limit, Aida clarified it for me:

> You see, we look around, flirt, and romanticize about boyfriends. And what if you like someone from the other curriculum? If you just flirt with them a little bit for a few days, that is OK. You do not even have to mention it to your parents. But if it goes over a month then it could become serious. Then you would want to get engaged, because you cannot imagine living without them anymore. And then you would want to marry them. And you might do that if you love them very much, even if your parents do not approve. And then you would have kids with them. And that is when the troubles start. How will you name the child? Will you baptize or circumcise the child? When children grow bigger, they do not know which side to take, and they become atheists…and they start taking drugs.

This quote demonstrates how deep the new culture of ethnic and religious homogeneity penetrates youth's approach to life, including the culture of dating and especially marriage. This student developed a whole plot of a possible life tragedy, the seed of which is in liking and dating someone of another ethnoreligious background. As she explains, liking, flirting, and dating the ethnic other could lead to one's unhappiness in life, the culmination of which is having children who are drug addicts! This culture of fear of dating across ethnic lines lead some students to even sign a petition against the reunification of the school in order to avoid the danger of mixing and subsequently falling in love with the ethnic others. Tea explains,

> Before they [Bosniaks] returned, we talked about that. We signed a petition—who wants them to come and who does not. I said that I did not want them to come [laughs]. I know that Ines [a Bosniak girl in a Croat curriculum and Tea's best friend at the school] said she wanted them to come. I mean, with my friends, I did not look at the difference if you are a Muslim or a Croat, this or that. What I did not want to happen tomorrow is to fall in love with someone of a different religion. I wanted to marry someone of my own religion.

Similarly to Aida and Tea, many other young women mentioned problems and issues that emerge from dating or marrying ethnic others. Some, such as Amna who often flirted with Croat boys in the bathroom, used these limited opportunities to educate the Croat youth about Islam. In those short interactions, she always mentioned her dedication to Islam, and she jokingly attempted to convert some of the Croat boys she liked to Islam, so they become religiously suitable for dating. One day, in the bathroom so full of cigarette smoke that I could barely see their bodies standing only two meters away from me, Amna taught Ivan how to recite several verses from the Koran so that they could date. Even though this was a joyful and joking performance, it hid much deeper rules of new interaction, and it suggested the only possible way through which this romantic relationship could develop for Amna, which is, only if Ivan would convert to Islam.

Because of the new dominant culture of nonmixing when dating, youth in B&H who live in mixed regions of the country are very careful not to date ethnoreligious others, because falling in love can lead to all sorts of social problems and obstacles. The majority of students I talked to had clearly defined views on this issue, which proves that their families, friends, teachers, and community transmit unambiguous messages to them in terms of who to date and marry. The words of Irfan, the religion (Islam) teacher in the Federal Curricula, demonstrates this well. While he criticized the emerging social distance among youth of two ethnic groups in Mostar, he also stressed the importance of endogamy, or marrying into one's social group:

> *I*: What do you teach your students in terms of mixed marriages?
> *F*: This question is hard to explain in one sentence. You know, that phenomenon [of mixed marriages]…it was evident in Bosnia before the war. Maybe the best answer to your question is if I tell you the story from my family, about my aunt, Catholic Ljilja, the wife of my *rehmeti amidža* Ahmo [deceased uncle Ahmo, God rest his soul]. They had a better marriage than the other two of my uncles. Her answer to that

question, when she was advising her children and children of her sister was: "Do not do what I did." So, she answered that question for me. And that is what I say to my students. Regardless of all the similarities in the mentality of the people, in their way of life, but…they [mixed marriages] are not a solution. They are more of a problem, both for the married couple and for their children. It is even a bigger problem for their children because of the reactions of the surrounding[s] in which they live. I do direct my students to look at [the] cultural and religious identity of a person when they choose the marriage partner. Choosing the partner from your own religious community is the best way to also spark recognition and the respect of the other. True, we do live in the world of a free choice; everyone is free to do what he or she wants and wishes. And if someone stresses their freedom to support mixed marriages, then they should not take away from me my right to suggest non-mixing to my students.

Another Croat teacher at the Gymnasium Mostar, herself married to a Serb, echoed Irfan's story of the Catholic aunt very closely:

I said to my husband that I would do the same thing again [marry him] and that I am not sorry about what I did. But I would not recommend it to others. Every community has its own problems, and one has to adjust himself or herself to that community and in that process give up a part of himself or herself. Every additional pressure on the community [unintelligible]…if a person can avoid it he should, because there are too many problems anyhow. I say all this to my students; it is wise to run away from temptations and challenges. Unfortunately, my husband and I did not have children, but if we did, how would we name it? Lazar [Serb name] or Ante [Croat name]? I did not say all this just like that… all societal problems land on mixed marriages. For example, we could not get jobs. And we paid a high price for our national identities—I suffered many insults from his side, as he did from mine.

These explicit messages transmitted through education in family and in school form new rules of proper social conduct in terms of who to date and who to marry. Students I got to know were aware of the fine line between what is allowed and what is forbidden. Under these rules, only "innocent" and short-term flirtation, or a one-night stand (which is allowed for boys) was socially tolerable. For girls like Tea, who absorbed these rules, the ethnically and religiously different boys of the same age cease to exist as potential boyfriends. Adisa explains this phenomenon: "*Hodati sa nekim* [to walk with someone—slang for dating]…hmm… No, that is not it…when you mix with them [Croats] it is almost like you are with some friend you never consider to have that kind of [romantic] relationship with…or it is as if you are hanging out with someone much older than you…something like that…Simply, that [dating] is not what you have on your mind."

Melita, who wanted to mix with the youth from the other curriculum, criticized situations such as the time when she and her friends were standing in the school's hallway and she observed, "Look at that boy, he is soooooo cute." And her friends said, "Yes, but he is Croat." Upset by this attitude, she went home and asked her parents, "What would you do if I came home and told you that I am seeing a Croat?" Melita's mother, Suzana, replied, "I would be happy because that means that he is also open-minded since he wants to date you." Families such as Melita's and Fedja's are rare in the socially devastated, ethnically divided, post-conflict Mostar in which the spirit of mixing has been altered and considerably contracted so that it excludes dating and marrying people from other ethnic and religious communities.

Conclusion

Simultaneously malleable and safeguarded forms of social interaction in post-conflict B&H cannot be captured under the existing concepts of reconciliation, integration, coexistence, and segregation, even though they are influenced by all of these discourses. These multifaceted types of social interactions that take place in the context of everyday life can best be captured under the local term of *miješanje*.

These new forms of social relations, neither too close nor too distanced, take place in formal and informal situations, and they shape and are shaped by the new boundaries of intimacy. Based on these rules, *miješanje* in post-conflict B&H does not mean full-scale intermingling, as it meant in the socialist era of mixed marriages. *Miješanje*, however, symbolizes curiosity, interaction, flirtation, possibility of friendship, and first seeds of trust, but it also embodies tension, symbolic and structural violence, fear, and uncertainty.

In addition to being an ethnographic account of a unified school in a particular history, this study is also a contribution to the existing literature in various fields. Firstly, in the domain of anthropology, this work might provoke a new interest in mixing as a social practice and as an analytic tool. By focusing on mixing, anthropologists could turn the existing primary categories (such as race, ethnicity, and class) inside out in order to describe everyday practices and interpretations in which people engage as they define themselves as members of different groups. Secondly, in the field of peace and conflict studies, mixing could shed new light at the continuum between antagonistic and passive coexistence and full-scale reconciliation. More concretely, *miješanje* signifies that time in social reorganization after the war when social circumstances are ripe for the transformation of passive coexistence into active tolerance. Therefore, mixing as an analytical concept helps us better explain phases of post-conflict social reconstruction, since it captures those "in-between" moments in everyday life when hatred, pain, and mistrust are first being confronted and contested through short dialogues, curiosity, and flirtation. Thirdly, this study is a contribution to the existing studies of the transition to democracy in the former Eastern Europe and beyond. I argue that the emerging practices of mixing best illustrate the nature of post-conflict democracy and its novel parameters of sociality and solidarity—the ones based on fragmentation and shrinking spaces for interethnic interaction. Ironically, my study suggests that it is the very nature of democratization in B&H that largely prevents materialization of interconnectedness, solidarity, and nationhood.

Finally, in the domain of policy, the importance of the moments of mixing should not be underestimated, but ways for expanding places of mixing should be among the main goals of the policy makers. Furthermore, if there is to be further integration in Mostar and B&H, the IC has to develop, in a dialogue with the moderate citizens of B&H, a new political design that would breach the exiting fragmentation and that would more successfully accommodate history of interconnectedness in B&H. Youth in B&H surely deserve that opportunity.

Notes

1. This research was supported by grants from the American Association of University Women, the Social Science Research Council, the United States Institute of Peace, Penfield, the New Europe College, and the Spencer Foundation. I am especially grateful to Aaron Vlasak for his intellectual contribution. I thankfully acknowledge the help of Stef Jansen, Kathleen Hall, Ritty Lukose, and Genevra Murray, and two anonymous reviewers in regards to various parts and versions of this paper. I would also like to acknowledge the support of the Department of Anthropology at the University of Wisconsin at Oshkosh where I received generous support for my work.
2. During the war, the term "Bosniak" replaced the term "Bosnian Muslim." While the two largely overlap, they are not entirely synonymous (see Bringa, 1993).
3. The ten cantons in FB&H fall into three groups: five where Bosniaks are the majority population, three Croatian-majority cantons, and two "mixed" cantons.
4. The IC in B&H are best described as a "loose coalition of international governmental institutions, national governments and non-governmental organizations that has bound itself to Bosnia and Herzegovina by the Dayton Accords and the period of reconstruction" (World Bank and Council of Europe, 1999, p. 2).

5. In this chapter, I do not discuss in-depth everyday practices and interpretations in which people engage as they define themselves as Croats, Serbs, or Bosniaks.
6. Please see World Bank and Council of Europe (1999) at http://www.seerecon.org/bosnia/documents/education_report.pdf
7. The bathrooms are unisex because the second bathroom on each floor is reserved for professors and is always locked.
8. The names of all informants have been changed in order to protect their identities.
9. "Literally 'insurgent' name taken by an extremist wing of the Croatian Party of Rights which accepted the patronage of fascist Italy in the interwar period; in 1941 the Ustashe were installed in power by the Nazis in the quisling 'Independent State of Croatia,' which included the whole B&H, and in which they pursued genocidal policies against Serb, Jewish, Roma and other minorities" (Lovrenović, 2001, p. 232).
10. Balija is a slang name used for Bosnian Muslims as an insult.
11. Srebrenica is an eastern Bosnian town in which a massacre of 7,000 Bosniak men by the Serb forces took place in the summer of 1995 under the eye of the United Nations.
12. Drežnica is small town near Mostar in which the massacre of the Croat civilians by the B&H Army took place in 1993.
13. *Raja* (Raya), "originally non-Ottoman subject people (Muslim as well as non-Muslim); by the nineteenth century generally meant non-Muslim subjects only; in modern time often just refers to the 'common people' (Lovrenović, 2001, p. 231). In urban slang, *raja* symbolizes a shared sense of humor, urban neighborliness, and belonging to a loose community of friends.

References

Botev, N., & Wagner, R. (1993). Seeing past the barricades: Ethnic intermarriage in Yugoslavia during the last three decades. *Anthropology of East Europe Review*, *11* (1/2). Retrieved on September 28, 2008, from http://condor.depaul.edu/~rrotenbe/aeer/aeer11_1/botev.html

Bringa, T. (1993). *Being Muslim the Bosnian way*. Princeton: Princeton University Press.

Campbell, D. (1999). Apartheid cartography: The political anthropology and spatial effects of international diplomacy in Bosnia. *Political Geography*, *18*, 395–435.

Chandler, D. (2000). *Bosnia: Faking democracy after Dayton*. London: Pluto Press.

Federalni Zavod za Statistiku. (1991). *Stanovnistvo Prema Općinama i Mjesnim Zajednicama*. Sarajevo: Author.

Gagnon, V. P. (1994). Reaction to the Special Issue of AEER war among the Yugoslavs. *Anthropology of East Europe Review*, *12* (1), 50–51.

Hayden, R. M. (1996a). Imagined communities and real victims: Self-determination and ethnic cleansing in Yugoslavia. *American Ethnologist*, *23*, 783–801.

Khan, A. (2004). *Callaloo nation: Metaphors of race and religious identity among South Asians in Trinidad*. Durham: Duke University Press.

Lovrenović, I. (2001). *Bosnia. A cultural history*. London: Saqi Books.

Malcolm, N. (1996). *Bosnia: A short history*. New York: New York University Press.

Organization for Security and Co-operation in Europe (OSCE). (2005). Gymnasium Mostar, Mostar's "other landmark": Reconstruction and revitalization efforts. Unpublished report. Mostar.

Taylor, C. (1994). *Multiculturalism, examining the politics of recognition*. Princeton: Princeton University Press.

Trappenburg, M. (2003). Against segregation: Ethnic mixing in liberal states. *Journal of Political Philosophy, 1* (3), 295–319.

Vetters, L. (2007). The power of administrative categories: Emerging notions of citizenship in the divided city of Mostar. *Ethnopolitics, 6* (2), 187–209.

Wimmen, H. (2003). Territory, nation, and the power of language: Implications of education reform in the Herzegovinian town of Mostar. *GSC Quarterly, 11*, 1–21.

World Bank and Council of Europe. (1999). *Education in Bosnia and Herzegovina governance, finance, and administration*. (Sarajevo). Retrieved on September 28, 2008, from http://www.seerecon.org/bosnia/documents/education_report.pdf

Chapter 8

The Cultural Psychology of American-based Coexistence Programs for Israeli and Palestinian Youth

Phillip L. Hammack

> I don't believe in peace. I believe peace is like giving up. And there's this thing in Islam. If someone dies for his own country, he's like, these are the best people. If you die for your country, you go straight to heaven....The whole Islamic population is supposed to fight for Palestine....The whole land is ours. It's like we're supposed to fight for every inch of the country. It's ours, and they took it by force. We're gonna take it back by force. If we can. But we, we can't take it back by force. We don't have money. We're not allowed to have an army, weapons, nothing. This is why we use the freedom fighters.
>
> —Ali, sixteen-year-old Palestinian Muslim, one year after participation in an American coexistence program

Ali, a young Palestinian Muslim, introduces a fundamental dilemma for peace education programs: How can identities attuned to peaceful coexistence be cultivated in the context of an ongoing intractable conflict? In the midst of intractability, what role can peace education assume? The ideological setting of Ali's life story at age sixteen, which would not seem to serve the interests of peace, presents a major challenge for theory and practice in peace education. Is it possible to educate for coexistence in the absence of policies that support peace (see Bar-Tal, 2004)? Or, rather, is it inevitable that the narrative conditions of conflict will only be reproduced by young Israelis and Palestinians (Bekerman & Maoz, 2005) until the day when a new "master" narrative of peace is born (Hammack, 2008)?

This chapter examines these challenging questions about peace education through a description of fieldwork conducted from 2003–2007 in two American-based coexistence programs for Israeli and Palestinian youth as well as with youth and their families in the region before and up to four years following program participation. My identity as a non-Jewish, non-Arab American psychologist positioned me as a "stranger" (Simmel, 1971) to the conflict and seemed to enhance the desire of youth to engage with me about their stories. Yet my American identity figured prominently in all of my interactions in the field, for both Israelis and Palestinians viewed me as someone to "win over"—the face of a global cosmopolitan Westerner who might spread word of the legitimacy of their fragile narratives.

Coexistence through Identity Transcendence: An American Cultural Model

A central argument I will develop in this chapter is that American-based efforts at peace education are fundamentally rooted in an American folk psychology about identity and intergroup relations. As a cultural psychologist, I am interested in the meaning embedded in acts (e.g., Bruner, 1990) and the way that identity is constructed through social interaction and practice (e.g., Holland, Lachicotte, Skinner, & Cain, 1998). I view cultural meaning systems as always being in dynamic states and not as static categories that can "predict" individual subjectivity (see Gjerde, 2004), yet I believe it is possible to describe a particular meaning system as it is actively deployed. This view of culture allows us to chart "cultural models" that provide a particular symbolic and discursive framework for the construction of meaning (see D'Andrade & Strauss, 1992).

I conducted fieldwork in two American-based coexistence programs: Seeds of Peace, located in the woods of rural Maine, and Hands of Peace, located in suburban Chicago, Illinois. The cultural model underlying both programs is characterized by (a) the framing of conflict as a problem primarily of individual prejudice and (b) the consequent conviction that intervention in individual personality development can effectively contribute to social change. In this model, the individual possesses power to affect the social structure of conflict. An emphasis on social policy or social structure is largely absent in this vision of the individual actor constructing the conditions of his or her own development.

The cultural model of both programs is closely linked to intellectual perspectives in American social science post-World War II. The programs represent experiments in "intergroup contact" and are thus traceable to the intellectual project of contact theory that emerged in the mid-twentieth century in American social psychology. Allport (1954) postulated that, under certain conditions, contact between groups in conflict will break down the barriers of prejudice and stereotypes. Allport's theory relies upon the notion that origins of conflict lie in the existence and proliferation of ethnocentric personalities (cf. Adorno, Frenkel-Brunswik, Levinson, & Sanford, 1950). As a consequence, Allport's approach suggests intervention at the level of the individual.

Allport's model was challenged by subsequent social psychological work in conflict and intergroup relations, such as realistic conflict theory (Sherif, 1958) and social identity theory (Tajfel & Turner, 1979). These perspectives challenged the notion that conflict is rooted in individual prejudice and personality by highlighting the material and social structural origins of conflict. Both challenged the notion that the individual possesses sufficient power to affect the larger system of power, identity, and intergroup relations. The theoretical and empirical work in these traditions instead revealed the significant influence of the collective on individual cognition and behavior.

Yet an American folk psychology that emphasizes the power of the individual endures (see Sampson, 1977). Such a model seems particularly pervasive in the American discourse on diversity and multiculturalism (e.g., Fowers & Davidov, 2006), which argues that increased individual sensitivity to multiculturalism will alleviate intergroup tensions in American society. In an American cultural frame, the role of structural and policy transformations is typically recognized but not necessarily prioritized over individual interventions to transform intergroup relations.

In American social psychology, a theory that sought to integrate earlier theories of intergroup relations emerged in the 1990s with common ingroup identity theory (e.g., Gaertner & Dovidio, 2000). This perspective recognized the premises of realistic conflict theory and social identity theory but argued that intergroup conflict could be reduced through the cultivation of a common, superordinate identity among individuals. A superordinate identity is meant to facilitate the recategorization of self and other such that a higher level of category inclusiveness is realized. For example, instead of Ali adhering to rigid categorizations of "Palestinians" and "Israelis," he might recognize through contact with Israelis that they share a common identity as "Israelis and Palestinians committed to peace" or even the larger category of "human beings." This common identity is not necessarily meant to threaten his social identity as a Palestinian. Rather, it becomes a "supplement" to Ali's identity that allows him to transcend the divisiveness of conflicting narratives between Palestinians and Israelis.

There is a clear connection between common ingroup identity theory and the American discourse on multiculturalism and identity that began to thrive in the 1990s (see Hollinger, 2006). The American discourse on identity diversity calls upon Americans to transcend their subgroup affiliations and to embrace the common American identity they share (e.g., Hornsey & Hogg, 2000). It is precisely this American discourse that frames the underlying philosophy of the two programs at which I conducted fieldwork.

In addition to the underlying model of identity and intergroup relations, another important aspect of American folk psychology is present in the design of these peace programs. Both programs rely on a cultural model of the life course that began to emerge in American psychology in the early twentieth century with the work of Hall (1904) but received its most significant momentum midcentury with the work of Erikson (1963, 1968; see also Kett, 1977). This cultural model relied on a concept of adolescence as a life-course moment ascribed significant power to repudiate a social order. With their reliance on this American notion of the cultural power of youth, the programs rely on an American cultural model of social change and the individual life course.

In sum, American-based coexistence programs are grounded in a distinctly American folk model of intergroup relations, identity diversity, and the life course. This grounding influences every aspect of curriculum in both subtle and obvious ways. I will briefly highlight the basic curricular structure of both programs to reveal these points of connection between cultural and philosophical grounding and practice.

Departing the Conflict: Curriculum of American-based Programs

The most obvious feature of the curriculum of both programs is the removal of the individual from the zone of conflict. Interestingly, even the idea that this removal is valuable or appropriate reveals the cultural psychology of the programs, for one of their primary notions is that individuals can escape the psychological confines of the conflict through physical removal. This foundational narrative speaks to the triumph of the individual over his or her environment—the individual may gain mastery over the environment once he or she recognizes the ease with which identity shifts with a change in context.

Hands of Peace and Seeds of Peace differ slightly in their approach to "cultural removal." Seeds of Peace is a traditional American summer camp located in an isolated, rural setting in which the construction of an entirely new cultural system is attempted (see Wallach, 2000). In this locale, a cultural system is constructed with norms, roles, rituals, and a clear ideological discourse about conflict, identity, and intergroup relations. There is an attempt to "neutralize" identity in discourse and practice through the policies and statements of authority figures regarding "equality" and through the use of a common uniform and common access to resources for all participants. The social structure of the program is thus designed to remove structural distinctions between Israelis and Palestinians that exist in the reality of the conflict. The result is a contrived but alluring social ecology in which young Israelis and Palestinians, liberated from the social structure of the conflict, can experiment with new roles and identities.

At Seeds of Peace, the curriculum is designed to facilitate a number of social psychological processes of identity challenge and transformation. Dialogue sessions conducted by professional facilitators represent the daily ritual in which social identity is typically most salient, since these meetings involve direct discussion of the conflict. Athletic and artistic activities are designed to offer opportunities for cross-group cooperation and collaboration, and major rituals contribute to the overall press to deaccentuate one's national identity and take on the superordinate identity of a "Seed." The notion that the intractability of conflict can be transcended at the individual level is pervasive in the discourse of the program with the ubiquity of the founder's "Make one friend" slogan. This view of intergroup contact is closely linked to approaches articulated by American social psychologists who focus on the role of personalization in shifting negative intergroup relations (e.g., Brewer & Miller, 1984; Miller, 2002; Pettigrew, 1997, 1998).

Hands of Peace is a coexistence program in which youth are integrated into an existing American suburban community. Participants reside with families and come together every day for two weeks for facilitated dialogue and activities designed to foster cross-group friendships and cooperation. Like Seeds of Peace, there are a number of rituals that serve to activate a cognitive process of identity recategorization. These rituals include participation in a teams course, religious services, and events such as a "culture night," in which each national group prepares a meal and performs songs and skits related to its culture. The idea is to expose participants to the legitimate identity diversity they all possess and, in the process, to try to cultivate a superordinate identity attuned to peaceful coexistence. Like Seeds of Peace, Hands of Peace has a program anthem it teaches all participants, featuring lyrics like "We are people from different nations, but now we're learning how to live as one."

While both programs seem to possess a curricular structure that at times accentuates the salience of social identity (e.g., dialogue sessions, religious services), the overarching aim of both programs is to encourage the transcendence of a polarizing and delegitimizing ingroup narrative. Through exposure to the other in the context of social support for intergroup contact, individuals experience the press of identity transcendence, just as they experience its antithesis in their daily lives in conflict.

Stories of Coexistence: Narrative Outcomes
Identity Transcendence

In addition to participant observation during the programs, I conducted interviews with participants immediately after the program and for a number of years following participation. Participants tended to construct narratives of identity transcendence immediately following program participation, in keeping with the goals of both programs. The immediate postprogram narratives of Ayelet and Israa illustrate this outcome:

> When I go home, I wanna tell everyone about all the Arab friends I made, and what amazing people they are, and how they're just like us. There's no difference really between Jews and Arabs....Listening to all of the stories of the Arabs, it made me realize why they do those things [like bombings]....We are all human beings....Growing up in Israel, I always knew there was a war, and suicide bombings, but I never understood the reason. Now, listening to the Palestinians....I see the whole picture, and now I understand myself and I'm proud of myself. (Ayelet, Jewish Israeli)

> Maybe I was, [before the program], losing hope of peace with the Israelis, when they do everything in Palestine...like checkpoints, separation wall and all these things. I was losing hope, and I was also very afraid to meet the Israelis and to sit with them in the same room and discuss political issues. But I was very interested to come and see their point of view and to tell the Americans and the Israelis, some of our suffering in Palestine....Then after having these two weeks, I start changing my point or looking to the Israelis, I look to them as humans....I looked to them as enemies, but now with feelings and with emotions as me, as well, as I find similar, in our personalities. And I started to have more hope to live with them in peace. And the Palestinians to live with Israelis in peace, as I lived here. As an example, I live here with Jewish Israelis and I have a great time with them, and I made some good friends. (Israa, Palestinian Muslim)

These immediate postprogram narratives reveal the success of these programs, as both of these young women detail their psychological transformation from a state of identity polarization to transcendence (Hammack, 2006).

The narratives of Israa and Ayelet are typical of youth interviewed immediately postprogram, when they are far from the conflict in both physical and mental space. Young Palestinians like Israa, who lives in the West Bank and thus routinely traverses the structural reality of conflict through checkpoints, experience in the United States a remarkable feeling of "freedom," particularly freedom of movement. For them, a dreamlike state of liberation from the occupation sets into their consciousness and ingratiates them to the American organizers of these ventures—people who made their transportation from the zone of conflict to a zone of peace and structural equality possible.

For Jewish Israelis like Ayelet, removal from the conflict is also psychologically liberating, though not for the same reasons as for young Palestinians. Young Jewish Israelis experience the conflict differently than the Palestinians, given the asymmetry of the conflict, in which Jewish Israelis serve the role of "occupier" (e.g., Gordon, 2008; Rouhana, 2004). What seems to be liberating for youth like Ayelet is the ability to experience a sense of existential security—that is, to live without the discourse of fear and threat that pervades Israeli society—while also being temporarily relieved of the role of "occupier." In a place of structural equality with Palestinians, young Israelis like Ayelet begin to realize the ways in which the social structure of conflict creates a discourse of identity polarization, and they are attracted to the allure of repudiating this discourse.

Narrative outcomes such as that of Ayelet and Israa represent the internalization of a superordinate identity, as both programs desire and as predicted by common ingroup identity theory. Yet, in presenting the narratives of Ayelet and Israa, I do not mean to suggest that such outcomes are universal among the young participants in these programs. The most notable axis upon which immediate outcome appeared to vary was *sex*, with outcomes of identity transcendence extremely uncommon for males.

The dynamics of gender roles in conflict influence identity development for Israeli and Palestinian youth. Aside from the basic connection between masculinity and nationalism that seems to endure across time and place (Nagel, 1998) and along with the patriarchal structure that characterizes many societies, there is something specific about gender and the Israeli-Palestinian conflict that would seem to suggest such an outcome. In Israeli society, the construction of masculinity is carefully deployed to serve the security needs of the state, and military service is institutionalized into the life course in such a way that young boys begin to prepare excitedly for service years in advance (see Golan, 1997; Kaplan, 2006). In Palestinian society, the occupation creates a situation of significant emasculation, in which the ability of men to fulfill their traditional social roles of economic provision and social leadership are essentially blocked (Johnson & Kuttab, 2001; Roy, 2004). Because of their involvement in political violence and movements, men routinely go through a period of prison sentence, which in fact serves as a site of education about the Palestinian cause (Barber, 1999; Peteet, 1994). The prison becomes just as much a critical life-course moment for the Palestinian man as military service is for the Israeli man. Thus, in the structural reality of conflict and in the patriarchal systems of both Israeli and Palestinian cultures, males serve as "guardians" of identity (Erikson, 1968).

Identity Accentuation

Social identity theory suggests a different set of predictions about what might occur as young Israelis and Palestinians engage in contact. In a direct challenge to an American social psychology that emphasized the possibility of the individual personality to combat ethnocentrism, Tajfel and Turner (1979) demonstrated through a series of rigorous experiments that mere categorization into meaningless groups activates a state of identity polarization—that is, contact situations might actually increase the salience of ingroup identity and intergroup polarization. The mechanism for this process is, they argue, rooted in the need for a positive social identity. It is important to note that the experiments of Tajfel and Turner were not conducted with individuals whose groups were already in a state of intractable conflict; thus this social psychological process is probably amplified when we consider contact between individuals from meaningful social categories already in a state of intractable conflict.

The immediate postprogram narrative of Roai, a sixteen-year-old Jewish Israeli, captures the outcome of identity accentuation:

> First of all, I felt like the program was somehow not equal, that somehow the Palestinians were more powerful and we heard so much of only their suffering and not *our* suffering as Israelis. What surprised me most about the program, talking with Palestinians, is the facts. I mean, I know facts, and they know facts, but it's not the same facts. They're changing the facts! I know the facts! I believe Israelis don't change the facts....I didn't change my mind about anything listening to the Palestinians, but it was interesting.

For Roai, participation in the coexistence program did not result in the recategorization of self and other from a state of identity polarization to transcendence. Consistent with social identity theory, Roai's social identity has become further accentuated through intergroup contact. In this state of accentuation, his role as a "guardian" of Israeli identity is clear: he perceives his ingroup narrative to have been too challenged and threatened by the experience of coexistence. His response is to amplify the extent to which he advocates that narrative and seeks its endurance.

This pattern of identity accentuation, in which youth came to integrate polarizing master narratives of identity more fully into their life stories, represented a common, immediate outcome for males. Identity accentuation was also the most common long-term outcome for all participants.

One year after his experience at Seeds of Peace, Mohammed reflected about its influence:

> I didn't, like, change, or accept the Israelis. I felt more like, I realized that I'm the real owner of this land....I was even more Palestinian—I *felt* more Palestinian—when I came back because I realized they don't really care. When I came back, it made me wanna read more about the conflict and about my people. But it also made me realize nothing's gonna change. All I can do is stay focused on my life, and just be proud to be a Palestinian cause you know you're the legitimate owner of this land. I always say "A day will come and everything will be like the way it should be from the beginning"—we'll have our land back, our country back—and if not, the end of the world will come soon, and people will be judged for what they did. That's it. I'm just living here, trying not to think about the conflict, but it's all around me.

Contact with Israelis increased Mohammed's sense of connection with an enduring, if fragile, Palestinian identity. The result is a personal narrative that appears to reproduce, rather than to repudiate, the narrative conditions of conflict.

Roai's narrative one year postprogram assumes similar thematic content. Roai suggests that contact exposed him to the Palestinian narrative of the conflict but that this exposure only seemed to confirm for him the illegitimacy of the Palestinian narrative. One year postprogram, Roai summarized his critical view of Hands of Peace as follows:

> The problem with the program is that, when you come back and end this program, you are going back to reality, and your reality is not the way it was in the program. The biggest problem is taking us out of Israel, and I think this is the main difference, in the reality of the program versus the reality in Israel. To be with the Palestinians inside a bubble, you know things and you remember things but in some way you can't hear things that are going on. But we're not touching. So when you're back here, you forget about things. The environment there is really kind and peaceful. You think in another way there than here.

Roai's eloquent critique is rooted precisely in the American cultural model of the program.

If programs that target young Israelis and Palestinians are to have any measure of success in repudiating a status quo of intractability, they cannot be entirely divorced from the reality of the conflict itself, for the allure of escapism is too great for participants. They long to be taken away from the conflict, to be removed from its inhibiting chains of ideological polarity and rigid insularity. They see the unjust social structure before them, and they long to acknowledge it. Yet as long as they remain in states of existential insecurity and as long as they are educated with the discourse of a master narrative that maintains a state of intractability and negative interdependence (Hammack, 2008; Kelman, 1999), the possibility for a truly transcendent experience seems unlikely.

What's Wrong with Identity? In Defense of Identity Accentuation

Upon considering identity accentuation as an outcome of such programs, the reader is left to debate the merits of any kind of contact situation for Israelis and Palestinians. If contact results in such an outcome, how can it be supported as a contribution to the larger project of peace education? In concluding this chapter, I want to suggest that, in fact, we ought to capitalize on identity accentuation and consider its possible benefits to conflict reduction, even if those benefits seem initially challenging to comprehend. But first, it is worth further consideration as to why identity accentuation occurs among these youth.

Why Accentuation?

Identity accentuation represents an expectable outcome for participants in these programs for at least three reasons. First, not only is the sociopolitical reality of the conflict a context in which identity accentuation thrives, but it also drives the conflict and constructs comforting discourses of identity that promote notions of exceptionalism and exclusive legitimacy. That is, the pervasive sense of existential insecurity in both Palestinian and Israeli societies creates the need for a coherent and distinctive master narrative that facilitates individual coping with the conflict (see Bar-Tal, 2007). Because basic needs for security and identity recognition are unmet in both societies, it makes sense that a sense of collective identity would need to be maintained at all costs, since identity itself is at stake for the group (Pettigrew, 2003).

Second, there is an obvious dissonance between the cultural context of conflict and the programs. The curriculum of both programs is oriented more toward the American cultural context of ethnocentrism and racism than it is toward the context of intractable conflict. As Bar-Tal (2004) argues, these divergent cultural contexts speak to different social psychological needs and different strategies for coexistence education. Coexistence education assumes a more limited role in the context of intractable conflict because it relies upon structural and political change for its effectiveness. In the absence of clear policy support for coexistence, it is extremely challenging to engage in coexistence education. When a conflict remains active and unresolved, as it does for Israelis and Palestinians, a larger cultural context and discourse of coexistence is absent.

Unlike the context of intractable conflict, the American cultural context is one in which pluralism and identity diversity represent central concerns. American society continues to be characterized by racism, ethnocentrism, and pervasive structural inequities, but social policies and social movements beginning in the mid-twentieth century have altered the discourse on identity politics in American society in profound ways. The same cannot be said in Israel and Palestine, where the absence of a final, comprehensive peace agreement constrains the discourse on identity and pluralism. The insecurity of identity for both Palestinians and Israelis creates a radically different lens through which to view intergroup relations when compared with Americans.

A cultural analysis of the curriculum and philosophy of both programs, however, suggests that they are more oriented to the American cultural context than to the Israeli-Palestinian. For example, the reliance on a common ingroup identity model, with specific rituals designed to instill a state of identity transcendence, is connected to the American need to internalize a common identity in the midst of diversity. In the context of an intractable conflict, identity distinction and recognition come to the forefront. Thus, it is not surprising that many program participants accentuate their social identities, for the dissonance between the cultural context of the program and the conflict only elevates their sense of existential insecurity, amplifying their need to identify with the fragile master narrative of the group.

A third explanation for the outcome of identity accentuation is perhaps the simplest: identity accentuation is a normal, expectable outcome of contact between groups. The vast literature in social identity theory has consistently demonstrated that mere categorization activates a sense of ingroup solidarity and identification that then drives behavior toward conflict. Brewer's (1991) optimal distinctiveness theory further explains the outcome of identity accentuation. She argues that individuals fundamentally strive to reconcile opposing needs for assimilation and differentiation from others. In reconciling these needs, they reach a level of optimal distinctiveness in their identities. In the context of intractable conflict, the need for a sense of distinctiveness in identity is probably greater because of the mutual perception of existential insecurity and the lack of mutual identity recognition.

What's Wrong with Identity Accentuation?

Intuitively, identity accentuation seems problematic for peace education. However, there are clear psychological benefits of identity accentuation for individuals in conflict zones. First, a stronger sense of group identification is associated with enhanced self-esteem (e.g., Phinney, 1991). Second, the ideological commitment associated with a strong sense of social identity facilitates coping with the conflict (e.g., Punamäki, 1996). Young people involved in or exposed to political violence attribute meaning to conflict-related events, which seems to buffer them from the negative psychological consequences of conflict (e.g., Barber, 2001).

While identity accentuation might be beneficial at the individual level, its implications for the social reproduction of conflict are troubling. Identity accentuation would seem to secure the reproduction of the narrative conditions of conflict—hardly a desired outcome for peace education. Yet if we view the fundamental problem of the Israeli-Palestinian conflict as one of identity nonrecognition, we can perhaps identify some value in identity accentuation.

The absence of recognition is characterized by delegitimization of mutual distinctiveness. That is, Israelis and Palestinians fail to recognize the legitimacy of one another and essentially deny each other's existence (see Bar-Tal, 1990a, 1990b). Until relatively recently, this explicit delegitimization was institutionalized in both societies (e.g., in educational materials; Oren & Bar-Tal, 2007). Bringing Israelis and Palestinians together to hear and to recognize the distinctiveness of their social identities might in fact represent the best that can be done during continued pervasive intractability. A model that embraces identity accentuation and views it as a necessary and useful process for individuals has been developed at the School for Peace in Israel (Halabi, 2004; Halabi & Sonnenschein, 2004).

Context and Peace Education: Implications of a Cultural Approach

A distinctly cultural approach to the study of peace education programs orients practitioners toward the ways in which programs themselves serve as sites for a new form of social practice and a new discourse on conflict. Through analysis of both participant experience and the philosophy and curriculum of American-based programs, the narrative outcomes of program participation allow for an interpretation of why this new practice and discourse fails to possess long-term salience for participants.

Seeds of Peace and Hands of Peace rely on an American folk model of intergroup relations that locates the source of conflict in the prejudiced individual. This emphasis is distinctly American in that it privileges the power of the individual in possibilities for social transformation. Conflict, in this frame, is more connected to individual prejudice than to structural inequities, the absence of social policies that promote coexistence, or the identity politics that constructs polarized narratives. As such, individual psychological transformations through acquaintanceship can contribute to peace-building efforts. Focusing on the distinction of American culture, we might connect this underlying philosophical orientation to the American myth of structural equality that each individual gets a fair chance at success and the "American dream" of happiness through economic achievement. I refer to this belief as a myth because it is clear that, according to social identity, access to resources and social capital is by no means standardized across groups in the United States. Racial and ethnic minorities have long been disenfranchised from economic and social advancement opportunities (Kimble, 2007; Lott & Bullock, 2007).

Although power and hegemony characterize intergroup relations in the United States, this myth of structural equality endures. Early social psychological research on intergroup relations produced in the United States seemed to believe in the ability to "neutralize" power in intergroup encounters (e.g., Allport, 1954), which is connected to mythology around power and identity in the American cultural context. There is no question that, in the context of these American-based programs, a belief in the ability to neutralize power endures. The programs are carefully conceived to create a context of equality among participants.

In keeping with this American model of intergroup relations, both programs rely on an American folk model of social change. Connected to their emphasis on *adolescence* as the key life-course moment of intervention, they emphasize a view of youth as "producers" rather than "products" of a particular social structure. The emphasis they place on the possibility of individual agency to effect the course of the conflict is not proportionate to the actual structural barriers created by conflict. This vision of youth in the process of social change relies on a "bottom-up" theory of how transformation actually occurs. Identity accentuation challenges this theory and suggests that, in the context of intractable conflict, recognition of the limitations to agency is essential.

I do not want to suggest, however, that the "problem" with these programs can be exclusively located in their curricula and their underlying philosophical orientation. There is an inherent challenge in coexistence education itself because of its tendency to create a context in which the conditions of conflict can so easily be reproduced. Coexistence education can serve a reproductive function by providing a forum for the reproduction of nationalist discourse (Bekerman, 2002; Bekerman & Maoz, 2005). Participants in these American-based programs are consumed with this unresolved battle over national identity recognition. As Bekerman and Maoz (2005) argue, this discursive struggle is the product of the nationalist era that began in the nineteenth century and spawned the rival movements of Zionism and Palestinian nationalism. But as borders come down and the pitfalls of nationalism are identified in global discussions of identity, Israelis and Palestinians appear to be "trapped" in an old discourse of "imagined communities" (Anderson, 1983). The fact that Israelis and Palestinians were never able to achieve stable, secure, and universally recognized national identities explains this inability to move beyond the discourse of nation, but coexistence education does not sufficiently challenge the artificiality of this discourse (Bekerman & Maoz, 2005).

The problem may indeed be one of temporal sequence if we consider the relationship between peace education and social change. Returning to Bar-Tal's (2004) argument, coexistence education lags behind political change and can only contribute minimally to conflict reduction absent a political resolution. The research discussed in this chapter supports the recognition that coexistence efforts cannot be undertaken with grand aspirations for social change.

The implications of this research for the programs themselves suggest that, first and foremost, they would benefit from greater reflexivity about their own cultural psychology. That is, the programs need to examine their missions, goals, philosophies, and curricula through a cultural lens. They also would benefit from greater recognition of the distinct sociopolitical realities of the United States versus those of Israel-Palestine and the ways in which these distinctions might affect program goals. Both programs need to have more modest, realistic goals that are sensitive to the social ecology of conflict. There is a need to theorize the relationship between individual psychological and social structural change in more complex, nuanced ways. For example, the integration of a policy- or action-oriented approach into the curriculum would recognize the need for structural and policy change if individual psychological changes are to have any meaningful social support. In other words, the programs would benefit from a more critical consciousness about the path to social change. An acknowledgement of the limitations of intergroup contact and of youth to contribute to social change would reorient these programs toward a more realistic view of their role in conflict transformation. Given such acknowledgement and recognition, the dissonance participants experience upon their return to the zone of conflict might diminish.

I close with the sentiments of Mohammed, now a nineteen-year-old college student in the West Bank. Four years after his participation in the coexistence program, he offers the following reflection:

> I think the programs are basically bullshit. It's all about making the Americans feel good about themselves, like they have to have something to do. It's like they're holding us like babies sometimes, thinking they can teach us. It's just like they are with everything in the world—Iraq, everything. I don't like this. I did this to do something for my country, for Palestine, and I think I did something good. But the only thing that keeps me going is knowing I can't control anything, not the situation, not anything. What will happen will happen, and in the end there will be justice. I have to believe in this. But me, I can't do anything to change the reality. And the Americans just never understood that.

Mohammed's account of the coexistence program is representative of many youth who come to recognize the cultural psychology of the program itself. As they attempt to make sense of the intensity of the experience and its dissonance from their lived experience, such youth come to view the programs as disconnected from the identity politics of the conflict.

In this chapter, I have argued that the reliance on an American cultural model diminishes the effectiveness of American-based coexistence programs to contribute to conflict reduction. The narratives of youth collected up to several years following participation suggests ideological content that reproduces, rather than repudiates, the narrative stalemate of the Israeli-Palestinian conflict. In this way, youth fulfill their roles as "guardians" of identity, and the possibilities of their identity development are constrained by the structural reality of conflict. Interventions that privilege the personal over the political might avoid a more substantive role in conflict reduction. A model that embraces identity accentuation as an inevitable developmental process associated with conflict might provide a more salient and less dissonant experience for youth. The principles of coexistence mandate a priori some modicum of secure and sustainable existence, which does not characterize the experience of Israelis and Palestinians. The voices of young people represented in this chapter reveal the formidable sense of insecurity that pervades the narratives of both groups. That we might allow these voices to transform our vision of the path to peace speaks to a recognition that the practice of peace education must be connected to the authentic possibilities of human development.

Acknowledgments

The research reported in this chapter was supported by fellowships from the United States Institute of Peace, the Spencer Foundation, and the Alfred P. Sloan Foundation. I thank Amal Ekaik, Abigail Jacobson, Brian Lobel, Razan Makhlouf, and Rami Mehdawi for research assistance in Israeli and Palestine. I thank my colleagues Manal Al-Tamimi, Abigail Jacobson, Elizabeth Shulman, and Scott Silk for our enlightening discussions of the research. I also thank administrators at both programs for permission to conduct the research, especially Gretchen Grad and Bill Taylor. Finally, I thank Bertram J. Cohler, Dan P. McAdams, Barbara Schneider, and Richard A. Shweder for their intellectual guidance during this project.

References

Adorno, T. W., Frenkel-Brunswik, E., Levinson, D.J., & Sanford, R.N. (1950). *The authoritarian personality*. New York: Harper & Brothers.
Allport, G. W. (1954). *The nature of prejudice*. Reading, MA: Perseus.
Anderson, B. (1983). *Imagined communities*. New York: Verso.
Barber, B. K. (1999). Youth experience in the Palestinian *Intifada*: A case study in intensity, complexity, paradox, and competence. In M. Yates & J. Youniss

(Eds.), *Roots of civic identity: International perspectives on community service and activism in youth* (pp. 178–204). New York: Cambridge University Press.

Barber, B. K. (2001). Political violence, social integration, and youth functioning: Palestinian youth from the *Intifada*. *Journal of Community Psychology, 29*, 259–280.

Bar-Tal, D. (1990a). Causes and consequences of delegitimization: Models of conflict and ethnocentrism. *Journal of Social Issues, 46*(1), 65–81.

Bar-Tal, D. (1990b). Israeli-Palestinian conflict: A cognitive analysis. *International Journal of Intercultural Relations, 14*, 7–29.

Bar-Tal, D. (2004). Nature, rationale, and effectiveness of education for coexistence. *Journal of Social Issues, 60*(2), 253–272.

Bar-Tal, D. (2007). Sociopsychological foundations of intractable conflicts. *American Behavioral Scientist, 50*(11), 1430–1453.

Bekerman, Z. (2002). The discourse of nation and culture: Its impact on Palestinian-Jewish encounters in Israel. *International Journal of Intercultural Relations, 26*, 409–427.

Bekerman, Z., & Maoz, I. (2005). Troubles with identity: Obstacles to coexistence education in conflict ridden societies. *Identity: An International Journal of Theory and Research, 5*(4), 341–358.

Brewer, M. B. (1991). The social self: On being the same and different at the same time. *Personality and Social Psychology Bulletin, 17*(5), 475–482.

Brewer, M. B., & Miller, N. (1984). Beyond the contact hypothesis: Theoretical perspectives on desegregation. In N. Miller & M.B. Brewer (Eds.), *Groups in contact: The psychology of desegregation* (pp. 281–302). Orlando, FL: Academic Press.

Bruner, J. (1990). *Acts of meaning.* Cambridge, MA: Harvard University Press.

D'Andrade, R. G., & Strauss, C. (Eds.). (1992). *Human motives and cultural models.* New York: Cambridge University Press.

Erikson, E. H. (Ed.). (1963). *The challenge of youth.* New York: Anchor.

Erikson, E. H. (1968). *Identity: Youth and crisis.* New York: Norton.

Fowers, B. J., & Davidov, B. J. (2006). The virtue of multiculturalism: Personal transformation, character, and openness to the other. *American Psychologist, 61*(6), 581–594.

Gaertner, S. L., & Dovidio, J. F. (2000). *Reducing intergroup bias: The common ingroup identity model.* Philadelphia, PA: Psychology Press/Taylor & Francis.

Gjerde, P. F. (2004). Culture, power, and experience: Toward a person-centered cultural psychology. *Human Development, 47*, 138–157.

Golan, G. (1997). Militarization and gender: The Israeli experience. *Women's Studies International Forum, 20*, 581–586.

Gordon, N. (2008). From colonization to separation: Exploring the structure of Israel's occupation. *Third World Quarterly, 29*(1), 25–44.

Halabi, R. (Ed.). (2004). *Israeli and Palestinian identities in dialogue: The School for Peace approach.* New Brunswick, NJ: Rutgers University Press.

Halabi, R., & Sonnenschein, N. (2004). The Jewish-Palestinian encounter in a time of crisis. *Journal of Social Issues, 60*(2), 373–388.

Hall, G. S. (1904). *Adolescence: Its psychology and its relation to physiology, anthropology, sociology, sex, crime, religion, and education.* Englewood Cliffs, NJ: Prentice-Hall.

Hammack, P. L. (2006). Identity, conflict, and coexistence: Life stories of Israeli and Palestinian adolescents. *Journal of Adolescent Research, 21*(4), 323–369.
Hammack, P. L. (2008). Narrative and the cultural psychology of identity. *Personality and Social Psychology Review, 12*(3), 222–247.
Holland, D., Lachicotte, W., Skinner, D., & Cain, C. (1998). *Identity and agency in cultural worlds*. Cambridge, MA: Harvard University Press.
Hollinger, D. A. (2006). *Postethnic America: Beyond multiculturalism* (Rev. ed.). New York: Basic Books.
Hornsey, M. J., & Hogg, M. A. (2000). Assimilation and diversity: An integrative model of subgroup relations. *Personality and Social Psychology Review, 4*(2), 143–156.
Johnson, P., & Kuttab, E. (2001). Where have all the women (and men) gone? Reflections on gender and the second Palestinian intifada. *Feminist Review, 69*, 21–43.
Kaplan, D. (2006). *The men we loved: Male friendship and nationalism in Israeli culture*. New York: Berghahn Books.
Kelman, H. C. (1999). The interdependence of Israeli and Palestinian national identities: The role of the other in existential conflicts. *Journal of Social Issues, 55*(3), 581–600.
Kett, J. F. (1977). *Rites of passage: Adolescence in America, 1790 to the present*. New York: Basic Books.
Kimble, J. (2007). Insuring inequality: The role of the Federal Housing Administration in the urban ghettoization of African Americans. *Law & Social Inquiry, 32*(2), 399–434.
Lott, B., & Bullock, H. (Eds.). (2007). *Psychology and economic injustice: Personal, professional, and political intersections*. Washington, DC: American Psychological Association Press.
Miller, N. (2002). Personalization and the promise of contact theory. *Journal of Social Issues, 58*(2), 387–410.
Nagel, J. (1998). Masculinity and nationalism: Gender and sexuality in the making of nations. *Ethnic and Racial Studies, 21*(2), 242–269.
Oren, N., & Bar-Tal, D. (2007). The detrimental dynamics of delegitimization in intractable conflicts: The Israeli-Palestinian case. *International Journal of Intercultural Relations, 31*, 111–126.
Peteet, J. (1994). Male gender and rituals of resistance in the Palestinian intifada: A cultural politics of violence. *American Ethnologist, 21*(1), 31–49.
Pettigrew, T. F. (1997). Generalized intergroup contact effects on prejudice. *Personality and Social Psychology Bulletin, 23*(2), 173–185.
Pettigrew, T. F. (1998). Intergroup contact theory. *Annual Review of Psychology, 49*, 65–85.
Pettigrew, T. F. (2003). Peoples under threat: Americans, Arabs, and Israelis. *Peace and Conflict: Journal of Peace Psychology, 9*(1), 69–90.
Phinney, J. S. (1991). Ethnic identity and self-esteem: A review and integration. *Hispanic Journal of Behavioral Sciences, 13*(2), 193–208.
Punamäki, R. (1996). Can ideological commitment protect children's psychosocial well-being in situations of political violence? *Child Development, 67*(1), 55–69.

Rouhana, N. N. (2004). Group identity and power asymmetry in reconciliation processes: The Israeli-Palestinian case. *Peace and Conflict: Journal of Peace Psychology, 10*(1), 33–52.

Roy, S. (2004). The Palestinian-Israeli conflict and Palestinian socioeconomic decline: A place denied. *International Journal of Politics, Culture and Society, 17*(3), 365–403.

Sampson, E. E. (1977). Psychology and the American ideal. *Journal of Personality and Social Psychology, 35*(11), 767–782.

Sherif, M. (1958). Superordinate goals in the reduction of intergroup conflict. *American Journal of Sociology, 63*(4), 349–356.

Simmel, G. (1971). The stranger. In D. N. Levine (Ed.), *Georg Simmel: On individuality and social forms* (pp. 143–149). Chicago: University of Chicago Press. (Original work published 1908)

Tajfel, H., & Turner, J. (1979). An integrative theory of intergroup conflict. In W. G. Austin & S. Worchel (Eds.), *The social psychology of intergroup relations* (pp. 33–47). Monterey, CA: Brooks/Cole.

Wallach, J. (2000). *The enemy has a face: The Seeds of Peace experience.* Washington, DC: United States Institute of Peace Press.

CHAPTER 9

Toward the Development of a Theoretical Framework for Peace Education Using the Contact Hypothesis and Multiculturalism

Ulrike Niens

Introduction

Ethnopolitical conflict and community divisions are significant phenomena in modern societies and are sometimes considered the modern variant of the cold war, which was regarded as endangering to world security in the second half of the last century. Education has long been acknowledged as a tool to promote social cohesion and peace; therefore, it gained increasing academic, public, and political attention, especially in the last two decades.

At an international level, the United Nations (UN) Decade of Human Rights for Human Rights Education (1995–2004) and the currently ongoing UN Decade of Sustainable Development Education (2005–2014) may be seen as signs of the importance attached to the role of education in national and international contexts. The overall aim of the current UN decade is to encourage changes in behavior that will create a more sustainable future in terms of environmental integrity, economic viability, and a just society for present and future generations. 'Cultural Diversity' as well as 'Peace and Human Security' belong to the eight key themes of the current Decade. The 2001 Universal Declaration on Cultural Diversity affirms even more directly "that respect for the diversity of cultures, tolerance, dialogue and cooperation, in a climate of mutual trust and understanding are among the best guarantees of international peace and security" (UNESCO Universal Declaration on Cultural Diversity, 2001, p. 12). At the national level, many countries have introduced various educational programs, including peace, reconciliation, citizenship, and human rights education, with the aim to facilitate relationships between diverse social groups and to foster social cohesion.

While education thus takes center place in the development of strategies and policies to manage ethnic and cultural diversity, the meaning of the term "peace education" often remains conceptually ambiguous and its role undefined. Furthermore, despite a wealth of academic and public interest in the area, peace education appears to be detached from relevant social scientific theories that may be used to underpin the development of a theoretically grounded framework of peace education that would support a tailored approach to educational systems, policies, and practice in different sociopolitical contexts.

While it is acknowledged that an interdisciplinary perspective may be required to fully understand the possible factors affecting the impact of peace education, including theories from a range of academic disciplines, such as anthropology, sociology, etc., it is the aim of this chapter to shed some light on the conceptualization of peace education and to explore how theoretical frameworks, based on frequently employed approaches from the political sciences and social psychology in particular, may be used to underpin the design of educational strategies for promoting social cohesion and peace in diverse societies at relative peace as well as those with community tensions or conflict.

In the following chapter, an attempt is made to explore peace education conceptually and to elicit gaps in the explanatory value of current theoretical conceptualizations of peace education, especially with regard to its application to various contexts characterized to a greater or lesser extent by peace, community tensions, or conflict. Drawing upon two theoretical perspectives on diversity and conflict, this chapter considers how multiculturalism and the contact hypothesis may be used to address these ambiguities and to underpin the development of peace education programs in various sociopolitical contexts ranging from relative peace to conflict. The chapter will conclude with implications of these perspectives for the development of a theoretical framework of peace education as well as for educational policies and practice and some final comments on the need for further theoretical development and research in this area.

Conceptualizing Peace Education

The UN declaration clearly acknowledges the potential role of education for the promotion of peace at an intergroup, national, and international level. Article 26 of the Universal Declaration of Human Rights states, "Education shall be directed to the full development of the human personality and to the strengthening of respect for human rights and fundamental freedoms. It shall promote understanding, tolerance and friendship among all nations, racial or religious groups, and shall further the activities of the United Nations for the maintenance of peace."

However, academics have long lamented a lack of conceptual clarity with regard to peace education (Salomon, 2002), which may be exemplified by Harris and Morrison's (2003) claim that "peace education is currently considered to be both a philosophy and a process" (p. 9). The term "peace education" has been used to describe a wide range of educational programs, including those that are concerned with conflict in interpersonal relationships (e.g., mediation training), those concerned with nonviolent behaviors in schools, and those concerned with intergroup relations at societal level (Reardon, 1997). Therefore, peace education can be seen as an umbrella term that covers various approaches to promoting harmonious relations between individuals and groups not only in societies emerging from violent conflict but also in other societies for the prevention of such conflicts. Depending on the sociopolitical context and the level of violence, Salomon (2002) differentiates between peace education in regions of intractable conflicts, regions of interethnic tensions, and regions of relative experienced tranquility. This broad understanding of peace education, which may be preventative or a strategy for dealing with tension and conflict, could be seen as a way of dealing with diversity and inclusion by promoting an awareness and appreciation of negative and positive peace (Galtung, 1969).

In recent years, attention has frequently been drawn to curricular subjects associated with equality and justice, social cohesion, and peace. Human rights education as well as citizenship education, which have been introduced into the formal school curricula of many societies across the world in the last decade (Davies, 2000a, 2000b), are undoubtedly closely related to peace education (Andreopoulos, 1997; Davies, 2005). Despite the specific challenges of implementing citizenship education in divided societies, including the lack of uniting national and cultural identity, governance, or commonly agreed goals (Smith, 2003), it may provide an opportunity to peacefully debate and negotiate identities, intergroup relations and political aspirations in societies with various degrees of political violence (Kerr, McCarthy, & Smith, 2002; Wylie, 2004). Similarly, human rights education has been proposed as a key element of peace building (Andreopoulos, 1997). Notwithstanding its potential to challenge inequality and injustice, human rights education may prove controversial as it may obscure the distinction between human rights legislation and social values (Ely-Yamin, 1993). Due to connotations of "passive peace" and religion, for example, peace education has also been considered as contentious "because of controversy surrounding the word 'peace'" (Harris, 2004, p. 8). However, I would argue that conceptualizing peace education as an umbrella category that incorporates community relations, citizenship, and human rights education may provide a framework that explicitly proposes peace as the main societal goal, which may be partly achieved through human rights and democratic citizenship as indicated in the UN declaration of human rights. To adopt such a comprehensive approach to peace education that is firmly based on the notion of the development of positive peace, which enables positive intergroup attitudes and democratic behaviors within society as a whole, it is necessary to reconsider its underpinning theoretical framework and, in turn, its applicability to various contexts of relative peace, community tension, or conflict.

THEORETICAL PERSPECTIVES ON MANAGING DIVERSITY IN SOCIETY

In education, two main perspectives on managing diversity in society can be identified, which have widely informed peace education policy and practice in different settings. Multicultural education is based on theories of pluralism and liberalism in the political sciences, which have been used to explore plural and monocultural education systems as well as various curricular developments, especially in the context of societies with relative peace or those with low levels of community tensions, and, as McGlynn and Bekerman (2007) point out, multicultural theories had relatively little impact on peace education in settings of sociopolitical conflict. In contrast, the contact hypothesis, which has been developed within social psychology, has been used to investigate the impact of intergroup contact on attitudes and identities, especially in the context of societies with community tensions and conflict as well as in the context of laboratory experiments. The following sections will review both perspectives before considering their implications for peace education in policy and practice.

MULTICULTURALISM

Political scientists have long debated the merits and disadvantages of various approaches to social inclusion and diversity in society and their impact on social cohesion and peace. Traditionally, strong nation-states supported the assimilation of immigrants into the majority culture and one unifying national identity was assumed, which superseded individual and group identities (Giddens, 1987). In the latter half of the twentieth century, multicultural ideas, which highlight the importance of group rights, took hold of Western nations' public and political debates and, eventually, policies and integration strategies (Kymlicka, 1995). In the United States, assimilation was strongly tied to the notion of a "melting pot" while multiculturalism was closely associated with the notion of a "salad bowl" (Gleason, 1964).

Habermas (1993) proposes two stages of assimilation, including political acculturation (i.e., acceptance of constitution) and social acculturation (i.e., acceptance of customs and cultures), whereby the state can request citizens only to adopt the first but not the second type of acculturation. Habermas' conceptualization of acculturation reflects understandings of patriotism and national identity (e.g., Feshbach, 1987; Kosterman & Feshbach, 1987) that emphasize respect of the nation as a political entity and pride of belonging to a particular nationhood, respectively. However, political acculturation, which is mainly based on cognitions and behaviors, may be criticized for underestimating the influence of identity and emotions on individuals' relationship with their social environment (Miller, 1995; Schnapper, 2002).

In recent years, especially since 9/11, multiculturalism as a policy to manage societal diversity has been severely criticized and public and political debates increasingly look at common values and social cohesion as necessary prerequisites for functioning, diverse, and peaceful democracies (Brubaker, 2001; Modood, 2005). Straddling the balance between assimilation and diversity is often seen as one of the most significant challenges the modern world must overcome to ensure sustainable peace (Taylor, 1991).

In many areas of public life, different approaches to multiculturalism are evident, which focus to varying degrees on societal unity or diversity. Kincheloe and Steinberg (1997) suggest four approaches to multiculturalism:

1. Monoculturalism: emphasis on one dominant culture
2. Liberal multiculturalism: emphasis on similarities between communities
3. Pluralist multiculturalism: emphasis on differences between communities
4. Critical multiculturalism: challenging inequalities between communities

Different approaches to multiculturalism in society are mirrored in strategies to managing diversity within the formal educational system, curricula, and school policies (Banks, 2006). Academics discuss which approaches can be most effectively applied to different educational contexts in various societies. In the United Kingdom, plural approaches used to be most prominent; however, in more recent years, in line with criticisms relating to social policies based on plural multiculturalism, questions have been asked relating to the potentially divisive nature of an educational system that emphasizes cultural differences and may neglect to highlight commonalities between various groups. In turn, there is skepticism about perceived forced assimilation, which may alienate minority groups. The Crick Report (Qualifications and Curriculum Authority, 1998), which focuses on social cohesion, and the Parekh Report (Runnymede Trust, 2000), which highlights pluralist strategies in dealings with diversity, represent examples of this educational debate (Olssen, 2004). However, discourses about the value of different strategies often take place in parallel with little overlap. Public debates may focus on faith schools and parental choice and the display of religious symbols (e.g., Burtonwood, 2002; Parker-Jenkins, Hartas, & Irving, 2004) or the impact of specific curricular subjects, such as citizenship education, on pupils' attitudes and behaviors (e.g., Banks, 2007; Osler & Starkey, 2000).

Divided societies are frequently characterized by plural education systems that have often been blamed for providing unequal opportunities and perpetuating community divisions and conflict (Bush & Saltarelli, 2000), despite opposition, for example, from advocates of faith schools (e.g., Gardner, Lawton & Cairns, 2005; Short, 2002). Even if schools are not openly propagating conflict, separate schooling itself may be regarded as emphasizing differences and thereby strengthening intergroup boundaries.

Research indicates that both, shared and separate, schools employ different approaches to diversity and community relations, based on notions of liberal, plural, or critical multiculturalism (McGlynn, in press; Schofield, 2001). While the emphasis on similarities between groups may lead to an avoidance of sensitive and controversial issues (Donnelly, 2004), approaches focusing on differences in shared schools may attract similar criticisms as separate education. Critical multiculturalism has been suggested to expand on the notion of plural multiculturalism; therefore, it employs explicit antiracist and antisectarian strategies, which may make it possible to deal with similarities and differences in a way that enables children and young people to confront prejudices in attitudes and behaviors (Nieto, 2004). In general, systematic research evidence that supports claims of the effectiveness of these approaches on changing young people's attitudes and behaviors is scarce.

CONTACT HYPOTHESIS

The assumption of the beneficial effects of shared schooling on children's attitudes and behaviors relating to community relations is often based on the notion that prejudices develop as a result of ignorance and fear and that contact with members of the other community may enable individuals to learn more about the other, to associate positive emotions and experiences with the other community, and thereby to reduce intergroup anxiety, which, in turn, is believed to increase self-esteem and positive attitudes to the other community. Most prominently, this assumption is captured in the contact hypothesis (Allport, 1954), which proposes that contact between members of opposing groups will promote positive intergroup attitudes in individuals and improve relationships between groups. While the contact hypothesis has often been cited to affirm suggestions of the beneficial effects of shared education, it has frequently been overlooked that specific conditions were stipulated as prerequisites of effective contact, which were rarely met in educational settings. Allport suggests that institutional support, equal status, cooperation, and superordinate goals are essential elements of successful intergroup contact, and research to date indicates that these conditions are necessary for contact to make a difference with regard to individuals' attitudes (Pettigrew & Tropp, 2006).

The contact hypothesis has since been further developed, and specific attention has been drawn to the central role of identity in intergroup relations, and thereby in intergroup contact situations. Three strategies, which differ in the way that identities are considered, have been proposed to introduce successful contact. The *decategorization model* (Brewer & Miller, 1984) calls for *interpersonal* contact between members of opposing groups. Hewstone and Brown (1986) suggest *intergroup contact* (i.e., contact in which group identities are highlighted, for example, in discussions of controversial issues) as the most effective means to achieve a reduction of intergroup conflict. Research clearly indicates the quality of contact to be of importance and the necessity for controversial issues to be discussed (Niens, Cairns, & Hewstone, 2003). Gaertner, Dovidio, Anastasio, Bachevan, and Rust (1993) propose *superordinate recategorization* (i.e., identification with broader social categories and the establishment of a common ingroup identity). More recently, Pettigrew (1998) advocates that it is the order in which contact approaches are introduced that matters in the successful implementation of contact programs. Thus, interpersonal contact could first be introduced, followed by intergroup contact, and, finally, a superordinate identity could be established. Relatively little systematic research has been conducted into the most effective sequence of contact approaches in various settings, and, in particular, systematic field research about the sequential introduction of different types of contact in natural settings of strained community relations is virtually nonexistent (Brewer, 1999).

The contact hypothesis has often been applied to analyze school systems. Separate schools may be seen as enshrining a culture of ignorance, which does not provide children and young people with the opportunity to meet others who are not from their own community's background (Dunn, 1986; Gallagher, 1989). Thus, shared education has been proposed as a way to promote contact between children from different communities and positive intergroup relations in society in the long term. In response, in various countries there have been movements advocating shared education, which caters to pupils from all communities in various countries, including Israel (e.g., Mor-Sommerfeld, Azaiza, & Hertz-Lazarowitz, 2007), Northern Ireland (e.g., Niens & Cairns, 2005), South Africa (e.g., Vandeyar & Esakov, 2007), and the United States (e.g., Schofield, 1991). In general, some empirical research results from Northern Ireland (Niens & Cairns, in press) and elsewhere (Dovidio,

Gaertner, & Kawakami, 2003; Pettigrew, 1998) indicates that contact in shared schools can be effective in fostering positive intergroup attitudes and identities if Allport's (1954) conditions of contact are upheld. Effectiveness also appears to depend upon a number of other factors, including the approach taken to diversity and inclusion, the educational and sociopolitical context, and the involvement of parents and the wider community in the affairs of the school.

There has been an ongoing debate about the age at which it may be useful to introduce programs aimed at promoting positive attitudes to other groups and peaceful intergroup relations in general. Some people propose that programs should be introduced as early as possible and provide young children with a rich and diverse environment in order for them to learn to value individual and collective differences and similarities (Connolly, Fitzpatrick, Gallagher, & Harris, 2006). In contrast, others maintain that educational programs, aimed at attitudinal change and identities, are more useful for children in their teens who have the cognitive capabilities to think in systematic and abstract terms (Piaget, 1965) and who have the moral understanding to engage in issues relating to equality and justice (Kohlberg, 1981). While research evidence clearly indicates that young children can correctly identify their membership in specific social groups and often display preferences for their own group (e.g., gender, Banerjee, 2005; nationality, Barrett, 2005; ethnicity, Connolly & Healy, 2004), the relationship of positive attitudes to the ingroup and negative attitudes toward the outgroup remains unclear, with some research suggesting that positive ingroup attitudes are associated with positive and other research suggesting an association with negative outgroup attitudes (Cameron, Alvarez, Ruble, & Fuligni, 2001). This ambiguity is mirrored in various debates focusing on the development of positive cultural, ethnic, or national identities, which entail positive affiliation to the ingroup without any negative outgroup associations (e.g., Brewer, 1999), in contrast to the attempt to decategorize such identities and to forge individual affiliations, which may be less emotive at the societal level.

IMPLICATIONS FOR PEACE EDUCATION THEORY, EDUCATIONAL PRACTICE, AND INDICATIONS FOR FUTURE RESEARCH

Conceptualizing peace education broadly, as a type of education that comprises community relations, citizenship, and human rights, may help to set a clear agenda for peace in a range of contexts experiencing relative peace, community divisions, or conflict. Multiculturalism and the contact hypothesis may offer complementary conceptual perspectives that may allow the development of a theoretical framework for peace education, which can enable its application to various levels of analysis. Multicultural theories and the contact hypothesis are frequently applied to different contexts of community divisions and conflict. The contact hypothesis focuses on bringing together communities that have little opportunity for contact in everyday life, with the aim to change individuals' attitudes and behaviors relating to the other community. Therefore, the contact hypothesis applies readily to the context of severe community divisions and conflict. However, it offers little insight into the development of democratic attitudes and behaviors in general, which are necessary for a society to maintain positive peace in the long term. In turn, multiculturalism deals with the management of communities that struggle to find a satisfactory balance between assimilation and maintenance of cultural identity in democratic societies, with the aim to facilitate social cohesion in democratic societies. Therefore, multiculturalism applies community divisions in contexts of relative peace. Yet, it gives little indication about how individuals and communities, in contexts of divided societies and conflict, may be enabled to learn about and interact with each other. The contact hypothesis could be regarded as providing a micro to meso-level of analysis (Pettigrew, 1986), which allows its application to school structures as shared or separate and to the development of effective implementation of contact programs. However, it offers little guidance on the development of effective educational policies that may promote positive attitudes at the societal and institutional level or on teaching methods, which may facilitate the development of democratic behaviors among pupils. In contrast, multicultural theories appear to provide mainly a micro and macro level of analysis, while plural and liberal perspectives are applicable to educational and school policies, and elicit suitable pedagogical strategies teachers may employ in shared and separate classrooms to promote positive attitudes and behaviors. The development of a theoretical framework of peace education, which incorporates current thinking about multicultural education and the contact hypothesis, may offer practical suggestions for the implementation of effective educational policies, curricula, and pedagogical tools that aim to promote active peace in a variety of settings, and further theoretical development and research in this area is necessary to guide good practice.

Synthesizing the contact hypothesis and multiculturalism into one theoretical framework for peace education raises a number of questions for education, which may need to be addressed in future research, relating to the role of superordinate identities, the most effective ways to introduce contact situations and to implement school policies to promote positive intergroup contact, and the pupils' age.

Contact research suggests the development of a superordinate identity, which overarches various group identities, as a crucial element of successful contact (Pettigrew, 1998). A superordinate identity, which comprises diverse community identities, should provide the consistency of various cultural traditions, languages and religions and, at the same time, offer a shared vision and positive future orientation for society as a whole. The assumption of a unifying superordinate identity, which enshrines diversity through cultural identities, is equally put forward by multicultural theorists (e.g., Banks, 2004) and clearly demonstrates the centrality of social, national, and cultural identifications. Research has shown that education may promote a shared sense of identity and belonging relating to the school among pupils; however, school identities are *sub*ordinate to community identities. Unless superordinate identities and shared societal goals, which are meaningful for all (or most) communities within society, are agreed upon and taken forward at the governmental level, it may be impossible for schools to develop contact programs that are effective in improving pupils' attitudes and community relations in general in the long term (cf. Bar-Tal, 2002). The question remains, what superordinate identity? Superordinate identities often do not feature on the public agenda, especially in divided societies. On the contrary, pluralistic policies may enshrine community divisions in their endeavor to ensure group distinctiveness, a balance of power between groups and peaceful relations (McGarry & O'Leary, 2004). In such contexts, how can one expect education to derive a meaningful superordinate identity if it is not reflected in reality?

Different types of contact may be equated to different approaches to educational practice in schools. In line with liberal multicultural approaches, which emphasize similarities between communities on the basis of the assumption that individual differences outweigh intergroup differences (despite the acknowledgment that minority rights need protection, Kymlicka, 2001), interpersonal contact highlights the uniqueness of each person and the individual's autonomy. In accordance with plural multicultural approaches, which highlight differences between communities due to the significance attached to collectivism and group rights, intergroup contact emphasizes collective identities. If both types of contact are important for successful contact to be established, schools may need to apply liberal and plural approaches to issues related to diversity and inclusion. Furthermore, given that quality of contact is essential for contact to make a difference, schools and curricula should encourage a critical multicultural approach that focuses on controversial issues, including consideration of equality and social justice. In the context of schools with diverse populations, which include pupils from opposing sections of society, research will need to explore how a threefold approach to intergroup contact, including interpersonal and intergroup dimensions as well as identity recategorization, can be implemented most effectively, taking into consideration a changing pupil population over time. In the context of divided school systems where community contacts would need to be forged across school boundaries, the question of how to implement a sustainable threefold approach to contact is even more difficult to answer.

Personal development theories and political socialization theories propose that education aimed at moral judgment, identity, and pro-social behavior may be most effective in the teenage years while research into the development of ingroup and outgroup attitudes indicates that exposure to people from diverse backgrounds may help even young children to become more open-minded. While exposure to diversity may be useful for younger children (e.g., at preschool or primary school level), more cognitively oriented programs specifically aimed at attitudinal and behavioral change might be more appropriate for post-primary schools. However, more research is required to clarify which age group is most suitable for the introduction of contact schemes and how they can be best adapted to suit children of various age groups.

Conclusion

It was the aim of this chapter to explore conceptualizations of peace education and to reflect upon the potential application of two theoretical perspectives—namely, multiculturalism and the contact hypothesis—for the development of a broad framework of peace education that is applicable to a variety of sociopolitical contexts experiencing relative peace, community tensions or conflict, and its implications on educational policy and practice. It has been argued that peace education can be regarded as an umbrella term that encompasses different educational programs aimed at promoting issues of equality and social justice, and this broad understanding of peace education provides a consistent framework, which allows its application to the range of political contexts that characterize societies. Using the contact hypothesis in conjunction with multiculturalism to underpin the development of such a broad theoretical framework for peace education may facilitate the development of effective and strategic educational initiatives, including educational structures, policies, and curriculum, in societies that not only differ in relation to the extent in which peace or conflict characterize everyday life but also those societies that equally strive to ensure a peaceful future.

References

I would like to thank Professor Ed Cairns, whose seminar presentation at Queen's University Belfast in 2007 provided the initial idea for writing this chapter.

Allport, G. W. (1954). *The nature of prejudice*. Reading, MA: Addison-Wesley.
Andreopoulos, G. (1997). Human rights education in the post-cold war context. In G. Andreopoulos & R. P. Claude (Eds.), *Human rights education for the twenty-first century* (pp. 9–20). Philadelphia: University of Pennsylvania Press.
Banerjee, R. (2005). Gender identity and the development of gender roles. In S. Ding & K. S. Littleton (Eds.), *Children's personal and social development*. Oxford: Blackwell.
Banks, J. A. (2004). Teaching for social justice, diversity and citizenship in a global world. *Educational Forum, 68*, 289–298.

Banks, J. A. (2006). Pluralism, ideology, and curriculum reform. In J. A. Banks (Ed.), *Race, culture, and education: The selected works of James A. Banks*. London: Routledge.

Banks, J. A. (2007). *Educating citizens in a multicultural society* (2nd ed.). New York: Teachers College Press.

Barrett, M. (2005). National identities in children and young people. In S. Ding & K. S. Littleton (Eds.), *Children's personal and social development* (pp. 181–220). Milton Keynes: Open University/Blackwell Publishing.

Bar-Tal, D. (2002). The elusive nature of peace education. In G. Salmon & B. Nevo (Eds.), *Peace education: The concept, principles, and practices around the world* (pp. 27–35). London: Lawrence Erlbaum.

Brewer, M. B. (1999). The psychology of prejudice: Ingroup love or outgroup hate? *Journal of Social Issues, 55*(3), 429–444.

Brewer, M. B., & Miller, N. (1984). Beyond the contact hypothesis: Theoretical perspectives on desegregation. In N. Miller & M. B. Brewer (Eds.), *Groups in Contact: The psychology of desegregation* (pp. 281–302). New York: Academic Press.

Brubaker, R. (2001). The return of assimilation? Changing perspectives on assimilation and its sequels in France, Germany, and the United States. *Ethnic & Racial Studies, 24*(4), 531–548.

Burtonwood, N. (2002). Political philosophy and the lessons for faith-based schools. *Educational Studies, 28*(3), 239–252.

Bush, K. D., & Saltarelli, D. (2000). *The two faces of education in ethnic conflict: Towards a peacebuilding education for children*. Florence: United Nations Children's Fund (UNICEF).

Cameron, J. A., Alvarez, J. M., Ruble, D. N., & Fuligni, A. J. (2001). Children's lay theories about ingroups and outgroups: Reconceptualizing research on prejudice. *Personality and Social Psychology Review, 5*(2), 118–128.

Connolly, P., Fitzpatrick, S., Gallagher, T., & Harris, P. (2006). Addressing diversity and inclusion in the early years in conflict-affected societies: A case study of the Media Initiative for Children—Northern Ireland. *International Journal for Early Years Education, 14*(3): 263–278.

Connolly, P., & Healy, J. (2004). *Children and the conflict in Northern Ireland: The experiences and perspectives of 3–11 year olds*. Belfast: Office of the First Minister and Deputy First Minister.

Davies, L. (2000a). *Citizenship education and human rights education: Key concepts and debates*. London: British Council.

Davies, L. (2000b). *Citizenship education and human rights education: An international overview*. London: British Council.

Davies, L. (2005). Teaching about conflict through citizenship education. *International Journal of Citizenship and Teacher Education, 1*(2), 17–34.

Donnelly, C. (2004). Constructing the ethos of tolerance and respect in an integrated school: the role of teachers. *British Educational Research Journal, 30*(2), 263–278.

Dovidio, J. F., Gaertner, S. L., & Kawakami, K. (2003). Intergroup contact: The past, present, and the future. *Group Processes & Intergroup Relations, 6*(1), 5–21.

Dunn, S. (1986). *Education and the conflict in Northern Ireland: A guide to the literature*. Coleraine: University of Ulster.
Ely-Yamin, A. (1993). Empowering visions: Towards a dialectical pedagogy of human rights. *Human Rights Quarterly, 15*(4), 640–685.
Feshbach, S. (1987). Individual aggression, national attachment, and the search for peace: Psychological perspectives. *Aggressive Behavior, 13*, 315–325.
Gaertner, S., Dovidio, J. F., Anastasio, P. A., Bachevan, B. A., & Rust, M. C. (1993). The common ingroup identity model: Recategorization and the reduction of intergroup bias. In W. Stroewe & M. Hewstone (Eds.), *European Review of Social Psychology, 4*, 1–26.
Gallagher, A. M. (1989). *Majority minority review 1: Education and religion in Northern Ireland*. Coleraine: University of Ulster.
Galtung, J. (1969). Violence, peace, and peace research. *Journal of Peace Research, 6*(3), 167–191.
Gardner, R., Lawton, D., & Cairns, J. (2005). *Faith schools: Consensus or conflict?* Abingdon: Routledge Falmer.
Giddens, A. (1987). Nation-states and violence. In A. Giddens (ed.), *Social Theory and Modern Sociology* (pp. 166–182). Cambridge: Polity Press.
Gleason, P. (1964). Symbol of fusion or confusion? *American Quarterly, 16*(1), 20–46.
Habermas, J. (1993). *Justification and application: Remarks on discourse ethics*. Cambridge: MIT Press.
Harris, I. (2004). Peace education theory. *Journal of Peace Education, 1*(1), 5–20.
Harris, I. M., & Morrison, M. L. (2003). *Peace education*. Jefferson, NC: McFarland.
Hewstone, M., & Brown, R. (1986). Contact is not enough: An intergroup perspective on the contact hypothesis. In M. Hewstone & R. Brown (Eds.), *Contact and conflict in intergroup encounters* (pp. 3–44). Oxford: Basil Blackwell.
Kerr, D., McCarthy, S., & Smith, A. (2002). Citizenship education in England, Ireland and Northern Ireland. *European Journal of Education, 37*(2), 179–191.
Kincheloe, J. L., & Steinberg, S. R. (1997). *Changing multiculturalism*. Philadelphia: Open University Press.
Kohlberg, L. (1981). *Essays on moral development, vol. I: The philosophy of moral development*. New York, NJ: Harper & Row.
Kosterman, R., & Feshbach, S. (1987). Toward a measure of patriotic and nationalistic attitudes. *Political Psychology, 10*, 257–274.
Kymlicka, W. (1995). *Multicultural citizenship*. New York: Oxford University Press.
Kymlicka, W. (2001). *Politics in the vernacular: Nationalism, multiculturalism, and citizenship*. Oxford: Oxford University Press.
McGarry, J., & O'Leary, B. (2004). Introduction: Consociational theory and Northern Ireland. In J. McGarry & B. O'Leary (Eds.), *The Northern Ireland conflict: Consociational engagements* (pp. 1–62). Oxford: Oxford University Press.

McGlynn, C. (in press). Negotiating difference in post-conflict Northern Ireland: An analysis of approaches to integrated education. *Multicultural Perspectives*.

McGlynn, C., & Bekerman, Z. (2007). The management of pupil difference in Catholic-Protestant and Palestinian-Jewish integrated education in Northern Ireland and Israel. *Compare, 37*(5), 689–703.

Miller, D. (1995). *On nationality*. Oxford: Oxford University Press.

Modood, T. (2005). *Remaking multiculturalism after 7/7*. Retrieved November 27, 2007, from http://www.opendemocracy.net/conflict-terrorism/multiculturalism_2879.jsp

Mor-Sommerfeld, A., Azaiza, F., & Hertz-Lazarowitz, R. (2007). Into the future: Towards bilingual education in Israel. *Education, Citizenship and Social Justice, 2*(1), 5–22.

Niens, U., & Cairns, E. (2005). Lessons learnt: Peace Education. *Theory Into Practice, 44*(4), 337–344.

Niens, U., & Cairns, E. (2008). Integrated education in Northern Ireland: A review. In D. Berliner & H. Kupermintz (Eds.), *Fostering Change in Institutions, Environments, and People: A Festschrift in Honor of Gavriel Salomon*. Mahwah, NJ: Lawrence Erlbaum.

Niens, U., Cairns, E., & Hewstone, M. (2003). Contact and conflict in Northern Ireland. In O. Hargie & D. Dickson (Eds.), *Researching the Troubles: Social science perspectives on the Northern Ireland conflict* (pp. 123–139). Edinburgh: Mainstream.

Nieto, S. (2004). Critical multicultural education and students' perspectives. In D. Gillborn & G. Ladson-Billings (Eds.), *The RoutledgeFalmer Reader in multicultural education* (pp. 179–200). London: RoutledgeFalmer.

Olssen, M. (2004). From the Crick Report to the Parekh Report: Multiculturalism, cultural difference, and democracy—the re-visioning of citizenship education. *British Journal of Sociology of Education, 25*(2), 179–192.

Osler, A., & Starkey, H. (2000). Citizenship, human rights and cultural diversity. In A. Osler (Ed.), *Citizenship and democracy in schools: Diversity, identity, equality* (pp. 3–17). Stoke on Trent: Trentham Books

Parker-Jenkins, M., Hartas, D., & Irving, B. (2004). *In good faith: Schools, religion and public funding*. Abingdon: Ashgate Press.

Pettigrew, T.F. (1986). The intergroup contact hypothesis reconsidered. In M. Hewstone & R. Brown (Eds.), *Contact and conflict in intergroup encounters* (pp. 169–195). Oxford: Basil Blackwell.

Pettigrew, T. F. (1998). Intergroup contact theory. *Annual Review of Psychology, 49*, 65–85.

Pettigrew, T. F., & Tropp, L. R. (2006). A meta-analytic test of intergroup contact theory. *Journal of Personality and Social Psychology, 90*(5), 751–783.

Piaget, J. (1965). *The moral judgment of the child*. New York: Free Press.

Qualifications and Curriculum Authority (QCA). (1998). *Education for citizenship and the teaching of democracy in schools (The Crick Report)*. London: Author.

Reardon, B. A. (1997). Human rights as education for peace. In G. Andreopoulos & R. P. Claude (Eds.), *Human rights education for the twenty-first century* (pp. 21–34). Philadelphia: University of Pennsylvania Press.

Runnymede Trust. (2000). *The future of multi-ethnic Britain: The Parekh Report*. London: Profile Books.

Salomon, G. (2002). The nature of peace education: Not all programs are created equal. In G. Salmon & B. Nevo (Eds.), *Peace education: The concept, principles, and practices around the world* (pp. 3–13). London: Lawrence Erlbaum.

Schnapper, D. (2002). Citizenship and national identity in Europe. *Nations and Nationalism, 8*(1), 1–14.

Schofield, J. W. (1991). School desegregation and intergroup relations: A review of the literature. *Review of Research in Education, 17*, 335–409.

Schofield, J. W. (2001). Maximizing the benefits of student diversity: Lessons from school desegregation research. In G. Orfield (Ed.), *Diversity challenged: Evidence on the impact of affirmative action* (pp. 99–109). Cambridge: Harvard Education.

Short, G. (2002). Faith-based schools: A threat to social cohesion? *Journal of Philosophy of Education, 36*(4), 559–572.

Smith, A. (2003). Citizenship education in Northern Ireland: Beyond national identity? *Cambridge Journal of Education, 33*(1), 15–31.

Taylor, D. M. (1991). The social psychology of racial and cultural diversity: Issues of assimilation and multiculturalism. In A.G. Reynolds (Ed.), *Bilingualism, multiculturalism and second language learning: The McGill Conference in honour of Wallace E. Lambert*. Hillsdale: Lawrence Erlbaum.

UNESCO Universal Declaration on Cultural Diversity (2001). Retrieved September 30, 2008, from http://unesdoc.unesco.org/images/0012/001271/127160m.pdf

Vandeyar, S., & Esakov, H. (2007). Color coded: How well do students of different race groups interact in South African schools? In Z. Bekerman & C. McGlynn (Eds.), *Addressing ethnic conflict through peace education: International perspectives* (pp. 63–76). New York: Palgrave Macmillan.

Wylie, K. (2004). Citizenship, identity and social inclusion: Lessons from Northern Ireland. *European Journal of Education, 39*(2), 237–248.

Chapter 10

Promoting Reconciliation through Community Relations Work
A Comparison among Young People in Belfast, Northern Ireland, and Vukovar, Croatia

Ankica Kosic and Jessica Senehi

Introduction

This chapter provides a conceptual framework for mapping cross-community work and projects that have been designed in more recent years to assist the process of reconciliation among young people in Northern Ireland (Belfast) and Croatia (Vukovar), and to analyze underlying sociopsychological assumptions of these interventions. The first part of the chapter briefly describes the historical background of conflicts in Northern Ireland and in Croatia (former Yugoslavia). It is followed by a description of some sociopsychological theories on the process of reconciliation among groups in post-conflict areas. In the last section, the nature of initiatives proposed to promote the reconciliation among youth in the cities of Belfast and Vukovar is examined through the prism of these sociopsychological theories.

Conflicts in Northern Ireland and Croatia

A broad range of subjective and objective factors have been identified as cues in the escalation of conflict in Northern Ireland and in Croatia (Kay & Olsen, 1993; O'Leary & McGarry, 1993). The conflict in Northern Ireland is most easily understood as a struggle between those who wish to see Northern Ireland remain part of the United Kingdom and those who wish to see the reunification of the island of Ireland, underpinned by historical, religious, political, economic, and psychological factors. Almost thirty years of conflict, called the "Troubles," characterized by sporadic fighting between paramilitary groups and terrorist attacks, resulted in high numbers of victims, many of whom were innocent civilians. Between 1966 and 1999, more than 3,500 people were killed and about fifty thousand were injured as the conflict spread beyond Northern Ireland's borders onto the British mainland (Hayes & McAllister, 2004). Despite all political solutions and changes at institutional level (e.g., the Belfast Agreement of 1998), Northern Irish society is still characterized by a high level of polarization between the two main communities. For example, currently 95 percent of schooling and 80 percent of social housing in Northern Ireland are segregated by religion (Schubotz & Robinson, 2006). In the Northern Irish context, people still have not come together at the interpersonal level and still tend to preserve exclusionist attitudes toward outsiders. There is still suspicion, enmity, and mistrust (Norman, 2003).

In mid-1991, a conflict escalated in areas of Croatia populated by large numbers of Serbs and continued until 1995. The cost of war was high among both groups in Croatia. An estimated six thousand to ten thousand people were killed, and more than thirteen thousand disappeared (Tanner, 1997). The city of Vukovar was almost completely destroyed, and the majority of Croats from Vukovar were expelled and spent years as refugees in other parts of Croatia or abroad. According to the last census conducted in 2001 by the Croatian Bureau of Statistics, the city's registered population was 31.670, consisting of 57.5 percent ethnic Croats and 32.9 percent ethnic Serbs, with other minorities making up 6.28 percent (Republic of Croatia Central Bureau of Statistics, 2008). Since the end of conflict in Croatia in 1995, the challenge of building sustainable coexistence between Croats and Serbs in Vukovar proves to be hard to achieve. In the present situation in Vukovar, most Croats and Serbs work in different places and frequent shops, café bars, and so on. Primary schools are separated by Croatian and Serbian, but secondary schools, since 2005, are semi-integrated in the sense that youth belonging to different ethnic groups go to the same schools but are in separate classes. There are many other problems, such as a disabled economy, a high unemployment rate, and human rights abuses (Amnesty International, 2007).

Conflict left a legacy of anger, bitterness, and hatred among the belligerent groups that is difficult to dissolve. Children and youth living in post-conflict areas grow up in an environment marked by a culture of negative attitudes, prejudices, and hatred. The questions remain: how are both countries to deal with such a past when new generations are concerned, and how do they move beyond the pattern of viewing the other side only through the prism of the suffering and pain of one's group?

Reconciliation through Contact and Interaction

Reconciliation in post-conflict areas requires changes at political, economic, juridical, educational, and at social-psychological levels. According to sociopsychological theories, fundamental to the reconciliation process is the restoration and rebuilding of relationships. It is argued that contact may lead to improved communication and better understanding between groups and, consequently, to greater cooperation and coexistence at the individual and group level (Hargie, Dickson & Nelson, 2003). These presumptions are based on the theory of contact hypothesis (Allport, 1954), which suggests that intergroup contact, under appropriate conditions, might help to alleviate conflict between groups and reduce mutual prejudice (Allport, 1954; for a review, see Pettigrew & Tropp, 2000). Favorable conditions include cooperative contact between equal-status members of the two groups in a situation that allows individuals to get to know each other on a friendly and prolonged, rather than a superficial, basis, to cooperate in achieving common goals, and to have a support of relevant social groups and institutions. However, contact with members belonging to the other community may be associated with social anxiety, especially in post-conflict areas.

In addition to contact theory, social psychology proposed that intergroup conflict may be reduced—and reconciliation promoted—through changes in the structure of social categorization. An improvement to intergroup relations, it is suggested, requires reducing the salience of existing ethnic and religious identities (Brewer & Miller, 1984). This, it has been proposed, can occur through a number of mechanisms, such as (a) decategorization, (b) recategorization, and (c) crossed categorization. The decategorization model (Brewer & Miller, 1984) suggests minimizing the use of category labels and, instead, interacting on an individual basis. It argues that, to achieve harmonious intergroup relations, group membership needs to be made *less* salient. The recategorization model (e.g., Gaertner, Dovidio, Anastasio, Bachman, & Rust, 1993) argues that intergroup prejudice can be reduced if perceivers reject the use of "us" and "them" in favor of a more inclusive, superordinate "we" category. Relationships that cut across ethnic, religious, or cultural lines help to combat the effects of narrow identity groups and harsh intolerance, and move individuals toward a wider sense of social identity. The third model on crossed categorization proposed that most realistic intergroup contexts involve several categorizations, some of which coincide and some of which cut across each other. Thus, "others" may be outgroup on one dimension but ingroup on another.

We are interested in exploring types of programs and interventions organized by civic organizations in Belfast and Vukovar with the aim to promote intergroup contact among young people and deal with salient ethnic and religious identities.

CROSS-COMMUNITY WORK WITH YOUNG PEOPLE IN BELFAST AND IN VUKOVAR

In Northern Ireland, a series of reforms aimed at promoting intercommunity dialogue have been introduced in recent years at policy, legislation, and infrastructure levels (see Fraser & Fitzduff, 1994). Changes at the macro level over the last decade in Northern Ireland have resulted in the proliferation of a broad range of community relations initiatives, programs, and organizations. The voluntary sector experienced substantial growth over the past years through access to a number of funding programs, especially the Eastern Union (EU) Peace I and II programs (Byrne, Irvin, Fissuh, & Cunningham, 2006).

In Croatia, there are approximately 360 associations dealing with children and youth. Vukovar is a small city, and the number of nongovernmental organizations (NGOs) is much smaller than in Belfast. Most organizations have been created upon the initiative of people from some NGOs in Western countries who have been working on transferring their experiences, skills, and knowledge to local communities and partners. By 2004, most international organizations and donors had gradually left the area, led by the assumption that mainstream organizations could now continue work on their own.

This chapter aims to explore the role of civic organizations and projects that have been designed in more recent years to assist the cross-community work with young people in Belfast and in Vukovar, with an objective of promoting peace education, breaking down enemy images, and reducing fear and distrust toward "the other side." A description was made of the types of civic organizations and of approaches used by them in promoting intercommunity contact and to deal with salient social (ethnic and religious) identity. Lastly, this study tries to assess the sustainability, strength, weakness, opportunities, and barriers for peace education through community relations work in these two contexts.

METHODOLOGY

In-depth interviews were conducted with twenty-five representatives of civic organizations in Belfast and with thirteen representatives in Vukovar. The interviewees were asked to describe themes of the areas and activities in which their organization has been involved, and strategies and methods of interventions. In addition, they were asked to concentrate on the assessment of the sustainability, strengths, weaknesses, opportunities, and barriers for peace education through community relations work in these two contexts. All interviews were audiotaped to draw upon experiences, transcribed, and subject to a content analysis. Analysis of interviews concentrates on discourses constructed around themes: (a) how they select the problem to deal with in their project's areas of intervention, (b) which sociopsychological strategies and methods are used in interventions, and (c) how they promote intergroup contact and deal with salient ethnic and religious identity.

Findings

Areas of Intervention

Our analysis of interviews promoted by civic organizations working with young people showed that most projects have been focused on (a) prevention and reducing of antisocial behavior, (b) improvement of socioeconomic situation through training and personal development, and (c) leisure activities.

Projects Aimed At Preventing and Reducing Antisocial Behavior among Youth
Many of the youth programs, especially in Belfast, have been set up to address specific issues of social exclusion and antisocial behavior. Over recent years, residents, community workers, political representatives, and the police have all noted the influence of young people in sustaining tension between communities (Hansson, 2005). Many interface communities in Belfast sporadically experience periods of tension and violence caused by young people (especially during the summer when young people are throwing stones across the wall). There are some events, such as parades and football matches that function as key triggers, that raise tensions and sectarianism between young people (Jarman & O'Halloran, 2001). In a recent study in Northern Belfast, Byrne, Conway, and Ostermeyer (2005) found that young people felt restrictions on their movements and feared the dangers of moving outside of their area. The 2003 Young Persons Behaviour and Attitudes Survey indicated that 21 percent of eleven- to sixteen-year-olds admitted to being "attacked, threatened, or rude to someone" in last twelve months (NISRA, 2003, p.1), suggesting that many young people have engaged in forms of anti-social behavior.

This is less the case in Vukovar; they do not enter into conflict on the street and there are no riots, but some problems have been registered in nightclubs and secondary schools where individuals or groups provoke others and express ethnic intolerance. These conflicts have been of a verbal type but, on a few occasions, have exploded into the use of violence.

However, conflict in young peoples' lives is not always directly related to sectarianism. Schools, families, and local communities are also contested spaces where young people can feel unsafe and vulnerable. In Belfast, youth workers come into contact with young people underachieving at school, teenage mothers and young fathers, those abusing drugs and alcohol, those with behavioral problems, and those involved in crime, paramilitary activities, and hooliganism. Vukovar also has problems with youth who suffer behavioral disorders and those who are addicted to drugs or alcohol, but only a small percentage of young people violate the law and accomplish criminal offences. Only one NGO in Vukovar has had a few short-term projects aimed at prevention of behavioral disorders, through work with parents, teachers, and children.

Improving the Socioeconomic Situation through Education, Training, and Personal Development

Some of the interviewees emphasized that sectarianism in Northern Ireland cannot be considered in isolation from other social problems. While economic prosperity, with wealth relatively equitably distributed, will not totally eliminate prejudice, there is a lot of evidence to suggest that in times and areas of economic scarcity, prejudicial behavior is likely to flourish. This was the rationale for including economic measures within the EU Peace II Program. About 39 percent of the Peace II Program was invested in specifically economic projects (Matic, Byrne, & Fissuh, 2008).

The economy in Northern Ireland has become the miracle economy of the Eastern Union with a tremendous growth rate (Morrow, 2005). Nevertheless, some areas of Belfast are suffering from a relatively high concentration of problems, such as unemployment, poor housing, and low income. In a changing employment market, it has become increasingly difficult for young people and adults with low academic achievement to secure skilled-labor jobs (Smyth, Fay, Brough, & Hamilton, 2004). The area of Vukovar has been, in the post-war period, one of the less-developed areas in the country, with a high unemployment rate.

It is mentioned in cross-community programs that economic initiatives can impact peace education and reconciliation on a number of different levels. On one level, economic measures can have an indirect impact by increasing prosperity, which reduces social exclusion and diverts attention away from political and sectarian issues to reduce intercommunity tensions. On the other level, economic initiatives can facilitate processes of engagement that have a direct impact on peace and reconciliation goals by building networks and facilitating relationships between communities.

Many projects in Belfast and Vukovar have focused on helping socially disadvantaged young people, especially those who leave school with no qualifications and who live in areas of high deprivation. These initiatives are designed to raise young people's expectations, hopes, and aspirations by using education and training to increase their skills to cope with a life of social disadvantages (see also Byrne, Thiessen & Fissuh, 2008). Here, the principle of individual empowerment is perceived as a key aspect of their work and an important condition for reducing intergroup negative attitudes.

Leisure Activities

Youth free time in Belfast and Vukovar is fairly disorganized. Most young people spend their free time watching TV programs or hanging out in café bars. One of the frequent comments made in relation to young people becoming involved in violent and antisocial behavior is that there are few resources available to them. Consequently, young people start drinking and engaging in antisocial behavior as a response to the boredom they feel (Hall, 2005). This has been repeatedly cited in the Belfast interviews in relation to trouble that breaks out during the summer holidays. Most disorders are related to problems caused by a relatively small number of young people who are under the influence of alcohol. Some young men in both cities feel that violence is the norm for settling conflicts and can play a role in maintaining their status and in building their tough reputation (Hansson, 2005). Communities in Belfast have realized that something must be done for young people to keep them constructively occupied and consequently far away from antisocial and criminal activities (Hansson, 2005; Jarman, 2006). Numerous programs have been established to distract young people from the interfaces, especially during periods of celebrations and parades. For example, many organizations promote programs to bring together young people from both communities for a range of outings, street events, arts, cultural events, and sporting activities as well as cross-community residential and holiday programs. Civic organizations in Vukovar are also aware of the need to help young people to improve the quality of life through involvement, for example, in cultural and sport activities, but very few initiatives have been promoted due to the impossibility of securing funding to organize these programs.

Arts and Cultural Projects

Cultural events and activities (e.g., music, cinema, storytelling, theater, visual arts, etc.) have great potential to attract people irrespective of ethnic origin, and are important tools in dealing with problems of salient social identity (Avruch, 1998; Cohen, 2005; Senehi, 1996, 2002).

Most cultural events provide a noncompetitive opportunity for interactive participation with members of the "other" community. Art and culture may be used as a good vehicle for the exploration of sensitive or difficult issues (e.g., history, identity, traditions, symbolism, divisions, etc.) and to tell a constructive story about the society (Senehi, 2002). Through the arts, communities can ask questions, challenge authority, have fun, and celebrate their own special identities.

The Arts and Culture Northern Ireland Survey (Stevenson, 2004), commissioned by the Arts Council Northern Ireland, found that a high proportion of young people between sixteen and twenty-four years of age had attended at least one arts or cultural event in the last year. However, there were higher levels of participation in arts and cultural activities among respondents living in less-deprived areas. It seems that many young people are reluctant to leave their district to attend cultural events organized in the city center or other districts.

Vukovar is still under reconstruction, and not all cultural venues have been rebuilt until now. Young people in Vukovar are eager for more cultural events, such as concerts, movies, etc., but very few have been offered to them until recently.

There is a general distinction between professional arts and community arts. Many cultural organizations in Belfast encourage the use of arts and popular culture as a tool for community development, and education for peace and reconciliation. Projects range from creative writing, festivals, and musical productions to theater, dancing, film, storytelling festivals (e.g., Ulster-American Storytelling Festival), and exhibitions. Some of the established projects require the participation of members of both communities over a sustained period of time.

Belfast has generated a number of substantial community drama activities over the past few years, such as "The Wedding" a theater production written by Jo Egan and Maureen Harkins. With the subject matter of mixed marriage, it provided a context in which attitudes and beliefs could be challenged with irony and humor. Some of the theater plays also run a summer schedule in Belfast's districts, with others in the city center. However, few theater companies work in schools where theater and storytelling could be used as teaching tools.

Music is an important instrument for bringing young people together through common interests, joint participation in music groups and orchestras, and concerts and festivals. In the past, different projects have been supported, which include young people from both communities playing music together, but less in Vukovar than in Belfast. Some concerts and music festivals have also been organized, attracting young people across borders (e.g., Exit Festival, which is organized every summer in Novi Sad, a city in Serbia not far from Vukovar, and has attracted not only young people from all over the former Yugoslavia but also from other European countries).

Sport Activities
Community divisions can often be reflected in the sporting domains as well. However, sports can also give young people a great opportunity to meet others from the other community. In divided communities after the violence, "mixed" teams and groups can be formed to play basketball, ice hockey, and volleyball as a way to recategorize identities and promote

dialogue among young people. Many community organizations in Belfast have sport programs. For example, since April 2006, the North Belfast Play Forum has promoted Midnight Street Soccer in which young people aged eight to seventeen years can participate in community football on Saturday nights from nine o'clock to midnight from March to June, August to November. For ten weeks, teams compete against other local teams. The games attract over five hundred participants each weekend, and hundreds more spectators. The games combine training, matches, and educational workshops that address different problems within and between communities, and helps to challenge stereotypes empirically. The football games usually avoid competition between community groups and promote mixed teams based on cooperation.

In Vukovar, sport activities have not been used as a means to promote intergroup relations. Young people sometimes gather at school sport terrains to play football or volleyball, but they remain always separate. No mixed teams have ever been formed in school sporting events or competitions. There are a few cases of Serbian children attending Croatian sports clubs, but none of Croatian children attending Serbian sports centers.

Sociopsychological Strategies and Methods Used in Interventions

The strategies used in cross-community programs may be divided into two categories: (a) single-identity work and (b) intergroup contact.

Single-identity Work

Single-identity work involves exploring and affirming issues related to cultural identity through workshops on differences concerning history, culture, religion, and politics. It is used more in programs promoted in Belfast than in Vukovar. In Northern Ireland, single-identity work is based on an assumption that communities (especially Protestant) are not confident about their identity and that most young people have limited information about the history and the conflict. Most of the interviewees in Belfast emphasized it is important to increase awareness of one's own cultural identity as well as to create an understanding that differences can be resolved through trust, respect, and tolerance. Moreover, they suggest that single-identity work may assist people in perceiving the diversity that exists in their own community and that their community is not homogeneous in attitudes about history, culture, and politics.

Interviewees mentioned that some project participants were reluctant about engaging in cross-community contacts (e.g., young people who had negative experiences in previous contact with the other community, etc.), and, therefore, single-identity work was noted as a useful first-step approach. However, in these cases, problems could arise in terms of motivating and maintaining their commitment. The tactics used to secure engagement and continued participation varied widely, but it is important to note that any kind of constraint imposed could instigate a negative reaction.

These initiatives are sometimes understood as a prelude to cross-community contact. However, little research has been carried out on the role of single-identity projects in creating the confidence in contact with the other community. Some scholars have pointed to a number of potential negative outcomes of single-identity work (e.g., Church, Visser, & Johnson, 2002): First, while engaged in an examination of their own cultural issues, participants might be inclined to reinforce their negative attitudes and stereotypes toward the "other." Second, the group could further entrench the righteous view of their own position. Third, the group could simultaneously develop sophisticated arguments about why they should not engage with the other community.

Promoting Intergroup Contact among Young People

Many organizations working to improve community relations among young people in Belfast and in Vukovar base their projects primarily on the theory that a friendly and cooperative contact with people and groups from the antagonist community will lead to tolerance and understanding. A variety of methodologies have been developed by community organizations in Belfast with the aim of bringing people together. Programs vary greatly in terms of the number of children involved, but most of them operate within a range of ten to fifteen children, as they try to have a balance between the number of Catholic and Protestant youth, which is not always easy to achieve. Participation is voluntary, but sometimes young people are selected through schools and other community institutions. Some of the participants are indicated by youth workers as "specific cases," having expressed negative attitudes towards the other community. They attend reunions several times a week for a few hours during the project's duration, usually from one to three years. Project leaders in Belfast mentioned difficulties in finding venues that can be comfortably used by different communities as a safe space, taking into account historical and existing fears about different locations. The objective of bringing groups together is to provide opportunities for young people to work in joint activities. There are discussion groups on the themes of common interest and concern, or those that unite them: school issues (e.g., canteen improvements, bullying, etc.), local issues (e.g., youth facilities), and larger social issues (e.g., sport, music, the arts, environmental issues, etc.). It is supposed that, through contact, young people may discover many of their beliefs, concerns, and experiences are similar. On the basis of their shared interest, common goals can be employed to create a condition of cooperation.

In Vukovar, very few cross-community projects have been promoted with aims to bring people together and have discussion and fun activities. The intercommunity groups have been organized around some volunteering and cultural activities (e.g., ecology, support to elderly people, and artistic and cultural activities). Participation of youth is on voluntary basis, and there is no concern about balance between the number of Croats and Serbs. In few cases, there was a predominance of one community and other members withdrew from participation.

During some weekends or holidays, groups of young people in Belfast spend time together at residential centers in Northern Ireland or in other locations in the Republic of Ireland, England, and Scotland. They take part in a variety of activities organized to promote fun. Residentials fulfill a key role in creating the conditions in which young people form friendships with those of the other community. Besides fun activities, each weekend has a particular theme for discussion.

Vukovar NGOs started more recently to organize residential programs, especially during summertime. For example, the project called "Run without frontiers" (Note: It symbolically refers to the Danube River) involved a group of ten youth from secondary schools in Vukovar and ten youth from Serbia, and brought them together to an ecological farm in a Croatian village near Vukovar. They not only actively participated in the work of the farm but also in a series of seminars on sociopsychological themes, such as stereotypes and prejudice, nonviolent resolution of conflicts, and the like. A project leader from Vukovar noted in her interview that "if you take children out from the local context—from Vukovar—then they are absolutely different. They do not care about divisions and borders; they do not need to think what they would say to their parents."

Most of the organizations in Belfast offer a trip to the United States for a cross-community holiday at the end of the project, which can act as a motivational factor to get young people involved in the project. Many holiday programs for children from Northern Ireland originated in the 1970s. The early emphasis of these cross-community projects was to provide children with an opportunity to spend the school holidays in a more peaceful environment. Grant aid for such programs has been available mostly from foundations in the United States. Usually two children from both religions stay with an American family who may be of a different religion. Many organizations, such as Corrymeela, the Peace People, Children Project, and others, have devoted themselves to promoting these projects. The interviewees emphasized that children benefit most from contact with a multicultural environment in the United States. The U.S. dimension enriches young people's experience of understanding diversity. It may open up their minds and make them aware that there is a wider world beyond Belfast and Northern Ireland and that prejudiced views need to be challenged and changed.

There are no programs of support of this type in Vukovar. Due to poor socioeconomic standards in the region, most young people do not have opportunities for educational, cultural, and tourist mobility outside the area. In secondary schools, recreational excursions, graduation trips, and other travels are noncompulsory extracurricular activities.

A significant part of intercommunity programs in Belfast concerns work on "sensitive issues." It includes themes that focus on the differences between communities and the problems arising from within them (e.g., cultural diversity, politics, human rights, etc.). Some programs bring groups of young people from the two communities together to listen to each other about their personal experiences related to the conflict. These initiatives give young people the opportunity to begin to see the other side's point of view. They try to teach young people that different cultural and religious perspectives, and even political preferences, can coexist within a society and that no group should regard it as their right to dominate or intimidate the other into adopting alternative beliefs and practices. They aim at developing the participants' abilities to move beyond "political correctness" and toward a more open dialogue, enabling them to identify ways in which they may contribute to the creation of a more tolerant and pluralist society.

In Vukovar, very few initiatives have been promoted of this type, especially when youth are concerned. The problem is that finding the funds to carry out such programs and finding experts able to focus on the development of such programs is difficult.

Interviewees suggest that bringing young people together in an environment where they can live, talk, work, and play together could help them break down the barriers of ignorance that have separated them. Some studies suggest that such projects influence social understandings and beliefs about the other group (Trew, 1989), whereas others suggest a more limited impact occurs (Cairns & Cairns, 1995; Hughes & Knox, 1997). The more critical studies expressed concern about the fact that, even where there was an apparent attitudinal change during cross-community projects, the attitudinal change was short-lived or context-specific. There are few possibilities to meet friends from the other community outside of activities promoted by the project; it is difficult for these young people to visit each others' homes.

Dealing with Problems of Social Anxiety and Salient Ethnic and Religious Identity

Social Anxiety

Project leaders are aware of the anxiety that may occur during contact with members of the other community, and in Belfast they try to address these fears and prejudices through single-identity work prior to contact. In Vukovar very limited attention has been given to this problem.

Many interviewees in Belfast and Vukovar noted that, regardless of background, many youth lack self-confidence and feel embarrassed in social interactions with whomever they talk. "Their verbal skills are very modest, and the range of topics they can discuss with others is limited" (Interview in Belfast). The anxiety and uncertainty management theory of effective communication (Gudykunst, 2005) assumes that the perception of effectiveness in communication with others reduces anxiety and eases communication. We may suppose that youth with a low perceived effectiveness in communication may avoid contact with others, especially with those belonging to the other community. Thus, a great importance should be given to the building of self-confidence and social skills. Many programs in Belfast are aware of this fact; however, it is less the case in Vukovar.

Salient Social (Ethnic and Religious) Identities

The concept of social identity is used broadly to refer to the psychological link between individuals and the social groups to which they belong. We all belong to several social categories and therefore may have a series of social identifications, one of which is salient at any given time. Conflicts reinforce the individual's membership with their ethnic or religious group and the ingroup bias. In Belfast and Vukovar, most people have strong ethnic and religious identities and there is often an obsession about the need to recognize the Other on the base of the ethnic and religious dimension. As described in the introduction, salient social identities may be reduced by strategies that are focused on decategorization; recategorization, or cross-categorization. Cross-community leaders assume that, if we let young people from opposing groups get to know each other as individuals, they will discover that the person from the outgroup whom they are in contact with is more similar to themselves than they originally thought and that pleasant interactions would lead toward decategorization of ethnic and religious identities. Some cross-community projects are focused on recategorization or development of awareness of a common identity (e.g., youth identity, European identity). It is supposed that these relationships that cut across ethnic and religious lines could help to combat the effects of narrow identity groups and harsh intolerance, and move individuals toward a wider sense of social identity. Many projects in Vukovar give attention to development of awareness on European identity and on understanding and acceptance of multiculturalism in Europe. This is realized through education (e.g., courses on foreign languages), thematic seminars, and awareness-raising campaigns. Less attention has been given to development of European identity in cross-community work in Belfast. Furthermore, arts and cultural activities may promote reconciliation through recategorization; for example, young people belonging to "opposite" communities form together some music groups, "new age" groups, and others that may help the creation of a common identity. The third model on cross-categorization suggests that most realistic intergroup contexts involve several categorizations, some of which coincide and some of which cut across each other. Projects oriented at developing professional expertise may increase awareness and contact among young people on the basis of their expertise or common interests.

Conclusions

This preliminary study has provided some insights into the nature of community relations work with young people in Belfast and Vukovar. A number of community projects have been undertaken in recent years to promote intercommunity dialogue among youth. The enormous efforts that individuals and communities put into these projects should be saluted and recognized. Different strategies and activities have been used, involving a relatively small number of participants, and with very few having a longitudinal developmental plan to follow young people after the termination of each project. In almost all of the categories, the strategy has been to improve community relations through cross-community contact. With studies on contact hypothesis we do not know, *per se*, if contact produces positive attitudes toward others, or if in fact individuals who engage in contact have already had a certain level of positive attitude toward relations with other groups, or at least an absence of negative attitude. Individuals who become involved in community relations projects are normally those who already uphold the values of a peaceful and equitable society.

Another concern deals with participant involvement in these coexistence projects, including the recruitment, commitment, and motivation of individuals who join these projects. There is the problem of how to attract unwilling individuals into cross-community contact groups. The individuals who have negative attitudes and perpetrate sectarianism in the society would be the least willing to become involved in cross-community reconciliation efforts. To counter this behavior, various methods are used to keep participants involved ranging from residential workshops to trips abroad. These methods can be considered as a carrot-and-stick approach, which raises concerns as to the reasons of participant involvement in coexistence projects.

It seems that the types of projects promoted in Belfast and Vukovar have been guided, not only by an analysis of needs in the context, but also by possibilities of obtaining funding. Furthermore, project leaders perceived that the increase in short-term funding over the past ten years has ushered in a spirit of competition into youth-work practice. They underlined in the interviews that funding application processes are often cumbersome and time-consuming. Thus, one of the recommendations is to regard the possibility of rendering the application procedure less complicated. The overall picture of community relations initiatives is somewhat fragmented, reflecting the development of disparate projects that are relatively isolated from one another (see Acheson, Williamson, Cairns, & Stringer, 2006).

A limited number of projects in Belfast and none in Vukovar cope with the issue of forgiveness and trauma among young people and of ways to deal with the past. Even if young people have had little, if any, direct personal experience of violence as a result of the conflict, they still have knowledge of how their community or their family members have suffered and been affected. This knowledge was internalized, and some assumed the hurt of a past experience on a very personal level. Such history was often used to explain and to justify their own and others' feelings, behaviors, and attitudes. In conflict and also in post-conflict time, there is a prevalent and dominant perceptual pattern where people view their group as being an innocent victim and the rival group as a guilty perpetrator of wrongdoings. Such stereotypical perceptions decrease the willingness for a dialogue with the other side and legitimize suspicion and hostility toward the outgroup. This chapter suggests that more attention should be given to the issue of perception of victimhood and collective responsibility to promote reconciliation in both countries, in Northern Ireland and in Croatia.

References

Research for this report was conducted in October and November 2006. The study is funded by the European Commission, Human Resources and Mobility Activity, Marie Curie Actions.

The authors would like to thank all project managers and community leaders in Belfast and Vukovar for their support and participation in the research, as well as all others who work to promote peace and reconciliation in post-conflict areas.

Acheson, N., Williamson, A., Cairns, E., & Stringer, M. (2006). *Voluntary action and community relations in Northern Ireland*. A report of a research funded by the Community Relations Council and the Office of First Minister and Deputy First Minister. University of Ulster.

Allport, G. W. (1954). *The nature of prejudice*. Reading, MA: Addison-Wesley.

Amnesty International. (2007). *Annual report for Croatia*. Retrieved April 20, 2008, from http://www.amnestyusa.org/annualreport.php?id=ar&yr=2007&c=HRV

Avruch, K. (1998). *Culture and conflict resolution*. Washington, DC: United States Institute of Peace Press.

Brewer, M. B., & Miller, N. (1984). Beyond the contact hypothesis: Theoretical perspectives on desegregation. In N. Miller & M. B. Brewer (Eds.), *Groups in contact: The psychology of desegregation* (pp. 281–302). Orlando, FL: Academic Press.

Byrne, J., Conway, M., & Ostermeyer, M. (2005). *Young people's attitudes and experiences of policing, violence and community safety in North Belfast*. Belfast: Northern Ireland Policing Board.

Byrne, S., Irvin, C., Fissuh, E., & Cunningham, C. (2006). People's perceptions of the role of economic assistance in conflict reduction in Northern Ireland. *Peace and Conflict Studies, 13*(2), 1–21.

Byrne, S., Thiessen, C., & Fissuh E. (in press). Economic assistance and peacebuilding in Northern Ireland. *Canadian Journal of Peace Research*.

Cairns, E., & Cairns, T. (1995). Children and conflict: A psychological perspective. In S. Dunn (Ed.), *Facets of the conflict in Northern Ireland* (pp. 97–113). Basingstoke: Macmillan.

Church, C., Visser, A., & Johnson, L. (2002). *Single identity work: An approach to conflict resolution in Northern Ireland* International Conflict Research (INCORE Working Paper). Derry: University of Ulster.

Cohen, C. (2005). Creative approaches to reconciliation. In M. Fitzduff & C. E. Stout (Eds.), *The psychology of resolving global conflicts: From war to peace: Vol. 2. Group and social factors*. Westport, CT: Praeger.

Fraser, H., & Fitzduff, F. (1994). *Improving community relations: A paper prepared for the Standing Advisory Commission on Human Rights*. Retrieved January 22, 2008, from http://cain.ulst.ac.uk/issues/community/frazer.htm

Gaertner, S. L., Dovidio, J. F., Anastasio, P. A., Bachman, B. A., & Rust, M. C. (1993). The common group identity model: Recategorization and the reduction of intergroup bias. *European Review of Social Psychology, 4*, 1–26.

Gudykunst, W. B. (2005). An anxiety/uncertainty management (AUM) theory of effective communication. In W. B. Gudykunst (Ed.), *Theorizing about intercultural communication* (pp. 281–322). Thousand Oaks, CA: Sage.

Hall, M. (2005). *Finding common ground. An exploration by young people from both sides of the East Belfast interface*. Farset Community Think Tanks Project. Pamphlet No. 52, Newtownabbey, Co. Antrim: Island Pamphlets.

Hansson, U. (2005). *Troubled youth? Young people, violence and disorder in Northern Ireland*. Belfast: Institute for Conflict Research.

Hargie, O., Dickson, D., & Nelson, S. (2003). A lesson too late for the learning? Cross-community contact and communication among university students. In O. Hargie & D. Dickson. (Eds.), *Researching the Troubles: Social science perspectives on the Northern Ireland conflict*. Edinburgh: Mainstream Press.

Hayes, B., & I. McAllister (2004). Who backs the bombers? *Fortnight, 425,* 11–12.

Hughes, J., & Knox, C. (1997). For better or worse? Community relations initiatives in Northern Ireland. *Peace and Change, 22,* 330–355.

Jarman, N. (2006). *Working at the interface: Good practice in reducing tension and violence*. Institute for Conflict Research. Belfast: Institute for Conflict Research. Retrieved January 22, 2008, from http://www.conflictresearch.org.uk/documents/Working%20at%20the%20Interface.pdf

Jarman, N., & O'Halloran, C. (2001). Recreational rioting: Young people, interface areas and violence. *Child Care in Practice, 7,* 2–16.

Kay, M., & Olsen, G. (1993). Bridge on the Sava: Ethnicity in Eastern Croatia, 1981–1991. War among the Yugoslavs [Special issue]. *Anthropology of East Europe Review, 11*(1/2), 54–62.

Matic, M., Byrne, S., & Fissuh E. (2007). Awareness and process: The role of the European Union Peace II Fund and the International Fund for Ireland in building the peace dividend in Northern Ireland. *Journal of Conflict Studies, 27*(1), 110–133.

Morrow, D. (2005). *Shaping our shared future. In shaping and delivering peace at local level? Learning from the experience of Peace II.* Belfast: Community Relations Council.

Norman, P. (2003). *The elusive quest: Reconciliation in Northern Ireland.* Belfast: Blackstaff Press.

Northern Ireland Statistics and Research Agency. (June 11, 2004). Young Person's Behavior and Attitudes Survey Bulleting 2003. Belfast: Central Survey Unit, NISRA Retrieved October 2, 2008, from http://archive.nics.gov.uk/dfp/040611a-dfp.htm

O'Leary, B., & McGarry, J. (1993). *The politics of antagonism: Understanding Northern Ireland.* London: Athlone.

Pettigrew, T. F., & Tropp, L. R. (2000). Does intergroup contact reduce prejudice? Recent meta-analytic findings. In S. Oskamp (Ed.), *Reducing prejudice and discrimination: Social psychological perspectives* (pp. 93–114). Mahwah, NJ: Erlbaum.

Republic of Croatia Central Bureau of Statistics. (2008). Retrieved May 29, 2008, from http://www.dzs.hr/

Schubotz, D., & Robinson, G. (2006). *Cross-community integration and mixing: does it make a difference?* Research Update 43. Retrieved January 22, 2008, from http://www.ark.ac.uk

Senehi, J. (1996). Language, culture and conflict: Storytelling as a matter of life and death. *Mind and Human Interaction, 7*(3), 150–164.

Senehi, J. (2002). Constructive storytelling: A peace process. *Peace and Conflict Studies, 9*(2), 41–63.

Smyth, M., Fay, M. T., Brough, J., & Hamilton, J. (2004). *The Impact of political conflict on children in Northern Ireland: A report on the community conflict impact on children study.* Belfast: Institute for Conflict Research.

Stevenson, G. (2004). *Arts and culture in Northern Ireland: 2004 baseline survey.* Retrieved April 24, 2008, from http://www.artscouncil-ni.org/departs/all/report/research/Gen%20Pop%20Survey.pdf

Tanner, M. (1997). *Croatia: A nation forced in war.* New Haven: Yale University Press.

Trew, K. (1989). Evaluating the impact of contact schemes for Catholic and Protestant children. In J. Harbison (Ed.), *Growing up in Northern Ireland* (pp. 131–160). Belfast: Northern Ireland Learning Resources Unit, Stranmillis College.

Part III

Curriculum and Pedagogy

Introduction

Michalinos Zembylas

Curriculum and pedagogy have often been ascribed the power of maintaining or subverting existing social and other conflicts (Apple, 1979; McLaren, 1989). For example, history curricula and textbooks in conflict areas have been analyzed in terms of constructing social and political contexts that encourage students to enact a conflicting ethos toward the enemy, or the Other (Cole, 2007; Davies, 2004). Undoubtedly, the economies of power and affect built through textbooks and curricula may contribute to the conservation of existing power relationships by securing prevailing social, political, and emotional norms in relation to the Other (Zembylas, 2008). Curriculum and pedagogy play a crucial role in the efforts to promote peace education policies and practices. Therefore, in-depth analyses of curricular and pedagogical work in relation to issues of conflict and peace are greatly needed; such analyses need to be aware of the multiple complexities and provide pedagogical resources for reconciling ethnic, racial, and religious differences in ways that foster understanding, social justice, and coexistence.

The chapters in this part pursue analytical, historical, and empirical explorations that attempt to provide responses to difficult questions about the larger purposes and social values that animate curricula and pedagogies, especially with regard to their role in advancing peace and social justice. The collection of chapters in this part offers many important and challenging ideas in the context of ongoing debates in peace education concerning the following questions: What are the pedagogical and curricular challenges for peace and social justice education? How do claims for recognition advance or prevent the creation of critical spaces for dialogue and deliberation? How can schools develop curricula and pedagogies that promote alterative historical consciousness that is not grounded in hatred and resentment? How could educational environments promote the learning of the Other's language as a means for peace and coexistence? And finally, can we envision and create a critical and emancipatory teacher education for peace education in the twenty-first century? The chapters in this part shed light on these sorts of questions, challenging the reader again and again with the tensions troubling peace educators and exploring some insightful possibilities of responding to such tensions. The authors of these chapters do not pretend to have better answers to these questions than those presented by others. However, they follow provocative lines of investigation that complicate the issues and enrich our perspectives.

Michalinos Zembylas, in his chapter, invokes the notion of *critical emotional praxis* as a critical tool for curriculum and pedagogy to analyze and sort through nationalistic narratives brought into the classroom. As he explains, critical emotional praxis is "critical thinking and action that questions the emotional, ethical, political, and pedagogical implications of our identifications with particular ideologies such as nationalism" (Chapter 11 in this volume). Through analyzing examples of his Greek-Cypriot university students' narratives, Zembylas highlights the students' emotional ambivalence with respect to efforts toward coexistence and peace in Cyprus. He argues that the use of critical emotional praxis in curriculum and pedagogy brings to surface these ambivalent feelings and helps educators to deal with the powerful, affective investments of past trauma and suffering.

In their chapter, Tamar Zelniker and her colleagues ground their work in personality and social psychology and focus on personal and group relations between Arab and Jewish students who are citizens of Israel. They describe their efforts in the context of an action research course to investigate how students' national identity definitions and religion influence their perception of negative and positive aspects of life on campus. The authors' findings over five years of conducting action research projects with their students point to the ways in which both Arab and Jewish students use hyphenated identities. The action research procedures that are followed combine two peace education strategies—integrated education and intergroup encounters—which have important implications for teacher education curricula and pedagogies in conflict areas.

Pilvi Torsti and Sirkka Ahonen present the results of a study on historical consciousness in postwar Bosnia and Herzegovina, exploring the contradiction between the divided nature promoted through curricula and the shared historical identity of young people. For this reason, they suggest that *deliberative communication*—grounded in Jürgen Habermas's work—can be helpful in problematizing such contradictions. The authors discuss the implications of deliberative communication for deliberative democracy in the context of history teaching in post-conflict situations.

Bekerman shows, through his long-standing ethnographic research in Palestinian-Jewish integrated schools in Israel, that Jews do not become bilingual. Bekerman is careful not to blame the teachers or the students but, instead, emphasizes how the Israeli sociopolitical context discourages the teaching and learning of Arabic as a second language. His research exposes multiple practices that could be judged as contradictory to the bilingual principles, yet these practices are also attuned to the macro-contextual levels in which bilingual education is embedded. The implications of this research for bilingual curricula and pedagogies are significant because language learning is shown to be strongly related to sociopolitical contexts, and thus it is not simply a matter of pedagogical methodology or content.

Finally, Candice C. Carter and Saloshna Vandeyar review two teacher education programs (one in South Africa and another in southern United States) in terms of instructional contexts, curriculum contents, and individual as well as collective participant behaviors. This comparative exploration points to some similarities and dissimilarities in these three domains. Some of the issues that are highlighted include the importance of courage, commitment, and compassion in the promotion of transformative learning. Comparison of these two contexts also evidence the value of critical theory and recognition of cultural capital; thus, Carter and Vandeyar argue that preparing teachers to engage with social or other conflicts needs to acknowledge the transformative impact of such ideas.

Taken together the chapters in this part demonstrate the importance of using different theoretical and methodological perspectives in the analyses of interrelations among peace education, coexistence, and social justice. The ideas that these diverse chapters provide inform peace education literature by enriching it with perspectives from multicultural education, bilingual education, social psychology, philosophy, history, and teacher education. By placing these chapters together in this particular part, it becomes readily apparent how important a diversity of theoretical and methodological approaches is in the field of peace education.All the chapters together offer a multiperspectival view on conflict and peace education and bring to light tensions related to the role of curriculum and pedagogy in the formation of practices and policies that promote peace, coexistence, and social justice.

References

Apple, M. (1979). *Ideology and curriculum*. London: Routledge.
Cole, E. (Ed.). (2007). *Teaching the violent past: History education and reconciliation*. Lanham, MD: Rowman & Littlefield.

Davies, L. (2004). *Education and conflict: Complexity and chaos.* London: RoutledgeFalmer.
McLaren, P. (2003). *Life in schools: An introduction to critical pedagogy in the foundations of education* (4th ed.). Boston: Allyn and Bacon.
Zembylas, M. (2008). *The politics of trauma in education.* New York: Palgrave Macmillan.

Chapter 11

Inventing Spaces for Critical Emotional Praxis
The Pedagogical Challenges of Reconciliation and Peace

Michalinos Zembylas

For several years, I have been involved in research that explores the emotional aspects of peace and reconciliation education in Cyprus. I have collected ethnographic data from Greek-Cypriot (G/C) students in higher education (who are mostly preservice kindergarten to sixth-grade teachers), focusing on their feelings for the political situation in Cyprus, their Turkish-Cypriot (T/C) compatriots, and their perceptions about the prospects of peace and reconciliation after decades of trauma and suffering as a result of the ongoing conflict between Greek Cypriots and Turkish Cypriots. Not surprisingly, this work has reiterated what previous studies have found (e.g., see Bryant, 1998, 2001, 2004; Hadjipavlou-Trigeorgis, 1998, 2007; Papadakis, 1995; Spyrou, 2001a, 2001b, 2002, 2006), that is, how educational practices have been systematically used to create nationalist subjects in Cyprus. Elementary and secondary school curricula and pedagogies implore students to remember the nation glories, honor the leaders and warriors who defended the lands and values of the nation, and to despise and hate the enemy.

The premise on which this chapter rests—that nationalistic education is a problem—is not new; that premise is not the most important contribution of this chapter. The more important contribution is the analysis and sorting through nationalistic narratives brought into the classroom, to figure out ways to disrupt those practices and invoke spaces for *critical emotional praxis* (Chubbuck & Zembylas, 2008; Zembylas, 2008). Critical emotional praxis is critical thinking and action that questions the emotional, ethical, political, and pedagogical implications of our identifications with particular ideologies, such as nationalism (see Boler & Zembylas, 2003; Zembylas, 2006). The notion of critical emotional praxis rests on three assumptions: First, it is grounded in an historical and political understanding of the role of emotions in conflict-ridden areas. Second, critical emotional praxis consists of the ability to question emotionally charged, cherished beliefs, exposing how privileged positions and comfort zones inform the ways in which one recognizes what and how he or she has been taught to see and act (or not to see and act), and empowering different ways of being with or for the Other. Finally, critical emotional praxis translates these emotional understandings into relationships, practices, and enactments that benefit teaching and learning for peace and reconciliation.

In addition to reiterating the finding about the nationalistic ideologies embedded in G/C schools, the ethnographic investigation of my students' emotions has revealed a novel component not previously found. This component is the students' emotional ambivalence with respect to efforts toward coexistence and peace in Cyprus: that is, feelings of hatred coexist with feelings of empathy; there are both feelings of loss and hope, anger and understanding, resentment and sympathy for my students' T/C compatriots. Rather than being negative hindrances to educational efforts toward coexistence, these ambivalent emotions and the struggle to cope with them are shown to be both significant and productive. Therefore, I argue that the notion of ambivalence may be helpful to educators who are struggling to find pedagogical ways that deal with the powerful, effective investments of past trauma and suffering, because it signifies openness, not closure. As I will suggest, although negative feelings about the Other are difficult to change, unraveling the ambivalent emotions creates possibilities for enriching educators' and students' perspectives on mutual understanding and solidarity with others.

The Conflict in Cyprus: The Case of an Ethnically Divided Country

Overview of the Context

The recent history of Cyprus has been dominated by the ethnic conflict between Greeks and Turks on the island, which goes back in time over a number of centuries. Looking at this history, one can easily find competing discourses within each side—that is, the G/C and the T/C side—about the Other. Each side constructs narratives that are different with respect to how the Other is portrayed, but the common themes focus on the violence, hatred, and historical trauma that one side has inflicted on the other. There is now much ethnographic evidence indicating how individuals as well as organized groups from both communities systematically attempt to nationalize suffering and highlight the need to remember what "the enemy" has committed in the past (Bryant, 2004; Cassia, 2006; Loizos, 1998; Papadakis, 1998).

Undoubtedly, there is a lot of lingering anger, resentment, and grief in both communities over the years, but the biggest problem, according to Kizilyürek (1993), is the mentality of "us and them" that continues to be dominant in both communities. The most powerful way of forming an "us and them" mentality is to idealize one's own group and demonize the other. Idealization and demonization are accomplished through myth-making—that is, accounts that justify the negative evaluation of other groups and glorify one's own nation (Aho, 1994). It is, therefore, argued that the intensification of national hatred in Cyprus shapes a sense that there is a commonality in being G/C or T/C with Greeks and Turks, respectively (Attalides, 1979; Kizilyürek, 1993; Mavratsas, 1996, 1999; Papadakis, 1998). In fact, school education promotes the use of more inclusive categories, such as Greeks or Turks, at the expense of more synthetic or hybrid ones, such as Greek- and Turkish-Cypriots (Spyrou, 2006; Theodossopoulos, 2006). Each group constructs its ethnic identity through learning to hate the other. Not surprisingly, then, memories of life before the conflicts between the two communities—that is, memories of friendly interethnic neighborhood relations—become part of a hidden discourse because they are at odds with the official nationalist discourse (Loizos, 1998).

Research Examples

In my research on the emotional aspects of peace and reconciliation in Cyprus, I have been primarily interested in the affective implications of my students' narratives about the Other, trauma, suffering, peace, reconciliation, and emotions of living in a conflict-ridden area. In this section, I provide examples that describe (a) the ambivalent feelings of students' narratives about peace, reconciliation, and the Other in Cyprus and (b) how these ambivalent feelings create openings for witnessing the Other's trauma and enacting critical emotional praxis. These examples are drawn from a series of ethnographic studies that I conducted over the last five years (see Zembylas, 2006, 2007a, 2007b, 2008; Zembylas & Karahasan, 2006).

As an instructor who teaches prospective teachers in this troubled part of the world, I see that a major aspect of my teaching is to convey the affective implications of narratives that revisit traumatic events of the past, such as war, violence, and ethnic conflict. In particular, I consider that nationalism—that is, idealizing one's own nation and vilifying others—and its affective implications remain largely unspoken and unacknowledged in public discourse, in the media, and in schools. As all educators in this historical and political context teach and work with narratives of traumatic events on an everyday basis, it is important to explore how teachers and students at all levels of the educational system may be educated toward an understanding of affect that encourages an alternative affective, ethical, and political response. Such a response would move beyond nationalistic reactions to trauma or mere recognition that the Other is different and would take into account alternative meanings of narratives about trauma as well as the possibility that the classroom might be a site for political transformation (Rak, 2003).

My students' personal narratives about trauma, suffering, peace, and reconciliation in Cyprus tell us what is obvious to an outside observer—that is, how there is a "memory industry" (Klein, 2000, p. 127) prevailing in Cyprus. These personal narratives highlight two important aspects in the circulation of stories that are woven through nationalist discourses of education. First, personal narratives of education provide significant evidence of the ways in which pedagogical practices are constructed around the politics of emotions (Abu-Lughod & Lutz, 1990), such as hatred, trauma, resentment, and anger. The theme of politics of emotions emphasizes how emotions are not simply an individual matter but are crucial to the formation of social norms and collective imaginations (Lupton, 1998; Lutz & Abu-Lughod, 1990). In other words, emotions circulate and play an important part in the constitution of collective identities and power relations within a community (Ahmed, 2004). In her study of personal narratives in Cyprus, Hadjipavlou-Trigeorgis (1998) emphasizes how personal feelings are political in the sense of how Cypriots' experiences or memories of past events are embedded in conflict-socializing processes and reflect the political reality in each community.

In my studies, in addition to those views that were adamant about feelings of hatred for the Turks, there were also narratives full of ambivalence and different workings of negative feelings about the Other, such as the following:

> I am aware that we grew up hating Turks. The schools, the church, the society certainly contributed in creating this perception. But I think it's impossible to overcome this feeling of bitterness and rage. That's just how I feel about it. Perhaps my feelings will change in the future....I know I shouldn't make generalizations and say that all Turks are bad people. But every time I make an effort to see things differently, all these images come to my mind: our occupied villages; pictures of our beautiful churches and historical monuments that Turks took from us; images of killings and destructions that we suffered during the Turkish invasion; our refugees....With all these images haunting us, how can

we ever live with them? I just hope that one day I'll be able to overcome these feelings. But right now, that's just how I feel. (male junior student)

In other words, there are students who problematize their feelings of hatred for Turkish Cypriots ("I know I shouldn't make generalizations and say that all Turks are bad people"). The ambivalence of hatred is bound up with the positing of an affective relationality between the "I" and the "we" (Ahmed, 2004). But the meaning of "we" is neither fixed nor univocal; in fact, there is some space left for new meanings of "we." Thus, understanding the Other becomes an affect and effect of identification and works to read the Other outside of stereotypes (Bhabha, 1994). This ambivalence also shows how the meaning of hatred is historical and political rather than simply individual and psychological. It is not easy to dismiss collective memories and imaginations; however, it is a pragmatic goal to begin imagining the capacity to reconcile with one's enemies.

Thus, in my students' narratives, the notion of the politics of trauma and hatred in Cyprus helps us understand the ways in which emotional practices, sociability, and power are interrelated both in everyday life contexts and in educational settings. In other words, students learn how to remember the past trauma and sustain negative emotions about the Other through everyday social and educational practices. Inevitably, then, the collective memory of fear, hatred, victimization, and dehumanization of the Other becomes a powerful symbol and an effective tool that strengthens the existing, conflicting ethos. Consequently, when the emotional elements of the politics of trauma and hatred are not accounted for in educational efforts, they risk perpetuating the existing, conflicting ethos. Personal narratives should not be discarded but considered in critical terms to help us relearn the wisdom of forgetting (Eppert, 2003) to remember that the weight of the past should not stand in the way of the future. Ricoeur (1999) reminds us that "the duty to remember is a duty to teach, whereas the duty to forget is a duty to go beyond anger and hatred" (p. 11).

What is interesting in some of my students' narratives is that forgetting is not presented as it is commonly understood—that is, as an omission that constitutes an unpatriotic thing to do—but rather as a dynamic movement toward developing new emotional connections between the two communities. This is more clearly seen in the following narrative:

No, I don't hate Turkish Cypriots. I don't have anything against them. I despise the Turks who invaded Cyprus and I despise the Greek Cypriot "super-patriots" who caused the military coup and gave Turkey the opportunity to invade Cyprus....Both Greek Cypriots and Turkish Cypriots suffered a lot. We caused a lot of suffering to them during the period [of] 1963 [to] 1974 but nobody talks about this in our side. So I see their perspective too. They've been refugees, they've had missing persons too, and they've lost loved ones....After the opening of the Green Line in 2003, I realize more and more how Turkish Cypriots look like us! I mean it's hard to tell if someone is Greek Cypriot or Turkish Cypriot! Can you imagine my surprise when I think someone is Greek Cypriot and then I hear them speak Turkish?...They are human beings just like us. They are not the monsters we have been taught in our schools, by our politicians for such a long time....Yes, despite what happened in the past, I think we can live together peacefully respecting each other, because Cyprus belongs to all Cypriots. (female sophomore student)

Therefore, another important aspect in these stories is that discussions of peace and reconciliation in Cyprus may be suppressed, yet not completely eliminated. These stories, such as the above narratives, are usually suppressed in the sense of being played down in favor of legitimating conflicting ethos and demonizing the Other. Although school curricula highlight the violent, traumatic aggression and loss and the cultivation of a deeply rooted fear that the enemy is simply waiting for another opportunity to inflict more pain and suffering, there are some openings left as a result of acquiring new experiences and learning how to see the Other differently.

Consequently, it is important to highlight the significance of lived experiences to understand the emotional depth and power of collective imaginations around memory and forgetting. Personal narratives tell us a lot about how individuals and social groups are engaged in the work of constructing their identities (Holstein & Gubrium, 2000). Such narratives reflect the political circumstances and the larger ideologies and hegemonies that lie behind them (Denzin, 1997). Therefore, narratives should not be dismissed, no matter how painful they are; all points of view must be heard and acknowledged. It is through finding ways to subvert the hegemony (Apple, 1979) of official narratives that educators and students in both communities will construct spaces for peace and reconciliation in educational settings.

There is now ample evidence around the world that, in areas of conflict, education is systematically used to demonize the enemy and legitimize particular nationalist narratives and agendas (Bekerman & McGlynn, 2007; Davies, 2004). The challenging question is, then, how should we, as educators, approach personal narratives that communicate suffering for past historical trauma and resentment for the Other? A pessimistic response would be that these narratives are so deeply embedded in a group's historical consciousness that nothing can disavow past memories of trauma and resentment. However, an alternative response that is more optimistic aspires toward a critical reconsideration of the representation of each other that goes beyond debates concerning memory and forgetting. I suggest that personal narratives can help us rethink the way we teach and learn, and teach us how to discontinue to be traumatically possessed by the past when we work through it (Eppert, 2003). Forgetting, therefore, argues Eppert, is not only bound up with obligation but also with an obligation implicated in peace and reconciliation.

Inventing Pedagogical Spaces for Critical Emotional Praxis

As Callahan (2004) explains, coping with the emotions that occur as a result of narratives about suffering and hatred requires more than dialogue. Ellsworth (1989), in fact, emphasizes that dialogue alone may simply heighten the emotions that result from an increased awareness of the existing power structures and the status quo. Teaching about or for peace and reconciliation, therefore, is not only a cognitive endeavor; it involves engaging in emotional reflection, finding one's own relationship to peace and reconciliation, and creating an empowered sense of agency to take action and transform one's beliefs and practices. If such emotions and the struggles to cope with them are understood and approached as significantly productive components of being a teacher or a student in a conflict ridden area, the positive growth and transformation required in that process are more likely.

The lessons learned from my studies on the emotional ambivalence of students' narratives about peace and reconciliation in Cyprus help shape the development of the notion of critical emotional praxis. Critical emotional praxis begins with the acknowledgment that enacting teaching and learning for peace and reconciliation presupposes an understanding of the role of emotion in the everyday lives of those who live in conflict-ridden areas. One way of examining the emotional implications of systems and practices in such areas is to consider how emotions work to differentiate between us and them (Ahmed, 2004). This differentiation is crucial in the politics of emotions and works to establish a distinction between legitimate and illegitimate lives—we have positive feelings for those we consider like us and negative feelings for those we see as other. Educators thus need to understand and care how issues of power, privilege, and nationalism depend on withholding particular emotional responses (such as grief, compassion, and caring) toward certain groups of people deemed other and less worthy. My students' understanding of this perspective is seen in their expressions of grief and compassion only for those considered to belong in the same group as them.

Critical emotional praxis calls on educators and students to unpack their cherished beliefs and comfort zones to deconstruct the ways in which they have learned to see and act. Educators and their students must recognize how emotions influence the ways in which one chooses to see and, conversely, not to see things (e.g., how compassion for the suffering of the Other often involves one's discomfort because one's own group is responsible for the other's suffering). Critical emotional praxis, therefore, builds on the work of those who argue that emotion theory in education needs to be politicized and thus address questions of otherness, difference, and power (Boler, 1999; Boler & Zembylas, 2003; Zembylas, 2005, 2007c).

The aim of an educator who is willing to enact critical emotional praxis is to analyze these "emotional landmines" (Boler, 2001, p. 1) created in the classroom and the community, to understand and challenge how they shape and mark one's sense of emotional attachment and identity. Developing the skills and knowledge to analyze how unjust practices teach people to feel the world through an ideological lens, often with little awareness that they are doing so, is an important step in identifying exploitation, violence, and nationalism. As is evident in my studies, my students' understandings about peace and reconciliation develop in conjunction with their ongoing reflection on their emotions about T/Cs. Despite the discomfort that this process creates, some students are able to feel the politics of emotions in the constitution of education in divided Cyprus; others have more difficulties. For example, in the excerpts shared earlier, both students seem to realize that larger political and ideological struggles in the public arena as well as in schooling are inextricable aspects of how they feel.

Finally, critical emotional praxis draws from the above emotional understandings and responds to the particular context in which a school is located, creating and enacting pedagogies that reconceptualize the emotional culture of a classroom or school. For example, the absence of an empathetic culture in the schooling is widely evident, whereas anger and resentment predominate in students' perceptions. Nevertheless, research shows that persistence and creativity in the efforts to enrich the empathetic culture of a classroom or school can indeed alter the emotional connections between communities, even in the face of larger political issues (Berlak, 2004; Zembylas, 2005, 2007c).

POSSIBILITIES FOR PEACE AND RECONCILIATION EDUCATION IN CYPRUS

Here I want to consider two ways to strengthen the potential for developing pedagogical spaces of critical emotional praxis for reconciliation and peace in divided Cyprus. The first way is to develop pedagogies that encourage empathetic communication through an understanding of Others' thinking and feeling. The second way is the need to develop pedagogies that construct citizenship education that accepts difference and the notion of hybrid identities by relaxing the emphasis on separate identities. I discuss these ways below.

The first role for pedagogies of reconciliation and peace in Cyprus is to engage both communities in relational empathy (Broome, 1991, 1993, 1997, 1998, 1999, 2001, 2003, 2004a, 2004b). The process of relational empathy can be useful in the development of shared meanings created through interpersonal encounters. Such pedagogies of empathetic communication would lead students to start thinking and feeling about the Other in different ways than those in the past. Instead of presenting the Other as the enemy or someone who cannot be trusted (as many of my students' narratives suggest), students should be encouraged to see the Other as a human being who has also been traumatized by past events and who has similar needs for security, rights, and homeland (as the ambivalent feelings of the two students' narratives from which I quoted earlier). In Cyprus there is an urgent need of pedagogies that are based on "empathy towards the suffering Other" (Theodossopoulos, 2006, p. 10). As Theodossopoulos asserts, humanizing processes, such as similar cultural characteristics between G/Cs and T/Cs and common predicaments, could be some of the things to stress when one teaches social studies.

Clearly, promoting relational empathy in the classroom is not an easy process and it often involves a lot of discomfort for students and teachers. To confront the trauma and suffering felt by students and their families in conflict-ridden areas, educators and students need to engage in what Boler (1999) calls *pedagogy of discomfort* or *pedagogy of suffering* (Martusewicz, 2001)—both examples of pedagogies that transform suffering into compassion and an "alternate criticality" (Burbules & Berk, 1999, p. 59) that opposes the hegemonic culture of conflict and suggests that we think and feel differently. This position is emotionally discomforting and unsettling for those who feel that pain and suffering belong only to them, but, under some circumstances, the discomfort felt acknowledges the creative potential of affect (Wang, 2005).

In the examples shared earlier, the two students seem to realize the transformative power of empathy; this perspective gives them a new outlook of emotional criticality because it makes them realize the importance of expanding their sense of self in relation to T/Cs. Although the second student is more positive than the first, they both attempt to see things from the other's point of view. As Zembylas and Boler (2002) further emphasize, a pedagogy of discomfort requires that individuals step outside of their comfort zones and recognize what and how one has been taught to *see* (or not to see) things. In Cyprus, a pedagogy of discomfort could be used as a powerful pedagogical tool to help teachers and students to step outside of their comfort zones and problematize the ways in which G/Cs and T/Cs have been taught to see the Other (e.g., through history textbooks, pedagogical practices, school rituals, celebrations, etc.), that is, to understand how education is so often politicized and one-sided (see also Boler & Zembylas, 2003).

In building empathy and reconciliation, a wide variety of alternative narratives need to be developed out of the mutually hostile trauma stories. It is important to deepen awareness and criticality in young people about how trauma stories can be used to teach fear, hate, and mistrust

(Ramanathapillai, 2006). All narratives, Kreuzer (2002) emphasizes, even the ones from the perpetrators of violence, need to be considered seriously, because they help us understand the emotional aspects of conflict and they point toward openings for strategic intervention. To build empathy and reconciliation, it is valuable to identify the narratives that evoke fear, hate, and mistrust and publicize the stories that show positive emotions emphasizing the humanity of the "enemy"—for example, stories of collaboration and caring among G/Cs and T/Cs. Telling positive stories can help rehumanize the Other, and they counteract the confrontational symbolical and emotional content of competing narratives that work hard to dehumanize the enemy. I suggest, therefore, that the promotion of empathy and reconciliation in curriculum and pedagogy is a critical component of developing alternative narratives about past traumas—narratives that contribute to changing the hegemonic conflictive ethos.

Second, another way of inventing pedagogical spaces for critical emotional praxis in Cyprus is to construct pedagogies that promote the idea of citizenship education based on accepting differences and hybrid identities. Bekerman and Maoz (2005; see also Bekerman, 2007) suggest that goals, such as peace and coexistence education, may be better achieved if the emphasis on separate identity and culture is somewhat relaxed. According to them, strengthening coexistence might not be achieved if alternative options to the ones dictated in the past are not pursued. As Edward Azar also notes, it is the perpetuation of "exclusionary myths, demonizing propaganda and dehumanizing ideologies" (in Miall, Ramsbotham, & Woodhouse, 2000, p. 75) that legitimize polarized trauma narratives. Educators and students should learn to be open to the possibility of transformation and the exploration of multiple ways of connecting with each other. Such connections will constitute a third space—a space that opposes nationalist sentiments and polarized trauma narratives and opens possibilities for reimagining the sense of community and identity. An important way that pushes such connections is to avoid becoming enclosed in past identities that have been historically associated with nationalism and struggle to invent a democratic citizenship that critically reconsiders past feelings of belonging.

It is important to emphasize that one need to be careful with claims about what kind of citizenship education is promoted, since much citizenship education has been geared to the strengthening of nationalism and patriotism (Davies, 2004). The question here is what citizenship education would look like to challenge nationalist ideologies. I want to argue that hybridity should be an important component of citizenship education in Cyprus. That is, Cypriot educators need to develop a notion of citizenship that takes into account difference. "The tendency," writes, Davies (2004), "is to view citizenship in terms of universals that everyone, despite or because of their differences, should try to recognise and respect" (p. 90). However, there are problems in an approach that tends to represent citizenship education as a homogenizing process. Spinner-Halev (2003) urges us to be particularly cautious about citizenship education in divided societies: "Education in divided societies has to begin with [a] different assumption than education in other societies. In divided societies, those divided by religion or nationality, where fear and perhaps hatred permeate these divisions, the group cannot be ignored" (p. 90).

Consequently, what I am trying to do as an educator is to provide opportunities for my students to encounter firsthand testimonies to ethnic hatred and atrocities conducted by both communities, as well as to create openings for students to expose acts of kindness and compassion enacted by both communities in the past or in the present. The intended effect of directing students to collect and examine such testimonies (e.g., through oral stories, interviews, and written records) is to invite students into bearing witness to one's own or another's trauma (Zembylas, 2006, 2008). That is, my intention is to constitute us responsible for one another as co-witnesses who engage in alternative versions of how past traumatic events make us feel and why. This pedagogical approach is set in motion by questions of how we and others feel about trauma narratives, feelings that we are eager to talk about and ones not easily acknowledged or expressed. In this way, the classroom-based community moves beyond traumatic feelings by using those as a springboard to think about emotions and nationalism politically and ethically.

Conclusion

To conclude, educational programs and pedagogies inspired by critical emotional praxis may offer two important things. First, they can provide a space where educators and students can question common-sense assumptions and the politics of hegemonic trauma narratives. Second, those programs and pedagogies may provide opportunities for traumatized students to work through feelings of trauma and rehumanize the Other. In Cyprus, where suffering has been experienced by all communities, educators may choose to use the lived experiences of one's own suffering to enhance his or her understanding of the suffering of the Other. This is not an easy task, especially because our "enemies" are implicated in our suffering (as we are in theirs). Suffering, in itself, does not necessarily lead to compassion or empathy; however, compassionate and empathetic attitudes can be nourished (Cohen, 1997). Through social and educational practices, our own experiences of suffering, and our memory and forgetting of them, we may enhance our capacity to form wise and compassionate responses to the suffering of others and help us take a critical stance toward the construction of our narratives.

References

Abu-Lughod, L., & Lutz, C. A. (1990). Introduction: Emotion, discourse, and the politics of everyday life. In C. Lutz & L. Abu-Lughod (Eds.), *Language and the politics of emotion* (pp. 1–23). Cambridge: Cambridge University Press.

Ahmed, S. (2004). *The cultural politics of emotion*. Edinburgh, UK: Edinburgh University Press.

Aho, J. A. (1994). *This thing of darkness: A sociology of the enemy*. Seattle: University of Washington Press.

Apple, M. (1979). *Ideology and curriculum*. London, Routledge.

Attalides, M. (1979). *Cyprus: Nationalism and international politics*. Edinburgh, UK: Q Press.

Bekerman, Z. (2007). Rethinking intergroup encounters: rescuing praxis from theory, activity from education, and peace/co-existence from identity and culture. *Journal of Peace Education, 4*(1), 21–37.

Bekerman, Z., & Maoz, I. (2005). Troubles with identity: Obstacles to coexistence education in conflict ridden societies. *Identity: An International Journal of Theory and Research, 5*, 341–357.

Bekerman, Z., & McGlynn, C. (Eds.). (2007). *Addressing ethnic conflict through peace education: International perspectives*. New York: Palgrave Macmillan.

Berlak, A. (2004). Confrontation and pedagogy: Cultural secrets and emotion in antioppressive pedagogies. In M. Boler (Ed.), *Democratic dialogue in education: Troubling speech, disturbing silence* (pp. 123–144). New York: Peter Lang.

Bhabha, H. (1994). *The location of culture*. London: Routledge.

Boler, M. (1999). *Feeling power: Emotions and education*. New York: Routledge.

Boler, M. (2001). *LoveOnLine: Educating eros in digital education*. Paper presented at the annual meeting of the American Educational Research Association, Seattle, WA.

Boler, M., & Zembylas, M. (2003). Discomforting truths: The emotional terrain of understanding differences. In P. Tryfonas (Ed.), *Pedagogies of difference: Rethinking education for social justice* (pp. 110–136). New York: Routledge.

Broome, B. (1991). Building shared meaning: Implications of a relational approach to empathy for teaching intercultural communication. *Communication Education, 40*, 235–249.

Broome, B. J. (1993). Managing differences in conflict resolution: The role of relational empathy. In D. J. Sandole & H. van der Merwe (Eds.), *Conflict resolution theory and practice: Integration and application* (pp. 97–111). New York: Manchester University Press.

Broome, B. J. (1997). Designing a collective approach to peace: Interactive design and problem-solving workshops with Greek-Cypriot and Turkish-Cypriot communities in Cyprus. *International Negotiation, 2*, 381–407.

Broome, B. J. (1998). Overview of conflict resolution activities in Cyprus: Their contribution to the peace process. *Cyprus Review, 10*, 47–66.

Broome, B. J. (1999). Inter-communal contacts help build links for the future of Cyprus. *Washington Reports on Middle East Affairs, 18*(6), 69–71.

Broome, B. J. (2001). Participatory planning and design in a protracted conflict resolution: Applications with citizen peace-building groups in Cyprus. *Systems Research and Behavioral Science, 18,* 1–9.

Broome, B. J. (2003). Responding to the challenges of third-party facilitation: Reflections of a scholar-practitioner in the Cyprus conflict. *Journal of Intergroup Relations, 26*(4), 24–43.

Broome, B. J. (2004a). Reaching across the dividing line: Building a collective vision for peace in Cyprus. *International Journal of Peace Research, 41,* 191–209.

Broome, B. J. (2004b). Building a shared future across the divide: Identity and conflict in Cyprus. In M. Fong & R. Chuang (Eds.), *Communicating ethnic and cultural identity* (pp. 275–294). Lanham, MD: Rowman and Littlefield.

Bryant, R. (1998). An education in honor: Patriotism and the schools of Cyprus. In V. Calotychos (Ed.), *Cyprus and its people: Nation, identity, and experience in an unimaginable community, 1955–1997* (pp. 69–84). Boulder, CO: Westview Press.

Bryant, R. (2001). An aesthetics of self: Moral remaking and Cypriot education. *Comparative Study of Society and History, 43,* 583–614.

Bryant, R. (2004). *Imagining the modern: The cultures of nationalism in Cyprus.* London: I. B. Tauris.

Burbules, N. C., & Berk, R. (1999). Critical thinking and critical pedagogy: Relations, differences, and limits. In T. Popkewitz & L. Fendler (Eds.), *Critical theories in education: Changing terrains of knowledge and politics* (pp. 45–65). New York: Routledge.

Callahan, J. L. (2004). Breaking the cult of rationality: Mindful awareness of emotion in the critical theory classroom. *New Directions for Adult and Continuing Education, 102,* 75–83.

Cassia, P. S. (2006). Guarding each other's dead, mourning one's own: The problem of missing persons and missing pasts in Cyprus. *South European Society and Politics, 11,* 111–128.

Chubbuck, S., & Zembylas, M. (2008). The emotional ambivalence of socially just teaching: A case study of a novice urban school teacher. *American Educational Research Journal, 45*(2), 274–318.

Cohen, C. E. (1997). *A poetics of reconciliation: The aesthetic mediation of conflict.* Unpublished doctoral dissertation, University of New Hampshire, Durham, New Hampshire.

Davies, L. (2004). *Education and conflict: Complexity and chaos.* New York: Routledge.

Denzin, N. (1997). *Interpretive ethnography: Ethnographic practices for the 21st century.* Thousand Oaks, CA: Sage.

Ellsworth, E. (1989). Why doesn't this feel empowering? Working through the repressive myths of critical pedagogy. *Harvard Educational Review, 59,* 297–324.

Eppert, C. (2003). Histories re-imagined, forgotten and forgiven: Student responses to Toni Morrison's *Beloved. Changing English, 10,* 185–194.

Hadjipavlou-Trigeorgis, M. (1998). Different relationships to the land: Personal narratives, political implications and future possibilities. In V. Calotychos (Ed.),

Cyprus and its people: Nation, identity, and experience in an unimaginable community, 1955–1997 (pp. 251–276). Boulder, CO: Westview Press.

Hadjipavlou-Trigeorgis, M. (2007). Multiple realities and the role of peace education in deep-rooted conflicts: The case of Cyprus. In Z. Bekerman & C. McGlynn (Eds.), *Addressing ethnic conflict through peace education: International perspectives* (pp. 35–48). New York: Palgrave Macmillan.

Holstein, J. A., & Gubrium, J. F. (2000). *The self we live by: Narrative identity in a postmodern world*. New York: Oxford University Press.

Kızılyürek, N. (1993). *Ulus ötesi Kıbrıs / I Kypros peran tou ethnous* [Cyprus beyond nation]. Nicosia: Kassulides.

Klein, K. L. (2000). On the emergence of memory in historical discourse. *Representations, 69*, 127–150.

Kreuzer, P. (2002). *Applying theories of ethno-cultural conflict and conflict resolution to collective violence in Indonesia*. Frankfurt: Peace Research Institute of Frankfurt.

Loizos, P. (1998). How might Turkish and Greek Cypriots see each other more clearly? In V. Calotychos (Ed.), *Cyprus and its people: Nation, identity, and experience in an unimaginable community, 1955–1997* (pp. 35–52). Boulder, CO: Westview Press.

Lupton, D. (1998). *The emotional self: A sociocultural exploration*. London: Sage.

Lutz, C., & Abu-Lughod, L. (Eds.). (1990). *Language and the politics of emotion*. Cambridge: Cambridge University Press.

Martusewicz, R. (2001). *Seeking passage*. New York: Teachers College Press.

Mavratsas, C. (1996). Approaches to nationalism: Basic theoretical considerations in the study of the Greek-Cypriot Case and a historical overview. *Journal of the Hellenic Diaspora, 22*, 77–102.

Mavratsas, C. (1999). National identity and consciousness in everyday life: Toward a sociology of knowledge of Greek-Cypriot nationalism. *Nations and Nationalism, 5*, 91–104.

Miall, H., Ramsbotham, O., & Woodhouse, T. (2000). *Contemporary conflict resolution: The prevention, management, and transformation of deadly conflicts*. Cambridge: Polity Press.

Papadakis, Y. (1995). Nationalist imaginings of war in Cyprus. In R. Hinde & H. Watson (Eds.), *War, a cruel necessity? The bases of institutionalized violence* (pp. 54–67). London: I. B. Tauris.

Papadakis, Y. (1998). Greek Cypriot narratives of history and collective identity: Nationalism as a contested process. *American Ethnologist, 25*, 149–165.

Rak, J. (2003). Do witness: *Don't: A Woman's Word* and trauma as pedagogy. *Topia, 10*, 53–71.

Ramanathapillai, R. (2006). The politicizing of trauma: A case study of Sri Lanka. *Peace and Conflict: Journal of Peace Psychology, 12*, 1–18.

Ricoeur, P. (1999). Memory and forgetting. In R. K. Earney & M. D. Ooley (Eds.), *Questioning ethics: Contemporary debates in philosophy* (pp. 5–11). New York: Routledge.

Spinner-Halev, J. (2003). Education, reconciliation and nested identities. *Theory and Research in Education, 1*, 51–72.

Spyrou, S. (2001a). Those on the other side: Ethnic identity and imagination in Greek-Cypriot children's lives. In H. B. Schwartzman (Ed.), *Children and*

anthropology: Perspectives for the 21st century (pp. 167–185). London: Bergin and Garvey.
Spyrou, S. (2001b). Being one and more than one: Greek Cypriot children and ethnic identity in the flow of everyday life. *Disclosure, 10*, 73–94.
Spyrou, S. (2002). Images of "the Other": The Turk in Greek Cypriot children's imaginations. *Race, Ethnicity and Education, 5*, 255–272.
Spyrou, S. (2006). Constructing "the Turk" as an enemy: The complexity of stereotypes in children's everyday worlds. *South European Society and Politics, 11*, 95–110.
Theodossopoulos, D. (2006). Introduction: The "Turks" in the imagination of the "Greeks." *South European Society & Politics, 11*, 1–32.
Wang, H. (2005). Aporias, responsibility, and im/possibility of teaching multicultural education. *Educational Theory, 55*, 45–59.
Zembylas, M. (2005). *Teaching with emotion: A postmodern enactment.* Greenwich, CT: Information Age Publishing.
Zembylas, M. (2006). Witnessing in the classroom: The ethics and politics of affect. *Educational Theory, 56*, 305–324.
Zembylas, M. (2007a). The politics of trauma: Empathy, reconciliation and education. *Journal of Peace Education, 4*(2), 207–224.
Zembylas, M. (2007b). The affective politics of hatred: Implications for education. *Intercultural Education, 18*(3), 177–192.
Zembylas, M. (2007c). *Five pedagogies, a thousand possibilities: Struggling for hope and transformation in education.* Rotterdam, The Netherlands: SensePublishers.
Zembylas, M. (2008). *The politics of trauma in education.* New York: Palgrave Macmillan.
Zembylas, M., & Boler, M. (2002). On the spirit of patriotism: Challenges of a "pedagogy of discomfort." Education and September 11 [Special issue]. *Teachers College Record On-line.* Retrieved September 29, 2008, from http://www.tcrecord.org
Zembylas, M., & Karahasan, H. (2006). The politics of memory and forgetting in pedagogical practices: Towards pedagogies of reconciliation and peace in divided Cyprus. *Cyprus Review, 18(2)*, 15–35.

Chapter 12

Arab and Jewish Students' Participatory Action Research at the University of Haifa
A Model for Peace Education

Tamar Zelniker, Rachel Hertz-Lazarowitz, Hilla Peretz, Faisal Azaiza, and Ruth Sharabany

National identity and religion have been core issues within the protracted conflict between Jews and Arabs in Israel. The dynamics of identity formation among Arabs and Jews in Israel reflect a complex political and historical context characterized by conflict such as the 1948 war, subsequent wars with neighboring Arab countries, and more recently, the "Intifada" of the Palestinians in the occupied territories. Since 1948, Israel has been a Jewish state with a Jewish majority, maintaining a moderate democracy, with only partial equality of civic rights for the Arab minority (White-Stephan, Hertz-Lazarowitz, Zelniker, & Stephan, 2004; Yiftachel, 2006).

It is not surprising that the tension between Arabs and Jews transpires to Israeli universities, notably, the University of Haifa (UH), where the percentage of Arab students is higher than in other universities and similar to their percentage in the population (20 percent). University campuses, in general, serve as a stage for social-political conflicts and activities. UH, with its makeup of student body, located in a mixed Jewish-Arab city, is a microcosm of the Israeli society and, thus, a natural setting for a social laboratory for studying the interactions between Jews and Arabs.

The school system in Israel is fully segregated for Jews and Arabs, unlike other countries suffering intractable conflicts, such as Northern Ireland, where part of the school system is integrated (Bekerman & McGlynn, 2007; McGlynn & Bekerman, 2007). Following segregated schooling until age eighteen, Israeli universities constitute the first instance of an integrated educational system where the two national groups meet and interact socially and academically. This new experience allows the students to reexamine their power, status, and identity (Hertz-Lazarowitz, 2006; Hurtado, 2005). Two main components of identity have been recognized by researchers studying national identity of the population in Israel: a civic component, which derives from the actual status of Jews and Arabs as citizens of Israel, and the national-ideological component, which includes nationality and religion for Jews, and nationality, religion, and language for Arabs. Persisting civic discrimination of the Arab minority, combined with mutual fear and mistrust as well as heightened levels of religiosity of both Jews and Arabs, led to ideological social-political transformations and redefinitions of identity among both national groups. Since 1967, the Arabs in Israel have undergone an intensive process of consolidation of their Palestinian national identity, which led to radicalization in their relation to the Israeli state and society. The stronger the process of modernization among the Arabs in terms of level of education exposure to media and standard of living, the stronger this process of elucidation of national identity (Abu Nimer, 2004; Ghanem, 2001; Hertz-Lazarowitz & Zelniker, 2004). Jewish identity has also undergone changes as a result of modernization and secularization. One perspective of identity research focused on the Zionist ethos, which involved the creation of the "New Israeli" returning from the Diaspora. The Jews launched a process of modernization in the state of Israel and embarked on a special effort to create a flourishing and a safe homeland, Zion, for global Jewry that had been victims during a long history of exile and massacres. Thus, a secure Jewish-Zionist state has become a cornerstone of identity for many Israeli Jews (Herman, 1970; Kimmerling & Moore, 1997).

Another perspective of identity research, a political-historical perspective, points out that the "Arabs of 1948" were called "Israeli-Arabs," an identity that was imposed on them by the Jewish majority (Abu Nimer, 2004; Abu Saad, 2006; Bishara, 1999; Hertz-Lazarowitz, Zelniker, White-Stephan, & Stephan, 2004). The consolidation of identity of Israel's Arab population was influenced by local, national, and regional factors as well as by religion. Over time, the Arabs have developed a Palestinian-Israeli identity, negotiating a civic-Israeli component and a national-Palestinian component. As they were deepening the process of modernizing, they were also involved in an intense drive to attain equal rights and resources. At the national-regional level, the Arabs support the dreams and aspirations of their fellow Palestinians for independence and for the establishment of a Palestinian state alongside Israel. In addition, in recent years, there has been a significant increase in levels of religiosity (Waardenburg, 2004) and the influence of the various factors yielded complex identity changes (Azaiza, Mor-Sommerfeld, & Hertz-Lazarowitz, 2007; Smooha, 2005).

According to the conflict hypothesis (Hofman & Rouhana, 1976), the Arab-Israeli conflict created a contradiction between civic identity and national identity. Later, Rouhana (1997) maintained that the Arabs in Israel adopted a Palestinian national identity in response to Israel's Jewish-Zionist character. He claims that, while this prevents them from identifying with the state's civic symbols and institutions, it fulfills their psychological need for a complete identity. Smooha (1992, 2005) assumed a separate continuum for civic and for national identity and suggested that combining the two identities entails a process of consolidation of complex identities shaped by both old and new components. A parallel, though less extensive process of identity change has taken place in the Jewish population. Smooha (2005) claims that secular Jews and left-wing Jews usually choose the shared identity term of "Israeli," whereas religious Jews and right-wing Jews tend to prefer the separating term "Jewish." In recent years, a growing number of Jews add the term "Jewish" to their "Israeli" identity (Levy & Katz, 2005).

Both national groups have been affected by a vast range of events perceived as crises, including extreme political and ideological changes, wars, the occupation of Gaza and West Bank, armed conflicts, and terror attacks, which led to changes in identities. Such changes entail taking on or adding identities that are more closely related to one's collective national goals and existence, such as Jewish and Zionist for Jews, and Palestinian for Arabs. These changes depict the expansion of identity definitions into multiple, hyphenated definitions, for example, Jewish-Israeli and Palestinian-Arab-living in Israel. Multiple identity definitions enable both Arabs and Jews to contain the different components of their identity as linked to different aspects (e.g., national and civic) of the complex, multifaceted, sociopolitical life in Israel and in the region. The same processes take place at the university, where students, as individuals and as a national collective, experience a multitude of positive and negative factors that give rise to multiple identities integrating nationality, religion, and ideology (Hertz-Lazarowitz et al., 2004; Maoz, 2002; Zelniker & Hertz-Lazarowitz, 2005). Fine (1994) and, more recently, Sirin and Fine (2007) proposed that certain groups may be "living on the hyphens" of multiple identities that exist simultaneously. We maintain that in Israel, such hyphenated identities include collective, individual, and unique constructs.

Recent studies on hyphenated identities have been launched at UH, which constitutes a multicultural, unique microcosm of the highly diverse groups within Israel. The university provides the opportunity for contact and dialogue and affords academic and social empowerment to both national groups.

We maintain that creating appropriate conditions for dialogue within the university can facilitate mutual understanding and respect, pursuit of justice, and coexistence. Accordingly, we utilized participatory action research (PAR), in which students participate as researchers. We conceptualize PAR as a paradigm suitable not only for research but also for peace education (PE).

Our work on coexistence and PE derives from personality and social psychology and focuses on personal and group relations between Arab and Jewish students who are citizens of Israel. Our PAR work on campus is designed to create academic spaces for dialogues, to promote research on identity and religion, and to advance recognition of and respect for each others' identity definitions, needs, and grievances. This chapter will point to theoretical perspectives and practices that guided our PE work and the knowledge and insights we gained from employing PAR in an academic setting.

Theoretical Background and Goals

Within the domain of PE, social psychology, and group relations, there are several theories that inform strategies of PE programs as well as experimental paradigms of psychologically and sociopolitically based research on coexistence and PE.

Among the theories, we note Lewin's dynamic field theory (Lewin, 1935), Allport's contact theory (Allport, 1954) elaborated by Pettigrew (1998), social identity theory (Tajfel & Turner, 1986), personal-psychodynamics process (Ben-Ari, 2004), dramaturgical model (Harré, 1979; Hertz-Lazarowitz, 1988), diversity and social equality model (Duarte & Smith, 2000), and narrative-based perceived histories and memories (Bruner, 2002; Salomon, 2004). Among PE strategies, we note integrative education (Bekerman & Maoz, 2005), intergroup encounters (Halabi & Sonnenschein, 2004; Maoz, 2002; Suleiman, 2004), and sharing personal narratives (Bar-on & Kassem, 2004). While different theoretical approaches are relevant to one or more of these strategies, it is not always possible to discern clear links between a particular theoretical approach and a particular strategy. We maintain that most of these theories constitute conceptual approaches rather than theoretical models in the scientific sense. Still, these conceptualizations have been influential in the development of major strategies employed in PE projects, including our own experimental paradigm, PAR, which is founded on intergroup relations and dialogue. We maintain that PAR meets necessary conditions stipulated by several theories, notably, the contact theory (Allport, 1954) and the diversity and social equality model (Duarte & Smith, 2000). Furthermore, within the university context, PAR combines significant elements of intergroup encounters as well as integrated education.

Our main research goal was to investigate how students' national identity definitions and religion influence their perception of negative and positive aspects of life on campus as well as their preference for segregation and integration. Students participating in the PAR research seminar were to define core issues, design the study, perform the research and, subsequently, discuss the significance of the results and their potential implications. Our underlying assumption was that, in addition to PAR being a suitable research paradigm, the process also constitutes PE within the students' natural learning environment. We planned to assess the impact of PAR as PE by using qualitative analyses of students' personal reflections at the closing stage of the seminar.

Our initial objective was to create the setting for dialogue among Jewish and Arab students within the natural learning environment of the university and to facilitate familiarization with core issues relevant to the conflict and coexistence between Arabs and Jews at UH. We anticipated that seminar students, being active participants in the research, would acquire knowledge and sensitivity to critical issues pertaining to individuals as well as to the collective of the other group.

We focused the dialogue on fundamental issues of the persisting conflict between Arabs and Jews. Those issues included national identity and religion and their contributions to the perception of the university as a site of national-political conflicts as compared to a site of potential advancement of PE and coexistence.

Within the seminar, PAR was expected to provide answers to our research questions and to function also as means of achieving PE, as we deem PE to be inherent in the process of PAR. At the university-wide level, relevant research results were to be disseminated to other teachers, students, and administrators at UH to ultimately improve conditions for dialogue, justice, and coexistence. The wide-ranging, long-term goal was to carry this knowledge and understanding to the population in Israel. It was assumed that our students would eventually hold leadership roles in the community and, thus, would influence wider circles of the population, promoting coexistence by advancing mutual understanding, respect, and pursuit for justice.

Participatory Action Research Seminars

Our research constitutes a series of studies conducted in a seminar at UH from 2001 until 2007. The research, carried out under the academic guidance of Hertz-Lazarowitz (2003), employed PAR, following the six stages of the group investigation model (Sharan & Hertz-Lazarowitz, 1980). In this process, students in the seminar (a) selected a relevant topic for investigation, (b) wrote personal stories and shared them, (c) conducted peer interviews and shared them with seminar participants, (d) formulated a complete research plan, (e) carried out the study and submitted a written paper, and (f) presented the results and discussed their insights and the implications of the study (Hertz-Lazarowitz, 2003).

In the first study (2001), seminar participants were twenty-one- to twenty-five-year old mostly third-year undergraduate students, taking courses in the faculty of education. In this PAR study, the students investigated instances of injustice and surveillance as experienced and interpreted by Arab and Jewish students on campus. Following PAR methodology, each seminar participant interviewed four other Jewish and Arab students, totaling eighty-six students. With Hebrew being the language of instructions at UH, all students master the Hebrew language, and, accordingly, the questionnaire was administered in Hebrew by the PAR students to Jewish as well as to Arab students at UH. The data yielded painful accounts of injustice in the course of interactions on campus. Many students, Arabs more so than Jews, complained about biased grading, unfair treatment by teachers, prejudiced conduct by security guards during security checks on campus, and inequitable policy and treatment with respect to their religious practices. The Arab students and their leadership stressed the need for greater fairness and justice to be exercised by university authorities in allocating academic resources. In general, Arab students attributed most acts of injustice to racism and disrespect, while Jewish students blamed most acts of injustice experienced on personal characteristics of the "others" and on the lack of sensitivity of the system. The leadership of the Jewish students who aspired to promote the Jewish-Israeli-Zionist characteristics of the campus, perceived the Arabs' political demonstrations and protests as a threat to the existence of UH as a Jewish-Israeli campus. The PAR seminar created a unique culture of dialogue around research design and findings that were relevant to the students' experiences (Hertz-Lazarowitz, 2003).

In 2002, a new group of PAR students opted to investigate both negative and positive aspects of life on campus. Each student in the seminar conducted four in-depth interviews, totaling seventy-four interviews. Categories for analyses developed in the seminar included positive and negative experiences on campus, analyzed in relation to the individual and to the group. Based on the interviews, one-hundred key statements were sorted into four categories: personal-positive ("I have friends from different groups"), group-positive ("Cultural exposure takes place on campus"), personal-negative ("I feel rejected"), and group-negative ("There is discrimination on campus"). A frequency analysis performed on these statements indicated that Arab and Jewish students had reasonably high and similar percentages of positive experiences. Although both groups acknowledged the occurrence of negative incidents, the rate of negative perception reported was higher among Arab participants than comparable rates among Jewish students. The overall picture in the 2002 study portrayed both positive and negative characteristics of life on campus. The findings served as the basis for dialogue and stimulated further reading and study.

In 2003, PAR students chose to study the impact of background variables, such as nationality and religion on social aspects of life on campus. An eighty-item Likert scale questionnaire based on the 2002 study was administered by seminar participants to 510 UH students on campus. As expected, nationality was found to have a significant effect on students' perceptions. In general, Arab students were more positive in their personal (e.g., friendship) and collective (e.g., multiculturalism) perception than the Jewish students, but they were also more negative in their personal (e.g., rejection) and collective (e.g., discrimination) perception. All students had somewhat higher scores on positive aspects than on negative aspects of campus life. Religion was also significant, with Jewish students being least negative and Muslim students most negative, with respect to both personal and collective attitudes. Of the Muslim students, those who included the term Palestinian in their identity were the most negative. However, the main finding of the 2003 study was that positive and negative perception can be contained simultaneously by the students (Hertz-Lazarowitz & Zelniker, 2004; Hertz-Lazarowitz et al., 2004).

In 2004, students in the PAR seminar added several variables related to the students' perception of life on campus. As in previous years, independent, background variables included national identity and religion and dependent variables included positive and negative perceptions of life on UH campus. Newly added dependent variables included students' preference for segregation and for integration. Parts of the 2004 study are presented in this chapter.

Method

Participants

PAR seminar participants consisted of twenty-five Israeli Arab and Jewish students at UH. Most of them were undergraduates in the faculty of education. Study participants consisted of 537 students of whom 171 were Jews and 366 Arabs. All participants were born in Israel, and their average age was 24.5 (SD = 4.6). Among the Arab students 66 percent were Muslims and 34 percent were Christians. A breakdown of additional demographic data was as follows: 60 percent women, 80 percent single, 80 percent undergraduates, 42.7 percent secular, 42.5 percent traditional, and 44.7 percent politically left-wing.

Measures

The questionnaire included items pertaining to students' background and their perceptions of the university. The three independent variables presented in this chapter were nationality (Jewish, Arab), religion (Christian, Jews, and Muslims), and national identity. Information regarding the first two variables was gathered from a personal background questionnaire. With respect to the definition of national identity, participants were asked, "How would you define your identity?" and were given twelve possible responses, including "other." These identity categories were developed over the years based on students' responses to open questions related to their identity (Hertz-Lazarowitz & Zelniker, 2004). Four dependent variables were derived from the 2003 questionnaire items rated on a five-point Likert scale (1 = low, 5 = high) condensed to four scales.

Positive perception: This scale measures students' perception of the university as a place of coexistence that facilitates the development of positive relationships between the different religious groups. The questionnaire included eleven items, for example, "The University provides an opportunity to get to know and accept different people." Reliability was $\alpha = 0.81$.

Negative perception: This scale measures students' perception of the university as a place that promotes disagreement and conflict between the different groups. Negative perception was measured using a ten-item questionnaire, for example, "The University is an environment which entails alienation and increases distancing between groups." Reliability was $\alpha = 0.83$.

Segregation: This scale refers to students' preference for values, norms, and behaviors of one's own ingroup over those of outgroup members (Berry, 1992). Segregation was measured by a five-item questionnaire, for example, "I prefer my friends to be only from my reference group." Reliability was $\alpha = 0.63$.

Integration: This scale refers to students' preferences for values, norms, and behaviors of ingroup members as well as outgroup members (Berry, 1992). Integration was measured by a five-item questionnaire, for example, "I would like to have friends both from my reference group (Jews or Arabs) and from the other group." Reliability was $\alpha = 0.63$.

Procedure

Twenty-five Israeli Arab and Jewish students administered the questionnaire to 537 students of whom 171 were Jews and 366 Arabs.

Results

Table 12.1 presents the distribution of identity definitions according to religion (Jewish, Christians, Muslims). The largest group of Jewish students (66 percent) defined themselves as Jewish Israeli, the largest group of Muslims (50 percent) defined themselves as Palestinian Arabs living in Israel, while the largest group of Christians (34 percent) defined themselves as Arab Israelis. Other descriptive findings indicate that the majority of Arab participants (58 percent) chose a definition that included the term "Palestinian" (a national-political identity), and the majority of the Jewish students (66 percent) chose a definition that included the term "Israeli" (a civic identity).

Based on civic, national, and political identity definitions, each national group was further divided into two grouped identity categories: "Jewish" (national definition) and "Israeli" (civic definition) for the Jews, and "Arab" (national definition) and "Palestinian" (political definition) for the Arabs. The distribution of grouped identity presented in Table 12.2 indicates that most Jewish students defined themselves as Israeli (66 percent), most Muslim Arabs defined themselves as "Palestinian" (66 percent), whereas most Christian Arabs defined themselves as "Arab" (57 percent).

The differences among the three religious groups for each of the four dependent variables were examined using ANOVA. The results presented in Table 12.3 show a significant effect on negative perception ($F = 27.91$; $p < .01$) and on integration ($F = 11.55$; $p < .01$). In both cases, post hoc analyses showed that there were no significant differences between Muslims and Christians and that both Arab groups had higher negative perception scores as well as higher integration scores than Jews. Thus, these differences can be attributed to nationality rather than to religion.

Finally, using one-way ANOVAS, we examined the effects of grouped identity on positive and negative perceptions and on segregation and integration. The results, presented in Table 12.4, indicate that grouped identity had a significant effect on negative perception ($F = -22.18$; $p < .01$) and integration ($F = 9.49$, $p < .01$). Post hoc analyses for negative perception indicate that the source of the effect was the significant difference between those students who defined themselves as Israeli, who had the lowest scores on negative perception ($M = 2.53$, $SD = .66$), and students in the other three groups, who defined themselves as Jewish, Arab, and Palestinian. The latter three groups did not differ significantly from each other. Post hoc analyses for integration show that the Arab group had the highest integration scores ($M = 3.16$, $SD = .70$) and the Israeli group had the lowest integration score ($M = 2.68$, $SD = .81$). While there were no significant differences between the two Jewish groups or between the two Arab groups, both Jewish groups had significantly lower scores than Arab students defining themselves as Arab, while the Israeli group had also significantly lower scores than the Palestinian group.

Discussion

Our main objectives were to advance a dialogue between Arab and Jewish students and study significant variables that shape the dialogue. We found that both Arab and Jewish students use hyphenated identities. Most Jewish students used the term Israeli in their definition, whereas most Arab students used the term Palestinian in their definition. Religion was found to be related to national grouped identity. Further research is necessary to investigate these potentially interesting relationships among the independent variables and their possible direct or indirect influence on the dependent variables. There were significant differences among national identity groups (grouped identity) on negative perception and preference for integration. As compared to Jewish students, Arab students not only had higher scores on integration but also higher scores on negative perception. Thus, while Arabs note positive aspects as much as Jews and

Table 12.1 Distribution of identity definitions for each religion

Religion	Identity	N	%
Jews	Jewish Zionist	15	9
	Jewish	43	25
	Jewish-Israeli	113	66
	Total Jews	171	100
Muslims	Arab	52	21
	Arab-Israeli	33	13
	Arab-Israeli Palestinian	32	13
	Palestinian	7	3
	Palestinian Arab living in Israel	123	50
	Total Muslims	247	100
Christians	Arab	28	23
	Arab-Israeli	40	34
	Arab-Israeli Palestinian	11	9
	Palestinian	4	3
	Palestinian Arab living in Israel	36	31
	Total Christians	119	100

$N = 537$

express greater leanings toward integration, they are also more critical of discrimination and injustice. Overall, both Jewish and Arab students perceive the university as a somewhat more positive than negative environment. It should be noted that differences in students' negative perception of the university and preferences for integration appear to be related to national grouped identity rather than religion. Qualitative aspects of the study, which include personal reflections students reported upon the completion of the seminar, are presently being analyzed. Initial results indicate that the different stages employed in PAR encouraged students to examine their own identity, reflect on the other group's needs and grievances, and reshape their positive and negative experiences relevant to their identity. The appropriateness of PAR as a means for advancing PE should be investigated in a separate study designed specifically for this purpose.

We propose that within a seminar context, PAR can be used as means for conducting research as well as achieving PE. We maintain that this is realizable because university campuses provide a natural environment for contact among different groups and an opportunity to set up conditions that promote constructive dialogue. With respect to campus-wide activities, present administrative regulations are not supportive of those aspects

Table 12.2 Distribution of grouped identity definitions for each religion

Religion		N	%
Jewish students	*Jewish*	58	34
	Israeli	113	66
	Total	171	100
Arabs-Muslims	*Arab*	85	34
	Palestinian	162	66
Arabs-Christians	*Arab*	68	57
	Palestinian	58	43
All Arab students	*Arab*	153	42
	Palestinian	213	58
	Total	366	100

N = 537

Table 12.3 ANOVA results for differences among religions on negative and positive perception, segregation and integration

Religion	Positive perception $M(SD)$	Negative perception $M(SD)$	Integration $M(SD)$	Segregation $M(SD)$
Jews	3.53 (.64)	2.66 (.69) [1]	2.74 (.77) [1]	3.18 (.85)
Muslims	3.42 (.56)	3.12 (.59) [2]	3.09 (.71) [2]	3.27 (66)
Christians	3.52 (.50)	2.98 (.56) [2]	2.99 (.72) [2]	3.12 (68)
F	2.51	27.91**	11.55**	1.96

* $p < .05$ ** $p < .01$
[1], [2], [3] Post-hoc results

of the dialogue that involve conflicts, voicing of grievances, and protests of injustice. University administrators, beset by wavering ambivalence, generally frown upon these activities. They often censure such protests that may be accompanied by the protestors' show of force perceived by the administration as a threat (Hertz-Lazarowitz, 1988, 2003). Such conditions discourage dialogue on deep-seated and painful issues that should be shared and discussed to improve understanding and advance justice and equality. Yet, educational activities such as PAR and PE are inherent in the free academic setting afforded by the university. We believe that the six stages of PAR provide the conditions and process for effective research and constructive dialogue between the two national groups as well as between students and faculty and UH administrators.

The PAR pedagogical procedure employed combines the two central PE strategies, integrated education and intergroup encounters, and is consistent with significant principles of theoretical approaches deemed

Table 12.4. ANOVA results for differences among grouped identities on the four scales

Segregation M (SD)	Integration M (SD)	Negative perception M (SD)	Positive perception M (SD)	Grouped identity:
3.26 (.82)	2.85[1,2] (.81)	2.92[2] (67.)	3.57 (67.)	Jewish
3.14 (.87)	2.68[1] (.75)	2.53[1] (66.)	3.51 (63.)	Israeli
3.20 (.66)	3.16[3] (.70)	3.08[2] (56.)	3.48 (50.)	Arab
3.24 (.73)	2.98[2,3] (.71)	3.08[2] (61.)	3.43 (57.)	Palestinian
.56	9.49**	*22.18*	1.18	F value

* $p < .05$ ** $p < .01$

[1], [2], [3] Post-hoc results

conducive to the advancement of PE. The main contact theory principles (Allport, 1954) include common goal, equal group status within situations, intergroup cooperation, and support of authorities. In line with these principles, PAR is conducted within a natural environment where Arab and Jewish students share common educational goals and have reasonably equal status as students in the seminar. The students engage in intergroup cooperation by means of joint planning and shared data and gain support of university authorities from the seminar teacher who leads the students through the different PAR stages. Finally, in line with two central principles stipulated by Duarte and Smith (2000), there is significant diversity among students and a fundamental aspiration for equality. These conditions and the gradual process of PAR, which entails the use of personal narratives, research, and open discussions, allow students to raise issues of a personal nature as well as issues they deem critical for their collective while shaping the dialogue.

The process, which lasts about half a year, is considerably longer than most intergroup encounters and enables a gradual development of a constructive dialogue. The outcome of our PAR work was passed on to students in subsequent years as well as to university teachers and administrators. However, the effect of the information on UH administration is intricate and challenging and requires continued communication and monitoring.

It should be noted that PAR, as performed in the seminar, yielded a pedagogical environment that constitutes a microcosm of the university, which provides the space for natural contact among different national and religious groups. The PAR seminar bears some resemblance to a focus group where PE processes are quite intense. The construction of the study and discussions of the results and their implications facilitated awareness and the rather rapid shaping of the dialogue among the groups. A similar PE process, albeit slower and more limited, is expected to take place on the campus at large.

Seminar discussions of research results furthered our own understanding of relevant variables. On the basis of these discussions, we identify two clusters of motives and goals that characterize university students in the process of shaping the dialogue: psychological-personal and political.

Psychological-personal motives: Some students focus on personal-psychological aspects of their life on campus and on their academic advancement and define themselves as apolitical. The dialogue enables them to develop friendships with individuals from the other national group, search for common goals and shared interests, and attain a more positive perception of the university. Having even one close friend from the other national group was found to predict positive perception of the university (Hertz-Lazarowitz et al., 2004; Pettigrew, 1998).

Political motives: Other students focus on political issues and conflicts and underscore the differences between the groups. They protest discrimination and injustices on national grounds and emphasize the need to rectify injustices. These students engage in political and administrative dialogues, negotiations, and demonstrations to achieve greater potency and justice.

As more students turn to perceive themselves as holding hyphenated identities, there is a potential for a new and creative dialogue, mutual respect, pursuit of equality, social justice, and partnership. We propose that in order for PE to be effective, whether employing PAR or other methods, it should be consistent with students' motives and goals. We maintain that PAR can provide the appropriate conditions, content, and process taking into account students' personal motives as well as their political goals. We believe that such a critical pedagogical process of group investigation will help students from the two national groups learn to live with the conflict while at the same time, take action to correct injustices by constructive and peaceful means.

As for the long-term, we expect our students to hold leadership roles in the educational system, government offices, and large corporations, to carry the dialogue, and to advance understanding and justice to larger segments of the population. The challenge facing the university community, faculty members, students, and management is to allow room for the different forms of dialogue presented here and to empower dialogues for PE as an institution policy, which will, in turn, advance the transformation of the university to a site of justice and peace.

References

Abu Nimer, M. (2004). Education for coexistence and Arab-Jewish encounters in Israel: Potential and challenges. *Journal of Social Issues, 60*(2), 405–422.

Abu Saad, I.(2006). State-controlled education and identity formation among the Palestinian Arab minority in Israel. *American Behavioral Scientist, 49*(8), 1085–1100.

Allport, G. W. (1954). *The nature of prejudice*. Reading, MA: Addison Wesley.

Azaiza, F., Mor-Sommerfeld, A., & Hertz-Lazarowitz, R. (2007). Into the future: Bilingual education in Israel: Manifesto. *Education, Citizenship and Social Justice,* 2(1), 5–22.

Bar-On, D., & Kassem, F. (2004). Storytelling as a way to work through intractable conflicts: The German-Jewish experience and its relevance to the Palestinian-Israeli context. *Journal of Social Issues,* 60(2), 289–306.

Bekerman, Z., & Maoz, I. (2005). Troubles with identities: Obstacles to coexistence education in conflict ridden societies. *Identity,* 5(4), 341–358.

Bekerman, Z., & McGlynn, C. (Eds.). (2007). *Addressing ethnic conflict through peace education: International perspectives.* New York: Palgrave Macmillan.

Ben-Ari, R. (2004). Coping with the Jewish-Arab conflict: A comparison among three models. *Journal of Social Issues,* 60(2), 307–322.

Berry, J. W. (1992). Acculturation and adaptation in a new society. *International Migration Review,* 30, 69–85.

Bishara, A. (Ed.). (1999). *Between "I" and "We": The construction of identities and Israel identity.* Jerusalem: Van Leer Institute and Hakibbutz Hameuchad.

Bruner, J. (2002). *Making stories.* New York: Farrar, Strauss, and Giroux.

Duarte, E. M., & Smith, S. (2000). *Foundational perspectives in multicultural education.* New York: Longman.

Fine, M. (1994). Working the hyphens: Reinventing the self and other in qualitative research. In N. Denzin & Y. S. Lincoln (Eds.), *Handbook of qualitative research* (pp. 70–82). Thousand Oaks, CA: Sage.

Ghanem. (2001). *The Palestinian-Arab minority in Israel 1948–2001: A political study.* Albany, NY: State University of New York Press.

Halabi, R., & Sonnenschein, N. (2004). The Jewish Palestinian encounter in a time of crisis. *Journal of Social Issues,* 60(2), 373–387.

Herman, S. N. (1970). *Israelis and Jews—the continuing of identity.* New York: Random House.

Harré, R. (1979). *Social being.* Oxford: Basil Blackwell.

HertzLazarowitz, R. (1988). Conflict on campus: A socialdrama perspective. In J. E. Hofman (Ed.), *ArabJewish relations in Israel* (pp. 271–301). Bristol: Wyndham Hall Press.

Hertz-Lazarowitz, R. (2003). Arab and Jewish youth in Israel: Voicing national injustice on camps. *Journal of Social Issues,* 59(1), 51–66.

Hertz-Lazarowitz, R. (2006). Acceptance and rejection at Haifa University: The source of conflict between Arab and Jews. In C. Daiute, Z. Beykont, C. Higson-Smith, & L. Nucci (Eds.), *Global perspectives on youth conflict and resilience.* New York: Oxford University Press.

Hertz-Lazarowitz, R., & Zelniker, T. (2004). Can peace education be enhanced via participatory research: Three case studies at Haifa University 2001–2003. *Peace Research,* 36(1), 119–134.

Hertz-Lazarowitz, R., Zelniker. T., White-Stephan, C., & Stephan, W. G. (2004). Arab-Jewish coexistence programs. *Journal of Social Issues,* 60(2), 237–452

Hofman, J. E., & Rouhana, N. (1976). Young Arabs in Israel: Some aspects of a conflicted social identity. *Journal of Social Psychology,* 99, 75–86.

Hurtado, S (2005). The next generation of diversity and intergroup relations research. *Journal of Social Issues,* 61(3), 595–610.

Kimmerling, B., & Moore, D. (1997). Collective identity as agency and structuration of society. *International Review of Sociology, 7*, 25–49.

Levy, S., & Katz, E. (2005). Dynamics of inter-group relations in Israel: 1967–2002. *Social Indicators Research, 74*(2), 295–312.

Lewin, K. (1935). *Principles of topological psychology* (F. & G. M. Heider, Trans.). New York: McGraw-Hill.

Maoz, I. (2002). Conceptual mapping and evaluation of peace education programs. In G. Salomon & B. Nevo (Eds.), *Peace education: The concept, principles and practices around the world* (pp. 185–197). Mahwah, NJ: Lawrence Erlbaum Associates.

McGlynn, C., & Bekerman, Z. (2007). The management of pupil difference in Catholic Protestant and Palestinian-Jewish integrated education in Northern Ireland and Israel. *Compare: A Journal of Comparative Education, 37*(5), 689–703.

Pettigrew, T. F. (1998). Intergroup contact: Theory, research and new perspectives. *Annual Review of Psychology, 49*, 65–85

Rouhana, N. (1997). *Identity in conflict: Palestinian citizen in an ethnic Jewish state*. New Haven, CT: Yale University Press.

Salomon, G. (2004). A narrative-based view of coexistence education. *Journal of Social Issues, 60*(2), 273–287.

Sharan, S., & Hertz-Lazarowitz, R. (1980). A group investigation method of cooperative learning in the classroom. In S. Sharan, P. Hare, C. Webb, & R. Hertz-Lazarowitz (Eds.), *Cooperation in education* (pp. 14–46). Provo, UT: Brigham Young University Press.

Sirin, S. R., & Fine, M. (2007). Hyphenated selves: Muslim American youth negotiating identities on the fault lines of global conflict. *Applied Developmental Science, 11*, 151–163.

Smooha, S. (1992). *Arabs and Jews in Israel*. Boulder: Westview Press.

Smooha, S. (2005). *Index of Arab-Jewish relations in Israel 2004*. Haifa: Jewish-Arab Center, University of Haifa; Jerusalem: The Citizens' Accord Forum between Jews and Arabs in Israel; Tel-Aviv: Friedrich Ebert Stiftung.

Suleiman, R. (2004). Planned encounters between Jewish and Palestinian Israelis: A social-psychological perspective. *Journal of social issues, 60*(2), 323–337.

Tajfel, H., & Turner, J.C. (1986). *The social identity theory of intergroup behavior*. In S. Worchel & W. G. Austin (Eds), *Psychology of intergroup relations* (pp. 7–24). Chicago: Nelson-Hall.

Waardenburg, J. (2004). Christians, Muslims, Jews and their religion. *Islam and Christian–Muslim Relations, 15*(1), 13–33.

White-Stephan, C., Hertz-Lazarowitz, R., Zelniker, T., & Stephan, W. (2004). Improving Arab Jewish relations in Israel: Theory and practice in coexistence educational programs. *Journal of Social Issues, 60*(2), 237–252.

Yiftachel, O. (2006). *Ethnocracy: Land and identity politics in Israel/Palestine*. Philadelphia: University of Pennsylvania Press.

Zelniker, T., & Hertz-Lazarowitz, R. (2005). School-Family Partnership for Coexistence (SFPC) in the city of Acre: Promoting Arab and Jewish parent's role as facilitators of children's literacy development and as agents of coexistence. *Language Culture and Curriculum, 18*(1), 114–138.

Chapter 13

Deliberative History Classes for a Post-conflict Society
Theoretical Development and Practical Implication through International Education in United World College in Bosnia and Herzegovina

Pilvi Torsti and Sirkka Ahonen

Introduction

A properly working civic society is a necessity for a post-conflict society. A capability for open dialogue and popular control of power defuse the negative spoils of a conflict. Where tension still lingers a new civic identity is in demand, one based on equal recognition of mutual fears, anxieties, and aspirations.

Bosnia and Herzegovina provides a lucid example of how the civic identity of the people is historically constructed: Pre-1992 to 1995, the three historical communities of the country coexisted and lived in mixed communities with the fourth (Yugoslav) historical community being in the process of getting constructed.[1] Post-1992 to 1995, three historical communities live in increasingly divided areas and foster deep suspicions of each other, even if the Dayton Peace Agreement negotiated in 1995 by the international community expected and forced them to maintain a multiethnic state (Torsti, 2003, pp. 107–109). Nor is the relationship between Bosnia-Herzegovinians and the international community working properly, as the Dayton Peace Agreement created dynamics that made Bosnian people overdependent on the international community (Chandler, 1999, p. 196). Above all, a substantial part of the Bosnian population regard themselves as being victimized by the leading countries of the European Union who did not interfere in time to prevent the atrocities of the war.

In the context of an international research project, Youth and History, into the historical construction of the civic identity of people, young Bosnians from all national groups of the country were asked how they relate to the past (Torsti, 2003). The key framing concept of the Youth and History research project was historical consciousness, conceptualized as the interaction between understanding of the past and the aspirations of future.

In this chapter, we will first present the results of Torsti's (2003) empirical study on historical consciousness and historical culture in postwar Bosnia and Herzegovina, paying special attention to the contradiction between the nationally divided historical culture and the shared historical identity of young people. Secondly, recognizing this contradiction, we will try to map the ethical and cognitive parameters of history education in a post-conflict society using Bosnia and Herzegovina as a case study. The core concept of our educational project scheme will be deliberative communication for a deliberative democracy, which we will regard as the necessary form of a post-conflict state. In this chapter, deliberative communication is first conceptualized and then discussed in the context of education in general and history education in particular. We then turn to a real classroom and discuss the applicability of deliberative communication, using the United World College (UWC) in Mostar and the International Baccalaureate Diploma Programme as an example. In conclusion, we shall discuss the possible wider lessons to be learned for history teaching in post-conflict situations.

One of the main recommendations—in a recent conference that addressed the challenges of teaching history in societies emerging from violent conflict—for educators, historians, social scientists, and education ministry officials from around the world, was the need to identify teaching methods that are most successful in promoting moral development and social agency as goals of history education (Cole & Barsalou, 2006). This chapter elaborates on deliberative communication as such a method in the context of Bosnia.

Our approach relies heavily on the idea of peace building education as presented in Bush and Saltarelli (2000), which suggest negotiation skills, conflict management, and noncompetitive dialogue as means of helping students to accept differences between and within groups, particularly in regions characterized by latent violence. Bosnia and Herzegovina is precisely such a region, and it is argued that deliberative communication is a feasible way of allowing students to articulate and accept differences.

The Historical Construction of Civic Identity among Young Bosnia-Herzegovinians

The extensive international Youth and History survey, conducted from 1995 to 1997, studied the understanding of the past, present, and future of the youth in various European countries (Angvik & von Borries, 1997). As a spin-off of the main survey, in 1999 to 2000 more than 900 eighth-grade pupils from all parts of Bosnia and Herzegovina representing all national groups filled the survey questionnaire. Torsti, co-author of this chapter, managed the survey in Bosnia and Herzegovina. In Torsti's analysis of the survey, the students were considered agents whose historically constructed ideas and concepts were at the focus of the attention. Such ideas and concepts were considered as presenting social facts present in post-war Bosnian society (Torsti, 2003).[3]

To contextualize such an analysis, we had to look at the postwar historical context in Bosnia and Herzegovina through the presence of history. Here, the focus was on school history textbooks and historical culture more generally. Historical culture is understood as part of the culture where people face the past and try to come to terms with it. It includes mechanisms and avenues where knowledge about the past can be produced, transmitted, presented, used and experienced within a society. Crucially important is the understanding that historical culture exists within society in several forms and ways and emerges through a group of channels from state approved memorials and curricula to the sphere of cultural institutions, architecture and mass consumption (Torsti, 2003, see also Hentilä, 2001 and Aronsson, 2000).

Divided Historical Culture and History Textbooks Surrounding the Youth[4]

Torsti's (2003) descriptive analysis of the presence of history in wartime and postwar Bosnia and Herzegovina illustrated the division of historical culture into three separate—and even opposing—cultures that had resulted from a dramatic and aggressive, conscious process.

First, the analysis of eighth-grade (the eighth grade was the last year of obligatory schooling at the time of the research) history textbooks used by the three Bosnian national communities in postwar Bosnia and Herzegovina demonstrated how presentations of the past among the three communities created hostile images of the country's other national groups. An "us-them" dichotomous representation of the parties was the most important finding of the extensive textbook analysis conducted by Torsti (2003). We could also note here that, while differing and even opposing each other in content, when dealing with such topics as the Second World War, the textbooks used by the three Bosnian communities also shared one characteristic: the recognition of connection between past and present. In particular, previous wars typically served as reference background for the recent conflict. The book used by the Bosnian Serbs, for example, referred to the Serb warrior myth stating how Serbs "had to defend their rights again with guns" in the context of the 1990s (Gac´es¯a, Mladenovic, Maksinovic, & Zivkovic´ 1997, p. 96). In a similar manner, the Bosniak textbooks stated how "the Serb-chetnik genocide on Muslims has deep roots," thus referring to the genocide as a typical historical fate of Bosnian Muslims (Imamovic´, Pelesic´, & Ganibegovic´, 1994, p. 96).

In conclusion it was stated that, while stereotypical images of different nations are quite typical in history textbooks, the concentration on enemy images of other national groups should be considered particularly problematic in the Bosnian context because the country's intention, as expressed in the Dayton Peace Agreement, is to be multicultural and multinational.

A recent study on history textbooks used in Bosnia and Herzegovina in 2007 applied the analysis suggested by Torsti (2003) and reconfirmed most of her findings related to textbooks used eight years earlier.[5] Thus, twelve years after the war, no substantial change has occurred in the history textbooks used by the three curricula in place in the area.

In addition to the history textbook analysis, the historical culture and its division in postwar Bosnia and Herzegovina were analyzed by Torsti (2003) to provide the full societal context for the Youth and History project analysis on the thinking of the young people in the postwar era. Three categories were identified in analysis: (1) the destruction and reconstruction of physical symbols (i.e., religious objects), (2) the division of national symbols and language, and (3) historical culture as illustrated through various cultural artifacts.

Tendencies among the differing historical cultures were uncovered. Among the Bosnian Serbs, the signaling aspect was crucial: historical culture was used to signal to others the mastering of territory or institutions. Destruction and forgetting the past was also characteristic. For example, the tourist brochures of Banja Luka, capital of Bosnian Serbs, "forgot" to mention the Turkish heritage and history of the city, but rather focused on the glorious future of the "Bosnian Serb capital." The forgetting was possible because of the destruction of all mosques (i.e., remnants of the Turkish past).

Among Bosnian Croats, language played a particular role in the construction of the separate historical culture. The construction of new buildings and other artifacts expressed the need to signal messages to others. As a whole, the creation of new culture was central, first through the identification with mother-Croatia (the state of Croatia) and secondly as part of Herzegovina.

The third variant of the historical culture prevalent among Bosniaks (Bosnian Muslims) and pro-Bosnia-orientated areas did not seem to stress the creation of a new culture and appeared unwilling to accept the inevitable changes in historical culture, for example, by describing the cities in tourist brochures as they were before the war rather than as they were in the postwar situation. Simultaneously, however, the third form of historical culture stressed the need for universal symbols of state and other forms of universality of Bosnia and Bosnians. The difficulty and artificiality of this process is seen in the fact that many of the new products (flag, national anthem) were imported from outside.

Similarities in the Historical Identity of Young Bosnians[6]

The reception of history in the societal and educational context described above was studied through the Youth and History descriptive statistic survey analysis of the answers from 907 pupils in the eighth grade to forty-eight questions, which, in total, included 280 items. The answers of the Bosnian national groups were compared to each other and to other European country samples. The main analyses were performed on single-item level using cross-tabulations and comparison of means as methods. The correlation coefficients were also used to detect the connections and associations between the variables. Constructs (scales and factors) were also built in some cases after the single-item level analyses.

The analysis showed that in most questions, the Bosnian national groups differed only marginally from one another in their responses. The differences among Bosnian national groups existed merely in the intensity of historical analysis, not in the dimensions of thinking. Based on detailed statistical tests and analyses, it could be stated that the thoughts and attitudes of young Bosnians as expressed in the Youth and History survey demonstrated that young Bosnians, Croats, and Serbs shared their representations to a large extent. This means that, for example, Bosnian Croat youth belonged together with their Bosnian peers rather than with the young people from Croatia proper. This result seems to suggest that opposing historical culture and textbooks cannot change the historically constructed identity, at least not overnight.

In the European comparison, Bosnians formed statistically a single group. The similarity was measured by a cluster analysis. Together, with the overall similarity of all Bosnian national groups, the most important conclusions of the Youth and History survey in Bosnia and Herzegovina in the European comparison illustrated great belief in future peace among all Bosnian national groups. Also, wars were not considered important factors of change in history.

Deliberative Communication as a New Frame of Classroom Discourse

Above, we have illustrated the contradiction between the divided historical culture and shared historical identity of young Bosnians when analyzed in the European comparison. This leads to a dilemma of enabling the development of education that would challenge the existing divided historical culture and segregated textbooks, and thereby make room for the recognition of the historically constructed shared identity of young Bosnians. Let us look at deliberative communication as a possible concept.[7]

Deliberative communication as an educational concept is founded on Dewey's (1980) ideas of a school as a miniforum of democracy and Habermas's (1984) theory of communicative action as the way to transform society. Deliberative communication means an open, multilateral human interaction, the purpose of the participants being not to persuade each other to refer to the will of the majority but to give voice to as many views as possible and to provide time and space for their elaboration and arbitration (i.e., deliberation). In such a communication, there are chances for everybody, not just for the fastest and the most articulate (Habermas, 1984). While Habermas regards deliberation as a criterion of democratic decision making, Dewey (1980) advocates deliberation specifically as a democratic classroom process.

The aim of deliberative communication is to reach a consensus, instead of a majority opinion, and the consensus would be based on symmetry in regard to the power relations of the participants. According to the premises of the theory, in a symmetric negotiation, coalitions to beat somebody's view are not appropriate. Neither are opportune compromises. Consensus means a genuine inclusion of the arguments of all participants.

Deliberation is a democratic way of meaning attribution. In the process of deliberation, the meaning of such concepts as "democracy," "nation," "human rights," "welfare state," and "collective security" is decided by different persons and groups through mutual exchange of experiences, aspirations, and value statements. Deliberation as meaning construction leads us to school education, in which making abstract concepts meaningful is one of the purposes (Englund, 2006).

In the Habermasian view, deliberative communication is a prerequisite of advanced democracy where the civic power of a person is not restricted to a vote on a ballot but expanded to her or his right and opportunity to present individual arguments and take part in the dialogue of argumentation. In a case of a multiethnic state, deliberative democracy implies preconditions for confidence building and peace. Deliberative communication is therefore one of the key concepts of sustainable civic education in a post-conflict society.[8]

Deliberative Communication in Schools: Schools as Public Spaces with a Preference for Pluralism

In the following section, theories of Dewey (1980) and Habermas (1984) are reflected on with regard to the constitution of post-conflict education, with references to the situation in today's Bosnia and Herzegovina. In an open society, school is one of the public arenas of free communication. Schools provide a place where individuals learn to come to terms with "the other" and may safely exchange views and aspirations across groups. For such a purpose, to provide an arena for deliberative communication, looking from our theoretical premises, a school has to meet the three requirements presented below.

The first requirement is that the basic schools are common to all children. This requirement is not fulfilled in today's Bosnia and Herzegovina, as schools are ethnically divided. Exceptions are rare. In the city of Mostar, one local gymnasium known as the "old Gymnasium" today is, after strong pressure and considerable material support by the international community, attended by both Croats and Bosniaks. Still, it is only the building and school administration that are common. The curricula are separate, and there are no structures that would support the creation of a common identity, "our school." Young Croats and Bosniaks have no opportunity to discuss their divergent views of the past and future in the classroom.

The second requirement concerns the concept of multiculturalism. All over Europe, the political doctrine of multiculturalism, one of the guiding educational principles of the 1980s, has recently been counteracted by a demand for integration. The multiculturalism of the 1980s implied the expansion of the cultural rights of the minorities. Minorities in society were expected to have their own cultural institutions, even if that meant a breach to norms of the mainstream culture and led, for instance, to segregated schools, Islamic schools being the most illustrative example. Today, in many Western countries, the pursuit of integration has been resumed for the sake of social harmony. However, often, the people who are asked to get integrated actually feel repressed. They claim to feel safe only within a frame of multiculturalism that allows for them to maintain their own (separate) cultural institutions. Multiculturalism, when understood under the umbrella of deliberative communication, means an opportunity for an open and regular encounter with the "other" within integrated institutions. Through deliberative communication, multiculturalism can be made into an asset rather than a risk in a society. In Bosnia and Herzegovina, multiculturalism is not part of schooling and the attempts of the international community have been focused on integration rather than on achieving true multiculturalism. Deliberative communication provides a theoretical frame for the accommodation of the principles of integration and multiculturalism at the same time.

The third requirement is intersubjectivity in communication. Dewey (1976) was the first educationalist to stress the potential of intersubjectivity in knowledge formation. He started with the assumption that the acquisition of knowledge starts from a problem and proceeds as a problem-solving process but pointed out that the process is not individual. It is in a social situation that different aspects of a problem are illuminated and a person's habitual view is challenged (Dewey). Deliberative communication in school is founded on the Deweyan view of education as a process rather than a substance. Education is seen as a process of deliberation between people with different experiences. The procedural aspect thus defines school as a democratic forum.[9]

Deliberative Communication in History Education: From Hegemonic Stories to a Dialogue of Stories

In the school subject history, traditional textbooks tend to provide a hegemonic representation and interpretation of the past. This is especially true about national history, which often is written as separate chapters or even as one separate book. The first part of this chapter brought up the segregation of one story into three hegemonic stories in the case of Bosnia and Herzegovina. In a deliberative classroom setting, the stories interact. In the case of Bosnia and Herzegovina, the Croat, Serb and Bosniak students would learn about each others' stories and compare them. For deliberation to take place, both the right and the opportunity to judge the foundations of the mutual stories are required. A reflection on the nature of historical knowledge guides us to find what is required for a good deliberative process in a history classroom (Ahonen, 1990).

Firstly, the students have the right to ask where from and how the historical knowledge is acquired. The requirement is fulfilled through the opportunity for critical work on historical evidence. Such work is not just a preliminary exercise but a constant dimension of the studies. Apart from being about truth, such work will teach the students to pay attention to the connotative nature of words and texts, especially in political documents.

Secondly, explanation of historical action in a deliberative classroom is based on a multiperspectival approach to history. The participants in a deliberation are free to apply their own point of view on the condition that they are open to the perspectives taken by other students. As the main rule, historical explanation is based on the intentions of the historical actors. Reenacting the intentions in their minds, the students practice the skill of empathizing with the opponent (Ahonen, 1990). Apart from being a method of history, such a skill is vital in the conflict-solving situations of the present time.

Thirdly, judging past acts requires a recognition of the transgenerational nature of human societies, that is to say, recognizing that the decisions and acts of today will be judged tomorrow. Even if history lessons are not meant for passing sentence and delivering penalties, there is an ethical dimension in human action, whether past or present. Honest and open deliberation is an attempt to fulfill the necessary requirement of objectivity in the judgment.

Even if the epistemological nature of historical knowledge is to be recognized in the classroom, history is not just a spin-off of history as an academic discipline. History fulfills a social function, as it serves the identity building of individuals and communities. In search of identity, members of a community tend to risk the intellectual requirements of a strict objectivity.[10] The solution to the problem is built into the concept of deliberative communication. If the students are not expected to conform to the mainstream collective identity but, instead, are given the freedom and informative resources to build their historical identity on their own transgenerational experience, neither their intellectual integrity nor their social needs will be violated. An open encounter with the historical identifications of their friends and open discussion therefore will not disrupt their positive identification with the past achievements of their affinity group.

A comparison between the characteristics of a traditional debate and a deliberative process illustrates the nature of deliberative communication as a pedagogical tool. While a debate is based on the opposition between defenders and critics of a certain interpretation of history, in deliberative communication the participants do not take opposite positions. They do not lock themselves in the positions of defense and opposition. Apart from bolstering their own story, they listen to the arguments of the other participants of the discussion. Through actively listening to each other, they will be able to embrace each others' stories. Deliberative communication spares the participants from ending up as winners and losers. Even if participants do not give up the appreciation and pride of their own past, their perspective to the past gets widened.

In short, the rules of deliberative history classroom are the following: (a) different stories of the past are disclosed and presented, (b) evidence for the stories is brought up and the reliability of that evidence is discussed, (c) a sustainable dialogue between the stories is established through the recognition of their respective validity.

We have developed the model of deliberative communication for the classroom discourse in a post-conflict situation, such as Bosnia and Herzegovina, where the only sustainable educational model can be one that allows a discussion in an open mode.[11] We shall now turn to presenting International Baccalaureate (IB) as one possible curriculum providing a context for deliberative communication in a classroom in Mostar, Bosnia and Herzegovina.

History Classrooms as a Road toward Deliberative Democracy in a Post-conflict Society: Example of International Education in the United World College in Mostar

In this chapter, we have demonstrated the contradiction discovered in the empirical research on historical culture and historical consciousness of young people in Bosnia and Herzegovina. Although aspirations for peace were shared, the culture of history was divided. This led us to study deliberative communication as a way to deal with divided history and as a means to bolster the historical consciousness in a post-conflict society. Deliberation is the way of a true civic society, where people identify with commonly shared liberties, opportunities, and values rather than with ethnic differences. For young people in Bosnia and Herzegovina, deliberative communication is a way to become socialized in an open society, where both information and arguments are expected to be transparent.

UWC, which opened in September 2006 as part of the Mostar Gymnasium, has been the first place since the war to teach history for sixteen- to eighteen-year-old students from all Bosnian national groups in the same classroom.[12] The curriculum is the International Baccalaureate Diploma Programme (IBDP), which is recognized as the world-leading international school-leaving certificate. Thus, the approach of international education[13] is being utilized to allow for a possibility of deliberation in classroom and history education.

We can see the suitability of the IB's approach in providing the curricular foundation for deliberative communication in education from basic features of international education defined by the former director general of the International Baccalaureate Office, George Walker (2002/2004). Among the features are the following requirements:

1. Students should be taught the art of negotiation.
2. Students should be taught to understand other nations' priorities.
3. Students should be taught awareness and understanding of the difference between national groups, for that provides the basis for tolerance.

In an international history classroom in Bosnia and Herzegovina, for example, the problem of nation-building in the areas inhabited by Bosniaks, leads to a deliberation about the meaning of the concept of "nation." Meaning is constructed through an intersubjective exchange of information and views. From this follows the discussion on the concept of "state" and "nation-state," which will, through the deliberation, be broadened into a meaning continuum of "ethnic-civic state."

The curriculum of the IB enables a multiperspectival and interactive approach to history. In the Bosnian context, the syllabus allows a choice of the Balkan area as a special focus of twentieth-century European history. This way the national story will be studied in the context of wider European and international developments. The combination of facing up to the native past and considering it from an international perspective can be healing for the historical traumas of a community.

In an international classroom with a deliberative approach and an open door to sensitive historical issues, young people are able to realize that their community is not alone in dealing with traumatizing memories. The memories can be dealt with, and the reconciliatory opportunities shared. The processing of collective memories in the classroom is in accordance with Dewey's (1976, 1980) appeal to schools to practice a "continuous reconstruction of experience," which Dewey considered to be a road to a better future society (Dewey). The classic educational legacy of Dewey thus meets the quest for international understanding as expressed in the IB curriculum.

Conclusion: Wider Lessons of Bosnia and United World College in Mostar for History Education in Post-conflict Situations

This chapter presented Torsti's (2003) empirical research, which concluded in a contradiction. A few years after the war in Bosnia and Herzegovina, the culture of history and history textbooks represented deeply divided national realities. Young people in Bosnia and Herzegovina representing all three national groups, however, demonstrated an historical identity that did not reflect national differences. This result creates a pedagogical challenge. The similarity of the historical identity of young Bosnians in terms of general values and attitudes toward the past suggests a possibility for mutual understanding. Yet, in the current segregated system and curriculum, that is hardly possible. Therefore, it seemed very important to develop a pedagogical tool and context that allows the young people to articulate their views and different stories as part of history education.

This led us to develop the concept of deliberative communication as an educational tool in this chapter. The concept was deduced from the theory of deliberative democracy as developed by Habermas.(1984) Deliberative communication incorporates the socioethical ideas of democracy and the inviolability of intellectual honesty. As post-conflict education is both an ethical project and a pursuit of truth, the process and atmosphere of learning is a matter of pedagogical innovation. All traces of manipulative practices are suspected of being conflict-feeding rather than conflict-reconciling.

In the development of the post-conflict history education in the pilot case of the UWC in Mostar, the deduction of educational principles from the concept of deliberative communication has proved feasible.

No contradictions between the deliberative approach and requirements of the existing multicultural situation or the curriculum of the IB have arisen. On the contrary, the IB curriculum, through the demands of in-depth studies and critical thinking, has proved a supportive context for the introduction of deliberative communication.

In regard to schools in other post-conflict countries, deliberative communication as such does not require an international curriculum like the IB. School curricula are normally written in national terms. In a post-conflict situation, however, the "nation" is most often ethnically, socially, politically, or religiously divided, and if education is expected not to accentuate or perpetuate the divisions, the school curriculum, both substantively and procedurally, has to be as inclusive as possible. In this chapter, deliberative communication was suggested to provide the procedural inclusiveness.

Concerning the role of international interventions in general, it has also been noted that, in many societies, history teaching has been suspended altogether immediately after conflict, for it may take a decade or more to reform history curricula and reach consensus as to what to teach. In such situations, assistance from "outsiders" can be vital (Cole & Barsalou, 2006, p. 1).

The curriculum development in the UWC in Mostar is in a pilot phase. Only after an empirical follow-up study will a conclusive evaluation of the pedagogical feasibility of deliberative communication be possible. The same applies for its possible impact on students. Today, we can only provide the logical arguments, originally based on the pragmatic theories of Dewey (1980) and Habermas (1984, 1996). We offer the arguments for the benefit of educators who want to respond to the challenges of a post-conflict situation in their countries.

NOTES

1. For example, the last census in Bosnia and Herzegovina as part of Yugoslavia in 1981 demonstrated the growing number of people declaring themselves as Yugoslavs. See Sells (1996, p. 8) and Almond (1994, p. 180).
2. Bosnia and Herzegovina suffered from a brutal conflict in 1992 to 1995. What started as an aggression of the Yugoslav army and Bosnian Serb paramilitary troops against the newly independent state of Bosnia and Herzegovina became characterized as a civil war in the latter years of the conflict. Of the approximately four million Bosnians, 50 percent became either refugees abroad or displaced within their country, over 100,000 people, most of them civilians, died, and tens of thousands went missing. The war ended in the Dayton Peace Agreement in November 1995, which managed to stop the war but created a very complicated state structure that, together with enormous material and human losses caused by the war, has caused the postwar notion to prevail inside the country,

which was last concluded by the report of International Crisis Group in 2007, which stated, "Bosnia remains unready for unguided ownership of its future—ethnic nationalism remains too strong" (Ensuring Bosnia's Future: February 2007). In education, the internationally created situation of thirteen ministers of education has remained in place (see Cole & Barsalou, 2006). For further analysis on the nature of post-conflict Bosnia and Herzegovina, see references in Torsti (2003, pp. 98–105), Crampton (2002, p. 268) and Chandler (1999).
3. The idea of "social facts" entails concepts, definitions, theories, and so forth, which involve collective intentionality and are formed by agents (individuals, groups, parties, etc.) within the social setting; see Collin (1997).
4. For the full analysis, see Torsti (2003, pp. 115–258).
5. Obrazovanje u Bosni i Hercegovini: Cemu ucimo djecu? Analiza sadrzaja udzbenika nacionalne grupe predmeta. [Education in Bosnia and Herzegovina: What do we teach to children? Analysis of the contents of textbooks in the national group of subjects] Program podrske obrazovanju [Program for educational support]. Fond otvoreno drustvo Bosni i Hercegovina. 2007.
6. For the full analysis, see Torsti (2003, pp. 259–322).
7. We could note here the conclusion of academic experts and educationalists with experience from post-conflict history teaching, which stresses the importance of pedagogy for the reform efforts. The way history is taught should take priority over curriculum revision in particular when resources are scarce. Also, pedagogical reform may be less controversial and threatening (and, therefore, more attractive) than attempts to change historical narratives through curriculum reform immediately after a conflict (Cole & Barsalou, 2006, pp. 1, 10). Deliberative communication is thus described in this chapter as a pedagogical tool for a post-conflict classroom situation.
8. For Habermas's thoughts about the relationship between deliberative democracy and education, see Habermas (1996).
9. For further understanding of what is meant by deliberative communication in education, note Swedish educationist Englund's suggestion for the main characteristics: (a) different views are confronted with one another, and arguments for them are given time and space to be articulated; (b) there is tolerance and respect for the concrete other, and participants learn to listen to the other; c) elements of collective will-formation are present—that is, endeavor to reach consensus or at least temporary agreement. (Englund, 2006, 512).
10. For more about identity building as a function of history education, see Ahonen (2001) and Ahonen (2005).
11. It has been suggested that, in cases such as Bosnia where the conflict has ended through international intervention, it is most likely that historical narratives at schools are simplified and biased and often controversial (Cole & Barsalou, 2006, p. 1). This further stresses the importance of open-mode discussion in history teaching.

12. For more on the UWC in Mostar, see http://www.uwc-ibo.org or http://www.uwc.org.
13. Attempts to define what is meant by international education have led to the idea of it as an inclusive umbrella term that can incorporate other more specific interpretations. We should note that international education is not a synonym to international schools, but rather a broader concept for an educational approach. The editorial preface of the *Education Review*'s special issue on international education used the following summary: "International, global, cross-cultural and comparative education are different terms used to describe education which attempts—in greater or lesser degree—to come to grips with the increasing interdependence that we face and to consider its relationship to learning" (Hayden, 2006, p. 5)

References

Ahonen, S. (1990). *The form of historical knowledge and the adolescent conception of it* (Research Report No. 80). Department of Teacher Education, University of Helsinki. Helsinki: Yliopistopaino.

Ahonen, S. (2001). The past, history and education. *Journal of Curriculum Studies, 33*(6), 737–751.

Ahonen, S. (2005). Historical consciousness, a valid paradigm for history education. *Journal of Curriculum Studies, 37*(1), 697–707.

Almond, M. (1994). *Europe's backyard war*. London: Heinemann.

Angvik, M., & von Borries, B. (Eds.). (1997). *Youth and history, a comparative European survey on historical consciousness and political attitudes among adolescents* (Vols. A–B). Hamburg: Körber Stiftung.

Aronsson, P. (2000). Historiekultur i förändring. In Aronsson, P. (Ed.), *Makten over Minnet. Historiekultur i Förändring* (pp. 7–33). Lund: Studentlitteratur.

Bush, K. D., and Saltarelli, D. (Ed.). (2000). *The two faces of education in ethnic conflict: Towards a peacebuilding education for children*. Florence: United National Children's Fund Innocenti Research Centre.

Chandler, D. (1999). *Faking democracy after Dayton*. London: Pluto Press.

Cole, E. A., & Barsalou, J. (2006, June). Unite or divide? The challenges of teaching history in societies emerging from violent conflict (United States Institute of Peace Special Report No. 163). Retrieved March 14, 2008, from http://www.usip.org

Collin, F. (1997). *Social reality*. London Routledge.

Crampton, R. (2002). *The Balkans since the Second World War*. London: Pearson Education Limited.

Dewey, J. (1976). The school and society. In J. Dewey (Ed.), *The middle works, 1899–1924* (J. A. Boydston, ed.) (Vol. 1, pp. 1–237). Chardondale, IL. Southern Illinois University Press. (Original work published 1899)

Dewey, J. (1980) Democracy and education. In J. Dewey (Ed.) *The Middle Works, 1899–1924* (J. A. Boydston, ed.) (Vol. 9, pp. 1–237). Chardondale, IL. Southern Illinois University Press. (Original work published 1916)

Englund, T. (2006). Deliberative communication: A pragmatist proposal. *Journal of Curriculum Studies, 38*(5), 503–520.

Gaćeša, Mladenovic, Maksinovic, & Zivković. (1997). *Istorija za 8. razred osnovne škole* [History for the eighth grade of primary school]. Beograd: Zavod za udžbenike i nastavna sredstva.

Habermas, J. (1984). *The theory of communicative action, Vol. 1: Reason and rationalisation of society* (T. McCarthy, Trans.). Boston: Beacon Press.

Habermas, J. (1996). *Between facts and norms: Contributions to a discourse theory of law and democracy* (W. Rehg, Trans.). Cambridge, MA: Polity Press.

Hayden, M. (2006). *Introduction to international education: International schools and their communities.* London: Sage Publications.

Hentilä, S. (2001). Historiapolitiikka–*Holocaust* ja historian julkinen käyttö. In Kalela, Jorma & Lindroos, Ilari (Eds.), *Jokapäiväinen historia* (pp. 26–49). Helsinki: Finnish Literary SOciety

Imamović, M., Pelesić, M., & Ganibegović M. (1994). *Historija za 8. razred osnovne škole* [History for the eighth grade of primary school]. Sarajevo: Republika Bosna i Hercegovina ministarstvo obrazovanja, nauke i kulture.

International Crisis Group. (2007, February). *Ensuring Bosnia's future: A new international engagement strategy* (Report No. 180). Europe: International Crisis Group.

Obrazovanje u Bosni i Hercegovini: Cemu ucimo djecu? Analiza sadrzaja udzbenika nacionalne grupe predmeta. Program podrske obrazovanju. Fond otvoreno drustvo Bosni i Hercegovina. 2007.

Sells, M. (1996). *The bridge betrayed: Religion and genocide in Bosnia.* Berkeley: University of California Press.

Torsti, P. (2003). *Divergent stories, convergent attitudes: A study on the presence of history, history textbooks and the thinking of youth in post-war Bosnia and Herzegovina.* Helsinki: Taifuuni.

Walker, G. (2002/2004). *To educate the nations, vol. 2: Reflections on an international education.* Suffolk: Peridot Press.

Chapter 14

"Yeah, It Is Important to Know Arabic—I Just Don't Like Learning It"

Can Jews Become Bilingual in the Palestinian-Jewish Integrated Bilingual Schools?

Zvi Bekerman

For the last decade, I have been studying integrated bilingual Palestinian-Jewish schools in Israel. Identity construction and cultural negotiation were the interests that brought me into this scene. However, I had little choice but to start paying attention to language because language was always marked in the activities I recorded. Language was marked because the teaching of both Arabic and Hebrew had been chosen as the main feature through which to mediate the encounter between the two populations involved, Jews and Palestinians, with their long history of conflict. It was assumed that the learning of the other group's language was essential in fostering outgroup recognition and tolerance. Over the course of my research, I continually returned to the following question: how could an educational environment so committed to bilingualism and so invested in efforts to achieve bilingualism fail for one group (Jews) while being so successful for the other (Palestinians)?

Implications reverberating from this question occupy the scope of this article. After offering a limited review of theoretical issues related to bilingual education, I will describe the sociopolitical context of the bilingual initiative. I will then analyze some of the ethnographic data gathered during the study. Finally, I will try and draw some conclusions regarding the potential of bilingual initiatives to overcome contextual constraints.

Bilingual Education and Contextual Limitations

Dual-language programs have been developing and increasing in number in the United States since the second half of the twentieth century (Freeman, Freeman, & Mercuri, 2005). There are a variety of models for dual-language programs. In particular, there are programs in which two language groups are simultaneously taught their two languages. There are also programs where two languages are taught to one language group. Regardless of the composition, research conducted on these programs has consistently shown their potential for developing high levels of academic achievement and cross-cultural awareness among participants (Gomez, Freeman, & Freeman, 2005; Howard & Christian, 2002; Thomas & Collier, 2002).

Dual-language programs aspire to reach high standards of academic achievement; their students are expected to reach high literacy levels in both languages (Torres-Guzmán, 2002). These programs also seek to promote positive cross-cultural attitudes among their participants (Lindholm-Leary 2001). Dual-language programs vary in terms of the percentage of first-language (L1) and second-language (L2) instruction with models ranging from a 90/10 to 50/50 rate of instruction in both languages; variation can also be found regarding language distribution within the curriculum (Jong, 2002). Research shows that these types of language implementation may result in qualitative differences regarding the language input to which native and English Language Learners (ELL) participants are exposed and, thus, on their achievements.

Literature pertaining to L2 acquisition posits that multiple factors play a significant role in improving student motivation in acquiring and learning a second language. These include the status of the L2 in the immediate social context, the cultural beliefs of students about the target language, its speakers and culture, and parental encouragement and parental attitudes toward the language being learned. Early studies by Gardener and Lambert (1972) considered motivation to learn a language as the primary force for enhancing or hindering the learning of a second language. The authors identified two classes of orientations—the integrative orientation and the instrumental orientation. The former describes the will to learn L2 so as to have contact and even identify with the L2 community. The latter refers to the desire to learn L2 for some practical goal. They suggested that the integrative orientation would achieve greater L2 competence. Later studies (Clement & Kruidenier, 1983, 1985) have suggested that these orientations might play similar roles depending on influences from the social milieu. More recent studies have added complexity to early schemes; intrinsic and extrinsic factors have problematized the rather simple instrumental and integrative divide (Noels, Pelletier, Clement, & Vallerand, 2003).

Educational contexts have also been shown to be as relevant as the social milieu in affecting learners' motivation. Factors relevant to the learning situation, such as school facilities, course books, learning situations, changes in the educational context, and teachers' attitudes and behaviors, have been shown to account for students' motivation or lack there of (Donitsa-Schmidt, Inbar, & Shohamy, 2004; Dornyei, 2001, 2003; Inbar, Donitsa-Schmidt, & Shohamy, 2000). Moreover, L2 learning—more than other school subjects—is considered to be deeply imbued in social and cultural contexts, making its learning a deeply social event. The learning process includes L2 culture as well as language learning (Williams, 1994).

Similar studies (Valdes, 1997) have pointed out that the success of these programs is dependent on the will of the native language majority population and their perceptions regarding the need of their children to become bilingual in a world going global. Tosi (1999) has shown the importance played by local conditions in individual communities as factors that contribute to language maintenance and revitalization. Close observations of dual-language practice have shown that contextual conditions seem to influence the use of the minority language by both ELL and native learners (Edelsky, 1996; McCollum, 1999). External social factors have been shown to influence social informal activities in dual-language programs exposing the students' preferences to interact with children from their ingroup when choosing, for example, with whom to sit or whom to invite home (Lambert & Cazabon, 1994). Other studies have shown the dominance of the L1 and native speakers in the dual-language classroom suggesting that this is a product of the dominance of L1 in the larger context (Amrein & Peña, 2000). Such conclusions point toward the possibility that these programs tend to replicate outside social and political realities (Amrein & Peña, 2000; Freeman, 1998; Valdes, 1998).

It has also been suggested that language plays a crucial role in social interaction and the transmission of cultural and social values (Fishman, 1970, 1997; Safran, 1999). As a symbolic system, language not only constructs social identity but also may solidify or revitalize national or ethnic identities and loyalties (Fishman, 1989; Haarmann, 1986; Smith, 1998). Thus, one may consider language to be a sociocultural resource used by nations to unify and separate national or ethnic groups into discrete speech communities, each with its own level of access to concomitant social resources and each loyal to its own divergent, linguistically constructed culture (Haslett, 1989; Scollon & Scollon, 1981).

Two comprehensive reviews (Genesee & Gandara, 1999; Slavin & Cooper, 1999) have examined the influence of bilingual and cooperative learning on prejudice, discrimination, and the acquisition of new cultural paradigms. Genesee and Gandara emphasize that, if bilingual education is to improve intergroup attitudes and relationships, explicit attention must be given to societally based intergroup factors. Slavin and Cooper point toward the relevance of stressing pedagogical factors, such as cooperative educational approaches, so as to create conditions for reframing cultural relations.

In bilingual programs, intergroup power relations play an important role in either reproducing or overcoming conditions that subordinate language minority students and their communities (Paulston, 1994; Ricento & Hornberger, 1996).

Recent studies conducted by Papademeter and Routoulas (2001) emphasize the ambivalence reflected in the views and opinions of minority immigrant groups toward bilingual and bicultural education. Bissoonauth and Offord (2001) suggest that the association of language with high status and prestige influences language use in multilingual societies. Obeng (2000) shows how attitudes encompassing a wide spectrum of values, beliefs, and emotions concerning language influence participants' perspectives toward languages in general and toward educational bilingual initiatives in particular.

Ricento (2000) has challenged researchers to integrate micro and macro levels of investigation so as to provide better explanations for language behavior than those currently available. This suggests that the ecology of language paradigm might be in need of further conceptual development to better serve the needs of language education planning in the future. It is toward this challenge that the following description and analysis work.

THE SOCIOPOLITICAL CONTEXT

The Israeli-Palestinian conflict can be traced to the beginning of Zionist colonialization of Palestine toward the end of the nineteenth century. Claimed by Jews to be the land of their birthright, this seemingly intractable conflict produced at least two dominant ideological discourses (one Jewish, one Palestinian) concerning control of the land and recognition of group sovereignty. Historically, the region was never autonomously controlled, having a long history of colonial and imperial rule (Khalidi, 1997). The 1948 war, called the War of Independence by Israelis, and the Naqbe (the Catastrophe) by Palestinians, was the first open military clash between Zionist and Palestinian nationalist movements. Palestinians in Israel (20 percent) are an indigenous minority, who formed the majority in Palestine (two-thirds of the population) until 1947.

The ongoing Israeli occupation of the Gaza strip and the West Bank since 1967 and the Intifada outbreaks in 1997 and 2000 brought about events that shattered the optimism for a peaceful solution that emerged after the Oslo agreements between the Israeli government and the Palestinian Liberation Organization (PLO) in 1993. It remains to be seen whether the recent disengagement from the Gaza strip holds any future promises; the 2006 second Lebanese war and the recent overtake by Hamas of the Gaza area of the Palestinian Authority leave little place for optimism.

In spite of Israel's declared goals of offering equal opportunity to all its citizens through the educational system, the gap between the Jewish and Palestinian sectors remains. For example, in 1991, 45.4 percent Palestinian and 67.3 percent Jewish children earned a matriculation diploma, while in 2001, the percentage increased to 59.1 percent and 69.7 percent, respectively (Statistical Abstract of Israel, 2002). As of today, Israel has no official multicultural educational policies. The Jewish curriculum focuses on national Jewish content and Jewish nation building, and the Palestinian curriculum is sanitized of any national Palestinian content (Rouhana, 1997). While Jewish students are called to engage in the collective Jewish national enterprise, Palestinian students are expected to accept the definition of Israel as a Jewish democratic state (Al-Haj, 2005; Gordon, 2005). All in all, the Palestinian educational system in Israel lacks the preferential support given by the government to the Jewish educational system, thus creating an enormous gap and leaving the Palestinian educational system behind.

Setting and Method

The school under study is the largest integrated school in Israel today. For the most part, the school uses the regular curriculum of the state school system with the major difference being that both Hebrew and Arabic are used as languages of instruction. The school has adopted what has been characterized as a strong additive bilingual approach, which emphasizes symmetry between both languages in all aspects of instruction (Garcia, 1997). In terms of aims and processes, it is to be assumed that the initiators of the bilingual project would agree with Skutnabb-Kangas and Garcia's (1995) three main benefits of an effective bilingual educational project: (1) a high level of multilingualism, (2) equal opportunity for academic achievement, and (3) a strong, positive multilingual and multicultural identity, including positive attitudes toward self and others. The school has adhered to an ideology that emphasizes the need to sustain symmetry at all organizational, curricular, and practical levels. They have been successful in sustaining this goal by securing the presence of a rather well-balanced body of students and the services of a well-balanced educational staff, both a Palestinian and a Jewish teacher in each class and a Palestinian and a Jewish school principal.

I have been researching this school through a long-standing ethnographic effort that included the gathering of information through field observations and videotaping of multiple classroom activities and school events (over two-hundred hours); interviewing representatives of all school stakeholders, principals, teachers, parents, and students (over 100 interviews were conducted); and the collection of school documents and curricular materials. The effort was conducted by a team that, at all times, included bilingual (Hebrew, Arabic) research assistants from both ethnic groups (Palestinians and Jews). Space constrains prevent me from going into much detail. Those interested in the methodological and descriptive details are encouraged to consult some of my previously published work (Bekerman, 2003a, 2003b, 2004, 2005; Bekerman & Maoz, 2005; Bekerman & Nir, 2006; Bekerman & Shhadi, 2003). In addition, other scholars who have researched these schools and their work should also be considered (Feuerverger, 1998; Glazier, 2003, 2004).

The school counted 254 children in the 2004 to 2005 academic year and 306 students for the 2005 to 2006 academic year (the years from which the data is rendered), with a total of ten and twelve classrooms, respectively. The classrooms ranged from kindergarten to sixth grade during the first year of our research and added the seventh grade (middle school) in the second year.

During the first year, our research focused on the first and third grades and continued into the second and fourth grades during the second year. The first-grade class had thirty-two children (fifteen Palestinians and seventeen Jews) and the third-grade class had twenty-nine children (thirteen Palestinians and sixteen Jews).

All six homeroom teachers who we observed hold degrees in education, three of them in special education. Three hold an MA degree and one was working toward it. Two of the Jewish teachers had an intermediate and high command of the Arabic language, which allowed them to feel rather at ease in the bilingual environment. Two had no command of the Arabic language, in this sense being more representative of the school's Jewish body of teachers.

Findings

On Language Practice

In this section we offer examples of events related to language use and how interactions and discourse were organized for Hebrew to be more prominent than Arabic.

The first scene is presented to give a sense of a very basic classroom exchange when only one teacher, in this case, the Palestinian teacher (PT), is present. The scene takes place in the first-grade class almost two months into the school year. Nun, the PT, has been dealing with some administrative issues and has now informed the class that Yod, the Jewish co-teacher, will not be coming in to school today. In lines 1 and 3, Nun speaks in Arabic. The loud intervention of a Jewish student (JS Girl/Boy) indicating she does not understand (line 4) the Arabic being spoken requires attention by the teacher. She can respond in one of two ways. Either she will translate some of the words used in the last sentence into Hebrew or, because a Palestinian student (PS Girl/Boy) has already hinted in Hebrew at the content of the conversation (see line 6), she will continue in Arabic. Which option will be preferred is difficult to predict, but when dealing with what might be understood as not such important issues, the second option will be preferred (as in the case below). What usually will not happen is that the call by a Jewish student will be left unattended. It is also important to remember that though we have records of Palestinian children not understanding Hebrew, we do not have records of loud intervention by Palestinian children demanding translation.

> DVD No. 9–28/10/04-Palestinian Teacher teaches alone 1st grade—Transcript lines 97–103
> 1 PT: ok Yod is sick today she will not come I will be with you alone
> 2 CLASS: no:::, yah:::
> 3 PT: please ((in English)) pay attention to me, help me seriously ok?
> 4 JSG: I DO NOT UNDERSTAND I DO NOT UNDERSTAND
> 5 TP: Y is sick, with fever
> 6 PSB: *Does she have fever in her head*
> 7 JSB: Virus
> 8 JSG: What, every body is sick in class now!
> 9 ((noise in class))
> 10 PT: ok, each one who has in his table children who are not here

Jewish students claim their language with ease.

In this next section, we see the PT starting a turn in Hebrew (line 2; underlined in English text), a Palestinian child taking a turn in Hebrew (line 3) and PT changing back into Arabic but integrating into her utterances Hebrew words (lines 4–5). The use of Hebrew by the PT seems to be preferred because otherwise a somewhat important message regarding the need to contact absent students will not be understood by the Jewish children. Still, in line 9 the Jewish child complains about not understanding. This statement brings Nun to integrate more Hebrew into her next turn (lines 10–11).

> DVD No. 9–28/10/04 - Palestinian Teacher teaches alone 1st grade -Transcript lines 166–182
> 1 PT: *I will sit, I ask not* (X) ((teacher sits H'comes in))
> 2 PSB: ((laughing)) one more child came in. one more child.

3 PT: you can see that I want to say a sentence and I can't. I can't say the sentence. From
4 today *each child that is missing, every child who is missing from school*, we want two children to
5 call
6 PSB: [me]
7 PSB: [why] two children and not one child
8 PT: we want two children do you know why, so if one forgets
9 JSG: I DO NOT UNDERSTAND
10 PT: *If a child does not come to school* each time, from us, two children, will call ask why
11 he didn't come to school why he did not come ok

When the two teachers are present in class, the Arabic language is managed somewhat differently. When together, the teachers complement each other. The PT still integrates a few Hebrew words but much less than in the above examples, and the JT does not necessarily translate but adds to what is being said by, for example, conceptualizing the activity as a wider referential context.

Our last example related to language use shows conversational give and take among four children in the third grade. Three Palestinians (two girls and one boy) and a Jewish boy are working together on an assignment where they were asked to describe some experiences from the vacation they just had. The example clearly shows the pattern of language use that regularly develops among mixed groups. Even in this specific case, where three out of the four participants were Palestinian, the *lingua franca* used by the group was Hebrew. The Palestinians are the ones who sustain the floor (almost 85 percent of the time) and, for the most part, lead the conversation and activity. The two Palestinian girls lead the activity. Both are good students, one of them among the best in class and known for her strong political awareness. The Palestinian and Jewish boys are average students, but the Jewish boy is outstanding in that he frequently declares his willingness to learn Arabic and has, on multiple occasions, expressed his interest in Palestinian culture.

National pride and commitment to recognizing alterity are much of what could be needed to secure Arabic use. But even under these extremely favorable circumstances, Arabic is displaced and the Palestinian children speak more Hebrew (their second language) than Arabic (their first) while the Jewish student speaks only in Hebrew.

From our first analysis of this scene, we tried to identify the conditions under which Arabic might make its appearance. The following points became apparent:

1. Arabic seems to be used when one of the Palestinians involved in the interaction does not understand the activity that has been assigned.

Most of the strings of conversation in the segment are started by one of the Palestinian girls explaining to the Palestinian boy what needs to be done.
2. When such a situation occurs and another Palestinian student joins the conversation, there is a good chance he will join in speaking Arabic. When the Jewish child is involved in the conversation, all three Palestinians speak Hebrew.
3. These rules are not fixed. However, they represent fairly well many of the events we recorded during formal activities in class (for informal activities, i.e., breaks, we have less information; although, when playing in mixed groups, Hebrew seems to dominate).

On Language Use

When discussing the field notes and our observations, we raised questions regarding the choice of language use made by participants in the school setting. We discussed our belief that the Jewish group seemed to evade the use of Arabic particularly among the students but also among the teachers. In our notes, we had fairly good descriptions to substantiate these statements. Nevertheless, we wanted to go more into detail, hoping to better understand what was going on and how these doings got done. We report here on the first results from our first detailed analysis. In the following, we offer a first feel of our data as a whole. To achieve this, we found it useful to use certain quantitative measures, however crude they may be.

The transcripts we counted included six hours of classroom activity in the first grade and a similar amount in the third grade. These hours include both the Palestinian and Jewish teachers. In the second and the fourth grades, we counted two hours of Palestinian-Jewish co-teaching. We also recorded the Palestinian and Jewish teachers working individually (alone) in class. In each case, we counted four hours of activity. The recordings we report on include a variety of subjects such as language, math, and memorial days (Remembrance Day for Yitzhak Rabin, Holocaust Day Memorial).

Regarding the language of choice of the participating teachers and students (Hebrew or Arabic), our findings show that the balance expected to be achieved between the languages is not attained. Out of the 2,511 utterances counted in the transcripts under analysis, Jewish teachers expressed themselves in Hebrew 2,456 (97.81 percent) times, in Arabic 26 (1.04 percent) times, and 29 (1.15 percent) times we counted events of code switching or code integration. In contrast, PTs used Arabic in 1,563 (70.09 percent) out of 2,230 utterances, Hebrew in 221 (9.91 percent) utterances, and code integration or switching on 446 (20.0 percent) occasions.

The children's linguistic behavior mirrored the teachers' and accentuated it. Out of a total of 2,608 utterances made by Jewish students, 2,490 (95.48 percent) were made in Hebrew, 84 (3.22 percent) in Arabic, and 34 (1.30 percent) using code switching or code integration. Out of the 1,540 utterances made by Palestinian students, 850 (55.19 percent) were made in Arabic, 672 (43.64 percent) were made in Hebrew, and 18 (1.17 percent) involved code switching or integration.

When we looked further into different segments of the transcripts, we realized that the averages in language choice for the PTs had changed throughout the years. For the PTs, the choice to speak in Arabic grew from first grade (55 percent) to second grade (80 percent), stayed steady during third grade, but fell to 60 percent in fourth grade. When the PTs taught alone, the average use of Arabic did not rise. Throughout, the Jewish teachers maintained their 95 percent use of Hebrew. Again, it is difficult to explain these findings, and it would be irresponsible to posit any final conclusions. Still, it could be assumed that the increased rate of Arabic use from the first to the third grade is a result of the fact that the Jewish children are starting to recognize the language, which allows the PT to use it more in their daily conversation. The decrease of Arabic use in fourth grade could be connected to a sense of despair by the PT and an acceptance that the Jewish children, given present circumstances, might not go much further in their language acquisition. The presence of the Palestinian cohort throughout does not change the situation because their goals (as described by their parents) do not support a bilingual endeavor for their Jewish peers; moreover, Palestinian bilingualism is anyway secured through the classroom practices.

The fact that when the PT teaches alone, the use of Arabic does not rise might be connected to the fact that (as in any other occasions) the use of Arabic by a PT is not dependant on her individual decision but is strongly related to the social context in which the language evolves. In our specific case, it is worth considering that although she is alone, and does not have to attune herself to her monolingual Jewish co-teacher; all other elements have remained the same. Both the Palestinian and the Jewish children have not changed and stick to their language behavior and expectations.

Children's language choices remained rather steady. Palestinian children chose Arabic 55 percent of the time, and Jewish children chose Hebrew 95 percent of the time. Palestinians decreased their choice for Arabic use as they grew older. In the first grade, we recorded 70 percent Arabic use, in the second grade, 56 percent Arabic use, and in the third grade 63 percent Arabic use. Finally, when a PT was alone in class, the Palestinian children averaged 66 percent turns in Arabic, and the Jewish children recorded a lower average use of Hebrew (87 percent). Possibly a good step toward increasing Jewish bilingualism would be longer periods where the PTs direct the class alone.

What Children, Teachers, and Parents Say

Jewish children in the first grade seemed to have a pretty realistic assessment of their knowledge of Arabic. Only two students said they know the language and the rest stated their difficulties and limitations, always adding that Arabic is not an easy language to learn. These difficulties did not seem to interfere with their sense that learning Arabic was important. With the exception of two students, all others, for different reasons ("because there are Arabs around," "because it is important to learn languages"), found learning Arabic important. Questions about Arabic at school allowed for some fascinating dialogues with the children. These dialogues revealed their deep understanding of the connection between politics and the school's curriculum ("it aims at allowing for coexistence and peace") and the connection between Arabic and Hebrew literacy and wider contexts ("Andi knows more Hebrew than I know Arabic because here in Jerusalem the majority speaks Hebrew").

When asked about their perception of the Hebrew language, Palestinian children in the same grade were generally very positive about the language. Some mentioned that Hebrew is a rather easy language to write ("the letters need not be connected"). Others mentioned the importance of knowing foreign languages or mentioned that Hebrew was helpful to get along with "security people," and one, rather surprisingly, said, "because if I learn a lot I will feel like a Jew later." This appreciation for Hebrew did not stand in the way of their understanding that learning Arabic was also very important to them because "it is our language." The one student who was not so convinced that learning Arabic was important stated "because I'm Arab and I need to know Hebrew."

Jewish children in the third grade testified as to having some knowledge of the Arabic language. Only one student said she knows Arabic well, and one other student said that he does not know it at all. From the students who stated that they know some Arabic, some mentioned that they like it but immediately added that it is difficult. Other students were even less enthusiastic. Still, they all believed it was important to learn Arabic. Their responses were more articulated and complex than the responses articulated in first grade. The students emphasized the possibilities that knowing Arabic afforded them in terms of communicating with Arab populations. Ein offered an answer that touched on problems of social justice and the need to offer recognition to the Palestinian minority. Dalet mentioned that she loves the Arabic language, but she just does not like learning it.

Palestinian children in the third grade agreed that the main characteristic that set the school apart from other schools was its bilingual and binational character. Learning Hebrew was important for them so they could speak to Jews, have Jewish friends, understand the news, and because "I have too, I'm Arab and I need to know Hebrew." Learning Arabic was important for more sentimental reasons: "It is our language." Other students, seemingly voicing their parents, emphasized the importance of knowing Hebrew for their future education when reaching the university and, even further, when joining the workforce.

Teachers in both groups expressed a strong belief in the bilingual agenda adopted by the school. Jewish teachers seemed to be much more ready to accept the reality, which was known to them all, that Jewish students were lacking the expected competencies in Arabic. They sounded saddened by this fact but explained it as a natural outcome of a non-supportive context. They also rested on the success they perceived the school was achieving in terms of guiding Jewish children on the path of recognition toward Palestinian culture. PTs strongly agreed with this last appreciation but expressed great dissatisfaction with the achievements of the Jewish cohort in Arabic. From their perspective, Arabic competency by the Jewish children was the most important entry point to the creation of a true dialogue among the children of both groups. They also emphasized that there could not be true cultural understanding if Arabic was not available to those interested in understanding it.

Jewish parents supported bilingualism as long as it did not harm educational excellence. They seemed satisfied with an educational initiative that allows them to substantiate their liberal positions and to offer their children cultural understanding and sensitivity toward the "other": "We did want our children to learn Arabic, but given the context it is difficult and it will be enough [for them and us] to get to know Arabic culture and tradition." If these goals were achieved, the lack of success in bilingual achievements could be forgiven.

Palestinian parents wanted the best education available for their children, given the present Israeli sociopolitical context. Israel's present sociopolitical conditions made it almost impossible for parents to dream about a soon-to-arrive, top-down, multicultural, multilingual policy. It is also not totally clear whether the parents would adopt such a policy if imposed. As members of the upper-middle socioeconomic sector of society, they perceived education as a means to mobility in a world going global. Thus, they preferred an English *lingua franca* and high Hebrew literacy to achieve the dreams for their children's future.

Discussion

As is the case in many bilingual programs, the bilingual school studied suffers from somewhat contradictory practices, perspectives, and expectations in relation to its goals. The current Israeli sociopolitical context seems to discourage the teaching and learning of Arabic as L2. Even when the monetary resources are available to create a nearly perfect bilingual environment with declared, across-the-board, ideological support, bilingualism for the Jewish population seems not able to take root.

The ethnographic data exposed multiple practices that could not only be judged as contradictory to the bilingual principles but also as being well-attuned to the macrocontextual levels within which bilingual education is embedded. Recent reports submitted to the schools by bilingual specialists have suggested the need to invest energies in helping the Jewish faculty gain bilingual competencies, in encouraging Jewish parents to support and encourage their children in the pursue of bilingualism and in enriching the presence of the Arabic language in the school context (its physical environment and its formal and informal activities). Though adopting these measures could in some ways benefit the cause of bilingualism, we should be careful not to find fault with the teachers and parents involved in our program. Blaming them for consciously or unconsciously conveying negative messages about the minority language in spite of their overt efforts to create a school environment and a curriculum that represent a balanced bilingual effort would be clutching at straws. If placed anywhere, the "blame" should more accurately be placed on an adaptive, wider, sociopolitical system in which Arabic carries little symbolic power. In Bourdieu's (1991) terms, it can be said that, in general, in Israel, speakers of Hebrew have more cultural capital in the linguistic market place than those who speak Arabic. It seems clear that the social milieu affects Jewish learners' motivations as much as it affects teachers' behaviors and attitudes toward the learning and teaching of Arabic as a L2. Jewish children do not even need to consider holding an integrative orientation, and the sociopolitical context offers no instrumental reason to support viewing Arabic as a second language as an asset. At their best, intrinsic and extrinsic factors fail to encourage the learning of Arabic by Jews. At their worst, extrinsic factors (given the present monocultural policies in the conflicted Israeli society) are oppositional to gaining Arabic literacy.

Given the nature of language learning as a deeply social event and the strong connection between language learning and social and cultural contexts, one can hope that the failure of the Jewish group to learn Arabic as a L2 will not be detrimental, in the long run, to the declared aims of the bilingual schools. In particular, the goal is to instill in their students a sense of cross-cultural awareness and tolerance toward the "other."

Note

"This study is part of a longstanding research project, supported by the Bernard Van Leer Foundation. I want to thank Julia Schlam for her critical insights and assistance when editing the manuscript."

References

Al-Haj, M. (2005). National ethos, multicultural education, and the new history textbooks in Israel. *Curriculum Inquiry, 35*(1), 48–71.

Amrein, A., & Peña, R. (2000). Asymmetry in dual language practice: Assessing imbalance in a program promoting equity [Electronic version]. *Education Policy Analysis Archives, 8*. Retrieved August 18, 2007, from http://epaa.asu.edu/epaa/v8n8.html

Bekerman, Z. (2003a). Never free of suspicion. *Cultural Studies Critical Methodologies, 3*(2), 136–147.

Bekerman, Z. (2003b). Reshaping conflict through school ceremonial events in Israeli Palestinian-Jewish Co-Education. *Anthropology & Education Quarterly, 34*(2), 205–224.

Bekerman, Z. (2004). Multicultural approaches and options in conflict ridden areas: Bilingual Palestinian-Jewish education in Israel. *Teachers College Record, 106*(3), 574–610.

Bekerman, Z. (2005). Complex contexts and ideologies: Bilingual education in conflict-ridden areas. *Journal of Language Identity and Education, 4*(1), 1–20.

Bekerman, Z., & Maoz, I. (2005). Troubles with identity: Obstacles to coexistence education in conflict ridden societies. *Identity, 5*(4), 341–358.

Bekerman, Z., & Nir, A. (2006). Opportunities and challenges of integrated education in conflict ridden societies: The case of Palestinian-Jewish schools in Israel. *Childhood Education, 82*(6), 324–333.

Bekerman, Z., & Shhadi, N. (2003). Palestinian Jewish bilingual education in Israel: Its influence on school students. *Journal of Multilingual and Multicultural Development, 24*(6), 473–484.

Bissoonauth, A., & Offord, M. (2001). Language use in Mauritian adolescents. *Journal of Multilingual and Multicultural Development, 25*(5), 381–400.

Bourdieu, P. (1991). *Language and symbolic power*. Cambridge: Harvard University Press.

Clement, R., & Kruidenier, B. G. (1983). Orientations in second language acquisition: The effects of ethnicity, milieu, and target language on their emergence. *Language Learning, 33*, 272–291.

Clement, R., & Kruidenier, B. G. (1985). Aptitude, attitude and motivation in second language proficiency: A test of Clement's model. *Journal of Language and Social Psychology, 4*(1), 21–37.

Donitsa-Schmidt, S., Inbar, O., & Shohamy, E. (2004). The effects of teaching spoken Arabic on students' attitudes and motivation in Israel. *The Modern Language Journal, 88*(ii), 217–228.

Dornyei, Z. (2001). *Teaching and researching motivation*. Harlow; UK: Pearson Education.

Dornyei, Z. (2003). Attitudes, orientations, and motivations in language learning: Advances in theory, research, and applications. *Language Learning, 53*(1), 3–32.

Edelsky, C. (1996). *With literacy and justice for all: Rethinking the social in language and education*. London, UK: Taylor & Francis.

Feuerverger, G. (1998). Neve Shalom/Wahat Al-Salam: A Jewish-Arab school for peace. *Teachers College Record, 99*, 692–730.

Fishman, J. A. (1970). *Sociolinguistics*. Rowley, MA: Newbury House.
Fishman, J. A. (1989). *Language and ethnicity in minority sociolinguistic perspective: Loyalty in the United States*. Clevedon: Multilingual Matters.
Fishman, J. A. (1997). Language and ethnicity: The view from within. In F. Coulmas (Ed.), *The handbook of sociolinguistics* (pp. 327–343). Oxford: Blackwell.
Freeman, R. D. (1998). *Bilingual education and social change*. Clevedon, UK: Multilingual Matters.
Freeman, Y. S., Freeman, D. E., & Mercuri, S. P. (2005). *Dual language essentials for teachers and administrators*. Portsmouth, NH: Heinemann.
Garcia, O. (1997). Bilingual education. In F. Coulmas (Ed.), *The handbook of sociolinguistics* (pp. 405–420). Oxford: Blackwell.
Gardener, R., & Lambert, W. (1972). *Attitudes and motivation in second language learning* Rowley, MA: Newbury House.
Genesee, F., & Gandara, P. (1999). Bilingual education programs: A cross national perspective. *Journal of Social Issues, 55*(4), 665–685.
Glazier, J. A. (2003). Developing cultural fluency: Arab and Jewish students engaging in one another's company. *Harvard Educational Review, 73*(2), 141–163.
Glazier, J. A. (2004). Collaborating with the "other": Arab and Jewish teachers teaching in each other's company. *Teachers College Rec, 106*(3), 611–633.
Gomez, L., Freeman, D., & Freeman, Y. (2005). Dual language education: A promising 50–50 model. *Bilingual research journal, 29*(1), 145–164.
Gordon, D. (2005). History textbooks, narratives, and democracy: A response to Majid Al-Haj. *Curriculum Inquiry, 35*(3), 367–376.
Haarmann, H. (1986). *Language in ethnicity: A view of basic ecological relations*. Berlin: Mouton de Gruyter.
Haslett, B. (1989). Communication and language. In S. Ting-Toomey & F. Korzenny (Eds.), *Language, communication, and culture* (pp. 19–34). London: Sage.
Howard, E. R., & Christian, D. (2002). *Two-way immersion 101: Designing and implementing a two-way immersion education program at the elementary level.* Santa Cruz, CA: Center for Research on Education, Diversity & Excellence, University of California.
Inbar, O., Donitsa-Schmidt, S., & Shohamy, E. (2000). Students' motivation as a function of language learning: The teaching of Arabic in Israel. In Z. Dornyei & R. Schmidt (Eds.), *Motivation and second language acquisition* (pp. 70–96). Honolulu, HI: University of Hawaii, Second language Teaching & Curriculum Center, 70–96.
Jong, E. J. d. (2002). Effective bilingual education: From theory to academic achievement in a two-way bilingual program. *Bilingual Research Journal, 26*(1), 65–86.
Khalidi, R. (1997). *Palestinian identity: The construction of modern national consciousness*. New York: Columbia University Press
Lambert, W. E., & Cazabon, M. T. (1994). *Students' views of the Amigos program* (Research Report No. 11) Santa Cruz: National Center for Research on Cultural Diversity and Second Language Learningo.
Lindholm-Leary, K. (2001). *Dual language education*. Clevedon, England: Multilingual Matters.
McCollum, P. (1999). Learning to value English: Cultural capital is a two-way bilingual program. *Bilingual Research Journal, 23*(2/3), 113–134.

Noels, K. A., Pelletier, L. G., Clement, R., & Vallerand, R. J. (2003). Why are you learning a second language? Motivational orientations and self-determination theory. *Language Learning, 53*(1), 33–64.

Obeng, S. G. (2000). Speaking the unspeakable: Discursive strategies to express language attitudes in Legon (Ghana) graffiti. *Research on Language and Social Interaction, 33*(3), 291–319.

Papademeter, L., & Routoulas, S. (2001). Social, political, educational, linguistic and cultural (dis-) incentives for languages education in Australia. *Journal of Multilingual and Multicultural Development, 22*(2), 134–151.

Paulston, C. (1994). *Linguistic Minorities in Multilingual Settings.* Amsterdam: John Benjamins.

Ricento, T. (2000). Historical and theoretical perspectives in language policy and planning. *Journal of Sociolinguistics, 4*(2), 196–213.

Ricento, T., & Hornberger, N. (1996). Unpeeling the onion: Language planning and policy and the ELT professional. *TESOL Quarterly, 30,* 401–428.

Rouhana, N. (1997). *Palestinian citizens in an ethnic Jewish state.* New Haven: Yale University Press.

Safran, W. (1999). Nationalism. In J. A. fishman (Ed.), *Handbook of language and ethnic identity* (pp. 77–93). Oxford: Oxford University Press.

Scollon, R., & Scollon, S. B. K. (1981). *Narrative, literacy and face in interethnic communication.* Norwood, NJ: Ablex Publishing Corporation.

Skutnabb-Kangas, T., & Garcia, O. (Eds.). (1995). *Multilingualism for all? General principles.* Lisse: Swets and Zeitlinger.

Slavin, R. E., & Cooper, R. (1999). Improving intergroup relations: Lessons learned from cooperative learning programs. *Journal of Social Issues, 55*(4), 647–663.

Smith, A. D. (1998). *Nationalism and modernism.* London: Routledge.

Statistical Abstract of Israel (2002). Central Bureau of Statistics, Jerusalem, Israel.

Thomas, W. P., & Collier, V. P. (2002). A national study of school effectiveness for language minority students' long-term academic achievement. Retrieved August 15, 2007, from http://crede.berkeley.edu/research/crede/pdf/rb10.pdf

Torres-Guzmán, M. E. (2002). *Dual language programs.* Washington, DC: National Clearinghouse for Bilingual Education.

Tosi, A. (1999). The notion of "community" in language maintenance. In G. Extra & L. Verhoeven (Eds.), *Bilingualism and migration* (pp. 325–343). Berlin: Mouton de Gruyter.

Valdes, G. (1997). Dual-language immersion programs: A cautionary note concerning the education of language minority students. *Harvard Educational Review, 67*(3), 391–429.

Valdes, G. (1998). The world outside and inside schools: Language and immigrant children. *Education Researcher, 27*(6), 4–18.

Williams, M. (1994). Motivation in foreign and second language learning: An interactive perspective. *Educational and Child Psychology, 11,* 77–84.

Chapter 15

Teacher Preparation for Peace Education in South Africa and the United States
Maintaining Commitment, Courage, and Compassion

Candice C. Carter and Saloshna Vandeyar

Introduction

This chapter reviews experiences with transformation of teacher candidates' knowledge and skills in societies where human diversity and social injustice were highly associated. Following descriptions of instructional situations and responses to challenges faced in them is a discussion about sustained conflict-focused instruction and corresponding student engagement. Compared are the contextual differences of teacher preparation in South Africa and the southern United States of America (USA), along with their effects. Recognized are commonalities in both instructional contexts beyond a shared vision of and commitment to peace through education. Student responses to transformative education highlighted crucial instructor dispositions for success with it.

Theoretical Foundation

Teacher education opens the window of pedagogical possibilities. It brings forth considerations about how learning occurs, as well as the purposes for it. Across its various models, education for peace holds constant a goal of fostering learning that will support social cohesion, equity, and environmental preservation as well as reconstruction where it is needed (Salomon & Nevo, 2002; Wenden, 2004). Social cohesion and mutual understanding between populations that are experiencing strife are goals of learning, along with multicultural accommodation (Melnick & Zeichner, 1997). Social justice education centers on transformation of inequitable opportunities that students learn to recognize and change as global citizens with local identities (Banks, 2008; Darling-Hammond, French, & Garcia-Lopez, 2002). While these foci have differed in emphasis when addressing the contextual conditions, such as structural inequality, that yield social inequities, they are grounded in a vision of societal harmony. Common across conceptions of education is the goal of transforming as well as learning about problems in society.

Transformative Pedagogy

Theoretical foundations of peace education evidence a clear focus on changing society through learning that supports the development of transformative knowledge, skills, and dispositions (Counts, 1932). Critical theory provides a lens for seeing the disparity in society and how its institutions contribute to the reproduction of power inequalities (Apple, 1995; McLaren, 2003). Transformation of inequities can occur through liberatory education (Freire, 1998). One useful concept for recognizing power disparity is cultural capital (Bourdieu, 1977). The accommodated communication norms of school participants who exhibit dominant culture are an example of how cultural capital helps reproduce advantages for those who exhibit such behaviors (Lareau & Horvat, 1999). Other practices, which are commonly grounded in cultural capital, produce the antecedents of structural violence. For example, labeling students to sort them into different hierarchies of instructional richness is an ostensibly well-intended practice that enables a focus on the learning capabilities expected of students (Hudak & Kihn, 2001). Yet, patterns of labeling commonly evidence structural violence through reduction in opportunity to learn for lower-class populations. The recognizable role such practices have in reproduction of inequity has spawned visionary pedagogies predicated on equitable access to education (Fine et al., 1998; Oakes, 1985; Page, 1991).

Vision, Commitment, and Courage

Peace education has at its core contextually responsive visions and efforts to manifest them (Harris & Morrison, 2003). A vision that sustains educators who commit to teaching for peace is a foundation of their practice that they pass on to their students (Hutchinson, 1996). Envisioning peace is a productive skill that enables transformation of violence at macro and micro levels. People who have made major transformations of violence in their society held fast to their dreams and visions, without clarity of the processes that would manifest their aspirations (Canfield et al., 2005). Along with a picture of a peaceful context, other keys of peacemaking are (a) commitment to working for the contextual change and (b) maintaining courage to face the often violent challenges in the transformation process (Diamond, 1999). Core to transformative teacher education is the sharing of a vision, a commitment to enacting it, and the courage to meet difficult challenges in those processes.

During circumstances that change, along with the society in which they are teaching, peace educators strive to exemplify the wide-awakeness that enables their pedagogical responsiveness (Greene, 1973). The many challenges educators experience, especially in peace education, highlight their crucial commitment to teaching. Discomfort with student responses to transformative content and activities is a catalyst for a teacher's self-work prior to and following lessons (Jacobson, 2003). When students challenge the knowledge and pedagogy of their teachers, courage is as necessary as commitment for sustaining peace education and recognizing what methods of it need to be changed for optimizing success with each group of students. Instructors in teacher education whose evaluations by their students are used in decisions about promotion or just continued employment have valid concerns about the effects of their pedagogy. Such situations underscore the need for care of themselves and of their students. One way educators advance professional self-care occurs through communication with other instructors in which they destress while they share community and possibilities for effective instruction. The collaborations of the instructors described in this chapter were part of that caring process. The need for care in education is clear, and imperative when educators feel a threat from their students, which occurs in experiential learning whereby the students learn to apply transformative concepts. Empathy and compassion, by other students as well as their instructors, for students who have psychological and social leaps to make in development are two tools for sustaining patience with and instruction of such students (Hoffman, 2000; Johnston, 2006; Lampert, 2003; Noddings, 1992). In recognition of missing awareness and skills of their students, peace-focused teacher educators develop learning activities that they hope will be facilitative of social amelioration through student development of the capacities to bring about interpersonal peace (Goldstein, 2002).

Experiential learning to address problems in their society, such as Dewey (1916) advocated, has often been more productive for teacher development than acquiring knowledge through banking activities. The banking model of education deposits information in students and typically retrieves it through recall activity (Freire, 1998). Transformative and social action approaches to multicultural diversity education are designed not for transmission of existing norms and knowledge. Rather, they are learning opportunities for changing cognitive and behavioral norms that sustain violence, about which teachers-in-training from dominant cultures often have insufficient awareness. Transcending norms that sustain violence occurs with emotional and experiential maturity (Galtung, 2000). Such maturity develops from direct experience with proactive transformation of conflict and reflection that follows it. With this awareness, teacher educators have been designing and implementing instruction that gives their students opportunities for not only recognizing conflicts that undermine peace but also for experiencing proactive ways in which those conflicts can be addressed (Eisler & Miller, 2004). For example, they bring to the attention of students the effects of white privilege and the need to redistribute opportunities for success, which are impeded by racism and colorism.

Social Contexts

Resulting from the common vision in different locations, peace education has a consistent goal of addressing structural violence, regardless of variations in different contexts for how that can be done. While human interactions vary due to cultural norms and variable rights for free speech, proactively responding to violence of any type involves deliberate behaviors that are contextually effective (Bekerman & McGlynn, 2007). As such, educational responses to forced ethnic and religious integration in schools have resulted with wide-ranging efforts in building social cohesion, understanding, and justice. While some educators have implemented the contact method of integration, which has not been very effective and occasionally counterproductive, others have been able to facilitate intercultural understanding through sustained discourse within diverse groups.

Communication is crucial in responding to conflict (Deutsch, Coleman, & Marcus, 2006). Yet, how and when to optimally engage in interpersonal discourse depends on cultural norms, the nature of the conflict, and felt readiness (Oetzel & Ting-Toomey, 2006). While successfully communicating in peace education about power relations and responsibilities for transforming them, educators incorporate self-knowledge as well as awareness of their students' needs (Hart & Hodson, 2004; Keating, 2007). The social contexts in which teacher educators enact peace education constrain their success when interactions with themselves and their students are fraught with negative thoughts and emotions. For example, self-doubt and lack of efficacy for managing classroom conversations about current issues can impede discussion facilitation, while fear of professional sanctions for accomplishing them are other impediments. Successful teacher educators develop strategies for accomplishing their goals with those constraints. One common picture of peace that many educators maintain is the facilitation of cross-cultural understanding and cooperation. Those are widespread goals for responding to the segregation and sectarianism that evidence structural violence. Teaching with strategies that work for students in the same class who have different languages and cultural norms is a bridge to peace in transformative education.

Background

Reviewed here are the two contexts where we engaged in and researched teacher education. Although we were affiliated in peace-focused teacher preparation, we separately designed instruction for preparation of teachers in societies where social class struggles and identity politics had resulted in official, yet limited, social reconstruction. Results of mandating greater opportunities for historically oppressed peoples in those regions resulted with resistance by their dominant cultures and restructuring of inequities along original identity and other social class lines. Needed in both contexts were successful practices for reconstructive education. Retrenchment of structural violence after forced school integration was a common issue we faced, as well as our need for transforming resistance of students. While South Africa had experienced as an outcome of revolution the most recent change of its political and social statutes supporting social reconstruction, in the USA a civil war followed by a civil rights movement that began a century later had not effectively redressed social and economic inequities, especially in its southern region. Regardless of the geographic and temporal distances of the two contexts, the challenges we faced in accomplishing peace education were similar.

South Africa

The African continent is rich in traditions of peace as well as recent initiatives for transforming conflict (Hoopers, 2000). The multitude of ways African cultures developed for peaceful conflict transformation are worthy of study. While Western psychologists explore the dynamics of self-concept as an antecedence of peace and violence, they find that indigenous customs across Africa include caring through intensive affirmation. Along with other methods of peaceful transformation, a study of *uMotho*, which is approximately translated to "humanness" (Ramose, 1996; Sharra, 2006), is worthwhile. As a legacy of colonialism in South Africa and the southern USA indigenous methods of peacemaking have been understudied. Sociological concepts, such as race and other identifiers, along with a focus on justice, have dominated discourse about conflict. During this study, there was a dearth of literature about commitment, courage, and caring as responses to violence by educators.

Historic Antecedents

In South Africa, "race remains the primary point of reference" (Soudien, 1994, p. 56; Soudien, Carrim, & Sayed, 2004). Under apartheid, the minority white population used four essentialized classifications—white, African, colored, and Indian—to distinguish rights and maintain their power (Moodley & Adam, 2004). The latter three identity categories were further homogenized through the common representation of blackness and, consequently, in postapartheid discourse, the black experience (Potgieter, 2002). Identities were considered rigid and fixed, with whiteness treated as morally, intellectually, and biologically superior, and blackness as subaltern. Education reflected this segregated and inequitable environment, with every aspect of schooling regulated according to race (Carrim, 1998; Sayed, 2001).

The need for rectification and parity in all aspects of education was imperative (Jansen, 2004; Sayed, 2001). Since 1994, various policies encouraged the process of desegregation (read: integration) in South Africa. The once segregated, bleached-out zones were being infused with different colors as white advantages were ostensibly ended. However, in many instances, they were retained through proxy. Examples included (a) maintaining the hegemonic institutional culture at many institutions by filling the lower ranks at historically white institutions with black appointees and (b) setting up structures that challenged the authority of the government, including school-governing bodies of former white public schools.

For many black laymen, the perception was that not much has changed for them since the advent of democracy. At the same time, many whites perceived a loss of privilege, as evident from a petition by a group of white students at the Union Buildings (Deon de Lange, 2006). The issue of affirmative action also unnerved a number of whites. Hence, there have been a large number of whites emigrating from South Africa.

Southern USA

Long after a civil war (in the 1860s) was fought in the USA, which officially outlawed slavery, social forms of resistance to those who become known as "coloreds" were entrenched so deeply that segregation became an acceptable norm in the southern USA. Separate facilities were designated for "white" and "colored" use. Unequally distributed public monies perpetuated structural violence based on people's physical and social characteristics. Political struggles were at their height in the 1960s when nonviolent protests succeeded in affecting political mandates for new civil rights of all citizens in the USA. Nevertheless, resistance to enacting those guaranteed rights remained. Inequality of educational opportunities was apparent in the social class reproduction that government-funded schools produced through a variety of ways.

Policy Variations

In response to inequitable learning opportunities that were particularly apparent along ethnic and cultural lines, education that accommodated and supported human diversity was advocated to different degrees across teacher education programs throughout the nation. Supplemental support programs, such as affirmative action, designed to advantage cultural minorities who are very underrepresented in universities, waxed and waned across regions of the country. Due to complaints of unfairness to others whose privileges were not officiated in policy, the state of Florida eliminated affirmative action at the close of the Twentieth Century. The variable support of those facing social and economic disadvantages in the USA mirrored the viewpoints of people who resented assistance programs for disadvantaged populations.

Diversity Education

Within teacher education courses that embodied four-year degree programs in the USA, learning about human diversity and methods of teaching diverse populations were created in the last two decades. Spaces for such instruction typically existed in one mandated course focused on multicultural education. Additionally, proactive teacher educators created such learning opportunities in other required "methods" courses for teacher certification. Recognizable factors contributing to such opportunities are institutional policies that advocate multicultural education as well as the associated motivation and skill of teacher educators. Motivation and skill, which are typically products of personal and professional experiences that build efficacy, as well as peacebuilding, are valuable for creating proactive responses to conflict in uncomfortable situations that occur while working with notions of social justice.

Common Agenda

In our different societies with ongoing systemic violence, especially racism, we provide diversity education with a common goal of conflict transformation; enabling recognition of and proactive responses to sources of intercultural violence. We incorporate critical theory and visioning of social cohesion through education. The wide-awakeness of our teacher candidates to their role in providing transformative education is one focus. Another includes the modeling of caring education that supports students who experience discomfort as a response to the transformative pedagogy, and those who have been victims of structural and interpersonal violence. Common concepts in our lessons are found in teacher education literature and peace education (Carter, 2008). Described in this chapter are student responses to one of those concepts, "white privilege" (McIntosh,

1989; Wise, 2005). Our research contributes comparative analysis to extant works on transformative education, especially those that include deconstruction of privilege as an antecedence of violence (Keating, 2007; Lea & Sims, 2008; Mezirow, 2000).

Research Methodology

For comparative inquiry in two different contexts of teacher preparation, we used a limited case study design (Merriam, 1998). With the components of description, explanation, and judgment, an evaluative case study provided us as participant researchers with a tool for examining and comparing our work in this domain of peace education. We were interested in contextual differences across nations and responses to them that advantaged and constrained transformative teaching and learning. Of particular interest was student responses to our instructional methods. We examined difficulties that our students and thus we had. One of our expectations was identification of outcomes from teacher preparation that might occur regardless of contextual differences. Another was association of our categorical identities with student resistance to critical theory. For example, how did our membership in dominant culture in the USA and dominated culture in South Africa associate with student engagement in the learning process? Ultimately, we reflected on how we maintained a care ethic after experiencing threatening student resistance to our transformative pedagogy.

Data Collection and Analysis

First collected for analysis were products of student learning. These included students' writings on the course topics and analytic charts that they created for working with the concepts in their course. Second, communication via e-mail by the instructors, in which they explained to each other how the students were experiencing their courses, provided narrative data. Reflective writing by the instructors, as emergent data resulting from their responses to students' learning behaviors, was also used for analysis. Their reflective writing documented observations of learning occurrences and instructor thoughts about them. Finally, in one course, anonymous evaluations of the teacher's instruction, done at the end of the semester, provided valuable information.

Data collection and analysis focused on three domains: (1) instructional milieu, including factors such as student and instructor characteristics that might have influenced learning, (2) curriculum contents, and (3) individual as well as collective participant behaviors. Those domains were associated with student learning about and engagement with conflict topics. Documented were the instructional milieus, including factors such as student and instructor characteristics that might have influenced learning. In the analysis, we compared our milieu, curricula, student responses to its use, and our reflective writings. We evaluated student engagement with concepts and their level of using them. In addition to the observational data we generated, evidence of student use came from written assignments they did, which described their application of transformative knowledge and skills.

Findings

We found some dissimilarities in the three domains we examined. Evident in the instructional milieus were temporal factors associated with regional history, in addition to our identity and experience distinctions. Curriculum differences included dimensions of conflict study and presence of revisionist history. Variation in participant behaviors reflected contextual differences in connection with their developmental readiness for critical analysis of individual and collective transformation.

Milieus

One difference was duration of time during which each of the societies had been culturally integrated through mandates. Whereas school integration occurred thirty years earlier in the USA than in South Africa, visions of teaching in such contexts differed. Several teacher candidates in South Africa openly expressed their plan to only teach in white schools like the ones they had attended. Such expressions were much less evident in the USA where a few middle-class students shared their plans to teach in suburban schools, which were mostly white, like them. The degrees of openness about visions of education, including participation in social transformation through school integration, were different only in the lesser amount of teacher candidates who demonstrated no interest in and resistance to cultural and social class border-crossing for participation in transformative education. The longer the duration of school integration policy, the less students demonstrated such resistance. The normality of social cohesion visions may influence visioning, or just open discourse about them when personal engagement in transformative teaching is not intended.

The instructor in the USA had a decade of experience with teaching a multicultural education course in teacher preparation, whereas such material was newly provided in the South African context. Both instructors differed in cultural identity within their societies; the one in the USA was of white, European heritage, and the one in South Africa was a native of Indian descent who represented a recent power change through her membership in a formerly subjugated, servant population. The instructor in the USA had the advantage of representing to the students, through her modeled actions and personal stories that she told, a personal quest for social justice as a member of dominant society. The instructor in South Africa faced a greater instructional challenge as her students became accustomed to her new authority position in their institution and national society.

Curriculum

Both instructors used similar and common course material in their shared quest to advance peace through teacher education. Similar curriculum content provided in each course included examples of social disparity and associated practices, which sustained it, in addition to learner diversity, which the teachers-in-training were prepared to accommodate in their future classrooms. Use of different languages that were commonly spoken in their regions demonstrated, in both contexts, an ethos of plurality through linguistic accommodation and respect for the dominated cultures whose language had been underrepresented. A new policy for use of 50 percent English and 50 percent Afrikaans in the South African university ensured inclusive communication of at least two of the eleven official languages in that country. However, in the USA, use of different languages in regular classrooms, versus designated bilingual ones that focus on teaching English, was voluntary. The conflict for students there of not understanding a language other than English in classroom discourse was one of several aspects of the unofficial curriculum.

Due to the greater duration of the course, analysis of social, economic, and political issues associated with diversity enabled more student engagement with conflict study in the USA. Students there had specific assignments that required their examination of multiple conflicts with analysis of each one from many perspectives. They were also required to complete a social action project in which they engaged in transformative work, much of which was responding to structural violence, including the removal of white privileges where they saw them present. The requirement for their direct experience with conflict work associated with human diversity underscored the importance of that skill while it developed their efficacy with transformative action. One conflict that occurred in the USA course was the ill feelings of white students who did not like reading only revisionist history in the course, which uses the voices and stories of dominated populations to present their experiences. Students explained their perception of disrespect for and scapegoating of white people when they read about the structural violence that revisionist history illustrates (Takaki,1993). Expressions of anger with the instructor in classroom discourse, and also in student evaluations of the instructor, happened every semester. Dissatisfaction with critical examination of power relations occurred to a greater degree in South Africa.

Participant Behaviors

Although student responses to the courses varied, in both contexts, many experienced dissonance in response to their instruction. Demonstrations of their need for developmental maturity ranged from their walking-out-of-class protests in South Africa to engagement in compassionate communication with their instructors about their personal need to feel respected when discussions of privilege occurred. While newness of the transforming society in South Africa was a source of insecurity for students, identification of continued complacency with structural violence in schools of the USA also had an unsettling effect. While being in the midst of current structural transformations is a source of discomfort, being given the responsibility to start them where needed was a psychological challenge for the teacher candidates, hence the importance of their experience with enactment of peace development closely following their wide-awakeness to the need for it.

An evident challenge in both places was student identification of their privileges, especially if they were from a low socioeconomic background. Another common challenge for students was finding proactive ways in which they could disrupt and transform social injustice. For many, it was a new skill to recognize conflicts around them and then take responsibility for addressing those problems, especially when the conflicts did not seem to directly concern themselves. Writing about the privileges they had and the effects helped the students expand their perceptions and sense of responsibility. Our triangulation of data produced in their class discussions, written assignments, and communications with us outside of class revealed a need for students to have models for their proactive engagement. They turned to their instructors and guest speakers for sharing true stories about such work. Students needed examples to which they could relate to see themselves in such situations and anticipate how they might accomplish their work.

Our responses to student engagement with difficult concepts included steadfastness and concern. Levels of comfort improved for students in both contexts where instruction invariably evidenced consistent caring for them, along with an evident commitment to transformative education. Our expressions of compassion included communication and temporal accommodation, or time for students to complete transformation-oriented assignments that were developmentally challenging for them. While caring for the students, we found self-care was crucial in our ability to maintain courage. When facing direct or indirect threats from students who were experiencing discomfort with the curriculum contents and our requirement to use the concepts in them, we used reflection and connection. After identification of the sources of discomfort that precipitated students' rude communication with us, we were able to identify their needs as well as ours. Connection with the students outside of class to continue conversations with them about their experiences helped us understand and work with them, which was also reciprocal. Additionally, connection with other colleagues who taught similar classes sustained our courage and expectation of success with transformative pedagogy.

CONCLUSION

The disposition capacities this study highlighted associate with student and instructor success in transformative learning. Valuable were internal and external compassion, with selves and others (Aronson, 2000; Miller, 2006; Whang & Nash, 2005). Compassionate communication facilitated community building in liberatory education (Pierce, 2004; Rosenberg, 2003; Sergiovanni, 1994). Courage in the face of perceived threats sustained the work and evidenced commitment, which was crucial for transformation of uncomfortable circumstances for learning, along with steadfastness when stress increased instructional challenges. Visions of a better society and world sustained commitments and courage to incorporate difficult issues and proactive responses to them. In the relatively short time that South Africans have had to affect transformation through education, their efforts are valuable for examination of peace education and its outcomes, and the depth of the vision there is worthy of study (Jansen, 2004).

While the recent social and political transformation in South Africa contributed to resistance in analysis of white privilege and other sources of differential power, the continued complicity in the southern USA with social injustice had normalized relations that students initially failed to recognize or acknowledge. Comparison of these two contexts evidenced the value of critical theory and recognition of cultural capital in liberatory education that identifies the sources of structural violence. Preparing teachers to recognize, address, and work with their students to transform societal conflicts presented challenges in both regions. Identification of their responses to those challenges may help and inspire teacher educators in similar situations. The movement of barriers to peace education are possible and worthy of the efforts that they require (Hagan & McGlynn, 2003).

Methods for optimal response to the contextual conditions that affect transformative education are continually being identified (Ball, 2006). This research illustrated processes which sustained multicultural and social justice strands of peace education in different world regions. Commitment, courage, and compassion were crucial in pedagogy, much as they have been in other methods of peace development.

REFERENCES

Apple, M. (1995). *Education and power* (2nd ed.). New York: Routledge.
Aronson, E. (2000). *Nobody left to hate: Teaching compassion after Columbine.* New York: Freeman.

Ball, A. F. (2006). *Multicultural strategies for education and social change. Carriers of the torch in the United States and South Africa*. New York: Teachers College Press.

Banks, J. A. (2008). Diversity, group identity, and citizenship education in a global age. *Educational Researcher, 37*(3), 129–139.

Bekerman, Z., & McGlynn, C. (Eds.). (2007). *Addressing ethnic conflict through peace education*. New York: Palgrave Macmillan.

Bourdieu, P. (1977). Cultural reproduction and social reproduction. In J. Karabel & H. Halsey (Eds.), *Power and ideology in education* (pp. 487–511). New York: Oxford University Press.

Canfield, J., Hansen, M. V., Carter, C. C., Palomares, S., Williams, L., & Winch, B. (Eds.). (2005). *Chicken soup for the soul: Stories for a better world*. Deerfield Beach, FL: Health Communications.

Carrim, N. (1998). Anti-racism and the "new" South African educational order. *Cambridge Journal of Education, 28*(3), 301–320.

Carter, C. C. (2008). Voluntary standards for peace education. *Journal of Peace Education 5*(2), 141–155.

Counts, G. S. (1932). *Dare the schools build a new social order?* New York: John Day.

Darling-Hammond, L., French, J., & Garcia-Lopez, S. (Eds.). (2002). *Learning to teach for social justice*. New York: Teachers College Press.

De Lange, D. (2006, Oktober 6). "Ons is ook afrikane," sê wit tukkies. *The Beeld*, 6 p. 1.

Deutsch, M., Coleman, P. T., & Marcus, E. C. (Eds.). (2006). *The handbook of conflict resolution: Theory and practice* (2nd ed.). San Francisco: Jossey-Bass.

Dewey, J. (1916). *Democracy and education*. New York: Macmillan.

Diamond, L. (1999). *The courage for peace. Daring to create harmony in ourselves and the world*. Berkley, CA: Conari.

Eisler, R., & Miller, R. (Eds.). (2004). *Educating for a culture of peace*. Portsmouth, NH: Heinemann.

Fine, M., Anand, B., Hancock, M., Jordan, C., & Sherman, D. (1998). *Off track: Classroom privilege for all* [video]. New York: Teachers College Press.

Freire, P. (1998). *Pedagogy of freedom. Ethics, democracy, and civic courage* (P. Clarke, Trans.). New York: Rowman & Littlefield.

Galtung, J. (2000, May). Maturity is needed. *Higher education for peace*. Proceedings of the Higher Education for Peace Conference in Tromsø, Norway, 8. Retrieved April 28, 2008, from http://www.peace2.uit.no/hefp/final_report/final_report.html

Goldstein, L. S. (2002). *Reclaiming caring in teaching and teacher education*. New York: Peter Lang.

Greene, M. (1973). *Teacher as stranger: Educational philosophy for the modern age*. Belmont, CA: Wadsworth.

Hagan, M., & McGlynn, C. W. (2003, September). Moving barriers: Promoting learning for diversity in initial teacher education. *Journal of Intercultural Education, 15*(4), 243–252.

Harris, I. M., & Morrison, M. L. (2003). *Peace education* (2nd ed.). Jefferson, NC: McFarland.

Hart, S., & Hodson, V. K. (2004). *The compassionate classroom: Relationship based teaching and learning.* Encinitas, CA: PuddleDancer Press.

Hoffman, M. L. (2000). *Empathy and moral development: Implications for caring and justice.* New York: Cambridge University Press.

Hoppers, C. O. (2000, May). An African culture of peace. *Higher education for peace.* Proceedings of the Higher Education for Peace Conference in Tromsø, Norway, 9. Retrieved April 28, 2008, from http://www.peace2.uit.no/hefp/final_report/final_report.html

Hudak, G., & Kihn, P. (Eds.). (2001). *Labeling, pedagogy and politics.* New York: Routledge.

Hutchinson, F. P. (1996). *Educating beyond violent futures.* New York: Routledge.

Jacobson, T. (2003). *Confronting our discomfort: Clearing the way for anti-bias in early childhood education.* Portsmouth, NH: Heinemann.

Jansen, J. (2004). Race, education and democracy after ten years: How far have we come? Prepared for the Institute for Democracy in South Africa, *Lessons from the field: A decade of democracy in South Africa.* Retrieved October 1, 2008, from http://chet.org.za/download/2733/issues_210704.doc

Johnston, D. K. (2006). *Education for a caring society: Classroom relationships and moral action.* New York: Teachers College Press.

Keating, A. (2007). *Teaching transformation: Transcultural classroom dialogues.* New York: Palgrave Macmillan.

Lampert, K. (2003). *Compassionate education: A prolegomena for radical schooling.* Lanham, MD: University Press of America.

Lareau, A., & Horvat, E. M. (1999). Moments of social in inclusion and exclusion: Race, class and cultural capital in family-school relations. *Sociology of Education 72,* 37–53.

Keating, A. (2007). *Teaching transformation: Transcultural classroom dialogues.* New York: Palgrave.

Lea, V., & Sims. E. J. (2008). *Undoing whiteness in the classroom: Critical educultural teaching approaches for social justice activism.* New York: Peter Lang.

McIntosh, P. (1989, July/August). White privilege: Unpacking the invisible knapsack. *Peace and Freedom, 3,* 10–12.

McLaren, P. (2003). *Life in schools: An introduction to critical pedagogy in the foundations of education* (4th ed.). New York: Longman.

Melnick, S. L., & Zeichner, K. M. (1997). Enhancing the capacity of teacher education institutions to address diversity issues. In J. I. King, E. R. Hollins, & W. C. Hayman (Eds.), *Preparing teachers for cultural diversity* (pp. 23–39). New York: Teachers College Press.

Merriam, S. B. (1998). *Qualitative research and case study applications in education.* San Francisco: Jossey-Bass

Mezirow, J. (2000). *Learning as transformation: Critical perspectives on a theory in progress.* San Francisco: Jossey-Bass.

Miller, J. P. (2006). *Educating for wisdom and compassion: Creating conditions for timeless learning.* Thousand Oaks, CA: Corwin.

Moodley, K. A, & Adam, H. (2004). Citizenship education and political literacy in South Africa. In J. Banks (Ed.), *Diversity and citizenship education: Global perspectives* (pp. 158–180). San Francisco: Jossey-Bass.

Noddings, N. (1992). *The challenge to care in school. An alternative approach to education.* New York: Teachers College Press.

Oakes, J. (1985). *Keeping track: How schools structure inequality.* New Haven, CT: Yale University.

Oetzel, J. G., & Ting-Toomey, S. (Eds.). (2006). *The SAGE handbook of conflict communication: Integrating theory, research and practice.* Thousand Oaks, CA: Sage.

Page, R. N. (1991). *Lower-track classrooms: A curricular and cultural perspective.* New York: Teachers College.

Pierce, P. (2004). From gladiator to midwife: Birthing "the beloved community" of partnership in a Black Studies course. In R. Eisler & R. Miller (Eds.), *Educating for a culture of peace* (pp. 181–188). Portsmouth, NH: Heinemann.

Potgieter, C. (2002). *Black academics on the move.* Pretoria: Centre for Higher Education.

Ramose, M. B. (1996). Specific African thought structures and their possible contribution to world peace. In H. Beck and G. Schmirber (Eds.), *Creative peace through encounter of world cultures* (pp. 211–235). New Delhi: Sri Satguru.

Rosenberg, M. B. (2003). *Nonviolent communication. A language of compassion* (2nd ed.). Encinitas, CA: PuddleDancer Press.

Salomon, G., & Nevo, B. (Eds.). (2002). *Peace education. The concept, principles, and practices around the world.* Mahwah, NJ: Lawrence Erlbaum.

Sayed, Y. (2001). Post-apartheid educational transformation: Policy concerns and approaches. In Y. Sayed & J. Jansen (Eds.), *Implementing education policies: The South African experience* (pp. 250–271). Cape Town: University of Cape Town Press.

Sergiovanni, T. J. (1994). *Building community in schools.* San Francisco: Jossey-Bass.

Sharra, S. L. (2006). Breaking the elephant's tusk: Teacher autobiography and methodology in peace education. *Journal of Stellar Peacemaking, 1* (3). Retrieved April 28, 2008, from http://www.jsp.st

Soudien, C. (1994). Equality and equity in South Africa: Multicultural education and change. *Equity & Excellence, 27*(3), 55–60.

Soudien, C., Carrim, N., & Sayed, Y. (2004). School inclusion and exclusion in South Africa: Some theoretical and methodological considerations. In M. Nkomo, C. McKinney, & L. Chisholm (Eds.), *Reflections on school integration* (pp. 19–43). Cape Town: HSRC Publishers.

Takaki, R. (1993). *A different mirror. A history of multicultural America.* Boston: Little Brown.

Wenden, A. L. (2004). *Education for a culture of social and ecological peace.* New York: State University of New York.

Whang, P. A., & Nash, C. P. (2005). Reclaiming compassion: Getting to the heart and soul of teacher education. *Journal of Peace Education, 2*(1), 79–92.

Wise, T. J. (2005). *White like me.* Brooklyn, NY: Soft Skull Press.

Contributors

Cheila Valera Acosta is a Dominican educator and social worker who has served as the director of the Facultad Latinoamericana de Ciencias Sociales (FLACSO) in Santo Domingo, the largest social-science research institute in the country. She received her master's degree in the social sciences at FLACSO Argentina and is currently completing her doctoral studies in political science at the University of Puerto Rico. She is the author of several books on educational politics, citizenship and education, and educational reform in the Caribbean.

Sirkka Ahonen is a professor emerita in social-studies education in the Department of Applied Sciences of Education at the University of Helsinki in Finland. Her research has focused on the nature of historical thinking, postcommunist history curricula in eastern central Europe, the formation of historical identity among young adults in Finland, and the role of school in the making of civic society in the Nordic countries. She is the author of *Clio Sans Uniform: A Study of Post-Marxist Transformation of the History Curricula in East Germany and Estonia, 1986–1991* (Finnish Historical Society,1992), and the coeditor of *Nordic Lights: Education for Nation and Civic Society in the Nordic Countries, 1850–2000* (Finnish Literary Society, 2001).

Faisal Azaiza is the head of the master's program at the School of Social Work, Faculty of Social Welfare and Health Sciences at the University of Haifa, where he is professor. He is also the head of the university's Jewish-Arab Center and a member of the Council for Higher Education in Israel. His research focus is the health and welfare of Israel's Arab population in terms of social needs, health problems, educational programs, and service-delivery systems.

Monisha Bajaj is assistant professor at Teachers College of Columbia University. Within the international and comparative education program at Teachers College, she coordinates a concentration for masters and doctoral students in peace education. Her research has examined peace and human rights education in diverse international contexts, including the Dominican Republic, Zambia, Tanzania, India, and the United States. She is the editor of the *Encyclopedia of Peace Education* (Information Age Publishing, 2008) and the author of a human rights education manual for Dominican teachers published by the United Nations Educational Scientific and Cultural Organisation (UNESCO) (2003), which she wrote as a Fulbright scholar in the Dominican Republic.

Zvi Bekerman teaches anthropology of education at the School of Education and the Melton Center at the Hebrew University of Jerusalem and is a research fellow at the Truman Institute for the Advancement of Peace at Hebrew University. His interests are in the study of cultural, ethnic, and national identity, including identity processes and negotiation during intercultural encounters, and in formal and informal learning contexts. He is the editor (with Seonaigh MacPherson) of the journal *Diaspora, Indigenous, ad Minority Education: An International Journal*. Among his recently published books are, with Ezra Kopelowitz, *Cultural Education-Cultural Sustainability: Minority, Diaspora, Indigenous and Ethno-Religious Groups in Multicultural Societies* (Routledge, 2008) and, with Diana Silberman-Keller, Henry A. Giroux, and Nicholas Burbules, *Mirror Images: Popular Culture and Education* (Peter Lang, 2008).

Candice C. Carter is an associate professor at the University of North Florida. Her research and scholarship topics include conflict transformation, peace policy, multicultural education, history and social-studies instruction, citizenship education, peace education, peace through arts, peace literature, and teacher training. She serves in many international and national peace education and policy organizations. She designs and facilitates peace education programs in all levels of education, including the interdisciplinary Conflict Transformation Program at the University of North Florida. She is the editor of the *Journal of Stellar Peacemaking*.

Pam Christie holds research and teaching positions at the University of Queensland (UQ) in Australia, the Cape Peninsula University of Technology (CPUT), and the University of the Witwatersrand in South Africa. She wrote her chapter in this volume under the auspices of the Australian Centre for Peace and Conflict Studies at UQ and the Faculty of Education at CPUT. She has published widely on education in South Africa. In addition to her current interests in peace education and human rights, she is also working on a number of projects on teacher education, classroom practice, and development.

Tony Gallagher is a professor at Queen's University and head of the School of Education. In 2004 he published *Education in Divided Societies* (Palgrave Macmillan), which reflects his main research interest, having worked in Northern Ireland, the Middle East, South East Europe, and parts of Asia. He has also published research on policies for social inclusion, the educational consequences of social disadvantage, and the effects of high-stakes testing. He is an International Fellow with Facing History and Ourselves, chair of Public Achievement (Northern Ireland), a member of Healing Through Remembering, and a member of the advisory board of the Northern Ireland Foundation.

Phillip L. Hammack is Assistant Professor of Psychology at the University of California, Santa Cruz. His research broadly investigates the particularity of identity development in cultural, social, and political contexts. With an emphasis on the ways in which possibilities of identity development are co-constituted by individuals and social structural realities, his work relies upon an interdisciplinary approach grounded in his training at the University of Chicago. Professor Hammack has served a number of professional roles in peace education programs, including positions related to group facilitation and program administration. Since 2003, he has conducted fieldwork with Israeli and Palestinian youth participants in peace education programs. In 2006 Professor Hammack was named a Peace Scholar by the United States Institute of Peace for his research with Israeli and Palestinian youth.

Rachel Hertz-Lazarowitz is a professor of social-educational psychology at the Faculty of Education at the University of Haifa in Israel. Her current research and action focus on "Arab and Jewish Life on a diverse Campus." With a team of researchers, she works on the development of interpersonal and intergroup relationships, positive and negative perception and attitudes, identity development, and academic and personal empowerment to understand the predictors of coexistence and conflict. She is a founding member (1979) of the International Association of the Study of Cooperation and an active researcher in the Center for Jews and Arabs at Haifa University.

Azra Hromadzic is a PhD candidate in cultural anthropology at the University of Pennsylvania. She is a recipient of several honors and awards, including the Penn Prize for Excellence in Teaching by Graduate Students. She published articles in German and English, and she presented her work at more than thirty conferences around the world. Her doctoral research titled "Emerging Citizens: Youth, Education, and Democratization in Post-conflict Bosnia and Herzegovina" is supported by research grants from the Social Science Research Council, the American Association of the University Women, the Spencer Foundation, the United States Institute of Peace, the New Europe College, and the University of Pennsylvania.

Ankica Kosic obtained her PhD in social psychology at the Faculty of Psychology at the University of Rome "La Sapienza" in 1999. In the period of 2001 to 2006, she worked as a Research Fellow at European University Institute in Italy, where she has been involved in a number of large-scale research projects. Currently, she is a Senior Marie Curie Research Fellow at the European Research Centre at the University of Kingston in the United Kingdom. Her research interest concerns the issues of immigrant integration, intergroup relationships, stereotypes and prejudice, and the process of reconciliation in post-conflict areas. She has published several articles in Italian and international journals, and book chapters.

Claire McGlynn lectures at the School of Education at Queen's University Belfast. Her research interests lie in gaining understanding of integrated education in Northern Ireland and in other countries damaged by ethnic conflict. Her published work covers the long-term impact of integrated education, the contribution of integrated education to society, multicultural approaches to integrated education, and teacher education for diversity. She edited *Addressing Ethnic Conflict through Peace Education* (Palgrave Macmillan, 2007) with Zvi Bekerman. She is program chair of the Peace Education Special Interest Group of the American Educational Research Association (AERA), a member of the editorial board of the *Journal of Peace Education*, and a member of council of the Peace Education Commission of the International Peace Research Association.

Elavie Ndura-Ouedraogo is an associate professor of education in the Initiatives in Educational Transformation program in the College of Education and Human Development at George Mason University. She holds degrees from Burundi, England, and the United States. Her interdisciplinary scholarship focuses on critical multicultural and peace education, and immigrants' acculturation. She edited *Seeds of New Hope: Pan-African Peace Studies for the Twenty-First Century* (Africa World Press, 2008) with Matt Meyer. She has contributed chapters to several books. Her scholarly articles have appeared in the *Harvard Educational Review*, *Peace and Change*, *Journal of Adult and Adolescent Literacy*, *Language, Culture and Curriculum*,

Multicultural Perspectives, Multicultural Education, American Secondary Education, Intercultural Education, Culture of Peace Online Journal, and other publications. She is actively engaged in outreach activities that further the cause of social justice and peace.

Ulrike Niens completed her PhD in psychology and worked as a researcher with the School of Psychology and the UNESCO Centre, School of Education, at the University of Ulster after receiving a psychology degree at the Free University of Berlin in Ulrike. Since 2006, Ulrike has been a lecturer in the School of Education at Queen's University Belfast. She is a member of the editorial board of *Peace & Conflict: The Journal of Peace Psychology* and *Peace & Conflict Review*. Her research interests focus on peace education, democracy, and reconciliation, and she has been involved in a number of research projects on this topic.

Paul Nolan works in the School of Education at Queen's University Belfast as a director of education with responsibility for adult learning programs. He began his career as a development officer in community education, working in disadvantaged areas of Belfast, and went on to become director of the Workers' Educational Association of Northern Ireland. In 2001 he moved to Queen's where he retains his interest in political education.

Hilla Peretz received her PhD, summa cum laude, from the University of Haifa. She recently completed a postdoctoral Research Fellow at the Whitman School of Management at Syracuse University in New York. Her research interests can be situated on the interface between two disciplinary areas: education studies and management studies. Specially, she focuses on training, leadership, values, and culture. She has written a number of papers and has presented these papers in a number of international academic conferences such as the *International Society of Work and Organizational Values* and the *American Educational Research Association*.

Jessica Senehi is associate director of the Arthur Mauro Centre for Peace and Justice St. Paul's College at the University of Manitoba, and assistant professor in the PhD program in Peace and Conflict Studies at the University of Manitoba. With Sean Byrne, she codirected *The North American Conflict Resolution Program: A Cross Cultural, Interdisciplinary Experiment in Peacebuilding* student exchange (supported by HRSDC). She has published a number of scholarly articles as well as *The Process of Storytelling: Building Community, Building Peace* and *VIOLENCE: Intervention and Prevention*. At the Hebrew

University of Jerusalem and Al Quds University, she is assessing the impact of the Jerusalem Stories Project on peace building. She is the founder, organizer, and executive director of Winnipeg's annual International Storytelling Festival as well as the academic institute Storytelling for Peacebuilding and Renewing Community.

Ruth Sharabany is associate professor in the Department of Psychology at the University of Haifa in Israel. She received her PhD from Cornell University, and is a developmental and clinical psychologist. She researches and publishes on friendship, intimacy, socialization, cross-cultural research, and kibbutz socialization. She coauthored, along with R. Josselson, A. Leiblich, R. Sharabany, and H. Wiseman, the book *Conversation as a method: Analyzing the relational world of people who were raised communally* (Sage, 1997). She is an associate editor of the *Journal of Social and Personal Relationship*. She has supervised clinical psychologists in different settings and is the chair of the postgraduate program of psychoanalytic psychology at the University of Haifa. She is also a member of the Graduate School council.

Ana Tomovska has recently obtained her PhD from the School of Education at Queen's University Belfast. She has obtained her bachelor's (First Class Honors) in psychology from the University "SS Cyril and Methodius" Skopje. Her current research is concentrated on exploring children's views and experiences of intergroup contact programs in conflict-affected societies. She is particularly interested in the interconnection of cultural and ethnic identity politics with issues of intercultural and peace education, promotion of social justice and cohesion, and social inclusion. She has been involved in a number of educational and research projects, presented her research in national and international conferences around the world, and is currently working on a number of publications.

Pilvi Torsti published her seminal work on history textbooks and uses of history in postwar Bosnia and Herzegovina, *Divergent Stories, Convergent Attitudes. A Study on the Presence of History, History Textbooks and the Thinking of Youth in post-War Bosnia and Herzegovina*, in 2003. Since then she has published, lectured, and presented broadly on former Yugoslavia, Bosnia, and history education. In 2005 to 2006, she worked as a founding program director of the United World College (UWC) and International Baccalaureate Initiative in Bosnia and Herzegovina, which set up the UWC in Mostar 2006. For this work, she earned two international peace awards. Currently, she works as a postdoctoral researcher at the University of Helsinki in Finland.

Tamar Zelniker is a cognitive psychologist in the Psychology Department at Tel-Aviv University. She is also a founding member of the academic program of studies of psychotherapy and human rights established in Gaza in 1996, and has been a member if its academic board (1996–2008). Her research focuses on cognitive development, theories of mind, and Jewish-Arab relations. She coedited "Arab-Jewish Coexistence Programs," a special issue of the *Journal of Social Issues*, with Rachel Hertz-Lazarowitz, Cookie White-Stephan, and Walter Stephan (2004).

Michalinos Zembylas is assistant professor of education at the Open University of Cyprus. His research interests are in the areas of educational philosophy and curriculum theory, and his work focuses on exploring the role of emotion and affect in curriculum and pedagogy. He is particularly interested in how affective politics intersect with issues of social-justice pedagogies, intercultural and peace education, and citizenship education. He is the author of numerous articles in international refereed journals as well as the books *Teaching With Emotion: A Postmodern Enactment* (Information Age Publishing, 2005), *Five Pedagogies, a Thousand Possibilities: Struggling for Hope and Transformation* (SensePublishers, 2007), and *The Politics of Trauma in Education* (Palgrave Macmillan, 2008).

Index

adolescence, 130, 139
adult learning, 66–67
African Great Lakes region, 30–32
Allport, Gordan, 94, 102–3, 105, 129, 151–52, 202
American, 127–41
antisocial behavior, 165–67
apartheid, 75–87, 252
Arabic, 181, 231, 235–43
Arab students, 180, 199, 202–10
authoritarianism, 45–46, 53
autonomy, 10, 12, 18, 20–22

Belfast, 161–62, 164–75
bilingual education, 181, 231–43
bilingualism, 181, 231, 240–43
bioecological system theory, 96
Bosnia and Herzegovina, 109–23, 180, 215–27
Bourdieu, Pierre, 90, 94, 96, 104–5, 243
Bronfenbrenner, Urie, 94, 96, 104–5
Burundi, 27–38

Catholic, 9, 13, 16–21, 45–46, 48, 54, 60, 64–66, 70, 170
children, 94–104
Christian, 17, 19, 70, 205–8
citizenship, 78, 81, 86, 146–48, 150, 152, 190, 192–93
civic education debate, 220, 223
civil society, 2, 6–7, 46, 50, 52, 54
civil war, 28, 31–37

coexistence, 111, 113, 122, 127–28, 130–31, 134, 136, 138–41, 162–63, 172, 174
coffee drinking, 109, 117–18
commitment, 181, 247–49, 251, 253, 257–58
communicative skills, 163, 173
communitarian social thesis, 10
community relations, 63–64, 68, 147, 150–52, 154, 164–65, 170–75 community work, 161, 164–65, 173–74
compassion, 181, 249, 257–58
conflict, 1–2, 5, 59, 62, 64, 69, 71–72, 127–41, 145–48, 150–53, 155, 231, 234, 243. *See also* conflict resolution; conflict society; ethnic conflict; violence
conflicting ethos, 183, 187–88
conflict resolution, 17–18, 45, 62, 64, 82, 85–86, 171, 225
conflict society, 43, 46, 53–54
contact hypothesis, 2, 21, 89–91, 93–94, 104–5, 129, 146, 148, 150–53, 155, 163, 174, 202, 210
contact programs, 95–105
courage, 181, 248–49, 251–52, 257–58
creativity, 76, 85–87
critical, 16–22
critical emotional praxis, 180, 184–85, 189–90, 192–93
critical multiculturalism, 149–50, 154

critical pedagogy, 51–53
critical theory, 181, 248, 253–54, 258
Croatia, 161–62, 164, 169, 171, 175
cultural capital, 181, 248, 258
cultural diversity, 9–11, 66
cultural psychology, 128, 130, 140
cultural transition, 233–34, 242–43
culture, 113, 119–20, 128, 131, 134, 138
Cyprus, 183–93

dating, 109, 118–22
Dayton Peace Agreement, 110–11, 215–16, 218, 226
decategorization, 163, 173
dehumanization, 187, 192–93
deliberative communication, 180–81, 216–17, 220–27
deliberative democracy, 181, 216, 220, 224–25, 227
dialogue, 131
discourse, 130–31, 133, 136, 138–39
diversity, 9, 11–12, 15, 145–50, 152, 154–55
divided societies, 147, 150, 153–54
Dominican Republic, 43–55
Dominico-Haitians, 43, 46–48, 55

education, 5–7, 27–32, 36–39, 60–61, 64–67, 70–71, 111, 115, 121
educational context, 231–35, 238, 240–43
educators, 28–32, 36–38
emotional ambivalence, 184–87, 189, 191
emotions, 183–93
ethnic conflict, 27–39, 44, 71, 110–11, 115
ethnicity, 62, 71
ethnic/religious identity, 163–65, 173–74
ethnography, 94, 97
exosystem, 95, 101

framework, 146, 148, 151–53, 155
Freire, Paulo, 48, 71

Good Friday Agreement, 13, 60–61, 68, 70
Greek Cypriots, 183–85, 187, 191–92
group-hopping, 35–36

habitus, 90, 96–97, 99–101
hatred, 184–87, 189, 193
Hebrew, 231, 235–43
historical culture, 216–20, 224–25
history education, 216–27
history teaching, 181, 216, 222–67
human rights, 43–55, 145–48, 152
human rights education (HRE), 6, 44–45, 47–49, 51–55
Hutu, 27–36, 38
hybridity, 185, 190, 192
hyphenated identities, 201, 207, 211

identity, 10–13, 18–22, 78, 86, 127–39, 141, 231, 233, 235, 251–52, 255. *See also* hyphenated identities; national identity
imaginary, 79–80, 84–86
inclusivity, 85
inequality, 79–86
integrated education, 6, 12–22
integration, 111, 122–23, 180–81, 200, 202, 205–10, 231, 234–35, 237–40, 255
interaction, 233, 236, 238
interethnic communities, 27–29, 36–39
intergroup contact, 163–65, 169–70
intergroup relations, 128–31, 134, 137–40
International Baccalaureate, 216, 223–26
International Education, 215, 224, 228
intractability, 71–72, 127
Israel, 199–211, 231, 234–43
Israeli, 127–29, 131–41

Index

Jewish, 69–70, 128, 132–34, 180, 199–210, 231, 234–43
justice, 75–77, 79, 82, 84–86

language, 181, 231–43
leadership, 14–21
learning culture, 64, 66
learning society, 59–61, 66–67, 69, 71–72
liberal, 15–21
liberal/critical, 16, 18, 20, 22
liberalism, 148–50, 153–54
liberal multiculturalism, 149–50, 154
liberal passive, 15, 16, 20–21
liberal/plural, 16, 17–18, 20, 22
liberal proactive, 15, 16, 19, 20–21
liberation theology, 48–49, 52

macrosystem, 95, 97
Mandela, Nelson, 75–77, 79
memory, 185–88, 193
mesosystem, 95–96, 99, 103, 105
microsystem, 95–96, 98–101, 103
military, 28–30, 33–36
militia, 33–36
mindfulness, 249–51, 253–54, 257
mixed marriages, 112–13, 119–22
mixing, 90, 109, 112–23
monoculturalism, 149
moral imagination, 76, 85
Mostar, 109–11, 113, 116–23, 216, 221, 223–26, 228
multicultural, 9–16, 22
multicultural education, 2, 6, 28–29, 38–39, 148, 153, 235, 242, 248–50, 253, 255, 258
multiculturalism, 91, 146, 148–50, 152–53, 155
Muslim, 70, 110, 118, 120, 127, 132, 137, 205–9, 218–19, 221

narratives, 180, 184–89, 191–93. *See also* youth narrative
nation, 110–13, 121, 123
national identity, 180, 199–207

nationalism, 180, 184–86, 189–90, 192–93
nation-building, 78–79
negative peace, 44–45, 86, 147
negotiations, 76–77
nongovernmental organizations (NGOs), 44, 49–52, 164, 166, 171
Northern Ireland, 59–72, 161–62, 164, 166, 168–69, 171–72, 175

occupation, 132–33, 201, 234–35

Palestinian, 127–29, 131–41, 231, 234–42
participatory action research (PAR), 202–11
participatory approach, 49peace, 11–13, 21–22, 127–33, 137–38, 140–41, 179–80, 183–86, 188–90, 192
peace education, 1–3, 28–29, 36–39, 43–46, 51–52, 54, 76, 82, 85–86, 89, 91–92, 146–48, 152–53, 155, 164–66, 180–81, 180, 202–3, 208–11, 216, 241. *See also* contact hypothesis
peace process, 59–62, 64–65, 67–71
perception of the university, 180, 201–11
plural, 15–21
plural inclusive, 16, 17, 19, 20–21
pluralism, 148–50, 153–54
pluralist multiculturalism, 149–50, 154
plurality, 256
plural limited, 16–17, 21
policy, 253, 255–56
positive peace, 44–45, 76, 85–86, 147–48, 153
post-conflict area, 161, 163, 175
post-conflict society, 27, 30–34, 37–39, 109, 111–12, 115–17, 122–23
poverty, 76, 79–84
power, 234, 243, 257

pre-conflict society, 43, 53–54
privilege, 250, 252–54, 256–58
progress, 71–72
Protestant, 9, 13, 16–21, 54, 60, 64–66, 70, 169–70

racism, 45–46
recategorization, 163, 173–74
reconciliation, 75–77, 80, 85–86, 91, 110–11, 122, 161, 163, 166, 168, 174–75, 183–86, 188–92
relational empathy, 190–92
religion, 199–209
Republic of Macedonia, 93–94, 97–102
responsibility, 86–87
rights, 76, 78, 81–82

second language, 232–33, 238, 242–43
sectarianism, 13, 18, 165–66, 174
security, 133, 136–37, 139, 141
segregation, 111–12, 122
single identity work, 169–70, 173
smoking, 114
social action, 249, 256
social cohesion, 10
social context, 95–101
social justice, 181, 247–48, 250–51, 253, 255–58
social psychology, 129, 131, 134, 136, 139
social reconstruction, 27–30, 36–39
socioeconomic empowerment, 165–67, 172
South Africa, 247, 251–52, 254–58
southern U.S., 251–52, 254–58
Structural Adjustment Program, 50
structural violence, 85–86, 248, 250–53, 256–58
students, 28–30, 34–38
suffering, 180, 183–89, 191, 193

teacher preparation, 247, 249–51, 253–55, 257–58
terrorism, 12, 149
theoretical development, 146, 153
transformation, 28–30, 36–39, 75–76
transformative pedagogy, 181, 247–51, 253–58
trauma, 180, 183–88, 191–93
Truth and Reconciliation Commission, 69–70, 75, 77, 85
Turkish Cypriots, 183–85, 187–88, 190–92
Tutsi, 27–29, 31–36, 38
Twa, 33

umbrella, 147, 155, 228
uMotho, 251
United Kingdom, 12, 149, 162
United Nations, 44, 47–48, 50–51, 53–54, 61, 145–47
United States, 11–12, 251–52, 254–58. *See also* southern U.S.
United World College, 216, 224–26
United World College in Mostar Youth and History, 216–19, 225–26
Universal Declaration of Human Rights (UDHR), 44–45
university pedagogical model, 209–11

victimhood, 91, 162, 175
violence, 5, 6, 9, 27, 29–30, 32–36, 39, 110, 112–13, 115–16, 122
Vukovar, 161–62, 164–75

women's rights, 49–52

young people, 161, 164–75
youth, 28–30, 32, 34–36, 39, 109, 111–12, 114–15, 119–23, 161–67, 170–75
youth narrative, 127–28, 130–34